AMERICA

AMERICA

A NARRATIVE HISTORY

FIFTH EDITION

GEORGE BROWN TINDALL
DAVID EMORY SHI

W · W · NORTON & COMPANY · NEW YORK · LONDON

FOR BRUCE AND SUSAN
AND FOR BLAIR

FOR
JASON AND JESSICA

The text of this book is composed in Fairfield Light,
with the display set in Torino.
Composition by Compset Inc.
Manufacturing by Courier.
Book design by Antonina Krass.
Cover illustration: Springfield Bicycle Club. Bicycle Camp.
Exhibition and Tournament. Springfield, Mass., USA, September 18, 19, 20, 1883.
Lithograph by Milton Bradley & Company.
Library of Congress, Prints and Photographs Division.
Cartographer: CARTO-GRAPHICS/Alice Thiede and William Thiede,
with relief maps from Mountain High Maps®, Digital Wisdom, Inc.

Acknowledgments and copyrights continue on p. A61,
which serves as a continuation of the copyright page.

The Library of Congress has cataloged the one-volume edition as follows:

Tindall, George Brown.
    America : A narrative history / George Brown Tindall,
David Emory Shi.—5th ed.
        p.   cm
    Includes bibliographical references (p.   ) and index.
    ISBN 0-393-97339-5
    1. United States—History.   I. Shi, David Emory.   II. Title.
    E178.1.T55   1999   98-41989
    973–dc21

W. W. Norton & Company, Inc., 500 Fifth Avenue, New York, N.Y. 10110
http://www.wwnorton.com

W. W. Norton & Company Ltd., 10 Coptic Street, London WC1A 1PU

5 6 7 8 9 0

CONTENTS

List of Maps • *xv*
Preface • *xix*

℘ART ONE / **A NEW WORLD**

1 | THE COLLISION OF CULTURES   5

PRE-COLUMBIAN INDIAN CIVILIZATIONS   7   •   EUROPEAN VISIONS OF
AMERICA   13   •   THE EXPANSION OF EUROPE   15   •   THE VOYAGES
OF COLUMBUS   17   •   THE GREAT BIOLOGICAL EXCHANGE   21   •
PROFESSIONAL EXPLORERS   24   •   THE SPANISH EMPIRE   26   •
THE PROTESTANT REFORMATION   36   •   CHALLENGES TO SPANISH
EMPIRE   40   •   FURTHER READING   46

2 | ENGLAND AND ITS COLONIES   47

THE ENGLISH BACKGROUND   48   •   SETTLING THE CHESAPEAKE   53   •
SETTLING NEW ENGLAND   65   •   INDIANS IN NEW ENGLAND   77   •
THE ENGLISH CIVIL WAR IN AMERICA   82   •   SETTLING THE CAROLINAS   84   •
SETTLING THE MIDDLE COLONIES AND GEORGIA   89   •   THRIVING COLONIES
102   •   FURTHER READING   103

3 | COLONIAL WAYS OF LIFE   105

THE SHAPE OF EARLY AMERICA   106   •   SOCIETY AND ECONOMY IN
THE SOUTHERN COLONIES   115   •   SOCIETY AND ECONOMY IN
NEW ENGLAND   129   •   SOCIETY AND ECONOMY IN THE MIDDLE COLONIES
143   •   COLONIAL CITIES   147   •   THE ENLIGHTENMENT   152   •
THE GREAT AWAKENING   156   •   FURTHER READING   162

4 | THE IMPERIAL PERSPECTIVE   165

ENGLISH ADMINISTRATION OF THE COLONIES   166   •   THE HABIT OF SELF-
GOVERNMENT   173   •   TROUBLED NEIGHBORS   177   •   THE COLONIAL
WARS   183   •   FURTHER READING   197

5 | FROM EMPIRE TO INDEPENDENCE   198

THE HERITAGE OF WAR   199   •   BRITISH POLITICS   201   •   WESTERN
LANDS   202   •   GRENVILLE AND THE STAMP ACT   205   •   FANNING THE
FLAMES   213   •   DISCONTENT ON THE FRONTIER   218   •   A WORSENING
CRISIS   220   •   SHIFTING AUTHORITY   228   •   INDEPENDENCE   234   •
FURTHER READING   239

*P*ART TWO / **BUILDING A NATION**

6 | THE AMERICAN REVOLUTION   245

1776: WASHINGTON'S NARROW ESCAPE   246   •   AMERICAN SOCIETY AT
WAR   249   •   1777: SETBACKS FOR THE BRITISH   254   •   1778: BOTH
SIDES REGROUP   258   •   THE WAR IN THE SOUTH   263   •   NEGOTIATIONS
269   •   THE POLITICAL REVOLUTION   272   •   THE SOCIAL REVOLUTION   276
•   THE EMERGENCE OF AN AMERICAN CULTURE   285   •   FURTHER
READING   290

7 | SHAPING A FEDERAL UNION   291

THE CONFEDERATION   292   •   ADOPTING THE CONSTITUTION   309
•   FURTHER READING   326

8 | The Federalists: Washington and Adams   327

A NEW NATION   327   •   HAMILTON'S VISION OF AMERICA   334   •   THE
REPUBLICAN ALTERNATIVE   342   •   CRISES FOREIGN AND DOMESTIC   345
•   LAND SETTLEMENT   352   •   TRANSFER OF POWER   •   357   •   THE
ADAMS YEARS   360   •   FURTHER READING   369

9 | Republicanism: Jefferson and Madison   371

JEFFERSON IN OFFICE   373   •   DIVISIONS IN THE REPUBLICAN PARTY   384
•   WAR IN EUROPE   387   •   THE WAR OF 1812   392   •   FURTHER
READING   407

10 | Nationalism and Sectionalism   408

ECONOMIC NATIONALISM   409   •   "GOOD FEELINGS"   414   •   CRISES AND
COMPROMISES   420   •   JUDICIAL NATIONALISM   424   •   NATIONALIST
DIPLOMACY   428   •   ONE-PARTY POLITICS   431   •   FURTHER READING   440

Part Three / AN EXPANSIVE NATION

11 | The Jacksonian Impulse   447

SETTING THE STAGE   448   •   NULLIFICATION   454   •   JACKSON'S INDIAN
POLICY   461   •   THE BANK CONTROVERSY   465   •   VAN BUREN AND THE NEW
PARTY SYSTEM   474   •   ASSESSING THE JACKSON YEARS   481   •   FURTHER
READING   483

12 | The Dynamics of Growth   485

AGRICULTURE AND THE NATIONAL ECONOMY   486   •   TRANSPORTATION
AND THE NATIONAL ECONOMY   492   •   THE GROWTH OF INDUSTRY   502
•   THE POPULAR CULTURE   514   •   IMMIGRATION   519   •   ORGANIZED
LABOR   529   •   JACKSONIAN INEQUALITY   532   •   FURTHER READING   534

13 | AN AMERICAN RENAISSANCE: RELIGION, ROMANTICISM, AND REFORM 536

RATIONAL RELIGION   537 • THE SECOND GREAT AWAKENING   539 • ROMANTICISM IN AMERICA   547 • THE FLOWERING OF AMERICAN LITERATURE   552 • EDUCATION   561 • SOME MOVEMENTS FOR REFORM   566 • FURTHER READING   579

14 | MANIFEST DESTINY 581

THE TYLER YEARS   582 • THE WESTERN FRONTIER   585 • MOVING WEST 595 • ANNEXING TEXAS   602 • POLK'S PRESIDENCY   606 • THE MEXICAN WAR   611 • FURTHER READING   621

𝒫ART FOUR / **A HOUSE DIVIDED**

15 | THE OLD SOUTH: AN AMERICAN TRAGEDY   627

DISTINCTIVENESS OF THE OLD SOUTH   628 • WHITE SOCIETY IN THE SOUTH   636 • BLACK SOCIETY IN THE SOUTH   646 • THE CULTURE OF THE SOUTHERN FRONTIER   657 • ANTISLAVERY MOVEMENTS   661 • FURTHER READING   670

16 | THE CRISIS OF UNION   673

SLAVERY IN THE TERRITORIES   674 • THE COMPROMISE OF 1850   682 • FOREIGN ADVENTURES   691 • THE KANSAS-NEBRASKA CRISIS   693 • THE DEEPENING SECTIONAL CRISIS   703 • THE CENTER COMES APART 713 • FURTHER READING   721

17 | THE WAR OF THE UNION   723

END OF THE WAITING GAME   724 • THE BALANCE OF FORCE   731 • THE WAR'S EARLY COURSE   734 • EMANCIPATION   754 • WOMEN AND THE WAR   760 • GOVERNMENT DURING THE WAR   763 • THE FALTERING CONFEDERACY   771 • THE CONFEDERACY'S DEFEAT   777 • A MODERN WAR   784 • FURTHER READING   786

18 | RECONSTRUCTION: NORTH AND SOUTH   789

THE WAR'S AFTERMATH   790   •   THE BATTLE OVER RECONSTRUCTION   796   •
RECONSTRUCTING THE SOUTH   807   •   THE RECONSTRUCTED SOUTH   812
•   THE GRANT YEARS   823   •   FURTHER READING   834

PART FIVE / GROWING PAINS

19 | NEW FRONTIERS: SOUTH AND WEST   839

THE NEW SOUTH   840   •   THE NEW WEST   857   •   FURTHER
READING   885

20 | BIG BUSINESS AND ORGANIZED LABOR   887

THE POST-CIVIL WAR ECONOMY   888   •   ENTREPRENEURS   898   •
A CHANGING ENVIRONMENT FOR WORKERS   908   •   UNION
ORGANIZATION   909   •   FURTHER READING   927

21 | THE EMERGENCE OF URBAN AMERICA   929

AMERICA'S MOVE TO TOWN   931   •   THE NEW IMMIGRATION   936
•   EDUCATION   948   •   THE RISE OF PROFESSIONALISM   953   •   POPULAR
CULTURE   954   •   THEORIES OF SOCIAL CHANGE   965   •   REALISM IN FACT
AND FICTION   969   •   THE SOCIAL GOSPEL   978   •   EARLY EFFORTS AT
URBAN REFORM   980   •   FURTHER READING   988

22 | GILDED-AGE POLITICS AND AGRARIAN REVOLT   989

PARADOXICAL POLITICS   990   •   CORRUPTION AND REFORM   994   •   THE
PROBLEMS OF FARMERS   1012   •   ECONOMIC DEPRESSION AND THE SILVER
SOLUTION   1023   •   FURTHER READING   1029

$\mathcal{P}$ART SIX / **MODERN AMERICA**

23 | AN AMERICAN EMPIRE   1035

TOWARD THE NEW IMPERIALISM   1036 • EXPANSION IN THE PACIFIC   1037 • DIPLOMATIC INCIDENTS IN THE 1880S AND 1890S   1041 • THE SPANISH-AMERICAN WAR   1042 • IMPERIAL RIVALRIES IN EAST ASIA   1058 • ROOSEVELT'S BIG STICK DIPLOMACY   1060 • FURTHER READING   1070

24 | THE PROGRESSIVE ERA   1072

ELEMENTS OF REFORM   1073 • THE FEATURES OF PROGRESSIVISM   1076 • ROOSEVELT'S PROGRESSIVISM   1084 • FROM ROOSEVELT TO TAFT   1092 • WILSON'S PROGRESSIVISM   1100 • THE LIMITS OF PROGRESSIVISM   1114 • FURTHER READING   1116

25 | AMERICA AND THE GREAT WAR   1117

WILSON AND FOREIGN AFFAIRS   1117 • AN UNEASY NEUTRALITY   1122 • AMERICA'S ENTRY INTO THE WAR   1134 • "THE DECISIVE POWER"   1142 • THE FIGHT FOR THE PEACE AT HOME AND ABROAD   1148 • LURCHING FROM WAR TO PEACE   1156 • FURTHER READING   1161

26 | THE MODERN TEMPER   1163

REACTION IN THE TWENTIES   1164 • THE ROARING TWENTIES   1173 • THE CULTURE OF MODERNISM   1185 • FURTHER READING   1194

27 | REPUBLICAN RESURGENCE AND DECLINE   1196

"NORMALCY"   1197 • THE NEW ERA   1207 • PRESIDENT HOOVER, THE ENGINEER   1217 • FURTHER READING   1230

28 | NEW DEAL AMERICA 1232

FROM HOOVERISM TO THE NEW DEAL 1233 • RECOVERY THROUGH
REGULATION 1243 • THE SECOND NEW DEAL 1251 • ROOSEVELT'S
SECOND TERM 1265 • THE LEGACY OF THE NEW DEAL 1276
• CULTURE IN THE THIRTIES 1278 • FURTHER READING 1284

29 | FROM ISOLATION TO GLOBAL WAR 1286

POSTWAR ISOLATIONISM 1287 • WAR CLOUDS 1295 • THE STORM
IN EUROPE 1305 • THE STORM IN THE PACIFIC 1313 • FURTHER
READING 1319

30 | THE SECOND WORLD WAR 1321

AMERICA'S EARLY BATTLES 1322 • MOBILIZATION AT HOME 1324
• SOCIAL EFFECTS OF THE WAR 1328 • THE ALLIED DRIVE TOWARD
BERLIN 1336 • LEAPFROGGING TO TOKYO 1352 • A NEW AGE IS
BORN 1358 • THE FINAL LEDGER 1371 • FURTHER READING 1373

$\mathscr{P}$ART SEVEN / **THE AMERICAN AGE**

31 | THE FAIR DEAL AND CONTAINMENT 1379

DEMOBILIZATION UNDER TRUMAN 1380 • THE COLD WAR 1388
• HARRY GIVES 'EM HELL 1400 • THE COLD WAR HEATS UP 1408
• FURTHER READING 1421

32 | THROUGH THE PICTURE WINDOW: SOCIETY AND CULTURE, 1945–1960 1423

PEOPLE OF PLENTY 1424 • A CONFORMING CULTURE 1438 • CRACKS
IN THE PICTURE WINDOW 1446 • ALIENATION AND LIBERATION 1450
• A PARADOXICAL ERA 1457 • FURTHER READING 1458

33 | CONFLICT AND DEADLOCK: THE EISENHOWER YEARS   1460

"TIME FOR A CHANGE"   1461   •   EISENHOWER'S HIDDEN-HAND
PRESIDENCY   1464   •   FOREIGN INTERVENTION   1471   •   REELECTION
AND FOREIGN CRISES   1480   •   DOMESTIC PROBLEMS   1485
•   FESTERING PROBLEMS ABROAD   1488   •   THE EARLY CIVIL RIGHTS
MOVEMENT   1492   •   ASSESSING THE EISENHOWER YEARS   1498
•   FURTHER READING   1499

34 | NEW FRONTIERS: POLITICS AND SOCIAL CHANGE IN THE 1960s   1501

THE NEW FRONTIER   1502   •   EXPANSION OF THE CIVIL RIGHTS
MOVEMENT   1509   •   FOREIGN FRONTIERS   1515   •   LYNDON JOHNSON
AND THE GREAT SOCIETY   1522   •   FROM CIVIL RIGHTS TO BLACK
POWER   1531   •   THE TRAGEDY OF VIETNAM   1535   •   SIXTIES
CRESCENDO   1543   FURTHER READING   1546

35 | REBELLION AND REACTION IN THE 1960s AND 1970s   1549

THE ROOTS OF REBELLION   1550   •   NIXON AND VIETNAM   1570
•   NIXON AND MIDDLE AMERICA   1577   •   NIXON TRIUMPHANT   1584
•   WATERGATE   1588   •   AN UNELECTED PRESIDENT   1593   •   THE
CARTER INTERREGNUM   1596   •   FURTHER READING   1603

36 | A CONSERVATIVE INSURGENCY   1605

THE REAGAN REVOLUTION   1606   •   REAGAN'S FIRST TERM   1611
•   REAGAN'S SECOND TERM   1619   •   THE BUSH YEARS   1633   •   THE
COMPUTER REVOLUTION   1643   •   FURTHER READING   1647

37 | CULTURAL POLITICS   1649

AMERICA'S CHANGING FACE   1650   •   CULTURAL CONSERVATISM   1655
•   BUSH TO CLINTON   1657   •   DOMESTIC POLICY IN CLINTON'S FIRST
TERM   1662   •   FOREIGN POLICY CHALLENGES   1668   •   REPUBLICAN
INSURGENCY   1673   •   CLINTON'S SECOND TERM   1679   •   FIN-DE-SIÈCLE
AMERICA   1686   •   FURTHER READING   1688

APPENDIX   A1

THE DECLARATION OF INDEPENDENCE   A3   •   ARTICLES OF CONFEDERATION A8   •   THE CONSTITUTION OF THE UNITED STATES   A16   •   PRESIDENTIAL ELECTIONS   A36   •   ADMISSION OF STATES   A44   •   POPULATION OF THE UNITED STATES   A45   •   IMMIGRATION TO THE UNITED STATES, FISCAL YEARS 1820–1990   A46   •   IMMIGRATION BY REGION AND SELECTED COUNTRY OF LAST RESIDENCE, FISCAL YEARS 1820–1989   A48   •   PRESIDENTS, VICE-PRESIDENTS, AND SECRETARIES OF STATE   A55

CREDITS   A61

INDEX   A69

MAPS

The First Migration 6
Pre-Columbian Indian Civilizations in Middle and
   South America 8
Pre-Columbian Indian Civilizations in North America 11
Norse Discoveries 14
Columbus's Voyages 20
Spanish and Portuguese Explorations 25
Spanish Explorations of the Mainland 32
English, French, and Dutch Explorations 41
Land Grants to the Virginia Company 54
Early Virginia and Maryland 64
Early New England Settlements 67
The West Indies, 1600–1800 71
Early Settlements in the South 85
The Middle Colonies 97
European Settlements and Indian Tribes in Early America 100–101
The African Slave Trade, 1500–1800 122
Atlantic Trade Routes 135
Major Immigrant Groups in Colonial America 145
The French in North America 181
Major Campaigns of the French and Indian Wars 189
North America, 1713 194
North America, 1763 195
The Frontier in the 1760s 203
Lexington and Concord, April 19, 1775 228
Major Campaigns in New York and New Jersey, 1776–1777 248
Major Campaigns of 1777: Saratoga and Philadelphia 254

Western Campaigns, 1776–1779 261

Major Campaigns in the South, 1778–1781 264

North America, 1783 271

Western Land Cessions, 1781–1802 295

The Old Northwest, 1785 297

The Vote on the Constitution 323

The Treaty of Greenville, 1795 349

Pinckney's Treaty, 1795 352

Election of 1800 367

Explorations of the Louisiana Purchase 381

The War of 1812: Major Northern Campaigns 397

The War of 1812: Major Southern Campaigns 399

The National Road, 1811–1838 413

Boundary Treaties, 1818–1819 416

The Missouri Compromise, 1820 423

Election of 1828 439

Indian Removal, 1820–1840 465

Election of 1840 480

Population Density, 1820 489

Population Density, 1860 489

Transportation West, About 1840 494–495

The Growth of Railroads, 1850 497

The Growth of Railroads, 1860 499

The Growth of Industry, 1840s 511

The Growth of Cities, 1820 513

The Growth of Cities, 1860 513

The Mormon Trek, 1830–1851 546

The Webster-Ashburton Treaty, 1842 584

Wagon Trails West 592

Election of 1844 608

The Oregon Dispute, 1818–1846 611

The Mexican War: Major Campaigns 616

Cotton Production, 1821 630

Population Growth and Cotton Production, 1821–1859 631

Slave Population, 1820 649

Slave Population, 1860 649

Compromise of 1850 687

The Gadsden Purchase, 1853 693

The Kansas-Nebraska Act, 1854 — 695
Election of 1856 — 703
Election of 1860 — 717
Secession, 1860–1861 — 727
First Bull Run, July 21, 1861 — 735
Campaigns in the West, February–April 1862 — 744
Campaigns in the West, August–October 1862 — 746
The Peninsular Campaign, 1862 — 747
Campaigns in Virginia and Maryland, 1862 — 753
Vicksburg 1863 — 772
Campaigns in the East, 1863 — 774
Grant in Virginia, 1864–1865 — 780
Sherman's Campaigns, 1864–1865 — 782
Reconstruction, 1865–1877 — 822
Election of 1876 — 831
Sharecropping and Tenancy, 1880–1900 — 834
The New West — 862–863
Indian Wars, 1864–1890 — 867
Transcontinental Railroad Lines, 1880s — 892
The Emergence of Cities, 1880 — 932
The Emergence of Cities, 1920 — 933
Women's Suffrage, 1896–1914 — 984
Election of 1896 — 1028
Spanish-American War: The Pacific, 1898 — 1049
Spanish-American War: The Caribbean, 1898 — 1051
U.S. Interests in the Pacific — 1054
U.S. Interests in the Caribbean — 1064
Election of 1912 — 1104
Europe at War, 1914 — 1123
The Western Front, 1918 — 1144
Europe after Versailles — 1152
Election of 1932 — 1236
The Tennessee Valley Authority — 1249
Aggression in Europe, 1935–1939 — 1300
Japanese Expansion before Pearl Harbor — 1314
Military Alliances in 1942 — 1338
War in Europe and Africa, 1942–1945 — 1342–1343
The War in the Pacific, 1942–1945 — 1354–1355

Occupation of Germany and Austria 1397
Election of 1948 1408
The Korean War, 1950 1413
The Korean War, 1950–1953 1413
Election of 1952 1463
Postwar Alliances: The Far East 1478
Postwar Alliances: Europe, North Africa, The Middle East 1482
Election of 1960 1506
Vietnam, 1966 1538
Election of 1968 1545
Election of 1980 1610
Election of 1988 1632

PREFACE

Just as history is never complete, neither is a historical textbook. We have learned much from the responses of readers and instructors to the first four editions of *America: A Narrative History.* Perhaps the most important and reassuring lesson is that our original intention has proved valid: to provide a compelling narrative history of the American experience, a narrative animated by human characters, informed by analysis and social texture, and guided by the unfolding of events. Readers have also endorsed the book's distinctive size and format. *America* is designed to be read and to carry a moderate price.

In a significant attempt to help students grasp the major themes and developments throughout the text, without compromising its intellectual integrity, *America* now contains a new pedagogical program. Part openers lay out the major ideas emphasized in upcoming chapters. Chapter organizers appear on the first page of each chapter and present key idea statements that serve as a guide through the narrative. "Making Connections" boxes appear on the final page of the text of each chapter to link significant events in the current chapter to issues in surrounding chapters. The new pedagogical program as well as the larger format and the two-color design result in an attractive, easy-to-read text that instructors and students should find inviting. The new map program also adds to the attractiveness of the book. Every map in the book has been reconsidered and redrawn, resulting in maps that are clearer and more helpful to the student.

The revisions incorporated in this new edition of *America* highlight aspects of popular culture, beginning with the culture of everyday life: how Americans spent their leisure time, what forms of recreation and entertainment they engaged in, and how the performing arts helped people to understand and deal with traumatic events such as wars and economic depressions. For example, we have incorporated new material dealing with the architecture of colonial homes, the role of taverns in eighteenth-century social life, the celebration of national holidays such as Independence Day, dueling as a manifestation of the cult of honor in the antebellum South, the emergence of professional sports and the performing arts, the popularity of minstrel shows and jazz, and the development of the radio, television, and film industries.

Taken together, these activities, as well as others like them, document the importance of popular culture in unifying a disparate nation. Such collective forms of social activity have served to democratize American life. As cultural life has become more inclusive, it has helped bridge social, racial, and ethnic differences. Such developments in popular culture in turn inform our understanding of major trends in social and political life. Thus, understanding how people of different economic and social classes gathered together at the same taverns and engaged in similar discussions and games helps explain how the diverse elements of the population were able to unite against British rule. Reading about how people of all classes went to the theater or to revival meetings both to watch and listen to what was being said and to socialize with others in the audience contributes to our knowledge of the public life. Likewise, seeing how the southern code of honor led men of all classes to take offense at the slightest perceived insult and to resort to violence to uphold their honor helps us to comprehend how people of the South were willing to resort to war to defend their land and honor. These forms of popular culture and others like them help expand and enrich our understanding of what "history" includes.

The Fifth Edition, like its predecessor, integrates social history into the narrative of American experience, detailing the folkways and contributions of those groups often underrepresented in historical treatments—women, blacks, and ethnic Americans. The Fifth Edition also continues to emphasize the importance of immigration and frontiers to the American experience. We have added a new section describing the journey on the Wilderness Trail into Kentucky, and how these hardy settlers staked out their frontier claims, built their homes, and dealt with their isolation and nurtured their sense of community. Another new section describes black migration to the West after the Civil War, including the efforts of whites to prevent African Americans from leaving the Old South and the difficulties encountered by the migrants who did reach Kansas and the Oklahoma Territory. A new section describes the origins of Sears & Roebuck as a mail-order giant, and how the Sears catalogue supplied the material and psychological needs of those in isolated areas. Also included in the Fifth Edition are new discussions of transportation in the cities and of how immigrants and native-born Americans began to participate in outdoor recreation as well as forming clubs and attending vaudeville and Wild West shows in the cities, and later going to football and baseball games.

In addition to new material dealing with popular culture, frontiers, and cities, the Fifth Edition includes new sections describing the difficulties faced by white women in the South during the Civil War, the treatment of minorities under the New Deal, developments in civil rights after World War II, how major league baseball was integrated, the problem of juvenile delinquency in the 1950s and the rise of rock 'n' roll music, new interpretations of Dwight Eisenhower and Ronald Reagan, a new section detailing the computer revolution, an expanded section on mistrust of government and the militia movement, a section on the "new economy" and Alan Greenspan's monetarist policies as supported by Bill Clinton, a section on the shift to the right of the Supreme Court and the narrowing of affirmative action programs, and a new section on the series of scandals that rocked the Clinton administration.

In preparing this Fifth Edition of *America,* we have benefited from the insights and suggestions of many people. The following scholars have provided close readings of the manuscript at various stages: Lucy Barber (University of California at Davis), Michael Barnhart (State University of New York at Stony Brook), Charles Eagles (University of Mississippi), Tera Hunter (Carnegie-Mellon University), Peter Kolchin (University of Delaware), Christopher Morris (University of Texas at Arlington), David Parker (Kennesaw State University), and Marilyn Westerkamp (University of California at Santa Cruz). Once again we thank our friends at W. W. Norton, especially Steve Forman, Jon Durbin, Sandy Lifland, and Candace Kooyoomjian, for their care and attention along the way.

—George B. Tindall
—David E. Shi

America

PART ONE

A NEW WORLD

Long before Christopher Columbus accidentally discovered the New World in his effort to find a passage to Asia, the tribal peoples he mislabeled "Indians" had occupied and shaped the lands of the Western Hemisphere. The first people to settle the New World were nomadic hunters and gatherers who migrated from northeastern Asia during the last glacial advance of the Ice Age, nearly 20,000 years ago. By the end of the fifteenth century, when Columbus began his voyage west, there were millions of Native Americans living in the Western Hemisphere. Over the centuries, they had developed stable, diverse, and often highly sophisticated societies, some rooted in agriculture, others in trade or imperial conquest.

The Native American cultures were, of course, profoundly affected by the arrival of peoples from Europe and Africa. They were exploited, enslaved, displaced, and exterminated. Yet this conventional tale of conquest oversimplifies the complex process by which Indians, Europeans, and Africans interacted. The Indians were more than passive victims; they were also trading partners and rivals of the transatlantic newcomers. They became enemies and allies, neighbors and advisers, converts and spouses. As such they fully participated in the creation of the new society known as America.

The Europeans who risked their lives to settle in the New World were themselves quite diverse. Young and old, men and women, they came from Spain, Portugal, France, Great Britain, the Netherlands, Italy, and the various German states. A variety of motives inspired them to undertake the transatlantic voyage. Some were adventurers and fortune seekers, eager to find gold and spices. Others were fervent Christians determined to create kingdoms of God in the New World. Still others were convicts, debtors, indentured servants, or political or religious exiles. Many were simply seeking higher wages and greater economic opportunity. A settler in Pennsylvania noted that "poor people (both men and women) of all kinds can here get three times the wages for their labour than they can in England or Wales."

Yet such enticements were not sufficient to attract enough workers to keep up with the rapidly expanding colonial economies. So the Europeans began to force Indians to work for them. But there were never enough of them to meet the unceasing demand. Moreover, they often escaped or were so obstreperous that several colonies banned their use. The Massachusetts legislature did so because Indians were of such "a malicious, surly and re-vengeful spirit; rude and insolent in their behavior, and very ungovern-able."

Beginning early in the seventeenth century, more and more colonists turned to the African slave trade for their labor needs. In 1619 white traders began transporting captured Africans to the English colonies. This development would transform American society in ways that no one at the time envisioned. Few Europeans during the colonial era saw the contra-diction between the New World's promise of individual freedom and the expanding institution of race slavery. Nor did they reckon with the prob-lems associated with introducing into the new society peoples they consid-ered alien and unassimilable.

The intermingling of peoples, cultures, and ecosystems from the three continents of Africa, Europe, and North America gave colonial American society its distinctive vitality and variety. In turn, the diversity of the envi-ronment and climate led to the creation of quite different economies and patterns of living in the various regions of North America. As the original settlements grew into prosperous and populous colonies, the transplanted Europeans had to fashion social institutions and political systems to man-age growth and control tensions.

At the same time, imperial rivalries among the Spanish, French, Eng-lish, and Dutch produced numerous intrigues and costly wars. The mon-archs of Europe had a difficult time trying to manage and exploit this fluid and often volatile colonial society. Many of the colonists, they discov-ered, brought with them to the New World a feisty independence that led them to resent government interference in their affairs. A British official in North Carolina reported that the residents of the Piedmont region were "without any Law or Order. Impudence is so very high [among them], as to be past bearing." As long as the reins of imperial control were loosely applied, the two parties maintained an uneasy partnership. But as the British authorities tightened their control during the mid–eighteenth cen-tury, they met resistance, which became revolt, and culminated in revolu-tion.

1 ∞ THE COLLISION OF CULTURES

he first Americans were Asians. Nearly 20,000 years ago, nomadic peoples from Siberia began crossing the Bering Strait to what is now Alaska, either by island-hopping or by walking across a broad land bridge (Beringia) from which the waters receded during the Ice Ages. They came in pursuit of deer and elephants (the extinct American mammoth), which they hunted over the ice sheets that covered the land. Driven by frigid weather, they drifted southward toward warmth. Once the ice sheets melted and the sea rose again, these migrants to the New World were cut off from the rest of

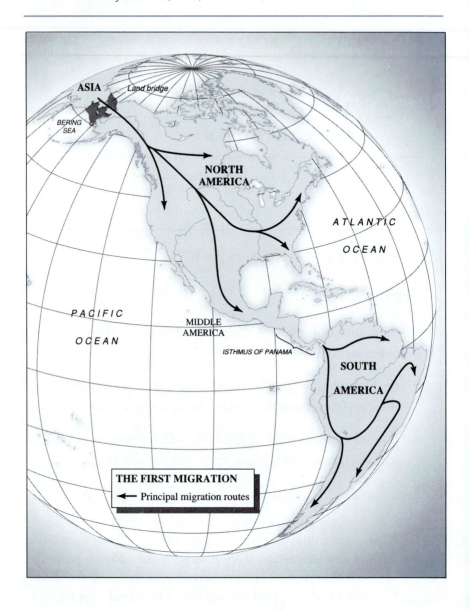

THE FIRST MIGRATION

← Principal migration routes

humanity (except for the short-lived Viking settlements on Greenland and Newfoundland) until Columbus arrived in 1492. Their story remains in the realm of prehistory, the domain of archeologists and anthropologists who must salvage an incomplete record from the rubble of the past: stone tools and weapons, bones, pottery, figurines, ancient dwellings, burial places, scraps of textiles and basketry, and finally bits of oral tradition and the reports of early explorers, all pieced together with the adhesive of informed guesswork.

PRE-COLUMBIAN INDIAN CIVILIZATIONS

Archeological digs add yearly to the sparse fragments of knowledge about the varied and complex societies of pre-Columbian America. The richest finds have been made on either side of the Isthmus of Panama, where Indian civilization peaked in the high altitudes of Mexico and Peru. Indeed, researchers have reconstructed a remarkable story of peoples who built great empires and a monumental architecture, supported by large-scale agriculture and a far-flung commerce: the Mayas, Toltecs, Aztecs, Incas, and others.

EARLY CULTURAL STAGES   By 1492 over 50 million people lived in the Western Hemisphere, about 4 million in what is now the United States. Their cultures ranged from those of Stone Age nomads to those of people in settled agricultural communities, although none of them ever achieved the sophistication of the cultures to the south.

Remnants of stone choppers and scrapers suggest the presence of people in the Americas long before the development, by about 9500 B.C., of projectile points for use on spears and, later, on arrows. As hunting and gathering became a way of life at around 5000 B.C., diet became more varied. It included a number of small creatures such as raccoons and opossums, along with fish and shellfish and wild plants: nuts, greens, berries, and fruits. The Indians then began to settle in permanent or semipermanent villages. They invented fiber snares, basketry, and mills for grinding nuts, and they domesticated the dog and the turkey.

A new cultural stage arrived with the introduction of farming and pottery. In these developments Middle Americans outpaced the tribes farther north and became the center of innovation and cultural diffusion. By about 5000 B.C., Indians of the Mexican highlands were consuming plant foods that became the staples of the New World: chiefly maize (Indian corn), beans, and squash, but also chili peppers, avocados, and pumpkins.

THE MAYAS, AZTECS, AND INCAS   By about 2000–1500 B.C., permanent towns dependent on farming had appeared in Mexico. The more settled life in turn provided leisure for more complex cultures, for the cultivation of religion, crafts, art, science, administration—and warfare. From about A.D. 300–900, Middle America reached the flowering of its classic cultures, with great centers of religion, gigantic pyramids, temple complexes, and courts for ceremonial games, all supported by the surrounding peasant villages. Moreover, the Mayas had developed enough mathematics (including a symbol for zero) and astronomy to devise a calendar more accurate than the one the Europeans were using at the time of Columbus.

About A.D. 900, the classic cultures collapsed, and the religious centers were abandoned. The disappearance of Mayan culture has baffled scholars. Pollen recovered from underground debris suggests that the Mayas overexploited the rain forest upon whose fragile ecosystem they

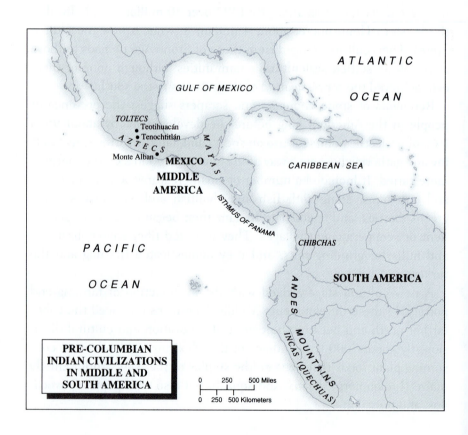

PRE-COLUMBIAN INDIAN CIVILIZATIONS IN MIDDLE AND SOUTH AMERICA

A fresco depicting the social divisions of Mayan society. The king, on the top step, is surrounded by nobles; below, prisoners are guarded by warriors.

depended for survival. Overpopulation also placed added strain on Mayan society. The primary factor, however, was unrelenting civil war among the Mayas themselves. Mayan war parties destroyed each other's cities and took prisoners who were then sacrificed to the gods in theatrical rituals. Whatever the reasons, the Mayas succumbed to the Toltecs, a warlike people who conquered most of the region in the tenth century. But around A.D. 1200, the Toltecs too mysteriously withdrew.

During the time of troubles that followed, the Aztecs arrived from somewhere to the northwest, founded the city of Tenochtitlán (now Mexico City) in 1325, and gradually expanded their control over central Mexico. When the Spaniards invaded in 1519, the Aztec Empire under Montezuma II ruled over perhaps 5 million people—estimates range as high as 20 million. They were held in fairly loose subjugation for the sake of trade and tribute. They also furnished captives to sacrifice on the altars of their bloodthirsty sun god, Huitzilopochtli (symbolized by the hummingbird), to feed and strengthen him for his daily journey across the sky.

Farther south, in what is now Colombia, the Chibchas built a similar empire on a smaller scale. Still farther south the Quechua peoples (better known by the name of their ruler, the Inca) by the fifteenth century

A wooden carving of a mother carrying a child, found in a Hopewell burial mound in southern Ohio.

controlled an empire that stretched a thousand miles along the Andes Mountains from Ecuador to Chile. It was connected by an elaborate system of roads and organized under an autocratic government that dominated life.

INDIAN CULTURES OF NORTH AMERICA   The Indians of the present-day United States reached the stage of agricultural settlements only in the last thousand years before Christ. There were three identifiable cultural peaks: the Adena-Hopewell culture of the Northeast (800 B.C.–A.D. 600); the Mississippian culture of the Southeast (A.D. 600–1500); and the Pueblo-Hohokam culture of the Southwest (400 B.C.–present). None of these developed as fully as the classic cultures of Middle America, although they showed strong influences from the Mayas, Aztecs, and Incas.

The Adena culture, centered in the Ohio Valley, was older but overlapped the similar Hopewell in the same area. The Adena-Hopewell peoples left behind enormous earthworks and burial mounds—sometimes elaborately shaped like great snakes, birds, or other animals. Evidence from the mounds suggests a developed social structure and a specialized division of labor. Moreover, an elaborate trade network spanned the continent. The Hopewellians made ceremonial blades from Rocky Mountain obsidian, bowls from seashells of the Gulf and

Atlantic, ornamental silhouettes of hands, claws, and animals from Appalachian mica, and breastplates and ornaments from copper found near Lake Superior. The Northeastern Indians at the time of colonization were distant heirs to the Hopewellians after their decline as a culture.

The Mississippian culture of the Southeast, centered in the central Mississippi Valley, probably derived its impulse from the Hopewellians, but reached its height later and under greater influence from Middle America—in its intensive agriculture, its pottery, its temple mounds (vaguely resembling pyramids), and its death cults, which involved human torture and sacrifice. The Mississippian culture peaked in the fourteenth and fifteenth centuries, and collapsed finally because of diseases transmitted from European contacts.

The Mississippian culture touched all the pre-Columbian peoples of the Southeast and also those far into the Midwest. As late as the eighteenth century, tribes of the Southeast still practiced their annual busk, or green corn ceremony, a ritual of renewal in which pottery was smashed, dwellings were cleaned out, all fires were quenched, and a new fire was kindled in the temple.

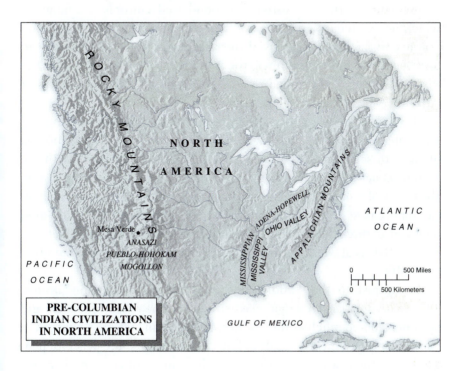

PRE-COLUMBIAN INDIAN CIVILIZATIONS IN NORTH AMERICA

Ruins of Anasazi cliff dwellings at Mesa Verde, Colorado. The circular chamber to the left is a ceremonial kiva.

The arid Southwest hosted irrigation-based cultures, elements of which persist today and heirs of which (the Hopis, Zunis, and others) still live in the adobe pueblos of their ancestors. The most widespread and best known of the cultures, the Anasazi ("the ancient ones," in the Navajo language), developed in the "four corners" where the states of Arizona, New Mexico, Colorado, and Utah now meet.

The Anasazis never gave up their traditional patterns of hunting and gathering, eating small mammals, rodents, reptiles, birds, and insects, along with seeds, mesquite beans, yucca fruits, and berries. With the coming of agriculture, they perfected techniques of "dry farming," using the traces of ground water and catching the runoff in garden terraces or, in some cases, extensive irrigation works. They lived in baked-mud adobe structures that were built four and five stories high and were often located, as at Mesa Verde, Colorado, in canyons underneath protective cliffs.

In contrast to the Middle American and Mississippian cultures, Anasazi society lacked a rigid class structure. The religious leaders and warriors labored much as the rest of the people. In fact, they engaged in warfare only as a means of self-defense (Hopi means "the peaceful people"), and there was little evidence of human sacrifice or human trophies. Toward the end of the thirteenth century a lengthy drought and the pressure of new arrivals from the north began to restrict the territory of the Anasazis. Into their peaceful world came the aggressive Navajos and Apaches, followed two centuries later by Spaniards marching up from the south.

Even the most developed Indian societies of the sixteenth century were ill equipped to resist the dynamic European cultures invading their world. There were large and fatal gaps in Indian knowledge and technology. Southwestern Indians had invented etching, but in the New World the wheel was found only on a few toys. The Indians of Mexico had copper and bronze but no iron except a few specimens of meteorites. Messages were conveyed by patterns in beads in the Northeast and by knotted cords among the Incas, but there was no true writing except for the hieroglyphs of Middle America. The Indians had domesticated dogs, turkeys, and llamas, but horses were unknown until the Spaniards came astride their enormous "dogs."

Disunity everywhere—civil disorders and rebellions plagued the Aztecs, Mayas, and Incas—left the peoples of the New World open to division and conquest. As it turned out, however, the centralized societies in the south were as vulnerable as the scattered tribes farther north. The capture or death of their rulers left them in disarray and subjection. The loosely organized tribes of North America (over one thousand in all) made the Europeans pay more dearly for their conquest, but when open conflict erupted, arrows and tomahawks were seldom a match for guns.

Despite such disadvantages, the Indians resisted European invaders for centuries. They displayed an amazing capacity for adapting to changing circumstances, incorporating European technology and weaponry, forging new alliances, changing their own community structures, and, in numerous instances, converting the Europeans to their way of life. For centuries, scholars glossed over the awkward fact that many Spanish, English, and French settlers had voluntarily joined Indian society or had chosen to stay after being captured.

European Visions of America

Long before Columbus, America lived in the fantasies of Europeans. The vast unknown beyond the sea held a prominent place in the

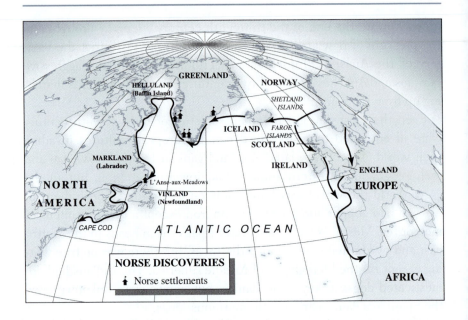

mythology of ancient Greece. In the west, toward the sunset which marked the end of day and symbolically the end of life, was supposedly an earthly paradise. The vision of America as a place of rebirth, a New Eden freed from the historic sins of the Old World, still colors the self-image of the American people.

Norse discoveries of the tenth and eleventh centuries are the earliest that can be verified, and even they have dissolved into legend. Like Eskimos crossing the Bering Strait to the east, the Norsemen went island-hopping across the North Atlantic to the west. Before about A.D. 870 they conquered Iceland from Irish settlers while other Vikings terrorized the coasts of Europe. Around 985 an Icelander named Erik the Red colonized the west coast of an icebound island he deceptively called Greenland—Erik was the New World's first real-estate booster—and about a year later a trader missed Greenland and sighted land beyond. Knowing of this, Thorvald Eriksson, son of Erik the Red, sailed out from Greenland about A.D. 1001 and sighted the coasts of Helluland (Baffin Island), Markland (Labrador), and Vinland (Newfoundland), where he settled for the winter. Speculation had long placed Vinland as far south as Rhode Island or Chesapeake Bay, but in 1963 a Norwegian investigator uncovered the ruins of a number of Norse houses at L'Anse-aux-Meadows, on the northern coast of Newfoundland. This almost surely was the Vinland of the Norse sagas.

The Norse discoveries of the New World are fascinating, but they have no connection to later American history unless Columbus heard of them, which is doubtful. The Norsemen withdrew from North America in the face of hostile natives, and the Greenland colonies vanished mysteriously in the fifteenth century. Nowhere in Europe had the forces yet developed that would impel adventurers and subdue the New World.

THE EXPANSION OF EUROPE

The age of discovery coincided with the opening of the modern period in European history. The expansion of Europe derived from, and in turn affected, the peculiar patterns and institutions that distinguished modern times from the medieval. These included the revival of learning and the rise of the inquiring spirit; the rise of trade, towns, and modern corporations; the decline of feudalism and the rise of national states; the Protestant Reformation and the Catholic Counter-Reformation; and, on the darker side, some old sins—greed, conquest, exploitation, oppression, racism, and slavery—that quickly defiled the fancied innocence of the New Eden.

RENAISSANCE GEOGRAPHY For more than two centuries before Columbus, the mind of Europe quickened with the fledgling Renaissance: the rediscovery of ancient classics, the rebirth of secular learning, the spirit of inquiry, all of which spread the more rapidly after Johann Gutenberg's invention of movable type around 1440. Learned Europeans of the fifteenth century held in almost reverential awe the authority of ancient learning. The age of discovery was especially influenced by the ancient understanding of geography. As early as the sixth century B.C., the Pythagoreans had taught the sphericity of the earth, and in the third century B.C., the earth's size was computed very nearly correctly. All this was accepted in Renaissance universities on the word of Aristotle, and the story that Columbus was trying to prove this theory is one of those durable falsehoods that will not disappear in the face of the evidence. No informed person at that time thought the earth was flat.

Progress in the art of navigation accompanied the revival of learning. The precise origin of the magnetic compass is unknown, but the principle was known by the twelfth century, and in the fifteenth century

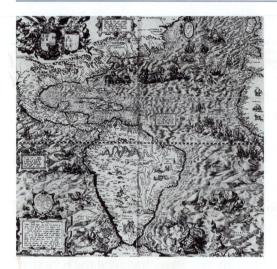

An engraved map of North, Central, and South America, compiled by Spanish pilot Diego Gutérrez in the mid–sixteenth century, details the region's geographical features, its peoples, and their settlements.

mariners employed the astrolabe and cross-staff long used by land-locked astronomers to sight stars and find the latitude. Steering across the open sea, however, remained a matter of dead reckoning. A ship's master set his course along a given latitude and calculated it from the angle of the North Star, or with less certainty the sun, estimating speed by the eye. Longitude remained a matter of guesswork, since accurate timepieces were needed to obtain it. Ship's clocks were too inaccurate until more precise chronometers were developed in the eighteenth century.

THE GROWTH OF TRADE, TOWNS, AND NATION-STATES The forces that would invade and reshape the New World found their focus in the rising towns, the centers of a growing trade that slowly broadened the narrow horizons of feudal Europe. In its farthest reaches, this trade moved either overland or through the eastern Mediterranean all the way to East Asia, whence Europeans imported medicine, silks, precious stones, dye-woods, perfumes, and rugs. There they also purchased the spices—pepper, nutmeg, clove—so essential to the preserving of food, especially in the countries of southern Europe, where the warm, humid climate accelerated spoilage. The trade gave rise to a merchant class and to the idea of corporations through which stockholders would share risks and profits.

The trade was both chancy and costly. Goods commonly passed from hand to hand, from ships to pack trains and back to ships along the way, subject to levies by all sorts of princes and potentates, with each middleman pocketing whatever he could. The Muslim world, from Spain across North Africa into Central Asia, lay athwart all the important trade routes, and this added to the hazards. Little wonder, then, that Europeans should dream of an all-water route to the riches of East Asia and the Indies. Travelers' stories also stirred interest in the Orient. The Venetian Marco Polo provided the most famous account in 1298–1299. Christopher Columbus had a Latin version, with margins heavily annotated in his own hand.

Another spur to exploration was the rise of national states, with kings and queens who had the power and the means to sponsor the search. The growth of the merchant class went hand in hand with the growth of centralized power. Merchants wanted uniform currencies, trade laws, and the elimination of trade barriers. They thus became natural allies of the sovereigns who could meet their needs. In turn, merchants and university-trained professionals supplied the monarchs with money, lawyers, and officials. The Crusades to capture the Holy Land (1095–1270) had also advanced the process of international trade and exploration. They had brought the West into contact with Eastern autocracy and had decimated the ranks of the feudal lords. And new means of warfare—the use of gunpowder and standing armies—further weakened the independence of the nobility. By 1492 the map of western Europe showed several united kingdoms: France, where in 1453 Louis XI had emerged from the Hundred Years' War as head of a unified state; England, where in 1485 Henry VII emerged victorious after thirty years of civil strife, the Wars of the Roses; Spain, where in 1469 Ferdinand of Aragon and Isabella of Castile united two great kingdoms in marriage; and Portugal, where even earlier, in 1385, John I had fought off the Castilians and assured national independence.

THE VOYAGES OF COLUMBUS

It was in Portugal, with the guidance of John's son, Prince Henry the Navigator, that exploration and discovery began in earnest. In 1422 Prince Henry sent out his first expedition to map the coast of Africa. Driven partly by the hope of outflanking the Islamic world, partly by the hope of trade, the Portuguese by 1446 reached Cape Verde, then the equator, and by 1482 the Congo River. In 1488 Bartholomew Diaz rounded the Cape of Good Hope at Africa's southern tip, and in 1498 Vasco da Gama went on to India.

Christopher Columbus meanwhile was learning his trade in the school of Portuguese seamanship. Born in 1451, the son of an Italian weaver, Columbus took to the sea at an early age, making up for his lack of formal education by teaching himself geography, navigation, and Latin. By the 1480s, Columbus—a tall, red-haired, long-faced man with a ruddy complexion, oval eyes, and a prominent nose—was an experienced seaman. Dazzled by the prospect of Asian riches, he hatched a scheme to reach the Indies (India, China, the East Indies, or Japan) by sailing west. After the courts of Portugal, England, and France showed little interest in his plan, Columbus won the support of Ferdinand and Isabella, the Spanish monarchs, and himself raised much of the money needed to finance the voyage. The legend that the queen had to hock the crown jewels is as spurious as the fable that Columbus set out to prove the earth was round.

Columbus chartered one seventy-five-foot ship, the *Santa María,* and the Spanish city of Palos supplied two smaller caravels, the *Pinta* and *Niña.* From Palos this little squadron, with eighty-seven officers and men, set sail westward for what Columbus thought was Asia. The first leg of the journey went well, but then the breeze lagged, the days

A 1493 woodcut depicting Columbus's discovery of America. At left is Spain's King Ferdinand, who with Queen Isabella authorized the expedition.

passed, and the crew began to grumble about their captain's farfetched plan. Columbus finally promised that the expedition would turn back if land were not sighted in three days.

Early on October 12, 1492, after thirty-three days at sea, a lookout on the *Santa María* yelled *"Tierra! Tierra!* [Land! Land!]" It was an island in the Bahamas that Columbus named San Salvador (Blessed Savior). According to Columbus's own reckoning he was near the Indies, so he called the island people *los Indios*. He described the "Indians" as naked people, "very well made, of very handsome bodies and very good faces." The Arawaks paddled out in dugout logs, which they called canoes, and offered gifts to the strangers. Their warm generosity and docile temperament led Columbus to write in his journal that "they invite you to share anything that they possess, and show as much love as if their hearts went with it." Yet he added that "with fifty men they could all be subjugated and compelled to do anything one wishes."

At the moment, however, Columbus was not interested in enslaving noble savages; he was seeking the Indies. He therefore continued to search through the Bahamian Cays down to Cuba, a place name that suggested Cipangu (Japan), and then eastward to the island he named Española (or Hispaniola, now the site of Haiti and the Dominican Republic), where he first found significant amounts of gold jewelry. Columbus learned of, but did not encounter until his second voyage, the fierce Caribs of the Lesser Antilles. The Caribbean Sea was named after them, and, because of their alleged bad habits, the word "cannibal" was derived from a Spanish version of their name (Caníbal).

On the night before Christmas the *Santa María* ran aground off Hispaniola, and Columbus, still believing he had reached Asia, decided to return home. He left about forty men behind in camp and seized a dozen natives to present as gifts to Spain's royal couple. When Columbus reached Palos, the news of his discovery spread rapidly throughout Europe, and Ferdinand and Isabella instructed him to prepare for a second voyage. They also set about shoring up their legal claim against Portugal's pretensions to the newly discovered lands. When the pope, who was Spanish, interceded on Spain's behalf, Spain and Portugal reached a compromise agreement called the Treaty of Tordesillas (1494), which drew an imaginary line west of the Cape Verde Islands and stipulated that the area west of the line would be a Spanish sphere of exploration and settlement.

Columbus returned across the Atlantic in 1493 with seventeen ships and some 1,200 men, as well as royal instructions to "treat the Indians very well and affectionately without causing them any annoyance whatever." Once back in the New World, Admiral Columbus discovered that the camp he had left behind was in chaos. The unsupervised soldiers had run amok, raping native women, robbing Indian villages, and, as Columbus's son later added, "committing a thousand excesses for which they were mortally hated by the Indians." The Indians finally struck back and killed ten Spaniards. A furious Columbus immediately launched a wholesale attack on the Indian villages. The Spaniards, armed with crossbows, guns, and ferocious dogs, decimated the native defenders and loaded 500 of them onto ships bound for the slave market in Spain.

Columbus thereafter ventured out across the Caribbean Sea. He found the Lesser Antilles, explored the coast of Cuba, discovered Jamaica, and finally returned to Spain in 1496. On a third voyage in 1498 Columbus found Trinidad and explored the northern coast of South America. He led a fourth voyage in 1502, during which he sailed along the coast of Central America, still looking in vain for Asia. Marooned on Jamaica more than a year, he finally returned to Spain in 1504. He died two years later.

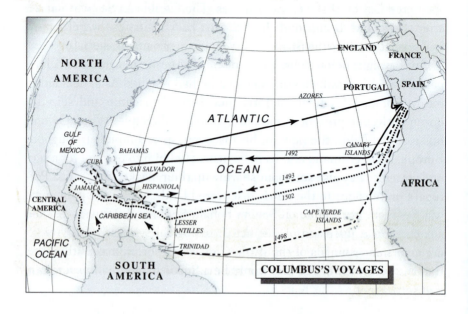

COLUMBUS'S VOYAGES

To the end, Columbus refused to believe that he had discovered anything other than outlying parts of Asia. Full awareness that a great land mass lay between Europe and Asia dawned on Europeans very slowly. By one of history's greatest ironies, this led the New World to be named not for its discoverer but, in what one writer has called a comedy of errors, for another Italian, Amerigo Vespucci.

Vespucci was a Florentine merchant and navigator sent to Spain as an agent of the ruling de Medici family. He knew Columbus and may have been among those who welcomed him back from the first voyage. He certainly helped outfit his ships for the second and third. Later, Vespucci himself made several voyages to the New World. Both he and Columbus used the expression "New World," but an Italian printer pulled it out of a Vespucci letter, and used it as the title of a Latin translation, *Mundus Novus*. Then, in 1507, the young geographer Martin Waldseemüller published a new Latin edition of Ptolemy's *Cosmography*. Out to make a name for himself, Waldseemüller appended another Vespucci letter which, either by design or by a printer's error, credited Vespucci with having reached South America in 1497, one year before Columbus did. For that reason Waldseemüller suggested that the new continent, "the fourth part of the world"—along with Europe, Asia, and Africa—be named "America" in his honor.

Actually, Amerigo Vespucci's first voyage began in 1499, and there is no firm evidence that he, any more than Columbus, ever believed he had touched anything more than a part of East Asia—or perhaps a continent to its southeast. So many writers and mapmakers followed Waldseemüller's idea, however, that the name was entrenched before Vespucci's right to the honor was questioned.

THE GREAT BIOLOGICAL EXCHANGE

The first European contacts with the New World began a diffusion of cultures, an exchange of such magnitude and pace as humanity had never known before. It was in fact more than a diffusion of cultures: it was a diffusion of distinctive biological systems. If anything, the plants and animals of the two worlds were more different than the people and their ways of life. Europeans, for instance, had never seen such creatures as the fearsome (if harmless) iguana, flying squirrels,

A tortoise, drawn by John White, one of the earliest English settlers in America.

fish with whiskers like cats, snakes that rattled "castanets," or anything quite like several other species: bison, cougars, armadillos, opossums, sloths, tapirs, anacondas, electric eels, vampire bats, toucans, Andean condors, and hummingbirds. Among the few domesticated animals, they could recognize the dog and the duck, but turkeys, guinea pigs, llamas, and alpacas were all new. Nor did the Native Americans know of horses, cattle, pigs, sheep, goats, and (maybe) chickens, which soon arrived from Europe in abundance. Yet, within a half century, whole islands of the Caribbean would be overrun by pigs, whose ancestors were bred in Spain.

The exchange of plant life worked an even greater change, a revolution in the diets of both hemispheres. Before the Great Discovery three main staples of the modern diet were unknown in the Old World: maize, potatoes (sweet and white), and many kinds of beans (snap, kidney, lima, and others). The white potato, although commonly called "Irish," actually migrated from South America to Europe and only reached North America with the Scotch-Irish immigrants of the 1700s. Other New World food plants included peanuts, squash, peppers, tomatoes, pumpkins, pineapples, sassafras, papayas, guavas, avocados, cacao (the source of chocolate), and chicle (for chewing gum). Europeans in turn soon introduced rice, wheat, barley, oats, wine grapes, melons, coffee, olives, bananas, "Kentucky" bluegrass, daisies, and dandelions to the New World.

The beauty of the exchange was that the food plants were more complementary than competitive. They grew in different soils and climates, or on different schedules. Indian corn, it turned out, could flourish almost anywhere—high or low, hot or cold, wet or dry. It spread quickly throughout the world. Before the end of the 1500s, American maize and sweet potatoes were staple crops in China. The green revolution exported from the Americas thus helped nourish a worldwide population explosion probably greater than any since the invention of agriculture. Plants domesticated by Native Americans now make up about a third of the world's food plants.

Europeans, moreover, adopted many Native American devices: canoes, snowshoes, moccasins, hammocks, kayaks, ponchos, dogsleds, and toboggans. The rubber ball and the game of lacrosse had Indian origins. New words entered the languages of Europeans: wigwam, teepee, papoose, succotash, hominy, tobacco, moose, skunk, opossum, woodchuck, chipmunk, tomahawk, hickory, pecan, raccoon, and hundreds of others—and new terms in translation: warpath, warpaint, paleface, medicine man, firewater. And the natives left the map dotted with place names of Indian origin long after they were gone, from Miami to Yakima, from Penobscot to Yuma.

There were still other New World contributions: tobacco and a number of other drugs, including coca (for cocaine and novocaine), curare (a muscle relaxant), and cinchona bark (for quinine), and one common medical device, the enema tube. But Europeans also exposed the New World inhabitants to exotic new illnesses they could not handle. Even minor European diseases such as measles turned killer in the bodies of Indians who had never encountered them and thus had built up no immunity. Major diseases such as smallpox and typhus killed all the more speedily. According to an account from the first English colony, sent by Sir Walter Raleigh on Roanoke Island, within a few days after Englishmen visited the Indian villages of the neighborhood "people began to die very fast, and many in short space. . . . The disease also was so strange that they neither knew what it was, nor how to cure it." Epidemics ravaged the native population. In central Mexico alone, some

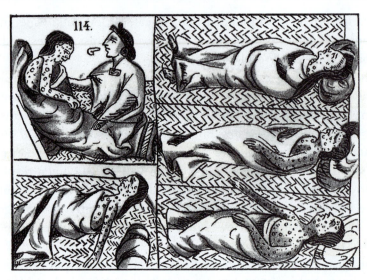

A devastating smallpox epidemic depicted in an Aztec manuscript.

8 million people, perhaps a third of the entire population, died of disease within a decade after the Spaniards arrived. In what is now Texas, one Spanish explorer noted, "half the natives died from a disease of the bowels and blamed us."

PROFESSIONAL EXPLORERS

Undeterred by new diseases and encouraged by Columbus's discoveries, professional explorers, mostly Italians, hired themselves out to the highest bidder to look for a western passage to Asia. They probed the shorelines of America during the early sixteenth century in the vain search for an opening, and thus increased by leaps and bounds European knowledge of the New World. The first to sight the North American continent was John Cabot, a Venetian whom Henry VII of England sponsored. Acting on the theory that China was opposite England, Cabot sailed across the North Atlantic in 1497. His landfall at what the king called "the new founde lande" gave England the basis for a later claim to all of North America. During the early sixteenth century, however, the English grew so preoccupied with internal divisions and conflicts with France that they failed to capitalize on Cabot's discoveries.

Only fishermen exploited the teeming waters of the Grand Banks. In 1513 the Spaniard Vasco Núñez de Balboa became the first European to sight the Pacific Ocean, but only after he had crossed the Isthmus of Panama on foot.

The Portuguese, meanwhile, went the other way. In 1498, while Columbus prowled the Caribbean, Vasco da Gama sailed around Africa and soon set up the trading posts of a commercial empire stretching from India to the Moluccas (or Spice Islands) of Indonesia. The Spaniards, however, reasoned that the line of demarcation established by the Treaty of Tordesillas ran around the other side of the earth as well. Hoping to show that the Moluccas lay near South America within the Spanish sphere, Ferdinand Magellan, a haughty Portuguese seaman in the employ of Spain, set out to find a passage through or around South America. Departing Spain in 1519, he found his way through the dangerous strait that now bears his name, then moved far to the north. On a journey far longer than he had anticipated, he touched upon Guam and eventually made a landfall in the Philippines, where he lost his life in a fight with the natives.

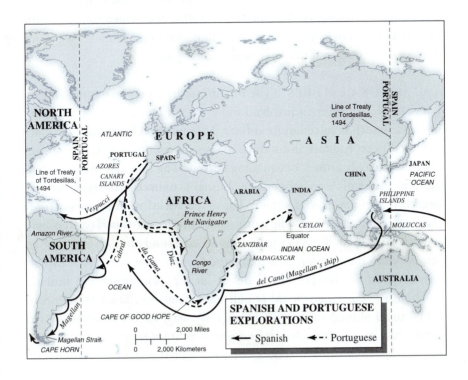

SPANISH AND PORTUGUESE EXPLORATIONS

← Spanish ◀-- Portuguese

Magellan's remaining crew members made their way to the Moluccas, picked up a cargo of spices, and returned to Spain in 1522. This first voyage around the globe quickened Spanish ambitions for empire in the East, but after some abortive attempts at establishing themselves there, the Spaniards, beset by war with France, sold Portugal their claims to the Moluccas. From 1565, however, Spaniards would begin to penetrate the Philippines, discovered by Magellan and named for the Spanish prince who became Philip II. In the seventeenth century, the English and the Dutch would oust Portugal from most of its empire, but for a century the East Indies were Portuguese.

THE SPANISH EMPIRE

During the sixteenth century, the New World was a Spanish preserve, except for the Portuguese colony of Brazil. The Caribbean Sea served as the funnel through which Spanish power entered the New World. After establishing colonies on Hispaniola and at Santo Domingo, which became the capital of the West Indies, the Spanish proceeded eastward to Puerto Rico (1508) and westward to Cuba (1511–1514). Their motives were explicit. Said one soldier: "We came here to serve God and the king, and also to get rich."

A CLASH OF CULTURES The encounter between Spaniards and Indians in North America involved more than a clash between different peoples. It also involved quite different forms of technological development. Where Indians used dugout canoes for transport, Europeans sailed on heavily armed, oceangoing vessels. The Spanish ships not only carried human cargo; they also brought with them steel swords, firearms, explosives, and armor. These advanced military tools struck fear into many Indians. A Spanish priest in Florida observed that gunpowder "frightens the most valiant and courageous Indian and renders him slave to the white man's command." Such weaponry helps explain why the Europeans were able to defeat far superior numbers of Indians.

The Europeans enjoyed other cultural advantages. The only domestic four-legged animal in North America, for example, was the dog. The Spaniards, on the other hand, brought with them horses, pigs, and cattle, all of which offered sources of food and leather. Horses provided

Cortés and an interpreter hold discussions with the Aztec emperor Montezuma at Tenochtitlán. In the foreground are deer, quail, and maize, gifts from the Aztecs to Cortés. Cortés's wiles would soon destroy Montezuma and enslave the Aztec nation.

greater speed in battle and also introduced a decided psychological advantage. "The most essential thing in new lands is horses," reported one of Coronado's soldiers. "They instill the greatest fear in the enemy and make the Indians respect the leaders of the army." Even more feared among the Indians were the greyhound dogs that the Spaniards used to guard their camps. Incredibly fast, they were trained to attack Indians, tearing their limbs away and scaring them into surrender.

CORTÉS'S CONQUEST   In the islands, Spaniards found only primitive cultures of hunters and gatherers. On the mainland, however, they discovered civilizations that were quite sophisticated but whose people were almost as vulnerable to European power and infectious diseases as were the people in the more primitive cultures. The first conquest of a major civilization on the mainland began in 1519, when Hernando Cortés and 600 men landed on the site of Vera Cruz, which he founded. Then, far exceeding his orders, Cortés's men set about a dar-

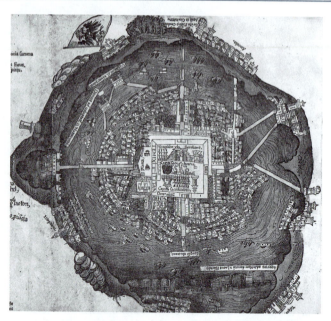

A map of Tenochtitlán, capital of the Aztec empire, drawn by Cortés, 1524.

ing conquest of the Aztec Empire. The 200-mile march from Vera Cruz through difficult mountain passes to the magnificent Aztec capital of Tenochtitlán (Mexico City), and the subjugation of the Aztecs, was one of the most remarkable—and tragic—feats in human history.

Cortés made the most of his few assets. An acute judge of character and a gifted diplomat as well as military leader, he landed in a region where the local Indians were still fighting off the spread of Aztec power and were ready to embrace new allies, especially those possessing strange animals (horses) and powerful weapons. By a combination of threats and deceptions, Cortés entered Tenochtitlán peacefully and made the emperor, Montezuma, his puppet. Cortés explained to Montezuma why the invasion was necessary: "We Spaniards have a disease of the heart that only gold can cure."

After taking all the gold the Aztecs had already gathered, the Spanish forced Montezuma to provide Indian laborers to mine more. This state of affairs lasted until the spring of 1520, when disgruntled Aztecs, regarding Montezuma as a traitor, rebelled, stoned him to death, and attacked Cortés's forces. The Spaniards lost about a third of their men as they fought their way out of the city. Their Indian allies remained loyal, however, and Cortés gradually regrouped. In 1521 he took the city again. After that, the resistance collapsed, and Cortés and his officers simply replaced the former Aztec overlords as rulers over the Indian empire.

In doing so, they set the style for other conquistadores to follow, who within twenty years had established a Spanish empire far larger than Rome's had ever been. Between 1522 and 1528, various lieutenants of Cortés conquered the remnants of Indian culture in Yucatán and Guatemala. In 1531 Francisco Pizarro led a band of soldiers down the Pacific coast from Panama toward Peru, where they attacked and subdued the Inca Empire. From Peru conquistadores (Spanish conquerors) extended Spanish authority through Chile by about 1553 and to the north, in present-day Colombia, in 1536–1538.

SPANISH AMERICA   The Spaniards sought to displace the "pagan" civilizations throughout the Americas with their Catholic-based culture. Believing that God was on their side in this cultural exchange, the Spaniards carried with them an intoxicating sense of mission that bred both intolerance and zeal. The conquistadores transferred to America a system known as the *encomienda,* whereby favored officers became privileged landowners who controlled Indian villages or groups of villages. As *encomenderos,* they were called upon to protect and care for the villages and support missionary priests. In turn, they could levy tribute in goods and labor. Spanish America therefore developed from the start a society of extremes: conquistadores and *encomenderos* who sometimes found wealth beyond the dreams of avarice, if more often just a crude affluence, and subject peoples who were held in poverty.

What were left of them, that is. By the mid-1500s Indians were nearly extinct in the West Indies, reduced more by European diseases than by Spanish brutalities. To take their place, as early as 1503 the colonizers began to transport slaves from Africa, the first in a wretched traffic that eventually would carry over 9 million people across the Atlantic in bondage. In all of Spain's New World empire, by one informed estimate, the Indian population dropped from about 50 million at the outset to 4 million in the seventeenth century, and slowly rose again to 7.5 million. Whites, who totaled no more than 100,000 in the mid–sixteenth century, numbered over 3 million by the end of the colonial period.

The Indians, however, did not always lack advocates. In many cases Catholic missionaries offered a sharp contrast to the conquistadores. Setting examples of self-denial, they ventured into remote areas, usually without weapons or protection, to spread the gospel—and often suffered martyrdom for their efforts. Among them rose defenders of the Indians, the most noted of whom was Bartolomé de las Casas, a priest in Hispaniola and later bishop of Chiapas, Guatemala, author of *A Brief Relation of the Destruction of the Indies* (1552). Las Casas won some limited reforms from the Spanish government, but ironically had a more lasting influence in giving rise to the so-called Black Legend of Spanish cruelty, which the enemies of Spain gleefully spread abroad, often as a cover for their own abuses.

From such violently contrasting forces, Spanish America gradually developed into a settled society. The independent conquistadores were replaced quickly by a second generation of bureaucrats and the *encomienda* was replaced by the *hacienda* (a great farm or ranch) as the claim to land became a more important source of wealth than the claim to labor. From the outset, in sharp contrast to the later English experience, the crown regulated every detail of colonial administration. After 1524 the Council of the Indies, directly under the crown, issued laws for America, served as the appellate court for civil cases arising in the colonies, and administered the bureaucracy.

The culture of Spanish America would be fundamentally unlike the English-speaking culture that would arise to the north. In fact, a difference already existed in pre-Columbian America, with largely nomadic tribes to the north and the more complex civilizations in Mesoamerica. On the latter world, the Spaniards imposed an overlay of their own peculiar ways, but without uprooting the deeply planted cultures they found. Catholicism, which for long centuries had absorbed pagan gods and transformed pagan feasts into such holy days as Christmas and Easter, in turn adapted Indian beliefs and rituals to its own purposes. The Mexican Virgin of Guadalupe, for instance, evoked memories of feminine divinities in native cults. Thus Spanish America, in the words of modern-day Mexican writer Octavio Paz, became a land of superimposed pasts. "Mexico City was built on the ruins of Tenochtitlán, the Aztec city that was built in the likeness of Tula, the Toltec city that was built in the likeness of Teotihuacán, the first great city on the American continent. Every Mexican bears within him this continuity, which goes back two thousand years."

SPANISH EXPLORATIONS   For more than a century after Columbus, no European power other than Spain had more than a brief foothold in the New World. Spain had the advantage not only of having sponsored the discovery, but of having stumbled onto those parts of America that would bring the quickest profits. While France and England struggled with domestic quarrels and religious conflict, Spain had forged an intense national unity. Under Charles V, heir to the throne of Austria and the Netherlands, and Holy Roman Emperor to boot, Spain dominated Europe as well as the New World. The treasures of the Aztecs and the Incas added to Spain's power, but they would prove to be a mixed blessing. The easy reliance on American gold and silver undermined the basic economy of Spain and tempted the government to live beyond its means, while American bullion contributed to price inflation throughout Europe.

For most of the colonial period, much of what is now the United States belonged to Spain, and Spanish culture has left a lasting imprint upon American ways of life. Spain's colonial presence lasted more than three centuries, much longer than either England's or France's, and its possessions were much more far-reaching. New Spain was centered in Mexico, but its frontiers extended from the Florida Keys to Alaska and included areas not currently thought of as formerly Spanish, such as the Deep South (Memphis was founded as San Fernando, Vicksburg as Nogales) and the lower Midwest. Hispanic place names—San Francisco, Santa Barbara, Los Angeles, San Diego, Tucson, Santa Fe, San Antonio, Pensacola, and St. Augustine—survive to this day, as do Hispanic influences in art, architecture, literature, music, law, and cuisine.

The Spanish encounter with Native American populations and their diverse cultures produced a two-way exchange by which the two societies blended, coexisted, and interacted. To be sure, each side was more concerned with preserving its own integrity and dealing with its own internal squabbles than with understanding the other. But even when locked in mortal conflict and riven with hostility and mutual suspicion, the two cultures necessarily affected each other. The imperative of survival forced both natives and conquerors to devise creative adaptations.

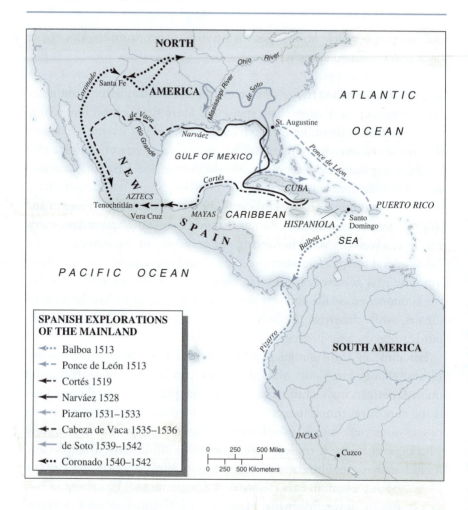

SPANISH EXPLORATIONS OF THE MAINLAND

◄··· Balboa 1513
◄ – Ponce de León 1513
◄ · Cortés 1519
◄ Narváez 1528
◄ ·· Pizarro 1531–1533
◄ – Cabeza de Vaca 1535–1536
◄ de Soto 1539–1542
◄··· Coronado 1540–1542

In other words, this frontier world, while permeated with violence, coercion, and intolerance, also produced mutual accommodation that enabled two living traditions to persist side by side. For example, the Pueblo Indians of the Southwest practiced two religious traditions simultaneously, adopting Spanish Catholicism while at the same time retaining the essence of their own inherited faith.

The "Spanish borderlands" of the southern United States preserve many reminders of the Spanish presence. The earliest known exploration (of Florida) was made in 1513 by Juan Ponce de León, then governor of Puerto Rico. Meanwhile, Spanish explorers skirted the Gulf coast from Florida to Vera Cruz, scouted the Atlantic coast from Cuba to Newfoundland, and established a short-lived colony on the Carolina coast.

Sixteenth-century knowledge of the interior came mostly from would-be conquistadores who sought but found little to plunder in the hinterlands. The first, Pánfilo de Narváez, landed in 1528 at Tampa Bay, marched northward to Appalachee, an Indian village in present-day Alabama, then back to the coast near St. Marks, where his party contrived crude vessels in hope of reaching Mexico. Wrecked on the coast of Texas, a few survivors under Núñez Cabeza de Vaca worked their way painfully overland and after eight years stumbled into a Spanish outpost in western Mexico.

Hernando de Soto followed their example. With 600 men he landed on the Florida west coast in 1539, hiked up as far as western North Carolina, then westward beyond the Mississippi, and up the Arkansas River. In the spring of 1542 de Soto died near the site of Memphis; the next year the survivors floated down the Mississippi, and 311 of the original band found their way to Mexico. In 1540 Francisco Vásquez de Coronado, inspired by rumors of gold, traveled northward into New Mexico and eastward across Texas and Oklahoma as far as Kansas. He returned in 1542 without gold but with a more realistic view of what lay in those arid lands.

The Spanish established provinces in North America not so much as commercial enterprises but as defensive buffers protecting their more lucrative trading empire in Mexico and South America. They were concerned about French traders infiltrating from Louisiana, English settlers crossing into Florida, and Russian seal hunters wandering down the California coast. Yet the Spanish settlements in what is today the United States never flourished. The Spaniards failed to realize that a prosperous and enduring colonial empire depended on self-sustaining economic development. Preoccupied with exploitive and extractive economic objectives, they never understood the central significance of developing a viable market economy. The primary reason why England and France surpassed Spain in the development of a presence in America was that Spain mistakenly assumed that developing a thriving trade in goods with the Native Americans was less important than the conversion of "heathens" and the vain search for gold and silver.

The first Spanish base in the present United States emerged in response to French encroachments on Spanish claims. In the 1560s French Huguenots (Protestants) established short-lived colonies in South Carolina and Florida. In 1565 a Spanish outpost, St. Augustine, became the first European town in the present-day United States, and is now its oldest urban center except for the pueblos of New Mexico. Spain's colony at St. Augustine included a fort, church, hospital, fish market, and over 100 shops and houses—all built decades before the first English settlements at Jamestown and Plymouth. While other outposts failed, St. Augustine survived as a defensive base perched on the edge of a continent.

THE SPANISH SOUTHWEST   The Spanish eventually established other permanent settlements in what is now New Mexico, Texas, and California. Eager to pacify rather than fight the far more numerous Indians of the region, the Spanish used religion as an effective instrument of colonial control. Missionaries representing the various monastic orders, particularly the Franciscans and Jesuits, ventured into the frontier to establish isolated Catholic missions where they taught Christianity to the Indians. After about ten years, a mission was secularized; its lands were divided among the converted Indians, the mission chapel became a parish church, and the inhabitants were given full Spanish citizenship—including the privilege of paying taxes. The soldiers who were sent to protect the missions were housed in *presidios,* or forts, while their families and the merchants accompanying the soldiers lived in adjacent villages.

The Franciscans were an order of celibate males founded in 1209. To be eligible for the order, applicants had to surrender all their personal property and live only on charitable contributions. In 1526 the Spanish monarchy ordered that at least two Franciscan friars accompany each colonial expedition to ensure that the "conquest be a Christian apostolic one and not a butchery," as Mexico's first bishop explained. The Franciscans not only wanted to save the souls of "heathen" Indians; they also sought to transform their cultures. They smashed, burned, or confiscated the objects deemed sacred by the Indians and suppressed spiritual rituals, ceremonial dances, and recreational sports native to the region.

The land that would later be called New Mexico was the first center of mission activity in the American Southwest. In 1598 Juan de Oñate, the wealthy son of a prominent family in Mexico, received a patent for the territory north of Mexico above the Rio Grande. With an expeditionary military force, he took possession of New Mexico, established a capital at San Gabriel, and sent out search parties looking for evidence

A friar forcing a native woman to weave.

of gold and silver deposits. He promised the Pueblo Indian leaders that Spanish dominion would bring them peace, justice, prosperity, and protection. Conversion to Catholicism offered even greater benefits: "an eternal life of great bliss" instead of "cruel and everlasting torment." One of Oñate's aides recorded that the Indians thereupon "spontaneously" agreed to become Spanish vassals and Christians.

Some Indians welcomed the missionaries as "powerful witches" capable of easing their burdens. Others tried to use the Spanish as allies against rival Indian tribes. Still others saw no alternative but to submit. The Indians living in Spanish New Mexico were required to pay tribute to their *encomenderos.* The annual tribute usually entailed a bushel of maize and a blanket or deer hide. But often Indians were required to perform personal tasks for the *encomenderos,* including sexual favors. Disobedient Indians were flogged, by both soldiers and priests.

Before the end of the province's first year, the Indians discovered that the Spanish were not keeping their promises of just treatment. They revolted, killing several soldiers and incurring Oñate's wrath. During three days of relentless fighting, the Spanish killed 500 Pueblo men and 300 women and children. Surviving women were enslaved. Pueblo males over the age of twenty-five had one foot severed in a public ritual intended to strike fear in the hearts of the Indians. Children were taken from their parents and placed under the care of a Franciscan mission where, Oñate remarked, "they may attain the knowledge of God and the salvation of their souls."

During the first three-quarters of the seventeenth century, Spanish New Mexico expanded very slowly. The hoped-for deposits of gold and silver failed to materialize, and a sparse food supply also helped dull interest among potential colonists. The Spanish king prepared to abandon the colony, only to realize that Franciscan missionaries had baptized so many Pueblo Indians that they could not be deserted. In 1608 the Spanish government decided to turn New Mexico into a royal province. The following year it dispatched a royal governor, and in 1610, at the same time that the English settlers were struggling to survive at Jamestown, the Spanish moved the capital of New Mexico to Santa Fe, the first seat of government in the present-day United States. By 1630 there were fifty Catholic churches and friaries in New Mexico and some 3,000 Spaniards.

The leader of the Franciscan missionaries claimed that 86,000 Pueblo Indians had been converted to Christianity. In fact, however, resentment among the Indians increased with time. In 1680 a charismatic Indian leader named Popé organized a massive rebellion that involved some 17,000 Indians living in separate villages spread across hundreds of miles. To coordinate the timing of the attacks, Popé sent ropes with knots in them to the outlying pueblos, each knot indicating how many days until the assault was to begin. When the Spanish intercepted two Indian messengers and discovered the ropes, Popé ordered the fighting to commence. Within a few weeks, the Spaniards had been driven from New Mexico. Almost 400 of the 2,500 Europeans were killed in the uprising. The outraged Indians burned churches, tortured and executed priests, and destroyed all relics of Christianity. It took fourteen years and four military assaults for the Spaniards to reestablish their control over New Mexico. Thereafter, except for sporadic raids by Apaches and Navajos, the Spanish exercised stable control over New Mexico. Spanish outposts on the Florida and Texas Gulf coasts and in California did not appear until the eighteenth century.

THE PROTESTANT REFORMATION

While Spain built her empire, a new movement was growing elsewhere in Europe, the Protestant Reformation. It would intensify na-

Martin Luther.

tional rivalries, and, by encouraging serious challenges to Catholic Spain's power, profoundly affect the course of early American history. When Columbus sailed in 1492, all of western Europe acknowledged the Catholic church and its pope in Rome. The unity of Christendom began to crack in 1517, however, when Martin Luther, a German monk and theologian, posted his "Ninety-five Theses" in protest against abuses in the church. He especially criticized the sale of indulgences, whereby priests would forgive sins in exchange for money or goods. Sinners, Luther argued, could win salvation neither by good works nor through the mediation of the church, but only by faith in the redemptive power of Christ and through a direct relationship to God—the "priesthood of all believers."

Lutheranism spread rapidly among the people and their rulers—some of them with an eye to seizing church properties. When the pope expelled Luther from the church in 1520, reconciliation became impossible. The German states fell into conflict over religious differences until 1555, when they finally patched up a peace whereby each prince determined the religion of his subjects. Most of northern Germany, along with Scandinavia, became Lutheran. The principle of close association between church and state thus carried over into Protestant lands, but Luther had unleashed volatile ideas that ran beyond his personal control.

Other Protestants pursued Luther's doctrine to its logical end and preached religious liberty for all. Further divisions on doctrinal matters led to the appearance of various sects such as the Anabaptists, who rejected infant baptism and favored the separation of church and state. Other offshoots, including the Mennonites, Amish, Dunkers, Familists, and Schwenkfelders, appeared later in America, but the more numerous like-minded groups would be Baptists and Quakers, who derived from English origins.

CALVINISM   Soon after Luther began his revolt, Swiss Protestants also challenged the authority of Rome. In Geneva the reform movement looked to John Calvin, a French scholar who had fled to Switzerland and who brought his adopted city under the sway of his beliefs. In his great theological work, *The Institutes of the Christian Religion* (1536), Calvin set forth a stern doctrine. All people, he taught, were damned by the original sin of Adam, but the sacrifice of Christ made possible their redemption. The experience of faith, however, was open only to those whom God had elected and thus predestined to salvation from the beginning of time. Predestination was a hard doctrine, but the infinite wisdom of God was beyond human understanding.

Calvin insisted upon strict morality and hard work, values that especially suited the rising middle class. Moreover, he taught that people serve God through any legitimate calling, and permitted lay members a share in the governance of the church through a body of elders and ministers called the presbytery. Calvin's doctrines became the basis for the beliefs of the German Reformed and Dutch Reformed churches, the Presbyterians in Scotland, some of the Puritans in England, and the Huguenots in France. Through these and other groups, Calvin exerted more effect upon religious belief and practice in the English colonies than did any other single leader of the Reformation.

John Calvin.

Queen Elizabeth I.

THE REFORMATION IN ENGLAND   In England the Reformation, like so many other things, followed a unique course. The Church of England, or Anglican church, took form through a gradual process of Calvinizing English Catholicism. Purely political reasons initially led to the rejection of papal authority. Henry VIII (1509–1547), the second of the Tudor dynasty, had in fact won from the pope the title of Defender of the Faith, for refuting Luther's ideas. But Henry's marriage to Catherine of Aragon had produced no male heir, and to marry again he required an annulment. In the past, popes had found ways to accommodate such requests, but Catherine was the aunt of Charles V, king of Spain and emperor of the Holy Roman Empire, whose support was vital to the church's cause on the continent. So the pope refused to grant an annulment. Unwilling to accept the rebuff, Henry severed the connection with Rome, named a new archbishop of Canterbury, who granted the annulment, and married the lively Anne Boleyn. In one of history's great ironies, she presented him not with the male heir he sought but with a daughter, who as Elizabeth I would reign from 1558 to 1603 over one of England's greatest eras.

Elizabeth could not be a Catholic, for in the Catholic view she was illegitimate. During her reign, therefore, the Church of England became Protestant, but in its own way. The structure of organization, the bishops and archbishops, remained much the same, but the doctrine and practice changed: the Latin liturgy became, with some changes, the English *Book of Common Prayer,* the cult of saints was dropped, and the clergy were permitted to marry. For the sake of unity the "Elizabethan Settlement" allowed some latitude in theology and other matters, but this did not satisfy all. Some tried to enforce the letter of the law, stressing traditional Catholic practices. Many others, however, especially those under Calvinist influence, wished to "purify" the church of all its Catholic remnants so that it more nearly fit their views of biblical authority. Some of these Puritans would leave England to build their own churches in America. Those who broke altogether with the Church of England were called Separatists. The religious controversies associated with the English Reformation so dominated the political life of the nation that interest in colonizing the New World was forced to the periphery of concern.

CHALLENGES TO SPANISH EMPIRE

The Spanish monopoly of New World colonies remained intact throughout the sixteenth century, but not without challenge from national rivals spurred now by the emotion unleashed by the Protestant Reformation. The French were the first to pose a serious threat as Huguenot seamen promised to build France into a major sea power. Spanish treasure ships from the New World were tempting targets for French privateers. In 1524 the French king sent an Italian named Giovanni da Verrazano in search of a passage to Asia. Sighting land (probably at Cape Fear, North Carolina), Verrazano ranged along the coast as far north as Maine. On a second voyage in 1538, his career met an abrupt end in the West Indies at the hands of the fierce Caribs.

Unlike the Verrazano voyages, those of Jacques Cartier about a decade later led to the first French effort at colonization. On three voyages Cartier explored the Gulf of St. Lawrence and ventured up the St. Lawrence River. Twice he got as far as present-day Montréal, and twice wintered at or near the site of Québec, near which a short-lived French colony appeared in 1542–1543. From that time forward, however, French kings lost interest in Canada. France after mid-century plunged into religious civil wars, and the colonization of Canada had to await the coming of Samuel de Champlain, the "Father of New France," after 1600.

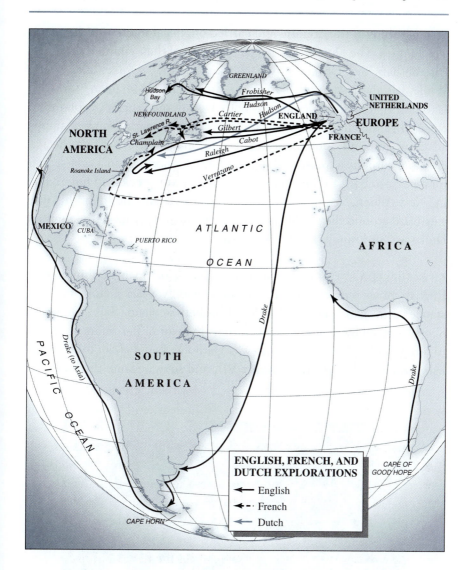

ENGLISH, FRENCH, AND
DUTCH EXPLORATIONS

← English
←-· French
← Dutch

From the mid-1500s, greater threats to Spanish power arose from the growing strength of the Dutch and English. The provinces of the Netherlands, which had passed by inheritance to the Spanish king, and which had become largely Protestant, rebelled against Spanish rule in 1567. A protracted and bloody struggle for independence ensued. Spain did not accept the independence of the Dutch Republic until 1648.

Almost from the beginning of the revolt, the Dutch "Sea Beggars," privateers working out of both English and Dutch ports, plundered

Spanish ships in the Atlantic and carried on illegal trade with the Spanish colonies. The Dutch "Sea Beggars" soon had their counterpart in the Elizabethan "Sea Dogges": John Hawkins, Francis Drake, and others. While Elizabeth steered a tortuous course to avoid open war with Catholic Spain, she encouraged both Dutch and English captains to engage in smuggling and piracy. In 1577 Drake embarked on his famous adventure around South America to raid Spanish towns along the Pacific and surprise a treasure ship from Peru. Continuing in a vain search for a passage back to the Atlantic, he spent seven weeks at Drake's Bay in "New Albion," as he called California. Eventually he found his way westward around the world and back home in 1580. Elizabeth knighted Drake as "Sir Francis" upon his return.

THE ARMADA'S DEFEAT   Such plundering of Spanish shipping by English privateers continued for some twenty years before circumstances provoked open war. In 1568 Elizabeth's cousin Mary, "Queen of Scots," ousted by Scottish Presbyterians in favor of her infant son, fled to refuge in England. Mary, who was Catholic, had a claim to the English throne by descent from Henry VII, and soon became the focus for

The defeat of the Spanish Armada, depicted in a contemporary English oil painting.

Spanish-Catholic intrigues to overthrow Elizabeth. Finally, after an abortive plot to kill Elizabeth and elevate Mary to the throne, Elizabeth yielded to the demands of her ministers and had Mary beheaded in 1587.

In revenge Spain's king, Philip II, decided to crush once and for all the Protestant power of the north and began to gather his ill-fated Armada, whereupon Francis Drake destroyed part of the Spanish fleet before it was ready to sail. His "singeing of the King of Spain's beard" postponed for a year the departure of the "Invincible Armada," which set out to invade England in 1588. The heavy Spanish galleons, however, could not cope with the smaller, faster English vessels. Drake and the English harried the Spanish ships through the English Channel on their way to the Netherlands, where the Armada was to pick up an invasion force. But caught up in a powerful "Protestant Wind" from the south, the storm-tossed fleet was swept into the North Sea instead. What was left of it finally found its way home around the British Isles, leaving wreckage scattered on the shores of Scotland and Ireland.

Defeat of the Armada marked the beginning of English naval supremacy and cleared the way for English colonization of America. It was the climactic event of Elizabeth's reign. England at the end of the sixteenth century was in the springtime of its power, filled with a youthful zest for new worlds and new wonders that were opening up before the nation.

ENGLISH EXPLORATIONS   A significant figure in channeling this energy was Richard Hakluyt, an Oxford clergyman, who became an active promoter of colonization. In 1584, at the request of Sir Walter Raleigh, he prepared for the queen *A Discourse of Western Planting* (first published three centuries later) in which he pleaded for colonies to accomplish diverse objects: to extend the reformed religion, to expand trade, to supply England's needs from her own dominions, to provide bases in case of war with Spain, to enlarge the queen's revenues and navy, to discover a Northwest Passage to the Orient, and to employ the growing number of people made idle by the surge of population growth. He lamented that England was "swarminge at this day with valiant youths rusting and hurtfull by lacke of employment."

The history of English colonization begins with Sir Humphrey Gilbert and his half-brother, Sir Walter Raleigh. In 1578 Gilbert, who had long been a confidant of the queen, secured a royal patent to possess and hold "heathen and barbarous landes countries and territories not actually possessed of any Christian prince or people." Significantly, the patent guaranteed to settlers and their descendants in such a colony the rights and privileges of Englishmen "in suche like ample manner and fourme as if they were borne and personally residaunte within our sed Realme of England." And laws had to be "agreable to the forme of the lawes and pollicies of England."

Gilbert, after two false starts, finally set out with a colonial expedition in 1583, intending to settle near Narragansett Bay (in present-day Rhode Island). He landed in Newfoundland, and took possession of the land for Elizabeth. With the season far advanced and his largest vessels lost, Gilbert resolved to return home. While in transit, however, his ship vanished, and he was never seen again.

RALEIGH'S LOST COLONY   The next year, 1584, Raleigh persuaded the queen to renew Gilbert's colonizing mission in his own name, and sent out a ship to reconnoiter a site. Sailing by way of the West Indies, they came to the Outer Banks of North Carolina and discovered Roanoke Island, where the soil seemed fruitful and the natives friendly. After several false starts, Raleigh in 1587 sponsored an expedition of

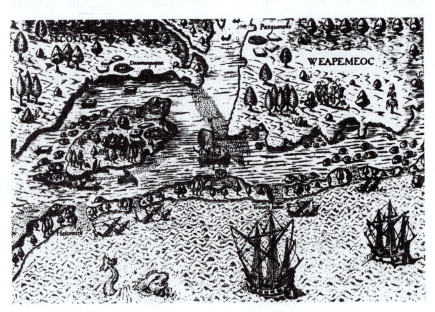

The English arrival at the Outer Banks, with Roanoke Island at left.

117 men, women, and children, under Governor John White. After a month in Roanoke, Governor White returned to England to get supplies, leaving behind his daughter Elinor and his granddaughter Virginia Dare, the first English child born in the New World. White, however, could not get back because of the war with Spain. He finally returned in 1590 to find the city of "Ralegh" abandoned and pillaged.

No trace of the "Lost Colonists" was ever found. Hostile Indians may have destroyed the colony, or hostile Spaniards—who certainly planned to attack—may have done the job. The most recent scientific research indicates that the "Lost Colony" fell prey to the region's worst drought in eight centuries. Tree-ring samples reveal that the colonists arrived during the driest seven-year period in 770 years. While some may have gone south, the main body of colonists appears to have gone north to the southern shores of Chesapeake Bay, as they had talked of doing, and lived there for some years until killed by local Indians. Unless some remnant of the Lost Colony did survive in the woods, there was still not a single English colonist in North America when Queen Elizabeth died in 1603.

MAKING CONNECTIONS

- The funding of the voyages of discovery by various European nations had implications for the settlement and control of the New World, as will be discussed in later chapters.

- This chapter features the settlement pattern and plundered wealth obtained by the Spanish in the New World, which will be contrasted in the next chapter with the patterns of English settlement and sources of wealth found in the New World.

- The next chapter describes how the Reformation and religious controversies in Europe led various religious groups to found their own settlements in the New World, where they did not face discrimination and persecution.

FURTHER READING

A fascinating study of Pre-Columbian migration is Brian M. Fagan's *The Great Journey: The Peopling of Ancient America* (1987). Alice B. Kehoe's *North American Indians: A Comprehensive Account* (1992) provides an encyclopedic treatment of Native Americans. An evocative portrait of the Aztecs can be found in Michael E. Smith's *The Aztecs* (1997). The best introduction to the prehistory of the American Southwest, its people, and archaeology is Stephen Plog's *Ancient Peoples of the American Southwest* (1997).

The conflict between Native Americans and Europeans is treated well in James Axtell's *The Invasion Within:The Contest of Cultures in Colonial North America* (1986) and *Beyond 1492: Encounters in Colonial North America* (1992). Karen O. Kupperman's *Settling with the Indians: The Meeting of English and Indian Cultures in America, 1580– 1640* (1980) stresses the racist nature of the conflict. Alfred W. Crosby's *Ecological Imperialism: The Biological Expansion of Europe, 900– 1900* (1986) explores the ecological effects of European settlement.

The most comprehensive overviews of European exploration are two volumes by Samuel E. Morison, *The European Discovery of America: The Northern Voyages,* A.D. *500–1600* (1971), and *The Southern Voyages, 1492–1616* (1974). David B. Quinn's *North America from Earliest Discovery to First Settlements* (1977) is also useful. A good outline of the forces of exploration is John H. Parry's *The Age of Renaissance* (1963).

The voyages of Columbus are surveyed in William D. Phillips, Jr., and Carla Rahn Phillips's *The Worlds of Christopher Columbus* (1992). David J. Weber examines Spanish colonization in *The Spanish Frontier in North America* (1993). For the French experience, see William J. Eccles's *France in America* (1972).

For background on the motives for English exploration and settlement, see Carl Bridenbaugh's *Vexed and Troubled Englishmen, 1590– 1642* (1968).

2 ✍ ENGLAND AND
ITS COLONIES

CHAPTER ORGANIZER

This chapter focuses on:

- the reasons for the founding of the different colonies in North America.

- the ways in which the British colonists and Native Americans adapted to each other's presence.

- the factors making for England's success in North America.

The England that Queen Elizabeth bequeathed to King James I, like the colonies it would plant, was a unique blend of elements. The language and the people themselves mixed Germanic and Latin ingredients. The Anglican church mixed Protestant theology and Catholic forms in a way unknown on the continent. And the growth of royal power paradoxically had been linked with the rise of English liberties, in which even Tudor monarchs took pride. In the course of their history, the English people have displayed a genius for "muddling through," a gift for the pragmatic compromise that defied logic but in the light of experience somehow worked.

THE ENGLISH BACKGROUND

Set off from continental Europe by the English Channel, England had safe frontiers after the union of the English and Scottish crowns in 1603. Such comparative isolation enabled England to develop institutions unlike those on the continent. By 1600 the decline of feudal practices was far advanced. The great nobles, decimated by the Wars of the Roses, had been brought to heel by Tudor monarchs and their ranks filled with men loyal to the crown. In fact the only nobles left, strictly speaking, were those who sat in the House of Lords. All others were commoners, and among their ranks the aristocratic pecking order ran through a great class of landholding squires, distinguished mainly by their wealth, and bearing the simple titles of "esquire" and "gentleman," as did many well-to-do townsmen. They in turn mingled freely and often intermarried with the classes of yeomen (small freehold farmers) and merchants.

ENGLISH LIBERTIES   It was to these middle classes that the Tudors looked for support and, for want of bureaucrats or a standing army, for local government. Chief reliance in the English counties was on the country gentlemen, who usually served as officials without pay. Government, therefore, allowed a large measure of local initiative. Self-rule in the counties and towns became a habit—one that, along with the offices of justice of the peace and sheriff, English colonists took along to the New World as part of their cultural baggage.

In the making of laws, the monarch's subjects consented through representatives in the House of Commons. Subjects could be taxed only with the consent of Parliament. By its control of the purse strings, Parliament drew other strands of power into its hands. This structure of powers formed a constitution that was not only not written in one place, but, for that matter, not fully written down at all. The Magna Carta (Great Charter) of 1215, for instance, had been a statement of privileges wrested by certain nobles from the king, but it became part of a broader assumption that the people as a whole had rights that even the monarch could not violate.

A further buttress to English liberty was the great body of common law, which had developed since the twelfth century in royal courts es-

The House of Commons in 1640.

tablished to check the arbitrary power of local nobles. Without laws to cover every detail, judges had to exercise their own ideas of fairness in settling disputes. Decisions once made became precedents for later decisions, and over the years a body of judge-made law developed, the outgrowth more of experience than of abstract logic. The courts evolved the principle that people could be arrested or their goods seized only upon a warrant issued by a court, and that individuals were entitled to a trial by a jury of their peers (their equals) in accordance with established rules of evidence.

ENGLISH ENTERPRISE   English liberties inspired a certain initiative and vigor of which prosperity and empire were born. The ranks of entrepreneurs and adventurers were constantly replenished by the younger sons of the squirearchy, cut off from the estate that the oldest son inherited by the law of primogeniture (or first born). The formation of joint-stock companies spurred commercial expansion. These companies were the ancestors of the modern corporation, in which stockholders shared the risks and profits, sometimes for a single venture but more and more on a permanent basis. In the late 1500s some of the larger companies managed to get royal charters that entitled them to monopolies in certain areas and even governmental powers in their outposts. Such companies would become the first instruments of colonization.

For all the vaunted glories of English liberty and enterprise, it was not the best of times for the common people. For more than two centuries, serfdom had been on the way to extinction, as the feudal duties of serfs were transformed into rents and the serfs themselves into tenants. But while tenancy gave a degree of independence, it also allowed landlords to increase demands, and, as the trade in woolen products grew, to enclose farmlands and evict the tenants in favor of sheep. The enclosure movement of the sixteenth century gave rise to the great numbers of sturdy beggars and rogues who peopled the literature of Elizabethan times and gained immortality in Mother Goose: "Hark, hark, the dogs do bark. The beggars have come to town." The needs of this displaced population became another argument for colonial expansion.

PARLIAMENT AND THE STUARTS   With the death of Elizabeth, who never married and did not give birth to an heir, the Tudor line ran out and the throne fell to the first of the Stuarts, whose dynasty spanned most of the seventeenth century, a turbulent time during which the English planted an overseas empire. In 1603 James VI of Scotland, son of the ill-fated Mary, Queen of Scots, and great-grandson of Henry VII, became James I of England—as Elizabeth had planned. A man of ponderous learning, James fully earned his reputation as the "wisest fool in all Christendom." He lectured the people on every topic but remained blind to English traditions and sensibilities. Where the Tudors had wielded absolute power through constitutional forms, James demanded a more consistent logic and promoted the theory of divine right, by which monarchs answered only to God for their actions. Where the Puritans hoped to find a Presbyterian ally in their opposition to Anglican trappings, they found instead a testy autocrat who promised to "harry them out of the land." He even offended Anglicans by deciding to end Elizabeth's war with Catholic Spain.

Charles I, who succeeded his father in 1625, proved even more stubborn about royal power. He ruled without Parliament from 1629 to 1640 and levied taxes by royal decree. In the religious arena, the archbishop of Canterbury, William Laud, directed a systematic persecution of Puritans but finally overreached himself when he tried to impose Anglican worship on Presbyterian Scots. In 1638 Scotland rose in revolt, and in 1640 Charles called Parliament to rally support and raise money for the defense of his kingdom. The "Long Parliament" impeached Laud instead, condemned to death the king's chief minister,

(Left) James I, the successor to Queen Elizabeth and the first of England's Stuart kings. (Right) Charles I, in a portrait by Van Dyck.

and abolished the king's "prerogative courts." In 1642, when the king tried to arrest five members of Parliament, civil war erupted between the "Roundheads," who backed Parliament, and the "Cavaliers," who supported the king.

In 1646 royalist resistance collapsed, and parliamentary forces captured the king. Parliament, however, could not agree on a permanent settlement. A dispute arose between Presbyterians and Independents (who preferred a congregational church government), and in 1648 the Independents purged the Presbyterians, leaving a "Rump Parliament" that then instigated the trial and execution of Charles I on charges of treason.

Oliver Cromwell, commander of the army, operated like a military dictator, ruling first through a council chosen by Parliament (the Commonwealth), and, after forcible dissolution of Parliament, as Lord Protector (the Protectorate). Cromwell extended religious toleration to all except Catholics and Anglicans, but his arbitrary governance and his moralistic codes provoked growing public resentment. When, after his death in 1658, his son proved too weak to carry on, the army once again took control, permitted new elections for Parliament, and in 1660 supported the restoration of the monarchy under Charles II, son of the martyred king.

Charles accepted as terms of the Restoration settlement the principle that he must rule jointly with Parliament. By tact or shrewd maneu-

*Oliver Cromwell, England's Lord
Protector from 1653 until his death
in 1658.*

vering, he managed to hold his throne. His younger brother, the duke of
York (who became James II upon succeeding to the throne in 1685) was
less flexible. He openly avowed Catholicism and assumed the same unyielding stance as the first two Stuarts. The people could bear it so long
as they expected one of his Protestant daughters, Mary or Anne, to succeed him. In 1688, however, the birth of a son who would be reared a
Catholic finally brought matters to a crisis. Leaders of Parliament invited Mary and her husband, William of Orange, a Dutch prince, to assume the throne jointly, and James fled the country.

By this "Glorious Revolution," Parliament finally established its freedom from royal control. Under the Bill of Rights, in 1689, William and
Mary gave up the prerogatives of suspending laws, erecting special
courts, keeping a standing army, or levying taxes except by Parliament's
consent. They further agreed to hold frequent legislative sessions and
allow freedom of speech in Parliament, freedom of petition to the
crown, and restrictions against excessive bail and cruel and unusual
punishments. The Toleration Act of 1689 extended a degree of freedom
of worship to all Christians except Catholics and Unitarians, although
dissenters from the established church still had few political rights. In
1701 the Act of Settlement ensured a Protestant succession through
Queen Anne (1702–1714). And by the Act of Union in 1707, England
and Scotland became the United Kingdom of Great Britain.

SETTLING THE CHESAPEAKE

During these eventful years all but one of the thirteen North American colonies had their start. In 1606 King James I chartered a Virginia Company with two divisions, the First Colony of London and the Second Colony of Plymouth. The London group could plant a settlement between the 34th and 38th parallels, the Plymouth group between the 41st and 45th parallels, and either between the 38th and 41st parallels, provided they kept a hundred miles apart. The stockholders expected a potential return from gold and other minerals; products, such as wine, citrus fruits, and olive oil, to free England from dependence on Spain; trade with the Indians; pitch, tar, potash, and other forest products needed for naval use; and perhaps a passage to East Asia. Some investors dreamed of finding another Aztec or Inca Empire. Few if any investors foresaw what the first English colony would actually become: a place to grow tobacco.

From the outset, the pattern of English colonization diverged significantly from the Spanish pattern, which was an autocratic model in which the Spaniards conquered highly sophisticated peoples and proceeded to regulate all aspects of colonial life. The English had a different model in their experience. While the interest in America was growing, the English were already involved in planting settlements, or "plantations," in Ireland, which the English had conquered by military force under Elizabeth. Within their own pale (or limit) of settlement in Ireland, the English set about transplanting their familiar way of life insofar as possible. The English would apply the same pattern as they settled North America, subjugating the Indians there as they had the Irish in Ireland. Yet, in America the English settled along the Atlantic seaboard, where the native populations were relatively sparse. There was no Aztec or Inca Empire to conquer and rule. The colonists thus had to establish their own communities within a largely wilderness setting.

VIRGINIA   The London group of the Virginia Company planted the first permanent colony in Virginia, named after Elizabeth I, the "Virgin Queen." On May 6, 1607, three ships carrying about 100 men reached Chesapeake Bay after four storm-tossed months at sea. They chose a

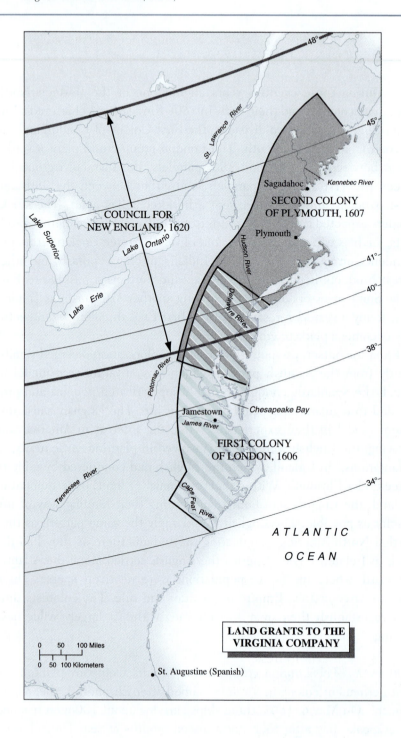

LAND GRANTS TO THE
VIRGINIA COMPANY

river with a northwest bend—in hope of a passage to Asia—and settled about 40 miles from the sea to hide from marauding Spaniards. One of the settlers noted that they found "fair meadows and goodly, tall trees, with such fresh waters running through the woods as I was almost ravished with the first sight thereof."

The river they called the James, and the colony, Jamestown. The sea-weary colonists began building a fort, thatched huts, a storehouse, and a church. They then set to planting, but most were either townsmen unfamiliar with farming or "gentleman" adventurers who scorned manual labor. They had come to find gold, not to establish a farm settlement. Ignorant of woodlore, they did not know how to exploit the area's abundant game and fish. Supplies from England were undependable, and only some effective leadership and their trade with the Indians, who taught the colonists to grow maize, enabled them to survive.

The Indians of the region were loosely organized. Wahunsonacock, called Powhatan by the English after the name of his tribe, was the chief of numerous Algonquian-speaking towns in eastern Virginia representing over 10,000 Indians. The Indians making up the so-called Powhatan Confederacy were largely an agricultural people who focused on the raising of several varieties of corn. They lived along rivers in fortified towns and resided in framed houses sheathed with bark. Despite occasional clashes with the colonists, the Indians of Virginia initially adopted a stance of nervous assistance and watchful waiting. Powhatan developed a lucrative trade with the colonists, exchanging corn for hatchets, swords, and muskets; he realized too late that the newcomers intended to expropriate his lands and subjugate his people. As one Indian said in 1608, "We hear you are come from under the World to take our World from us."

The colonists, as it happened, had more than a match for Powhatan in Captain John Smith, a swashbuckling soldier of fortune with rare powers of leadership and self-promotion. The story goes that earlier in his career, while fighting with the Austrians against the Turks in Hungary, he had beheaded three Turks in hand-to-hand challenges staged in front of a Turkish fortress. Thereafter Smith was wounded, captured, and enslaved in Turkey, but he freed himself by killing his overseer. After fleeing across Russia and sailing in a pirate ship off the coast of Africa, the twenty-four-year-old Smith was "befriended by a gentlewoman" who facilitated his return to England in 1604.

Captain Smith taketh the King of Pamaunkee prisoner, *1608, from John Smith's map of "Ould Virginia," 1624.*

The Virginia Company, understandably impressed by Smith's exploits, appointed him a member of the resident council to manage the new colony in America. It was a wise decision. With the colonists on the verge of starvation, Smith imposed strict discipline and forced all to labor, noting that "he that will not work shall not eat." Smith also bargained with the Indians and explored and mapped the Chesapeake region. Through his efforts, Jamestown survived, but Smith's dictatorial acts did not endear him to many of the colonists. One called him "ambitious, unworthy, and vainglorious."

In 1609 the Virginia Company moved to reinforce the Jamestown colony. A new charter redefined the colony's boundaries and replaced the largely ineffective council with an all-powerful governor whose council was only advisory. The company then lured new investors and attracted new settlers with the promise of free land after seven years of labor. The company in effect had given up hope of prospering except through the sale of lands which would rise in value as the colony grew. The governor, the noble Lord De La Warr (Delaware), sent as interim governor Sir Thomas Gates. In 1609 Gates set out with a fleet of nine vessels and about 500 passengers and crew. On the way Gates was shipwrecked on Bermuda, where he and the other survivors wintered in comparative ease, subsisting on fish, fowl, and wild pigs. (Their story was transformed by William Shakespeare into his play *The Tempest*.)

Most of the fleet, however, did reach Jamestown. Some 400 settlers overwhelmed the remnant of about 80. All chance that John Smith might control things was lost when he suffered a gunpowder burn and sailed back to England. The consequence was anarchy and the "starving time" of the winter of 1609–1610, during which most of the colonists, weakened by hunger, fell prey to pestilence. By May 1610, when Gates and his companions made their way to Jamestown on two small ships built in Bermuda, only about 60 remained alive. All poultry and livestock (including horses) had been eaten, and one man was even said to have dined on his wife. Jamestown was falling into ruins and was abandoned.

In June 1610, as the colonists made their way down the river, the new governor, Lord Delaware, providentially arrived with three ships and 150 men, whereupon instead of leaving Virginia, the colonists returned to Jamestown and created the first new settlements upstream at Henrico (Richmond) and two more downstream near the mouth of the river. It was a critical turning point for the colony, whose survival required a combination of stern measures and not a little luck. When Lord Delaware returned to England in 1611, Gates took charge of the colony and established a strict system of *Lawes Divine, Moral, and Martiall,* inaccurately called "Dale's Code," after Thomas Dale who en-

A 1609 handbill of the Virginia Company attempts to lure settlers to Jamestown.

forced them as marshal. Severe even by the standards of a ruthless age, the code enforced a militaristic discipline needed for survival. The new colonial regime also assaulted the local Indians. English soldiers attacked Indian villages and destroyed their crops. One commander reported that they marched a captured Indian queen and her children to the river where they "put the Children to death . . . by throwing them overboard and shooting out their brains in the water."

Over the next seven years, the colony limped along until it gradually found a reason for being: tobacco. In 1612 John Rolfe had begun to experiment with the harsh Virginia tobacco. Eventually he got hold of some seed for the more savory Spanish varieties, and by 1616 the weed had become an export staple.

Meanwhile Rolfe had made another contribution to stability by marrying Pocahontas, the daughter of Powhatan. Pocahontas (a nickname usually translated as "frisky"—her given name was Matowaka) had been a familiar figure in Jamestown almost from the beginning. In 1607, then only eleven, she figured in perhaps the best-known story of the settlement, her plea for the life of John Smith, who credited to his own charm what was perhaps the climax to a ritual threat of execution—that is, a bit of playacting to impress Smith with Powhatan's authority. In 1613, however, on a foray to extort corn from the Indians, settlers captured Pocahontas and held her for ransom. To fend off the crisis, Rolfe

In this engraving from John Smith's Generall Historie, *Pocahontas pleads with her father to spare John Smith's life.*

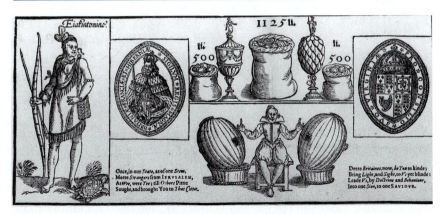

The Virginia Company recommended that prospective settlers bring to America these "provisions necessary to sustain themselves."

proposed marriage to Pocahontas, Powhatan agreed, and a wary peace ensued. By now Pocahontas had been baptized in the Anglican church, and she was given a new name, "Lady Rebecca." In 1616 Rolfe took Rebecca and their infant son Thomas to London, where the young princess drew excited attention from the royal family and curious Londoners. But only a few months after arriving, Rebecca grew gravely ill and died at the age of twenty. Distinguished Virginians still boast of their descent from the Indian "princess."

In 1618 Sir Edwin Sandys, a prominent member of Parliament, became head of the company and set about making a series of reforms. First of all he inaugurated a new "headright" policy: anyone who bought a share in the company and who could transport himself to Virginia could have fifty acres, and fifty more for any servants he might send or bring. The following year, 1619, was memorable in several ways. The company now relaxed the tight regimen of the *Lawes* and promised that the settlers should have the "rights of Englishmen," including a representative assembly.

A new governor arrived with instructions to put the new order into effect, and on July 30, 1619, the first General Assembly of Virginia, including the governor, six councilors, and twenty-two burgesses, met in the church at Jamestown and deliberated for five days, "sweating & stewing, and battling flies and mosquitoes." It was an eventful year in two other respects. The promoters also saw a need to send out wives for the men. During 1619 a ship arrived with ninety young women who were to be sold to likely husbands of their own choice for the cost of transportation (about 125 pounds of tobacco). And a Dutch man-of-war, according to an ominous note in John Rolfe's diary, stopped by and dropped off "20 Negars," the first blacks known to have reached English America.

The profitable tobacco trade intensified the settlers' lust for land. They especially coveted Indian fields because they had already been cleared and were ready to be planted. In 1622 the Indians, led by Opechancanough, Powhatan's brother and successor, tried to repel the land-grabbing English. They killed some 350 colonists, including John Rolfe, only to provoke a vengeful counterattack. John Smith denounced the Indian assault as a "massacre" and dismissed the "savages" as "cruel beasts" whose "brutishness" exceeded that of wild animals. Others declared that the dead colonists certified the English claim to the lands of the New World: "We who hitherto have had no more ground than their [Indian] waste, and our purchase . . . may now by right of War, and law of Nations, invade the Country, and destroy them who sought to destroy us." Whatever moral doubts had earlier plagued English settlers were now swept away. "We shall enjoy their cultivated places. . . . Now their cleared grounds in all their villages (which are situated in the fruitfulest places of the land) shall be inhabited by us."

The English thereafter sought to wipe out the Indian presence along their frontier. In 1623 Captain William Tucker and a band of soldiers met with Indian leaders to negotiate a settlement. After signing a treaty, Tucker invited the Indians to drink a toast to celebrate their truce. The Indians drank the proffered wine, only to realize too late that it had been poisoned. Two hundred Indians died from the doctored brew. The soldiers then burned Indian villages and plundered the corn, killed another fifty, and "brought home part of their heads." This process of "continual incursions" into Indian territory persisted throughout the decade.

Yet the English foothold in Virginia remained tenuous. Some 14,000 men, women, and children had migrated to the colony since 1607, but the population in 1624 stood at a precarious 1,132. Despite the broad initial achievements of the company, after about 1617 a handful of insiders had appropriated large estates and began to monopolize the indentured workers. Some made fortunes from the tobacco boom, but

most of the thousands sent out died before they could prove themselves. At the behest of Sandys's opponents, the king appointed a commission to investigate the running of the colony by the London Company, and on the recommendation of the commission a court dissolved
the company. In 1624 Virginia became a royal colony.

The king did not renew instructions for an assembly, but his governors found it impossible to rule the troublesome Virginians without
one. Annual assemblies met after 1629, although they were not recognized by the crown for another ten years. After 1622, relations with the
Indians continued in a state of what the governor's council called "perpetual enmity" until the aging Opechancanough staged another concerted attack in 1644. The English suffered as many casualties as they
had twenty-two years before, but put down the uprising with such fe-
rocity that nothing quite like it happened again.

Sir William Berkeley, who arrived as governor in 1642, presided over
the colony's growth for most of the next thirty-four years. The brawling
populace of men on the make over which he held sway was a far cry
from the cultivated gentry of the next century. But among them were
the Byrds, Carters, Masons, and Randolphs who made the fortunes that
nurtured the celebrated aristocrats of later generations.

During the 1630s and 1640s the instability and turmoil of Virginia's
early days gave way to a more settled and stable period. Tobacco prices
peaked, and the large planters began to consolidate their economic
gains through political action. They assumed key civic roles as justices
of the peace and sheriffs, helped initiate internal improvements such as
roads and bridges, supervised elections, and collected taxes. They also
formed the able-bodied males into local militias. Despite the presence
of a royal governor, the elected assembly continued to assert its sovereignty, making laws for the colony and resisting the governor's encroachments.

Virginia at mid-century continued to serve as a magnet for new settlers. Indentured servants streamed into the colony. As the sharp rise in
tobacco profits leveled off, planters began to grow corn and raise cattle.
The increase in the food supply helped lower mortality rates and fuel
the rapid rise in population. By 1650 there were 15,000 residents of
Virginia. As servants fulfilled their indentures, they gained access to
land. Many former servants became planters in their own right. Women
typically improved their status through marriage. If they outlived their

husbands—and many did—they inherited the property and often increased their wealth through second and even third marriages.

The relentless stream of new white settlers exerted constant pressure on Indian lands and produced unwanted economic effects. The increase in the number of planters resulted in a dramatic rise in production. This in turn caused the cost of land to soar and the price of tobacco to plummet. To sustain their competitive advantage, the largest planters bought up the most fertile lands along the coast, thereby forcing freed servants to become tenants or to claim less fertile lands along the frontier. In either case, they found themselves at a disadvantage. Tenants grew dependent on planters for land and credit, while small farmers along the frontier became more vulnerable to Indian attacks.

The plight of common folk worsened after 1660, when a restored monarchy under Charles II instituted new trade regulations for the colonies. By 1676 a fourth of the free white men in Virginia were landless. Vagabonds roamed the roads, squatting on private property, working at odd jobs, or poaching game or engaging in other petty crimes in order to survive. Alarmed by the growing social unrest, the large planters controlling the assembly lengthened the indentures, passed more stringent vagrancy laws, stiffened punishments, and stripped the landless of their political rights. But such efforts only increased social unrest.

BACON'S REBELLION   A variety of simmering tensions—caused by depressed tobacco prices, rising taxes, and crowds of freed servants greedily eyeing Indian lands—contributed to the tangled events that have come to be labeled Bacon's Rebellion. Just before the outbreak, Governor William Berkeley had remarked in a letter: "How miserable that man is that Governes a People where six parts of seaven at least are Poore, Endebted, Discontented and Armed."

The discontent turned to violence in 1675 when a petty squabble between a frontier planter and the Doeg Indians on the Potomac led to the murder of the planter's herdsman, and in turn to retaliation by frontier militiamen who killed ten or more Doegs and, by mistake, fourteen Susquehannocks. Soon a force of Virginia and Maryland militiamen laid siege to the Susquehannocks, murdered five chieftains who came out to negotiate, and then let the enraged survivors escape to take their revenge on frontier settlements. Scattered attacks continued on down to the James River, where Nathaniel Bacon's overseer was killed.

By then, their revenge accomplished, the Susquehannocks pulled back. What followed had less to do with a state of war than with a state of hysteria. Berkeley proposed that the assembly support a series of forts along the frontier. But that would not slake the thirst for revenge—nor would it open new lands to settlement. Besides, it would be expensive. Some thought Berkeley was out to preserve a profitable fur trade, although there is no evidence that he was deeply involved personally.

In 1676 Nathaniel Bacon defied Governor Berkeley's authority by assuming command of a group of frontier vigilantes. The tall, slender, twenty-nine-year-old Bacon, a graduate of Cambridge University, had been in Virginia only two years, but he had been well set up by an English father relieved to get his vain, ambitious, hot-tempered son out of the country. Later historians would praise Bacon as the "Torchbearer of the Revolution" and leader of the first struggle of common man versus aristocrat, of frontier versus Tidewater. In part this was true. The rebellion he led was largely a battle of servants, small farmers, and even slaves against Virginia's wealthy planters and political leaders. But Bacon was also the spoiled son of a rich squire who had a talent for trouble. It was his ruthless assaults against peaceful Indians rather than any commitment to democratic principles that brought him into conflict with the governing authorities.

Bacon was early in the line of one lamentable American tradition. Indians, he said, were "all alike," in that they were "wolves, tigers, and bears" who preyed upon "our harmless and innocent lambs," and therefore were fair game. After threatening to kill the governor and members of the assembly if they tried to intervene, the headstrong Bacon began preparing for a total war against all the local Indians. To prevent any governmental interference, he ordered the governor arrested. Berkeley's forces resisted—but only feebly—and Bacon's men burned Jamestown. Bacon, however, could not savor the victory long; he fell ill and died of swamp fever a month later.

Governor Berkeley quickly regained control and subdued the leaderless rebels. In the process, he hanged twenty-three men and confiscated several estates. When his men captured one of Bacon's closest lieutenants, Berkeley gleefully exclaimed: "I am more glad to see you than any man in Virginia. Mr. Drummond, you shall be hanged in half an hour." For such severity, the king recalled Berkeley to England, and a

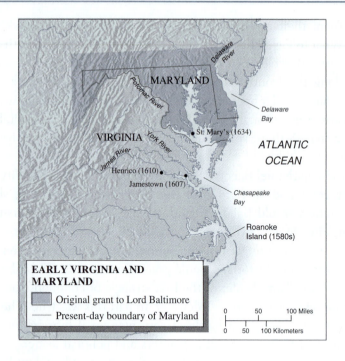

EARLY VIRGINIA AND MARYLAND

Original grant to Lord Baltimore

Present-day boundary of Maryland

royal commission made treaties of pacification with the remaining Indians, some of whose descendants still live in Virginia on tiny reservations guaranteed them in 1677. The fighting opened new lands to the colonists and confirmed the power of an inner group of established landholders who sat in the council.

MARYLAND   In 1634, ten years after Virginia became a royal colony, a neighboring settlement appeared on the northern shores of Chesapeake Bay. Named Maryland in honor of Queen Henrietta Maria, it was granted to Lord Baltimore by King Charles I and became the first proprietary colony—that is, it was owned by an individual, not a joint-stock company. Sir George Calvert, the first Lord Baltimore, had announced in 1625 his conversion to Catholicism and sought the colony as a refuge for English Catholics who were subjected to discrimination at home. His son, Cecilius Calvert, the second Lord Baltimore, actually founded the colony. The charter gave the proprietor powers similar to those of an independent monarch, though the charter specified that the laws must be in accordance with those of England. References to religion were vague except for a mention that chapels should be established according to the ecclesiastical law of England.

In 1634 Calvert planted the first settlement in Maryland at St. Mary's on a small stream near the mouth of the Potomac. St. Mary's in fact was already there, a native settlement purchased from friendly Indians along with the cleared fields around it. Calvert brought Catholic gentlemen as landholders, but a majority of the servants were Protestants. The charter gave Calvert power to make laws with the consent of the freemen (all property holders). The first legislative assembly met in 1635, and divided into two houses in 1650, with governor and council sitting separately. This was instigated by the predominantly Protestant freemen—largely servants who had become landholders, or immigrants from Virginia. The charter also empowered the proprietor to grant huge manorial estates, and Maryland had some sixty before 1676, but the Lords Baltimore soon found that to draw settlers they had to offer small farms. The colony was meant to rely on mixed farming, but its fortunes, like those of Virginia, soon came to depend on tobacco.

Settling New England

PLYMOUTH   Far to the north of the Chesapeake Bay colonies, quite different settlements were taking shape. In 1607 the Plymouth group of the Virginia Company founded a colony at Sagadahoc on the Kennebec River in what is now Maine. The settlement, however, survived only one winter, after which interest in the northern region of America waned. Reports of rich cod fisheries off the New England coast helped revive interest, and in 1620 the Virginia Company reorganized itself into the Council for New England. But before the Council could mount its own colonizing expedition, a band of settlers initially headed for Virginia strayed off course and made landfall at Cape Cod. There they decided to establish a colony, naming it Plymouth after the English port from which they embarked.

The Pilgrims who established Plymouth colony belonged to the most uncompromising sect of Puritans, the Separatists, who had severed all ties with the Church of England. They stemmed from a congregation established at Scrooby in eastern England, members of which had slipped away to Holland in 1607 to escape persecution. The Calvinistic Dutch granted them asylum and toleration, but restricted them mainly to unskilled labor. After ten years in the Dutch city of Leyden, they had wearied of the struggle. Watching their children take up Dutch habits and customs, drifting away to become sailors, soldiers, or worse, so that "their posterity would be in danger to degenerate and be corrupted," they longed for English ways and the English flag. If they could not have them at home, perhaps they might transplant them to the New World. King James would not promise outright toleration if they set up a colony, but he did agree to leave them alone, or, as he put it, to "connive at them."

The Leyden group secured a land patent from the Virginia Company and set up a joint-stock company. In 1620, 101 men, women, and children, led by William Bradford, crammed aboard the three-masted *Mayflower*. Their ranks included both "saints" (people recognized as having been elected by God for salvation) and "strangers" (those yet to receive the gift of grace). The latter group included John Alden, a cooper, and Miles Standish, a soldier hired to organize their defenses. A stormy voyage led them to Cape Cod, far north of Virginia. Heading south, they encountered rough waters and turned back to seek safety at

A sixteenth-century oceangoing vessel.

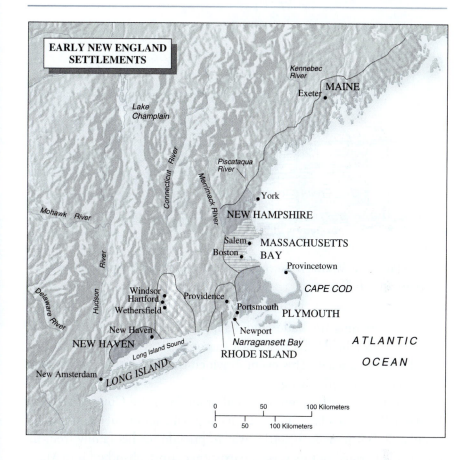

EARLY NEW ENGLAND SETTLEMENTS

Kennebec River

MAINE

Exeter

Lake Champlain

Piscataqua River

Connecticut River

Merrimack River

Mohawk River

York

NEW HAMPSHIRE

Salem MASSACHUSETTS
Boston BAY

Provincetown

CAPE COD

Hudson River

Windsor
Hartford Providence
Wethersfield

Portsmouth PLYMOUTH

Delaware River

New Haven

Newport

NEW HAVEN

Long Island Sound

Narragansett Bay

ATLANTIC

RHODE ISLAND

OCEAN

New Amsterdam LONG ISLAND

| 0 | 50 | 100 Kilometers |

| 0 | 50 | 100 Kilometers |

Provincetown. "Being thus arrived at safe harbor, and brought safe to land," William Bradford wrote, "they fell upon their knees and blessed the God of Heaven who had brought them over the vast and furious ocean." Since they were outside the jurisdiction of any organized government, forty-one of the Pilgrim leaders entered into a formal agreement to abide by laws made by leaders of their own choosing—the Mayflower Compact.

On December 26 the *Mayflower* reached Plymouth harbor and stayed there until April to give shelter and support while the Pilgrims built and occupied their dwellings amid the winter snows. Nearly half the colonists died of exposure and disease, but friendly relations with the neighboring Wampanoag Indians proved their salvation. In the spring of 1621 the colonists met Squanto, an Indian who spoke English and showed them how to grow maize. By autumn the Pilgrims had a bumper crop of

The Plymouth Meetinghouse, built in 1683 with funds from the sale of confiscated Indian lands.

corn, a flourishing fur trade, and a supply of lumber for shipment. To celebrate, they held a harvest feast in company with Chief Massasoit and the Wampanoags. This event provided the inspiration for what has since become Thanksgiving.

In 1621 Plymouth received a land grant from the Council for New England. Two years later it gave up its original communal economy, and stipulated that now each settler was to provide for his family from his own land. Throughout its separate existence, until absorbed into Massachusetts in 1691, the Plymouth colony remained in the anomalous position of holding a land grant but no charter of government from any English authority. The government grew instead out of the Mayflower Compact, which was neither exactly a constitution nor a precedent for later constitutions. Rather it was the obvious recourse of a group that had made a covenant (or agreement) to form a church and that believed God had made a covenant with them to provide a way to salvation. Thus the civil government grew naturally out of the church government, and the members of each were identical at the start. The signers of the compact at first met as the General Court, which chose the governor and his assistants (or council). Later others were admitted as members, or "freemen," but only church members were eligible. Eventually, as the colony grew, the General Court became a body of representatives from the various towns.

MASSACHUSETTS BAY   The Plymouth colony's population never rose above 7,000, and after ten years it was overshadowed by its larger neighbor, the Massachusetts Bay colony. It, too, was originally intended to be a holy commonwealth made up of religious folk bound together in the harmonious worship of God and the pursuit of their "callings." Like the Pilgrims, the Puritans who colonized Massachusetts Bay were primarily Congregationalists who sought to form self-governing churches with membership limited to "visible saints"—those who could demonstrate receipt of the gift of God's grace. But unlike the Plymouth Separatists, the Puritans who settled Massachusetts Bay were still hopeful that they could help to reform the Church of England and therefore they were called Non-Separating Congregationalists.

In 1628 a group of Puritans and merchants formed the New England Company and got a land patent from the Council for New England. To confirm its legality, the company turned to Charles I, who issued a charter in 1629 under the new name of the Massachusetts Bay Company. Leaders of the company at first looked upon it mainly as a business venture, but a majority faction led by John Winthrop, a well-to-do lawyer from East Anglia recently discharged from a government job, resolved to use the colony as a refuge for persecuted Puritans and as an instrument for building a "wilderness Zion" in America.

Governor John Winthrop, in whose vision the Massachusetts Bay colony would be as "a city upon a hill."

Winthrop was a courageous, resolute leader who reflected the strengths and weaknesses of Puritanism, a movement determined to rid the Church of England of its Catholic trappings. By 1629 Winthrop was forty years of age, had a large family, and found himself in control of a floundering estate that could not support his seven sons. Even more unsettling to him was the heightened persecution of Puritans and other dissenters by the Stuart monarchy. Hence he eagerly supported the idea of establishing a spiritual plantation in the New World, and he agreed to head up the enterprise.

Winthrop shrewdly took advantage of a fateful omission in the charter for the Massachusetts Bay Company: the usual proviso that the company maintain its home office in England. Winthrop's group took its charter with them, thereby transferring the entire government of the colony to Massachusetts Bay, where they hoped to ensure Puritan control. By the Cambridge Agreement of 1629, twelve leaders resolved to migrate on these conditions, and the company's governing body agreed.

In 1630 the *Arbella,* with Governor John Winthrop and the charter aboard, embarked with six other ships for Massachusetts. In a lay sermon, "A Model of Christian Charity," delivered on board, Winthrop told his fellow Puritans "we must consider that we shall be a city upon a hill"—an exemplary beacon to all people of what a godly community could be. They first landed at Salem, a struggling settlement with an air of failure. Winthrop thereupon told the group to return to the ships. They then sailed south to Charlestown. By the end of the year seventeen ships bearing 1,000 more colonists arrived. As settlers—both Puritan and non-Puritan—poured into the region, Boston became the new colony's chief city and capital.

The *Arbella* migrants proved to be the vanguard of a massive movement, the Great Migration, that carried some 80,000 men, women, and children away from their homeland to new settlements around the world over the next decade. Fleeing persecution and economic depression at home, they gravitated to Ireland, the Netherlands, and the Rhineland. But the majority traveled to the New World. They went not only to New England and the Chesapeake, but now also to new English settlements in the Lesser Antilles: St. Christopher, Barbados, Nevis, Montserrat, and Antigua.

The transfer of the Massachusetts charter, whereby an English trading company evolved into a provincial government, was a unique ven-

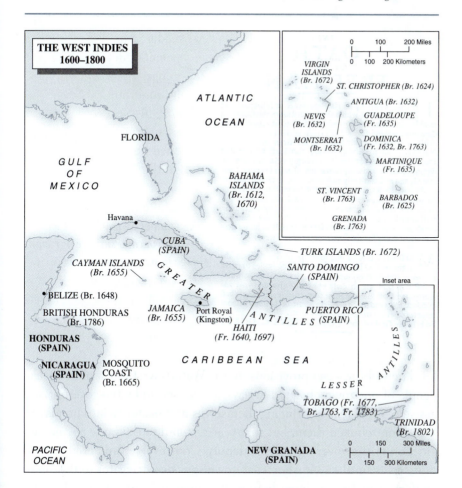

THE WEST INDIES
1600–1800

VIRGIN ISLANDS (Br. 1672)

ST. CHRISTOPHER (Br. 1624)

ATLANTIC

OCEAN

ANTIGUA (Br. 1632)

FLORIDA

NEVIS (Br. 1632)

GUADELOUPE (Fr. 1635)

GULF OF MEXICO

BAHAMA ISLANDS (Br. 1612, 1670)

MONTSERRAT (Br. 1632)

DOMINICA (Fr. 1632, Br. 1763)

MARTINIQUE (Fr. 1635)

ST. VINCENT (Br. 1763)

BARBADOS (Br. 1625)

Havana

CUBA (SPAIN)

GRENADA (Br. 1763)

TURK ISLANDS (Br. 1672)

CAYMAN ISLANDS (Br. 1655)

G R E A T E R

SANTO DOMINGO (SPAIN)

Inset area

BELIZE (Br. 1648)

BRITISH HONDURAS (Br. 1786)

JAMAICA (Br. 1655)

Port Royal (Kingston)

A N T I L L E S

PUERTO RICO (SPAIN)

HONDURAS (SPAIN)

HAITI (Fr. 1640, 1697)

NICARAGUA (SPAIN)

MOSQUITO COAST (Br. 1665)

CARIBBEAN SEA

L E S S E R

A N T I L L E S

TOBAGO (Fr. 1677, Br. 1763, Fr. 1783)

TRINIDAD (Br. 1802)

PACIFIC OCEAN

NEW GRANADA (SPAIN)

ture in colonization. Under this royal charter, power in the company rested with the General Court, which elected the governor and assistants. The General Court consisted of shareholders, called freemen (those who had the "freedom of the company"), but only a few besides Winthrop and his assistants had such status. This suited Winthrop and his friends, but then over 100 settlers asked to be admitted as freemen. Rather than risk trouble, the inner group invited applications and finally admitted 118 in 1631, stipulating that only church members could become freemen.

At first the freemen had no power except to choose assistants, who in turn chose the governor and deputy governor. The procedure violated provisions of the charter, but Winthrop kept the document hidden and

THE
OATH OF A
FREE-MAN

I A.B. being by Gods Providence an Inhabitant and FREEMAN within the Iurifdiction of this Common wealth; doe freely acknowledge myfelfe to be fubject to the Government thereof.
AND therefore doe here fweare by the Great and Dreadful NAME of the Everliving GOD, that I will be true and faithfull to the fame, and will accordingly yield affiftance & fupport thereunto with my perfon and eftate as in equity I am bound; and will alfo truly endeavour to maintaine & preferve all the liberties & priviledges thereof, fubmitting myfelfe to the wholefome Lawes & Orders made and eftablifhed by the fame. +++ AND further that I will not Plot or practife any evill againft it, or confent to any that fhall fo doe: but will timely difcover and reveal the fame to lawfull authority now here eftablifhed, for the fpeedy preventing thereof.

MOREOVER I doe folemnly bind myfelfe in the fight of GOD, that when I fhall be called to give my voyce touching any fuch matter of this State in which FREEMEN are to deale +++ I will give my vote and fuffrage as I fhall judge in mine own confcience may beft conduce and tend to the publicke weale of the body without refpect of perfon or favour of any man.
So help me GOD in the LORD IESVS CHRIST.

The Oath of a Free-Man: "I will give my vote and suffrage as I shall judge in mine own conscience . . ." (1639).

few knew of the exact provisions. In the Watertown Protest of 1632, the people of one town objected to paying taxes levied by the governor and assistants "for fear of bringing themselves and posterity into bondage." Winthrop rebuked them, but that year restored to the body of freemen election of the governor and his deputy. Controversy simmered for two more years until 1634, when each town sent two delegates to Boston to confer on matters coming before the General Court. There they demanded to see the charter, which Winthrop reluctantly produced, and they read that the power to pass laws and levy taxes rested in the General Court. Winthrop argued that the body of freemen had grown too large, but when it met, the General Court responded by turning itself into a representative body with two or three deputies to represent each town. They also chose a new governor, and Winthrop did not resume the office until three years later.

A final stage in the evolution of the government, a two-house legislature, came in 1644 when, according to Winthrop, "there fell out a great business upon a very small occasion." The "small occasion" pitted a poor widow against a well-to-do merchant over ownership of a stray sow. The General Court, being the supreme judicial as well as legislative body, was the final authority in the case. Popular sympathy and the deputies favored the widow, but the assistants disagreed. The case was finally settled out of court, but the assistants feared being outvoted on some greater occasion. They therefore secured a separation into two houses, and Massachusetts thenceforth had a bicameral assembly, the deputies and assistants sitting apart, with all decisions requiring a majority in each house.

Thus over a period of fourteen years the Massachusetts Bay Company, a trading corporation, evolved into the governing body of a commonwealth. Membership in a Puritan church replaced the purchase of stock as the means of becoming a freeman, which was to say, a voter. The General Court, like Parliament, became a representative body of two houses: the House of Assistants corresponding roughly to the House of Lords, and the House of Deputies to the House of Commons. The charter remained unchanged, but practice under the charter was quite different from the original expectation.

RHODE ISLAND   More by accident than design Massachusetts became the staging area for the rest of New England as new colonies grew out of religious quarrels within the fold. Young Roger Williams, who arrived in 1631, was among the first to cause problems, precisely because he was the purest of Puritans, troubled by the failure of Massachusetts Nonconformists to repudiate the Church of England entirely. He held a brief pastorate in Salem, then tried Separatist Plymouth. Governor Bradford found Williams to be gentle and kind in his personal relations as well as a charismatic speaker. But he charged that Williams "began to fall into strange opinions," specifically questioning the king's right to confiscate Indian lands. Williams then returned to Salem. Williams's belief that a true church must have no truck with the unregenerate led him eventually to the conclusion that no true church was possible, unless perhaps consisting of his wife and himself—and he may have had doubts about her.

But eccentric as some of Williams's beliefs may have been, they led him to principles that later generations would honor for other reasons. The purity of the church required complete separation of church and state and freedom from coercion in matters of faith. "Forced worship," he declared, "stinks in God's nostrils." Williams therefore questioned the authority of government to impose an oath of allegiance and rejected laws imposing religious conformity. Such views were too ad-

Religious quarrels within the Puritan fold led to the founding of new colonies. Here a seventeenth-century cartoon shows wrangling sects tossing a Bible in a blanket.

vanced even for the radical church of Salem, which finally removed him, whereupon Williams retorted so hotly against churches that were "ulcered and gangrened" that the General Court in 1635 banished him to England. Governor Winthrop, however, out of personal sympathy, permitted him to slip away with a few followers among the Narraganset Indians, whom he had befriended. In 1636 Williams established the town of Providence at the head of Narragansett Bay, the first permanent settlement in Rhode Island, and the first in America to legislate freedom of religion.

Anne Hutchinson quarreled with the Puritan leaders for different reasons. The articulate, strong-willed, and intelligent wife of a prominent merchant, she raised thirteen children, served as a healer and midwife, and hosted meetings in her Boston home to discuss sermons. Soon, however, the discussions turned into forums for Hutchinson to provide her own commentaries on religious matters. She claimed to have experienced direct revelations from the Holy Spirit that convinced her that only two or three Puritan ministers actually preached the appropriate "covenant of grace." The others, she claimed, were deluded and incompetent; the "covenant of works" they promoted led people to believe that good conduct would ensure salvation.

Hutchinson's beliefs were provocative for several reasons. Puritan theology was grounded in the Calvinist doctrine that people could be saved only by God's grace rather than through their own willful actions. But Puritanism in practice also insisted that ministers were necessary to interpret God's will for the people so as to "prepare" them for the possibility of their being selected for salvation. In challenging the very legitimacy of the ministerial community as well as the hard-earned assurances of salvation enjoyed by current church members, Hutchinson was undermining the stability of an already fragile social system. Moreover, her critics likened her claim of direct revelations from the Holy Spirit to the antinomian heresy, technically a belief that one is freed from obeying the moral law by one's own faith and by God's grace. And what made the situation worse in the male-dominated society of seventeenth-century New England was that a *woman* had made such charges and assertions. Mrs. Hutchinson had both offended authority and sanctioned a disruptive individualism.

A pregnant Hutchinson was hauled before the General Court in 1637, and for two days she verbally sparred on equal terms with the presiding magistrates and testifying ministers. Her skillful deflections of the charges and her ability to cite chapter-and-verse defenses of her actions led an exasperated Governor Winthrop at one point to explode: "We do not mean to discourse with those of your sex." He found Hutchinson to be "a woman of haughty and fierce carriage, of a nimble wit and active spirit, and a very voluble tongue." As the trial continued, an overwrought Hutchinson was eventually lured into convicting herself by claiming direct divine inspiration—blasphemy in the eyes of orthodox Puritans.

Banished in 1638 as a leper not fit for "our society," Hutchinson settled with her family and a few followers on an island south of Providence, near what is now Portsmouth, Rhode Island. But the arduous journey had taken its toll. Hutchinson grew sick and her baby was stillborn, leading her critics back in Massachusetts to assert that the "monstrous birth" was God's way of punishing her for her sins. Hutchinson's spirits never recovered. After her husband's death in 1643, she moved to Long Island, then under Dutch jurisdiction, and the following year she and five of her children were massacred during an Indian attack. Her fate, wrote a vindictive Winthrop, was "a special manifestation of divine justice."

Thus the colony of Rhode Island and Providence Plantations, the smallest in America, grew up in Narragansett Bay, as a refuge for dissenters who agreed that the state had no right to coerce religious belief. In 1640 they formed a confederation and in 1643 secured their first charter. Roger Williams lived until 1683, an active and beloved citizen of the commonwealth he founded in a society which, during his lifetime at least, lived up to his principles of religious freedom and a government based on the consent of the people.

CONNECTICUT   Connecticut had a more orthodox beginning than did Rhode Island. In 1633, a group from Plymouth settled in the Connecticut River valley. Three years later Thomas Hooker led three entire church congregations from Massachusetts Bay to the Connecticut River towns of Wethersfield, Windsor, and Hartford, which earlier arrivals had laid out the previous year.

For a year the settlers in the river towns were governed under a commission from the Massachusetts General Court, but the inhabitants organized the self-governing colony of Connecticut in 1637. The impulse to organize came when representatives of the towns met to consider ways of meeting the danger of attack from the Pequot Indians, who lived east of the river.

In 1639 the Connecticut General Court adopted the "Fundamental Orders of Connecticut," a series of laws that provided for a government like that of Massachusetts, except that voting was not limited to church members. New Haven had by then appeared within the later limits of Connecticut. A group of English Puritans, led by their minister and a wealthy merchant, had migrated first to Massachusetts and then, seeking a place to establish themselves in commerce, to New Haven on Long Island Sound in 1638. Mostly city dwellers, they found themselves reduced to hardscrabble farming, despite their intentions. The New Haven colony became the most rigorously Puritan of all. Like all the other offshoots of Massachusetts, it too lacked a charter and maintained a self-governing independence until 1662, when it was absorbed into Connecticut under the terms of that colony's first royal charter.

NEW HAMPSHIRE AND MAINE   To the north of Massachusetts, most of what are now New Hampshire and Maine was granted in 1622 by the Council for New England to Sir Ferdinando Gorges and Captain John Mason and their associates. In 1629 Mason and Gorges divided their territory at the Piscataqua River, Mason taking the southern part which he named New Hampshire, and Gorges taking the northern part, which became the province of Maine. In the 1630s Puritan immigrants began filtering in, and in 1638 the Reverend John Wheelwright, one of

Anne Hutchinson's group, founded Exeter. Maine consisted of a few scattered settlements, mostly fishing stations, like York.

An ambiguity in the Massachusetts charter brought the proprietorships into doubt, however. The charter set the boundary three miles north of the Merrimack River, and the Bay colony took that to mean north of the river's northernmost reach, which gave it a claim on nearly the entire Gorges-Mason grant. During the English time of troubles in the early 1640s, Massachusetts took over New Hampshire, and in the 1650s extended its authority to the scattered settlements in Maine. This led to lawsuits with the heirs of the proprietors, and in 1678 English judges and the Privy Council decided against Massachusetts in both cases. In 1679, New Hampshire became a royal colony, but Massachusetts bought out the Gorges heirs and continued to control Maine as its proprietor. A new Massachusetts charter in 1691 finally incorporated Maine into Massachusetts.

INDIANS IN NEW ENGLAND

The English settlers who poured into New England found not a "virgin land" of uninhabited wilderness but a developed region populated by over 100,000 Indians. To the white colonists, the Native Americans represented both an alien race and an impediment to their economic and spiritual goals. To the Indians, the newcomers seemed like magical monsters. As one Indian leader explained, the white adventurers "strike awe and terror to our hearts." But the interactions of the two cultures were more complex than the conventional story of conquest and subjugation. Indians coped with the newcomers and changing circumstances in a variety of different ways. Some resisted, others sought accommodation, and still others grew dependent on European culture. In some areas, Indians survived and even flourished in concert with European settlers over long periods of time and with varying degrees of advantage. In other areas, land-hungry newcomers quickly displaced or decimated the native populations. The interactions of the two cultures thus involved misunderstandings, the mutual need for trade and adaptation, and sporadic outbreaks of epidemics and warfare.

In general, the English colonists adopted a quite different strategy for dealing with the Native Americans than that of the French and the

Dutch. Merchants from France and the Netherlands were preoccupied with exploiting the fur trade. To do so they established permanent trading outposts among the Indians. This led them to establish amicable relations with the far more numerous Indians in the region. In contrast, the English colonists were more interested in fish and farms. They were quite willing to manipulate and exploit Indians rather than deal with them on an equal footing. Their goal was subordination rather than reciprocity.

THE NEW ENGLAND INDIANS   In Maine the Abenakis were mainly hunters and gatherers dependent upon the natural offerings of the land and waters. The men did the hunting and fishing while the women retrieved the dead game and prepared it for eating. Women were also responsible for setting up and breaking camp, gathering fruits and berries, and raising the children. The Algonquian tribes of southern New England—the Massachusetts, Nausets, Narragansets, Pequots, and Wampanoags—were more horticultural. Their highly developed agricultural system centered on three primary crops: corn, beans, and pumpkins. While the men still hunted, fished, or traded surplus grain, women planted crops in regularly spaced mounds or "hills" so as to al-

Native Americans fishing, in an engraving by Theodor de Bry based on a watercolor by John White.

low the roots of the plants to intertwine and thereby protect the young tendrils from wind and birds.

For centuries the Indians had used the "slash-and-burn" technique to transform densely wooded forests into fields or parklike hunting preserves. They set fires to burn the underbrush and to nourish the soil. This not only facilitated planting but also allowed for the emergence of succulent new plants that enticed deer. Burning the thick underbrush under the forest canopy also made it easier for Indians to track game and to gather nuts and berries.

The Indians' dependence on nature for their survival shaped their religious beliefs. They believed in a Creator who provided them with the land and its bountiful resources. Many rituals, ceremonies, and taboos acknowledged their dependence on the gods. Rain dances, harvest festivals, and sacrificial offerings bespoke a culture whose fate was dependent on supernatural powers.

Initially, the coastal Indians helped the white settlers develop a subsistence economy. They taught the Europeans how to plant corn and to use fish for fertilizer. They also developed a flourishing trade with the newcomers, exchanging furs for manufactured goods and "trinkets." Although often portrayed as a monolithic group, the various Indian tribes of New England often fought among themselves, usually over disputed land. Had they been able to forge a solid alliance, they would have been better able to resist the encroachments of white settlers. As it was, they not only were fragmented but also vulnerable to the infectious diseases carried on board the ships transporting European settlers to the New World. Epidemics of smallpox soon devastated the Indian population, leaving the coastal areas "a widowed land." Between 1610 and 1675, the Abenakis declined from 12,000 to 3,000, and the southern New England tribes from 65,000 to 10,000. Governor William Bradford of Plymouth reported that the Indians "fell sick of the smallpox, and died most miserably." By the hundreds, they died "like rotten sheep."

Many of the Puritan leaders interpreted these epidemics as divine harvests intended to clear the region of Indians and thereby facilitate white settlement. After all, they reasoned, the Indians were heathens doing the devil's work. They must be rooted out. Those Indians who survived the epidemics and refused to yield their lands were often dislodged by force. In 1636 white settlers in Massachusetts accused a Pequot of murdering a colonist. Joined by Connecticut colonists, they ex-

The Puritans and their Indian allies, the Narragansets, mount a ferocious attack on the Pequots at Mystic, Connecticut (1637).

acted their revenge by setting fire to a Pequot village on the Mystic River. As the Indians fled their burning huts, the Puritans shot and killed them—men, women, and children. In less than an hour, all but seven escapees were dead.

Sassacus, the Pequot chief, then organized the survivors among his followers and attacked the whites. During the Pequot War of 1637, the colonists and their Narraganset allies indiscriminately killed hundreds of Pequots in their village near West Mystic, in the Connecticut River valley. A white participant described the horrible scene: "Many were burnt in the fort, men, women, and children. . . . There were about four hundred souls in this fort, and not above five of them escaped out of our hands. Great and doleful was the bloody sight." The magisterial Puritan minister Cotton Mather described the slaughter as a "sweet sacrifice" and "gave the praise thereof to God." Only a few colonists regretted the massacre. Roger Williams warned that the lust for land would become "as great a God with us English as God Gold was with the Spanish." With poignant clarity, Pequot survivors recognized the motives of the English settlers: "We see plainly that their chiefest desire is to deprive us of the privilege of our land, and drive us to our utter ruin."

Indeed, the white colonists captured most of the surviving Pequots and sold them into slavery in Bermuda. Under the terms of the Treaty of Hartford (1638), the Pequot nation was declared dissolved.

After the Pequot War, the prosperous fur trade contributed to peaceful relations between whites and the remaining Indians, but the relentless growth of the colony and the decline of the animal population began to reduce the eastern tribes to relative poverty. The colonial government repeatedly encroached upon the Indian settlements, forcing them to acknowledge English laws and customs. Colonial leaders argued that the Indians should be deprived of their land because they were not using it as efficiently as the English would. One colonist explained that the Indians "are not industrious, neither have they art, science, skill, or faculty to use either the land or the commodities of it, but all spoils, rots, and is marred for want of manuring, gathering, ordering, etc." At the same time that colonial leaders expropriated Indian lands, Puritan missionaries sought to convert the tribes. One missionary, John Eliot, translated the Bible into the Algonquian language. By 1675 hundreds of converts had settled in special "praying Indian" towns.

The era of fairly peaceful coexistence that began with the Treaty of Hartford came to an end during the last quarter of the seventeenth century. In 1675 Philip (Metacom), chief of the Wampanoags and the

The official seal of the Massachusetts Bay colony after 1675. The Indian is depicted as saying, "Come over and help us."

son of Massasoit, who had helped the original Pilgrims, forged an alliance among the remaining tribes of southern New England—the Narragansets, Mohegans, and Wampanoags. The spark that set New England ablaze resulted from the murder of Sassamon, a "praying Indian" who had attended Harvard, later strayed from the faith while serving Metacom, and then returned to the Christian fold. The officials of Plymouth colony tried and executed three Wampanoags for the murder of Sassamon. In retaliation the Indians attacked and burned colonial settlements throughout Massachusetts and Plymouth colony.

Both sides suffered incredible losses. It is estimated that some 20,000 people were killed in what came to be called either King Philip's War or Metacomet's War. Within a year, the Indians were threatening Boston itself. Finally, however, depleted supplies and the casualty toll wore down Indian resistance. Philip's wife and son were captured and sold into slavery. Some of the tribes surrendered, a few succumbed to disease, while others fled to the west. Those who remained behind were forced to resettle in villages supervised by white settlers. Philip initially escaped, only to be hunted down and killed in 1676. Sporadic fighting continued in Maine and New Hampshire for several more years.

THE ENGLISH CIVIL WAR IN AMERICA

Before 1640 English settlers in New England and around Chesapeake Bay had established two great beachheads on the Atlantic coast, separated by the Dutch colony of New Netherland in between. After 1640, however, the struggle between king and Parliament distracted attention from colonization, and migration dwindled to a trickle of emigrants for more than twenty years. During the time of civil war and Oliver Cromwell's Puritan dictatorship, the struggling colonies were left pretty much to their own devices, especially in New England where English Puritans saw little need to intervene.

In 1643 four of the New England colonies—Massachusetts Bay, Plymouth, Connecticut, and New Haven—formed the New England Confederation to provide joint defense against the Dutch, French, and Indians. They also agreed to support the Christian faith, to render up fugitives, and to settle disputes through the machinery of the Confederation. Two commissioners from each colony met annually to transact business. In some ways the Confederation behaved like a sovereign power. It made treaties, and in 1653 it voted a war against the Dutch who were supposedly stirring the Indians against Connecticut. Massachusetts, far from the scene of trouble, failed to cooperate, which greatly weakened the Confederation. But the commissioners continued to meet annually until 1684, when Massachusetts lost its charter.

Virginia and Maryland remained almost as independent as New England. At the behest of Governor William Berkeley, the Virginia burgesses in 1649 denounced the execution of Charles and recognized his son, Charles II, as the lawful king. In 1652, however, the assembly yielded to parliamentary commissioners and overruled the governor. In return for the surrender, the commissioners let the assembly choose its own council and governor, and the colony grew rapidly in population during its years of independent government—some of the growth came from the arrival of royalists who found a friendly haven in the Old Dominion, despite its capitulation to the English Puritans.

The parliamentary commissioners who won the submission of Virginia proceeded to Maryland, where the proprietary governor faced particular difficulties with his Protestant majority, largely Puritan but including some earlier refugees from Anglican Virginia. At the governor's suggestion, the assembly had passed, and the proprietor had accepted, the Maryland Toleration Act of 1649, an assurance that Puritans would not be molested in their religion. In 1652 the commissioners revoked the Toleration Act and deprived Lord Baltimore of his governmental rights, though not of his lands and revenues. Still, the more extreme Puritan elements were dissatisfied and a brief clash in 1654 brought civil war to Maryland, deposing the governor. But the Calverts had a remarkable skill at retaining favor. Oliver Cromwell took the side of Lord Baltimore and restored him to full rights in 1657, whereupon the Toleration Act was reinstated. The act deservedly stands as a landmark to human liberty, albeit enacted more out of expediency than conviction, although it limited toleration to those who professed belief in the Holy Trinity.

Cromwell let the colonies go their own way, but he was not indifferent to the nascent empire. He fought trade wars with the Dutch and harassed England's traditional enemy, Catholic Spain, in the Caribbean. In 1655 he sent out an expedition that wrested Jamaica from the Spaniards, thereby improving the odds for English privateers and pirates who pillaged Spanish ships—and often any others that chanced by.

The Restoration of King Charles II in England led to an equally pain-less restoration of previous governments in the colonies. The process involved scarcely any change, since little had occurred under Cromwell. Emigration rapidly expanded the populations in Virginia and Maryland. Fears of reprisals against Puritan New England proved unfounded, at least for the time being. Agents hastily dispatched by the colonies won reconfirmation of the Massachusetts charter in 1662 and the very first royal charters for Connecticut and Rhode Island in 1662 and 1663. All three retained their status as self-governing corporations. Plymouth still had no charter, but it went unmolested. New Haven, however, disappeared as a separate entity, absorbed into the colony of Connecticut.

SETTLING THE CAROLINAS

The Restoration of Charles II opened a new season of enthusiasm for colonial expansion, directed mainly by royal favorites. Within twelve years the English had conquered New Netherland, had settled Carolina, and very nearly filled out the shape of the colonies. In the middle region formerly claimed by the Dutch, four new colonies sprang into being: New York, New Jersey, Pennsylvania, and Delaware. Without exception the new colonies were proprietary, awarded by the king to men who had remained loyal, or had brought about his restoration, or in one case to whom he was indebted. In 1663 he granted Carolina to eight prominent allies who became Lords Proprietors of the region.

NORTH CAROLINA   Carolina was from the start made up of two widely separated areas of settlement, which finally became separate colonies. The northernmost part, long called Albemarle, had been entered as early as the 1650s by stragglers who drifted southward from Virginia. For half a century Albemarle remained a remote scattering of settlers along the shores of Albemarle Sound, isolated from Virginia by the Dismal Swamp and lacking easy access for oceangoing vessels. Its reputation had long suffered from the belief that it served as a rogues' harbor for the outcasts of Virginia. Albemarle had no governor until 1664, no assembly until 1665, and not even a town until a group of French Huguenots founded the village of Bath in 1704.

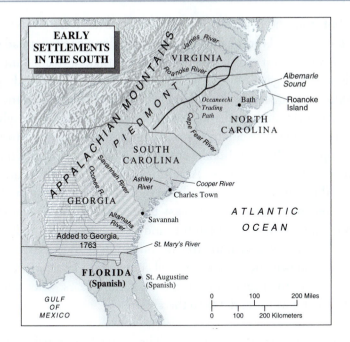

EARLY
SETTLEMENTS
IN THE SOUTH

VIRGINIA

James River

Roanoke River

Albemarle
Sound

APPALACHIAN MOUNTAINS

PIEDMONT

*Occaneechi
Trading
Path*   Bath

Roanoke
Island

Cape Fear River

NORTH
CAROLINA

SOUTH
CAROLINA

Savannah River

Oconee R.

Ashley
River   *Cooper River*

Charles Town

GEORGIA

*Altamaha
River*   Savannah

ATLANTIC

OCEAN

Added to Georgia,
1763   *St. Mary's River*

FLORIDA
(Spanish)   St. Augustine
(Spanish)

0   100   200 Miles

0   100   200 Kilometers

GULF
OF
MEXICO

SOUTH CAROLINA   The eight Lords Proprietors to whom the king gave Carolina neglected Albemarle from the outset, and focused on more promising sites to the south. They sought settlers who had already been seasoned in the colonies, and from the outset Barbadians showed a lively interest, for the rise of large-scale sugar production in Barbados had persuaded small planters to try their luck elsewhere. In 1669 three ships left London with about 100 settlers recruited in England. The expedition sailed first to Barbados, to pick up more settlers, then north to Bermuda. They settled in South Carolina at a place several miles up the Ashley River, where Charles Town (later known as Charleston) remained from 1670 to 1680, when it was moved across and downstream to Oyster Point, overlooking Charleston Harbor. There, as proud Charlestonians later claimed, the Ashley and Cooper Rivers "join to form the Atlantic Ocean."

The government of this colony rested on one of the most curious documents of colonial history, the "Fundamental Constitutions of Carolina," drawn up by one of the proprietors, Lord Ashley-Cooper, with the help of his secretary, the philosopher John Locke. Its cumbersome frame of government and its provisions for an elaborate nobility had little effect in the colony except to encourage a practice of large land grants, but from the beginning smaller "headrights" were given to every immigrant who paid for the cost of transit. The provision that had greatest effect was a grant of religious toleration, designed to encourage immigration, which gave South Carolina a greater degree of indulgence (extending even to Jews and heathens) than either England or any other colony except Rhode Island and, once it was established, Pennsylvania.

For two decades the South Carolina proprietors struggled to find a staple crop. The first profitable enterprise was a flourishing trade in deerskins and Indian slaves. Ambitious Barbadians dominated the colony and organized a major trade in Indian slaves, whom the Westo Indians obligingly drove to the coast for shipment to the Caribbean. The first major export other than furs and slaves was cattle, and a staple crop was not developed until the introduction of rice in the 1690s. South Carolina became a separate royal colony in 1719. North Carolina remained under the proprietors' rule for ten more years, when they surrendered their governing rights to the crown.

THE SOUTHERN INDIAN TRADE   The major Indian tribes in Florida, the Carolinas, Georgia, and what is today Alabama and Mississippi—the Apalachee, Timucua, Catawba, Cherokee, Chickasaw, Choctaw, Creek, and Tuscarora—combined farming with hunting and fishing to produce a thriving culture. They clustered in matrilineal clans (in which authority and property descended through the maternal line). The women raised beans, potatoes, and especially corn. The men hunted, traded, and made war. Beginning in the late seventeenth century, the Creeks developed a flourishing trade with the British settlers, exchanging deerskins for manufactured goods—hoes, copper kettles, knives, beads, blankets, and clothing.

In the late seventeenth century English merchants—mostly illiterate adventurers—began traveling southward from Virginia down the Occaneechi trading path into the Piedmont region of Carolina, where they developed a prosperous exchange with the Catawbas. By 1690 traders from Charleston, South Carolina, made their way up the Savannah River to arrange deals with the Cherokees, Creeks, and Chickasaws. Between 1699 and 1715 Carolina exported an average of 54,000 deerskins per year. The voracious demand for the soft skins almost exterminated the deer population.

The growing trade with the English exposed the Indians to contagious diseases that decimated their population. Commercial activity

An Indian village in North Carolina, in an engraving by
Theodor de Bry based on a sketch by John White.

also entwined the Indians in a dependent relationship that would prove
disastrous to their traditional way of life. Eager to receive more finished
goods, weapons, and ammunition, the Indians became pliable trading
partners, easily manipulated by wily English entrepreneurs and government officials. The English traders began providing the Indians with
firearms and rum as incentives to convince them to capture rival tribes-
men to be sold as slaves.

During the early eighteenth century, Indians equipped with British
weapons and led by English soldiers crossed into Spanish territory in
south Georgia and north Florida. They were intent upon destroying
Spanish missions and capturing Indian slaves from the Timucua and
Apalachee tribes. One large campaign destroyed thirteen missions,
killed several hundred Indians and Spaniards, and enslaved over three
hundred Indian men, women, and children. By 1710 the Florida tribes
were on the verge of extinction.

One white Carolinian rationalized enslaving Indians by arguing that
"it both serves to lessen their numbers before the French can arm them,
and it is a more Effectuall way of Civilizing and Instructing [them] than
all of the efforts used by the French missionaries." In 1708, when the
total population of South Carolina was 9,580, including 2,900 blacks,

A contemporary print depicting seven "Chiefs of the Cherokee Indians" who had been taken from Carolina to England in 1730.

there were 1,400 Indian slaves. Because the captive Indians frequently escaped or revolted, many were relocated to New England or the West Indies.

The continuing Indian trade led to repeated troubles. In 1711 the Tuscaroras in North Carolina were goaded by the Iroquois to abandon their accommodating ways and oust the Europeans. The catalyst for their uprising was the severe punishment of a Tuscarora accused of a petty offense. In a vengeful outburst, the Tuscaroras captured and killed a white colonist, then assaulted several plantations. When South Carolina dispatched a relief expedition of whites and Indian allies, the Tuscaroras held out in forts of their own. But in 1713 they succumbed to a massive assault. Hundreds of Tuscaroras were killed and over four hundred enslaved. Most of the survivors of this Tuscarora War retreated north, where they joined the Iroquois League.

Two years later, in 1715, Creeks, Choctaws, and members of smaller tribes organized a more massive revolt against English control. This Yamasee War began when Indians killed several English traders, including the Indian agent for South Carolina. The English attributed the attacks to French and Spanish intrigues, but it now seems likely that the Indians acted on their own. The English colonists won out by playing the Indians against one another, convincing the Cherokees to join their side. When the Creek leaders visited the Cherokees in an effort to gain their support, the Cherokees killed them, an incident that engendered hatred between the two tribes for years thereafter.

The Yamasee War ended in 1717, but infighting among the Indians continued. For the next ten years or so, the Creeks and Cherokees engaged in a costly blood feud, much to the delight of the English. One Carolinian explained that their challenge was to figure "how to hold both as our friends, for some time, and assist them in cutting one another's throats without offending either. This is the game we intend to play if possible." The French played the same brutal game, doing their best to excite hatred between the Choctaws and the Chickasaws.

SETTLING THE MIDDLE COLONIES AND GEORGIA

NEW NETHERLAND BECOMES NEW YORK Charles II resolved early to pluck out that old thorn in the side of the English colonies— New Netherland. The Dutch colony was older than New England, and had been planted when the two Protestant powers enjoyed friendly relations in opposition to Catholic Spain. The Dutch East India Company (organized in 1602) had hired an English captain, Henry Hudson, to seek the elusive passage to China. Sailing along the upper coast of North America in 1609, Hudson had discovered Delaware Bay and explored the river named for him, to a point probably beyond Albany, where he and a group of Mohawks made merry with brandy. From the contact stemmed a lasting trade relation between the Dutch and the Iroquois nations. In 1614 the Dutch established fur-trading posts on Manhattan Island and upriver at Fort Orange (later Albany). In 1626 Governor Peter Minuit purchased Manhattan from the resident Indians, and a Dutch fort appeared at the lower end of the island. The village of New Amsterdam, which grew up around the fort, became the capital of New Netherland.

Dutch settlements gradually dispersed in every direction where furs might be found. In 1638 a Swedish trading company established Fort Christina at the site of the present Wilmington and scattered a few hundred settlers up and down the Delaware River. The Dutch, at the time allied to the Swedes in the Thirty Years' War, made no move to challenge the claim until 1655, when a force outnumbering the entire Swedish colony subjected them without bloodshed to the rule of New Netherland. The chief contribution of the short-lived New Sweden to

New Amsterdam in 1667.

American culture was the idea of the log cabin, which the Swedes and a few Finnish settlers had brought from the woods of Scandinavia.

Like the French, the Dutch were interested mainly in the fur trade rather than agricultural settlements. In 1629, however, the Dutch West India Company (organized in 1621) provided that any stockholder might obtain a large estate (a patroonship) if he peopled it with fifty adults within four years. The patroon was obligated to supply cattle, tools, and buildings. His tenants, in turn, paid him rent, used his grist-mill, gave him first option on surplus crops, and submitted to a court he established. It amounted to transplanting the feudal manor into the New World, and met with as little luck as similar efforts in Maryland and South Carolina. Volunteers for serfdom were hard to find when there was land to be had elsewhere; most settlers took advantage of the company's provision that one could have as farms (*bouweries*) all the lands one could improve.

The colony's government was under the almost absolute control of a governor sent out by the Dutch West India Company, subject to little check from his council or from the directors back in Holland. The governors were mostly stubborn autocrats, either corrupt or inept, especially at Indian relations. They depended on a small professional garrison for defense, and the inhabitants (including a number of English on Long Island) showed almost total indifference in 1664 when Governor Peter Stuyvesant called them to arms against a threatening British fleet. Almost defenseless, old soldier Stuyvesant blustered and stomped about on his wooden leg, but finally surrendered without a shot and stayed on quietly at his farm in what had become the colony of New York.

The plan of conquest had been hatched by the king's brother, the duke of York and Albany, later King James II. As lord high admiral and an investor in the African trade, he had already harassed Dutch shipping and forts in Africa. When he and his advisers counseled that New Netherland could easily be conquered, Charles II simply granted the region to his brother as proprietor, permitted the hasty gathering of an invasion force, and the English transformed New Amsterdam into New York and Fort Orange into Albany. The Dutch, however, left a permanent imprint on the land and the language: the Dutch vernacular faded away but place names such as Block Island, Wall Street (the original wall was for protection against Indians), and Broadway (*Breede Wegh*) remained, along with family names like Rensselaer, Roosevelt, and Van Buren. The Dutch presence lingered in the Dutch Reformed church; in words like *boss, cookie, crib, snoop, stoop, spook,* and *kill* (for creek); and in the legendary Santa Claus and Rip Van Winkle.

THE IROQUOIS LEAGUE   One of the most significant effects of European settlement in North America during the seventeenth century was the intensification of warfare between Indian peoples. The same combination of forces that decimated the Indian population of New England and the Carolinas affected the tribes around New York City and the lower Hudson Valley. Dissension among the Indians and susceptibility to infectious disease left them vulnerable to exploitation by whites and by other Indians.

In the interior of New York, however, a different situation arose. There the Iroquois (an Algonquian term signifying "snake" or "terrifying man") nation would eventually forge a strong alliance, a league so strong and numerous that the outnumbered Dutch and, later, English traders were forced to work with the Indians in exploiting the lucrative fur trade. Initially, the Mahicans (an offshoot of the Pequots) supplied the Dutch with pelts. By 1625, however, the game animals in the Mahican territory had been hunted almost to extinction, so the Dutch turned to the Iroquois, a federation of five tribes that spoke related languages—the Mohawk, Oneida, Onondaga, Cayuga, and Seneca (a sixth tribe, the Tuscaroras, joined them from Carolina in 1712)—for supplies of fur and for allies.

By the early 1600s, some fifty sachems (chiefs) governed the 12,000 members of the Iroquois League. The sachems made decisions for all the villages and served to minimize tribal rivalries and dissension within the confederacy. The well-organized, firmly knit Iroquois tribes lived in rectangular "long houses" sheathed in bark. These multifamily dwellings could house fifty or sixty members of an extended family. Iroquois men hunted deer, bear, and beaver; women grew corn, beans, and squash. They used belts of colored beads, known as wampum, to symbolize words intended to certify treaties or record transactions with other Indians and whites. The rejection or return of a wampum belt meant that its message or proposal was unacceptable. Although a patriarchal society, the Iroquois granted considerable powers to women, who controlled the nominations for the tribal councils and could remove ineffective or corrupt leaders.

When the Iroquois began to deplete the local game during the 1640s, they used firearms supplied by their Dutch trading partners to seize the Canadian hunting grounds of the neighboring Hurons and Eries. During the so-called Beaver Wars, the Iroquois defeated the western tribes and thereafter hunted the region to extinction. Other Indian nations such as the Fox, Sauk, and Kickapoo fled in terror at the approach of

Iroquois wampum belts.

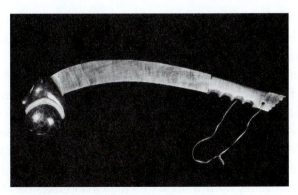

An Onondaga (Iroquois) war club.

the Iroquois. The lucrative trade in pelts led the Iroquois to emphasize the warrior-hunter ideal as the masculine archetype.

Iroquois men were proud, ruthless warriors. Participation in a war party served as the crucial rite of passage for young men. They fought opponents to gain status and revenge and to ease the grief caused by the death of friends and relatives. Their skill and courage in battle determined their social status. A warrior's success was not only measured by his fighting prowess but also by his ability to take prisoners and bring them back alive for adoption or ritual execution. This helps explain the Indian preference for surprise attacks and ambushes rather than conventional frontal assaults.

If captured themselves, the Iroquois expected to be tortured. They, in turn, tortured, roasted, and occasionally ate their foes. A captive slated for execution was daubed with red and black paint, given a death feast, and invited to recite his own feats in war. On the appointed day he was tied to a stake, and villagers of all ages then took turns burning him with red-hot objects. A courageous victim was expected to endure such torments stoically, but few could do so for long. Eventually the prisoner was scalped, hot sand was thrown onto the exposed skull, and a hatchet blow to the neck ended his suffering.

While providing profitable new hunting grounds, wars against other Indian tribes depleted the Iroquois population. This led them to replace lost relatives by allowing elder women to "adopt" able-bodied captives after they had been tortured so as to break their allegiance to their native group or culture. In 1657 a French missionary noted that "more

Foreigners than natives of the country" resided in Iroquoia. By the 1660s more than two-thirds of the residents of some Iroquois villages were adoptees.

During the second half of the seventeenth century, the relentless search for furs and captives led Iroquois war parties to range far and wide across what is today eastern North America. They gained control over a huge area from the St. Lawrence River to Tennessee and from Maine to Michigan. These wars helped reorient the political relationships in the whole eastern half of the continent, especially in the area from the Ohio Valley northward across the Great Lakes basin. Besieged by the Iroquois League, the western tribes forged defensive alliances with the French.

For over twenty years warfare raged across the Great Lakes region. In the 1690s the French and their Indian allies gained the advantage over the Iroquois. They destroyed their crops and villages, infected them with smallpox, and reduced the male population by more than a third. Facing extermination, the Iroquois made peace with the French in 1701. They claimed to be tired of serving the English as a "Pack of Hounds" to harass the French. During the first half of the eighteenth century, they maintained a shrewd neutrality between the two rival European powers that enabled them to play the British off against the French, all the while creating a thriving fur trade for themselves.

NEW JERSEY   Shortly after the conquest of New Netherland, still in 1664, the duke of York granted his lands between the Hudson and the Delaware Rivers to Sir George Carteret and Lord John Berkeley (brother of Virginia's governor), and named the territory for Carteret's native island of Jersey. In 1676, by mutual agreement, the colony was divided by a diagonal line into East and West New Jersey, with Carteret taking the east. Finally in 1682 Carteret sold out to a group of twelve, including William Penn, who in turn brought into partnership twelve more proprietors, for a total of twenty-four! In East New Jersey, peopled at first by perhaps 200 Dutch who had crossed the Hudson, new settlements gradually arose: some disaffected Puritans from New Haven founded Newark, Carteret's brother brought a group to found Elizabethtown (Elizabeth), and a group of Scots founded Perth Amboy. In the west, which faces the Delaware River, a scattering of Swedes, Finns, and Dutch remained, soon to be overwhelmed by swarms of

English Quakers. In 1702 East and West New Jersey were united as a single royal colony.

PENNSYLVANIA AND DELAWARE   The Quaker sect, as the Society of Friends was called in ridicule (because they told their followers to "tremble at the word of the Lord"), became the most influential of many radical groups that sprang from the turbulence of the English Civil War. Founded by George Fox in about 1647, the Quakers carried further than any other group the doctrine of individual inspiration and interpretation—the "inner light," they called it. They discarded all formal sacraments and formal ministry, refused deference to persons of rank, used the familiar "thee" and "thou" in addressing everyone, refused to take oaths because that was contrary to Scripture, and embraced pacifism. Quakers were subjected to intense persecution—often in their zeal they seemed to invite it—but never inflicted it on others. Their toleration extended to complete religious freedom for all, of whatever belief or disbelief, and to the equality of the sexes and the full participation of women in religious affairs.

In 1673 George Fox returned from a visit to America with the vision of a Quaker commonwealth in the New World and enticed others with

A Quaker meeting. The presence of women is evidence of Quaker views on the equality of the sexes.

his idea. The entrance of Quakers into New Jersey encouraged Quakers to migrate, especially to the Delaware River side. And soon, across the river, arose William Penn's Quaker commonwealth, the colony of Pennsylvania.

Penn was the son of Admiral Sir William Penn, who had supported Parliament in the Civil War and had led Cromwell's conquest of Jamaica but later helped in the Restoration. Young William was reared as a proper gentleman, but as a student at Oxford he had turned to Quakerism. Upon his father's death, Penn inherited a substantial estate, including a claim of £16,000 his father had lent the crown. Whether in settlement of the claim or out of simple friendship, he got from Charles II in 1681 proprietary rights to a tract extending westward from the Delaware River for 5 degrees of longitude and from the "beginning" of the 43rd degree on the north to the "beginning" of the 40th degree on the south. The land was named, at the king's insistence, for Penn's father: Pennsylvania (literally Penn's Woods). The boundary overlapped lands granted to both New York and Maryland. The New York boundary was settled on the basis of the duke of York's charter at 42° North, but the Maryland boundary remained in question until 1767 when a compromise line (nineteen miles south of the 40th parallel) was surveyed by Charles Mason and Jeremiah Dixon—the celebrated Mason-Dixon line.

When Penn assumed control of the area, there was already a scattering of Dutch, Swedish, and English settlers on the west bank of the Delaware. But Penn also soon made vigorous efforts to bring in more

William Penn, the Quaker who founded the Pennsylvania colony in 1681.

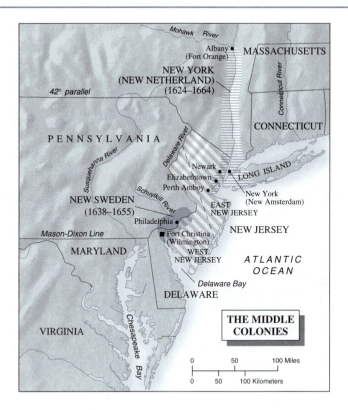

settlers. He published glowing descriptions of the colony, which were translated into German, Dutch, and French. By the end of 1681, Penn had about 1,000 settlers in his province, and in October of the next year arrived himself with 100 more. By that time, a town was growing up at the junction of the Schuylkill and Delaware Rivers. Penn called it Philadelphia (the City of Brotherly Love). Because of the generous terms on which Penn offered land, because indeed he offered aid to emigrants, the colony grew rapidly.

The relations between the Indians and the Quakers were cordial from the beginning, because of the Quakers' friendliness and because of Penn's careful policy of purchasing land titles from the Indians. Penn even took the trouble to learn the language of the Delawares, something few colonists even tried. For some fifty years, the settlers and the natives lived side by side in peace, in relationships of such trust that Quaker farmers sometimes left their children in the care of Indians when they were away from home.

The government, which rested on three Frames of Government promulgated by Penn, resembled that of other proprietary colonies, except that the freemen (taxpayers and property owners) elected the councilors as well as the assembly. The governor had no veto—although Penn, as proprietor, did. "Any government is free . . . where the laws rule and the people are a party to the laws," Penn wrote in the 1682 Frame of Government. He hoped to show that a government could run in accordance with Quaker principles, that it could maintain peace and order without oaths or wars, and that religion could flourish without an established church and with absolute freedom of conscience. Because of its tolerance, Pennsylvania became a refuge not only for Quakers but for a variety of dissenters—as well as Anglicans—and early reflected the ethnic mixture of Scotch-Irish and Germans that became common to the middle colonies and the southern backcountry. Penn himself stayed only four years in the colony.

In 1682 the duke of York also granted Penn the area of Delaware, another part of the Dutch territory. At first Delaware became part of Pennsylvania, but after 1701 it was granted the right to choose its own assembly. From then until the American Revolution it had a separate assembly but the same governor as Pennsylvania.

GEORGIA   Georgia was the last of the British continental colonies to be established, half a century after Pennsylvania. During the seventeenth century, English settlers pushed southward into the borderlands between the Carolinas and Florida. They brought with them their African slaves and a desire to win over the Indian trade from the Spanish. Each side used guns, goods, and rum to influence the Indians, and the Indians, in turn, effectively played off the English against the Spanish in order to gain the most favorable terms.

In 1732 George II gave the land between the Savannah and Altamaha Rivers to the twenty-one trustees of Georgia. In two respects Georgia was unique among the colonies: it was set up as both a philanthropic experiment and a military buffer against Spanish Florida. General James E. Oglethorpe, who accompanied the first colonists as resident trustee, represented both concerns: as a soldier who organized the defenses, and as a philanthropist who championed prison reform and sought a colonial refuge for the poor and religiously persecuted.

A view of Savannah in 1734. The town's layout was carefully planned.

In 1733 a band of 120 colonists founded Savannah near the mouth of the Savannah River. Carefully laid out by Oglethorpe, the old town with its geometrical pattern and its numerous little parks remains a monument to the city planning of a bygone day. A group of Protestant refugees from Austria began to arrive in 1734, followed by a number of Germans and German-speaking Moravians and Swiss, who made the colony for a time more German than English. The addition of Highland Scots, Portuguese Jews, Welsh, and others gave the early colony a cosmopolitan character much like that of Charleston.

As a buffer against Florida the colony succeeded, but as a philanthropic experiment it failed. Efforts to develop silk and wine production had little success. Land holdings were limited to 500 acres, rum was prohibited, and the importation of slaves was forbidden, partly to leave room for servants brought on charity, partly to ensure security. But the utopian rules soon collapsed. The regulations against rum and slavery were widely disregarded, and finally abandoned. By 1759 all restrictions on landholding were removed.

In 1753 the trustees' charter expired, and the province reverted to the crown. As a royal colony, Georgia acquired for the first time an ef-

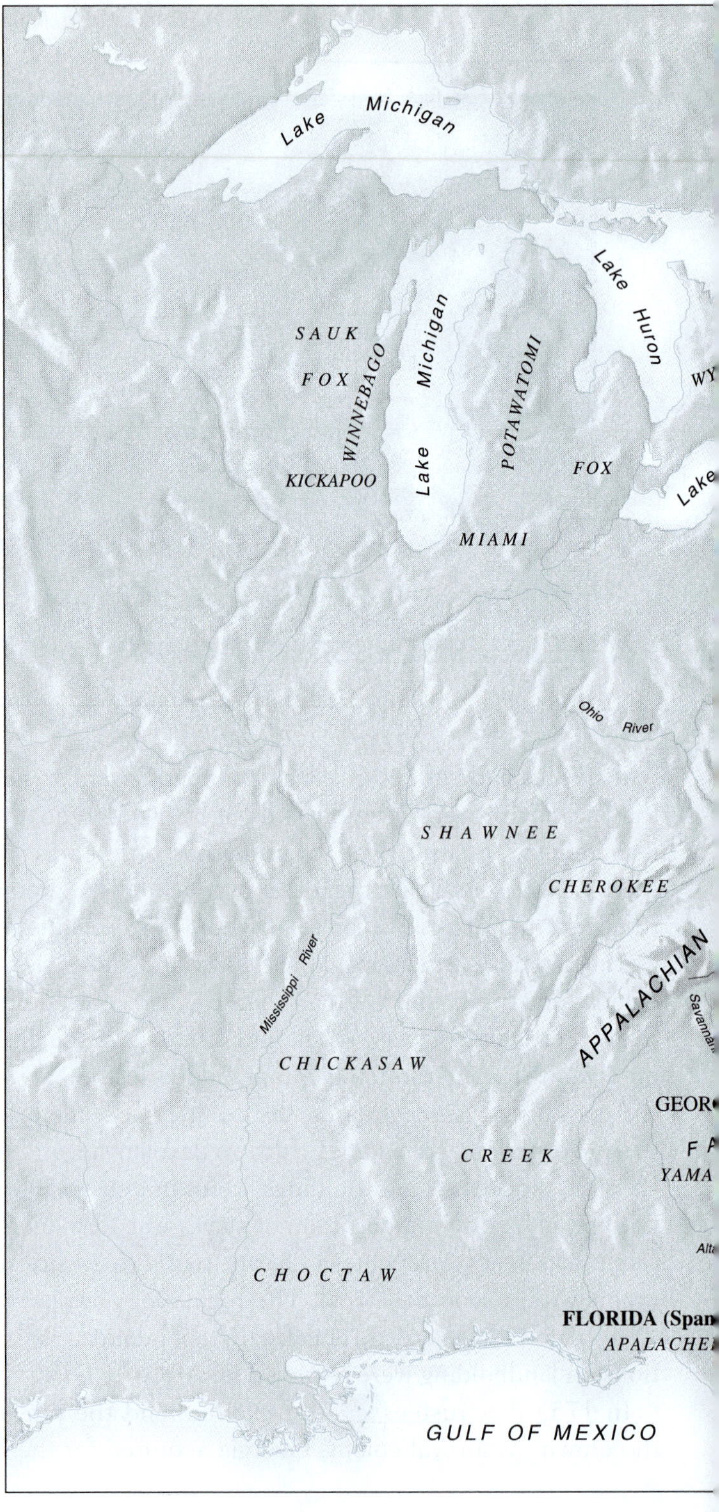

Lake Michigan
Lake Michigan
Lake Huron
Lake
SAUK
FOX
WINNEBAGO
KICKAPOO
POTAWATOMI
FOX
MIAMI
WY
Ohio River
SHAWNEE
CHEROKEE
APPALACHIAN
Mississippi River
CHICKASAW
CREEK
CHOCTAW
FLORIDA (Span
APALACHE
GULF OF MEXICO

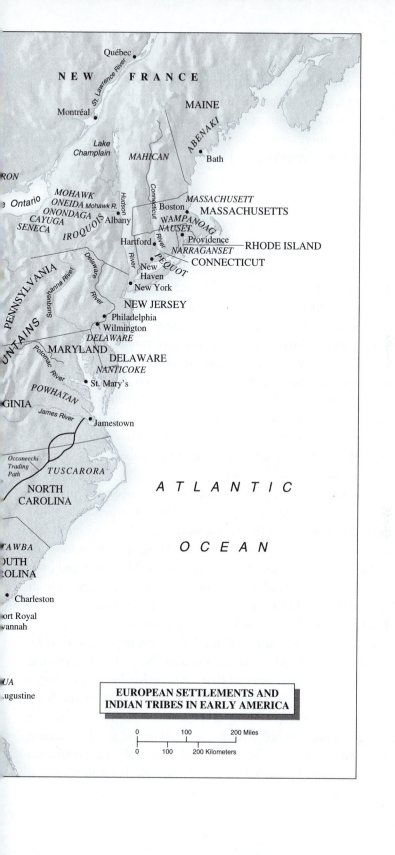

Québec

NEW   FRANCE

MAINE

Montréal

St. Lawrence River

ABENAKI

Lake
Champlain   *MAHICAN*   Bath

RON

e Ontario   *MOHAWK*
              ONEIDA Mohawk R.   *MASSACHUSETT*
          ONONDAGA   Boston   MASSACHUSETTS
        CAYUGA   Albany   *WAMPANOAG*
      SENECA   *NAUSET*
              IROQUOIS   Providence ── RHODE ISLAND
                        Hartford   *NARRAGANSET*
                               PEQUOT ── CONNECTICUT
                           New
                           Haven
                        New York

Hudson
Connecticut
River
River

PENNSYLVANIA   NEW JERSEY

Delaware
Susquehanna River   Philadelphia
Susquehanna   *River*   Wilmington
                           DELAWARE
UNTAINS   MARYLAND   DELAWARE
          Potomac   *NANTICOKE*
            River   St. Mary's

POWHATAN

GINIA   *James River*   Jamestown

Occaneechi
Trading
Path   *TUSCARORA*
          NORTH
          CAROLINA   ATLANTIC

AWBA
UTH   OCEAN
OLINA

Charleston
ort Royal
vannah

UA
ugustine

EUROPEAN SETTLEMENTS AND
INDIAN TRIBES IN EARLY AMERICA

0   100   200 Miles

0   100   200 Kilometers

fective government. The province developed slowly over the next decade, but grew rapidly in population and wealth after 1763. Instead of wine and silk, as was Oglethorpe's plan, Georgians exported rice, indigo, lumber, naval stores, beef, and pork, and carried on a lively trade with the West Indies. The colony had become a commercial success.

THRIVING COLONIES

By the early eighteenth century, the English had outstripped both the French and the Spanish in the New World. The centralized control imposed by the monarchs of Spain and France got them off the mark more quickly but eventually brought about their downfall because it hobbled innovation and responsiveness to new circumstances. The British acted by private investment and with a minimum of royal control. Not a single colony was begun at the direct initiative of the crown. In the English colonies, poor immigrants had a much greater chance of getting at least a small parcel of land. The English, unlike their rivals, welcomed people from a variety of nationalities and dissenting sects who came in search of a new life or a safe harbor. And a degree of self-government made the English colonies more responsive to new circumstances—if sometimes stalled by controversy.

The compact pattern of English settlement contrasted sharply with the pattern of Spain's far-flung conquests or France's far-reaching trade routes to the interior by way of the St. Lawrence and Mississippi Rivers (discussed in Chapter 4). Geography reinforced England's bent for concentrated occupation and settlement of its colonies. The rivers and bays that indented the coasts served as veins of communication along which colonies first sprang up, but no great river offered a highway to the far interior. About a hundred miles back in Georgia and the Carolinas, and nearer the coast to the north, the "fall line" of the rivers presented rocky rapids that marked the head of navigation and the end of the coastal plain. About a hundred miles beyond that, and farther back in Pennsylvania, stretched the rolling expanse of the Piedmont, literally the foothills. And the final backdrop of English America was the Appalachian Mountain range, some 200 miles from the coast in the south, reaching down to the coast at points in New England, with only one significant break—up the Hudson-Mohawk Valley of New York. For 150 years the farthest outreach of settlement stopped at the slopes of the mountains. To the east lay the wide expanse of ocean, which served as a highway for the transit of civilization from Europe to America, but also as a barrier beyond which civilization took to new paths in a new environment.

MAKING CONNECTIONS

- What we now know about the early settlements sets the stage for regional differences in social patterns discussed in the next chapter.

- This chapter contains the observation that in founding its American colonies, "the British acted by private investment and with a minimum of royal control." This will change in Chapter 4 as England begins to take control of the American colonies.

- Later relations between colonists and Native Americans, described in Chapter 4, had their roots in the history of these early settlements.

FURTHER READING

Bernard Bailyn's multivolume work *The Peopling of British North America*, the first two volumes of which have appeared (*The Peopling of British North America: An Introduction*, 1986, and *Voyagers to the West: A Passage in the Peopling of America on the Eve of the Revolution*, 1986), provides a comprehensive view of European migration. Carl Bridenbaugh's *Vexed and Troubled Englishmen, 1590–1642* (1968) helps explain why so many sought a new home in a strange land. English constitutional traditions and their effect on the colonists are examined in Edmund S. Morgan's *Inventing the People: The Rise of Popular Sover-*

eignty in England and America (1988). Jack P. Greene provides a brilliant synthesis of British colonization in *Pursuits of Happiness: The Social Development of Early Modern British Colonies and the Formation of American Culture* (1988). Carl Bridenbaugh's *Jamestown, 1544–1699* (1980) traces the English experience on the Chesapeake. See Daniel K. Richter's *The Ordeal of the Longhouse: The Peoples of the Iroquois League in The Era of European Colonization* (1992) for a history of the northeastern Iroquois Nation.

A succinct overview on Puritanism can be found in Alan Simpson's *Puritanism in Old and New England* (1955). Andrew Delbanco's *The Puritan Ordeal* (1989) is a powerful study of the tensions inherent in the Puritan outlook. Useful works on the problem of dissent in a theocracy include Edmund S. Morgan's *Roger Williams, the Church, and the State* (1967) and Emery Battis's *Saints and Sectaries: Anne Hutchinson and The Antinomian Controversy in Massachusetts Bay Colony* (1962).

The pattern of settlement in the middle colonies is illuminated in Barry Levy's *Quakers and the American Family: British Settlement in the Delaware Valley* (1988). Randall Balmer's *A Perfect Babel of Confusion: Dutch Religion and English Culture in the Middle Colonies* (1989) describes how the English conquest of New Netherlands intensified the cultural complexity of the middle colonies. The influence of Quakers can be studied through Gary B. Nash's *Quakers and Politics: Pennsylvania, 1681–1726* (1968).

Settlement of the areas along the South Atlantic is traced in Wesley F. Craven's *The Southern Colonies in the Seventeenth Century, 1607–1689* (1949) and Clarence L. Ver Steeg's *Origins of a Southern Mosaic* (1975). Robert M. Weir's *Colonial South Carolina* (1983) covers the activities of the Lords Proprietors. For a study of race and the settlement of South Carolina, see Peter Wood's *Black Majority: Negroes in Colonial South Carolina from 1670 through the Stono Rebellion* (1975). Those interested in the colonization of Georgia should consult *Oglethorpe in Perspective: Georgia's Founder after Two Hundred Years* (1989), edited by Phinizy Spalding and Harvey H. Jackson. A brilliant book on relations between the Catawba Indians and their black and white neighbors is James H. Merrell's *The Indians' New World: Catawbas and Their Neighbors from European Contact through the Era of Removal* (1989).

3 ❧ COLONIAL WAYS OF LIFE

CHAPTER ORGANIZER

This chapter focuses on:

- the social and economic differences among the southern, middle, and New England colonies.

- how various groups of people of different genders, races, and classes fit into colonial society.

- the impact of the Enlightenment and the Great Awakening on the American colonies.

The process of carving a new civilization out of an abundant yet menacing and violent frontier was largely the story of thousands of diverse folk engaged in the everyday tasks of building homes, planting crops, raising families, enforcing laws, and worshipping their God. Those who colonized America during the seventeenth and eighteenth centuries were part of a massive pattern of social migration occurring throughout Europe and Africa. Everywhere, it seemed, people were moving from farms to villages, from villages to cities, and from homelands to colonies. They came from varied locales—the streets of London and other cities in southern and central England, the farms of Yorkshire and the Scottish Highlands, the villages of Germany, Switzerland, and Protestant Ireland, and the savannas and jungles of West Africa. They moved for different reasons. Most were responding to powerful social and economic forces, as rapid population growth and the rise of commercial agriculture squeezed people off the land. Many traveled in search of political security or religious freedom. Africans were moved to new lands against their will.

America's settlers were mostly young (over half were under twenty-five), and mostly male. Almost half were indentured servants or slaves, and during the eighteenth century England would transport some 50,000 convicted felons to the North American colonies. About a third of the settlers came with their families, but most arrived alone. A very few were wealthy, but more were impoverished. Most were of the "middling sort," neither very rich nor very poor. Whatever their status or ambition, however, this extraordinary mosaic of ordinary yet adventurous people was primarily responsible for creating the American institutions and values we have all inherited.

THE SHAPE OF EARLY AMERICA

BRITISH FOLKWAYS   The vast majority of early settlers came from the British Isles. They clustered in four mass migrations from distinct regions of Britain over the seventeenth and eighteenth centuries. The first involved some 20,000 Puritans who settled Massachusetts between 1629 and 1641, most of whom hailed from the East Anglian counties east of London. A generation later, a smaller group of wealthy Royalist cavaliers and their indentured servants migrated from southern England to Virginia. These English aristocrats, mostly Anglicans, were already beneficiaries of severe social inequalities and so had few qualms about the introduction of African slavery. The third migratory wave brought some 23,000 Quakers from the North Midlands of England to the Delaware Valley colonies of West Jersey, Pennsylvania, and Delaware. They imported with them a social system that was distinctive for its sense of spiritual equality, suspicion of class distinctions and powerful elites, and a commitment to plain living and high thinking. The fourth and largest surge of colonization occurred between 1717 and 1775 and included hundreds of thousands of Celtic Britons and Scotch-Irish from northern Ireland, the Scottish Lowlands, and the northern counties of England; these were mostly coarse, feisty, clannish folk who settled in the rugged backcountry along the Appalachian Mountains.

It was long assumed that the strenuous demands of the American frontier environment served as a great "melting pot" that stripped such immigrants of their native identities and melded them into homogeneous Americans. Yet for all of the transforming effects of the New World, the persistence of disparate British ways of life was remarkable. Although most British settlers spoke a common language and shared the Protestant faith, they carried with them—and retained—sharply different cultural attitudes and customs from their home regions. They spoke distinct dialects, cooked different foods, named and raised their children differently, adopted different educational philosophies and attitudes toward time, adopted different architectural styles, engaged in disparate games and forms of recreation, and organized their societies differently.

Echoes of these divergent regionally based folkways still resonate through American culture. People in the South prefer fried foods in part because their ancestors from southern and western England did so. People in the hollows of Appalachia who manufacture "moonshine" are simply continuing a pattern of home distilling begun in the borderlands of northern Britain.

In gender relations, religious practices, criminal propensities, and dozens of other ways, many American customs in the 1990s still reflect age-old British customs. Of course, such cultural continuity is not unique to British Americans. Enduring folkways are also evident among the descendants of settlers from Africa, Europe, Latin America, the Middle East, and Asia. Americans thus constitute a mosaic rather than a homogeneous mass, and they share a quite varied social and cultural heritage.

SEABOARD ECOLOGY   One of the cherished legends of American history has it that those settling British America arrived to find an unspoiled wilderness little touched by human activity. But that was not the case. For thousands of years, Indian hunting practices had produced what one scholar has called the "greatest known loss of wild species" in the continent's history. The Indians had burned forests and dense undergrowth in order to provide cropland, to ease travel through hardwood forests, and to make way for grasses, berries, and other forage

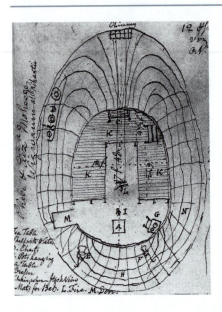

A sketch of Niantic wigwams in 1761, by Ezra Stiles.

for the animals they hunted. Indians worked cleared lands for six to eight years until the nutrients in the soil were depleted, and then they moved on to new areas. This migratory "slash-and-burn" agriculture increased the rate at which plant nutrients were recycled and also allowed more sunlight to reach the forest floor. These conditions in turn created rich soil and ideal grazing grounds for elk, deer, turkey, bear, moose, and beaver. Nutrients from the topsoil also fertilized the streams and helped produce teeming schools of sturgeon, smelt, and small herrings called alewives. Indian farming practices also halted the normal forest succession and, especially in the Southeast, created large stands of longleaf pines, still the most common source of timber in the region.

Equally important in shaping the ecosystem of America was the European attitude toward the environment. Where the Native Americans tended to be migratory, considering land and animals as communal resources to be shared and consumed only as necessary, many European colonizers viewed natural resources as privately owned commodities to be sold for profit. Settlers thus quickly set about evicting Indians, clearing, fencing, improving, and selling land, growing surpluses, and trapping game for commercial use. These practices transformed the seaboard environment. In many places—Plymouth, for instance, or St.

Mary's, Maryland—settlers occupied the sites of former Indian towns, and maize, corn, beans, and squash quickly became colonial staples, along with new crops brought from Europe.

In time a more dense population of humans and their domestic animals created a new landscape of fields, meadows, fences, barns, and houses. Such innovations further altered the ecology of the New World environment. Colonists brought with them new domesticated animals—pigs, sheep, cattle, and horses—as well as new weeds and pests such as dandelions, black flies, and cockroaches. Animal crowding forced further deforestation. So, too, did the ravenous demand for timber to construct ships and houses, a demand that devoured many of the white oak, white pine, cedar, and hickory trees in the East.

There followed consequences no one had anticipated. Because cleared and grazed land is warmer, drier, and more compacted, it is more easily subject to flooding and erosion. Foraging cattle, sheep, horses, and pigs gradually changed the distribution of trees, shrubs, and grasses. The transformed landscape made regions such as New England sunnier, windier, and colder than they had been before colonization. And many Indians, far from being passive observers in this frenzy of environmental change, contributed to the process by trading furs for metal or glass trinkets. This ravaged the populations of large mammals that had earlier been central to Indian culture—and to the ecological balance. By 1800 the physical environment of the eastern seaboard had changed markedly from what it had been in 1600.

POPULATION GROWTH   England's first footholds in America were bought at a fearful price. But once the brutal seasoning time was past and the colony was on its feet, Virginia and all its successors grew rapidly. After the last major Indian uprising in 1644, Virginia's population quadrupled from about 8,000 to 32,000 over the next thirty years, then more than doubled, to 75,000, by 1704. Throughout the mainland colonies the yearly growth rate during the eighteenth century ran about 3 percent. In 1625 the English colonists numbered little more than 2,000 in Virginia and Plymouth together; by 1700 the population in the colonies was perhaps 250,000, and during the eighteenth century it doubled at least every twenty-five years. By 1750 the number of colonists had passed 1 million; by 1775 it stood at about 2.5 million. In 1700 the English at home outnumbered the colonists by about 20 to 1;

by 1775, on the eve of the American Revolution, the ratio had fallen to 3 to 1.

The prodigious increase of colonial population did not go unnoticed. Benjamin Franklin of Pennsylvania, a keen observer of many things, published in 1751 his *Observations Concerning the Increase of Mankind* in which he pointed out two facts of life that distinguished the colonies from Europe: land was plentiful and cheap; labor was scarce and dear. Just the opposite conditions prevailed in the Old World. From this reversal of conditions flowed many if not most of the changes that European culture underwent in the New World—not the least being that good fortune beckoned the immigrant and induced the settlers to replenish the earth with large families. Where labor was scarce, children could lend a hand, and once they were grown could find new land for themselves if need be. Colonists tended, as a result, to marry and start new families at an earlier age.

BIRTHRATES AND DEATH RATES   Given the better economic prospects in the colonies, a greater proportion of American women married and the birthrate remained much higher than in Europe. Where in England the average age at marriage for women was twenty-five or twenty-six, in America it dropped to twenty or twenty-one. Men also married younger in the colonies than in the Old World. The birthrate rose accordingly, since those who married earlier had time for about two additional pregnancies during the childbearing years. In eighteenth-century Virginia, William Byrd II of Westover asserted, matrimony thrived "so excellently" that "an Old Maid or an Old Bachelor are as scarce among us and reckoned as ominous as a Blazing Star." And early marriage remained common. The most "antique Virgin" Byrd knew was his twenty-year-old daughter.

Equally responsible for the burgeoning population in the colonies was a much lower death rate in the New World. After the difficult first years of settlement, infants generally had a better chance to reach maturity, and adults had a better chance to reach old age. In seventeenth-century New England, apart from childhood mortality, men could expect to reach seventy and women nearly that age.

This longevity resulted from several factors. Since the land was more bountiful, famine seldom occurred after the first year, and while the winters were more severe than in England, firewood was plentiful. Be-

Mr. John Freake, and Mrs. Elizabeth Freake and Baby Mary. Elizabeth married John at age nineteen; Mary, born when Elizabeth was thirty-two, was the Freakes' eighth and last child.

ing younger on the whole—the average age in the new nation in 1790 was sixteen!—Americans were less susceptible to disease than were Europeans. More widely scattered, they were also less exposed to disease. This began to change, of course, as population centers grew and trade and travel increased. By the mid–eighteenth century, the colonies were beginning to have levels of contagion much like those in Europe.

The greatest variations on these patterns occurred in the earliest testing times of the southern colonies. During the first century after the Jamestown settlement, until about 1700, a high rate of mortality and a chronic shortage of women meant that the population increase there could be sustained only by immigration. In the southern climate, English settlers proved vulnerable to malaria, dysentery, and a host of other diseases. The mosquito-infested rice paddies of the Carolina Tidewater were notoriously unhealthy. And ships that docked at the Chesapeake tobacco plantations brought in with their payloads unseen cargoes of smallpox, diphtheria, and other infections. Given the higher mortality, families were often broken by the early death of parents. One consequence was to throw children on their own at an earlier age. Another was probably to make the extended family support network, if not the extended household, more important in the South.

SEX RATIOS AND THE FAMILY   Whole communities of religious or ethnic groups migrated more often to the northern colonies than to the southern, bringing more women in their company. There was no mention of any women at all among the first arrivals at Jamestown. Virginia's seventeenth-century sex ratio of two or three white males to each female meant that many men never married, although nearly every adult woman did. Counting only the unmarried, the ratio went to about eight men for every woman. In South Carolina around 1680 the sex ratio stood at about three to one, but since about three-quarters of the women were married, it was something like seven to one for singles.

A population made up largely of bachelors without strong ties to family and to the larger community made for instability of a high order in the first years. And the high mortality rates of the early years further loosened family ties. While the first generations in New England proved to be long-lived, and many more children there knew their grandparents than in the motherland, young people in the seventeenth-century South were apt never to see their grandparents, and in fact to lose one or both of their parents before reaching maturity. But after a time of seasoning, immunities built up. Eventually the southern colonies reverted to a more even sex ratio and family sizes approached those of New England.

"A little commonwealth." This eighteenth-century American family shows the "stairstep" pattern of childbearing, in which children were born at approximately two-year intervals.

Survival was the first necessity, and for the 90 to 95 percent of colonists who farmed, a subsistence or semi-subsistence economy remained the foundation of being. Not only food, but shelter, implements, utensils, furnishings, and clothing had to be made at home from the materials at hand. As the primary social and economic unit, the family became a "little commonwealth" which took on functions performed by the community in other times and places. Production, religion, learning, health care, and other activities centered on the home. Fathers taught sons how to farm, hunt, and fish. Mothers taught daughters how to tend to the chickens, the gardens, and the countless household chores that fell to the women of that time.

WOMEN IN THE COLONIES   Most colonists brought to America deeply rooted convictions concerning the inferiority of women. As one preacher stressed, "the woman is a weak creature not endowed with like strength and constancy of mind." Their prescribed role in life was clear: to obey and serve their husbands, nurture their children, and endure the taxing labor required to maintain their households. John Winthrop insisted that a "true wife" would find true contentment only "in subjection to her husband's authority." His sister, Lucy Winthrop Downing, accepted such a subordinate position. In a letter to her brother, she confessed: "I am but a wife and therefore it is sufficient for me to follow my husband."

Even high-spirited women such as Virginia's Lucy Parke Byrd submitted to their husbands' absolute authority. The imperious patrician William Byrd II managed his wife's estate without consulting her, kept a tenacious grip on his property—even to the point of forbidding her to borrow a book from his library without explicit permission—and saw fit to interfere in her own field of domestic management. In his secret diary he recorded their stormy relationship:

> [April 7] I reproached my wife with ordering the old beef to be kept and the fresh beef to be used first, contrary to good management, on which she was pleased to be very angry . . . then my wife came and begged my pardon and we were friends again. . . .
> [April 8] My wife and I had another foolish quarrel about my saying she listened at the top of the stairs . . . she came soon after and begged my pardon.

[April 9] My wife and I had another scold about mending my shoes, but it was soon over by her submission.

Both social custom and legal codes ensured that most women, like Lucy Byrd, remained deferential. In most colonies they could not vote, preach, hold office, attend public schools or colleges, bring lawsuits, make contracts, or own property.

WOMEN'S WORK   In the eighteenth century, "women's work" typically involved activities in the house, garden, and yard. Farm women usually rose at four in the morning and prepared breakfast by five-thirty. They then fed and watered the livestock, awakened the children, churned butter, tended the garden, prepared lunch, played with the children, worked the garden again, cooked dinner, milked the cows, got the children ready for bed, and cleaned the kitchen before retiring about nine. Women also combed, spun, spooled, wove, and bleached wool for clothing, knitted linen and cotton, hemmed sheets, pieced quilts, made candles and soap, chopped wood, hauled water, mopped floors, and washed clothes. Martha Ballard, a farm woman in Maine,

Prudence Punderson's needlework, "The First, Second, and Last Scene of Mortality" (c. 1776), shows the domestic path, from cradle to coffin, followed by most colonial women.

reported in her diary that when a sheep returned from the pasture with a gash in its neck, she "drest it with Tarr," and when a lamb was born with its "entrails hanging out," she sewed it up.

Despite the conventional mission of women to serve in the domestic sphere, the scarcity of labor opened opportunities. Quite a few women by necessity or choice went into gainful occupations. In her role as a paid midwife, for example, Martha Ballard delivered almost 800 babies. In the towns women commonly served as tavern hostesses and shopkeepers, but occasionally women also worked as doctors, printers, upholsterers, glaziers, painters, silversmiths, tanners, and shipwrights—often, but not always, widows carrying on their husbands' trades. Some managed plantations, again usually carrying on in the absence of husbands.

The New World environment did generate slight improvements in the status of women. The acute shortage of women in the early years made them more highly valued than in Europe, and the Puritan emphasis on well-ordered family life led to laws protecting wives from physical abuse and allowing for divorces. In addition, colonial laws allowed wives greater control over property that they had contributed to a marriage or that was left after a husband's death. But the central notion of female subordination and domesticity remained firmly entrenched in the New World. As a Massachusetts boy maintained in 1662, the superior aspect of life was "masculine and eternal; the feminine inferior and mortal."

SOCIETY AND ECONOMY IN THE SOUTHERN COLONIES

CROPS The southern colonies had one unique advantage—the climate. They could grow exotic staples (market crops) prized by the mother country. Virginia, as Charles I put it, was "founded upon smoke." By 1619 tobacco production had reached 20,000 pounds, and in the year of the Glorious Revolution, 1688, it was up to 18 million pounds. "In Virginia and Maryland," wrote Governor Leonard Calvert in 1729, "Tobacco as our Staple is our All, and indeed leaves no room for anything else."

Working the tobacco crop (late eighteenth century).

After 1690 rice was as much the staple in South Carolina as tobacco in Virginia or sugar in Barbados. The rise and fall of tidewater rivers made the region ideally suited to a crop that required alternate flooding and draining of the fields.

In the 1740s, another exotic staple appeared—indigo, the blue dye-stuff which found an eager market in the British woolens industry. An enterprising young woman named Eliza Lucas, daughter of the governor of Antigua, produced the first crop on her father's Carolina plantation, left in her care when she was only seventeen. She thereby founded a major industry, and as the wife of Charles Pinckney, later brought forth a major family dynasty that flourished in the golden age of Charleston.

The southern woods provided harvests of lumber and naval stores (tar, pitch, and turpentine) as well. From their early leadership in the latter trade, North Carolinians would later earn the nickname of Tar Heels. In the interior, a fur trade flourished, and in the Carolinas, there was a cattle industry that presaged the later industry on the Great Plains—with cowboys, roundups, brandings, and long drives to market.

English customs records showed that for the years 1698–1717 South Carolina and the Chesapeake colonies enjoyed a favorable balance of trade with England. But the surplus revenues earned on American goods sold to England were more than offset by "invisible" charges: freight payments to shippers, profits, commissions, storage charges, and interest payments to English merchants, insurance premiums, inspection and customs duties, and outlays to purchase indentured servants and slaves. Thus began a pattern that would plague the southern staple-crop system into the twentieth century. Planter investments went into land and slaves while the profitable enterprises of shipping, trade, investment, and manufacture fell under the sway of outsiders.

LAND   Land could be had almost for the asking throughout the colonial period, although many a frontier squatter ignored the formalities of getting a deed. In colonial law, land titles rested ultimately upon grants from the crown, and in colonial practice, the evolution of land policy in the first colony set patterns that were followed everywhere save in New England. In 1618 the Virginia Company, lacking any assets other than land, sold each investor a fifty-acre "share-right" and gave each settler a "headright" for paying his own way or for bringing in others. When Virginia became a royal colony in 1624, the headright system continued to apply, administered by the governor and his council. Lord Baltimore adopted the same practice in Maryland, and successive proprietors in the other southern and middle colonies adopted variations on the plan.

As time passed, certain tracts were put up for sale and throughout the colonies special grants (often sizable) went to persons of rank or persons who had performed some meritorious service, such as fighting the Indians. With the right connections, persons or groups might amass handsome estates and vast speculative tracts in the interior, looking toward future growth and rising land values. But by the early 1700s, acquisition of land was commonly by purchase under more or less regular conditions of survey and sale by the provincial government.

If one distinctive feature of the South's staple economy was a good market in England, another was a trend toward large-scale production. Those who planted tobacco soon discovered that it quickly exhausted the soil, thereby giving an advantage to the planter who had extra fields to rotate in beans and corn or to leave fallow. With the increase of the tobacco crop, moreover, a fall in prices meant that economies of scale might come into play—the large planter with lower cost per unit might still make a profit. Gradually he would extend his holdings along the

An idyllic view of a Tidewater plantation. Note the easy access to oceangoing vessels.

riverfronts, and thereby secure the advantage of direct access to the oceangoing vessels that moved freely up and down the waterways of the Chesapeake, discharging goods from London and taking on hogsheads of tobacco. So easy was the access, in fact, that the Chesapeake colonies never required a city of any size as a center of commerce, and the larger planters functioned as merchants and harbormasters for their neighbors.

LABOR   Voluntary indentured servitude accounted for probably half the white settlers (mostly from England, Ireland, or Germany) in all the colonies outside New England. The name derived from the indenture, or contract, by which a person promised to work for a fixed number of years in return for transportation to the New World. Usually one made the contract with a shipmaster who would then sell it to a new master upon arrival. Not all went voluntarily. The London underworld developed a flourishing trade in "kids" and "spirits," who were "kidnapped" or "spirited" into servitude. After 1717, by act of Parliament, convicts guilty of certain crimes could escape the hangman by "transportation" to the colonies. Most of these, like Moll Flanders, the lusty heroine of Daniel Defoe's novel, seem to have gone to the Chesapeake Bay region.

In due course, however, usually after four to seven years, the indenture ended and the servant claimed the freedom dues set by custom and law—money, tools, clothing, food, and occasionally small tracts of land. Some did very well for themselves. In 1629 seven members of the Virginia legislature were former indentured servants. Others, including Benjamin Franklin's maternal grandmother, married the men who bought their services. Many servants died before completing their indenture, however, and recent evidence suggests that most of those who served their term remained relatively poor thereafter. With the increase of the colonies, servants had a wider choice of destination. Pennsylvania became more often the chosen land, "one of the best poor man's countries in the world," in the verdict of a judge at the time.

SLAVERY Most captive Africans had no choice over their fate and served for life. Slavery evolved in the Chesapeake after 1619, when a Dutch vessel dropped off twenty Africans in Jamestown. Some of the first were treated as indentured servants, with a limited term. Court

An advertisement from the Virginia Gazette, *October 4, 1779, for indentured servants. These people secured a life in America, but for a steep price. Servants endured years of labor before a contract ended and allowed them their freedom.*

records indicate that black and white servants occasionally escaped together. A Virginia court, for instance, declared that six white servants and a "negro Servant" who had run away from their masters be given "thirty-nine lashes well layed on." Those African servants who worked out their term of indenture gained freedom and a fifty-acre parcel of land. They themselves sometimes acquired slaves and white indentured servants. Gradually, however, with rationalizations based on color difference or heathenism, the practice of hereditary life service became the custom of the land. By the 1660s, colonial assemblies recognized slavery by laws that later expanded into elaborate and restrictive slave codes.

The sugar islands of the French and British Antilles and the cane fields of Portuguese Brazil had the most voracious appetite for human cargoes, using them up in the tropical heat on the average within seven years. By 1675 the English West Indies had over 100,000 slaves, while the colonies in North America had only about 5,000. But as staple crops became established on the American continent, the demand for slaves grew. As readily available lands diminished, Virginians were less eager to bring in indentured servants who would lay claim to them at

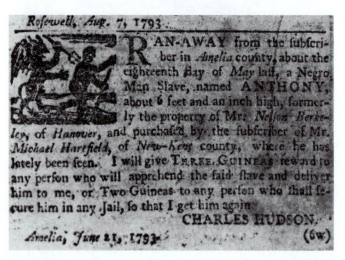

A notice for a runaway slave in the *Virginia Gazette and General Advertiser. Most of these ads included woodcut illustrations; here, a runaway is shown being chased by a devil and its pitchfork.*

PERCENTAGE OF AFRICAN AMERICANS IN THE TOTAL POPULATION OF THE BRITISH COLONIES, 1660–1780

Year	New England	Middle Colonies	Upper South	Lower South	West Indies
1660	1.7	11.5	3.6	2.0	42.0
1700	1.8	6.8	13.1	17.6	77.7
1740	2.9	7.5	28.3	46.5	88.0
1780	2.0	5.9	38.6	41.2	91.1

Source: U.S. Bureau of the Census, *Historical Statistics of the United States, Colonial Times to 1970* (Washington, D.C.: U.S. Government Printing Office, 1975), 2:1168 (Ser.Z1-19).

the end of their service. Though British North America took less than 5 percent of the total slave imports to the Western Hemisphere during the more than three centuries of that squalid traffic—400,000 out of some 9,500,000—it offered better chances for survival if few for human fulfillment. The natural increase of black immigrants in America approximated that of whites by the end of the colonial period. By that time, every fifth American was either an African or a descendant of one.

Slavery was recognized in the laws of all the colonies, but flourished in the Tidewater South—one colony, South Carolina, had a black majority through most of the eighteenth century. By one estimate, about 40 percent of the slaves imported into North America came in through Sullivan's Island in Charleston Harbor, which was to African Americans what New York's Castle Garden and Ellis Island were later to millions of European immigrants or what San Francisco's Angel Island was to Asians.

AFRICAN ROOTS Slaves are so often lumped together as a social group that their great ethnic diversity is overlooked. They came from lands as remote from each other as Angola and Senegal, on the west coast of Africa, and they spoke Mandingo, Ibo, Kongo, and other tongues. Still, the many peoples of Africa did share similar kinship and political systems. Not unlike Native American cultures, African societies were often matrilineal. Property and political status descended through the mother rather than the father. When a couple married, the wife did not leave her family; the husband left his family to join that of his bride.

West African tribes were organized hierarchically. Priests and the nobility lorded over the masses of farmers and craftspeople. Below the
masses were the slaves, typically war captives, criminals, or debtors.
African slaves, however, did have certain rights. They could marry, be
educated, and have children. Their servitude was not permanent, nor
were children automatically slaves by virtue of their parentage, as would
be the case in North America.

West Africans were predominantly agricultural people. Their economy centered on hunting, fishing, planting, and animal husbandry. Men
and women typically worked alongside one another in the fields. Religious belief served as the spine of West African life. All tribal groups believed in a supreme Creator and an array of lesser gods tied to specific
natural forces such as rain, fertility, and animal life. West Africans were
pantheistic in that they believed that spirits resided in trees, rocks, and

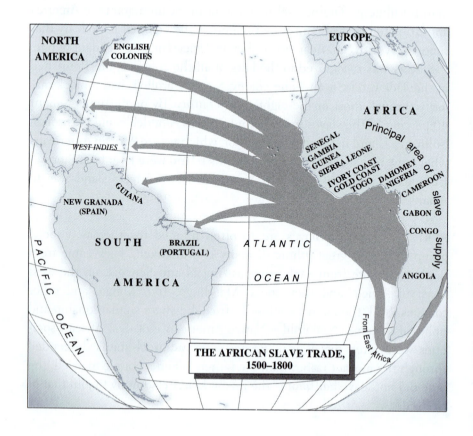

THE AFRICAN SLAVE TRADE,
1500–1800

Neck and wrist irons used to subdue slaves during the passage from Africa.

streams. People who died were also subjects of reverence because they served as mediators between the living and the gods.

When captured by the slave traders, the Africans were herded together, frequently branded with a company mark, and packed tightly in slave ships, where they endured a four- to six-week Atlantic passage so brutal that one in seven captives died en route. Once in America, they were thrown indiscriminately together and treated like work animals. Some "saltwater" slaves rebelled against their new masters, resisting work orders, sabotaging crops and tools, or running away to the frontier. In a few cases they organized rebellions that were ruthlessly suppressed. "You would be surprised at their perseverance," noted one white planter. "They often die before they can be conquered." Those still alive when captured frequently faced ghastly retribution. After rounding up slaves who participated in the Stono uprising in South Carolina in 1739, enraged planters "Cutt off their heads and set them up at every Mile Post."

SLAVE CULTURE   With the odds so heavily stacked against resistance, most slaves resigned themselves to the overwhelming authority of the "peculiar institution." Yet in the process of being forced into lives of bondage, diverse blacks from diverse homelands forged a new identity as African Americans, while at the same time leaving entwined in

The survival of African culture among American slaves is evident in this late-eighteenth-century painting of a South Carolina plantation. The musical instruments, pottery, and clothing are of African origin, probably Yoruba.

the fabric of American culture more strands of African heritage than historians and anthropologists can ever disentangle. Among them were new words that entered the language, such as *tabby, tote, cooter, goober, yam,* and *banana,* and the names of the Coosaw, Peedee, and Wando Rivers.

More important were African influences in music, folklore, and religious practices. On one level, slaves used such cultural activities to distract themselves from their servitude; on another level, they used songs, stories, and sermons as coded messages expressing their distaste for masters or overseers. Slave religion, a unique blend of African and Christian beliefs, was frequently practiced in secret. Its fundamental theme was deliverance: God would eventually free them from slavery and open up the gates to Heaven's promised land.

The planters, however, sought to strip slave religion of its liberationist hopes. They insisted that being "born again" had no effect upon their workers' status as slaves. In 1667 the Virginia legislature declared that "the conferring of baptism does not alter the condition of the person as to his bondage or freedom."

Africans brought to America powerful kinship ties. Even though most colonies outlawed slave marriages, many masters realized that slaves would work harder and be more stable if allowed to form families. Though many families were broken up when members were sold, slave culture retained its powerful domestic ties. It also developed gender roles distinct from those of white society. Most slave women were by necessity field workers as well as wives and mothers responsible for household affairs. Since they worked in close proximity to black men, they were treated more equally than most of their white counterparts.

Most of the slaves were fated to become fieldhands, but not all did. Many of those from the lowlands of Africa used their talents as boatmen in the coastal waterways. Some had linguistic skills that made them useful interpreters. Others tended cattle and swine in the wilderness, or hacked away at the forests and operated sawmills. In a society forced to construct itself, they became skilled artisans: blacksmiths, carpenters, coopers, bricklayers, and the like. Some entered domestic service as cooks or maids.

Slavery and the growth of a biracial South had economic, political, and cultural effects far into the future, and set America on the way to tragic conflicts. Questions about the beginnings of slavery still have a bearing on the present. Did a deep-rooted color prejudice lead to slavery, for instance, or did the existence of slavery produce the prejudice? Clearly, slavery evolved because of the desire for a supply of controlled labor, and the English adopted a trade established by the Portuguese and Spanish more than a century before—the very word "Negro" is Spanish for "black." But while English settlers often enslaved Indian captives, they did not bring their European captives into slavery. Color was the crucial difference, or at least the crucial rationalization.

The English associated the color black with darkness and evil; they stamped the different appearance, behavior, and customs of Africans as "savagery." At the very least, such perceptions could soothe the consciences of people who traded in human flesh. On the other hand, most of the qualities that colonial Virginians imputed to blacks to justify slavery were the same qualities that the English assigned to their own poor to explain *their* status: their alleged bent for laziness, improvidence, treachery, and stupidity, among other shortcomings. Similar traits, moreover, were imputed by ancient Jews to the Canaanites and by the Mediterranean peoples of a later date to the Slavic captives sold among

An English tobacco label depicting black labor.

them. The names Canaanite and Slav both became synonymous with slavery—the latter lingers in our very word for it. Such expressions would seem to be the product of power relationships and not the other way around. Dominant peoples repeatedly assign ugly traits to those they bring into subjection.

THE GENTRY   By the early eighteenth century, Virginia and South Carolina were moving into the golden age of the Tidewater gentry, leaving the more isolated and rustic colony of North Carolina as "a valley of humiliation between two mountains of conceit." The first rude huts of Jamestown had given way to frame and brick houses, but it was only as the seventeenth century yielded to the eighteenth that the stately country seats in the Georgian, or "colonial," style began to emerge along the banks of the great rivers. In South Carolina the mansions along the Ashley, Cooper, and Wando Rivers boasted spacious gardens and avenues of moss-draped live oaks.

The new aristocracy patterned its provincial lifestyle after that of the English country gentleman. The great houses became centers of sumptuous living and legendary hospitality to neighbors and passing strangers. In their zest for the good life, the planters kept in touch with the latest refinements of London style and fashion, living on credit extended for the next year's crop and the years' crops beyond that, to such a degree that in the late colonial period Thomas Jefferson called the Chesapeake gentry "a species of property annexed to certain English mercantile houses." Dependence on outside capital remained a chronic southern problem far beyond the colonial period.

In season the carriages of the Chesapeake elite rolled to the villages of Annapolis and Williamsburg, and the city of Charleston became the center of political life and high fashion where aristocrats could patronize the taverns, silversmiths, cabinetmakers, milliners, and tailors. Through much of the year, the outdoors beckoned planters to the pleasures of hunting, fishing, and riding. Gambling on horse races, cards, and dice became consuming passions for men and women alike. But a few cultivated high culture. William Byrd II of Westover pursued learning with a passion. He built a library of some 3,600 volumes and often rose early to keep up his Latin, Greek, and Hebrew. The Pinckneys of the Carolina low country, when they were at home, practiced their musical instruments and read from such authors as Virgil, Milton, Locke, Addison, Pope, and Richardson. These families commonly sent their sons—and often their daughters—abroad for an education, usually to England, sometimes to France.

RELIGION After 1642 Virginia Governor William Berkeley decided that the colony was to be Anglican, and he passed laws requiring "all

South Carolina planters at leisure (1754).

nonconformists . . . to depart the colony with all conveniency." Puritans and Quakers were hounded out of the colony. By the end of the seventeenth century, Anglicanism predominated in the region, and it proved especially popular among the large landholders. In the early eighteenth century, it became the established church in all the South—and some counties of New York and New Jersey, despite the presence of many dissenters. In the new environment, however, the Anglican church evolved into something quite unlike the state church of England. The scattered population and the absence of bishops made centralized control difficult.

In practice therefore, if not in theory, the Anglican churches became as independent of any hierarchy as the Puritans of New England. Governance fell to lay boards of vestrymen, who chose the ministers, and usually held them on a tight rein by granting short-term contracts. In Virginia ministerial salaries depended on the taxes paid in the parish, and the salary fluctuated with the price of tobacco. Standards were often lax, and the Anglican clergy around the Chesapeake became notorious for its "sporting parsons," addicted to fox-hunting, gambling, drunkenness, and worse. Few among the conscientious and upright Anglican ministers preached fire-and-brimstone sermons. Their congregations showed little toleration for being chastised from the pulpit. One minister lamented that the powerful planters removed any preacher who

The elegant pulpit at Christ's Church, an eighteenth-century Anglican church in Williamsburg, Virginia.

"had the courage and resolution to preach against any Vices taken into favor by the leading Men of his Parish."

It has often been said that Americans during the seventeenth century took religion more seriously than at any time since. That may have been true, but it is important to remember how many early Americans were not active communicants. One estimate holds that fewer than one in fifteen residents of the southern colonies were church members. There the tone of religious belief and practice was different from that in Puritan New England or Quaker Pennsylvania. As in England, colonial Anglicans tended to be more conservative, rational, and formal in their forms of worship than their Puritan, Quaker, or Baptist counterparts. Anglicans tended to stress collective rituals over personal religious experience.

SOCIETY AND ECONOMY IN NEW ENGLAND

TOWNSHIPS In contrast to the seaboard planters who transformed the English manor into the southern plantation, the Puritans transformed the English village into the New England town, although there were several varieties. Land policy in New England had a stronger social and religious purpose than elsewhere. Towns shaped by English precedent and Puritan policy also fitted the environment of a rockbound land, confined by sea and mountains and unfit for large-scale cultivation.

Unlike the pattern in the southern colonies or in Dutch New York, few individual settlers in New England received huge tracts of land. The standard system was one of township grants to organized groups. A group of settlers, often gathered already into a church, would petition the General Court for a town (what elsewhere was commonly called a "township") and then divide it according to a rough principle of equity—those who invested more, or had larger families or greater status, might receive more land—retaining some pasture and woodland in common and holding some for later arrivals. In some early cases the towns arranged each settler's land in separate strips after the medieval practice, but with time land was commonly divided into separate farms to which landholders would move, away from the close-knit village. Still later, by the early eighteenth century, the colonies used their remaining land as a source of revenue by selling townships to proprietors whose purpose, more often than not, was speculation and resale.

DWELLINGS AND DAILY LIFE   The first colonists in New England arrived to find what one called a "hideous and desolate wilderness, full of wild beasts & wild men." Forced first to live in caves, tents or "English wigwams," they soon built simple, small frame houses clad with hand-split clapboards. The roofs were steeply pitched to reduce the buildup of snow and were covered with thatched grasses or reeds. By 1654 one settler could declare that "the Lord hath been pleased to turn all the wigwams, huts, and hovels the English dwelt in at their first coming into orderly, fair, and well-built houses, well furnished."

By the end of the seventeenth century, most New England homes were plain but sturdy dwellings centered on a fireplace. Some had glass windows brought from England. The interior walls were often plastered and whitewashed, but the exterior boards were rarely painted. It was not until the eighteenth century that most houses were painted, and they were usually a dark "Indian red." New England homes were not commonly painted white until the nineteenth century. The interiors

This frame house, commonly known as a "saltbox house," had two stories in the front, but only one story in back because of its steeply pitched roof. This design prevented the accumulation of snow during New England winters.

were dark, illuminated only by candles or oil lamps, both of which were expensive; most people usually went to sleep soon after sunset. With no form of pest control other than swatting, innumerable ants and roaches, flies and mosquitoes, lived with the residents.

Family life revolved around the main room on the ground floor, called the "hall." Here meals would be cooked in a large fireplace. Pots would be suspended on an iron rod over the fire, and food would be served at a table made of rough-hewn planks called "the board." The father was sometimes referred to as the "chair man" because he sat in the only chair (hence the origin of the term "chairman of the board"). The rest of the family usually stood to eat or sat on stools or benches. People in colonial times ate with their hands and with wooden spoons. Forks were not introduced until the eighteenth century. The fare was usually corn, boiled meat, and vegetables washed down with beer, cider, rum, or milk. Wine was rare and expensive, served only on special occasions. Corn bread was a daily staple, as was cornmeal mush, known as "hasty pudding." Colonists also relished "succotash," an Indian meal of corn and kidney beans cooked in bear grease.

Residents in New England homes would bathe near the fire in the hall, using water brought in buckets from an outside well. The hall would be cluttered with items such as a spinning wheel, a hand loom for weaving cloth, a churn for making butter and cheese, and a cup-board and chest. In many homes the hall also served as the master bed-room. Husband and wife would sleep on a "jack bed" built into the cor-ner, thus requiring only a single post for support. A trundle bed for young children would be stored under the jack bed.

Below the main floor of a New England house was a cellar for storing food and other supplies for the long winters. Above the hall was a loft where older children might sleep on bedrolls. As families grew more af-fluent, they might add "lean-to" rooms to the backs of the houses, the first addition usually being a separate kitchen, thus enabling them to turn the hall into a parlor, or "best room" for entertaining visitors.

ENTERPRISE   The life of New England farmers consisted of hard-scrabble subsistence. Simply clearing the glacier-scoured soil of rocks might require sixty days of hard labor per acre. The growing season was short, and no exotic staples grew in that harsh climate. The crops and livestock were those familiar to the English countryside: wheat, barley,

Newfoundland fishery, 1705. For centuries, the rich fishing grounds in the eastern waters provided New Englanders with a prosperous industry.

oats, some cattle, swine, and sheep. By the end of the seventeenth cen-tury, New England farmers were developing some surpluses for export but never any staples that met the demands of the English market.

With virgin forests ready for conversion into masts, lumber, and ships, and rich fishing grounds that stretched northward to Newfound-land, it is little wonder that New Englanders turned to the sea for their livelihood. The Chesapeake region afforded a rich harvest of oysters, but New England, by its proximity to waters frequented by cod, mack-erel, halibut, and other varieties, became the more important maritime center. Whales, too, abounded in New England waters and supplied oil for lighting and lubrication, as well as ambergris, a secretion used in perfumes.

The fisheries, unlike the farms, supplied a staple of export to Europe, while lesser grades of fish went to the West Indies as food for slaves. Fisheries encouraged the development of shipbuilding, and experience at seafaring spurred commerce. This in turn encouraged wider contacts in the Atlantic world and a degree of materialism and cosmopolitanism that clashed with the Puritan credo of plain living and high thinking. In

1714 an anxious Puritan deplored the "great extravagance that people are fallen into, far beyond their circumstances, in their purchases, buildings, families, expenses, apparel, generally in the whole way of living."

By the mid–seventeenth century, shipyards had developed at Boston, Salem, Dorchester, Gloucester, Portsmouth, and other towns. New England remained the center of shipbuilding throughout the colonial period. Lumber provided not only raw material for ships but a prime cargo. As early as 1635 what may have been the first sawmill appeared at Portsmouth, New Hampshire. Sawmills soon abounded throughout the colonies, often together with gristmills using the same source of waterpower.

TRADE By the end of the seventeenth century, the colonies had become part of a great North Atlantic connection, trading not only with the British Isles and the British West Indies, but also—and often illegally—with Spain, France, Portugal, Holland, and their colonies from America to the shores of Africa. Out of necessity the colonists had to import manufactured goods from Britain and Europe: hardware, machinery, paint, instruments of navigation, various household items. The

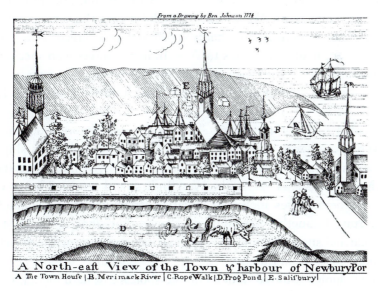

Newburyport, Massachusetts, in 1774.

colonies thus served as an important market for English goods from the mother country. The central problem for the colonies was to find the means of paying for the imports—the eternal problem of the balance of trade.

The mechanism of trade in New England and the middle colonies differed from that of the South in two respects: their lack of staples to exchange for English goods was a relative disadvantage, but the abundance of their own shipping and mercantile enterprise worked in their favor. After 1660, in order to protect English agriculture and fisheries, the English government raised prohibitive duties against certain major colonial exports: fish, flour, wheat, and meat, while leaving the door open to timber, furs, and whale oil, products in great demand in the home country. As a consequence, New York and New England in the years 1698–1717 bought more from England than they sold there, incurring an unfavorable trade balance.

The northern colonies met the problem partly by using their own ships and merchants, thus avoiding the "invisible" charges for trade and transport, and by finding other markets for the staples excluded from England, thus acquiring goods or bullion to pay for imports from the mother country. American lumber and fish therefore went to southern Europe, Madeira, and the Azores for money or in exchange for wine; lumber, rum, and provisions went to Newfoundland; and all of these and more went to the West Indies, which became the most important outlet of all. American merchants could sell fish, bread, flour, corn, pork, bacon, beef, and horses to West Indian planters who specialized in sugarcane. In return they got money, sugar, molasses, rum, indigo, dyewoods, and other products, much of which went eventually to England.

This gave rise to the famous "triangular trade" (more a descriptive convenience than a rigid pattern) in which New Englanders shipped rum to the west coast of Africa and bartered for slaves, took the slaves on the "Middle Passage" to the West Indies, and returned home with various commodities including molasses, from which they manufactured rum. In another version they shipped provisions to the West Indies, carried sugar and molasses to England, and returned with manufactured goods from Europe.

The colonies suffered from a chronic shortage of hard money, which drifted away to pay for imports and invisible charges. Various expedi-

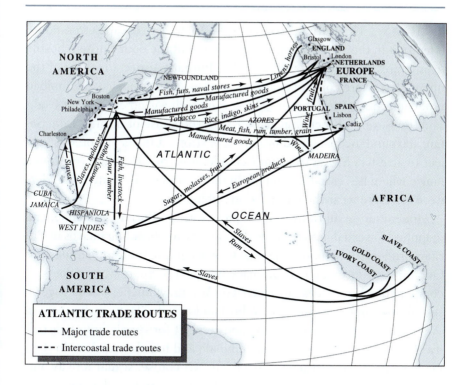

ATLANTIC TRADE ROUTES
— Major trade routes
--- Intercoastal trade routes

ents met the shortage of currency: the use of wampum or commodities, the monetary value of which colonial governments tried vainly to set by law. Promissory notes of individuals or colonial treasurers often passed as a crude sort of paper money. Most of the colonies at one time or another issued bills of credit, on promise of payment later (hence the dollar "bill"), and most set up land banks that issued paper money for loans to farmers on the security of their lands, which were mortgaged to the banks. Colonial farmers began to recognize that an inflation of paper money led to an inflation of crop prices, and therefore asked for more and more paper. Thus began in colonial politics what was to become a recurrent issue in later times, the question of currency inflation. Whenever the issue arose, debtors commonly favored growth in the money supply, which would make it easier for them to settle accounts, whereas creditors favored a limited money supply, which would increase the value of their capital. In 1751 Parliament outlawed legal-tender paper money in New England, and in 1764 throughout the colonies.

RELIGION   The Puritans had come to America to escape error, not to tolerate it in their New Zion. Yet the picture of the dour Puritan, hostile to anything that gave pleasure, is false. Puritans, especially those of the upper class, wore colorful clothing, enjoyed secular music, and imbibed prodigious quantities of rum. "Drink is in itself a good creature of God," said the Reverend Increase Mather, "but the abuse of drink is from Satan." If found incapacitated by reason of strong drink, a person was subject to arrest. A Salem man, for example, was tried for staggering into a house where he "eased his stomak in the Chimney." Repeated offenders were forced to wear the letter "D" in public.

Moderation in all things except piety was the Puritan guideline, and it applied to sexual activity as well. Contrary to prevailing images of Puritan prudery, they quite openly acknowledged natural human desires. One minister stressed that intimacy between partners was a necessary component of a successful marriage. Any unwillingness to engage in sexual intercourse on the part of husband or wife "Denies all reliefe in Wedlock unto Human necessity: and sends it for supply unto Beastiality." Churches occasionally expelled male and female members for failing to satisfy their partner's sexual needs. Of course, sexual activity outside the bounds of marriage was strictly forbidden, but like most social prohibitions it may have provoked transgression. New England court records are filled with cases of adultery and fornication. A man found guilty of coitus with an unwed woman could be jailed, whipped, fined, disenfranchised, and forced to marry the woman. Women offenders were also jailed and whipped, and in some cases adulterers were forced to wear the letter "A" in public. In part the abundance of sex offenses is explained by the disproportionate number of men in the colonies. Many were unable to find a wife and were therefore tempted to satisfy their sexual desires outside of marriage.

The Puritans who settled Massachusetts, unlike the Separatists of Plymouth, proposed only to form a purified version of the Anglican church. They believed that they could remain loyal to the Church of England, the unity of church and state, and the principle of compulsory uniformity. But their remoteness from England led them to adopt a congregational form of church government identical with that of the Pilgrim Separatists, and for that matter little different from the practice of southern Anglicans.

Certain aspects of the Puritan faith were pregnant with meaning for the future. In the Puritan's version of Calvin's theology, God had voluntarily entered into a covenant, or contract, with people through which they could secure salvation. By analogy, therefore, an assembly of true Christians could enter into a church covenant, a voluntary union for the common worship of God. From this it was a fairly short step to the idea of a voluntary union for purposes of government. The history of New England affords examples of several such limited steps toward constitutional government: the Mayflower Compact, the Cambridge Agreement of John Winthrop and his followers, the Fundamental Orders of Connecticut, and the informal arrangements whereby the Rhode Island settlers governed themselves until they secured a charter in 1663.

The covenant theory contained certain kernels of democracy in both church and state, but democracy was no part of Puritan political thought, which like so much else in Puritan belief began with original sin. Humanity's innate depravity made government necessary. "If people be governors," asked the Reverend John Cotton, "who shall be governed?" The Puritan was dedicated to seeking not the will of the people but the will of God, and the ultimate source of authority was the Bible. But the Bible had to be known by right reason, which was best applied by those trained to the purpose. Hence most Puritans deferred to an intellectual elite for a true knowledge of God's will. Church and state were but two aspects of the same unity, the purpose of which was to carry out God's will on earth. The New England way might thus be summarized in the historian Perry Miller's phrase as a kind of "dictatorship of the regenerate."

The church exercised a pervasive influence over the life of the town, but unlike the Church of England it technically had no temporal power. Thus while Puritan New England has often been called a theocracy, the church was entirely separated from the state—except that the residents were taxed for its support. And if not all inhabitants were church members, all were nonetheless required to attend church services. So complete was the consensus of church member and nonmember that the communities of New England have been called peaceable kingdoms.

It was a peace, however, under which bubbled a volcano of soul-searching. Puritans were assailed by doubts, by a fear of falling away from godly living, by the haunting fear that despite their best outward efforts they might not be among God's elect. Add such concerns to the long winters that kept the family cooped up during the dark, cold months, and one has a formula for seething resentments and recriminations that, for the sake of peace in the family, had to be projected outward toward neighbors. The New Englanders of those peaceable kingdoms therefore built a reputation as the most litigious people on the face of God's earth, continually quarreling over fancied slights, business dealings, and other issues, and building in the process a flourishing legal profession.

DIVERSITY AND SOCIAL STRAINS   Despite long-enduring myths, New England towns were not always pious, harmonious, static, and self-sufficient peasant utopias populated by praying Puritans. Many communities were founded not as religious farming utopias but as secular centers of fishing, trade, or commercial agriculture, and the animating concerns of residents in such towns tended to be more entrepreneurial than spiritual. After a Puritan minister delivered his first sermon to a congregation in the fishing port of Marblehead, a crusty fisherman admonished him: "You think you are preaching to the people of the Bay. Our main end was to catch fish." Similar priorities appeared in highly commercialized inland towns such as Springfield, Massachusetts. There, too, material opportunity rather than religious communalism governed individual behavior. Yet such acquisitive individualism, while generating marked social inequalities, was accompanied by growing social stability as an economic elite came to exercise paternalistic control over town affairs.

In many of the godly backwoods communities, social strains increased as time passed, a consequence primarily of population pressure on the land and rising disparities of wealth. "Love your neighbor," said Benjamin Franklin's Poor Richard, "but don't pull down your fence." Initially, among the first settlers, fathers exercised strong authority over sons through their control of the land. They kept the sons and their families in the town, not letting them set up their own households or get title to their farmland until they reached middle age. In New England, as elsewhere, fathers tended to subdivide their land among all the male children. But by the eighteenth century, with land scarcer, the younger sons were either getting control of property early or moving on. Often they were forced out, with family help and blessings, to seek land

School Street, Salem, around 1765. The mansion of a wealthy merchant dominates this street scene in Salem, a prosperous port town.

elsewhere or new kinds of work in the commercial cities along the coast or inland rivers. With the growing pressure on land in the settled regions, poverty and social tension increased in what had once seemed a country of unlimited opportunity.

Interestingly enough, however, in seaport towns such as Salem, Marblehead, and Gloucester, settled by contentious English immigrants eager to succeed, community and family life grew more cohesive, stable, and visibly religious with the passage of time, the growth of population, and the advance of prosperity. Increasing concentrations of wealth enabled a social and economic elite to coalesce and dominate the political process. Aspects of the original Puritan vision—civic consciousness, deference to leaders and institutions, church membership, and family authority—remained strong well into the eighteenth century. Rather than witnessing a decline from communitarian standards, these maritime communities attained greater equilibrium as time passed.

Yet sectarian disputes and religious indifference were on the rise in many communities. The emphasis on a direct accountability to God, which lay at the base of all Protestant theology, itself caused a persistent tension and led believers to challenge authority in the name of private conscience. Massachusetts repressed such heresy in the 1630s, but it resurfaced during the 1650s among Quakers and Baptists, and in

1659–1660 the colony hanged four Quakers who persisted in returning after they were expelled. These acts caused such revulsion—and an investigation by the crown—that they were not repeated, although heretics continued to face harassment and persecution.

More damaging to the Puritan utopia was the increasing worldliness of New England, which placed growing strains on church discipline. More and more children of the "visible saints" found themselves unable to give the required testimony of regeneration. In 1662 an assembly of ministers at Boston accepted the "Half-Way Covenant," whereby baptized children of church members could be admitted to a "halfway" membership and secure baptism for their own children in turn. Such members, however, could neither vote in church nor take communion. A further blow to Puritan control came with the Massachusetts royal charter of 1691, which required toleration of dissenters and based the right to vote in public elections on property rather than on church membership.

THE DEVIL IN NEW ENGLAND   The strains accompanying Massachusetts's transition from Puritan utopia to royal colony reached an unhappy climax in the witchcraft hysteria at Salem Village (now the town of Danvers) in 1692. Belief in witchcraft was widespread throughout Europe and New England in the seventeenth century. Prior to the dra-

Three "notorious witches" hanged in Chelmsford, England, 1589. In New England, a century later, more than thirty people were hanged during a period of "witchcraft hysteria."

matic episode in Salem, almost three hundred New Englanders (mostly middle-aged women) had been accused as witches, and more than thirty had been hanged. New England was, in the words of Cotton Mather, "a country . . . extraordinarily alarum'd by the wrath of the Devil."

Still, the outbreak in Salem was distinctive in its scope and intensity. Salem Village was about eight miles from the larger Salem Town, a thriving port. A contentious community made up of independent farm families and people who depended on the commercial activity of the port, Salem Village struggled to free itself from the influence and taxes of Salem proper. The tensions that arose apparently made the residents especially susceptible to the idea that the devil was at work in the village.

During the winter of 1691–1692, several adolescent girls began meeting in the kitchen of the town minister, the Reverend Samuel Parris. There they gave rapt attention to the voodoo stories told by Tituba, Parris's West Indian slave. As the days passed, the entranced girls began to behave oddly—shouting, barking, groveling, and twitching for no apparent reason. A doctor concluded that the girls were bewitched. When asked who was tormenting them, the girls replied that three women— Tituba, Sarah Good, and Sarah Osborne—were Satan's servants.

Authorities thereupon arrested the three women. At a special hearing before the magistrates, the "afflicted" girls rolled on the floor in convulsive fits as the accused women were questioned. In the midst of the hearing, Tituba shocked listeners by not only confessing to the charge but also divulging the names of many others in the community who she claimed were also performing the devil's work. Soon thereafter, dozens more girls and young women began to experience the same violent contortions. The accusations spread throughout the community. Within a few months, the Salem Village jail was filled with townspeople—men, women, and children—accused of practicing witchcraft.

At the end of May the authorities arrested Martha Carrier. A farmer had testified that several of his cattle suffered "strange deaths" soon after he and Carrier had an argument. Little Phoebe Chandler added that she had been stricken with terrible stomach pains soon after she heard Carrier's voice telling her she was going to be poisoned. Even Carrier's own children testified against her: they reported that their mother had recruited them as witches. But the most damning testimony was provided by several young girls. When they were brought into the hearing room, they began writhing in agony at the sight of Carrier. They claimed that they could see the devil whispering in her ear. Carrier declared that it was "a shameful thing that you should mind these folks that are out of their wits. I am wronged." A few days later she was hanged. Rebecca Nurse, a pious seventy-one-year-old matriarch of a large family went to the gallows in July. George Jacobs, an old man whose servant girl accused him of witchcraft, dismissed the whole chorus of accusers as "bitch witches." He was hanged in August.

But as the net of accusation spread wider, extending far beyond the confines of Salem, leaders of the Massachusetts Bay colony began to worry that the witch-hunts were out of control. The governor intervened when his own wife was accused of serving the devil. He disbanded the special court in Salem and ordered the remaining suspects released. A year after it had begun, the fratricidal event was finally over. Nineteen people (including some men married to women who had been convicted) had been hanged; one man—the stubborn Giles Corey—was pressed to death by heavy stones, and more than one hundred others were jailed. Nearly everybody responsible for the Salem executions later recanted, and nothing quite like it happened in the colonies again.

What explains the witchcraft hysteria at Salem? Some have argued that it may have represented nothing more than a contagious exercise in adolescent imagination intended to enliven the dreary routine of everyday life. Yet it was adults who pressed the formal charges against the accused and provided most of the testimony. This has led some scholars to speculate that long-festering local feuds and property disputes may have triggered the prosecutions.

More recently, historians have focused on the most salient fact about the accused witches: almost all of them were women. Many of the accused women, it turns out, had in some way defied the traditional roles assigned to females. Some had engaged in business transactions outside the home; others did not attend church; some were curmudgeons. Most of them were middle-aged or older and without sons or brothers. They thus stood to inherit property and live as independent women. The notion of autonomous spinsters flew in the face of prevailing social conventions.

Whatever the precise cause, there is little doubt that the witchcraft hysteria reflected the peculiar social dynamics of the Salem community. Late in 1692, as the hysteria in Salem subsided, several of the afflicted girls were traveling through nearby Ipswich when they encountered an old woman resting on a bridge. "A witch!" they shouted and began writhing as if possessed. But the people of Ipswich were unimpressed. Passersby showed no interest in the theatrical girls. Unable to generate either sympathy or curiosity, the girls picked themselves up and continued on their way.

SOCIETY AND ECONOMY IN THE MIDDLE COLONIES

AN ECONOMIC MIX   Both geographically and culturally the middle colonies stood between New England and the South, blending their own influences with elements derived from the older regions on either side. In so doing they more completely reflected the diversity of colonial life and more fully foreshadowed the pluralism of the later American nation than the regions on either side. Their crops were those of New England but more bountiful, owing to better land and a longer growing season, and they developed surpluses of foodstuffs for export to the plantations of the South and the West Indies: wheat, barley, oats, and other cereals, flour, and livestock. Three great rivers—the Hudson, Delaware, and Susquehanna—and their tributaries gave the middle colonies ready access to their backcountry and to the fur trade of the interior, where New York and Pennsylvania long enjoyed friendly relations with the Iroquois, Delaware, and other tribes. As a consequence the region's commerce rivaled that of New England, and indeed Philadelphia in time supplanted Boston as the largest city of the colonies.

Land policies followed the headright system of the South. In New York the early royal governors carried forward, in practice if not in name, the Dutch device of the patroonship, granting to influential favorites vast estates on Long Island and up the Hudson and Mohawk Valleys. These realms most nearly approached the Old World manor. They were self-contained domains farmed by tenants who paid fees to use the landlords' mills, warehouses, smokehouses, and wharfs. But with free land available elsewhere, New York's population languished, and the new waves of immigrants sought the promised land of Pennsylvania.

AN ETHNIC MIX   In the makeup of their population the middle colonies stood apart from both the mostly English Puritan settlements and the biracial plantation colonies to the South. In New York and New Jersey, for instance, Dutch culture and language lingered for some time, along with the Dutch Reformed church. Along the Delaware River the few Swedes and Finns, the first settlers, were overwhelmed by the influx of English and Welsh Quakers, followed in turn by the Germans and Scotch-Irish.

The Germans came mainly from the Rhineland, a region devastated by incessant war. (Keep in mind that until German unification in 1871, ethnic Germans—those Europeans speaking German as their native language—lived in a variety of areas and principalities in central Europe.) Penn's brochures on the bounties of Pennsylvania circulated in German translation, and his promise of religious freedom brought a response from persecuted sects, especially the Mennonites, German Baptists whose beliefs resembled those of the Quakers. In 1683 a group of Mennonites founded Germantown near Philadelphia. They were but the vanguard of a swelling migration in the eighteenth century that included Lutherans, Reformed Calvinists, Moravians, Dunkers, and others, a large proportion of whom paid their way as indentured servants, or "redemptioners," as they were commonly called. West of Philadelphia they created a belt of settlement in which the "Pennsylvania Dutch" (a corruption of *Deutsch,* meaning German) predominated, as well as a channel for the dispersion of German populations throughout the colonies.

The more aggressive Scotch-Irish began to arrive later and moved still farther out in the backcountry. "Scotch-Irish" is an enduring misnomer for Ulster Scots, Presbyterians transplanted from Scotland to confiscated lands in northern Ireland to give that country a more Protestant tone. The Ulster plantation dated from 1607 to 1609, the years when Jamestown was fighting for survival. A century later the Ulster Scots, mostly Presbyterians, were on the move again, in flight both from Anglican persecution and from economic disaster caused by English tariffs. These and other "border Britons" constituted a truly mass migration. Between 1717 and 1775, over a quarter million of them left northern England, southern Scotland, and northern Ireland for America. This time they looked mainly to Pennsylvania and the fertile valleys stretching southwestward into Virginia and Carolina.

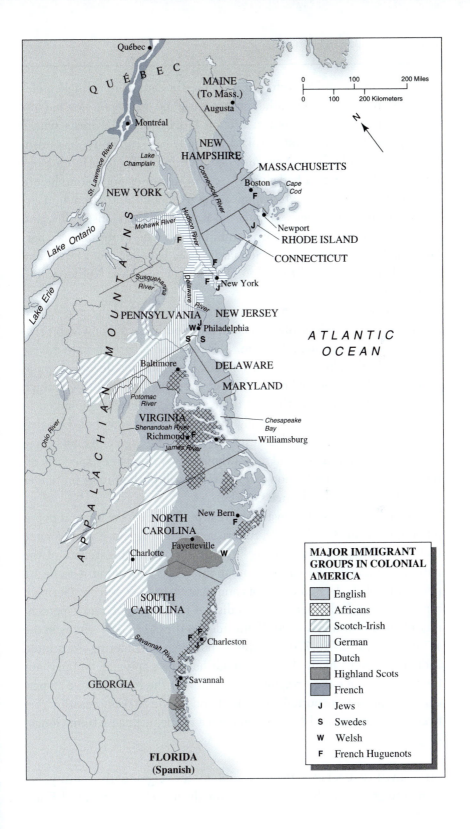

Québec

Québec •

QUÉBEC

St. Lawrence River

Montréal •

Lake Champlain

NEW YORK

Lake Ontario

Mohawk River

Lake Erie

APPALACHIAN MOUNTAINS

Susquehanna River

Ohio River

PENNSYLVANIA

Baltimore •

Potomac River

VIRGINIA

Shenandoah River

Richmond •**F**

James River

NORTH CAROLINA

Charlotte •

Fayetteville •

SOUTH CAROLINA

Savannah River

F F
•
Charleston •

GEORGIA

J • Savannah

FLORIDA
(Spanish)

MAINE
(To Mass.)

Augusta •

NEW
HAMPSHIRE

Connecticut River

MASSACHUSETTS

Boston •
F

Cape Cod

J

Newport

RHODE ISLAND

CONNECTICUT

F

Hudson River

Delaware River

F

F J • New York

NEW JERSEY

J
W • Philadelphia
S S

DELAWARE

MARYLAND

Chesapeake Bay

• Williamsburg

New Bern •
F

W

ATLANTIC
OCEAN

0   100   200 Miles
0   100   200 Kilometers

N

**MAJOR IMMIGRANT
GROUPS IN COLONIAL
AMERICA**

English
Africans
Scotch-Irish
German
Dutch
Highland Scots
French

J Jews
S Swedes
W Welsh
F French Huguenots

The Germans and Scotch-Irish became the largest non-English elements in the colonies, but other groups enriched the population in New York and the Quaker colonies: French Huguenots (Calvinists whose privilege of toleration was revoked in France in 1685), Irish, Welsh, Swiss, Jews, and others. New York had inherited from the Dutch a tradition of toleration that had given the colony a motley population before the English conquest: French-speaking Walloons and French, Germans, Danes, Portuguese, Spaniards, Italians, Bohemians, Poles, and others, including some New England Puritans. The Protestant Netherlands had given haven to the Sephardic Jews expelled from Spain and Portugal, and enough of them found their way into New Netherland to found a synagogue there.

What could be said of Pennsylvania as a refuge for the persecuted might be said as well of Rhode Island and South Carolina, which practiced a similar religious toleration. Newport and Charleston, like New York and Philadelphia, became centers of minuscule Jewish populations. French Huguenots made their greatest mark on South Carolina, more by their enterprise than by their numbers, and left implanted in the life of the colony such family names as Huger, Porcher, DeSaussure, Legare, Lanneau, and Lesesne. A number of Highland Scots came directly from their homeland rather than by way of Ulster, especially after suppression of a rebellion in 1745 on behalf of the Stuart pretender to the throne, "Bonnie Prince Charlie."

The eighteenth century was the great period of expansion and population growth in British North America, and during those years a large increase of the non-English stock took place. A rough estimate of the national origins of the white population as of 1790 found it to be 61 percent English, 14 percent Scots and Scotch-Irish, 9 percent German, 5 percent Dutch, French, and Swedish, 4 percent Irish, and 7 percent miscellaneous or unassigned. If one adds to the 3,172,444 whites in the 1790 census the 756,770 nonwhites, not even considering uncounted Indians, it seems likely that only about half the populace, and perhaps fewer, could trace their origins to England. Of the blacks about 75 percent had been transported from the bend of the African coastline between the Senegal and Niger Rivers; most of the rest came from Congo-Angola.

THE BACKCOUNTRY Pennsylvania in the eighteenth century became the great distribution point for the diverse ethnic groups of European origin, just as the Chesapeake Bay region and Charleston became the distribution points for African peoples. Before the mid–eighteenth century, population in the Pennsylvania backcountry was coming up against the Appalachian barrier and, following the line of least resistance, the Scotch-Irish and Germans filtered southward along what came to be called the Great Philadelphia Road, the primary internal migration route during the colonial period. It headed west from the port city, traversing Chester and Lancaster counties, and turned southwest at Harris' Ferry (now Harrisburg), where it crossed the Susquehanna. Continuing south across western Maryland, it headed down the Shenandoah Valley of Virginia, and on into the Carolina and Georgia backcountry. Germans were first in the upper Shenandoah Valley, and to the south of them Scotch-Irish filled the lower valley. Migrants continued to move into the Carolina and Georgia backcountry, while others found their way up from Charleston.

Along the fringes of the frontier were commonly found the Scotch-Irish, who had acquired in their homeland and in Ulster a stubborn fighting spirit that brooked no nonsense from the "savages" of the woods. Theirs was a lonely life of scattered settlements, isolated log cabins set on plots of land that the pioneer owned or at least occupied, furnished with crude furniture hacked out with axe and adze and pieced together with pegs. With time, of course, neighborhoods grew up within visiting distance, animal and Indian trails broadened into wagon roads, and crossroads stores grew up into community gathering places where social intercourse could be lubricated with the whiskey that was omnipresent on the Scotch-Irish frontier.

The backcountry of the Piedmont, and something much like it on up to northern New England (Maine, New Hampshire, and what would become Vermont), became a fourth major region that stretched the length of the colonies across the boundaries separating the political units. Government was slow to reach these remote settlements, and the system of "every man for himself" sometimes led frontier communities into conditions of extreme disorder.

COLONIAL CITIES

During the seventeenth century the colonies remained in comparative isolation, evolving subtly distinctive ways and unfolding separate histories. Boston and New York, Philadelphia and Charleston were more likely to keep in closer touch with London than with each other. The Carolina upcountry had more in common with the Pennsylvania backcountry than either had with Charleston or Philadelphia. Since commerce was their chief reason for being, colonial cities hugged the coastline or, like Philadelphia, sprang up on rivers where oceangoing vessels could reach them. Never holding more than 10 percent of the colonial population, they exerted a disproportionate influence in commerce, politics, and civilization. By the end of the colonial period Philadelphia, with some 30,000 people, was the largest city in the colonies and second only to London in the British Empire. New York, with about 25,000, ranked second; Boston numbered 16,000; Charleston, 12,000; and Newport, Rhode Island, 11,000.

THE SOCIAL AND POLITICAL ORDER   The upper crust of urban society were the merchants who bartered the products of American farms and forests for the molasses and rum of the West Indies, the wines of Madeira, the manufactured goods of Europe, and the slaves of Africa. Their trade in turn stimulated the sail makers, instrument makers, and ship chandlers who supplied vessels leaving port. After the merchants, who constituted the chief urban aristocracy, came a middle class of retailers, innkeepers, and artisans who met a variety of needs. Almost two-thirds of urban adult male workers were artisans, people who made

The Rapalje Children *by John Durand, circa 1768. These children of a wealthy Brooklyn merchant wear garb typical of upper-crust urban society.*

Fighting a fire in colonial New York, 1762.

their living at handicrafts. They included carpenters and coopers (barrel makers), shoemakers and tailors, silversmiths and blacksmiths, sail makers, stonemasons, weavers, and potters. At the bottom of the pecking order were sailors and unskilled workers.

Class stratification in the cities became more pronounced as time passed. One study of Boston found that in 1687 the richest 15 percent of the population owned 52 percent of the taxable wealth; by 1771 the top 15 percent owned about 67 percent and the top 5 percent owned some 44 percent of the wealth. In Philadelphia the concentration of wealth was even more pronounced.

Problems created by urban growth are nothing new. Colonial cities had traffic requiring not only paved streets and lighting but regulations to protect children and animals in the streets from reckless riders. Regulations restrained citizens from tossing their garbage into the streets. Fires that on occasion swept through closely packed buildings led to preventive standards in building codes, restrictions on burning rubbish, and the organization of fire companies. Crime and violence made necessary more police protection. And in cities the poor became more visible than in the countryside. Colonists brought with them the English principle of public responsibility. The number of Boston's poor receiving public assistance rose from 500 in 1700 to 4,000 in 1736, New

York's from 250 in 1698 to 5,000 in the 1770s. Most of it went to "outdoor" relief in the form of money, food, clothing, and fuel, but almshouses also appeared in colonial cities.

Town governments were not always equal to their multiple tasks. Of the major cities, Boston and Newport had the common New England system of town meetings and selectmen, while New York after 1791 had an elected council responsive to the citizens, although its mayor and other officials were still appointed by the governor. Philadelphia, however, fell under a self-perpetuating closed corporation in which the common run of citizens had no voice, and colonial Charleston never achieved status as a municipal corporation at all, but remained under the thumb of the South Carolina assembly.

THE URBAN WEB   Transit within and between cities was difficult at first. The first roads were likely to be Indian trails, which themselves often followed the tracks of bison through the forests. The trails widened with travel, then were made roads by order of provincial and local authorities. Land travel at first had to go by horse or by foot. The first stagecoach line for the public, opened in 1732, linked Burlington and Perth Amboy, New Jersey, connecting by water to Philadelphia and New York, respectively. That same year a guidebook published in Boston gave roads connecting from Boston through Providence, New York, Philadelphia, and eventually on to Williamsburg and Charleston, with connecting branches. From the main ports good roads might reach thirty or forty miles inland, but all were dirt roads subject to washouts and mudholes. There was not a single hard-surfaced road during the entire colonial period, aside from city streets.

Taverns were an important adjunct of colonial travel, since movement by night was too risky. By the end of the seventeenth century, there were more taverns in America than any other business. Indeed, they became the most important social institution in the colonies—and the most democratic. By 1690 there were fifty-four taverns in Boston alone, half of them operated by women. In rural areas or along the main roads, the first taverns were called "ordinaries." They were simply farmhouses that offered travelers something potent to drink and a bed in a corner or hayloft. In the coastal cities, they tended to be seedy grogshops along the waterfront, catering to sailors and prostitutes, or large and even elegant establishments in the uptown commercial districts with proper English names such as the Green Dragon, the Black Horse, the Blue Bell, or the Golden Lion.

Like private clubs today, colonial taverns and inns were places to drink, relax, read the newspaper, play cards or billiards, gossip about people or politics, learn news from travelers, or conduct business. Local ordinances regulated and licensed the taverns, setting their prices and usually prohibiting them from serving liquor to blacks, Indians, servants, or apprentices. Some ordinances regulated how much liquor could be served to a customer, lest he become "bereaved or disabled in the use of his understanding."

To be sure, such regulations were often ignored. A young John Adams recorded in his diary that the Boston taverns were always "full of People, drinking Drams, Phlip, Toddy, Carousing, Swearing." He added that "here [in such taverns] diseases, vicious habits, bastards, and legislators are frequently begotten." What Adams called "phlip" was an especially potent brew made up of molasses, beer, and rum. A red-hot iron was plunged into the concoction, making the liquor foam and tinging its flavor with the bitterness of burnt sugar. In 1726 a concerned Bostonian wrote a letter to the community declaring that "the abuse of strong

A tobacconist's trade card from 1770 captures the atmosphere of taverns in the late eighteenth century. Here, men in a Philadelphia tavern share conversation while they drink ale and smoke pipes.

Drink is becoming Epidemical among us, and it is very justly Supposed . . . that the Multiplication of Taverns has contributed not a little to this Excess of Riot and Debauchery." Yet the taverns continued to proliferate, and by the mid–eighteenth century they would become the gathering place for protests against British rule.

Postal service through the seventeenth century was almost nonexistent—people entrusted letters to travelers or sea captains. Massachusetts set up a provincial postal system in 1677, and Pennsylvania in 1683. Under a parliamentary law of 1710, the postmaster of London named a deputy in charge of the colonies and a postal system eventually extended the length of the Atlantic seaboard. Benjamin Franklin, who served as deputy postmaster from 1753 to 1774, speeded up the service with shorter routes and night-traveling post riders, and he increased the volume by inaugurating lower rates.

More reliable deliveries gave rise to newspapers in the eighteenth century. Before 1745 twenty-two newspapers had been started, seven in New England, ten in the middle colonies, and five in the South. An important landmark in the progress of freedom of the press was John Peter Zenger's trial for seditious libel for publishing criticisms of New York's governor in his newspaper, the *New York Weekly Journal*. Zenger was imprisoned for ten months and brought to trial in 1735. The established rule in English common law held that one might be punished for criticism that fostered "an ill opinion of the government." The jury's function was only to determine whether the defendant had published the opinion. Zenger's lawyer startled the court with his claim that the editor had published the truth—which the judge ruled an unacceptable defense. The jury, however, agreed with the assertion and held the editor not guilty. The libel law remained standing as before, but editors thereafter were emboldened to criticize officials more freely.

The Enlightenment

DISCOVERING THE LAWS OF NATURE   Through their commercial contacts, newspapers, and other activities, the cities became the centers for the dissemination of fashion and ideas. In the world of ideas a new fashion was abroad: the Enlightenment. During the seventeenth century, Europe experienced a scientific revolution in which the old Ptolemaic view of an earth-centered universe was overthrown by the new heliocentric (sun-centered) system of Polish astronomer Nicolaus Copernicus. A climax to the revolution came with Sir Isaac Newton's *Principia* (*Mathematical Principles of Natural Philosophy,* 1687), which set forth his theory of gravitation. Newton depicted a mechanistic universe moving in accordance with natural laws that could be grasped by human reason and explained by mathematics. Newton implied that natural laws governed all things—the orbits of the planets and also the orbits of human relations: politics, economics, and society. Reason could make people aware, for instance, that the natural law of supply and demand governed economics or that natural rights to life, liberty, and property determined the limits and functions of government.

Much of enlightened thought could be reconciled with established beliefs—the idea of natural law existed in Christian theology, and religious people could reason that the rational universe of Copernicus and Newton simply demonstrated the glory of God. Puritan leaders accepted Newtonian science from the start. Yet when people carried it to its ultimate logic, as the Deists did, the idea of natural law left God eliminated or at best reduced to the position of a remote Creator—as the French *philosophe* Voltaire put it, the master clockmaker who planned the universe and set it in motion. Evil in the world, in this view, resulted not from original sin and innate depravity so much as it did from an imperfect understanding of the laws of nature. Humanity, the English philosopher John Locke argued in his *Essay on Human Understanding* (1690), is largely the product of the environment, the mind being a blank tablet on which experience is written. The way to improve both society and human nature was by the application and improvement of Reason—which was the highest Virtue (enlightened thinkers often capitalized both words).

THE ENLIGHTENMENT IN AMERICA   However interpreted, such ideas profoundly affected the climate of thought in the eighteenth century. The premises of Newtonian science and the Enlightenment, moreover, fitted the American experience. In the New World people no longer moved solely in the worn grooves of tradition that defined the roles of priest or peasant or noble. Much of their experience had already been directed by observation, experiment, and the need to think anew. America was therefore receptive to the new science. Anybody who pretended to a degree of learning revealed a curiosity about natural philosophy, and some carried it to considerable depth.

John Winthrop, Jr., three times governor of Connecticut, wanted to establish industries and mining in America. These interests led to his work in chemistry and membership in the Royal Society of London. He owned probably the first telescope brought to the colonies. His cousin, John Winthrop IV, was a professional scientist, Hollis Professor of Mathematics and Natural Philosophy at Harvard, who introduced to the colonies the study of calculus and ranged over the fields of astronomy, geology, chemistry, and electricity. David Rittenhouse of Philadelphia, a clockmaker, became a self-taught scientist who built probably the first telescope made in America. John Bartram of Philadelphia spent a lifetime traveling and studying American plant life, and gathered in Philadelphia a botanical garden now part of the city's park system.

FRANKLIN'S INFLUENCE   Benjamin Franklin stood apart as the person who epitomized the Enlightenment, in the eyes of both Americans and Europeans. Born in Boston in 1706, he was the son of a candle and soap maker. Apprenticed to his older brother, a printer, Franklin left home at the age of seventeen, bound for Philadelphia. There, before he was twenty-four, he owned a print shop, where he edited and published the *Pennsylvania Gazette,* and when he was twenty-seven he brought out *Poor Richard's Almanac,* filled with homely maxims on success and happiness. Before he retired from business at the age of forty-two,

Benjamin Franklin. By the time he retired from business at the age of forty-two, Franklin had, among other things, owned a print shop, edited and published a newspaper, established a fire company, and invented the lightning rod and Franklin stove.

Franklin, among other achievements, had founded a library, set up a fire company, helped start the academy that became the University of Pennsylvania, and started a debating club that grew into the American Philosophical Society. After his early retirement, he intended to devote himself to public affairs and the sciences.

The course of events allowed Franklin less and less time for science, but that was his passion. Franklin's *Experiments and Observations on Electricity* (1751) went through many editions in several languages and established his reputation as a leading thinker and experimenter. His speculations extended widely to the fields of medicine, meteorology, geology, astronomy, physics, and other aspects of science. He invented the Franklin stove, the lightning rod, and a glass harmonica for which Mozart and Beethoven composed. The triumph of this untutored genius confirmed the Enlightenment trust in the powers of Nature.

EDUCATION IN THE COLONIES   For the colonists at large, education in the traditional ideas and manners of society—even literacy itself—remained primarily the responsibility of family and church, and one not always accepted. The modern conception of universal free education was slow in coming and failed to win universal acceptance until the twentieth century. Yet there is evidence of a widespread concern almost from the beginning that steps needed to be taken lest the children of settlers grow up untutored in the wilderness.

Conditions in New England proved most favorable for the establishment of schools. The Puritan emphasis on Scripture reading, which all Protestants shared in some degree, implied an obligation to ensure literacy. The great proportion of highly educated people in Puritan New England (Massachusetts probably had a greater proportion of college graduates in the early seventeenth century than in the twentieth) ensured a common respect for education. And the compact towns of that region made schools more feasible than among the scattered people of the southern colonies. In 1647 the colony enacted the famous "ye olde deluder Satan" Act (designed to thwart the Evil One), which required every town of fifty or more families to set up a grammar school (a Latin school that could prepare a student for college). Although the act was widely evaded, it did signify a serious purpose to promote education. Massachusetts Bay set an example that the rest of New England emulated.

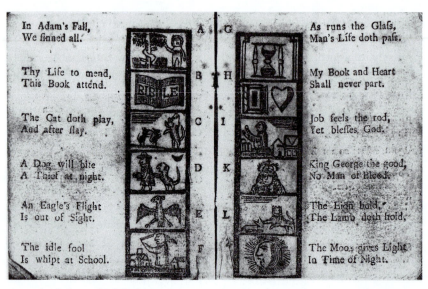

In Adam's Fall, We finned all.	A G	As runs the Glafs, Man's Life doth pafs.
Thy Life to mend, This Book attend.	B H	My Book and Heart Shall never part.
The Cat doth play, And after flay.	C I	Job feels the rod, Yet bleffes God.
A Dog will bite A Thief at night.	D K	King George the good, No Man of Blood.
An Eagle's Flight Is out of Sight.	E L	The Lion bold, The Lamb doth hold.
The idle fool Is whipt at School.	F	The Moon gives Light In Time of Night.

From the "Rhymed Alphabet" of The New England Primer, *first published in America in the 1680s.*

The Dutch in New Netherland were nearly if not equally as interested in education as the New England Puritans. In Pennsylvania the Quakers never heeded William Penn's instructions to establish public schools, but they did respect the usefulness of education and financed a number of private schools teaching practical as well as academic subjects. In the southern colonies efforts to establish schools were hampered by the more scattered populations, and in parts of the backcountry by indifference and neglect. Some of the wealthiest planters and merchants of the Tidewater sent their children to England or hired tutors, who in some cases would also serve the children of neighbors. In some places wealthy patrons or the people collectively managed to raise some kind of support for "old field" schools and academies at the secondary level.

THE GREAT AWAKENING

STIRRINGS Amid the new currents of learning and the Enlightenment, many people seemed to be drifting away from the old moorings of piety. Despite the belief that the Lord had allowed great Puritan and

Quaker merchants of Boston and Philadelphia to prosper, there remained a haunting fear that the devil had lured them into the vain pursuit of worldly gain, deism, and skepticism. And out along the fringes of settlement there grew up a great backwater of the unchurched. On the frontier, people had no minister to preach or administer sacraments or perform marriages. According to some, these pioneers lapsed into a primitive and sinful life, little different from the heathens who lurked in the woods. By the 1730s, the sense of falling-away provoked a revival of faith, which became known as the Great Awakening. Within a few years, the wave of evangelism that characterized the Great Awakening would sweep the colonies from one end to the other.

In 1734–1735 a remarkable spiritual revival occurred in the congregation of Jonathan Edwards, a Congregationalist minister in Northampton, in western Massachusetts. One of America's most brilliant philosophers and theologians, Edwards was the only son among eleven children. He entered Yale in 1716 at age thirteen and was graduated valedictorian four years later. While a college student, he developed a mystical religious strain. In 1726 Edwards was called to serve the Congregational church in Northampton. There he found the congregation's spirituality at low ebb. "Licentiousness for some years greatly prevailed among the youth of the town: there were many of them much addicted to night walking and frequenting the tavern, and lewd practices wherein some by their example exceedingly corrupted others." He was convinced that Christians had become too preoccupied with making

The Reverend Jonathan Edwards awoke many congregants to their plight in sermons such as "Sinners in the Hands of an Angry God."

and spending money, and that religion had become too intellectual, thereby losing its animating emotional force. "Our people," he said, "do not so much need to have their heads stored as to have their hearts touched." He added that he considered it a "reasonable thing to endeavor to fright persons away from hell." His own vivid descriptions of the torments of hell and the delights of heaven helped rekindle spiritual fervor among his congregants. By 1735 he could report that "the town seemed to be full of the presence of God; it never was so full of love, nor of joy."

About the same time, William Tennent, the Irish-born Presbyterian revivalist, set up a "Log College" in Neshaminy, Pennsylvania, for the education of ministers to serve the Scotch-Irish Presbyterians around Philadelphia. The Log College specialized in turning out zealots who proclaimed the need for revival. Among the most successful of these was Tennent's son, Gilbert. He became the leader of the so-called New Light faction and eventually helped raise funds for the College of New Jersey (now Princeton University), of which he was a trustee. Critics scorned Tennent and his fellow backwoods evangelists, branding them "half educated enthusiasts," but two of these rustic preachers later became presidents of Princeton.

The true catalyst of the Great Awakening, however, was a twenty-seven-year-old English minister, George Whitefield, whose reputation as a spellbinding evangelist in the Wesleyan revivals then under way in England preceded him to the colonies. Congregations were lifeless, he claimed, "because dead men preach to them." Too many ministers were "slothful shepherds and dumb dogs." His objective was to restore the fires of religious fervor to American congregations. In the autumn of 1739 he arrived in Philadelphia, and late in that year preached to crowds in the area of as many as 6,000. After visiting Georgia, he made a triumphal procession northward to New England, drawing great crowds and releasing "Gales of Heavenly Wind" that blew gusts throughout the colonies.

Young and magnetic, possessed of a golden voice, Whitefield in the pulpit was a dramatic actor who impersonated the agonies of the damned and the joys of the regenerate. He enthralled audiences with his unparalleled eloquence. Even the skeptical Ben Franklin, who went to see the show in Philadelphia, found himself so carried away that he emptied his pockets into the collection plate. The English revivalist

George Whitefield's dramatic eloquence roused American congregants, leading many to experience a religious rebirth.

urged his listeners to experience a "new birth"—a sudden, emotional moment of conversion and salvation—and warned of the dangers of a ministry that had not experienced such rebirth. By the end of his sermon, one listener reported, the entire congregation was "in utmost Confusion, some crying out, some laughing, and Bliss still roaring to them to come to Christ, as they answered, *I will, I will, I'm coming, I'm coming.*"

Jonathan Edwards took advantage of the commotion stirred up by Whitefield to spread his own revival gospel. In his view, a religion of the heart was central to true faith. The Christian, Edwards explained, "does not merely rationally believe that God is glorious, but he had a sense of the gloriousness of God in his heart." Edwards, however, was never given to the excesses of Whitefield. He acknowledged that religion should not be reduced to sheer emotionalism, nor should it shift its focus from the grace of God to the intensity of an individual's conversion experience. Instead, he sought to use his remarkable powers as a theologian and preacher to remind people of the sovereignty of God and the irresistible attraction of his glory, beauty, and love.

The Awakening in New England reached its peak in 1741, when Edwards delivered his most famous sermon at Enfield, Massachusetts. Entitled "Sinners in the Hands of an Angry God," it represented a devout appeal to repentance. Edwards reminded the congregation that hell was real and that God's vision was omnipotent, his judgment certain. He noted that God "holds you over the pit of hell, much as one holds a spider, or some loathsome insect, over the fire, abhors you, and is dreadfully provoked . . . he looks upon you as worthy of nothing else, but to be cast into the fire." But for all the terror of his theme, Edwards did not rant or engage in theatrics. Instead, he delivered the carefully reasoned sermon in a soft, solemn voice and a calm manner. When he finished, he had to wait several minutes for the congregation to quiet down before leading them in a closing hymn.

Edwards and Whitefield inspired many imitators, some of whom carried the fiery language to extremes. Once unleashed, spiritual enthusiasm is hard to control. In many ways the Awakening backfired on those who had intended it to bolster church discipline and social order. Some of the revivalists began to court those at the bottom of the social scale—laborers, seamen, servants, and farm folk. The Reverend James Davenport, for instance, a fiery itinerant New England Congregationalist, set about shouting, raging, and stomping on the devil, beseeching his listeners to renounce the established clergy and become the agents of their own salvation. The churched and unchurched flocked to hear his mesmerizing sermons. Seized by the terror and ecstasy, they groveled on the floor or lay unconscious on the benches, to the chagrin of more decorous churchgoers. One never knew, the more traditional clergymen warned, whence came these enthusiasms—perhaps they were devilish delusions intended to discredit the true faith.

PIETY AND REASON   Everywhere the Awakening brought splits, especially in the more Calvinistic churches. Presbyterians divided into the "Old Side" and "New Side"; Congregationalists into "Old Lights" and "New Lights." New England religious life would never be the same. The more traditional clergy found its position being undermined as church members chose sides and either dismissed their ministers or deserted them. Many of the "New Lights" went over to the Baptists, and others flocked to Presbyterian or, later, Methodist groups, which in turn divided and subdivided into new sects.

New England Puritanism disintegrated amid the revivals of the Great Awakening. The precarious tension in which the founders had held the elements of emotionalism and reason was now sundered. In consequence, New England attracted more and more Baptists, Presbyterians, Anglicans, and other denominations, while the revival frenzy scored its most lasting victories along the frontiers of the middle and southern colonies. In the more sedate churches of Boston, moreover, the principle of rational religion gained the upper hand in a reaction against the excesses of revival emotion. Boston ministers such as Charles Chauncey and Jonathan Mayhew reexamined Calvinist theology and found it too forbidding and irrational that people could be forever damned by predestination. The rationality of Newton and Locke, the idea of natural law, crept more and more into their sermons. They were already on the road to Unitarianism and Universalism.

In reaction to taunts that the "born-again" revivalist ministers lacked learning, the Awakening gave rise to the denominational colleges that became so characteristic of American higher education. The three colleges already in existence had grown earlier from religious motives: Harvard, founded in 1636, because the Puritans dreaded "to leave an illiterate ministry to the church when our present ministers shall lie in the dust"; the College of William and Mary, in 1693, to serve James Blair's purpose of strengthening the Anglican ministry; and Yale College, in 1701, set up to educate the Puritans of Connecticut, who felt that Harvard was drifting from the strictest orthodoxy. The College of New Jersey, later Princeton University, was founded by Presbyterians in 1746 as successor to William Tennent's Log College. In close succession came King's College (1754) in New York, later Columbia University, an Anglican institution; the College of Rhode Island (1764), later Brown University, Baptist; Queen's College (1766), later Rutgers, Dutch Reformed; and Congregationalist Dartmouth (1769), the outgrowth of an earlier school for Indians. Among the colonial colleges, only the University of Pennsylvania, founded as the Philadelphia Academy in 1754, arose from a secular impulse.

The Great Awakening, like the Enlightenment, set in motion powerful currents that still flow in American life. It implanted in American culture the evangelical principle and the appeal of revivalism. The movement weakened the status of the old-fashioned clergy and encouraged believers to exercise their own judgment, and thereby weakened habits of deference generally. By encouraging the proliferation of denominations it heightened the need for toleration of dissent. But in some respects the counterpoint between the Awakening and the Enlightenment, between the principles of spirit and reason, led by different roads to similar ends. Both movements emphasized the power and right of individual decision making, and both aroused millennial hopes that America would become the promised land in which people might attain the perfection of piety or reason, if not of both.

MAKING CONNECTIONS

- This chapter contains hints of tensions in colonial Virginia society; such tensions would periodically come to a head, as in Bacon's Rebellion, discussed in Chapter 2.

- During the imperial crisis of the 1760s and 1770s, the ideas of the Great Awakening and especially the Enlightenment helped shape the American response to British actions and thereby contributed to a revolutionary mentality.

FURTHER READING

The diversity of colonial societies may be seen in David Hackett Fischer's *Albion's Seed: Four British Folkways in America* (1989). Other useful works include Richard F. Hofstadter's *America at 1750: A Social Portrait* (1971), and James A. Henretta's *The Evolution of American Society, 1700–1815* (1973). Also see Jack P. Greene's *Imperatives, Behaviors, and Identities: Essays in Early American Cultural History* (1992).

Until recently Puritan communities received the bulk of scholarly attention. Studies of the New England town include Darrett B. Rutman's *Winthrop's Boston: Portrait of a Puritan Town, 1630–1649* (1965) and Kenneth A. Lockridge's *A New England Town: The First One Hundred Years* (2nd ed., 1985). John Frederick Martin's *Profits in the Wilderness: Entrepreneurship and the Founding of New England Towns in the Seventeenth Century* (1991) indicates that economic concerns rather than spiritual motives were driving forces in many New England towns.

Paul S. Boyer and Stephen Nissenbaum's *Salem Possessed* (1974) connects the notorious witch trials to changes in community structure.

For an interdisciplinary approach, see John Demos's *Entertaining Satan: Witchcraft and the Culture of Early New England* (1982). Bernard Rosenthal challenges many myths concerning the Salem witch trials in *Salem Story: Reading the Witch Trials of 1692* (1993).

Of the more recent works dealing with New England society, see Janice Knight's *Orthodoxies in Massachusetts: Rereading American Puritanism* (1994), and Stephen Innes's *Creating the Commonwealth: The Economic Culture of Puritan New England* (1995).

Discussions of women in the New England colonies can be found in Laurel Ulrich's *Good Wives: Image and Reality in the Lives of Women in Northern New England, 1650–1750* (1982), Joy Buel and Richard Buel, Jr.'s *The Way of Duty* (1984), and Carol Karlsen's *The Devil in the Shape of a Woman: Witchcraft in Colonial New England* (1987). John Demos describes family life in *A Little Commonwealth: Family Life in Plymouth Colony* (1970).

For the social history of the southern colonies, see Allan Kulikoff's *Tobacco and Slaves: The Development of Southern Cultures in the Chesapeake, 1680–1800* (1986) and *Colonial Chesapeake Society* (1988), edited by Lois Green Carr. Family life along the Chesapeake is described in Gloria L. Main's *Tobacco Colony* (1982) and Daniel B. Smith's *Inside the Great House: Planter Family Life in Eighteenth-Century Chesapeake Society* (1980).

Edmund S. Morgan's *American Slavery, American Freedom: The Ordeal of Colonial Virginia* (1975) examines Virginia's social structure, environment, and labor patterns in a biracial context. More specific on the racial nature of the origins of slavery are Winthrop D. Jordan's *White over Black: American Attitudes toward the Negro* (1968) and David B. Davis's *The Problem of Slavery in Western Culture* (1986). Philip D. Curtin's *The Atlantic Slave Trade* (1969) is a valuable quantitative study. On the interaction of the cultures of blacks and whites, see Mechal Sobel's *The World They Made Together: Black and White Values in Eighteenth Century Virginia* (1987). Black viewpoints are presented in Timothy H. Breen and Stephen Innes's *"Myne Owne Ground": Race and Freedom on Virginia's Eastern Shore, 1640–1676* (1980). David W. Galenson's *White Servitude in Colonial America* (1981) looks at the indentured labor force.

Henry F. May's *The Enlightenment in America* (1976) examines intellectual trends in eighteenth-century America. Lawrence A. Cremin's

American Education: The Colonial Experience, 1607–1783 (1970) surveys educational developments.

On the Great Awakening, see Edwin S. Gaustad's *The Great Awakening in New England* (1957) and Patricia U. Bonomi's *Under the Cope of Heaven: Religion, Society, and Politics in Colonial America* (1986). The political impact of the new religious enthusiasm is shown in Rhys Isaac's *The Transformation of Virginia, 1740–1790* (1982). Patricia J. Tracy's *Jonathan Edwards, Pastor* (1980) stresses the Northampton minister's relations to his community.

4 THE IMPERIAL PERSPECTIVE

CHAPTER ORGANIZER

This chapter focuses on:

- England's changing policies in the political and economic administration of the colonies.

- how colonial governments were structured.

- the relations between English colonists and their neighbors in North America: the French and the Indians.

he British differed from the Spanish and French in the degree of autonomy they allowed their colonies in the Western Hemisphere. Unlike New France and New Spain, New England was in effect a self-governing community. Unlike the French and Spanish, the English were unwilling to incur the expenses of a vast colonial bureaucracy. The constant struggle between Parliament and the Stuart kings prevented England from perfecting either a systematic colonial policy or effective agencies of imperial control. After the Restoration of the Stuart monarchy in 1660, a more comprehensive plan of colonial administration slowly emerged, but even so it lacked coherence and efficiency.

As a result of inefficient—and often lax—colonial administration by the mother country, Americans grew accustomed to loose and often paradoxical imperial policies. For instance, the British government granted home rule to the settlements along the Atlantic coast and then sought to keep them from exercising it. It regarded the English colonists as citizens, but it refused to grant them the privileges of citizenship. It insisted that the settlers contribute to the expense of maintaining the colonies, but it refused to allow them a voice in the shaping of administrative policies. Such inconsistencies made tensions inevitable. By the mid–eighteenth century, when Britain tried to impose on its American colonies the kind of controls that were reaping such profits in India, it was too late. British Americans had developed a far more powerful sense of their rights than any other colonial people, and they were determined to assert and defend those rights.

ENGLISH ADMINISTRATION OF THE COLONIES

Throughout the colonial period, the king was the source of legal authority in America, and land titles derived ultimately from royal grants. All colonies except Georgia received charters from the king before the Glorious Revolution of 1688, when the crown lost supremacy to Parliament. The colonies therefore continued to stand as "dependencies of the crown," and the important colonial officials held office at the pleasure of the crown. After King George granted a group of investors a charter for the new colony of Georgia in 1732, its status conformed to the established practice.

The king exercised his power through the Privy Council, a body of some thirty to forty advisers appointed by and responsible solely to him, and this group became the first agency of colonial supervision. But the Privy Council was too large and too busy to keep track of the details. So in 1634 Charles I entrusted colonial affairs to eleven of its members, the Lords Commissioners for Plantations in General, with William Laud, archbishop of Canterbury, as its head. The Laud Commission grew in part out of the troubles following the dissolution of the Virginia Company and in part out of Laud's design to impose political and religious conformity on New England. In 1638 his commission ordered Massachusetts to return its charter and answer charges that colonial officials had violated its provisions. Sir Ferdinando Gorges, appointed governor-general of New England, planned to subdue the region by force if necessary, and might have quashed the Puritan experiment except for the troubles at home that prevented further action. The Civil War in England, which lasted from 1642 to 1649, was followed by Oliver Cromwell's Puritan Commonwealth and Protectorate, and both developments gave the colonies a respite from efforts at royal control.

THE MERCANTILE SYSTEM   Cromwell showed little passion for colonial administration, but he had a lively concern for colonial trade, which had fallen largely to Dutch shipping during the upheavals in England. Therefore, in 1651 Parliament adopted a Navigation Act that excluded nearly all foreign shipping from the English and colonial trade. The act required that all goods imported into England or the colonies must arrive on English ships and that the majority of the crew must be English. In all cases colonial ships and crews qualified as English. The act excepted European goods, which might come in ships of the country that produced the goods, but only from the place of origin or the port from which they were usually shipped.

On economic policy, if nothing else, Restoration England under Charles II followed the lead of Cromwell and all the other major European powers of the seventeenth and eighteenth centuries. The new Parliament adopted the mercantile system, or mercantilism, which assumed that economies could not grow by themselves and that the total of the world's gold and silver remained essentially fixed, with only a nation's share in that wealth subject to change. Thus a nation could gain wealth only at the expense of another country—by seizing its gold and silver and dominating its trade. To get and keep gold and silver, the government had to direct all economic activities, limiting foreign imports and preserving a favorable balance of trade. This required the government to encourage manufacturers, through subsidies and monopolies if need be, to develop and protect its own shipping, and to make use of colonies as sources of raw materials and markets for its finished goods.

The Navigation Act of 1660 gave Cromwell's act of 1651 a new twist. Ships' crews now had to be not just a majority but three-quarters English, and certain specified goods were to be shipped only to England or other English colonies. The list of "enumerated" goods initially included tobacco, cotton, indigo, ginger, dyewoods, and sugar. Rice, hemp, masts and spars, copper ores, and furs, among other items, were later added to the list. Not only did England (and its colonies) become the sole outlet for these colonial exports, but three years later the Navigation Act of 1663 sought to make England the funnel through which all colonial imports had to be routed. The act was sometimes called the Staple Act because it made England the staple (market or trade center) for all goods sent to the colonies. Virtually everything shipped from Europe to America had to stop off in England, be landed, and duty paid on it before reshipment. A third major act rounded out the trade system. The Navigation Act of 1673 (sometimes called the Plantation Duty Act) required that every captain loading enumerated articles give bond to land them in England, or if they were destined for another colony, that he pay on the spot a duty roughly equal to that paid in England.

ENFORCING THE NAVIGATION ACTS   The Navigation Acts supplied a convenient rationale for a colonial system: to serve the economic needs of the mother country. Yet enforcement was spotty. During the reign of Charles I a bureaucracy of colonial administrators began to emerge, but it took shape slowly and incompletely. After the Restoration of 1660, supervision of colonial affairs fell once again to the Privy Council, or rather to a succession of its committees. In 1675 Charles II introduced some order into the chaos when, as his father had done before, he designated certain privy councilors the Lords of Trade. The Lords of Trade were to make the colonies abide by the mercantile system and to seek out ways to make them more profitable to England and the crown. To these ends, they served as the clearinghouse for all colonial affairs, building up a bureaucracy of colonial experts. The Lords of Trade named governors, wrote or reviewed the governors' instructions, and handled all reports and correspondence dealing with colonial affairs.

Within five years of the Plantation Duty Act, between 1673 and 1678, collectors of customs appeared in all the colonies, and shortly thereafter a surveyor general of the customs in the American colonies was named. The most notorious of these, insofar as resentful colonists were concerned, was Edward Randolph, the first man to make an entire career in the colonial service and the nemesis of insubordinate colonials for a quarter century.

Randolph arrived at Boston in 1676 to demand that Massachusetts answer complaints that it had usurped the proprietary rights in New Hampshire and Maine. Randolph submitted a report bristling with hos-

This view of eighteenth-century Boston shows the importance of shipping and its regulation in the colonies, especially in Massachusetts Bay.

tility. The Bay colony had not only ignored royal wishes, it had tolerated violations of the Navigation Acts, refused appeals from its courts to the Privy Council, and had operated a mint in defiance of the king's prerogative. Massachusetts officials had told him, Randolph reported, "that the legislative power is and abides in them solely to act and make laws by virtue" of their charter. The Lords of Trade began legal proceedings against the colonial charter in 1678. Meanwhile Randolph returned in 1680 to inaugurate the royal colony of New Hampshire, then set up shop as the king's collector of customs in Boston, whence he dispatched repeated accounts of colonial recalcitrance. Eventually, in 1684, the Lords of Trade won a court decision that annulled the charter of Massachusetts. The Puritan utopia was fast becoming a lost cause.

THE DOMINION OF NEW ENGLAND Temporarily, the government of Massachusetts Bay was placed in the hands of a special royal commission. Then in 1685 Charles II died, to be succeeded by his brother, the duke of York, as James II, the first Catholic sovereign since the death of Queen Mary in 1558. James II asserted his prerogatives more forcefully than his brother had. The new king readily approved a proposal to create a Dominion of New England and to place under its sway all colonies south through New Jersey.

The Dominion was to have a government named altogether by royal authority, a governor and council that would rule without any assembly. The royal governor, Sir Edmund Andros, appeared in Boston in 1686 to establish his rule, which he soon extended over Connecticut and Rhode Island, and in 1688 over New York and East and West New Jersey. Andros was a soldier, accustomed to taking—and giving—orders. He seems to have been honest, efficient, and loyal to the crown, but tactless in circumstances that called for the utmost diplomacy—the uprooting of long-established institutions in the face of popular hostility.

A rising resentment greeted Andros's measures, especially in Massachusetts. Taxation was now levied without the consent of the General Court, and when residents of one seaboard town protested against taxation without representation, a number of them were imprisoned or fined. Andros suppressed town governments, enforced the trade laws, and subdued smuggling. Most ominous of all, Andros and his lieutenants took over one of the Puritan churches for Anglican worship in Boston. Puritan leaders believed, with good reason, that he was conspiring to break their power and authority.

But the Dominion was scarcely established before the Glorious Revolution of 1688 erupted. James II, like Andros in New England, had aroused resentment by instituting arbitrary measures and, what was more, by openly parading his Catholic faith. The birth of a son, sure to be reared a Catholic, put the opposition on notice that James's system

King James II (1685–1688).

would survive him. The Catholic son, rather than the Protestant daughters, Mary and Anne, would be next in line for the throne. Parliamentary leaders, their patience exhausted, invited Mary and her husband, the Dutch leader, William of Orange, to assume the throne as joint monarchs. James, seeing his support dwindling, fled the country.

THE GLORIOUS REVOLUTION IN AMERICA   When news reached Boston that William had landed in England, Boston staged its own Glorious Revolution, as bloodless as that in England. Andros and his councilors were arrested, and Massachusetts reverted to its former government. In rapid sequence the other colonies that had been absorbed into the Dominion followed suit. All were permitted to retain their former status except Massachusetts and Plymouth which, after some delay, were united under a new charter in 1691 as the royal colony of Massachusetts Bay.

In New York, however, events took a different course. There, Andros's lieutenant-governor was deposed by a group led by a German immigrant, Jacob Leisler, who assumed the office of governor pending word from England. For two years he kept the province under his control with the support of the militia. Finally, in 1691, the king appointed a new governor. When Leisler hesitated to turn over authority, he was charged with treason. Leisler and his son-in-law were hanged on May 16, 1691. Four years too late, in 1695, Parliament exonerated them of all charges. For years to come Leisler and anti-Leisler factions would poison the political atmosphere of New York.

The new monarchs made no effort to restore the Dominion of New England. But the crown salvaged a remnant of that design by bringing more colonies under royal control through the appointment of governors in Massachusetts, New York, and Maryland. Maryland, however, reverted to proprietary status in 1715 after the fourth Lord Baltimore became Anglican. Pennsylvania had an even briefer career as a royal colony, 1692–1694, before reverting to Penn's proprietorship. New Jersey became a royal province in 1702, South Carolina in 1719, North Carolina in 1729, and Georgia in 1752.

The Glorious Revolution had significant long-term effects on American history in that the Bill of Rights and the Toleration Act, passed in England in 1689, influenced attitudes and the course of events in the colonies. Even more significant, the overthrow of James II set a precedent for revolution against the monarch. In defense of that action the philosopher John Locke published his *Two Treatises on Government* (1690), which had an enormous impact on political thought in the colonies. The *First Treatise* refuted theories of the divine right of kings. The more important *Second Treatise* set forth Locke's contract theory of government, which claimed that people were endowed with certain natural rights to life, liberty, and property. In a state of nature, prior to the implementation of a government, such rights went without safeguard. This led people to establish governments among themselves. Kings were parties to such agreements, and obligated to protect the property and lives of their subjects. When they failed to do so, the people had the right—in extreme cases—to overthrow the monarch and change their government.

The idea that governments emerged by contract out of a primitive state of nature is of course hypothetical, not an account of actual events. But in the American experience governments had actually grown out of contractual arrangements such as Locke described: the Mayflower Compact, the Cambridge Agreement, the Fundamental Orders of Connecticut. The royal charters themselves constituted a sort of contract between the crown and the settlers. Locke's writings understandably appealed to colonial readers, and his philosophy probably had more influence in America than in England.

AN EMERGING COLONIAL SYSTEM   The accession of William and Mary to the English throne provoked a refinement of the existing Navigation Acts. In 1696 two developments created at last the semblance, and to some degree the reality, of a coherent colonial system. First, the Navigation Act of 1696 required colonial governors to enforce the Navigation Acts, allowed customs officials to use "writs of assistance" (general search warrants that did not have to specify the place to be searched), and ordered that accused violators be tried in admiralty courts, which Edward Randolph had recommended because juries habitually refused to convict their peers. Admiralty cases were decided by judges whom the governors appointed.

Second, also in 1696, William III created the Lords of Trade and Plantations (the Board of Trade) to take the place of the Lords of Trade. Colonial officials were required to report to the board, and its archives constitute the largest single collection of materials on colonial relations with the mother country from that time on. The Board of Trade investigated the enforcement of the Navigation Acts and recommended ways to limit colonial manufactures and to encourage the production of raw materials. At the board's behest, Parliament enacted a bounty for the production of ship timber, masts, hemp, rice, indigo, and other commodities. The board examined all colonial laws and made recommendations for their disallowance by the crown. In all, 8,563 colonial laws eventually were examined and 469 of them were actually disallowed.

SALUTARY NEGLECT   From 1696 to 1725 the Board of Trade worked vigorously toward subjecting the colonies to a more efficient royal control. After the death of Queen Anne in 1714, however, its energies waned. The throne went in turn to the Hanoverian monarchs, George I (1714–1727) and George II (1727–1760), German princes who were next in the Protestant line of succession by virtue of descent from James I. Under these monarchs, the cabinet (a kind of executive committee in the Privy Council) emerged as the central agency of administration. Robert Walpole, as first minister (1721–1742), deliberately followed a policy that the philosopher Edmund Burke later called "a wise and salutary neglect." The Board of Trade became chiefly an agency of political patronage, studded with officials who took an interest mainly in their salaries.

THE HABIT OF SELF-GOVERNMENT

Government within the colonies, like colonial policy, evolved without plan. In broad outline the governor, council, and assembly in each colony corresponded to the king, lords, and commons of the mother country. At the outset, all the colonies except Georgia had begun as projects of trading companies or feudal proprietors holding charters from the crown, but eight colonies eventually relinquished or forfeited their charters and became royal provinces. In these the crown named the governor. In Maryland, Pennsylvania, and Delaware the governor remained the choice of a proprietor, although each had an interim period of royal government. Connecticut and Rhode Island were the last of the corporate colonies; they elected their own governors to the end of the colonial period. In the corporate and proprietary colonies, and in Massachusetts, the charter served as a rough equivalent to a written constitution. Rhode Island and Connecticut in fact kept their charters as state constitutions after independence. Over the years certain anomalies appeared as colonial governments diverged from that of England. On the one hand, the governors retained powers and prerogatives that the king had lost in the course of the seventeenth century. On the other hand, the assemblies acquired powers, particularly with respect to appointments, that Parliament had yet to gain.

POWERS OF THE GOVERNORS   The crown never vetoed acts of Parliament after 1707, but the colonial governors still held an absolute veto and the crown could disallow (in effect, veto) colonial legislation on advice of the Board of Trade. With respect to the assembly, the governor still had the power to determine when and where it would meet, to prorogue (adjourn or recess) sessions, and to dissolve the assembly for new elections or to postpone elections indefinitely at his pleasure. The crown, however, had to summon Parliament every three years and call elections at least every seven, and could not prorogue sessions. The royal or proprietary governor, moreover, nominated for life appointment the members of his council (except in Massachusetts, where they were chosen by the lower house), and the council functioned as both the upper house of the legislature and the highest court of appeal within the colony. With respect to the judiciary, in all but the charter colonies the governor held the prerogative of creating courts and of naming and dismissing judges, powers explicitly denied the king in England. Over time, however, the colonial assemblies generally made good their claim that courts should be created only by legislative authority, although the crown repeatedly disallowed acts to grant judges life tenure in order to make them more independent.

As chief executive the governor could appoint and remove officials, command the militia and naval forces, and grant pardons. In these respects his authority resembled the crown's, for the king still exercised executive authority and had the power generally to name all administrative officials. This often served as a powerful means of royal influence in Parliament, since the king could appoint members or their friends to lucrative offices. While the arrangement might seem a breeding ground for corruption or tyranny, it was often viewed in the eighteenth century as a stabilizing influence, especially by the king's friends. But it was an influence less and less available to the governors. On the one hand, colonial assemblies nibbled away at their power of appointment; on the other hand, the authorities in England more and more drew the control of colonial patronage into their own hands.

POWERS OF THE ASSEMBLIES   Unlike the governor and council, who were appointed by an outside authority, either king or proprietor, the colonial assembly was elected. Whether called the House of Burgesses (Virginia), of Delegates (Maryland), of Representatives (Massachusetts), or simply "assembly," the lower houses were chosen by popular vote in counties or towns or, in South Carolina, parishes. Although the English Toleration Act of 1689 did not apply to the colonies, religious tests for voting tended to be abandoned thereafter (the Massachusetts charter of 1691 so specified) and the chief restriction left was a property qualification, based on the notion that only men who held a

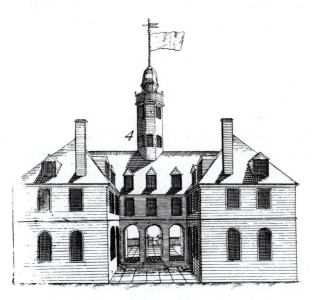

The Virginia Capitol, depicted here in the eighteenth century, "was an architectural representation of the British constitution as adapted for use in the colonies." In the upper story of one wing sat the King's Council, the upper legislative house. Immediately below, the governor and council sat as the General Court, the highest judicial body. Across from the Court sat the House of Burgesses, the body of elected representatives.

"stake in society" could vote responsibly. Yet the property qualifications generally set low hurdles in the way of potential voters. Property holding was widespread, and a greater proportion of the population could vote in the colonies than anywhere else in the world of the eighteenth century.

Women, children, Indians, and blacks were excluded from the political process—as a matter of course—and continued to be excluded for the most part into the twentieth century, but the qualifications excluded few adult free white males. Virginia, which at one time permitted all freemen to vote, in the eighteenth century required only the ownership of twenty-five acres of improved land or one hundred acres of wild land, or the ownership of a "house" and part of a lot in town, or a service in a five-year apprenticeship in Williamsburg or Norfolk. Qualifications for membership in the assembly ran somewhat higher, and officeholders tended to come from the more well-to-do—a phenomenon not unknown today—but there were exceptions. One unsympathetic colonist observed in 1744 that the New Jersey assembly "was chiefly composed of mechanicks and ignorant wretches; obstinate to the last degree."

Colonial politics of the eighteenth century mirrored English politics of the seventeenth. In one case, there had been a tug-of-war between king and Parliament, ending with the supremacy of Parliament, confirmed by the Glorious Revolution. In the other case, colonial governors were still trying to wield prerogatives that the king had lost in England. The assemblies knew this; they also knew the arguments for the "rights" and "liberties" of the people and their legislative bodies, and against the dangers of despotic power. A further anomaly in the situation was the undefined relationship of the colonies to Parliament. The colonies had been created by authority of the crown and their governmental connections ran to the crown, yet Parliament on occasion passed laws that applied to the colonies and were tacitly accepted by the colonies.

By the early eighteenth century, the assemblies, like Parliament, held two important strands of power—and they were perfectly aware of the parallel. First, they held the power of the purse strings in their right to vote on taxes and expenditures. Second, they held the power to initiate legislation and not merely, as in the early history of some colonies, the right to act on proposals from the governor and council. They used these powers to pull other strands of power into their hands when the chance presented itself. Governors in most colonies were held on a tight leash by the assembly's control of salaries, his own and others, which were voted annually and sometimes not at all.

Assemblies, because they controlled finance, demanded and often got the right to name tax collectors and treasurers. Then they stretched the claim to cover public printers, Indian agents, supervisors of public works and services, and other officers of the government. By specifying how appropriations should be spent, they played an important role even in military affairs and Indian relations, as well as other matters. Indeed, in the choice of certain administrative officers they pushed their power beyond that of Parliament in England, where appointment remained a crown prerogative.

All through the eighteenth century, the assemblies expanded their power and influence, sometimes in conflict with the governors, sometimes in harmony with them, and often in the course of routine business passing laws and setting precedents the collective significance of which neither they nor the imperial authorities fully recognized. Once established, however, these laws and practices became fixed principles, parts of the "constitution" of the colonies. Self-government became first a habit, then a "right."

TROUBLED NEIGHBORS

SPANISH AMERICA IN DECLINE   By the start of the eighteenth century, the Spanish ruled over a huge colonial empire spanning North America. Yet their settlements in the borderlands north of Mexico were a colossal failure when compared to the colonies of the other European powers. In 1821, when Mexico declared its independence without firing a shot and the Spanish withdrew from North America, the most populated Hispanic settlement, Santa Fe, had only 6,000 residents. The next largest, San Antonio and St. Augustine, totaled only 1,500 each.

The Spanish failed to create thriving North American colonies for several reasons. Perhaps the most obvious was that the region lacked the gold and silver as well as the large native populations that attracted Spanish priorities to Mexico and Peru. In addition, the Spanish were distracted by their need to control the perennial unrest in Mexico among the natives and *mestizos* (people of mixed Indian and European ancestry). Moreover, those Spaniards who led the colonization effort in the borderlands were so preoccupied with military and religious exploitation that they never devoted enough attention to the factors necessary for producing viable settlements with self-sustaining economies. Only rarely, for example, did the Spanish send many women to their colonies in North America. They never understood that the main factor in creating successful communities was a thriving market economy. Instead they concentrated on building missions and forts and looking—in vain—for gold. Where the French and the English built their Indian policies around trading relationships (including firearms), Spain emphasized conversion to Catholicism, forbade manufacturing within the colonies, and strictly limited trade with the natives.

NEW FRANCE   Permanent French settlement in the New World differed considerably from both the Spanish and the English models. The French settlers were predominantly male but much smaller in number than the English and Spanish settlers. About 40,000 French colonists came to the New World over the seventeenth and eighteenth centuries. The relatively small French population proved to be an advantage in forcing the French to develop cooperative relationships with the Indians. Unlike the English settlers, the French established trading outposts rather than farms, mostly along the St. Lawrence River, on lands not claimed by Indians. They thus did not have to confront initial hostility. In addition, the French served as effective mediators between rival Great Lakes tribes. This diplomatic role gave them much more local authority and influence than their English counterparts, who disdained such mediation, had along the Atlantic coast. The heavily outnumbered and disproportionately male French settlers sought to integrate themselves with Indian culture rather than to displace it. They also encouraged the Indians to embrace Catholicism and hate the English. This more fraternal bond between the French and the Indians proved to be a source of strength in the wars with the English, enabling New France to survive until 1760, despite the lopsided disparity in numbers between the two colonial powers.

French exploration began with the explorer Samuel de Champlain, who landed on the shores of the St. Lawrence River in 1603, and two years later at Port Royal, Acadia (later Nova Scotia). Champlain led an-

Samuel de Champlain firing his harquebus at a group of Mohawks, killing two chiefs (1609).

other expedition in 1608, during which he founded Québec, a year after the Jamestown landing. While Acadia remained a remote outpost, New France expanded well beyond Québec, from which Champlain pushed his explorations up the great river and into the Great Lakes as far as Lake Huron, and southward to the lake that still bears his name. There, in 1609, he joined a band of Huron and Algonquian allies in a fateful encounter, fired his harquebus into the ranks of their Iroquois foes, and kindled a hatred that pursued New France to the end. Shortly afterward the Iroquois had a more friendly meeting with Henry Hudson near Albany and soon acquired their own firearms from Dutch, and later English, traders. The Iroquois now stood as a buffer against French designs to move toward the English of the middle colonies and as a constant menace on the flank of the French waterways to the interior.

Until his death in 1635 Champlain governed New France under a trading company whose charter imposed a fatal weakness that hobbled New France to its end. The company won a profitable monopoly of the fur trade, but it had to limit the population to French Catholics. Neither the enterprising, seafaring Huguenots (French Protestants) of coastal France nor foreigners of any faith were allowed to populate the country. Great land grants went to persons who promised to bring set-

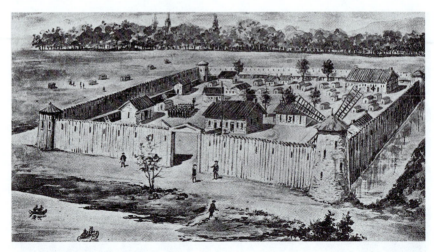

Sketch of Fort Rémy, built in 1671.

tlers to work the land under feudal tenure. The colony therefore remained a scattered patchwork of dependent peasants, Jesuit missionaries, priests, soldiers, officials, and *coureurs de bois* (literally, runners of
the woods), who ranged the interior in quest of furs.

In 1663 King Louis XIV and his chief minister, Jean Baptiste Colbert,
changed New France into a royal colony and pursued a plan of consolidation and stabilization. Colbert dispatched new settlers, including
shiploads of young women to lure disbanded soldiers and traders into
settled matrimony. He sent out tools and animals for farmers, nets for
fishermen, and tried to make New France self-sufficient in foodstuffs.
The population grew from about 4,000 in 1665 to about 15,000 in
1690. Still, Louis de Baude, Count Frontenac, who was governor from
1672 to 1682 and 1689 to 1698, held to a grand vision of French empire in the interior, spurring on the fur traders and missionaries and
converting their outposts into military stations in the wilderness: Fort
Detroit appeared at the far end of Lake Erie, Fort Michilimackinac at
the far end of Lake Huron.

FRENCH LOUISIANA From the Great Lakes French explorers moved
southward. In 1673 Louis Jolliet and Père Jacques Marquette, a Jesuit
priest, ventured into Lake Michigan, up the Fox River from Green Bay,
then down the Wisconsin to the Mississippi, and on as far as the
Arkansas River. Satisfied that the great river flowed to the Gulf of Mex-

ico, they turned back for fear of meeting with Spaniards. Nine years later Robert Cavalier, sieur de La Salle, went all the way to the Gulf of Mexico and named the country Louisiana after King Louis XIV of France.

Settlement of the Louisiana country finally began in 1699 when Pierre le Moyne, sieur d'Iberville, landed a colony near Biloxi, Mississippi. The main settlement then moved to Mobile Bay and in 1710 to the present site of Mobile, Alabama. For nearly half a century the dri-

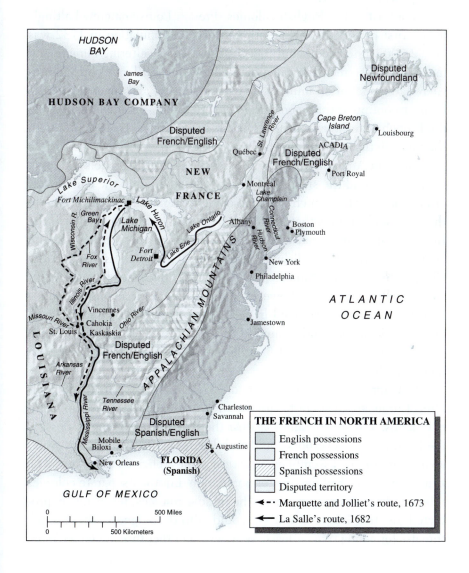

THE FRENCH IN NORTH AMERICA

☐ English possessions
☐ French possessions
▨ Spanish possessions
☐ Disputed territory
◄ ‑ ‑ Marquette and Jolliet's route, 1673
◄ La Salle's route, 1682

ving force in Louisiana was Jean Baptiste le Moyne, sieur de Bienville, a younger brother of Iberville. Bienville arrived with the first settlers in 1699, when he was only eighteen, and left the colony for the last time in 1743, when he was sixty-two. Sometimes called the "Father of Louisiana," he served periodically as governor or acting governor and always as adviser during those years. In 1718 he founded New Orleans, which shortly thereafter became the capital. Louisiana, first a royal colony, then a proprietary and then a corporate colony, again became a royal province in 1731.

In contrast to the English colonies, French Louisiana grew haltingly in the first half of the eighteenth century. Its population in 1732 was only 2,000 whites and about 3,800 slaves. The sweltering climate and mosquito-infested environment enticed few new settlers. Poorly administered, dependent on imports for its sustenance, and expensive to defend, it continued throughout the century to be a financial liability to the French government. It never became the thriving trade center with the Spanish that its founders had envisioned.

"France in America had two heads," the historian Francis Parkman wrote, "one amid the snows of Canada, the other amid the canebrakes of Louisiana." The French thus had one enormous advantage: access to the great water routes that led to the heartland of the continent. In the Illinois region, scattered settlers began farming the fertile soil, and courageous priests established missions at places such as Terre Haute ("high land") and Des Moines ("some monks"). Because of geography as well as deliberate policy, however, French America remained largely a howling wilderness traversed by a mobile population of traders, trappers, missionaries—and, mainly, Indians. In 1750 when the English colonials numbered about 1.5 million, the French population was no more than 80,000.

Yet in some ways the French had the edge on the British. They offered European goods in return for furs, encroached far less upon Indian lands, and so won allies against the English who came to possess the land. French governors could mobilize for action without any worry about quarreling assemblies or ethnic and religious diversity. The British may have had the greater population, but their separate colonies often worked at cross purposes. The middle colonies, for instance, protected by the Iroquois buffer, could afford to ignore the French threat—for a long time at least. Whenever conflict threatened, colonial assemblies seized the moment to extract new concessions from their governors. Colonial merchants, who built up a trade supplying food-stuffs to the French, persisted in smuggling supplies even in wartime.

THE COLONIAL WARS

French and British colonists clashed from the beginning of settlement. The Acadians fought with English settlers in Maine. Only a thin stretch of woods separated New England from Québec and Montréal, and an English force briefly occupied Québec from 1629 to 1632. Between New York and Québec, Lake Champlain supplied an easy water route for invasion in either direction, but the Iroquois stood athwart the path. Farther south, the mountainous wilderness widened into an almost impenetrable buffer. On the northernmost flank, the isolated Hudson Bay Company offered British competition for the fur trade of the interior, and both countries laid claim to Newfoundland. On the southernmost flank, the British and French jockeyed for position in the Caribbean sugar islands.

But for most of the seventeenth century, the two continental empires developed in relative isolation from each other, and for most of that century the homelands remained at peace with each other. After the Restoration, Charles II and James II pursued a policy of friendship with

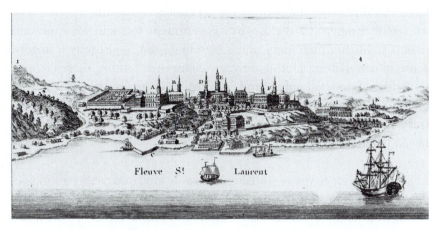

A view of Québec, the spires of its cathedrals and seminaries soaring high (1740s).

Louis XIV. The Glorious Revolution of 1688, however, worked an abrupt reversal in English diplomacy. William III, the new king, as leader of the Dutch Republic had fought a running conflict against the ambitions of Louis XIV. His ascent to the throne brought England almost immediately into a Grand Alliance against Louis in the War of the League of Augsburg, sometimes called the War of the Palatinate and known in the colonies simply as King William's War (1689–1697).

This was the first of four great European and intercolonial wars over the next sixty-four years: the War of the Spanish Succession (Queen Anne's War, 1702–1713), the War of the Austrian Succession (King George's War, 1744–1748), and the Seven Years' War (the French and Indian War, which lasted nine years in America, 1754–1763). In all except the last, the battles in America were but a sideshow to greater battles in Europe, where British policy pivoted on keeping a balance of power against the French. The alliances shifted from one fight to the next, but Britain and France were pitted against each other every time.

Thus for much of the century, the colonies were embroiled in wars and rumors of wars. The effect on much of the population was devastating. New England, especially Massachusetts, suffered probably more than the rest, for it was closest to the centers of French population. It is estimated that 900 Boston men (about 2.5 percent of the eligible males) died in the fighting. This meant that the city was faced with assisting a large population of widows and orphans. Even more important, these prolonged conflicts had profound consequences for Britain that later would reshape the contours of its relationship with America. The wars with France led the English government to incur an enormous debt, establish a huge navy and a standing army, and excite a jingoist sense of nationalism. During the early eighteenth century, these changes in British financial policy and political culture provoked critics to charge that traditional liberties were being usurped by a tyrannical central government. After the French and Indian War, American colonists began making the same point.

KING WILLIAM'S WAR In King William's War, scattered fighting occurred in the Hudson Bay posts, most of which fell to the French, and in Newfoundland, which also fell to a French force. The French aroused their Indian allies to join in scattered raids along the northern

EUROPEAN WARS ALSO FOUGHT IN NORTH AMERICA

European War	Major Participants	Colonial War	American Dates	Treaty
War of the League of Augsburg (War of the Palatinate) (1689–1697)	England and Holland *vs.* France	King William's War	1689–1697	Treaty of Ryswick (1697)
War of the Spanish Succession (1701–1714)	England, Austria, and Holland *vs.* France and Spain	Queen Anne's War	1702–1713	Peace of Utrecht (1713)
War of the Austrian Succession (1740–1748)	England and Austria *vs.* France and Prussia	King George's War	1744–1748	Treaty of Aix-la-Chapelle (1748)
Seven Years' War (1756–1763)	England and Prussia *vs.* France, Spain, Austria, and Russia	French and Indian War	1754–1763	Peace of Paris (1763)

frontier. In Massachusetts, Captain William Phips, who was about to become the first royal governor, organized an expedition that took Acadia. Various expeditions against French Canada failed to coalesce, and the war finally degenerated into a series of frontier raids. It ended ingloriously with the Treaty of Ryswick (1697), which returned the colonies to their prewar status.

QUEEN ANNE'S WAR   Fighting resumed only five years later. The War of the Spanish Succession was known to the colonists as Queen Anne's War. It saw the French and Spanish allied against the English. This time the Iroquois, tired of fighting the French, remained neutral. The brunt of this war fell on New England, South Carolina, and Florida. Between 1706 and 1713, a sporadic border war raged between South Carolina and Spanish Florida, and the English with Yamasee and Creek allies took the war nearly to St. Augustine.

South Carolina's Indian allies in fact constituted most of a force that responded to North Carolina's call for help in the Tuscarora War (1711–1713). The Tuscaroras, a numerous people who had long led a settled life in the Tidewater, suddenly found their lands invaded in 1709 by German and Swiss settlers. The war began when the Tuscaroras assaulted the new settlements. It ended when slave merchants of South Carolina mobilized their Indian allies, killed about 1,000 Tuscaroras and enslaved another 700. The survivors found refuge in the north, where they became the sixth nation of the Iroquois Confederacy.

In New England, the exposed frontier from Maine to Massachusetts suffered repeated raids during Queen Anne's War. In the winter of 1704, French and Indian forces sacked several Massachusetts villages, including Deerfield. The settlers were either slaughtered or taken on desperate marches through the snow to captivity among the Indians or the Canadians.

In the complex Peace of Utrecht (1713), Louis XIV recognized British title to the Hudson Bay, Newfoundland, Acadia (now Nova Scotia), and St. Christopher, as well as the British claim to sovereignty over the Iroquois. (Nobody consulted the Iroquois.) The French renounced any claim to special privileges in the commerce of Spanish or Portuguese America. Spain agreed not to transfer any of its American territory to a third party, and granted to the British the *asiento*, a contract for supplying Spanish America with 4,800 slaves annually over a period of

An Iroquois warrior in an eighteenth-century French etching.

thirty years. This opened the door for British smuggling, a practice that grew into a major cause of friction and, eventually, of renewed warfare.

In the South, the frontier flared up once more shortly after the war. The former Yamasee and Creek allies, outraged by the continuing advance of British settlement, attacked the Charleston colony. The Yamasee War of 1715 was the southern equivalent of King Philip's War in New England, a desperate struggle that threatened the colony's very existence. Once again, however, the Indians were unable to present a united front. The Cherokees remained neutral for the sake of their fur trade, and the defeated Yamasees retired into Florida, leaving open the country in which the new colony of Georgia appeared eighteen years later.

KING GEORGE'S WAR   The third great international war began in 1739 with a preliminary bout between England and Spain, called the War of Jenkins' Ear in honor of an English seaman who lost an ear to a Spanish soldier and exhibited the shriveled member as part of a campaign to arouse London against Spain's rudeness to smugglers.

The war began with a great British disaster, a grand expedition against Porto Bello in Panama, for which thousands of colonists volunteered and in which many died of yellow fever. One of the survivors, Lawrence Washington of Virginia, memorialized the event by naming his estate Mount Vernon after the ill-starred but popular admiral in command. Along the southern frontier the new colony of Georgia, less than a decade old, now served its purpose as a military buffer. General James Oglethorpe staged a raid on St. Augustine and later fought off Spanish counterattacks, but Charleston remained secure.

In 1744 France entered the war, which merged with another general European conflict, the War of the Austrian Succession, or King George's War in the colonies. Once again border raids flared along the northern frontier. Governor William Shirley of Massachusetts mounted an expedition against French Canada and conquered Fort Louisbourg on Cape Breton after a long siege. It was a costly conquest, but the war ended in stalemate. In the Treaty of Aix-la-Chapelle (1748) the British exchanged Louisbourg for Madras, which the French had taken in India.

Thereafter, the focus of attention turned to the Ohio Valley. French traders had moved westward to the Great Lakes and down the Mississippi, but the Ohio, with short portages from Lake Erie to its headwaters, would make a shorter connecting link for French America. During the 1740s, however, fur traders from Virginia and Pennsylvania had also begun to exploit that disputed region. Not far behind were the Pennsylvania and Virginia land speculators. "The English," one French agent warned the Indians, "are much less anxious to take away your peltries than to become masters of your lands." Virginians had organized several land companies, most conspicuously the Ohio Company, to which the king granted 200,000 acres along the upper Ohio in 1749, with a promise of 300,000 more.

The French resolved to act before the British advance became a dagger pointed at the continental heartland. In 1749 French scouts proceeded down the Allegheny and Ohio Rivers to spy out the land, woo the Indians, and bury leaden plates with inscriptions stating the French claim. Engravings hardly made the soil French, but in 1753 a new governor, the Marquis Duquesne, arrived in Canada and set about making good on the claim with a chain of forts in the region.

THE FRENCH AND INDIAN WAR   When news of these trespasses reached Williamsburg, the governor sent out an emissary to warn off the French. An ambitious young adjutant-general of the Virginia militia, Major George Washington, whose older brothers owned a part of the Ohio Company, volunteered for the mission. With a few companions

Washington made his way to Fort Le Boeuf and returned with a polite but firm French refusal. The governor then sent a small force to erect a fort at the strategic fork where the Allegheny and Monongahela Rivers meet to form the great Ohio. No sooner had the English started than a larger French force appeared, ousted them, and proceeded to build Fort Duquesne (now Pittsburgh) on the same strategic site.

Meanwhile, Washington had been organizing a force of volunteers, and in the spring of 1754 he went out with an advance guard and a few Indian allies. Near Great Meadows they skirmished with a French detachment. It marked the first bloodshed of a long—and finally decisive—war that reached far beyond America. Washington retreated with his prisoners and hastily constructed a stockade, Fort Necessity, which soon fell under siege by a larger French force from Fort Duquesne. On July 4, 1754, Washington surrendered and was permitted to withdraw with his survivors. With that disaster in the backwoods a great world

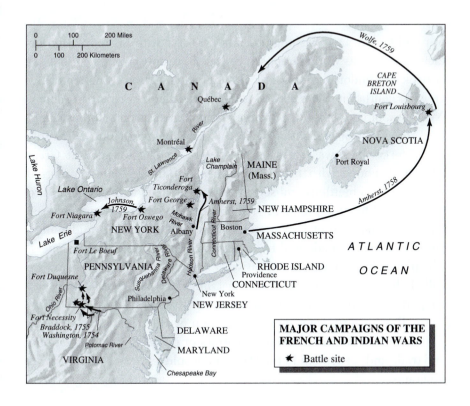

Benjamin Franklin's symbol of the need to unite the colonies against the French in 1754 would become popular again twenty years later, when the colonies faced a different threat.

war had begun, but Washington came out of it with his reputation intact—and he was world famous at the age of twenty-two.

Back in London the Board of Trade already had taken notice of the growing conflict in the backwoods and had called a meeting in Albany, New York, of commissioners from all the colonies as far south as Maryland to confer on precautions. The Albany Congress (June 19 to July 10, 1754), which was sitting when the first shots sounded at Great Meadows, ended with little accomplished. The delegates conferred with Iroquois chieftains and sent them away loaded with gifts in return for some halfhearted promises of support. The congress is remembered mainly for the Plan of Union worked out by a committee under Benjamin Franklin and adopted by unanimous vote of the commissioners. The plan called for a chief executive, a kind of supreme governor to be called the President-General of the United Colonies, appointed and supported by the crown, and a supreme assembly called the Grand Council, with forty-eight members chosen by the colonial assemblies. This federal body would oversee matters of defense, Indian relations, and trade and settlement in the West and would levy taxes to support its programs.

It must have been a good plan, Franklin reasoned, since the assemblies thought it gave too much power to the crown and the crown thought it gave too much to the colonies. At any rate the assemblies either rejected or ignored the plan. Only two substantive results came out of the congress. Its idea of a supreme commander for British forces in America was adopted, as was its advice that a New Yorker who was a friend of the Iroquois be made British superintendent of the northern Indians.

In London the government decided to force a showdown in America. In 1755 the British fleet captured Nova Scotia and expelled most of its French population. Some 5,000–7,000 Acadians who refused to take an oath of allegiance to the British crown were scattered through the colonies from Maine to Georgia. Impoverished and homeless, many of them desperately found their way to French Louisiana, where they became the Cajuns (a corruption of "Acadians") whose descendants still preserve elements of the French language along the remote bayous and in many urban centers.

The backwoods, however, became the scene of one British disaster after another over the next three years. In 1755 a new British commander-in-chief, General Edward Braddock, arrived in Virginia with two regiments of regulars. With the addition of some colonial troops, including George Washington as a volunteer staff officer, Braddock hacked a road through the wilderness from the upper Potomac to the vicinity of Fort Duquesne. Hauling heavy artillery to surround the French fort, along with a wagon train of supplies, Braddock's men achieved a great feat of military logistics and were on the verge of success when, seven miles from Fort Duquesne, the surrounding woods suddenly came alive with Indians and Frenchmen in Indian costume. Beset on three sides by concealed enemies, the British forces panicked and retreated in disarray, abandoning most of their artillery and supplies. Braddock lost his life in the encounter, and his second in command directed the remaining British regulars to the safety of Philadelphia.

A WORLD WAR   For two years, war raged along the frontier without becoming the cause of war in Europe. In 1756, however, the colonial war merged with what became the Seven Years' War in Europe. There, Empress Maria Theresa of Austria, still brooding over the loss of terri-

Amherst's attack on Louisbourg, July 1758, depicted on a French map.

tory in the previous conflict, worked a diplomatic revolution by bringing Austria's old enemy France, as well as Russia, into an alliance against Frederick the Great of Prussia. Britain, ever mindful of the European balance of power, now deserted Austria to ally with Frederick. The onset of war brought into office a new British government with the eloquent William Pitt as head of the ministry. Pitt's ability and assurance ("I know that I can save England and no one else can") instilled confidence at home and abroad.

British sea power soon began to cut off French reinforcements and supplies to the New World—and the trading goods with which they bought Indian allies. Pitt improved the British forces, gave command to young men of ability, and carried the battle to the enemy. In 1758 the tides began to turn. Fort Louisbourg fell. The Iroquois, sensing the turn of fortunes, pressed their dependents, the Delawares, to call off the frontier attacks on English settlements.

In 1759 the war reached its climax in a three-pronged offensive against the French in Canada, along what had become the classic invasion routes: via Niagara, Lake Champlain, and up the St. Lawrence. On the Niagara expedition the British were joined by a group of Iroquois, and they captured Fort Niagara, which virtually cut the French lifeline to the interior. On Lake Champlain, General Jeffrey Amherst took Fort

George and Fort Ticonderoga, then paused to refortify and await reinforcements for an advance northward.

Meanwhile, the most decisive battle was shaping up at Québec. There, British forces led by General James Wolfe waited out the advance of General Louis Joseph de Montcalm and his French infantry until they were within close range, then loosed a simultaneous volley followed by one more that devastated the French ranks—and ended French power in North America for all time. News of the victory reached London along with similar reports from India, where English forces had reduced French outposts one by one and established the base for an expanding British control of India. It was the *annus mirabilis,* the miraculous year 1759, during which Great Britain secured an empire "on which the sun never set."

The war dragged on until 1763, but the rest was a process of mopping up. In the South, where little significant action had occurred, belated hostility flared up between the settlers and the Cherokee nation. A force of British regulars and provincials broke Cherokee resistance in 1761. In the North, just as peace was signed, a chieftain of the Ot-

With Québec in the background, France kneels before a victorious Britain (1763).

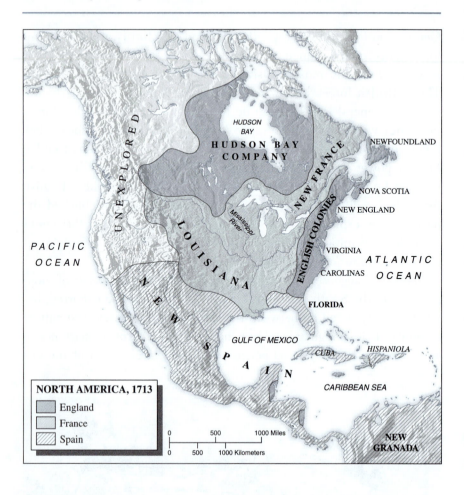

NORTH AMERICA, 1713

England
France
Spain

0   500   1000 Miles

0   500   1000 Kilometers

tawas, Pontiac, conspired to confederate all the Indians of the frontier and launched a series of attacks that were not completely suppressed until the end of 1764, after the backwoods had been ablaze for ten years.

In 1760 King George II died, and his grandson ascended to the throne as George III. He resolved to seek peace and forced Pitt out of office. Pitt had wanted to carry the fight to the enemy by declaring war on Spain before the French could bring that other Bourbon monarchy into the conflict. He was forestalled, but Spain belatedly entered in 1761 and during the next year met the same fate as the French: in 1762 British forces took Manila in the Philippines and Havana in Cuba.

THE PEACE OF PARIS   The Peace of Paris of 1763 brought an end to the war and to French power in North America. Britain took all French North American possessions east of the Mississippi River (except New Orleans) and all of Spanish Florida. The English invited the Spanish settlers to remain and practice their Catholic religion, but few accepted the offer. The Spanish king ordered them to evacuate the colony and provided free transportation to Spanish possessions in the Caribbean. Within a year most of the Spaniards sold their property at bargain prices to English speculators and began an exodus to Cuba and Mexico.

In compensation for the loss of Florida, Spain received Louisiana (New Orleans and all French land west of the Mississippi River) from

France. Unlike the Spanish in Florida, however, few of the French settlers left Louisiana after 1763. The French government encouraged them to stay and work with their new Spanish governors to create a bulwark against further English expansion. Spain would hold title to Louisiana for nearly four decades, but would never succeed in erasing its French roots. The French-born settlers always outnumbered the Spanish.

The loss of Louisiana left France with no territory on the continent of North America. In the West Indies, France gave up Tobago, Dominica, Grenada, and St. Vincent. British power reigned supreme over North America east of the Mississippi.

But a fatal irony would pursue the British victory. In gaining Canada the British government put in motion a train of events that would end twenty years later with the loss of all the rest of British North America. France, humiliated in 1763, thirsted for revenge. In London, Benjamin Franklin, agent for the colony of Pennsylvania (1764–1775), found the French minister inordinately curious about America and suspected him of wanting to ignite the coals of controversy. Less than three years after Franklin left London, and only fifteen years after the conquest of New France, he would be in Paris arranging an alliance on behalf of Britain's rebellious colonists.

MAKING CONNECTIONS

- Although the British victory in the French and Indian War brought the colonies and England closer together in some ways, it was also an important factor in the approach of the American Revolution, as demonstrated in Chapter 5.

- One of the great struggles of the Revolution would be transforming the British colonies described in this chapter into the American states as described in Chapter 6.

FURTHER READING

The economics motivating colonial policies are covered in John J. McCusker and Russell R. Menard's *The Economy of British America, 1607–1789*, rev. ed. (1991). The problems of colonial customs administration are explored in Michael Kammen's *Empire and Interest: The American Colonies and the Politics of Mercantilism* (1970).

Jack P. Greene's *The Quest for Power* (1963) describes the politics of the southern colonies, and Richard P. Johnson's *Adjustment to Empire* (1981) examines New England. The Andros crisis and related topics are treated in Jack M. Sosin's *English America and the Revolution of 1688* (1982). Stephen S. Webb's *The Governors-General: The English Army and the Definition of the Empire, 1569–1681* (1979) argues that the crown was more concerned with military administration than with commercial regulation, and Webb's *1676: The End of American Independence* (1984) shows how the Indian wars undermined the autonomy of colonial governments.

The early Indian wars are treated in Jill Lepore's *The Name of War: King Philip's War and the Origins of American Identity* (1998) and Francis Jennings's *The Invasion of America* (1975). See also Jennings's *The Ambiguous Iroquois Empire* (1984) and *Empire of Fortune: Crowns, Colonies, and Tribes in the Seven Years War in America* (1988) and Richard Aquila's *The Iroquois Restoration: Iroquois Diplomacy on the Colonial Frontier, 1701–1754* (1983). Gregory Evans Dowd describes the unification efforts of Indians east of the Mississippi in *A Spirited Resistance: The North American Indian Struggle for Unity, 1745–1815* (1992).

A good introduction to the imperial phase of the colonial conflicts is Howard H. Peckham's *The Colonial Wars, 1689–1762* (1964). More analytical is Douglas Leach's *Arms for Empire: A Military History of the British Colonies in North America* (1973). Fred Anderson's *A People's Army* (1984) is a social history of the Seven Years' War.

5 ~ FROM EMPIRE

TO INDEPENDENCE

---

*S*eldom if ever since the days of Elizabeth had England thrilled with such pride as in the closing years of the Great War for Empire. In 1760 the vigorous, young George III ascended to the throne. Three years later the Peace of Paris confirmed the possession of a great new British empire spanning the globe. Most important, the Peace of Paris effectively ended the French imperial domain in North America. This in turn influenced the future development of the vast region between the Appalachian Mountains and the Mississippi River and from the Gulf of Mexico to Hudson Bay. The maturing mainland colonies began to experience dynamic agricultural and com-

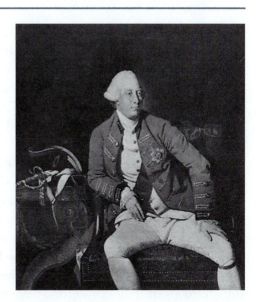

George III, at age thirty-three, the young king of a victorious empire.

mercial growth that enormously increased their importance to the British economy. Yet the North American colonies remained both extra-ordinarily diverse in composition and outlook and peculiarly averse to cooperative efforts. That they would manage to unify themselves and declare independence in 1775 was indeed surprising.

THE HERITAGE OF WAR

In 1763 the colonists shared in the patriotic zeal generated by the great victory over the French. But the moment of euphoria masked festering resentments and new problems that were the heritage of the war. Underneath the pride in the British Empire an American nationalism was maturing. Americans were beginning to think and speak of themselves more as Americans than as English or British. With a great new land to exploit, they could look to the future with confidence.

Many Americans had a new sense of importance after fighting a vast world war with such success. Some harbored resentment, justified or not, at the haughty air of British soldiers and slights received at their hands, and many in the early stages of the war lost their awe of British soldiers, who were at such a loss in frontier fighting. Recent studies of the Seven Years' War reveal that many Americans became convinced as well of their moral superiority to their British allies. Ninety percent of the New England provincial soldiers were probably volunteers, and most of them were sons of prosperous and pious farm families. The proportion of volunteers was lower in New York and much lower in Virginia until pay rates and bounties were raised in a successful effort to boost recruitment.

At least one-third of military-age New England males participated in the fighting. For them, army life was both a revelation and an opportunity. From their isolated farms they converged to form huge army camps—hives of thousands of strangers living in overcrowded and disease-infested conditions. Although they admired the courage and discipline of British redcoats under fire, New Englanders abhorred the carefree cursing, whoring, and Sabbath breaking they observed among British troops. But most upsetting were the daily "shrieks and cries" resulting from the brutal punishments imposed by the British leaders on their wayward men. Minor offenses might earn hundreds of lashes, and a thousand was the standard punishment for desertion. One American soldier recorded in his diary in 1759 that "there was a man whipped to death belonging to the Light Infantry. They say he had twenty-five lashes after he was dead." The war thus heightened the New Englanders' sense of their separate identity and of their greater worthiness to be God's chosen people.

Imperial forces nevertheless had borne the brunt of the war and had won it for the American colonists, who had supplied men and materials, sometimes reluctantly, and who persisted in trading with the enemy. Molasses in the French West Indies, for instance, continued to draw New England ships like flies. The trade was too important for the colonists to give up, but was more than Pitt could tolerate. Along with naval patrols, one important means of disrupting this trade was the use of "writs of assistance," general search warrants that allowed officers to enter any place during daylight hours to seek evidence of illegal trade. In 1760 Boston merchants hired James Otis to fight the writs in the courts. He lost, but in the process advanced the provocative argument that any act of Parliament that authorized such "instruments of slavery" violated the British constitution and was therefore void. This was a radical idea for its time. Otis sought to overturn a major tenet of the English legal system, namely that acts of Parliament were by their very nature constitutional.

The peace that secured an empire in 1763 also laid upon the British ministry a burden of new problems. How should the British manage the defense and governance of the new possessions? What should they do about the western lands inhabited by Indians but coveted by whites? How were they to service an unprecedented debt built up during the war and bear the new burdens of administration and defense? And— the thorniest problem of all, as it turned out—what role should the colonies play in all this? The problems were of a magnitude and complexity to challenge men of the greatest statemanship and vision, but those qualities were rare among the ministers of George III.

BRITISH POLITICS

In the British politics of the day nearly everybody called himself a Whig, even King George. Whig had been the name given to those who opposed James II, led the Glorious Revolution of 1688, and secured the Protestant Hanoverian succession in 1714. The Whigs were the champions of liberty and parliamentary supremacy, but with the passage of time Whiggism had drifted into complacency. The dominant group of landholding Whig families was concerned mostly with the pursuit of personal gain and with local questions rather than great issues of statecraft. In the absence of party organization, parliamentary politics hinged on factions bound together by personal loyalties, family connections, and local interests, and on the pursuit of royal patronage.

In the administration of government, an inner "cabinet" of the king's ministers had been supplanting the unwieldy Privy Council as the center of power since the Hanoverian succession. The kings still had the prerogative of naming their ministers. They used it to form coalitions of men who controlled enough factions in the House of Commons to command majorities for the government's measures, though the king's ministers were still technically responsible to the king rather than to parliamentary majorities.

Throughout the 1760s, the king turned first to one and then to another leader, ministries came and went, and the government fell into instability just as the new problems of empire required creative solutions. Ministries rose and fell because somebody offended the king or because somebody's friend failed to get a job. Colonial policy remained marginal to the chief concerns of British politics. The result was inconsistency and vacillation followed by stubborn inflexibility.

WESTERN LANDS

No sooner was peace arranged in 1763 than events thrust the problem of the western lands upon the government in an acute form. The Indians of the Ohio region, skeptical that their French friends were helpless and fully expecting the reentry of English settlers, grew restless and receptive to the warnings of Pontiac, chief of the Ottawas. In 1763 Pontiac's effort to seize Fort Detroit was betrayed and failed, but the western tribes joined his campaign to reopen frontier warfare and within a few months wiped out every British post in the Ohio region except Fort Detroit and Fort Pitt. A relief force lifted the siege of Fort Pitt, and Pontiac abandoned the attack on Fort Detroit, but the outlying settlements suffered heavy losses before British forces could stop the attacks. Pontiac himself did not agree to peace until 1766.

THE PROCLAMATION OF 1763   To keep the peace on the frontier and to keep earlier promises to the Delawares and Shawnees, the ministers in London postponed further settlement. The immediate need was to stop Pontiac's warriors and reassure the Indians. There were influential fur traders, moreover, who preferred to keep the wilderness as a game preserve. The pressure for expansion into Indian-held territory might ultimately prove irresistible—British and American speculators were already dazzled by the prospects—but there would be no harm in a pause while things settled down and a new policy evolved. The king's ministers therefore brought forward, and the king signed, the Royal Proclamation of 1763. The order drew a Proclamation Line along the crest of the Appalachians beyond which settlers were forbidden to go and colonial governors were forbidden to authorize surveys or issue land grants. It also established the new British colonies of Quebec and East and West Florida, the last two consisting mainly of small settlements at St. Augustine and St. Marks, respectively.

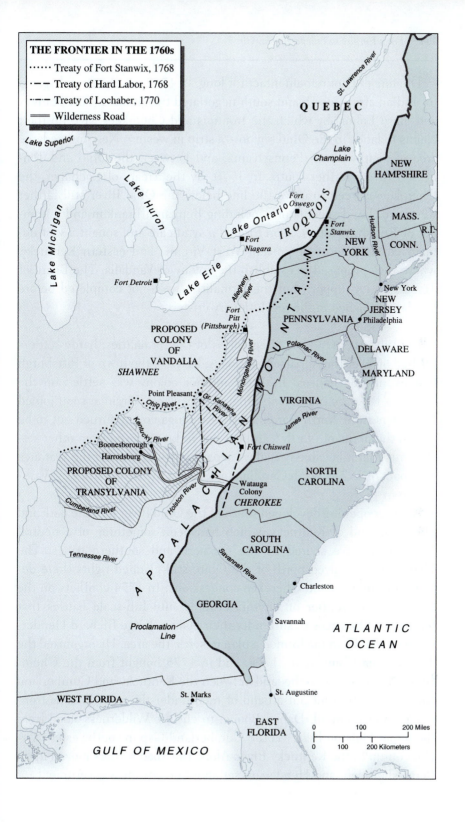

THE FRONTIER IN THE 1760s
- ·········· Treaty of Fort Stanwix, 1768
- – · – Treaty of Hard Labor, 1768
- –··– Treaty of Lochaber, 1770
- ═══ Wilderness Road

Lake Superior

Lake Michigan

Lake Huron

St. Lawrence River

QUEBEC

Lake Champlain

NEW HAMPSHIRE

Lake Ontario

Fort Oswego

IROQUOIS

MASS.

Fort Stanwix

Hudson River

R.I.

Fort Niagara

NEW YORK

CONN.

Lake Erie

Fort Detroit

Allegheny River

New York

NEW JERSEY

Fort Pitt (Pittsburgh)

PENNSYLVANIA

Philadelphia

PROPOSED COLONY OF VANDALIA

Monongahela River

Potomac River

DELAWARE

SHAWNEE

MARYLAND

Point Pleasant

Gr. Kanawha River

VIRGINIA

Ohio River

James River

Kentucky River

Boonesborough

Harrodsburg

Fort Chiswell

PROPOSED COLONY OF TRANSYLVANIA

Holston River

Watauga Colony

NORTH CAROLINA

CHEROKEE

Cumberland River

Tennessee River

SOUTH CAROLINA

Savannah River

A P P A L A C H I A N   M O U N T A I N S

Charleston

GEORGIA

Proclamation Line

Savannah

ATLANTIC OCEAN

WEST FLORIDA

St. Marks

St. Augustine

EAST FLORIDA

| 0 | 100 | 200 Miles |

| 0 | 100 | 200 Kilometers |

GULF OF MEXICO

The line did not remain intact for long. In 1768 the chief royal agents for Indian affairs north and south negotiated two treaties (Fort Stanwix and Hard Labor) by which the Iroquois and Cherokees gave up their claims to lands in the Ohio region—a strip in western New York, a large area of southwestern Pennsylvania, and between the Ohio and Tennessee Rivers farther south. In 1770, by the Treaty of Lochaber, the Cherokees agreed to move the line below the Ohio River still farther westward. Land speculators, including Benjamin Franklin and a number of British investors, soon formed a syndicate and sought a vast domain covering most of present West Virginia and eastern Kentucky, where they proposed to establish the colony of Vandalia. The Board of Trade lent its support, but the formalities were not completed before Vandalia vanished in the revolutionary crisis.

SETTLERS PUSH WEST   Regardless of the formalities, hardy settlers pushed on over the Appalachian ridges; by 1770 the town of Pittsburgh had twenty log houses. In 1769 another colony was settled on the Watauga River by immigrants from southwestern Virginia, soon joined by settlers from North Carolina. The Watauga colony turned out to be within the limits of North Carolina, but so far removed from other settlements that it became virtually a separate republic under the Watauga Compact of 1772; North Carolina took it into the new district of Washington in 1776.

Another opening developed south of the Ohio River into the dark and bloody ground of Kentucky, which had been something of a neutral hunting preserve shared by the northern and southern tribes. The Shawnees, who lived north of the Ohio, still claimed rights there despite the Iroquois and Cherokee concessions. In 1774 conflicts on the northwestern frontier of Virginia erupted into full-scale battles that forced the Shawnees to surrender their claims. Judge Richard Henderson of North Carolina formed a plan to settle the area. He organized the Transylvania Company in 1774, and in 1775 bought from the Cherokees a dubious title to the land between the Kentucky and Cumberland Rivers. Next he sent out a band of men under the most famous frontiersman of them all, Daniel Boone, to cut the Wilderness Road from the upper Holston River via the Cumberland Gap in southwestern Virginia on up to the Kentucky River. Along this road settlers moved up to Boonesborough, and Henderson set about organizing a government for his colony of Transylvania. But his claim was weak. Transylvania sent a delegation to the Continental Congress, which refused to receive it, and in 1776 Virginia responded to a petition from the Harrodsburg settlers and organized much of present Kentucky into a county of Virginia.

GRENVILLE AND THE STAMP ACT

GRENVILLE'S COLONIAL POLICY   Just as the Proclamation of 1763 was being drafted, a new British ministry had begun to grapple with the problems of imperial finances. The new first minister and first lord of the Treasury, George Grenville, was much like the king: industrious, honest, and hardheaded. Grenville took for granted the need for redcoats to defend the frontier, although the colonies had been left mostly to their own devices before 1754. He also wanted to keep a large army in America to avoid a rapid demobilization that would retire a large number of influential officers and thereby provoke political criticism at home. But he faced sharply rising costs for American defense, on top of an already staggering debt. He had already tried to find new revenues at

The Great Financier, or British Economy for the Years 1763, 1764, 1765. *A cartoon critical of Grenville's tax policies. America, depicted as an Indian (at left), groans under the burden of new taxes.*

home, one result being a cider tax so unpopular that it helped to drive him briefly out of office. It would not be the last time that British or American officials would learn that liquor taxes stirred deadly passions.

Because there was a large tax burden at home and a much lighter one in the colonies, Grenville reasoned that the Americans were obligated to share the cost of their own defense. He also learned that the American customs service was grossly inefficient. Evasion and corruption were rampant. Grenville directed absentee customs agents to pack themselves off to America and cease hiring deputies. He issued stern orders to colonial officials and set the British navy to patrolling the coasts. In Parliament he secured an Act for the Encouragement of Officers Making Seizures (1763), which set up a new maritime or vice-admiralty court in Halifax (replacing the ineffectual admiralty courts established in 1696) with jurisdiction over all the colonies, a court that had both original and appellate jurisdiction, but had no juries of colonists sympathetic to smugglers. The period of salutary neglect in the enforcement of the Navigation Acts was coming to an end, causing great annoyance to American shippers.

Strict enforcement of the old Molasses Act of 1733 posed a serious threat to New England's mercantile prosperity, which in turn created markets for British goods. The sixpence-per-gallon duty had been set prohibitively high, not for purposes of revenue but to prevent trade with the French sugar islands. Yet the rum distilleries consumed more molasses than the British West Indies provided, and as the governor of Massachusetts wrote to the king: "Even illegal trade, where the balance is in favor of British subjects, makes its final return to Great Britain." Grenville recognized that the sixpence duty, if enforced, would be ruinous to a major colonial enterprise. So he put through a new Revenue Act of 1764, commonly known as the Sugar Act, which cut the duty in half, from sixpence to threepence per gallon. This, he believed, would reduce the temptation to smuggle or to bribe the customs officers. In addition the Sugar Act levied new duties on imports of foreign textiles, wines, coffee, indigo, and sugar. The act, Grenville estimated, would bring in about £45,000 a year that would go "toward defraying the necessary expenses of defending, protecting, and securing, the said colonies and plantations." For the first time Parliament had adopted duties frankly designed to raise revenues in the colonies and not merely intended to regulate trade.

Another of Grenville's new regulatory measures had an important impact on the colonies: the Currency Act of 1764. The colonies faced a chronic shortage of hard money, which kept going out to pay debts in England. To meet the shortage, they resorted to issuing their own paper money. British creditors, however, feared payment in such a depreciated currency. To alleviate their fears, Parliament in 1751 had forbidden the New England colonies to make their currency legal tender. Now Grenville extended the prohibition to all the colonies. The result was a decline in the value of existing paper money, since nobody was obligated to accept it in payment of debts, even in the colonies. The deflationary impact of the Currency Act, combined with new duties and stricter enforcement, delivered a severe shock to a colonial economy already suffering a postwar business decline.

THE STAMP ACT   But Grenville's new plan to make Americans pay for British expenses remained incomplete. The Sugar Act would defray only a fraction of the cost of maintaining the 10,000 soldiers to be stationed along the western frontier. He had in mind still another measure to raise money in America, a stamp tax. On February 13, 1765, Grenville laid his proposal before Parliament, and the act passed the Commons easily. It created revenue stamps and required that they be fixed to printed matter and legal documents of all kinds: newspapers, pamphlets, broadsides, almanacs, bonds, leases, deeds, licenses, insurance policies, ship clearances, college diplomas, even dice and playing cards. The requirement would go into effect on November 1, 1765.

That same year Grenville completed his new system of colonial regulations when he put through the Quartering Act. In effect it was still another tax. This act required the colonies to supply British troops with provisions and to provide them with barracks or submit to their use of inns and vacant buildings. It applied to all colonies, but affected mainly New York, headquarters of the British forces.

THE IDEOLOGICAL RESPONSE   The cumulative effect of Grenville's measures raised colonial suspicions to a fever. Unwittingly, this plodding minister of a plodding king had stirred up a storm of protest and set in motion a profound exploration of English traditions and imperial relations. The radical ideas of the minority "Real Whigs" slowly began to take hold in the colonies. These ideas derived from various sources but above all from John Locke's justification of the Glorious Revolution, his *Two Treatises on Government* (1690). Locke and other "Real Whigs" viewed English history as a struggle by Parliament to preserve life, liberty, and property against royal tyranny.

Their religious heritage and what Patrick Henry called "the lamp of experience" also convinced them that human nature is corruptible and lusts after power. The safeguard against abuses, in the view of those in England who called themselves "Real Whigs," was not to rely on human goodness but to check power with power so as to preserve individual liberty. And the British constitution had embodied these principles in a mixed government of kings, lords, and commons, each serving as a check on the others.

But in 1764 and 1765 the colonists felt that Grenville and Parliament had loosed upon them the very engines of tyranny from which Parliament had rescued England in the seventeenth century. A standing army was the historic ally of despots, and now with the French gone and Pontiac subdued, several thousand British soldiers remained in the colonies. For what purpose—to protect the colonists or to subdue them? It was beginning to seem clear that it was the latter. Among the fundamental rights of English people were trial by jury and the presumption of innocence, but the new vice-admiralty courts excluded juries and put the burden of proof on the defendant. Most important, Englishmen had the right to be taxed only by their elected representatives. Parliament claimed that privilege in England, and the colonial assemblies had long exercised it in America. Now Parliament was usurping the assemblies' power of the purse strings.

THE QUESTION OF REPRESENTATION In a flood of colonial pamphlets, speeches, and resolutions, debate on the Stamp Act turned mainly on the point expressed in a slogan familiar to all Americans: "no taxation without representation," a cry that had been raised years before in response to the Molasses Act of 1733. In 1764 James Otis, now a popular leader in the Massachusetts assembly, set forth the argument in a pamphlet, *The Rights of the British Colonists Asserted and Proved.* Grenville had one of his subordinates prepare an answer, which developed the ingenious theory of "virtual representation." If the colonies had no vote in Parliament, his reasoning went, neither did most Englishmen who lived in boroughs that had developed since the last apportionment. Large cities had grown up that had no right to elect a member, while old boroughs with little or no population still returned members. Nevertheless, each member of Parliament represented the interests of the whole country and indeed the whole empire. Charleston, South Carolina, for instance, had fully as much representation as Manchester, England.

Many colonial critics considered virtual representation nonsense, justified neither by logic nor by their own experience. In America, to be sure, the apportionment of assemblies failed to keep pace with the westward movement of population, but it was based more nearly on population and—in contrast to British practice—each member was expected to live in the district he represented. In a pamphlet widely circulated during 1765, Daniel Dulany, a young lawyer of Maryland, suggested that even if the theory had any validity for England, where the interests of electors might be closely tied to those of nonelectors, it had none for colonists 3,000 miles away, whose interests differed and whose distance made it impossible for them to influence members of Parliament.

PROTEST IN THE COLONIES   The Stamp Act became the chief target of colonial protest. Unlike the Sugar Act, which affected mainly New England, the Stamp Act imposed a burden on all the colonists who did any kind of business. And it affected most of all the articulate elements in the community: merchants, planters, lawyers, printer-editors—all strategically placed to influence public opinion.

Through the spring and summer of 1765, popular resentment found outlet in mass meetings, parades, bonfires, and other demonstrations. To be sure, only a minority engaged in such public protests. They included farmers, artisans, laborers, businessmen, dock workers, and seamen alarmed at the disruption of business. Lawyers, editors, and merchants such as Christopher Gadsden of Charleston and John Hancock of Boston took the lead or lent support. North Carolina's governor reported the mobs to be composed of "gentlemen and planters." The militants began to call themselves Sons of Liberty. They met underneath "Liberty Trees"—in Boston a great elm on Hanover Square, in Charleston a live oak.

One day in mid-August, nearly three months before the effective date of the Stamp Act, an effigy of Boston's stamp agent swung from the

In protest of the Stamp Act, which was to take effect the next day, the Pennsylvania Journal *appeared with the skull and crossbones on its masthead.*

Liberty Tree. In the evening a mob carried it through the streets, destroyed the stamp office, and used the wood to burn the effigy. Somewhat later another mob sacked the homes of Lieutenant-Governor Thomas Hutchinson and the local customs officer. Thoroughly shaken, the Boston stamp agent resigned his commission, and stamp agents throughout the colonies were hounded out of office. Loyalists deplored such riotous violence, arguing that the American rebels were behaving more tyrannically than the British.

By November 1, its effective date, the Stamp Act was a dead letter. Business went on without the stamps. Newspapers appeared with a skull and crossbones in the corner where the stamp belonged. After passage of the Sugar Act, a movement had begun to boycott British goods. Now colonists adopted non-importation agreements to exert pressure on British merchants. Americans knew that they had become a major market for British products. By shutting off imports, they could exercise real leverage. Homegrown sage and sassafras took the place of British tea. Homespun garments became the fashion as symbols of colonial defiance. In this regard, the non-importation movement offered landmark opportunities for women to participate in political agitation.

The widespread protests encouraged the idea of colonial unity, as colonists discovered that they had more in common with each other than with London. The Virginia House of Burgesses had struck the first blow against the Stamp Act in the Virginia Resolves, a series of resolutions inspired by young Patrick Henry's "torrents of sublime eloquence." Virginians, the burgesses declared, were entitled to the rights of Englishmen, and Englishmen could be taxed only by their own representatives. Virginians, moreover, had always been governed by laws passed with their own consent. Newspapers spread the resolutions throughout the colonies, along with even more radical statements that were kept out of the final version, and other assemblies hastened to copy Virginia's example. In 1765, the Massachusetts House of Representatives issued a circular letter inviting the various assemblies to send delegates to confer in New York on appeals for relief from the king and Parliament.

Nine responded, and from October 7 to 25, the Stamp Act Congress of twenty-seven delegates conferred and issued expressions of colonial sentiment: a Declaration of the Rights and Grievances of the Colonies, a petition to the king for relief, and a petition to Parliament for repeal of the Stamp Act. The delegates acknowledged that the colonies owed a "due subordination" to Parliament and recognized its right to regulate colonial trade, but they questioned Parliament's right to levy taxes, which were a free gift granted by the people through their representatives. Grenville responded by denouncing the colonists as "ungrateful."

REPEAL OF THE ACT The storm had scarcely broken before Grenville's ministry was out of office, dismissed not because of the colonial turmoil but because he had fallen out with the king over the appointment of offices. The king installed a new minister, the marquis of Rockingham, leader of the "Rockingham Whigs," the "Old Whig" faction, which included people who sympathized with the colonists' views. Pressure from British merchants who feared the economic consequences of the non-importation movement bolstered Rockingham's resolve to repeal the Stamp Act, but he needed to move carefully in order to win a majority. Simple repeal was politically impossible without some affirmation of parliamentary authority. When Parliament assembled early in the year, William Pitt demanded that the Stamp Act be repealed "absolutely, totally, and immediately," but urged that Britain's authority

The Repeal, or the Funeral Procession of Miss America-Stamp *(1766).*
Grenville carries the dead Stamp Act in its coffin. In the background, trade with
America starts up again.

over the colonies "be asserted in as strong terms as possible," except on
the point of taxation. Rockingham steered a cautious course, and seized
upon the widespread but false impression that Pitt accepted the principle of "external" taxes on trade but rejected "internal" taxes within the
colonies. Benjamin Franklin, summoned before Parliament for interrogation in what was probably a rehearsed performance, helped to further
the false impression that this was the colonists' view as well, an impression easily refuted by reference to the colonial resolutions of the previous year.

In 1766 Parliament repealed the Stamp Tax, but at the same time
passed the Declaratory Act, which asserted the full power of Parliament
to make laws binding the colonies "in all cases whatsoever." It was a cunning evasion that made no concession with regard to taxes, but made no
mention of them either. It left intact in the minds of many members the
impression that a distinction had been drawn between "external" taxes
on trade and "internal" taxes within the colonies, and that impression
would have fateful consequences for the future. For the moment, however, the Declaratory Act seemed little if anything more than a gesture to
save face. Amid the rejoicing and relief on both sides of the Atlantic
there were no omens that the quarrel would be reopened within a year.

To be sure, the Sugar Act remained on the books, but Rockingham reduced the molasses tax from threepence to a penny a gallon.

FANNING THE FLAMES

Meanwhile, the king continued to have his ministers play musical chairs. Rockingham fell because he lost the confidence of the king, and his own administration suffered a paralyzing fragmentation. The king invited Pitt to form a ministry that included the major factions of Parliament. The ill-matched combination—which Edmund Burke compared to pigs gathered at a trough—would have been hard to manage even if Pitt had remained in charge, but the old warlord began to slip over the fine line between genius and madness. For a time in 1767 the guiding force in the ministry was the witty and reckless Charles Townshend, chancellor of the Exchequer, whose "abilities were superior to those of all men," according to Horace Walpole, "and his judgement below that of any man." The erratic Townshend took advantage of Pitt's absence to reopen the question of colonial taxation and seized upon the notion that "external" taxes were tolerable to the colonies—not that he believed it for a moment.

THE TOWNSHEND ACTS   In 1767 Townshend put his plan through the House of Commons, and a few months later he died, leaving behind a bitter legacy: the Townshend Acts. First, he sought to bring the New York assembly to its senses. That body had defied the Quartering Act and refused to provide beds or supplies for the king's troops. Parliament, at Townshend's behest, suspended all acts of the assembly until it yielded. New York protested but finally caved in, inadvertently confirming the British suspicion that too much indulgence had encouraged colonial bad manners. Townshend followed up with the Revenue Act of 1767, which levied duties ("external taxes") on colonial imports of glass, lead, paint, paper, and tea. Third, he set up a Board of Customs Commissioners at Boston, the colonial headquarters of smuggling. Finally, he reorganized the vice-admiralty courts, providing four in the continental colonies—at Halifax, Boston, Philadelphia, and Charleston.

The Townshend duties did increase government revenues, but the intangible costs were greater. The duties taxed goods exported from England, indirectly hurting British manufacturers, and had to be collected in colonial ports, increasing collection costs. But the greater cost was a new drift into ever-greater conflict. The Revenue Act of 1767 posed a more severe threat to colonial assemblies than Grenville's taxes, for Townshend proposed to apply these revenues to pay governors and other officers and thereby release them from financial dependence on the colonial assemblies.

DICKINSON'S *LETTERS*   The Townshend Acts surprised the colonists, and this time the storm gathered more slowly than it had two years before. Once again citizens resolved to resist, to boycott British goods, to wear homespun, to develop their own manufactures. Once again the colonial press spewed out expressions of protest, most notably the essays of John Dickinson, a Philadelphia lawyer who hoped to resolve the dispute by persuasion. Late in 1767 his twelve *Letters of a Pennsylvania Farmer* (as he chose to style himself) began to appear in the *Pennsylvania Chronicle,* from which they were copied in other papers and in pamphlet form. His argument repeated with greater detail and more elegance what the Stamp Act Congress had already said. The colonists held that Parliament might regulate commerce and collect duties incidental to that purpose, but it had no right to levy taxes for revenue, whether they were internal or external. Dickinson used the language of moderation throughout. "The cause of Liberty is a cause of too much dignity to be sullied by turbulence and tumult," he argued. The colonial complaints should "speak at the same time the language of affliction and veneration." Such conciliatory language led John Adams to dismiss Dickinson as a "piddling genius."

SAMUEL ADAMS AND THE SONS OF LIBERTY   But the affliction grew and the veneration waned. British ministers could neither conciliate moderates like Dickinson nor cope with firebrands such as Samuel Adams of Boston, who was now emerging as the supreme genius of revolutionary agitation. Born in 1722, Adams graduated from Harvard and soon thereafter inherited the family brewery, which he quickly ran into bankruptcy. The lure of monetary gain never intoxicated him. His distant cousin John Adams described Sam as a "universal good character," a "plain, simple, decent citizen, of middling stature, dress, and manners," who prided himself on his frugality and his distaste for ceremony

Samuel Adams, an organizer of the Sons of Liberty.

and display. Politics, not profits, was his abiding passion, and he spent most of his time debating political issues with sailors, roustabouts, and stevedores at local taverns. Often dressed in a dingy red coat and ink-stained shirt, he would bring his huge Newfoundland dog to the tavern and, while eating raw oysters and fish chowder, engage in animated discussions about British rule. Adams grew obsessed with the conviction that Parliament had no right to legislate at all for the colonies, that Massachusetts must return to the spirit of its Puritan founders and defend itself from a new conspiracy against its liberties.

While other men tended their private affairs, Sam Adams was whipping up the Sons of Liberty and organizing protests in the Boston town meeting and the provincial assembly. Early in 1768 he and James Otis formulated another Massachusetts circular letter, which the assembly dispatched to the other colonies. The letter restated the illegality of parliamentary taxation, warned that the new duties would be used to pay colonial officials, and invited the support of other colonies. In London the earl of Hillsborough, just appointed to the new office of secretary of state for the colonies, made matters only worse. He ordered the assembly to withdraw the letter. The assembly refused and was dissolved. The consequence was simply more discussion of the need for colonial cooperation.

The new Board of Customs Commissioners at Boston further confirmed Adams's suspicions of British intentions. Customs officers had been unwelcome in Boston since the arrival of Edward Randolph a century before. But the irascible Randolph was at least honest. His successors cultivated the fine art of what one historian has called "customs racketeering." Under the Sugar Act, collectors profited from illegal cargoes and exploited technicalities. One ploy was to neglect certain requirements, then suddenly insist on a strict adherence. In 1768, for example, they set a trap for Sam Adams's friend and patron John Hancock, a well-to-do merchant. On the narrow ground that Hancock had failed to post a bond before loading his sloop *Liberty* (previously he had always posted bond after loading), they seized the ship. A mob gathered to prevent its unloading. The commissioners towed the ship to Castle William in the harbor and called for the protection of British troops.

In 1768 two regiments of redcoats arrived in Boston. They were not there to protect the frontiers. On the day the soldiers arrived, a convention of delegates from Massachusetts towns declared their "aversion to an unnecessary Standing Army, which they look upon as dangerous to their Civil Liberty." To members of Parliament the illegal convention smacked of treason, but it gave them little reason to believe that any colonial jury would ever convict the likes of Sam Adams. As a consequence, Parliament recommended that the king get information on "all treasons" committed in Massachusetts and return the accused to England for trial.

The king never acted on the suggestion, but the threat was unmistakable. In 1769 the Virginia assembly passed a new set of resolves reasserting its exclusive right to tax Virginians, challenging the constitutionality of an act that would take a man across the ocean for trial, and calling upon the colonies to unite in the cause. Virginia's royal governor promptly dissolved the assembly, but the members met independently, dubbed themselves a "convention" after Boston's example, and adopted a new set of nonimportation agreements. Once again, as with the Virginia Resolves against the Stamp Act, most of the other assemblies followed the example.

In London, events across the Atlantic still evoked only marginal interest. The king's long effort to reorder British politics to his liking was coming to fulfillment, and that was the big news. In 1769 new elections for Parliament finally produced a majority of the "King's Friends." And George III found a minister to his taste in Frederick, Lord North, the plodding chancellor of the Exchequer who had replaced Townshend. In 1770 the king installed a cabinet of the King's Friends, with North as first minister. North, who venerated the traditions of Parliament, was no stooge for the king, but the two worked in harmony.

THE BOSTON MASSACRE   The impact of colonial boycotts on English commerce had persuaded Lord North to modify the Townshend Acts, just in time to halt a perilous escalation of conflict. The presence of soldiers in Boston had been a constant provocation. Bostonians copied the example of the customs officers and indicted soldiers on technical violations of local law. Crowds heckled and ridiculed the "lobster backs."

On March 5, 1770, in the square before the customs house, a group of rowdies began taunting and snowballing the sentry on duty. His call for help brought reinforcements. Then somebody rang the town firebell, drawing a larger crowd to the scene. At their head, or so the story goes, was Crispus Attucks, a runaway mulatto slave who had worked for some years on ships out of Boston. Finally a soldier was knocked down,

Paul Revere's partisan engraving of the Boston Massacre.

rose to his feet, and fired into the crowd. When the smoke cleared, five people lay on the ground dead or dying, and eight more were wounded. The cause of resistance now had its first martyrs, and the first to die was Crispus Attucks. Governor Thomas Hutchinson, at the insistence of a mass meeting in Faneuil Hall, moved the soldiers out of town to avoid another incident. Those involved in the shooting were indicted for murder, but they were defended by John Adams, Sam's cousin, who thought they were the victims of circumstance, provoked, he said, by a "motley rabble of saucy boys, negroes and mulattoes, Irish teagues and outlandish Jack tars." All were acquitted except two, who were convicted of manslaughter and branded on their thumbs.

The so-called Boston Massacre sent shock waves up and down the colonies, and the unrest caught the attention of British officials. Late in April 1770 Parliament repealed all the Townshend duties save one. The cabinet, by a fateful vote of five to four, had advised keeping the tea tax as a token of parliamentary authority. Colonial diehards insisted that pressure should be kept on British merchants until Parliament gave in altogether, but the non-importation movement soon faded. Parliament, after all, had given up the substance of the taxes, with one exception, and much of the colonists' tea was smuggled in from Holland anyway.

For two years thereafter discontent simmered down, and suspicions began to fade on both sides of the ocean. The Stamp Act was gone, as were all the Townshend duties except that on tea. But most of the Grenville-Townshend innovations remained in effect: the Sugar Act, the Currency Act, the Quartering Act, the vice-admiralty courts, the Board of Customs Commissioners. The redcoats had left Boston, but they remained nearby, and the British navy still patrolled the coast. Each remained a source of irritation and the cause of occasional incidents. There was still tinder awaiting a spark, and the rebellious among the colonists promoted continuing conflicts. As Sam Adams stressed, "Where there is a spark of patriotick fire, we will enkindle it."

DISCONTENT ON THE FRONTIER

Many American colonists had no interest in the disputes over British regulatory policy raging along the seaboard. Parts of the back-country stirred with quarrels that had nothing to do with the Stamp and

Townshend Acts. Rival land claims to the east of Lake Champlain pitted New York against New Hampshire, and the Green Mountain Boys led by Ethan Allen against both. Eventually the denizens of the area would set up shop on their own as the state of Vermont, created in 1777 although not recognized as a member of the Union until 1791. In Pennsylvania sporadic quarrels broke out with land claimants who held grants from Virginia and Connecticut, whose boundaries under their charters overlapped those granted to William Penn, or so they claimed.

A more dangerous division in Pennsylvania arose when a group of frontier ruffians took the law into their own hands. Outraged at the lack of frontier protection during Pontiac's rebellion because of pacifist Quaker influence in the assembly, a group called the "Paxton Boys" took revenge by massacring peaceful Conestoga Indians in Lancaster County; then they threatened the so-called Moravian Indians, a group of Christian converts near Bethlehem. When the Indians took refuge in Philadelphia, some 1,500 Paxton Boys marched on the capital, where Benjamin Franklin talked them into returning home by promising that more protection would be forthcoming.

Farther south, frontier folk of South Carolina had similar complaints about the lack of settled government and the need for protection against horse thieves, cattle rustlers, and Indians. Backcountry residents organized societies called "Regulators" to administer vigilante justice in the region and refused to pay taxes until they gained effective government. In 1769 the assembly finally set up six new circuit courts in the region, but still did not respond to the backcountry's demand for representation in the legislature.

In North Carolina the protest was less over the lack of government than over the abuses and extortion inflicted by appointees from the eastern part of the colony. Farmers felt especially oppressed at the refusal either to issue paper money or to accept produce in payment of taxes, and in 1766 they organized to resist. Efforts of these Regulators to stop seizures of property and other court proceedings led to more disorders and an enactment of a bill that made the rioters guilty of treason. In the spring of 1771 Governor William Tryon led 1,200 militiamen into the Piedmont center of Regulator activity. There he met and defeated some 2,000 ill-organized Regulators in the Battle of Alamance, in which eight were killed on each side. One insurgent was executed on the battlefield, twelve others were convicted of treason, and six were hanged. While this went on, Tryon's men ranged through the backcountry, forcing some 6,500 Piedmont settlers to sign an oath of allegiance.

These internal disputes and revolts within the colonies illustrate the fractious diversity of opinion and outlook evident among Americans on the eve of the Revolution. Colonists were of many minds about many things, including British rule. The disputatious frontier in colonial America also helped convince British authorities that the colonies were inherently unstable and that they required even keener and firmer oversight, even to the extent of using military force to ensure civil stability.

A WORSENING CRISIS

Two events in 1772 further eroded the colonies' fragile relationship with the mother country. Near Providence, Rhode Island, a British schooner, the *Gaspee,* patrolling for smugglers, accidentally ran aground. A crowd from the town boarded the ship, removed the crew, and set fire to the vessel. A commission of inquiry was formed with authority to hold suspects (for trial in England, it was rumored, under an old statute passed during the reign of Henry VIII), but no witnesses could be found. Four days after the burning, on June 13, 1772, Governor Thomas Hutchinson told the Massachusetts assembly that his salary thenceforth would come out of the customs revenues. Soon thereafter word came that judges of the Superior Court would be paid from the same source and no longer be dependent on the assembly for their income. The assembly expressed a fear that this portended "a despotic administration of government."

The existence of the *Gaspee* commission, which bypassed the courts of Rhode Island, and the independent salaries for royal officials in Massachusetts both suggested to the residents of other colonies that the same might be in store for them. The discussion of colonial rights and parliamentary encroachments regained momentum. To keep the pot boiling, Sam Adams convinced the Boston town meeting to form a Committee of Correspondence, which issued a statement of rights and grievances and invited other towns to do the same. Committees of Correspondence sprang up across Massachusetts and spread into other colonies. In 1773 the Virginia assembly proposed the formation of such committees on an intercolonial basis, and a network of the committees

Massachusetts governor Thomas Hutchinson found himself at the center of the imperial crisis in 1772 and 1773.

spread across the colonies, mobilizing public opinion and keeping colonial resentments at a simmer. In unwitting tribute to their effectiveness, a Massachusetts Loyalist called the committees "the foulest, subtlest, and most venomous serpent ever issued from the egg of sedition."

THE BOSTON TEA PARTY   Lord North soon provided the colonists with the occasion to bring resentment from a simmer to a boil. In 1773 he undertook to help some friends through a little difficulty. North's scheme was a clever contrivance, perhaps too clever, designed to bail out the East India Company, which was foundering in a spell of bad business. The company had in its British warehouses some 17 million pounds of tea. Under the Tea Act of 1773 the government would refund the British duty of twelve pence per pound on all that was shipped to the colonies and collect only the existing threepence duty payable at the colonial port. By this arrangement colonists could get tea more cheaply than English buyers could. North, however, miscalculated in assuming that price alone would govern colonial reaction. Even worse, he permitted the East India Company to serve retailers directly through its own agents or consignees, bypassing the wholesalers who had handled it before. Once that kind of monopoly was established, colonial merchants began to wonder, how soon would the precedent apply to other commodities?

The Committees of Correspondence, backed by colonial merchants, alerted people to the new danger. The government, they said, was trying

Americans throwing the Cargoes of the Tea Ships into the River, at Boston, *1773.*

to purchase colonial acquiescence with cheap tea. Before the end of the year, large consignments of tea went out to major colonial ports. In New York and Philadelphia popular hostility forced company agents to resign. When no one received the tea, it went back to England. In Charleston it was unloaded into warehouses—and later sold to finance the Revolution. In Boston, however, Governor Hutchinson and Sam Adams engaged in a test of will. The ships' captains, alarmed by the radical opposition, proposed to turn back. Hutchinson, who had two sons who were consignees and who stood to profit from the tea, demanded that the tea be landed and the duty paid. On November 30, 1773, the Boston town meeting warned officials not to assist the landing of the tea. But they were legally bound to seize the cargo after twenty days in port, which in this case fell on December 16. On that night in December a group of men hastened to Griffin's Wharf where, thinly disguised as Mohawk Indians, they boarded the three ships and threw the 342 chests of tea overboard—cheered on by a crowd along the shore. Like those who had burned the *Gaspee,* they remained parties unknown— except to hundreds of Bostonians. One participant later testified that Sam Adams and John Hancock were there. About £15,000 worth of tea, a substantial sum in 1773, went to the fish.

Given a more deft response from London, the Boston Tea Party might easily have undermined the radicals' credibility. Many people, especially merchants, were aghast at the wanton destruction of property. A town meeting in Bristol, Massachusetts, condemned the action. Ben Franklin called on his native city to pay for the tea and apologize. But the British authorities had reached the end of their patience. They were now convinced that the very existence of the empire was at stake. The rebels in Boston had instigated what could become a widespread effort to evade royal authority and imperial regulations. A firm response was required. "The colonists must either submit or triumph," George III wrote to Lord North, and North strove to make the king's judgment a self-fulfilling prophecy.

THE COERCIVE ACTS   In 1774 Parliament enacted four measures designed by North to discipline Boston. The Boston Port Act closed the port from June 1, 1774, until the city paid for the lost tea. An Act for the Impartial Administration of Justice let the governor transfer to England the trial of any official accused of committing an offense in the line of duty—no more redcoats would be tried on technicalities. A new Quartering Act directed local authorities to provide lodging for soldiers, in private homes if necessary. Finally, the Massachusetts Government Act made the colony's council and law-enforcement officers all appointive rather than elected; sheriffs would select jurors; and no town meeting could be held without the governor's consent, except for the annual election of town officers. In May, General Thomas Gage replaced Hutchinson as governor and assumed command of British forces. Massachusetts now had a military governor.

These actions were designed to isolate Boston and make an example of the colony. Instead they galvanized colonial unity and emboldened resistance. "Your scheme yields no revenue," Edmund Burke had warned his fellow members of Parliament; "it yields nothing but discontent, disorder, disobedience. . . ." At last, it seemed to the colonists, their worst fears were being confirmed. If these "Intolerable Acts," as the colonists labeled the Coercive Acts, were not resisted, they would eventually be applied to the other colonies.

Further confirmation of British designs came with news of the Quebec Act, passed in June. The act provided that the government to the north in Canada would not have a representative assembly and would

The Able Doctor, or America Swallowing the Bitter Draught. *This 1774 engraving shows Lord North, with the Boston Port Act in his pocket, pouring tea down America's throat. America spits it back.*

be instead led by an appointed governor and council. It also gave a privileged position to the Catholic church. The measure was actually designed to deal with the peculiar milieu of a predominantly French colony unused to representative assemblies, but it seemed merely another indicator of tyrannical designs for the rest of the colonies. In addition, colonists pointed out that they had lost many lives in an effort to liberate the trans-Appalachian West from the control of French Catholics. Now the British seemed to be protecting papists at the expense of their own colonists. What was more, the act placed within the boundaries of Quebec the western lands north of the Ohio River, lands that Pennsylvania, Virginia, and Connecticut claimed.

Meanwhile, colonists rallied to the cause of besieged Boston, taking up collections and sending provisions. In Williamsburg, when the Virginia assembly met in May, a young member of the Committee of Correspondence, Thomas Jefferson, proposed to set aside June 1, the effective date of the Boston Port Act, as a day of fasting and prayer in Virginia. The governor immediately dissolved the assembly, whose members retired to the Raleigh Tavern and drew up a resolution for a "Continental Congress" to make representations on behalf of all the colonies. Similar calls were coming from Providence, New York, Philadelphia, and elsewhere, and in June the Massachusetts assembly suggested a meeting in Philadelphia in September. Shortly before George Washington left to represent Virginia at the gathering, he wrote to a friend: "the crisis is arrived when we must assert our rights, or submit to every imposition, that can be heaped upon us, till custom and use shall make us as tame and abject slaves, as the blacks we rule over with such arbitrary sway."

THE CONTINENTAL CONGRESS   On September 5, 1774, the First Continental Congress assembled in Philadelphia. There were fifty-five members representing twelve continental colonies, all but Georgia, Quebec, Nova Scotia, and the Floridas. Peyton Randolph of Virginia was elected president and Charles Thomson, "the Sam Adams of Philadelphia," became secretary, but not a member. The Congress agreed to vote by colonies, although Patrick Henry urged the members to vote as individuals on the grounds that they were not Virginians or New Yorkers or whatever, but Americans. In effect, the delegates functioned as a congress of ambassadors, gathered to join forces on common policies and neither to govern nor to rebel but to adopt and issue a series of resolutions and protests.

The Congress gave serious consideration to a plan of union introduced by Joseph Galloway of Pennsylvania. He proposed to set up a central administration of a governor-general appointed by the crown and a grand council chosen by the assemblies to regulate "general affairs." All measures dealing with America would require approval of both this body and Parliament. The plan was defeated by a vote of only six to five. Meanwhile a silversmith from Boston, Paul Revere, had come riding in from Massachusetts with the radical Suffolk Resolves, which the Congress proceeded to endorse. The resolutions declared the Intolerable Acts null and void, urged Massachusetts to arm for defense, and called for economic sanctions against British commerce.

In place of Galloway's plan, the Congress adopted a Declaration of American Rights, which conceded only Parliament's right to regulate commerce and those matters that were strictly imperial affairs. It proclaimed once again the rights of Americans as English citizens, denied Parliament's authority with respect to internal colonial affairs, and proclaimed the right of each assembly to determine the need for British

Goods from around the world could be found in a Philadelphia shop in 1772: Jamaica spirits, Madeira wines, molasses, souchong tea, cloves, Florence oil.

troops within its own province. In addition the Congress sent the king a petition for relief and issued addresses to the people of Great Britain and the colonies.

Finally the Continental Congress adopted the Continental Association of 1774, which recommended that every county, town, and city form committees to enforce a boycott on all British goods. These committees would become the organizational and communications network for the Revolutionary movement, connecting every locality to the leadership. The Continental Association also included provisions for the nonimportation of British goods (implemented in 1774) and the nonexportation of American goods to Britain (to be implemented in 1775 unless colonial grievances were addressed).

In taking its bold stand, the Congress had adopted what later would be called the dominion theory of the British Empire, a theory long implicit in the assemblies' claim to independent authority but more recently formulated in two widely circulated pamphlets by James Wilson of Pennsylvania (*Considerations on the Nature and Extent of the Legislative Authority of the British Parliament*) and Thomas Jefferson of Virginia (*Summary View of the Rights of British America*). Each tract had argued that the colonies were not subject to Parliament but merely to the crown; each colony, like England itself, was a separate realm, a point further argued in the *Novanglus Letters* of John Adams, published in Massachusetts after the Congress adjourned.

In London the king fumed. He wrote his prime minister that the "New England colonies are in a state of rebellion," and "blows must decide whether they are to be subject to this country or independent." British critics of the American actions reminded the colonists that Parliament had absolute sovereignty. Power could not be shared. Parliament could not abandon its claim to authority in part without abandoning it altogether. Only a few members of Parliament were ready to comprehend, much less accept, the colonists' "liberal and expanded thought," as Jefferson called it. In the House of Commons, Edmund Burke, in a brilliant speech on conciliation, urged merely an acceptance of the American view on taxation as consonant with English principles. The real question, he argued, was "not whether you have the right to render your people miserable; but whether it is not your interest to make them happy."

But Parliament rejected the notion of compromise. Instead it declared Massachusetts in rebellion, forbade the New England colonies to trade with any nation outside the empire, and excluded New Englanders from the North Atlantic fisheries. Lord North's Conciliatory Resolution, adopted February 27, 1775, was as far as they would go. Under its terms, Parliament would refrain from any measures but taxes to regulate trade and would grant to each colony the duties collected within its boundaries, provided the colonies would contribute voluntarily to a quota for defense of the empire. It was a formula, Burke said, not for peace but for new quarrels.

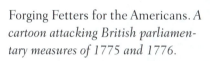

Forging Fetters for the Americans. *A cartoon attacking British parliamentary measures of 1775 and 1776.*

SHIFTING AUTHORITY

Events were already moving beyond conciliation. All through late 1774 and early 1775 the patriot defenders of American rights were seizing the initiative. The uncertain and unorganized Loyalists, if they did not submit to nonimportation agreements, found themselves confronted with persuasive committees of "Whigs," with tar and feathers at the ready. The Continental Congress urged each colony to mobilize its militia units. The militia, as much a social as a military organization in the past, now took to serious drill in formations, tactics, and marksmanship, and organized special units of Minute Men ready for quick mobilization. Everywhere royal and proprietary officials were losing control as provincial congresses assumed authority and colonial militias organized, raided military stores, and gathered arms and gunpowder. But British military officials remained smugly confident. Major John Pitcairn wrote home from Boston in 1775: "I am satisfied that one active campaign, a smart action, and burning two or three of their towns, will set everything to rights."

LEXINGTON AND CONCORD Pitcairn soon had his chance. On April 14, 1775, Gage received secret orders to suppress the "open rebellion" that existed in the colony. Gage determined to capture and arrest leaders of the Provincial Congress and to seize the militia's supply depot at Concord, about twenty miles away. On the night of April 18 Lieutenant-Colonel Francis Smith and Major Pitcairn gathered 700

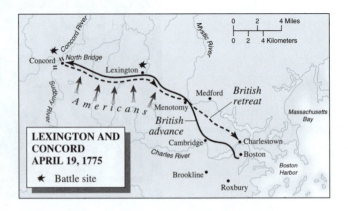

The Retreat. *An American cartoon showing the retreat of British forces at Lexington and Concord, April 1775.*

men on Boston Common and set out by way of Lexington. When local patriots got wind of the plan, Boston's Committee of Safety sent Paul Revere and William Dawes by separate routes on their famous ride to spread the alarm. Revere reached Lexington about midnight and alerted John Hancock and Sam Adams, who were hiding there. Joined by Dawes and Dr. Samuel Prescott, who had been visiting in Lexington, Revere rode on toward Concord. A British patrol intercepted the trio, but Prescott slipped through with the warning.

At dawn on April 19 the British advance guard found Captain John Parker and about seventy Minute Men lined up on the dewy Lexington green. Parker apparently intended only a silent protest, but Pitcairn rode onto the green, swung his sword, and brusquely yelled: "Disperse, you damned rebels! You dogs, run!" The Americans had already begun quietly backing away when someone fired a shot, whereupon the British soldiers loosed a volley into the Minute Men, then charged them with bayonets, leaving eight dead and ten wounded. One wounded American patriot, whose wife and son were watching the spectacle, crawled 100 yards to die on his front doorstep.

The British officers hastily brought their men under control and led them to Concord. There the Americans already had carried off most of their munitions, but the British destroyed what they could. At Concord's North Bridge the growing American forces inflicted fourteen casualties on a British platoon, and by about noon the British began marching back to Boston. By then, however, the road back had turned into a gauntlet of death as the embattled farmers from "every Middlesex village and farm" sniped from behind stone walls, trees, barns, houses, all the way back to Charlestown peninsula. By nightfall the redcoat survivors were safe under the protection of the fleet and army at Boston, having suffered over 250 casualties along the way, and the Americans nearly a hundred. A British general reported to London that the rebels had earned his respect: "Whoever looks upon them as an irregular mob will find himself much mistaken."

THE SPREADING CONFLICT   The war had begun. When the Second Continental Congress convened at Philadelphia on May 10, 1775, British-held Boston was under siege by the Massachusetts militia. On the very day that Congress met, Fort Ticonderoga in New York fell to a force of Green Mountain Boys under hotheaded Ethan Allen of Vermont and Massachusetts volunteers under Benedict Arnold of Connecticut. Two days later the colonial force took Crown Point, north of Ticonderoga.

The Continental Congress, with no legal authority and no resources, met amid reports of spreading warfare and had little choice but to assume the de facto role of a revolutionary government. On June 15 it named George Washington general and commander-in-chief of a Continental army. He accepted on the condition that he receive no pay. The Congress fastened on Washington because his service in the French and Indian War made him one of the most experienced officers in America. The fact that he was from populous and influential Virginia heightened his attractiveness. To finance the enterprise the Congress resorted to a familiar colonial expedient, printing paper money.

On June 17, the very day that Washington was commissioned, the colonials and British forces engaged in their first major fight, the Battle of Bunker Hill. While the Congress deliberated, both American and British forces in and around Boston had grown. Militiamen from Rhode Island, Connecticut, and New Hampshire joined in the siege. British reinforcements included three major-generals—Sir William Howe, Sir Henry Clinton, and John Burgoyne. On the day before the battle, American forces used picks and shovels to fortify the high ground of Charlestown peninsula, overlooking Boston. Breed's Hill was the battle location, nearer to Boston than Bunker Hill, the site first chosen (and the source of the battle's erroneous name).

The Battle of Bunker Hill and the burning of Charlestown peninsula.

The rebels were spoiling for a fight. As Joseph Warren, a dapper Boston physician, put it, "the British say we won't fight; by heavens, I hope I shall die up to my knees in blood!" He soon got his wish. With civilians looking on from rooftops and church steeples, the British commander, General Thomas Gage, ordered a conventional frontal assault in the blistering heat, with 2,200 British troops moving in tight formation through tall grass. The Americans, pounded by naval guns, watched from behind their hastily built earthworks as the waves of brightly uniformed British troops advanced up the hill. The militiamen waited until the attackers came within fifteen to twenty paces, then loosed a shattering volley. The militiamen cheered as they watched the greatest soldiers in the world retreating in panic.

Within a half hour, however, the British had reformed and attacked again. Another sheet of flame and lead greeted them, and the vaunted redcoats retreated a second time. Still, the proud British generals were determined not to let such ragtag rustics humiliate them. On the third attempt, when the colonials began to run out of gunpowder and were forced to throw stones, a bayonet charge ousted them. The British took the high ground, but at the cost of 1,054 casualties. Colonial losses were about 400. "A dear bought victory," recorded General Clinton; "another such would have ruined us."

The Battle of Bunker Hill had two profound effects. First, the high number of British casualties made the English generals more cautious in subsequent encounters with the Continental army. Second, Congress recommended after the battle that all able-bodied men enlist in the militia. This tended to divide the male population into Patriot and Loyalist camps. A middle ground was no longer tenable.

In early March 1776, American forces occupied Dorchester Heights to the south of Boston and brought the city under threat of bombardment with cannon and mortars. General William Howe, who had replaced Gage as British commander, retreated by water to Halifax, Nova Scotia. The last British forces, along with fearful American Loyalists, embarked on March 17, 1776. By that time British power had collapsed nearly everywhere, and the British forces faced not the suppression of a rebellion but the reconquest of a continent.

While American forces held Boston under siege, the Continental Congress pursued the dimming hope of a compromise settlement. On July 5 and 6, 1775, the delegates issued two major documents: an appeal to the king thereafter known as the Olive Branch Petition, and a Declaration of the Causes and Necessity of Taking Up Arms. The Olive Branch Petition, written by John Dickinson, professed continued loyalty to George III and begged him to restrain further hostilities pending a reconciliation. The Declaration, also largely Dickinson's work, traced the history of the controversy, denounced the British for the unprovoked assault at Lexington, and rejected independence but affirmed the colonists' purpose to fight for their rights rather than submit to slavery. When the Olive Branch Petition reached London, the outraged king refused even to look at it. On August 22 he declared the American colonists "as open and avowed enemies." The next day he issued a proclamation of rebellion.

Before the end of July 1775 the Congress authorized an attack on British troops in Quebec in the vain hope of rallying support from the French inhabitants in Canada. One force, under Richard Montgomery, advanced by way of Lake Champlain; another, under Benedict Arnold, struggled through the Maine woods. Together they held Quebec under siege from mid-September until their final attack was repulsed on December 30, 1775. Montgomery was killed in the battle and Arnold wounded.

In the South, Virginia's Governor Dunmore raised a Loyalist force, including slaves recruited on promise of freedom, but met defeat in December 1775. After leaving Norfolk he returned on January 1, 1776, and burned most of the town. In North Carolina, Loyalist Highland Scots, joined by some former Regulators, lost a battle with a Patriot force at Moore's Creek Bridge. The Loyalists had set out for Wilmington to join an expeditionary force under Lord Cornwallis and Sir Henry Clinton. That plan frustrated, the British commanders decided to attack Charleston instead, but the Patriot militia there had partially finished a palmetto log fort on Sullivan's Island (later named in honor of its commander, Colonel William Moultrie). When the British fleet attacked on June 28, 1776, the spongy palmetto logs absorbed the naval fire, and Fort Moultrie's cannon returned it with devastating effect. The fleet, with over 200 casualties and every ship damaged, was forced to retire. South Carolina honored the palmetto tree by putting it on its state flag.

As the fighting spread north into Canada and south into Virginia and the Carolinas, the Continental Congress assumed, one after another, the functions of government. It appointed commissioners to negotiate treaties of peace with Indian tribes, organized a Post Office Department with Benjamin Franklin as postmaster-general, and authorized formation of a navy and a marine corps.

Still, the delegates continued to hold back from the seeming abyss of independence. Yet through late 1775 and early 1776 word came of one British action after another that proclaimed rebellion and war. In December 1775 a Prohibitory Act declared the colonies closed to all commerce. The king and cabinet also recruited mercenaries in Europe. Eventually almost 30,000 Germans served, about 17,000 of them from the principality of Hesse-Kassel, and "Hessian" became the name applied to them all. Parliament remained deaf to the warnings of members that the reconquest of America would not only be costly in itself but that the effort might lead to another great war with France and Spain.

COMMON SENSE   In 1776 Thomas Paine's pamphlet *Common Sense* was published anonymously in Philadelphia. Paine had arrived there from England thirteen months before. Coming from a humble Quaker background, Paine had distinguished himself chiefly as a drifter, a failure in marriage and business. At age thirty-seven he set sail for America with a letter of introduction from Benjamin Franklin and the purpose of setting up a school for young ladies. When that did not work out, he moved into the political controversy as a freelance writer, and with

Common Sense proved himself the consummate Revolutionary rhetorician. Until his pamphlet appeared, the squabble had been mainly with Parliament; few colonists considered independence an option. Paine, however, directly attacked allegiance to the monarchy, which had remained the last frayed connection to Britain, and refocused the hostility previously vented on Parliament. The common sense of the matter, it seemed, was that King George III and the King's Friends bore the responsibility for the malevolence toward the colonies. Americans should consult their own interests, abandon George III, and declare their independence: "The blood of the slain, the weeping voice of nature cries, 'TIS TIME TO PART."

INDEPENDENCE

Within three months, more than 150,000 copies of Paine's pamphlet were in circulation, an enormous number for the time. *"Common Sense* is working a powerful change in the minds of men," George Washington said. A visitor to North Carolina's Provincial Congress could "hear nothing praised but *Common Sense* and independence." One by one the provincial governments authorized their delegates in the Continental Congress to take the final step. On June 7 Richard Henry Lee of Virginia moved "that these United Colonies are, and of right ought to be, free and independent states. . . ." Lee's resolution passed on July 2, a date that "will be the most memorable epoch in the history of America," John Adams wrote to his wife, Abigail. The memorable date, however, became July 4, 1776, when the Congress adopted Thomas Jefferson's Declaration of Independence, a statement of political philosophy that retains its dynamic force to the present day.

JEFFERSON'S *DECLARATION* Although Jefferson is often called the "author" of the Declaration of Independence, he is more accurately termed its draftsman. In June 1776 the Continental Congress appointed a committee of five men—Jefferson, Benjamin Franklin, John Adams, Robert Livingston of New York, and Roger Sherman of Connecticut—to develop a public explanation of the reasons for colonial discontent and to provide a rationale for independence. John Adams convened the committee on June 11. The group asked Adams and Jefferson to produce a first draft, whereupon Adams deferred to Jefferson because of the thirty-three-year-old Virginian's reputation as an eloquent writer.

During two days in mid-June 1776, on the second floor of his rented lodgings at Seventh and Market Streets in Philadelphia, Jefferson used a quill pen and a portable desk to write the first statement of American grievances and principles. He later explained that his purpose was "not to find out new principles, or new arguments, never before thought of, not merely to say things which had never been said before; but to place before mankind the common sense of the subject, in terms so plain and firm as to command their assent. . . ." He intended his words to serve as "an expression of the American mind, and to give to that expression the proper tone and spirit called for by the occasion."

Jefferson did not write in a vacuum. Between April and early July 1776, over ninety local "declarations" of independence had already been issued by Massachusetts towns; by militias in New York and Pennsylvania; and by counties, grand juries, and provincial congresses throughout the colonies. During his two-day drafting exercise, Jefferson drew primarily upon two sources: his own draft preamble to the Virginia Constitution written a few weeks earlier, and George Mason's draft of

Thomas Jefferson's draft of the Declaration of Independence.

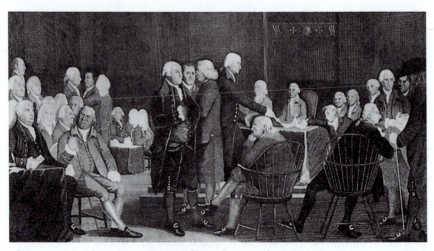

The Continental Congress votes Independence, July 2, 1776.

Virginia's Declaration of Rights, which appeared in Philadelphia news-papers in mid-June. It was Mason's text that stimulated many of Jefferson's most famous phrases. Mason had written that "all men are born equally free and independent, and have certain inherent natural Rights, . . . among which are the Enjoyment of Life and Liberty, with the Means of acquiring and possessing Property, and pursuing and obtaining Happiness and Safety."

Jefferson shared his draft with the committee members, and they made several minor revisions to the opening paragraphs and to his listing of the charges against King George III. For example, the committee replaced Jefferson's phrase "sacred & undeniable" truths with "self-evident" truths. They submitted the document to the entire Congress on June 28, whereupon it was tabled until July 1. Off and on during the next three days, the legislators turned themselves into a Committee of the Whole to consider the draft. They made eighty-six changes in Jefferson's declaration, including shortening its overall length by one-fourth. Most of the revisions dealt with the section summarizing British colonial policy over the previous fifteen years, but the Congress did see fit to insert two references to God. Jefferson regretted many of the changes, believing his colleagues had "mangled" the document. He especially criticized the decision to delete his attack on the British people rather than simply the monarchy and ministry. He also attacked the deletion of his statement about British promotion of the slave trade. But overall the legislative editing improved the declaration, making it more concise, accurate, and coherent—and, as a result, more powerful.

The Declaration of Independence constitutes an eloquent restatement of John Locke's contract theory of government—the theory, in Jefferson's words, that governments derived "their just Powers from the consent of the people," who were entitled to "alter or abolish" those that denied their "unalienable rights" to "life, Liberty, and the pursuit of Happiness." The appeal was no longer simply to "the rights of Englishmen" but to the broader "laws of Nature and Nature's God." Parliament, which had no proper authority over the colonies, was never mentioned by name. The enemy was a king who had "combined with others to subject us to a jurisdiction foreign to our constitution, and unacknowledged by our laws. . . ." The document set forth "a history of repeated injuries and usurpations, all having in direct object the establishment of an absolute Tyranny over these States." The "Representatives of the United States of America," therefore, declared the thirteen "United Colonies" to be "Free and Independent States."

"WE ALWAYS HAD GOVERNED OURSELVES" So it had come to this, thirteen years after Britain acquired domination of North America. In explaining the causes of the Revolution, historians have advanced many theories and explanations: trade regulation, the restrictions on western lands, the tax burden, the mounting debts to British merchants, the fear of an Anglican bishop, the growth of a national consciousness, the lack of representation in Parliament, ideologies of Whiggery and the Enlightenment, the evangelistic impulse, the abrupt shift from a mercantile to an "imperial" policy after 1763, class conflict, and revolutionary conspiracy.

Each of them separately and all of them together are subject to challenge, but each contributed something to collective grievances that rose to a climax in a gigantic failure of British statesmanship. A conflict between British sovereignty and American rights had come to a point of confrontation that adroit statesmanship might have avoided, side-stepped, or outflanked. Irresolution and vacillation in the British ministry finally gave way to the stubborn determination to force an issue long permitted to drift. The colonists, conditioned by the Whig interpretation of history, saw these developments as the conspiracy of a corrupted oligarchy—and finally, they decided, of a despotic king—to impose an "absolute Tyranny."

Perhaps the last word on causes of the Revolution should belong to an obscure participant, Levi Preston, a Minute Man from Danvers, Massachusetts. Asked sixty-seven years after Lexington and Concord about British oppressions, he responded, as his young interviewer reported later: " 'What were they? Oppressions? I didn't feel them.' 'What, were you not oppressed by the Stamp Act?' 'I never saw one of those stamps. . . . I am certain I never paid a penny for one of them.' 'Well, what then about the tea-tax?' 'Tea-tax! I never drank a drop of the stuff; the boys threw it all overboard.' 'Then I suppose you had been reading Harrington or Sidney and Locke about the eternal principles of liberty.' 'Never heard of 'em. We read only the Bible, the Catechism, Watts's Psalms and Hymns, and the Almanack.' 'Well, then, what was the matter? and what did you mean in going to the fight?' 'Young man, what we meant in going for those redcoats was this: we always had governed ourselves, and we always meant to. They didn't mean we should.' "

In July 1776, on the day independence was proclaimed, a band of Patriots pulled down a statue of George III in New York City, expressing the end of Britain's rule over America.

MAKING CONNECTIONS

- The American revolutionary rhetoric was important not only for fighting the American Revolution; it also provided the framework for the creation of new American governments. This will be discussed in the next two chapters.

- The section titled "Discontent on the Frontier" shows the tension between people in the more urban eastern areas of several states and those on the western frontier. These same tensions will reappear in several future chapters—for example, in the Federalist/Antifederalist debate over ratification of the Constitution (in Chapter 7).

FURTHER READING

For a narrative survey of the events leading to the Revolution, see Edward Countryman's *The American Revolution* (1985). For the perspective of Great Britain on the imperial conflict, see Sir Lewis Namier's *England in the Age of the American Revolution* (2nd ed., 1961) and Ian Christie, *Crisis of Empire* (1966).

The intellectual foundations for revolt are traced in Bernard Bailyn's *The Ideological Origins of the American Revolution* (1967) and in John Phillip Reid's *Constitutional History of the American Revolution: The Authority of Rights* (1987). To understand how these views were connected to organized protest, see Pauline Maier's *From Resistance to Revolution: Colonial Radicals and the Development of American Opposition to Britain, 1765–1776* (1972). The transfer of allegiance from king to Congress is examined in Jerrilyn Marston's *King and Congress: The Transfer of Political Legitimacy, 1774–1776* (1987).

Profiles of the Revolutionary generation of leaders can be found in Bernard Bailyn's *Faces of Revolution: Personalities and Themes in the*

Struggle for American Independence (1990), in Pauline Maier's *The Old Revolutionaries: Political Lives in the Age of Samuel Adams* (1980), and in A. J. Langguth's *Patriots: The Men Who Started the American Revolution* (1988).

A number of books deal with specific events in the chain of crisis. Oliver M. Dickerson's *The Navigation Acts and the American Revolution* (1951) stresses the change from trade regulation to taxation in 1764. Edmund S. Morgan and Helen M. Morgan's *The Stamp Act Crisis* (rev. ed., 1962) gives the colonial perspective on that crucial event. Also valuable are Hiller B. Zobel's *The Boston Massacre* (1970), Benjamin W. Labaree's *The Boston Tea Party* (1964), and David Ammerman's *In the Common Cause: American Response to the Coercive Acts of 1774* (1974). Thomas Doerflinger's *A Vigorous Spirit of Enterprise: Merchants and Economic Development in Revolutionary Philadelphia* (1986) describes the role of that influential group in the imperial crisis.

Pauline Maier's *American Scripture: Making the Declaration of Independence* (1997) is the best analysis of the framing of that document. For accounts of the imperial controversy at the colony level, see Edward Countryman's *A People in Revolution* (1981), on New York; Richard L. Bushman's *King and People in Provincial Massachusetts* (1985); James H. Hutson's *Pennsylvania Politics, 1746–1770* (1972); Rhys Isaac's *The Transformation of Virgina, 1740–1790* (1982), and A. Roger Ekirch's *"Poor Carolina": Politics and Society in Colonial North Carolina, 1729–1776* (1981).

Events west of the Appalachians are chronicled concisely by Jack M. Sosin in *The Revolutionary Frontier, 1763–1783* (1967). Military affairs in the early phases of the war are handled in John W. Shy's *Toward Lexington: The Role of the British Army in the Coming of the American Revolution* (1965) and in other works listed in Chapter 6.

PART TWO

BUILDING
A NATION

The signing of the Declaration of Independence generated great excitement among the rebellious colonists. Yet a stern reality tempered their celebrations. It was one thing for Patriot leaders to declare American independence from British authority; it was quite another to win it on the battlefield. Barely a third of the colonists actively supported the Revolution, the political stability of the new nation was uncertain, and George Washington found himself in command of a poorly supplied, ragtag army.

Yet the Revolutionary movement would persevere and prevail. The skill and fortitude of Washington and his lieutenants enabled the American armies to exploit their geographic advantages. Equally important was the intervention of the French on behalf of the Revolutionary cause. The Franco-American Alliance proved to be decisive. After eight years of sporadic fighting and heavy human and financial losses, the British gave up the fight and their American colonies.

In the midst of the Revolutionary turmoil, the Patriots faced the daunting task of forming new governments for themselves. Their deeply engrained resentment of British imperial rule led them to decentralize power and place sovereignty in the individual states. As Thomas Jefferson declared, "Virginia, Sir, is my country." Such local ties help explain why the colonists focused their attention on creating new state constitutions rather than a national government. The Articles of Confederation, ratified in 1781, provided only the semblance of national authority. All final power to make and execute laws remained with the states.

After the end of the Revolutionary War in 1783, the flimsy political bonds authorized by the Articles of Confederation proved inadequate to the needs of the new—and expanding—nation. This realization led to the calling of the Constitutional Convention in 1787. The process of drafting and ratifying the new constitution prompted a debate about the relative significance of national power, local control, and individual freedom that has provided the central theme of American political thought ever since.

The American Revolution, however, involved much more than the apportionment of political power. It also unleashed social forces and posed social questions that would help to reshape the very fabric of American culture. What would be the role of women, blacks, and Native Americans in the new republic? How would the contrasting economies of the various regions of the new United States be developed? Who would control and facilitate access to the vast territories to the west of the original thirteen *states? How would the new republic relate to the other nations of the world?*

These controversial questions helped foster the creation of the first national political parties in the United States. During the 1790s, Federalists led by Alexander Hamilton and Republicans led by Thomas Jefferson and James Madison engaged in a heated debate about the political and economic future of the new nation. With Jefferson's election as president in 1800, the Republicans gained the upper hand in national politics for the next quarter century. In the process they presided over a maturing American society that aggressively expanded westward at the expense of the Native Americans, ambivalently embraced industrial development, fitfully engaged in a second war with Great Britain, and ominously witnessed a growing sectional controversy over slavery.

6 THE AMERICAN REVOLUTION

CHAPTER ORGANIZER

This chapter focuses on:

- American and British military strategies and the Revolutionary War's major turning points.

- the effect of the war on the home front.

- the American Revolution considered as a "social revolution," in matters of social equality, slavery, the rights of women, and religious freedom.

- the beginnings of a distinctive American culture.

Few foreign observers thought that the upstart American revolutionaries could win a war against the world's greatest empire—and the Americans did lose most of the battles of the Revolution. But they eventually forced the British to sue for peace and grant their independence, an unlikely result that reflects the tenacity of the Patriots as well as the peculiar difficulties facing the British as they tried to conduct a far-flung campaign thousands of miles from home. The costly military commitments they maintained elsewhere around the globe further complicated the British situation.

Fighting in the New World, however, was not an easy task for either side. The Americans had to create a military force from scratch, one capable of opposing the foremost army in the world. Recruiting, supplying, equipping, training and paying soldiers were monumental challenges, especially for a fledgling nation in the midst of forming its first governments. Yet the perseverance of the revolutionaries bore fruit, as war-weariness and political dissension in London hampered British efforts to suppress the rebel forces.

Like all major military events, the Revolution had unexpected consequences affecting political, economic, and social life. It not only secured American independence, generated a new sense of nationalism, and created a unique system of self-governance; it also began a process of societal definition and change that has yet to run its course. The turmoil of Revolution upset traditional class and social relationships and helped transform the lives of people who have long been relegated to the periphery of historical concern—blacks, women, and Indians. In important ways, then, the Revolution was much more than simply a war for independence. It was an engine for political experimentation and social change.

1776: WASHINGTON'S NARROW ESCAPE

On July 2, 1776, the day that Congress voted for independence, British redcoats landed on the undefended Staten Island. They were the vanguard of a gigantic effort to reconquer America and the first elements of an enormous force that gathered around New York Harbor over the next month. By mid-August General William Howe, with the support of a fleet under his older brother, Admiral Richard, Lord Howe, had some 32,000 men at his disposal, the largest single force ever mustered by the British in the eighteenth century. Washington transferred most of his men from Boston, but he could gather only about 19,000 Continentals and militiamen. This was too small a force to defend New York, but Congress wanted it held. This forced Washington to expose his men to entrapments from which they escaped more by luck and Howe's caution than by any strategic genius of the American commander. Washington was still learning the art of generalship, and the New York campaign afforded some expensive lessons.

General William Howe, commander-in-chief of His Majesty's forces in America.

FIGHTING IN NEW YORK AND NEW JERSEY   The first conflicts took place on Long Island, where the Americans wanted to hold Brooklyn Heights, from which the city might be bombarded. By invading and occupying New York, the British hoped to sever New England from the rest of the rebellious colonies. Howe inflicted heavy losses in early battles and forced Washington to evacuate Long Island to reunite his dangerously divided forces. A timely rainstorm, with strong winds and high tides, kept the British fleet out of the East River and made possible a withdrawal to Manhattan under cover of darkness.

Had Howe moved quickly, he could have trapped Washington's army in lower Manhattan. The main American force of 6,000 men, however, withdrew northward to mainland New York, traveled up to Harlem Heights, White Plains, and Peekskill, crossed the Hudson River, and then retreated slowly across New Jersey and over the Delaware River into Pennsylvania. In the retreat marched a British volunteer, Thomas Paine. Having opened an eventful year with his inspiring pamphlet *Common Sense,* he now composed in Newark *The American Crisis,* in which he penned an immortal line:

> These are the times that try men's souls: The summer soldier and the sunshine patriot will, in this crisis, shrink from the service of his country; but he that stands it NOW deserves the love and thanks of man and woman. Tyranny, like Hell, is not easily conquered. Yet we

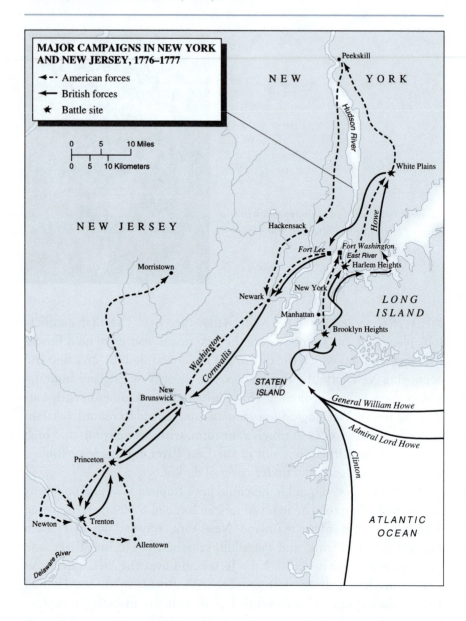

MAJOR CAMPAIGNS IN NEW YORK AND NEW JERSEY, 1776–1777

◄-- American forces
◄— British forces
★ Battle site

0   5   10 Miles
0   5   10 Kilometers

NEW YORK

Peekskill

Hudson River

White Plains

NEW JERSEY

Hackensack

Howe

Fort Lee

Fort Washington
East River
Harlem Heights

Morristown

Newark

New York

LONG ISLAND

Manhattan

Washington

Cornwallis

Brooklyn Heights

STATEN ISLAND

New Brunswick

General William Howe

Admiral Lord Howe

Princeton

Clinton

Newton

Trenton

ATLANTIC OCEAN

Allentown

Delaware River

have this consolation with us, that the harder the conflict, the more glorious the triumph.

The pamphlet, ordered read in the American army camps, bolstered the shaken morale of the Patriots—as events would soon do more decisively.

General Howe, firmly—and luxuriously—based in New York (which the British held throughout the war), established outposts in New Jer-

George Washington at Princeton, *by Charles Willson Peale.*

sey and to the east at Newport, and settled down to wait out the winter. Washington, however, was not yet ready to go into winter quarters. Instead he seized the initiative. On Christmas night 1776, he slipped across the icy Delaware River, with some 2,400 men. Near dawn at Trenton, the Americans surprised a garrison of 1,500 Hessians (German mercenaries) still befuddled from too much holiday rum. It was a total rout from which only 500 royal soldiers escaped death or capture. Only six of Washington's men were wounded, one of whom was Lieutenant James Monroe, the future president. At nearby Princeton on January 3 the Americans repelled three regiments of British redcoats before taking refuge in winter quarters at Morristown, in the hills of northern New Jersey. The campaigns of 1776 had ended, after repeated defeats, with two minor victories that bolstered the Patriot cause. Howe had missed his great chance, indeed several chances, to bring the rebellion to a speedy end. Grumbled one British officer, the Americans had "become a formidable enemy," even though they had yet to win a full-scale conventional battle.

AMERICAN SOCIETY AT WAR

CHOOSING SIDES   Since the end of the French and Indian War, the colonies had required all adult males between the ages of fifteen and sixty to enroll in their local militia company. They attended a monthly drill and turned out on short notice for emergencies. When fighting erupted between the British and revolutionaries, members of community militias chose sides.

Opinion among the colonists concerning the war divided in three ways: Patriots or Whigs (as the revolutionaries called themselves), Tories (as Patriots called the Loyalists, recalling the diehard defenders of royal prerogative in England), and an indifferent middle group swayed mostly by the better organized and more energetic radicals. That the Loyalists were numerous is evident from the departure during or after the war of roughly 100,000 of them, or more than 3 percent of the total population. But the Patriots were probably the largest of the three groups. There was a like division in British opinion. The aversion of so many Englishmen to the war was one reason for the government's hiring German mercenaries.

Estimating how many Americans remained loyal to Britain was a central concern of English military planners, for they based many of their decisions on such figures. Through most of the war, in New Jersey and in other colonies, the British would be chasing the elusive Tory majority that Loyalists kept telling them was out there waiting only for British regulars to show the flag. Often they miscalculated. Generally, American Tories were concentrated in the seaport cities, but they came from all walks of life. Governors, judges, and other royal officials were almost all Loyalists; most Anglican ministers also preferred the mother country; colonial merchants might be tugged one way or the other, depending on how much they had benefited or suffered from mercantilist regulation; the great planters were swayed one way by dependence on British bounties, another by their debts to British merchants. In the backcountry of New York and the Carolinas, many humble folk rallied to the crown. Where planter aristocrats tended to be Whig, as in North Carolina, backcountry farmers (many of them recently Regulators) leaned to the Tories.

In few places, however, were there enough Tories to assume control without the presence of British troops, and nowhere for very long. Time and again the British forces were frustrated by both the failure of Loyalists to materialize in strength and the collapse of Loyalist militia units once regular detachments pulled out. Even more disheartening was what one British officer called "the licentiousness of the troops, who committed every species of rapine and plunder," and thereby converted potential friends into enemies. British and Hessian regulars, brought up in a hard school of warfare, tended to treat all civilians as hostile.

The inability of the British to use Loyalists effectively as pacification troops led them to abandon areas once they had conquered them. Because Patriot militias quickly returned whenever the British left an area, any Loyalists in the region faced a difficult choice: either accompany the British and leave behind their property or stay behind and face the wrath of the Patriots. In addition, the British policy of offering slaves their freedom in exchange for their loyalty and even arming many of them to fight against the Americans served to alienate large numbers of neutral or even Tory planters.

The Patriot militia kept springing to life whenever redcoats appeared nearby, and all adult white males, with few exceptions, were obligated under state law to serve when called. With time, even the most apathetic would be pressed into a commitment, if only to turn out for drill. And sooner or later nearly every colonial county experienced military action that would call for armed resistance. The war itself, then, whether through British and Loyalist behavior or the call of the militia, mobilized the apathetic into at least an appearance of support for the American cause. Once made, this commitment was seldom reversed.

"One of those ubiquitous American frontiersmen-turned-soldier," second from right. Sketches of the American militia by a French soldier at Yorktown.

MILITIA AND ARMY   American militiamen served two purposes. They constituted a home guard, defending their own communities, and they also helped augment the Continental army. In the backcountry, the militia engaged in the kind of fighting that had become habitual when they were colonists. Dressed in hunting shirts and armed with muskets with long, grooved barrels, they preferred to ambush their opponents or engage them in hand-to-hand combat rather than fight in traditional formations. They also tended to kill unnecessarily and torture prisoners. To repel an attack, the militia somehow materialized; the danger past, it evaporated, for there were chores to do at home. They "come in, you cannot tell how," George Washington said in exasperation, "go, you cannot tell when, and act you cannot tell where, consume your provisions, exhaust your stores, and leave you at last at a critical moment."

The Continental army, by contrast, was on the whole well trained. Unlike the professional soldiers in the British army, Washington's troops were citizen-soldiers, mostly poor native-born Americans, or immigrants who had been indentured servants or convicts. Many found camp life debilitating and combat horrifying. As General Nathanael Greene, Washington's ablest commander, pointed out, few had ever engaged in mortal combat, and they were hard pressed to "stand the shocking scenes of war, to march over dead men, to hear without concern the groans of the wounded."

Desertions grew as the war dragged on, and the army fluctuated in size from around 10,000 troops to as high as 20,000 and as low as 5,000. At times Washington could put only 2,000 to 3,000 men in the field. Regiments were organized state by state, and the states were supposed to keep them filled with volunteers, or conscripts if need be, but Washington could never be sure that his requisitions would be met.

PROBLEMS OF FINANCE AND SUPPLY   The Congress found it difficult to supply the army. None of the states provided more than a part of its share, and Congress reluctantly let army agents take supplies directly from farmers in return for certificates promising future payment. Many of the states found a ready source of revenue in the sale of abandoned Loyalist estates. Nevertheless, the Congress and the states fell short of funding the war's cost, and resorted to printing paper money.

Congress did better at providing munitions than at providing other supplies. In 1777 Congress established a government arsenal at Spring-

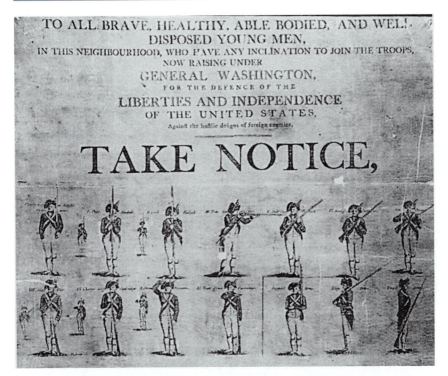

A poster recruiting soldiers for the Continental army. The Congress appealed to those interested in "viewing the different parts of this beautiful continent, in the honourable and truly respectable character of a soldier," and then returning home "with his pockets FULL of money and his head COVERED with laurels."

field, Massachusetts, and during the war, states offered bounties for the manufacture of guns and powder. Still, most munitions were supplied either by capture during the war or by importation from France, where the government was all too glad to help rebels against its British arch-enemy.

During the harsh winter at Morristown (1776–1777), Washington's army very nearly disintegrated as enlistments expired and deserters fled the hardships. Only about 1,000 Continentals and a few militiamen stuck it out. With the spring thaw, however, recruits began arriving to claim the bounty of $20 and 100 acres of land offered by Congress to those who would enlist for three years or for the duration of the conflict, if less. With some 9,000 regulars Washington began sparring and feinting with Howe in northern New Jersey. Howe had been making other plans, however, and so had other British officers.

1777: Setbacks for the British

Divided counsels, overconfidence, poor communications, and indecision plagued British planning for the campaigns of 1777. After the removal of General Gage during the siege of Boston, "Gentleman Johnny" Burgoyne took command of the northern armies. He proposed to bisect the colonies. His men would advance southward from Canada to the Hudson while another force moved eastward from Oswego down the Mohawk River Valley. Howe, meanwhile, would lead a third force up the Hudson from New York City. Howe in fact had proposed a simi-

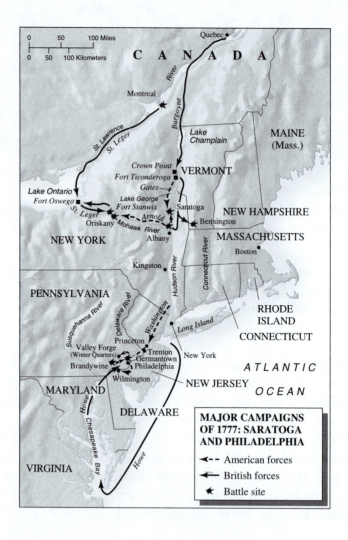

MAJOR CAMPAIGNS
OF 1777: SARATOGA
AND PHILADELPHIA

◄- - American forces
◄— British forces
★ Battle site

The vainglorious General John Burgoyne, commander of England's northern forces. Burgoyne and most of his British troops surrendered to the Americans at Saratoga on October 17, 1777.

lar plan, combined with an attack on New England. Had he stuck to it, he might have cut the colonies in two and delivered them a disheartening blow. But he changed his mind and decided to move against the Patriot capital, Philadelphia, expecting that the Pennsylvania Tories would then rally to the crown and secure the colony.

Washington, sensing Howe's purpose, withdrew most of his men from New Jersey to meet the new threat. At Brandywine Creek, south of Philadelphia, Howe pushed Washington's forces back on September 11, and fifteen days later occupied Philadelphia. Washington counterattacked against a British encampment at Germantown on October 4, but reinforcements from Philadelphia under General Lord Cornwallis arrived in time to repulse the attack. Washington retired into winter quarters at Valley Forge while Howe and his men remained for the winter in the relative comfort of Philadelphia, twenty miles away. Howe's plan had succeeded, up to a point. He had taken Philadelphia—or as Benjamin Franklin put it, Philadelphia took him. But the Tories there proved fewer than he expected, and his decision to move on Philadelphia from the south, by way of Chesapeake Bay, put his forces even farther away from Burgoyne. Meanwhile, Burgoyne was stumbling into disaster in the north.

SARATOGA   After concluding his marching orders by declaring "This Army must not Retreat," Burgoyne moved southward from Canada to-

General Horatio Gates in a portrait by Rembrandt Peale.

ward Lake Champlain in 1777 with about 7,000 men, his mistress, and a baggage train that included some thirty carts filled with his personal belongings and a large supply of champagne. Such heavily laden forces had a difficult time traversing the wooded and marshy terrain. He sent part of his forces down the St. Lawrence River with Lieutenant-Colonel Barry St. Leger, and at Oswego they were joined by a force of Iroquois allies. This combined force headed east toward Albany.

The American army in the north, like Washington's army at Morristown, had dwindled during the winter. When Burgoyne brought his cannon to bear on Fort Ticonderoga, the Continentals prudently abandoned the fort, but with substantial loss of powder and supplies. An angry Congress thereupon fired the American commander and replaced him with Horatio Gates, a favorite of the New Englanders. Fortunately for the American forces, Burgoyne delayed at Ticonderoga, thereby enabling reinforcements to arrive from the south and New England.

The more mobile Americans inflicted two serious reversals on the British forces. At Oriskany, New York, on August 6, 1777, a band of militia repulsed an ambush by Tories and Indians under St. Leger, and gained time for General Benedict Arnold to bring a thousand Continentals to the relief of Fort Stanwix. The Indians, convinced they faced an even greater force than they actually did, deserted, and the Mohawk

Valley was secured for the Patriot forces. To the east, at Bennington, Vermont (August 16), a body of New England militia led by Colonel John Stark repulsed a British foraging party with heavy losses. Stark had pledged that morning: "We'll beat them before night, or Molly Stark will be a widow." As American reinforcements continued to gather, and after two other defeats by the Americans, Burgoyne pulled back to Saratoga, where General Horatio Gates's forces surrounded him.

On October 17, 1777, Burgoyne, resplendent in his scarlet, gold, and white uniform, surrendered to the plain, blue-coated Gates, and most of his 5,700 soldiers were imprisoned in Virginia. Gates allowed Burgoyne himself to go home, where he received an icy reception. Gates was ecstatic. He wrote his wife: "If old England is not by this lesson taught humility, then she is an obstinate old slut, bent upon her ruin."

ALLIANCE WITH FRANCE   In early December 1777, news of the American triumph reached London and Paris, where it was celebrated almost as if it were a French victory. Its impact made Saratoga a decisive turning point in the war. The French foreign minister, the comte de Vergennes, had watched the developing Anglo-American crisis with great anticipation and had sent a special agent to Philadelphia to encourage the colonists and hint at French aid.

In 1776 the French had taken their first step toward aiding the colonists, sending fourteen ships with military supplies to America; most of the Continental army's powder in the first years of the war came from this source. The Spanish government added a donation, and soon established its own supply company.

Word of the American victory at Saratoga led to the signing in early 1778 of two treaties: a Treaty of Amity and Commerce, in which France recognized the United States and offered trade concessions, including important privileges to American shipping, and a Treaty of Alliance. Under the latter both parties agreed, first, that if France entered the war, both countries would fight until American independence was won; second, that neither would conclude a "truce or peace" without "the formal consent of the other first obtained"; and third, that each guaranteed the other's possessions in America "from the present time and forever against all other powers." France further bound itself to seek neither Canada nor other British possessions on the mainland of North America.

The British Lion Engaging Four Powers. *The American Revolution sparked a world war, as this British cartoon suggests: "Behold the Dutch and Spanish Currs, / Perfidious Gallus in his Spurs, / And Rattlesnake, with head upright, / The British Lion join to fight; / He scorns the Bark, the Hiss, the Crow, / That he's a Lion soon they'll know."*

By June 1778 British vessels had fired on French ships, and the two nations were at war. In 1779, after extracting French promises to help it regain territories taken by the British in previous wars, Spain entered the war as an ally of France, but not of the United States. In 1780 Britain declared war on the Dutch, who persisted in a profitable trade with the French and Americans. The embattled farmers at Lexington and Concord had indeed fired the "shot heard round the world." Like Washington's encounter with the French in 1754, it was the start of another world war, and the fighting now spread to the Mediterranean, Africa, India, the West Indies, and the high seas.

1778: BOTH SIDES REGROUP

After Saratoga, Lord North knew that the war was unwinnable, but the king refused to let him either resign or make peace. On March 16, 1778, the House of Commons adopted a program that in effect granted all the American demands prior to independence. Parliament repealed the Townshend tea duty, the Massachusetts Government Act, and the Prohibitory Act, which had closed the colonies to commerce, and sent peace commissioners to Philadelphia to negotiate an end to hostilities. But the American Congress refused to begin any negotiations until Britain recognized American independence or withdrew its forces.

Unbeknownst to the British peace commissioners, the crown had already authorized the evacuation of British troops from Philadelphia, a withdrawal that further weakened what little bargaining power they had. After Saratoga, General Howe had resigned his command and Sir Henry Clinton had replaced him, with orders to pull out of Philadelphia, and if necessary, New York, but to keep Newport. He was to supply troops for an expedition in the South, where the government believed a latent Tory sentiment in the backcountry needed only the British presence for its release. The ministry was right, up to a point, but the sentiment turned out once again, as in other theaters of war, to be weaker than it seemed.

For Washington's army at Valley Forge, the winter of 1777–1778 was a season of suffering far worse than the previous winter at Morristown. The American force, encamped near Philadelphia, endured unrelenting cold, hunger, and disease. Many soldiers deserted or resigned their commissions, leading Washington to warn Congress that unless substantial supplies were forthcoming, the army "must inevitably be reduced to one or other of these three things: starve, dissolve, or disperse." The winter witnessed dissension in Congress and the army. Some critics wanted to make Washington the scapegoat for the Patriots' plight, but there was never any concerted effort to replace him.

Desperate for relief, Washington ordered two of his generals, Nathanael Greene and Henry Lee, to organize foraging expeditions. Their troops crossed the Delaware River into New Jersey and on into Delaware and the eastern shore of Maryland, confiscating horses, cattle, and livestock in exchange for "receipts" to be honored by the Continental Congress. By March the once gaunt troops at Valley Forge saw their strength restored. Their improved health enabled Washington to begin a training program designed to bring unity to his motley array of forces. Because few of the regimental commanders had any formal military training, their troops lacked leadership, discipline, and skill. To remedy this defect, Washington turned to an energetic Prussian soldier of fortune, Frederick William Augustus Henry Ferdinand, baron von

Steuben. He used an interpreter and frequent profanity to instruct the troops, teaching them close-order drill, how to march in formations, and how to handle their weapons. By the end of March the ragtag soldiers were beginning to resemble a professional army.

As winter drew to an end the army's morale stiffened when Congress promised extra pay and bonuses after the war. The good news from France helped as well. As General Clinton's British forces withdrew eastward toward New York, Washington pursued them across New Jersey. On June 28 he engaged the British in an indecisive battle at Monmouth Court House. But the Battle of Monmouth was significant for revealing Washington's temper and leadership qualities. In the midst of the fighting, he discovered that his potbellied subordinate, General Charles Lee, was retreating rather than attacking as ordered. Infuriated, Washington swore at Lee "till the leaves shook the trees," at one point calling him a "damned poltroon." Then Washington rallied the troops just in time to stave off defeat. Clinton slipped away into New York while Washington took up a position at White Plains, north of the city. From that time on, the northern theater, scene of the major campaigns and battles in the first years of the war, settled into a long stalemate, interrupted by minor and mostly inconclusive engagements.

ACTIONS ON THE FRONTIER The one major American success of 1778 occurred far from the New Jersey battlefields. Out to the west the British under Colonel William Hamilton at Forts Niagara and Detroit had incited frontier Tories and Indians to raid western settlements and offered to pay bounties for American scalps. To end such attacks, young George Rogers Clark took 175 frontiersmen and a flotilla of flatboats down the Ohio River early in 1778, marched through the woods, and on the evening of July 4 took Kaskaskia by surprise. The French inhabitants, terrified at first, "fell into transports of joy" at news of the French alliance. Then, without bloodshed, Clark took Cahokia (opposite St. Louis), Vincennes, and some minor outposts in what he now called the county of Illinois in the state of Virginia. After the British retook Vincennes, Clark marched his men (almost half French volunteers) through icy rivers and flooded prairies, sometimes in water neck deep, and laid siege to an astonished British garrison there. Then Clark, the hardened woodsman, tomahawked Indian captives in sight of the fort to show that the British afforded them no protection. He spared the

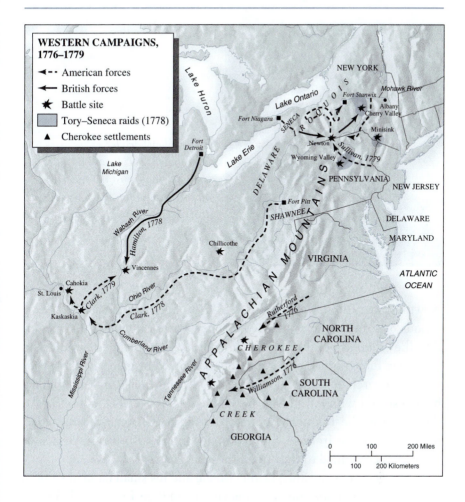

WESTERN CAMPAIGNS,
1776–1779

◄-- American forces
◄— British forces
✶ Battle site
▨ Tory–Seneca raids (1778)
▲ Cherokee settlements

British captives when they surrendered, however. Clark is often credited with having conquered the West for the new nation, but there is no evidence that the peace negotiators in 1782 had yet heard of his exploits.

While Clark's captives traveled eastward, a much larger American expedition moved through western Pennsylvania to attack Iroquois strongholds in western New York. There the Tories and Indians had terrorized frontier settlements all through the summer of 1778. Led by the charismatic Mohawk Joseph Brant, the Iroquois killed hundreds of militiamen along the Pennsylvania frontier. In response, Washington dispatched an expedition of 4,000 men under General John Sullivan. At

The Mohawk leader Thayendanegea (Joseph Brant), who fought against the Americans in the Revolution. Portrait painted by Gilbert Stuart in 1786.

Newton (now Elmira) on August 29, 1779, Sullivan defeated the only serious opposition and proceeded to carry out Washington's instruction that the Iroquois country be not "merely overrun but destroyed." The American force burned about forty Seneca and Cayuga villages together with their orchards and food supplies, leaving many of the Indians homeless and without enough provisions to survive. The action broke the power of the Iroquois federation for all time, but it did not completely pacify the frontier. Sporadic encounters with various tribes of the region continued to the end of the war.

In the Kentucky territory, Daniel Boone and his small band of settlers risked constant attack from the Shawnees and their British and Tory allies. During the Revolution, they survived frequent ambushes, at least seven skirmishes, and three pitched battles. In 1778 Boone and some thirty men, aided by their wives and children, held off an assault by more than 400 Indians at Boonesborough. Thereafter, Boone himself was twice shot and twice captured. Indians killed two of his sons, a brother, and two brothers-in-law. His daughter was captured and another brother was wounded four times. Despite such ferocious fighting and dangerous circumstances, the white settlers refused to leave Kentucky.

In early 1776 a delegation of northern Indians—Shawnees, Delawares, and Mohawks—had talked the Cherokees into striking at frontier settlements in Virginia and the Carolinas. Swift retaliation followed as South Carolina forces burned the lower Cherokee towns and destroyed all the corn they could get their hands on. Virginia and North Carolina militia brought a similar destruction upon the middle and upper towns. Once again, in 1780, a Virginia–North Carolina force wrought destruction on the Cherokees, killing twenty-nine Indians and burning over 1,000 towns and 50,000 bushels of corn, along with other supplies, lest the Indians go to the aid of General Cornwallis. By weakening the major Indian tribes along the frontier, the American Revolution, among its other results, cleared the way for rapid settlement of the trans-Appalachian West after the war.

THE WAR IN THE SOUTH

At the end of 1778 the focus of British action shifted suddenly to the south. The whole region from Virginia southward had been free from major action since 1776. Now the British would test King George's belief that a sleeping Tory power in the South needed only the presence of a few redcoats to awaken it. General Clinton decided to take Savannah, Georgia, and roll northward, gathering momentum from the Loyalist countryside. For a while the idea seemed to work, but it ran afoul of two developments: first, the Loyalist strength was less than estimated; and second, the British forces behaved so harshly that they drove even Loyalists into rebellion.

SAVANNAH AND CHARLESTON   In November 1778 Clinton dispatched units under Lieutenant-Colonel Archibald Campbell from New York and New Jersey to join General Augustin Prevost's Florida Rangers in attacking Savannah. So small was the defending force of Continentals and militia that the British quickly overwhelmed the Patriots, took the town, and brushed aside opposition in the interior. There followed a byplay of thrust and parry between British and South Carolinian forces until the redcoats under Prevost finally drove toward Charleston, plundering plantation houses along the way.

The seesaw campaign took a major turn when General Clinton accompanied by General Charles Cornwallis brought new naval and land forces southward to join a massive amphibious attack that bottled up American general Benjamin Lincoln on the Charleston peninsula. On May 12, 1780, Lincoln surrendered the city and its 5,500 defenders, the greatest single American loss of the war. At this point Congress,

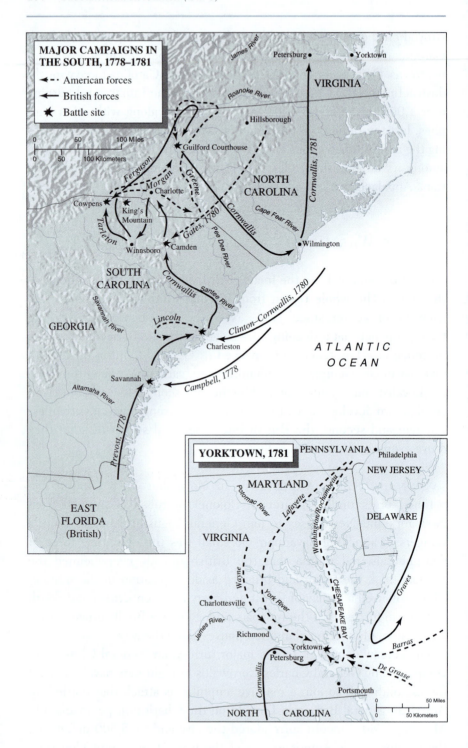

MAJOR CAMPAIGNS IN THE SOUTH, 1778–1781

- American forces
- British forces
- ★ Battle site

0   50   100 Miles
0   50   100 Kilometers

James River
Petersburg
Yorktown
Roanoke River
VIRGINIA
Hillsborough
Guilford Courthouse
Ferguson
Morgan
Greene
NORTH CAROLINA
Cornwallis, 1781
Charlotte
Cowpens
King's Mountain
Tarleton
Cornwallis
Cape Fear River
Winnsboro
Camden
Gates, 1780
Pee Dee River
Wilmington
SOUTH CAROLINA
Cornwallis
Santee River
Savannah River
GEORGIA
Lincoln
Clinton–Cornwallis, 1780
Charleston
ATLANTIC OCEAN
Savannah
Campbell, 1778
Altamaha River
Prevost, 1778
EAST FLORIDA (British)

YORKTOWN, 1781

PENNSYLVANIA
Philadelphia
NEW JERSEY
MARYLAND
Potomac River
Washington/Rochambeau
Lafayette
DELAWARE
VIRGINIA
Wayne
York River
Graves
Charlottesville
CHESAPEAKE BAY
James River
Richmond
Yorktown
Barras
Petersburg
De Grasse
Cornwallis
Portsmouth
0   50 Miles
0   50 Kilometers
NORTH   CAROLINA

against Washington's advice, turned to the victor of Saratoga, Horatio Gates, to take command and sent him south. Clinton returned to New York and left General Cornwallis in charge of the British troops in the South. Cornwallis led three columns from Charleston to subdue the Carolina interior and surprised Gates's force at Camden, South Carolina, routing his new army, which retreated all the way back to Hillsborough, North Carolina, 160 miles away. It had come to pass as Gates's friend and neighbor Charles Lee had warned after Saratoga: "Beware that your Northern laurels do not turn to Southern willows."

THE CAROLINAS   From the point of view of British imperial goals, the southern colonies were ultimately more important than the northern ones because they produced valuable staple crops such as tobacco, indigo, and naval stores. The war in the Carolinas eventually involved not only opposing British and American armies, but also degenerated into brutal guerrilla-style civil conflicts between local Loyalists and local Patriots. Such infighting brought chaos.

Cornwallis had South Carolina just about under control, but his subordinates Banastre Tarleton and Patrick Ferguson, who mobilized Tory militiamen, overreached themselves in their effort to subdue the Whigs. "Tarleton's Quarter" became bywords for savagery, because "Bloody Tarleton" gave little quarter to vanquished foes. Ferguson sealed his own doom when he threatened to march over the mountains and hang the leaders of the Watauga country. Instead the feisty "overmountain men" went after Ferguson and, allied with other backcountry Whigs, caught him and his Tories on King's Mountain, just inside South Carolina. There, on October 7, 1780, they routed his force. By then feelings were so strong that American irregulars continued firing on Tories trying to surrender and later inflicted indiscriminate slaughter on Tory prisoners. King's Mountain was the turning point of the war in the South. By proving that the British were not invincible, it emboldened small farmers to join guerrilla bands under partisan leaders such as Francis Marion, "the Swamp Fox," and Thomas Sumter, "the Gamecock."

While the overmountain men were closing in on Ferguson, Congress had chosen a new commander for the southern theater, General Nathanael Greene, the "fighting Quaker" of Rhode Island. A man of infinite patience, skilled at managing men and saving supplies, careful to avoid needless risks, he was suited to a war of attrition against the British forces. From Charlotte, where he arrived in December 1780, Greene moved his army eastward toward the Pee Dee River. As a diversion he sent General Daniel Morgan with about 700 men on a sweep to the west of Cornwallis's headquarters at Winnsboro.

Taking a position near Cowpens, a cow-grazing area in northern South Carolina, Morgan found himself swamped by militia units joining him faster than he could provide for them. Tarleton caught Morgan and his men on January 17, 1781, with the rain-swollen Broad River at their backs—a position Morgan took deliberately to force the green militiamen to stand and fight. Once the battle was joined, Tarleton mistook a readjustment in the American line for a militia panic, and rushed his men into a destructive fire. Tarleton and a handful of cavalry escaped, but more than 100 of his men were killed and more than 700 were taken prisoner.

Morgan then fell back into North Carolina, linked up with Greene's main force at Guilford Courthouse (now Greensboro), and then led Cornwallis on a wild goose chase up to the Dan River. Once the Americans had crossed, the British could not follow, for their supplies were running low. Cornwallis was forced to draw back to Hillsborough. When reinforcements from Virginia and the Carolinas arrived, Greene returned to Guilford Courthouse and offered battle on March 15, 1781. Having inflicted heavy losses, the Americans prudently withdrew to fight another day.

Cornwallis marched off toward the coast at Wilmington to lick his wounds and take on new supplies. Greene then resolved to go back into South Carolina in the hope of drawing Cornwallis after him or forcing the British to give up the state. There he joined forces with the guerrillas already active on the scene, and in a series of brilliant actions kept losing battles while winning the war: "We fight, get beat, rise, and fight again," he said. By September 1781 he had narrowed British control in the Deep South to Charleston and Savannah, although for more than a year longer Whigs and Tories slashed at each other "with savage fury" in the backcountry, where there was "nothing but murder and devastation in every quarter," Greene said.

Meanwhile Cornwallis had headed north away from Greene, reasoning that Virginia must be eliminated as a source of reinforcement before the Carolinas could be subdued. In May 1781 he marched north into

A crowd parading through Philadelphia prior to burning an effigy of Benedict Arnold as "Spy Traytor" (1780).

Virginia. There, since December 1780, Benedict Arnold, now a *British* general, was engaged in a war of maneuver against American forces under the French marquis de Lafayette and the Prussian baron von Steuben. Arnold, until September 1780, had been American commander at West Point. Overweening in ambition, lacking in moral scruples, and a reckless spender on his fashionable wife, Arnold had nursed a grudge against Washington over an official reprimand for his extravagances as commander of reoccupied Philadelphia. Traitors have a price, and Arnold had found his: he had crassly plotted to sell out the West Point garrison to the British, and he even suggested how they might capture Washington himself. Only the fortuitous capture of the British go-between, Major John André, had ended Arnold's plot. Forewarned that his plan had been discovered, Arnold had joined the British in New York while the Americans hanged André as a spy.

YORKTOWN When Cornwallis linked up with Arnold at Petersburg, their combined forces rose to 7,200, far more than the small American force there. The arrival of American reinforcements under Anthony Wayne and the marquis de Lafayette led Cornwallis to pick Yorktown as a defensible site. There appeared to be little reason to worry about a siege, since Washington's main land force seemed preoccupied with attacking New York and the British navy controlled American waters.

To be sure, there was a small American navy, but it was no match for the British fleet. Yet American privateers distracted and wounded the British fleet. Most celebrated were the exploits of Captain John Paul

Jones. Off England's coast on September 23, 1779, Jones won a desperate battle with a British frigate, which he captured and occupied before his own ship sank. This was the occasion for his stirring and oft-repeated response to a British demand for surrender: "I have not yet begun to fight."

Still, such heroics were little more than nuisances to the British. But at a critical point, thanks to the French navy, the British lost control of the Chesapeake waters. Indeed, it is impossible to imagine an American victory in the Revolution without the assistance of the French. As long as the British navy maintained supremacy at sea, the Americans could not hope to force a settlement to their advantage. For three years Washington had waited to get some military benefit from the French alliance. In July 1780 the French had finally landed a force of about 6,000 at Newport, which the British had given up to concentrate on the South, but the French army under the comte de Rochambeau and the French navy under the comte de Barras had sat there for a year, blockaded by the British fleet.

Then, in 1781, the elements for combined action suddenly fell into place. In May, as Cornwallis moved into Virginia, Washington persuaded Rochambeau to join forces for an attack on New York. The two armies linked up in July, but before they could strike at New York, word came from the West Indies that Admiral de Grasse was bound for the Chesapeake with his entire French fleet and some 3,000 soldiers. Washington and Rochambeau immediately set out toward Yorktown, all the while preserving the semblance of a flank movement against New York. Meanwhile, Barras slipped out of the British barricade at Newport and also headed south toward Chesapeake Bay.

On August 30 de Grasse's fleet reached Yorktown, and he landed his troops to join the American force already watching Cornwallis. On September 6, the day after a British fleet appeared, de Grasse gave battle and forced the British to give up the effort to relieve Cornwallis, whose fate was quickly sealed. De Grasse then sent ships up the Chesapeake to ferry down Washington's and Rochambeau's armies, which brought the total American and French forces to more than 16,000, or better than double the size of Cornwallis's army.

The siege began on September 28. At one point during the attack, Washington and his staff came under fire as they observed the action. A worried aide suggested to the commanding general that perhaps he should "step back a little." Washington tersely replied: "Colonel Cobb,

British troops grounding their arms at the surrender at Yorktown in 1781.

if you are afraid, you have the liberty to step back." On October 14 two major redoubts guarding the left of the British line fell to French and American attackers, the latter led by Washington's aide Alexander Hamilton. A British counterattack failed to retake them. Later that day a squall forced Cornwallis to abandon a desperate plan to escape across the York River. On October 17, 1781, four years to the day after Saratoga, Cornwallis sued for peace, and on October 19 the British force of more than 7,000 marched out, their colors cased, as the British band played somber tunes along with the English nursery rhyme "The World Turned Upside Down." Cornwallis himself claimed to be too "ill" to appear. His dispatch to his superior was telling: "I have the mortification to inform your Excellency that I have been forced to . . . surrender the troops under my command."

NEGOTIATIONS

Whatever lingering hopes of victory the British may have harbored vanished at Yorktown. "Oh God, it's all over," Lord North groaned at news of the surrender. On February 27, 1782, the House of Commons voted against continuing the war, and on March 5 authorized the crown

American Commissioners of the Preliminary Peace Negotiations with Great Britain, *a painting by Benjamin West. From left, John Jay, John Adams, Benjamin Franklin, Henry Laurens, and Franklin's nephew, William Temple Franklin (1782).*

to make peace. On March 20 Lord North resigned. The new ministry included old friends of the Americans headed by the duke of Rockingham, who had brought about repeal of the Stamp Act. The new colonial minister, Lord Shelburne, became chief minister after Rockingham's death in September and directed negotiations with American commissioners.

The Continental Congress named a five-man commission to negotiate a peace treaty. Only three members of the commission were active, however: John Adams, who was on state business in the Netherlands; John Jay, minister to Spain; and Benjamin Franklin, already in Paris. Franklin and Jay did most of the work.

The French commitment to Spain complicated matters. Spain and the United States were both allied with France, but not with each other. America was bound by its alliance to fight on until the French made peace, and the French were bound to help the Spanish recover Gibraltar from England. Unable to deliver Gibraltar, or so the tough-minded Jay reasoned, the French might try to bargain off American land west of the Appalachians in its place. Fearful that the French were angling for a separate peace with the British, Jay persuaded Franklin to play the same game. Ignoring their instructions to consult fully with the French, they agreed to further talks with the British. On November 30, 1782, the talks produced a preliminary treaty with Great Britain. If it violated the spirit of the alliance, it did not violate the strict letter of the treaty with France, for the French minister was notified the day before

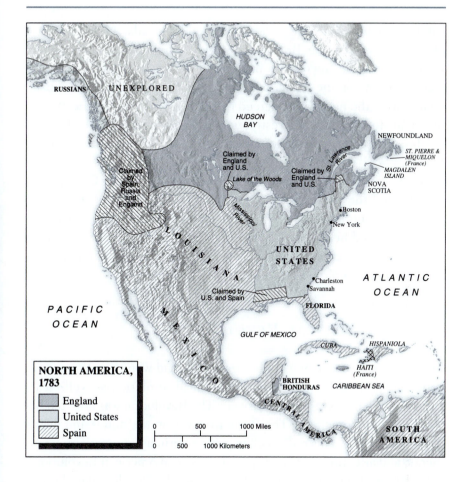

NORTH AMERICA, 1783

England
United States
Spain

RUSSIANS   UNEXPLORED

HUDSON BAY

NEWFOUNDLAND

Claimed by England and U.S.

Lake of the Woods

Claimed by England and U.S.

St. Lawrence River

ST. PIERRE & MIQUELON *(France)*

MAGDALEN ISLAND

NOVA SCOTIA

Claimed by Spain, Russia and England

Mississippi River

UNITED STATES

•Boston
•New York

L O U I S I A N A

ATLANTIC OCEAN

•Charleston
•Savannah

Claimed by U.S. and Spain

FLORIDA

PACIFIC OCEAN

M E X I C O

GULF OF MEXICO

CUBA   HISPANIOLA

HAITI *(France)*

BRITISH HONDURAS   CARIBBEAN SEA

C E N T R A L   A M E R I C A

SOUTH AMERICA

0   500   1000 Miles

0   500   1000 Kilometers

it was signed, and final agreement still depended on a Franco-British settlement.

THE PEACE OF PARIS   Early in 1783 France and Spain gave up on Gibraltar and reached an armistice with Britain. The final signing of the Peace of Paris came on September 3, 1783. In accord with the bargain already struck, Great Britain recognized the independence of the United States and agreed to a Mississippi River boundary to the west. Both the northern and southern borders left ambiguities that would require further definition. Florida, as it turned out, passed back to Spain. The British further granted Americans the "liberty" of fishing off Newfoundland and in the St. Lawrence Gulf, and the right to dry their catches on the unsettled Atlantic coast of Canada. On the matter of debts, the best the British could get was a promise that British merchants should "meet with no legal impediment" in seeking to collect them. And on the tender point of Loyalists whose estates had been confiscated, the negotiators agreed that Congress would "earnestly recommend" to the states the restoration of confiscated property. Each of the last two points was little more than a face-saving gesture for the British.

On November 24 the last British troops left New York City, and on December 4 they evacuated Staten Island and Long Island. That same day Washington took leave of his officers in New York. On December 23 he appeared before the Continental Congress, meeting in Annapolis, to resign his commission. Before the end of the next day he was back at Mount Vernon, home in time for Christmas.

THE POLITICAL REVOLUTION

REPUBLICAN IDEOLOGY The Americans had won their War for Independence. Had they undergone a political revolution as well? Years later, John Adams offered one answer: "The Revolution was effected before the war commenced. The Revolution was in the minds and hearts of the people. . . . This radical change in the principles, opinions, sentiments, and affections of the people, was the real American Revolution." Yet Adams's observation ignores the fact that the Revolutionary War itself served as the catalyst for a prolonged internal debate about what new forms of government would best serve an independent republic. The conventional British model of mixed government sought to balance monarchy, aristocracy, and the common people and thereby protect individual liberty. Because of the more democratic nature of their society, however, Americans knew that they must derive new political assumptions and institutions. They had no monarchy or aristocracy. Yet how could sovereignty reside in the common people? How could Americans ensure the survival of a republican form of government, long assumed to be the most fragile? The war thus provoked a spate of state constitution-making that remains unique in human history.

A struggle for the rights of English citizens became a fight for independence in which those rights found expression in governments that

America Triumphant and Britannia in Distress (*1782*).

were new, yet deeply rooted in the colonial experience and the prevailing viewpoints of Whiggery and the Enlightenment. With the Loyalists displaced or dispersed, such ideas as the contract theory of government, the sovereignty of the people, the separation of powers, and natural rights found their way into the new frames of government that were devised while the fight went on—amid other urgent business.

The very idea of republican government was a radical departure in that day. Americans began to see themselves in a new light, no longer the rustic provincials in a backwater of European culture but rather the embodiment of the civic virtue deemed necessary to the success of a republican form of government. As free citizens of a republic, Americans would cast off the corruptions of the Old World and usher in a new reign of liberty and virtue, not only for themselves but for all peoples. The new American republic, in other words, would endure as long as the majority of the people were virtuous and willingly placed the good of society above the self-interest of individuals. Herein lay the hope and the danger of the new American experiment in popular government: even as leaders enthusiastically fashioned new state constitutions, they feared that their experiments in republicanism would fail because of a lack of civic virtue.

NEW STATE CONSTITUTIONS   Most of the political experimentation between 1776 and 1787 occurred at the state level. Innovations
devised in the state constitutional conventions created the core principle of the American political system: representative government defined in written constitutions in which the people are sovereign and
delegate limited authority to the government. In addition, the states initiated bills of rights guaranteeing particular individual rights, and fashioned procedures for constitutional conventions that have also remained an essential part of the American political system. In sum, the
innovations at the state level during the Revolution created a reservoir
of ideas and experience that formed the basis for the creation of the
federal constitution in 1787.

At the onset of the fighting every colony saw the departure of governors and other officials, and usually the expulsion of Loyalists from the
assemblies, which then assumed power as provincial "congresses" or
"conventions." But they were acting as revolutionary bodies without any
legal basis for the exercise of authority. In two of the states this presented little difficulty. Connecticut and Rhode Island, which had been
virtually little republics as corporate colonies, simply purged their charters of any reference to colonial ties. Massachusetts followed their example until 1780.

In the other states the prevailing notions of social contract and popular sovereignty led to written constitutions that specified the framework
and powers of government. One of the lessons of the Revolution was
the danger of relying on the vague body of law and precedent that made
up the unwritten constitution of Britain. Constitution-making in fact
had begun even before independence. In 1776 Congress advised the
colonies to set up new governments "under the authority of the people."
At first the authority of the people was exercised by legislatures, which
simply adopted constitutions and implemented them. But they had little more status than ordinary statutory law, it could be argued, since the
people had no chance to express their wishes directly.

When the Massachusetts assembly hastily submitted a constitution
to the towns for approval, however, it was rejected. Massachusetts
thereupon invented what became a standard device for American constitution-making: a body separate from and superior to the legislature to
exercise the people's sovereignty. In 1779–1780 Massachusetts elected
a special convention, chosen for the specific purpose of making a con-

stitution. The invention of the constitutional convention was an altogether original contribution to the art of government, and one that other states copied. The resultant document went out to the town meetings with the provision that two-thirds or more would have to ratify it, which they did.

The first state constitutions varied mainly in detail. They formed governments much like the colonial governments, with elected governors and senates instead of appointed governors and councils. Generally they embodied, sometimes explicitly, a separation of powers as a safeguard against abuses. Most of them also included a bill of rights that protected the time-honored rights of petition, freedom of speech, trial by jury, freedom from self-incrimination, and the like. Most tended to limit the powers of governors and increase the powers of the legislatures, which had led the people in their quarrels with the colonial governors. Pennsylvania went so far as to eliminate the governor and upper house of the legislature altogether. It had an executive council of twelve, including a president, and operated until 1790 with a unicameral legislature limited only by a house of "censors" who reviewed its work every five years.

THE ARTICLES OF CONFEDERATION The central government, like the state governments, grew out of an extralegal revolutionary body. The Continental Congress exercised governmental powers without any constitutional sanction before March 1781. Plans for a permanent frame of government were started very early, however. Richard Henry Lee's motion for independence included a call for a plan of confederation. As early as July 1776, a committee headed by John Dickinson produced a draft constitution, the "Articles of Confederation and Perpetual Union." For more than a year Congress debated the articles in between more urgent matters and finally adopted them in November 1777, subject to ratification by all the states. All states ratified promptly except Maryland, which stubbornly insisted that the seven states claiming western lands should cede them to the authority of Congress. Maryland did not relent until early 1781, when Virginia gave up its claims under the old colonial charter to the vast region north of the Ohio River. New York had already relinquished a dubious claim based on its "jurisdiction" over the Iroquois, and the other states eventually abandoned their charter claims, although Georgia did not until 1802.

When the Articles of Confederation became effective in March 1781, they did little more than legalize the status quo. "The United States in Congress Assembled" had a multitude of responsibilities but little authority to carry them out. The Congress was intended not as a legislature, nor as a sovereign entity unto itself, but as a collective substitute for the monarch. In essence, it was to be a plural executive rather than a parliamentary body. It had full power over foreign affairs and questions of war and peace; it could decide disputes between the states; it had authority over coinage, postal service, and Indian affairs, and responsibility for the government of the western territories. But it had no courts and no power to enforce its resolutions and ordinances upon either states or individuals. It also had no power to levy taxes, but had to rely on requisitions, which state legislatures could ignore at their will.

The states, after their battles with Parliament, were in no mood for a strong central government. The Congress in fact had less power than the colonists had once accepted in Parliament, since it could not regulate interstate and foreign commerce. For certain important acts, moreover, a "special majority" was required. Nine states had to approve measures dealing with war, privateering, treaties, coinage, finances, or the army and navy. Unanimous approval of the states was needed to levy tariffs (often called "duties") on imports. Amendments to the articles also required unanimous ratification by all the states. The Confederation had neither an executive nor a judicial branch; there was no administrative head of government (only the president of the Congress, chosen annually) and no federal courts.

For all its weaknesses, however, the Confederation government represented the most pragmatic structure for the new nation. After all, the Revolution on the battlefields had yet to be won, and America's statesmen could not risk the prolonged and divisive debates over the distribution of power that other forms of government would have provoked.

The Social Revolution

Americans forged a consensus on the general frame of government—the forms grew so naturally out of experience and the prevalent theories. On other points, however, there was sharp disagreement. Political revolutions easily spawn social revolutions. Just as the Great

Awakening brought with it unintended social effects, the turmoil from the Revolution allowed long pent-up frustrations among the lower ranks to find expression. What did the Revolution mean to those workers, servants, farmers, and freed slaves who participated in the Stamp Act demonstrations, supported the boycotts, idolized Tom Paine, and fought with Washington and Greene?

Many laboring folk hoped that the Revolution would remove, not reinforce, the elite's traditional political and social advantages. The more conservative Patriots would have been content to replace royal officials with the rich, the well-born, and the able, and let it go at that. But more radical elements raised the question not only of home rule but of who should rule at home.

EQUALITY AND ITS LIMITS   This spirit of equality found outlet in several directions, one of which was simply a weakening of old habits of deference. A Virginia gentleman told of being in a tavern when a rough group of farmers came in, spitting and pulling off their muddy boots without regard to the sensibilities of the gentlemen present: "The spirit of independence was converted into equality," he wrote, "and every one who bore arms, esteems himself upon a footing with his neighbors. . . . No doubt each of these men considers himself, in every respect, my equal." No doubt each did.

In this watercolor by Benjamin Latrobe, a gentleman played billiards with artisans, suggesting that "the spirit of independence was converted into equality."

What was more, participation in the army or militia excited people who had taken little interest in politics before. The large number of new political opportunities afforded by the creation of state governments led more ordinary citizens into participation than ever before. The social base of the new legislatures was thus much broader than that of the old assemblies.

Men fighting for their liberty found it difficult to justify denying other white men the rights of suffrage and representation. The property qualifications for voting, which already admitted an overwhelming majority of white males, were lowered still further. In Pennsylvania, Delaware, North Carolina, Georgia, and Vermont, any male taxpayer could vote, although officeholders usually had to meet higher property requirements. Men who had argued against taxation without representation now questioned the denial of proportionate representation for the backcountry, which generally enlarged its presence in the legislatures. More often than not the political newcomers were men of lesser property and little formal education. All states concentrated much power in a legislature chosen by a wide suffrage, but not even Pennsylvania, which adopted the most radical of the state constitutions, went quite so far as universal manhood suffrage.

New developments in land tenure that grew out of the Revolution extended the democratic trends of suffrage requirements. Confiscations resulted in the seizure of Tory estates by all the state legislatures. These properties, however, were of small consequence in contrast to the unsettled areas formerly at the disposal of crown and proprietors, now in the hands of popular assemblies. Much of this land was now used for bonuses to veterans of the war. Moreover, western lands, formerly closed by the Proclamation of 1763 and the Quebec Act of 1774, were soon thrown open for settlers.

THE PARADOX OF SLAVERY   The Revolutionary generation of leaders was the first to confront the issue of slavery and to consider abolishing it. The principles of liberty and equality had clear implications for enslaved blacks. Jefferson's draft of the Declaration of Independence had indicted the king for having violated the "most sacred rights of life and liberty of a distant people, who never offended him, captivating them into slavery in another hemisphere," but the clause was deleted "in complaisance to South Carolina and Georgia." The clause was in fact inaccurate in completely ignoring the implication of American slaveholders and slave traders in the traffic. Before the Revolution, only Rhode Island, Connecticut, and Pennsylvania had halted the importation of slaves. After independence, all the states except Georgia stopped the traffic, although South Carolina later reopened it.

Black soldiers or sailors were present at most of the major battles, from Lexington to Yorktown; most were on the Loyalist side. Lord Dunmore, governor of Virginia, anticipated a general British policy in 1775 when he promised freedom to slaves, as well as indentured servants, who would bear arms for the Loyalist cause. Taking alarm at this, General Washington at the end of 1775 reversed the policy of excluding blacks from American forces—except the few already in militia companies—and Congress quickly approved. Only two states, South Carolina and Georgia, held out completely against the policy, but by a rough estimate few blacks, probably no more than about 5,000, were admitted to the total American forces of about 300,000, and most of those were free blacks from northern states. They served mainly in white units, although Massachusetts did organize two all-black companies, and Rhode Island organized one.

Slaves who served in the cause of independence won their freedom and in some cases land bounties. But the British army, which carried off probably tens of thousands of slaves during the war, was a greater instrument of emancipation than the American forces. Most of the newly freed blacks found their way to Canada or to British colonies in the Caribbean. American Whigs showed no mercy to blacks who were caught aiding or abetting the British cause. A Charleston mob hanged and then burned Thomas Jeremiah, a free black who was convicted of telling slaves that the British "were come to help the poor Negroes." White Loyalists who were caught stirring up slave militancy were tarred and feathered.

In the northern states, which had fewer slaves than the southern states, the doctrines of liberty led swiftly to emancipation for all either during the fighting or shortly afterward. Vermont's Constitution of 1777 specifically forbade slavery. The Massachusetts Constitution of 1780 proclaimed the "inherent liberty" of all. In 1780 Pennsylvania provided that all children born thereafter to slave mothers would become free at age twenty-eight, after enabling their owners to recover their initial cost. In 1784 Rhode Island provided freedom for all children of slaves

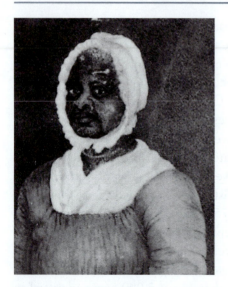

Elizabeth Freeman, born in Africa around 1742, was sold as a slave to a Massachusetts family. She won her freedom by claiming in court that the "inherent liberty" of all applied to slaves as well.

born thereafter, at age twenty-one for males, eighteen for females. New York lagged until 1799 in granting freedom to mature slaves born after enactment, but an act of 1817 set July 4, 1827, as the date for emancipation of all remaining slaves.

In the states south of Pennsylvania, emancipation was less popular. Yet even there slaveholders like Washington, Jefferson, Patrick Henry, and others expressed moral qualms. Jefferson wrote in his *Notes on Virginia* (1785): "Indeed I tremble for my country when I reflect that God is just; that his justice cannot sleep forever." But he, like many other white southerners could not bring himself to free his slaves. In the southern states, antislavery sentiment went no further than a relaxation of the manumission laws under which owners might free their slaves as individual acts. It is estimated that some 10,000 slaves in Virginia were manumitted during the 1780s. A much smaller number would be shipped back to Africa during the early nineteenth century. By the outbreak of the Civil War in 1861, approximately half of the blacks living in Maryland were free.

Manumission, of course, freed slaves by the action of a white owner. But slaves, especially in the upper South, also earned freedom through their own actions during the Revolutionary era, frequently by running away. They often gravitated to the growing number of African-American communities in the North. Because of emancipation laws in the northern states, and with the formation of free black neighborhoods in the

North and in several southern cities, runaways found refuge and the opportunities for new lives. Many of these free blacks used the egalitarian rhetoric spawned by the Revolution to speak out against the evils of slavery. It is estimated that 55,000 slaves fled to freedom during the Revolution.

THE STATUS OF WOMEN   The logic of liberty applied to the status of women as much as to that of blacks. Women in the colonies had remained essentially confined to the domestic sphere during the eighteenth century. They could not vote or preach or hold office. Few had access to formal education. Although both single and married women could own property and execute contracts, in several colonies married women could not legally own real or personal property—even their own clothes—and they had no legal rights over their children. Divorces were extremely difficult to obtain.

Initially, women predicted that the Revolution would do little to improve their social status. Soon after the fighting started, Margaret Livingston of New York wrote her sister that "our Sex are doomed to be obedient in every stage of life so that we shant be gainers by this contest."

Yet the Revolutionary ferment offered women new opportunities and engendered in many a new outlook. The war drew women at least tem-

Frontispiece from Lady's Magazine, 1792. *"The Genius of the Ladies Magazine, accompanied by the Genius of Emulation, who carries in her hand a laurel crown, approaches Liberty, and kneeling, presents her with a copy of the Rights of Woman."* The Lady's Magazine *reprinted extensive extracts from Mary Wollstonecraft's A Vindication of the Rights of Woman (1792).*

A woodcut of Hannah Snell, which appeared in the book Life and Adventures of a Female Soldier.

porarily into new pursuits. They plowed fields and melted down pots and pans to make shot. Esther Reed of Philadelphia organized a ladies' association that raised money to provide comforts for the troops. Women supported the armies in various roles, such as handling supplies, serving as couriers, and working as camp followers—cooking, cleaning, and nursing the soldiers. Wives often followed their husbands to camp, and on occasion took their places in the line, as Margaret Corbin did at Fort Washington when her husband fell at his artillery post, or Mary Ludwig Hays (better known as Molly Pitcher) did when her husband collapsed of heat exhaustion. An exceptional case was that of Deborah Sampson, who joined a Massachusetts regiment as "Robert Shurtleff" and served from 1781 to 1783 by the "artful concealment" of her sex.

To be sure, most women retained the circumscribed domestic outlook that had long been imposed on them by society. But a few free-spirited reformers argued that only educated and independent mothers could raise children fit for republican citizenship. Some demanded equal treatment. In an essay entitled "On the Equality of the Sexes," written in 1779 and published in 1790, Judith Sargent Murray of Gloucester, Massachusetts, stressed the importance of mutuality in marriage: "Mutual esteem, mutual friendship, mutual confidence, begirt about by mutual forbearance." Murray and others insisted that women were perfectly capable of excelling outside the domestic sphere.

Early in the Revolutionary struggle, Abigail Adams, one of the most learned, spirited, and independent women of the time, wrote to her husband John: "In the new Code of Laws which I suppose it will be necessary for you to make I desire you would remember the Ladies. . . . Do not put such unlimited power into the hands of the Husbands." Since men were "Naturally Tyrannical," she wrote, "why then, not put it out of the power of the vicious and the Lawless to use us with cruelty and indignity with impunity." Otherwise, "If particular care and attention is not paid to the Ladies we are determined to foment a Rebellion, and will not hold ourselves bound by any Laws in which we have no voice, or Representation."

Husband John expressed surprise that women might be discontented, but he clearly knew the privileges enjoyed by males and was determined to retain them: "Depend upon it, we know better than to repeal our Masculine systems." Thomas Jefferson was of one mind with Adams on this matter. When asked about women's voting rights, he replied that "the tender breasts of ladies were not formed for political convulsion."

The legal status of women did not improve dramatically as a result of the Revolutionary ferment, even though in Pennsylvania and parts of New England divorces were somewhat easier to obtain after the Revolution. One Connecticut woman, for instance, successfully brought suit against her husband on the grounds that he "rendered her life miserable by frequent beating with brutal violence, almost constant intoxication and lascivious conduct with several lewd women." But married women in most of the states still forfeited control of their own property to their husbands, and women gained no permanent political rights. Under the 1776 New Jersey constitution, which neglected to specify an exclusively male franchise because the delegates apparently took the distinction for granted, women who met the property qualifications for voting exercised the right until they were denied access early in the nineteenth century.

FREEDOM OF RELIGION   The Revolution also set in motion a transition from the toleration of religious dissent to a complete freedom of religion in the separation of church and state. The Anglican church, established in five colonies and parts of two others, was especially vulnerable because of its association with the crown and because dissenters outnumbered Anglicans in most states except Virginia. And all but Virginia removed tax support for the church before the fighting was over. In 1776 the Virginia Declaration of Rights guaranteed the free ex-

The Congregational church developed a national presence in the early nineteenth century, and Lemuel Haynes, depicted here, was its first black preacher.

ercise of religion, and in 1786 the Virginia Statute of Religious Freedom (written by Thomas Jefferson) declared that "no man shall be compelled to frequent or support any religious worship, place or ministry whatsoever" and "that all men shall be free to profess, and by argument to maintain, their opinions in matters of religion." These statutes and the Revolutionary ideology that spawned them helped shape the course that religion would take in the new United States: pluralistic and voluntary rather than state supported and monolithic.

In churches as well as in government, the Revolution set off a period of constitution-making, as some of the first national church bodies emerged. In 1784 the Methodists, who at first were an offshoot of the Anglicans, came together in a general conference at Baltimore under Bishop Francis Asbury. The Anglican church, rechristened Episcopal, gathered in a series of meetings which by 1789 had united the various dioceses in a federal union; in 1789 the Presbyterians also held their first general assembly in Philadelphia. The following year, the Catholic church had its first bishop in the United States when John Carroll was named bishop of Baltimore. Other churches would follow in the process of coming together on a national basis.

EMERGENCE OF AN AMERICAN CULTURE

The Revolution helped generate among some Americans a sense of common nationality. As early as the Stamp Act Congress of 1765, Christopher Gadsden, leader of the Charleston radicals, had said: "There ought to be no New England man, no New Yorker, known on the Continent; but all of us Americans." In the First Continental Congress, Patrick Henry asserted that such a sense of identity had come to pass: "The distinctions between Virginians, Pennsylvanians, New Yorkers, and New Englanders are no more. I am not a Virginian but an American."

The concrete experience of the war reinforced the rhetoric. Soldiers who went to fight in other states broadened their horizons. John Marshall, future chief justice, served first in the Virginia militia and then in the Continental army in the Middle States and endured the winter of 1777–1778 at Valley Forge. He later wrote: "I found myself associated with brave men from different states who were risking life and everything valuable in a common cause. I was confirmed in the habit of considering America as my country and Congress as my government." The Revolution thus marked the start of a national consciousness and a national tradition.

ART IN THE NEW NATION The Revolution provided the first generation of native artists with inspirational subjects. It also filled them with high expectations that individual freedom would release creative energies and vitalize both commerce and the arts. In fact, the late eighteenth century did witness a sudden efflorescence of the arts.

Ironically, the best American painters of the time spent all or most of the Revolution in England, studying with Benjamin West of Pennsylvania and John Singleton Copley of Massachusetts, both of whom had set up shop in London before the outbreak of war. Even John Trumbull, who had served in the siege of Boston and the Saratoga campaign, somehow managed a visit to London during the war before returning to help supply the Continentals. Later he adopted patriotic themes in *The Battle of Bunker Hill*, and in his four panels in the Capitol Rotunda in Washington: *The Declaration of Independence*, *The Surrender of General Burgoyne*, *Surrender of Lord Cornwallis*, and *The Resignation of General Washington*. Charles Willson Peale, who fought at Trenton and Prince-

Surrender of Lord Cornwallis. *John Trumbull completed his painting of the pivotal British surrender at Yorktown in 1794.*

ton and survived the winter at Valley Forge, produced a virtual portrait gallery of Revolutionary War figures. Over twenty-three years he painted George Washington seven times from life and produced in all sixty portraits of him.

INDEPENDENCE DAY One of the first ways to forge a national consciousness was through the annual celebration of the new nation's independence from Great Britain. On July 2, 1776, when the Second Continental Congress had resolved "that these United Colonies are, and of right ought to be, free and independent states," John Adams had written his wife Abigail that future generations would remember that date as their "day of deliverance." Adams realized that celebrating of the birth of the nation would help to unite a disparate republic. People, he predicted, would celebrate the occasion with "solemn acts of devotion to God Almighty" and with "pomp and parade, with shows, games, sports, guns, bells, bonfires and illuminations [fireworks] from one end of this continent to the other, from this time forward, forever more."

Adams got everything right but the date. Americans fastened not upon July 2 but July 4 as their Independence Day. To be sure, it was on the Fourth that Congress formally adopted the Declaration of Independence and ordered it to be printed and distributed within the states, but America by then had been officially independent for two days. The Declaration of Independence was not read in public until July 8 and was not copied onto parchment and signed by the delegates until August 2. In fact, the last of the fifty-six delegates to sign the document, Thomas McKean of Delaware, waited until 1777 to do so!

As luck would have it, July 4 became Independence Day by accident. In 1777 Congress forgot about any acknowledgment of the first anniversary of independence until July 3, when it was too late to honor July 2. As a consequence, the Fourth won by default.

In 1777, in the midst of the Revolutionary War, the Patriots of Boston marked the first full year of independence with great gusto. At dawn, ships in Boston Harbor fired a "grand salute" to the new day. In the afternoon, a prominent minister preached a patriotic sermon to the state legislature. Afterward, Governor John Hancock proposed thirteen toasts from the balcony of the statehouse, one for each of the new states.

Similar activities occurred throughout the new nation. Independence Day quickly became the most popular and most important public ritual in the United States. Huge numbers of people from all walks of life suspended their normal routines in order to devote a day to parades, formal orations, and fireworks displays. In the process, the infant republic began to create its own myth of national identity that transcended local or regional concerns. "What a day!" exclaimed the editor of the *Southern Patriot* in 1815. "What happiness, what emotion, what virtuous triumph must fill the bosoms of Americans!"

As time passed, however, the celebrations of Independence Day would focus more and more on popular entertainment and recreation rather than on solemn remembrance. Yet, Independence Day would remain a national holiday, one that would unite the elite and the masses, people of the cities and the backcountry, in a celebration that went beyond local identity to forge a feeling of national unity.

EDUCATION   The most lasting cultural effect of postwar nationalism may well have been its mark on education. In the colonies there had been a total of nine colleges, but once the Revolution was over, eight more sprang up in the 1780s and six in the 1790s. Several of the state constitutions had provisions for state universities. Georgia's was the first chartered, in 1785, but the University of North Carolina (chartered in 1789) was the first to open, in 1795.

Even more important, the Revolution provided the initial impetus for state-supported public school systems. Many of the founders believed that the survival of the new nation depended upon instilling in the public an appreciation for the fragility of republican government and its utter dependence on private and civic virtue. They viewed public schools as the best institutions for such moral and civic development. In such schools, as Pennsylvania's Benjamin Rush maintained, American children not only would become literate but would also learn to choose the public good over all private interests and concerns.

Jefferson agreed that public education would serve as the very "keystone of our arch of government," and in 1779 he introduced his "Bill for the More General Diffusion of Knowledge" into the Virginia assembly. It included an elaborate plan for the state to fund elementary schools for all free persons, and higher education for the talented, up through a state university. Several years later Samuel Adams proposed the same in Massachusetts. Yet almost every one of these schemes for public schools came to naught. Wealthy critics opposed spending tax money on schools that would mingle their sons "in a vulgar and suspicious communion" with the masses. The spread of public schools would have to wait for a more democratic climate.

Education played an important role in broadening and deepening the sense of nationalism, and no single element was as important, perhaps, as the spelling book, an item of almost universal use. Noah Webster prepared an elementary speller published in 1783. By 1890 more than 60 million copies of his "Blue Back Speller" had been printed, and the book continued to sell well into the twentieth century. In his preface Webster issued a cultural Declaration of Independence: "The country," he wrote, "must, in some future time, be as distinguished by the superiority of her literary improvements, as she already is by the liberality of her civil and ecclesiastical constitutions."

American nationalism embodied a stirring idea. This first new nation, unlike the Old World nations of Europe, was not rooted in antiquity. Its people, except for the Indians, had not inhabited it over the centuries, nor was there any nation of a common ethnic descent. "The American national consciousness," one observer wrote, "is not a voice crying out of the depth of the dark past, but is proudly a product of the enlightened present, setting its face resolutely toward the future."

Many people, at least since the time of the Pilgrims, had thought America to be singled out for a special identity, a special mission. Jonathan Edwards said God had chosen America as "the glorious renovator of the world," and still later John Adams proclaimed the opening of America "a grand scheme and design in Providence for the illumination and the emancipation of the slavish part of mankind all over the earth." This sense of mission was neither limited to New England nor rooted solely in Calvinism. From the democratic rhetoric of Jefferson, to the pragmatism of Washington, to heady toasts bellowed in South Carolina taverns, patriots everywhere articulated a special American leadership role in human history. The mission was now a call to lead the world toward liberty and equality. Meanwhile, however, Americans had to address more immediate problems created by their new nationhood. The Philadelphia doctor and scientist Benjamin Rush issued a prophetic statement in 1787: "The American war is over: but this is far from being the case with the American Revolution. On the contrary, but the first act of the great drama is closed."

MAKING CONNECTIONS

- The American Revolution was the starting point for the foreign policy of the United States. Many of the specific foreign concerns that will be discussed in Chapters 8 and 9 sprang from issues directly relating to the Revolution.

- Much of what became Jacksonian Democracy (introduced in Chapter 10) can be traced to social and political movements associated with the American Revolution.

- The Articles of Confederation, the document that established the first national government for the United States, saw the new nation through the Revolution; but within a few years the Articles were discarded in favor of a new government, set forth in the Constitution.

FURTHER READING

The Revolutionary War is the subject of Colin Bonwick's *The American Revolution* (1991), Theodore Draper's *A Struggle for Power: The American Revolution* (1996), and Gordon S. Wood's *The Radicalism of the American Revolution* (1991). David Hackett Fischer's *Paul Revere's Ride* (1994) details the events surrounding the immediate outbreak of fighting, while Jeremy Black's *War for America: The Fight for Independence, 1775–1783* (1991) focuses on the war itself.

On the social history of the Revolutionary War, see John W. Shy's *A People Numerous and Armed* (1976), Charles Royster's *A Revolutionary People at War* (1979), Lawrence D. Cress's *Citizens in Arms* (1982), and E. Wayne Carp's *To Starve the Army at Pleasure: Continental Army Adminstration and American Political Culture, 1775–1783* (1984). Colin G. Calloway tells the neglected story of the Indian experiences in the Revolution in *The American Revolution in Indian Country: Crisis and Diversity in Native American Communities* (1995).

Why some Americans remained loyal to the crown is the subject of Bernard Bailyn's *The Ordeal of Thomas Hutchinson* (1974), Robert M. Calhoon's *The Loyalists in Revolutionary America, 1760–1781* (1973), and Mary Beth Norton's *The British-Americans* (1972).

A superb community-level study of revolutionary change is Robert A. Gross's *The Minutemen and Their World* (1976). The definitive study of African Americans during the Revolutionary era remains Benjamin Quarles's *The Negro in the American Revolution* (1961). Mary Beth Norton's *Liberty's Daughters* (1980) and Linda K. Kerber's *Women of the Republic* (1980) document the role women played in securing independence. Joy D. Buel and Richard Buel, Jr.'s *The Way of Duty* (1984) shows the impact of the Revoluton on one New England family.

The standard introduction to the diplomacy of the Revolutionary era is Jonathan R. Dull's *A Diplomatic History of the American Revolution* (1985). Richard B. Morris's *The Peacemakers* (1965) examines more closely the negotiations for the Peace of Paris.

7  SHAPING A FEDERAL UNION

CHAPTER ORGANIZER

This chapter focuses on:

- the achievements and weaknesses of the Confederation government.

- the issues involved in writing the Constitution.

- the debate over ratifying the Constitution.

n an address to fellow graduates at the Harvard commencement in 1787, young John Quincy Adams lamented "this critical period" when the country was "groaning under the intolerable burden of . . . accumulated evils." The same phrase, the "critical period," has often been used to label the history of the United States under the Articles of Confederation. Fear of a central authority dominated this period. Yet, while there were weaknesses of the Confederation, there were also major achievements. Moreover, lessons learned under the Confederation would serve well in the formulation of a new Constitution, and in the balancing of central and local authority under that Constitution.

THE CONFEDERATION

The Congress of the Confederation had little governmental authority. "It could ask for money but not compel payment," as one historian wrote, "it could enter into treaties but not enforce their stipulations; it could provide for raising of armies but not fill the ranks; it could borrow money but take no proper measures for repayment; it could advise and recommend but not command." The Congress was virtually helpless to cope with problems of diplomacy and postwar depression that would have challenged the resources of a much stronger government. It was not easy to find men of stature to serve in such a body, and often hard to gather a quorum of those who did. Yet in spite of its handicaps, the Confederation Congress somehow managed to survive and to lay important foundations for the future. It concluded the Peace of Paris in 1783. It created the first executive departments. And it formulated principles of land distribution and territorial government that guided expansion all the way to the Pacific coast.

Throughout most of the War for Independence the Congress remained distrustful of executive power. It assigned administrative duties to its committees and thereby imposed a painful burden on conscientious members. At one time or another John Adams, for instance, served on some eighty committees. In 1781, however, Congress began to set up three departments: Foreign Affairs, Finance, and War. Each was to have a single head responsible to Congress. Given time and stability, Congress and the department heads might have evolved into something like the parliamentary cabinet system. As it turned out, these agencies were the forerunners of the government departments that came into being later under the Constitution.

FINANCE   As yet, however, there was neither president nor prime minister, only the presiding officer of Congress and its secretary, Charles Thomson, who served continuously from 1774 to 1789. The closest thing to an executive head of the Confederation was Robert Morris, who as superintendent of finance in the final years of the war became the most influential figure in the government. He wanted to make both himself and the Confederation more powerful. He envisioned a coherent program of taxation and debt management to make the government financially stable; "a public debt supported by public

Robert Morris, the most influential figure in the Confederation government, in a portrait by Charles Willson Peale.

revenue will prove the strongest cement to keep our confederacy together," he confided to a friend. It would wed to the support of the federal government the powerful influence of the public creditors. Morris therefore welcomed the chance to enlarge the debt by issuing new government bonds in settlement of wartime claims. Because of the government's precarious finances, these securities brought only ten to fifteen cents on the dollar, but with a sounder Treasury—certainly with a tax power—they could be expected to rise in value, creating new capital with which to finance banks and economic development.

In 1781, as part of his plan, Morris secured a congressional charter for the Bank of North America, which would hold government deposits, lend money to the government, and issue bank notes. Though a national bank, it was in part privately owned and was expected to turn a profit for Morris and other shareholders, in addition to performing a public service. But Morris's program depended ultimately on a secure income for the government, and it foundered on the requirement of unanimous state approval for amendments to the Articles of Confederation. Local interests and the fear of a central authority—a fear strengthened by the recent quarrels with king and Parliament—hobbled action.

To carry their point, Morris and his nationalist friends in 1783 risked a dangerous gamble. Washington's army, encamped at Newburgh on the Hudson River, had grown restless in the final winter of the war. Their pay was late as usual, and experience gave them reason to fear that claims to bounties and life pensions for officers might never be honored once their services were no longer needed. A delegation of officers traveled to Philadelphia with a petition for redress. Soon they found themselves drawn into a scheme to line up the army and public creditors with nationalists in Congress and confront the states with the threat of a coup d'état unless they yielded more power to Congress. Alexander Hamilton, congressman from New York and former aide to General Washington, sought to bring his old commander into the plan.

Washington sympathized with the purpose. If congressional powers were not enlarged, he had told a friend, "the band which at present holds us together, by a very feeble thread, will soon be broken, when anarchy and confusion must ensue." But Washington was just as deeply convinced that a military coup would be both dishonorable and dangerous. When he learned that some of the plotters had planned an unauthorized meeting of officers, he confronted the conspirators. Drawing his spectacles from his pocket, he began: "I have grown not only gray but blind in the service of my country." When he had finished his dramatic and emotional address, his officers unanimously adopted resolutions denouncing the recent "infamous propositions," and the so-called Newburgh Conspiracy came to a sudden end.

A body of Pennsylvania recruits provided a sorry aftermath to the quiet dispersal of troops at war's end. Their pay in arrears, about eighty militiamen mutinied, marched from Lancaster to Philadelphia, and with reinforcements from regiments there conducted a threatening demonstration in front of Independence Hall. When state authorities failed to provide a guard for fear the militia would join the mutiny, the Congress after three days fled to Princeton, later adjourned to Annapolis, then Trenton, and in 1785 finally settled in New York. Moving from place to place, often unable to muster a quorum, the Congress grew increasingly impotent.

The Confederation never did put its finances in order. The Continental currency had long since become a byword for worthlessness. It was never redeemed. The debt, domestic and foreign, grew from $11 million to $28 million as Congress paid off citizens' and soldiers' claims. Each year Congress ran a deficit on its operating expenses.

LAND POLICY   The one source from which Congress might hope ultimately to draw an independent income was the sale of western lands. Throughout the Confederation period, however, that income remained more a fleeting promise than an accomplished fact. The Confederation nevertheless dealt more effectively with the western lands than with anything else. There Congress had direct authority, at least on paper.

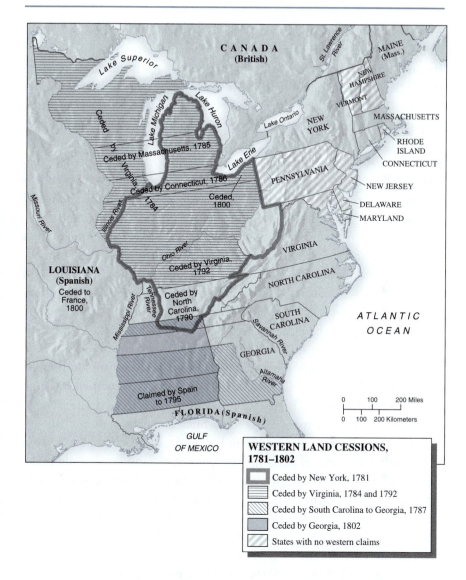

Lake Superior

CANADA
(British)

St. Lawrence River

MAINE
(Mass.)

NEW HAMPSHIRE

Lake Michigan

Lake Huron

VERMONT

Lake Ontario

NEW YORK

MASSACHUSETTS

Ceded by Massachusetts, 1785

Lake Erie

RHODE ISLAND

CONNECTICUT

Ceded by Virginia, 1784

Ceded by Connecticut, 1786

PENNSYLVANIA

NEW JERSEY

Ceded, 1800

DELAWARE

MARYLAND

Missouri River

Illinois River

Ohio River

Ceded by Virginia, 1792

VIRGINIA

NORTH CAROLINA

LOUISIANA
(Spanish)

Ceded to France, 1800

Tennessee River

Mississippi River

Ceded by North Carolina, 1790

SOUTH CAROLINA

Savannah River

ATLANTIC OCEAN

GEORGIA

Altamaha River

Claimed by Spain to 1795

FLORIDA (Spanish)

GULF OF MEXICO

0   100   200 Miles

0   100   200 Kilometers

WESTERN LAND CESSIONS, 1781–1802

Ceded by New York, 1781

Ceded by Virginia, 1784 and 1792

Ceded by South Carolina to Georgia, 1787

Ceded by Georgia, 1802

States with no western claims

Thinly populated by Indians, French settlers, and a growing number of American squatters, the region north of the Ohio River had long been the site of overlapping claims by colonies and speculators. In 1784 Virginia's cession of lands north of the Ohio was complete, and by 1786 all states had abandoned their claims in the area except for a 120-mile strip along Lake Erie, which Connecticut held until 1800 as its "Western Reserve," in return for giving up its claims in the Wyoming Valley of Pennsylvania.

As early as 1779 Congress had made a commitment in principle not to treat the western lands as colonies. The delegates resolved instead that western lands ceded by the states "shall be . . . formed into distinct Republican states," equal in all respects to other states. Between 1784 and 1787 policies for the development of the West emerged in three major ordinances of the Confederation Congress. These documents, which rank among its greatest achievements—and among the most important in American history—set precedents that the United States would follow in its expansion all the way to the Pacific. Thomas Jefferson in fact was prepared to grant self-government to western states at an early stage, when settlers would meet and choose their own officials. Under Jefferson's ordinance of 1784, when the population equaled that of the smallest existing state, the territory would achieve full statehood.

In the Land Ordinance of 1785 the delegates outlined a plan of land surveys and sales that would eventually stamp a rectangular pattern on much of the nation's surface, a pattern still visible from the air in many parts of the country because of the layout of roads and fields. Wherever Indian titles had been extinguished, the Northwest was to be surveyed into townships six miles square along east-west and north-south lines. Each township in turn was divided into 36 lots (or sections) one mile square (or 640 acres). The 640-acre sections were to go at auction for no less than $1 per acre, or $640 total. Such terms favored land speculators, of course, since few common folk had that much money or were able to work that much land. In later years new land laws would make smaller plots available at lower prices, but in 1785 Congress was faced with an empty Treasury. In each township, however, Congress did reserve the income from the sixteenth section for the support of schools— a significant departure at a time when public schools were rare.

In seven ranges to the west of the Ohio River, an area in which recent treaties had voided Indian titles, surveying began. But before any land sales occurred a group of speculators from New England presented cash-poor Congress with a seductive offer. Organized in Boston, the group took the name of the Ohio Company and sent the Reverend Manasseh Cutler to present their plan. Cutler proved a persuasive lobbyist, and in 1787 Congress voted a grant of 1.5 million acres for about $1 million in certificates of indebtedness to Revolutionary War veterans. The arrangement had the dual merit, Cutler argued, of reducing the debt and encouraging new settlement and sales. Further, to ensure passage the lobbyist cut in several congressmen on another deal, the Scioto Company, which got an option on 5 million acres more.

THE NORTHWEST ORDINANCE   Spurred by the plans for land sales and settlement, Congress drafted a more specific frame of territorial government to replace Jefferson's ordinance of 1784. The new plan backed off from Jefferson's recommendation of early self-government. Because of the trouble that might be expected from squatters who were clamoring for free land, the Northwest Ordinance of 1787 required a period of colonial tutelage. At first the territory fell subject to a governor, a secretary, and three judges, all chosen by Congress. Eventually there would be three to five territories in the region, and when any one had 5,000 free male adults it could choose an assembly, and Congress would name a council of five from ten names proposed by the assembly. The governor would have a veto, and so would Congress.

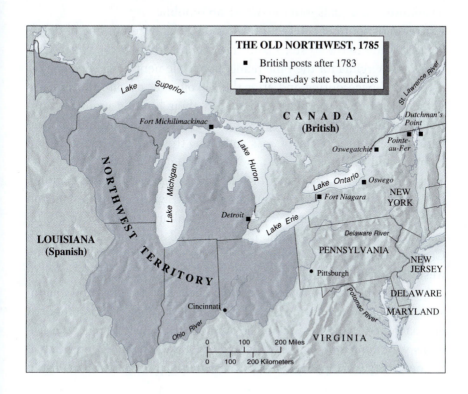

THE OLD NORTHWEST, 1785
- British posts after 1783
— Present-day state boundaries

The resemblance to the old royal colonies is clear, but there were two significant differences. For one, the Ordinance anticipated statehood when any territory's population reached 60,000. At that point a convention could be called to draft a state constitution and apply to Congress for statehood. For another, it included a Bill of Rights that guaranteed religious freedom, representation in proportion to population, trial by jury, habeas corpus, and the application of common law. Finally, the Ordinance excluded slavery permanently from the Northwest—a proviso Jefferson had failed to get accepted in his ordinance of 1784. This proved a fateful decision. As the progress of emancipation in the existing states gradually freed all slaves above the Mason-Dixon line, the Ohio River boundary of the Old Northwest extended the line between freedom and slavery all the way to the Mississippi.

The Northwest Ordinance had a larger importance beyond establishing a formal procedure for transforming territories into states. It represented a sharp break with the imperialistic assumption behind European expansion into the Western Hemisphere. The new states were to be admitted as equals into the American republic.

The lands south of the Ohio River followed a different line of development. Title to the western lands remained with Georgia, North Carolina, and Virginia for the time being, but settlement proceeded at a far more rapid pace during and after the Revolution, despite the Indians' fierce resentment of encroachments on their hunting grounds. Substantial centers of population grew up around Harrodsburg and Boonesboro in the Kentucky Blue Grass and along the Watauga, Holston, and Cumberland Rivers, as far west as Nashborough (Nashville). In the Old Southwest active movements for statehood arose early. North Carolina tentatively ceded its western claims in 1784, whereupon the Holston settlers formed the short-lived state of Franklin, which became little more than a bone of contention between rival speculators until North Carolina reasserted control in 1789, shortly before the cession of its western lands became final.

Indian claims too were being extinguished. The Iroquois and Cherokees, badly battered during the Revolution, were in no position to resist encroachments. By the Second Treaty of Fort Stanwix (1784), the Iroquois were forced to cede land in western New York and Pennsylvania. In the Treaty of Hopewell (1785), the Cherokees gave up all claims in

South Carolina, much of western North Carolina, and large portions of present-day Kentucky and Tennessee. Also in 1785 the major Ohio tribes dropped their claim to most of Ohio, except for a chunk bordering the western part of Lake Erie. The Creeks, pressed by the state of Georgia to cede portions of their lands in 1784–1785, went to war in the summer of 1786 with covert aid from Spanish Florida. When Spanish aid diminished, however, the Creek chief traveled to New York and in 1791 finally struck a bargain that gave the Creeks favorable trade arrangements with the United States but that did not restore the lost lands.

TRADE AND THE ECONOMY   In its economic life, as in planning westward expansion, the young nation dealt vigorously with difficult problems. Congress had little to do with achievements in the economy, but neither could it bear the blame for an acute economic contraction between 1770 and 1790, the result primarily of the war and separation from the British Empire. Although farmers enmeshed in local markets maintained their livelihood during the Revolutionary era, commercial agriculture dependent upon trade with foreign markets suffered a severe downturn. The southern Tidewater suffered a loss of slave labor, much of it carried off by the British. Chesapeake planters also lost their lucrative foreign markets. Tobacco was especially hard hit. The British decision to close its West Indian colonies to American trade devastated what had been a thriving commerce in timber, wheat, and other foodstuffs. Returns from indigo and naval stores declined with the loss of British bounties.

Merchants suffered even more wrenching adjustments than the farmers. Cut out of the British mercantile system, they had to find new outlets for their trade. Circumstances that impoverished some enriched those who financed privateers, supplied the armies on both sides, and hoarded precious goods while demand and prices soared. By the end of the war, a strong sentiment for free trade had developed in both Britain and America. In the memorable year 1776, the Scottish economist Adam Smith brought out *The Wealth of Nations,* a classic manifesto against mercantilism. Some British statesmen embraced the new gospel, but the public and Parliament still clung to the conventional wisdom of mercantilism for many years to come.

After the war British trade with America did resume, and American ships were allowed to deliver American products and return to the United States with British goods. American ships could not carry British goods anywhere else, however. The pent-up demand for familiar goods created a vigorous market in exports to America, fueled by British credits and the hard money that had come into America from foreign aid, the expenditures of foreign armies, or wartime trade and privateering. The result was a quick cycle of postwar boom and bust, a buying spree followed by a money shortage and economic troubles that lasted several years.

In colonial days the chronic trade deficit with Britain had been offset by the influx of coins from trade with the West Indies. Now American ships found themselves excluded altogether from the British West Indies. The islands, however, still demanded wheat, fish, lumber, and other products from the mainland, and American shippers had not lost their talent for smuggling, at which the islanders connived. Already American shippers had begun exploring new outlets, and by 1787 their seaports were flourishing more than ever. Freed from colonial restraints, they now had the run of the seven seas. Trade treaties opened

A rare glimpse of a construction site in 1800, from William Birch's series The City of Philadelphia As It Appeared in the Year 1800.

Merchants' Counting House. *Americans involved in overseas trade, such as the merchants depicted here, were sharply affected by the dislocations of war.*

new markets with the Dutch (1782), Swedes (1783), Prussians (1785), and Moroccans (1787), and American shippers found new outlets on their own in Europe, Africa, and Asia. The most spectacular new development, if not the largest, was trade with China. It began in 1784–1785, when the *Empress of China* sailed from New York to Canton and back, around the tip of South America. Profits from its cargo of silks and tea encouraged the outfitting of other ships that carried ginseng root and other American goods to exchange for the luxury goods of East Asia.

By 1790 American commerce and exports had far outrun the trade of the colonies. Merchants had more ships than before the war. Farm exports were twice what they had been. Although most of the exports were the products of forests, fields, and fisheries, during and after the war more Americans had turned to small-scale manufacturing, mainly for domestic markets. By 1787 a summary of major American enterprises included dozens of products from ships and ironwork to shoes, textiles, and soap.

DIPLOMACY   The achievements of the flourishing young nation are more visible in hindsight than they were then. Until 1787 the short-

The Savages Let Loose, or the Cruel Fate of the Loyalists. *A British comment on the treatment of Loyalists in the peace settlement of 1783.*

comings and failures remained far more apparent—and the advocates of a stronger central government were extremely vocal on the subject. In diplomacy, there remained the nagging problems of relations with Great Britain and Spain, both of which still kept posts on American soil and conspired with Indians and white settlers in the West. The British, despite the peace treaty of 1783, held on to a string of forts along the Canadian border. From these they kept a hand in the fur trade and a degree of influence with the Indian tribes, whom they were suspected of stirring up to make sporadic attacks on the frontier. They gave as a reason for their continued occupation the failure of Americans to pay their prewar debts to British creditors. They conveniently ignored the point that the peace treaty had included only a face-saving gesture that committed Congress to recommend that the states place no legal impediment in the way of their collection. Impediments continued nonetheless. According to one Virginian, a common question in his state was: "If we are now to pay the debts due to British merchants, what have we been fighting for all this while?"

Another major irritant was the confiscation of Loyalist property. The peace treaty had encouraged Congress to stop confiscations, to guarantee immunity to Loyalists for twelve months, during which they could return and wind up their affairs, and to recommend that the states give back confiscated property. Persecutions, even lynchings, of Loyalists still occurred until after the end of the war. Some Loyalists returned unmolested, however, and once again took up their lives in their former homes. By the end of 1787, moreover, at the request of Congress, all the states had rescinded the laws that were in conflict with the peace treaty.

With Spain, the chief issues were the southern boundary and the right to navigate the Mississippi. According to the preliminary treaty with Britain, the United States claimed a line as far south as the 31st parallel; Spain held out for the line running eastward from the mouth of the Yazoo River (at 32°28′N), which it claimed as the traditional boundary. The American treaty with Britain had also specified the right to navigate the Mississippi River to its mouth. Still, the international boundary ran down the middle of the river most of its length, and the Mississippi was entirely within Spanish Louisiana in its lower reaches. The right to navigation was a matter of importance because of the growing settlements in Kentucky and Tennessee, but in 1784 Louisiana's Spanish governor closed the river to American commerce and began to intrigue with the Creeks, Choctaws, Chickasaws, and other Indians of the Southwest against the American settlers and with the settlers against the United States. General James Wilkinson, a Kentucky land speculator, further enriched himself with Spanish gold in return for his promise to conspire for secession of the West and perhaps its annexation by Spain. Wilkinson, however, was a professional conniver with an instinct for trouble, whose loyalties ran mainly to his own pocketbook. He was not the only man on the make who was double-dealing with the Spaniards.

THE CONFEDERATION'S PROBLEMS The problems of trans-Appalachian settlers, however, seemed remote from the everyday concerns of most Americans. What touched them more closely were economic troubles and the currency shortage. Merchants who found themselves excluded from old channels of imperial trade began to agitate for reprisals. State governments, in response, laid special tonnage duties on British vessels and special tariffs on the goods they brought. State action alone, however, failed to work because of lack of unifor-

American craftsmen, such as this cabinetmaker, sought tariffs against foreign goods that competed with theirs.

mity among all the states. British ships could be diverted to states whose duties were less restrictive. The other states tried to meet this problem by taxing British goods that flowed across state lines, creating an impression that states were involved in commercial war with each other. Although these duties seldom affected American goods, there was a clear need, it seemed to commercial interests, for a central power to regulate trade.

Mechanics (skilled workers who made, used, or repaired tools and machines) and artisans (skilled workers who made products) were developing an infant industry. Their products ranged from crude iron nails to the fine silver bowls of Paul Revere. They wanted to take reprisals against British goods as well as British ships. They sought, and in various degrees obtained from the states, tariffs against foreign goods that competed with theirs. The country would be on its way to economic independence, they argued, if only the money that flowed into the country were invested in domestic manufactures instead of being paid out for foreign goods. Nearly all the states gave some preference to American goods, but again the lack of uniformity in their laws put them at cross purposes, and so urban mechanics along with merchants were drawn into the movement for a stronger central government in the interest of uniform regulation.

The shortage of cash and other economic difficulties gave rise to more immediate demands for paper currency as legal tender, for postponement of tax and debt payments, and for laws to "stay" the foreclosure of mortgages. Farmers who had profited during the war found themselves squeezed by depressed crop prices and mounting debts while merchants sorted out and opened up their new trade routes. Creditors demanded hard money, but it was in short supply—and paper money was almost nonexistent after the depreciation of the Continental currency. The result was an outcry for relief, and around 1785 the demand for new paper money became the most divisive issue in state politics. Debtors demanded the addition of paper money as a means of easing repayment, and farmers saw it as a way to raise commodity prices.

In 1785–1786 seven states (Pennsylvania, New York, New Jersey, South Carolina, Rhode Island, Georgia, and North Carolina) provided for issues of paper money. It served in five of these states—Pennsylvania, New York, New Jersey, South Carolina, and Rhode Island—as a means of credit to hard-pressed farmers through state loans on farm mortgages. It was variously used to fund state debts and to pay off the claims of veterans. In spite of the cries of calamity at the time, the money never seriously depreciated in Pennsylvania, New York, and South Carolina.

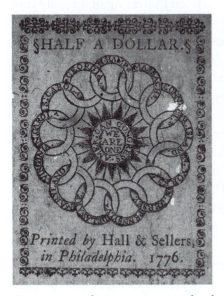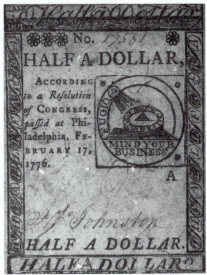

Congress issued paper currency as legal tender because of a shortage of hard money.

In Rhode Island, however, the debtor party ran wild. In 1786 the Rhode Island legislature issued more paper money than any other state in proportion to population, and declared it legal tender in payment of all debts. Creditors fled the state to avoid being paid in worthless paper, merchants closed their doors while mobs rioted against them, and a "forcing act" denied trial by jury and levied fines against anyone who refused to take the money at face value. Eventually the state's supreme court ruled the law unconstitutional, the first time a court exercised the doctrine of judicial review in holding a state law unconstitutional. The forcing act was then repealed and the legal tender clause finally repealed in 1789.

SHAYS'S REBELLION   Newspapers throughout the country ran accounts of the developments in Rhode Island. The little commonwealth, stubbornly independent since the days of Roger Williams, became the prime example of democracy run riot—until its riotous neighbor, Massachusetts, provided the final proof (some said) that the country was poised on the brink of anarchy: Shays's Rebellion. There, the trouble was not too much paper money but too little, as well as too much taxation.

After 1780, Massachusetts had remained in the grip of a rigidly conservative regime, which levied ever-larger poll and land taxes to pay off a heavy war debt, held mainly by wealthy creditors in Boston. The taxes fell most heavily upon beleaguered farmers and the poor in general. When the Massachusetts legislature adjourned in 1786 without providing either paper money or any other relief from taxes and debts, three western counties erupted into spontaneous revolt.

Armed bands closed the courts and prevented foreclosures. A ragtag "army" of some 1,200 disgruntled farmers under Daniel Shays, a destitute farmer and war veteran, advanced upon the federal arsenal at Springfield, Massachusetts, in 1787. Shays and his followers sought a more flexible monetary policy, laws allowing them to use corn and wheat as money, and the right to postpone paying taxes until the depression lifted.

A small militia force, however, scattered the debtor army with a single volley that left four dead. General Benjamin Lincoln, a hero of the Revolution, arrived soon after with reinforcements from Boston and routed the remaining Shaysites. The rebel farmers nevertheless had a

Led by Daniel Shays, a band of disgruntled farmers attacked the federal arsenal at Springfield, Massachusetts, in January 1787, but were repulsed by the militia.

victory of sorts. The new state legislature included members sympathetic to the agricultural crisis. They omitted direct taxes the following year, lowered court fees, and exempted clothing, household goods, and tools from the debt process. But a more important consequence was the impetus the rebellion gave to conservatism and nationalism.

Rumors, at times deliberately inflated, greatly exaggerated the extent of this pathetic rebellion of desperate men. The rebels were linked to the conniving British and accused of seeking to pillage the wealthy. What was more, the uprising set an ominous example. "There are combustibles in every State," George Washington wrote, "which a spark might set fire to." Panic set in among the republic's elite. New York's Gouverneur Morris was typically blunt: "The mob begin to think and reason. Poor reptiles! They bask in the sun and ere noon they will bite, depend upon it. The gentry begin to fear this." In a letter to Jefferson, Abigail Adams was equally anxious. She tarred the Shaysites as "Ignorant, restless desperadoes, without conscience or principles . . . mobbish insurgents [who]are for sapping the foundation" of the struggling young government.

Jefferson disagreed. If Adams and others were overly critical of Shays's Rebellion, Jefferson was, if anything, too complacent. From his post in Paris, he wrote to a friend back home: "The tree of liberty must be refreshed from time to time with the blood of patriots and tyrants." Abigail Adams was so infuriated by Jefferson's position that she stopped corresponding with him for months.

CALLS FOR A STRONGER GOVERNMENT   Well before the outbreaks in New England, the advocates of a stronger central authority had come to demand a convention to revise the Articles of Confederation. Self-interest led bankers, merchants, and mechanics to promote a stronger central government. Many public-spirited men saw it as the only alternative to anarchy. Gradually people were losing the fear of a tyrannical central authority as they saw evidence that tyranny might come from other quarters, including the common people themselves.

By the mid-1780s, in fact, several prominent political spokesmen had become convinced that the new state governments were being run by uneducated entrepreneurs pursuing selfish economic and petty political interests. Men of humble origins and parochial points of view were allegedly displacing the "wise and virtuous" from seats of power. Such inexperienced and frequently uncouth legislators were passing an avalanche of legislation merely to serve particular interest groups and constituents rather than the general welfare. They were printing excessive amounts of paper money and passing "stay" laws (laws that granted stays, or postponements, on debt payments) preventing judicial action against debtors.

Such developments led many of the Revolutionary leaders to revise their assessment of American character. "We have, probably," concluded George Washington in 1786, "had too good an opinion of human nature in forming our confederation." The following year James Madison reported to Jefferson that America was displaying "symptoms . . . truly alarming, which have tainted the faith of most orthodox republicans." People were stretching the meaning of liberty far beyond what he and others had envisioned. He found a "spirit of *locality*" rampant in the state legislature that was destroying the "aggregate interests of the community." Even worse, he saw people taking the law and other people's property into their own hands. Such developments led Madison and others to revise their assumptions about republican virtue. At any given time, they decided, only a distinct minority could be relied upon to set aside their private interests in favor of the common good. These so-called Federalists concluded that the new republic must now depend for its success on the constant virtue of the few rather than the public-spiritedness of the many.

In 1785 commissioners from Virginia and Maryland had met at Mount Vernon on Washington's invitation to promote commerce and economic development and to settle outstanding questions about the navigation of the Potomac and Chesapeake Bay. Washington had a personal interest in the river flowing by his door: it was a potential route to the West, with its upper reaches close to the upper reaches of the Ohio, where his military career had begun thirty years before. The delegates agreed on interstate cooperation, and Maryland suggested a further pact with Pennsylvania and Delaware to encourage water communication between the Chesapeake and the Ohio River; the Virginia legislature agreed, and at Madison's suggestion invited all thirteen states to send delegates for a general discussion of commercial problems. Nine states named representatives, but those from only five appeared at the Annapolis Convention in 1786—neither the New England states nor the Carolinas and Georgia were represented. Apparent failure soon turned into success, however, when the alert Alexander Hamilton, representing New York, presented a resolution for still another convention in Philadelphia to consider all measures necessary "to render the constitution of the Federal Government adequate to the exigencies of the Union."

ADOPTING THE CONSTITUTION

THE CONSTITUTIONAL CONVENTION   After stalling for several months, Congress fell in line in 1787 with a resolution endorsing a convention "for the sole and express purpose of revising the Articles of Confederation." By then five states had already named delegates; before the meeting, called to begin on May 14, 1787, six more states had acted. New Hampshire delayed until June, and its delegates arrived in July. Fearful of consolidated power, tiny Rhode Island kept aloof throughout. (Critics labeled the fractious little state "Rogue Island.") Virginia's Patrick Henry, an implacable foe of centralized government, claimed to "smell a rat" and refused to represent his state. Twenty-nine delegates from nine states began work on May 25. Altogether the state legislatures elected seventy-three men. Fifty-five attended at one time or another, and after four months, thirty-nine signed the Constitution they had drafted.

The durability and flexibility of that document testify to the remarkable quality of the men who made it. Thomas Jefferson, who was serving abroad as minister to France, later referred to the Convention as an assembly of "demi-gods." The delegates were surprisingly young: forty-two was the average age. Farmers, merchants, lawyers, bankers, many of them were widely read in history, law, and political philosophy. They were familiar with the writings of Locke and Montesquieu, aware of the confederacies of the ancient world, and at the same time practical men of experience, tested in the fires of the Revolution. Twenty-one had served in the conflict, seven had been state governors, most of them had been members of the Continental Congress, and eight had signed the Declaration of Independence.

The magisterial Washington served as presiding officer, but participated little in the debates. Eighty-one-year-old Benjamin Franklin, the oldest delegate, also said little from the floor but did provide a wealth of experience, wit, and common sense behind the scenes. More active in the debates were James Madison, the ablest political philosopher in the group; Massachusetts's dapper Elbridge Gerry, a Harvard graduate who

A session of the Constitutional Convention with George Washington presiding.

earned the nickname "Old Grumbletonian" because, as John Adams once said, he "opposed everything he did not propose"; George Mason, the irritable author of the Virginia Declaration of Rights and a slave-owning planter with a deep-rooted suspicion of all government; the eloquent, arrogant New York aristocrat Gouverneur Morris, who harbored a venomous contempt for the masses; Marylander Luther Martin, the ardent spokesman for states' rights whose speeches were fueled by his fiery temper and frequent drunkenness; Scots-born James Wilson of Pennsylvania, one of the ablest lawyers in the new nation and next in importance at the convention only to Washington and Madison; and Roger Sherman of Connecticut, a self-trained lawyer adept at negotiating compromises. John Adams, like Jefferson, was serving abroad. Also conspicuously absent during most of the Convention was thirty-two-year-old Alexander Hamilton, the staunch nationalist who regretfully went home when the other two New York delegates walked out because of their states'-rights principles.

All the participants acknowledged that Madison emerged as the central figure at the Convention. Small of stature—barely over five feet tall—and frail in health, the thirty-six-year-old Madison was a studious bachelor descended from wealthy slave-owning Virginia planters. He suffered from chronic headaches and was painfully shy. Being jilted as a young man by his sixteen-year-old fiancée in favor of a medical student only heightened his natural aloofness. (She had sealed her farewell letter with rye dough as "a profession of indifference.") Crowds made him nervous, and he hated to use his high-pitched voice in public, much less in open debate.

But the Princeton graduate who had found the practice of law too "coarse and dry" possessed a keen, agile mind with a voracious appetite for learning, and the convincing eloquence of his arguments proved to be decisive. "Every person seems to acknowledge his greatness," wrote one delegate. Madison arrived in Philadelphia with trunks full of books and a head full of ideas. He had been preparing for the Convention for months and probably knew more about historic forms of government than any other delegate.

For the most part, the delegates' differences on political philosophy fell within a narrow range. On certain fundamentals they generally agreed: that government derived its just powers from the consent of the people, but that society must be protected from the tyranny of the ma-

James Madison was only thirty-six when he assumed a major role in the drafting of the Constitution. This miniature is by Charles Willson Peale (c. 1783).

jority; that the people at large must have a voice in their government, but that checks and balances must be provided to keep any one group from arrogating power; that a stronger central authority was essential, but that all power was subject to abuse. They assumed with Madison that if people were "angels, no government would be necessary." Even the best people were naturally selfish, and government, therefore, could not be founded altogether upon a trust in goodwill and virtue. Yet by a careful arrangement of checks and balances, by checking power with countervailing power, the Founding Fathers hoped to devise institutions that could constrain individual sinfulness and channel self-interest to benefit the public good.

THE VIRGINIA AND NEW JERSEY PLANS   At the outset the delegates unanimously elected Washington president of the Convention. One of the first decisions was to meet behind closed doors in order to discourage outside pressures and theatrical speeches to the galleries. The secrecy of the proceedings was remarkably well kept, and knowledge of the debates comes mainly from Madison's extensive notes. It was Madison, too, who drafted the proposals that set the framework of the discussions. These proposals, which came to be called the "Virginia Plan," embodied a revolutionary idea for the delegates to scrap their instructions to revise the Articles of Confederation and to submit an entirely new document to the states. The plan proposed separate legislative, executive, and judicial branches, and a truly national government to make laws binding upon individual citizens and upon states as well. Congress would be divided into two houses, a lower one chosen by popular vote and an upper house chosen by the lower house from nominees of the state legislatures. Congress could disallow state laws under the plan and would itself define the extent of its and the states' authority.

On June 15 delegates submitted the "New Jersey Plan," which proposed to keep the existing structure of equal representation of states in a unicameral Congress, but to give it power to levy taxes and regulate commerce and authority to name a plural executive (with no veto) and a Supreme Court. The different plans presented the Convention with two major issues: whether to amend the Articles or draft a new document, and whether to have congressional representation by states or by population. On the first point the Convention voted to work toward a national government as envisioned by the Virginians. Regarding the powers of this government there was little disagreement except in the details. Experience with the Articles had persuaded the delegates that an effective central government, as distinguished from a confederation, needed the power to levy taxes, to regulate commerce, to raise an army and navy, and to make laws binding upon individual citizens. The lessons of the 1780s suggested to them, moreover, that in the interest of order and uniformity the states must be denied certain powers: to issue money, abrogate contracts, make treaties, wage war, and levy tariffs.

But furious disagreements then arose. The first clash in the Convention involved the issue of representation, and it was resolved by the "Great Compromise," sometimes called the "Connecticut Compromise," proposed by Roger Sherman, which gave both groups their way. The more populous states won apportionment by population in the House of Representatives; the states that sought to protect state power won equality in the Senate, with the vote by individuals and not by states.

An equally contentious struggle ensued between northern and southern delegates over slavery and the regulation of trade, an omen of sectional controversies to come. Slavery, Madison's secretary noted, was a "distracting question" to most of the delegates rather than a compelling moral dilemma. Few if any of the framers of the Constitution even considered the notion of abolition, and they carefully avoided using the term "slavery" in the final document. In this they reflected the prevailing attitudes among white Americans. Most agreed with South Carolina's canny John Rutledge when he asserted: "Religion and humanity

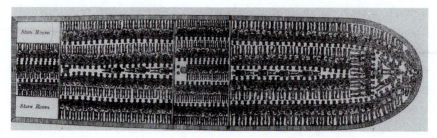

This cross-sectional view of the British slave ship Brookes *shows the abominably crowded conditions the "cargo" endured in the international slave trade.*

[have] nothing to do with this [slavery] question. Interest alone is the governing principle of nations."

The interest of southern delegates, with slaves so numerous in their states, dictated that slaves be counted as part of the population in determining the number of their representatives. Northerners were willing to have slaves counted in deciding each state's share of direct taxes, but not for purposes of representation. On this issue the Confederation Congress had supplied a handy precedent when it sought an amendment to make population rather than land values the standard for fiscal requisitions. The proposed amendment to the Articles would have counted three-fifths of the slaves for this purpose. The delegates, with little dissent, agreed to incorporate the same three-fifths ratio in the new Constitution as a basis for apportioning both representatives and direct taxes.

A more sensitive issue involved an effort to prevent the central government from stopping the Atlantic slave trade. Virginia's George Mason, himself a slave owner, condemned the "infernal traffic," which his state had already outlawed. He argued that the issue concerned "not the importing states alone but the whole union." People in the western territories were "already calling out for slaves for their new lands." He feared that they would "fill the country" with slaves. Such a development would bring forth "the judgment of Heaven" on the country. Southern delegates were quick to challenge Mason's reasoning. They argued that the continued importation of slaves was vital to their states' economies.

To resolve the question, the delegates established a time limit. Congress could not forbid the foreign slave trade before 1808, but it could levy a tax of $10 a head on all slaves imported. In both provisions, a sense of delicacy—and hypocrisy—dictated the use of euphemisms. The Constitution spoke of "free Persons" and "all other persons," of "such persons as any of the States Now existing shall think proper to admit," and of persons "held to Service of Labor." The odious word "slavery" did not appear in the Constitution until the Thirteenth Amendment (1865) abolished the "peculiar institution" by name.

The final decision on the slave trade was linked to a compromise on the question of the broader congressional power to regulate commerce. Northern states, where the merchant and shipping interests were most influential, were prepared to give Congress unlimited powers. The southerners, however, feared that navigation acts favoring American shipping might work at the expense of getting southern commodities to market by reducing foreign competition with northern shippers. Southerners therefore demanded that navigation acts be passed only by a two-thirds vote, but finally traded this demand for a prohibition on congressional power to levy export taxes and for a twenty-year, instead of a ten-year, delay on the power to prohibit the slave trade.

If the delegates found the slavery issue distracting, they considered irrelevant any discussion of the legal or political role of women under the new Constitution. The Revolutionary rhetoric of liberty prompted some women to demand political equality. "The men say we have no business" with politics, Eliza Wilkinson of South Carolina observed as the Constitution was being framed, "but I won't have it thought that because we are the weaker sex as to bodily strength we are capable of nothing more than domestic concerns." Her complaint, however, fell on deaf ears. There was never any formal discussion of women's rights at the Convention. The new nationalism still defined politics and government as outside the realm of female endeavor.

The Constitution also said little about the processes of immigration and naturalization, and most of what it said was negative. In Article II, Section 1, it prohibited any future immigrant from becoming president, limiting that office to a "natural born Citizen." In Article I, Sections 2 and 3, respectively, it stipulated that no person could serve in the House of Representatives who had not "been seven Years a Citizen of the United States" or in the Senate who had not "been nine Years a Citizen." On the matter of defining citizenship, the Constitution gave Congress the authority "to establish an uniform Rule of Naturalization," but offered no further guidance on the matter. As a result, naturalization policy has changed significantly over the years in response to fluctuating social attitudes and political moods. In 1790 the first Congress passed a naturalization law that allowed "free white persons" who had been in the country for as little as two years to be made naturalized citizens in any court. This meant that persons of African descent were denied federal citizenship. It was left to individual states to determine whether free blacks were citizens. And because Indians were not "free white persons," they were also treated as aliens rather than citizens. Not until 1924 would Congress grant citizenship to American Indians.

THE SEPARATION OF POWERS   The details of governmental structure embedded in the Constitution, while causing disagreement, caused far less trouble than the basic issues pitting the large against the small states and the northern against the southern states. Existing state constitutions, several of which already separated powers among legislative, executive, and judicial branches, set an example that reinforced the Convention's resolve to disperse power with checks and balances. Although the Founding Fathers hated royal tyranny, most of them also feared the people and favored various mechanisms to check public passions. Some delegates displayed a thumping disdain for any democratizing of the political system. Hamilton once called the people "a great beast," and Elbridge Gerry asserted that most of the nation's problems "flow from an excess of democracy."

These elitist views were accommodated by the Constitution's mixed legislative system, which acknowledged the "genius of the people," as George Mason phrased it. The lower house was designed to be closest to voters, who elected it every two years. It would be, according to Mason, "the grand repository of the democratic principle of the Government." House members should "sympathize with their constituents, should think as they think, & feel as they feel; and for these purposes should even be residents among them." The upper house, or Senate, its members elected by state legislatures, was intended to be more detached from the voters. Staggered six-year terms prevented the choice of a majority in any given year, and thereby further isolated senators from the passing fancies of public passion.

The decision that a single person be made the chief executive caused the delegates "considerable pause," according to Madison. George Mason protested that this would create a "fetus of monarchy." Indeed, several of the chief executive's powers actually exceeded those of the British monarch. This was the sharpest departure from the recent experience in state government, where the office of governor had commonly been diluted because of the recent memory of struggles with the colonial executives. The president had a veto over acts of Congress, subject to being overridden by a two-thirds vote in each house, although the royal veto had long since fallen into complete disuse. The president was commander-in-chief of the armed forces and responsible for the execution of the laws. The chief executive could make treaties with the advice and consent of two-thirds of the Senate, and had the power to appoint diplomats, judges, and other officers with the consent of a Senate majority. The president was instructed to report annually on the state of the nation and was authorized to recommend legislation, a provision that presidents eventually would take as a mandate to form and promote extensive programs.

But the president's powers were limited in certain key areas. The chief executive could neither declare war nor make peace; those powers were reserved for Congress. Unlike the British king, moreover, the president could be removed. The House could impeach (indict) the chief executive—and other civil officers—on charges of treason, bribery, or "other high crimes and misdemeanors," and the Senate could remove an impeached president by a two-thirds vote upon conviction. The presiding officer at the trial of a president would be the chief justice, since the usual presiding officer of the Senate (the vice-president) would have a personal stake in the outcome.

The Convention's nationalists—men like Madison, James Wilson, and Hamilton—wanted to strengthen the independence of the executive by entrusting the choice to popular election. At least in this instance, the nationalists, often accused of being the aristocratic party, favored a bold new departure in democracy. But an elected executive was still too far beyond the American experience. Besides, a national election would have created enormous problems of organization and voter qualification. Wilson suggested instead that the people of each state choose presidential electors equal to the number of their senators and representatives. Others proposed that the legislators make the choice. Finally, the Convention voted to let the legislature decide the method in each state. Before long nearly all the states were choosing the electors by popular vote, and the electors were acting as agents of party will,

Signing the Constitution, September 17, 1787. *Thomas Pritchard Rossiter's painting shows George Washington presiding over what Thomas Jefferson called "an assembly of demi-gods."*

casting their votes as they had pledged before the election. This method diverged from the original expectation that the electors would deliberate and make their own choices.

On the third branch of government, the judiciary, there was surprisingly little debate. Both the Virginia and New Jersey Plans had called for a Supreme Court, which the Constitution established, providing specifically for a chief justice of the United States and leaving up to Congress the number of other justices. Although the Constitution nowhere authorized the courts to declare laws void when they conflicted with the Constitution, the power of judicial review was implied, and was soon exercised in cases involving both state and federal laws. Article VI declared the federal constitution, federal laws, and treaties to be the "supreme law of the land," state laws or constitutions to the contrary notwithstanding. At the time the advocates of states' rights thought this a victory, since it eliminated the proviso in the Virginia Plan for Congress to settle all conflicts with state authority. As it turned out, however, the clause became the basis for an important expansion of judicial review.

While the Constitution extended vast new powers to the national government, the delegates' mistrust of unchecked power is apparent in repeated examples of countervailing forces: the separation of the three branches of government, the president's veto, the congressional power of impeachment and removal, the Senate's power over treaties and appointments, the courts' implied right of judicial review. In addition, the new frame of government specifically forbade Congress to pass bills of attainder (criminal condemnation by legislative act) or ex post facto laws (laws adopted after the event to make past deeds criminal). It also reserved to the states large areas of sovereignty—a reservation soon made explicit by the Tenth Amendment. By dividing sovereignty between the people and the government, the framers of the Constitution provided a distinctive contribution to political theory. That is, by vesting ultimate authority in the people, they divided sovereignty *within* the government. This constituted a dramatic break with the colonial tradition. The British had always insisted that the sovereignty of the king-in-Parliament was indivisible.

The most glaring defect of the Articles of Confederation, the rule of unanimity that defeated every effort to amend them, led the delegates to provide a less forbidding though still difficult method of amending the new Constitution. Amendments could be proposed either by two-thirds vote of each house or by a convention specially called, upon application of two-thirds of the legislatures. Amendments could be ratified by approval of three-fourths of the states acting through their legislatures or special conventions. The national convention has never been used, however, and state conventions have been called only once—to ratify the repeal of the Eighteenth Amendment, which had established Prohibition.

THE FIGHT FOR RATIFICATION   The final article of the Constitution provided that it would become effective upon ratification by nine states (not quite the three-fourths majority required for amendment). After fighting off efforts to censure the Convention for exceeding its authority, the Congress submitted its work to the states on September 28, 1787.

In the ensuing political debate, advocates of the new Constitution, who might properly have been called Nationalists because they preferred a strong central government, assumed the more reassuring name of Federalists. Opponents, who favored a more decentralized federal system, became Antifederalists. The initiative that the Federalists took in assuming their name was characteristic of the whole campaign. They got the jump on their critics. Their leaders had been members of the

Convention and were already familiar with the document and the arguments on each point. They were not only better prepared but better organized, and on the whole, made up of the more articulate elements in the political community.

Historians have hotly debated the motivation of the advocates of the new Constitution. For more than a century the tendency prevailed to idolize the Founding Fathers. In 1913, however, Charles A. Beard's book *An Economic Interpretation of the Constitution* advanced the shocking thesis that the Philadelphia "assembly of demi-gods" was made up of men who had a selfish economic interest in the outcome.

Beard argued that the delegates represented an economic elite of speculators in western lands, holders of depreciated government securities, and creditors whose wealth was mostly in "paper": mortgages, stocks, bonds, and the like. The holders of western lands and government bonds would benefit from a stronger government. Creditors generally stood to gain from the prohibitions against state currency issues and against the impairment of contract, provisions clearly aimed at the paper money issues and stay laws that were then effective in many states.

Beard's thesis provided a useful antidote to unquestioning hero worship, and still contains a germ of truth, but he exaggerated. Most of the delegates, according to evidence unavailable to Beard, had no compelling stake in paper wealth, and most were far more involved in landholding. Many prominent nationalists, including the "Father of the Constitution," James Madison had no western lands, bonds, or much other personal property. Some opponents of the Constitution, on the other hand, held large blocks of land and securities. Economic interests certainly figured in the process, but they functioned in a complex interplay of state, sectional, group, and individual interests that turned largely on how well people had fared under the Confederation.

Charles A. Beard hardly made a new discovery in finding that people are selfish, but it would be simplistic to attribute all human action to hidden economic interest. One must give some credence to the possibility that people mean what they say and are often candid about their motives, especially in large matters of public affairs. The most notable circumstance of the times in fact was that, unlike so many revolutions, the American Revolution led not to general chaos and terror but to "an outbreak of constitution-making." From the 1760s through the 1780s there occurred a prolonged debate over the fundamental issues of gov-

ernment, which in its scope and depth—and in the durability of its outcome—is without parallel.

THE FEDERALIST   Among the supreme legacies of that debate was
The Federalist, a collection of essays originally published in the New
York press between 1787 and 1788. Instigated by Alexander Hamilton,
the eighty-five articles published under the name "Publius" included
about fifty by Hamilton, thirty by James Madison, and five by John Jay.
The authorship of some selections remains in doubt. Written in support
of ratification, the essays defended the principle of a supreme national
authority, but at the same time sought to reassure doubters that the
people and the states had little reason to fear usurpations and tyranny
by the new government.

In perhaps the most famous single essay, No. 10, Madison argued
that the very size and diversity of the country would make it impossible
for any single faction to form a majority that could dominate the government. This contradicted prevailing notions of republican forms of government. Republics, the conventional wisdom of the times insisted,
could survive only in small, homogeneous countries like Switzerland
and the Netherlands. Large republics, on the other hand, would fragment into anarchy and tyranny through the influence of factions. Quite
the contrary, Madison insisted. Given a balanced federal polity, they
could work in large and diverse countries probably better. "Extend the
sphere," he wrote, "and you take in a greater variety of parties and interests; you make it less probable that a majority of the whole will have a
common motive to invade the rights of other citizens."

The Federalists insisted that the new union would contribute to prosperity, in part to link their movement with the economic recovery already under way. The Antifederalists, however, talked more of the dangers of power in terms that had become familiar during the long
struggles with Parliament and the crown. They noted the absence of a
bill of rights protecting the rights of individuals and states. They found
the process of ratification highly irregular, as it was—indeed, illegal under the Articles of Confederation. Not only did Patrick Henry refuse to
attend the Constitutional Convention, he demanded later (unsuccessfully) that it be investigated as a conspiracy. The Antifederalist leaders—George Mason, Henry, and Richard Henry Lee of Virginia, George
Clinton of New York, Sam Adams and Elbridge Gerry of Massachusetts, Luther Martin of Maryland—were often men whose careers and

reputations had been established well before the Revolution. The Federalist leaders were more likely to be younger men whose careers had begun in the Revolution—men such as Hamilton, Madison, and Jay.

The disagreement between the two groups, however, was more over means than ends. Both sides, for the most part, agreed that a stronger national authority was needed, and that it required an independent income to function properly. Both were convinced that the people must erect safeguards against tyranny, even the tyranny of the majority. Few of its supporters liked the Constitution in its entirety, but they felt that it was the best obtainable; few of its opponents found it unacceptable in its entirety. Once the new government had become an accomplished fact, few wanted to undo the work of the Philadelphia convention.

THE DECISION OF THE STATES   Ratification gained momentum before the end of 1787, and several of the smaller states were among the first to act, apparently satisfied that they had gained all the safeguards they could hope for in equality of representation in the Senate. New Jersey and Georgia voted unanimously in favor. Massachusetts, still sharply divided in the aftermath of Shays's Rebellion, was the first state in which the outcome was close. There the Federalists carried the day by winning over two hesitant leaders of the popular party. They dangled before John Hancock the possibility of becoming vice-president, and won the acquiescence of Samuel Adams when they agreed to rec-

RATIFICATION OF THE CONSTITUTION

Order of Ratification	State	Date of Ratification
1	Delaware	December 7, 1787
2	Pennsylvania	December 12, 1787
3	New Jersey	December 18, 1787
4	Georgia	January 2, 1788
5	Connecticut	January 9, 1788
6	Massachusetts	February 7, 1788
7	Maryland	April 28, 1788
8	South Carolina	May 23, 1788
9	New Hampshire	June 21, 1788
10	Virginia	June 25, 1788
11	New York	July 26, 1788
12	North Carolina	November 21, 1789
13	Rhode Island	May 29, 1790

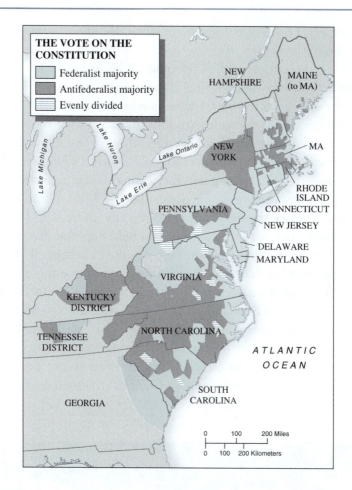

THE VOTE ON THE CONSTITUTION

- Federalist majority
- Antifederalist majority
- Evenly divided

ommend amendments designed to protect human rights, including one that would specifically reserve to the states all powers not granted to the new government. Massachusetts approved by 187 to 168 on February 7, 1788.

New Hampshire was the ninth to ratify, and the Constitution could now be put into effect, but the union could hardly succeed without the approval of Virginia, the most populous state, or New York, with the third highest population, which occupied a key position geographically. Both states harbored strong opposition groups. In Virginia Patrick Henry became the chief spokesman of backcountry farmers who feared the powers of the new government, but wavering delegates were won over by the same strategem as in Massachusetts. When it was proposed that the Convention should recommend a bill of rights, Edmund Randolph, who had refused to sign the finished document, announced his conversion to the cause.

Virginia's convention ratified on June 25 by a vote of 89 to 79. In New York, as in New Hampshire, Hamilton and the other Federalists worked for a delay, in the hope that action by New Hampshire and Virginia would persuade the delegates that the new framework would go into effect with or without New York. On July 26, 1788, they carried the day by the closest margin thus far, 30 to 27. North Carolina stubbornly withheld action until amendments comprising a bill of rights were actually submitted by Congress. On November 21, 1789, North Carolina joined the new government, which was already under way, 194 to 77. Rhode Island, true to form, continued to hold out, and did not relent until May 29, 1790. Even then the vote was the closest of all, 34 to 32.

Upon notification that New Hampshire had become the ninth state to ratify, the Confederation Congress began to draft plans for an orderly transfer of power. On September 13, 1788, it selected New York City as the seat of the new government and fixed the date for elections. March 4, 1789, was the date set for the meeting of the new Congress. Each state would set the date for electing the first members of Congress. On October 10, 1788, the Confederation Congress transacted its last business and passed into history.

Washington, holding the Constitution, and Franklin, with liberty cap, drive the Federal chariot as thirteen freemen, representing the states, pull it toward ratification (1788).

"Our constitution is in actual operation," the elderly Ben Franklin wrote to a friend; "everything appears to promise that it will last; but in this world nothing is certain but death and taxes." George Washington was even more uncertain about the future under the new plan of government. He had told a fellow delegate as the Convention adjourned: "I do not expect the Constitution to last for more than twenty years."

The Constitution has lasted much longer, of course, and in the process it has provided a model of republican government whose features have been repeatedly borrowed by other nations through the years. Yet what makes the American Constitution so distinctive is not its specific provisions but its remarkable harmony with the particular "genius of the people" it governs. The Constitution has been neither a static abstraction nor a "machine that would go of itself," as the poet James Russell Lowell would later assert. Instead it has provided a flexible system of government that presidents, legislators, judges, and the people have adjusted to changing social, economic, and political circumstances. In this sense the Founding Fathers not only created "a more perfect Union" in 1787; they engineered a frame of government whose resilience has enabled later generations to continue to perfect their republican experiment. But the framers of the Constitution failed in one significant respect. In skirting the issue of slavery so as to cement the union, they unknowingly allowed tensions over the "peculiar institution" to reach the point where there would be no political solution—only civil war.

MAKING CONNECTIONS

- The debate about the nature of the national government, and its relation to the people and the states reemerged in the Kentucky and Virginia Resolutions (Chapter 8), the Hartford Convention (Chapter 9), and the Nullification Crisis (Chapter 11).

- Slavery, viewed by the delegates to the Constitutional Convention as little more than a "distracting question," soon became a major political problem—especially after the Missouri Compromise (in Chapter 10).

Further Reading

A good overview of the Confederation period is Richard B. Morris's *The Forging of the Union, 1781–1789* (1987). Another useful analysis of this period is Richard Buel, Jr.'s *Securing the Revolution: Ideology in American Politics, 1789–1815* (1974). Relevant chapters of Gordon S. Wood's *The Creation of the American Republic, 1776–1787* (1969) trace the changing contours of political philosophy during these years.

David P. Szatmary's *Shays' Rebellion: The Making of an Agrarian Insurrection* (1980) covers that fateful incident. For a fine account of cultural change during the period, see Joseph J. Ellis's *After the Revolution: Profiles of Early American Culture* (1979) and Oscar Handlin and Lillian Handlin's *A Restless People: America in Rebellion, 1770–1787* (1982).

Excellent treatments of the post-Revolutionary era include Edmund S. Morgan's *Inventing the People* (1988), Michael Kammen's *Sovereignty and Liberty* (1988), and Forrest McDonald's *Novus Ordo Seclorum: The Intellectual Origins of the Constitution* (1985). Among the better collections of essays on the Constitution are *Toward a More Perfect Union* (1988), edited by Neil L. York, and *The Framing and Ratification of the Constitution* (1987), edited by Leonard W. Levy and Dennis J. Mahoney.

Bruce Ackerman's *We the People: Foundations* (1990) examines Federalist political principles. For the Bill of Rights that emerged from the ratification struggles, see Robert A. Rutland's *The Birth of the Bill of Rights, 1776–1791* (1955).

Michael Kammen's *A Machine That Would Go of Itself: The Constitution in American Culture* (1986) is a comprehensive cultural history of the Constitution that shows how it has become revered by the American public.

8 THE FEDERALISTS:

WASHINGTON AND ADAMS

ith the adoption of the new Constitution came the task of establishing a central government that would more effectively deal with the problems of the vast new nation. The election of the first president, the writing of a bill of rights, and various domestic and foreign crises faced the fledgling nation.

A NEW NATION

The framers of the Constitution sought to create a new federal government capable of administering a rapidly expanding territory and

Venerate the Plough. *Medal of the Philadelphia Society for the Promotion of Agriculture (1786).*

population. In 1789 the United States and the western territories covered an area from the Atlantic Ocean to the Mississippi River and included almost 4 million people. This vast new nation harbored distinct regional differences. New England remained a region of small farms and bustling seaports, but it was on the verge of developing a small-scale manufacturing sector. The Middle States boasted the most well-balanced economy, the largest cities, and the most diverse collection of ethnic and religious groups. The South was an agricultural region more ethnically homogeneous and increasingly dependent on slave labor. By 1790 the southern states were exporting as much tobacco as they had been before the Revolution, and new farm commodities such as grains, indigo, and hemp helped diversify the economy. Most important, however, was the surge in cotton production. Between 1790 and 1815, the annual production of cotton rose from less than 3 million pounds to 93 million pounds.

Overall, the United States in 1790 was predominantly a rural society. Eighty percent of households were involved in agricultural production. Only a few cities had more than 5,000 people. The first national census, taken in 1790, reported that there were 750,000 African Americans, almost one-fifth of the population. Most of the them lived in the five southernmost states. Less than 10 percent of the blacks lived outside the South. Most African Americans, of course, were slaves, but there were many free blacks as a result of the Revolutionary turmoil. In fact, the proportion of free blacks to slaves was never higher than in 1790.

The 1790 census did not even include the many Indians still living east of the Mississippi River. Most Americans still viewed the Native Americans as those peoples whom the Declaration of Independence dismissed as "merciless Indian savages." It is estimated that there were over eighty tribes totaling perhaps as many as 150,000 persons in 1790. In the Old Northwest along the Great Lakes, the British continued to arm the Indians and encouraged them to resist American encroachments. Between 1784 and 1790, Indians killed or captured some 1,500 settlers in Kentucky alone. Such bloodshed generated a ferocious reaction. "The people of Kentucky," observed an official frustrated by his inability to negotiate a treaty between whites and Indians, "will carry on private expeditions against the Indians and kill them whenever they meet them, and I do not believe there is a jury in all Kentucky that will punish a man for it." In the South the five most powerful tribes—the Cherokees, Chickasaws, Choctaws, Creeks, and Seminoles—numbered between 50,000 and 100,000. They steadfastly refused to recognize American authority and used Spanish-supplied weapons to thwart white settlement.

Only about 125,000 whites and blacks lived west of the Appalachians in 1790. But that was soon to change. The great theme of nineteenth-century American history would be the ceaseless stream of migrants flowing westward from the Atlantic seaboard. By foot, horse, boat, and wagon, pioneers and adventurers headed west. Kentucky, still a part of Virginia but destined for statehood in 1792, harbored 75,000 settlers in 1790. In 1776 there had been only 150 pioneers.

Rapid population growth, cheap land, and new economic opportunities fueled this phenomenon. Although immigrants contributed significantly to the rising numbers, the extraordinary growth rate resulted primarily from natural increase. The average white woman gave birth to eight children, and the white population doubled approximately once every twenty-two years. This made for a very young population on average. In 1790 almost half of all white Americans were under the age of sixteen.

A NEW GOVERNMENT   The men who drafted the Constitution knew that many questions were left unanswered, and they feared that putting the new frame of government into practice would pose unexpected challenges. On the appointed date, March 4, 1789, the new Congress of the United States, meeting in New York, could muster only eight senators and thirteen representatives. A month passed before both chambers gathered a quorum. Only then could the temporary presiding officer of the Senate count the ballots and certify the foregone conclusion that George Washington, with sixty-nine votes, was the unanimous choice of the electoral college for president. John Adams, with thirty-four votes, the second-highest number, became vice-president.

Washington was a reluctant president. He described his unanimous election as "the event which I have long dreaded." He greeted the news with "a heart filled with distress" because he imagined "the ten thousand embarrassments, perplexities and troubles to which I must again be exposed." He told a friend as he prepared to assume office in New York that he felt like a "culprit who is going to the place of his execution." Yet Washington felt compelled to serve because he had been "summoned by my country." A self-made man with little formal education, Washington brought to his new office a remarkable capacity for

President Washington's inauguration, April 30, 1789, at Federal Hall in New York City.

moderation and mediation that helped keep the infant republic from disintegrating.

GOVERNMENTAL STRUCTURE   During the summer of 1789, Congress authorized executive departments corresponding in each case to those already formed under the Confederation. To head the Department of State, Washington named Thomas Jefferson, recently back from his mission to France. To head the Department of the Treasury, Washington picked his old wartime aide Alexander Hamilton, now a prominent lawyer in New York. The new position of attorney-general was occupied by Edmund Randolph, former governor of Virginia.

Almost from the beginning Washington routinely called these men to sit as a group for discussion and advice on matters of policy. This was the origin of the president's cabinet, an advisory body for which the Constitution made no formal provision—except insofar as it provided for the heads of departments. The office of vice-president also took on what would become its typical character. "The Vice-Presidency," John Adams wrote his wife, Abigail, was the most "insignificant office . . . ever . . . contrived."

The structure of the court system, like that of the executive departments, was left to Congress, except for a chief justice and Supreme Court. Congress determined to set the membership of the highest court at six, the chief justice and five associate justices, and it created thirteen federal district courts. From these, appeals might go to one of three circuit courts, composed of two Supreme Court justices and the district judge, meeting twice a year in each district. Members of the Supreme Court, therefore, became itinerant judges riding the circuit during a good part of the year. All federal cases originated in the district court, and if appealed on issues of procedure or legal interpretation, went to the circuit courts and from there to the Supreme Court.

Washington named John Jay as the first chief justice, and he served until 1795. Born in New York City in 1745, Jay graduated from King's College (now Columbia University). His distinction as a lawyer led New York to send him as its representative to the First and Second Continental Congresses. After serving as president of the Continental Congress in 1779, Jay became the American minister in Spain. While in Europe, he helped John Adams and Benjamin Franklin negotiate the Treaty of Paris in 1783. After the Revolution, Jay served as secretary of

John Jay as chief justice of the Supreme Court (1794).

foreign affairs. He then joined Madison and Hamilton as coauthor of the *The Federalist* and became one of the most effective champions of the Constitution.

THE BILL OF RIGHTS   In the new House of Representatives, James Madison made a bill of rights a top priority. The lack of such provisions had been one of the Antifederalists' major objections to the Constitution as originally proposed. At first Madison believed that the proposals for a bill of rights were "unnecessary and dangerous." He feared that any list of rights would be incomplete. Madison and other Federalists also worried that specifying such rights might imply the existence of a parallel set of powers never meant to be delegated to the central government. Or, as Alexander Hamilton phrased it in the eighty-fourth paper of *The Federalist,* "Why declare things should not be done which there is no power to do?" Yet the fear of arbitrary federal power would not die. In the end, however, Madison recognized the need to allay the fears of Antifederalists and to meet the moral obligation imposed by those ratifying conventions that had approved the Constitution with the understanding that amendments would be offered.

Madison viewed a bill of rights as "the most dramatic single gesture of conciliation that could be offered the remaining opponents of the government." Those "opponents" included prominent Virginians George Mason and Richard Henry Lee as well as artisans, small traders, and backcountry farmers who expressed a profound egalitarianism. These "poor and middling" folk were skeptical that even the "best men" were capable of subordinating self-interest to the good of the Republic. They believed that all people were prone to corruption; that no one could be trusted. Therefore, a bill of rights must protect the liberties of all against the encroachments of a few.

The first eight Amendments were modeled after the Virginia Declaration of Rights that George Mason had written in 1776. These provided safeguards for certain rights of individuals: freedom of religion, press, speech, and assembly; the right to keep and bear firearms; the right to refuse to house soldiers in private homes; protection against unreasonable searches and seizures; the right to refuse to testify against oneself; the right to a speedy public trial before an impartial jury and to have legal counsel present; and protection against cruel and unusual punishment.

The Ninth and Tenth Amendments addressed themselves to the demand for specific statements that the enumeration of rights in the Constitution "shall not be construed to deny or disparage others retained by the people" and that "powers not delegated to the United States by the Constitution, nor prohibited by it to the States, are reserved to the States respectively, or to the people." The Tenth Amendment was taken almost verbatim from the Articles of Confederation. The House adopted, in all, seventeen amendments; the Senate, after conference with the House, adopted twelve; the states in the end voted separately on each proposed amendment and ratified ten, which constitute the Bill of Rights, effective December 15, 1791. The Bill of Rights provided no rights or legal protection to blacks.

RAISING A REVENUE   Revenue was the new federal government's most critical need, and the Congress undertook a revenue measure as another of the first items of business. Madison proposed a modest tariff (tax on imports) for revenue only, but the demands of manufacturers in the northern states for higher duties to protect them from foreign competition forced a compromise that imposed higher tariffs on certain listed items. Madison linked the tariff to a proposal for a mercantile system that would levy extra tonnage duties on foreign ships, an especially heavy duty on countries that had no commercial treaty with the United States.

Madison's specific purpose was to wage economic war against Great Britain, which had no such treaty but had more foreign trade with the new nation than any other country. Northern businessmen, however, were in no mood for a renewal of economic pressures, for fear of disrupting the economy. Secretary of the Treasury Hamilton agreed with them. In the end the only discrimination built into the Tonnage Act of 1789 was between American and all foreign ships: American ships paid a duty of 6¢ per ton; American-built but foreign-owned ships paid 30¢; and foreign-built and -owned ships paid 50¢ per ton.

The disagreements created by the trade measures were portents of quarrels yet to come. Should economic policy favor Britain or France? The more persistent question was whether tariff and tonnage duties should penalize farmers in the interest of northern manufacturers and shipowners. By imposing a tax on imports, tariffs and tonnage duties resulted in higher prices on goods bought by Americans, most of whom were tied to the farm economy. This raised a basic and perennial question: Should these rural consumers be forced to subsidize the nation's infant manufacturing sector? This issue became a sectional question of South versus North.

HAMILTON'S VISION OF AMERICA

The tariff and tonnage duties, linked as they were to other issues, marked but the beginning of the effort to get the country on a sound fiscal basis. Thirty-four-year-old Alexander Hamilton seized the initiative.

Alexander Hamilton, secretary of the treasury from 1789 to 1795.

The first secretary of the treasury was a protégé of the president, a younger man who had been Washington's aide during four years of the Revolution. Born out of wedlock on a Caribbean island and deserted by a ne'er-do-well father, Hamilton was left an orphan at thirteen by the death of his mother. With the help of friends and relatives, he found his way at seventeen to New York, attended King's College (later Columbia University), and entered the Revolutionary army, where he became a favorite of George Washington. He studied law, passed the bar examination, established a legal practice in New York, and became a self-made aristocrat, serving as collector of revenues and member of the Confederation Congress. An early convert to nationalism, he had a major role in promoting the Constitutional Convention. Shrewd, energetic, and determined, Hamilton had limitless ambition. As he recognized at age fourteen, "To confess my weakness, my ambition is prevalent."

In a series of classic reports submitted to Congress in the two years from January 1790 to December 1791, Hamilton outlined his program for government finances and the economic development of the United States. The reports were soon adopted, with some alterations in detail but little in substance. The last of the series, the Report on Manufactures, outlined a program of protective tariffs and other governmental supports of business. This eventually would become government policy, despite much brave talk of free enterprise and free trade.

ESTABLISHING THE PUBLIC CREDIT   Hamilton submitted the first and most important of his reports to the House of Representatives in 1790 at the invitation of that body. This First Report on the Public Credit, as it has since been called, made two key recommendations: first, funding of the federal debt at face value, which meant that those citizens holding government bonds could exchange them for new interest-bearing bonds; and second, the federal government's assumption of state debts from the Revolution to the amount of $21 million.

The funding scheme was controversial because many farmers and soldiers in immediate need of money had sold their securities for a fraction of their value to speculators who were eager to buy them up after reading Hamilton's First Report. These common folk argued that they should be reimbursed for their losses; otherwise, the speculators would gain a windfall from the new government's funding of bonds at face value. Hamilton sternly resisted such pleas. The speculators, he ar-

336 · *The Federalists: Washington and Adams (Ch. 8)*

gued, had "paid what the commodity was worth in the market, and took the risks." Therefore, they should reap the benefits. In fact, Hamilton insisted, the government should do all it could to win over the financial community because it represented the bedrock of a successful nation.

The report provoked lengthy debates before its substance was adopted. Then in short order came three more reports: a Second Report on Public Credit, which included a proposal for an excise tax on liquor to aid in raising revenue to cover the nation's debts. Another report recommended a national bank and a national mint—which was established in 1792. Finally, the Report on Manufactures proposed an extensive program of government aid and encouragement to the development of manufacturing enterprises.

Hamilton's program was substantially the one Robert Morris had urged upon the Confederation a decade before, and which Hamilton had strongly endorsed at the time. "A national debt," he had written Morris in 1781, "if it is not excessive, will be to us a national blessing; it will be a powerful cement of our union. It will also create a necessity for keeping up taxation to a degree which without being oppressive, will be a spur to industry." Payment of the national debt, in short, would be not only a point of national honor and sound finance, ensuring the country's credit for the future; it would also be an occasion to assert a federal taxing power and thus instill respect for the authority of the national government. Not least, the plan would win the new government the support of wealthy, influential creditors.

SECTIONAL DIFFERENCES EMERGE Madison, who had been Hamilton's close ally in the movement for a stronger government, broke with him over the matter of a national debt. Madison did not question that the debt should be paid; he was troubled, however, that speculators and "stock-jobbers" would become the chief beneficiaries. That the far greater portion of the debt was held north of the Mason-Dixon line further troubled him. Madison, whom Hamilton had expected to take the lead for his program in the House, therefore advanced an alternative plan to give a larger share to the first owners than to the later speculators. "Let it be a liberal one in favor of the present holders," Madison conceded. "Let them have the highest price which has prevailed in the market; and let the residue belong to the original sufferers." Madison's opposition touched off a vigorous debate, but Hamilton carried his point by a margin of three to one when the House brought it to a vote.

Madison's opposition to the assumption of state debts got more support, however, and set up a division more clearly along sectional lines. The southern states, with the exception of South Carolina, had whittled down their debts. New England, with the largest unpaid debts, stood to be the greatest beneficiary of the assumption plan. Rather than see Virginia victimized, Madison held out an alternative. Why not, he suggested, have the government assume state debts as they stood in 1783 at the conclusion of the peace? Debates on this point deadlocked the whole question of debt funding and assumption through much of 1790.

The stalemate finally ended in that year when Hamilton accosted Thomas Jefferson on the steps of the president's home and suggested a compromise. The next evening, at a dinner arranged by Jefferson, Hamilton and Madison reached an understanding. In return for northern votes in favor of locating the permanent national capital on the Potomac, Madison pledged to seek enough southern votes to pass the assumption, with the further arrangement that those states with smaller debts would get in effect outright grants from the federal government to equalize the difference. With these arrangements, enough votes were secured to carry Hamilton's funding and assumption schemes. The capital would be moved to Philadelphia for ten years, after which time it would be settled at a Federal City on the Potomac, the site to be chosen by the president.

A NATIONAL BANK   By this vast program of funding and assumption, Hamilton had called up from nowhere, as if by magic, a great sum of capital. As he put it in his original report, a national debt "answers most of the purposes of money." Transfers of government bonds, once the debt was properly funded, would be "equivalent to payments in specie." This feature of the program was especially important in a country that had, from the first settlements, suffered a shortage of hard money. Having established the public credit, Hamilton moved on to a related measure essential to his vision of national greatness. He called for a national bank, which by issuance of bank notes (paper money) might provide a uniform currency. Government bonds held by the Bank would back up the value of its new bank notes, needed as a medium of exchange because of the chronic shortage of specie. The national bank, chartered by Congress, would remain under governmental surveillance, but private investors would supply four-fifths of the $10 million capital and name twenty of the twenty-five directors; the government would

The First Bank of the United States in Philadelphia. Proposed by Hamilton, the Bank opened in 1791.

provide the other fifth of the capital and name five directors. Government bonds would be received in payment for three-fourths of the stock in the Bank, and the other fourth would be payable in gold and silver.

The Bank, Hamilton explained, would serve many purposes. Its notes would become a stable currency, uniform in value because redeemable in gold and silver upon demand. Moreover, the Bank would provide a source of capital for loans to fund the development of business and commerce. Bonds, which might otherwise be stowed away in safes, would instead become the basis for a productive capital by backing up bank notes available for loan at low rates of interest, the "natural effect" of which would be "to increase trade and industry." What is more, the existence of the Bank would serve certain housekeeping needs of the government: a safe place to keep its funds, a source of "pecuniary aids" in sudden emergencies, and the ready transfer of funds to and from branch offices through bookkeeping entries rather than shipment of metals.

Once again Madison rose to lead the opposition, arguing that he could find no basis in the Constitution for such a bank. That was enough to raise in President Washington's mind serious doubts as to the constitutionality of the measure, which Congress passed fairly quickly over Madison's objections. Before signing the bill into law, therefore, the president sought the advice of his cabinet, where he found an equal division of opinion. The result was the first great and fundamental debate on constitutional interpretation. Should there be a strict or a broad construction of the document? Were the powers of Congress only those explicitly stated or were others implied? The argument turned chiefly on Article I, Section 8, which authorized Congress to "make all laws which shall be necessary and proper for carrying into execution the foregoing Powers."

Such language left room for disagreement and led to a confrontation between Jefferson and Hamilton. Jefferson pointed to the Tenth Amendment, which reserved to the states and the people powers not delegated to Congress. "To take a single step beyond the boundaries thus specially drawn around the powers of Congress, is to take possession of a boundless field of power, no longer susceptible of any definition." A bank might be a convenient aid to Congress in collecting taxes and regulating the currency, but it was not, as Article I, Section 8, specified, *necessary*.

In a long report to the president, Hamilton countered that the power to charter corporations was included in the sovereignty of any government, whether or not expressly stated. The word "necessary," he explained, often meant no more than "needful, requisite, incidental, useful, or conducive to." And in a classic summary, he expressed his criterion on constitutionality: "This criterion is the *end*, to which the measure relates as a *mean*. If the *end* be clearly comprehended within any of the specified powers, collecting taxes and regulating the currency, and if the measure have an obvious relation to that *end*, and is not forbidden by any particular provision of the Constitution, it may safely be deemed to come within the compass of the national authority."

The president, influenced by the fact that the matter came within the jurisdiction of the secretary of the treasury, accepted Hamilton's argument and signed the bill. In doing so, he had indeed, in Jefferson's words, opened up "a boundless field of power," which in coming years would lead to a further broadening of implied powers with the approval of the Supreme Court. Under John Marshall, the Court would eventually adopt Hamilton's words almost verbatim. On July 4, 1791, the Bank's stock was put up for sale and in what seemed to Jefferson a "delirium of speculation" sold out within a few hours, with hundreds of buyers turned away. It cost the government itself nothing until later, for its subscription of $2 million was immediately returned by the Bank in a loan of the same amount, with ten years for repayment.

ENCOURAGING MANUFACTURES   Hamilton's imagination and his ambitions for the new country were as yet unexhausted. In the last of his great reports, the Report on Manufactures, he set in place the capstone of his design: the active encouragement of manufacturing to provide productive uses for the new capital created by his funding, assumption, and banking schemes. Hamilton believed that several advantages would flow from the development of manufactures: the diversification of labor in a country given over too much to farming; greater use of machinery; paid work for those not ordinarily employed outside the home, such as women and children; the promotion of immigration; a greater scope for the diversity of talents in business; more ample and various opportunities for entrepreneurial activity; and a better domestic market for agricultural products.

To secure his ends, Hamilton proposed to use the means to which other countries had resorted, and which he summarized: protective tariffs on foreign goods, or in Hamilton's words, "protecting duties," which in some cases might be put so high as to deter imports altogether; restraints on the export of raw materials; bounties and premiums to encourage certain industries; tariff exemptions for the raw materials needed for American manufacturing, or "drawbacks" (rebates) to manufacturers where duties had been levied for revenue or other purposes; encouragements to inventions and discoveries; regulations for the inspection of commodities; and finally, the encouragement of internal improvements in transportation, including the development of roads, canals, and navigable streams.

Some of Hamilton's tariff proposals were enacted in 1792. Otherwise the program was filed away—but not forgotten. It became an arsenal of arguments for the advocates of manufactures in years to come, in Europe as well as in America. Hamilton denied that there was any necessary economic conflict between the northern and southern regions of the Union. If, as seemed likely, the northern and middle states should become the chief scenes of manufacturing, they would create robust markets for agricultural products, some of which the southern states were peculiarly qualified to produce. North and South would both ben-

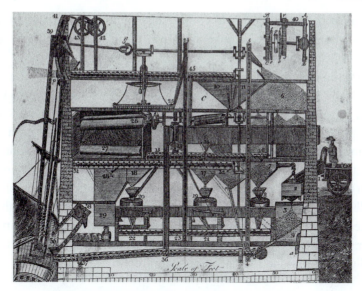

Hamilton's Report on Manufactures proposed tariffs on foreign products to encourage American manufacturing and innovation, as represented by this mechanized grain elevator patented by a Delaware resident in 1795.

efit, he argued, as more commerce moved between these regions than across the Atlantic, thus strengthening the Union.

HAMILTON'S ACHIEVEMENT   Largely owing to the skillful Hamilton, the Treasury Department, which employed half or more of the civil servants at the time, largely as customs agents, was established on a basis of integrity and efficiency. The department began to retire the Revolutionary War debt, and foreign capital began to flow in once again. Prosperity, so elusive in the 1780s, began to flourish once again, although President Washington cautioned against attributing "to the Government what is due only to the goodness of Providence."

Hamilton was inclined toward a truly nationalist outlook, and he focused his energies on the rising power of commercial capitalism. In fact, he would have favored a much stronger central government, including a federal veto on state action, even a constitutional monarchy if that had been practicable. Hamilton believed that throughout history a minority of the strong dominated the weak. There was always a ruling group, perhaps military or aristocratic, and Hamilton had the foresight to see now the rising power of commercial capitalism. He was in many ways a classic Whig who, like Britain's ruling oligarchy of the eighteenth century, favored government by the rich and well-born.

Hamilton never understood or appreciated the people of the small villages and farms, the people of the frontier. They were foreign to his world, despite his own humble beginnings in the Caribbean islands. Along with the planters of the South, common folk would be at best only indirect beneficiaries of his programs. Below the Potomac, the Hamiltonian vision excited little enthusiasm except in South Carolina, which had a large state debt to be assumed and a concentration of mercantile interests at Charleston. There were, in short, a vast number of people who were drawn into opposition to Hamilton's new engines of power. In part they were southern, in part backcountry, and in part a politically motivated faction opposing Hamilton in New York.

THE REPUBLICAN ALTERNATIVE

This split over the Hamiltonian program provided the seeds of the first national political parties. Hamilton became the embodiment of the party known as the Federalists; Madison and Jefferson became the leaders of those who took the name Republicans and thereby implied that the Federalists really aimed at a monarchy. Parties were slow in developing, or at least in being acknowledged as legitimate. All the political philosophers of the age deplored the spirit of party or faction. The concept of a loyal opposition, of a two-party system as a positive good, was yet to be formulated. Parties, or factions, as the eighteenth century knew them, smelled of corruption. As Jefferson once declared, "If I could not go to heaven but with a party I would not go there at all."

Neither side in the disagreement over national policy deliberately set out to create a party system. But there were important differences of both philosophy and self-interest that simply would not dissolve. At the outset Madison, who had worked with Hamilton to build a national government, assumed leadership of Hamilton's opponents in the Congress. The states meant more to Madison than to Hamilton, who would just as soon have seen a consolidated central government. Madison, like Thomas Jefferson, was rooted in Virginia, where opposition to the funding schemes flourished.

After the compromise that had assured the assumption of state debts, Madison and Jefferson moved into ever more resolute opposition to Hamilton's policies: his effort to place an excise tax on whiskey, which laid a burden especially on the trans-Appalachian farmers, whose grain was best transported in liquid form; his proposal for the national bank; and his Report on Manufactures. As the differences built, hostility between Jefferson and Hamilton grew and festered, to the distress of President Washington. Jefferson, the temperamentally shy and retiring secretary of state, then emerged as the leader of the opposition to Hamilton's policies; Madison continued to direct the anti-Hamilton forces in Congress.

Thomas Jefferson, twelve years Hamilton's senior, was in most respects his opposite. In contrast to Hamilton, Jefferson was to the manor born, his father a successful surveyor and land speculator, his mother a Randolph, from one of the First Families in Virginia. Jefferson developed a breadth of cultivated interests that ranged perhaps more widely in science, the arts, and the humanities than those of any contemporary, even Franklin. Jefferson read or spoke seven languages. He was an architect of distinction (Monticello, the Virginia Capitol, and the University of Virginia are monuments to his talent), a man who understood mathematics and engineering, an inventor, an agronomist. He knew music and practiced the violin, although some wit said only Patrick Henry played it worse.

Thomas Jefferson. A portrait by Charles Willson Peale (1791).

Philosophically, Hamilton and Jefferson represented polar visions of the character of the Union and defined certain fundamental issues of American life that still echo two centuries later. Hamilton foresaw a diversified capitalistic economy, agriculture balanced by commerce and industry, and was thus the better prophet. Jefferson feared the growth of crowded cities divided into a capitalistic aristocracy on the one hand and a deprived proletariat on the other. Hamilton feared anarchy and loved order; Jefferson feared tyranny and loved liberty.

What Hamilton wanted for his country was a strong central government actively encouraging capitalistic enterprise. What Jefferson wanted was a republic made up primarily of small farmers: "Those who labor in the earth," he wrote, "are the chosen people of God, if ever he had a chosen people, whose breasts He has made His peculiar deposit for genuine and substantial virtue." Jefferson did not oppose all forms of manufacturing. What he feared was that the unlimited expansion of commerce and industry would produce a class of wage laborers who were dependent on others for their livelihood and therefore subject to political manipulation and economic exploitation.

Where Hamilton was the old-fashioned English Whig, Jefferson, who spent several years in France, was the enlightened *philosophe,* the natural radical and reformer who attacked the aristocratic relics of entail and primogeniture in Virginia, opposed an established church, proposed an elaborate plan for public schools, prepared a more humane criminal code, and was instrumental in eliminating slavery from the Old Northwest, although he kept the slaves he had inherited. On his tomb were finally recorded the achievements of which he was proudest: author of the Declaration of Independence and the Virginia Statute of Religious Freedom, and founder of the University of Virginia.

In their quarrel, Hamilton unwittingly identified Jefferson more and more in the public mind as the leader of the opposition to his policies; Madison was still a relatively obscure congressman whose central role in the Constitutional Convention was unknown. In the summer of 1791 Jefferson and Madison set out on a "botanizing" excursion up the Hudson, a vacation that many Federalists feared was a cover for consultations with Governor George Clinton, the Livingstons, and Aaron Burr, leaders of the faction in New York that opposed the aristocratic party of the DeLanceys, Van Rensselaers, and Philip Schuyler, Hamilton's father-in-law. While the significance of that single trip was blown out of proportion, there did ultimately arise an informal alliance of Jeffersonian Republicans in the South and New York that would become a constant if sometimes divisive feature of the party and its successor, the Democratic party.

Still, there was no opposition to Washington, who longed to end his exile from Mount Vernon and even began drafting a farewell address, but was urged by both Hamilton and Jefferson to continue in public life. He was the only man who could transcend party differences and hold things together with his unmatched prestige. In 1792 Washington was unanimously reelected, but in the scattering of second votes the Republican Clinton got fifty electoral votes to John Adams's seventy-seven.

CRISES FOREIGN AND DOMESTIC

In Washington's second term the problems of foreign relations came to center stage, brought there by the consequences of the French Revolution, which had begun during the first months of his presidency. Americans followed the tumultuous events in France with almost universal sympathy, up to a point. By the spring of 1792, though, the experiment in liberty, equality, and fraternity had transformed itself into a monster. France plunged into war with Austria and Prussia. The Revolution began devouring its own children along with its enemies during the Terror of 1793–1794.

After the execution of King Louis XVI in 1793, Great Britain entered into the coalition of monarchies at war with the French Republic. For the next twenty-two years Britain and France were at war, with only a brief respite, until the final defeat of the French forces under Napoleon in 1815. The war presented Washington, just beginning his second term, with an awkward decision. By the treaty of 1778, the United States was a perpetual ally of France, obligated to defend her possessions in the West Indies.

But Americans wanted no part of the war. They were determined to maintain their lucrative trade with both sides in the European conflict. Of course, the combatants resented and resisted America's profitable neutrality. For their part, Hamilton and Jefferson found in the neutrality policy one issue on which they could agree. Where they differed was in how best to implement the policy. Hamilton had a simple and direct answer to this problem: declare the alliance invalid because it was made with a government that no longer existed. Jefferson preferred to delay and use the alliance as a bargaining point with the British. In the end, however, Washington followed the advice of neither. Taking a middle course, on April 22, 1793, the president issued a neutrality proclamation that evaded even the word "neutrality." It simply declared the United States "friendly and impartial toward the belligerent powers" and warned American citizens that "aiding or abetting hostilities" or other un-neutral acts might be prosecuted.

CITIZEN GENÊT   At the same time, Washington accepted Jefferson's argument that the United States should recognize the new French government (becoming the first country to do so) and receive its new ambassador, Citizen Edmond Charles Genêt. Early in 1793 Genêt landed at Charleston, where he immediately organized a Jacobin Club to support that faction of French revolutionaries. Along the route to Philadelphia the enthusiasm of his sympathizers gave Genêt an inflated notion of his potential, not that he needed much encouragement. In Charleston he engaged privateers to bring in British prizes, and in Philadelphia he continued the process. He intrigued with frontiersmen and land speculators, including George Rogers Clark, with an eye to an attack on Spanish Florida and Louisiana.

Genêt quickly became an embarrassment even to his Republican friends. Jefferson decided that the French minister had overreached himself when he violated a promise not to outfit a captured British ship as a privateer. Such actions could have provoked a British declaration of war against the United States. When, finally, Genêt threatened in a moment of anger to appeal his cause directly to the American people over the head of their president, the cabinet unanimously agreed that he had to go, and in August 1793 Washington demanded his recall. Meanwhile a new party of radicals had gained power in France and sent over its own minister with a warrant for Genêt's arrest. Instead of returning to risk the guillotine, Genêt sought asylum, married the daughter of Governor Clinton, settled down as a country gentleman on the Hudson, and died years later an American citizen.

Genêt's foolishness and the growing excesses of the French radicals were fast cooling American support for their revolution. To Hamilton's followers it began to resemble their worst nightmares of democratic anarchy and infidelity. The French made it hard even for Republicans to retain sympathy, but they swallowed hard and made excuses. "The liberty of the whole earth was depending on the issue of the contest," the genteel Jefferson wrote, "and . . . rather than it should have failed, I would have seen half the earth devastated." Nor did the British make it easy for Federalists to rally to their side. Near the end of 1793 they informed the American government that they intended to occupy their northwestern posts indefinitely and began to seize the cargoes of American ships with provisions for or produce from the French islands.

Despite the offenses by both sides, the French and British causes polarized American opinion. In the contest, it seemed, one either had to be a Republican and support liberty, reason, and France, or become a Federalist and support order, religious faith, and Britain. The division gave rise to some curious loyalties: slaveholding planters joined the cheers for Jacobin radicals who dispossessed aristocrats in France, and supported the protest against British seizures of New England ships; Massachusetts shippers still profited from the British trade and kept quiet. Boston, once a hotbed of revolution, became a bastion of Federalism.

JAY'S TREATY Early in 1794 the Republican leaders in Congress were gaining support for commercial retaliation to bring the British to their senses, when the British gave Washington a timely opening for a settlement. They stopped seizing American brigs and schooners, and on April 16, 1794, Washington named Chief Justice John Jay as a special envoy to Great Britain. Jay left with instructions to settle all major issues: to get the British out of the northwestern posts, to secure reparations for the losses of American shippers, compensation for slaves carried away in 1783, and a commercial treaty that would legalize American commerce with the British West Indies.

To win his objectives, Jay accepted the British definition of neutral rights: that naval stores were contraband, that provisions could not go in neutral ships to enemy ports, and the "Rule of 1756," by which trade that was prohibited in peacetime because of mercantilist restrictions could not be opened in wartime. Britain also gained most-favored-nation treatment in American commerce and a promise that French privateers would not be outfitted in American ports. Finally, Jay conceded

A 1794 watercolor of Fort Detroit, a major center of Indian trade that the British agreed to evacuate in Jay's Treaty.

that the British need not compensate Americans for the slaves who escaped during the war and that the old American debts to British merchants would be adjudicated and paid by the American government. In return for these concessions, he won three important points: British evacuation of the northwestern posts by 1796, reparations for the seizures of American ships and cargoes in 1793–1794, and legalization of trade with the British West Indies. But the last of these (Article XII) was so hedged with restrictions that the Senate eventually struck it from the treaty.

Public outrage greeted the terms of the treaty. Even Federalist shippers, ready for settlement on almost any terms, were disappointed at the limitations on their privileges in the West Indies. But much of the outcry was simply expression of disappointment by Republican partisans who sought an escalation of conflict with "perfidious Albion." Some of it was the outrage of Virginia planters at the concession on debts to British merchants and the failure to get reparations for lost slaves. Given the limited enthusiasm of Federalists—Washington himself wrestled with doubts over the treaty—Jay remarked that he could travel across the country by the light of his burning effigies. Yet the Senate debated the treaty in secret, and in the end quiet counsels of moderation prevailed. Without a single vote to spare, Jay's Treaty got the necessary two-thirds majority on June 24, 1795, with Article XII (the provision regarding the West Indies) expunged.

Washington still hesitated but finally signed the treaty as the best he was likely to get and out of fear that a refusal would throw the United States into the role of a French satellite. In the House, opponents went so far as to demand that the president produce all papers relevant to the treaty, but the president refused on the grounds that treaty approval was solely the business of the Senate. He thereby set an important precedent of executive privilege (a term not used at the time), and the House finally relented, supplying the money to fund the treaty by a close vote.

THE FRONTIER STIRS   Other events also had an important bearing on Jay's Treaty, adding force to the importance of its settlement of the Canadian frontier and strengthening Spain's conviction that it too needed to reach a settlement of long-festering problems along America's southwestern frontier. While Jay was haggling in London, frontier conflict with Indians escalated, with American troops twice crushed by northwestern Indians. At last, Washington named General Wayne, known as "Mad Anthony," to head an expedition into the Northwest Territory. In the fall of 1793 Wayne marched into Indian country with some 2,600 men, built Fort Greenville, and with reinforcements from Kentucky, went on the offensive in 1794.

In August 1794, some 2,000 Shawnee, Ottawa, Chippewa, and Potawatomi warriors, reinforced by some Canadian militia, attacked Wayne's troops at the Battle of Fallen Timbers, but this time the Americans were

ready and repulsed them. The Indians suffered heavy losses. American detachments then laid waste their fields and villages. The Indians finally agreed to the Treaty of Greenville, signed in August 1795. In the treaty, at the cost of a $10,000 annuity, the United States bought from twelve tribes the rights to the southeastern quarter of the Northwest Territory (now Ohio and Indiana) and enclaves at the sites of Vincennes, Detroit, and Chicago.

THE WHISKEY REBELLION   Wayne's forces were still mopping up after the Battle of Fallen Timbers when the administration resolved on another show of strength in the backcountry against the so-called Whiskey Rebellion. Hamilton's excise tax on liquor, levied in 1791, had excited strong feeling among frontier farmers because it taxed their staple crop. The frontiersmen considered the tax another part of Hamilton's scheme to pick the pockets of the poor to enrich fat speculators. All through the backcountry, from Georgia to Pennsylvania and beyond, the tax gave rise to resistance and evasion.

In the summer of 1794 the rumblings of discontent broke into open rebellion in the four western counties of Pennsylvania, where vigilantes,

Washington as commander-in-chief reviews the troops mobilized to quell the Whiskey Rebellion in 1794.

mostly of Scots or Irish descent, organized to terrorize revenuers and taxpayers. They blew up the stills of those who paid the tax, robbed the mails, stopped court proceedings, and threatened an assault on Pittsburgh. On August 7, 1794, President Washington issued a proclamation ordering them home and calling out 12,900 militiamen from Virginia, Maryland, Pennsylvania, and New Jersey. Getting no response from the "Whiskey Boys," he issued a proclamation on September 24 for suppression of the rebellion.

Under the command of General Henry Lee, "a force larger than any Washington had ever commanded" in the Revolution marched out from Harrisburg across the Alleghenies with Hamilton in their midst, itching to smite the insurgents. But the rebels vaporized like corn mash when the heat was applied, and the troops met with little opposition. By dint of great effort and much marching, they finally rounded up twenty barefoot, ragged prisoners whom they paraded down Market Street in Philadelphia and clapped into prison. Eventually two of these were found guilty of treason, but were pardoned by Washington on the grounds that one was a "simpleton" and the other "insane." The government had made its point and gained "reputation and strength," according to Hamilton, by suppressing a rebellion that, according to Jefferson, "could never be found." The use of force, however, led many who sympathized with the frontiersmen to become Republicans, who scored heavily in the next Pennsylvania elections. Nor was it the end of whiskey rebellions, which continued in an unending war of wits between moonshiners and revenuers.

PINCKNEY'S TREATY   While these stirring events were transpiring in Pennsylvania, Spanish intrigues among the Creeks, Choctaws, Chickasaws, and Cherokees in the Southwest were keeping up the same turmoil the British had fomented along the Ohio. In Tennessee, settlers reacted by burning and leveling Indian villages. The defeat of their Indian allies, combined with Britain's concessions in the north and worries about possible American intervention in Louisiana, led the Spanish to enter into treaty negotiations with the Americans. United States minister Thomas Pinckney won acceptance of a boundary at the 31st parallel, free navigation of the Mississippi, the right to deposit goods at New Orleans for three years with promise of renewal, a commission to settle American claims against Spain, and a promise on each side to refrain

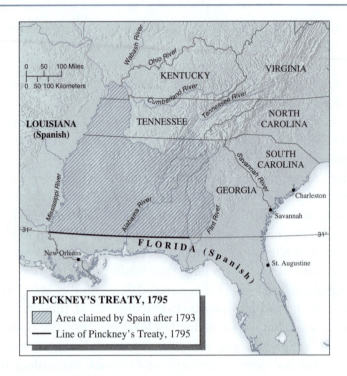

Map labels:

Wabash River

Ohio River

0 50 100 Miles

0 50 100 Kilometers

KENTUCKY

VIRGINIA

Cumberland River

Tennessee River

LOUISIANA
(Spanish)

TENNESSEE

NORTH
CAROLINA

SOUTH
CAROLINA

Savannah River

Mississippi River

Alabama River

Flint River

GEORGIA

Charleston

Savannah

31°

31°

FLORIDA (Spanish)

New Orleans

St. Augustine

PINCKNEY'S TREATY, 1795

▨ Area claimed by Spain after 1793

— Line of Pinckney's Treaty, 1795

from inciting Indian attacks on the other. Ratification of the Pinckney Treaty ran into no opposition. In fact, it was immensely popular, especially among westerners eager to use the Mississippi River to transport their crops to market.

LAND SETTLEMENT

Now that Jay and Pinckney had settled things with Britain and Spain, and General Wayne in the Northwest and the Tennessee settlers in the South had smashed the Indians, the West was open for a renewed surge of settlers. New lands, ceded by the Indians in the Treaty of Greenville, revealed Congress once again divided on land policy. There were two basic viewpoints on the matter, one that the public domain should serve mainly as a source of revenue, the other that it was more important to accommodate settlers with low prices, maybe free land, and get the country settled. In the long run, the evolution of policy would be from the first toward the second viewpoint, but for the time being the government's need for revenue took priority.

LAND POLICY   Opinions on land policy, like other issues, separated
Federalists from Republicans. Federalists involved in speculation might
prefer lower land prices, but the more influential Federalists like Hamilton and Jay preferred to build the population of the eastern states first,
lest the East lose political influence and lose a labor force important to
the future growth of manufactures. Men of their persuasion favored high
land prices to enrich the Treasury, sale of relatively large parcels of land
to speculators rather than small amounts to actual settlers, and the development of compact settlements. In addition to his other reports,
Hamilton had put out one on the public lands, in which he emphasized
the need for governmental revenues. Jefferson and Madison were reluctantly prepared to go along for the sake of reducing the national debt,
but Jefferson expressed hope for a plan by which the lands could be
more readily settled. In any case, he suggested, frontiersmen would do
as they had done before: "They will settle the lands in spite of everybody." The Daniel Boones of the West, always moving out beyond the
settlers and surveyors, were already proving him right.

For the time, however, Federalist policy prevailed. In the Land Act of
1796 Congress resolved to extend the rectangular surveys ordained in

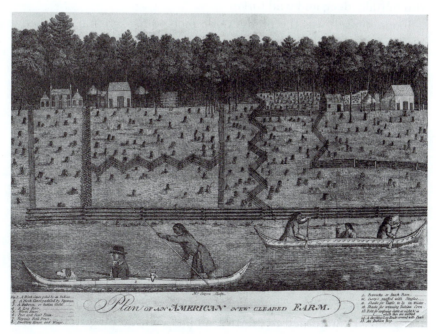

A newly cleared American farm.

1785, but it doubled the price to $2 per acre, with only a year in which to complete payment. Half the townships would go in 640-acre sections, making the minimum cost $1,280, and alternate townships would be sold in blocks of eight sections, or 5,120 acres, making the minimum cost $10,240. Either was beyond the means of most ordinary settlers, and a bit much even for speculators, who could still pick up state lands at lower prices. By 1800 government land offices had sold fewer than 50,000 acres under the act. Continuing pressures from the West led to the Land Act of 1800, which reduced the minimum sale to 320 acres and spread the payments over four years. Thus with a down payment of $160 one could get a farm. All lands went for the minimum price if they did not sell at auction within three weeks. Under the Land Act of 1804 the minimum unit was reduced to 160 acres, which became the traditional homestead, and the price per acre went down to $1.64.

THE WILDERNESS TRAIL   The lure of western lands led thousands of settlers to follow Daniel Boone into the territory known as Kentucky or "Kaintuck"—from the Cherokee name Ken-ta-ke ("great meadow"). In the late eighteenth century, Kentucky was a farmer's fantasy and a hunter's paradise, with its fertile soils and abundant forests teeming with buffalo, deer, and wild turkey.

Boone himself was the product of a pioneer background. Born on a small farm in 1734 in central Pennsylvania, the son of hard-working Quakers, he was one of eleven children. By the age of twelve Daniel was an experienced farmer, accomplished woodsman, and deadeye marksman. In 1750 the Boone family moved to the Yadkin valley of North Carolina. There Daniel emerged as the region's greatest hunter, trading animal skins for salt and other family needs. In 1756 he married Rebecca Bryan, a seventeen-year-old daughter of a neighbor. She would eventually bear ten children.

After hearing numerous reports about the territory over the mountains, Boone set out alone to find a trail into Kentucky in 1769. Armed with a long rifle, tomahawk, and hunting knife, dressed in a hunting shirt, deerskin leggings, and moccasins, he found what was called the Warriors Path, a narrow foot trail that buffalo, deer, and Indians had worn along the steep ridges. It took him through the Cumberland Gap. For two years thereafter, Boone explored the region, living off the plentiful game. He returned to North Carolina with exciting stories about the riches of Kentucky.

Daniel Boone Escorting Soldiers through the Cumberland Gap *by George Caleb Bingham.*

In 1773 Boone led the first group of settlers through the Appalachian Mountains at Cumberland Gap in southwestern Virginia. But an Indian attack forced them to turn back against Boone's wishes. Two boys, including Boone's oldest son, were tortured before being killed. Two years later, Boone and thirty woodsmen used axes to widen the Warriors Path into what became known as the Wilderness Road, a passage that more than 300,000 settlers would use over the next twenty-five years. At a point where a branch of the Wilderness Road intersected with the Kentucky River, near what is now Lexington, Boone built a settlement known as Boonesborough. His family joined him there in an area known as Transylvania.

Although subject to frequent Indian attacks, a steady stream of settlers, mostly Scotch-Irish folk from Pennsylvania, Virginia, and North Carolina, poured into Kentucky during the last quarter of the eighteenth century. Upon their arrival, they typically bought a piece of land from a speculator who preceded them or from a government agent. Many veterans of the Revolutionary War received land grants in Kentucky as compensation for their military service. The pioneers who settled on land that had not been surveyed were called squatters because they had no official title to the land. After the land was surveyed, they were eligible to buy it under rights of ownership called squatters' rights.

The backcountry settlers came on foot or on horseback, often leading a mule or cow that carried their few tools and possessions. On a good day they might cover fifteen miles. The journey was grueling. Near a creek or spring they would buy a parcel or stake out a claim and mark its boundaries by chopping notches into "witness trees." They then would build a lean-to or half-camp for temporary shelter and clear the land for planting. The larger trees could not be felled with an axe. Instead they were "girdled." A cut would be made around the trunk and the tree would be left to die. Because this often took years, a farmer had to plant and hoe around a field filled with stumps and trees.

The pioneers grew melons, beans, turnips, and other vegetables, but corn was the preferred crop because it kept well and had so many uses. Ears were roasted and eaten on the cob, and kernels were ground into meal for making mush, hominy grits, hoecake and "johnnycake" (a dry biscuit suitable for travelers that was originally called journeycake). Pigs and cows provided pork and milk, butter and cheese. Many of the frontier families also built crude stills to manufacture a potent whiskey known as "corn likker."

Eventually, the pioneers constructed small but sturdy log cabins to replace their temporary shelters. Because no man could lift the heavy logs alone, neighbors would converge for a house-raising, one of the primary social events on the frontier. On the appointed day, families would arrive with tools and food. While the men cut, notched, and placed the logs, women and children would fill or "chink" the spaces in between with wood slivers kept in place by a mixture of clay and moss. The floors were usually made of dirt, but some settlers added a wooden floor by splitting logs into puncheons and laying them next to each other, flat side up. A stone fireplace with a log chimney lined with clay would be built at one end of the cabin. Windows were kept to a minimum for security purposes. The final task was to install a heavy plank door hung on leather hinges. A string made of deerskin was tied to the latch and hung on the outside of the door. At night the latchstring would be pulled inside and the door barred. The latchstring hanging outside the door became a symbol of frontier hospitality. To this day, some people assure friends that their "latchstring is always out."

Frontier settlements developed a variety of social events to combat their isolation and nurture their sense of community. In addition to house-raisings and wedding parties, corn-husking contests also brought farm families together. Foot races and wrestling or shooting matches provided added entertainment. Competing marksmen would take aim at the head of a nail pounded into a board. Hence the winner was the one who "hit the nail on the head." At the end of the day everyone would gather for a common meal. Afterward, stories might be told around a bonfire, or people would dance and sing while a fiddler played.

TRANSFER OF POWER

By 1796 President Washington had decided that two terms in office were enough. Tired of the political quarrels and the venom of the partisan press, he was ready to retire once and for all to Mount Vernon. He would leave behind a formidable record of achievement: the organization of a national government with demonstrated power, a secure national credit, the recovery of territory from Britain and Spain, a stable northwestern frontier, and the admission of three new states: Vermont (1791), Kentucky (1792), and Tennessee (1796).

The Washington family at Mount Vernon, with one of the family's slaves in the background, in a sketch by Benjamin Latrobe (1797).

WASHINGTON'S FAREWELL   With the help of Jay and especially Hamilton, Washington set about preparing a valedictory address, using a draft prepared by Madison four years before. Washington's farewell address, dated September 17, 1796, stated first his resolve to decline being considered for a third term. After that, most of the message dwelled on the need for unity among the American people in backing their new government. Washington decried the spirit of sectionalism. "In contemplating the causes which may disturb our union," he wrote in one prescient passage, "it occurs as a matter of serious concern that any ground should have been furnished for characterizing parties by geographical discriminations—*Northern* and *Southern, Atlantic* and *Western*—whence designing men may endeavor to excite a belief that there is a real difference of local interests and views." He decried as strongly the spirit of party, while acknowledging a body of opinion that parties were "useful checks upon the administration of the government, and serve to keep alive the spirit of liberty." From the natural tendency of men there would always be enough spirit of party, however, to serve that purpose. The danger was partisan excess: "A fire not to be quenched, it demands a uniform vigilance to prevent its bursting into a flame, lest, instead of warming, it should consume."

In foreign relations, Washington said, America should show "good faith and justice toward all nations" and avoid either "an habitual hatred or an habitual fondness" for other countries. Europe, he noted, "has a set of primary interests which to us have none or a very remote relation. Hence she must be engaged in frequent controversies, the causes of which are essentially foreign to our concerns." The United States should keep clear of those quarrels. It was, moreover, "our true policy to steer clear of permanent alliances with any portion of the foreign world." A key word here is "permanent." Washington enjoined against any further permanent arrangements like the one with France, still technically in effect. He did not speak of "entangling alliances"—that phrase would be used by Thomas Jefferson in his first inaugural address—and in fact specifically advised that "we may safely trust to temporary alliances for extraordinary emergencies." Washington's warning against permanent foreign entanglements thereafter served as a fundamental principle in American foreign policy until the early twentieth century.

Washington himself had not escaped the "baneful effects" of the party spirit, for during his second term the Republican press came to link him with the Federalist partisans. For the first time in his long career Washington was subjected to sustained, and often scurrilous, criticism. According to the editor of the *Philadelphia Aurora,* the president was "a man in his political dotage" and "a supercilious tyrant." Washington never responded to such abuse in public but in private he went into towering rages. This criticism hastened his resolve to retire. On the eve of that event the *Aurora* proclaimed that "this day ought to be a Jubilee in the United States. . . . If ever a nation was debauched by a man, the American Nation has been debauched by Washington."

THE ELECTION OF 1796   With Washington out of the race, the United States had its first partisan election for president. The logical choice of the Federalists would have been Washington's protégé Hamilton, the chief architect of their programs. But Hamilton's policies had left scars and made enemies. Nor did he suffer fools gladly, a common affliction of Federalist leaders, including the man on whom the choice fell. In Philadelphia, a caucus of Federalist congressmen chose John Adams as heir apparent, with Thomas Pinckney of South Carolina, fresh from his triumph in Spain, as nominee for vice-president. As expected, the Republicans drafted Jefferson and added geographical balance to the ticket with Aaron Burr of New York.

The rising strength of the Republicans, fueled by the smoldering resentment toward Jay's Treaty, very nearly swept Jefferson into office, and perhaps would have but for the public appeals of the French ambassador for his election—an action that backfired. Then, despite a Federalist majority among the electors, Alexander Hamilton thought up an impulsive scheme that very nearly threw the election away after all. Thomas Pinckney, Hamilton thought, would be more subject to influence than the strong-minded Adams. He therefore sought to have South Carolina Federalists withhold a few votes from Adams and bring Pinckney in first. The Carolinas more than cooperated—they divided their vote between Pinckney and Jefferson—but New Englanders got wind of the scheme and dropped Pinckney. The upshot of Hamilton's intrigue was to cut Pinckney out of both offices and elect Jefferson vice-president with sixty-eight votes, second to Adams's seventy-one.

THE ADAMS YEARS

Adams had behind him a distinguished career as a Massachusetts lawyer, a leader in the Revolutionary movement and the Continental Congress, a diplomat in France, Holland, and Britain, and as vice-president. His political philosophy fell somewhere between Jefferson's and Hamilton's. He shared neither the one's faith in the common people nor the other's fondness for an aristocracy of "paper wealth." He favored the classic mixture of aristocratic, democratic, and monarchical elements, though his use of "monarchical" interchangeably with "executive" exposed him to the attacks of Republicans who saw a monarchist in every Federalist. Yet Adams's fondness for titles and protocol arose from a reasoned purpose, to exploit the human "thirst for distinction." Although he tried to play the role of distinguished executive, he was always haunted by a feeling that he was never properly appreciated—and he may have been right. Yet, on the overriding issue of his administration, war and peace, he kept his head when others about him were losing theirs—probably at the cost of his reelection.

WAR WITH FRANCE   Adams inherited from Washington his cabinet—the precedent of changing personnel with each new administra-

John Adams.

tion had not yet been set—and with them an intraparty division, for three of the department heads looked to Hamilton for counsel: Timothy Pickering at the State Department, Oliver Wolcott at the Treasury Department, and Joseph McHenry at the War Department. Adams also inherited a menacing quarrel with France, a byproduct of the Jay Treaty. When Jay accepted the British position that food supplies and naval stores—as well as war matériel—were contraband subject to seizure, the French reasoned that American cargoes in the British trade were subject to the same interpretation and loosed their corsairs in the West Indies with even more devastating effect than the British had in 1793–1794. By the time of Adams's inauguration in 1797, the French had plundered some 300 American ships and had broken diplomatic relations. As ambassador to Paris, James Monroe had become so pro-French and so hostile to the Jay Treaty that Washington had felt impelled to remove him for his indiscretions. France then had refused to accept Monroe's replacement, Charles Cotesworth Pinckney (brother of Thomas Pinckney), and ordered him out of the country.

Adams immediately acted to restore relations in the face of an outcry for war from the "High Federalists," including Secretary of State Pickering. Hamilton agreed with Adams on this point and approved his last-ditch effort for a settlement. In 1797 Pinckney returned to Paris with John Marshall (a Virginia Federalist) and Elbridge Gerry (a Massachusetts Republican) for further negotiations. After long, nagging delays, the three commissioners were accosted by three French counterparts (whom Adams labeled X, Y, and Z in his report to Congress), agents of Foreign Minister Talleyrand, a past master of the diplomatic shakedown. The three French diplomats delicately let it be known that negotiations could begin only if there were a loan of $12 million, a bribe of $250,000 to the five directors then heading the government, and suitable apologies for remarks recently made in Adams's message to Congress.

Such bribes were common eighteenth-century diplomatic practice—Washington himself had bribed a Creek chieftain and ransomed American sailors from Algerian pirates, each at a cost of $100,000—but Talleyrand's price was high merely for a promise to negotiate. The answer, according to the commissioners' report, was "no, no, not a sixpence." When the XYZ Affair was reported in Congress and the public press, this was translated into the more stirring slogan: "Millions for defense

A cartoon indicating the anti-French feeling generated by the XYZ Affair. The three American ministers at left reject the "Paris Monster's" demand for money.

but not one cent for tribute." Thereafter, the expressions of hostility toward France rose in a crescendo—even the most partisan Republicans were hard put to make any more excuses, and many of them joined a cry for war. Yet Adams resisted a formal declaration of war; the French would have to bear the onus for that. Congress, however, authorized the capture of armed French ships, suspended commerce with France, and renounced the alliance of 1778, which was already a dead letter.

In 1798 George Logan, a Pennsylvania Quaker, visited Paris at his own expense, hoping to head off war. He did secure the release of some American seamen and won assurances that a new American ambassador would be welcomed. The fruits of his mission, otherwise, were widespread denunciation and passage of the Logan Act (1799), which still forbids private citizens to negotiate with foreign governments without official authorization.

Adams proceeded to strengthen American defenses. An American navy had ceased to exist at the end of the Revolution. Except for revenue cutters of the Treasury Department, no armed ships were available when Algerian brigands began to prey on American commerce in 1794. As a result Congress had authorized the arming of six ships.

These were incomplete in 1796 when Washington bought peace with the Algerians, but Congress allowed work on three to continue: the *Constitution,* the *United States,* and the *Constellation,* all completed in 1797. In 1798 Congress authorized a new Department of the Navy. By the end of 1798 the number of naval ships had increased to twenty and by the end of 1799 to thirty-three. But before the end of 1798 an undeclared naval war had begun in the West Indies with the French capture of an American schooner.

While the naval war went on, a new army was authorized in 1798 as a 10,000-man force to serve three years. Adams called Washington from retirement to be its commander, agreeing to Washington's condition that he name his three chief subordinates. Washington sent in the names of Hamilton, Charles C. Pinckney, and Henry Knox. In the old army the three ranked in precisely the opposite order, but Washington insisted that Hamilton be his second in command. Adams relented, but resented the slight to his authority as commander-in-chief. The rift among Federalists thus widened further. Because of Washington's age, the choice meant that Hamilton would command the army in the field, if it ever took the field. But recruitment went slowly until well into 1799, by which time all fear of French invasion was dispelled. Hamilton continued to dream of imperial glory, though, planning the seizure of Louisiana and the Floridas to keep them out of French hands, and even the invasion of South America, but these remained Hamilton's dreams.

Peace overtures began to come from Talleyrand by the autumn of 1798, before the naval war was fully under way. Adams decided to act on the information and took it upon himself, without consulting the cabinet, to name the American minister to the Netherlands, William Vans Murray, as special envoy to Paris. The Hamiltonians, infected with a virulent attack of war fever, fought the nomination but finally compromised, in the face of Adams's threat to resign, on a commission of three envoys. After a long delay they left late in 1799 and arrived to find themselves confronting a new government under First Consul Napoleon Bonaparte. By the Convention of 1800, they won the best terms they could from the triumphant Napoleon. In return for giving up all claims of indemnity for American losses, they got official suspension of the 1778 perpetual alliance with France and the end of the quasi war. The Senate ratified, contingent upon outright abrogation of the alliance, and the agreement became effective on December 21, 1801.

THE WAR AT HOME   The real purpose of the French crisis all along, the more ardent Republicans suspected, was to create an excuse to put down the domestic opposition. The Alien and Sedition Acts of 1798 lent credence to their suspicions. These four measures, passed in the wave of patriotic war fever, limited freedom of speech and the press and the liberty of aliens. Proposed by Federalists in Congress, they did not originate with Adams but had his blessing. Three of the four acts reflected hostility to foreigners, especially the French and Irish, a large number of whom had become active Republicans and were suspected of revolutionary intent. The Naturalization Act lengthened from five to fourteen years the residence requirement for citizenship. The Alien Act empowered the president to deport "dangerous" aliens on pain of imprisonment. The Alien Enemy Act authorized the president in time of declared war to expel or imprison enemy aliens at will. Finally, the Sedition Act defined as a high misdemeanor any conspiracy against legal measures of the government, including interference with federal officers and insurrection or riot. What is more, the law forbade writing, publishing, or speaking anything of "a false, scandalous and malicious" nature against the government or any of its officers.

Considering what Federalists and Republicans said about each other, the act, applied rigorously, could have caused the imprisonment of nearly the whole government. In practice, however, the purpose was transparently partisan, designed to punish Republicans, whom Federalists could scarcely distinguish from Jacobins and traitors. To be sure, partisan Republican journalists were resorting to scandalous lies and misrepresentations, but so were Federalists; it was a time when both sides seemed afflicted with paranoia. But the fifteen indictments brought under the act, with ten convictions, were all directed at Republicans.

In the very first case one unfortunate was fined $100 for wishing out loud that the wad of a salute cannon might hit President Adams in his rear. The most conspicuous targets of prosecution were Republican editors and a Republican congressman, Matthew Lyon of Vermont, a rough-and-tumble Irishman who published censures of Adams's "continual grasp for power" and "unbounded thirst for ridiculous pomp, foolish adulation, and selfish avarice." For such libels Lyon got four months and a fine of $1,000, but from his cell he continued to write articles and letters for the Republican papers. The few convictions under the act only created martyrs to the cause of freedom of speech and the press, and exposed the vindictiveness of Federalist judges.

Republican representative Matthew Lyon and the Connecticut Federalist Roger Griswald go at each other on the floor of the House (1798). Lyon soon became a target of the Sedition Act.

Lyon and the others based a defense on the unconstitutionality of the Sedition Act, but Federalist judges were scarcely inclined to entertain such notions. It ran against the Republican grain, anyway, to have federal courts assume the authority to declare laws unconstitutional. To offset the Alien and Sedition Acts, therefore, Jefferson and Madison conferred and brought forth drafts of what came to be known as the Kentucky and Virginia Resolutions. These passed the legislatures of the two states in 1798, while further Kentucky Resolutions, adopted in 1799, responded to counterresolutions from northern states. These resolutions, much alike in their arguments, denounced the Alien and Sedition Acts as unconstitutional and advanced what came to be known as the state-compact theory. Since the Constitution arose as a compact among the states, the resolutions argued, it followed logically that the states should assume the right to say when Congress had exceeded its powers. The Virginia Resolutions, drafted by Madison, declared that states "have the right and are in duty bound to interpose for arresting the progress of the evil." The second set of Kentucky Resolutions, in restating the states' right to judge violations of the Constitution, added: "That a nullification of those sovereignties, of all unauthorized acts done under color of that instrument, is the rightful remedy."

These doctrines of interposition and nullification, revised and edited by later theorists, were destined to be used for causes unforeseen by the authors of the Kentucky and Virginia Resolutions. (Years later Madison would disclaim the doctrine of nullification as developed by John C. Calhoun, but his own doctrine of "interposition" would resurface as late as the 1950s as a device to oppose racial integration.) At the time, it seems, both men intended the resolutions to serve chiefly as propaganda, the opening guns in the political campaign of 1800. Neither Kentucky nor Virginia took steps to nullify or interpose its authority against enforcement of the Alien and Sedition Acts. Instead both called upon the other states to help them win a repeal. Jefferson counseled against any thought of violence, which was "not the kind of opposition the American people will permit." He assured a fellow Virginian that "the reign of witches" would soon end, that it would be discredited by the arrival of the tax collector more than anything else.

REPUBLICAN VICTORY   As the presidential election of 1800 approached, grievances were mounting against Federalist policies: taxation to support an unneeded army; the Alien and Sedition Acts, which cast the Federalists as anti-liberty; the lingering fears of "monarchism"; the hostilities aroused by Hamilton's programs; the suppression of the Whiskey Rebellion; and Jay's Treaty. When Adams decided for peace in 1800, he probably doomed his one chance for reelection, a wave of patriotic war fever with a united party behind him. His decision gained him much goodwill among the people at large, but left the Hamiltonians unreconciled and his party divided. In 1800 the Federalists summoned enough unity to name as their candidates Adams and Charles C. Pinckney; they agreed to cast all their electoral votes for both. But the Hamiltonians continued to snipe at Adams and his policies, and soon after his renomination Adams removed two of them from his cabinet. Hamilton struck back with a pamphlet questioning Adams's fitness to be president, citing his "disgusting egotism." Intended for private distribution among Federalist leaders, the pamphlet reached the hands of Aaron Burr, who put it in general circulation.

Jefferson and Burr, as the Republican candidates, once again represented the alliance of Virginia and New York. Jefferson, perhaps even more than Adams, became the target of vilification as a Jacobin and an atheist. His election, Americans were warned, would bring "dwellings in flames, hoary hairs bathed in blood, female chastity violated . . . children writhing on the pike and halberd." Jefferson kept quiet, refused to answer the attacks, and directed the campaign by mail from his home at Monticello. He was advanced as the farmers' friend, the champion of states' rights, frugal government, liberty, and peace.

Adams proved more popular than his party, whose candidates generally fared worse than the president, but the Republicans edged him out by seventy-three electoral votes to sixty-five. The decisive states were New York and South Carolina, either of which might have given the victory to Adams. But in New York Burr's organization won control of the legislature, which cast the electoral votes. In South Carolina, Charles Pinckney (cousin to the Federalist Pinckneys) won over the legislature by well-placed promises of Republican patronage. Still, the result was not final, for Jefferson and Burr had tied with seventy-three votes each, and the choice of the president was thrown into the House of Representatives, where Federalist diehards tried vainly to give the election to Burr. This was too much for Hamilton, who opposed Jefferson but held a much lower opinion of Burr. Eventually the deadlock was broken when a confidant of Jefferson assured a Delaware congressman that Jefferson would refrain from wholesale removals of Federalists and uphold the new fiscal system. The representative resolved to vote for Jefferson, and several other Federalists agreed simply to cast blank ballots,

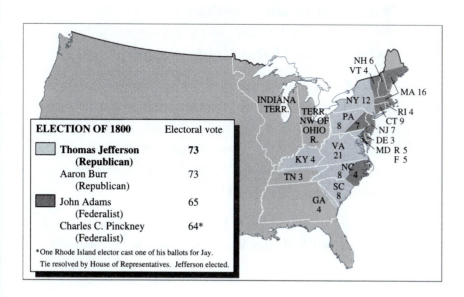

ELECTION OF 1800   Electoral vote

Thomas Jefferson   **73**
(Republican)

Aaron Burr   73
(Republican)

John Adams   65
(Federalist)

Charles C. Pinckney   64*
(Federalist)

*One Rhode Island elector cast one of his ballots for Jay.

Tie resolved by House of Representatives. Jefferson elected.

NH 6
VT 4
MA 16
INDIANA TERR.
NY 12
RI 4
TERR. NW OF OHIO R.
PA 8
7
CT 9
NJ 7
DE 3
VA 21
MD R 5
F 5
KY 4
NC 8   4
TN 3
SC 8
GA 4

permitting Jefferson to win without any of them actually having to vote for him.

Before the Federalists relinquished power to the Jeffersonian Republicans on March 4, 1801, their "lame-duck" Congress passed the Judiciary Act of 1801. Intended to ensure Federalist control of the judicial system, this act provided that the next vacancy on the Supreme Court should not be filled, created sixteen circuit courts with a new judge for each, and increased the number of attorneys, clerks, and marshals. Before he left office, Adams named John Marshall to the vacant office of chief justice and appointed good Federalists to all the new positions, including forty-two justices of the peace for the new District of Columbia. The Federalists, defeated and destined never to regain national power, had in the words of Jefferson "retired into the judiciary as a stronghold." The election of 1800 marked a turning point in American political history. It was the first time that one political party, however ungracefully, relinquished power to the opposition party.

MAKING CONNECTIONS

- Thomas Jefferson's Republican philosophy offered a strong alternative to Hamilton's Federalism. As the next chapter shows, however, once the Republicans got into power, they adopted a number of Federalist principles and positions.

- The Bank of the United States and the protective tariff continued to be controversial. The Bank was renewed for another twenty years in 1816, the same year in which the first truly protective tariff was passed (Chapter 10), but in the 1830s the Bank was eliminated, and the tariff became a major source of sectional conflict (Chapter 11).

- The foreign policy crises with England and France described in this chapter will lead to the War of 1812, discussed in Chapter 9.

FURTHER READING

The best introduction to the early Federalists remains John C. Miller's *The Federalist Era, 1789–1800* (1960). Other works analyze the ideological debates among the nation's first leaders. Richard Buel, Jr.'s *Securing the Revolution: Ideology in American Politics, 1789–1815* (1974), Joyce Appleby's *Capitalism and a New Social Order* (1984), Drew McCoy's *The Elusive Republic: Political Economy in Jeffersonian America* (1982) and *The Last of the Fathers: James Madison and the Republican Legacy* (1989), and Stanley Elkins and Eric McKitrick's *The Age of Federalism* (1993) trace the persistence and transformation of ideas first fostered during the Revolutionary crisis. John F. Hoadley's *Origins of American Political Parties, 1789–1803* (1986) is superb.

The 1790s may also be understood through the views and behavior of national leaders. See the following biographies: Forrest McDonald, *Alexander Hamilton: A Biography* (1979), Richard Brookhiser's *Founding Father: Rediscovering George Washington* (1996), Joseph J. Ellis's *Passionate Sage: The Character and Legacy of John Adams* (1993). For a female perspective, see Phyllis Lee Levin's *Abigail Adams* (1991) and Edith B. Gelles's *Portia: The World of Abigail Adams* (1992). The opposition viewpoint is the subject of Lance Banning's *The Jeffersonian Persuasion: Evolution of a Party Ideology* (1978).

Federalist foreign policy is explored in Jerald A. Comb's *The Jay Treaty* (1970), William C. Stinchcombe's *The XYZ Affair* (1980), and Felix Gilbert's *To the Farewell Address: Ideas of Early American Foreign Policy* (1961).

For specific domestic issues, see Thomas Slaughter's *The Whiskey Rebellion: Frontier Epilogue to the American Revolution* (1986) and Harry Ammon's *The Genêt Mission* (1973). Patricia Watlington's *The Partisan Spirit: Kentucky Politics, 1779–1792* (1972) examines the Kentucky Resolutions. The treatment of Indians in the Old Northwest is explored in Richard H. Kohn's *Eagle and Sword: The Federalists and the Creation of the Military Establishment in America, 1783–1802* (1975). For the Alien and Sedition Acts, consult James Morton Smith's *Freedom's Fetters: The Alien and Sedition Laws and American Civil Liberties* (1966). Daniel Sisson's *The American Revolution of 1800* (1974) is useful on that important election.

Several books focus on social issues of the post–Revolutionary period, including *Keepers of the Revolution: New Yorkers at Work in the Early Republic* (1992), edited by Paul A. Gilje and Howard B. Rock, Ronald Schultz's *The Republic of Labor: Philadelphia Artisans and the Politics of Class, 1720–1830* (1993), and Peter Way's *Common Labour: Workers and the Digging of North American Canals, 1780–1860* (1993).

The African-American experience in the Revolutionary era is detailed in Mechal Sobel's *The World They Made Together: Black and White Values in Eighteenth-Century Virginia* (1988) and Gary B. Nash's *Forging Freedom: The Formation of Philadelphia's Black Community, 1720–1840* (1988).

9   REPUBLICANISM:
JEFFERSON AND MADISON

CHAPTER ORGANIZER

This chapter focuses on:

- the domestic policies of the Republicans in power.

- political divisions in the early republic.

- the causes and effects of the War of 1812.

On March 4, 1801, Thomas Jefferson, tall and thin, with ill-fitting clothes, red hair, and a ruddy complexion, became the first president to be inaugurated in the new federal city, Washington, District of Columbia. Washington was still a motley array of buildings around two centers, Capitol Hill and the Executive Mansion. Between them was a swampy wilderness, still full of stumps and mudholes, but with a stone walkway that offered a vantage from which to shoot duck, snipe, and partridge. The Congress, having met in eight different towns and cities since 1774, had at last found a permanent home, but as yet enjoyed few amenities. There were only two places of amusement, one a racetrack, the other a theater filled with "tobacco smoke, whiskey breaths, and other stenches, mixed up with the effluvia

This Plan of the City of Washington *(1800) shows the detailed gridwork pattern of "Grand Avenues and Streets."*

of stables, and miasmas of the canal." Practically deserted much of the year, the town came to life only when Congress assembled.

Jefferson's informal inauguration befitted the primitive surroundings. The new president left his lodgings and walked two blocks to the unfinished Capitol, entered the Senate chamber, took the oath from Chief Justice John Marshall, read his inaugural address in a barely audible voice, and returned to his boardinghouse for dinner with the guests at the common table. A tone of simplicity and conciliation ran through his inaugural address: "We are all Republicans—we are all Federalists. If there be any among us who would wish to dissolve this Union or to change its republican form, let them stand undisturbed as monuments of the safety with which error of opinion may be tolerated where reason is left free to combat it." Jefferson concluded with a summary of the "essential principles" that would guide his administration: "Equal and exact justice to all men . . . ; peace, commerce, and honest friendship with all nations, entangling alliances with none . . . ; freedom of religion; freedom of the press; and freedom of person, under the protection of the habeas corpus; and trial by juries impartially selected. . . . The wisdom of our sages and the blood of our heroes have been devoted to their attainment."

JEFFERSON IN OFFICE

The deliberate display of republican simplicity at Jefferson's inauguration set the style of his administration. He took pains to avoid the occasions of pomp and circumstance that had characterized Federalist administrations and which to his mind suggested the trappings of kingship. Presidential messages went to Congress in writing lest they resemble the parliamentary speech from the throne. The practice also allowed Jefferson, a notoriously bad public speaker, to exploit his skill as a writer.

Jefferson discarded the coach and six in which Washington and Adams had gone to state occasions and rode about the city on horseback, often by himself. But this was, at least in part, therapy recommended by a doctor, and in part because Washington's rutted streets were hardly the place for a carriage. Dinners at the White House were held around a circular table, so that none should take precedence. At social affairs the new president simply ignored the rules of protocol for what he called the rule of *pele mele,* in which the only custom observed was that the ladies went ahead of the men. "When brought together in society, all are perfectly equal," Jefferson affirmed.

Jefferson liked to think of his election as the "Revolution of 1800," but the margin had been close and the policies that he followed were more conciliatory than revolutionary. His overwhelming reelection in 1804 attests to the popularity of his philosophy. Perhaps the most revolutionary thing about Jefferson's presidency was the orderly transfer of power in 1801, an uncommon event in the world of that day. "The changes of administration," a Washington lady wrote in her diary, "which in every age have most generally been epochs of confusion, villainy and bloodshed, in this our happy country take place without any species of distraction, or disorder."

Jefferson placed in policy-making positions men of his own party, and he was the first president to pursue the role of party leader, cultivating congressional support at his dinner parties and otherwise. In the cabi-

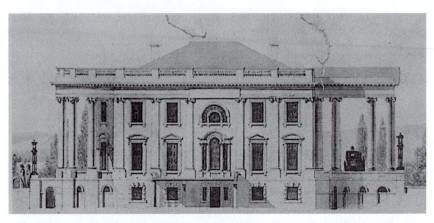

A watercolor of the president's house during Jefferson's term in office. Jefferson called it "big enough for two emperors, one pope, and the grand lama in the bargain."

net, the leading figures were Secretary of State James Madison, a long-time neighbor and political ally, and Secretary of the Treasury Albert Gallatin, a Swiss-born Pennsylvania Republican whose financial skills had won him the respect of Federalists. In an effort to cultivate Federalist New England, Jefferson chose men from that region for the positions of attorney-general, secretary of war, and postmaster-general.

In lesser offices, however, Jefferson refrained from wholesale removal of Federalists, preferring to wait until vacancies appeared. But the pressure from Republicans was such that he often yielded and removed Federalists, trying as best he could to assign some other than partisan causes for the removals. In one area, however, he managed to remove the offices rather than the appointees. In 1802 Congress repealed the Judiciary Act of 1801, and so abolished the circuit judgeships and other offices to which Adams had made his "midnight appointments." A new judiciary act restored to six the number of Supreme Court justices, and set up six circuit courts, each headed by a justice.

MARBURY V. MADISON   Adams's "midnight appointments" sparked the case of *Marbury* v. *Madison* (1803), the first in which the Supreme Court declared a federal law unconstitutional. The case involved the appointment of one William Marbury as justice of the peace in the District of Columbia. Marbury's appointment letter, or commission, signed by President Adams two days before he left office, was still undelivered when Madison took office as secretary of state, and Jefferson directed him to withhold it. Marbury then sued for a court order (a writ of mandamus) directing Madison to deliver his commission.

The Court's unanimous opinion, written by John Marshall, held that Marbury deserved his commission, but then denied that the Court had jurisdiction in the case. Section 13 of the Judiciary Act of 1789, which gave the Court original jurisdiction in mandamus proceedings, was unconstitutional, the Court ruled, because the Constitution specified that the Court should have original jurisdiction only in cases involving ambassadors or states. The Court, therefore, could issue no order in the case. With one bold stroke Marshall had chastised the Jeffersonians while avoiding an awkward confrontation with an administration that might have defied his order. At the same time, he established the precedent that the Court could declare a federal law invalid on the grounds that it violated provisions of the Constitution.

PARTISAN SQUABBLES   The Court's decision, about which Jefferson could do nothing, confirmed his fear of the judges' partisanship. In 1804 Republicans used the impeachment power against two of the most partisan Federalist judges, and succeeded in ousting one of the two. The Republican House brought impeachments against District Judge John Pickering of New Hampshire and Supreme Court Associate Justice Samuel Chase. Pickering was clearly insane, which was not a high crime or misdemeanor, but he was also given to profane and drunken harangues from the bench, which the Senate quickly decided was an impeachable offense. In any event he was incompetent.

The case against Justice Chase was a more complicated matter. That he was highhanded and intemperate there was no question. Chase had presided at the sedition trials of two Republican editors, ordering a marshal to strike off the jury panel "any of those creatures or persons called democrats." He once attacked the Maryland Constitution from the bench because it granted manhood suffrage, under which "our republican Constitution will sink into a mobocracy." But neither Jefferson nor the best efforts of John Randolph of Roanoke as prosecutor for the House could persuade two-thirds of the senators that Chase's vindictive partisanship constituted "high crimes and misdemeanors." His removal might have set off the partisanship of Republicans in a political carnival of reprisals. His acquittal discouraged further efforts at impeachment, however, which Jefferson pronounced a "farce," after the failure to remove Chase.

DOMESTIC REFORMS   Aside from this setback, however, Jefferson's first term was a succession of triumphs in both domestic and foreign affairs. He did not set out to dismantle Hamilton's program. Under Treasury Secretary Gallatin's tutoring, he learned to accept the national bank as an essential convenience, and he did not push a measure for the Bank's repeal which more dogmatic Republicans sponsored. It was too late of course to undo Hamilton's funding and debt assumption operations, but none too soon in the opinion of both Jefferson and Gallatin to begin retiring the resultant federal debt. At the same time, Jefferson won the repeal of the whiskey tax and other Federalist excises, much to the relief of backwoods distillers, drinkers, and grain farmers.

Without the excise taxes, frugality was all the more necessary to a government dependent for revenue chiefly on tariffs and the sale of western lands. Happily for the Treasury, both activities flourished. The European war brought a continually increasing traffic to American shipping and thus revenues to the federal Treasury. At the same time, settlers flocked into the western lands, which were coming more and more within their reach. The admission of Ohio in 1803 increased to seventeen the number of states.

By the "wise and frugal government" promised in the inaugural address, Jefferson and Gallatin reasoned, the United States could live within its income, like a prudent farmer. The basic formula was simple: cut back expenses on the military. A standing army menaced a free soci-

Cincinnati in 1800, twelve years after its founding. Though its population was only about 750, its inhabitants were already promoting Cincinnati as "the metropolis of the north-western territory."

ety anyway. It therefore should be kept to a minimum and the national defense left, in Jefferson's words, to "a well-disciplined militia, our best reliance in peace, and for the first moments of war, till regulars may relieve them." The navy, which the Federalists had already reduced after the quasi war with France, ought to be reduced further. Coastal defense, Jefferson argued, should rely on fortifications and a "mosquito fleet" of small gunboats.

In 1807 Jeffersonian reforms culminated with an act that outlawed the foreign slave trade as of January 1, 1808, the earliest date possible under the Constitution. At the time South Carolina was the only state that still permitted the trade, having reopened it in 1803. But for years to come an illegal traffic would continue. By one informal estimate perhaps 300,000 slaves were smuggled into the United States between 1808 and 1861.

THE BARBARY PIRATES   Issues of foreign relations intruded on Jefferson early in his term, when events in the Mediterranean quickly gave him second thoughts about the need for a navy. On the Barbary Coast of North Africa the rulers of Morocco, Algiers, Tunis, and Tripoli had for years practiced piracy and extortion. After the Revolution, American shipping in the Mediterranean became fair game, no longer protected by British payments of tribute. The new American government yielded up protection money too, first to Morocco in 1786, then to the others in the 1790s. In 1801, however, the pasha of Tripoli upped his demands and declared war on the United States by the symbolic gesture of chopping down the flagpole at the United States consulate. Rather than give in to this, Jefferson sent warships to blockade Tripoli.

A wearisome war dragged on until 1805, punctuated in 1804 by the notable exploit of Lieutenant Stephen Decatur, who slipped into Tripoli Harbor by night and set fire to the frigate *Philadelphia,* which had been captured (along with its crew) after it ran aground. The pasha finally settled for $60,000 ransom and released the *Philadelphia's* crew, whom he had held hostage for more than a year. It was still tribute, but less than the $300,000 the pasha had demanded at first, and much less than the cost of war.

THE LOUISIANA PURCHASE   It was an inglorious end to a shabby affair, but well before it was over, events elsewhere had led to the greatest single achievement of the Jefferson administration. The Louisiana

Purchase of 1803 more than doubled the territory of the United States. It included the entire Mississippi Valley west of the river itself. Louisiana, settled by the French, had been ceded to Spain in 1763. Since that time the dream of retaking Louisiana had stirred in French minds. In 1800 Napoleon Bonaparte secured its return in exchange for a promise (never fulfilled) to set up a Spanish princess and her husband in Italy as rulers of an enlarged Tuscany. When unofficial word of the deal reached Washington in 1801, Jefferson hastened Robert R. Livingston, the new minister to France, on his way. Spain in control of the Mississippi outlet was bad enough, but Napoleon in control could only mean serious trouble. "There is on the globe one single spot the possessor of which is our natural and habitual enemy," Jefferson wrote Livingston: "The day that France takes possession of New Orleans . . . we must marry ourselves to the British fleet and nation," an unhappy prospect for Jefferson.

But Spain still held the Floridas. Long and frustrating talks dragged out into 1803, while Spanish forces remained in control in Louisiana, awaiting the arrival of the French. Early that year James Monroe was sent to assist Livingston in Paris, but no sooner had he arrived than Napoleon's minister, Talleyrand, surprised Livingston by asking if the United States would like to buy the whole of Louisiana. Livingston, once he regained his composure, snapped up the offer.

Napoleon's motives in the whole affair can only be surmised. At first he seems to have thought of a New World empire, but that plan took an ugly turn in French Saint Domingue (later Haiti). There during the 1790s the revolutionary governments of France had lost control to a slave revolt. In 1802 Napoleon sent a force to subdue the island. By a ruse of war the French captured the black leader, Toussaint l'Ouverture, but then fell victim to guerrillas and yellow fever. Napoleon's plan may have been discouraged too by the fierce American reaction when the Spanish governor of Louisiana closed the Mississippi River to American traffic in 1802, on secret orders from Madrid. In the end Napoleon's purpose seems to have been simply to cut his losses, turn a quick profit, mollify the Americans, and go back to reshaping the map of Europe.

By the treaty of cession, dated April 30, 1803, the United States obtained the Louisiana Territory for about $15 million. The treaty was vague in defining the boundaries of Louisiana. Its language could be stretched to provide a tenuous claim on Texas and a much stronger

In 1802 Toussaint l'Ouverture led the slave revolt on Saint Domingue (later Haiti) depicted in this engraving.

claim on West Florida, from Baton Rouge on the Mississippi past Mobile to the Perdido River on the east. When Livingston asked about the boundaries, Talleyrand responded: "I can give you no direction. You have made a noble bargain for yourselves, and I suppose you will make the most of it."

The turn of events had presented Jefferson with a noble bargain, a great new "empire of liberty," but also with a constitutional dilemma. Nowhere did the Constitution even mention the purchase of territory. By a strict construction, which Jefferson had professed, no such power existed. Jefferson at first thought to resolve the matter by offering an amendment, but his advisers argued against delay lest Napoleon change his mind. The power to purchase territory, they reasoned, resided in the power to make treaties. Jefferson relented, trusting, he said, "that the good sense of our country will correct the evil of loose construction when it shall produce ill effects." New England Federalists boggled at the prospect of new states that would probably strengthen the Jeffersonian party, and centered their fire on a proviso that the inhabitants be "incorporated in the Union" as citizens. In a reversal that anticipated many future reversals on constitutional issues, Federalists found themselves arguing strict construction of the Constitution while Republicans brushed aside such scruples in favor of implied power.

The Senate ratified the treaty by an overwhelming vote of 26 to 6, and on December 20, 1803, American officials took formal possession of Louisiana from a French agent who had taken over from Spanish authorities only three weeks before. For the time being the Spanish kept West Florida, but within a decade that area would be ripe for the plucking. In 1808 Napoleon put his brother on the throne of Spain. With the Spanish colonial administration in disarray, American settlers in 1810 staged a rebellion in Baton Rouge and proclaimed the Republic of West Florida, which was quickly annexed and occupied by the United States as far eastward as the Pearl River. In 1812 the state of Louisiana absorbed the region—still known today as the Florida parishes. In 1813, with Spain itself a battlefield for French and British forces, Americans took over the rest of West Florida, now the Gulf coast of Mississippi and Alabama. Legally, the American government has claimed ever since, all these areas were included in the original Louisiana Purchase.

EXPLORING THE CONTINENT   As an amateur scientist long before he was president, Jefferson had nourished an active curiosity about the Louisiana country, its geography, its flora and fauna, its prospects for trade and agriculture. In 1803 he asked Congress for $2,500 to send an exploring expedition to the Far Northwest, beyond the Mississippi, in what was still foreign territory. Although Jefferson was keenly interested in mapping the trans-Mississippi wilderness and collecting scientific information, as well as promoting the fur trade and trade with the Indians of the interior, he explained to Congress that the expedition would be "for the purpose of extending the foreign commerce of the United States." He realized that Congress would not approve a merely scientific foray. Congress approved, and Jefferson assigned as commanders twenty-nine-year-old Meriwether Lewis, who as the president's private secretary had been groomed for the job, and another Virginian, William Clark, the much younger brother of George Rogers Clark.

In 1804 the "Corps of Discovery," numbering nearly fifty, set out from St. Louis to ascend the Missouri River. Forced to live off the land, they quickly adapted themselves to a new environment. Local Indians introduced them to new clothes made from deer hides and taught them new hunting techniques. Six months later, near the Mandan Sioux villages in what later became North Dakota, they built Fort Mandan and wintered there in relative comfort, sending back downriver a barge

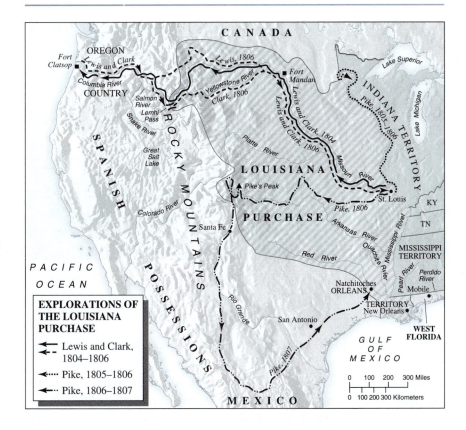

loaded with specimens such as the prairie dog, previously unknown to science, and the magpie, previously unknown in America. Jefferson kept the great horns of a wapiti (elk) to display at Monticello.

In the spring Lewis and Clark added to the main party a French guide, who was little help, and his remarkable Shoshone wife, Sacajawea ("Canoe Launcher"), who proved an enormous help as interpreter with the Indians of the region, and set out once again upstream. At the head of the Missouri they took the north fork, thenceforth the Jefferson River, crossed the Continental Divide at Lemhi Pass, and in dugout canoes descended the Snake and Columbia Rivers to the Pacific. Near the later site of Astoria at the mouth of the Columbia they built Fort Clatsop, in which they spent another winter. The following spring, they split into two parties, with Lewis heading back by almost the same route, and Clark going by way of the Yellowstone River. They rejoined each other at the juncture of the Missouri and Yellowstone Rivers, re-

Lewis and Clark holding a council with the Indians, from a book of engravings of the Lewis and Clark expedition (c. 1812).

turning together to St. Louis in 1806, having been gone nearly two and a half years.

No longer was the Far West unknown country. Although it was nearly a century before a good edition of the *Journals of Lewis and Clark* appeared in print, many of their findings came out piecemeal, including an influential map in 1814. Convinced that they had found a practical route for the China trade, Lewis and Clark were among the last to hold out hope for a water route through the continent. Their reports of friendly Indians and abundant pelts quickly attracted traders and trappers to the region, and also gave the United States a claim to the Oregon country by right of discovery and exploration.

While Lewis and Clark were gone, Jefferson sent Lieutenant Zebulon Pike to find the source of the Mississippi River. He mistakenly picked a tributary, later discoveries showed, but contributed to knowledge of the upper Mississippi Valley. Then, during 1806–1807, he went out to the headwaters of the Arkansas River as far as Colorado. He discovered Pike's Peak but failed in an attempt to climb it, and made a roundabout return by way of Santa Fe, courtesy of Spanish soldiers who captured his party. Pike's account, while less reliable and less full than that of Lewis and Clark, appeared first and gave Americans their first overall picture of the Great Plains and Rocky Mountains. It also contributed to the widespread belief that the arid regions of the West constituted a Great American Desert, largely unfit for human habitation.

POLITICAL SCHEMES   Jefferson's policies, including the Louisiana Purchase, brought him almost solid support in the South and West. Even New Englanders were moving to his side. By 1809 John Quincy Adams, the son of the second president, would become a Republican! Die-hard Federalists read the handwriting on the wall. The acquisition of a vast new empire in the West would reduce New England to insignificance in political affairs, and along with it the Federalist cause. Under the leadership of Senator Thomas Pickering, a group of ardent Massachusetts Federalists called the Essex Junto considered seceding from the Union, an idea that would simmer in New England circles for another decade.

Soon they hatched a scheme to link New York with New England and contacted Vice-President Aaron Burr, who had been on the outs with the Jeffersonians. Their plan depended on Burr's election as governor of New York, but in 1804, Burr lost to the regular Republican candidate. The extreme Federalists, it turned out, could not even hold members of their own party to the plan, which Hamilton bitterly opposed on the grounds that Burr was "a dangerous man, and one who ought not to be trusted with the reins of government."

When Hamilton's remarks appeared in the public press, Burr's demand for an explanation led to a duel in 1804 at Weehawken, New Jersey. On a grassy ledge above the Hudson River, Burr shot Hamilton through the heart. Hamilton personally opposed dueling, but his romantic streak and sense of honor compelled him to demonstrate his courage, long since established beyond any question at Yorktown. He went to his death, as his son had done in a similar affair the previous year, determined not to fire at his opponent. Burr had no such scruples. The death of Hamilton ended both Pickering's scheme and Burr's political career—but not his intrigues.

Meanwhile the presidential campaign of 1804 got under way when a congressional caucus of Republicans renominated Jefferson and chose George Clinton for vice-president. Opposed by the Federalists Charles C. Pinckney and Rufus King, Jefferson and Clinton won 162 of 176 electoral votes. Jefferson's policy of conciliation had made him a national rather than a sectional candidate.

DIVISIONS IN THE REPUBLICAN PARTY

RANDOLPH AND THE *TERTIUM QUID*   Freed from a strong opposition—Federalists made up only a quarter of the new Congress—the majority began to lose its cohesion. Cracks appeared in the Republican facade, portents of major fissures that would finally split the party as the Federalists faded into oblivion. John Randolph, a Jeffersonian mainstay in the first term, became the most conspicuous of the dissidents. Randolph was a powerful combination of principle, eccentricity, and rancor. Famous for his venomous assaults delivered in a shrill soprano voice, the Virginian congressman strutted about the House floor with a whip in his hand, a symbol that he flourished best in opposition. Few colleagues had the stomach for his tongue-lashings.

Randolph, too much a loner for any leadership roles, became the crusty spokesman for a shifting group of "Old Republicans," whose adherence to party principles had rendered them more Jeffersonian than Jefferson himself. Their philosopher was John Taylor of Caroline, a Virginia planter-pamphleteer whose theories of states' rights and strict construction had little effect at the time but delighted the secessionists of later years. Neither Randolph nor Taylor could accept his leader's pragmatic gift for adjusting principle to circumstance.

Randolph first began to smell a rat in the case of the Yazoo Fraud, a land scheme that originated in Georgia but entangled speculators from all over. In 1795 the Georgia legislature had sold to four land companies, in which some of the legislators were involved, 35 million acres in the Yazoo country (Mississippi and Alabama) for $500,000 (little more than a penny an acre). A new legislature rescinded the sale the following year, but not before some of the land claims had been sold to third parties. When Georgia finally ceded its western lands to federal authority in 1802, Jefferson sought a compromise settlement of the claims. But Randolph managed to block passage of the necessary measures and in the ensuing quarrels was removed as Speaker of the House. The snarled Yazoo affair plagued the courts and Congress for another decade. Finally, in the case of *Fletcher* v. *Peck* (1810), Chief Justice Marshall ruled that the original sale, however fraudulent, was a legal contract. Marshall held that the repeal impaired the obligation of contract and was therefore unconstitutional. Final settlement came in 1814 when Congress awarded $4.2 million to the speculators.

Randolph's definitive break with Jefferson came in 1806, when the president sought an appropriation of $2 million for a thinly disguised bribe to the French to win their influence in persuading Spain to yield the Floridas to the United States. "I found I might co-operate or be an honest man—I have therefore opposed and will oppose them," Randolph said. Thereafter he resisted Jefferson's initiatives almost out of reflex. Randolph and his colleagues were sometimes called "Quids," or the *Tertium Quid* (the "third something"), and their dissents gave rise to talk of a third party, neither Republican nor Federalist. But they never got together. Some of the dissenters in 1808 backed James Monroe against James Madison for the presidential succession, but the campaign quickly fizzled. The failure of the Quids would typify the experience of almost all third-party movements thereafter.

THE BURR CONSPIRACY   John Randolph may have become enmeshed in dogma, but Aaron Burr was never one to let principle stand in the way. Sheer brilliance and opportunism carried him to the vice-presidency. With a leaven of discretion he might easily have become heir apparent to Jefferson, but a taste for intrigue was the tragic flaw in his character. Caught up in the dubious schemes of Federalist diehards in 1800 and again in 1804, he ended his political career once and for all when he killed Hamilton. Even Hamilton's archenemies abhorred Burr's act. "No one wished to get rid of Hamilton that way," John Adams muttered. Indicted in New York and New Jersey for murder and

Aaron Burr.

heavily in debt, the vice-president went first to Spanish-held Florida. Once the furor subsided, he boldly returned to Washington to preside over the Senate. As long as he stayed out of New York and New Jersey, he was safe. Groused one senator: "We are indeed fallen on evil times."

But Burr focused his attention less on the Senate than on a cockeyed scheme to carve out a personal empire for himself in the West. What came to be known as the Burr Conspiracy was hatched when Burr met with General James Wilkinson, an old friend with a tainted Revolutionary War record who was a spy for the Spanish. Just what he and Burr were up to probably will never be known. The most likely explanation is that they sought to organize a secession of Louisiana and set up an independent republic. Earlier Burr had solicited British support for his scheme to separate "the western part of the United States in its whole extent."

Whatever the goal, Burr succeeded in having Wilkinson appointed governor of the Louisiana Territory. In the summer of 1805 Burr himself sailed downriver from Pittsburgh on a lavishly outfitted flatboat, leaving behind him a wake of rumors. By the summer of 1806, he was in Lexington, Kentucky, recruiting adventurers. Meanwhile, rumors began to reach Jefferson, and so did a letter from General Wilkinson warning of "a deep, dark, wicked, and wide-spread conspiracy." Wilkinson had apparently developed cold feet and now feigned ignorance of the whole affair.

In early 1807, as Burr neared Natchez, he learned that Wilkinson had betrayed him and that Jefferson had ordered his arrest. He set out cross-country for Pensacola, but was caught and taken off to Richmond for a trial, which, like the conspiracy, had a stellar cast. Charged with treason by the grand jury, Burr was brought for trial before Chief Justice Marshall. The case revealed both Marshall and Jefferson at their partisan worst. Marshall decided that the "hand of malignity" was grasping at Burr, while Jefferson, determined to get a conviction at any cost, published relevant affidavits in advance and promised pardons to conspirators who helped convict Burr. Marshall in turn was so indiscreet as to attend a dinner given by the chief defense counsel at which Burr himself was present.

The case established two major constitutional precedents. First, Jefferson ignored a subpoena requiring him to appear in court with certain papers in his possession. He refused, as George Washington had refused, to submit papers to the Congress on grounds of executive privilege. Both believed that the independence of the executive branch would be compromised if the president were subject to a court writ. The second major precedent was the rigid definition of treason. On this Marshall adopted the strictest of constructions. Treason under the Constitution consists of "levying war against the United States or adhering to their enemies" and requires "two witnesses to the same overt act" for conviction. Since the prosecution failed to produce two witnesses to an overt act of treason by Burr, the jury found him not guilty.

Whether or not Burr escaped his just deserts, Marshall's strict construction of the Constitution protected the United States, as the authors of the Constitution clearly intended, against the capricious judgments of "treason" that governments through the centuries have used to terrorize dissenters. As to Burr, with further charges pending, he skipped bail and took refuge in France, but returned unmolested in 1812 to practice law in New York. He survived to a virile old age. At age eighty, shortly before his death, he was divorced on grounds of adultery.

War in Europe

Oppositionists of whatever stripe were more an annoyance than a threat to Jefferson. The more intractable problems of his second term involved the renewal of the European war in 1803, which helped resolve the problem of Louisiana but put more strains on Jefferson's desire to avoid "entangling alliances" and the quarrels of Europe. In 1805 Napoleon's crushing defeat of Russian and Austrian forces at Austerlitz left him in control of western Europe. The same year, Admiral Nelson's defeat of the French and Spanish fleets in the Battle of Trafalgar secured Britain's control of the seas. The war resolved itself into a battle of elephant and whale, Napoleon dominant on land, the British dominant on the water, neither able to strike a decisive blow at the other, and neither restrained by an overly delicate sense of neutral rights or international law.

HARASSMENT BY BRITAIN AND FRANCE For two years after the renewal of hostilities, American shippers reaped the benefits, taking over trade with the French and Spanish West Indies. But in the case of the *Essex* (1805), a British court ruled that the practice of shipping French and Spanish goods through American ports while on their way elsewhere did not neutralize enemy goods. Such a practice violated the British Rule of 1756, under which trade closed in time of peace remained closed in time of war. Goods shipped in violation of the rule, the British held, were liable to seizure at any point under the doctrine of continuous voyage. In 1807 the commercial provisions of Jay's Treaty expired and James Monroe, ambassador to Great Britain, failed to get a renewal satisfactory to Jefferson. After that, the British interference with American shipping increased, not just to keep supplies from Napoleon's continent but also to hobble competition with British merchant ships.

In a series of Orders in Council adopted in 1806 and 1807, the British ministry set up a "paper blockade" of Europe that barred all trade between England and Europe. Moreover, vessels headed for continental ports were required to get licenses and were subject to British inspection. It was a "paper blockade" because even the powerful British navy was not large enough to monitor every European port. Napoleon retaliated with his "Continental System," proclaimed in the Berlin Decree of 1806 and the Milan Decree of 1807. In the Berlin Decree, he declared his own paper blockade of the British Isles and barred British ships from ports under French control. In the Milan Decree, he ruled that neutral ships that complied with British regulations were subject to seizure when they reached continental ports. The situation presented American shippers with a dilemma. If they complied with the demands of one side, they were subject to seizure by the other.

The risks were daunting, but the prospects for profits were so great that shippers ran the risk. For seamen the danger was heightened by a renewal of the practice of impressment. The use of press gangs to kidnap men in British (and colonial) ports was a long-standing method of recruitment for the British navy. The seizure of British subjects from American vessels became a new source of recruits, justified on the principle that British subjects remained British subjects for life: "Once an Englishman, always an Englishman." Mistakes might be made, of course, since it was sometimes hard to distinguish British subjects from Americans; indeed a flourishing trade in fake citizenship papers arose in American ports. Impressment was mostly confined to merchant vessels, but on at least two occasions before 1807, vessels of the American navy had been stopped on the high seas and seamen removed.

In the summer of 1807, the British frigate *Leopard* accosted an American naval vessel, the frigate *Chesapeake,* just outside territorial waters off Norfolk, Virginia. After the *Chesapeake's* captain refused to be searched, the *Leopard* opened fire, killing three Americans and wounding eighteen. The *Chesapeake,* caught unready for battle, was forced to strike its colors (lowering the flag was a sign of surrender). A British search party seized four men, one of whom was later hanged for desertion from the British navy. Soon after the *Chesapeake* limped back into Norfolk, the *Washington Federalist* editorialized: "We have never, on any occasion, witnessed . . . such a thirst for revenge. . . ." Public wrath was so aroused that Jefferson could have had war on the spot. Had Congress been in session, he might have been forced into war. But Jefferson, like Adams before him, resisted the war fever and suffered politically as a result. One Federalist called Jefferson a "dish of skim milk curdling at the head of our nation."

THE EMBARGO   Jefferson resolved to use public indignation as the occasion for an effort at "peaceable coercion." In 1807, in response to his request, Congress passed the Embargo Act, which stopped all export of American goods and prohibited American ships from leaving for foreign ports. The constitutional basis of the embargo was the power to regulate commerce, which in this case Republicans interpreted broadly as the power to prohibit commerce. "Let the example teach the world that our firmness equals our moderation," said the *National Intelligencer,* "that having resorted to a measure just in itself, and adequate to its object, we will flinch from no sacrifices which the honor and good of the nation demand from virtuous and faithful citizens."

Jefferson's embargo, however, failed from the beginning for want of the will to make the necessary sacrifices. The idealistic spirit that had made economic pressures effective in the pre-Revolutionary crises was lacking. Trade remained profitable despite the risks, and violation of the embargo was almost laughably easy. Lax enforcement and loopholes in the act permitted ships to leave port under the pretense of engaging in coastal trade or whaling, or under an amendment passed a few months after the act for the purpose of bringing home American property stored in foreign warehouses. Some 800 ships left on such missions, but few of them returned before the embargo expired. Trade across the Canadian border flourished. As it turned out, France was little hurt by the act. The lack of American cotton hurt some British manufacturers and

Preparation for War to Defend Commerce. *In 1806 and 1807 American shipping was caught in the crossfire of war between Britain and France.*

workers, but they carried little weight with the government, and British shippers benefited. With American ports closed, they found a new trade in Latin American ports thrown open by the colonial authorities when Napoleon occupied the mother countries of Spain and Portugal.

The coercive effect was minimal, and the embargo revived the moribund Federalist party in New England, which renewed the charge that Jefferson was in league with the French. At the same time, agriculture in the South and West suffered for want of outlets for grain, cotton, and tobacco. After fifteen months of ineffectiveness, Jefferson finally accepted failure and in 1809 signed a repeal of the embargo shortly before he relinquished the "splendid misery" of the presidency.

In the election of 1808 the succession passed to another Virginian, Secretary of State James Madison. Clinton was again the candidate for vice-president. The Federalists, backing Charles C. Pinckney and Rufus King of New York, revived enough as a result of the embargo to win 47 votes to Madison's 122.

THE DRIFT TO WAR Madison's presidency was entangled in foreign affairs from the beginning. Still insisting on neutral rights and freedom of the seas, he pursued Jefferson's policy of "peaceable coercion" by different but no more effective means. In place of the embargo Congress had substituted the Non-Intercourse Act, which reopened trade with all countries except France and Great Britain and authorized the president to reopen trade with whichever of these gave up its restrictions. British minister David Erskine assured Madison's secretary of state that Britain would revoke its restrictions in 1809. With that assurance, Madison reopened trade with Britain, but Erskine had acted on his own and the foreign secretary, repudiating his action, recalled him. Nonintercourse resumed, but it proved as ineffective as the embargo. In the vain search for an alternative, Congress in 1810 reversed its ground and adopted a measure introduced by Nathaniel Macon of North Carolina,

This 1807 Federalist cartoon compares Washington (left) to Jefferson (right). Washington is flanked by the British lion and the American eagle, while Jefferson is flanked by a snake and a lizard. Below Jefferson are volumes by French philosophers.

Macon's Bill Number 2, which reopened trade with the warring powers but provided that, if either dropped its restrictions, non-intercourse would be restored with the other.

This time Napoleon took a turn at trying to bamboozle Madison. Napoleon's foreign minister, the duc de Cadore, informed the American minister in Paris that he had withdrawn the Berlin and Milan Decrees, but the carefully worded Cadore letter had strings attached: revocation of the decrees depended on withdrawal of the British Orders in Council. The strings were plain to see, but either Madison misunderstood or, more likely, went along in hope of putting pressure on the British. In response to the Cadore letter, he restored non-intercourse with the British. The British refused to give in, but Madison clung to his policy despite Napoleon's continued seizure of American ships. The seemingly hopeless effort did indeed finally work. With more time, with more patience, with a transatlantic cable, Madison's policy would have been vindicated without resort to war. On June 16, 1812, the British foreign minister, facing economic crisis, announced revocation of the Orders in Council. Britain preferred not to risk war with the United States on top of its war with Napoleon. But on June 1 Madison had asked for war, and by June 18, 1812, the Congress concurred without knowing of the British repeal.

THE WAR OF 1812

CAUSES   The main cause of the war—the demand for neutral rights—seems clear enough. Neutral rights dominated Madison's war message and provided the salient reason for a mounting hostility toward the British. Yet the geographical distribution of the congressional vote for war raises a troubling question. The preponderance of the vote for war came from members of Congress representing the farm regions from Pennsylvania southward and westward. The maritime states of New York and New England, the region that bore the brunt of British attacks on American trade, gave a majority against the declaration of war. One explanation for this seeming anomaly is simple enough. The farming regions suffered damage to their markets for grain, cotton, and tobacco, while New England shippers made profits in spite of British restrictions.

Tecumseh, the Shawnee leader who tried to unite the tribes in defense of their lands. He was killed in 1813 at the Battle of the Thames.

Other plausible explanations for the sectional vote, however, include frontier Indian depredations, which were blamed on the British, western land hunger, and the desire for new lands in Canada and the Floridas. Indian troubles were endemic to a rapidly expanding West. Land-hungry settlers and speculators kept moving out ahead of government surveys and sales in search of fertile acres. The constant pressure to open new lands repeatedly forced or persuaded Indians to sign treaties they did not always understand, causing stronger resentment among tribes that were losing more and more of their lands. It was an old story, dating from the Jamestown settlement, but one that took a new turn with the rise of two Shawnee leaders, Tecumseh and his twin brother Tenskwatawa, "the Prophet."

Tecumseh saw with blazing clarity the consequences of Indian disunity. From his base on the Tippecanoe River in northern Indiana, he traveled from Canada to the Gulf of Mexico in his efforts to form a confederation of tribes to defend Indian hunting grounds, insisting that no land cession was valid without the consent of all tribes, since they held the land in common. His brother supplied the inspiration of a religious revival, calling upon the Indians to worship the "Master of Life," to resist the white man's liquor, and lead a simple life within their means. By 1811 Tecumseh had matured his plans and headed south to win the Creeks, Cherokees, Choctaws, and Chickasaws to his cause.

Governor William Henry Harrison learned of Tecumseh's plans, met with him twice, and pronounced him "one of those uncommon geniuses who spring up occasionally to produce revolutions and overturn the es-

The Battle of Tippecanoe, November 7, 1811, was won by William Henry Harrison and his troops while Tecumseh was away.

tablished order of things." In the fall of 1811, Harrison decided that Tecumseh must be stopped. He gathered a thousand troops and set out to attack Tecumseh's capital, Prophet's Town, on the Tippecanoe River, while the leader was away. The Indians attacked Harrison's encampment on the Tippecanoe River, although Tecumseh had warned against any fighting in his absence. The Shawnees lost a bloody engagement that left about a quarter of Harrison's men dead or wounded. Only later did Harrison realize that he had inflicted a defeat on the Indians, who had become demoralized and many of whom had fled to Canada. Harrison then burned their town and destroyed all its supplies. Tecumseh's dreams went up in smoke, and Tecumseh himself fled to British protection in Canada.

The Battle of Tippecanoe reinforced suspicions that the British were inciting the Indians. Actually the incident was mainly Harrison's doing. With little hope of help from war-torn Europe, Canadian authorities had steered a careful course, discouraging warfare but seeking to keep the Indians' friendship and fur trade. To eliminate the Indian menace, American frontiersmen reasoned, they needed to remove its foreign support, and they saw Upper Canada as a pistol pointing at the United States. Conquest of Canada would accomplish a twofold purpose. It would eliminate British influence among the Indians and open a new empire for land-hungry Americans. It was also the only place, in case of war, where the British were vulnerable to American attack. East Florida, still under the Spanish flag, posed a similar threat. Spain was too weak or unwilling to prevent sporadic Indian attacks across the frontier. The British were also suspected of smuggling through Florida and intriguing with the Indians on the southwest border.

Such concerns helped generate a war fever. In the Congress that assembled in late 1811, a number of new members from southern and western districts began to clamor for war in defense of "national honor." Among them were Henry Clay of Kentucky, who became Speaker of the House, Richard M. Johnson of Kentucky, Felix Grundy of Tennessee, and John C. Calhoun of South Carolina. John Randolph of Roanoke christened these "new boys" the "War Hawks." After they entered the House, Randolph said, "We have heard but one word—like the whip-poor-will, but one eternal monotonous tone—Canada! Canada! Canada!"

PREPARATIONS   As it turned out, the War Hawks would get neither Canada nor Florida. For James Madison had carried into war a country that was ill-prepared both financially and militarily. In 1811, despite earnest pleas from Treasury Secretary Gallatin, Congress had let the twenty-year charter of the Bank of the United States expire. A combination of strict-constructionist Republicans and Anglophobes, who feared the large British interest in the Bank, did it in. Also, many state banks were mismanaged, resulting in deposits lost through bankruptcy. Trade had approached a standstill and tariff revenues had declined. Loans were needed for about two-thirds of the war costs while northeastern opponents to the war were reluctant to lend money. Government bonds were difficult to float.

The military situation was almost as bad. War had been likely for nearly a decade, but Republican austerities had prevented preparations. When the war began the army numbered only 6,700 men, ill trained, poorly equipped, and led by aging officers. Most of the senior officers were veterans of the Revolution. One young Virginia officer named Winfield Scott, destined for military distinction, commented that most of the veteran commanders "had very generally slunk into either sloth, ignorance, or habits of intemperate drinking."

The navy, on the other hand, was in comparatively good shape, with able officers and trained men whose seamanship had been tested in the fighting against France and Tripoli. Its ships were well outfitted and seaworthy—all sixteen of them. In the first year of the war it was the navy that produced the only American victories in isolated duels with British vessels, but their effect was mainly an occasional lift to morale. Within a year the British had blockaded the coast, except for New England, where they hoped to cultivate antiwar feeling, and most of the little American fleet was bottled up in port.

THE WAR IN THE NORTH   The only place where the United States could effectively strike at the British was Canada. Madison's best hope was a quick attack on Quebec or Montreal to cut Canada's lifeline, the St. Lawrence River. Instead, the old history of the indecisive colonial wars was repeated, for the last time.

The administration opted for a three-pronged drive against Canada: along the Lake Champlain route toward Montreal, with General Henry Dearborn in command; along the Niagara River, with forces under General Stephen Van Rensselaer; and into Upper Canada (north of Lake Erie and Lake Ontario) from Detroit, with General William Hull and some 2,000 men. In 1812, Hull marched his men across the Detroit River but was pushed back to Detroit by the British under General Isaac Brock. Sickly and senile, Hull procrastinated in Detroit while his position worsened and the news arrived that Fort Michilimackinac had surrendered. The British commander cleverly played upon Hull's worst fears. Gathering what redcoats he could to parade in view of Detroit's defenders, he announced that thousands of Indian allies were at the rear and that once fighting began he would be unable to control them. Fearing massacre, Hull surrendered his entire force.

Along the Niagara front, General Van Rensselaer was more aggressive. An advance party of 600 Americans crossed the Niagara River and worked their way up the bluffs on the Canadian side. The stage was set for a major victory, but the New York militia refused to reinforce Van Rensselaer's men, claiming that their military service did not obligate them to leave the country. They complacently remained on the New York side and watched their outnumbered countrymen fall to a superior force across the river.

On the third front, the old invasion route via Lake Champlain, the trumpet once more gave an uncertain sound. General Dearborn led his army north from Plattsburgh toward Montreal. He marched them up to the border, where the militia once again stood on its alleged constitu-

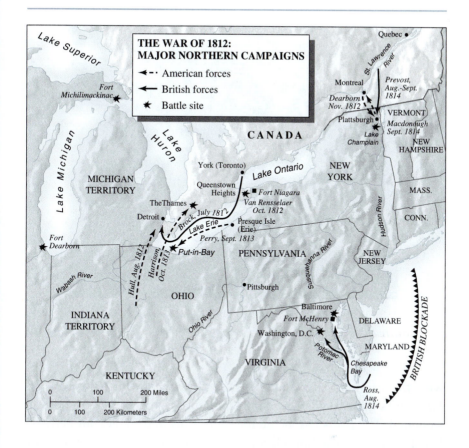

THE WAR OF 1812:
MAJOR NORTHERN CAMPAIGNS

◄·· American forces

◄— British forces

★ Battle site

tional rights and refused to cross, and then marched them back to Plattsburgh.

Madison's navy secretary now pushed vigorously for American control of inland waters. At Presque Isle (Erie), Pennsylvania, twenty-eight-year-old Commodore Oliver H. Perry, already a fourteen-year veteran who had seen action against Tripoli, was fetching hardware up from Pittsburgh and building ships from the wilderness lumber. By the end of the summer Perry had superior numbers and set out in search of the British, whom he found at Lake Erie's Put-in-Bay, on September 10, 1813. After completing the preparations for battle, Perry told an aide: "This is the most important day of my life."

It was indeed. Two British warships used their superior weapons to pummel the *Lawrence,* Perry's flagship, at long distance. Blood flowed on the deck so freely that the sailors slipped and fell as they wrestled

John Bull stung to agony by the *Wasp* and *Hornet, two Ameri-can ships with early victories in the War of 1812.*

with the cannon. After four hours of intense shelling, none of the *Lawrence*'s guns was left working, and most of the crew were dead or wounded. The British expected the Americans to turn tail, but Perry refused to quit. He had himself rowed to another vessel, carried the battle to the enemy, and finally accepted surrender of the entire British squadron. Hatless, begrimed, and bloodied, Perry then sent to General William Henry Harrison the long-awaited message: "We have met the enemy and they are ours."

American naval control of waters in the region soon made Upper Canada untenable to the British. They gave up Detroit, and when they took a defensive stand at the Battle of the Thames (October 5), General Harrison inflicted a defeat that eliminated British power in Upper Canada and released the Northwest from any further threat. In the course of the battle Tecumseh fell, and his dream of Indian unity died with him.

THE WAR IN THE SOUTH   In the Southwest, too, the war flared up in 1813. On August 30 the Creeks attacked Fort Mims, on the Alabama River above Mobile, killing almost half the people in the fort. The news found Andrew Jackson home in bed recovering from a street brawl with

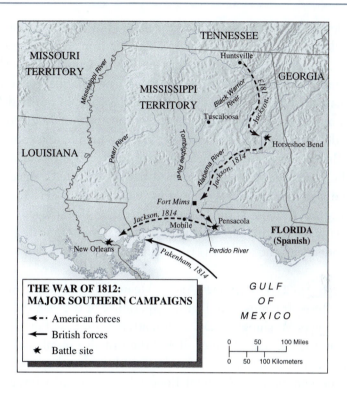

THE WAR OF 1812:
MAJOR SOUTHERN CAMPAIGNS

◄─·· American forces
◄─── British forces
★ Battle site

Thomas Hart Benton, later a senator from Missouri. As major-general of the Tennessee militia, Jackson summoned about 2,000 volunteers and set out on a campaign that utterly crushed the Creek resistance. The decisive battle occurred on March 27, 1814, at the Horseshoe Bend of the Tallapoosa River, in the heart of the upper Creek country. In the Treaty of Fort Jackson, the Creeks ceded two-thirds of their lands to the United States, including part of Georgia and most of Alabama.

Four days after the Battle of Horseshoe Bend, Napoleon's empire collapsed. Now free to deal with America, the British developed a three-fold plan of operations for 1814. They would launch a two-pronged invasion of America via Niagara and Lake Champlain to increase the clamor for peace in the Northeast; extend the naval blockade to New England, subjecting coastal towns to raids; and seize New Orleans to cut the Mississippi River, lifeline of the West.

MACDONOUGH'S VICTORY   The main British effort focused on a massive invasion via Lake Champlain. From the north General George Prevost, governor-general of Canada, advanced with the finest army yet assembled on American soil: fifteen regiments of regulars, plus militia and artillerymen, a total of about 15,000. The front was saved only by Prevost's vacillation and the superb ability of Commodore Thomas Macdonough, commander of the American naval squadron on Lake Champlain. A land assault might have taken Plattsburgh and forced Macdonough out of his protected position nearby, but England's army bogged down while its flotilla engaged Macdonough in a deadly battle.

The British concentrated their superior firepower on Macdonough's ship, the *Saratoga*. With his starboard battery disabled, Macdonough executed a daring maneuver known as "winding ship." He turned the *Saratoga* around while at anchor and brought its undamaged side into action with devastating effect. The *Saratoga* had to be scuttled, but the battle ended with the entire British flotilla either destroyed or captured.

FIGHTING IN THE CHESAPEAKE   Meanwhile, however, American forces suffered the most humiliating experience of the war, the capture and burning of Washington, D.C. With attention focused on the Canadian front, the Chesapeake Bay offered the British a number of inviting targets, including Baltimore, now the fourth-largest city in America. Under the command of General Robert Ross, a British force landed without opposition in 1814 at Benedict, Maryland, and headed for Washington, forty miles away. To defend the capital the Americans had a force of about 7,000, including only a few hundred regulars and 400 sailors. At Bladensburg, Maryland, the American militia melted away in the face of the smaller British force.

The British marched unopposed into Washington, where British officers ate a meal prepared for President and Mrs. Madison, who had joined the other refugees in Virginia. The British then burned the White House, the Capitol, and all other government buildings except the Patent Office. A tornado the next day compounded the damage, but a violent thunderstorm dampened both the fires and the enthusiasm of the British forces, who left to prepare a new assault on Baltimore.

The attack on Baltimore was a different story. With some 13,000 men, chiefly militia, American forces fortified the heights behind the city. About 1,000 men held Fort McHenry, on an island in the harbor. When the British finally came into sight of the city, they halted in the face of American defenses. All through the following night the fleet bombarded Fort McHenry to no avail, and the invaders abandoned the

The British bombardment of Fort McHenry in Baltimore Harbor, September 1814.

attack on the city as too costly a risk. Francis Scott Key, a Washington lawyer, watched the siege from a vessel in the harbor. The sight of the flag still in place at dawn inspired him to draft the verses of "The Star-Spangled Banner." Later revised and set to the tune of an English drinking song, it was immediately popular and eventually became the national anthem.

THE BATTLE OF NEW ORLEANS   The British failure at Baltimore followed by three days their failure on Lake Champlain, and their offensive against New Orleans had yet to run its course. Along the Gulf coast Andrew Jackson had been busy shoring up the defenses of Mobile and New Orleans. Without authorization, he invaded Spanish Florida and took Pensacola to end British intrigues there. Back in Louisiana, he began to erect defenses on the approaches to New Orleans, anticipating a British approach by the interior to pick up Indian support and control the Mississippi. Instead the British fleet, with some 8,000 European veterans under General Sir Edward Pakenham, took up positions on a level plain on the banks of the Mississippi just south of New Orleans.

Pakenham's painfully careful approach—he waited until all his artillery was available—gave Jackson time to build earthworks bolstered by cotton bales for protection. It was an almost invulnerable position, but Pakenham, contemptuous of Jackson's force of frontier militiamen, Creole aristocrats, free blacks, and pirates, rashly ordered his veterans forward in a frontal assault at dawn on January 8, 1815. His redcoats ran into a murderous hail of artillery shells and deadly rifle fire. Before the British withdrew, about 2,000 had been wounded or killed, including Pakenham himself, whose body, pickled in a barrel of rum, was returned to the ship where his wife awaited news of the battle.

The Battle of New Orleans occurred after a peace treaty had already been signed. But this is not to say that it was an anticlimax or that it had no effect on the outcome of the war, for the treaty was yet to be ratified and the British might have exploited the possession of New Orleans had they won it. The battle did assure ratification of the treaty as it stood, and both governments acted quickly.

THE TREATY OF GHENT Peace efforts had begun in 1812 even before hostilities got under way. The British, after all, had repealed their Orders in Council two days before the declaration of war and confidently expected at least an armistice. Secretary of State Monroe, however, told the British that they would have to give up the outrage of impressment as well. Meanwhile Czar Alexander of Russia offered to mediate the dispute, hoping to relieve the pressure on Great Britain, his ally against France. Madison sent Albert Gallatin and James Bayard to

Andrew Jackson's defeat of the British at New Orleans, January 1815.

join John Quincy Adams, American ambassador to Russia, in St. Petersburg. They arrived in 1813, but the czar was at the war front, and they waited impatiently for six months. At that point, the British refused mediation and instead offered to negotiate directly. Madison then appointed Henry Clay and Jonathan Russell to join the other three commissioners in talks that finally got under way in the Flemish city of Ghent in August.

In contrast to the array of talent gathered in the American contingent, the British diplomats were nonentities, really messengers acting for the Foreign Office, which was more concerned with the effort to remake the map of Europe at the Congress of Vienna. The Americans had more leeway to use their own judgment, and sharp disagreements developed that had to be patched up by Albert Gallatin. The sober Adams and the hard-drinking, poker-playing Clay, especially, rubbed each other the wrong way. The American delegates at first were instructed to demand that the British abandon impressment and paper blockades, and to get indemnities for seizures of American ships. The British opened the discussions with demands for territory in New York and Maine, removal of American warships from the Great Lakes, an autonomous Indian buffer state in the Northwest, access to the Mississippi River, and abandonment of American fishing rights off Labrador and Newfoundland. If the British insisted on such a position, the Americans informed them, the negotiations would be at an end.

But the British were stalling, awaiting news of victories to strengthen their hand. The news of American victory on Lake Champlain arrived in October and weakened the British resolve. Their will to fight was further eroded by a continuing power struggle at the Congress of Vienna, by the eagerness of British merchants to renew trade with America, and by the war-weariness of a tax-burdened public. The British finally decided that the game was not worth the cost. One by one demands were dropped on both sides until the envoys agreed to end the war, return the prisoners, restore the previous boundaries, and settle nothing else. The questions of fisheries and disputed boundaries were referred to commissions for future settlement. The Treaty of Ghent was signed on Christmas Eve of 1814.

THE HARTFORD CONVENTION   While the diplomats converged on a peace settlement, an entirely different kind of meeting took place in

Hartford, Connecticut. An ill-fated affair, the Hartford Convention represented the climax of New England's disaffection with "Mr. Madison's war." New England had managed to keep aloof from the war and extract a profit from illegal trading and privateering. New England shippers monopolized the import trade and took advantage of the chance to engage in active trade with the enemy. After the fall of Napoleon, however, the British extended their blockade to New England, occupied Maine, and conducted several raids along the coast. Even Boston seemed threatened. Instead of rallying to the American flag, however, Federalists in the Massachusetts legislature on October 5, 1814, voted for a convention of New England states to plan independent action.

On December 15 the Hartford Convention assembled with delegates chosen by the legislatures of Massachusetts, Rhode Island, and Connecticut, with two delegates from Vermont and one from New Hampshire: twenty-two in all. The convention included an extreme group, Timothy Pickering's "Essex Junto," who were prepared for secession from the Union, but it was controlled by a more moderate group led by Harrison Gray Otis, who wanted only a protest in language reminiscent of Madison's Virginia Resolutions of 1798. As the ultimate remedy for their grievances, they proposed seven constitutional amendments designed to limit Republican influence: abolishing the three-fifths compromise, requiring a two-thirds vote to declare war or admit new states, prohibiting embargoes lasting more than sixty days, excluding the foreign-born from federal offices, limiting the president to one term, and forbidding successive presidents from the same state.

Their call for a later convention in Boston carried the unmistakable threat of secession if the demands were ignored. Yet the threat quickly evaporated. When messengers from Hartford reached Washington, they found the battered capital celebrating the good news from Ghent and New Orleans. The consequence was a fatal blow to the Federalist party, which never recovered from the stigma of disloyalty and narrow provincialism stamped on it by the Hartford Convention.

THE WAR'S AFTERMATH For all the fumbling ineptitude with which the War of 1812 was fought, it generated an intense feeling of patriotism. Despite the standoff with which it ended at Ghent, the American public nourished a sense of victory, courtesy of Andrew Jackson and his men at New Orleans as well as the heroic exploits of American frigates

We Owe Allegiance to No Crown.
The War of 1812 generated a new
feeling of nationalism.

in their duels with British ships. Under Republican leadership, the nation had survived a "Second War of Independence" against the greatest power on earth, and emerged with new symbols of nationhood and a new gallery of heroes. The war also launched the United States toward economic independence, as the interruption of trade encouraged the growth of American manufactures. After forty years of independence, it dawned on the world that the new republic might be here to stay, and that it might be something more than a pawn in European power games.

As if to underline the point, Congress authorized a quick, decisive blow at the pirates of the Barbary Coast. During the War of 1812 they had again set about plundering American ships. On March 3, 1815, little more than two weeks after the Senate ratified the Treaty of Ghent, Congress sent Captain Stephen Decatur with ten vessels to the Mediterranean. He first seized two Algerian ships and then sailed boldly into the harbor of Algiers. On June 30, 1815, the dey of Algiers agreed to cease molesting American ships and to give up all American prisoners. Decatur's show of force induced similar treaties from Tunis and Tripoli. This time there was no tribute; this time, for a change, the Barbary pirates paid indemnities for the damage they had done. This time victory put an end to the piracy and extortion in that quarter, permanently.

One of the strangest results of a strange war and its aftermath was a reversal of roles by the Republicans and Federalists. Out of the wartime experience the Republicans had learned some lessons in nationalism. Certain needs and inadequacies revealed by the war had "Federalized" Madison, or "re-Federalized" this Father of the Constitution. Perhaps, he reasoned, a peacetime army and navy would not be such an unmitigated evil. Madison now preferred to keep something more than a token force. The lack of a national bank had added to the problems of financing the war. Now Madison wanted it back. The rise of new industries during the war led to a clamor for increased tariffs. Madison went along. The problems of overland transportation in the West had revealed the need for internal improvements. Madison agreed, but on that point kept his constitutional scruples. He wanted a constitutional amendment. So while Madison embraced nationalism and broad construction of the Constitution, the Federalists took up the Jeffersonians' position of states' rights and strict construction. It was the first great reversal of roles in constitutional interpretation. It would not be the last.

MAKING CONNECTIONS

- Jefferson's embargo and the War of 1812 encouraged the beginnings of manufacturing in the United States, an important subject in Chapter 12.

- The Federalist party collapsed because of its opposition to the War of 1812. But as the next chapter shows, Republicans did not prosper as much as might have been expected in the absence of political opposition.

- The American success in the War of 1812 (a moral victory at best) led to a tremendous sense of national pride and unity, a spirit analyzed in the next chapter.

FURTHER READING

Marshall Smelser's *The Democratic Republic, 1801–1815* (1968) presents an overview of the Republican administrations. The standard biography of Jefferson is Joseph J. Ellis's *American Sphinx: The Character of Thomas Jefferson* (1997). On the life of Jefferson's friend and successor, see Drew R. McCoy's *The Last of the Fathers: James Madison and the Republican Legacy* (1989). McCoy's *The Elusive Republic* (1982) discusses the political economy of these years in the context of republicanism; Joyce Appleby's *Capitalism and a New Social Order* (1984) minimizes the impact of republican ideology.

Linda K. Kerber's *Federalists in Dissent: Imagery and Ideology in Jeffersonian America* (1970) explores the Federalists while out of power. The concept of judicial review and the courts can be studied in Richard E. Ellis's *The Jeffersonian Crisis* (1971). On John Marshall, see G. Edward White's *The Marshall Court and Cultural Change, 1815–1835* (1991). Milton Lomask's two-volume *Aaron Burr: The Years from Princeton to Vice President, 1756–1805* (1979) and *The Conspiracy and the Years of Exile, 1805–1836* (1982) trace the career of that remarkable American.

For the Louisiana Purchase, consult Alexander De Conde's *This Affair of Louisiana* (1976). For a captivating account of the Lewis and Clark expedition, see Stephen Ambrose's *Undaunted Courage: Meriwether Lewis, Thomas Jefferson and the Opening of the American West* (1996). Bernard W. Sheehan's *Seeds of Extinction* (1973) is more analytical about the Jeffersonians' Indian policy and opening of the West.

Burton Spivak's *Jefferson's English Crisis: Commerce, the Embargo, and the Republican Revolution* (1979) discusses Anglo-American relations during Jefferson's administration; Clifford L. Egan's *Neither Peace nor War* (1983) covers Franco-American relations. An excellent revisionist treatment of the events that brought on war in 1812 is J. C. A. Stagg's *Mr. Madison's War* (1983). The war itself is the focus of Donald R. Hickey's *The War of 1812: A Forgotten Conflict* (1989). See also David Curtis Skaggs and Gerard T. Altoff's *A Signal Victory: The Lake Erie Campaign, 1812–1813* (1997).

10 ᕫ NATIONALISM AND SECTIONALISM

CHAPTER ORGANIZER

This chapter focuses on:

- the elements of the "Era of Good Feelings."

- how economic policies, diplomacy, and judicial decisions reflected the nationalism of these years.

- the various issues that promoted sectionalism.

- the fate of the Republican party after the collapse of the Federalists.

*A*mid the jubilation after the War of 1812 Americans began to transform their young nation. Hundreds of thousands of people began to stream westward at the same time that what had been a largely local economy was being transformed into a national market. The dispersion of plantation slavery and the cotton culture into the Old Southwest—Georgia, Alabama, Mississippi, Louisiana, and Texas—disrupted family ties and transformed social life. In the North and West, meanwhile, a dynamic middle class began to emerge and grow within towns and cities. Such dramatic changes prompted strident political debates over economic policies, transportation improvements, and the extension of slavery into the new territories. In the process the nation began to divide into three powerful regional blocs—North, South, and West—whose shifting coalitions shaped the political landscape until the Civil War.

ECONOMIC NATIONALISM

Immediately after the War of 1812, Americans experienced a new surge of nationalism. An abnormal economic prosperity after the war fed a feeling of well-being and enhanced the prestige of the national government. Jefferson's embargo ironically had given impulse to the factories that he abhorred. The idea spread that the country needed a more balanced economy of farming, commerce, and manufacturing. After a generation of war, shortages of farm products in Europe forced up the prices of American products and stimulated agricultural expansion, indeed, a wild speculation in farmlands. Southern cotton, tobacco, and rice came to account for about two-thirds of American exports. At the same time, the postwar market was flooded with cheap English goods that planters and farmers could buy. The new American manufacturers would seek protection from this competition.

The Union Manufactories of Maryland in Patapsco Falls, Baltimore County, c. 1815. *A textile mill begun during the embargo of 1807; by 1825 the Union Manufactories would employ over 600 people.*

President Madison, in his first annual message to Congress after the war, recommended several steps toward strengthening the government: better fortifications, a permanent army and a strong navy, a new national bank, effective protection of the new infant industries, a system of canals and roads for commercial and military use, and to top it off, a great national university. "The Republicans have out-Federalized Federalism," one New Englander remarked. Congress responded by authorizing a standing army of 10,000 and strengthening the navy as well.

THE BANK OF THE UNITED STATES   The trinity of economic nationalism—proposals for a second national bank, protective tariff, and internal improvements—inspired the greatest controversies. After the national bank expired in 1811, the country had fallen into a financial muddle. State-chartered banks mushroomed with little or no control, and their bank notes (paper money) flooded the channels of commerce with currency of uncertain value. Because hard money had been so short during the war, many state banks had suspended specie (gold or silver) payments in redemption of their notes, thereby depressing their value. The absence of a central bank had been a source of financial embarrassment to the government, which had neither a ready means of floating loans nor a way of transferring funds across the country.

The Second Bank of the United States.

Madison and most younger Republicans salved their constitutional scruples about a national bank with a dash of pragmatism. The issue, Madison said, had been decided "by repeated recognitions . . . of the validity of such an institution in acts of the legislative, executive, and judicial branches of the Government, accompanied by . . . a concurrence of the general will of the nation." In 1816 Congress adopted over the protest of Old Republicans provision for a new Bank of the United States (B.U.S.), which would be located in Philadelphia. Modeled after Hamilton's bank, it differed chiefly in that it was capitalized at $35 million instead of $10 million. Once again the charter ran for twenty years, and the government owned a fifth of the stock and named five of the twenty-five directors, with the Bank serving as the government depository for federal funds. Its bank notes were accepted in payments to the government. In return for its privileges the Bank had to take care of the government's funds without charge, lend the government $5 million on demand, and pay the government a cash bonus of $1.5 million.

The debate on the Bank, then and later, was colorful and bitter, and it helped to set the pattern of regional alignment for most other economic issues. Missouri senator Thomas Hart Benton predicted that the currency-short western towns would be at the mercy of a centralized eastern bank. "They may be devoured by it any moment! They are in the jaws of the monster! A lump of butter in the mouth of a dog! One gulp, one swallow, and all is gone!"

The debate was also noteworthy because of the leading roles played by the great triumvirate of John C. Calhoun of South Carolina, Henry Clay of Kentucky, and Daniel Webster of New Hampshire, later of Massachusetts. Calhoun, still in his youthful phase as a War Hawk nationalist, introduced the measure and pushed it through, justifying its constitutionality by citing the congressional power to regulate the currency, and pointing to the need for a uniform circulating medium. Clay, who had helped to kill Hamilton's bank in 1811, now confessed that he had failed to foresee the evils that resulted, and asserted that circumstances had made the Bank indispensable. Webster, on the other hand, led the opposition of the New England Federalists, who did not want the banking center moved from Boston to Philadelphia. Later, after he moved from New Hampshire to Massachusetts, Webster would return to Congress as the champion of a much stronger national power, while events would carry Calhoun in the other direction.

A PROTECTIVE TARIFF   The shift of capital from commerce to manufactures, begun during the embargo of 1807, had speeded up during the war. Peace in 1815 brought a sudden renewal of cheap British imports and generated pleas for the protection of infant American industries. The self-interest of the manufacturers, who as yet had little political impact, was reinforced by a patriotic desire for economic independence from Britain. New England shippers and southern farmers opposed the movement, but both sections had sizable minorities who believed that the promotion of industry enhanced both sectional and national welfare.

The Tariff of 1816, the first intended more for the protection of industry against foreign competition than for revenue, easily passed in Congress. The South and New England both split their votes, with New England registering a majority of its votes for the tariff and the South registering a majority of its votes against the bill, and the Middle States and Old Northwest cast only five negative votes altogether. Nathaniel Macon of North Carolina opposed the tariff and defended the Old Republican doctrine of strict construction. The power to protect industry, Macon said, like the power to establish a bank, rested on the idea that there were implied powers embedded in the Constitution; Macon worried that such implied powers might one day be used to abolish slavery. The minority of southerners who voted for the tariff, led by Calhoun, had good reason to expect that the South might itself become a manufacturing center. South Carolina was then developing a few textile mills. According to the census of 1810, the southern states had approximately as many manufacturers as New England. Within a few years, however, New England moved ahead of the South, and Calhoun went over to Macon's views against protection. The tariff then became a sectional issue, with manufacturers, wool processors, and food, sugar, and hemp growers favoring higher tariffs, while planters and shipping interests favored lower duties.

INTERNAL IMPROVEMENTS   The third major issue of the time involved internal improvements: the building of roads and the development of water transportation. The war had highlighted the shortcomings of existing facilities. Troop movements through the western wilderness proved very difficult, and settlers found that unless they located near navigable waters, they were cut off from trade and limited to a frontier subsistence.

The federal government had entered the field of internal improvements under Jefferson. He and both of his successors recommended an amendment to give the federal government undisputed power in the field. But lacking that, the constitutional grounds for federal action rested mainly on provision for national defense and expansion of the postal system. In 1803, when Ohio became a state, Congress decreed that 5 percent of the proceeds from land sales in the state would go to building a National Road from the Atlantic coast into Ohio and beyond as the territory developed. In 1806 Jefferson signed a measure for a survey, and construction of the National Road began in 1811.

Originally called the Cumberland Road, it was the first federally financed interstate road network. By 1818 it was open from Cumberland, Maryland, to Wheeling on the Ohio River. Construction stopped temporarily during the business panic of 1819, but by 1838 the road extended all the way to Vandalia, Illinois. By reducing transportation costs and opening up new markets, the National Road and other privately financed turnpikes helped accelerate the commercialization of agriculture.

In 1817 John C. Calhoun put through the House a bill to place in a fund for internal improvements the $1.5 million bonus the Bank of the United States had paid for its charter, as well as all future dividends on the government's bank stock. Opposition centered in New England and the South, which expected to gain least, and support came largely from the West, which badly needed good roads. On his last day in office

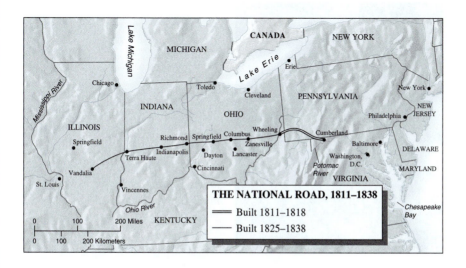

THE NATIONAL ROAD, 1811–1838
— Built 1811–1818
— Built 1825–1838

Madison vetoed the bill. While sympathetic to its purpose, he could not overcome his "insuperable difficulty . . . in reconciling the bill with the Constitution" and suggested instead a constitutional amendment. Internal improvements remained for another hundred years, with few exceptions, the responsibility of states and private enterprise. Then and later Congress supported river and harbor improvements, and scattered post roads, but nothing of a systematic nature. The federal government did not enter the field on a large scale until passage of the Federal Highways Act of 1916.

"Good Feelings"

JAMES MONROE   As Madison approached the end of a turbulent tenure, he, like Jefferson, turned to a fellow Virginian, another secretary of state, as his successor: James Monroe. In the Republican caucus Monroe won the nomination, then overwhelmed his Federalist opponent, Rufus King of New York, 183 to 34 in the electoral college. The "Virginia dynasty" continued. Like three of the four presidents before him, Monroe was a Virginia planter, but with a difference: he came from the small-planter group. At the outbreak of the Revolution he was just beginning college at William and Mary. He joined the army at the age of sixteen, fought with Washington at Trenton, and later studied law with Jefferson.

James Monroe, portrayed as he entered the presidency in 1816.

Monroe never displayed the depth of his Republican predecessors in scholarship or political theory, but what he lacked in intellect he made up in dedication to public service. His soul, Jefferson said, if turned inside out, would be found spotless. Monroe served in the Virginia assembly, as governor of the state, in the Confederation Congress and United States Senate, and as minister to Paris, London, and Madrid. Under Madison, he had been secretary of state, and twice doubled as secretary of war. Tall, rawboned Monroe, with his powdered wig, cocked hat, and knee breeches, was the last of the Revolutionary generation to serve in the White House and the last president to dress in the old style.

Firmly grounded in Republican principles, Monroe failed to keep up with the onrush of the new nationalism. He accepted as accomplished fact the Bank and the protective tariff, but during his tenure there was no further extension of economic nationalism. Indeed, there was a minor setback. He permitted the National (or Cumberland) Road to be carried forward, but in his veto of the Cumberland Road Bill (1822) he denied the authority of Congress to collect tolls to pay for its repair and maintenance. Like Jefferson and Madison, he also urged a constitutional amendment to remove all doubt about federal authority in the field of internal improvements.

Whatever his limitations, Monroe surrounded himself with some of the ablest young Republican leaders. John Quincy Adams became secretary of state. William Crawford of Georgia continued as secretary of the treasury. John C. Calhoun headed the War Department after Henry Clay refused the job in order to stay on as Speaker of the House. The new administration found the country in a state of well-being: America was at peace and the economy was flourishing. Soon after his 1817 inauguration, Monroe embarked on a goodwill tour of New England. In Boston, lately a hotbed of wartime dissent, a Federalist paper commented on the president's visit under the heading "Era of Good Feelings." The label became a popular catchphrase for Monroe's administration, and one that historians seized upon later. Like many a maxim, it conveys just enough truth to be sadly misleading. A resurgence of factionalism and sectionalism erupted just as the postwar prosperity collapsed in the Panic of 1819.

For two years, however, general harmony reigned, and even when the country's troubles returned, little of the blame fell on Monroe. In 1820 he was reelected without opposition. The Federalists were too weak to put up a candidate. Monroe won all the electoral votes except for three abstentions and one vote from New Hampshire for John Quincy Adams. The Republican party was dominant—for the moment. In fact, it was about to follow the Federalists into oblivion. Amid the general political contentment of the era, the first parties were fading away, but rivals for the succession soon commenced the process of forming new parties.

IMPROVING RELATIONS WITH BRITAIN   Adding to the prevailing contentment after the war was a growing rapprochement with the recent enemy. American shippers resumed trade with Britain (and India). The Treaty of Ghent had left unsettled a number of minor disputes, but subsequently two important compacts—the Rush-Bagot Agreement of 1817 and the Convention of 1818—removed several potential causes of irritation. In the first, effected by an exchange of notes between Acting Secretary of State Richard Rush and British minister Charles Bagot, the threat of naval competition on the Great Lakes vanished with an arrangement to limit forces there to several revenue cutters. Although the exchange made no reference to the land boundary between the countries, its spirit gave rise to the tradition of an unfortified border, the longest in the world.

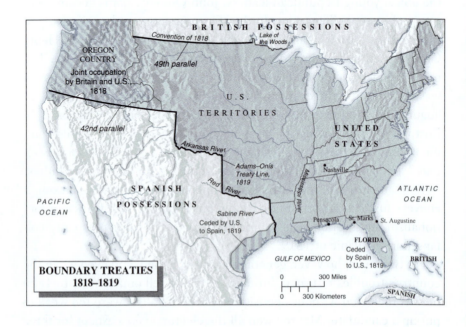

The Convention of 1818 covered three major points. The northern limit of the Louisiana Purchase was settled by extending the national boundary along the 49th parallel west from Lake of the Woods to the crest of the Rocky Mountains. West of that point the Oregon Country would be open to joint occupation by the British and Americans, but the boundary remained unsettled. The right of Americans to fish off Newfoundland and Labrador, granted in 1783, was acknowledged once again.

The chief remaining problem was Britain's exclusion of American ships from the West Indies in order to reserve that lucrative trade for British ships. The Commercial Convention of 1815 did not apply there, and after the War of 1812 the British had once again closed the door. This remained a chronic irritant, and the United States retaliated with several measures. Under a Navigation Act of 1817, importation of West Indian produce was restricted to American vessels or vessels belonging to West Indian merchants. In 1818 American ports were closed to all British vessels arriving from a colony that was legally closed to vessels of the United States. In 1820 Monroe approved an act of Congress that specified total non-intercourse—with British vessels, with all British colonies in the Americas, and even in goods taken to England and reexported. The rapprochement with Britain therefore fell short of perfection.

EXTENSION OF BOUNDARIES   The year 1819 was one of the more fateful years in American history. Controversial efforts to expand American territory, a sharp financial panic, a tense debate over the extension of slavery, and several landmark Supreme Court cases combined to bring an unsettling end to the "Era of Good Feelings." The new nationalism reached a climax with the acquisition of Florida and the extension of the southwestern boundary to the Pacific, but nationalism quickly began to run afoul of domestic crosscurrents that would set up an ever-widening swirl in the next decades.

In the calculations of global power, it was perhaps long since reckoned that Florida would someday pass to the United States. Spanish sovereignty was more a technicality than an actuality, and extended little beyond St. Augustine on the east coast and Pensacola and St. Marks on the Gulf. The province had been a thorn in the side of the United States during the recent war as a center of British intrigue, a haven for

Portrait of an escaped slave who lived with the Seminoles in Florida.

Creek refugees, who were beginning to take the name Seminole ("runaway" or "separatist"), and a harbor for runaway slaves and criminals. Florida also stood athwart the outlets of several important rivers flowing to the Gulf.

Spain, once dominant in the Americas, was now a declining power suffering from both internal and colonial revolt, unable to enforce its obligations under the Pinckney Treaty of 1795 to pacify the frontiers. In 1816 American forces clashed with a group of escaped slaves who had taken over a British fort on the Appalachicola River. Seminoles were soon fighting white settlers in the area, and in 1817 Americans burned a Seminole border settlement, killed five of its inhabitants, and dispersed the rest across the border into Florida.

At this point Secretary of War Calhoun authorized a campaign against the Seminoles, and he summoned General Andrew Jackson from Nashville to take command. Jackson's orders allowed him to pursue the offenders into Spanish territory, but not to attack any Spanish post. A frustrated Jackson pledged to President Monroe that if the United States wanted Florida, he could wind up the whole controversy in sixty days. All he needed was private, unofficial word, which might be sent through Tennessee representative John Rhea. Soon afterward Jackson indeed got a letter from Rhea, and claimed that it transmitted cryptically the required authority, although Monroe always denied any such intention. The truth about the Rhea letter, which Jackson destroyed (at Monroe's request, he said), remains a mystery.

In any case, when it came to Spaniards or Indians, few white Tennesseans—and certainly not Andrew Jackson—were likely to bother

Andrew Jackson, victor at the Battle of New Orleans, Indian fighter, and future president.

with technicalities. Jackson pushed eastward through Florida, reinforced by Tennessee volunteers and a party of friendly Creeks, taking a Spanish post and skirmishing with the Seminoles, destroying their settlements. Jackson hanged two of their leaders without any semblance of a trial. Having mopped up the region from the Appalachicola to the Suwannee, he then turned west and seized Pensacola and returned home to Nashville. The whole episode had taken about four months; the Florida panhandle was in American hands by 1818.

The news of Jackson's exploits aroused anger in Madrid and concern in Washington. Spain demanded the return of its territory, reparations, and the punishment of Jackson, but Spain's impotence was plain for all to see. Monroe's cabinet was at first prepared to disavow Jackson's action, especially his direct attack on Spanish posts. Calhoun, as secretary of war, was inclined, at least officially, to discipline Jackson for disregard of orders—a stand that caused bad blood between the two men later—but privately confessed a certain pleasure at the outcome. In any case a man as popular as Jackson was almost invulnerable. And he had one important friend, Secretary of State John Quincy Adams, who realized that Jackson had strengthened his hand in negotiations already under way with the Spanish minister. American forces withdrew from Florida, but negotiations resumed with the knowledge that the United States could take Florida at any time.

With the fate of Florida a foregone conclusion, Adams now turned his eye on a larger purpose, a definition of the western boundary of the

Louisiana Purchase and—his boldest stroke—extension of a boundary to the Pacific coast. In lengthy negotiations, Adams gradually gave ground on claims to Texas, but stuck to his demand for a transcontinental line. Agreement finally came early in 1819. Spain ceded all of Florida in return for American assumption of private American claims against Spain up to $5 million. The western boundary of the Louisiana Purchase would run along the Sabine River and then in stair-step fashion up to the Red River, along the Red, and up to the Arkansas River. From the source of the Arkansas it would go north to the 42nd parallel and thence west to the Pacific coast. A dispute over land claims held up ratification for another two years, but those claims were revoked and final ratifications were exchanged in 1821. Florida became a territory, and its first governor was briefly Andrew Jackson. In 1845 Florida achieved statehood.

CRISES AND COMPROMISES

THE PANIC OF 1819   Adams's Transcontinental Treaty was a triumph of foreign policy and the climactic event of the postwar nationalism. Even before it was signed in 1819, however, two thunderclaps signaled the end of the brief "Era of Good Feelings" and gave warning of stormy weather ahead: the financial Panic of 1819 and the controversy over statehood for Missouri. The occasion for the panic was the sudden collapse of cotton prices in the English market. At one point in 1818 cotton had soared to 32½¢ a pound. The pressure of high prices forced British textile mills to turn away from American sources to cheaper East Indian cotton, and by 1819 cotton averaged only 14.3¢ per pound at New Orleans. The price collapse set off a decline in the demand for other American goods and suddenly revealed the fragility of the prosperity that had begun after the War of 1812.

Since 1815 a speculative bubble had grown, with expectations that expansion would go on forever. But American industry struggled to find markets for its goods. Even the Tariff of 1816 had not been enough to eliminate British competition. What was more, businessmen, farmers, and land jobbers had inflated the bubble with a volatile expansion of credit. The sources of this credit were both government and banks. Under the Land Act of 1800 the government extended four years' credit to those who bought western lands. After 1804 one could buy as little as 160 acres at a minimum price of $1.64 per acre (although in auctions the best lands went for more). In many cases speculators took up large tracts, paying only one-fourth down, and then sold them to settlers with the understanding that the settlers would pay the remaining installments. With the collapse of prices, and then of land values, both speculators and settlers found themselves caught short.

The reckless practices of state banks compounded the inflation of credit. To enlarge their loans they issued bank notes far beyond their means of redemption, and at first were under little pressure to promise redemption in specie. Even the Second Bank of the United States, which was supposed to introduce some order to the financial arena, was at first caught up in the mania. Its first president yielded to the contagion of get-rich-quick fever that was sweeping the country. The proliferation of branches, combined with little supervision from Philadelphia, carried the Bank into the same reckless extension of loans that state banks had pursued. In 1819, just as alert businessmen began to take alarm, a case of extensive fraud and embezzlement in the Baltimore branch came to light. The disclosure prompted the appointment of Langdon Cheves, former congressman from South Carolina, as the Bank's president and the establishment of a sounder policy.

Cheves reduced salaries and other costs, postponed dividends, restrained the extension of credit, and presented for redemption the state bank notes that came in, thereby forcing the state-chartered banks to keep specie reserves. Cheves rescued the Bank from near-ruin, but only by putting heavy pressure on state banks. State banks in turn put pressure on their debtors, who found it harder to renew old loans or get new ones. In 1823, his job completed, Cheves relinquished his position to Nicholas Biddle of Philadelphia. The Cheves policies were the result rather than the cause of the Panic, but they pinched debtors, who found it all the more difficult to meet their obligations. Hard times lasted about three years, and the Bank took much of the blame in the popular mind. The Panic passed, but resentment of the Bank lingered. It never fully regained the confidence of the South and the West.

THE MISSOURI COMPROMISE   Just as the Panic spread over the country, another cloud appeared on the horizon, the onset of a sectional controversy over slavery. By 1819 the country had an equal number of slave and free states, eleven of each. The line between them was defined by the southern and western boundaries of Pennsylvania and the Ohio River. Although slavery still lingered in some places north of the line, it was on the way to extinction there. Beyond the Mississippi, however, no move had been made to extend the dividing line across the Louisiana Purchase territory, where slavery had existed from the days when France and Spain had colonized the area. At the time the Missouri Territory embraced all of the Louisiana Purchase except the state of Louisiana (1812) and the Arkansas Territory (1819). In the westward rush of population, the old French town of St. Louis became the funnel through which settlers pushed on beyond the Mississippi. These were largely settlers from the South who brought their slaves with them.

In 1819 the House of Representatives was asked to approve legislation enabling Missouri to draft a state constitution, its population having passed the minimum of 60,000. At that point Representative James Tallmadge, Jr., a New York congressman, introduced a resolution prohibiting the further introduction of slaves into Missouri, which already had some 10,000 slaves, and providing freedom at age twenty-five for those born after the territory's admission as a state. After brief but fiery exchanges, the House passed the amendment on an almost strictly sectional vote. The Senate rejected it by a similar tally, but with several northerners joining in the opposition. With population at the time growing faster in the North, a balance between the two sections could be held only in the Senate. In the House, slave states had 81 votes while free states had 105; a balance was unlikely ever again to be restored in the House.

Maine's application for statehood made it easier to arrive at an agreement. Since colonial times Maine had been the northern province of Massachusetts. The Senate linked its request for separate statehood with Missouri's and voted to admit Maine as a free state and Missouri as a slave state, thus maintaining the balance between free and slave states in the Senate. An Illinois senator further extended the compromise by an amendment to exclude slavery from the rest of the Louisiana Purchase north of 36°30′N, Missouri's southern border. Slavery thus would continue in the Arkansas Territory and in the state of Missouri, and be excluded from the remainder of the area. But that was country that Zebulon Pike's reports had persuaded the public was the Great American Desert, unlikely ever to be settled. For this reason the arrange-

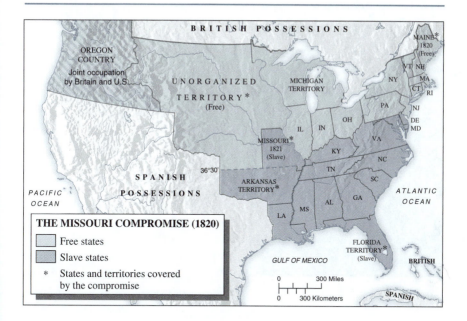

THE MISSOURI COMPROMISE (1820)

□ Free states
■ Slave states
* States and territories covered by the compromise

ment seemed to be a victory for the slave states. By a very close vote it passed the House on March 2, 1820.

Then another problem arose. The proslavery elements that dominated Missouri's constitutional convention inserted in the proposed new state constitution a proviso excluding free blacks and mulattoes from the state. This clearly violated the requirement of Article IV, Section 2, of the Constitution: "The Citizens of each State shall be entitled to all Privileges and Immunities of Citizens in the Several States." Free blacks were citizens of many states, including the slave states of North Carolina and Tennessee where, until the mid-1830s, they also voted.

The renewed controversy threatened final approval of Missouri's admission until Henry Clay formulated a "Second Missouri Compromise." Admission of Missouri as a state depended on assurance from the Missouri legislature that it would never construe the offending clause in such a way as to sanction denial of privileges that citizens held under the Constitution. It was one of the more artless dodges in American history, for it required the legislature to affirm that the state constitution did not mean what it clearly said, but the compromise worked. The Missouri legislature duly adopted the pledge, while denying that the legislature had any power to bind the people of the state. On August

Henry Clay.

10, 1821, President Monroe proclaimed the admission of Missouri as the twenty-fourth state. For the moment, the controversy subsided. "But this momentous question," the aging Thomas Jefferson wrote to a friend after the first compromise, "like a firebell in the night awakened and filled me with terror. I considered it at once as the knell of the Union."

JUDICIAL NATIONALISM

JOHN MARSHALL, CHIEF JUSTICE Meanwhile nationalism still flourished in the Supreme Court, where Chief Justice John Marshall preserved Hamiltonian Federalism for yet another generation. Marshall, a survivor of the Revolution and a distant cousin of Thomas Jefferson, was among those who had been forever nationalized by the experience. In later years he said: "I was confirmed in the habit of considering America as my country and Congress as my government." The habit persisted through a successful legal career punctuated by service in Virginia's legislature and ratifying convention, as part of the "XYZ" mission to France, and as a member of Congress. Never a judge before he became chief justice in 1801, he established the power of the Supreme Court by his force of mind and crystalline logic.

Chief Justice John Marshall, pillar of judicial nationalism.

During Marshall's early years on the Court (altogether he served thirty-four years), he affirmed the principle of judicial review. In *Marbury* v. *Madison* (1803) and *Fletcher* v. *Peck* (1810), the Court first struck down a federal law and then a state law as unconstitutional. In the cases of *Martin* v. *Hunter's Lessee* (1816) and *Cohens* v. *Virginia* (1821), the Court assumed the right to take appeals from state courts on the grounds that the Constitution, laws, and treaties of the United States could be kept uniformly the supreme law of the land only if the Court could review decisions of state courts. In the first case, the Court overruled Virginia's confiscation of Loyalist property, because this violated treaties with Great Britain; in the second, it upheld Virginia's right to forbid the sale of lottery tickets.

PROTECTING CONTRACT RIGHTS   In the fateful year 1819, Marshall and the Court made two more decisions of major importance in checking the states and building the power of the central government: *Dartmouth College* v. *Woodward* and *McCulloch* v. *Maryland*. The Dartmouth College case involved an attempt by the New Hampshire legislature to alter a provision in Dartmouth's charter, under which the college's trustees became a self-perpetuating board. In 1816 the state's Republican legislature, offended by this relic of monarchy and even more by the Federalist majority on the board, placed Dartmouth under a new board named by the governor. The original trustees sued, lost in the state courts, but with Daniel Webster as counsel won on appeal to the Supreme Court. The charter, Marshall said for the Court, was a valid contract that the legislature had impaired, an act forbidden by the Constitution. This implied a new and enlarged definition of *contract* that seemed to put private corporations beyond the reach of the states that chartered them. But thereafter states commonly wrote into charters and general laws of incorporation provisions making them subject to modification. Such provisions were then part of the "contract."

STRENGTHENING THE FEDERAL GOVERNMENT   Marshall's single most important interpretation of the constitutional system appeared in the case of *McCulloch v. Maryland*. McCulloch, a clerk in the Baltimore branch of the Bank of the United States, failed to affix state revenue stamps to bank notes as required by a Maryland law taxing the notes. Indicted by the state, McCulloch, acting for the Bank, appealed to the Supreme Court, which handed down a unanimous judgment upholding the power of Congress to charter the Bank and denying any right of the state to tax the Bank. In a lengthy opinion Marshall rejected Maryland's argument that the federal government was the creature of sovereign states. Instead, he argued, it arose directly from the people acting through the conventions that ratified the Constitution. While sovereignty was divided between the states and the national government, the latter, "though limited in its powers, is supreme within its sphere of action."

Marshall then went on to endorse the doctrine of broad construction and implied powers set forth by Hamilton in his bank message of 1791. The "necessary and proper" clause, he argued, did not mean "absolutely indispensable." The test of constitutionality he summed up in almost the same words as Hamilton: "Let the end be legitimate, let it be within the scope of the Constitution, and all means which are appropriate, which are plainly adapted to that end, which are not prohibited, but consistent with the letter and spirit of the Constitution, are constitutional."

Maryland's effort to tax the national bank conflicted with the supreme law of the land. One great principle that "entirely pervades the Constitution," Marshall wrote, was "that the Constitution and the laws made in pursuance thereof are supreme: that they control the Constitution and laws of the respective states, and cannot be controlled by them." The tax therefore was unconstitutional, for the "power to tax involves the power to destroy"—which was precisely what the legislatures of Maryland and several other states had in mind with respect to the Bank.

REGULATING INTERSTATE COMMERCE   Marshall's last great decision, *Gibbons* v. *Ogden* (1824), established national supremacy in regulating interstate commerce. In 1808 Robert Fulton and Robert Livingston, who pioneered commercial use of the steamboat, won from the New York legislature the exclusive right to operate steamboats on the state's waters. From them in turn Aaron Ogden received exclusive right

Deck Life on the *Paragon,* 1811–1812. *The* Paragon, *"a whole floating town," was the third steamboat operated on the Hudson by Robert Fulton and Robert R. Livingston. Fulton said the* Paragon *"beats everything on the globe, for made as you and I are we cannot tell what is in the moon."*

to navigation across the Hudson between New York and New Jersey. Thomas Gibbons, however, operated a coastal trade under a federal license and came into competition with Ogden. On behalf of a unanimous Court, Marshall ruled that the monopoly granted by the state conflicted with the federal Coasting Act under which Gibbons operated. Congressional power to regulate commerce, the Court said, "like all others vested in Congress, is complete in itself, may be exercised to its utmost extent, and acknowledges no limitations other than are prescribed in the Constitution."

The opinion stopped just short of stating an exclusive federal power over commerce, and later cases would clarify the point that states had a concurrent jurisdiction so long as it did not come into conflict with federal action. For many years there was in fact little federal regulation of commerce, so that in striking down the monopoly created by the state Marshall had opened the way to extensive development of steamboat navigation and, soon afterward, steam railroads. Economic expansion was often consonant with judicial nationalism.

NATIONALIST DIPLOMACY

THE NORTHWEST   In foreign affairs, too, nationalism continued to be an effective force. Within two years after final approval of John Quincy Adams's Transcontinental Treaty, the secretary of state was able to draw another important transcontinental line. In 1819 Spain had abandoned its claim to the Oregon Country above the 42nd parallel. Russia, however, had claims along the Pacific coast as well. In 1741 Vitus Bering, in the employ of Russia, had explored the strait that now bears his name, and in 1799 the Russian-American Company had been formed to exploit the resources of Alaska. In 1821 the Russian czar claimed the Pacific coast as far south as 51°, which in the American view lay within the Oregon Country.

In 1823 Secretary of State Adams contested "the right of Russia to any territorial establishment on this continent." The American government, he informed the Russian minister, assumed the principle "that the American continents are no longer subjects for any new European colonial establishments." His protest resulted in a treaty signed in 1824 whereby Russia, which had more pressing concerns in Europe, accepted the line of 54°40′ as the southern boundary of its claim. In 1825 a similar agreement between Russia and Britain gave the Oregon Country clearly defined boundaries, although it was still subject to joint occupation by the United States and Great Britain under their agreement of 1818. In 1827 both countries agreed to extend indefinitely the provision for joint occupation, subject to termination by either power.

LATIN AMERICA   Adams's disapproval of further colonization also had clear implications for Latin America. One consequence of the Napoleonic Wars and French occupation of Spain and Portugal had been a series of wars of liberation in Latin America. Within little more than a decade after the flag of rebellion was first raised in 1811, Spain had lost almost its entire empire in the Americas. All that was left were the islands of Cuba, Puerto Rico, and Santo Domingo. The only other European possessions in the Americas, 330 years after Columbus, were Russian Alaska, British Canada, British Honduras, and Dutch, French, and British Guiana.

That Spain could not regain her empire seems clear enough in retrospect. The British navy would not permit it, because Britain's trade with the area was too important. For a time, however, European victors over Napoleon sought to restore "legitimacy" everywhere. The great European peace conference, the Congress of Vienna (1814–1815), returned that continent, as nearly as possible, to its status before the French Revolution and set out to make the world safe for monarchy. To that end the major powers (Great Britain, Prussia, Russia, and Austria) set up the Quadruple Alliance (it became the Quintuple Alliance after France entered in 1818) to police the European continent. In 1821 the Alliance, with Britain dissenting, authorized Austria to put down liberal movements in Italy. The British government was no champion of liberal revolution, but neither did it feel impelled to police the entire continent. In 1822, when the allies met in the Congress of Verona, they authorized France to suppress the constitutionalist movement in Spain and to restore the monarchy.

THE MONROE DOCTRINE   In 1823 French troops crossed the Spanish border, put down the rebels, and restored the king to absolute authority. Rumors began to circulate that France would also try to restore the Spanish king's power over Spain's American empire. Monroe and

Secretary of War Calhoun were alarmed at the possibility, although John Quincy Adams took the more realistic view that such action was unlikely. After breaking with the Quintuple Alliance, British foreign minister George Canning sought to reach an understanding with the American minister to London that the two countries would jointly undertake to forestall action by the Quadruple Alliance against Latin America.

Monroe at first agreed, with the support of his sage advisers Jefferson and Madison. Adams, however, urged upon Monroe and the cabinet the independent course of proclaiming a unilateral policy against the restoration of Spain's colonies. "It would be more candid," Adams said, "as well as more dignified, to avow our principles explicitly to Russia and France, than to come in as a cockboat in the wake of the British man-of-war." Adams knew that the British navy would stop any action by the Quadruple Alliance in Latin America, and he suspected that the Alliance had no real intention to intervene anyway. The British, moreover, wanted the United States to agree not to acquire any more Spanish territory, including Cuba, Texas, or California, but Adams preferred to avoid such a commitment.

Monroe incorporated the substance of Adams's views in his annual message to Congress in 1823. The Monroe Doctrine, as it was later called, comprised four major points: (1) that "the American continents . . . are henceforth not to be considered as subjects for future colonization by any European powers"; (2) the political system of European powers was different from that of the United States, which would "consider any attempt on their part to extend their system to any portion of this hemisphere as dangerous to our peace and safety"; (3) the United States would not interfere with existing European colonies; and (4) the United States would keep out of the internal affairs of European nations and their wars.

At the time the statement drew little attention either in the United States or abroad. The Monroe Doctrine, not even so called until 1852, became one of the cherished principles of American foreign policy, but for the time being it slipped into obscurity for want of any occasion to invoke it. In spite of Adams's affirmation, the United States came in as a cockboat in the wake of the British man-of-war after all, for the effectiveness of the doctrine depended on British naval supremacy. The doctrine had no standing in international law. It was merely a statement of intent by an American president to the Congress, and did not even draw enough interest at the time for European powers to renounce it.

ONE-PARTY POLITICS

Almost from the start of Monroe's second term the jockeying for the presidential succession had begun. Three members of Monroe's cabinet were active candidates: Secretary of War John Calhoun, Secretary of the Treasury William Crawford, and Secretary of State John Quincy Adams. Henry Clay, longtime Speaker of the House, also hungered after the office. And on the fringes of the Washington scene a new force appeared in the person of Andrew Jackson, the scourge of the British, Spaniards, Creeks, and Seminoles, the epitome of what every frontiersman admired, who was elected a senator from Tennessee in 1823. All were Republicans, for again no Federalist stood a chance, but they were competing in a new political world, complicated by the crosscurrents of nationalism and sectionalism. With only one party there was in effect no party, for there existed no generally accepted method for choosing a "regular" candidate.

PRESIDENTIAL NOMINATIONS   Selection by congressional caucus, already under attack in 1816, had disappeared in the wave of unanimity that reelected Monroe in 1820 without the formality of a nomination. The friends of Crawford sought in vain to breathe life back into "King Caucus," but only a minority of congressmen appeared in answer to the call. They duly named Crawford for president, but the endorsement was so weak as to be more a handicap than an advantage. Crawford was in fact the logical successor to the Virginia dynasty, a native of the state though a resident of Georgia. He had flirted with nationalism, but swung back to states' rights and strict construction, and assumed leadership of a faction, called the Radicals, that included Old Republicans and those who distrusted the nationalism of Adams and Calhoun. Crawford's candidacy floundered from the beginning, for the candidate had been stricken in 1823 by some unknown disease that left him half-paralyzed and half-blind. His friends protested that he would soon be well, but he never did fully recover.

The presidential "race" of 1824, with Clay and Jackson in the foreground, Adams at far right.

Long before the rump caucus met in early 1824, indeed for two years before, the country had broken out in a rash of presidential endorsements by legislatures and public meetings. In 1822 the Tennessee legislature named Andrew Jackson. In 1824 a mass meeting of Pennsylvanians added their endorsement. Jackson, who had previously kept silent, responded that while the presidency should not be sought, it could not with propriety be declined. The same meeting named Calhoun for vice-president, and Calhoun accepted. The youngest of the candidates, he was content to take second place and bide his time. Meanwhile, the Kentucky legislature had named its favorite son, Henry Clay, in 1822. The Massachusetts legislature named Adams in 1824.

Of the four candidates, only two had clearly defined programs, and the outcome was an early lesson in the danger of being committed on the issues too soon. Crawford's friends emphasized his devotion to the "principles of 1798," states' rights and strict construction. Clay, on the contrary, took his stand for the "American System": he favored the national bank, the protective tariff, and a national program of internal improvements to bind the country together and build its economy. Adams was close to Clay, openly dedicated to internal improvements but less strongly committed to the tariff. Jackson, where issues were concerned, carefully avoided commitment. His managers hoped that, by being all things to all men, Jackson could capitalize on his popularity as the hero of the Battle of New Orleans.

THE "CORRUPT BARGAIN" The outcome turned on personalities and sectional allegiance more than on issues. Adams, the only northern candidate, carried New England, the former bastion of Federalism, and most of New York's electoral votes. Clay took Kentucky, Ohio, and Missouri. Crawford carried Virginia, Georgia, and Delaware. Jackson swept the Southeast, plus Illinois and Indiana, and, with Calhoun's support, the Carolinas, Pennsylvania, Maryland, and New Jersey. All candidates got scattered votes elsewhere. In New York, where Clay was strong, his supporters were outmaneuvered by the Adams forces in the legislature, which still chose the presidential electors.

The result was inconclusive in both the electoral vote and the popular vote, wherever the state legislature permitted the choice of electors by the people. In the electoral college Jackson had 99 votes, Adams 84, Crawford 41, Clay 37. In the popular vote the trend ran about the same: Jackson 154,000, Adams 109,000, Crawford 47,000, and Clay 47,000. Whatever might have been said about the outcome, one thing seemed apparent. It was a defeat for Clay's American System: New England and New York opposed him on internal improvements, the South and Southwest on the protective tariff. Sectionalism had defeated the national program.

Yet the advocate of the American System now assumed the role of president-maker, as the election was thrown into the House of Representatives, where Speaker Clay's influence was decisive. Clay had little trouble in choosing, since he regarded Jackson as unfit for the office. "I cannot believe," he muttered, "that killing 2,500 Englishmen at New Orleans qualifies for the various, difficult and complicated duties of the Chief Magistracy." He eventually threw his support to Adams. The final vote in the House, which was by state, carried Adams to victory with thirteen votes to Jackson's seven and Crawford's four.

It was a costly victory, for the result united Adams's foes and crippled his administration before it got under way. There is no evidence that Adams entered into any bargain with Clay to win his support. Still the charge was made and widely believed after Adams made Clay his secretary of state, and thus put him in the office from which three successive presidents had risen. Adams's Puritan conscience could never quite overcome a sense of guilt at the maneuverings that were necessary to gain his election, but a "corrupt bargain" was too much out of character for credence. Yet credence it had with a large number of people, and on that cry a campaign to elect Jackson next time was launched almost immediately after the 1824 decision. The Crawford people, including Martin Van Buren, the "Little Magician" of New York politics, soon moved into the Jackson camp. So too did the new vice-president, John Calhoun of South Carolina, who ran on both the Adams and the Jackson tickets but favored the general from Tennessee.

JOHN QUINCY ADAMS'S PRESIDENCY   John Quincy Adams was one of the ablest men, hardest workers, and finest intellects ever to enter the White House. Yet he lacked the common touch and the politician's gift for maneuver. A stubborn man who saw two brothers and two sons die from alcoholism, he suffered from chronic bouts of depression that provoked in him a grim self-righteousness and self-pity, self-doubts, and self-loathing, qualities that did not endear him to fellow politicians. He once confessed that others perceived him as "obstinate and dogmatical, and *pedantic.*" His idealism also irritated the party faithful. He refused to play the game of patronage, arguing that it would be dishonorable to dismiss "able and faithful political opponents to provide for my own partisans." In four years he removed only twelve officeholders. His first annual message to Congress included a grandiose blueprint for national development, set forth in such a blunt way that it became a disaster of political ineptitude.

In the boldness and magnitude of its conception, the Adams plan outdid those of both Hamilton and Clay. The central government, the

John Quincy Adams, a president of great intellect but without the common touch.

president proposed, should promote internal improvements, set up a national university, finance scientific explorations, build astronomical observatories, and create a new Department of the Interior. To refrain from using broad federal powers, Adams insisted, "would be treachery to the most sacred of trusts." Officers of the government, he said, should not "fold up our arms and proclaim to the world that we are palsied by the will of our constituents."

Whatever grandeur of conception the message to Congress had, it was obscured by an unhappy choice of language. For a minority president to demean the sovereignty of the voter was tactless enough. For the son of John Adams to cite the example "of the nations of Europe and of their rulers" was downright suicidal. At one fell swoop he had revived all the Republican suspicions of the Adamses and served to define a new party system. The minority who cast their lot with Adams and Clay were turning into National-Republicans; the opposition, the growing party of Jacksonians, were the Democratic-Republicans, who would eventually drop the name Republican and become Democrats.

Adams's headstrong plunge into nationalism and his refusal to play the game of politics condemned his administration to utter frustration. Congress ignored his domestic proposals, and in foreign affairs the triumphs that he had scored as secretary of state had no sequels. The climactic effort to discredit Adams came on the tariff issue. The Panic of 1819 had provoked calls for a higher tariff in 1820, but the effort failed by one vote in the Senate. In 1824 the advocates of protection renewed the effort, with greater success. The Tariff of 1824 favored the Middle Atlantic and New England manufacturers with higher duties on woolens, cotton, iron, and other finished goods. Clay's Kentucky won a tariff on hemp, and a tariff on raw wool brought the wool-growing interests to the support of the measure. Additional revenues were provided by duties on sugar, molasses, coffee, and salt. The tariff on raw wool was in obvious conflict with that on manufactured woolens, but the two groups got together and reached an agreement.

At this point Jackson's supporters saw a chance to advance their candidate through an awkward scheme hatched by John Calhoun. The plan was to present a bill with such outrageously high tariffs on raw materials that the manufacturers of the East would join the commercial interests there, and, with the votes of the agricultural South and Southwest, defeat the measure. In the process Jackson men in the Northeast could take credit for supporting the tariff, and Jackson men, wherever it fitted their interests, could take credit for opposing it—while Jackson himself remained in the background. Virginia's John Randolph saw through the ruse. The bill, he asserted, "referred to manufactures of no sort or kind, but the manufacture of a President of the United States."

The complicated scheme helped elect Jackson, but in the process Calhoun became a victim of his own scheming. The high tariffs ended up becoming law. Calhoun calculated neither upon the defection of Van Buren, who supported a crucial amendment to satisfy the woolens manufacturers, nor upon the growing strength of manufacturing interests in New England. Daniel Webster, now a senator from Massachusetts, explained that he was ready to deny all he had said against the tariff because New England had built up her manufactures on the understanding that the protective tariff was a settled policy.

When the bill passed on May 11, 1828, it was Calhoun's turn to explain his newfound opposition to the gospel of protection, and nothing so well illustrates the flexibility of constitutional principles as the switch in positions by Webster and Calhoun. Back in South Carolina, Calhoun prepared the *South Carolina Exposition and Protest* (1828), which was issued anonymously along with a series of resolutions by the South Carolina legislature. In that document Calhoun declared that a state could nullify an act of Congress that it found unconstitutional.

JACKSON SWEEPS IN   Thus far the stage was set for the election of 1828, which might more truly be called a revolution than that of 1800. But if the issues of the day had anything to do with the election, they were hardly visible in the campaign, in which politicians on both sides reached depths of scurrilousness that had not been plumbed since 1800. Jackson was denounced as a hot-tempered and ignorant barbarian, co-conspirator with Aaron Burr, a participant in repeated duels and frontier brawls, a man whose fame rested on his reputation as a killer. In addition, his enemies dredged up the old story that Jackson had lived in adultery with his wife Rachel before they had been legally married; in fact they had lived together for two years in the mistaken belief that her divorce from a former husband was final. As soon as the official divorce had come through, Jackson and Rachel had been remarried. But such distinctions escaped his opponents. One anti-Jackson newspaper asked, "Ought a convicted adulteress and her paramour husband to be placed in the highest offices of this free and Christian land?" Rachel's worry

Jackson is to be President, and you will be HANGED. *This anti-Jackson cartoon, published during the 1828 campaign, shows him as a frontier ruffian.*

over this humiliation and her probable reception in Washington may have contributed to an illness from which she died before her husband took office, and it was one thing for which Jackson could never forgive his enemies. "May God Almighty forgive her murderers," he pleaded at her funeral, "as I know she forgave them. I never can." Jackson blamed Clay and Adams for not restraining their supporters from having made such scurrilous charges against his family.

The Jacksonians, however, got in their licks against Adams, condemning him as a man who had lived his adult life on the public treasury, who had been corrupted by foreigners in the courts of Europe, and who had allegedly delivered up an American girl to serve the lust of Czar Alexander I while serving as minister to Russia. They called him a gambler and a spendthrift for having bought a billiard table and a chess set for the White House, and a puritanical hypocrite for despising the common people and warning Congress to ignore the will of its constituents. He had finally reached the presidency, the Jacksonians claimed, by a corrupt bargain with Henry Clay.

In the campaign of 1828 Jackson held most of the advantages. As a military hero he had some claim on patriotism. As a son of the West he was almost unbeatable there. As a planter and slaveholder he had the trust of southern planters. Debtors and local bankers who hated the national bank turned to Jackson. In addition, his vagueness on the issues protected him from attack by various interest groups. Not least of all, Jackson benefited from a spirit of democracy in which the common folk were no longer satisfied to look to their betters for leadership, as they had done in the lost world of Thomas Jefferson. It had become politically fatal to be labeled an aristocrat. Jackson's coalition now included even a seasoning of young Federalists eager to shed the stigma of aristocracy and get on in the world.

Since the Revolution and especially since 1800, white male suffrage had been gaining ground. The traditional story has been that a surge of Jacksonian Democracy came out of the West like a great wave, supported mainly by small farmers, leading the way for the East. But there were other forces working in the older states toward a wider franchise: the Revolutionary doctrine of equality, and the feeling on the parts of the workers, artisans, and small merchants of the towns, as well as small farmers and landed gentry, that a democratic ballot provided a means to combat the rising commercial and manufacturing interests. From the beginning Pennsylvania had opened the ballot box to all adult males who paid taxes; by 1790 Georgia and New Hampshire had similar arrangements. Vermont, in 1791, became the first state with universal manhood suffrage, having first adopted it in 1777. Kentucky, admitted in 1792, became the second. Tennessee (1796) had only a light taxpaying qualification. New Jersey in 1807, and Maryland and South Carolina in 1810, abolished property and taxpaying requirements, and the new states of the West after 1815 came in with either white manhood suffrage or a low taxpaying requirement. Connecticut (1818),

Jackson Forever!

The Hero of Two Wars and of Orleans!

The Man of the People!

HE WHO COULD NOT BARTER NOR BARGAIN FOR THE

PRESIDENCY!

Who, although *"A Military Chieftain,"* valued the purity of Elections and of the Electors, MORE than the Office of PRESIDENT itself! Although the greatest in the gift of his countrymen, and the highest in point of dignity of any in the world,

BECAUSE

It should be derived from the

PEOPLE!

No Gag Laws! No Black Cockades! No Reign of Terror! No Standing Army or Navy Officers, when under the pay of Government, to browbeat, or

KNOCK DOWN

Old Revolutionary Characters, or our Representatives while in the discharge of their duty. To the Polls then, and vote for those who will support

OLD HICKORY

AND THE ELECTORAL LAW.

This 1828 handbill identifies Jackson, "The Man of the People," with the democratic impulse of the time.

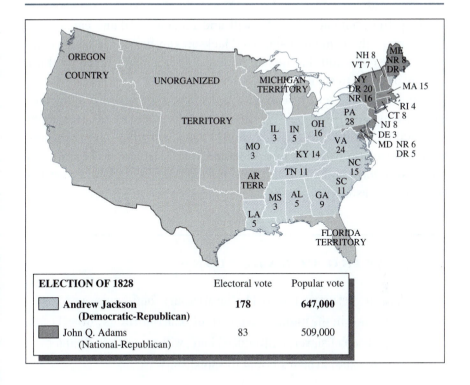

ELECTION OF 1828	Electoral vote	Popular vote
Andrew Jackson (Democratic-Republican)	**178**	**647,000**
John Q. Adams (National-Republican)	83	509,000

Massachusetts (1821), and New York (1821) all abolished their property requirements.

Along with the broadening of the suffrage went a liberalization of other features of government. Representation was reapportioned more nearly in line with population. An increasing number of officials, even judges, were named by popular vote. Final disestablishment of the Congregational church in New England came in Vermont (1807), New Hampshire (1817), Connecticut (1818), Maine (1820), and Massachusetts (1834). In 1824 six state legislatures still chose the presidential electors. By 1828 the popular vote prevailed in all but South Carolina and Delaware, and by 1832 in all but South Carolina.

The spread of the suffrage brought a new type of politician to the fore: the man who had special appeal to the masses or knew how to organize the people for political purposes, and who became a vocal advocate of the people's right to rule. Jackson fitted the ideal of this new political world, a leader sprung from the people rather than an aristocratic leader of the people, a frontiersman of humble origin who had scrambled up the political ladder by will and tenacity. "Adams can write," went one of the campaign slogans, "Jackson can fight." He could write too, but he once said that he had no respect for a man who could think of only one way to spell a word.

When the 1828 returns came in, Jackson won by a comfortable margin. The electoral vote was 178 to 83, and the popular vote was about 647,000 to 509,000 (the figures vary). Adams won all of New England, except for one of Maine's nine electoral votes, sixteen of the thirty-six from New York, and six of the eleven from Maryland. All the rest belonged to Jackson.

MAKING CONNECTIONS

- Thomas Jefferson referred to the Missouri Compromise as "a firebell in the night." He was right. The controversy over the expansion of slavery, introduced here, will reappear in Chapter 14's discussion of Texas and the Mexican War.

- John Quincy Adams's National-Republicans, who could trace some of their ideology back to the Federalists, will be at the core of the Whig coalition that opposes Jackson in Chapter 11.

- Several of the issues on which the nation united during the "Era of Good Feelings"—the Bank and the protective tariff, for example—will become much more divisive, as discussed in the next chapter.

FURTHER READING

The standard overview of the Era of Good Feelings remains George Dangerfield's *The Awakening of American Nationalism, 1815–1828* (1965). The gathering sense of a national spirit, hindered by an equally growing sectionalism, can be traced in Daniel J. Boorstin's *The Americans: The Nationalist Experience* (1965).

For discussions of the American System, see Bray Hammond's *Banks and Politics in America from the Revolution to the Civil War* (1957) and George R. Taylor's *The Transportation Revolution, 1815–1860* (1951). A classic overview of the economic trends of the period is Douglas C. North's *The Economic Growth of the United States, 1790–1860* (1961).

The political temper of the times is treated in biographical studies of principal figures: Irving Bartlett's *Daniel Webster* (1981) and *John C. Calhoun: A Biography* (1993), Noble Cunningham's *The Presidency of James Monroe* (1996), Clement Eaton's *Henry Clay and the Art of American Politics* (1957), Paul C. Nagel's *John Quincy Adams: A Public Life, A Private Life* (1997), and Jean Edward Smith's *John Marshall: Definer of a Nation* (1997).

A stimulating synthesis of economic, social, and political developments is Sean Wilentz's *Chants Democratic: New York City and the Rise of the American Working Class, 1788–1850* (1983). The emergence of slavery as the most divisive sectional issue is treated in Donald L. Robinson's *Slavery in the Structure of American Politics, 1765–1820* (1971).

On diplomatic relations during James Monroe's presidency, see Williams Earl Weeks's *John Quincy Adams and American Global Empire* (1992). For relations after 1812, see Ernest R. May's *The Making of the Monroe Doctrine* (1975) and Dexter Perkin's *A History of the Monroe Doctrine* (1955).

Background on Andrew Jackson can be obtained from works cited in Chapter 11. The campaign that brought Jackson to the White House is analyzed in Robert V. Remini's *The Election of Andrew Jackson* (1963).

PART THREE

AN EXPANSIVE NATION

The election of Andrew Jackson signaled a new era in American history. By 1828 the United States was no longer an infant nation hugging the Atlantic coast. The maturing republic now included twenty-four states and almost 13 million people. Many Americans were on the move during the early nineteenth century. They formed a relentless migratory stream that spilled over the Appalachian Mountains, spanned the Mississippi River, and in the 1840s, reached the Pacific Ocean. Wagons, canals, flatboats, steamboats, and eventually railroads helped expedite the westward migration.

The feverish expansion of the United States into new western territories brought Americans into conflict with Native Americans, Mexicans, and the British. Only a few people, however, expressed moral reservations about displacing others. Most Americans believed it was the "manifest destiny" of the United States to spread across the entire continent—at whatever cost and at whomever's expense. Americans generally believed that they enjoyed the blessing of Providence in their efforts to consolidate the entire continent under their control.

While most Americans during the Jacksonian era continued to earn their living from the soil, textile mills and manufacturing plants began to dot the landscape and transform the nature of work and the pace of life. By mid-century the United States was emerging as one of the world's major industrial powers. In addition, the lure of cheap land and plentiful jobs, as well as the promise of political equality and religious freedom, attracted hundreds of thousands of immigrants from Europe. These newcomers, mostly from Germany and Ireland, faced ethnic prejudices, religious persecution, and language barriers that made assimilation into American culture all the more difficult.

All these developments gave to American life in the second quarter of the nineteenth century its dynamic and fluid quality. The United States, said the philosopher-poet Ralph Waldo Emerson, was "a country of beginnings, of projects, of designs, of expectations." A restless optimism characterized the period. People of lowly social status who heretofore had accepted their lot in life now strove to climb the social ladder and enter the political arena. The patrician democracy espoused by Jefferson and Madison gave way to the frontier democracy promoted by the Jacksonians. Americans were no longer content to be governed by a small, benevolent aristocracy of talent and wealth. They began to demand—and obtain—government of, by, and for the people.

The fertile economic environment during the antebellum era helped foster the egalitarian idea that individuals (except African Americans, Native Americans, and women) should have an equal opportunity to better themselves and should be granted political rights and privileges. In America, observed a journalist in 1844, "One has as good a chance as another according to his talents, prudence, and personal exertions."

The exuberant individualism embodied in such mythic expressions of economic equality and political democracy also spilled over into the cultural arena during the Jacksonian era. The so-called romantic movement applied democratic ideals to philosophy, religion, literature, and the fine arts. In New England, Ralph Waldo Emerson and Henry David Thoreau joined other transcendentalists in espousing a radical individualism. Other reformers were motivated more by a sense of spiritual mission than democratic individualism. In striving to enhance personal morality and the general welfare, mostly middle-class reformers sought to introduce public-supported schools, abolish slavery, promote temperance, and improve the lot of the disabled, insane, and imprisoned. Their efforts helped ameliorate some of the problems created by the frenetic pace of economic growth and territorial expansion. But the reformers made little headway against slavery. It would take a brutal civil war to dislodge America's "peculiar institution."

11 ∽ THE JACKSONIAN
IMPULSE

CHAPTER ORGANIZER

This chapter focuses on:

- the social and political context of the Jackson/Van Buren administrations.

- Andrew Jackson's attitudes and actions concerning the tariff (and nullification), Indian policy, and the Bank of the United States.

- the rise of a new party system (Democrats and Whigs).

*T*he election of Andrew Jackson initiated a new era in American politics and social development. He was the first president not to come from a prominent colonial family. As a self-made soldier-politician-land speculator from the backcountry, he symbolized a sea change in the social temper. The nation he prepared to govern was vastly different from that led by Washington and Jefferson. In 1828 the United States boasted twenty-four states and nearly 13 million people, many of them recent arrivals from Germany and Ireland. An incredible surge in foreign demand for cotton and other goods, along with British investment in American enterprises, helped fuel a revolution in transportation and an economic boom. Textile factories sprouted like mushrooms across the New England countryside, their ravenous spinning looms fed by cotton grown in the newly cultivated lands of Alabama and Mississippi. This fluid new economic environment fostered a mad scramble for material gain and political advantage. People of all ranks and backgrounds engaged in a frenzied effort to acquire wealth and thereby gain social status and prestige.

The Jacksonians sought to democratize economic opportunity and political participation. Yet to call the Jacksonian era the "age of the common man," as many historians have done, is misleading. While political participation increased during the Jacksonian era, most of the common folk remained *common* folk. The period never produced true economic and social equality. Power and privilege, for the most part, remained in the hands of an "uncommon" elite. Jacksonians in power proved to be as opportunistic and manipulative as the patricians they displaced. And they never embraced the principle of material equality. "Distinctions in society will always exist under every just government," Andrew Jackson observed. "Equality of talents, or education, or of wealth cannot be produced by human institutions." He and other Jacksonians wanted every American to have an equal chance to compete in the economic marketplace and political arena, but they never sanctioned equality of results. "True republicanism," one commentator declared, "requires that every man shall have an equal chance—that every man shall be free to become as unequal as he can." But in the afterglow of Jackson's election victory, few observers troubled with such distinctions. It was time to celebrate the commoner's ascension to the presidency.

SETTING THE STAGE

INAUGURATION Inauguration day, March 4, 1829, was balmy after a bitterly cold winter. When Jackson, a sixty-one-year-old widower, emerged from his lodgings, dressed in black out of respect to his late wife Rachel, who had died in December, a great crowd filled both the east and west slopes of Capitol Hill. After Chief Justice Marshall administered the oath, the new president, plagued by a persistent cough and severe headaches, delivered his inaugural address in a voice so low that few in the crowd of 15,000 spectators could hear it. It mattered little, for Jackson's advisers had eliminated anything that might give of-

All Creation Going to the White House. *The scene following Jackson's inauguration as president, according to satirist Robert Cruikshank.*

fense. On the major issues of the tariff, internal improvements, and the Bank of the United States, Jackson remained vague. Only a few points foreshadowed policies that he would pursue: he favored retirement of the national debt, a proper regard for states' rights, a "just" policy toward Indians, and rotation in federal offices, which he pronounced "a leading principle in the republican creed"—a principle his enemies would dub the "spoils system."

After his speech Jackson mounted his horse and rode to the White House, where a reception was scheduled for all who chose to come. The boisterous party that followed evoked the climate of turmoil that seemed always to surround Jackson. The revelers pushed into the White House, surged through the rooms, jostled the waiters, broke dishes, leaped onto the furniture—all in an effort to shake the president's hand or at least get a glimpse of him. To one observer, "the reign of 'King Mob' seemed triumphant."

As a fighter, horse trader, land speculator, and frontier lawyer, Andrew Jackson symbolized the rugged new western temperament. A fellow law student described him as a "most roaring, rollicking, game-cocking, horse-racing, card-playing, mischievous fellow." His father had died before he was born, and his mother scratched out a meager living as a housekeeper. Jackson grew to be proud, gritty, short-tempered, and a good hater. During the Revolution, when he was a young boy, his mother died, two of his brothers were killed by redcoats, and the young Jackson suffered a scar from a British officer's saber that he carried with him for life. He also carried with him the conviction that it was not enough for a man to be right; he had to be tough as well, a quality that inspired his soldiers to nickname him "Old Hickory." During a duel with a man reputed to be the best shot in Tennessee, Jackson nevertheless let his opponent fire first. For his gallantry Jackson received a bullet wedged next to his heart. But he straightened himself, patiently took aim, and killed his aghast foe. "I should have hit him," Jackson claimed, "if he had shot me through the brain."

APPOINTMENTS AND POLITICAL RIVALRIES   To the office seekers who made up much of the restless crowd at the inaugural, Jackson held out high expectations that he planned to "turn the rascals out" and let the people rule. So it seemed when he set forth a reasoned defense of rotation in office. The duties of government were simple, he said. Democratic principles supported the idea that a man should serve a term in government, then return to the status of private citizen, for office-holders who stayed too long grew corrupt. And democracy, he argued, "is promoted by party appointments by newly elected officials."

Jackson hardly foresaw how these principles would work out in practice, and it would be misleading to link him too closely with the "spoils system," which took its name from an 1832 partisan assertion by Democratic senator William L. Marcy of New York: "To the victor belong the spoils." Jackson in fact behaved with great moderation compared to the politicians of New York and Pennsylvania, where the spoils of office nourished extensive political machines. And a number of his successors made many more partisan appointments. During his first year in office Jackson replaced only about 9 percent of the appointed officials in the federal government, and during his entire term fewer than 20 percent.

Jackson's administration was from the outset a house divided between the partisans of Secretary of State Martin Van Buren of New York and those of Vice-President John C. Calhoun of South Carolina. Much of the political history of the next few years would turn upon the rivalry of the two, as each man jockeyed for position as Jackson's successor. It soon became clear that Van Buren held most of the advantages, fore-

Cartoon depicting Jackson as a demon dangling political plums before office seekers.

most among them his skill at timing and tactics. Jackson, new to political administration, leaned heavily on him for advice and for help in soothing the ruffled feathers of rejected office seekers. Van Buren had perhaps more skill at maneuvering than Calhoun, and certainly more freedom to maneuver, because his home base of New York was more secure politically than Calhoun's base in South Carolina.

But Calhoun, a man of towering intellect, humorless outlook, and apostolic zeal, could not be taken lightly. A visitor remarked after a three-hour discussion with the bushy-browed Calhoun, "I hate a man who makes me think so much . . . and I hate a man who makes me feel my own inferiority." Perhaps Henry Clay described Calhoun best: "tall, careworn, with furrowed brow, haggard and intensely gazing, looking as if he were dissecting the last abstraction which sprung from a metaphysician's brain." Since returning from Washington to his South Carolina plantation in 1825, Calhoun had nurtured his crops and his ardent love for his native region. Now as vice-president he was determined to defend southern interests against the worrisome advance of northern industrialism and abolitionism.

John C. Calhoun.

THE EATON AFFAIR   In his battle with Calhoun over political power, Van Buren had luck on his side. Fate handed him a trump card: the succulent scandal of the Peggy Eaton affair. The daughter of an Irish tavern owner, Peggy Eaton was a vivacious widow whose husband had supposedly committed suicide upon learning of her affair with Tennessee senator John Eaton. Her marriage to Eaton, three months before he became Jackson's secretary of war, had scarcely made a virtuous woman of her in the eye of the proper ladies of Washington. Floride Calhoun, the vice-president's wife, especially objected to Peggy Eaton's lowly origins and unsavory past. She pointedly snubbed her, and other cabinet wives followed suit.

Peggy's plight reminded Jackson of the gossip that had pursued his own Rachel, and he pronounced Peggy "chaste as a virgin." To a friend he wrote: "I did not come here to make a Cabinet for the Ladies of this place, but for the Nation." His cabinet members, however, were unable to cure their wives of what Van Buren dubbed "the Eaton Malaria." Van Buren, though, was a widower, and therefore free to lavish on poor Peggy all the attention that Jackson thought was her due. The amused John Quincy Adams looked on from afar and noted in his diary that Van Buren had become the leader of the party of the frail sisterhood. Mrs. Eaton herself finally wilted under the chill and withdrew from society. The outraged Jackson came to link Calhoun with what he called a conspiracy against her and drew even closer to Van Buren.

INTERNAL IMPROVEMENTS   While capital society weathered the chilly winter of 1829–1830, Van Buren delivered some additional blows

King Andrew the First. *Opponents considered Jackson's Maysville veto an abuse of power. This cartoon shows King Andrew Jackson trampling on the Constitution, internal improvements, and the Bank of the United States.*

to Calhoun. It was easy to bring Jackson into opposition to internal improvements and thus to federal programs with which Calhoun had long been identified. Jackson did not oppose road building per se, but he had the same constitutional scruples as Madison and Monroe about federal aid to local projects. In 1830 the Maysville Road Bill, passed by Congress, offered Jackson a happy chance for a dual thrust at both Calhoun and Clay. The bill authorized the government to buy stock in a road from Maysville to Clay's hometown of Lexington. The road lay entirely within the state of Kentucky, and though part of a larger scheme to link up with the National Road via Cincinnati, it could be viewed as a purely local undertaking. On that ground Jackson vetoed the bill as unconstitutional, to widespread popular acclaim.

Yet while Jackson continued to oppose federal aid to local projects, he supported interstate projects such as the National Road, as well as road building in the territories, and river and harbor bills, the "pork barrels" from which every congressman tried to pluck a morsel for his district. Even so, Jackson's attitude toward the Maysville Road set an important precedent, on the eve of the railroad age, for limiting federal initiative in internal improvements. Railroads would be built altogether by state and private capital at least until 1850.

NULLIFICATION

CALHOUN'S THEORY There is a fine irony to Calhoun's plight in the Jackson administration, for Calhoun was now in midpassage from his early phase as a War Hawk nationalist to his later phase as a states'-rights sectionalist—and open to thrusts on both flanks. Conditions in his home state had brought on this change. Suffering from agricultural depression, South Carolina lost almost 70,000 people to emigration during the 1820s and was fated to lose nearly twice that number in the 1830s. Most South Carolinians blamed the protective tariff, a series of taxes placed on imports, which tended to raise the price of manufactured goods. Insofar as tariffs discouraged the sale of foreign goods in the United States, they reduced the ability of British and French traders to acquire the American money and bills of exchange with which to buy American cotton. This worsened already existing problems of low cotton prices and exhausted lands. Compounding the South Carolinians' malaise was a growing reaction against the North's criticism of slavery. Hardly had the country emerged from the Missouri controversy when Charleston was thrown into panic by the Denmark Vesey slave insurrection of 1822, though the Vesey plot was put down before it got very far.

The unexpected passage of the Tariff of 1828 (called the "Tariff of Abominations" by its critics) left Calhoun no choice but to join those in opposition or give up his home base. Calhoun's *South Carolina Exposition and Protest* (1828), written in opposition to that tariff, actually had been an effort to check the most extreme states'-rights advocates with a fine-spun theory in which nullification stopped short of secession from the Union. The unsigned statement accompanied resolutions of the South Carolina legislature protesting the tariff and urging its repeal. Calhoun, it was clear, had not entirely abandoned his earlier nationalism. He wanted to preserve the Union by protecting the minority rights that the agricultural and slaveholding South claimed. The fine balance he struck between states' rights and central authority was actually not as far removed from Jackson's own philosophy as it might seem, but growing tension between the two men would complicate the issue. The flinty Jackson, in addition, was determined to draw the line at any defiance of federal law.

Nor would Calhoun's theory permit any state to take up such defiance lightly. The procedure of nullification or interposition, whereby a state could interpose state authority and in effect repeal a federal law, would follow that by which the original thirteen states had ratified the Constitution. A special state convention, like the ratifying conventions embodying the sovereign power of the people, could declare a federal law null and void within the state's borders because it violated the Constitution, the original compact among the states. One of two outcomes would then be possible. Either the federal government would have to abandon the law, or it would have to get a constitutional amendment removing all doubt as to its validity. The immediate issue was the constitutionality of a tariff designed mainly to protect American industries against foreign competition. The South Carolinians argued that the Constitution authorized tariffs for revenue only.

THE WEBSTER-HAYNE DEBATE   South Carolina leaders had proclaimed their dislike for the tariff, but they had postponed any action against its enforcement, awaiting with hope the election of 1828 in which antitariff Calhoun was the Jacksonian candidate for vice-president. There the issue stood until 1830, when the great Webster-Hayne debate sharpened the lines between states' rights and the Union.

The immediate occasion for the debate, however, was the question of public lands. The federal government still owned immense tracts of unsettled land, and the issue of their fate elbowed its way onto center stage of sectional debate. Late in 1829 Senator Samuel A. Foot of Connecticut, an otherwise obscure figure, proposed that the federal government restrict land sales in the West. When the Foot Resolution came before the Senate in 1830, Thomas Hart Benton of Missouri denounced it as a sectional attack designed to hamstring the settlement of the West so that the East might maintain its supply of cheap factory labor. Robert Y. Hayne of South Carolina took Benton's side. Hayne saw in the issue a chance to strengthen the alliance of South and West reflected in the vote for Jackson. Perhaps by supporting a policy of cheap lands in the West, the southerners could gain western support for lower tariffs. The government, said Hayne, endangered the Union by imposing any policy that would cause a hardship on one section to the benefit of another. The use of public lands as a source of revenue to the central government would create "a fund for corruption—fatal to the sovereignty and independence of the states."

Daniel Webster of Massachusetts rose to defend the East. Possessed of a thunderous voice and a theatrical flair, Webster was widely recog-

The eloquent Massachusetts senator Daniel Webster stands to rebut the argument for nullification in the Webster-Hayne debate.

nized as the nation's foremost orator and lawyer. Legend had it that he could out-argue the devil, and his striking physical presence enhanced his rhetorical skills. Webster had the torso of a bull, and his huge head, with its craggy brows overhanging dark eyes, commanded attention. With the gallery hushed, Webster denied that the East had ever shown a restrictive policy toward the West. He then rebuked those southerners who, he said, "habitually speak of the Union in terms of indifference, or even of disparagement." Hayne had raised the false specter of "Consolidation!—That perpetual cry, both of terror and delusion—consolidation!" Webster had adroitly lured Hayne into defending states' rights and upholding the doctrine of nullification instead of pursuing a coalition with the West.

Hayne took the bait. Himself an accomplished speaker, he launched into a defense of the *South Carolina Exposition,* appealed to the example of the Virginia and Kentucky Resolutions of 1798, and called attention to the Hartford Convention, in which New Englanders had taken much the same position against majority measures as South Carolina did. The Union constituted a compact of the states, he argued, and the federal government, which was their "agent," could not be the judge of its own powers, else its powers would be unlimited. Rather, the states remained free to judge when their agent had overstepped the bounds of its constitutional authority. The right of state interposition was "as full and complete as it was before the Constitution was formed."

In rebuttal to the state-compact theory, Webster defined a nationalistic view of the Constitution. From the beginning, he asserted, the American Revolution had been a crusade of the united colonies rather than of each separately. True sovereignty resided in the people as a whole, for whom both federal and state governments acted as agents in their respective spheres. If a single state could nullify a law of the general government, then the Union would be a "rope of sand," a practical absurdity. Instead the Constitution had created a Supreme Court with the final jurisdiction on all questions of constitutionality. A state could neither nullify a federal law nor secede from the Union. The practical outcome of nullification would be a confrontation leading to civil war.

Hayne may have had the better of the argument historically in advancing the state-compact theory, but the Senate galleries and much of the country at large thrilled to the eloquence of "the God-like Daniel." Webster's closing statement became an American classic, reprinted in school texts and committed to memory by schoolchild orators: "When my eyes shall be turned to behold, for the last time, the sun in heaven, may I not see him shining on the broken and dishonored fragments of a once glorious Union. . . . Let their last feeble and lingering glance, rather, behold the gorgeous ensign of the republic . . . blazing on all its ample folds, as they float over the sea and over the land . . . Liberty and Union, now and forever, one and inseparable." In the practical world of coalition politics Webster had the better of the argument, for the Union and majority rule meant more to westerners, including Jackson, than the abstractions of state sovereignty and nullification. As for the public lands, the Foot Resolution was soon defeated anyway. And whatever one might argue about the origins of the Union, its evolution would more and more validate Webster's position.

THE RIFT WITH CALHOUN   As yet, however, the enigmatic Jackson had not spoken out on the issue. Jackson, like Calhoun, was a slave-holder, albeit a westerner, and might be expected to sympathize with South Carolina, his native state. Soon all doubt was removed, at least on the point of nullification. On April 13, 1830, the Jefferson Day Dinner was held in Washington to honor the birthday of the former president. It was a party affair, but the Calhounites controlled the arrangements with an eye to advancing their own doctrine. Jackson and Van Buren were invited as a matter of course, and the two agreed that Jackson should present a toast proclaiming his opposition to nullification. When his turn came, after twenty-four toasts, many of them extolling states' rights, Jackson raised his glass, pointedly stared at Calhoun, and announced: "Our Union—It must be preserved!" Calhoun, who followed, trembled so that he spilled some of the amber fluid from his glass (according to Van Buren), but tried quickly to retrieve the situation with a toast to "The Union, next to our liberty most dear! May we all remember that it can only be preserved by respecting the rights of the States and distributing equally the benefit and the burden of the Union!" But Jackson had set off a bombshell that exploded the plans of the states'-righters.

Nearly a month afterward a final nail was driven into the coffin of Calhoun's presidential ambitions. On May 12, 1830, Jackson first saw a letter containing final confirmation of reports that had been reaching him of Calhoun's stand in 1818, when as secretary of war he had proposed to discipline Jackson for his Florida invasion. A tense correspondence between Jackson and Calhoun followed, and ended with a curt note from Jackson cutting it off. "Understanding you now," Jackson

The Rats Leaving a Falling House. *During his first term Jackson was beset by dissension within his administration. Here "public confidence in the stability and harmony of this administration" is toppling.*

wrote two weeks later, "no further communication with you on this subject is necessary."

As a result of the growing rift between the two proud men, Jackson resolved to remove all Calhoun partisans from the cabinet. Before the end of the summer of 1831 the president had a new cabinet entirely loyal to him. He then named Van Buren, who had resigned from the cabinet, minister to Great Britain, and Van Buren departed for London. The friends of Van Buren now urged Jackson to repudiate his previous intention of serving only one term. It might be hard, they felt, to get the nomination in 1832 for the New Yorker, who had been charged with intrigues against Calhoun, and the still-popular Carolinian might yet carry off the prize.

Jackson relented and in the fall of 1831 announced his readiness for one more term, with the idea of returning Van Buren from London in time to win the presidency in 1836. But in 1832, when the Senate reconvened, Van Buren's enemies opposed his appointment as minister, and gave Calhoun, as vice-president, a chance to reject the nomination by a tie-breaking vote. "It will kill him, sir, kill him dead," Calhoun told Senator Thomas Hart Benton. Benton disagreed: "You have broken a minister, and elected a Vice-President." So, it turned out, he had. Calhoun's vote against Van Buren provoked popular sympathy for the New Yorker, who returned from London and would soon be nominated to succeed Calhoun.

Now that his presidential hopes were blasted, Calhoun came forth as the public leader of the nullificationists. These South Carolinians thought that, despite Jackson's gestures, tariff rates remained too high. Jackson accepted the principle of using tariffs to protect new American industries from foreign competition. Nevertheless, he had called upon Congress in 1829 to modify duties by reducing tariffs on goods "which cannot come in competition with our own products." Late in the spring of 1830 Congress lowered duties on consumer products such as tea, coffee, salt, and molasses. That and the Maysville veto, coming at about the same time, mollified a few South Carolinians, but nullifiers regarded the two actions as "nothing but sugar plums to pacify children." By the end of 1831 Jackson was calling for further reductions to take the wind out of the nullificationists' sails, and the Tariff of 1832, pushed through by John Quincy Adams (back in Washington as a congressman), cut rates again. But tariffs on cottons, woolens, and iron remained high.

THE SOUTH CAROLINA ORDINANCE   In the South Carolina state elections of 1832, attention centered on the nullification issue. The nullificationists took the initiative in organization and agitation, and the Unionist party was left with a distinguished leadership but only small support, drawn chiefly from the merchants of Charleston and the small farmers of the upcountry. A special session of the legislature called for the election of a state convention, which overwhelmingly adopted an ordinance of nullification that repudiated the tariff acts of 1828 and 1832 as unconstitutional and forbade collection of the duties in the state after February 1, 1833. The reassembled legislature then provided that any citizen whose property was seized by federal authorities for failure to pay the duty could get a state court order to recover twice its value. The legislature also chose Hayne as governor and elected Calhoun to succeed him as senator. Calhoun promptly resigned as vice-president in order to defend nullification on the Senate floor.

JACKSON'S FIRM RESPONSE   In the crisis South Carolina found itself standing alone, despite the sympathy expressed elsewhere. Jackson's response was measured and firm, but not rash—at least not in public. In private he threatened to hang Calhoun and all other traitors—and later expressed regret that he had failed to hang at least Calhoun. In his annual message on December 4, 1832, Jackson announced his firm intention to enforce the tariff, but once again urged Congress to lower the rates.

On December 10 Jackson followed up with his Nullification Proclamation, which characterized the doctrine of nullification as an "impractical absurdity." He said in part: "I consider, then, the power to annul a law in the United States, assumed by one state, incompatible with the existence of the Union, contradicted expressly by the letter of the Constitution, unauthorized by its spirit, inconsistent with every principle on which it was founded, and destructive of the great object for which it was formed." He appealed to the people of his native state not to follow false leaders: "The laws of the United States must be executed. . . . Those who told you that you might peaceably prevent their execution, deceived you; they could not have been deceived themselves. . . . Their object is disunion. But be not deceived by names. Disunion by armed force is treason."

CLAY'S COMPROMISE Jackson sent General Winfield Scott to Charleston Harbor with reinforcements of federal soldiers. A ship of war and seven revenue cutters appeared in the harbor, ready to enforce the tariff before ships had a chance to land their cargoes. The nullifiers mobilized the state militia while unionists in the state organized a volunteer force. In 1833 the president requested from Congress a "Force Bill" specifically authorizing him to use the army to compel compliance with federal law in South Carolina. Under existing legislation he already had such authority, but this affirmation would strengthen his hand. At the same time he supported a bill in Congress that would have lowered tariff duties substantially within two years.

The nullifiers postponed enforcement of their ordinances in anticipation of a compromise. Passage of the bill depended on the support of Henry Clay, who finally yielded to those urging him to save the day. On February 12, 1833, he brought forth a plan to reduce the tariff gradually until 1842, by which time the rate on cotton would be cut in half. It was less than South Carolina would have preferred, but it got the nullifiers out of the corner into which they had painted themselves.

On March 1, 1833, the compromise tariff and the Force Bill were passed by Congress, and the next day Jackson signed both. The South Carolina convention then met and rescinded its nullification of the tariff acts. In a face-saving gesture, it then nullified the Force Bill, for which Jackson no longer had any need. Both sides were able to claim victory. Jackson had upheld the supremacy of the Union, and South Carolina had secured a reduction of the tariff. Calhoun, worn out by the controversy, returned to his plantation. "The struggle, so far from being over," he ominously wrote, "is not more than fairly commenced."

JACKSON'S INDIAN POLICY

During the 1820s and 1830s the United States was fast becoming a multicultural nation of peoples from many different countries. As economic growth reinforced the institution of slavery and accelerated westward expansion, policy makers struggled to preserve white racial homogeneity and hegemony. "Next to the case of the black race within our bosom," declared former president James Madison, "that of the red

[race] on our borders is the problem most baffling to the policy of our country."

Andrew Jackson, however, saw nothing baffling about Indian policy. His attitude toward Indians was the typically western one, that they were barbarians and better off out of the way. Jackson had already done his part in the Creek and Seminole Wars to chastise Indians and separate them from their lands. By the time of his election in 1828 he was fully in accord with the view that a "just, humane, liberal policy toward Indians" dictated moving them onto the plains west of the Mississippi River. The policy was by no means new or original with Jackson; the idea had emerged gradually after the Louisiana Purchase in 1803. It had been formally set forth in 1823 by Calhoun, as secretary of war. By now it was generally accepted that a permanent solution to the Indian "problem" would involve their removal and resettlement in the "Great American Desert," which white settlers would never covet, since it was thought fit mainly for horned toads and rattlesnakes.

INDIAN REMOVAL   In response to a request by Jackson, Congress in 1830 approved the Indian Removal Act. Jackson's presidency saw some ninety-four removal treaties negotiated. By 1835 he was able to announce that the policy had been carried out or was in process of completion for all but a handful of Indians. The policy was effected with remarkable speed, but even that was too slow for state authorities in the South and Southwest. Unlike the Ohio Valley–Great Lakes region, where the flow of white settlement had constantly pushed the Indians westward before it, in the Old Southwest settlement moved across Kentucky and Tennessee and down the Mississippi, surrounding the Creeks, Choctaws, Chickasaws, Seminoles, and Cherokees. These tribes had over the years taken on many of the features of white society. The Cherokees even had such products of "white civilization" as a constitution, a written language, and black slaves.

Most of the northern tribes were too weak to resist the offers of Indian commissioners who, if necessary, used bribery and alcohol to woo the chiefs, and there was, on the whole, remarkably little resistance. In Illinois and Wisconsin Territory an armed clash sprang up in 1832, which came to be known as the Black Hawk War, when the Sauk and Fox under Chief Black Hawk sought to reoccupy some lands they had abandoned in the previous year. Facing famine and hostile Sioux west of the Mississippi, they were simply seeking a place to raise a corn crop. The Illinois militia mobilized to expel them, chased them into Wisconsin Territory, and massacred women and children as they tried to escape across the Mississippi. The Black Hawk War came to be remembered later, however, less because of the atrocities inflicted on the Indians than because the participants included two native Kentuckians later pitted against each other: Lieutenant Jefferson Davis of the regular army and Captain Abraham Lincoln of the Illinois volunteers.

In the South two nations, the Seminoles and Cherokees, put up a stubborn resistance. The Seminoles of Florida fought a protracted guerrilla war in the Everglades from 1835 to 1842. But most of the vigor went out of their resistance after 1837, when their leader, Osceola, was seized by treachery under a flag of truce, imprisoned, and left to die at Fort Moultrie near Charleston Harbor. After 1842 only a few hundred Seminoles remained, hiding out in the swamps. Most of the rest had been banished to the West.

THE CHEROKEES' TRAIL OF TEARS   The Cherokees had by the end of the eighteenth century fallen back into the mountains of northern Georgia and western North Carolina, onto land guaranteed to them in 1791 by treaty with the United States. But when Georgia ceded its western lands in 1802, it did so on the ambiguous condition that the United States extinguish all Indian titles within the state "as early as the same can be obtained on reasonable terms." In 1827 the Cherokees, relying on their treaty rights, adopted a constitution in which they declared pointedly that they were not subject to any other state or nation. In 1828 Georgia responded with a law stipulating that after June 1, 1830, the authority of state law would extend over the Cherokees living within the boundaries of the state.

The discovery of gold in 1829 whetted the whites' appetite for Cherokee lands and brought bands of rough prospectors into the country. The Cherokees sought relief in the Supreme Court, but in *Cherokee Nation v. Georgia* (1831) John Marshall ruled that the Court lacked jurisdiction because the Cherokees were a "domestic dependent nation" rather than a foreign state in the meaning of the Constitution. Marshall added, however, that the Cherokees had "an unquestionable right" to their lands "until title should be extinguished by voluntary cession to the United States." In 1830 a Georgia law had required whites in the terri-

Elias Boudinot, editor of the Cherokee Phoenix, *signed the Indian removal treaty in 1835 and was subsequently murdered.*

tory to get licenses authorizing their residence there, and to take an oath of allegiance to the state. Two New England missionaries among the Indians refused and were sentenced to four years at hard labor. On appeal their case reached the Supreme Court as *Worcester* v. *Georgia* (1832), and the Court held that the Cherokee Nation was "a distinct political community" within which Georgia law had no force. The Georgia law was therefore unconstitutional.

Six years earlier Georgia had faced down President Adams when he tried to protect the rights of the Creeks. Now Georgia faced down the Supreme Court with the tacit consent of another president. Jackson is supposed to have said privately: "Marshall has made his decision, now let him enforce it!" Whether or not he put it so bluntly, Jackson did nothing to enforce the decision. In the circumstances there was nothing for the Cherokees to do but give in and sign a treaty, which they did in 1835. They gave up their lands in the Southeast in exchange for tracts in the Indian Territory west of Arkansas, $5 million from the federal government, and expenses for transportation.

By 1838 some 12,000 Cherokees had departed on the "Trail of Tears" westward, following the Choctaws, Chickasaws, Creeks, and Seminoles on a journey marked by the cruelty and neglect of soldiers and private contractors, and scorn and pilferage by whites along the way. A few held out in the mountains and acquired title to federal lands in North Carolina; thenceforth they were the "Eastern Band" of the Cherokees. Some Seminoles were able to hide out in the Everglades, and a few of

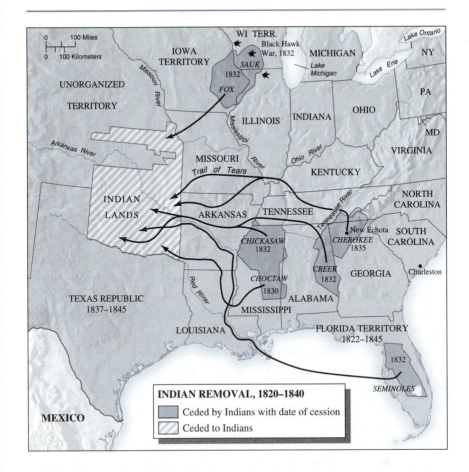

INDIAN REMOVAL, 1820–1840

- Ceded by Indians with date of cession
- Ceded to Indians

the others remained scattered in the Southeast, especially mixed-blood Creeks who could pass for white. Only 8,000 of the exiles survived the forced march to Oklahoma.

THE BANK CONTROVERSY

THE BANK'S OPPONENTS   The overriding national issue in the campaign of 1832 was neither Jackson's Indian policy nor South Carolina's obsession with nullification. It was the question of rechartering the Bank of the United States (B.U.S.). On the Bank issue, as on others, Jackson had made no public commitment, but his personal opposition to the Bank was already formed. Jackson had absorbed the western attitude of hostility toward the Bank after the Panic of 1819, and held to a conviction that it was unconstitutional no matter what Marshall had said in *McCulloch* v. *Maryland*. Banks in general had fed a speculative mania, and Jackson, suspicious of all banks, preferred a hard-money policy.

Under the management of Nicholas Biddle, the Bank of the United States had prospered and grown. Coming from a well-to-do Philadelphia family, Biddle was brilliant. He was valedictorian of his Princeton class at age fifteen. He had little acquaintance with business when Monroe appointed him a government director of the Bank, but he proved a quick study. By the time he became president of the Bank in 1823 Biddle was well versed in banking.

The Bank had facilitated business expansion and supplied a stable currency by forcing state banks to keep a specie reserve (gold or silver) on hand to back their paper currency. The Bank also acted as the collecting and disbursing agent for the federal government, which held one-fifth of the Bank's $35 million capital stock. From the start, this combination of private and public functions caused problems for the B.U.S. As the government's revenues soared, the Bank became the most powerful lending institution in the country, a central bank, in effect, whose huge size enabled it to determine the amount of available credit for the nation.

Arrayed against the Bank were powerful enemies: some of the state and local banks that had been forced to reduce their volume of paper money, debtor groups that suffered from the reduction, and businessmen and speculators "on the make," who wanted easier credit. States'-rights groups questioned the Bank's constitutionality, though Calhoun, who had sponsored the original charter and valued the Bank's function of regulating the currency, was not among them. Financiers on New York's Wall Street resented the supremacy of the Bank on Philadelphia's Chestnut Street.

Many westerners and workingmen, like Jackson, felt in their bones that the Bank was, in Thomas Hart Benton's word, a "Monster," a monopoly controlled by a few of the wealthy with power that was irreconcilable with a democracy. "I think it right to be perfectly frank with you," Jackson told Biddle in 1829. Jackson distrusted all forms of paper money. "I do not dislike your Bank any more than all banks." Jackson was perhaps right in his instinct that the Bank lodged too much power in private hands, but mistaken in his understanding of the Bank's policies. By issuing paper money of its own, the Bank provided a stable and uniform currency for the expanding economy as well as a regulating mechanism controlling the pace of growth.

Biddle at first tried to conciliate Jackson and appointed a number of Jackson men to branch offices of the Bank. In his first annual message (1829), however, Jackson questioned the Bank's constitutionality and asserted (whatever the evidence to the contrary) that it had failed to maintain a sound and uniform currency. Jackson talked of a compromise, perhaps a bank completely owned by the government with its operations confined chiefly to government deposits, its profits payable to the government, and its authority to set up branches in any state, dependent on the state's wishes. But Jackson would never commit himself on the precise terms of compromise. The defense of the Bank was left up to Biddle.

BIDDLE'S RECHARTER EFFORT The Bank's twenty-year charter would run through 1836, but Biddle could not afford the uncertainty of waiting until then for a renewal. He pondered whether to force the issue of recharter before the election of 1832 or after. On this point, leaders of the National-Republicans, especially Clay and Webster (who was legal counsel to the Bank as well as a senator), argued that the time to move was before the election. Clay, already the candidate of the National-Republicans, proposed to make the Bank the central election issue. Friends of the Bank held a majority in Congress, and Jackson would risk loss of support in the election if he vetoed a renewal. But they failed to grasp the depth of prejudice against the Bank, and succeeded mainly in handing to Jackson a popular issue on the eve of the election. "The Bank," Jackson told Martin Van Buren in May 1832, "is trying to kill me. But I will kill it."

Both houses passed the recharter by comfortable margins, but without the two-thirds majority needed to override a veto. On July 10, 1832, Jackson vetoed the bill, sending it back to Congress with a ringing denunciation of monopoly and special privilege. Jackson argued that the Bank was unconstitutional, whatever the Court and Congress said. "The opinion of the judges has no more authority over Congress than the opinion of Congress had over the judges, and on that point the President is independent of both." Besides, there were substantive objec-

Jackson battling the hydra-headed Bank of the United States.

tions aside from the question of constitutionality. Foreign stockholders in the Bank had an undue influence. The Bank had shown favors to members of Congress and exercised an improper power over state banks. The bill, he argued, demonstrated that "Many of our rich men have not been content with equal protection and equal benefits, but have besought us to make them richer by act of Congress." An effort to overrule the veto failed in the Senate, thus setting the stage for a nationwide financial crisis.

CAMPAIGN INNOVATIONS   The year 1832 witnessed another presidential election. For the first time a third party entered the field. The Anti-Masonic party was, like the Bank, the object of strong emotions then sweeping the new democracy. The group had grown out of popular hostility toward the Masonic order, members of which were suspected of having kidnapped and murdered a New Yorker for revealing the "secrets" of his lodge. Opposition to a fraternal order was hardly the foundation on which to build a lasting party, but the Anti-Masonic party had three important "firsts" to its credit: in addition to being the first third party, it was the first party to hold a national nominating convention and the first to announce a platform, all of which it accomplished in 1831 when it nominated William Wirt of Maryland for president.

The major parties followed its example by holding national conventions of their own. In December 1831 the delegates of the National-Republican party assembled in Baltimore to nominate Henry Clay for president and John Sergeant of Pennsylvania, counsel to the Bank and chief advocate of the recharter strategy, for vice-president. Jackson endorsed the idea of a nominating convention for the Democratic party (the name "Republican" was now formally dropped) to demonstrate popular support for its candidates. To that purpose the convention, also meeting at Baltimore, adopted the two-thirds rule for nomination (which prevailed until 1936, when it became a simple majority), and then named Martin Van Buren as Jackson's running mate. The Democrats, unlike the other two parties, adopted no formal platform at their first convention, and relied to a substantial degree on hoopla and the personal popularity of the president to carry their cause.

George Caleb Bingham's Verdict of the People *depicts the increasingly democratic politics of the early to mid–nineteenth century.*

The outcome was an overwhelming endorsement of Jackson in the electoral college by 219 votes to 49 for Clay, and a less overwhelming but solid victory in the popular vote, by 688,000 to 530,000. William Wirt carried only Vermont, with several electoral votes. South Carolina, preparing for nullification and unable to stomach either Jackson or Clay, delivered its eleven votes to Governor John Floyd of Virginia.

REMOVAL OF GOVERNMENT DEPOSITS   Jackson interpreted his election as a mandate to proceed further against the Bank. He asked Congress to investigate the safety of government deposits in the Bank, since one of the current rumors told of empty vaults, carefully concealed. After a committee had checked, the Calhoun and Clay forces in the House of Representatives passed a resolution affirming that government deposits were safe and could be continued. The resolution passed on March 2, 1833, by chance the same day that Jackson signed the compromise tariff and the Force Bill. With the nullification issue out of the way, however, Jackson was free to wage his unrelenting war on the Bank, that "hydra of corruption," which still had nearly four years to run on its charter. Despite the House study and resolution, Jackson now resolved to remove all government deposits from the Bank.

When Secretary of the Treasury Louis McLane opposed removal of the government deposits and suggested a new and modified version of the Bank, Jackson again shook up his cabinet. He kicked McLane upstairs to head the State Department, which Edward Livingston left to become minister to France. To take McLane's place at the Treasury Department he chose William J. Duane of Philadelphia, but by some oversight Jackson failed to explore Duane's views fully or advise him of the presidential expectations. Duane was anti-Bank, but he was consistent in his convictions. Dubious about banks in general, he saw no merit in removing deposits from the Bank of the United States for redeposit in countless state banks. Jackson summarily dismissed Duane and moved Attorney-General Roger Taney to the Treasury Department, where the new secretary gladly complied with the presidential wishes, which corresponded to his own views.

Taney continued to draw on governmental accounts with Biddle's bank, and to deposit all new federal receipts in state banks. By the end of 1833 there were twenty-three state banks that had the benefit of federal deposits, "pet banks" as they came to be called. Transferring the

The Downfall of Mother Bank. *In this pro-Jackson cartoon, the Bank crumbles and Jackson's opponents flee in the face of the heroic president's removal of government deposits.*

government's deposits was a highly questionable action under the law, and the Senate voted to censure Jackson for his actions. Biddle refused to surrender. "This worthy President," he declared, "thinks that because he has scalped Indians and imprisoned Judges he is to have his way with the Bank. He is mistaken." Biddle ordered that the B.U.S. curtail loans throughout the nation and demand the immediate redemption of state bank notes in specie as fast as possible. He sought to bring the economy to a halt, create a sharp depression, and reveal to the nation the importance of maintaining the Bank. By 1834 the tightness of credit was creating complaints of business distress, which was probably exaggerated by both sides in the Bank controversy for political effect: Biddle to show the evil consequences of the withdrawal of deposits, Jacksonians to show how Biddle abused his power.

Biddle's contraction policy unwittingly unleashed, however, a speculative binge encouraged by the deposit of government funds in the pet state banks. With the restraint of Biddle's bank removed, the state banks gave full rein to their wildcat tendencies. (The term "wildcat," used in this sense, originated in Michigan, where one of the fly-by-night banks featured a panther, or wildcat, on its worthless notes.) New banks mushroomed, printing bank notes with abandon for the purpose of lending to speculators. Sales of public lands rose from 4 million acres in 1834 to 15 million in 1835 and to 20 million in 1836. At the same time the states plunged heavily into debt to finance the building of roads and canals, inspired by the success of New York's Erie Canal. By 1837 total state indebtedness had soared to $170 million, a very large sum for that time. The supreme irony of Jackson's war on the Bank was that it sparked the speculative mania that he most feared.

FISCAL MEASURES   The surge of cheap money reached its greatest extent in 1836, when events combined suddenly to deflate it. Most important among these were the Distribution Act and the Specie Circular. Distribution of the government's surplus funds to the states had long been a pet project of Henry Clay. One of its purposes was to eliminate the federal surplus, thus removing one argument for cutting the tariff. Much of the surplus, however, resulted from the "land office business" in western real estate, and was therefore in the form of bank notes that had been issued to speculators. Many westerners thought that the solution to the surplus was simply to lower the price of land; southerners preferred to lower the tariff—but such action would now upset the compromise achieved in the Tariff of 1833. For a time the annual surpluses could be applied to paying off the government debt, but the debt, reduced to $7 million by 1832, was entirely paid off by 1835.

Still the federal surplus continued to mount. Clay again proposed distribution, but Jackson had constitutional scruples about the process. Finally, a compromise was worked out whereby the government would distribute most of the surplus as loans to the states. To satisfy Jackson's scruples the funds were technically "deposits," but in reality they were never demanded back. Distribution was to be in proportion to each state's representation in the two houses of Congress, and was to be paid out in quarterly installments, beginning in 1837.

The Specie Circular, issued by the secretary of the treasury at Jackson's order, applied the president's hard-money conviction to the sale of public lands. According to his order, the government would accept only gold or silver in payment for land. The purposes declared in the circular were to "repress frauds," to withhold support "from the monopoly of the public lands in the hands of speculators and capitalists," and to discourage the "ruinous extension" of bank notes and credit.

Irony dogged Jackson to the end on this matter. Since few actual settlers could get their hands on specie, they were now left all the more at the mercy of speculators for land purchases. Both the Distribution Act and the Specie Circular put many state banks in a precarious plight. The distribution of the surplus to the state governments resulted in federal funds being withdrawn from the state banks. In turn, the state banks had to call in a large part of their loans in order to make the transfer of federal funds to the state governments. This caused greater disarray among the already chaotic state banking community. At the same time, the new requirement that only hard money be accepted for federal land purchases put an added strain on the supplies of gold and silver.

BOOM AND BUST   But the boom and bust cycle of the 1830s had causes larger even than Andrew Jackson, causes that were beyond his control. The inflation of mid-decade was rooted not so much in a prodigal expansion of bank notes, as it seemed at the time, but in an increase of specie payments from England and France, and especially from Mexico, for investment and for the purchase of American cotton and other products. At the same time, British credits enabled Americans to buy British goods without having to export specie. Meanwhile, the flow of hard cash to China, where silver had been much prized, decreased. The Chinese now took in payment for their goods British credits, which they could in turn use to cover rapidly increasing imports of opium from British India.

Contrary to appearances, therefore, the reserves of specie in American banks kept pace with the increase of bank notes, despite reckless behavior on the part of some banks. But by 1836 a tighter British economy caused a decline in British investments and in British demand for American cotton just when the new western lands were creating a rapid increase in cotton supply. Fortunately for Jackson, the Panic of 1837 did not break until he was out of the White House and safely back at the Hermitage, his plantation near Nashville, Tennessee. His successor would serve as the scapegoat.

In May 1837 New York banks suspended specie payments on their bank notes, and fears of bankruptcy set off runs on banks around the country, many of which were soon overextended. A brief recovery followed in 1838, stimulated in part by a bad wheat harvest in England, which forced the British to buy American wheat. But by 1839 that stimulus had passed. The same year a bumper cotton crop overloaded the market, and a collapse of cotton prices set off a depression from which the economy did not fully recover until the mid-1840s.

VAN BUREN AND THE NEW PARTY SYSTEM

THE WHIG COALITION   Before the crash, however, the Jacksonian Democrats reaped a political bonanza. Jackson had downed the dual monsters of nullification and the Bank, and the people loved him for it. The hard times following the contraction of the economy turned people against Biddle and the B.U.S., but not against Jackson. The president exclaimed: "I have obtained a glorious triumph . . . and put to death that mammoth of corruption." But his opponents began in 1834 to pull together a new coalition of diverse elements united chiefly by their hostility to Jackson. The imperious demeanor of that champion of democracy had given rise to the name of "King Andrew I." His followers therefore were "Tories," supporters of the king, and his opponents became "Whigs," a name that linked them to the patriots of the American Revolution. This diverse coalition clustered around its center, the National-Republican party of John Quincy Adams, Clay, and Webster. Into the combination came remnants of the Anti-Masons and Democrats who for one reason or another were alienated by Jackson's stands on the bank or states' rights. Of the forty-one Democrats in Congress who had voted to recharter the Bank, twenty-eight joined the Whigs by 1836.

Whiggery always had about it an atmosphere of social conservatism and superiority. The core Whigs were the supporters of Henry Clay, men who supported his "American System." In the South the Whigs enjoyed the support of the urban banking and commercial interests, as well as their planter associates, owners of most of the slaves in the region. In the West, farmers who valued internal improvements joined the Whig ranks. Most states'-rights supporters eventually dropped away, and by the early 1840s the Whigs were becoming more clearly the party of Henry Clay's nationalism, even in the South. Unlike the Democrats, who attracted Catholics from Germany and Ireland, Whigs tended to be native-born and British-American evangelical Protestants—Presbyterians, Baptists, and Congregationalists—who were active in promoting social reforms such as abolitionism and temperance.

THE ELECTION OF 1836   By the presidential election of 1836 a new two-party system was emerging out of the Jackson and anti-Jackson forces, a system that would remain in fairly even balance for twenty years. In 1835, eighteen months before the election, the Democrats held their second national convention and nominated Jackson's hand-picked successor, Vice-President Martin Van Buren. The Whig coalition, united chiefly in its opposition to Jackson, held no convention but adopted a strategy of multiple candidacies, hoping to throw the election into the House of Representatives.

The result was a free-for-all reminiscent of 1824, except that this time one candidate stood apart from the rest. It was Van Buren against the field. The Whigs put up three favorite sons: Daniel Webster, named by the Massachusetts legislature; Hugh Lawson White, chosen by anti-Jackson Democrats in the Tennessee legislature; and William Henry Harrison of Indiana, nominated by a predominantly Anti-Masonic convention in Harrisburg, Pennsylvania. In the South the Whigs made heavy inroads on the Democratic vote by arguing that Van Buren would be soft on antislavery advocates and that the South could trust only a southerner—that is, White—as president. In the popular vote Van Buren outdistanced the entire Whig field, with 765,000 votes to 740,000 votes for the Whigs, most of which were cast for Harrison. Van Buren had 170 electoral votes, Harrison 73, White 26, and Webster 14.

Jackson urging on his hand-picked successor, Martin Van Buren, in his battle with William Henry Harrison, 1836.

Martin Van Buren, the "Little Magician."

Martin Van Buren, the eighth president, was the first of Dutch ancestry and at the age of fifty-five the first born under the Stars and Stripes. Son of a tavernkeeper in Kinderhook, New York, he had been schooled in a local academy, read law, and entered politics. Although he kept up a limited legal practice, he had been for most of his adult life a professional politician, so skilled in the arts of organization and manipulation that he came to be known as the "Little Magician." In 1824 he supported Crawford, then switched to Jackson in 1828, but continued to look to the Old Republicans of Virginia as the southern anchor of his support. After a brief tenure as governor of New York, he resigned to join the cabinet, and because of Jackson's favor became vice-president.

THE PANIC OF 1837   Van Buren owed much of his success to good luck. But once he had climbed to the top of the greased pole, luck suddenly deserted him. Van Buren had inherited Jackson's favor and many of his followers, but he also inherited a financial panic. An already precarious economy was tipped over into crisis by depression in England, which resulted in a drop in the price of cotton from 17½¢ to 13½¢ a pound, and caused English banks and investors to cut back their commitments in the New World and to refuse extensions of loans. This was a particularly hard blow, because much of America's economic expansion depended on European—and mainly English—capital. On top of everything else, in 1836 there had been a failure of the wheat crop, the export of which in good years helped offset the drain of payments abroad. As creditors hastened to foreclose, the inflationary spiral went into reverse. States curtailed ambitious plans for roads and canals, and in many cases felt impelled to repudiate their debts. In the crunch, a

The Times. *This anti-Jacksonian cartoon depicts the effects of the depression of 1837: a panic at a state bank, beggars in the street.*

good many of the wildcat banks succumbed, and the government itself lost some $9 million it had deposited in pet banks.

The working classes, as always, were particularly hard hit during the economic slump, and they largely had to fend for themselves. By the fall of 1837, one-third of the workforce was jobless, and those still fortunate enough to have jobs saw their wages cut by 30 to 50 percent within two years. At the same time, prices for food and clothing soared. As winter approached in 1837, a journalist reported that in New York City there were 200,000 people "in utter and hopeless distress with no means of surviving the winter but those provided by charity." There was no government aid; churches and voluntary societies were the major sources of support for the indigent.

Van Buren's advisers and supporters were inclined to blame speculators and bankers, but at the same time to expect that the evildoers would get what they deserved in a healthy shakeout that would bring the economy back to stability. Van Buren did not believe that he or the government had any responsibility to rescue hard-pressed farmers or businessmen or to provide public relief. He did feel obliged to keep the government itself in a healthy financial situation, however. To that end he called a special session of Congress in 1837, which quickly voted to postpone indefinitely the distribution of the surplus because of a probable upcoming deficit, and also approved an issue of Treasury notes to cover immediate expenses.

AN INDEPENDENT TREASURY   Van Buren believed that the government should cease risking its deposits in shaky banks and set up an Independent Treasury. Under this plan the government would keep its funds in its own vaults and do business entirely in hard money. Van Buren observed that the founders of the republic had "wisely judged that the less government interferes with private pursuits the better for the general prosperity." Webster's response typified the Whig reaction: "I feel . . . as if this could not be America when I see schemes of public policy proposed, having for their object the convenience of Government only, and leaving the people to shift for themselves." The Whiggish approach, presumably, would have been some kind of Hamiltonian program of government promotion of economic development, perhaps in the form of tariff or currency legislation. Good Jacksonians disapproved of such programs, at least when they were run from Washington.

The Independent Treasury Act provoked opposition from a combination of Whigs and conservative Democrats who feared deflation. It took Van Buren several years of maneuvering to get what he wanted. Calhoun signaled a return to the Democratic fold, after several years of flirting with the Whigs, when he came out for the Independent Treasury Act. Van Buren gained western support by backing a more liberal land policy. Congress finally passed the Independent Treasury Act on July 4, 1840. Although it lasted little more than a year before the Whigs repealed it in 1841, it would be restored in 1846.

The drawn-out struggle over the Treasury was only one of several that kept Washington preoccupied through the Van Buren years. A flood of petitions for Congress to abolish slavery and the slave trade in the District of Columbia brought on tumultuous debate, especially in the House of Representatives. Border incidents growing out of a Canadian insurrection in 1837 and a dispute over the Maine boundary kept British-American animosity at a simmer, but General Winfield Scott, the president's ace troubleshooter, managed to keep the hotheads in check along the border. The spreading malaise of the time was rooted in the depressed condition of the economy, which lasted through Van Buren's entire term. Fairly or not, the administration became the target of growing discontent. The president won renomination easily enough, but could not get the Democratic convention to agree on his vice-presidential choice, which the convention left up to the Democratic electors.

THE "LOG CABIN AND HARD CIDER" CAMPAIGN   The Whigs got an early start on their campaign when they met at Harrisburg, Pennsylvania, on December 4, 1839, to choose a candidate. Clay expected 1840 to be his year and had soft-pedaled talk of his American System in the interest of building broader support. Although he led on the first ballot, the convention was of a mind to look for a Whiggish Jackson, as it were, a military hero who could enter the race with few known political convictions or enemies. One possibility was Winfield Scott, but the delegates finally turned to William Henry Harrison. His credentials were impressive: victor at the Battle of Tippecanoe against the Shawnees in 1811, former governor of the Indiana Territory, briefly congressman and senator from Ohio, more briefly minister to Colombia. Another advantage of Harrison's was that the Anti-Masons liked him. To rally their states'-rights wing, the Whigs chose for vice-president John Tyler of Virginia, a close friend of Clay.

The Whigs prevailed in their "Log Cabin and Hard Cider" campaign of 1840.

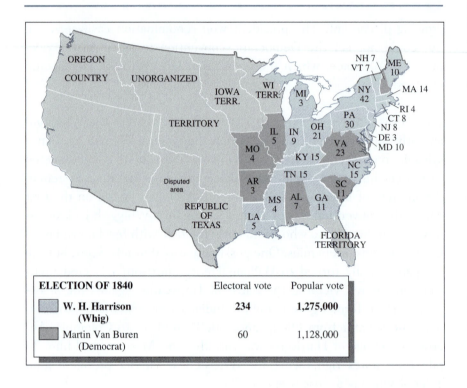

ELECTION OF 1840	Electoral vote	Popular vote
W. H. Harrison (Whig)	**234**	**1,275,000**
Martin Van Buren (Democrat)	60	1,128,000

The Whigs had no platform. That would have risked dividing a coalition united chiefly by opposition to the Democrats. But they had a slogan, "Tippecanoe and Tyler too," that went trippingly on the tongue. And they soon had a rousing campaign theme, which a Democratic paper unwittingly supplied them when the *Baltimore Republican* declared sardonically "that upon condition of his receiving a pension of $2,000 and a barrel of cider, General Harrison would no doubt consent to withdraw his pretensions, and spend his days in a log cabin on the banks of the Ohio." The Whigs seized upon the cider and log cabin symbols to depict Harrison as a simple man sprung from the people. Actually, he sprang from one of the first families of Virginia and lived in a commodious farmhouse.

Substituting spectacle for argument, the Whig "Log Cabin and Hard Cider" campaign featured such sublime irrelevancy as the country had never seen before. Portable log cabins rolled through the streets along with barrels of potable cider. All the devices of hoopla were mobilized: placards, emblems, campaign buttons, floats, effigies, great rallies, and a campaign newspaper, *The Log Cabin*. Building on the example of the

Jacksonians' campaign to discredit John Quincy Adams, the Whigs pictured Van Buren, who unlike Harrison really did come from humble origins, as an aristocrat living in luxury at "the Palace."

"We have taught them to conquer us!" the *Democratic Review* lamented. The Whig party had not only learned its lessons well, it had learned to improve on its teachers in the art of campaigning. "Van! Van! Is a Used-up Man!" went one of the campaign refrains, and down he went by the thumping margin of 234 votes to 60 in the electoral college. In the popular vote it was closer: 1,275,000 for Harrison; 1,128,000 for Van Buren.

ASSESSING THE JACKSON YEARS

The Jacksonian impulse had altered American politics permanently. Long-standing ambivalence about political parties had been purged in the fires of political conflict, and mass political parties had arrived to stay. They were now widely justified as a positive good. By 1840 both parties were organized down to the precinct level, and the proportion of adult white males who voted in the presidential election tripled, from 26 percent in 1824 to 78 percent in 1840. That much is beyond dispute, but the phenomenon of Jackson, the great symbol for an age, has inspired among historians conflicts of interpretation as spirited as those among his supporters and opponents at the time.

The earliest historians of the Jackson era belonged largely to an eastern elite nurtured in a "Whiggish" culture, men who could never quite forgive Jackson for the spoils system, which in their view excluded the fittest from office. A later school of "progressive" historians depicted Jackson as the leader of a vast democratic movement that welled up in the West and mobilized a farmer-labor alliance to sweep the "Monster" Bank into the dustbin of history. Some historians have recently focused attention on local power struggles in which the great national debates of the time often seemed empty rhetoric or at most snares to catch the voters. One view of Jackson makes him out to be essentially a frontier opportunist for whom democracy "was good talk with which to win the favor of the people."

Yet there seems little question that, whatever else Jackson and his supporters had in mind, they followed an ideal of republican virtue, of returning to the Jeffersonian vision of the Old Republic in which gov-

Andrew Jackson in 1845. Jackson died shortly after this daguerreotype was taken.

ernment would leave people largely to their own devices. In the Jacksonian view the alliance of government and business was always an invitation to special favors and an eternal source of corruption. The national bank was the epitome of such evil. The right policy for government, at the national level in particular, was to refrain from granting special privileges and to let free competition in the marketplace regulate the economy.

In the bustling world of the nineteenth century, however, the idea of a return to agrarian simplicity was a futile exercise in nostalgia. Instead, free enterprise policies opened the way for a host of aspiring entrepreneurs eager to replace the established economic elite with a new order of free enterprise capitalism. And in fact there was no great conflict in the Jacksonian mentality between the farmer or planter who delved in the soil and the independent speculator and entrepreneur who won his way by other means. Jackson himself was all these things. What the Jacksonian mentality could not foresee was the degree to which, in a growing country, unrestrained enterprise could lead to new economic combinations, centers of gigantic power largely independent of governmental regulation. But history is forever pursued by unintended consequences. Here the ultimate irony would be that the laissez-faire rationale for republican simplicity eventually became the justification for the growth of unregulated centers of economic power far greater than any ever wielded by Biddle's bank.

> **MAKING CONNECTIONS**
>
> • This chapter analyzes the political side of "Jacksonian Democracy." Chapter 12 concludes with an assessment of the accuracy of that term from social and economic perspectives.
>
> • John C. Calhoun, Henry Clay, and Daniel Webster, three of the statesmen described in this chapter, continued for many years to be the major spokesmen for their positions. The last great debate for the three, over the Compromise of 1850, is discussed in Chapter 16.

FURTHER READING

A recent survey of events covered in the chapter is Daniel Feller's *The Jacksonian Promise: America, 1815–1840* (1995). A more political focus can be found in Harry L. Watson's *Liberty and Power: The Politics of Jacksonian America* (1990). Lee Benson's *The Concept of Jacksonian Democracy* (1961) remains an important revisionist interpretation. Edward Pessen's *Jacksonian America: Society, Personality, and Politics* (rev. ed., 1979) stresses the lack of genuine democracy in society and politics.

A still valuable standard introduction to the development of political parties of the 1830s is Richard P. McCormick's *The Second Party System* (1966). For an outstanding analysis of women in New York City during the Jacksonian period, see Christine Stansell's *City of Women: Sex and Class in New York, 1789–1860* (1986). In *Chants Democratic: New York City and the Rise of the American Working Class, 1788–1850* (1984), Sean Wilentz analyzes the social basis of working-class politics. John Marszalek's *The Petticoat Affair: Manners, Mutiny, and Sex in Andrew Jackson's White House* (1997) assesses the Peggy Eaton controversy.

The best biography of Jackson remains Robert V. Remini's three-volume work: *Andrew Jackson: The Course of American Empire, 1767–1821* (1977), *Andrew Jackson: The Course of American Freedom, 1822–*

1832 (1981), and *Andrew Jackson: The Course of American Democracy, 1833–1845* (1984). On Jackson's successor, consult John Niven's *Martin Van Buren: The Romantic Age of American Politics* (1983). Studies of other major figures of the period include John Niven's *John C. Calhoun and the Price of Union* (1988), Merrill Peterson's *The Great Triumvirate: Webster, Clay, and Calhoun* (1987), and Robert Remini's *Henry Clay: Statesman for the Union* (1992) and *Daniel Webster: The Man and His Time* (1997).

The political philosophies of Jackson's opponents are treated in Daniel W. Howe's *The Political Culture of the American Whigs* (1979) and William P. Vaughn's *The Antimasonic Party in the United States, 1826–1843* (1983).

Two studies of the impact of the Bank controversy are William G. Shade's *Banks or No Banks: The Money Question in the Western States, 1832–1865* (1972) and James R. Sharp's *The Jacksonians versus the Banks: Politics in the States after the Panic of 1837* (1970). Daniel Feller's *The Public Lands in Jacksonian Politics* (1984) is a good introduction to that important topic.

The outstanding book on the nullification issue remains William W. Freehling's *Prelude to Civil War: The Nullification Controversy in South Carolina, 1816–1836* (1966). John M. Belohlavek's *"Let the Eagle Soar!": The Foreign Policy of Andrew Jackson* (1985) is a thorough study of Jacksonian diplomacy. Ronald N. Satz's *American Indian Policy in the Jacksonian Era* (1974) surveys that tragedy; Michael P. Rogin's *Fathers and Children: Andrew Jackson and the Subjugation of the American Indian* (1975) is a psychological interpretation of Jackson's Indian policy.

12 ⚬ THE DYNAMICS OF GROWTH

CHAPTER ORGANIZER

This chapter focuses on:

- the expansion of agriculture, industry, and transportation.

- patterns of immigration at mid-century.

- the status of labor unions.

he Jacksonian-era political debate between democratic and elitist elements was rooted in a profound transformation of American social and economic life. Between 1815 and 1850, the United States expanded all the way to the Pacific coast. An industrial revolution in the Northeast began to reshape the contours of the economy and propel an unrelenting process of urbanization. In the West an agricultural empire began to emerge based upon the foundation of corn, wheat, and cattle. In the South cotton became king, and its reign came to depend on an expanding institution of slavery. At the same time, innovations in transportation—horse-drawn wagons, canals, steamboats, and railroads—conquered time and space and knit together a national market. An economy based primarily on small-scale farming and local commerce matured into a far-flung capitalist marketplace entwined with world markets. These economic developments in turn generated changes in every other area of American life, from politics to the legal system, from the family to social values.

AGRICULTURE AND THE NATIONAL ECONOMY

The first stage of industrialization brought with it an expansive commercial and urban outlook that by the end of the century would supplant the agrarian philosophy espoused by Thomas Jefferson and many others. "We are greatly, I was about to say fearfully, growing," John C. Calhoun told his congressional colleagues in 1816, and many other statesmen shared his ambivalent outlook. Would the republic retain its virtue and cohesion amid the turmoil of commercial development? In the brief period of good feelings after the War of 1812, however, such a troublesome question was easily brushed aside. Economic opportunities seemed available to Americans everywhere, and nowhere more than in Calhoun's native South Carolina. The reason was cotton, the new staple crop of the South, which was spreading from South Carolina and Georgia into the new lands of Mississippi, Alabama, Louisiana, and Arkansas.

COTTON Cotton had been used from ancient times, but the industrial revolution and its spread of textile mills created a rapidly growing market for the fluffy fiber. Cotton had remained for many years rare and expensive because of the need for hand labor to separate the lint from the tenacious seeds. But by the mid-1780s in coastal Georgia and South Carolina a long-fiber Sea Island cotton was being grown commercially that could easily be separated from its shiny black seeds by squeezing it through rollers. Sea Island cotton, like the rice and indigo of the colonial Tidewater, had little chance, though, in the soil and climate of the upcountry. And the green seed of the upland cotton clung to the lint so stubbornly that the rollers crushed the seed and spoiled the fiber. One person working all day could manage to separate little if any more than a pound by hand. Cotton could not yet be king.

The rising cotton kingdom of the lower South came to birth at a plantation called Mulberry Hill in coastal Georgia, the home of Mrs. Nathanael Greene, widow of the Revolutionary War hero. At Mulberry Hill, discussion often turned to the promising new crop and to speculation about better ways to remove the seeds. In 1792, on the way to a job as a tutor

Whitney's cotton gin revolutionized the South's economy and breathed new life into slavery.

in South Carolina, young Eli Whitney, recently graduated from Yale, visited fellow graduate Phineas Miller, who was overseer at Mulberry Hill. Catharine Greene noticed her visitor's mechanical aptitude, which had been nurtured in boyhood by the needs of a Massachusetts farm. When she suggested that young Whitney devise a mechanism for removing the seed from upland cotton, he mulled it over and solved the problem in ten days. In the spring of 1793, his job as a tutor quickly forgotten, Whitney had a working model of a cotton gin (short for engine). With it one person could separate fifty times as much cotton as could be done by hand. The device was an "absurdly simple contrivance," too much so as it turned out. A simple description was all any skilled worker needed to make a copy, and by the time Whitney and Miller had secured a patent in 1794, a number of copies were already in use. As a consequence, the two men were never able to make good on the promise of riches that the gin offered, and spent most of their modest gains in expensive lawsuits.

Although Whitney realized little profit from his idea, he had unwittingly begun a revolution. Green-seed cotton first engulfed the up-country hills of South Carolina and Georgia, and after the War of 1812 migrated into the former Creek, Choctaw, and Chickasaw lands to the west. Cotton production soared, and in the process planters found a new and profitable use for slavery. Planters migrated westward with their gangs of workers in tow, and a profitable trade began to develop in the sale of slaves from the coastal South to the West. The cotton culture became a way of life that tied the Old Southwest to the coastal Southeast in a common interest.

Not the least of the cotton gin's revolutionary consequences, although less apparent at first, was that cotton became almost immediately a major export commodity. Cotton exports averaged about $9 million in value from 1803 to 1807, about 22 percent of the value of all exports; from 1815 to 1819 they averaged over $23 million, or 39 percent of the total; and from the mid-1830s to 1860 they accounted for more than half the value of all exports. The South supplied the North both raw materials and markets for manufactures. Income from the North's role in handling the cotton trade then provided surpluses for capital investment.

FARMING THE WEST   The westward flow of planters and their slaves to Alabama and Mississippi during these flush times mirrored another migration through the Ohio Valley and the Great Lakes region, where the Indians had been steadily pushed westward. "Old America seems to be breaking up and moving westward," an English traveler observed in 1817 as he watched the migrants make their way along westward roads in Pennsylvania. Family groups, stages, light wagons, and riders on horseback made up "a scene of bustle and business, extending over three hundred miles, which is truly wonderful." In 1800 some 387,000 settlers were counted west of the Atlantic states; by 1810, 1,338,000 lived over the mountains; by 1820, 2,419,000. By 1860 more than half the nation's population resided in trans-Appalachia, and the restless movement had long since spilled across the Mississippi and touched the shores of the Pacific.

North of the expanding cotton belt in the Gulf states, the fertile woodland soils, riverside bottom lands, and black loam of the prairies drew farmers from the rocky lands of New England and the leached, exhausted soils of the Southeast. A new land law of 1820, passed after the Panic of 1819, eliminated the credit provisions of the 1800 act but reduced the minimum price from $1.64 to $1.25 per acre and the minimum plot from 160 to 80 acres. The settler could get a place for as little as $100, and over the years the proliferation of state banks made it pos-

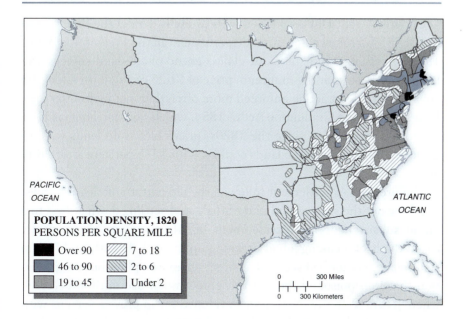

POPULATION DENSITY, 1820
PERSONS PER SQUARE MILE

sible to continue buying on credit. Even that was not enough for westerners, who began a long—and eventually victorious—agitation for further relaxation of the land laws. They favored preemption, the right of squatters to purchase land at the minimum price, and graduation, the progressive reduction of the price on lands that did not sell.

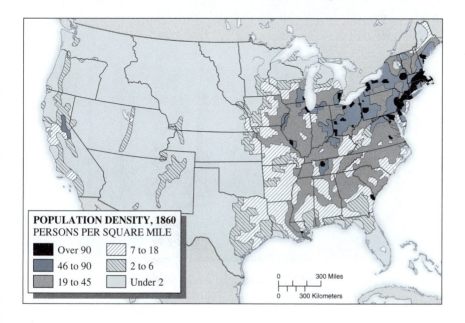

POPULATION DENSITY, 1860
PERSONS PER SQUARE MILE

Congress eventually responded with two bills. Under the Preemption Act of 1830, a renewable law made permanent in the Preemption Act of 1841, squatters could stake out claims ahead of the land surveys and later get 160 acres at the minimum price of $1.25 per acre. In effect the law recognized a practice enforced more often than not by frontier vigilantes. Under the Graduation Act of 1854, which Senator Thomas Hart Benton had promoted since the 1820s, prices of unsold lands were to go down in stages until the lands could sell for 12½¢ per acre after thirty years.

The progress of settlement followed the old pattern of clearing trees, grubbing out the stumps and underbrush, and settling down at first to a crude subsistence. The development of effective iron plows greatly eased the backbreaking job of breaking up the soil. As early as 1797 an American inventor had secured a patent on an iron plow, but a superstition that iron poisoned the soil prevented much use until after 1819, when Jethro Wood of New York developed an improved version with separate parts that could be replaced without buying a whole new plow. The prejudice against iron suddenly vanished, and the demand for plows grew so fast that Wood, like Whitney, could not supply the need and spent much of his remaining fifteen years fighting against patent

American Log Cabin, 1822. *For those who settled the Midwest, it was necessary to clear trees and brush before the land was suitable for farming.*

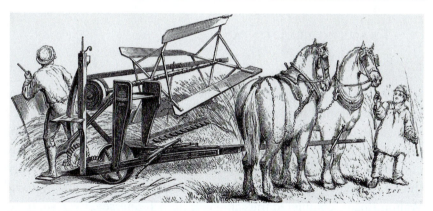

McCormick's Reaping Machine. *This illustration appeared in the catalogue of the Great Exhibition at the Crystal Palace in London, 1851. The plow eased the transformation of rough plains into fertile farm land, and the reaping machine accelerated farm production.*

infringements. The iron plow was a special godsend to those farmers who first ventured into the sticky black loams of the treeless prairies. Further improvements would follow, including John Deere's steel plow (1837) and the chilled-iron and steel plow of John Oliver (1855).

By the 1840s new mechanical seeders replaced the need to sow seed by hand. Even more important, Cyrus Hall McCormick of Virginia invented a primitive grain reaper in 1834, a development as significant to the agricultural economy of the Old Northwest as the cotton gin was to the South. After tinkering with his machine for almost a decade, McCormick applied for a patent in 1841. Six years later he moved to Chicago and built a manufacturing plant for his reapers and mowers. Within a few years he had sold thousands of new machines, transforming the scale of American agriculture. Using a hand-operated sickle, a farmer could harvest half an acre of wheat a day; with a McCormick reaper two people could work twelve acres a day.

McCormick's success attracted other manufacturers and inventors, and soon there were mechanical threshers to separate the grains of wheat from the straw. Farming remained, as it still is, a precarious vocation, subject to the whims of climate, the assault of insects, and the fluctuations of foreign markets, but by the 1850s it had become a major commercial activity. As the volume of agricultural products soared, prices dropped, income rose, and the standard of living for many farm families in the Old Northwest improved.

TRANSPORTATION AND
THE NATIONAL ECONOMY

NEW ROADS   Transportation improvements helped spur the development of a national market. As settlers moved west, there developed a stronger demand for better roads. In 1795 the Wilderness Road, along the trail blazed by Daniel Boone twenty years before, was opened to covered-wagon and stagecoach traffic, thereby easing the route through the Cumberland Gap into Kentucky and along the Knoxville and Old Walton Roads, completed the same year, into Tennessee. Even so, travel was difficult at best. Stagecoaches crammed with as many as a dozen people crept along at four miles per hour. One early stage rider said he alternately walked and rode and "though the pain of riding exceeded the fatigue of walking, yet . . . it refreshed us by varying the weariness of our bodies." South of these roads there were no such major highways. South Carolinians and Georgians pushed westward on whatever trails or rutted roads had appeared.

To the northeast a movement for graded and paved roads (macadamized with crushed stones packed down) gathered momentum after completion of the Philadelphia-Lancaster Turnpike in 1794 (the term derives from a pole or pike at the tollgate, turned to admit the traffic). By 1821 some 4,000 miles of turnpikes had been completed, mainly connecting eastern cities. Western traffic moved along the Frederick Turnpike to Cumberland and thence along the National Road, to Wheeling on the Ohio River in 1818, then to Columbus in the Northwest Territory and on to Vandalia, Illinois, by about mid-century. This 600-mile road passed through an eighty-foot-wide clearing. The road itself was twenty feet wide. Another route went along the old Forbes Road from Philadelphia to Pittsburgh. Another used the Mohawk and Genesee Turnpike from the Massachusetts state line through Albany to Buffalo, whence one could take ship for points on the Great Lakes.

WATER TRANSPORT   Once turnpike travelers had reached the Ohio River, they could float westward in comparative comfort. At Pittsburgh, Wheeling, and other points the emigrants could buy flatboats, commonly of two kinds: an ark with room for living quarters, possessions, and perhaps some livestock; or a keelboat—similar but with a keel. For

Steamers at the levee at St. Paul, Minnesota, 1859.

large flatboats—a capacity of forty tons was common—crews were available for hire. At the destination the boat could be used again or sold for lumber. In the early 1820s an estimated 3,000 flatboats went down the Ohio every year, and for many years after that the flatboat remained the chief conveyance for heavy traffic downstream.

By the early 1820s the turnpike boom was giving way to new developments in water transportation: the river steamboat and the canal barge, which carried bulk commodities far more cheaply than did covered wagons on the National Road. As early as 1787 one inventor had launched a steamboat on the Delaware River, but no commercially successful steamboat appeared until Robert Fulton and Robert R. Livingston sent the *Clermont* up the Hudson River to Albany in 1807. Thereafter, the use of the steamboat spread rapidly to other eastern rivers and to the Ohio and Mississippi, opening nearly half a continent to water traffic.

By 1836, 361 steamboats navigated the western waters, reaching ever farther up the tributaries that connected to the Mississippi. By the 1840s, shallow-draft, steam-powered ships that traveled *on* rather than *in* the water became the basis of the rivermen's boast that the boats were "so built that when the river is low and the sandbars come out for air, the first mate can tap a keg of beer and run the boat four miles on the suds." These boats ventured into far reaches of the Mississippi Val-

TRANSPORTATION WEST, ABOUT 1840

〰 Canals ═ Roads
— Navigable rivers

ley, up such rivers as the Wabash, the Monongahela, the Cumberland, the Tennessee, the Missouri, and the Arkansas.

The durable flatboat, however, still carried to market most of the western wheat, corn, flour, meal, bacon, ham, pork, whiskey, soap and candles (the byproducts of slaughterhouses), lead from Missouri, copper from Michigan, wood from the Rockies, and ironwork from Pittsburgh. But the steamboat, by bringing two-way traffic to the Mississippi Valley, created a continental market and an agricultural empire that became the new breadbasket of America. Farming evolved from a subsistence level to the ever greater production of valuable staples. Along with the new farmers came promoters, speculators, and land boomers. Villages at strategic trading points along the streams evolved into centers of commerce and urban life. The port of New Orleans grew in the 1830s and 1840s to lead all others in exports.

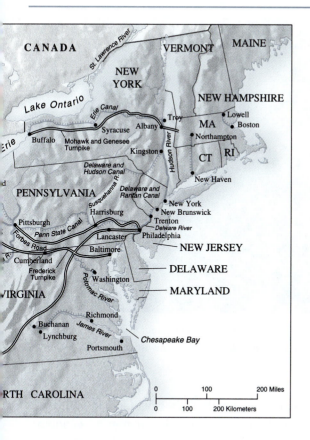

But by then the Erie Canal was drawing eastward much of the trade that once went down to the Gulf, and this would have major economic and political consequences, tying together the West and East while further isolating the Deep South. In 1817 the New York legislature endorsed Governor De Witt Clinton's dream of connecting the Hudson River with Lake Erie. Eight years later, in 1825, the canal was open for its entire 350 miles from Albany to Buffalo; branches soon put most of the state within reach of the canal. The completion of the canal reduced travel time from New York City to Buffalo from twenty days to six, and the cost of moving a ton of freight plummeted from $100 to $5. After 1828 the Delaware and Hudson Canal linked New York with the anthracite fields of northeastern Pennsylvania. The speedy success of the New York system inspired a mania for canals that lasted more than a decade and resulted in the completion of about 3,000 miles of water-

Constructing the Erie Canal, 1820. *When the Erie Canal opened in 1825 it allowed flatboats to carry freight eastward directly from the Great Lakes to New York State.*

ways by 1837. But no canal ever matched the spectacular success of the Erie, which rendered the entire Great Lakes region an economic tributary to the port of New York. With the further development of canals spanning Ohio and Indiana from north to south, much of the upper Ohio Valley also came within the economic sphere of New York.

RAILROADS   The Panic of 1837 and the subsequent depression cooled the canal fever. Some states that had borrowed heavily to finance canals had to repudiate their debts. The holders of repudiated bonds had no recourse. Meanwhile, a new and more versatile form of transportation was gaining on the canal: the railroad. Vehicles that ran on iron rails had long been in use, especially in mining, but now came a tremendous innovation—the use of steam power—as the steam locomotive followed soon after the steamboat. As early as 1814 the first practical steam locomotive was built in England. In 1825, the year the Erie Canal was completed, the world's first commercial steam railway began operations in England. By the 1820s the port cities of Baltimore, Charleston, and Boston were alive with schemes to tap the hinterlands by rail.

On July 4, 1828, Baltimore got the jump on other cities when Charles Carroll, the last surviving signer of the Declaration of Independence, laid the first stone in the roadbed of the Baltimore and Ohio (B&O) Railroad. Four years later the roadbed reached seventy-three miles west of Baltimore. The Charleston and Hamburg Railroad, started in 1831 and finished in 1833, was at that time the longest railroad under single management in the world. It reached westward 136 miles to the hamlet of Hamburg, opposite Augusta, where Charleston merchants hoped to divert traffic from the Savannah River.

By 1840 the railroads, with a total of 3,328 miles, had outdistanced the canals by just two miles. Over the next twenty years, though, railroads grew nearly tenfold to cover 30,626 miles; more than two-thirds of this total was built in the 1850s. If the automobile was to be the catalyst for the explosion of suburbs, the railroad was responsible for a tremendous increase in the size of American cities. Rail lines were laid out to connect cities with one another; the small towns and villages were bypassed. Several major east-west lines appeared, connecting Boston to Albany and Albany to Buffalo; combined in 1853, these lines became the New York Central. In 1851 the Erie Railroad spanned southern New York; by 1852 the Pennsylvania Railroad connected Philadelphia and Pittsburgh; in 1853 the B&O finally reached Wheeling on the Ohio. By then New York had connections all the way to Chicago, and in two years to St. Louis. Before 1860 the Hannibal and St. Joseph had crossed the state of Missouri. Farther south, despite Charleston's early start on both canals and railroads and despite the brave dream of a line to tap western commerce at Cincinnati, the network of railroads still had many gaps in 1860. By 1857 Charleston, Savannah, and Norfolk connected by way of lines into Chattanooga and thence along a single line to Memphis, the only southern route that connected the east coast and the Mississippi. In 1860 the North and South had only three major links: at Washington, Louisville, and Cairo, Illinois.

Travel on the early railroads was a risky venture. Iron straps on top of wooden rails, for instance, tended to work loose and curl up into "snakesheads" that sometimes pierced railway coaches. Wood was used for fuel too, and the sparks often caused fires along the way or damaged passengers' clothing. An English traveler reported seeing a lady's shawl ignited on one trip. She found in her own gown thirteen holes "and in my veil, with which I saved my eyes, more than could be counted." Cre-

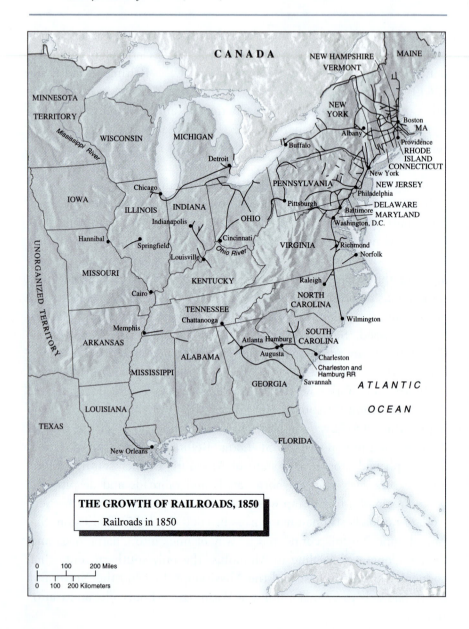

THE GROWTH OF RAILROADS, 1850

—— Railroads in 1850

```
0    100    200 Miles
0    100    200 Kilometers
```

ation of the "spark arrester" and the use of coal alleviated but never overcame the hazard. Land travel, whether by stagecoach or train, was a jerky, bumpy, wearying ordeal.

Water travel, where available, offered far more comfort, but railroads gained supremacy over other forms of transport because of their economy, speed, and reliability. They averaged ten miles per hour, more than

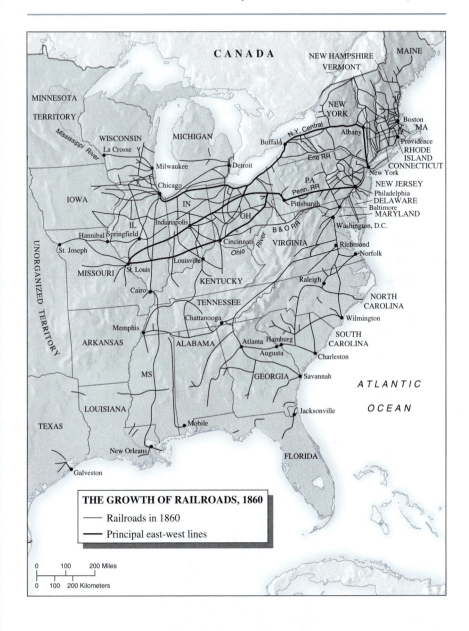

THE GROWTH OF RAILROADS, 1860

— Railroads in 1860

— Principal east-west lines

twice as fast as stagecoaches and four times as fast as water travel. By 1859, railroads had reduced the cost of transportation services by $150 million to $175 million, accounting for a saving that amounted to some 4 percent of the gross national product. By 1890, the saving would increase to almost 15 percent. Railroads provided indirect benefits by encouraging settlement and the expansion of farming. During the antebellum period, the reduced costs brought on by the railroads aided the expansion of farming more than manufacturing, since manufacturers in the Northeast, especially New England, had better access to water transportation. The railroads' demand for iron and equipment of various kinds, however, did provide an enormous market for the industries that made these capital goods. And the ability of railroads to operate year round in all kinds of weather gave them an advantage in carrying finished goods, too.

OCEAN TRANSPORT   For oceangoing traffic, the start of service on regular schedules was the most important change of the early 1800s. In the first week of 1818 ships of the Black Ball Line inaugurated a weekly transatlantic packet service between New York and Liverpool. Beginning with four ships in all, the Black Ball Line thereafter had one ship leaving each port monthly at an announced time. With the economic recovery in 1822, the packet business grew in a rush. By 1845 some fifty-two transatlantic lines ran square-riggers on schedule from New York, with three regular sailings per week. Many others ran in the coastwise trade, to Charleston, Savannah, New Orleans, and elsewhere.

The same year, 1845, witnessed a great innovation with the launching of the first clipper ship, the *Rainbow*. Built for speed, the sleek clip-

Clipper ship at the New York docks, 1840s.

pers were the nineteenth-century equivalent of the supersonic jetliner. They doubled the speed of the older merchant vessels, and trading companies rushed to purchase them. Long and lean, with taller masts and more sails, they cut dashing figures during their brief but colorful career, which lasted less than two decades. What provoked the clipper boom was the lure of Chinese tea, a drink long coveted in America but in scarce supply. The tea leaves were a perishable commodity that had to reach market quickly, and the new clippers now made this possible. Even more important, the discovery of California gold in 1848 lured thousands of prospectors and entrepreneurs from the Atlantic seaboard. These new settlers generated an urgent demand for goods, and the clippers met the need. In 1854 the *Flying Cloud* took eighty-nine days and eight hours to make the distance from New York to San Francisco, around Cape Horn, a speed that steamships took several decades to equal. But clippers, while fast, lacked ample cargo space, and after the Civil War would give way to the steamship.

THE ROLE OF GOVERNMENT   The massive internal improvements of the era were the product of both state government and private initiatives, sometimes undertaken jointly and sometimes separately. Private investment accounted for nearly all the turnpikes in New England and the Middle States. Elsewhere states invested heavily in turnpike companies and in some cases, notably South Carolina and Indiana, themselves built and owned the turnpikes. Canals were to a much greater extent the product of state investment, and more commonly state owned and operated. The Panic of 1837, however, caused states to pull back and leave railroad development mainly to private corporations. Most of the railroad capital came from private sources. Still, government had an enormous role in railroad development. Several states of the South and West built state-owned lines, although they generally looked to private companies to handle actual operations and in some cases sold the lines. States and localities along the routes invested in railroad corporations and granted loans; states were generous in granting charters and tax concessions.

The federal government helped too, despite the constitutional scruples of some officials against direct involvement. The government bought stock in turnpike and canal companies, and after the success of the Erie, extended land grants to several western states for the support of canal projects. Congress provided for railroad surveys by government engineers, and reduced the tariff duties on iron used in railroad con-

Trade and Commerce Quilt, 1830. *In this panel, passengers on a steamboat watch a sailor at work.*

struction. In 1850 Senator Stephen A. Douglas of Illinois and others prevailed on Congress to extend a major land grant to support a north-south line connecting Chicago with Mobile, Alabama. Grants of three square miles on alternate sides for each mile of railroad subsidized the building of the Illinois Central and the Mobile and Ohio Railroads. Regarded at the time as a special case, the 1850 grant set a precedent for other bounties that totaled about 20 million acres by 1860—a small amount compared to the grants for transcontinental lines in the Civil War decade.

THE GROWTH OF INDUSTRY

While the South and West developed the agricultural basis for a national economy, the Northeast was laying foundations for an industrial revolution. Technology in the form of the cotton gin, the harvester, and improvements in transportation had quickened agricultural development and to some extent decided its direction. But technology altered the economic landscape even more profoundly by giving rise to the factory system.

EARLY TEXTILE MANUFACTURES   At the end of the colonial period, manufacturing remained in the household or handicraft stage of development, or at most the "putting-out" stage, in which the merchant capitalist would distribute raw materials (say, leather patterns for shoes) to be worked up at home, then collected and sold. Farm families themselves had to produce much of what they needed in the way of crude implements, shoes, and clothing, and in their simple workshops inventive genius was sometimes nurtured. As a boy Eli Whitney had set up a forge to make nails in his father's rural workshop. The transition from such production to the factory was slow, but one for which a base had been laid before 1815.

In the eighteenth century Great Britain had jumped out to a long head start in industrial production. The foundations of Britain's advantage were the development of iron smelting by coke when sufficient wood was lacking; the invention of the steam engine in 1705 and its improvement by James Watt in 1765; and a series of inventions that mechanized the production of textiles, including John Kay's flying shuttle (1733), James Hargreaves's spinning jenny (1764), Richard Arkwright's "water frame" (1769), and Samuel Crompton's spinning mule (1779). The water frame was a water-powered spinning machine that twisted carded cotton into thread. The spinning mule could do the work of 200 spinners. Britain carefully guarded its hard-won secrets, forbidding the export of machines or descriptions of them, even restricting the departure of informed mechanics. But the secrets could not be kept. In 1789 Samuel Slater arrived in America from England with the plan of a water frame in his head. He contracted with an enterprising merchant-manufacturer in Rhode Island to build a mill in Pawtucket, and in this little mill, completed in 1790, nine children turned out a satisfactory cotton yarn, which was then worked up by the putting-out system.

The beginnings in textile production were slow and faltering until Jefferson's embargo in 1807 stimulated domestic production. Policies adopted during the War of 1812 restricted imports and encouraged the merchant capitalists of New England to switch their resources into manufacturing. New England, it happened, had the distinct advantage of its many rivers that provided waterpower and water transportation. By 1815 textile mills numbered in the hundreds. A flood of British imports after the War of 1812 dealt a temporary setback to the infant industry, but the foundations of textile manufacture were laid, and they spurred the growth of garment trades and a machine-tool industry to build and service the mills.

New England Factory Village, *1830. Mills and factories gradually transformed the New England landscape in the early nineteenth century.*

TECHNOLOGY IN AMERICA   The practical bent of Americans was one of the outstanding traits noted by foreign visitors. In Europe, where class consciousness prevailed, Alexis de Tocqueville wrote, people confined themselves to "the arrogant and sterile researches of abstract truths, whilst the social condition and institutions of democracy prepare them [Americans] to seek immediate and useful practical results of the sciences." In 1814 Dr. Jacob Bigelow, a Harvard botanist, began to lecture on "The Elements of Technology," a word he did much to popularize. In his book of the same title he argued that technology constituted the chief superiority of moderns over the ancients, effecting profound changes in ways of living.

One of the most striking examples of the connection between pure research and innovation was in the work of Joseph Henry, a Princeton physicist. His research in electromagnetism provided the basis for Samuel F. B. Morse's invention of the telegraph and for electrical motors later on. In 1846 Henry became head of the new Smithsonian Institution, founded with a bequest from the Englishman James Smithson "for the increase and diffusion of knowledge among men." The year 1846 also saw the founding of the American Association for the Advancement of Science.

It would be difficult to exaggerate the importance of science and technology in changing the ways people live. All aspects of life—the social, cultural, economic, and political—were and are shaped by it. To cite but a few examples: improved transportation and a spreading market economy combined with innovations in canning and refrigeration to provide people a more healthy and varied diet. Fruit and vegetables, heretofore available only during harvest season, could be shipped in much of the year. Scientific breeding of cattle helped make meat and milk more abundant.

Technological advances also helped improve living conditions: houses were larger, better heated, and better illuminated. Although working-class residences had few creature comforts, the affluent were able to afford indoor plumbing, central heating, gas lighting, bathtubs, iceboxes, and sewing machines. Even the lower classes were able to afford new coal-burning cast-iron cooking stoves that facilitated the preparation of more varied meals and improved heating. The first sewer systems began to help rid city streets of human and animal waste, while underground water lines enabled fire companies to use hydrants rather than bucket brigades. Machine-made clothes fit better and were cheaper than homespun; newspapers and magazines were more abundant and affordable, as were clocks and watches. Invention often brought about completely new enterprises, the steamboat and the railroad being the most spectacular, without which the pace of development would have been slowed immeasurably.

Eli Whitney, whose cotton gin had deeply influenced the development of the South, also developed a basic principle that promoted the industrial growth of the North—mass production. In 1799 he won a government contract for the manufacture of muskets, and in his shop at New Haven developed machine tools to make parts with such precision as to be virtually identical. In a shop twenty miles away, Simeon North began the same year with a contract for pistols. No one can say with assurance which man was the inventor. It was in fact more an evolution in machine tools than an invention, and the original idea seems to have been French. Its perfection, however, was an original American contribution.

Most basic inventions were imports from Europe. Preservation of food by canning, for instance, was unknown before the early nineteenth century, when Americans learned of a new French discovery that food

Daguerreotype of the First Telegraph, *1844. Invented by Samuel Morse, the telegraph epitomized the practical bent of American technology, ultimately enabling Americans to communicate cross-country.*

stayed fresh when cooked in airtight containers. By 1820 major canneries were in existence in Boston and New York. At the end of the 1830s glass containers were giving way to the "tin can" (tin-plated steel) brought in from England, and these were eventually used to market Gail Borden's new invention—a process for condensed milk.

A spate of inventions in the 1840s generated dramatic changes in American life. In 1844 Charles Goodyear patented a process for vulcanizing rubber, which made it stronger and more elastic. In the same year the first intercity telegraph message was transmitted from Baltimore to Washington on the device Samuel Morse had invented back in 1832. The telegraph was slow to catch on at first, but in 1861, seventeen years after that demonstration, with the completion of connections to San Francisco, an entire continent had been wired for instant communication. In 1846 Elias Howe invented the sewing machine, soon improved by Isaac Merritt Singer. The sewing machine, incidentally, actually slowed the progress of the factory. Since it was adapted to use in the home, it gave the "putting-out" system a new lease on life in the clothing industry.

THE LOWELL SYSTEM   Before the 1850s the factory still had not become typical of American industry. Handicraft and domestic production (putting-out) remained common. In many industries they stayed for decades the chief agencies of growth. Hatmaking in Danbury, Connecticut, and shoemaking in eastern Massachusetts, for instance, grew mainly by the multiplication of small shops and their gradual enlargement. Not until the 1850s did either begin to adopt power-driven machinery, usually a distinctive feature of the factory system.

The factory system sprang full-blown upon the American scene at Waltham, Massachusetts, in 1813, in the plant of the Boston Manufacturing Company, formed by the Boston Associates, including Francis Cabot Lowell. Their plant was the first factory in which the processes of spinning and weaving by power machinery were brought under one roof, mechanizing every process—from raw material to finished cloth. In 1822 the Boston Associates developed a new center at a village, renamed Lowell, where the Merrimack River fell thirty-five feet. At this "Manchester of America" the Merrimack Manufacturing Company developed a new plant similar to the Waltham mill.Companies organized on the Waltham plan produced by 1850 a fifth of the nation's total output of cotton cloth. The chief features of this plan were large capital investment, the concentration of all processes in one plant under unified

The cotton mills at Lowell, Massachusetts, 1852.

management, and specialization in a relatively coarse cloth requiring minimum skill by the workers.

The founders of the enterprise sought to establish at Lowell an industrial center compatible with republican values of plain living and high thinking. During the early decades of the nineteenth century, Jefferson and others had claimed that urban-industrial development threatened a republican form of government rooted in self-reliant agrarianism. Sensitive to this view, Lowell's owners insisted that they could design model factory centers and communities that would strengthen rather than corrupt the social fabric. To avoid the drab, crowded, and wretched life of English mill villages, they located American mills in the countryside and established an ambitious program of paternal supervision for the workers.

The operatives in the Lowell factories were mostly young women from New England farm families. Employers preferred women because they could pay them less than men. Moreover, by the 1820s there was a surplus of females in the region because so many men had migrated westward in search of cheap land and new economic opportunities. As many of the household goods produced by daughters gave way to the "store-bought" goods of a market economy, young farm women faced diminishing prospects for employment as well as for marriage. The chance to escape the routine of farm life and to earn cash money to help the family or improve their own circumstances also drew many women workers to the Lowell mills. As one female mill worker explained, she was working because of "a father's debts . . . to be paid, an aged mother to be supported, a brother's ambition to be aided."

In the early 1820s a steady stream of single women began flocking toward Lowell and the other mill towns cropping up across the region. To reassure worried parents, the mill owners promised to provide the "Lowell girls" with tolerable work, prepared meals, secure and comfortable housing, moral discipline, and a variety of educational and cultural opportunities such as lectures and evening classes.

Initially the "Lowell idea" worked pretty much according to plan. Visitors commented on the well-designed mills with their lecture halls and libraries. The laborers appeared "healthy and happy." The women workers lived in dormitories staffed by matronly supervisors who rigidly enforced mandatory church attendance, temperance regulations, and curfews. Despite their thirteen-hour day and six-day workweek tending the knitting looms, some of the women found the time and energy to form study groups, publish a literary magazine, and attend lectures by Ralph Waldo Emerson and other luminaries of the era. But Lowell soon lost its innocence as it experienced mushrooming growth. By 1840 there were thirty-two mills and factories in operation, and the blissful rural town had become a bustling, grimy, bleak industrial city.

Other factory centers began sprouting up across New England, displacing forests and farms and engulfing villages, filling the air with smoke, noise, and stench. As early as 1832 the writer Washington Irving lamented that the "march of mechanical invention is driving everything poetical before it." Between 1820 and 1840 the number of Americans engaged in manufactures increased eightfold, and the number of city dwellers more than doubled.

Booming growth transformed the Lowell experiment in industrial republicanism. By 1846 a concerned worker told those young farm women thinking about taking a job in a factory that they would do well not to leave their "homes in the country. It will be better for you to stay at home on your fathers' farms than to run the risk of being ruined in a manufacturing village." The problem of the degeneration of morals attributed to life in the factory towns was accompanied by the emergence of class consciousness and labor unrest among the supposedly contented workers.

During the 1830s, as textile prices and mill wages dropped, relations between workers and managers rapidly deteriorated. A new generation of owners and foremen began stressing efficiency and profit margins over community values. They worked their machines and operatives at a faster pace, and the women workers organized strikes to protest deteriorating working conditions. In 1834, for instance, they unsuccessfully "turned out" (struck) against the mills after learning of a sharp cut in their wages. Visitors noted the growing similarity between Lowell and the dismal factory towns of England immortalized in Dickens's *Hard Times*.

The "Lowell girls" drew attention less because they were typical than because they were special. An increasingly common pattern for industry was the family system, sometimes called the Rhode Island or Fall River system, which prevailed in textile manufactures outside of northern New England. The Rhode Island factories, which relied on waterpower, often were built in unpopulated areas, and part of their con-

Women Workers inside a Textile Mill. *Although mill work once provided women with an opportunity for independence and education, conditions soon deteriorated as profits took precedence over the workers.*

struction included tenements or mill villages. Whole families might be hired, the men for heavy labor, the women and children for the lighter work. Like the Lowell model, the Rhode Island system promoted paternalism. Employers dominated the life of the mill villages, often setting rules of good behavior. Wages under the system are hard to establish, for employers frequently paid in goods from the company store. The hours of labor often ran from sunup to sunset, and longer in winter—a sixty-eight- to seventy-two-hour week. Such hours were common on the farms of the time, but in factories the work was more intense and offered no seasonal letup. The labor of children, common on the farm, excited little censure from communities still close to the soil. A common opinion at the time regarded the provision of gainful employment for the women and children of the "lower orders" as a community benefit.

CORPORATIONS AND INDUSTRY   Early American manufacturing firms usually took the form of individual proprietorships, family enterprises, or partnerships. However, the growing scale and complexity of business affairs led more and more firms to "incorporate" ownership. The success of the Boston Associates at Waltham and Lowell, and the

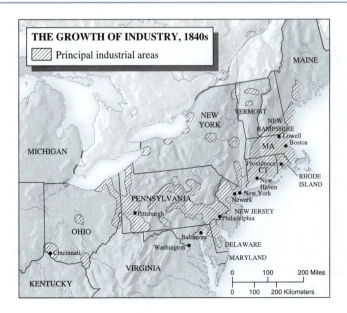

THE GROWTH OF INDUSTRY, 1840s

Principal industrial areas

growth of larger units, particularly in textiles, brought the corporate form into greater use. But until 1860 most manufacturing was carried on by unincorporated enterprises.

The corporate organization was more common for banking, turnpike, canal, and railroad companies, since many people then believed that the form should be reserved for such quasi-public and quasi-monopolistic functions. The irregular practices of wildcat banks also gave corporations a bad name in local communities throughout the period. Corporations were regarded with suspicion as the beneficiaries of special privileges, and as threats to individual enterprises. It would be years before corporations were widely regarded as agencies of free enterprise.

While most of the country remained wedded to agriculture, industry was heavily concentrated in the Northeast. In southern New England, especially its coastal regions, and along the Hudson and Delaware Rivers, the concentration of industry rivaled that in any of the industrialized parts of Britain and exceeded that in most parts of Europe. In all, American industry in 1860 employed 1,311,000 workers in 140,000 establishments; with a capital investment of just over $1 billion, output amounted to $1.9 billion (up significantly from 1810's total output of $149 million), of which the value added by manufacturing was $854 million.

A photograph of Boston in 1860 made from an aerial balloon.

INDUSTRY AND CITIES   The rapid growth of commerce and industry impelled a rapid growth of cities. Using the census definition of "urban" as places with 8,000 inhabitants or more, the proportion of urban population grew from 3 percent in 1790 to 16 percent in 1860. Modern cities have served three major economic functions: they have been centers of trade and distribution, centers of manufacturing, and centers of administration. Until near the mid–nineteenth century American cities grew mainly in response to the circumstances of transportation and trade. Because of their strategic locations, the four great Atlantic seaports of New York, Philadelphia, Baltimore, and Boston held throughout the pre–Civil War period the relative positions of leadership they had gained by the end of the Revolution. New Orleans became the nation's fifth-largest city from the time of the Louisiana Purchase. Its focus on cotton exports, to the neglect of imports, however, eventually caused it to lag behind its eastern competitors. New York outpaced all its competitors and the nation as a whole in its population growth. By 1860 it was the first American city to reach a population of more than a million, largely because of its superior harbor and its unique access to commerce.

Pittsburgh, at the head of the Ohio River, was already a center of iron production by 1800, and Cincinnati, at the mouth of the Little Miami, soon surpassed all other meatpacking centers, with pork a specialty. Louisville, because it stood at the falls of the Ohio, became an impor-

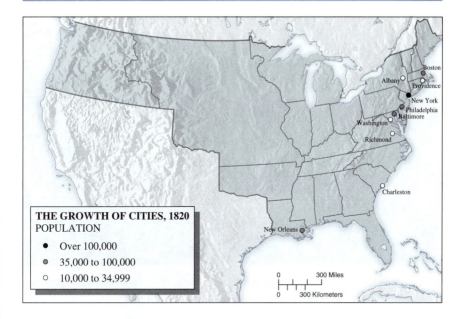

THE GROWTH OF CITIES, 1820
POPULATION
● Over 100,000
◉ 35,000 to 100,000
○ 10,000 to 34,999

tant stop for trade and remained so after the short Louisville and Portland Canal bypassed the falls in 1830. On the Great Lakes the leading cities also stood at important breaking points in water transportation: Buffalo, Cleveland, Detroit, Chicago, and Milwaukee. Chicago was well

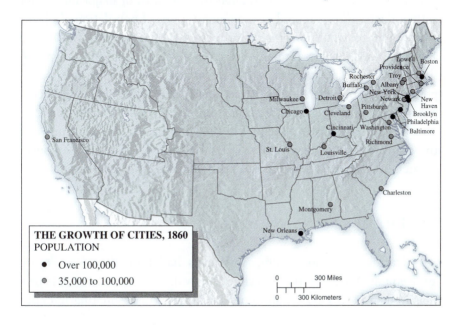

THE GROWTH OF CITIES, 1860
POPULATION
● Over 100,000
◉ 35,000 to 100,000

Broadway and Canal Street, New York City, 1836. *New York's economy and industry and those of many cities rapidly grew before the 1840s.*

located to become a hub of both water and rail transportation on into the trans-Mississippi West. During the 1830s St. Louis tripled in size mainly because most of the trans-Mississippi fur trade was funneled down the Missouri River. By 1860 St. Louis and Chicago were positioned to challenge Boston and Baltimore for third and fourth places.

Before 1840 commerce dominated the activities of major cities, but early industry often created new concentrations of population at places convenient to waterpower or raw materials. During the 1840s and 1850s, however, the stationary steam engine and declining transportation costs more and more offset the advantages of locations near waterpower and resources, and the attractions of older cities were enhanced: pools of experienced labor, capital, warehousing and trading services, access to information, the savings of bulk purchasing and handling, and the many amenities of city life. Urbanization thus was both a consequence of economic growth and a positive force in its promotion.

THE POPULAR CULTURE

During the colonial era, Americans had little time for play or amusement. Their priority was sheer survival. In rural areas people participated in barn raisings and corn-husking parties, shooting matches and foot races, while on the seacoast people sailed and fished. In colonial cities people attended balls, sleigh rides, picnics, and played "parlor games" at home—billiards, cards, and chess.

By the early nineteenth century, however, a more settled and more urban society could indulge in more diverse forms of recreation. As more people moved into cities in the first half of the nineteenth century, they began to create a distinctive urban culture. Laborers and shopkeepers sought new forms of leisure and entertainment as pleasant diversions from their long workdays.

URBAN RECREATION   In working-class neighborhoods at mid-century, young men formed volunteer fire companies and fraternal societies whose primary activities were drinking and gambling. The more affluent and educated people viewed leisure time as an opportunity for self-improvement and attended lectures by prominent figures such as Ralph Waldo Emerson and minister Henry Ward Beecher. Circuses began touring the country. Foot races, horse races, and boat races began attracting thousands of spectators. Nearly 100,000 people attended a horse race at Union Track on Long Island.

So-called blood sports were also a popular form of amusement. Cockfighting and dogfighting at saloons attracted excited crowds and frenzied betting. Prizefighting (also known as boxing) eventually displaced the animal contests. Imported from Britain, boxing surged into prominence at mid-century, and then, as now, proved popular with all

A Day at the Races. *Pictured here is Peytona and Fashion's great match for a $20,000 purse, Union Course, Long Island, May 13, 1845.*

Bare Knuckles. *Blood sports emerged as popular entertainment in the cities for men of all social classes.*

social classes. The early contestants tended to be Irish or English immigrants, often sponsored by a neighborhood fire company, fraternal association, or street gang. Prizefighting, like many other professional sports, became a popular vehicle for the immigrant working poor to better their condition.

In the antebellum era, contestants fought with bare knuckles, and the results were brutal. A match ended only when a contestant could not continue. One such bout in 1842 lasted 119 rounds and ended when one fighter died in his corner. Such mortal matches prompted clergymen to condemn prizefighting, and several cities outlawed the practice, only to see it reappear as an underground activity.

THE PERFORMING ARTS   The most popular form of indoor entertainment was theatrical. During the first half of the nineteenth century, the theater played the popular role that movie houses would provide in the first half of the twentieth century. People of all classes flocked to opera houses and theaters to watch a wide spectrum of performances: Shakespeare's tragedies, "blood and thunder" melodramas, comedies, minstrels, operas, magic shows, acrobatic troupes, and local pageants.

The audiences were predominantly young and middle-aged men. "Respectable" women were deterred from attending because of the boisterous atmosphere and the prevailing cult of domesticity that kept women in the home. Most antebellum theaters divided the classes and races into separate seating areas. In the orchestra pit directly in front of the stage were men from the "middling" class. The more affluent patrons, those of the "first respectability and fashion," sat in the first two tiers of boxes. The third tier of boxes usually hosted prostitutes and their pimps and clients, on whose patronage the theaters depended for their profits. Above the boxes, in the upper reaches of the balcony, were the "cheap seats," occupied by artisans, mechanics, apprentices, servants, and blacks.

Behavior in antebellum theaters was raucous and at times disorderly. People went to the theater not simply to watch the performances but also to socialize, to see and be seen, to talk business and gossip. Patrons were participants as well as spectators. Audiences cheered the heroes and heroines and hissed the villains. They often joined the actors in reciting famous passages or yelled out the punch lines for familiar jokes. If an actor did not meet expectations, audiences would hurl epithets, nuts, eggs, fruit, shoes, or chairs. A riot broke out in 1817 when an English actor at a New York theater refused to stop his prepared performance and comply with patrons' demands that he sing "Black-Eyed Susan." New York's Astor Place riot of 1849, provoked by a violent quarrel between rival American and English actors, and fed by seething anti-English feelings among Irish Americans living in New York, resulted in thirty-one deaths.

By mid-century, the arbiters of taste dealt with the problem of cultural rowdiness by creating separate theaters for the genteel elite and for laboring folk. As historian Lawrence Levine has remarked, the theaters and opera houses "no longer functioned as an expressive form that embodied all classes within a shared public space." Theaters grew darker, quieter, and more secure; audiences grew more affluent and passive.

MINSTREL SHOWS   The 1830s witnessed the emergence of the first uniquely American form of mass entertainment: the blackface minstrel show. Rooted in an old tradition of folk theatricals, the minstrel shows featured white performers made up as blacks. "Minstrelsy" drew upon African-American subjects and reinforced prevailing racial stereotypes. It featured banjo and fiddle music, "shuffle" dances, and low-brow humor. Between the 1830s and 1870s, the minstrel shows were immensely popular throughout the nation, especially among northern

Minstrel Show at the American Theater in New York City, 1833. *Thomas "Daddy" Rice performing in blackface as Jim Crow imitated African-American songs and dances. Minstrel shows enjoyed national popularity but reinforced racial stereotypes.*

working-class ethnics and southern whites, who were eager to flaunt their presumed superiority to blacks. The shows expanded to include entire troupes of performers who would tour the country, often using riverboats as their means of transportation, giving performances that would include jokes, sentimental songs, dances, comedy routines, and skits.

The two most famous minstrel performers were George Washington Dixon, who invented a character named "Zip Coon," and Thomas "Daddy" Rice, who popularized a song-and-dance routine called "Jump Jim Crow." Wearing ragged clothes, Rice would perform a shuffle dance while singing, "I jump 'jis so / An' ev'y time I turn about I jump Jim Crow." Rice claimed that the inspiration for his act was an old Louisville slave belonging to Jim Crow whom he saw entertaining other workers at a livery stable. Also famous were the Christy Minstrels, who toured the country with a show that always began with a master of ceremonies exchanging jokes with the two star performers, Mr. Bones and Mr. Tambo, whose names were derived from the two instruments they played, the tambourine and polished wood "bones," which sounded like castanets.

The most popular minstrel songs were written by a young composer named Stephen Foster. Born into a Scotch-Irish family in Pittsburgh on July 4, 1826, Foster was a self-taught musician who could pick up any tune by ear. By age fourteen he was composing songs on the piano. In 1846 he composed a song named "Oh! Susanna." It immediately became a national favorite, and by 1849 there were fifteen different editions of the sheet music in print. The popularity of "Oh! Susanna" catapulted Foster into the national limelight, and he followed it with equally popular tunes such as "Massa's in de Cold, Cold Ground," "Old Folks at Home" (popularly known as "Way Down upon the Suwanee River"), "Old Black Joe," and "My Old Kentucky Home," all of which perpetuated the sentimental myth of contented slaves, and none of which used actual African-American melodies.

Although antebellum minstrel shows usually portrayed slaves as blissfully contented and caricatured free blacks in the North as superstitious buffoons who preferred slavery to freedom, minstrelsy represented more than an expression of virulent racism and white exploitation of black culture; it also provided a medium for the expression of authentic African-American art forms.

IMMIGRATION

Amid all the new economic growth and urban development, one condition of American life carried over beyond the mid–nineteenth century: land remained plentiful and relatively cheap, while labor was scarce and relatively dear. A decline in the birthrate coinciding with the onset of industry and urbanization reinforced this condition. The United States remained a strong magnet for immigrants, offering them chances to take up farms in the country or jobs in the cities. Glowing reports from early arrivals who made good reinforced romantic views of American opportunity and freedom. "Tell Miriam," one immigrant wrote back, "there is no sending children to bed without supper, or husbands to work without dinner in their bags." A German immigrant in Missouri applauded the "absence of overbearing soldiers, haughty clergymen, and inquisitive tax collectors."

During the forty years from the outbreak of the Revolution until the end of the War of 1812, immigration had slowed to a trickle. The

French Revolution and the Napoleonic Wars restricted travel until 1815. Within a few years, however, packet lines had begun to cross the North Atlantic, and competing shippers who needed westbound payloads kept the transatlantic fares as low as $30 per person. One informed estimate revealed that from 1783 to 1819 total arrivals numbered about 250,000, or something under 7,000 per year. Thereafter the pace followed just behind the growth of business. For two decades the numbers rose steadily: 10,199 in 1825; 23,322 in 1830; 84,066 in 1840. After 1845 the tempo picked up rapidly. During the 1830s, total arrivals had numbered fewer than 600,000. In the 1840s almost three times as many, or 1.7 million, immigrated, and during the 1850s 2.6 million more came. The years from 1845 to 1854 saw the greatest proportionate influx of immigrants in American history, 2.4 million, or about 14.5 percent of the total population in 1845.

During the early 1800s most European immigrants entered the United States through the Port of New York. Ships would discharge passengers at wharves, and the newcomers would immediately have to fend for themselves in their alien environment. Before long thieves, thugs, and wily con men began preying upon the new arrivals. The infectious diseases that many of the immigrants brought with them also aroused popular concern. In 1855 the problems associated with the immigrants' arrival in America provoked the New York state legislature to lease Castle Garden, at the southern tip of Manhattan, for use as an immigration receiving center. Inside the depot, clerks would record the names, nationalities, and destinations of the new arrivals, physicians would give them a cursory physical exam, and labor bureau representatives would assist them in seeking jobs.

THE IRISH   In 1860 America's population was 31 million, with more than one of every eight foreign-born. The largest groups among them were 1.6 million Irish, 1.2 million Germans, and 588,000 British (mostly English). The Irish had a long-standing reason for migrating from their country: resentment of British rule, British landlords, British Protestantism, and British taxes. But what caused so many Irish to flee their homeland in the nineteenth century was the onset of a prolonged depression that brought immense social hardship. The most densely populated country in Europe, Ireland was so ravaged by the economic collapse that in rural areas the average age at death declined to nineteen.

In 1847, nearly 214,000 Irish emigrated to the United States and Canada aboard ships of the White Star Line and other companies. Thirty percent of these immigrants died on board, despite company promises of "unusually spacious, well lighted, ventilated, and warmed" steerage accommodations.

By the 1830s, the number of Irish migrants to America was growing quickly, and after an epidemic of potato rot in 1845 brought famine to rural Ireland that killed more than a million peasants, the flow of Irish immigrants to Canada and the United States rose to a flood. Buoyed by the promise of a better life in America, the immigrants braved the Atlantic crossing, in crowded and unsanitary conditions. Thousands died of dysentery, typhus, and malnutrition during the six-week ocean crossing. So many people died on the leaky, crowded vessels that they came to be called "coffin ships." In 1847 alone, 40,000 Irish perished aboard the overcrowded ships. "If crosses and tombs could be erected on water," lamented the United States commissioner for immigration, "the whole route of the emigrant vessels from Europe to America would long since have assumed the appearance of a crowded cemetery."

In 1847 Irish arrivals numbered above 100,000, and Irish immigration stayed above that level for eight years, reaching a peak of 221,000 in 1851. By 1850 the Irish constituted 43 percent of the foreign-born population in the United States. Unlike the German immigrants, who were predominantly male, the Irish newcomers were more evenly apportioned by sex; in fact a slight majority of them were women, most of them single young adults. Most of the Irish arrivals had been tenant farmers, but their rural sufferings left them little taste for farm work and little money to travel or buy land in America. Great numbers of the men hired on with construction gangs building the canals and rail-ways—about 3,000 set to work on the Erie Canal as early as 1818. Others worked in iron foundries, steel mills, warehouses, and ship-yards. Many Irish women found jobs as domestic servants, laundresses, or textile mill workers in New England. In 1845 the Irish constituted only 8 percent of the workforce in the Lowell mills; by 1860 they made up 50 percent. Although there were substantial Irish communities in New Orleans, Vicksburg, and Memphis, relatively few immigrants dur-ing the Jacksonian era found their way into the South, where land was expensive and industries scarce. The widespread use of slaves also left few opportunities in the region for free manual laborers.

Too poor to move inland, most of the destitute Irish congregated in the eastern cities, in or near their port of entry. By the 1850s the Irish made up over half the populations of Boston and New York City, and they were almost as prominent in Philadelphia. They clustered in murky slums and around Catholic churches, both of which became fa-miliar features of the urban scene. Life in America beat starvation at home, but their new situation was anything but comfortable. Irish new-comers crowded into filthy, poorly ventilated tenements, plagued by high rates of crime, infectious disease, prostitution, alcoholism, and in-fant mortality. The archbishop of New York City at mid-century de-scribed the Irish as "the poorest and most wretched population that can be found in the world."

But many enterprising Irish immigrants seized opportunities in their new environment to forge remarkable success stories. Twenty years af-ter arriving in New York, Alexander T. Stewart became the owner of America's largest department store and thereafter accumulated vast real-estate holdings in Manhattan. Michael Cudahy, who began work in a Milwaukee meatpacking business at age fourteen, became head of the Cudahy Packing Company and developed the process for the summer curing of meats under refrigeration. Dublin-born Victor Herbert emerged as one of America's most revered composers, and Irish dancers and playwrights came to dominate the American stage. Irishmen were equally successful in the boxing arena and on the baseball diamond.

These accomplishments did little to quell the acute anti-Irish senti-ments prevalent in nineteenth-century America. Irish immigrants confronted demeaning stereotypes and intense anti-Catholic prejudices. It was commonly assumed that the Irish were ignorant, filthy, clannish folk incapable of assimilation. George Templeton Strong, a prominent New York civic leader, expressed the contempt felt by many of his peers toward the Irish when he said: "Our Celtic fellow citizens are almost as remote from us in temperament and constitution as the Chinese." Many employers felt the same way, and "No Irish Need Apply" signs sprouted in every eastern city. But the Irish could be equally contemptuous of other groups, such as free African Americans who competed with them for low-status jobs. In 1850 the *New York Tribune* expressed consternation at the fact that the Irish, having themselves escaped from "a galling, degrading bondage" in their homeland, typically voted against any proposal for equal rights for the Negro and frequently arrived at the polls shouting, "Down with the Nagurs! Let them go back to Africa, where they belong." For their part, many African Americans viewed the Irish with equal disdain. In 1850 a slave expressed a common sentiment: "My Master is a great tyrant, he treats me badly as if I were a common Irishman."

In part because of the hostility they faced, the Irish communities in American cities retained much of their ethnic and cultural identity. Neighborhood newspapers, churches, political groups, saloons, volunteer fire companies, and fraternal associations such as the Friendly Sons of St. Patrick bolstered a sense of community. Especially popular were Irish militia companies with colorful names: the Jasper Greens, Napper Tandy Light Artillery, and Irish Rifles. The Hibernian Society and the Shamrock Society aided Irish immigrants, and Irish newspapers such as the *Boston Pilot* remain in circulation today.

Experienced at organized resistance to rent and tax collectors in their homeland, the Irish after becoming naturalized citizens formed powerful blocs of voters and found their way into American politics more quickly than any other immigrant group. Drawn mainly to the party of Jackson, they set a crucial pattern of identification with the Democrats that other ethnic groups by and large followed. In Jackson the Irish immigrants found a hero. Himself the son of Irish colonists, he was also popular for having defeated the hated British at New Orleans. In addition, the Irish loathing of aristocracy, which they associated with British rule, attracted them to the party claiming to represent "the common man." Although property requirements initially kept most Irish Ameri-

Anti-immigrant cartoon showing drunken Irish and German immigrants making off with a ballot box.

cans from voting, a New York state law extended the franchise in 1821, and five years later the state removed the property qualification altogether. In 1828 masses of Irish voters made the difference in the election between Jackson and John Quincy Adams. One newspaper expressed alarm at this new force in politics: "Every thing in the shape of an Irishman was drummed to the polls and their votes made to pass. . . . It was emphatically an Irish triumph. The foreigners have carried the day." Although women, African Americans, and Native Americans still could not vote, the Irish newcomers were able to use the franchise to exert a remarkable political influence.

Perhaps the greatest collective achievement of the Irish immigrants was stimulating the growth of the Catholic church in the United States. Years of persecution had instilled in Irish Catholics a fierce loyalty to the doctrines of the church, leading one Irish American to proclaim that religion "overrides all other sovereigns, and has the supreme authority over all the affairs of the world." Such passionate attachment to Catholicism generated both community cohesion among Irish Americans and fears of Romanism among American Protestants. By 1860 Catholics had become the largest single denomination in the United States.

THE GERMANS During the eighteenth century, Germans had responded to William Penn's offer of free religious expression and cheap, fertile land by coming in large numbers to America. As a consequence, when a new wave of German migration formed in the 1830s, there were still large enclaves of Germans in Pennsylvania and Ohio who had preserved their language and cultures, and in the Old World style had clustered in agricultural villages.

The new German migration took on a markedly different cast. It peaked in 1854, just a few years after the crest of Irish arrivals, when 215,000 Germans disembarked in American ports. These immigrants included a large number of learned, cultured professional people—doctors, lawyers, teachers, engineers—some of them refugees from the failed German revolutions of 1830 and 1848. In addition to an array of political opinions ranging from laissez-faire conservatism to Marxism, the Germans brought with them a variety of religious preferences. A third of the new arrivals were Catholic, most were Protestants (usually Lutherans), and a significant number were Jewish or freethinking atheists or agnostics. By the end of the century, some 250,000 German Jews had emigrated to America.

Unlike the Irish, the Germans settled more in rural areas than cities, and they included many independent farmers, skilled workers, and shopkeepers who arrived with some means to get themselves established in skilled jobs or on the land. More so than the Irish, they migrated in families and groups rather than as individuals, and this clannish quality helped them better sustain elements of German language and culture in their New World environment. More of them also tended to return to their native country. About 14 percent of the Germans eventually went back to their homeland, compared to 9 percent of the Irish.

Among the German immigrants who prospered in the New World were Ferdinand Schmacher, who began peddling oatmeal in glass jars in Ohio and eventually formed the Quaker Oats Company; Heinrich Steinweg, a piano maker from Lower Saxony, who in America changed his name to Steinway and became famous for the quality of his pianos; and Levi Strauss, a Jewish tailor who followed the gold rushers to California and began making long-wearing work pants that later were dubbed blue jeans or Levi's. Carl Schurz, another German immigrant, became a general in the Union army, represented Missouri in the Sen-

German Beer Garden, New York, *1825. German immigrants settled their own communities and retained traditions from their homeland.*

ate, and served as secretary of the interior under President Hayes. Major centers of German settlement developed in Missouri and southwestern Illinois (around St. Louis), in Texas (near San Antonio), in Ohio, and in Wisconsin (especially around Milwaukee). The larger German communities developed traditions of bounteous food, beer, and music along with German *Turnvereine* (gymnastic societies), sharpshooter clubs, fire engine companies, and kindergartens.

THE BRITISH, SCANDINAVIANS, AND CHINESE   Among the British immigrants too were large numbers of professionals, independent farmers, and skilled workers. Some British workers, such as Samuel Slater, helped transmit the technology of British factories into the United States. Two other groups that began to arrive in some number during the 1840s and 1850s were just the vanguard of greater numbers to come. Annual arrivals from Scandinavia did not exceed 1,000 until 1843, but by 1860 a total of 72,600 Scandinavians lived in America. The Norwegians and Swedes gravitated to Wisconsin and Minnesota, where the climate and woodlands reminded them of home. By the 1850s, the sudden development of California was bringing in Chinese who, like the Irish in the East, did the heavy work of construction. Infinitesimal in numbers until 1854, the Chinese in America numbered 35,500 by 1860.

NATIVISM   America had always been a land of immigrants, but the welcome accorded them had often been less than cordial. For many natives these waves of strangers in the land posed a threat of unknown languages and mysterious customs. The flood of Irish and German Catholics aroused Protestant hostility to "popery." A militant Protestantism growing out of the revivals in the early nineteenth century heated up the climate of opinion. There were fears of political radicalism among the Germans and of voting blocs among the Irish, but above all hovered the menace of unfamiliar religious practices. Catholic authoritarianism was widely perceived as a threat to hard-won liberties, religious and political.

In the 1830s nativism was conspicuously on the rise. Samuel F. B. Morse, already at work on his telegraph, took time out from his painting and inventing to write two books claiming that Catholicism in America was a plot of foreign monarchs to undermine American liberty before its revolutionary message affected their own people. In 1836 he ran for mayor of New York on a Native American ticket, and his books went through numerous editions.

At times this hostility rekindled the spirit of the wars of religion. In 1834 a series of anti-Catholic sermons by Lyman Beecher, a popular Congregational minister who served as president of Lane Seminary in Cincinnati, aroused feelings to the extent that a mob attacked and burned the Ursuline Convent in Charlestown, Massachusetts. In 1844 armed clashes between Protestants and Catholics in Philadelphia ended with about 20 killed and 100 injured. Sporadically, the nativist spirit took organized form in groups that proved their patriotism by hating foreigners and Catholics.

As early as 1837 a Native American Association was formed in Washington, but the most significant such group was the Order of the Star Spangled Banner, founded in New York in 1849. Within a few years this group had grown into a formidable third party. In 1854 delegates from thirteen states gathered to form the American party, which had the trappings of a secret fraternal order. Members pledged never to vote for any foreign-born or Catholic candidate. When asked about the organization, they were to say "I know nothing." In popular parlance the American party became the Know-Nothing party. For a season it seemed that the American party might achieve major-party status. In state and local campaigns during 1854 the Know-Nothings carried one election after another. They swept the Massachusetts legislature, winning all but two seats in the lower house. That fall they elected more than forty congressmen. For a while they threatened to control New England, New York, and Maryland, and showed strength elsewhere, but the anti-Catholic movement subsided when slavery became the focal issue of the 1850s (it would be exploited again by the new Republican party).

The Know-Nothings demanded the exclusion of immigrants and Catholics from public office and the extension of the period for naturalization from five to twenty-one years, but the party never gathered the political strength to effect such legislation. Nor did Congress act during the period to restrict immigration in any way. The first federal law on immigration, passed in 1819, enacted only safety and health regulations regarding supplies and the number of passengers on immigrant ships. This and subsequent acts designed to protect immigrants from overcrowding and unsanitary conditions were, however, poorly enforced.

A Know-Nothing cartoon showing the Catholic church attempting through Irish immigration to control American religious and political life.

ORGANIZED LABOR

As early as the colonial period, craftsmen had formed fraternal and mutual-benefit societies, much like the medieval guilds, through which they regulated a system for training apprentices. These organizations continued to flourish well into the national period. After the Revolution, however, organizations of journeymen carpenters, masons, shipfitters, tailors, printers, and cordwainers (as shoemakers were called) became concerned with wages, hours, and working conditions and began to back up their demands with such devices as the strike and the closed shop (in which only union members could work). These organizations were local, often largely social in purpose, and frequently lasted only for the duration of the dispute.

During the 1820s and 1830s, artisans who emphasized quality and craftsmanship for a custom trade found it hard to meet the competitive conditions created by the high production and low prices of mass production in factories. At this time, few workers belonged to unions, but a growing fear that they were losing status led artisans of the major cities into intense activity in labor politics and unions.

EARLY UNIONS   Early labor unions faced serious legal obstacles. Unions were prosecuted as unlawful conspiracies. In 1806, for instance, Philadelphia shoemakers were found guilty of a "combination to raise their wages." The decision broke the union. Such precedents were used for many years to hamstring labor organizations until the Massachusetts Supreme Court made a landmark ruling in the case of *Commonwealth* v. *Hunt* (1842). In this case the court ruled that forming a trade union was not in itself illegal, nor was a demand that employers hire only members of the union.

Until the 1820s, labor organizations took the form of local trade unions, confined to one city and one craft. During the ten years from 1827 to 1837, organization on a larger scale began to take hold. In 1834 the National Trades' Union was set up to federate the city societies. At the same time national craft unions were established by the shoemakers, printers, combmakers, carpenters, and hand-loom weavers, but all the national groups and most of the local ones vanished in the economic collapse of 1837.

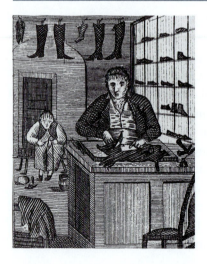

The Shoemaker, *from* The Book of Trades, *1807. When bootmakers and shoemakers in Philadelphia went on strike in 1806, a court found them guilty of a "conspiracy to raise their wages."*

LABOR POLITICS   With the removal nearly everywhere of property qualifications for voting, labor politics flourished briefly. In this, as in other respects, Philadelphia was in the forefront. A Working Men's party, formed there in 1828, gained the balance of power in the city council that fall. This success inspired other Working Men's parties in New York, Boston, and about fifteen states. The Working Men's parties were broad reformist groups devoted to the interests of labor, but they faded quickly because of the inexperience of labor politicians, which left the parties prey to manipulation by political professionals, because some of their issues were also espoused by the major parties, and because of their vulnerability to attack on grounds of extreme radicalism or dilettantism.

Once the parties had faded, many of their supporters found their way into a radical wing of the Jacksonian Democrats. This wing became the Equal Rights party and in 1835 acquired the name "Locofocos" when their opponents from New York City's regular Democratic organization, Tammany Hall, turned off the gas lights at one of their meetings and the Equal Rights supporters produced candles, lighting them with the new friction matches known as Locofocos. The Locofocos soon faded as a separate group, but they endured as a radical faction within the Democratic party.

While the labor parties elected few candidates, they did succeed in drawing notice to their demands, many of which attracted the support of middle-class reformers. Above all they promoted free public education and the abolition of imprisonment for debt, causes that won widespread popular support. The labor parties and unions actively promoted the ten-hour workday. In 1836 President Jackson established the ten-hour workday at the Philadelphia Navy Yard in response to a strike, and in 1840 President Van Buren extended the limit to all government offices and projects. In private jobs the ten-hour workday became increasingly common, although by no means universal, before 1860. Other reforms put forward by the Working Men's parties included mechanics' lien laws, to protect workers against nonpayment of wages; reform of a militia system that allowed the rich to escape service with fines but forced the poor to face jail terms; the abolition of "licensed monopolies," especially banks; measures to ensure hard money and to protect workers against inflated bank-note currency; measures to restrict competition from prison labor; and the abolition of child labor.

LABOR AND REFORM   After the Panic of 1837, the nascent labor movement went into decline, and during the 1840s, the focus of its radical spirit turned toward the promotion of cooperative societies. During the 1830s, there had been sporadic efforts to provide self-employment through producers' cooperatives, but the movement began to catch on after the iron molders of Cincinnati set up a successful shop in 1848. Soon the tailors of Boston had a cooperative workshop that employed thirty to forty men. New York was an especially strong center, with cooperatives among tailors, shirtmakers, bakers, shoemakers, and carpenters. Consumer cooperatives became much more vigorous and involved more people. The New England Protective Union, formed in 1845, organized a central purchasing agency for co-op stores and by 1852 was buying more than $1 million worth of goods while affiliated stores were doing in excess of $4 million in trade.

Most people were drawn to the producers' and consumers' movement for practical reasons: to reduce their dependence on employers or to reduce the cost of purchases. After peaking in the early 1850s, however, the cooperatives went into decline. The high mobility of Americans and the heterogeneous character of the population as immigration increased created unfavorable conditions. Insufficient capital and weak, inexperienced management also plagued the cooperative movement.

THE REVIVAL OF UNIONS   Unions began to revive with improved business conditions in the early 1840s. Still, the unions remained local, weak, and given to sporadic activity. Often they came and went with a single strike. The greatest single labor dispute before the Civil War came on February 22, 1860, when shoemakers at Lynn and Natick, Massachusetts, walked out for higher wages. Before the strike ended, it had spread through New England, involving perhaps twenty-five towns and 20,000 workers. It stood out also because the workers won. Most of the employers agreed to wage increases, and some also agreed to recognize the union as a bargaining agent.

This reflected the growing tendency of workers to view their unions as permanent. Workers began to emphasize the importance of union recognition and regular collective-bargaining agreements. They also shared a growing sense of solidarity. In 1852 the National Typographical Union revived the effort to organize skilled crafts on a national scale. Others followed, and by 1860 about twenty such organizations had appeared, although none was strong enough as yet to do much more than hold national conventions and pass resolutions.

JACKSONIAN INEQUALITY

During the years before the Civil War, the United States had begun to develop a distinctive working class, most conspicuously in the factories and the ranks of common labor, often including many Irish or German immigrants. More and more craftsmen, aware that they were likely to remain wage earners, joined unions to protect their interests. But the American legend of "rags to riches," the image of the self-made man, was a durable myth. Speaking to the Senate in 1832, Henry Clay claimed that almost all the successful factory owners he knew were "enterprising self-made men, who have whatever wealth they possess by patient and diligent labor." The legend had just enough basis in fact to gain credence. John Jacob Astor, the wealthiest man in America, worth more than $20 million at his death in 1848, came of humble if not exactly destitute origins. Son of a minor official in Germany, he arrived in 1784 with little or nothing, made a fortune first on the western fur trade, then parlayed that into a large fortune in New York real estate. But his and similar cases were more exceptional than common.

Research by social historians on the rich in major eastern cities shows that while men of moderate means could sometimes run their inheritances into fortunes by good management and prudent speculation, those who started with the handicaps of poverty and ignorance seldom made it to the top. In 1828 the top 1 percent of New York's families (owning $34,000 or more) held 40 percent of the wealth, and the top 4 percent held 76 percent. Similar circumstances prevailed in Philadelphia, Boston, and other cities.

A supreme irony of the times was that "the age of the common man," "the age of Jacksonian Democracy," seems actually to have been an age of increasing social distinctions. Years before, the colonists had brought to America conceptions of a social hierarchy that during the eighteenth century corresponded imperfectly with the developing reality. In the late eighteenth century, slavery aside, American society probably approached equality more closely than any society with a similar-size population anywhere else in the world. During the last half of the 1700s, one historian has argued, social mobility was higher than either before or since. By the time popular egalitarianism caught up with reality, however, reality was moving back toward greater inequality.

Why this happened is difficult to say, except that the boundless wealth of the untapped frontier narrowed as the land was occupied and claims on various opportunities were staked out. Such developments took place in New England towns even before the end of the seventeenth century. But despite growing social distinctions, it seems likely

Newest Fashions for Women, 1828. *During the Jackson years, social distinctions developed between the working classes and the wealthy. These morning, walking, and evening dresses* (pictured from left to right) *would be for the wives of the rich.*

that the white population of America, at least, was better off than the general run of European peoples. New frontiers, both geographical and technological, raised the level of material well-being for all.

MAKING CONNECTIONS

- Eli Whitney's invention of the cotton gin had a profound effect on southern economic and social development. Chapter 15 describes the economy and society of the Old South in greater detail.

- The westward migration traced in this chapter will increase tremendously in the 1840s, a trend discussed in Chapter 14.

- As this chapter demonstrates, the birth and expansion of railroads in the first half of the nineteenth century were an important part of "The Dynamics of Growth." Chapter 16 shows how a proposal for the first transcontinental railroad had an unexpected side effect: it intensified the debate over the spread of slavery westward.

FURTHER READING

On economic development in the nation's early decades, see Stuart W. Bruchey's *Enterprise: The Dynamic Economy of a Free People* (1990). The classic study of transportation and economic growth is George R. Taylor's *The Transportation Revolution, 1815–1860* (1951). A fresh view is provided in Sarah H. Gordon's *Passage to Union: How the Railroads Transformed American Life, 1829–1929* (1997).

The impact of technology is traced in David J. Jeremy's *Transatlantic Industrial Revolution: The Diffusion of Textile Technologies between Britain and America, 1790–1830s* (1981) and Merritt R. Smith's *Harper's Ferry Armory and the New Technology: The Challenge of Change* (1977). The evolution of the nation's postal system is ably recounted in Richard R. John's *Spreading the News: The American Postal System from Franklin to Morse* (1996).

Paul Johnson's *A Shopkeeper's Millennium: Society and Revivals in Rochester, New York, 1815–1837* (1978) studies the role religion played in the emerging industrial order. The attitude of the worker during this time of transition is surveyed in Edward E. Pessen's *Most Uncommon Jacksonians: The Radical Leaders of the Early Labor Movement* (1967). Detailed case studies of working communities include Anthony F. C. Wallace's *Rockdale: The Growth of an American Village in the Early Industrial Revolution* (1978); Thomas Dublin's *Women at Work: The Transformation of Work and Community in Lowell, Massachusetts, 1826–1860* (1979); Stephan Thernstrom's *Poverty and Progress: Social Mobility in a Nineteenth-Century City* (1964), on Newburyport, Massachusetts; and Sean Wilentz's *Chants Democratic* (1984), on New York City. Walter Licht's *Working for the Railroad: The Organization of Work in the Nineteenth Century* (1983) is rich in detail.

For a fine treatment of urbanization, see Charles N. Glaab and A. Theodore Brown's *A History of Urban America* (1976). A valuable case study is Edward K. Spann's *The New Metropolis: New York City, 1840–1857* (1981). On immigration, see Michael Coffey and Terry Golway, *The Irish in America* (1997). The rise of an indigenous American musical tradition is detailed in Ken Emerson's *Doo-Dah! Stephen Foster and the Rise of American Popular Culture* (1997).

13. AN AMERICAN RENAISSANCE: RELIGION, ROMANTICISM, AND REFORM

CHAPTER ORGANIZER

This chapter focuses on:

- the rise of new religious movements.

- the development of a distinctive American literary culture.

- the variety of social reform movements.

The American novelist Nathaniel Hawthorne once lamented "the difficulty of writing a romance about a country where there is no shadow, no antiquity, no mystery, no picturesque and gloomy wrong." Unlike nations of the Old World, rooted in shadow and mystery, entwined in historic cultures and traditions, the United States was an infant nation swaddled in the ideas of the Enlightenment. Those ideas, most vividly set forth in Jefferson's Declaration of Independence, had in turn a universal application that would influence religion, literature, and various social reform movements.

RATIONAL RELIGION

In the eyes of many if not most American citizens, the "first new nation" had a mission to stand as an example to the world, much as John Winthrop's "city upon a hill" had once stood as an example to erring humanity. The concept of America as having a special mission in fact still carried spiritual overtones, for the religious fervor quickened in the Great Awakening had reinforced the idea of national purpose. In turn the sense of high calling infused the national character with an element of perfectionism—and an element of impatience when reality fell short of expectations. The combination of religious belief and social idealism brought major reforms and advances in human rights. It also brought disappointments that at times festered into cynicism and alienation.

DEISM   The currents of the Enlightenment and the Great Awakening, now mingling, now parting, flowed on into the nineteenth century and in different ways eroded the remnants of Calvinist orthodoxy. As time passed, the image of a just but stern God promising predestined hellfire and damnation gave way to a more optimistic religious outlook. Enlightenment rationalism increasingly stressed humankind's inherent goodness rather than depravity, and it encouraged a belief in social progress and the promise of individual perfectibility.

Many leaders of the Revolutionary War era, such as Thomas Jefferson and Benjamin Franklin, became deists, even while nominally attached to existent churches. Deism, which arose in eighteenth-century Europe, carried the logic of Sir Isaac Newton's image of the world as a smoothly operating machine to its logical conclusion. The God of the deist had planned the universe, built it, set it in motion, and then left it to its own fate. By the use of reason people might grasp the natural laws governing the universe. Thomas Paine in *The Age of Reason* (1794) defined deistic religious duties as "doing justice, loving mercy and endeavoring to make our fellow creatures happy," a message of Quaker-like simplicity. But ever the controversialist, Paine felt obliged to assail the "superstition" of the Scriptures and the existing churches—"human inventions set up to terrify and enslave mankind and monopolize power and profit."

Orthodox believers could hardly distinguish such doctrine from atheism, but Enlightenment rationalism soon began to make deep inroads into American Protestantism. The old Puritan churches around Boston proved most vulnerable to the logic of the Enlightenment. A strain of rationalism had run through Puritan belief in its stress on the need for right reason to interpret the Scriptures. Boston's progress—or some would say degeneration—from Puritanism to prosperity had persuaded many affluent families that they were anything but sinners in the hands of an angry God. Drawn toward more consoling and less strenuous doctrines, some went back to the traditional rites of the Episcopal church. More of them simply dropped or qualified their adherence to Calvinism while remaining in the Congregational churches.

UNITARIANISM AND UNIVERSALISM   By the end of the eighteenth century, many New Englanders were drifting into Unitarianism, a belief that emphasized the oneness and benevolence of God, the inherent goodness of humankind, and the primacy of reason and conscience over established creeds and confessions. People were not inherently depraved, Unitarians stressed; they were capable of doing tremendous good, and *all* were eligible for salvation. One stale jest had it that Unitarians believed in the fatherhood of God, the brotherhood of man, and the neighborhood of Boston. Boston was very much the center of the movement, and it flourished chiefly within Congregational churches that kept their standing in the established order until controversy began to smoke them out. During the early nineteenth century, more and more liberal churches accepted the name of Unitarian.

William Ellery Channing of Boston's Federal Street Church emerged as the most inspiring Unitarian leader. "I am surer that my rational nature is from God," he said, "than that any book is an expression of his will." The American Unitarian Association in 1826 had 125 churches (all but 5 of them in Massachusetts). That same year, when the Presbyterian minister Lyman Beecher moved to Boston, he lamented: "All the literary men of Massachusetts were Unitarian; all the trustees and professors of Harvard College were Unitarian; all the elite of wealth and fashion crowded Unitarian churches."

A parallel movement, Universalism, attracted a different social group: working-class people of more humble status. In 1779 John Murray, who had come from England as a missionary for the new doctrine, founded the first Universalist church at Gloucester, Massachusetts. In 1794 a Universalist convention in Philadelphia organized the sect. Universalism stressed the salvation of all men and women, not just a predestined few. God, they taught, was too merciful to condemn anyone to eternal punishment. The unregenerate would suffer in proportion to their sins, but eventually all souls would come into harmony with God. "Thus, the Unitarians and Universalists were in fundamental agreement," wrote one historian of religion, "the Universalists holding that God was too good to damn man; the Unitarians insisting that man was too good to be damned."

THE SECOND GREAT AWAKENING

By the end of the eighteenth century, Enlightenment secularism had made deep inroads into American thought. Yet for all the impact of rationalism, Americans remained a profoundly religious people—as they have ever since. There was, the perceptive French visitor Alexis de Tocqueville observed, "no country in the world where the Christian religion retains a greater influence over the souls of men than in America." Around 1800, however, fears that secularism was indeed taking root sparked a revival that soon grew into a Second Awakening.

An early revivalist leader, Timothy Dwight, became president of Yale College in 1795 and struggled to purify a place which, in Lyman Beecher's words, had turned into "a hotbed of infidelity," where students openly discussed French radicalism, deism, and things even worse. Like his grandfather, Jonathan Edwards, "Pope Timothy" had the gift of moving both mind and spirit, of reaching both the lettered and the unlettered. The result was a series of revivals that swept the student body and spread to all of New England as well. "Wheresoever students were found," wrote a participant in the 1802 revival, "the reigning impression was, 'surely God is in this place.'"

After its founding in 1808, Jedidiah Morse's Andover Seminary reinforced theological orthodoxy and the revival spirit so forcefully that its location came to be known as "Brimstone Hill." Morse lambasted "the insidious encroachments of *innovation*—that evil and beguiling spirit which is now stalking to and fro in the earth, seeking whom it may devour." To avoid Harvard's fate, Morse and his associates made professors assent to an Andover Creed of double-distilled Calvinism. The religious intensity and periodic revivals at Andover and Yale had their counterparts in many colleges for the next fifty years, since most were under the control of evangelical denominations.

Religious Camp Meeting, c. 1839. *Religious revivals at times so infused people with religious fervor that they went into trances or jerked and twitched. These revivals served as an outlet for pent-up emotion and provided isolated people with social interaction.*

REVIVALS ON THE FRONTIER   In its frontier phase the Second Awakening, like the first, generated great excitement and strange manifestations. It gave birth, moreover, to a new institution, the camp meeting, in which the fires of faith were repeatedly rekindled. Missionaries found ready audiences among lonely frontier folk hungry for spiritual intensity and a sense of community. Religious revivals have long been a mainstay of popular culture. They combine emotional fervor with a spirit of social equality that binds participants together. In the backwoods and in small rural hamlets, the traveling revival was as welcome an event as the traveling circus. And at times they were equally acrobatic.

Among the established sects, the Presbyterians were entrenched among the Scotch-Irish from Pennsylvania to Georgia. They gained further from the Plan of Union worked out in 1801 with the Congregationalists of Connecticut and later with other states. Since the two groups agreed on doctrine and differed mainly on the form of church government, they were able to form unified congregations and call a minister from either church. The result through much of the Old Northwest was that New Englanders became Presbyterians by way of the "Presbygational" churches.

The Baptists embraced a simplicity of doctrine and organization that appealed especially to the common people of the frontier. Their theology was grounded in the infallibility of the Bible and the recognition of humankind's innate depravity. But they replaced the Calvinist notion of predestination with the concept of universal redemption and highlighted the ritual of adult baptism. They also explicitly stressed the equality of all men and women before God, regardless of one's wealth, social standing, or educational training. Since each congregation was its own highest authority, a frontier church need appeal to no hierarchy before setting up shop and calling a minister or naming one of its own. Sometimes whole congregations moved across the mountains as a body. As Theodore Roosevelt later described it: "Baptist preachers lived and worked exactly as their flocks. . . . they cleared the ground, split rails, planted corn, and raised hogs on equal terms with their parishioners."

The Methodists, who shared with Baptists an emphasis on salvation by free will, established a much more centralized church structure, which ironically may have been the most effective evangelical method of all: the circuit rider who sought out people in the most remote areas with the message of salvation as a gift free for the taking. The system began with Francis Asbury, a tireless British-born revivalist who scoured the trans-Appalachian frontier for lost souls, traversing fifteen states, preaching some 25,000 sermons while defying hostile Indians and suffering through harsh winters. Asbury established a mobile evangelism perfectly suited to the frontier environment and the new democratic age.

Peter Cartwright emerged as the most successful Methodist "circuit rider," and he grew justly famous for his highly charged sermons. He recalled stopping at a decaying Baptist church in frontier Kentucky: "While I was preaching, the power of God fell on the assembly, and there was an awful shaking among the dry bones. Several fell to the floor and cried for mercy. . . . I believe if I had opened the doors of the Church then, all of them would have joined the Methodist Church." Cartwright typified the Methodist disdain for an educated clergy, at one point arguing that it was "the illiterate Methodist preachers [who] actually set the world on fire." He was right. By the 1840s the Methodists had grown into the largest Protestant church in the country.

The Great Revival spread quickly through the West and into more settled regions back East. Camp meetings were held typically in late summer or fall, when farm work slackened. People came from far and wide, camping in wagons, tents, or crude shacks. Blacks, whether slave or free, were allowed to set up their own adjacent camp revivals, often separated from the white camp by a plank partition. On the final meeting day of the week, the wall would be taken down, enabling both groups to join in a song festival and a "marching ceremony." The largest camp meetings tended to be ecumenical affairs, with Baptist, Methodist, and Presbyterian ministers working as a team.

The crowds often numbered in the thousands, and the unrestrained atmosphere made for chaos. People participated actively in the services. If a particular hymn or sermon excited someone, they would cry, shout, dance, or repeat the phrase. One visitor at a Kentucky camp revival described it as a "scene of confusion that could scarce be put into human language." A Methodist minister reported that Presbyterians, not being accustomed to such tumultuous religious practices, were particularly susceptible to emotional seizures. Inflamed by the Holy Spirit, they often "went into great excess, and downright wildness." Mass excitement swept up even the most skeptical onlookers, and infusions of the spirit moved participants to strange manifestations. Some went into trances; others contracted the "jerks," laughed the "holy laugh," babbled in unknown tongues, or got down on all fours and barked like dogs to "tree the Devil."

But to dwell on the bizarre aspects of the camp meetings would be to distort an institution that offered a redemptive social outlet to isolated rural folk. This was especially true for women, for whom the camp meetings provided an alternative to the rigors and loneliness of frontier domesticity. Camp meetings also brought a more settled community life through the churches they spawned, and they helped spread a more democratic faith among the frontier people.

THE "BURNED-OVER DISTRICT" Regions swept by such revival fevers might be compared to forests devastated by fire. In 1830–1831 alone, the number of churches in New England grew by one-third. Lyman Beecher called the Awakening of 1831 "the greatest work of God, and the greatest revival of religion, that the world has ever seen." Western New York from Lake Ontario to the Adirondacks and including Rochester experienced such intense levels of evangelical activity that it was labeled the "Burned-Over District."

The most successful evangelist in the "Burned-Over District" was a lawyer named Charles Grandison Finney. In 1839 he preached for six months in Rochester and helped generate 100,000 conversions. Raised in the backwoods of New York, he never heard the name of God mentioned in his home except in profanity. He left home to study law and then began his legal practice in Adams, New York. While visiting the local Presbyterian church, he scoffed when he heard the parishioners praying for revival. Yet Finney's conscience began to gnaw at him. He could not eat or sleep. Finally, one evening in 1821, he fled to the woods on the edge of town and a "mighty baptism of the Holy Ghost overwhelmed him." The next day he announced a new profession: "I have a retainer from the Lord Jesus Christ to plead his case," he told a caller. In 1823 Finney was ordained and for the next decade he subjected the Burned-Over District to yet another scorching.

Finney wrestled with an age-old question that had plagued Protestantism for centuries: What role can the individual play in earning salvation? Orthodox Calvinists had long argued that people could neither earn nor choose salvation on their own accord. Grace was a gift of God, a predetermined decision incapable of human understanding or control. In contrast, Finney insisted that the only thing preventing conversion was the individual. And what most often discouraged individual conversion was the terrifying loneliness of the decision. Finney sought to combat such discomfort and bolster the courage of the ambivalent. He transformed revivals into collective conversion experiences in which spectacular public events displaced private communion and the unregenerate were brought into intense public contact with praying Christians.

Finney did not shrink from comparing his methods to those of politicians who used advertising and showmanship to get attention. "New measures are necessary from time to time to awaken attention and bring the gospel to bear on the public mind." To those who challenged such use of emotion Finney had a frank answer: "The results justify my methods." He carried the methods of the frontier revival into the cities of the East and as far as Great Britain. His gospel combined faith and good works: one led to the other. "All sin consists in selfishness," he said, "and all holiness or virtue, in disinterested benevolence." In 1835 Finney took the chair of theology in the new Oberlin College, founded by pious New Englanders in Ohio's Western Reserve. Later he served as its president. From the start Oberlin radiated a spirit of reform predicated on faith; it was the first college in America to admit either women or blacks, and it was a hotbed of antislavery doctrine.

Yet the ardor aroused by revivals led to narrow sectarian bickerings, repeated schisms, and the phenomenon known as "come-outism," which further multiplied the sects—a result almost always noted by foreign travelers. Revivals created a tremendous demand for preachers, which was met by ordaining men who lacked proper educational credentials. Independent congregations sprang up that recognized no authority other than the Bible. A movement arose independently in western Pennsylvania in 1809 led by Thomas and Alexander Campbell. The Campbellites adopted the name "Christian" and the practice of baptism by immersion. In 1832 a movement started in Lexington, Kentucky, to unite these churches as the Disciples of Christ.

THE MORMONS   The Burned-Over District gave rise to several new religious departures, of which the most important was the Church of Jesus Christ of Latter-day Saints, or the Mormons. The founder, Joseph Smith, Jr., born in Vermont, was the fourth child of wandering parents who finally settled in the village of Palmyra, New York. In 1820 young Smith (then fourteen) had a vision of "two Personages, whose brightness and glory defy all description." They identified themselves as the Savior and God the Father and cautioned him that all existing beliefs were false. About three years later, Smith claimed, an angel led the seventeen-year-old to a hill near his father's farm in upstate New York where he found the Book of Mormon engraved on golden tablets in "reformed Egyptian." Four years later, with the aid of magic stones, he rendered into English what he found to be a lost section of the Bible. This was the story of ancient Hebrews who had inhabited the New World and to whom Jesus had made an appearance.

On the basis of this revelation, Smith began forming his own church in 1830, and within a few years he had gathered converts by the thousands, most of them New Englanders. They found in Mormonism the promise of a pure kingdom of Christ in America and an alternative to the social turmoil and the degrading materialism of the era. Most of the first Mormons were poor farm folk who moved often in search of better lands and lives. Many were believers in popular magic and conjuring; indeed, Smith himself was descended from a long line of village magicians, and both his parents experienced dreams and visions similar to

The Mormon temple sits atop the highest hill in Nauvoo, Illinois, which the Mormons built into a city of 20,000 inhabitants in the early 1840s.

his. The early Mormons were ecstatic worshippers. They fainted at their gatherings, spoke in tongues, healed the sick, interpreted lost languages, levitated, saw visions of the future, and received revelations directly from God.

From the outset the Mormon saints upset the "gentiles" with their close-knit community and their assurance of righteousness. In their search for a refuge from persecution, the Mormons moved from New York to Kirtland, Ohio, where Smith was tarred and feathered, then to several places in Missouri, and finally in 1839 to Commerce, Illinois, which they renamed Nauvoo. There they settled and grew rapidly in number for some five years. In 1844 a crisis arose when dissidents accused Smith of justifying polygamy. Non-Mormons in the neighboring counties attacked Nauvoo, and Smith and his brother Hyrum were arrested. On June 27, 1844, an anti-Mormon lynch mob stormed the feebly defended jail and shot both Joseph and Hyrum Smith.

In Brigham Young, the remarkable successor to Joseph Smith, the Mormons found a leader of uncommon qualities: strong-minded, intelligent, and decisive. After the murder of Smith, Young patched up an unsure peace with the neighbors by promising an early exodus from Nauvoo. Before the year was out, Young had chosen a new land near the Great Salt Lake in Utah, then part of Mexico, guarded by mountains to

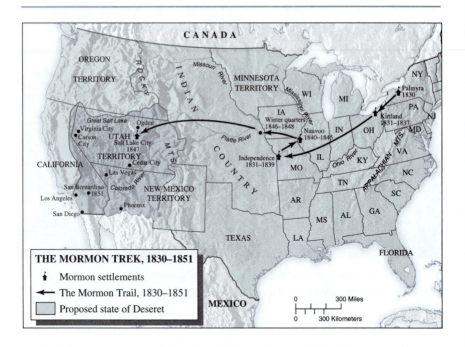

THE MORMON TREK, 1830–1851

- ♦ Mormon settlements
- ← The Mormon Trail, 1830–1851
- ▢ Proposed state of Deseret

the east and north, deserts to the west and south, yet itself fed by mountain streams. Despite its isolation, it was close enough to the Oregon Trail for the saints to prosper by trade with passing gentiles.

Brigham Young trusted God, but made careful preparations. As a result, the Mormon trek was better organized and less burdensome than most of the overland migrations of the time. Early in 1846 a small band of courageous believers crossed the frozen Mississippi River into Iowa to set up the Camp of Israel, the first in a string of way stations along the route. By the fall of 1846, all 15,000 of the migrants had reached the prepared winter quarters on the Missouri River, where they paused until the first bands set out the next spring for the Promised Land.

The first arrivals at Salt Lake in 1847 found only "a broad and barren plain hemmed in by mountains . . . the paradise of the lizard, the cricket and the rattlesnake." Young tapped the ground with his cane and announced that their new holy city would be built on the spot, "laid out perfectly square, north and south, east and west." By the end of 1848, the Mormons had developed an efficient irrigation system, and over the next decade, they brought about the greening of the desert. The Mormons had scarcely arrived when their land became part of the United

States. They organized at first their own state of Deseret (meaning "land of the honey bee," according to Young) with ambitious boundaries that reached the Pacific in southern California. But the Utah Territory, which Congress created, afforded them almost the same control, with Governor Young the chief political and theocratic authority. By 1869 some 80,000 Mormons had settled in Utah. Today there are 9 million Mormons, and it is the fastest growing religion in the world.

ROMANTICISM IN AMERICA

The revival of emotional piety during the early 1800s represented a widespread tendency throughout the Western world to accentuate the stirrings of the spirit over the dry logic of reason and the allure of material gain. Another great victory of heart over head was the romantic movement in thought, literature, and the arts. By the 1780s, a revolt was brewing in Europe against the well-ordered world of the Enlightened thinkers. Were there not, after all, more things in this world than reason and logic could box up and explain: moods, impressions, and feelings; mysterious, unknown, and half-seen things? Americans also took readily to the romantics' emphasis on individualism, idealizing now the virtues of common people, now the idea of original or creative genius in the artist, the author, or the great personality.

Where the Enlightened thinkers of the eighteenth century had scorned the Middle Ages, the romantics now looked back to the period with fascination. America, lacking a feudal history, nonetheless had an eager audience for the novels of Sir Walter Scott and copied the Gothic style in architecture. Even more congenial to the American scene were the new themes in art. In contrast to well-ordered classical scenes, romantic artists such as Thomas Cole (1801–1848) and Thomas Doughty (1793–1856) preferred wild and misty landscapes.

The German philosopher Immanuel Kant gave the worldwide romantic movement a summary definition in the title of his *Critique of Pure Reason* (1781), an influential book that emphasized the limits of human science and reason in explaining the universe. People have innate conceptions of conscience and beauty, the romantics believed, and religious impulses too strong to be dismissed as illusions. In those areas in which science could neither prove nor disprove concepts, people were

Kaaterskill Falls, 1825, *by Thomas Cole.*

justified in having faith. The impact of such ideas elevated intuitive knowledge at the expense of rational knowledge.

TRANSCENDENTALISM   The most intense expression of such romantic ideals was the transcendentalist movement of New England, which drew its name from its emphasis on those things that transcended (or rose above) the limits of reason. Transcendentalism, said one of its chroniclers, assumed "certain fundamental truths not derived from experience, not susceptible of proof, which transcend human life, and are perceived directly and intuitively by the human mind." If transcendentalism drew much from Kant, it was also rooted in New England Puritanism, to which it owed a pervasive moralism. It also had a close affinity with the Quaker doctrine of the inner light. The inner light, a gift from God's grace, was transformed into intuition, a faculty of the mind.

An element of mysticism had always lurked in Puritanism, even if viewed as a heresy—Anne Hutchinson, for instance, had been banished for claiming direct revelations from God. The reassertion of mysticism had something in common, too, with the meditative religions of Asia—with which New England now had a flourishing trade. Transcendentalists steeped themselves in the teachings of the Buddha, the Mo-hammedan Sufis, the Upanishads, and the Bhagavad Gita.

In 1836 an informal discussion group soon named the Transcenden-tal Club began to meet at the homes of members in Boston and Con-cord. It drew at different times clergymen such as Theodore Parker, George Ripley, and James Freeman Clarke; writers such as Henry Thor-eau, Bronson Alcott, Nathaniel Hawthorne, and Orestes Brownson; and learned women such as Elizabeth and Sophia Peabody and Mar-garet Fuller. Fuller edited the group's quarterly review, *The Dial* (1840–1844), for two years before the duty fell to Ralph Waldo Emerson, soon to become the acknowledged high priest of transcendentalism.

EMERSON   More than any other person, Emerson spread the tran-scendentalist gospel. Sprung from a line of New England ministers, he set out to be a Unitarian parson, then quit the "cold and cheerless" de-nomination before he was thirty. After travel to Europe, where he met England's great literary lights, Emerson settled in Concord to take up the life of an essayist, poet, and popular speaker on the lecture circuit, preaching the good news of optimism, self-reliance, and the individual's unlimited potential. Having found pure reason "cold as a cucumber" and discovered that the "ideal is truer than the actual," he was deter-mined to *transcend* the limitations of inherited conventions and of ratio-

Ralph Waldo Emerson.

nalism in order to penetrate the inner recesses of the self. As he once explained, transcendentalism meant a belief in a realm "a little beyond" the rational world.

Emerson's lectures and writings hold the core of the transcendentalist worldview. His notable lecture, "The American Scholar," delivered at Harvard in 1837, urged young Americans to put aside their awe of European culture and explore their own new world. It was "our intellectual Declaration of Independence," said one observer.

Emerson's lecture on "The Over-soul" set forth a kind of pantheism, in which the souls of all individuals commune with the great universal soul, of which they are part and parcel. His essay on "Self-Reliance" (1841) has a timeless appeal to youth with its message of individualism and the cultivation of one's personality. Like most of Emerson's writings, it is crammed with pungent quotations:

> Whoso would be a man, must be a nonconformist. . . . Nothing is at last sacred but the integrity of your own mind. . . . It is easy in the world to live after the world's opinion; it is easy in solitude to live after our own; but the great man is he who in the midst of a crowd keeps with perfect sweetness the independence of solitude. . . . A foolish consistency is the hobgoblin of little minds, adored by little statesmen and philosophers and divines. . . . Speak what you think now in hard words and tomorrow speak what tomorrow thinks in hard words again, though it contradict everything you said today. . . . To be great is to be misunderstood.

THOREAU Emerson's young friend and Concord neighbor, Henry David Thoreau, practiced the reflective self-reliance that Emerson preached. "I like people who can do things," Emerson stressed, and Thoreau, fourteen years his junior, could do many things well—carpentry, masonry, painting, surveying, sailing, gardening. The philosophical son of a pencil-maker father and domineering, abolitionist mother, Thoreau displayed a sense of uncompromising integrity, outdoor vigor, and tart individuality that Emerson found captivating. "If a man does not keep pace with his companions," Thoreau wrote, "perhaps it is because he hears a different drummer."

Thoreau himself marched to a different drummer all his life. After Harvard, where he exhausted the resources of the library in gargantuan bouts of reading, and after a brief stint as a teacher in which he got in

Henry David Thoreau, author of the American classics Walden *and "Civil Disobedience."*

trouble for refusing to cane students, Thoreau settled down to eke out a living through his family's cottage industry of pencil making. But he made frequent escapes to drink in the beauties of nature. He showed no interest in the contemporary scramble for wealth. It too often corrupted the pursuit of happiness. "The mass of men," he wrote, "lead lives of quiet desperation."

Determined himself to practice plain living and high thinking, Thoreau boarded with the Emersons for a time and then embarked on an experiment in self-reliance. On July 4, 1845, he took to the woods to live in a cabin he had built on Emerson's land beside Walden Pond. He wanted to see how far he could free himself from the complexities and hypocrisies of modern commercial life, and to devote his time to observation, reflection, and writing. His purpose was not to lead a hermit's life. He frequently walked the mile or so to town to dine with his friends, and he often welcomed guests at his cabin. "I went to the woods because I wished to live deliberately," he wrote in *Walden, or Life in the Woods* (1854), "and not, when I came to die, discover that I had not lived."

While Thoreau was at Walden Pond, the Mexican War erupted. Believing it an unjust war to advance the cause of slavery, he refused to pay his state poll tax as a gesture of opposition, for which he was put in jail (for only one night; an aunt paid the tax). The incident was so trivial as to be almost comic, but out of it grew the classic essay "Civil Disobedience" (1849), which was later to influence the passive-resistance movements of Mahatma Gandhi in India and Martin Luther King, Jr., in the American South. "If the law is of such a nature that it requires you to be an agent of injustice to another," Thoreau wrote, "then, I say, break the law. . . ."

The broadening ripples of influence more than a century after Thoreau's death show the impact a contemplative person can have on the world of action. Thoreau and the transcendentalists primarily supplied the force of an animating idea: people must follow their consciences. Though these thinkers attracted only a small following among the public at large in their own time, they inspired reform movements and were the quickening force for a generation of writers that produced the first great classic age of American literature.

The Flowering of American Literature

The half-decade of 1850–1855 saw the publication of *Representative Men* by Emerson, *Walden* by Thoreau, *The Scarlet Letter* and *The House of the Seven Gables* by Nathaniel Hawthorne, *Moby-Dick* by Herman Melville, and *Leaves of Grass* by Walt Whitman. As the critic F. O. Mathiessen wrote in his book *American Renaissance*: "You might search all the rest of American literature without being able to collect a group of books equal to these in imaginative quality."

HAWTHORNE   Nathaniel Hawthorne, the supreme writer of the New England group, never shared the sunny optimism of his neighbors or their perfectionist belief in reform. A sometime resident of Concord, but a native and longtime inhabitant of Salem, he was haunted by the knowledge of evil bequeathed to him by his Puritan forebears—one of whom had been a judge at the Salem witchcraft trial. After college at Bowdoin, he worked in obscurity in Salem, gradually began to sell a few stories, and finally earned a degree of fame with his collection of *Twice-Told Tales* (1837). In these, as in most of his later work, he presented powerful moral allegories. His central themes examined sin and its consequences: pride and selfishness, secret guilt, selfish egotism, the impossibility of rooting sin out of the human soul. His greatest novels ex-

Nathaniel Hawthorne, author of The Scarlet Letter.

plored such burdens. In *The Scarlet Letter* (1850), Hester Prynne, an adulteress tagged with a badge of shame by the Puritan authorities, won redemption by her suffering, while the Reverend Arthur Dimmesdale was destroyed by his gnawing guilt and Roger Chillingworth by his obsession with vengeance.

DICKINSON   The flowering of New England featured, too, a foursome of poets who shaped the American imagination in a day when poetry was still accessible to a wide public: Henry Wadsworth Longfellow, John Greenleaf Whittier, Oliver Wendell Holmes, Sr., and James Russell Lowell. A fifth poet, Emily Dickinson, the most original and powerful of the lot, remained a white-gowned recluse in her second-story bedroom in Amherst, Massachusetts. As she once prophetically wrote, "Success is counted sweetest / By those who ne'er succeed." Only two of her almost 1,800 poems had been published (anonymously) before her death in 1886, and the full corpus of her work remained unknown for years thereafter. Born in Amherst in 1830, the child of a prominent, stern father and gentle mother, she received a first-rate secondary education and then attended the new Mount Holyoke Female Seminary. Neither she nor her sister married, and they both lived out their lives in their parents' home.

Perhaps it was Emily's severe eye trouble during the 1860s that induced her solitary withdrawal from the larger society; perhaps it was the aching despair generated by her unrequited love for a married minister. Whatever the reason, her intense isolation led her to focus her writings on her own shifting psychic state. Her themes were elemental: life, death, fear, loneliness, nature, and, above all, God, a "Force illegible," a "distant, stately lover."

IRVING AND COOPER   A noted British critic asked in 1820: "In the four quarters of the Globe, who reads an American book?" Quoted out of context, the question rubbed Americans the wrong way, but the critic, an admirer of American institutions, foresaw a future flowering in the new country. He did not have long to wait, for within a year Washington Irving's *The Sketch Book* (1820) and James Fenimore Cooper's *The Spy* (1821) were drawing wide notice in Britain as well as in America.

Irving in fact stood as a central figure in the American literary world from the time of his satirical *Diedrich Knickerbocker's A History of New York* (1809) until his death fifty years later. He showed that an American could, after all, make a career of literature. During those years a flood of histories, biographies, essays, and stories poured from his pen. Irving was the first American writer to show that authentic American themes could draw a wide audience. Yet, as Melville later noted, he was less a creative genius than an adept imitator. Even the most "American" of his stories, "Rip Van Winkle" and "The Legend of Sleepy Hollow," drew heavily on German folk tales.

Cooper, a country gentleman, got his start as a writer on a bet with his wife that he could write a better novel than one they had just read. In *The Pioneers* (1823), Cooper introduced Natty Bumppo, an eighteenth-century frontiersman destined to be the hero of five novels collectively labeled *The Leather-Stocking Tales*. Natty Bumppo, a crack shot also known as Hawkeye, and his Indian friend Chingachgook, the epitome of the noble savage, took their place among the most unforgettable heroes of world literature. The tales of man pitted against nature in the backwoods, of hairbreadth escapes and gallant rescues, were the first successful romances of frontier life, and they served as models for the later cowboy novels and movies set in the Far West.

POE AND THE SOUTH   By the 1830s and 1840s, new major talents had come on the scene. Edgar Allan Poe, born in Boston but reared in Virginia, was a literary genius and probably the most important American writer of the times. The tormented, heavy-drinking Poe was a master of Gothic horror in the short story and the inventor of the detective story and its major conventions. He judged prose by its ability to pro-

Edgar Allan Poe, perhaps the most inventive American writer of the period.

voke emotional tension, and since he considered fear to be the most powerful emotion, he focused his efforts on making the grotesque and supernatural seem disturbingly real to his readers. Anyone who has read "The Tell-Tale Heart" or "The Pit and the Pendulum" can testify to his success.

Among southern authors, William Gilmore Simms best exemplified the genteel man of letters. Editor and writer in many genres, he wrote poems, novels, histories, biographies, essays, short stories, and drama. The peak of his achievement was in two novels published in 1835: *The Yemassee,* a story of Indian war in 1715, and *The Partisan,* first of seven novels about the Revolution in South Carolina. In his own time, Simms was the preeminent southern author and something of a national figure, but he finally dissipated his energies in politics and the defense of slavery. He went down steadily in critical esteem, and most critics would agree with his own epitaph, that he had "left all his better works undone."

MELVILLE   Herman Melville was a New Yorker whose reputation went into a decline after his initial successes. In the twentieth century Melville's reputation was dramatically revived, elevating him into the literary pantheon occupied by only the finest American authors. Born of distinguished ancestry on both sides, Melville suffered a sharp reversal of fortunes when his father died a bankrupt. After taking various odd jobs, he shipped out as a seaman at age twenty. Some time later, after eighteen months aboard a whaler, he arrived in the South Seas and jumped ship with a companion in the Marquesas Islands. After several weeks spent with a friendly tribe in the valley of the Typees, he signed on to an Australian whaler, jumped ship again in Tahiti, and finally returned home as a seaman aboard a frigate of the United States Navy. An embroidered account of his exotic adventures in *Typee* (1846) became an instant popular success, which he repeated in *Omoo* (1847), based on his stay in Tahiti.

So many readers took his accounts as fictional (as in part they were) that Melville was inspired to write novels of nautical adventures, and he produced one of the world's great novels in *Moby-Dick* (1851). In the story of Captain Ahab and his obsessive quest for the white whale that had caused the loss of his leg, Melville explored the darker recesses of the soul just as his good friend Hawthorne had done. The book was aimed at two audiences. On one level it was a ripping good yarn of adventure on the high seas. But Ahab's single-minded mission to slay the evildoer turned the captain himself into a monster of destruction who sacrificed his ship, his crew, and himself to his folly, leaving as the one survivor the narrator of the story. Unhappily, neither the public nor the critics at the time accepted the novel on either level. After that

Whaling Ship "Maria," *c. 1850. Harpooning whales, as described by Herman Melville in* Moby-Dick.

Melville's career wound down into futility. He supported himself for years with a job in the New York Custom House and turned to poetry, much of which, especially the Civil War *Battle-Pieces* (1866), gained acclaim in later years.

WHITMAN   The most provocative American writer during the antebellum period was Walt Whitman, a remarkably vibrant personality who disdained inherited conventions and artistic traditions. There was something elemental in Whitman's character, something bountiful and generous and compelling—even his faults and inconsistencies were ample. Born on a Long Island farm, he moved with his family to Brooklyn and from the age of twelve worked mainly as a handyman and journalist, frequently taking the ferry across the river to booming, bustling Manhattan. The city fascinated him, and he gorged himself on the urban spectacle—shipyards, crowds, factories, shop windows. From such material he drew his editorial opinions and poetic inspiration, but he remained relatively obscure until the first edition of *Leaves of Grass* (1855) caught the eye and aroused the ire of readers. Emerson found it "the most extraordinary piece of wit and wisdom that America has yet contributed," but more conventional critics shuddered at Whitman's explicit sexual references and groused at his indifference to rhyme and meter as well as his buoyant egotism.

The jaunty Whitman, however, refused to conform to genteel notions of art, and he spent most of his career working on his gargantuan *Leaves*

Walt Whitman.

of Grass, enlarging and reshaping it in successive editions. The growth of the book he identified with the growth of the country. While he celebrated America, Whitman also set out to "celebrate myself and sing myself." To his generation he was a startling figure with his frank sexual references and homoerotic overtones. He also stood out from the pack of fellow writers in rejecting the idea that a woman's proper sphere was in a supportive and dependent role.

FEMININE FICTION   In both poetry and fiction the antebellum reading public most loved edifying poems or "romances" that celebrated pious domestic life. Between 1830 and 1850, over 1,000 fictional works were published in the United States, and most of them revolved around domestic topics—courtship, marriage, religion, home management, child-rearing, and education. Such hearthside literature, redolent with an evangelical moralism and glazed with a meringue of sentimentalism, was intended to shore up the eroding strength of orthodox religious beliefs and conventional social and gender roles. The most popular of these novels were written by women, many of whom unapologetically viewed their fictions as idealizing sermons. As one of them confessed, "I mean always to write a good, pure, natural story, such as mothers are willing their daughters should read and such as will do good instead of harm."

Such saccharine fiction appealed not only to thousands of women readers but also to anxious male moralists who eagerly enlisted the aid of women in restoring the stabilizing social influence of the church and the family. They also wanted to channel female energies toward their "proper sphere" and away from organized efforts to promote political and legal equality for women or to allow women into the male workplace. The patriarchal message was clear: women were to accept their role as self-denying, submissive protectors of the hearth now that husbands were too busy with commercial affairs to attend to such traditional priorities.

THE POPULAR PRESS   The renaissance in literature coincided with a massive expansion in the popular press. The steam-driven Napier press, introduced from England in 1825, could print 4,000 sheets of newsprint in an hour. Richard Hoe of New York improved on it, inventing in

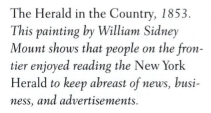

The Herald in the Country, *1853.*
This painting by William Sidney
Mount shows that people on the fron-
tier enjoyed reading the New York
Herald *to keep abreast of news, busi-*
ness, and advertisements.

1847 the Hoe rotary press, which printed 20,000 sheets an hour. Like
many advances in technology, this was a mixed blessing. The high cost
of such a press made it harder for a person of small means to break into
publishing. On the other hand it expedited production of cheap newspapers, magazines, and books.

The availability of daily newspapers costing only a penny each transformed daily reading into a form of popular entertainment. Circulation
soared in every city. The "penny dailies," explained one editor, "are to be
found in every street, lane, and alley; in every hotel, tavern, counting-
house, [and] shop." As readership soared, the content of newspapers expanded beyond political news and commentary to include social gossip,
sports, and sensational crime and accident reports. The *New York Sun,*
in 1833 the first successful penny daily, and others like it often ignored
the merely important in favor of scandals and sensations, true or false.
James Gordon Bennett, a native of Scotland, perfected this style on the
New York Herald, which he founded in 1835. His innovations drew
readers by the thousands: the first Wall Street column, the first society
page (which satirized the well-to-do until it proved more gainful to
show readers their names in print), pictorial news, telegraphic news,
and great initiative in getting scoops. Eventually, however, the *Herald*
suffered from dwelling so much on crime, sex, and depravity in general.

The chief beneficiary of a rising revulsion against the gutter press was the *New York Tribune,* founded as a Whig organ in 1841. Horace Greeley, who became the most important journalist of the era, announced that it would be a cheap but decent paper avoiding the "matters which have been allowed to disgrace the columns of our leading Penny Papers." And despite occasional lapses, Greeley's "Great Moral Organ" typically amused its readers with wholesome human-interest stories. Greeley also won a varied following by plugging the reforms of the day. Socialism, land reform, feminism, abolitionism, temperance, the protective tariff, internal improvements, improved methods of agriculture, vegetarianism, spiritualism, trade unions—all got a share of attention. The *Tribune,* moreover, set a new standard in reporting literary news. In 1856 the *Tribune* became the first daily to have a regular book-review column. For a generation it was probably the most influential paper in the country. By 1860 its weekly edition had a national circulation of 200,000. Meanwhile, the number of newspapers around the country grew from about 1,200 in 1833 to some 3,000 in 1860.

Magazines found a growing market too. *Niles' Weekly Register* (1811–1849) of Baltimore and Washington, founded by the printer Hezekiah Niles, was an earlier version of the twentieth-century news magazine. *Niles' Weekly Register* provided accurate reports on the War of 1812 and made a reputation for good and unbiased coverage of public events—all of which make it a basic source for historians. The *North American Review* of Boston (1815–1940), started by a young Harvard graduate, achieved high standing among scholarly readers. Its editor adorned the journal with materials on American history and biography. It also featured coverage of European literature.

Harper's Magazine (1850–present), originally the organ of the publishers Harper and Brothers, pirated the output of popular English writers in the absence of an international copyright agreement. Gradually, however, faced with an outcry against the practice, *Harper's* began paying for fresh contributions and published original material by American authors. *Frank Leslie's Illustrated Newspaper* (1855–1922) in New York used large and striking pictures to illustrate its material, and generally followed its founder's motto: "Never shoot over the heads of the people." *Leslie's* and a vigorous competitor of somewhat higher quality, *Harper's Illustrated Weekly* (1857–1916), appeared in time to provide a thoroughgoing pictorial record of the Civil War.

EDUCATION

Literacy in Jacksonian America was surprisingly widespread, given the condition of public education. By 1840, according to census data, some 78 percent of the total population and 91 percent of the white population could read and write. Ever since the colonial period, in fact, Americans had had the highest literacy rate in the Western world. Most children learned their letters from church or private "dame" schools, from formal tutors, or from their families.By 1830, no state had a school system in the modern sense, although Massachusetts had for nearly two centuries required towns to maintain schools. Some major cities had the resources to develop real systems on their own. For instance, the Public School Society of New York, established in 1805, built a model system of free schools in the city, with state aid after 1815.

A scattered rural population, however, did not lend itself so readily to the development of schools. In 1860, for instance, Louisiana had a population density of 11 per square mile and Virginia 14, while Massachusetts had 127. In many parts of the country, as in South Carolina after 1811, the state provided some aid to schools for children of indigent parents, but such institutions were normally stigmatized as "pauper schools," to be shunned by the better sort.

EARLY PUBLIC SCHOOLS   By the 1830s the demand for public schools was rising fast. Reformers argued that popular government presupposed a literate and informed electorate. Workers also wanted free schools to give their children an equal chance to pursue the American dream. In 1830 the Working Men's party of Philadelphia called for "a system of education that shall embrace equally all the children of the state, of every rank and condition." Education, it was argued, would improve manners and at the same time lessen crime and poverty.

Horace Mann of Massachusetts stood out in the early drive for statewide school systems. Trained as a lawyer, he sponsored the creation of a state board of education, which he then served as secretary. Mann went on to sponsor many reforms in Massachusetts, including the first state-supported "normal school" for the training of teachers, a state association of teachers, and a minimum school year of six months. He repeatedly defended the school system as the way to social stability and equal opportunity. It had never happened, he argued, and never could happen, that an educated people could be permanently poor. "Education then, beyond all other devices of human origin, is a great equalizer of the conditions of men—the balance wheel of the social machinery."

In the South the state of North Carolina led the way toward state-supported education. There Calvin H. Wiley played a role like that of Mann, building from a law of 1839 that provided support to localities willing to tax themselves for the support of schools. As the first state superintendent of public instruction he traveled to every county, drumming up support for the schools. By 1860, as a result of his activities, North Carolina enrolled more than two-thirds of its white school population for an average term of four months. But the educational pattern in the South continued to reflect the aristocratic pretensions of the region: the South had a higher percentage of college students than any other region, but a lower percentage of public school students. And the South had some 500,000 white illiterates, more than half the total number in the country.

For all the effort to establish state-supported schools, conditions for public education were seldom ideal. Funds were insufficient for buildings, books, and equipment; teachers were poorly paid, and often so poorly prepared as to be little ahead of their charges in the ability to read, write, and do arithmetic. In many a rural schoolhouse the teacher's first task was to thrash the huskiest youth in the class in order to establish authority. The teachers, consequently, were at first mostly men, often young men who did not regard teaching as a career but as a means of support while preparing for a career as a lawyer or preacher, or as part-time work during slack seasons on the farm. With the encouragement of educational reformers, however, teaching was beginning to be regarded as a profession. As the schools multiplied and the school term lengthened, women increasingly entered the field.

Most students going beyond the elementary grades went to private academies, often subsidized by church and public funds. Such schools, begun in colonial days, multiplied until there were in 1850 more than 6,000 of them. In 1821 the Boston English High School opened as the first free public secondary school, set up mainly for students not going on to college. By a law of 1827 Massachusetts required a high school in every town of 500; in towns of 4,000 or more the school had to offer

Latin, Greek, rhetoric, and other college preparatory courses. Public high schools became well established in school systems only after the Civil War. In 1860 there were barely 300 in the whole country.

POPULAR EDUCATION   Beyond the schools there grew up many societies and institutes to inform the general public: mechanics' and workingmen's "institutes," "young men's associations," "debating societies," "literary societies," and such. Outstanding in the field was the Franklin Institute, founded at Philadelphia in 1824 to inform the public mainly in the fields of science and industry. Similar institutes were sponsored by major philanthropists such as Francis Cabot Lowell in Boston, George Peabody in Baltimore, and Peter Cooper in New York. Some cities offered evening classes to those who could not attend day schools. The most widespread and effective means of popular education, however, was the lyceum movement, which aimed to diffuse knowledge through public lectures. Professional agencies provided speakers and performers of all kinds, in literature, science, music, humor, travel, and other fields.

Akin to the lyceum movement and ultimately reaching more people was the movement for public libraries. Benjamin Franklin's Philadelphia Library Company (1731) had given impulse to the growth of subscription or association libraries. In 1803 Salisbury, Connecticut, opened a free library for children and in 1833 Peterborough, New Hampshire, established a tax-supported library open to all. The opening of the Boston Public Library in 1851 was a turning point. By 1860 there were approximately 10,000 public libraries (not all completely free) housing some 8 million volumes.

HIGHER EDUCATION   The post-Revolutionary proliferation of colleges continued after 1800 with the spread of small church schools and state universities. Nine colleges had been founded in the colonial period, all of which survived; but not many of the fifty that sprang up between 1776 and 1800 lasted. Of the seventy-eight colleges and universities in 1840, fully thirty-five had been founded after 1830, almost all as church schools. A post-Revolutionary movement for state universities flourished in those southern states that had had no colonial university. Federal policy abetted the spread of universities into the West. When Congress granted statehood to Ohio in 1803, it set aside two

Greek Class at the Western Reserve Eclectic Institute at Hiram, Ohio, *1853. At front right are the young James A. Garfield and his future wife, Lucretia Randolph.*

townships for the support of a state university and kept up that policy in other new states.

The coexistence of state and religious schools, however, set up conflicts over funding and curriculum. Beset by the need for funds, as colleges usually were, denominational schools often competed with tax-supported schools. Regarding curricula, many of the church schools emphasized theology at the expense of science and the humanities. On the other hand, America's development required broader access to education and programs geared to vocations. The University of Virginia, "Mr. Jefferson's University," founded in 1819 within sight of Monticello, introduced in 1826 a curriculum modeled after Jefferson's own view that education ought to combine pure knowledge with "all the branches of science useful *to us, and at this day."* The model influenced the other new state universities of the South and West.

Technical education grew slowly. The United States Military Academy at West Point, founded in 1802, and the Naval Academy at Annapolis, opened in 1845, trained a limited number of engineers. More learned technical skills through practical experience with railroad and canal companies, and apprenticeship to experienced technologists.

Similarly, most aspiring lawyers went to "read law" with an established attorney, and doctors served their apprenticeships with practicing physicians. The president of Brown University remarked that there were forty-two theological schools and forty-seven law schools, but none to provide "the agriculturalist, the manufacturer, the mechanic, and the merchant with any kind of professional preparation." There were few schools of this sort before 1860, but a promise for the future came in 1855 when Michigan and Pennsylvania each established an agricultural and mechanical college, now Michigan State and Pennsylvania State.

Elementary education for girls met with general acceptance, but training beyond that level did not. Many men and women thought higher education unsuited to a woman's destiny in life. Some did argue that education would produce better wives and mothers, but few were ready yet to demand equality on principle. Progress began with the academies, some of which taught boys and girls alike. Good "female seminaries" like those founded by Emma Willard at Troy, New York

The George Barrell Emerson School, Boston, *c. 1850. Although higher education for women initially met with some resistance, female seminaries like this one were started in the 1820s and 1830s and taught women mathematics, physics, and history, as well as music, art, and the social amenities.*

(1824), and Mary Lyon at Mount Holyoke, Massachusetts (1836), prepared the way for women's colleges. Many of them, in fact, grew into such colleges, but Georgia Female College (later Wesleyan College) at Macon, chartered in 1836, first offered women the A.B. in 1840. The curricula in female seminaries usually differed from the courses in men's schools, giving more attention to the social amenities and such "embellishments" as music and art. Vassar, opened at Poughkeepsie, New York, in 1865, is usually credited with being the first women's college to give priority to academic standards. In general the West gave the greatest impetus to coeducation, with state universities in the lead. But once admitted, women students remained in a subordinate status. At Oberlin College in Ohio, for instance, they were expected to clean male students' rooms and were not allowed to speak in class or recite at graduation exercises. Coeducation did not mean equality.

SOME MOVEMENTS FOR REFORM

The urge to eradicate evil from nineteenth-century America had its roots in the widespread American sense of mission, which in turn drew upon rising faith in human perfectibility. Belief in perfectibility had both evangelical and liberal bases. Transcendentalism, the spirit of which infected even those unfamiliar with the philosophy, offered a romantic faith in the individual and the belief that human intuition led to right thinking.

Few areas of life escaped the attention of the reformers, however trivial or weighty: observance of the Sabbath, dueling, crime and punishment, the hours and conditions of work, poverty, vice, care of the handicapped, pacifism, foreign missions, temperance, women's rights, the abolition of slavery. Some crusaders challenged a host of evils; others focused on pet causes. One Massachusetts reformer, for example, insisted that "a vegetable diet lies at the basis of all reforms."

The greatest dietary reformer of the age, however, was Sylvester Graham, who started as a temperance speaker in 1830 and moved on to champion a natural diet of grains, vegetables, and fruits, and abstinence from alcohol, coffee, tea, tobacco, and many foods. The Graham cracker is one of the movement's legacies to later times. Graham's ideas evolved into a way of life requiring proper habits of dress, hygiene, sex, and mind. The movement became a major industry, sponsoring health clubs, camps, sanitariums, magazines, and regular lecture tours by Graham.

TEMPERANCE   The temperance crusade was perhaps the most widespread of all, with the possible exception of the public school movement. The cause drew its share of prigs, but it also drew upon concern over a real problem. The census of 1810 reported some 14,000 distilleries producing 25 million gallons of spirits each year. With a hard-drinking population of just over 7 million, the "alcoholic republic" was producing well over three gallons per year for every man, woman, and child, not counting beer, wine, and cider. And the census takers no doubt missed a few stills. William Cobbett, an English reformer who traveled in the United States, noted in 1819 that one could "go into hardly any man's house without being asked to drink wine or spirits, even *in the morning.*"

The temperance movement rested on a number of arguments. First and foremost was the religious concern that "soldiers of the cross" lead blameless lives. The bad effects of distilled beverages on body and mind were noted by the respected physician Benjamin Rush as early as 1784. The dynamic new economy, with factories and railroads moving on strict schedules, made tippling by the labor force a far greater problem than it had been in a simple economy. Humanitarians emphasized the relations between drinking and poverty. Much of the movement's propaganda focused on the sufferings of innocent mothers and children. "Drink," said a pamphlet from the Sons of Temperance, "is the prolific source (directly or indirectly) of nearly all the ills that afflict the human family."

In 1826 a group of ministers in Boston organized the American Society for the Promotion of Temperance. The society worked through lecturers, press campaigns, prize essay contests, and the formation of local and state societies. A favorite device was to ask each person who took the pledge to put by his or her signature a T for Total Abstinence. With that a new word entered the language: "teetotaler."

In 1833 the society called a national convention in Philadelphia, where the American Temperance Union was formed. The convention revealed internal tensions, however: Was the goal moderation or total abstinence, and if the latter, abstinence merely from liquor or also from wine, cider, and beer? Should activists work by persuasion or by legisla-

The Way of Good & Evil. *Intemperance was one of the steps on the way of evil, leading to "everlasting punishment."*

tion? Like nearly every movement of the day, temperance had a wing of perfectionists who rejected prudence. They would brook no compromise with Demon Rum and carried the day with a resolution that the liquor traffic was morally wrong and ought to be prohibited by law. The union, at its spring convention in 1836, called for abstinence from all alcoholic beverages—a costly victory that caused moderates to abstain from the movement instead.

The demand for the prohibition of alcoholic beverages led in the 1830s and thereafter to experiments with more stringent regulations and local option laws. In 1838 Massachusetts forbade the sale of spirits in lots of less than fifteen gallons, thereby cutting off sales in taverns and to the poor—who could not handle it as well as their betters, or so their betters thought. After repeal of the law in 1840, prohibitionists in Massachusetts turned to the towns, about a hundred of which were dry by 1845. In 1839 Mississippi restricted sales to no less than a gallon, but the movement went little further in the South. In 1846 Maine enacted a law against sales of less than twenty-eight gallons; five years later Maine forbade the manufacture or sale of *any* intoxicants. By 1855 thirteen states had such laws. Rum-soaked New England had gone legally dry, along with New York and parts of the Midwest. But most of the laws were poorly drafted and vulnerable to court challenge. Within a few years they survived only in northern New England. Still, between 1830 and 1860, the temperance agitation drastically reduced Americans' per-capita consumption of alcohol.

PRISONS AND ASYLUMS   The sublime optimism of the age, the liberal belief that people were innately good and capable of improvement, brought major changes in the treatment of prisoners, the handicapped, and dependent children. Public institutions arose dedicated to the treatment and cure of social ills. Earlier these had been "places of last resort," David Rothman wrote in *The Discovery of the Asylum.* Now they "became places of first resort, the preferred solution to the problems of poverty, crime, delinquency, and insanity." Removed from society, the needy and deviant could be made whole again. Unhappily, this ideal kept running up against the dictates of convenience and economy. The institutions had a way of turning into breeding grounds of brutality and neglect.

In the colonial period prisons were usually places for brief confinement before punishment, which was either death or some kind of pain or humiliation: whipping, mutilation, confinement in stocks, branding, and the like. A new attitude began to emerge after the Revolution. American reformers argued against the harshness of the penal code and asserted that the certainty of punishment was more important than its severity. Society, moreover, would benefit more from the prevention than the punishment of crime.

Gradually the idea of the penitentiary developed. It would be a place where the guilty experienced penitence and underwent rehabilitation, not just punishment. An early model of the new system, widely copied, was the Auburn Penitentiary, commissioned by New York in 1816. The prisoners at Auburn had separate cells and gathered for meals and group labor. Discipline was severe. The men were marched out in lockstep and never put face to face or allowed to talk. But prisoners were at least reasonably secure from abuse by other prisoners. The system, its advocates argued, had a beneficial effect on the prisoners and saved money since the workshops supplied prison needs and produced goods for sale at a profit. By 1840 there were twelve prisons of the Auburn type.

It was still more common, and the persistent curse of prisons, however, for inmates to be thrown together willy-nilly. In an earlier day of corporal punishments, jails housed mainly debtors. But as practices changed, debtors found themselves housed with convicts. Without provision for food, furniture, or fuel, the debtors would have expired but for charity. The absurdity of the system was so obvious that the tardiness of reform seems strange. New York in 1817 made $25 the minimum for which one could be imprisoned, but no state eliminated the practice altogether until Kentucky acted in 1821. Other states gradually fell in line, but it was still more than three decades before debtors' prisons became a thing of the past.

The reform impulse also found outlet in the care of the insane. The Pennsylvania Hospital (1752), one of the first in the country, had a provision in its charter that it should care for "lunaticks," but before 1800 few hospitals provided care for the mentally ill. One notable exception was the hospital opened in Williamsburg in 1759 specifically for treatment of the mentally ill. The insane were usually confined at home with hired keepers or in jails and almshouses. In the years after 1815, how-

The Pennsylvania Hospital was one of the few in eighteenth-century America to care for the mentally ill. It is depicted here in 1767.

ever, asylums that housed the disturbed separately from criminals began to appear. Early efforts led to such optimism that a committee reported to the Massachusetts legislature in 1832 that with the right treatment "insanity yields with more readiness than ordinary diseases." These high expectations gradually faded with experience.

The most important figure in arousing the public conscience to the plight of these unfortunates was Dorothea Lynde Dix. A pious, withdrawn, almost saintly Boston schoolteacher, she was called upon to instruct a Sunday-school class at the East Cambridge House of Correction in 1841. There she found a roomful of insane persons completely neglected and left without heat on a cold March day. She then commenced a two-year investigation of jails and almshouses in Massachusetts. In a memorial to the state legislature in 1843, she reported on "the *present* state of insane persons confined within the Commonwealth, in *cages, closets, cellars, stalls, pens! Chained, naked, beaten with rods, and lashed into obedience!*" Keepers of the institutions dismissed her charges as "slanderous lies," but she won the support of leading reformers. From Massachusetts, she carried her campaign throughout the country and abroad. By 1860 she had persuaded twenty states to heed her advice. Of Dorothea Dix it was truly said that "Few persons have ever had such far-reaching effect on public policy toward reform."

WOMEN'S RIGHTS   While Dorothea Dix stood out as an example of the opportunity reform gave middle-class women to enter public life, Catharine Beecher, a leader in the education movement and founder of women's schools in Connecticut and Ohio, published a guide prescribing the domestic sphere for women. *A Treatise on Domestic Economy* (1841) became the leading handbook of what historians have labeled the "cult of domesticity." While Beecher upheld high standards in women's education, she also accepted the prevailing view that the "woman's sphere" was the home and argued that young women should be trained in the domestic arts. Her guide, designed for use also as a textbook, led prospective wives and mothers through the endless rounds from Monday washing to Saturday baking, with instructions on health, food, clothing, cleanliness, care of domestics and children, gardening, and hundreds of other household details. Such duties, Beecher emphasized, should never be taken as "petty, trivial or unworthy" since "no statesman . . . had more frequent calls for wisdom, firmness, tact, discrimination, prudence, and versatility of talent."

The American Woman's Home, *1869. This is an illustrated page from Catharine Beecher's book. Although Beecher believed in the importance of educating women, she argued that women should remain in the home and be skilled in the domestic arts of cooking, cleaning, and child rearing.*

The social custom of assigning the sexes different roles, of course, did not spring full-blown into life during the nineteenth century. In earlier agrarian societies, gender-based functions were closely tied to the household and often overlapped. As the more complex economy of the nineteenth century matured, economic production came to be increasingly separated from the home, and the home in turn became a refuge from the outside world, with separate and distinctive functions for men and women. Some have argued that the home became a trap for women, a prison that hindered fulfillment. But others have noted that it often gave women a sphere of independence in which they might exercise a degree of initiative and leadership. The so-called cult of domesticity idealized a woman's moral role in civilizing husband and family.

The official status of women during this period remained much as it had been in the colonial era. Legally, a woman was unable to vote and, after marriage, was denied control of her property and even of her children. A wife could not make a will, sign a contract, or bring suit in court without her husband's permission. Her legal status was like that of a minor, a slave, or a free black. Gradually, however, women began to protest their status, and men began to listen. The organized movement for women's rights had its origins in 1840, when the American antislavery movement split over the question of women's right to participate.

American women decided then that they needed to organize on behalf of their own emancipation too.

In 1848 two prominent moral reformers and advocates of women's rights, Lucretia Mott, a Philadelphia Quaker, and Elizabeth Cady Stanton, a graduate of Troy Seminary who refused to be merely "a household drudge," decided to call a convention to discuss "the social, civil, and religious condition and rights of women." The hastily organized Seneca Falls Convention, the first of its kind, issued on July 19, 1848, a clever paraphrase of Jefferson's Declaration, the Declaration of Sentiments, mainly the work of Mrs. Stanton, who was also the wife of a prominent abolitionist and the mother of seven.

The document proclaimed the self-evident truth that "all men and women are created equal," and the attendant resolutions said that all laws that placed women "in a position inferior to that of men, are contrary to the great precept of nature, and therefore of no force or authority." Such language was too strong for most of the thousand delegates, and only about a third of them signed it. Ruffled male editors lampooned the women activists as being "love-starved spinsters" and "petticoat rebels." Yet the Seneca Falls gathering represented an important first step in the evolving campaign for women's rights.

From 1850 until the Civil War, the women's rights leaders held annual conventions and carried on a program of organizing, lecturing, and petitioning. The movement had to struggle in the face of meager funds and antifeminist women and men. Its success resulted from the work of a few undaunted women who refused to be overawed by the odds against them. Susan B. Anthony, already active in temperance and anti-slavery groups, joined the crusade in the 1850s. At age seventeen she had angrily noted, "What an absurd notion that women have not intellectual and moral faculties sufficient for anything else but domestic concerns!" Unlike Stanton and Mott, Anthony was unmarried and therefore able to devote most of her attention to the women's crusade. As one observer put it, Mrs. Stanton "forged the thunderbolts and Miss Anthony hurled them." Both were young when the movement started and both lived into the twentieth century, focusing after the Civil War on demands for women's suffrage. Many of the feminists like Elizabeth Stanton, Lucretia Mott, and Lucy Stone had supportive husbands, and the movement won prominent male champions such as Emerson, Whitman, William Ellery Channing, and William Lloyd Garrison.

Elizabeth Cady Stanton (left) *and Susan B. Anthony* (right). *Mrs. Stanton "forged the thunderbolts and Miss Anthony hurled them."*

The fruits of the movement ripened slowly. Women did not gain the ballot, but there were some legal gains. The state of Mississippi, seldom regarded as a hotbed of reform, was in 1839 the first to grant married women control over their property; by the 1860s eleven more states had such laws.

Still, the only jobs open to educated women in any numbers were nursing and teaching, both of which extended the domestic roles of health care and nurture into the world outside. Both brought relatively lower status and pay than "man's work" despite the skills, training, and responsibility involved. Against the odds, a hardy band of women carved out professional careers.

Harriet Hunt of Boston was a teacher who, after nursing her sister through a serious illness, set up shop in 1835 as a self-taught physician and persisted in medical practice although twice rejected by Harvard Medical School. Voted into Geneva Medical College in western New York as a joke, Elizabeth Blackwell of Ohio had the last laugh when she finished at the head of her class in 1849. She founded the New York Infirmary for Women and Children and later had a long career as a professor of gynecology in the London School of Medicine for Women.

An intellectual prodigy among women of the time—the derisory term was "bluestocking"—was Margaret Fuller. A precocious child, she was force-fed education by a father who taught her Latin when she was six.

Margaret Fuller, one of the great American intellectuals of her time.

As a young adult she moved confidently in the literary circles of Boston and Concord, edited *The Dial* for two years, and became literary editor and critic for Horace Greeley's *New York Tribune*. From 1839 to 1844, she conducted "conversations" with the cultivated ladies of Boston. From this classroom-salon emerged many of the ideas that went into her book *Woman in the Nineteenth Century* (1845), a plea for removal of all intellectual and economic disabilities. Minds and souls were neither masculine nor feminine, she argued. Genius had no sex. "What woman needs," Fuller contended, "is not as a woman to act or rule, but as a nature to grow, as an intellect to discern, as a soul to live freely and unimpeded, to unfold such powers as were given her when we left our common home."

UTOPIAN COMMUNITIES   Amid the pervasive climate of reform during the Jacksonian era, the quest for utopia flourished. Plans for new communities had long been an American passion, at least since the Puritans set out to build a Wilderness Zion. The visionary communes of the nineteenth century often had purely economic and social objectives, but those rooted in religion proved most durable.

More than a hundred utopian communities sprang up between 1800 and 1900. Among the most durable were those founded by the Shakers, officially the United Society of Believers in Christ's Second Appearing. Ann Lee Stanley (Mother Ann) reached New York State with eight followers in 1774. Believing religious fervor a sign of inspiration from the Holy Ghost, Mother Ann and her followers had strange fits in which

Shaker Dance. *The Shakers, who were officially named the United Society of Believers in Christ's Second Appearing, participated in ritual dances, as shown in this illustration.*

they saw visions and prophesied. These manifestations later evolved into a ritual dance—hence the name Shakers. Shaker doctrine held God to be a dual personality: in Christ the masculine side was manifested, in Mother Ann the feminine element. Mother Ann preached celibacy to prepare Shakers for the perfection that was promised them. The church would first gather in the elect, and eventually in the spirit world convert and save all humankind.

Mother Ann died in 1784, but the group found new leaders. From the first community at Mount Lebanon, New York, the movement spread to new colonies in New England, and soon afterward into Ohio and Kentucky. By 1830 about twenty groups were flourishing. In Shaker communities all property was held in common. Governance of the colonies was concentrated in the hands of select groups chosen by the ministry, or "Head of Influence" at Mount Lebanon. To outsiders this might seem almost despotic, but the Shakers emphasized equality of labor and reward, and members were free to leave at will. The Shakers' farms were among the leading sources of garden seed and medicinal herbs, and many of their manufactures, including clothing, household items, and especially furniture, were prized for their simple beauty. By the mid–twentieth century, however, few members remained alive; they had reached the peak of activity in the years 1830–1860.

John Humphrey Noyes, founder of the Oneida Community, was the son of a Vermont congressman. Educated at Dartmouth and then Yale Divinity School, he discovered true religion at one of Charles G. Finney's revivals and entered the ministry. He was forced out, however, when he concluded that with true conversion came perfection and a complete release from sin. In 1836 he gathered a group of "Perfectionists" around his home in Putney, Vermont. Ten years later Noyes announced a new doctrine of complex marriage, which meant that every man in the community was married to every woman and vice versa. "In a holy community," he claimed, "there is no more reason why sexual intercourse should be restrained by law, than why eating and drinking should be." Authorities thought otherwise, and Noyes was arrested for practicing his "free love" theology. He fled to New York and in 1848 established the Oneida Community, which numbered more than 200 by 1851.

The communal group eked out a living with farming and logging until the mid-1850s, when the inventor of a new steel trap joined the community. Oneida traps were soon known as the best in the country. The community then branched out into sewing silk, canning fruits, and making silver spoons. The spoons were so popular that, with the addition of knives and forks, tableware became the Oneida specialty. In 1879, however, the community faced a crisis when Noyes fled to Canada to avoid prosecution for adultery. The members then abandoned universal marriage, and in 1881 decided to convert into a joint-stock company, the Oneida Community, Ltd., which remains today a successful flatware company.

In contrast to these religious-based communities, Robert Owen's New Harmony was based on a secular principle. A British capitalist who worried about the social effects of the factory system, Owen built a model factory town, supported labor legislation, and set forth a scheme for a model community in his pamphlet *A New View of Society* (1813). Later he snapped at a chance to buy the town of Harmony, Indiana, and promptly christened it New Harmony.

In 1825 a varied group of about 900 colonists gathered in New Harmony for a period of transition from Owen's ownership to the new system of cooperation. After only nine months' trial, Owen turned over management of the colony to a town meeting of all residents and a council of town officers. The high proportion of learned participants generated a certain intellectual electricity about the place. For a time it looked like a brilliant success, but New Harmony soon fell into discord. Every idealist wanted his or her own patented plan put into practice. In 1827 Owen returned from a visit to England to find New Harmony insolvent. The following year he dissolved the project and sold or leased the lands on good terms, in many cases to the settlers. All that remained he turned over to his sons, who stayed and became American citizens.

The 1840s brought a flurry of interest in the ideas of Fourieristic socialism. Charles Fourier, a Frenchman, proposed to reorder society into small units, or "phalanxes," ideally of 1,620 members. All property would be held in common, and each phalanx would produce that for which it felt itself best suited; the joy of work and communal living would supply the incentive. The phalanxes would eventually cover the earth and displace capitalism. The first such community in America, the Sylvania Phalanx in northern Pennsylvania, was founded with Horace Greeley's help in 1842 and lasted but a year. Sylvania picked up 2,300 acres of remote and infertile land at little cost. During their only season, about 100 members produced just eleven bushels of grain on the four acres of arable land. Greeley lost $5,000. In all some forty or fifty phalanxes sprang up, but they lasted on the average only about two years.

Brook Farm was surely the most celebrated of all the utopian communities because it had the support of Emerson, Fuller, and countless other well-known literary figures of New England. Nathaniel Hawthorne, a member, later memorialized its failure in his novel *The Blithedale Romance* (1852). George Ripley, a Unitarian minister and transcendentalist, conceived of Brook Farm as a kind of early-day "think tank," combining high thinking and plain living. The place survived, however, mainly because of an excellent community school that drew tuition-paying students from outside. In 1844 Brook Farm converted itself into a phalanx, but when a new central building burned down on the day of its dedication in 1846, the community spirit expired in the embers.

Utopian communities, with few exceptions, quickly ran out of steam. Soon after Hawthorne left Brook Farm he wrote: "It already looks like a dream behind me." His life there was "an unnatural and unsuitable, and therefore an unreal one." Such experiments, performed in relative isolation, had little effect on the real world outside, where reformers wrestled with the sins of the multitudes. Among all the targets of reformers' wrath, one great evil would finally take precedence over the others— human bondage. The paradox of American slavery coupled with American freedom, of "the world's fairest hope linked with man's foulest crime," in Herman Melville's words, would inspire the climactic crusade of the age, abolitionism, one that would ultimately move to the center of the political stage and sweep the nation into an epic struggle.

MAKING CONNECTIONS

- The antislavery campaign, especially its abolitionist aspect, was related to the reform movements in this chapter. It is discussed following the section on slavery in Chapter 15.

- Chapter 17 shows how the Civil War had a significant impact on the status of women in American society, a continuation of a theme discussed here.

FURTHER READING

Russel B. Nye's *Society and Culture in America, 1830–1860* (1974) provides a wide-ranging survey. On the reform impulse, consult Ronald G. Walter's *American Reformers, 1815–1860* (1978). Revivalist religion is treated in Nathan O. Hatch's *The Democratization of American Christianity* (1989), and Christine Heyrman's *Southern Cross: The Beginnings of the Bible Belt* (1997). On the Mormons, see Leonard J. Arrington's *Brigham Young: American Moses* (1985).

The best introduction to transcendentalist thought is Paul Boller's *American Transcendentalism, 1830–1860* (1974). A more recent treatment is Carlos Baker's *Emerson Among the Eccentrics: A Group Portrait* (1997). Several good works describe various aspects of the antebellum reform movement. For temperance, see W. J. Rorabaugh's *The Alcoholic Republic: An American Tradition* (1979) and Barbara Leslie Epstein's *The Politics of Domesticity: Women, Evangelism, and Temperance in Nineteenth-Century America* (1981). Stephen Nissenbaum's *Sex, Diet, and Debility in Jacksonian America* (1980) looks at health reform. On prison reform and other humanitarian projects, see David J. Rothman's

The Discovery of the Asylum (1971), Gerald N. Grob's *Mental Institutions in America* (1973), and Charles Rosenberg's *The Care of Strangers: The Rise of America's Hospital System* (1987), and Thomas J. Brown's biography, *Dorothea Dix: New England Reformer* (1998).

Lawrence A. Cremin's *American Education: The National Experience, 1783–1876* (1980) traces early school reform. For other views, see Stanley K. Schultz's *The Culture Factory: Boston Public Schools, 1789–1860* (1973) and Carl F. Kaestle and Eric Foner's *Pillars of the Republic* (1983).

On women during the antebellum period, see Nancy F. Cott's *The Bonds of Womanhood: "Woman's Sphere" in New England, 1780–1835* (1977) and Ellen C. DuBois's *Feminism and Suffrage: The Emergence of an Independent Women's Movement in America, 1848–1869* (1978). Also valuable are Shirley Samuels's *The Culture of Sentiment: Race, Gender, and Sentimentality in Nineteenth-Century America* (1992), Jeanne Boydston's *The Limits of Sisterhood: The Beecher Sisters on Women's Rights and Woman's Sphere* (1988), and Mary P. Ryan's *Women in Public: Between Banners and Ballots, 1825–1880* (1990).

A small but growing literature on ideals of masculinity and changing roles of men in the nineteenth century includes David Leverenz's *Manhood and the American Renaissance* (1989), Mark C. Carnes's *Secret Ritual and Manhood in Victorian America* (1989), Mary Ann Clawson's *Constructing Brotherhood: Class, Gender, and Fraternalism* (1989), and E. Anthony Rotundo's *American Manhood: Transformations in Masculinity from the Revolution to the Modern Era* (1993). Changing ideals of the family in the nineteenth century are described in Steven Mintz and Susan Kellogg's *Domestic Revolutions: A Social History of American Family Life* (1988).

Michael Fellman's *The Unbounded Frame: Freedom and Community in Nineteenth-Century American Utopianism* (1973) surveys the utopian movements. Specific experiments are treated in Robert D. Thomas's *The Man Who Would Be Perfect* (1977), on John Humphrey Noyes; J. F. C. Harrison's *Robert Owen and the Owenites in Britain and America: The Quest for the New Moral World* (1969), on Robert Owen; Maren L. Carden's *Oneida* (1969); and Henri Desroche's *The American Shakers: From Neo-Christianity to Pre-Socialism* (1971). Lawrence Foster's *Religion and Sexuality* (1981) discusses the Oneida, Shaker, and Mormon communities.

14 ∞ MANIFEST DESTINY

*D*uring the 1840s the westering impulse, the quest for a better chance and more living room, continued to excite the American imagination. "If hell lay to the west," one pioneer declared, "Americans would cross heaven to get there." That may or may not have been true, but millions of Americans were willing to cross the Mississippi River and experience unrelenting hardships in order to conquer new frontiers and express their "providential destiny" to subdue the entire continent. By 1860 some 4.3 million people had settled in the trans-Mississippi West.

Of course, most of these settlers and adventurers sought to exploit the many economic opportunities afforded by the new lands. Trappers and farmers, miners and merchants, hunters, ranchers, teachers, domestics, and prostitutes, among others, headed west seeking their fortunes. Others sought religious freedom or new converts to Christianity.

Whatever the reason, they formed an unceasing migratory stream flowing across the Great Plains and the Rocky Mountains. The Indian and Mexican inhabitants of the region soon found themselves swept aside by successive waves of American settlement. In 1858 President James Buchanan could report that the nation was bound east and west "by a chain of Americans which can never be broken."

THE TYLER YEARS

When William Henry Harrison took office in 1841, elected like Jackson mainly on the strength of his military record and his lack of a public stand on key issues, the Whig leaders expected him to be a figurehead, a tool in the hands of Webster and Clay. Webster became secretary of state. Clay, who preferred to stay in the Senate, saw the cabinet filled with his friends. Within a few days of the inauguration, signs of strain appeared between Harrison and Clay, whose disappointment at missing the nomination had made him peevish. But the quarrel never had a chance to develop, for Harrison served the shortest term of any president—after the longest inaugural address. At the inauguration, held on a chilly and rainy day, he caught cold. The pleadings of office seekers in the following month filled his days and sapped his strength. On April 4, 1841, exactly one month after the inauguration, he died of pneumonia at age sixty-eight.

Thus John Tyler of Virginia, the first vice-president to succeed on the death of a president, served practically all of Harrison's term. And if there was ambiguity about where Harrison stood, there was none about Tyler's convictions. At age fifty-one, the thin, fragile Virginian was the youngest president to date, but he already had a long career behind him as legislator, governor, congressman, and senator, and his opinions on all the important issues had been forcefully stated and were widely known. Although officially a Whig, at an earlier time he might have been called an Old Republican; he was stubbornly opposed to everything associated with Clay's American System—protective tariffs, a national bank, and internal improvements at national expense—and in favor of strict construction and states' rights.

When asked about the concept of nationalism, Tyler replied that he had "no such word in my political vocabulary." Once a Democrat, he had broken with the party over Jackson's stand on a state's right to nullify federal laws and Jackson's imperious use of executive authority. Tyler had been chosen to "balance" the ticket, with no expectation that he would wield power. Acid-tongued John Quincy Adams said that Tyler was "a political sectarian of the slave-driving, Virginian, Jeffersonian school, principled against all improvement, with all the interests and passions and vices of slavery rooted in his moral and political constitution—with talents not above mediocrity, and a spirit incapable of expansion to the dimensions of the station upon which he has been cast."

DOMESTIC AFFAIRS   Given more finesse on Clay's part, he might have bridged the divisions among the Whigs over financial issues. But for once, driven by disappointment and ambition, the "Great Compromiser" lost his instinct for compromise. When Congress met in special session in 1841, Clay introduced a series of resolutions designed to supply the platform that the party had evaded in the previous election. The chief points were repeal of the Independent Treasury Act, establishment of a Third Bank of the United States, distribution to the states of proceeds from public land sales, and a higher tariff. Clay then set out to push his program through Congress. "Tyler dares not resist me. I will drive him before me," he said.

Tyler, it turned out, was not easily driven. Although he agreed to allow the repeal of the Independent Treasury Act and signed a higher tariff bill in 1842, Tyler vetoed Clay's bill for a new national bank. This provoked Tyler's entire cabinet, with the exception of Webster, to resign, in an unprecedented action. Tyler replaced the defectors with anti-Jackson Democrats like himself who had become Whigs. Irate congressional Whigs expelled him, and Democrats viewed him as an untrustworthy "renegade." By 1842 Clay's program was in ruins. Even his successes were temporary—a Democratic Congress and president in 1846 restored the Independent Treasury and cut the tariff, leaving preemption (which legalized the frontier tradition of "squatters' rights") as the only major permanent achievement of the Whigs, something that had been no part of Clay's original scheme. If the program was in ruins, however, Clay's leadership of his party was fixed beyond question, and Tyler had become a president without a party.

FOREIGN AFFAIRS   In foreign relations, on the other hand, developments of immense significance were taking place. Several unsettled issues had arisen to trouble relations between Britain and the United States. In the 1830s Canadian nationalists rebelled against British rule, and many of them took refuge across the border in the United States. They viewed their American bases as safe havens, and used an American ship called the *Caroline* to bring them supplies. In 1837 Canadian militia loyal to England seized the *Caroline* and set it afire. In the course of the incident, one American was killed. The British ignored all protests, but President Van Buren sent federal troops to prevent frontier violations in either direction.

Another issue between the two nations involved the suppression of the African slave trade, which both the United States and Britain had outlawed in 1808. Congress failed to provide funds for American participation in the African slave patrol. In 1841 Prime Minister Palmerston asserted the right of British patrols off the coast of Africa to board and search vessels flying the American flag to see if they carried slaves. But the American government, mindful of the impressments and seizures during the Napoleonic Wars, refused to accept it. Relations were further strained late in 1841 when American slaves on the *Creole,* bound from Hampton Roads to New Orleans, mutinied and sailed into Nassau, where the British set them free. Secretary of State Webster demanded that the slaves be returned as American property, but the British refused.

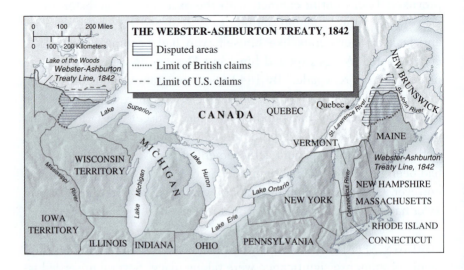

THE WEBSTER-ASHBURTON TREATY, 1842

Fortunately at this point a new British ministry decided to accept Webster's overtures for negotiations and sent Lord Ashburton to Washington. The Maine boundary was settled in what Webster later called "the battle of the maps." Webster settled for about seven-twelfths of the contested lands along the Maine boundary, and except for Oregon, which remained under joint occupation, he settled the other border disputes by accepting the existing line between the Connecticut and St. Lawrence Rivers, and by compromising on the line between Lake Superior and Lake of the Woods. The Webster-Ashburton Treaty (1842) also provided for joint patrols off Africa to suppress the slave trade.

THE WESTERN FRONTIER

In the early 1840s, the American people were no more stirred by the quarrels of Tyler and Clay over such issues as banking, tariffs, and distribution, important as they were, than students of history would be at a later date. What stirred the blood was the mounting evidence that the "empire of freedom" was hurdling the barriers of the "Great American Desert" and the Rocky Mountains, reaching out toward the Pacific coast. In 1845, an eastern editor gave a name to this bumptious spirit of expansion. "Our manifest destiny," he wrote, "is to overspread the continent allotted by Providence for the free development of our yearly multiplying millions." At its best this much-trumpeted notion of "Manifest Destiny" offered a moral justification for American expansion, a prescription for what an enlarged United States could and should be. At its worst it was a cluster of flimsy rationalizations for naked greed and imperial ambition. Whatever the case, hundreds of thousands of people began streaming into the Far West during the 1840s and after.

The western frontier across the Mississippi River differed radically from previous western frontiers encountered by settlers from the East. Here was a new environment as well as a new culture. The Great Plains and the Far West were already occupied by Indians and Mexicans, peoples who had lived in the region for centuries and had established their own distinctive customs and ways of life.

WESTERN INDIANS   Historians estimate that over 325,000 Indians inhabited the Southwest, the Great Plains, California, and the Pacific

Northwest in 1840, when the great migration of white settlers began to pour into the region. These Native Americans were divided into more than 200 different tribes, each with its own language, religion, economic base, kinship practices, and system of governance. Some were primarily farmers; others were nomadic hunters who preyed upon game animals as well as other Indians.

Some twenty-three tribes resided in the Great Plains, a vast grassland stretching from the Mississippi River west to the Rocky Mountains and from Canada to Mexico. This region had been virtually devoid of a human presence until the Spaniards introduced the horse and gun in the late sixteenth century. Prior to the advent of horses, Indians relied upon dogs as their beast of burden—other than women, who carried whatever the dogs could not. A horse could carry seven times as much weight as a dog. Even more important, a horse dramatically increased the mobility of the Plains Indians, enabling them to leave their villages and follow the great buffalo herds. They used buffalo meat for food and transformed the skins into clothing, bedding, and teepee coverings. The

Buffalo Lancing in the Snow Drifts, c. 1860s. *This painting by George Catlin shows the Sioux hunting buffalo.*

bones and horns served as tools and utensils. Even buffalo manure could be dried and used for fuel.

Plains Indians such as the Arapaho, Blackfoot, Cheyenne, Kiowa, and Sioux were horse-borne nomads; they moved across the grasslands with the buffalo herds, carrying their teepees with them. Disputes over buffalo and hunting grounds provoked clashes between rival tribes, which helps explain the cult of the warrior among the Plains Indians. Scalping or killing an enemy would earn praise from elders and feathers for their ceremonial headdresses. The most revered chiefs were allowed to wear eagle-feather warbonnets. Yet chiefs exercised only modest authority over their followers. As Chief Low Horn, a Blackfoot, explained, the chiefs "could not restrain their young men ... their young men were wild, and ambitious, in their turn to be braves and chiefs. They wanted by some brave act to win the favor of their young women, and bring scalps and horses to show their prowess."

Several quite different Indian tribes lived to the south and west of the Plains Indians. In the arid region including what is today Arizona, New Mexico, and southern Utah were the peaceful Pueblo tribes—Acoma, Hopi, Laguna, Taos, Zia, Zuni. They were sophisticated farmers who lived in adobe villages along rivers that they used to irrigate their crops of corn, beans, and squash. The word *pueblo* comes from the Spanish term for "village." Their rivals were the Apache and Navajo, warlike hunters who roamed the countryside in small bands and preyed upon the Pueblos. They, in turn, were periodically harassed by their powerful enemies, the Comanches.

To the north, in the Great Basin between the Rocky Mountains and the Sierra Nevada range, Indians such as the Paiutes and Gosiutes struggled to survive in the harsh, arid region of what is today Nevada, Utah, and eastern California. They traveled in family groups and subsisted on berries, pine nuts, insects, and rodents. West of the mountains, along the California coast, the Indians lived in small villages. They gathered wild plants and acorns and were quite adept at fishing in the rivers and bays. More than 100,000 Indians lived in coastal California in the 1840s.

The Indian tribes living along the northwest Pacific coast—the Nisqually, Spokane, Yakima, Chinook, Klamath, and Nez Percé (pierced noses)—enjoyed the most abundant natural resources and the most temperate climate. The ocean and rivers provided bountiful supplies of seafood—whales, seals, salmon, crabs. The lush forests just east of the coast harbored game, berries, and nuts. And the majestic stands of fir, redwood, and cedar offered wood for cooking and shelter.

All these Indian tribes eventually felt the unrelenting pressure of white expansion. Because Indian life on the Plains depended on the buffalo, the influx of white settlers posed a direct threat to their cultural survival. In an 1846 petition to President Polk, the Sioux protested that "for several years past the Emigrants going over the Mountains from the United States have been the cause that Buffalo in great measure left our hunting grounds, thereby causing us to go into the Country of Our Enemies to hunt, exposing our lives daily for the necessary subsistence of our wives and children and getting killed on several occasions." But the federal government turned a deaf ear to such pleas for assistance. It continued to build a string of frontier forts to protect the advancing settlers, and it sought to use treaties to gain control of new lands. When officials of the Indian Bureau could not coerce, cajole, or confuse Indian leaders into selling title to their tribal lands, fighting ensued. And after the discovery of gold in California in 1848, the tidal wave of white expansion flowed all the way to the west coast.

In 1851 U.S. officials invited the Indian tribes from the northern Plains to a conference held in a grassy valley along the North Platte River, near Ft. Laramie in what is now southeastern Wyoming. Almost 10,000 Indians—men, women, and children—attended the treaty council. What made the huge gathering even more remarkable is that so many of the tribes were at war with one another.

After nearly three weeks of heated discussions and after bestowing on the chiefs a mountain of gifts, federal negotiators and tribal leaders agreed to what became known as the Ft. Laramie Treaty. The American government promised to provide an annual cash payment to the Indians as compensation for the damages caused by wagon trains traversing their hunting grounds. In exchange, the Indians agreed to stop harassing white caravans, to allow federal forts to be built, and to confine themselves to a specified area "of limited extent and well-defined boundaries." Specifically, the Indians were restricted to lands north and south of a corridor through which passed the Overland Trail.

As the first comprehensive treaty with the Plains Indians, this agreement foreshadowed the "reservation" concept of Indian management.

Several tribes, however, refused to accept the treaty provisions. The most powerful tribe, the Lakota Sioux, reluctantly signed the agreement but thereafter failed to abide by its restrictions. "You have split my lands and I don't like it," declared Black Hawk, a Sioux chief at Ft. Laramie. "These lands once belonged to the Kiowas and the Crows, but we whipped these nations out of them, and in this we did what the white men do when they want the lands of the Indians."

THE SPANISH WEST AND MEXICAN REVOLUTION As American settlers moved westward, they also encountered Spanish-speaking peoples. Many whites were as contemptuous of these people as they were of Indians. Senator Lewis Cass, the expansionist from Michigan, expressed the sentiment of many Americans during a debate over the annexation of New Mexico. "We do not want the people of Mexico," he declared, "either as citizens or as subjects. All we want is a portion of territory . . . with a population, which would soon recede, or identify itself with ours." He viewed Mexicans as ignorant, indolent, and conniving. The vast majority of the Spanish-speaking people in what is today the American Southwest resided in New Mexico. Most of these were of mixed Indian and Spanish blood and were poor ranch hands or small farmers and herders.

Church interior, Las Trampas, New Mexico, constructed around 1760.

The Spanish had been less successful in colonizing Arizona and Texas than they had been in New Mexico and Florida. The Yuma and Apache Indians in Arizona and the Comanches and Apaches in Texas thwarted efforts to establish Catholic missions. After years of fruitless missionary efforts among the Pueblo Indians, one Spaniard complained that "most" of them "have never forsaken idolatry, and they appear to be Christians more by force than to be Indians who are reduced to the Holy Faith." By 1790, the Hispanic population in Texas numbered only 2,510 while in New Mexico it exceeded 20,000.

In 1807 French forces occupied Spain and imprisoned the king. This created both consternation and confusion throughout Spain's colonial possessions, including Mexico. Miguel Hidalgo y Costilla, a *creole* (Europeans born in the New World) Mexican priest, took advantage of the fluid situation to organize a revolt of Indians and *mestizos* (people of mixed Indian and white ancestry) against Spanish rule in Mexico. But the poorly organized uprising failed miserably. In 1811 Spanish troops captured Hidalgo and executed him. Other Mexicans, however, continued to yearn for independence. In 1820, Mexican creoles again tried to liberate themselves from Spanish authority. By then, the Spanish forces in Mexico had lost much of their cohesion and dedication. Facing a growing revolt, the last Spanish officials withdrew from Mexico in 1821, and it became an independent nation.

Mexican independence unleashed tremors throughout the Southwest. In New Mexico and Arizona, American fur traders streamed into the region and developed a lucrative commerce in beaver pelts. Wagon trains carrying American settlers began to make their way from St. Louis along the Santa Fe Trail. In California, American entrepreneurs flooded into the now-Mexican province and soon became a powerful force for change; by 1848 Americans made up half of the non-Indian population. In Texas, American adventurers decided to promote their own independence from a newly independent—and chaotic—Mexican government. Suddenly, it seemed, the Southwest was a ripe new frontier for American exploitation and settlement.

THE ROCKIES AND OREGON COUNTRY In the Northwest, the western frontier consisted of the Nebraska, Washington, and Oregon Territories. Fur traders were especially drawn to the Missouri River with its many tributaries. The heyday of the mountain fur trade began in 1822 when a Missouri businessman sent his first trading party to the

George Caleb Bingham's Fur Traders Descending the Missouri, *1845.*

upper Missouri River. By the mid-1820s, there developed the "rendezvous system," in which trappers, traders, and Indians from all over the Rocky Mountain country gathered annually at some designated place, usually in or near the Grand Tetons, in order to trade. But by 1840 the great days of the western fur trade were over. The streams no longer teemed with beavers.

During the 1820s and 1830s, the fur trade had sired a uniquely reckless breed of "mountain men" who deserted civilization for the pursuit of the beaver and reverted to a primitive existence in the wilderness, sometimes in splendid isolation, sometimes in the shelter of primitive forts, and sometimes among the Indians. They were the first to find their way around in the Rocky Mountains, and they pioneered the trails over which settlers by the 1840s were beginning to flood the Oregon Country and trickle across the border into California.

Beyond the mountains, the Oregon Country stretched from the 42nd parallel north to 54°40′, between which Spain and Russia had given up their rights, leaving Great Britain and the United States as the only claimants. Under the Convention of 1818, the two countries had agreed to "joint occupation." Until the 1830s, however, joint occupation had been a legal technicality, because the only American presence was the occasional mountain man who wandered into the Pacific slope or the infrequent trading vessel from Boston, Salem, or New York.

Word of Oregon's fertile soil, temperate climate, and magnificent forests gradually spread eastward. By the late 1830s, in the midst of economic hard times after the Panic of 1837, a trickle of emigrants was

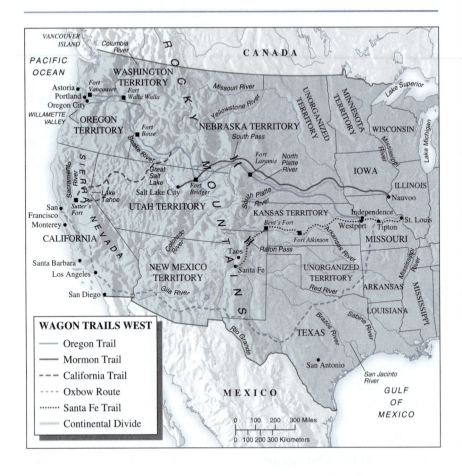

flowing along the Oregon Trail. Soon, "Oregon Fever" spread like a contagion. In 1841 and 1842 the first sizable wagon trains made the trip, and in 1843 the movement became a mass migration. By 1845 there were about 5,000 settlers in the Willamette Valley of Oregon.

CALIFORNIA   California was also an alluring attraction for new settlers and entrepreneurs. It first felt the influence of European culture in 1769, when Spain grew concerned about Russian fur and seal traders moving south along the Pacific coast from their base in Alaska. To thwart Russian intentions, Spain sent a naval expedition to explore and settle the region. The Spanish discovered San Francisco Bay and constructed *presidios* (military garrisons) at San Diego and Monterey. Even more important, Franciscan friars led by Junipero Serra established a mission at San Diego.

Over the next fifty years Franciscans built twenty more missions, spaced a day's journey apart along the coast from San Diego to San Francisco. There they converted Indians and established thriving agricultural estates. As in Mexico, the Spanish monarchy awarded huge land grants in California to a few ex-soldiers and colonists, who turned the grants into profitable cattle ranches. The Indians were left with the least valuable land, and most of them subsisted as farmers or artisans serving the missions. By 1803, 40 percent of California's Native American population had embraced Catholicism. Friars encouraged the piety and diligence of these "Mission Indians" with whippings, causing some to flee the jurisdiction of the church. Within three decades infectious diseases transmitted by European settlers ravaged the Indian population, leaving only a third as many by 1833 as in 1803.

For all of its rich natural resources, California remained thinly populated by Indians and mission friars well into the nineteenth century. It was a simple, almost feudal, agrarian society, without schools, industry, or defenses. In 1821, when Mexico wrested its independence from Spain, Californians took comfort in the fact that Mexico City was so far away that it would exercise little effective control over its farthest state. During the next two decades, Californians, including many recent

Ferriage of the Platte, July 1849. This sketch shows overlanders improvising their own ferry to get their wagons across the Platte River en route to Oregon.

American arrivals, staged ten revolts against the governors dispatched to lord over them.

Yet Mexican rule did produce a dramatic change in California history. In 1824, Mexico passed a colonization act that granted hundreds of huge "rancho" estates to Mexican settlers. With free labor extracted from Indians, who were treated like slaves, the *rancheros* lived a life of self-indulgent luxury and ease, roaming their lands, gambling, horse-racing, bull-baiting, and dancing. These freebooting *rancheros* soon cast covetous eyes on the vast estates controlled by the Franciscan missions. In 1833–1834, they convinced the Mexican government to confiscate the California missions, exile the Franciscan friars, release the Indians from church control, and make the mission lands available to new settlement. Within a few years, some 700 huge new rancho grants of 4,500 to 50,000 acres were issued along the coast from San Diego to San Francisco. Organized like feudal estates, these California ranches resembled southern plantations. But the death rate for Indian workers was twice as high as that of slaves in the Deep South.

Few accounts of life in California, however, took note of the brutalities inflicted on the Indians. Instead they portrayed the region as a proverbial land of milk and honey, ripe for development. Such a natural paradise could not long remain a secret, and Americans had already been visiting the Pacific coast in search of profits and land. By the late 1820s, American trappers wandered in from time to time, and American ships began to enter the "hide and tallow" trade. The ranchos of California produced cowhide and beef tallow in large quantity, and both products enjoyed a brisk demand, cowhides mainly for shoes and the tallow chiefly for candles. Ships from Boston, Salem, or New York, well stocked with trade goods, struggled southward around Cape Horn and northward to the customs office at the California capital of Monterey. From there the ships worked their way down the coast, stopping to sell their goods and take on return cargoes.

By the mid-1830s, shippers began setting up representatives in California to buy the hides and store them until a company ship arrived. One of these agents, Thomas O. Larkin at Monterey, would play a leading role in the American acquisition of California. Larkin stuck pretty much to his trade, operating a retail business on the side, while others branched out and struck it rich in ranching. The most noteworthy of the traders, however, was not American, but Swiss. John A. Sutter had

Sutter's Fort, renamed Fort Sacramento during the Mexican War.

tried the Santa Fe trade first, then found his way to California via Oregon, Hawaii, and Alaska. In Monterey he persuaded the Mexican governor to give him land on which to plant a colony of Swiss émigrés.

At the juncture of the Sacramento and American Rivers (later the site of Sacramento) Sutter built an enormous enclosure that guarded an entire village of settlers and shops. At New Helvetia (Americans called it Sutter's Fort), completed in 1843, no Swiss colony materialized, but the baronial estate became the mecca for Americans bent on settling the Sacramento country. It stood at the end of what became the most traveled route through the Sierras, the California Trail, which forked off the Oregon Trail and led through the mountains near Lake Tahoe. By the start of 1846 there were perhaps 800 Americans in California, along with some 8,000–12,000 Californios of Spanish descent.

MOVING WEST

Most of the western pioneers during the second quarter of the nineteenth century were American-born whites from the upper South and Midwest. A few blacks joined in the migration. One settler remembered seeing "a Negro woman . . . trampling along through heat and dust, carrying a cast-iron black stove on her head, with her provisions and a blanket piled on top . . . bravely pushing on for California." Although some emigrants traveled by sea to California, most went overland. Between 1841 and 1867, some 350,000 men, women, and children made the arduous trek to California or Oregon, while hundreds of thousands of others settled along the way in Colorado, Texas, Arkansas, and other areas. Americans of diverse ethnic origin and religious persuasion moved westward, and their encounters with the people they found there made for a volatile mix.

THE SANTA FE TRAIL   After gaining its independence in 1821, the new government of Mexico was much more interested in trade with Americans than Spain had been. In Spanish-controlled Santa Fe, in fact, all commerce with the United States had been banned. After 1821, however, trade flourished. Hundreds of entrepreneurs made the thousand-mile trek from St. Louis to Santa Fe, forging a route that became known as the Santa Fe Trail. These American traders braved deserts, mountains, and the threat of Indian attacks. Soon, Mexican traders began leading caravans east to Missouri. By the 1830s, there was so much commercial activity between Mexico and St. Louis that the Mexican silver peso became the primary medium of exchange in Missouri.

As they streamed into Santa Fe, American traders discovered the weakness of Mexico's control over its northern borderlands, and the Americans developed contempt for the "mongrel" population of the region. From the 1820s on, however, that population had begun to include a few Americans who lingered in Santa Fe or Taos, using them as jumping-off points for hunting and trapping expeditions northward and westward.

The traders along the Santa Fe Trail pioneered more than a new trail. They showed that heavy wagons could cross the plains and the mountains, and they developed the technique of organized caravans for common protection.

THE OVERLAND TRAIL   As on the Santa Fe Trail, people bound for Oregon and California traveled in caravans of wagons. But on the Overland Trail (also known as the Oregon Trail), most of the people were settlers rather than traders. They traveled mostly in family groups and came from all over the United States. The wagon trains followed the trail west from Independence, Missouri, along the North Platte River into what is now Wyoming, through South Pass down to Fort Bridger (abode of a celebrated mountain man, Jim Bridger), then down the Snake River to the Columbia River, and along the Columbia to their goal in the fertile Willamette Valley. They usually left Missouri in late spring, completing the grueling 2,000-mile trek in six months. Traveling in ox-drawn, canvas-covered wagons nicknamed "prairie schooners," they jostled their way across the dusty or muddy trails and traversed rugged mountains at the rate of about fifteen miles per day. The first wagon trains, usually consisting of ten to twenty wagons, departed in 1841. By 1845, some 5,000 people were making the arduous journey annually. The discovery of gold in California in 1848 brought some 30,000 pioneers along the Oregon Trail in 1849. By 1850, the peak year of travel along the trail, the number had risen to 55,000.

Contrary to popular myth, the Indians rarely attacked wagon trains. Less than 4 percent of the fatalities associated with the Overland Trail experience were the result of Indian attacks. More often, the Indians either allowed the settlers to pass through their tribal lands unmolested or demanded payment. The Sioux were especially shrewd toll keepers, who "in every case get the best of the bargain," observed one overlander. Many wagon trains never encountered a single Indian, and others received generous aid from Indians who served as guides, advisers, or traders. The Indians, one woman pioneer noted, "proved better than represented." To be sure, as the number of pioneers increased dramatically during the 1850s, tensions between overlanders and Indians increased, but never to the degree portrayed in Western novels and films.

Still, the journey west was incredibly difficult. Few who embarked on their western quest were adequately prepared for the ordeals they were to face. The carcasses of mules, oxen, and wagons from previous groups signaled the difficulties they would confront. The diary of Amelia Knight, who set out for Oregon in 1853 with her husband and their seven children, reveals the mortal threats along the trail: "Chatfield quite sick with scarlet fever. A calf took sick and died before breakfast. Lost one of our oxen; he dropped dead in the yoke. I could hardly help shedding tears. Yesterday my eighth child was born." Cholera claimed many lives. On average there was one grave every eighty yards along the trail between the Missouri River and the Willamette Valley. Some 20,000 pioneers died in all.

The never-ending routine of necessary chores and grinding physical labor on the Overland Trail took its toll on once-buoyant spirits. This

Life on the trail: "Father & Mother went into St. Joseph's, bought another tent, heavy canvas for the boys and men to sleep in, using the other tent for an eating place. They also bought a small sheet iron stove, cut a hole in the tent for the pipe, then when it was raining, we could warm up a pot of beans, make a kettle of soup or a pot of coffee, sometimes a pot of mush." Mary Hite, age 13, 1853.

was especially true for women, whose labors went on day and night. Uprooting their families and journeying west placed a distinctive burden on wives and mothers accustomed to the comforts of middle-class domesticity. The hardships of trail life shattered the conventional notion of the settled home as the family's moral center and nursery. The diary of one woman settler records with great poignancy the trail's wearying regimen: "I have done a washing. Stewed apples, made pies and a rice pudding, and mended our wagon cover. Rather tired." The next day brought more of the same: "Baked biscuits, stewed berries, fried meat, boiled and mashed potatoes, and made tea for supper, afterward baked bread. Thus you see I have not much rest." Another woman complained that, unlike the men, who smoked and talked together after supper, "we *have no time for sociability*." All was "hurry scurry." There "is no rest in such a journey."

Initially, the pioneers along the Overland Trail adopted the same division of labor used back East. Women cooked, washed, sewed, and monitored the children while men drove the wagons, tended the horses and cattle, and handled the heavy labor. But the unique demands of the trail

Gathering Buffalo Chips. *Women on the Overland Trail not only had to cook and wash and take care of their children but also had to gather dried buffalo dung for fuel as their wagons crossed the treeless plains.*

soon dissolved such neat distinctions and posed new tasks. Women found themselves gathering buffalo dung for fuel, pitching in to help dislodge a wagon mired in mud, helping to construct a makeshift bridge, or participating in a variety of other unladylike activities. Yet only rarely did menfolk assume conventional female roles. Most of the older women strove to keep distinct the traditional boundaries between men's and women's work, and quarrels frequently erupted. One woman reported that there was "not a little fighting" in their group, "invariably the outcome of disputes over divisions of labor."

The hard labor of the trail understandably provoked tensions within families and powerful yearnings for home. Many a tired pioneer could identify with the following comment in a girl's journal: "Poor Ma said only this morning, 'Oh, I wish we had never started.' She looks so sorrowful and dejected." Another woman wondered "what had possessed my husband, anyway, that he should have thought of bringing us away out through this God forsaken country." Some turned back, but most continued on. And once in Oregon or California they set about establishing stable communities. Noted one settler:

Friday, October 27.—Arrived at Oregon City at the falls of the Willamette.
Saturday, October 28.—Went to work.

THE DONNER PARTY   The most tragic story along the Overland Trail
involved the party led by George Donner, a prosperous sixty-two-year-
old farmer from Illinois, who led his family and a train of other settlers
along the Oregon Trail in 1846. They made every mistake possible.
They started too late in the year, overloaded their wagons, and took a
foolish shortcut to California across the Wasatch Mountains in the
Utah Territory. In the Wasatch, the Donner party was joined by another
group of thirteen pioneers, bringing the total to eighty-seven. Finding
themselves lost on their "shortcut," they had to backtrack before finally
finding their way across the Wasatch and into the desert leading to the
Great Salt Lake. Crossing the desert exacted a terrible toll. They lost
over 100 oxen and were forced to abandon several wagons and their
precious supplies. Tempers flared as the tired and hungry travelers
trudged on. One leader of the party killed a young teamster and was expelled, leaving his wife and children behind.

By the time the Donner party reached Truckee Lake at the base of
Truckee Pass, the last mountain barrier before reaching the Sacramento
Valley, the group had grown surly. They knew that they must cross the
pass before the next major snowfall hemmed them in, but they were too
late. A two-week-long snowfall trapped them in two separate camps. By
December eighty-one settlers, half of them children, were marooned,
and there was only enough meat to last through the end of the month.
Seventeen of the strongest members decided to cross the pass on their
own, only to be trapped by more snow on the western slope. Two members died of exposure and starvation. Just before he died, Uncle Billy
Graves urged his daughters to eat his body. The daughters were appalled by the prospect of cannibalism, but a day later they saw no other
choice. The group struggled on, and, when two more died, they, too,
were consumed. Only seven lived to reach the Sacramento Valley.

Four search parties were then dispatched to save the rest of the Donner party. Back at the main camps at Alder Creek and Truckee Lake,
the survivors slaughtered and ate the last of the livestock, then proceeded to boil hides and bones. One family killed their dog. When the
rescue party finally reached them, they discovered a grisly scene. Thirteen people had died, and cannibalism had become so commonplace

that one pioneer noted casually in his diary that "Mrs. Murphy said here yesterday that she thought she would commence on Milt and eat him. It is distressing. Saturday the 27th a beautiful morning." As the rescuers led the forty-seven survivors over the pass, George Donner, so weakened that he was unable to walk, stayed behind to die. His wife chose to remain with him.

THE PATHFINDER   Despite the hardships and dangers of the overland crossing, the Far West proved an irresistible attraction. The premier press agent for California, and the Far West generally, was John Charles Frémont, "the Pathfinder"—who mainly found paths that the mountain men showed him. Born in Savannah, Georgia, and raised in the South, he had a relentless love of the outdoors and an exuberant, charismatic personality. Frémont studied at the College of Charleston before being commissioned a second lieutenant in the United States Topographical Corps in 1838. In the early 1840s his new father-in-law, Missouri senator Thomas Hart Benton, arranged the explorations toward Oregon that made Frémont famous. In 1842 he mapped the Oregon Trail—and met Christopher "Kit" Carson, one of the most knowledgeable of the mountain men, who became his frequent associate and the most famous frontiersman after Daniel Boone. In 1843–1844 Frémont, typically clad in deerskin shirt, blue army trousers, and moccasins, went on to Oregon, then made a heroic sweep down the eastern

John Charles Frémont, the Pathfinder.

slopes of the Sierras, headed southward through the central valley of California, bypassed the mountains in the south, and returned via Great Salt Lake. His reports on both expeditions, published together in 1845, gained a wide circulation and helped excite the interest of easterners.

TALKS TO ANNEX CALIFORNIA   American presidents, beginning with Jackson, tried to acquire at least northern California, down to San Francisco Bay, by purchase from Mexico. Jackson reasoned that as a free state California could balance the future admission of Texas as a slave state. But Jackson's agent had to be recalled after a clumsy effort to bribe Mexican officials. Tyler's minister to Mexico resumed talks, but they ended abruptly after a bloodless comic-opera conquest of Monterey by the commander of the American Pacific Fleet, who had heard a false rumor of war.

Rumors flourished that the British and French were scheming to grab California, though neither government actually had such intentions. Political conditions in Mexico left the remote territory in near anarchy much of the time, as governors came and went in rapid succession. Amid the chaos substantial Californios reasoned that they would be better off if they cut ties to Mexico altogether. Some favored an independent state, perhaps under French or British protection. A larger group, led by a Sonoma cattleman, admired the balance of central and local authority in the United States and felt their interests might best be served by American annexation. By the time the Americans were ready to fire the spark of rebellion in California, there was little will in Mexico to resist.

ANNEXING TEXAS

AMERICAN SETTLEMENTS   America's lust for land was most clearly at work in the most accessible of all the Mexican borderlands, Texas. More Americans resided there than in all the other coveted regions combined. In fact, Texas was rapidly turning into an American province, for Mexico welcomed American settlers there as a means of stabilizing the border.

First and foremost among the promoters of Anglo-American settlement was Stephen F. Austin, a Missouri resident who gained from Mexico a huge land grant originally given to his father by Spanish authorities. Before Mexican independence from Spain was fully won, he had started a colony on the lower Brazos River late in 1821, and by 1824 more than 2,000 hardy souls had settled on his lands. In 1825, under a National Colonization Law, the state of Coahuila-Texas offered large tracts to *empresarios,* large ranchers, who promised to sponsor immigrants. Most of the newcomers were southern farmers drawn to rich new cotton lands going for only a few cents an acre. As a young woman settler recalled, "I was a young thing then, but 5 months married, my husband . . . failed in Tennessee. . . . I was ready to go anywhere . . . freely consented. . . . Texas fever rose then . . . there we must go. There without much reflection, we did go." By 1830 the coastal region of eastern Texas had about 20,000 white settlers and 1,000 black slaves brought in to work the cotton.

At that point the Mexican government grew alarmed at the flood of strangers threatening to engulf the province, and it forbade further immigration. But illegal American immigrants moved across the long border as easily as illegal Mexican immigrants would later cross over in the other direction. By 1835 the American population had grown to around 30,000, about ten times the number of Mexicans in Texas. Friction mounted in 1832 and 1833 as Americans organized conventions to demand a state of their own. Instead of granting the request, General Santa Anna, who had seized power in Mexico, dissolved the national congress late in 1834, abolished the federal system, and became dictator of a centralized state. Texans rose in rebellion and summoned a convention which, like the earlier Continental Congress, adopted a "Declaration of Causes" for taking up arms. On March 2, 1836, the Texans declared their independence as Santa Anna approached with an army of conquest.

INDEPENDENCE FROM MEXICO   The Mexican army delivered its first blow at San Antonio, where it assaulted a small garrison of Texans and American volunteers, led by Lieutenant-Colonel William B. Travis of South Carolina, holed up behind the adobe walls of an abandoned mission, the Alamo. Among the most celebrated of the volunteers was Davy Crockett, the Tennessee frontiersman who had fought Indians under Andrew Jackson and then served as a congressman. Full of bounce and brag, he was thoroughly expert at killing with his trusty rifle, "Old Betsy." As he once told his men, "Pierce the heart of the enemy as you

Sam Houston.

would a feller that spit in your face, knocked down your wife, burnt up your houses, and called your dog a skunk! Cram his pesky carcass full of thunder and lightning like a stuffed sassidge . . . and bite his nose off into the bargain."

On February 23, 1836, Santa Anna demanded that the 189 defenders at the Alamo surrender. They answered with a cannon shot. The 5,000 Mexicans then launched a series of frontal assaults. For twelve days they were repulsed with fearful losses.

Then, on March 6, the defenders of the Alamo were awakened by the sound of Mexican bugles playing the dreaded "Deguello" ("no mercy to the defenders"). Soon thereafter Santa Anna's men attacked from every side. They were twice repulsed, but on the third try, as the defenders ran low on ammunition, the Mexicans broke through the battered north wall and swarmed through the breach. Colonel Travis was killed by a bullet to the forehead. Davy Crockett and the other frontiersmen used their muskets as clubs, but they too were slain. The notorious slave smuggler, Indian fighter, and inventor of the Bowie knife, Jim Bowie, his pistols emptied, his famous knife bloodied, and his body riddled by Mexican bullets, lay dead on his cot. Santa Anna ordered the wounded Americans put to death and their bodies burned with the rest. The only survivors were sixteen women, children, and servants. It was a complete victory for the Mexicans, but a costly one. The defenders of the Alamo gave their lives at the cost of 1,544 Mexicans, and their heroic stand inspired the rest of Texas to fanatical resistance. While Santa

Anna dictated a glorious victory declaration, his aide wrote in his diary: "One more such 'glorious victory' and we are finished."

The commander-in-chief of the Texas forces was Sam Houston, a Tennessee frontiersman who had learned war under the tutelage of Andrew Jackson at Horseshoe Bend, had later represented the Nashville district in Congress, and had moved to Texas only three years before. Houston beat a strategic retreat eastward, gathering reinforcements as he went, including volunteer recruits from the United States. Just west of the San Jacinto River he finally paused near the site of the city that later bore his name, and on April 21, 1836, surprised a Mexican encampment there. The Texans charged, yelling "Remember the Alamo," overwhelmed the Mexican force within fifteen minutes, and took Santa Anna prisoner. The Mexican dictator bought his freedom for the price of a treaty recognizing Texan independence, with the Rio Grande as the boundary. The Mexican Congress repudiated the treaty, but the war was at an end.

THE MOVE FOR ANNEXATION The Lone Star Republic then drafted a constitution, made Houston its first president, and voted almost unanimously for annexation to the United States as soon as the opportunity arose. Houston's old friend Jackson was still president, but even Old Hickory could be discreet when delicacy demanded it. The addition of a new slave state at a time when Congress was beset with abolitionist petitions threatened a serious sectional quarrel that might endanger the election of Van Buren, his hand-picked successor. Worse than that, it raised the specter of war with Mexico. Jackson kept his counsel and even delayed recognition of the Texas Republic until his last day in office. Van Buren shied away from the issue of annexation during his entire term as president.

Rebuffed in Washington, Texans turned their thoughts to a separate destiny. Under President Mirabeau Bonaparte Lamar, elected in 1838, they began to talk of expanding to the Pacific as a new nation that would rival the United States. France and Britain extended formal recognition to the new Texas Republic and began to develop trade relations. Texas supplied them with an independent source of cotton, new markets, and promised also to become an obstacle to American expansion. The British, who had emancipated the slaves in their colonies in 1833, hoped Texans might embrace abolition in exchange for British protection against any Mexican effort to reassert its sovereignty over Texas.

Most Texans, however, had never abandoned their hopes of annexation to the United States. Reports of growing British influence in Texas created anxieties in the United States government and among southern slaveholders, who became the chief advocates of annexation. Secret negotiations with Texas began in 1843, and that April John C. Calhoun, Tyler's secretary of state, completed a treaty that went to the Senate for ratification.

Calhoun chose this moment also to send the British minister a letter instructing him on the blessings of slavery and stating that annexation of Texas was needed to foil the British abolitionists. Publication of the note fostered the claim that annexation was planned less in the national interest than to promote the expansion of slavery. It was so worded, one observer wrote Jackson, as to "drive off every northern man from the support of the measure." Sectional division, plus fear of a war with Mexico, contributed to the Senate's overwhelming rejection of the treaty. Solid Whig opposition was the most important factor behind its defeat.

POLK'S PRESIDENCY

THE ELECTION OF 1844   Prudent leaders in both political parties had hoped to keep the divisive issue of Texas out of the 1844 campaign. Clay and Van Buren, the leading candidates, had reached the same conclusion about Texas: when the treaty was submitted to the Senate, they both wrote letters opposing annexation because it would create the danger of war. Both letters, dated three days apart, appeared in separate Washington newspapers on April 27, 1844. Clay's "Raleigh letter" (written while he was on a southern tour) added that annexation was "dangerous to the integrity of the Union . . . and not called for by any general expression of public opinion." The outcome of the Whig convention in Baltimore seemed to bear out his view. Party leaders showed no qualms about Clay's stance. The convention nominated him unanimously, and the Whig platform omitted any reference to Texas.

The Democratic convention was a different story. Van Buren's southern supporters, including Jackson, abandoned him because of his opposition to Texas annexation. With the convention deadlocked, on the eighth ballot expansionist forces brought forward James K. Polk of Tennessee, and on the ninth ballot he became the first "dark horse" candidate to win a major-party nomination. The party platform took an unequivocal stand favoring expansion, and to win support in the North and West as well as in the South, it linked the questions of Oregon and Texas: "our title to the whole of the territory of Oregon is clear and unquestionable," the party proclaimed, and called for "the reoccupation of Oregon and the reannexation of Texas."

The combination of southern and western expansionism offered a winning strategy that was so popular that Clay began to hedge his statement on Texas. While he still believed the integrity of the Union was the chief consideration, he had "no personal objection to the annexation of Texas" if it could be achieved "without dishonor, without war, with the common consent of the Union, and upon just and fair terms." His explanation seemed clear enough, but prudence was no match for spread-eagle oratory and the emotional pull of Manifest Destiny. The net result of Clay's stand was to turn more antislavery votes to the Liberty party, which increased its count from about 7,000 in 1840 to more than 62,000 in 1844. In the western counties of New York, the Liberty party drew enough votes away from the Whigs to give the state to Polk. Had he carried New York, Clay would have won the election by seven electoral votes. Polk won a narrow plurality of 38,000 popular votes na-

James K. Polk.

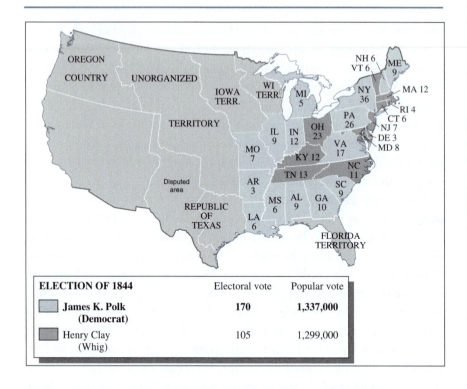

ELECTION OF 1844	Electoral vote	Popular vote
James K. Polk (Democrat)	170	1,337,000
Henry Clay (Whig)	105	1,299,000

tionwide (the first president since John Quincy Adams to win without a majority) but a clear majority of the electoral college, 170 to 105.

"Who is James K. Polk?" the Whigs scornfully asked in the campaign. But the man was not as obscure as they implied. He was a dark horse only in the sense that he was not a candidate before the convention. Born near Charlotte, North Carolina, trained in mathematics and the classics at the University of North Carolina, Polk had moved to Tennessee as a young man. A successful lawyer and planter, he had entered politics early, served fourteen years in Congress (four as Speaker of the House) and two as governor of Tennessee.

Young Hickory, as his partisans liked to call him, was a short, slender man with a shock of long, grizzled hair, probing gray eyes, and a seemingly permanent grimace. He had none of Jackson's charisma, but shared Jackson's prejudices and made up for his lack of color by stubborn determination and hard work, which destroyed his health during four years in the White House.

POLK'S PROGRAM   In domestic affairs "Young Hickory" Polk hewed to the principle of the old hero, but the new Jacksonians subtly reflected the growing influence of the slaveholding South within the party. Abolitionism, Polk warned, could bring the dissolution of the Union. Antislavery northerners had already begun to drift away from the Democratic party, which they complained was coming to represent the slaveholding interest.

Polk's major objectives were tariff reduction, reestablishment of the Independent Treasury, settlement of the Oregon question, and the acquisition of California. He gained them all. The Walker Tariff of 1846, in keeping with Democratic tradition, reduced the tariff. In the same year Polk persuaded Congress to restore the Independent Treasury, which the Whigs had eliminated. Twice Polk vetoed internal-improvements bills. In each case his blows to the American System of Henry Clay's Whigs satisfied the urges of the slaveholding South, but at the cost of annoying northern protectionists and westerners who needed internal improvements.

THE STATE OF TEXAS Polk's chief concern was geographic expansion. He privately vowed to acquire California, and New Mexico as well, preferably by purchase. The acquisition of Texas was already under way when Polk took office. In his final months in office President Tyler, taking Polk's election as a mandate to act, asked Congress to accomplish annexation by joint resolution, which required only a simple majority in each house and avoided the two-thirds Senate vote needed to ratify a treaty. Congress had read the election returns too, and after a bitter debate over slavery, the resolution passed by votes of 27 to 25 in the Senate and 120 to 98 in the House. Tyler signed the resolution on March 1, 1845, offering to admit Texas to statehood. The new state with its own consent might be divided into as many as five states in the near future. A Texas convention accepted the offer, and the voters of Texas ratified the action. The new state formally entered the Union on December 29, 1845.

OREGON Meanwhile, the Oregon issue heated up as expansionists aggressively insisted that Polk abandon previous offers to settle on the 49th parallel and stand by the platform pledge to take all of Oregon. The expansionists were prepared to risk war with Britain while relations with Mexico were simultaneously moving toward the breaking point. "Fifty-four forty or fight," they declared. "All of Oregon or none." In his inaugural address, Polk claimed that the American title to Oregon was "clear and unquestionable," but privately he favored a prudent compromise. War with Mexico was brewing; the territory up to 54°40′ seemed of less importance than Puget Sound or the ports of California, on which the British also were thought to have an eye. Since Monroe, each administration had offered to extend the boundary along the 49th parallel. In 1845 Polk renewed the offer, only to have it refused by the British minister, Richard Pakenham.

Polk withdrew the offer and went back to his claim to all of Oregon. Fortunately for Polk, the British government had no enthusiasm for war over that remote wilderness at the cost of profitable trade relations with the United States. From the British viewpoint, the only land in dispute all along had been between the 49th parallel and the Columbia River. But now the fur trade of the region was a dying industry. In 1846 the British government submitted a draft treaty to extend the border along the 49th parallel and through the main channel south of Vancouver Island and to keep the right to navigate all of the Columbia River. On June 15 Secretary of State James Buchanan and British minister Pakenham signed it, and three days later it was ratified in the Senate. The

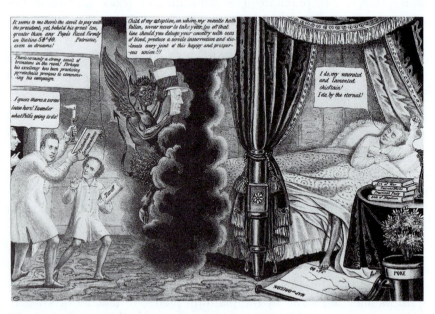

The devil advising Polk to pursue 54°40′ even if "you deluge your country with seas of blood, produce a servile insurrection, and dislocate every joint of this happy and prosperous union."

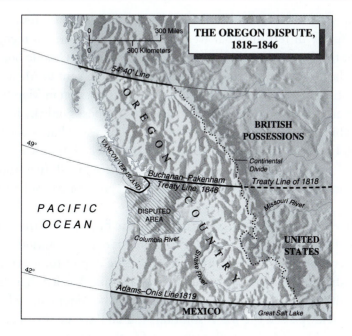

THE OREGON DISPUTE, 1818–1846

only opposition came from a group of expansionists representing the Old Northwest who wanted more. Most of the country was satisfied. Southerners cared less about Oregon than about Texas, and northern business interests valued British trade more than they valued Oregon. Besides, the country was already at war with Mexico.

THE MEXICAN WAR

THE OUTBREAK OF WAR   On March 6, 1845, two days after Polk took office, the Mexican ambassador broke off relations and left for home to protest the annexation of Texas. When an effort at negotiation failed, Polk focused his efforts on unilateral initiatives. Already he was fostering American intrigues in California. He wrote Consul Thomas O. Larkin in Monterey that he would make no effort to induce California into the Union, but "if the people should desire to unite their destiny with ours, they would be received as brethren." Larkin, who could take a hint, began to line up Americans and sympathetic Californios. Meanwhile Polk ordered American troops under General Zachary Taylor to take up positions on the Rio Grande in the new state of Texas. These positions lay in territory that was doubly disputed: Mexico recognized neither the American annexation of Texas nor the Rio Grande boundary.

The last hope for peace died when John Slidell, sent to Mexico City to negotiate a settlement, finally gave up on his mission in March 1846. Polk then resolved that he could achieve his purposes only by force. He won cabinet approval of a war message to Congress. That very evening, May 9, the news arrived that Mexicans had attacked American soldiers north of the Rio Grande. Eleven Americans were killed, five wounded, and the remainder taken prisoner. Polk's provocative scheme had worked.

In his war message Polk could now take the high ground that a declaration of war would be a response to aggression, a recognition that war had been forced upon the United States. "The cup of forbearance had been exhausted" before the incident; now, he said, Mexico "has invaded our territory, and shed American blood upon the American soil." Congress quickly passed the war resolution, and Polk signed the declaration of war on May 13, 1846. But support for the war was guarded. The House authorized a call for 50,000 volunteers and a war appropriation of $10 million, but sixty-seven Whigs voted against that measure, another token of rising opposition to the war.

OPPOSITION TO THE WAR In the Mississippi Valley, where expansion fever ran high, the war was immensely popular. In New England, however, there was less enthusiasm for "Mr. Polk's War." Whig opinion ranged from lukewarm to hostile. John Quincy Adams, who voted against participation, called it "a most unrighteous war." An obscure one-term congressman from Illinois named Abraham Lincoln, upon taking his seat in 1847, began introducing "spot resolutions," calling on Polk to name the spot where American blood had been shed on American soil, implying that American troops may, in fact, have been in Mexico when fired upon.

Many New Englanders believed that the war was the work of proslavery southerners seeking new territories and denounced the conflict as a war of conquest. But before the war ended some antislavery men had a change of heart about the war. Mexican territory seemed so unsuited to plantation staples that they endorsed expansion in hope of enlarging the area of free soil. Manifest Destiny exerted a potent influence even on those who opposed the war.

PREPARING FOR BATTLE   Both the United States and Mexico approached the war ill prepared. American policy had been incredibly reckless, risking war with both Britain and Mexico while doing nothing to strengthen the armed forces until war came. At the outset of war, the regular army numbered barely over 7,000, in contrast to the Mexican force of 32,000. Before the war ended, the American force grew to 104,000, of whom about 31,000 were regular army troops and marines. Most of these were six- and twelve-month volunteers from the West. Illinois provided enough men for fourteen regiments, even though its quota was only four. One editor explained the outpouring of citizen soldiers: "We had to show the Mexicans that a people without being military, may be *warlike.*" The volunteer militia companies, often filled with frontier toughs, lacked uniforms, standard equipment, and discipline. One observer watched a band of such recruits with "torn and dirty shirts—uncombed heads—unwashed faces" trying to drill, "all hollowing, cursing, yelling like so many incarnate fiends." Repeatedly, despite the best efforts of the commanding generals, these undisciplined forces engaged in plunder, rape, and murder.

Nevertheless, being used to a rough-and-tumble life, the motley American troops outmatched larger Mexican forces, which had their own problems with training, discipline, and munitions. Many of the Mexicans were pressed into service or recruited from prisons, and they made less than enthusiastic fighters. Mexican artillery pieces were generally obsolete, and the powder was so faulty that American soldiers could often dodge cannonballs that fell short and bounced ineffectively along the ground.

The United States entered the war without even a tentative plan of action, and politics complicated things. What Polk wanted, Thomas Hart Benton wrote later, was "a small war, just large enough to require a treaty of peace, and not large enough to make military reputations, dangerous for the presidency." Winfield Scott, general-in-chief of the army, was a politically ambitious Whig. Nevertheless Polk named him at first to take charge of the Rio Grande front. When Scott quarreled with Polk's secretary of war, however, the exasperated president withdrew the appointment.

There now seemed a better choice. General Zachary Taylor's men had scored two victories over Mexican forces north of the Rio Grande, at Palo Alto (May 8) and Resaca de la Palma (May 9). On May 18 Taylor crossed the river and occupied Matamoros, which a demoralized and

Zachary Taylor.

bloodied Mexican army had abandoned. These quick victories brought Taylor instant popularity, and the president responded willingly to the demand that he be made commander for the conquest of Mexico. "Old Rough and Ready" Taylor, a bowlegged, squatty, and none-too-handsome man of sixty-one, seemed unlikely stuff from which to fashion a hero and impressed Polk as less of a political threat than Scott. Without a major battle, he had achieved Polk's main objective, the conquest of Mexico's northern provinces.

ANNEXATION OF CALIFORNIA   Along the Pacific coast, conquest was under way before definite news of the Mexican War arrived. Near the end of 1845, John C. Frémont brought out a band of sixty frontiersmen, ostensibly on another exploration of California and Oregon. When the Mexican commandant at Monterey ordered him out of the Salinas Valley, Frémont at first dug in his heels and refused to go, but he soon changed his mind and headed for Oregon. In 1846 he and his men again moved south, this time into the Sacramento Valley. Americans in the area fell upon Sonoma on June 14, proclaimed the "Republic of California," and hoisted the hastily designed Bear Flag, a grizzly bear and star painted on white cloth—a version of which became the state flag.

Frémont endorsed the Bear Flag Republic and again set out for Monterey. Before he arrived, John D. Sloat, the commodore of the Pacific Fleet, having heard of the outbreak of hostilities with Mexico, sent a party ashore to raise the American flag and proclaim California a part of the United States. The Republic of California had lasted less than a month, and most Californians of whatever origin welcomed a change that promised order in preference to the confusion of the unruly Bear Flaggers.

Before the end of July a new commodore, Robert F. Stockton, began preparations to move against southern California. As senior officer on the scene, Stockton enlisted Frémont's band as the California Battalion and gave Frémont the rank of major. Stockton sent this group down to San Diego, but they were too late to overtake the fleeing Mexican loyalists. In a more leisurely fashion, Stockton occupied Santa Barbara and Los Angeles. By mid-August resistance had dissipated. On August 17 Stockton declared himself governor, with Frémont as military commander in the north.

By August another expedition was closing on Santa Fe. On August 18 Stephen Kearny and his men entered Santa Fe, which had been abandoned by an irresolute Mexican governor who had fled with its defenders. After setting up a civilian governor, Kearny divided his remaining force, leading 300 men west toward California. On October 6 they encountered a band of frontiersmen under Frémont's old helper, Kit Carson, who was riding eastward with news that California had already fallen. Kearny sent 200 of his men back and with the remaining 100 pushed west with Carson serving as a reluctant guide.

The Battle of the Plains of Mesa took place just before American forces entered Los Angeles. This sketch was made at the scene.

But after Carson's departure from the coast, the picture had changed. In southern California, where most of the poorer Mexicans and Mexicanized Indians resented American rule, a rebellion broke out. By the end of October, the rebels had ousted the token American force in southern California. Kearny walked right into this rebel zone when he arrived. At San Diego he met up with Stockton and joined him in the reconquest of southern California, which they achieved after two brief clashes when they entered Los Angeles on January 10, 1847. Rebel forces capitulated three days later.

TAYLOR'S BATTLES   Both California and New Mexico had been taken before General Zachary Taylor fought his first major battle in northern Mexico. Having waited for more men and munitions, he fi-

THE MEXICAN WAR:
MAJOR CAMPAIGNS

◄-- U.S. forces   ◄— Mexican forces

★ Battle site

--- Line set by Treaty of
    Guadalupe Hidalgo, 1848

nally moved out of his Matamoros base in September 1846 and headed southward toward the heart of Mexico. His first goal was the fortified city of Monterrey, which he took after a five-day siege. Polk, however, was none too happy with the easy terms of surrender to which Taylor agreed, or with Taylor's growing popularity. The whole episode merely confirmed the president's impression that Taylor was too passive to be trusted further with the major campaign. Besides, his victories, if flawed, were leading to talk of Taylor as the next Whig candidate for president.

Yet Polk's grand strategy was itself flawed. Having never seen the Mexican desert, he wrongly assumed that Taylor could live off the country and need not depend on resupply. Polk therefore misunderstood the general's reluctance to strike out across several hundred miles of barren land just north of Mexico City. On another point the president was simply duped. The old dictator Santa Anna, forced out in 1844, got word to Polk from his exile in Havana that in return for the right considerations he could bring about a settlement of the war. Polk in turn assured the Mexican leader that Washington would pay well for any territory taken through a settlement. In August 1846, after another change in the Mexican government, Santa Anna was permitted to pass through the American blockade into Vera Cruz. Soon he was again in command of the Mexican army and then was named president once more. Polk's intrigue unintentionally put perhaps the ablest Mexican general back in command of the enemy army, where he busily organized his forces to strike at Taylor.

By then another American front had been opened, and Taylor was ordered to wait in place. In October 1846 Polk and his cabinet decided to move against Mexico City by way of Vera Cruz. Polk would have preferred a Democratic general, but for want of a better choice named Winfield Scott to the field command. In January 1847 Taylor was required to give up most of his regulars to Scott's force gathering at Tampico. Taylor, miffed at his reduction to a minor role, disobeyed orders and advanced beyond Saltillo.

There, near the hacienda of Buena Vista, Santa Anna met Taylor's untested volunteers with a large but ill-trained and tired army. The Mexican general invited the outnumbered Americans to surrender. "Tell him to go to hell," Taylor replied. In the hard-fought Battle of Buena Vista (February 22–23, 1847), Taylor saw his son-in-law, Colonel Jefferson Davis, the future president of the Confederacy, lead a regiment that broke up a Mexican cavalry charge. Neither side could claim victory on the strength of the outcome, but Taylor was convinced that only his lack of regulars prevented him from striking a decisive blow. In any case it was the last major action on the northern front, and Taylor was granted leave to return home.

SCOTT'S TRIUMPH   Meanwhile, the long-planned assault on the enemy capital had begun on March 9, 1847, when Scott's army landed on the beaches south of Vera Cruz. It was the first major amphibious operation by American military forces, and was carried out without loss. Vera Cruz surrendered on March 27 after a week-long siege. Scott then set out on the route taken by Cortés more than 300 years before. Santa Anna tried to set a trap for him at the mountain pass of Cerro Gordo, but Scott's men took more than 3,000 prisoners, large quantities of equipment and provisions, and the Mexican president's personal effects.

On May 15 Scott's men entered Puebla, the second-largest Mexican city. There Scott lost about a third of his army because men whose twelve-month enlistments had expired felt free to go home, leaving Scott with about 7,000 troops in all. There was nothing to do but hang on until reinforcements and new supplies came up from the coast. Finally, after three months, with his numbers almost doubled, Scott set out on August 7 through the mountain passes into the valley of Mexico, cutting his supply line to the coast. The aging duke of Wellington, following the campaign from England, predicted Scott "is lost—he cannot capture the city and he cannot fall back upon his base."

Scott, however, directed a brilliant flanking operation around the lakes and marshes that guarded the eastern approaches to Mexico City. After a series of battles in which they overwhelmed Mexican defenses, American forces entered Mexico City on September 13, 1847, and within three days mopped up the remnants of resistance. At the National Palace a battalion of marines ran up the American flag and occupied the "halls of Montezuma." News of the victory generated great excitement. "A military ardor pervades all ranks," declared novelist Herman Melville from his New York home. "Nothing is talked of but the 'Halls of the Montezuma.'"

But victory came at a high price. After witnessing the fighting around Mexico City, a young American lieutenant described the scene in a letter to his wife. "I had no idea until a few days past," he reported, "what horrible sights a battlefield presented." He noted that the "road and its vicinity on both sides, for the most of three miles, were covered with the dead and dying, bodies without heads, arms, legs, and disfigured in every possible way!" He closed his letter by exclaiming: "Oh, it was awful and I can never forget this day."

THE TREATY OF GUADALUPE HIDALGO   After the fall of the capital, Santa Anna resigned and a month later left the country. Meanwhile Polk had appointed as chief peace negotiator Nicholas P. Trist, chief clerk of the State Department and a Virginia Democrat of impeccably partisan credentials. Formal talks got under way on January 2, 1848, at the village of Guadalupe Hidalgo just outside the capital, and dragged on through the month. By the Treaty of Guadalupe Hidalgo, signed on February 2, 1848, Mexico gave up all claims to Texas above the Rio Grande and ceded California and New Mexico to the United States. In return the United States agreed to pay Mexico $15 million and assume the claims of American citizens against Mexico up to a total of $3¼ million.

Polk submitted the treaty to the Senate. A growing movement to annex all of Mexico had impelled him to hold out for more. But as Polk confided to his diary, rejecting the treaty would be too risky. If he should reject a treaty made in accord with his own original terms in order to gain more territory, "the probability is that Congress would not grant either men or money to prosecute the war." In that case he might eventually have to withdraw the army and lose everything. The treaty went to the Senate, which ratified it on March 10, 1848. By the end of July, the last remaining American soldiers had boarded ship in Vera Cruz.

THE WAR'S LEGACIES   The seventeen-month-long Mexican War had cost the United States 1,721 killed, 4,102 wounded, and far more—11,155—dead of disease, mostly dysentery and chronic diarrhea. It remains the deadliest war in American military history in terms of the percentage of combatants killed. Out of every 1,000 soldiers in Mexico, some 110 died. The next highest death rate would be in the Civil War, with 65 out of every 1,000 participants. The military and naval expenditures totaled $98 million.

The United States acquired more than 500,000 square miles of territory (more than a million counting Texas), including the great Pacific harbors of San Diego, Monterey, and San Francisco, with uncounted millions in mineral wealth. Except for a small addition by the Gadsden Purchase of 1853, these annexations rounded out the continental United States. After the treaty was ratified, Polk wrote in his diary: "There will be added to the United States an immense empire, the value of which twenty years hence it would be difficult to calculate." A prominent Mexican, Porfirio Díaz, later to become president of Mexico, expressed a different view: "Alas, poor Mexico! So far from God and so close to the United States!"

Several important "firsts" are associated with the Mexican War: the first successful offensive American war, the first major amphibious operation, the first occupation of an enemy capital, the first in which martial law was declared on foreign soil, the first in which West Point graduates played a major role, and the first reported by modern war correspondents. It was also the first significant combat experience for a group of junior officers who would later serve as leading generals during the Civil War: Robert E. Lee, Ulysses S. Grant, Thomas "Stonewall" Jackson, George B. McClellan, George Pickett, Braxton Bragg, George Meade, and others.

Initially, the victory in Mexico provoked a surge of national pride. American triumphs "must elevate the *true* self-respect of the American people," Walt Whitman exclaimed. Others were not so sure. Ralph Waldo Emerson rejected war "as a means of achieving America's destiny," but he then accepted the annexation of new territory by force with the explanation that "most of the great results of history are brought about by discreditable means."

As the years passed, the Mexican War was increasingly seen as a war of conquest provoked by a president bent on expansion. One might argue that Polk merely hastened, and possibly achieved at less cost in treasure and human misery, what the march of the restless frontier would soon have achieved anyway. For a brief season, the glory of conquest added luster to the names of Zachary Taylor and Winfield Scott. Despite Polk's best efforts, he had manufactured the next, and last, two Whig candidates for president. One of them, Taylor, would replace him in the White House, with the storm of sectional conflict already on the horizon.

MAKING CONNECTIONS

- This chapter opens with the brief administration of William Henry Harrison, the first Whig president. The collapse of the Whig party is detailed in Chapter 16.

- The West developed quickly after the expansionist policies of the 1840s. Chapter 19 takes the story to the 1890s.

- This chapter ends with the observation of "the storm of sectional conflict already on the horizon." Chapter 16's discussion of "The Crisis of Union" traces the relationship between the Mexican War and the Civil War more explicitly.

FURTHER READING

For background on Whig programs and ideas, see Richard P. McCormick's *The Second American Party System: Party Formation in the Jacksonian Era* (1966). Several works help interpret the expansionist impulse. Frederick Merk's *Manifest Destiny and Mission in American History* (1963) remains a classic. A more recent treatment of expansionist ideology is Thomas R. Hietala's *Manifest Design: Anxious Aggrandizement in Late Jacksonian America* (1985).

The best survey of western expansion is Richard White's *"It's Your Misfortune and None of My Own": A New History of the American West* (1991). Robert M. Utley's *A Life Wild and Perilous: Mountain Men and the Paths to the Pacific* (1997) tells the dramatic story of the rugged pathfinders who found corridors over the Rocky Mountains. The movement of settlers to the West is ably documented in John Mack Faragher's *Women and Men on the Overland Trail* (1979). The best account of the California gold rush is Malcolm J. Rohrbough's *Days of Gold: The California Gold Rush and the American Nation* (1997).

Gene M. Brack's *Mexico Views Manifest Destiny, 1821–1846* (1975) takes Mexico's viewpoint on American designs on the West. On James K. Polk, see John H. Schroeder's *Mr. Polk's War* (1973). The best survey of the military conflict is John S. D. Eisenhower's *So Far from God: The U.S. War with Mexico, 1846–1848* (1989). For a textured account of the soldier's life in the war, see Richard Bruce Winders's *Mr. Polk's Army: The American Military Experience in the Mexican War* (1997). John S. D. Eisenhower's *Agent of Destiny: The Life and Times of General Winfield Scott* (1997) illuminates the greatest American soldier between George Washington and Ulysses S. Grant.

An excellent analysis of the diplomatic aspects of Mexican-American relations is David M. Pletcher's *The Diplomacy of Annexation: Texas, Oregon, and the Mexican War* (1973). On California, see Kevin Starr's *Americans and the California Dream, 1850–1915* (1973). On Oregon, see Earl Pomeroy's *The Pacific Slope: A History of California, Oregon, Washington, Idaho, Utah, and Nevada* (1965).

PART FOUR

A HOUSE DIVIDED

Of all the regions of the United States during the first half of the nineteenth century, the South was the most distinctive. Southern society remained fundamentally rural and agricultural long after the rest of the nation embraced the urban industrial revolution. By 1860 a southern white was only one-third as likely as a northern white to work at a non-farm job, live in a city, or be foreign-born. Likewise, the southern elite's tenacious desire to preserve and expand the institution of slavery muted social reform impulses in the South and ignited a prolonged political controversy that would end in civil war.

The rapid and relentless settlement of the western territories set in motion a ferocious competition between North and South for political influence in the burgeoning West. Would the new states in the West be "slave" or "free"? The issue of allowing slavery into the new territories involved more than humanitarian concern for the plight of enslaved blacks. By the 1840s, North and South had developed quite different economic interests. The North wanted high tariffs on imported manufactures to "protect" its infant industries from foreign competition. Southerners, on the other hand, favored free trade because they wanted to import British goods in exchange for the cotton they provided British textile mills.

A series of ingenious political compromises glossed over the fundamental differences between the sections during the first half of the nineteenth century. But abolitionists refused to give up their crusade against slavery. Moreover, a new generation of national political leaders emerged in the 1850s, men from both North and South who were less willing to seek political compromises. The continuing debate over allowing slavery into the new western territories kept sectional tensions at a fever pitch. By the time Abraham Lincoln was elected in 1860, many Americans had decided with the new president that the nation could not survive half-slave and half-free; something had to give.

In a last ditch effort to preserve the institution of slavery, eleven southern states seceded from the union and created a separate Confederate nation. This, in turn, prompted northerners such as Lincoln to support a civil war to preserve the Union. No one realized in 1861 how prolonged and costly the war between the states would become. Over 630,000 soldiers and sailors died of wounds or disease. The colossal carnage caused even the most seasoned observers to blanch in disbelief. As President Lincoln confessed in his second inaugural address, no one expected the war to become so "fundamental and astonishing."

Nor did people envision how sweeping the war's effects would be on the future of the country. The northern victory in 1865 restored the Union and in the process helped to accelerate America's transformation into a modern nation-state. National power and a national consciousness began to displace the sectional emphases of the antebellum era. A Republican-led Congress pushed through legislation to foster industrial and commercial development and western expansion. In the process, the United States began to leave behind the Jeffersonian dream of a decentralized agrarian republic.

The Civil War also ended slavery. Yet the actual status of the four million freed blacks remained precarious. How would they fare in a society built on slavery? In 1865 the daughter of a Georgia planter expressed her concern about such issues when she wrote in her diary that "there are sad changes in store for both races. I wonder the Yankees do not shudder to behold their work" ahead in trying to "reconstruct" the defeated South.

The former slaves found themselves legally free, but most were without property, homes, education, or training. Although the Fourteenth Amendment (1867) set forth guarantees for the civil rights of African Americans and the Fifteenth Amendment (1870) provided that black males could vote, local authorities found ingenious—and often violent—ways to avoid the spirit and letter of these new laws.

The restoration of the former Confederate states to the Union did not come easily. Much bitterness and resistance remained among the vanquished. Although Confederate leaders were initially disenfranchised, they continued to exercise considerable authority in political and economic matters. Indeed, in 1877 the last federal troops were removed from the occupied South, and former Confederates gleefully declared themselves "redeemed" from the stain of occupation. By the end of the nineteenth century, most states of the former Confederacy had devised a system of legal discrimination that re-created many aspects of slavery.

15 THE OLD SOUTH:

AN AMERICAN TRAGEDY

CHAPTER ORGANIZER

This chapter focuses on:

- industry and agriculture in the Old South.

- southern society, black and white.

- the antislavery movement and southern reactions to it.

Southerners, a North Carolina editor once wrote, are "a mythological people, created half out of dream and half out of slander, who live in a still legendary land." Most Americans, including southerners, carry in their minds an assorted baggage of myths about the South. But the main burden of southern mythology is carried in those especially pernicious images of the Old South set during the nineteenth-century sectional conflict: the idealized picture of kindly old massa with his mint julep on the white-columned porch, happy "darkies" singing in fields, coquettish belles wooed by slender gallants underneath the moonlight and magnolias.

There are other elements in the traditional myth. Off in the piney woods and erosion-gutted red clay hills, away from the plantation elite, dwelt a depraved group known as the poor white trash: the crackers, hillbillies, and sand-hillers. Somewhere in the myth the respectable small farmer so often praised by Jefferson and Jackson was lost from sight, perhaps neither romantic enough nor outrageous enough to fit in. He was absent too from the image of the Benighted South, in which the plantation myth simply appeared in reverse, as a pattern of corrupt opulence resting on human exploitation. Gentle old massa became the arrogant, haughty, imperious potentate, the very embodiment of sin, the central target of antislavery attack. He kept a slave mistress; he bred blacks like cattle and sold them "down the river" to certain death in the sugar mills, separating families if that suited his purpose, while southern women suffered in silence the guilty knowledge of their men's infidelity. The "happy darkies" in this picture became white men in black skins, an oppressed people longing for freedom, the victims of countless atrocities, forever seeking a chance to follow the North Star to freedom. The masses of the white folks were, once again, poor whites, relegated to ignorance and degeneracy by the slavocracy.

These pictures are overdrawn stereotypes, but myths are hard to shake, partly because they have roots in reality. To comprehend the distinctiveness of the Old South requires first identifying the forces and factors that gave it a sense of unity. Efforts to do so usually turn on two lines of thought: the causal effects of environment (geography and climate), and the causal effects of human decisions and actions. The hot, humid weather fostered the growing of staple crops, and thus encouraged the plantation system and black slavery. These developments in turn brought sectional conflict and civil war.

DISTINCTIVENESS OF THE OLD SOUTH

While geography was and is a key determinant of southern folkways, explanations that involve human agency are more persuasive. In the 1830s many observers found the origins of southern distinctiveness in the institution of slavery. The resolve of slaveholders to retain control of their socioeconomic order created a sense of racial unity that muted class conflict among whites. Yet, the biracial character of the population influenced far more. In shaping patterns of speech and folklore, of music, religion, literature, and recreation, black southerners immeasurably influenced and enriched the region's development.

The South differed from other sections, too, in its high proportion of native population, both white and black. Despite a great diversity of origins in the colonial population, the South drew few immigrants after the Revolution. One reason was that the main shipping lines went to northern ports; another, that the prospect of competing with slave labor deterred immigrants. After the Missouri Controversy of 1819–1821, the South became more and more a conscious minority, its population growth lagging behind that of other sections, its "peculiar institution" of slavery more and more an isolated and odious thing in Western civilization. Attitudes of defensiveness strongly affected its churches. The religious culture of the white South retreated from the liberalism of the Revolutionary War era into orthodoxy, which provided one line of defense against new doctrines of any kind, while black southerners found in a similar religious culture a refuge from the hardships of their lot, a promise of release on some future day of Jubilee.

The South also differed in its architecture, its penchant for fighting, for guns, and for the military, and its country-gentleman ideal. The preponderance of farming remained a distinctive regional characteristic, whether pictured as the Jeffersonian small farmer living by the sweat of his brow or the lordly planter dispatching his slave gangs. But in the end what made the South distinctive was its people's belief, and other people's belief, that they *were* distinctive.

STAPLE CROPS   The idea of the Cotton Kingdom is itself something of a mythic stereotype. Although cotton was the most important of the

Slave quarters on a South Carolina plantation.

staple, or market, crops, it was a latecomer. Tobacco, the first staple crop, had earlier been the mainstay of Virginia and Maryland, and common in North Carolina. After the Revolution, pioneers carried it over the mountains into Kentucky and as far as Missouri. Indigo, an important crop in colonial South Carolina, vanished with the loss of British bounties for this source of a valuable blue dye, but rice growing continued in a coastal strip that lapped over into North Carolina and Georgia. Rice growing was limited to the Tidewater because it required frequent flooding and draining of the fields, and along that sector of the coast the tides rose and fell six or seven feet. Since rice growing required substantial capital for floodgates, ditches, and machinery, the plantations that grew rice were large and relatively few in number.

Sugar, like rice, called for a heavy capital investment in machinery to grind the cane, and was limited in extent because the cane was extremely susceptible to frost. An influx of refugees from the revolution in Haiti helped the development of a sugar belt centered along the Mississippi River above New Orleans. Some sugar grew in a smaller belt of

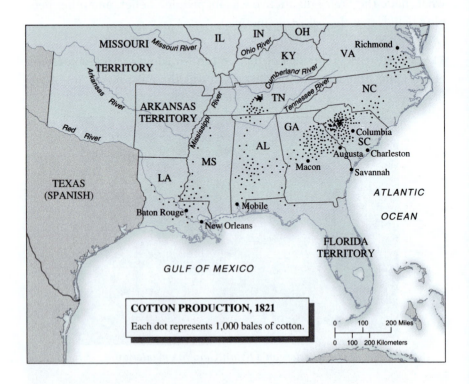

COTTON PRODUCTION, 1821

Each dot represents 1,000 bales of cotton.

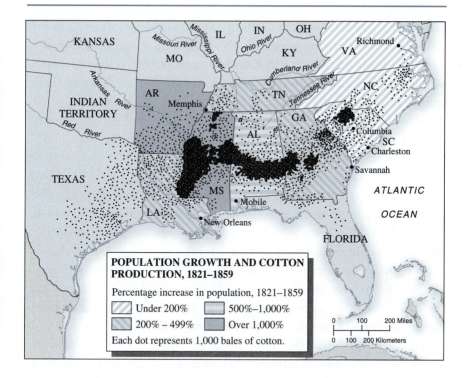

POPULATION GROWTH AND COTTON PRODUCTION, 1821–1859

Percentage increase in population, 1821–1859

Under 200%   500%–1,000%

200% – 499%   Over 1,000%

Each dot represents 1,000 bales of cotton.

eastern Texas, but it was always something of an exotic growth, better suited to a tropical climate. Since it needed the prop of a protective tariff, it produced the anomaly in southern politics of pro-tariff congressmen from Louisiana. Hemp had something of the same effect in the Kentucky Blue Grass region and northwestern Missouri. Both flax and hemp were important to backcountry farmers at the end of the colonial era. Homespun clothing was most apt to be linsey-woolsey, a combination of linen and wool. But flax never developed more than a limited commercial market, and that mostly for linseed oil. Hemp, on the other hand, developed commercial possibilities in rope and cotton baling cloth, and canvas for sails.

Cotton, the last of the major staples, eventually outpaced all the others put together. At the end of the War of 1812, annual cotton production was estimated at less than 150,000 bales; in 1860 it was reported at 4 million. Two things accounted for the growth: the voracious market for American cotton in British and French textiles, and the cultivation of new lands in the Southwest. Much of the story of the southern people—white and black—from 1820 to 1860 was their movement to fertile cotton lands farther west. By 1860 the center of the cotton belt stretched from eastern North Carolina through the fertile Alabama-Mississippi black belts (so called for the color of the soil), on to Texas, and up the Mississippi Valley as far as southern Illinois. Cotton prices fell sharply after the Panic of 1837, and remained below 10¢ a pound through most of the 1840s, but they advanced above 10¢ late in 1855 and stayed there until 1860, reaching 15¢ in 1857.

AGRICULTURAL DIVERSITY The focus on cotton and the other cash crops has obscured the degree to which the South fed itself from its own fields. With 30 percent of the country's area in 1860, and 39 percent of its population, the slave states produced 52 percent of the nation's corn, 29 percent of the wheat, 19 percent of the oats, 19 percent of the rye, 10 percent of the white potatoes, and 94 percent of the sweet potatoes. The upper South in many areas practiced general farming in much the same way as the Northwest. Cyrus McCormick first tested his harvester in the wheatfields of Virginia. Corn grew everywhere, but went less into the market than into local consumption, as feed and fodder, as hoecake and grits. On many farms and plantations the rhythms of the growing season permitted the labor force to alternate attention between the staples and the food crops.

Livestock added to the diversity of the farm economy. In 1860 the South had half of the nation's cattle, over 60 percent of the swine, nearly 45 percent of the horses, 52 percent of the oxen, 90 percent of the mules, and nearly 33 percent of the sheep, the last mostly in the upper South. Cattle herding prevailed on the southern frontier at one time, and persisted in areas less suited to farming, such as the piney woods of the coastal plains, the Appalachians, and the Ozarks and their foothills. Plantations and farms commonly raised livestock for home consumption.

Yet the picture was hardly one of unbroken prosperity. The South's staple crops quickly exhausted the soil, and open row crops such as tobacco, cotton, and corn left the bare ground in between subject to leaching and erosion. By 1800 much of eastern Virginia had abandoned tobacco, and in some places had turned to scrabbling wheat from the soil for the northern market. In low-country South Carolina, Senator Robert Y. Hayne spoke of "Fields abandoned; and hospitable mansions

Planting sweet potatoes on the Hopkinson plantation, Edisto Island, South Carolina, April 1862.

of our fathers deserted." The older farming lands had trouble competing with the newer soils farther west. But western lands too began to show wear and tear. By 1855 an Alabama senator noted: "Our small planters, after taking the cream off their lands . . . are going further west and south in search of other virgin lands which they may and will despoil and impoverish in like manner." This of course happened all along the frontier.

So the Southeast and then the Old Southwest faced a growing sense of economic crisis as the century advanced. Proposals to deal with it followed two lines. Some argued for agricultural reform and others for diversification through industry and trade. Edmund Ruffin of Virginia stands out as perhaps the greatest of the reformers. After studying the chemistry of soils, he reasoned that most exhausted soils of the upper South had acid conditions, which needed to be neutralized before they could become productive again. He turned his plantations into laboratories in which he discovered that marl from a shell deposit in eastern Virginia did the trick. Ruffin published the results in his *Essay on Calcareous Manures* (1832). Such publications and farm magazines in general, however, reached but a minority of farmers, mostly the larger and more successful planters.

MANUFACTURING AND TRADE   By 1840 many thoughtful southerners concluded that by staking everything on agriculture the region
had wasted chances in manufacturing and trade. The census of 1810
had shown the South with more various and numerous manufactures
than New England. The War of 1812 provided the South some stimulus
for manufacturing, but the momentum ebbed in the postwar flood of
British imports. Then cotton growing swept everything before it. The
proliferation of textile manufacturing in Britain led to a seemingly limitless demand for American cotton. As the cotton mania deflected concern with industry, the South became increasingly dependent on northern manufacturing and trade. Cotton and tobacco were exported mainly
in northern vessels. Southerners also relied on connections in the
North for imported goods. The South became, economically if not formally, a kind of colonial dependency of the North. The merchants of
northern cities, a southerner said, "export our . . . valuable productions,
and import our articles of consumption and from this agency they derive a profit which has enriched them . . . at our expense."

Along with the call for direct trade in southern ships went a movement for a more diversified economy, for native industries to balance
agriculture and trade. Southern publicists called attention to the section's great resources: its raw materials, labor supply, waterpower, wood
and coal, and markets. In Richmond, Virginia, the Tredegar Iron Works
grew into the most important single manufacturing enterprise in the
Old South. It used mostly slave labor to produce cannon, shot, and
shell, axes, saws, bridge materials, boilers, and steam engines, including locomotives.

The Tredegar Iron Works in Richmond, Virginia.

Daniel Pratt of Alabama built Prattville, which grew into a model of diversified industry. Prattville ultimately had a gristmill, a shingle mill, a carriage factory, foundries, a tin mill, and a blacksmith shop. Pratt then launched into the iron business and coal mining, while on the side experimenting with vineyards and truck farming. He used both black and white labor, but his approach was paternalistic. Profits from his company store went into churches, schools, a library, an art gallery, and a printing establishment—and into handsome dividends.

Pratt and others directed a program of industry that gathered momentum in the 1850s, and in its extent and diversity belied the common image of a strictly agricultural South. Manufactures were supplemented by important extractive industries such as coal, iron, lead, copper, salt, and gold, the last chiefly in North Carolina and Georgia. In manufacturing, the slave states altogether in 1860 had 22 percent of the country's plants, 17 percent of its labor, 20 percent of the capital invested, 17 percent of the wages generated, and 16 percent of the output—an impressive showing but still not up to the South's 30 percent of the population. Also, southern industry was concentrated in the border states, where economic conditions resembled those of neighboring states to the north—cheap labor, raw materials, capital investment, urban markets, and good transportation.

ECONOMIC DEVELOPMENT   During the antebellum years, there were two major explanations generally put forward for the lag in southern industrial development. First, blacks were presumed unsuited to factory work, perhaps because they supposedly could not adjust to the discipline of work by the clock. Second, the ruling orders of the Old South were said to have developed a lordly disdain for the practice of trade, because a certain aristocratic prestige derived from owning land and slaves, and from conspicuous consumption. But any argument that black labor was incompatible with industry simply flew in the face of the evidence, since factory owners bought or hired slave operatives for just about every kind of manufacture. Given the opportunity, a number of blacks displayed managerial skills as overseers.

One should not take at face value the legendary indifference of aristocratic planters to profits. More often than not the successful planter was a driving newcomer bent on maximizing profits. While the profitability of slavery has been a long-standing subject of controversy, in recent years economic historians have concluded that slaves on the average supplied about a 10 percent return on their cost. Then, as now, this was an enticing profit margin. Slave ownership was, moreover, a reasonable speculation, for slave prices tended to move upward. By a strictly hardnosed and hardheaded calculation, slaves and cotton lands were the most profitable investments available at the time in the South. Some slaveholders, particularly in the newer cotton lands of the Southwest, were rich beyond the dreams of avarice.

WHITE SOCIETY IN THE SOUTH

If an understanding of the Old South must begin with a knowledge of social myths, it must end with a sense of tragedy. White southerners had won short-term gains at the costs of both long-term development and moral isolation in the eyes of the world. The concentration on land and slaves, and the paucity of cities and immigrants, deprived the South of the dynamic bases of innovation. The slaveholding South hitched its wagon not to a star, but to the world (largely British) demand for cotton, which had not slackened from the start of the industrial revolution. During the late 1850s, it seemed that prosperity would never end. The South, "safely entrenched behind her cotton bags . . . can defy the world—for the civilized world depends on the cotton of the South," said a Vicksburg newspaper in 1860. "No power on earth dares to make war upon it," said James H. Hammond of South Carolina. "Cotton is king." The only perceived threat to King Cotton was the growing antislavery sentiment. What southern boosters could not perceive was an imminent slackening of the cotton market. The heyday of expansion in British textiles was over by 1860, but by then the Deep South was locked into cotton production for generations to come.

THE PLANTERS Although great plantations were relatively few in number, they set the tone of economic and social life in the South. What distinguished the plantation from the farm, in addition to its size, was the use of a large labor force, under separate control and supervision, to grow primarily staple crops (cotton, rice, tobacco, and sugarcane) for profit. A clear-cut distinction between management and labor

Photographs front and rear of the Stirrup Branch plantation, Bishopville, South Carolina, June 1857. Posed in front of the house is the family of Capt. James Rembert, the plantation owner. Assembled by rank at the rear of the house are the family slaves, with uniformed house servants, a foreman named Nero, two yard keepers, and a cook.

set the planter apart from the small slaveholder, who often worked side by side with his or her slaves at the same tasks.

If, to be called a planter, one had to own 20 slaves, only 1 out of every 30 whites in the South in 1860 was a planter. Fewer than 11,000 owned 50 or more slaves, and the owners of over 100 numbered 2,292. The census enumerated only 11 with 500 slaves and just 1 with as many as 1,000. Yet this small, privileged elite tended to think of its class interest as the interest of the entire South, and to perceive themselves as community leaders in much the fashion of the English gentry. The planter group, making up under 4 percent of the adult white males in the South, owned more than half the slaves, produced most of the cotton, tobacco, and hemp, and all of the sugar and rice. The total number of slaveholders was only 383,637, out of a total white population of 8 million. But assuming that each family numbered five people, the whites with some proprietary interest in slavery came to 1.9 million, or roughly one-fourth of the white population. While the preponderence of southern whites belonged to the small farmer class, the presumptions of the planters were seldom challenged. Too many small farmers aspired to become planters themselves.

Often the planter did live in the splendor that legend attributed to him, with the wealth and leisure to cultivate the arts of hospitality, good manners, learning, and politics. More often the scene was less charming. Some of the mansions on closer inspection turned out to be modest houses with false fronts. A style of housing derived from the frontier log cabin grew to be surprisingly common. The one-room cabin would expand by building a second room with a sheltered open "dog trot" in the middle. As wealth increased, larger houses evolved from the plain log cabin, and the dog trot grew into a central hall from the front to the rear of the house. In larger houses, halls to one or both sides might be added.

The planter commonly had less leisure than legend would suggest, for he in fact managed a large enterprise. At the same time he often served as the patron to whom workers appealed the actions of their foremen. The quality of life for the slaves was governed far more by the attitude of the master than by the formal slave codes, which were seldom strictly enforced except in times of troubles.

THE PLANTATION MISTRESS   The mistress of the plantation, like the master, seldom led a life of idle leisure. She supervised the domestic household in the same way the planter took care of the business, overseeing food, linens, housecleaning, the care of the sick, and a hundred other details. Mary Boykin Chesnut of South Carolina complained that "there is no slave like a wife."

The wives of all but the most wealthy planters were expected to supervise all the domestic activities of the household and manage the slaves to boot. A transplanted New Yorker living on a plantation in North Carolina observed that her mother-in-law "works harder than any Northern farmer's wife I know." The son of a Tennessee slaveholder remembered that his mother and grandmother were "the busiest women I ever saw." One of the most frustrating realities for the plantation mistress was the lack of personal freedom and leisure occasioned by the complex demands of her "separate sphere" of genteel domesticity. "These women have less chance to live their own lives than if they were African missionaries," wrote Chesnut. "They have a swarm of blacks about them like children under their care." One white woman, having stayed up all night helping deliver a slave baby, complained to a friend about her relentless routine: "It is the slaves who own me. Morning, noon, and night, I'm obliged to look after them, to doctor them, and attend to them in every way."

White women living within a slave-owning culture also confronted a double standard in terms of moral and sexual behavior. While they were expected to behave as chaste exemplars of Christian piety and sexual discretion, their husbands, brothers, and sons followed an unwritten rule of self-indulgent hedonism. "God forgive us," Mary Chesnut wrote in her diary, "but ours is a monstrous system. Like the patriarchs of old, our men live all in one house with their wives and their concubines; and the mulattoes one sees in every family partly resemble the white children. Any lady is ready to tell you who is the father of all the mulatto children in everybody's household but her own. Those, she seems to think, drop from the clouds."

Such a double standard both illustrated and reinforced the arrogant authoritarianism displayed by many male planters. Chesnut said that her father-in-law lorded over his plantation household. He was "as absolute a tyrant as the Czar of Russia . . . or the Sultan of Turkey." Another white woman complained that the men in her family treated everyone else as lesser people. Yet for all of their complaints and burdens, few plantation mistresses engaged in public criticism of the prevailing social order and racist climate.

THE MIDDLE CLASS   Overseers on the largest plantations generally came from the middle class of small farmers or skilled workers, or were younger sons of planters. Most aspired to become slaveholders themselves, and sometimes rose to that status, but others were constantly on the move in search of better positions. Their interests did not always coincide with the long-term interests of the planter. "Overseers are not interested in raising negro children, or meat, in improving land, or improving productive qualities of seed or animals," a Mississippi planter complained. "Many of them do not care whether property has depreciated or improved, so they make a crop to boast of." Occasionally there were black overseers, but the highest management position to which a slave could aspire was usually that of driver, placed in charge of a small group of slaves with the duty of getting them to work without creating dissension.

The most numerous white southerners were the small farmers (yeomen), those who lived with their families in modest two-room cabins rather than columned mansions. They raised a few hogs and chickens, grew some corn and cotton, and traded with neighbors more than stores. The men in the family focused their energies on outdoor labors. Women also worked in the fields during harvest time, but most of their days were spent attending to domestic chores. Many of these "middling" farmers owned a handful of slaves, but most owned none. The most prosperous of these small farm families generally lived in the mountain-sheltered valleys from the Shenandoah of Virginia down to northern Alabama, areas with rich soil but without ready access to markets, and so less suitable for staple crops or slave labor. But most of the South's small farms were located in the midst of the plantation economy.

In North Carolina in 1860, for instance, 70 percent of the farmers held less than 100 acres, and they were scattered throughout the state. These and other southern farmers were typically mobile folk, willing to pull up stakes and move west or southwest in pursuit of better land. They tended to be fiercely independent and suspicious of government authority, and they overwhelmingly identified with the party of Andrew Jackson and the spiritual fervor of evangelical Protestantism. Some southern farmers resented the planter elite because it controlled the most fertile land, the commodity markets, and the political machinery. Most of them, however, admired and envied the slaveholding aristocracy. And even though only a minority of the middle-class farmers owned slaves, most of them supported the slave system. They feared that the slaves, if freed, would compete with them for land, and they also enjoyed the privileged status that racially based slavery afforded them. As one farmer told a northern traveler, "Now suppose they [the slaves] was free. You see they'd all think themselves as good as we." Such sentiments pervaded the border states as well as the Deep South. Kentucky, for example, held a popular referendum on the issue of slavery in 1849, and the voters, most of whom owned no slaves, resoundingly endorsed the "peculiar institution."

THE "POOR WHITES" Outside observers often had trouble telling yeomen apart from the true "poor whites," a degraded class crowded off onto the least desirable land. Stereotyped views of southern society had prepared many travelers to see only planters and "poor whites," and many a small farmer living in rude comfort, his wealth concealed in cattle and swine off foraging in the woods, was mistaken for "white trash." The type was a familiar one from the frontier days, living on the fringes of polite society. One observer wrote in 1860: "There is no . . . method by which they can be weaned from leading the lives of vagrom-men, idlers, and squatters, useless to themselves and to the rest of mankind." The "poor whites" were characterized by a pronounced lankness and sallowness, given over to hunting and fishing, to hound dogs and moonshine whiskey.

Speculation had it that they were descended from indentured servants or convicts transported to the colonies, or that they were the weakest of the frontier population, forced to take refuge in the sand land, the pine barrens, and the swamps after having been pushed aside by the more enterprising and successful. But the problem was less heredity than environment, the consequence of infections and dietary deficiencies that gave rise to a trilogy of "lazy diseases": hookworm, malaria, and pellagra, all of which produced an overpowering lethargy. Many poor whites displayed a morbid craving to chew clay, from which they got the name "dirt eaters"; the cause was a dietary deficiency, although a folklore grew up about the nutritional and medicinal qualities of certain clays. Around 1900 modern medicine discovered the causes and cures for these diseases. By 1930 they had practically disappeared, taking with them many stereotypes of poor whites.

PROFESSIONALS AND OTHERS   Professional people, including lawyers, doctors, and editors, stood in close relationship to the planter and
merchant classes that they served and to which they sometimes belonged. Manufacturers held their own with the planters, as did merchants, often called brokers or factors, who handled the planters' crops
and acted as purchasing agents for their needs, supplying credit along
the way. Many professionals bought their way into the slaveholding
class, and many eventually acquired farms of their own.

There was a degree of fluidity and social mobility in the class structure of the white South. Few indeed were the "cotton snobs" who
lorded over the lower orders. Planters were acknowledged as the social
models and natural leaders. Yet those who aspired to public office, especially, could not afford to take a lordly attitude, for every southern
state by 1860 allowed universal white male suffrage. The voters, while
perhaps showing deference to their "betters," could nevertheless pick
and choose among them at election time.

Other groups stood farther from the mainstream. The mountain people of Appalachia engaged in subsistence farming, employed few or no
slaves, and in attitude stood apart from the planter society, sometimes
in open hostility toward it. Scattered in many of the flatland counties
were small groups who sometimes fell even below the poor whites in
the social scale. In some places the advance of the frontier had left behind pockets of Indians with whom passing whites and escaped slaves
eventually mingled.

HONOR AND VIOLENCE IN THE OLD SOUTH   From colonial times,
most southern white males prided themselves on adhering to a moral
code centered on a prickly sense of honor. It was honor, writes historian
Bertram Wyatt-Brown, that provided "the psychological and social un-
derpinnings of Southern culture." Such a preoccupation with honor
was common among Germanic and Celtic peoples (Scottish, Irish,
Scotch-Irish, Cornish, and Welsh) from whom most white southerners
were descended. It flourished in hierarchical rural societies where face-
to-face relations governed social manners.

The dominant ethical code for the southern white elite derived from
Protestant religion, classical philosophy, and medieval chivalry, and it
depended upon a rigidly hierarchical social system, where one's status
was defined by those above and below. Its elements included a combat-

ive sensitivity to slights; loyalty to family, locality, state, and region; deference to elders and social "betters"; and an almost theatrical hospitality. It manifested itself in a fierce defense of female purity, a propensity to magnify personal insults into capital offenses, and in public statements such as the following toast proposed by a South Carolina politician: "*The Palmetto State*: Her sons bold and chivalrous in war, mild and persuasive in peace, their spirits flushed with resentment for wrong."

Southern white women played an important role in the culture of honor. Indeed, they were the object of masculine chivalry and the subjects of male rule. The mythic southern "lady" was placed on a pedestal celebrating domestic devotion. While men cultivated and defended their *honor,* women paraded and protected their *virtue.* The southern lady presided over the morals and manners of the household—while submitting to patriarchal authority. She willingly subordinated her own individuality in order to serve her husband and their children. A southern lady, according to the prevailing standard, was to remain sexually pure, spiritually pious, and domestically submissive—all the while she managed the household.

Many women embraced this exalted, yet sacrificial mythology and its attendant duties. "We owe it to our husbands, children, and friends," wrote Louisiana's Caroline Merrick (who married at age fifteen), "to represent as nearly as possible the ideal which they hold so dear." According to the prevailing ideology of womanhood, southern ladies reinforced exaggerated gallantry and martial honor in their men. When young Sam Houston joined the army to fight in the War of 1812, his mother handed him the family musket, saying: "Never disgrace it; for remember, I had rather all my sons should fill one honorable grave, than that one of them should turn his back to save his life." She then gave him a ring with the word "Honor" inscribed on it. Almost fifty years later, as war broke out between North and South, an Alabama belle broke her engagement because her fiancé refused to enlist in the Confederate army before their wedding. She then sent him a skirt and female undergarments, admonishing him, "Wear these or volunteer."

The preoccupation of southern white men with a sense of honor steeped in violence found outlets in several popular rituals. Like their Scotch-Irish and English ancestors, white southerners loved to hunt, ride, and to gamble—over cards, dice, horse racing, and cockfighting. All such activities provided arenas for masculine camaraderie as well as competition. To engage in such competitive events constituted a rite of passage of sorts for young southern males. In some respects southern society itself revolved around such public recreation. During horse race week in Charleston, South Carolina, for instance, courts, schools, and shops shut down so as to enable all to participate. Some viewed the gambling on such sports as more reputable than other economic exchanges. As the South Carolina gentleman-philosopher, William Grayson, declared, "A gambling debt is a debt of honor, but a debt due a tradesman is not."

Southern men of all social classes were preoccupied with an often reckless manliness. As a northern traveler observed, "the central trait of the 'chivalrous southerner' is an intense respect for virility." The duel constituted the ultimate public expression of personal honor and manly courage. Although not confined to the South, dueling was much more common there than in the rest of the young nation, a fact that gave rise to the observation that southerners will be polite until they are angry enough to kill you. Dueling was outlawed in the northern states after Aaron Burr killed Alexander Hamilton in 1804, and a number of southern states and counties banned the practice as well—but the prohibition was rarely enforced.

Amid the fiery debates over nullification, abolitionism, or the fate of slavery in the territories during the antebellum era, clashing political opinions often provoked duels. In Virginia, a state senator and a state representative killed each other in a duel. Many of the most prominent southern leaders engaged in duels—congressmen, senators, governors, editors, and planters. The roster of participants included Andrew Jackson, Henry Clay, Sam Houston, Jefferson Davis, William Crawford, John Randolph, and Albert Sidney Johnston.

Southerners were easily provoked. A traveler to the region explained that the "smallest breach of courtesy, no matter how unintentional; the slightest suggestion of unfairness in a business deal; even a moment's awkwardness—were sufficient grounds for a challenge." Yet the ready prospect of mortal combat, the advocates of dueling argued, encouraged gentlemen to exercise greater care in their use of language and in their relations with others. A dueling society, southerners assumed in the early nineteenth century, was a more polite—and honorable—society.

Personal honor sometimes took precedence over personal survival, as in the 1826 duel between then Secretary of State Henry Clay and Con-

Southern Duels. *A duel at Half-Way House in New Orleans is pictured in this illustration from* Harper's Weekly, *July 14, 1886. Men participated in duels to defend their honor and express their courage in response to slights and insults.*

gressman John Randolph of Virginia. Their feud grew out of disagreements over American foreign policy. The night before the duel, Randolph, an eccentric, lifelong bachelor, resolved "to receive without returning Clay's fire; nothing shall induce me to harm a hair of his head. I will not make his wife a widow, or his children orphans. Their tears would be shed over his grave, but when the sod of Virginia rests on my bosom there is not in this wide world one individual to pay his tribute upon me."

True to his word, Randolph fired into a stump behind Clay, while Clay's shot missed as well. Clay asked for a second round. His next shot pierced the coat Randolph was wearing. Randolph then fired into the air and violated the "no-talking rule" by declaring "I will not fire at you, Mr. Clay. You owe me a coat." Clay reportedly replied, "I am glad the debt is no more." They then shook hands and their quarrel ended.

An elaborate series of strict rules and procedures governed duels. Only gentlemen, not laborers, mechanics, or blacks, were eligible to use pistols on the field of honor. Gentlemen were presumed to be planters, military officers, or professors. The status of ministers, newspaper editors, physicians, and bankers was less certain. Whatever the case, people of the "lesser sort" were denied access to the dueling field; they were to be dealt with by caning or horsewhipping.

So many duels and deaths occurred in the South that "anti-dueling societies" emerged to lobby against the social ritual. Most states outlawed the practice, but to little avail. As a grand jury in Savannah, Georgia, noted in 1819, "the frequent violations of the law to prevent dueling have made the practice fashionable and almost meritorious among its chivalrous advocates." Judges were reluctant to punish their fellow "gentlemen" for upholding their honor. In many cases, duelists simply agreed to stage their contest in an adjoining state. It was not until after the Civil War that dueling fell into widespread disgrace and began a rapid decline. Humorist Mark Twain deserves the last word: "I thoroughly disapprove of duels. If a man should challenge me, I would take him kindly and forgivingly by the hand and lead him to a quiet place and kill him."

BLACK SOCIETY IN THE SOUTH

"FREE PERSONS OF COLOR" In the Old South, "free persons of color" occupied an uncertain status, balanced somewhere between slavery and freedom, subject to legal restrictions not imposed on whites. State laws prohibited them from serving on juries or testifying against whites. In the seventeenth century, a few blacks had been freed on the same basis as indentured servants. Over the years, some slaves were able to purchase their freedom, while some gained freedom as a reward for service in American wars. Others were simply freed by conscientious masters, either in their wills or during their lifetimes.

The free persons of color included a large number of mulattoes. In urban centers like Charleston and especially New Orleans, "colored" society became virtually a third caste, a new people who occupied a status somewhere between black and white. Some of them built substantial fortunes and even became slaveholders. They often operated inns serving a white clientele. Jehu Jones, for instance, was the "colored" proprietor of one of Charleston's best hotels, which he bought in 1815 for $13,000. In Louisiana a mulatto, Cyprien Ricard, bought an estate that had ninety-one slaves for $250,000. In Natchez William Johnson, son of a white father and mulatto mother, operated three barbershops and owned 1,500 acres of land and several slaves.

Yarrow Mamout was an African Muslim who was sold into slavery, purchased his freedom, acquired property, and settled in Georgetown (now part of Washington, D.C.). Charles Willson Peale executed this portrait of Mamout in 1819, when Mamout was over one hundred years old.

William Ellison, a freed slave of partial white ancestry who lived in Stateburg, South Carolina, prospered as a cotton-gin maker. In 1816, at the age of twenty-six, he purchased his own freedom from his white master (who may have been his father). By the start of the Civil War, he had become the wealthiest free black in South Carolina, owner of a thriving business, an 800-acre plantation, and some sixty slaves. He was so indifferent to the plight of other blacks that he commonly sold his slaves' female babies because he believed they were unprofitable in his business. Like other successful mulattoes, Ellison distanced himself from the slaves and displayed a snobbish preoccupation with gradations of color. As a member of Charleston's "brown aristocracy," he looked down upon black people. During the Civil War, Ellison supported the Confederacy.

Black slaveholders were a tiny minority. The 1830 census revealed that only 3,775 free blacks, about 2 percent of the total free black population, owned 12,760 slaves. Although most of these black slave owners were in the South, some also lived in Rhode Island, Connecticut, Illinois, New Jersey, New York, and the border states. Some blacks owned slaves for humanitarian purposes. One minister, for instance, bought slaves and then enabled them to purchase their freedom from him on easy terms. Most often, black slaveholders were free blacks who bought their own family members with the express purpose of later freeing them. But many blacks engaged in slavery for purely selfish rather than humanitarian reasons. Like their white counterparts, they participated in slave auctions and advertised for the return of runaways.

This badge, issued in Charleston, South Carolina, was worn by a free black so he would not be mistaken for someone's property.

Most free blacks were not slave owners. Men were usually skilled artisans (blacksmiths, carpenters, cobblers), farmers, or common laborers. The increase in their numbers slowed as southern legislatures put more and more restrictions on the right to free slaves, but by 1860 there were 262,000 free blacks in the slave states, a little over half the national total of 488,000. They were most numerous in the upper South. In Maryland the number of free blacks very nearly equaled the number still held in slavery; in Delaware free blacks made up 92 percent of the black population.

THE TRADE IN SLAVES   The slaves stood at the bottom of the social hierarchy. Some Indians, themselves subject to brutal discrimination, owned African slaves. In fact, the practice became so widespread that when the Civil War erupted, most southern tribes supported the Confederacy. From the first census in 1790 to the eighth in 1860, the number of slaves had grown from 698,000 to almost 4 million. The rise in the slave population occurred mainly through a natural increase, the rate of which was very close to that of whites at the time. When the African slave trade was outlawed in 1808, it seemed to many a step toward the extinction of slavery, but the expansion of the cotton belt, with its voracious appetite for workers, soon created such a vested interest in slaves as to dash such hopes. Shutting off the import of slaves only added to the value of those already present. Prices for prime fieldhands ranged between $300 and $400 in the 1790s, rose to $1,000–$1,300 in the 1830s, peaked just before the onset of depression in 1837, and rose again in the great prosperity of the 1850s to $1,500–$2,000. Slaves with special skills cost even more.

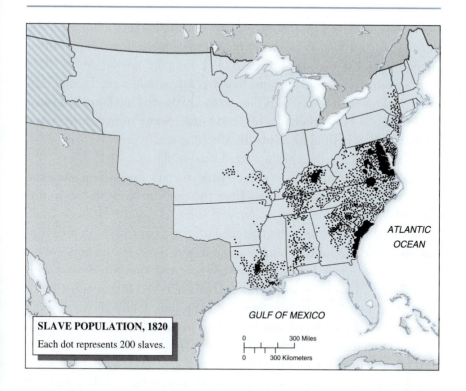

ATLANTIC
OCEAN

GULF OF MEXICO

SLAVE POPULATION, 1820

Each dot represents 200 slaves.

0   300 Miles

0   300 Kilometers

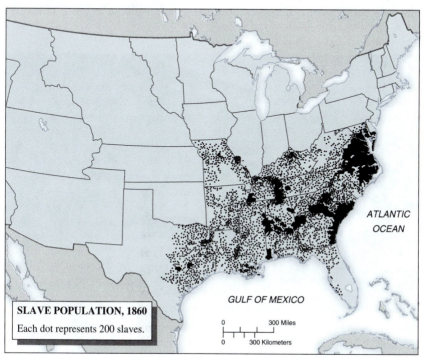

ATLANTIC
OCEAN

GULF OF MEXICO

SLAVE POPULATION, 1860

Each dot represents 200 slaves.

0   300 Miles

0   300 Kilometers

The rise in slave value tempered some of the harsher features of the peculiar institution. Valuable slaves, like valuable livestock, justified some minimal standards of care. "Massa was purty good," one ex-slave recalled later. "He treated us jus' 'bout like you would a good mule." Another said his master "fed us reg'lar on good, 'stantial food, jus' like you'd tend to you hoss, if you had a real good one." Some owners hired wage laborers, often Irish immigrants, for ditching and other dangerous work rather than risk the lives of the more valuable slaves.

The end of the foreign slave trade gave rise to a flourishing domestic trade, with slaves moving mainly from the used-up lands of the Southeast into the booming new country of the Old Southwest. The trade peaked just before 1837, then slacked off, first because of depression, then because agricultural reform and recovery renewed the demand for slaves in the upper South. Many slaves moved south and west with their owners, but there also developed an organized business with brokers, slave pens, and auctioneers. Franklin and Armfield, the leading traders, had their offices and collecting pens in Alexandria, Virginia, where they fattened and spruced up slaves for the auction block.

While the mainstream of the trade moved southwestward, every town of any size had public auctioneers and dealers willing to buy and sell slaves—along with other merchandise—or handle sales on a commis-

The offices of Price, Birch & Co., dealers in slaves, Alexandria, Virginia.

sion. The worst aspect of the slave trade was the dissolution of families. Only Louisiana and Alabama (from 1852) forbade separating a child under ten from its mother, and no state forbade separation of husband from wife. Many such sales are matters of record, and although the total number is controversial, it took only a few to damage the morale of all.

PLANTATION SLAVERY   Most slaves labored on plantations. The preferred jobs were those of household servants and skilled workers, including blacksmiths and carpenters. Others might get special assignments as, say, boatmen or cooks. Fieldhands were usually housed in one- or two-room wooden shacks with dirt floors, some without windows. Of food there was usually a rough sufficiency, but one slave recalled that "de flour dat we make the biscuits out of wus de third-grade sorts." A set of clothes was distributed twice a year, but shoes were generally provided only in winter. On larger plantations there was sometimes an infirmary and regular sick call, but most planters resorted to doctors mainly in cases of severe sickness. Based on detailed records from eleven plantations in the lower South during the antebellum era,

Domestic Industry. *The preferred jobs on plantations were those of household servants or skilled workers. These slaves are grinding corn, doing fieldwork, and spinning cotton.*

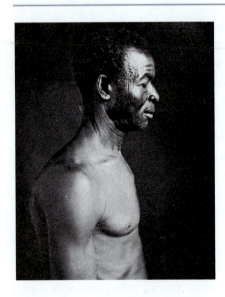

Jack (Driver), Guinea. Plantation of
B.F. Taylor, Esq. Columbia, S.C.
1850.

scholars have calculated that more than half of all slave babies died in
the first year of life, a mortality rate more than twice that of whites.

Fieldhands worked long hours from dawn to dusk, or "from kin [see]
to kaint." The slave codes gave little protection from long hours. South
Carolina's limit of fifteen hours in winter and sixteen in summer exceeded the hours of daylight most of the year. The slave codes adopted
in each state concerned themselves mainly with the owner's interests,
and subjected the slaves not only to his governance but to surveillance
by patrols of county militiamen, who struck fear into the slave quarters
by abusing slaves found at large. Evidence suggests that a majority of
both planters and small farmers used the whip, which the slave codes
authorized. The difference between a good owner and a bad one, according to one ex-slave, was the difference between one who did not
"whip too much" and one who "whipped till he's bloodied you and blis-
tered you."

A male slave's ultimate recourse was rebellion or flight, but most recognized the futility of such measures, with whites wielding the power
and weapons. Female slaves rarely saw escape as an option, concerned
as they were with pregnancies and child-raising responsibilities. "Slavery is terrible for men; but it is far more terrible for women," declared
Harriet Jacobs, a North Carolina slave. In the nineteenth century only

three slave insurrections drew much notice, and two of those were betrayed before they got under way. In 1800 a slave named Gabriel on a plantation near Richmond hatched a plot involving perhaps a thousand others to seize key points in Richmond and start a general slaughter of whites. Twenty-five of the slave conspirators were executed and ten others deported to the West Indies.

The Denmark Vesey plot in Charleston, discovered in 1822, was believed to be a plan of a free black to fall upon the white population of the town, seize ships in the harbor, and head for Santo Domingo. In this case thirty-five slave rebels were executed and thirty-four deported. The Vesey insurrection, however, remains an enigma. Some contemporaries in Charleston and historians since believed it had less to do with insurrection than with white hysteria, which fabricated a plot from rumors and the testimony of frightened slaves out to save their own skins by incriminating others.

Only the Nat Turner insurrection of 1831 in rural Southampton County, Virginia, got beyond the planning stage. Turner, a black overseer, was also a religious exhorter who professed a divine mission in leading the movement. The revolt began when a small group killed those in Turner's master's household and set off down the road repeating the process at other farmhouses, where other slaves joined in. Before it ended at least fifty-five whites were killed. Eventually trials resulted in seventeen hangings and seven deportations, but the militia killed large numbers of slaves indiscriminately in the process of putting down the rebels.

Slaves more often retaliated against oppression by malingering or by outright sabotage. There were constraints on such behavior, however, for laborers would likely eat better on a prosperous plantation than on one they had reduced to poverty. And the shrewdest slaveholders knew that they would more likely benefit from holding out rewards than from inflicting pain. Plantations based on the profit motive fostered between slaves and owners mutual dependency as well as natural antagonism. And in an agrarian society where personal relations counted for much, blacks could win concessions that moderated the harshness of slavery, permitting them a certain degree of individual and community development.

FORGING THE SLAVE COMMUNITY   To generalize about slavery is to miss elements of diversity from place to place and from time to time.

The experience could be as varied as people are. Slaves were victims, there was no question about that. But to stop with so obvious a perception would be to miss an important story of endurance and achievement. If ever there was a melting pot in American history, the most effective may have been that in which Africans from a variety of ethnic, linguistic, and tribal origins fused into a new community and a new culture as African Americans.

Members of the slave community were bound together in helping and protecting one another, which in turn created a sense of cohesion and pride. Slave culture incorporated many African survivals, especially in areas where whites were few. Among the Gullah blacks of the South Carolina and Georgia coast, a researcher found as late as the 1940s more than 4,000 words still in use from the languages of twenty-one African tribes. But the important point, as another researcher put it, was not survivals that served "as quaint reminders of an exotic culture sufficiently alive to render the slaves picturesquely different but little more." The point was one of transformations in a living culture. Elements of African cultures thus "have continued to exist . . . as dynamic, living, creative parts of life in the United States," and have interacted with other cultures in which they came in contact.

SLAVE RELIGION AND FOLKLORE   Among the most important manifestations of slave culture was its religion, a mixture of African and Christian elements. In this slaves could find both balm for the soul and release for their emotions. Most Africans brought with them a concept of a Creator, or Supreme God, whom they could recognize in Jehovah, and lesser gods whom they might identify with Christ, the Holy Ghost, and the saints, thereby reconciling their earlier beliefs with the new Christian religion. Alongside the church they maintained beliefs in spirits (many of them benign), magic, and conjuring. Belief in magic is in fact a common human response to conditions of danger or helplessness.

Slaves found great comfort in the church. Masters sought to instill lessons of Christian humility and obedience, but blacks could identify their plight with that of the Israelites in Egypt or of the God who suffered as they did. And the ultimate hope of a better world gave solace in this one. Some owners encouraged religious meetings among their slaves, many of them believing that a Christian slave would be a better slave. "Church was what they called it," one former slave remembered, "but all that [white] preacher talked about was for us slaves to obey our masters and not to lie and steal."

Such a manipulated Christianity alienated many slaves, and most sought to create a genuine faith that spoke to their own spiritual and human needs. This required many of them to worship in secret, stealing away from their quarters to hold "bush meetings." A slave preacher explained that the "way in which we worshiped is almost indescribable. The singing helped provoke a certain ecstasy of emotion, clapping of hands, tossing of heads, which would continue without cessation about half an hour. The old house partook of the ecstasy; it rang with their jubilant shouts, and shook in all its joints."

The preachers and exhorters who sprang up in the slave world commonly won the acceptance of the owners if only because efforts to get rid of them proved futile. The peculiar cadences of their exhortations, chants, and spirituals were to the whites at best exotic but fundamentally mystifying. The ecstatic "ring shout," in which the celebrants moved rhythmically in a circle, was not a dance—as whites tended to believe—because, the worshippers said, they never crossed their feet. Because whites so widely misperceived slave religion, one historian has called it the "invisible institution" of the antebellum South.

Slaves found the Bible edifying in its tributes to the poor and oppressed, and they embraced its promise of salvation through Jesus. Likewise, the lyrics in religious "spirituals" helped slaves endure the strain of field labor and provided them with a code with which to express their own desire for freedom on earth. The articulate former slave, Frederick Douglass, stressed that "slaves sing most when they are most unhappy," and such spirituals offered them deliverance from their worldly woes.

African cultural forms influenced a music of great rhythmic complexity, forms of dance and body language, spirituals and secular songs, and folk tales. Among oppressed peoples humor often becomes a means of psychological release, and there was a lively humor in the West African "trickster tales" of rabbits, tortoises, or Anansi the spider—relatively weak creatures who outwitted stronger animals. African-American folklore tended to be realistic in its images of wish fulfillment. Until after emancipation there were few stories of superhuman heroes, except for tales about captive Africans who escaped slavery by flying back home across the ocean.

Lynchburg Negro Dance, 1853. *Slaves successfully maintained some aspects of their African culture, incorporating it into their religion, music, and dance.*

THE SLAVE FAMILY   Slave marriages had no legal status, but slave owners generally seem to have accepted marriage as a stabilizing influence on the plantation. Sometimes they performed marriages themselves or had a minister celebrate a formal wedding with all the trimmings. A common practice was the "broomstick wedding," in which the couple jumped over a broomstick, a custom of uncertain origin. But whatever the formalities, the norm for the slave community as for the white was the nuclear family of parents and children, with the father regarded as head of the family. Slaves also displayed a lively awareness of the extended family of cousins. Most slave children were socialized into their culture through the nuclear family, which afforded some degree of independence from white influence.

Slaves were not always allowed to realize this norm. In some cases the matter of family arrangements was ignored or left entirely up to the slaves on the assumption that black females were simply promiscuous—a convenient rationalization for white sexual exploitation, to which the presence of so many mulattoes attested. The census of 1860 reported 412,000 persons of mixed ancestry in the United States, or about 10 percent of the black population, probably a drastic undercount. Planters and their sons often took sexual advantage of female

Several generations of a family raised in slavery. Plantation of J. J. Smith, Beaufort, South Carolina, 1862.

slaves. They sometimes clumsily defended such abuse on the grounds that the practice protected the chastity of white women.

THE CULTURE OF THE SOUTHERN FRONTIER

There was substantial social and cultural diversity within the South during the three decades before the Civil War. The antebellum southern frontier, for example, was a quite different region from the more settled areas in the states along the Atlantic seaboard. Of all the many frontiers that have combined to produce a distinctive American culture, the Old Southwest is perhaps the least well known. It included the states and territories west of the Georgia-Alabama border—Alabama, Mississippi, Louisiana, Texas, and Arkansas—as well as the frontier areas in Tennessee, Kentucky, and Florida.

Largely unsettled until the 1820s, this region bridged the South and the West, exhibiting characteristics of both areas. Raw and dynamic, filled with dangers, uncertainties, and opportunities, it served as a powerful magnet, luring thousands of settlers from Virginia and the Carolinas when the seaboard economy faltered during the 1820s and 1830s. By the 1830s, the bulk of cotton production was occurring in the lower South. The migrating southerners carved out farms, built churches, raised towns, and eventually brought culture and order to a raw frontier. As they took up new lives and occupations, these southern pioneers transplanted many practices and institutions from the coastal states. But they also fashioned a distinct new set of cultural values and social customs.

THE DECISION TO MIGRATE   Young white men aspiring to be planters, usually in their twenties, responded to the siren call of fertile soil in the Southwest. The agricultural economy of the upper South suffered from depressed commodity prices and soil exhaustion by the Jacksonian era. Large farm families, especially, struggled to provide each child with sufficient land and resources to subsist and maintain the family legacy. Thus, the dwindling economic opportunities available in the Carolinas and Virginia as well as restrictive kinship ties led many to migrate to the Southwest. As one young pioneer explained, he did not want to "creep and crawl in North Carolina like a poor sloth" when he could amass a fortune in the Southwest. Like their northern counterparts, restless southern sons of the planter and professional elite wanted to make it on their own, to be "self-made men," economically self-reliant and socially independent. To them speculative profit-seeking was more enticing than family stability. A North Carolinian expected to "rise and soar like an eagle" in the Southwest because he would be freed from the strictures of his family circle, which he perceived as holding him back.

Women were underrepresented among migrants to the Old Southwest. Few were interested in relocating to a disease-ridden, violent, and primitive frontier. The new region did not offer them independence or adventure. And their never-ending routine of domestic tasks would only increase in the frontier environment. In general, women regretted more than men the loss of kinship ties that migration would entail. To them a stable family life was more important than the prospect of material gain. As a Carolina woman prepared to depart for Alabama, she confided to a friend that "you *cannot* imagine the state of despair that I am in." Another said that "my heart bleeds within me" at the thought of the "many tender cords [of kinship] that are now severed forever." Others feared that life on the frontier would produce a "dissipation" of morals.

They heard vivid stories of frontier lawlessness, drunkenness, gambling, and miscegenation.

Slaves had many of the same reservations about moving west. Almost a million captive blacks joined in the migration to the Southwest during the antebellum era, most of them making the journey in the 1830s. Like the white women, they feared the harsh working conditions and torpid heat and humidity of the Southwest. They also were despondent at the breaking up of their family ties. As Frederick Douglass observed, the "removal" of a slave to the Southwest was considered a form of psychological "death." When a young slave girl left Virginia for the Southwest, her mother ran after the wagon, eventually fell down and rolled "over on de groun' jes' acryin'." She never saw her daughter again.

JOURNEY AND SETTLEMENT   Most of the migrants to the Southwest headed for the fertile lands of Alabama, Mississippi, and central Tennessee. The typical trek was about 500 miles. Along rough roads and trails, the pioneers averaged fifteen miles per day, occasionally staying overnight in taverns, more often camping in the open air amid panthers, bears, and wolves. At times the route was clogged with people. One traveler said that often he would see "an uninterrupted line of walkers, wagons, and carriages." Slaves traveled on foot, tied or chained together. Many drowned while fording rivers; others contracted mortal illnesses along the way.

Once in the Southwest, the pioneers bought land that had been appropriated from the Indians. Parcels of 640 acres sold for as little as $2 an acre. Land in Alabama's black belt brought higher prices. As cotton prices soared in the 1830s, aspiring planters bought as much land and as many slaves as possible. As a result, the average size of farms and plantations in the Southwest was larger than that in the Carolinas and Virginia.

But the Southwest was much more unhealthy than the Carolina Piedmont. The hot climate, contaminated water, and poor sanitation spawned an epidemic of diseases. Malaria was especially endemic to the region. Women and slaves also found their harsh new surroundings uninviting. Life in tents and rude log cabins made many newcomers yearn for the material comforts they had left behind. A male settler reported that "all the men is very well pleased but the women is not very satisfied." The physical and social isolation on the frontier was a disheartening new reality. After starting a homestead in Alabama, Mary Drake regretted the loss of her "large and respectable circle of relations" in North Carolina. Many decided to return home or move farther west.

A MASCULINE CULTURE   The southern frontier environment provoked important changes in sex roles, and relations between men and women became even more inequitable. Frontier life lent itself to the psychology of "manly independence" that many male pioneers eagerly sought. Young adult males indulged themselves in activities that would have generated disapproval in the more settled seaboard society. They drank, gambled, fought, and indulged their sexual desires. According to one disheartened observer, the typical young male settler, his "desires and appetites . . . unrestrained," became an embarrassment and source of sorrow to his family back East. In 1834 a South Carolina migrant urged his brother to move west and join him because "you can live like a fighting cock with us." A few years later he implored another brother to leave the seaboard because he had too much potential "to hang around Mother and drivel away your life."

Alcohol consumption hit new heights along the southwestern frontier. Most plantations had their own stills to manufacture whiskey, and alcoholism ravaged frontier families. Masculine violence was also commonplace. A Virginian who settled in Mississippi fought in fourteen duels and killed ten men in the process. The frequency of fights, stabbings, shootings, and murders shocked visitors. So, too, did the propensity of white men to take sexual advantage of slave women. An Alabama woman married to a lawyer and politician was outraged by the "beastly passions" of the white men who fathered slave children and then sold them like livestock. She also recorded in her diary instances of men regularly beating their wives with whips and drinking to excess. Wives, it seems, had little choice but to endure such mistreatment because, as one woman wrote about a friend whose husband abused her, she was "wholly dependent upon his care."

CELIA   Occasionally a single historical incident can encapsulate the larger web of laws and customs within a society. Such is the case with the story of a teenaged slave girl named Celia. Robert Newsom migrated from Virginia to the Southwest in the early 1820s and eventually established a prosperous 800-acre homestead. He owned a half dozen slaves, including Celia. Newsom told his family that he had bought her to serve as a domestic servant. But immediately after purchasing Celia, while driving her back to his farm, Newsom raped her. For the next five years he treated Celia as his mistress. During that time she gave birth to two children, presumably his offspring. In a fit of tortured generosity, Newsom built Celia a separate, comfortable brick cabin fifty yards from the main house. But the anguish and humiliation she suffered took its toll. When Celia privately appealed to Newsom's two grown daughters to intervene on her behalf and put a stop to their father's sexual advances, they turned a deaf ear.

Desperate for relief from her tormentor, Celia resolved in 1855 to resist his next assault, with words if possible, with a club if necessary. Soon thereafter, Newsom again entered her cabin, ignored her impassioned appeal, and kept advancing until she struck him on the head. After he fell to the floor, she clubbed him to death. As she later explained, "the Devil got into me, and I struck him with the stick until he was dead." Celia then burned the body, pulverized the bones, and convinced one of Newsom's grandsons to help her discard the ashes. She eventually was accused of the crime and confessed. Her attorneys, all of them slaveowners, argued that the right of white women to defend their sexual honor against assault should be extended to slaves as well. The judge and jury, however, disagreed, and Celia was hanged.

ANTISLAVERY MOVEMENTS

EARLY OPPOSITION TO SLAVERY   From the Revolution to the early 1830s, few southern whites showed much disposition to defend the peculiar institution. But in the oft-used figure of speech, they had the wolf by the ears and could not let go. The specter of racial intermarriage and possible race war convinced many whites that slavery must be maintained despite its evils. Such scattered antislavery groups and publications as existed in those years in fact were found mainly in the upper South.

The emancipation movement accelerated with the formation of the American Colonization Society in 1817. The society proposed to return freed slaves to Africa. Its supporters included such prominent figures as James Madison, James Monroe, Henry Clay, John Marshall, and Daniel

Webster, and it appealed to diverse opinions. Some backed it as an anti-slavery group, while others saw it as a way to bolster slavery by getting rid of potentially troublesome free blacks. Articulate elements of the free black community denounced it from the start. America, they stressed, was now their native land.

In 1821, nevertheless, agents of the society acquired from local chieftains in West Africa a parcel of land that became the nucleus of a new country. In 1822 the first freed slaves arrived there, and twenty-five years later the society relinquished control to the independent republic of Liberia. But given its uncertain purpose, the colonization movement received only meager support from either antislavery or proslavery elements. In all, up to 1860 only about 15,000 blacks migrated to Africa, approximately 12,000 with the help of the Colonization Society. The number was infinitesimal compared to the number of slave births.

FROM GRADUALISM TO ABOLITIONISM   Meanwhile in the early 1830s the antislavery movement took a new departure. Its initial efforts to promote a gradual end to slavery through prohibiting it in the territories and encouraging manumission gave way to demands for immediate abolition. In 1831, William Lloyd Garrison began publication in Boston of a new antislavery newspaper, *The Liberator.* Garrison, who rose from poverty in Newburyport, Massachusetts, had been apprenticed to a newspaperman and had edited a number of papers. In the first issue of his new paper he renounced "the popular but pernicious doctrine of

William Lloyd Garrison.

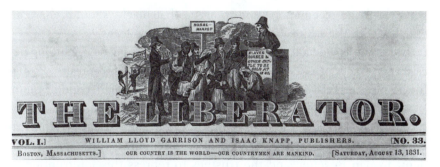

Masthead of William Lloyd Garrison's The Liberator. *This antislavery newspaper aroused great passions on both sides of the slavery issue.*

gradual emancipation" and vowed: "I will be as harsh as truth, and as uncompromising as justice." Circulation was never very large, but copies went to papers with much wider circulations. In the South, literate blacks would more likely encounter Garrison's ideas in the local papers than in the few copies of *The Liberator* that found their way to them.

Slaveholders' outrage mounted higher after the Nat Turner insurrection in August 1831. Garrison, they assumed, bore a large part of the responsibility for the affair, but there is no evidence that Nat Turner had ever heard of him, and Garrison said that he had not a single subscriber in the South at the time. What is more, however violent his language, Garrison was a pacifist, opposed to the use of violence.

A period of organization followed these events. In 1832 Garrison and his followers set up the New England Anti-Slavery Society. In 1833 two wealthy New York merchants, Arthur and Lewis Tappan, founded a similar group in their state and the same year took the lead in starting a national society, called the American Anti-Slavery Society, with the help of Garrison and a variety of other antislavery people. They hoped to exploit the publicity gained by the British antislavery movement, which that same year had induced Parliament to end slavery, with compensation to slaveholders, throughout the British Empire.

The American Anti-Slavery Society conceded the right of each state to legislate on its domestic institutions, but set a goal of convincing fellow citizens "that Slaveholding is a heinous crime in the sight of God, and that the duty, safety, and best interests of all concerned, require its *immediate abandonment,* without expatriation." The society went beyond the issue of emancipation to argue that blacks should "share an equality with the whites, of civil and religious privileges."

The group issued a barrage of propaganda for its cause, including periodicals, tracts, agents, lecturers, organizers, and fund-raisers. Probably its most effective single agent was Theodore Dwight Weld of Ohio, a convert and disciple of the great evangelist Charles Grandison Finney. In 1834 Weld led a group of students at Lane Theological Seminary in Cincinnati in a protracted discussion of abolition. Efforts of its president, Lyman Beecher, and the trustees to repress this interruption of normal routine led to a mass secession from Lane and the start of a new theological school at the recently opened Oberlin College near Cleveland. The move won the financial and moral support of the Tappans.

Weld and a number of the "Lane rebels" set out to evangelize the country for abolition. Weld earned the reputation of troublemaker and "the most mobbed man in the United States," but at the same time he displayed a genius for turning enemies into disciples.

THE MOVEMENT SPLITS   As the movement spread, debates over tactics inevitably grew. The Garrisonians, mainly New Englanders, were radicals who felt that American society had been corrupted from top to bottom and needed universal reform. Garrison embraced just about every important reform movement that came down the pike in those years: antislavery, temperance, pacifism, and women's rights. Deeply affected by the perfectionism of the times, he refused to compromise principle for expediency, to sacrifice one reform for another. Abolition was not enough. He opposed colonization of freed slaves and stood for equal rights. He broke with the organized church, which to his mind was in league with slavery. The federal government, with its Fugitive Slave Law, was all the more so. The Constitution, he said, was "a covenant with death and an agreement with hell." Garrison therefore refused to vote. He was, however, prepared to collaborate with those who did, or with those who disagreed with him on other matters.

Other reformers saw American society as fundamentally sound and concentrated their attention on purging it of slavery. Garrison struck them as an impractical fanatic. A showdown came in 1840 on the issue of women's rights. Women had joined the abolition movement from the start, but largely in groups without men. The activities of the Grimké sisters brought the issue of women's rights to center stage.

Sarah and Angelina Grimké, daughters of a prominent South Carolina family, had broken with their parents and moved north to embrace antislavery, feminism, and other reforms. Their publications included Angelina's *Appeal to the Christian Women of the South* (1836), calling on southern women to speak and act against slavery, and Sarah's *Letter on the Equality of the Sexes and the Condition of Women* (1838). Having attended Theodore Weld's school for antislavery apostles in New York (Angelina later married Theodore), they set out speaking to women in New England and slowly widened their audiences to "promiscuous assemblies" of both men and women. Such unseemly behavior inspired the Congregational clergy of Massachusetts to chastise the Grimké sisters for engaging in unfeminine activity. And it provoked Catharine Beecher to remind the activist sisters that women occupied "a subordinate relation in society to the other sex" and should therefore limit their activities to the "domestic and social circle." Angelina Grimké rejected such conventional arguments. "It is a woman's right," she insisted, "to have a voice in all laws and regulations by which she is to be governed, whether in church or in state."

The debate over the role of women in the antislavery movement crackled and simmered until it finally exploded at the Anti-Slavery Society's meeting in 1840. There the Garrisonians insisted on the right of women to participate equally in the organization, and carried their point. They did not commit the group to women's rights in any other way, however. Contrary opinion, mainly from the Tappans' New York group, ranged from outright antifeminism to simple fear of scattering shots over too many reforms. The New Yorkers broke away to form the American and Foreign Anti-Slavery Society. Weld, who had probably done more than anybody else to build the movement, declined to go with either group. Like the New Yorkers, he preferred to focus on slavery as the central evil of the times, but he could not accept their "antiwoman" attitude, as he saw it. Discouraged by the bickering, he drifted away from the movement he had done so much to build and into a long-term teaching career.

BLACK ANTISLAVERY ACTIVITY   White antislavery men also balked at granting full recognition to black abolitionists of either sex. Often blindly patronizing, white leaders expected African Americans to take a back seat in the movement. Not all blacks were easily manipulated,

Frederick Douglass (left) and Sojourner Truth (right) were both leading abolitionists.

however, and most became exasperated at whites' tendency to value purity over results, to strike a moral posture at the expense of action. Despite the invitation to form separate black groups, black leaders were active in the white societies from the beginning. Three attended the organizational meeting of the American Anti-Slavery Society in 1833, and some became outstanding agents for the movement, notably the former slaves who could speak from firsthand experience. Garrison pronounced such men as Henry Bibb and William Wells Brown, both escapees from Kentucky, and Frederick Douglass, who fled Maryland, "the best qualified to address the public on the subject of slavery."

Douglass, blessed with an imposing frame and a gift of eloquence, became the best-known black man in America. "I appear before the immense assembly this evening as a thief and a robber," he told a Massachusetts group in 1842. "I stole this head, these limbs, this body from my master, and ran off with them." Fearful of capture after publishing his *Narrative of the Life of Frederick Douglass* (1845), he left for an extended lecture tour of the British Isles and returned two years later with enough money to purchase his freedom. He then started an abolitionist newspaper for blacks, the *North Star,* in Rochester, New York.

Douglass's *Narrative* was but the best known among a hundred or more such accounts. Escapees often made it out on their own—Douglass borrowed a pass from a free black seaman—but many were aided by the Underground Railroad, which grew in legend into a vast system to conceal runaways and spirit them to freedom, often over the Canadian border. Levi Coffin, a North Carolina Quaker who moved to Cincinnati and did help many fugitives, was the reputed president. Actually, there seems to have been more spontaneity than system about the matter, and blacks contributed more than was credited in the legend. A few intrepid refugees actually ventured back into slave states to organize escapes. Harriet Tubman, the most celebrated, went back nineteen times.

Equally courageous was the articulate black female abolitionist Sojourner Truth. Born in New York State in 1797, Isabella Baumfree renamed herself in 1843 after experiencing a mystical conversation with God, who told her "to travel up and down the land" preaching the sins of slavery. She did just that, crisscrossing the country during the 1840s and 1850s, exhorting audiences about abolitionism and women's rights. Having been a slave until she fled to freedom in 1827, Sojourner Truth was able to speak with added conviction and knowledge about the evils of the "peculiar institution" and the inequality of women. As she told a gathering of the Ohio Women's Rights Convention in 1851, "I have plowed, and planted, and gathered into barns, and no man could head me—and ar'n't I a woman? I have borne thirteen children, and seen 'em mos' all sold off into slavery, and when I cried out with a mother's grief, none but Jesus heard—and ar'n't I a woman?" Through such compelling testimony, Sojourner Truth demonstrated the powerful intersection of abolitionism and women's rights agitation, and in the process she tapped the distinctive energies that women brought to reformist causes. "If the first woman God ever made was strong enough to turn the world upside down all alone," she concluded her address to the Ohio gathering, "these women together ought to be able to turn it back, and get it right side up again!"

REACTIONS TO ANTISLAVERY   Garrison, Douglass, Weld, and other abolitionists had to face down hostile crowds who disliked blacks or found antislavery agitation bad for business. In 1837 a hostile mob in Alton, Illinois, killed the antislavery editor Elijah P. Lovejoy, giving the movement a martyr to both abolition and freedom of the press.

By then proslavery southerners, by seeking to suppress discussion of emancipation, had already given abolitionists ways to link antislavery with the cause of civil liberties for whites. In the summer of 1835 a mob destroyed several sacks of abolitionist literature in the Charleston post office. The postmaster had announced that he would not try to deliver such matter. Bitter debates in Congress ensued. President Jackson wanted a law against handling "incendiary literature," but Congress failed to oblige him. The postmaster-general, nevertheless, did nothing about forcing delivery.

One shrewd political strategy, promoted by Weld, was to deluge Congress with petitions for abolition in the District of Columbia. Most such petitions were presented by former president John Quincy Adams, elected to the House from Massachusetts in 1830. In 1836, however, the House adopted a rule to lay abolition petitions automatically on the table, in effect ignoring them. Adams, "Old Man Eloquent," stubbornly fought this "gag rule" as a violation of the First Amendment, and hounded its supporters until the gag rule was finally repealed in 1844.

Meanwhile, in 1840, the year of the schism in the antislavery movement, a small group of abolitionists called a convention in Albany, New York, and launched the Liberty party with James G. Birney, onetime slaveholder of Alabama and Kentucky, as its candidate for president. Birney, converted to the cause by Weld, had tried without success to publish an antislavery paper in Danville, Kentucky. He then moved it to Ohio and in 1837 became executive secretary of the American Anti-Slavery Society. In the 1840 election he polled only 7,000 votes, but in 1844 his total rose to 60,000, and from that time forth an antislavery party contested every national election until Abraham Lincoln won the presidency.

THE DEFENSE OF SLAVERY   Birney was but one among a number of southerners propelled north during the 1830s by the South's growing hostility to emancipationist ideas. Antislavery in the upper South had its last stand in 1831–1832 when the Virginia legislature debated a plan of gradual emancipation and colonization, then rejected it by a vote of 73 to 58. Thereafter, leaders of southern thought worked out an elaborate intellectual defense of slavery, presenting it as a positive good rather than, in the words of Tennessee's constitutional convention of 1834, "a great evil" that "the wisest heads and most benevolent hearts" had not been able to eliminate.

The evangelical churches, which had widely condemned slavery at one time, gradually turned proslavery. Ministers of all denominations joined in the argument. Had not the patriarchs of the Old Testament held people in bondage? Had not Noah, upon awakening from a drunken stupor, cursed Canaan, son of Ham, from whom the Negroes were descended? Had not Saint Paul advised servants to obey their masters and told a fugitive servant to return to his master? And had not Jesus remained silent on the subject, at least so far as the Gospels reported his words? In 1843–1844 disputes over slavery split two great denominations along sectional lines and led to the formation of the Southern Baptist Convention and the Methodist Episcopal Church, South. Presbyterians, the only other major denomination to split, did not divide until the Civil War.

A more fundamental feature of the proslavery argument stressed the intrinsic inferiority of blacks. Most whites, blind and deaf to the complexity of black culture, assumed that the evidence of their eyes and ears confirmed their own superiority. The weight of scientific opinion, often prejudiced on such matters, was on their side, but it is doubtful that many felt the need of science to prove what seemed so obvious to them. Stereotyping the poor and powerless as inferior is an old and seemingly ineradicable human habit.

Other arguments took a more "practical" view of slavery. Not only was slavery profitable, it was a matter of social necessity. Jefferson, for instance, in his *Notes on Virginia* (1785), had argued that emancipated slaves and whites could not live together without risk of race war growing out of the recollection of past injustices. What is more, it seemed clear that blacks could not be expected to work under conditions of freedom. They were too shiftless and improvident, the argument went, and in freedom would be a danger to themselves as well as to others. White workmen, on the other hand, feared their competition. Whites were also struck with fear by the terrible example of the bloody rebellion in Santo Domingo.

A new argument arose in the late 1850s. Some began to defend slavery as being better for the workers, since it provided them with security in sickness and old age, than was the "wage slavery" of northern industry, which exploited workers for profit and then cast them away. Within one generation, such ideas had triumphed in the white South over the post-Revolutionary apology for slavery as an evil bequeathed by the forefathers. Opponents of the orthodox faith in slavery as a positive good were either silenced or exiled. Freedom of thought in the Old South had become a victim of the nation's growing obsession with slavery.

MAKING CONNECTIONS

- The abolition movement never represented the majority of northerners. As Chapter 16 shows, however, by the end of the 1850s most voters in the North could support the idea of limiting the expansion of slavery westward, if not the abolition of it in the southern states.

- The Civil War brought great changes to southerners, both black and white. Chapter 17 describes the effect of the war on southern society.

- There are revealing comparisons between the Old South of this chapter and the New South of Chapter 19.

FURTHER READING

Those interested in the problem of discerning myth and reality in the southern experience should consult William R. Taylor's *Cavalier and Yankee: The Old South and American National Character* (1961) and W. J. Cash's *The Mind of the South* (1941). Two recent efforts to understand the mind of the Old South and its defense of slavery are Eugene D. Genovese's *The Slaveholders' Dilemma: Freedom and Progress in Southern Conservative Thought, 1820–1860* (1992) and Eric H. Walther's *The Fire-Eaters* (1992).

Contrasting analyses of the plantation system are Eugene D. Genovese's *The World the Slaveholders Made* (1969) and Gavin Wright's *The Political Economy of the Cotton South* (1978). Stephanie McCurry's *Masters of Small Worlds: Yeoman Households, Gender Relations, and the Political Culture of the Antebellum South Carolina Low Country* (1995) greatly enriches our understanding of households, religion, and political culture.

Other essential works on southern culture and society include Bertram Wyatt-Brown's *Honor and Violence in the Old South* (1986),

Elizabeth Fox-Genovese's *Within the Plantation Household: Black and White Women of the Old South* (1988), Suzanne Lebsock's *The Free Women of Petersburg* (1984), Catherine Clinton's *The Plantation Mistress: Woman's World in the Old South* (1982), Joan Cashin's *A Family Venture: Men and Women on the Southern Frontier* (1991), and Theodore Rosengarten's *Tombee: Portrait of a Cotton Planter* (1987).

William J. Cooper, Jr.'s *Liberty and Slavery: Southern Politics to 1860* (1983) and Robert F. Durden's *The Self-Inflicted Wound* (1985) cover southern politics of the era. For a look at the role of religion in southern political life, see Mitchell Snay's *Gospel of Disunion: Religion and Separatism in the Antebellum South* (1993).

A provocative discussion of the psychology of black slavery can be found in Stanley M. Elkins's *Slavery: A Problem in American Institutional and Intellectual Life* (3rd ed., 1976). John W. Blassingame's *The Slave Community: Plantation Life in the Antebellum South* (2nd ed., 1979), Eugene D. Genovese's *Roll, Jordan, Roll: The World the Slaves Made* (1974), and Herbert G. Gutman's *The Black Family in Slavery and Freedom, 1750–1925* (1976) all stress the theme of a persisting and identifiable slave culture. Discussions of the diversity of the experience of slavery in particular places can be found in John C. Inscoe's *Mountain Masters: Slavery and the Sectional Crisis in Western North Carolina* (1989) and Randolph B. Campbell's *An Empire for Slavery: The Peculiar Institution in Texas, 1821–1865* (1989).

On the question of slavery's profitability, see Robert W. Fogel and Stanley L. Engerman's *Time on the Cross: The Economics of Negro Slavery* (2 vols., 1974), which argues that not only did planters benefit financially from bondage, but the slaves themselves incorporated a Victorian work ethic based on incentives. Herbert G. Gutman reviewed this controversy in *Slavery and the Numbers Game* (1975). See also Robert Fogel's reflections on the subject in *Without Consent or Contract* (1992).

Other works on slavery include Lawrence W. Levine's *Black Culture and Black Consciousness: Afro-American Folk Thought from Slavery to Freedom* (1977), Albert J. Raboteau's *Slave Religion: The "Invisible Institution" in the Antebellum South* (1978), Dorothy Sterling's *We Are Your Sisters* (1984), Deborah Gray White's *Ar'n't I a Woman? Female Slaves in the Plantation South* (1985), and Joel Williamson's *The Crucible of Race* (1985). Charles Joyner's *Down by the Riverside* (1984) offers a vivid reconstruction of one slave community. Editors Alonzo Johnson and Paul Jersild have compiled insightful essays dealing with slave culture in *"Ain't Gonna Lay My 'Ligion Down": African American Religion in the South* (1996).

Useful surveys of abolitionism include Ronald G. Walters's *The Antislavery Appeal: American Abolitionism after 1830* (1976) and James B. Stewart's *Holy Warriors: The Abolitionists and American Slavery* (1976). William S. McFeely's *Frederick Douglass* (1990) portrays the most eminent black male abolitionist while Nell Painter's *Sojourner Truth: A Life, A Symbol* (1996) profiles the leading female activist. For the proslavery argument as it developed in the South, see Larry Tise's *Proslavery: A History of the Defense of Slavery in America, 1701–1840* (1988), and James Oakes's *The Ruling Race: A History of American Slaveholders* (1982). The problems southerners had in justifying slavery are explored in Drew G. Faust's *A Sacred Circle: The Dilemma of the Intellectual in the Old South, 1840–1860* (1977), Kenneth S. Greenberg's *Masters and Statesmen: The Political Culture of American Slavery* (1985), and Carl N. Degler's *The Other South: Southern Dissenters in the Nineteenth Century* (1974).

16 ✑ THE CRISIS OF UNION

CHAPTER ORGANIZER

This chapter focuses on:

* the politicization of slavery.

* how the Compromise of 1850 and the Kansas-Nebraska Act reflected sectional tensions.

* the rise of a third generation party system: Republicans and Democrats.

* the specific events that led to the secession of the southern states.

ohn C. Calhoun and Ralph Waldo Emerson had little else in common, but both men sensed in the Mexican War the omens of a greater disaster. Mexico was "the forbidden fruit; the penalty of eating it would be to subject our institutions to political death," Calhoun warned. "The United States will conquer Mexico," Emerson conceded, "but it will be as the man swallows the arsenic. . . . Mexico will poison us." Wars, as both men knew, have a way of corrupting ideals and breeding new wars, often in unforeseen ways. Like Britain's conquest of New France, America's winning of the Southwest gave rise in turn to quarrels over newly acquired lands. In each case the quarrels set in train a series of disputes: Britain's eighteenth-century crisis of empire had its counterpart in America's nineteenth-century crisis of union.

SLAVERY IN THE TERRITORIES

THE WILMOT PROVISO   The Mexican War was less than three months old when the seeds of a new conflict began to sprout. On August 8, 1846, a sweltering House of Representatives reassembled to clear its calendar for adjournment. A freshman Democrat from Pennsylvania, David Wilmot, delivered a provocative speech. He favored expansion, Wilmot explained, even the annexation of Texas as a slave state. But slavery had come to an end in Mexico, and if new territory should be acquired, "God forbid that we should be the means of planting this institution upon it." Drawing upon the words of the Northwest Ordinance, he proposed that in lands acquired from Mexico, "neither slavery nor involuntary servitude shall ever exist in any part of said territory."

Proposed as an amendment to an appropriations bill, the Wilmot Proviso was never a law, but it politicized slavery once and for all. For a generation, since the Missouri controversy of 1819–1821, the issue had been lurking in the wings, kept there most of the time by politicians who feared its disruptive force. From that day forth, for two decades the question would never be far from center stage.

The House immediately adopted the Wilmot Proviso, but the Senate refused to concur. When Congress reconvened in 1846, Polk prevailed on Wilmot to withhold his amendment, but by then others were ready to take up the cause. When a New York congressman revived the proviso, he signaled a revolt by the Van Burenites in concert with the antislavery forces of the North. Once again the House approved the amendment. Once again the Senate refused to do so. In one form or another Wilmot's idea kept cropping up. Abraham Lincoln later recalled that during one term as congressman, 1847–1849, he voted for it "as good as forty times."

John Calhoun meanwhile devised a thesis to counter the proviso and set it before the Senate in four resolutions on February 19, 1847. The Calhoun Resolutions, which never came to a vote, argued that since the territories were the common possession of the states, Congress had no right to prevent any citizen from taking slaves into them. To do so would violate the Fifth Amendment, which forbade Congress to deprive any person of life, liberty, or property without due process of law, and slaves were property. By this clever stroke of logic, Calhoun took that basic guarantee of liberty, the Bill of Rights, and turned it into a basic guarantee of slavery. The irony was not lost on his critics, but the point became established southern dogma—echoed by his colleagues and formally endorsed by the Virginia legislature.

Senator Thomas Hart Benton of Missouri, himself a slaveholder but also a Jacksonian nationalist, found in Calhoun's resolutions a set of abstractions "leading to no result." Wilmot and Calhoun between them, he said, had fashioned a pair of shears. Neither blade alone would cut very well, but joined together they could sever the ties of union.

POPULAR SOVEREIGNTY   Many others, like Benton, refused to be polarized, seeking to bypass the brewing conflict. President Polk was among the first to suggest extending the Missouri Compromise dividing free and slave territory at latitude 36°30′ all the way to the Pacific. Senator Lewis Cass of Michigan suggested that the citizens of a territory "regulate their own internal concerns in their own way," like the citizens of a state. Such an approach would combine the merits of expediency and democracy. It would take the issue out of the national arena and put it in the hands of those directly affected.

Popular sovereignty, or squatter sovereignty, as the idea was also called, had much to commend it. Without directly challenging the slaveholders' access to the new lands, it promised to open them quickly to non-slaveholding farmers who would almost surely dominate the territories. With this tacit understanding, the idea prospered in Cass's Old Northwest, where Stephen A. Douglas of Illinois and other prominent Democrats soon endorsed it. Popular sovereignty, they hoped, might check the magnetic pull toward the opposite poles of Wilmot and Calhoun and thereby preserve the Union.

When the Mexican War ended in 1848, the question of bondage in the new territories was no longer hypothetical—unless one reasoned, as many did, that their arid climate excluded plantation crops and therefore excluded slavery. For Calhoun, who leaned to that opinion, that was beside the point, since the right to carry slaves into the territories was not to be yielded. In fact, there is little reason in retrospect to credit the argument that slavery had reached its natural limits of expansion. Slavery had been adapted to occupations other than plantation agriculture. Besides, on irrigated lands, cotton later became a staple crop of the Southwest.

Nobody doubted that Oregon would become free soil, but it too was drawn into the growing controversy. Territorial status, pending since 1846, was delayed because its provisional government had excluded slavery. To concede that provision would imply an authority drawn from the powers of Congress, since a territory was created by Congress. Finally, a Senate committee proposed to let Oregon exclude slavery but to deny the territories of California and New Mexico any power to legislate at all on the subject, thus passing the issue to the courts. The question of slavery, previously outlawed under Mexican rule, could rise on appeal to the Supreme Court and thus be kept out of the political arena. The Senate accepted this, but the House rejected it, and finally an exhausted Congress let Oregon organize without slavery, but postponed decision on the Southwest. Polk signed the bill on the principle that Oregon was north of 36°30'.

Polk had promised to serve only one term; exhausted and having reached his major goals, he refused to run again in 1848. At the Democratic convention Lewis Cass won the presidential nomination, but the party refused to endorse the "squatter sovereignty" plan. Instead it simply denied the power of Congress to interfere with slavery in the states and criticized all efforts to bring the question before Congress. The Whigs devised an even more artful shift. Once again, as in 1840, they passed over their party leader, Clay, for a general, Zachary Taylor, whose fame and popularity had grown since the Battle of Buena Vista. He was a legal resident of Louisiana who owned more than a hundred slaves, an apolitical figure who had never voted in a national election. Once again, as in 1840, the party adopted no platform at all.

THE FREE-SOIL COALITION   But the antislavery impulse was not easily squelched. Wilmot had raised a standard to which a broad coalition could rally. People who shied away from abolitionism could readily endorse the exclusion of slavery from the territories. The Northwest Ordinance and the Missouri Compromise supplied honored precedents. By doing so, moreover, one could strike a blow for liberty without caring about slavery itself, or about the slaves. One might simply want free soil for white farmers, while keeping the unwelcome blacks far away in the South, where they belonged. Free soil, therefore, rather than abolition, became the rallying point—and also the name of a new party.

Three major groups entered the free-soil coalition: rebellious Democrats, antislavery Whigs, and members of the Liberty party, which dated from 1840. Disaffection among the Democrats centered in New York, where the Van Burenite "Barnburners" squared off against the pro-administration "Hunkers" in a factional dispute that had as much to do with personal ambitions as with local politics. Each group gave the other its name, the one for its alleged purpose to rule or ruin like the farmer who burned his barn to get rid of the rats, the other for hankering or "hunkering" after office.

As their conflict grew, however, the Barnburners seized on the free-soil issue as a means of winning support. When the Democratic convention voted to divide the state's votes between contesting delegations, they bolted the party and named Van Buren as their candidate for president on a free-soil platform. Other Wilmot Democrats, including Wilmot himself, joined the revolt. Among the Whigs, revolt centered in Massachusetts where a group of "Conscience" Whigs battled the "Cotton" Whigs. The latter, according to Charles Sumner, belonged to a coalition of northern businessmen and southern planters, "the lords of the lash and the lords of the loom." Conscience Whigs rejected the slaveholder, Taylor. The third group in the coalition, the abolitionist Liberty party, had already nominated Senator John P. Hale of New Hampshire for president.

In August these groups—Barnburners, Conscience Whigs, and Liberty party followers—organized the Free Soil party in a convention at Buffalo. Its presidential nomination went to Martin Van Buren, while the vice-presidential nomination went to Charles Francis Adams, a Conscience Whig. The old Jacksonian and the son of John Quincy Adams made strange bedfellows indeed! The Liberty party was rewarded with a platform plank that pledged the government to abolish slavery whenever such action became constitutional, but the party's main principle was the Wilmot Proviso, and it entered the campaign with the catchy slogan of "free soil, free speech, free labor, and free men."

Its impact on the election was mixed. The Free Soilers split the Democratic vote enough to throw New York to Taylor, and the Whig vote

Independent Gold Hunter on His Way to California, *c. 1850. Once the discovery of gold in California was confirmed by President Polk, those interested in seeking their fortune quit their jobs and headed West.*

enough to give Ohio to Cass, but Van Buren's total of 291,000 votes was far below the popular totals of 1,361,000 for Taylor and 1,222,000 for Cass. Taylor won with 163 to 127 electoral votes, and both major parties retained a national following. Taylor took eight slave states and seven free; Cass just the opposite, seven slave and eight free.

THE CALIFORNIA GOLD RUSH   Meanwhile a new dimension had been introduced into the question of the territories. On January 24, 1848, gold was discovered in California. The word spread quickly, and Polk's confirmation of the discovery in his last annual message, on December 5, 1848, turned the gold fever into a worldwide epidemic. Word of limitless gold deposits in California, Polk said, "would scarcely command belief were they not corroborated by authentic reports." Throughout the rest of the nation, men quit their jobs or sold their businesses and headed west in 1849 and after. These "Forty-niners" were often termed "Argonauts," after the band of adventurers in Greek mythology who went in search of the Golden Fleece.

The California gold rush constituted the greatest mass migration in American history to that point. During 1849 some 80,000 gold seekers reached California, half of them Americans, and by 1854, the number would top 300,000. So many men left their families that people began to worry about the cohesion of society. The "Forty-niners" included people from every social class and from every state and territory, including slaves brought by their owners. Most went overland; the rest went by way of Panama or Cape Horn. Along the western slopes of the Sierra Nevada, they thronged the valleys and canyons.

After touring the gold region, the territorial governor reported that the influx of newcomers had "entirely changed the character of Upper California." The village of San Francisco, which grew rapidly into a city, mushroomed from 459 to 20,000 residents in a few months. The influx quickly reduced the 14,000 Mexicans in 1849 to a minority, and sporadic conflicts with the Indians of the Sierra Nevada foothills decimated the native peoples. In 1850 Americans accounted for 68 percent of the population, but there was also a cosmopolitan array of "Sydney Ducks" from Australia, "Kanakas" from Hawaii, "Limies" from London, "Paddies" from Ireland, "Coolies" from China, and "Keskydees" from France (who were always asking "Qu'est-ce qu'il dit?"—"What did he say?").

California News by William Sidney Mount, 1850. *During the California gold rush, San Francisco quickly became a cosmopolitan city as the population increased almost fifty-fold in a few months.*

Gold Miners, *c. 1850. Daguerreotype of miners panning for gold at their claim.*

THE MINING FRONTIER   Of all the many frontiers in the American experience, the mining frontier was perhaps the most exceptional and unstable. Unlike the land-hungry pioneers who traversed the overland trails, the miners were mostly unmarried young men from a variety of places, representing a wide spectrum of ethnic and cultural backgrounds. Few miners were interested in permanent settlement. They wanted to strike it rich and return home. The mining camps in California valleys, canyons, and along creek beds thus sprang up like mushrooms and disappeared almost as rapidly. As soon as rumors of a new strike made the rounds, miners converged on the area, joined soon thereafter by a hodgepodge of merchants and camp followers. Then, when no more gold was found, they picked up and moved on.

The mining shantytowns were disorderly and often lawless communities where vigilante justice prevailed and leisure time revolved around saloons and gambling halls. One newcomer reported that "in the short space of twenty-four days, we have had murders, fearful accidents, bloody deaths, a mob, whippings, a hanging, an attempt at suicide, and a fatal duel." Within six months of arriving in California in 1849, one in every five of the gold seekers was dead. The gold fields and mining towns were so dangerous that insurance companies refused to provide coverage. The town of Marysville had seventeen murders in one week, prompting the citizenry to form a vigilante committee. Everyone carried weapons—usually pistols or bowie knives. Suicides were common, and disease was rampant. Cholera and scurvy plagued every camp. With so many uprooted young men thrown together with criminals and vice peddlers, the primary forms of entertainment were gambling and alcohol.

Women were as rare as liquor was abundant. In 1850 less than 8 percent of California's total population was female, and even fewer women hazarded life in the mining camps. Those who did could demand quite a premium for their work as cooks, laundresses, entertainers, and prostitutes. One woman arrived in Sacramento to discover that a biscuit could be sold for $10. That night she dreamed of getting rich herself by feeding the miners, imagining "crowds of bearded miners striking gold from the earth with every blow of the pick, each one seeming to leave a share for me." Women from back East who rarely had a suitor suddenly found themselves smothered with attention in the mining country. Another female immigrant noted that she had "men come forty miles over the mountains, just to look at me, and I never was called a handsome woman, in my best days, even by my most ardent admirers."

In the polyglot mining camps, the Americans often looked with disdain upon the Hispanics ("greasers") and Chinese ("chinks"), who were most often employed as wage laborers to help in the panning process, separating gold from sand and gravel. But the Americans focused their contempt on the Indians. In the mining culture it was not a crime to kill Indians or work them to death. American miners tried several times to outlaw foreigners in the mining country but had to settle for a tax on foreign miners that was applied to Mexicans in express violation of the treaty ending the Mexican War.

CALIFORNIA STATEHOOD   As civic leaders emerged within the burgeoning California population, they grew increasingly frustrated by the inability of military authorities to maintain law and order. In this context the new president, Zachary Taylor, thought he saw an ideal opportunity to use California statehood as a lever to end the stalemate in Congress caused by the slavery issue. Born in Virginia, raised in Kentucky, he had been a soldier most of his adult life. Constantly on the move, he had acquired a home in Louisiana and a plantation in Mississippi. Southern Whigs had rallied to his support, expecting him to uphold the cause of slavery. Instead they had turned up a southern man with Union principles, who had no more use for Calhoun's proslavery abstractions than Jackson had for his nullification doctrine. Innocent of politics Taylor might be, but "Old Rough and Ready" had the direct mind of the soldier he was. Slavery should be upheld where it existed, he felt, but he had little patience with abstract theories about slavery in territories where it probably could not exist. Why not make California and New Mexico into states immediately, he reasoned, and bypass the whole issue?

But the Californians, in need of organized government, were already ahead of him. By December 1849, without consulting Congress, California had a free-state government in operation. New Mexico responded more slowly, but by 1850 Americans there had adopted another free-state constitution. The Mormons around Salt Lake, meanwhile, drafted a basic law for the imperial state of Deseret, which embraced most of the Mexican cession, including a slice of the coast from Los Angeles to San Diego.

In Taylor's annual message on December 4, 1849, he endorsed immediate statehood for California and enjoined Congress to "abstain from . . . those exciting topics of sectional character which have hitherto produced painful apprehensions in the public mind." The new Congress, however, was in no mood for simple solutions.

THE COMPROMISE OF 1850

The spotlight fell on the Senate, where a stellar cast enacted one of the great dramas of American politics, the Compromise of 1850: the triumvirate of Clay, Calhoun, and Webster, with a supporting cast that included William Seward, Stephen A. Douglas, Jefferson Davis, and Thomas Hart Benton. Seventy-three-year-old Henry Clay once again took the role of "Great Compromiser," which he had played in the Missouri and nullification controversies.

THE GREAT DEBATE   In January 1850 Clay presented a package of eight resolutions that wrapped up solutions to all the disputed issues. He proposed to (1) admit California as a free state, (2) organize the remainder of the Southwest without restriction as to slavery, (3) deny Texas its extreme claim to a Rio Grande boundary up to its source, (4) compensate Texas for this by assuming the Texas debt, (5) uphold slavery in the District of Columbia, but (6) abolish the slave trade across its boundaries, (7) adopt a more effective fugitive slave act, and (8) deny congressional authority to interfere with the interstate slave trade. His proposals, in substance, became the Compromise of 1850, but only after a prolonged debate, the most celebrated, if not the greatest, in the annals of Congress—and the final great debate for Calhoun, Clay, and Webster. Calhoun, already dying, would be gone on March 31, and Clay and Webster two years later, in 1852.

On February 5–6 Clay summoned all his eloquence in a defense of the settlement. In the interest of "peace, concord and harmony," he called for an end to "passion, passion—party, party—and intemperance." California should be admitted on the terms that its own people had approved. As to the remainder of the new lands, he told northerners: "You have got what is worth more than a thousand Wilmot provisos. You have nature on your side." Secession, he warned southerners, would inevitably bring on war. Even a peaceful secession, however unlikely, would gain none of the South's demands. Slavery in the territories and the District, the return of fugitives—all would be endangered.

The debate continued sporadically through February, with Sam Houston rising to the support of Clay's compromise, and Jefferson Davis defending the slavery cause on every point. Taylor believed that slavery in the South could best be protected if southerners avoided injecting the issue into the dispute over new territories. Unlike Calhoun, he did not believe the new western territories were suitable for slave-based agriculture. Because in his mind the issue of bringing slaves into the territories was moot, he continued to urge the Congress to admit California and New Mexico without reference to slavery. But few others embraced such a simple solution.

On March 4 Calhoun left his sickbed to sit in the Senate chamber, a gaunt figure with his cloak draped about his shoulders, as a colleague read the "sentiments" he had "reduced to writing." "I have, Senators, believed from the first that the agitation of the subject of slavery would, if not prevented by some timely and effective measure, end in disunion," said Calhoun. Neither Clay's compromise nor Taylor's efforts would serve the Union. The South needed simply an acceptance of its

Daniel Webster, in a daguerreotype made around the time of the Compromise of 1850.

rights: equality in the territories, the return of fugitive slaves, and some guarantee of "an equilibrium between the sections." The last, while not spelled out in the speech, referred to Calhoun's notion of a "concurrent majority" by which each section could gain security through a veto power, perhaps through a dual executive.

Three days later Calhoun returned to hear Daniel Webster. The "Godlike Daniel," long since acknowledged the supreme orator of an age of superb oratory, no longer possessed the thunderous voice of his youth, nor did his shrinking frame project its once magisterial aura, but he remained a formidable presence. His weathered face showed signs of worry and sorrow as he addressed the hushed Senate. He chose as his central theme the preservation of the Union: "I wish to speak today, not as a Massachusetts man, not as a Northern man, but as an American. . . . I speak today for the preservation of the Union. Hear me for my cause." The extent of slavery was already determined, he insisted, by the Northwest Ordinance, by the Missouri Compromise, and in the new lands by the law of nature. The Wilmot Proviso was superfluous: "I would not take pains to reaffirm an ordinance of nature nor to re-enact the will of God." Both sections, to be sure, had legitimate grievances: on the one hand, the excesses of "infernal fanatics and abolitionists" in the North; and on the other hand, southern efforts to expand slavery and heap southern slurs on northern workingmen. But "Secession! Peaceable secession! Sir, your eyes and mine are never destined to see that miracle." Instead of looking into such "caverns of darkness," let "men enjoy the fresh air of liberty and union. Let them look to a more hopeful future."

The March 7 speech was a supreme gesture of conciliation, and Webster had knowingly brought down a storm upon his head. New England antislavery leaders lambasted this new "Benedict Arnold" who had betrayed his region. But Webster had also revived hopes of compromise in both North and South. Georgia's Senator Toombs found "a tolerable prospect for a proper settlement of the slavery question, probably along the lines backed by Webster."

On March 11 William Seward, freshman Whig senator from New York, gave the antislavery reply to Webster. As the confidant of Taylor, he might have been expected to defend the president's program. Instead he stated his own view that compromise with slavery was "radically wrong and essentially vicious." There was, he said, "a higher law than the Constitution," thus leaving some doubt whether he was floor leader for Zachary Taylor or for God.

In mid-April a select Committee of Thirteen bundled Clay's suggestions (insofar as they concerned the Mexican cession) into one comprehensive bill, which the committee reported to the Senate early in May. The measure was quickly dubbed the "Omnibus Bill" because it resembled the contemporary vehicle that carried many riders. Taylor continued to oppose Clay's compromise, and the two men came to an open break that threatened to split the Whig party wide open. Another crisis loomed when word came near the end of June that New Mexico was applying for statehood, with Taylor's support, and with boundaries that conflicted with the Texas claim to the east bank of the Rio Grande.

TOWARD A COMPROMISE   On July 4, 1850, friends of the Union staged a grand rally at the base of the unfinished Washington Monument. Taylor went to hear the speeches, lingering in the hot sun. Back at the White House he quenched his thirst with iced water and milk, ate some cherries, cucumbers, or cabbage, and contracted cholera morbus (a gastrointestinal affliction). Five days later he was dead. The outcome of the sectional quarrel, had he lived, probably would have been different, whether for better or worse one cannot know. In a showdown Taylor had put everyone on notice that he would be as resolute as Jackson. "I can save the Union without shedding a drop of blood," he said. On the other hand, a showdown might have provoked civil war ten years before it came, years during which the northern states gained in population and economic strength.

Millard Fillmore, whose support of the Compromise of 1850 helped the Union muddle through the crisis.

Taylor's sudden death, however, strengthened the chances of compromise. The soldier in the White House was followed by a politician, Millard Fillmore. The son of a poor farmer in upper New York, Fillmore had come up through the school of hard knocks. Largely self-educated, he had made his own way in the profession of law and the rough-and-tumble world of New York politics. Experience had taught him caution, which some thought was indecision, but he had made up his mind to support Clay's compromise and had so informed Taylor. It was a strange switch. Taylor, the Louisiana slaveholder, had been ready to make war on his native region; Fillmore, who southerners thought was antislavery, was ready to make peace.

At this point young Senator Stephen A. Douglas of Illinois, a rising star of the Democratic party, rescued Clay's faltering compromise. Short and stocky, brash and brilliant, Douglas was known as the "Little Giant." His strategy was in fact the same one that Clay had used to pass the Missouri Compromise thirty years before. Reasoning that nearly everybody objected to one or another provision of the Omnibus Bill, Douglas worked on the principle of breaking it up into six (later five) separate measures. Few members were prepared to vote for all of them, but from different elements Douglas hoped to mobilize a majority for each.

It worked. Thomas Hart Benton described the sequel. The separate items were like "cats and dogs that had been tied together by their tails for months, scratching and biting, but being loose again, every one of them ran off to his own hole and was quiet." By September 20, Fillmore

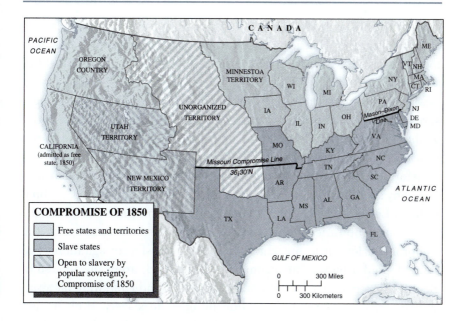

COMPROMISE OF 1850

- Free states and territories
- Slave states
- Open to slavery by popular sovereignty, Compromise of 1850

had signed the last of the five measures into law. The Union had muddled through, and the settlement went down in history as the Compromise of 1850. For the time it defused an explosive situation and settled each of the major points at issue.

First, California entered the Union as a free state, ending forever the old balance of free and slave states. *Second,* the Texas and New Mexico Act made New Mexico a territory and set the Texas boundary at its present location. In return for giving up its claims east of the Rio Grande, Texas was paid $10 million, which secured payment of the Texas debt and brought a powerful lobby of bondholders to the support of compromise. *Third,* the Utah Act set up another territory. The territorial act in each case omitted reference to slavery except to give the territorial legislature authority over "all rightful subjects of legislation" with provision for appeal to federal courts. For the sake of agreement the deliberate ambiguity of the statement was its merit. Northern congressmen could assume that territorial legislatures might act to exclude slavery on the unstated principle of popular sovereignty. Southern congressmen assumed that they could not.

Fourth, a new Fugitive Slave Act put the matter wholly under federal jurisdiction and stacked the cards in favor of slave-catchers. *Fifth,* as a gesture to antislavery forces, the slave trade, but not slavery itself, was abolished in the District of Columbia. The spectacle of chained-together slaves passing through the streets of the capital was brought to an end.

Millard Fillmore's message to Congress pronounced the five measures making up the Compromise of 1850 "a final settlement." Still, doubts lingered that either North or South could be reconciled to the measures permanently. In the South the disputes of 1846–1850 had transformed the abstract doctrine of secession into a movement animated by such "fire-eaters" as Robert Barnwell Rhett of South Carolina, William Lowndes Yancey of Alabama, and Edmund Ruffin of Virginia.

But once the furies aroused by the Wilmot Proviso were spent, the compromise left little on which to focus a proslavery agitation. The state of California was an accomplished fact, and, ironically, tended to elect proslavery men to Congress. New Mexico and Utah were far away, and in any case at least hypothetically open to slavery. Both in fact adopted slave codes, but the census of 1860 reported no slaves in New Mexico and only twenty-nine in Utah. The Fugitive Slave Act was something else again. It was the one clear-cut victory for the cause of slavery, but a Pyrrhic victory if ever there was one.

THE FUGITIVE SLAVE ACT   Southern insistence on the Fugitive Slave Act had presented abolitionists their greatest gift since the gag rule, giving them a new focus for agitation and one that was far more charged with emotion. The Fugitive Slave Act did more than strengthen the hand of slave-catchers; it offered a strong temptation to kidnap free blacks. The law denied alleged fugitives a jury trial and provided that special commissioners got a fee of $10 when they certified delivery of an alleged slave but only $5 when they refused certification. In addition federal marshals could require citizens to help in enforcement; violators could be imprisoned for up to six months and fined $1,000.

"This filthy enactment was made in the nineteenth century, by people who could read and write," Ralph Waldo Emerson marveled in his journal. He advised neighbors to break it "on the earliest occasion." The occasion soon arose in many places. Within a month of the law's enactment, claims were filed in New York, Philadelphia, Harrisburg, Detroit, and other cities. Trouble soon followed. In Detroit only military force stopped the rescue of an alleged fugitive by an outraged mob in October 1850.

CAUTION!!

COLORED PEOPLE

OF BOSTON, ONE & ALL,

You are hereby respectfully CAUTIONED and advised, to avoid conversing with the

Watchmen and Police Officers of Boston,

For since the recent ORDER OF THE MAYOR & ALDERMEN, they are empowered to act as

KIDNAPPERS

AND

Slave Catchers,

And they have already been actually employed in KIDNAPPING, CATCHING, AND KEEPING SLAVES. Therefore, if you value your LIBERTY, and the *Welfare of the Fugitives* among you, *Shun* them in every possible manner, as so many *HOUNDS* on the track of the most unfortunate of your race.

Keep a Sharp Look Out for KIDNAPPERS, and have TOP EYE open.

APRIL 24, 1851.

A notice to the free blacks of Boston to avoid the "watchmen and police officers" who "are empowered to act as kidnappers and slave catchers," 1851.

There were relatively few such incidents, however. In the first six years of the fugitive act, only three fugitives were forcibly rescued from the slave-catchers. On the other hand, probably fewer than 200 were returned to bondage during the same years. More than that were rescued by stealth, often through the Underground Railroad. Still, the Fugitive Slave Act had the tremendous effect of widening and deepening the antislavery impulse in the North.

UNCLE TOM'S CABIN   Antislavery forces found their most persuasive appeal not in the Fugitive Slave Act but in the fictional drama of Harriet Beecher Stowe's *Uncle Tom's Cabin* (1852), a combination of unlikely saints and sinners, stereotypes, and melodramatic escapades—and a smashing commercial success. The long-suffering Uncle Tom, the villainous Simon Legree, the angelic Eva, the desperate Eliza taking her child to freedom across the icy Ohio River—all became stock characters of the American imagination. Slavery, seen through Stowe's eyes, subjected its victims either to callous brutality or, at the hands of spendthrift masters, to the indignity of bankruptcy. It took time for the novel to work its effect on public opinion, however. Neither abolitionists nor fire-eaters fought for their sections at the time. The country was enjoying a surge of prosperity, and the course of the presidential campaign in 1852 reflected a common desire to lay sectional quarrels to rest.

"The Greatest Book of the Age." Uncle Tom's Cabin, *as this advertisement indicates, was a tremendous commercial success.*

THE ELECTION OF 1852   The Democrats, despite a fight over the nomination, had some success in papering over the divisions within their party. As their nominee for president they turned finally to Franklin Pierce of New Hampshire. The platform pledged the Democrats to "abide by and adhere to a faithful execution of the acts known as the Compromise measures." The candidates and the platform generated a surprising reconciliation of the party's factions. Pierce rallied both the southern rights' men and the Van Burenite Barnburners, who at least had not burned their bridges with the Democrats. The Free Soilers, as a consequence, mustered only 156,000 votes for John P. Hale in contrast to the 291,000 they got for Van Buren in 1848.

The Whigs were less fortunate. They repudiated the lackluster Fillmore, who had faithfully supported the Compromise, and once again tried to exploit martial glory. It took fifty-three ballots, but the convention finally chose Winfield Scott, the hero of Mexico City, a native of Virginia backed mainly by northern Whigs. The convention dutifully endorsed the Compromise, but with some opposition from the North. Scott, an able commander but politically inept, had gained a reputation for antislavery and nativism, alienating German and Irish ethnic voters. In the end Scott carried only Tennessee, Kentucky, Massachusetts, and Vermont. Pierce overwhelmed him in the electoral college 254 to 42, although the popular vote was close: 1.6 million to 1.4 million.

Pierce, an undistinguished but handsome and engaging figure, a former congressman, senator, and brigadier in Mexico, was, like Polk, touted as another "Young Hickory." But the youngest president turned out to be made of more pliable stuff, unable to dominate the warring factions of his party. Just after the election Pierce wrote a poignant letter to his wife in which he expressed his frustration at the prospect of keeping North and South together. "I can do no right," he sighed. "What am I to do, wife? Stand by me." By the end of his first year in office, the leaders of his own party had decided he was a failure. By trying to be all things to all people, Pierce looked more and more like a "Northern man with Southern principles."

FOREIGN ADVENTURES

CUBA   Foreign diversions now distracted attention from domestic quarrels. Cuba, one of Spain's earliest and one of its last possessions in the New World, continued to be an object of American desire. In the early 1850s a crisis arose over expeditions launched against Cuba from American soil. Spanish authorities retaliated against these provocations by harassing American ships. In 1854 the Cuban crisis expired in one final outburst of braggadocio, the Ostend Manifesto. That year the Pierce administration instructed Pierre Soulé, the American minister in Madrid, to offer $130 million for Cuba, which Spain peremptorily spurned. Soulé then joined the American ministers to France and Britain in drafting the Ostend Manifesto. It declared that if Spain, "actuated by stubborn pride and a false sense of honor refused to sell," then the United States must ask itself, "does Cuba, in the possession of Spain, seriously endanger our internal peace and existence of our cherished Union?" If so, "then, by every law, human and divine, we shall be justified in wresting it from Spain. . . ." Publication of the supposedly confidential dispatch left the administration no choice but to disavow what northern opinion widely regarded as a "slaveholders' plot."

DIPLOMATIC GAINS IN THE PACIFIC   In the Pacific, American diplomacy scored some important achievements. American trade with China dated from 1785, but was allowed only through the port of Canton. In 1844 the United States and China signed the Treaty of Wanghsia, which opened four ports, including Shanghai, to American trade and for the first time granted America "extraterritoriality," or special privileges, including the right of Americans in China to remain subject to their own law. The Treaty of Tientsin (1858) opened eleven more ports and granted Americans the right to travel and trade throughout China. American Protestant missionaries also developed a keen interest in China. About fifty were already there by 1855, and for nearly a century China remained far and away the most active mission field for Americans.

Japan meanwhile had remained for two centuries closed to American trade. Moreover, American whalers wrecked on the shores of Japan had been forbidden to leave the country. Mainly in their interest President Fillmore entrusted a special Japanese expedition to Commodore Matthew Perry, who arrived in Tokyo in 1853. Japan's actual ruler, the Tokugawa shogun, was already under pressure from merchants and the educated classes to seek wider contacts in the world. He agreed to deliver Perry's letter to the emperor. Negotiations followed, and in the Treaty of Kanagawa (1854) Japan agreed to an American consulate, promised good treatment to castaways, and permitted visits in certain ports for supplies and repairs. Broad commercial relations came after the first envoy, Townsend Harris, negotiated the Harris Convention of 1858, which opened five ports to American trade and made certain tariff concessions. In 1860 a Japanese diplomatic mission, the first to enter a Western country, visited the United States for three months.

A Japanese view of Commodore Perry's landing in Yokohama Harbor.

THE KANSAS-NEBRASKA CRISIS

During the 1850s, the only land added to the United States was a barren stretch of some 30,000 square miles south of the Gila River in present New Mexico and Arizona. This Gadsden Purchase of 1853, in which the United States paid Mexico $10 million, was made to acquire land offering a likely route for a Pacific railroad. The idea of building a railroad linking together the new continental domain of the United States, though a great national goal, spawned sectional rivalries in still another quarter and reopened the slavery issue. Among the many transcontinental routes projected, the four most important were the northern route from Milwaukee to the Columbia River, a central route from St. Louis to San Francisco, another from Memphis to Los Angeles, and a more southerly route from New Orleans to San Diego via the Gadsden Purchase.

DOUGLAS'S PROPOSAL   In 1852 and 1853 Congress debated and dropped several likely proposals. For various reasons, including terrain, climate, and sectional interest, Secretary of War Jefferson Davis favored the southern route and encouraged the Gadsden Purchase. Any other route, moreover, would go through the Indian country which stretched from Texas to the Canadian border.

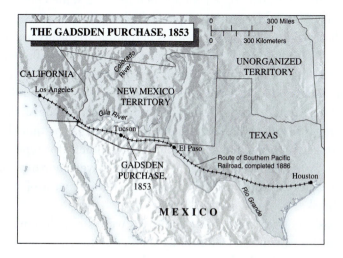

THE GADSDEN PURCHASE, 1853

0   300 Miles
0   300 Kilometers

CALIFORNIA

Los Angeles

Colorado River

NEW MEXICO TERRITORY

Gila River

Tucson

El Paso

UNORGANIZED TERRITORY

TEXAS

Route of Southern Pacific Railroad, completed 1886

Houston

GADSDEN PURCHASE, 1853

Rio Grande

MEXICO

Stephen Douglas.

Stephen A. Douglas of Illinois had an even better idea: he thought that Chicago should be the eastern terminus. Since 1845, therefore, Douglas and others had offered bills for a new territory in the lands west of Missouri and Iowa, bearing the Indian name Nebraska. In 1854, as chairman of the committee on territories, Senator Douglas reported yet another Nebraska bill, which became the Kansas-Nebraska Act. Unlike the others this one included the entire unorganized portion of the Louisiana Purchase to the Canadian border. At this point fateful connections began to transform his proposal from a railroad bill to a proslavery bill. To carry his point Douglas needed the support of southerners, and to win that support he needed to make some concession on slavery. This he did by writing popular sovereignty into the bill in language that specified that "all questions pertaining to slavery in the Territories, and in the new states to be formed therefrom are to be left to the people residing therein, through their appropriate representatives."

It was a clever dodge, since the Missouri Compromise would still exclude slaves until the territorial government had made a decision. Southerners quickly spotted the barrier, and Douglas as quickly made two more concessions. He supported an amendment for repeal of the Missouri Compromise insofar as it excluded slavery north of 36°30', and then agreed to organize two territories, Kansas, west of Missouri; and Nebraska, west of Iowa and Minnesota.

Douglas's motives are unclear. Railroads were surely foremost in his mind, but he was influenced also by the desire to win support for his bill in the South, by the hope that popular sovereignty would quiet the

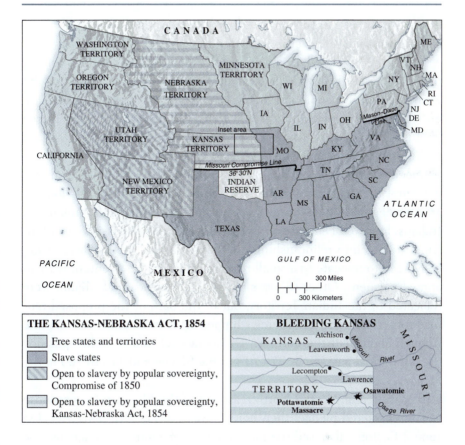

THE KANSAS-NEBRASKA ACT, 1854

- Free states and territories
- Slave states
- Open to slavery by popular sovereignty, Compromise of 1850
- Open to slavery by popular sovereignty, Kansas-Nebraska Act, 1854

BLEEDING KANSAS

slavery issue and open the Northwest, or by a chance to split the Whigs. But he had blundered, had damaged his presidential chances, and had set his country on the road to civil war. The tragic flaw in his plan was his failure to appreciate the depth of antislavery feelings. Douglas himself preferred that the territories become free. Their climate and geography excluded plantation agriculture, he reasoned, and he could not comprehend how people could get so wrought up over abstract rights. Yet he had in fact opened the possibility that slavery might gain a foothold in Kansas.

The agreement to repeal the Missouri Compromise was less than a week old before six antislavery congressmen published a protest, the "Appeal of the Independent Democrats." The tone of moral indignation that pervaded their protest quickly spread among those who opposed Douglas. The document arraigned his bill "as a gross violation of a sacred pledge," and as "part and parcel of an atrocious plot" to create "a dreary region of despotism, inhabited by masters and slaves." They called upon their fellow citizens to protest against this "atrocious crime."

Across the North, editorials, sermons, speeches, and petitions echoed this indignation. What had been radical opinion was fast becoming the common view of people in the North. But Douglas had the votes and, once committed, forced the issue with tireless energy. President Pierce impulsively added his support. Southerners lined up behind Douglas, with notable exceptions such as Texas senator Sam Houston, who denounced the violation of two solemn compacts: the Missouri Compromise and the confirmation of the territory to the Indians "as long as grass shall grow and water run." He was not the only one to think of the Indians, however. Federal agents were already busy hoodwinking or bullying Indians into relinquishing their land claims. The Delaware were convinced to relocate to a small reservation and to rest content with an annual payment. Other tribes, such as the Shawnee and Miami, were relocated to the Indian Territory, out of the path of the proposed railroad routes. Douglas and Pierce whipped reluctant Democrats into line (though about half the northern Democrats refused to yield), pushing the bill to final passage by 37 to 14 in the Senate and 113 to 100 in the House.

Very well, many in the North reasoned, if the Missouri Compromise was not a sacred pledge, then neither was the Fugitive Slave Act. On June 2 Boston witnessed the most dramatic demonstration against the act. After several attempts had failed to rescue a fugitive named Anthony Burns, a force of soldiers and marines dispatched by President Pierce marched him to a waiting ship through streets lined with people shouting "Kidnappers!" past buildings draped in black, while church bells tolled across the city. The event cost the federal government $14,000. Burns was the last to be returned from Boston, and was himself soon freed through purchase by the black community of Boston. New Englanders blamed Pierce for this sorry episode. One sent a letter to the White House that read: "To the chief slave-catcher of the United States. You damned, infernal scoundrel, if only I had you here in Boston, I would murder you!"

THE EMERGENCE OF THE REPUBLICAN PARTY What John Calhoun had called the cords holding the Union together had already begun to part. The national church organizations of Baptists and Methodists, for instance, had split over slavery by 1845. The national parties, which had created mutual interests transcending sectional issues, were beginning to buckle under the strain. The Democrats managed to postpone disruption for yet a while, but their congressional delegation lost heavily in the North, enhancing the influence of the southern wing.

The strain of the Kansas-Nebraska Act, however, soon destroyed the Whig party. Southern Whigs now tended to abstain from voting, while Northern Whigs moved toward two new parties. One was the new American (Know-Nothing) party, which had raised the banner of native Americanism and the hope of serving the patriotic cause of Union. More Northern Whigs joined with independent Democrats and Free Soilers in spontaneous antislavery coalitions with a confusing array of names, including "Anti-Nebraska," "Fusion," and "People's party." These coalitions finally united in 1854 under the name "Republican," evoking the memory of Jefferson.

"BLEEDING" KANSAS   After passage of the Kansas-Nebraska Act, attention swung to the plains of Kansas, where opposing elements gathered to stage a rehearsal for civil war. All agreed that Nebraska would be free, but Kansas soon exposed the potential for mischief in popular sovereignty. The ambiguity of the law, useful to Douglas in getting it passed, only added to the chaos. The people of Kansas were "perfectly free to form and regulate their domestic institutions in their own way, subject only to the Constitution." That in itself invited conflicting interpretations, but the law was completely silent as to the time of decision, adding to each side's sense of urgency about getting control of the territory.

The settlement of Kansas therefore differed from the usual pioneering efforts. Groups sprang up North and South to hurry right-minded settlers westward. In fact, however, few New Englanders migrated to Kansas. Most of the settlers were from Missouri and surrounding states. Although few of them owned slaves, they were not sympathetic to militant abolitionism. Racism was prevalent even among non-slaveholding whites. Many of the Kansas settlers wanted to keep all blacks, slave or free, out of the territory. "I kem [sic] to Kansas to live in a free state," declared a minister, "and I don't want niggers a-trampin' over my grave." By 1860, there were only 627 African Americans in the territory.

When Kansas's first governor arrived in 1854, he found several thousand settlers already there. He ordered a census and scheduled an election for a territorial legislature in 1855. When the election took place, several thousand "Border Ruffians" crossed over from Missouri, illegally swept the polls for proslavery forces, and vowed to kill every "God-damned abolitionist in the Territory." The governor denounced the vote as a fraud, but did nothing to alter the results, for fear of being killed. The legislature expelled the few antislavery members, adopted a drastic slave code, and made it a capital offense to aid a fugitive slave and a felony even to question the legality of slavery in the territory.

Free-state advocates rejected this "bogus" government and moved directly toward application for statehood. In 1855 a constitutional convention, the product of an extralegal election, met in Topeka, drafted a state constitution excluding both slavery and free blacks from Kansas, and applied for admission to the Union. By 1856 a free-state "governor" and "legislature" were functioning in Topeka; thus there were now two governments in the territory. But the prospect of getting any government to command general authority in Kansas seemed dim, and both sides began to arm.

Finally, confrontation began to slip into conflict. In May 1856 a proslavery mob entered the free-state town of Lawrence and destroyed newspaper presses, set fire to the free-state governor's private home, stole property that was not nailed down, and trained five cannon on the Free State Hotel, demolishing it.

The "sack of Lawrence" resulted in just one casualty, but the excitement aroused a fanatical Free-Soiler named John Brown, who had a history of instability. A companion described him as one "impressed with the idea that God had raised him up on purpose to break the jaws of the wicked." Two days after the sack of Lawrence, Brown set out with four sons and three other men toward Pottawatomie Creek, site of a proslavery settlement, where they dragged five men from their houses and hacked them to death in front of their screaming families, ostensibly as revenge for the deaths of free-state men.

The Pottawatomie Massacre (May 24–25, 1856) set off a guerrilla war in the territory that lasted through the fall. On August 30, Missouri ruffians raided the free-state settlement at Osawatomie. They looted the houses, burned them to the ground, and shot John Brown's son Frederick through the heart. The elder Brown, who barely escaped, looked back at the site being devastated by "Satan's legions," and muttered, "God sees it." He then swore to his surviving sons and followers:

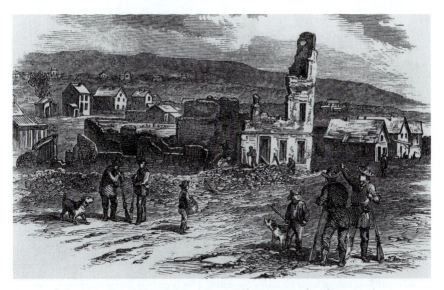

Ruins of the Free State Hotel (*Emigrant Aid Company headquarters*), *Lawrence, Kansas, 1856.*

"I have only a short time to live—only one death to die, and I will die fighting for this cause." Altogether, by the end of 1856 Kansas lost about 200 killed and $2 million in property destroyed during the territorial civil war.

VIOLENCE IN THE SENATE Violence in Kansas spilled over into Congress, where angry legislators began to trade recriminations, coming to the verge of blows. On May 22, 1856, the day after the sack of Lawrence, two days before the Pottawatomie Massacre, a sudden flash of violence on the Senate floor electrified the whole country. Just two days earlier Senator Charles Sumner of Massachusetts had finished an inflammatory speech on "The Crime against Kansas." Sumner, elected five years earlier by a coalition of Free Soilers and Democrats, was a man of principle with limited tolerance for opinions different from his own.

His speech was an exercise in studied insult. The proslavery Missourians who crossed into Kansas, Sumner charged, were "hirelings picked from the drunken spew and vomit of an uneasy civilization." Their treatment of Kansas was "the rape of a virgin territory," he said, "and it may be clearly traced to a depraved longing for a new slave State,

"Bully" Brooks's attack on Charles Sumner. The incident worsened the strains on the Union.

the hideous offspring of such a crime. . . ." Senator A. P. Butler of South Carolina became a special target of his censure. Butler, Sumner charged, had "chosen a mistress . . . who . . . though polluted in the sight of the world, is chaste in his sight—I mean the harlot, Slavery." Sumner said that Butler betrayed "an incapacity of accuracy," a constant "deviation of truth."

Sumner's rudeness might well have backfired had it not been for Butler's nephew Preston S. Brooks, a fiery-tempered congressman from Edgefield, South Carolina. For two days Brooks brooded over the insult to his uncle, Senator Butler. Knowing that Sumner would refuse a challenge to a duel, he considered but rejected the idea of taking a horsewhip to him. Finally, on May 22, he found Sumner writing at his Senate desk after an adjournment, accused him of libel against South Carolina and Butler, and commenced beating him about the head with a cane while stunned colleagues looked on. Sumner, struggling to rise, wrenched the desk from the floor and collapsed.

Brooks had satisfied his rage, but in doing so had created a martyr for the antislavery cause. Like so many other men in those years, he betrayed the zealot's gift for snatching defeat from the jaws of victory. For two and a half years Sumner's empty seat was a solemn reminder of the violence done to him. Some thought the senator was feigning injury, others that he really was physically disabled. In fact, although his injuries were bad enough, including two gashes to the skull, he seems to have suffered a psychosomatic shock that left him incapable of functioning. When the House censured Brooks, he resigned, went home to Edgefield, and returned after being triumphantly reelected. His admirers presented him with new canes. Southerners who never would have done what Brooks did now hastened to make excuses for him. Northerners who never would have said what Sumner said now hastened to his defense. The news of Sumner's beating drove John Brown "crazy," his eldest son remembered, *"crazy."* Men on each side, appalled at the behavior of the other, decided that North and South had developed into different civilizations with incompatible standards of honor. "I do not see," Ralph Waldo Emerson confessed, "how a barbarous community and a civilized community can constitute one state. We must either get rid of slavery, or get rid of freedom."

SECTIONAL POLITICS   Within the span of five days in May of 1856 "Bleeding Kansas," "Bleeding Sumner," and "Bully Brooks" had set the tone for another presidential year. The major parties could no longer evade the slavery issue. Already in February it had split the hopeful American party wide open. Southern delegates, with help from New York, killed a resolution to restore the Missouri Compromise, and nominated Millard Fillmore for president. Later, what was left of the Whig party endorsed the same candidate.

At its first national convention the new Republican party passed over its leading figure, William H. Seward, who was awaiting a better chance in 1860. Following the Whig tradition, they sought out a military hero, John C. Frémont, the "Pathfinder" and leader in the conquest of California. The Republican platform owed much to the Whigs too. It favored a transcontinental railroad and, in general, more internal improvements. It condemned the repeal of the Missouri Compromise, the Democratic policy of expansion, and "those twin relics of barbarism— Polygamy and Slavery." The campaign slogan echoed that of the Free Soilers: "Free soil, free speech, and Frémont." It was the first time a major party platform had taken a stand against slavery.

The Republican position on slavery, the historian Eric Foner has argued, developed from an ideology of free labor. "Political antislavery was not merely a negative doctrine, an attack on southern slavery and the society built on it," Foner wrote; "it was an affirmation of the superiority of the social system of the North—a dynamic expanding capitalist society, whose achievements and destiny were almost wholly the result of the dignity and opportunities which it offered the average laboring man." Such a creed, he argued, could accommodate a variety of opinions on race, economics, or other issues, but it was "an ideology which blended personal and sectional interest with morality so perfectly that it became the most potent political force in the nation."

The Democrats, meeting two weeks earlier in June, had rejected Pierce, the hapless victim of so much turmoil. Douglas too was left out because of the damage done by his Kansas-Nebraska Act. The party therefore turned to James Buchanan of Pennsylvania, who had long sought the nomination. The party and its candidate nevertheless hewed to Pierce's policies. The Democratic platform endorsed the Kansas-Nebraska Act and nonintervention. Congress, it said, should not interfere with slavery in either states or territories. The party reached out to its newly acquired ethnic voters by condemning nativism and endorsing religious liberty.

The campaign of 1856 resolved itself into two sectional campaigns. The "Black Republicans" had few southern supporters, and only a handful in the border states, where fears of disunion held many Whigs in line. Buchanan thus went into the campaign as the candidate of the only remaining national party. Although Fillmore won a larger vote in the South than Scott had, the slave states were safe for Buchanan. Frémont swept the northernmost states with 114 electoral votes, but Buchanan added five free states to his southern majority for a total of 174: Pennsylvania, New Jersey, Illinois, Indiana, and California.

Few presidents before Buchanan had a broader experience in politics and diplomacy. His career went back to 1815, when he started as a Federalist legislator in Pennsylvania before switching to Jackson's party in the 1820s. He had been in Congress for over twenty years, minister to Russia and Britain, and Polk's secretary of state in between. His long quest for the presidency had been built on a southern alliance, and his political debts reinforced his belief that saving the Union depended on concessions to the South. Republicans charged that he lacked the backbone to stand up to the southerners who dominated the Democratic majorities in Congress. His choice of four slave-state and only three free-state men for his cabinet seemed another bad omen.

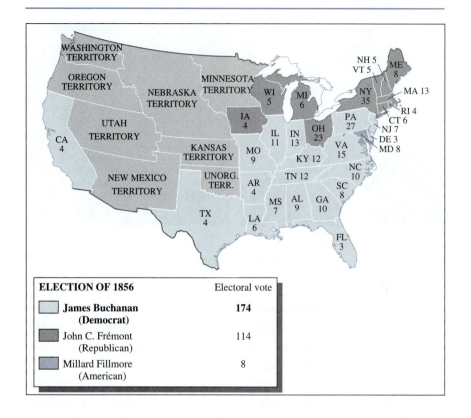

ELECTION OF 1856	Electoral vote
James Buchanan (Democrat)	**174**
John C. Frémont (Republican)	114
Millard Fillmore (American)	8

THE DEEPENING SECTIONAL CRISIS

An old saying has it that troubles cluster in threes. In 1856, the sack of Lawrence, the Brooks-Sumner affair, and the Pottawatomie Massacre came in quick succession. During Buchanan's first six months in 1857, he encountered the Dred Scott decision, new troubles in Kansas, and a business panic.

THE DRED SCOTT CASE   On March 6, 1857, two days after the inauguration, the Supreme Court rendered a decision in the long-pending case of *Dred Scott v. Sandford.* Dred Scott, born a slave in Virginia about 1800, had been taken to St. Louis and sold to an army surgeon, who took him as body servant to Fort Armstrong, Illinois, then to Fort Snelling in the Wisconsin Territory (later Minnesota), and finally returned him to St. Louis in 1838. After his master's death in 1843 Scott apparently had tried to buy his freedom. In 1846, with help from white friends, he brought suit in Missouri courts claiming that residence in

Dred Scott (left) *and Chief Justice Roger B. Taney* (right). *The Supreme Court's decision on Dred Scott's suit for freedom fanned the flames of discord.*

Illinois and the Wisconsin Territory had made him free. A jury decided in his favor, but the state supreme court ruled against him. When the case rose on appeal to the Supreme Court, the country anxiously awaited its opinion on the issue of slavery in the territories.

Each of the nine justices filed a separate opinion, except one who concurred with Chief Justice Roger B. Taney of Maryland. By different lines of reasoning, seven justices ruled that Scott remained a slave. The aging Taney, whose opinion represented the Court, ruled that Scott lacked legal standing because he lacked citizenship. Taney argued that one became a federal citizen either by birth or by naturalization, which ruled out any former slave. He further argued that no state had ever accorded citizenship to blacks—a statement demonstrably in error. At the time the Constitution was adopted, Taney further said, blacks "had for more than a century been regarded as . . . so far inferior, that they had no rights which the white man was bound to respect."

To clarify further the definition of Scott's status, Taney moved to a second major question. Residency in a free state had not freed Scott since, in line with precedent, the decision of the state court governed. This left the question of residency in a free territory. On this point Taney argued that the Missouri Compromise had deprived citizens of property in slaves, an action "not warranted by the constitution." He strongly implied, but never said explicitly, that the compromise had violated the due-process clause of the Fifth Amendment, as Calhoun had earlier argued. The upshot was that the Supreme Court had declared an act of Congress unconstitutional for the first time since *Marbury* v. *Madison* (1803), and a major act for the first time ever. Congress had repealed the Missouri Compromise in the Kansas-Nebraska Act three years earlier, but the decision now challenged popular sovereignty. If Congress itself could not exclude slavery from a territory, then presumably neither could a territorial government created by act of Congress.

By this decision the Supreme Court had thought to settle a question that Congress had dodged ever since the Wilmot Proviso surfaced. But far from settling it, it had only fanned the flames of dissension. Little wonder that Republicans protested: the Court had declared their program unconstitutional. It had also reinforced the suspicion that the slavocracy was hatching a conspiracy. Were not all but one of the justices who joined Taney southerners? And had not Buchanan chatted with the chief justice at the inauguration and then urged the people to accept the early decision as a final settlement, "Whatever this may be"? (Actually, Buchanan already knew the outcome because two other justices had spilled the beans in private letters.) Besides, if Dred Scott were not a citizen and had no standing in court, there was no case before it. The majority ruling was an *obiter dictum*—a statement not essential to deciding the case and therefore not binding, "entitled to just so much moral weight as would be the judgment of a majority of those congregated in any Washington bar-room."

Proslavery elements, of course, greeted the Court's opinion as binding. Now the fire-eaters among them were emboldened to yet another demand. It was not enough to deny Congress the right to interfere with slavery in the territories; Congress had an obligation to protect the property of slaveholders, making a federal slave code the next step. The idea, first broached by Alabama Democrats in the "Alabama Platform" of 1848, soon became orthodox southern doctrine.

THE LECOMPTON CONSTITUTION   Out in Kansas, meanwhile, the struggle continued. Just before Buchanan's inauguration the proslavery legislature called for an election of delegates to a constitutional convention. Since no provision was made for a referendum on the constitution, however, the governor vetoed the measure and the legislature overrode his veto. The Kansas governor resigned on the day Buchanan took office, and the new president replaced him with Robert J. Walker. A native Pennsylvanian who had made a political career in Mississippi and a former member of Polk's cabinet, Walker had greater prestige than his predecessors, and like contemporaries such as Houston of Texas, Foote of Mississippi, and Benton of Missouri, put the Union above slavery. In Kansas he scented a chance to advance the cause of both the Union and his party. Under popular sovereignty, fair elections would produce a state that would be both free and Democratic.

Walker arrived in 1857, and with Buchanan's approval, pledged to the free-state elements that the new constitution would be submitted to a fair vote. But in spite of his pleas, he arrived too late to persuade free-state men to vote for convention delegates in elections they were sure had been rigged against them. Later, however, Walker did persuade the free-state leaders to vote in the election of a new territorial legislature.

As a result a polarity arose between an antislavery legislature and a proslavery constitutional convention. The convention, meeting at Lecompton, drew up a constitution under which Kansas would become a slave state. A referendum on the document was cunningly contrived so that voters could not vote against the proposed constitution. They could only accept it "with slavery" or "with no slavery," and even the latter meant that property in slaves already in Kansas would "in no measure be interfered with." The vote was set for December 21, 1857, with rules and officials chosen by the convention.

Although Kansas had only about 200 slaves at the time, free-state men boycotted the election on the claim that it too was rigged. At this point President Buchanan took a fateful step. Influenced by southern

President James Buchanan, whose support of the Lecompton constitution drove another wedge into the Democratic party.

advisers and politically dependent upon southern congressmen, he decided to renege on his pledge to Walker and support the action of the Lecompton Convention. Walker resigned, and the election went according to form: 6,226 for the constitution with slavery, 569 for the constitution without slavery. Meanwhile, the acting governor had convened the antislavery legislature, which called for another election to vote the Lecompton constitution up or down. Most of the proslavery settlers boycotted this election, and the result on January 4, 1858, was overwhelming: 10,226 against the constitution, 138 for the constitution with slavery, 24 for the constitution without slavery.

The combined results suggested a clear majority against slavery, but Buchanan stuck to his support of the Lecompton constitution, driving another wedge into the Democratic party. Senator Douglas, up for re-election, could not afford to run as a champion of Lecompton. He broke dramatically with the president in a tense confrontation, but Buchanan persisted in trying to drive Lecompton "naked" through the Congress. In the Senate, administration forces held firm, and in 1858 Lecompton was passed. In the House, enough anti-Lecompton Democrats combined to put through an amendment for a new and carefully supervised popular vote in Kansas. Enough senators went along to permit passage of the House bill. Southerners were confident the vote would favor slavery, because to reject slavery the voters would have to reject the constitution, which would postpone statehood until the population reached 90,000. On August 2, 1858, Kansas voters nevertheless rejected Lecompton by 11,300 to 1,788. With that vote Kansas, now firmly in the hands of its antislavery legislature, largely ended its role in the sectional controversy.

THE PANIC OF 1857 The third crisis of Buchanan's first half year in office, a financial crisis, broke in August 1857. It was brought on by a reduction in demand for American grain caused by the end of the Crimean War (1854–1856), a surge in manufacturing that outran the growth of markets, and the continued weakness and confusion of the state bank-note system. Failure of the Ohio Life Insurance and Trust Company on August 24, 1857, precipitated the panic, which was followed by a depression from which the country did not emerge until 1859.

Everything in those years seemed to get drawn into the vortex of sectional conflict, and business troubles were no exception. Northern businessmen tended to blame the depression on the Democratic Tariff of 1857, which had set rates on imports at their lowest level since 1816. The agricultural South weathered the crisis better than the North. Cotton prices fell, but slowly, and world markets for cotton quickly recovered. The result was an exalted notion of King Cotton's importance to the world, and apparent confirmation of the growing argument that the southern system was superior to the free-labor system of the North.

DOUGLAS VS. LINCOLN   Amid the recriminations over Dred Scott, Kansas, and the depression, the center could not hold. The Lecompton battle put severe strains on the most substantial cord of union that was left, the Democratic party. To many, Douglas seemed the best hope, one of the few remaining Democratic leaders with support in both sections. But now Douglas was being whipsawed between the extremes. Kansas-Nebraska had cast him in the role of "doughface," a southern sympathizer. His opposition to Lecompton, the fraudulent fruit of popular sovereignty, however, had alienated him from Buchanan's southern junta. But for all his flexibility and opportunism, Douglas had convinced himself that popular sovereignty was a point of principle, a bulwark of democracy and local self-government. In 1858 he faced reelection to the Senate against the opposition of Buchanan Democrats and Republicans. The year 1860 would give him a chance for the presidency, but first he had to secure his home base in Illinois.

To oppose him, Illinois Republicans named Abraham Lincoln of Springfield, the lanky, rawboned former Whig state legislator and one-term congressman, a moderately prosperous small-town lawyer. Lincoln's early life had been the hardscrabble existence of the frontier farm. Born in a Kentucky log cabin in 1809, raised on frontier farms in Indiana and Illinois, the young Lincoln had the wit and will to rise above his coarse beginnings. With less than twelve months of sporadic schooling he learned to read, studied such books as came to hand, and eventually developed a prose style as muscular as the man himself. He worked at various farm tasks, operated a ferry, and made two trips down to New Orleans as a flatboatman. Striking out on his own, he managed a general store in New Salem, Illinois, learned surveying, served in the Black Hawk War (1832), won election to the legislature in 1834 at the age of twenty-five, read law, and was admitted to the bar in 1836.

As a Whig regular, Lincoln adhered to the economic philosophy of Henry Clay. He abhorred slavery but was no abolitionist. He did not be-

lieve the two races could coexist as equals. But he did oppose any further extension of slavery into new territories, assuming that over time it
would die a "natural death." Slavery, he said in the 1840s, was a vexing
but "minor question on its way to extinction." Lincoln stayed in the legislature until 1842, and in 1846 won a term in Congress. After a single
term he retired from active politics to cultivate his law practice in
Springfield.

In 1854 the Kansas-Nebraska debate drew Lincoln back into the political arena. When Douglas appeared in Springfield to defend popular
sovereignty, Lincoln spoke in refutation from the same platform. In
Peoria he repeated the performance of what was known thereafter as
the "Peoria speech." This speech began the journey toward his appointment with destiny, preaching an old but oft-neglected doctrine: hate
the sin but not the sinner.

> When Southern people tell us they are no more responsible for the origin
> of slavery, than we; I acknowledge the fact. When it is said that
> the institution exists; and that it is very difficult to get rid of it, in any
> satisfactory way, I can understand and appreciate the saying. . . .
>
> But all this, to my judgment, furnishes no more excuses for permitting
> slavery to go into our own free territory, than it would for reviving the
> African slave trade by law.

At first Lincoln held back from the rapidly growing Republican party,
but in 1856 he joined it, getting over 100 votes for its vice-presidential
nomination, and gave some fifty speeches for the Frémont ticket in Illinois and nearby states. By 1858 he was the obvious choice to oppose
Douglas for the Senate seat, and Douglas knew he was up against a formidable foe. Lincoln resorted to the classic ploy of the underdog: he
challenged the favorite to debate with him. Douglas had little relish for
drawing attention to his opponent, but agreed to meet him in seven
places around the state.

Thus the legendary Lincoln-Douglas debates took place, from August
21 to October 15, 1858. As they mounted the platform, the two men
could not have presented a more striking contrast in appearance. Lincoln was well over six feet tall, sinewy, and craggy-featured, with a singularly long neck and deep-set, brooding, even melancholy eyes. Unas-
suming in manner, dressed in homely, well-worn clothes, and walking
with a shambling gait, he lightened his essentially serious demeanor

with a refreshing sense of humor. To sympathetic observers he conveyed an air of simplicity, sincerity, and common sense. Douglas, on the other hand, was short, rotund, bulb-nosed, stern, and cocky, attired in the finest custom-tailored suits, and possessed of supreme self-confidence. A man of considerable abilities and even greater ambition, he strutted to the platform with the pugnacious air of a predestined champion.

At the time and since, much attention focused on the second debate, at Freeport, where Lincoln asked Douglas how he could reconcile popular sovereignty with the Dred Scott ruling that citizens had the right to carry slaves into any territory. Douglas's answer, thenceforth known as the Freeport Doctrine, was to state the obvious. Whatever the Supreme Court might say about slavery, it could not exist anywhere unless supported by local police regulations.

Douglas tried to set some traps of his own. It is standard practice, of course, to put extreme constructions upon an adversary's stand. Douglas intimated that Lincoln belonged to the fanatical sect of abolitionists who planned to carry the battle to the slave states, just as Lincoln intimated the opposite about his opponent. Douglas accepted, without any apparent qualms, the conviction of black inferiority that most whites, North and South, shared at the time, and sought to pin on Lincoln the stigma of advocating racial equality. The question was a hot potato, which Lincoln handled with caution. There was "A physical difference between the white and black races," and it would "forever forbid the two races living together on terms of social and political equality," he said. But Lincoln insisted that blacks did have an "equal" right to freedom and the fruits of their labor. He favored the containment of slavery where it existed so that "the public mind shall rest in the belief that it is in the course of ultimate extinction." But the basic difference between the two men, Lincoln insisted, lay in Douglas's professed indifference to the moral question of slavery: "He says he 'don't care whether it is voted up or voted down' in the territories. . . . Any man can say that who does not see anything wrong in slavery, but no man can logically say it who does see a wrong in it; because no man can logically say he don't care whether a wrong is voted up or down. . . ."

If Lincoln had the better of the argument, at least in the long view, Douglas had the better of the election. Still, according to the Constitution, the voters actually had to choose a legislature, which would then elect the senator. Lincoln men won the larger total vote, but its distribution gave Douglas the legislature, 54 to 41. As the returns trickled in from the fall elections in 1858—there was still no common election date—they recorded one loss after another for Buchanan men. When the elections were over, the administration had lost control of the House. But the new Congress would not meet in regular session until late 1859.

JOHN BROWN'S RAID   After the Lecompton fiasco the slavery issue was no longer before Congress in any direct way. The gradual return of prosperity in 1859 offered hope that the storms of the 1850s might yet pass. But the sectional issue still haunted the public mind, and like lightning on the horizon, warned that a storm was still pending. In October 1859 John Brown once again surfaced. Since the Pottawatomie Massacre in 1856, he had led a furtive existence, engaging in fundraising and occasional bushwhacking. His commitment to abolish the "wicked curse of slavery," meanwhile, had intensified to a fever pitch. Self-righteous and demanding, he was driven by a sense of crusading zeal. His penetrating gray eyes, flowing beard, and religious certainty evoked images of a vengeful Abraham and struck fear into supporters and opponents alike.

On October 16, 1859, Brown made his supreme gesture. From a Maryland farm he crossed the Potomac with about twenty men, including five blacks, and under cover of darkness occupied the federal arse-

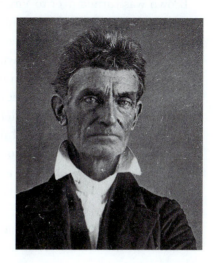

John Brown.

nal in Harper's Ferry, Virginia (now West Virginia). He planned to arm the many slaves who would flock to his cause, set up a black stronghold in the mountains of western Virginia, and provide a nucleus of support for slave insurrections across the South.

What he actually did was to take the arsenal by surprise, seize a few hostages, and hole up in the engine house until he was surrounded by militiamen and townspeople. The next morning Brown sent his son Watson and another supporter out under a white flag, but the enraged crowd shot them both. Intermittent shooting continued, and another Brown son was wounded. He begged his father to kill him so as to end his suffering, but the righteous Brown, befuddled and distraught by the unexpected collapse of his glorious insurrection, lashed out: "If you must die, die like a man." A few minutes later the son was dead.

That night Lieutenant-Colonel Robert E. Lee, U.S. Cavalry, arrived with his aide, Lieutenant J. E. B. Stuart, and a force of marines. The following morning, on October 18, Stuart and his troops broke down the barricaded doors and rushed into the engine house. A young lieutenant found Brown kneeling with his rifle cocked. Before the pious patriarch could fire, the marine plunged his dress sword into him with such force that the blade bent back double. He then used the hilt to beat Brown unconscious. By then the siege was over. Altogether Brown's men killed four people (including one marine) and wounded nine. Of their own force, ten died (including two of Brown's sons), seven were captured, and five escaped.

Brown was turned over to Virginia authorities, quickly tried for treason against the state and conspiracy to incite insurrection, convicted on October 31, and hanged on December 2 at Charlestown. Six others died on the gallows later. If Brown had failed in his purpose—whatever it was—he had achieved two things. He had become a martyr for the antislavery cause, and he had set off panic throughout the slaveholding South. At his sentencing he delivered one of the classic American speeches: "Now, if it is deemed necessary that I should forfeit my life for the furtherance of the ends of justice, and mingle my blood further with the blood of my children and with the blood of millions in this slave country whose rights are disregarded by wicked, cruel, and unjust enactments, I say, let it be done."

When Brown, still unflinching, met his end, there were solemn observances in the North. "That new saint," Ralph Waldo Emerson said, "will make the gallows as glorious as the cross." William Lloyd Garrison, the lifelong pacifist, now wished "success to every slave insurrection at the South and in every slave country." By far the gravest effect of Brown's raid was to leave proslavery southerners in no mood to distinguish between John Brown and the Republican party. All through the fall and winter of 1859–1860, rumors of conspiracy and insurrection swept the region. Every northern visitor, commercial traveler, or schoolteacher came under suspicion, and many were driven out. "We regard every man in our midst an enemy to the institutions of the South," said the *Atlanta Confederacy,* "who does not boldly declare that he believes African slavery to be a social, moral, and political blessing."

THE CENTER COMES APART

THE DEMOCRATS DIVIDE   Thus amid emotional hysteria and impossible demands the nation ushered in the year of another presidential election, destined to be the most fateful in its history. Four years earlier, in a moment of euphoria, the Democrats had settled on Charleston,

PROGRESSIVE DEMOCRACY—PROSPECT OF A SMASH UP.

Prospect of a Smash Up. *This 1860 cartoon shows the Democratic party—the last remaining national party—about to be split by sectional differences and the onrushing Republicans led by Lincoln.*

South Carolina, as the site for their 1860 convention. Charleston in April, with the azaleas ablaze, was perhaps the most enticing city in the United States, but the worst conceivable place for such a meeting, except perhaps Boston. It was a hotbed of extremist sentiment, and lacked adequate accommodations for the crowds thronging in. South Carolina itself had chosen a remarkably moderate delegation, but the extreme southern rights' men held the upper hand in the delegations from the Gulf states.

Douglas's supporters reaffirmed the platform of 1856, which simply promised congressional noninterference with slavery. Southern firebrands, however, were now demanding federal protection for slavery in the territories. Buchanan supporters, hoping to stop Douglas, encouraged the strategy. The platform debate reached a heady climax when the Alabama extremist William Yancey informed the northern Democrats that their error had been the failure to defend slavery as a positive good. An Ohio senator offered a blunt reply: "Gentlemen of the South," he said, "you mistake us—you mistake us. We will not do it."

When the southern planks lost, Alabama's delegates walked out of the convention, followed by those representing the other Gulf states, Georgia, South Carolina (except for two stubborn upcountry Unionists), and parts of the delegations from Arkansas and Delaware. This pattern foreshadowed with some fidelity the pattern of secession, in which the Deep South left the Union first. The convention then decided to leave the overwrought atmosphere of Charleston and reassemble in Baltimore on June 18. The Baltimore convention finally nominated Douglas on the 1856 platform. The Charleston seceders met first in Richmond, then in Baltimore, where they adopted the slave-code platform defeated in Charleston, and named Vice-President John C. Breckinridge of Kentucky for president. Thus another cord of union had snapped: the last remaining national party had fragmented.

LINCOLN'S ELECTION   The Republicans meanwhile gathered in Chicago. There everything suddenly came together for "Honest Abe" Lincoln, "the Railsplitter," the uncommon common man. Lincoln had suddenly emerged in the national view during his senatorial campaign two years before, and had since taken a stance designed to make him available for the nomination. He was strong enough on the containment of slavery to satisfy the abolitionists, yet moderate enough to seem less threatening than they were. In 1860 he had gone East to address an audience of influential Republicans at the Cooper Union in New York City, where he emphasized his view of slavery "as an evil, not to be extended, but to be tolerated and protected only because of and so far as its actual presence among us makes that toleration and protection a necessity."

At the Chicago convention, New York's William H. Seward was the early leader, but he had been tagged, perhaps wrongly, as an extremist for his earlier statements about an "irrepressible conflict" and a "higher law." On the first ballot Lincoln finished in second place. On the next ballot he drew almost even with Seward, and when he came within one and a half votes of a majority on the third count, Ohio quickly switched four votes to put him over the top.

The platform foreshadowed future policy better than most. It denounced John Brown's raid as "among the gravest of crimes," and promised the "maintenance inviolate of the right of each state to order and control its own domestic institutions." The party reaffirmed its resistance to the extension of slavery, and in an effort to gain broader support, endorsed a protective tariff for manufacturers, free homesteads for farmers, a more liberal naturalization law, and internal improvements, including a Pacific railroad. With this platform, Republicans made a strong appeal to eastern businessmen, western farmers, and the large immigrant population.

Both major conventions revealed that opinion tended to become more radical in the upper North and Deep South. Attitude followed latitude. In the border states a sense of moderation, perhaps reflecting the fear that they would bear the brunt of any calamity, aroused the diehard Whigs there to make one more try at reconciliation. Meeting in Baltimore a week before the Republicans met in Chicago, they reorganized into the Constitutional Union party and named John Bell of Tennessee for president. Their only platform was "the Constitution of the Country, the Union of the States, and the Enforcement of the Laws."

Of the four candidates, not one was able to command a national following, and the campaign evolved into a choice between Lincoln and Douglas in the North, Breckinridge and Bell in the South. One consequence of these separate campaigns was that each section gained a false impression of the other. The South never learned to distinguish Lincoln from the radicals; the North failed to gauge the force of southern intransigence—and in this Lincoln was among the worst. He stubbornly refused to offer the South assurances or to amplify his position, which he said was a matter of public record.

The one man who tried to break through the veil that was falling between the sections was Douglas, who tried to mount a national campaign. Only forty-seven, but already weakened by drink, ill health, and disappointments, he wore himself out in one final glorious campaign. Early in October 1860, at Cedar Rapids, Iowa, he learned of Republican state victories in Pennsylvania and Indiana. "Mr. Lincoln is the next President," he said. "We must try to save the Union. I will go South." Down through the hostile areas of Tennessee, Georgia, and Alabama Douglas carried appeals on behalf of the Union. "I do not believe that every Breckinridge man is a disunionist," he said, "but I do believe that every disunionist is a Breckinridge man." He was in Mobile when the election came.

By midnight of November 6 Lincoln's victory was clear. In the final count he had about 39 percent of the total popular vote, but a clear majority with 180 votes in the electoral college. He carried every one of the eighteen free states, and by a margin enough to elect him even if the

Abraham Lincoln, Republican candidate for president, June 1860.

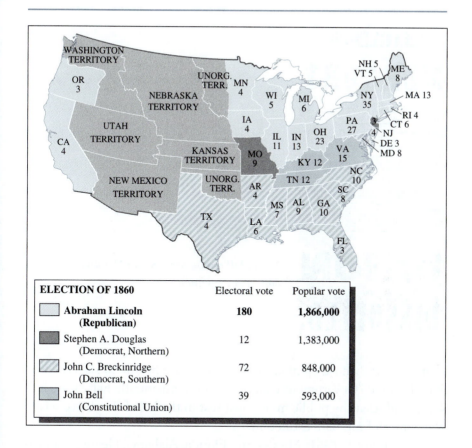

ELECTION OF 1860	Electoral vote	Popular vote
Abraham Lincoln (Republican)	**180**	**1,866,000**
Stephen A. Douglas (Democrat, Northern)	12	1,383,000
John C. Breckinridge (Democrat, Southern)	72	848,000
John Bell (Constitutional Union)	39	593,000

votes for the other candidates had been combined. Among all the candidates, only Douglas had electoral votes from both slave and free states, but his total of 12 was but a pitiful remnant of Democratic Unionism. He ran last. Bell took Virginia, Kentucky, and Tennessee for 39 votes, and Breckinridge swept the other slave states to come in second with 72.

SECESSION OF THE DEEP SOUTH Soon after the election, the South Carolina legislature, which had assembled to choose the state's electors, set a special election for December 6 to choose delegates to a convention. In Charleston on December 20, 1860, the convention unanimously voted an Ordinance of Secession, declaring the state's ratification of the Constitution repealed and the union with other states dissolved. A Declaration of the Causes of Secession reviewed the threats to slavery, and asserted that a sectional party had elected to the presi-

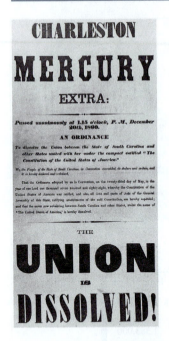

A handbill announcing South Carolina's seces-sion from the Union.

dency a man "whose opinions and purposes are hostile to slavery," who had declared "Government cannot endure permanently half slave, half free," and "that the public mind must rest in the belief that Slavery is in the course of ultimate extinction."

By February 1, 1861, Mississippi, Florida, Alabama, Georgia, Louisi-ana, and Texas had declared themselves out of the Union. Texas was the last to act because its governor, staunch old Jacksonian Sam Houston, had refused to assemble the legislature for a convention call, but seces-sionist leaders called an irregular convention that authorized secession. Only there was the decision submitted to a referendum, which the se-cessionists carried handily. On February 4, a convention of the seven states met in Montgomery; on February 7, they adopted a provisional constitution for the Confederate States of America, and two days later they elected Jefferson Davis its president. He was inaugurated February 18, with Alexander Stephens of Georgia as vice-president.

In all seven states of the southernmost tier, a solid majority had voted for secessionist delegates, but their combined vote would not have been a majority of the presidential vote in November. What happened, it seemed, was what often happens in revolutionary situations: a determined and decisive group acted quickly in an emotionally charged climate and carried its program against a confused and indecisive opposition. Trying to decide whether or not a majority of the whites actually favored secession probably is beside the point—a majority were vulnerable to the decisive action of the secessionists.

BUCHANAN'S WAITING GAME   History is full of might-have-beens. A bold stroke, even a bold statement, by the lame-duck president at this point might have changed things. But there was no Jacksonian will in Buchanan. Besides, a bold stroke might simply have hastened the conflict. No bold stroke came from Lincoln either, nor would he consult with the administration during the long months before his inauguration on March 4. He inclined all too strongly to the belief that secession was just another bluff and kept his public silence.

Buchanan followed his natural bent, the policy on which he had built a career: make concessions, seek a compromise to mollify the South. In his annual message on December 3, Buchanan made a forthright argument that secession was illegal, but that he lacked authority to coerce a state. "Seldom have we known so strong an argument come to so lame and impotent a conclusion," the *Cincinnati Enquirer* editorialized. There was, however, a hidden weapon in the president's reaffirmation of a duty to "take care that the laws be faithfully executed" insofar as he was able. If the president could enforce the law upon all citizens, he would have no need to "coerce" a state. Indeed his position became the policy of the Lincoln administration, which fought a war on the theory that individuals but not states as such were in rebellion.

Buchanan held firmly to his resolve, with some slight stiffening by the end of December 1860, when secession became a fact and the departure of two southerners removed the region's influence in his cabinet. He would retain positions already held, but he would make no effort to assert federal authority provocatively. As the secessionists seized federal property, arsenals, and forts, this policy soon meant holding to isolated positions at Fort Pickens in Pensacola Harbor, some remote islands off southern Florida, and Fort Sumter in Charleston Harbor.

On the day after Christmas the small garrison at Fort Moultrie had been moved into the nearly completed Fort Sumter by Major Robert Anderson, a Kentucky Unionist. Anderson's move, designed to achieve both disengagement and greater security, struck South Carolina authorities as provocative, a violation of an earlier "gentleman's agreement" that the administration would make no changes in its arrangements, and commissioners of the newly "independent" state peremptorily demanded withdrawal of all federal forces.

They had overplayed their hand. Buchanan's cabinet, with only one southerner left, insisted it would be a gross violation of duty, perhaps grounds for impeachment, for the president to yield. His backbone thus stiffened, he sharply rejected the South Carolina ultimatum to withdraw: "This I cannot do: this I will not do." His nearest approach to coercion was to dispatch a steamer, *Star of the West,* to Fort Sumter with reinforcements and provisions. As the ship approached Charleston Harbor, Carolina batteries at Fort Moultrie and Morris Island opened fire and drove it away on January 9. It was in fact an act of war, but Buchanan chose to ignore the challenge. He decided instead to hunker down and ride out the remaining weeks of his term, hoping against hope that one of several compromise efforts would yet prove fruitful.

LAST EFFORTS AT COMPROMISE   Forlorn efforts at compromise continued in Congress until the dawn of inauguration day. On December 18 Senator John J. Crittenden of Kentucky had proposed a series of amendments and resolutions, the central features of which were the recognition of slavery in the territories south of 36°30′and guarantees to maintain slavery where it already existed. Meanwhile a peace conference met in Willard's Hotel in February 1861, at the call of the Virginia legislature. Twenty-one states sent delegates and former president John Tyler presided, but the convention's proposal, substantially the same as the Crittenden Compromise, failed to win the support of either house of Congress. The only compromise proposal that met with any success was an amendment guaranteeing slavery where it existed. Many Republicans, including Lincoln, were prepared to go that far to save the Union, but they were unwilling to repudiate their stand against slavery in the territories. As it happened, after passing the House, the amendment passed the Senate without a vote to spare, by 24 to 12, on the dawn of inauguration day. It would have become the Thirteenth Amendment, with the first use of the word "slavery" in the Constitution, but the states never ratified it. When a Thirteenth Amendment was ratified in 1865, it did not guarantee slavery—it abolished slavery.

MAKING CONNECTIONS

- Through the 1850s, most of the debate over slavery concerned the expansion of slavery into the territories; with Lincoln's Emancipation Proclamation, discussed in the next chapter, the issue shifted to slavery itself.

- Many of the Radical Republicans who designed Reconstruction (Chapter 18) had been antislavery Republicans before the war.

- The proposed transcontinental railroad that brought about the Kansas-Nebraska crisis would finally be completed in 1869 (Chapter 20).

FURTHER READING

The best surveys of the forces and events leading to the Civil War include James M. McPherson's *Battle Cry of Freedom: The Civil War Era* (1988), Stephen B. Oates and Buz Wyeth's *The Approaching Fury: Voices of the Storm, 1820–1861* (1997), and Bruce Levine's *Half Slave and Half Free: The Roots of the Civil War* (1992). The most recent narrative of the political debate leading to secession is Michael A. Morrison's *Slavery and the American West: The Eclipse of Manifest Destiny and the Coming of the Civil War* (1997). Interpretive analyses can be found in Eric Foner's *Politics and Ideology in the Age of the Civil War* (1980) and Joel H. Silbey's *The Partisan Imperative: The Dynamics of American Politics before the Civil War* (1985).

Mark Stegmaier's *Texas, New Mexico, and the Compromise of 1850: Boundary Dispute and Sectional Crisis* (1996) probes that crucial dispute while Michael F. Holt's *The Political Crisis of the 1850s* (1978) traces the demise of the Whigs. Eric Foner shows how events and ideas combined in the formation of a new political party in *Free Soil, Free Labor, Free Men: The Ideology of the Republican Party before the Civil War* (1970). A more straightforward study of the rise of the Republicans is

William E. Gienapp's *The Origins of the Republican Party, 1852–1856* (1987). The economic, social, and political crises of 1857 are examined in Kenneth Stampp's *America in 1857: A Nation on the Brink* (1990).

Robert W. Johannsen's *Stephen A. Douglas* (1973) analyzes the issue of popular sovereignty. A more national perspective is provided in James A. Rawley's *Race and Politics: "Bleeding Kansas" and the Coming of the Civil War* (1969). On the role of John Brown in the sectional crisis, see Stephen B. Oates's *To Purge This Land with Blood: A Biography of John Brown* (2nd ed., 1984). Two other issues that divided the nation can be studied in Stanley W. Campbell's *The Slave Catchers* (1970), on attempts to enforce the Fugitive Slave Act, and Don E. Fehrenbacher's *Slavery, Law, and Politics* (1981), on the Dred Scott case.

An excellent study on the South's journey to secession is William Freehling's *The Road to Disunion* (1990). Studies of southern states include J. Mills Thornton's *Politics and Power in a Slave Society: Alabama, 1800–1860* (1978), Michael P. Johnson's *Toward a Patriarchal Republic: The Secession of Georgia* (1977), and Steven A. Channing's *Crisis of Fear: Secession in South Carolina* (1970). For developments in the border states, see Daniel W. Croft's *Reluctant Confederates: Upper South Unionists in the Secession Crisis* (1989).

On Lincoln's role in the coming crisis of war, see Don E. Fehrenbacher's *Prelude to Greatness* (1962). Harry V. Jaffa's *Crisis of the House Divided* (1959) details the Lincoln-Douglas debates, and Maury Klein's *Days of Defiance: Sumter, Secession, and the Coming of the Civil War* (1997) treats the Fort Sumter controversy.

17 ☙ THE WAR OF THE UNION

CHAPTER ORGANIZER

This chapter focuses on:

- the main course and major strategies of the Civil War.

- how the war affected the home front, North and South.

- the reasons for, and results of, Lincoln's Emancipation Proclamation.

*D*uring the four long months between his election and inauguration, Lincoln said little about future policies and less about past positions. "If I thought a repetition would do any good I would make it," he wrote to an editor in St. Louis. "But my judgment is it would do positive harm. The secessionists per se, believing they had alarmed me, would clamor all the louder." So he stayed in Springfield until mid-February 1861, biding his time. He then boarded a train for a long, roundabout trip, and began to drop some hints to audiences along the way. To the New Jersey legislature, which responded with prolonged cheering, he said: "The man does not live who is more devoted to peace than I am. . . . But it may be necessary to put the foot down." At the end of the journey, reluctantly yielding to rumors of plots against his life, he passed unnoticed on a night train through Baltimore and slipped into Washington before daybreak on February 23.

The furtive end to Lincoln's journey reinforced the fears of eastern sophisticates that the man lacked style. Lincoln, to be sure, had no formal education or training in the rules of etiquette. His tall frame shambled awkwardly, and he had an unseemly penchant for telling funny stories. But the qualities that had first called him to public attention would soon manifest themselves. His prose, at least, had style—and substance. So did his politics. What Nathaniel Hawthorne called Lincoln's "Yankee shrewdness" guided him through the traps laid for the unwary in Washington. Whatever else people might think of him, they soon learned that he was not easily dominated.

END OF THE WAITING GAME

At the end of 1860, as Abraham Lincoln prepared to take office and the possibility of civil war captured the attention of a divided nation, no one imagined that a conflict of horrendous scope and intensity awaited them. On both sides, people believed that the fighting would be a lark, that it would be over in little more than a month, and that their daily lives would go on as usual.

LINCOLN'S INAUGURATION   In his inaugural address, Lincoln repeated his pledge not "to interfere with the institution of slavery in the States where it exists. I believe I have no lawful right to do so, and I have no inclination to do so." But the immediate question had shifted from slavery to secession, and most of the speech emphasized Lincoln's view that "the Union of these States is perpetual." The Union, he asserted, preceded the Constitution itself, dating from the Articles of Association in 1774. It was "matured and continued" by the Declaration of Independence and the Articles of Confederation. Yet even if the United States were only a contractual association, "no State upon its own mere motion can lawfully get out of the Union." Lincoln promised to hold areas belonging to the federal government, collect taxes, and deliver the mails unless repelled, but beyond that "there will be no invasion, no using of force against or among the people anywhere." In the final paragraph of the speech, Lincoln offered an eloquent appeal for regional harmony:

I am loath to close. We are not enemies, but friends. We must not be enemies. Though passion may have strained, it must not break our bonds of affection. The mystic chords of memory, stretching from every battlefield and patriot grave to every living heart and hearthstone all over this broad land, will yet swell the chorus of the Union, when again touched, as surely they will be, by the better angels of our nature.

Lincoln not only entered office amid the gravest crisis yet faced by a president, but he also faced unusual problems of transition. Republicans, in power for the first time, crowded Washington, hungry for office. Four of the seven new cabinet members had been rivals for the presidency: William H. Seward at the State Department, Salmon P. Chase at the Treasury Department, Simon Cameron at the War Department, and Edward Bates as attorney-general. Four were former Democrats and three were former Whigs. They formed a group of better-than-average ability, though most were so strong-minded they thought themselves better qualified to lead than Lincoln. Only later did they acknowledge with Seward that "he is the best man among us."

THE FALL OF FORT SUMTER For the time being, Lincoln's combination of firmness and moderation differed little in effect from his predecessor's stance. Harsh judgments of Buchanan's waiting game overlook the fact that Lincoln kept it going. Indeed, his only other choices were to accept secession as an accomplished fact or to use force right away. On the day after he took office, however, word arrived from Charleston that time was running out. Major Robert Anderson, in charge of Fort Sumter, had supplies for a month to six weeks, and Confederates were encircling the fort with a "ring of fire."

Events moved quickly to a climax in the next two weeks. On April 4, 1861, Lincoln decided to resupply the sixty-nine men at Fort Sumter. Two days later, he notified the governor of South Carolina that "an attempt will be made to supply Fort Sumter with provisions only. . . ." On April 9, President Jefferson Davis and his cabinet in Montgomery decided against permitting Lincoln to maintain the status quo.

On April 11, Confederate general Pierre G. T. Beauregard, a dapper Creole from Louisiana who had taught artillery to Anderson at West Point, demanded a speedy surrender of Sumter. Major Anderson refused, but he said his supplies would be used up in three more days. With the relief ships approaching, Anderson received an ultimatum to yield. He again refused, and at 4:30 A.M. on April 12 the shelling of Fort Sumter began. After more than thirty hours, his ammunition exhausted, Anderson agreed to give up, and on April 14 he lowered the flag. Although over 3,000 shells hit the fort, the only fatalities were two men killed in an explosion during a final salute to the colors, the first in a melancholy train of war dead.

The guns of Charleston signaled the end of the waiting game. "So Civil War is inaugurated at last," observed New York lawyer George Templeton Strong. "God defend the right." Equally committed was South Carolina's Mary Chesnut: "Woe to those who began this war if they were not in bitter earnest." On the day after Anderson's surrender, Lincoln called upon the loyal states to supply 75,000 militiamen to subdue a combination "too powerful to be suppressed by the ordinary course of judicial proceedings." Volunteers rallied around the flag at the recruiting stations. On April 19, Lincoln proclaimed a blockade of southern ports which, as the Supreme Court later ruled, confirmed the existence of war.

TAKING SIDES   In the free states and the Confederate states, Lincoln's proclamation reinforced the patriotic fervor of the day. In the upper South it brought dismay, and another wave of secession that swept four more states into the Confederacy. Many in those states abhorred both abolitionists and secessionists, but faced with a call for troops to suppress their sister states, decided to abandon the Union. Virginia acted first. Its convention passed an Ordinance of Secession on April 17. The Confederate Congress then chose Richmond as its new capital, and the government moved there in June.

Three other states followed Virginia in little over a month: Arkansas on May 6, Tennessee on May 7, and North Carolina on May 20. All four of the holdout states, especially Tennessee and Virginia, had areas (mainly in the mountains) where both slaves and secessionists were scarce and where Union support ran strong. In Tennessee the mountain counties would supply more volunteers to the Union than to the Confederate cause. Unionists in western Virginia, bolstered by a Federal army from Ohio under General George B. McClellan, contrived a loyal government of Virginia that formed a new state. In 1863 Congress ad-

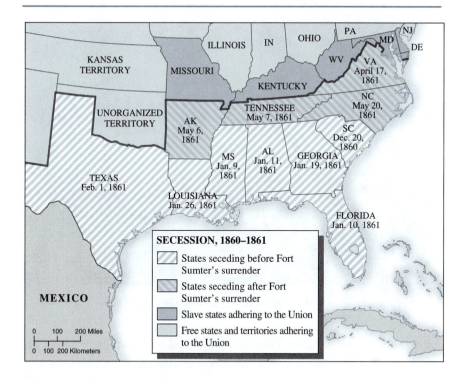

SECESSION, 1860–1861

States seceding before Fort Sumter's surrender

States seceding after Fort Sumter's surrender

Slave states adhering to the Union

Free states and territories adhering to the Union

mitted West Virginia to the Union with a constitution that provided for gradual emancipation of the few slaves there.

Of the other slave states, Delaware, with but a token number of slaves, remained firmly in the Union, but Maryland, Kentucky, and Missouri went through bitter struggles for control. The secession of Maryland would have isolated Washington within the Confederacy. In fact Baltimore's mayor for a time did cut all connections to the capital. A mob attacked the Sixth Massachusetts Regiment on its way through Baltimore and killed four. To hold the state Lincoln took drastic measures of dubious legality: he suspended the writ of habeas corpus (under which judges could require arresting officers to produce their prisoners and justify their arrest) and rounded up pro-Confederate leaders and threw them in jail. The fall elections ended the threat of Maryland's secession by returning a solidly Unionist majority in the state.

Kentucky, native state of both Lincoln and Davis, harbored divided loyalties. But spring elections for a state convention returned a thumping Unionist majority, and the state legislature proclaimed Kentucky's

U.S. Volunteers Attacked by the Mob, *St. Louis, Missouri, 1861.*

"neutrality" in the conflict. Lincoln recognized the strategic value of his native state, situated on the south bank of the Ohio. "I think to lose Kentucky is nearly the same as to lose the whole game," he said. He promised to leave the state alone so long as the Confederates did likewise, and he reassured its citizens that a war against secession was not a war against slavery. Kentucky's fragile neutrality lasted until September 3, when a Confederate force occupied several towns. General Ulysses S. Grant then moved Union soldiers into Paducah. Thereafter, Kentucky, though divided in allegiance, for the most part remained with the Union. It joined the Confederacy, some have said, only after the war.

Lincoln's effort to hold a middle course in Missouri ran afoul of the maneuvers of less patient men in the state. Unionists there had a numerical advantage, but there were many Confederate sympathizers. For a time the state, like Kentucky, kept an uneasy peace. But elections for a convention brought an overwhelming Union victory, while a pro-Confederate militia under the state governor began to gather near St. Louis. In the city Unionist forces rallied, and on May 10 they surprised and disarmed the militia at its camp. They pursued the pro-Confederate forces into the southwestern part of the state, and after a temporary setback on August 10, the Unionists pushed the Confederates back again, finally breaking their resistance at the Battle of Pea Ridge (March 6–8, 1862), just over the state line in Arkansas. Thereafter border warfare continued in Missouri, pitting against each other rival bands of gunslingers who kept up their feuding and banditry for years after the war was over.

A "BROTHERS' WAR"   Robert E. Lee epitomized the agonizing choice facing many residents of the border states. Son of "Lighthorse Harry" Lee, a Revolutionary War hero, and married to a descendant of Martha Washington, Lee had served in the United States Army for thirty years. Now a colonel and master of Arlington, an estate that faced Washington across the Potomac, he was summoned by General Winfield Scott, another Virginian, and offered command of the Federal forces in the field. After a sleepless night pacing the floor, Lee told Scott that he could not go against his "country," meaning Virginia. Although Lee failed to "see the good of secession," he could not "raise my hand against my birthplace, my home, my children." Lee resigned his commission, retired to his estate, and soon answered a call to the Virginia—later the Confederate—service.

Soldier Group. *Neither side in the Civil War was prepared for the magnitude of this first of "modern" wars.*

The conflict sometimes became literally a "brothers' war." At Hilton Head, South Carolina, Percival Drayton commanded a Federal gunboat while his brother led Confederate land forces. Franklin Buchanan, who commanded the *Virginia* (formerly the *Merrimack*), sank the Union ship *Congress* with his brother on board. John J. Crittenden of Kentucky had a son in each army. J. E. B. Stuart of the Confederate cavalry was chased around the peninsula below Richmond by his Federal father-in-law. Lincoln's attorney-general had a son in the Confederate army, and Mrs. Lincoln herself had a brother, three half-brothers, and three brothers-in-law in the Confederate forces.

Many southerners made great sacrifices to remain loyal to the Union. Some left their native region once the fighting began. Others who remained in the South found ways to support the Union. In every Confederate state except South Carolina, whole regiments were organized to fight for the Union. Some 100,000 men from the southern states fought against the Confederacy. One out of every five soldiers from Arkansas killed in the war fought for the Union side. Of course, some of these southern "Tories" changed sides out of expediency rather than loyalty. Confederate soldiers who had been captured occasionally chose to switch sides and serve on the Indian frontier rather than remain in prison.

Others, however, never embraced the Confederate cause. Many of the loyalists were Irish or German immigrants who had no love for slavery or the planter elite. In the Fredericksburg—San Antonio region of Texas, German Americans opposed secession and the war once fighting erupted. The Confederate state government declared six counties in open rebellion in 1862 and sent in troops to suppress Union sentiment. Any German who criticized the Rebel cause was hanged, shot, or whipped. Confederate cavalry units caught one group of Germans trying to escape to Mexico and killed thirty-four of them. In south Texas almost a thousand Texas-Mexicans fought against Confederate troops. Northwest Arkansas was also a Unionist stronghold. In late 1861, Confederate forces executed several members of the Arkansas Peace Society because they opposed secession and the war. Other members were forced to join the Confederate army. Whatever their motives, these and other southern loyalists played a significant role in helping the Union cause.

THE BALANCE OF FORCE

Shrouded in an ever-thickening mist of larger-than-life mythology, the Union triumph in the Civil War has acquired the mantle of inevitability. The Confederacy's fight for independence, on the other hand, has taken on the aura of a romantic lost cause, doomed from the start by the region's sparse industrial development, smaller pool of able-bodied men, paucity of capital resources and warships, and spotty transportation network. But in 1861 the military situation was by no means so clear-cut. For all of the South's obvious disadvantages, it initially enjoyed a captive labor force, superior officers, the prospects of foreign assistance, and the benefits of fighting a defensive campaign on familiar territory. Jefferson Davis and other Confederate leaders were genuinely confident that their cause would prevail on the battlefield. "If we husband our means and make a judicious use of our resources," Davis predicted in 1861, "it would be difficult to fix a limit to the period during which we could conduct a war against the adversary we now encounter." In short, the outcome of the Civil War was not inevitable: it was determined as much by human decisions and human willpower as by physical resources.

ECONOMIC ADVANTAGES   The South seceded in part out of a growing awareness of its minority status in the nation; a balance sheet of the sections in 1860 shows the accuracy of that perception. The Union held twenty-three states, including four border slave states, while the Confederacy had eleven, claiming also Missouri and Kentucky. Ignoring conflicts of allegiance within various states, which might roughly cancel each other out, the population count was about 22 million in the Union to 9 million in the Confederacy, and about 3½ million of the latter were slaves. The Union therefore had an edge of about four to one in potential human resources. To help redress the imbalance, the Confederacy mobilized 80 percent or more of its military-age white males, and a third of them would die during the prolonged war.

An even greater advantage for the North was its industrial development. The states that joined the Confederacy produced just 7.4 percent of the nation's manufactures on the eve of the war. What made the dis-

Gun Foundry *by John Ferguson Weir, 1867. The North had an advantage in industrial development and turned out most of the nation's firearms in foundries like this one.*

parity even greater was that little of this was in heavy industry. The only iron industry of any size in the Confederacy was the Tredegar Iron Works in Richmond, which had long supplied the United States Army. Tredegar's existence strengthened the Confederacy's will to defend its capital. Yet the Union states, in addition to making most of the country's shoes, textiles, and iron products, turned out 97 percent of the firearms and 96 percent of the railroad equipment. They had most of the trained mechanics, most of the shipping and mercantile firms, and the bulk of the banking and financial resources.

Even in farm production the northern states overshadowed the rural South, for most of the North's population was still rooted in the soil. As the progress of the war upset southern agricultural output, northern farms managed to increase theirs, despite the loss of workers to the army. The Confederacy produced enough to meet minimal needs, but the disruption of transport caused shortages in many places. One consequence was that the North produced a surplus of wheat for export at a time when drought and crop failures in Europe created a critical demand. King Wheat supplanted King Cotton as the nation's main export, becoming the chief means of acquiring foreign money and bills of exchange to pay for imports from abroad.

The North's advantage in transport weighed heavily as the war went on. The Union had more wagons, horses, and ships than the Confederacy, and an impressive edge in railroads: about 20,000 miles to the South's 10,000. The actual discrepancy was even greater, for southern railroads were mainly short lines built to different gauges (widths), and had few replacements for rolling stock that broke down or wore out. The Confederacy had only one east-west connection, between Memphis and Chattanooga. The latter was an important rail hub with connections via Knoxville into Virginia and down through Atlanta to Charleston and Savannah. But the North already had an extensive railroad network. Three major lines gave western farmers an outlet to the eastern seaboard and greatly lessened their former dependence on the Mississippi River.

MILITARY ADVANTAGES   Against the weight of such odds the wonder is that the Confederacy managed to survive for four years. Yet at the start certain factors evened the odds. The most important of these was geography: the Confederates could fight a defensive war on their own territory. In addition, the South had more experienced military leaders. A number of circumstances had given rise to a strong military tradition in the South: the long-standing Indian danger, the fear of slave insurrection, and a history of expansionism. Military careers had prestige, and military schools multiplied in the antebellum years, the most notable West Points of the South being The Citadel and Virginia Military Institute. West Point itself drew many southerners, producing an army corps dominated by men from the region.

At the start of the war, Union seapower relied on about 90 ships, though only 42 were in active service and most were at distant stations. But under the able guidance of Secretary Gideon Welles, the Union navy eventually grew to 650 vessels of all types. It never completely sealed off the South, but it raised to desperate levels the hazards of blockade running. On the inland waters navy gunboats and transports played an even more direct role in ultimately securing the Union's control of the Mississippi and its larger tributaries, which provided easy routes into the center of the Confederacy.

THE WAR'S EARLY COURSE

Amid the furies of passion after the fall of Fort Sumter, partisans on both sides hoped that the war might end with one sudden bold stroke, the capture of Washington or the fall of Richmond. Strategic thought at the time remained under the spell of Napoleon, holding that everything would turn on one climactic battle in which a huge force, massed against an enemy's point of weakness, would demoralize its armies and break its will to resist. Such ideas had been instilled in a generation of West Point cadets, but these lessons neglected the massive losses Napoleon had suffered, losses that finally turned his victories into defeat.

General Winfield Scott, the seventy-five-year-old commander of the Union army, saw a long road ahead. He proposed to use the navy to blockade the long Atlantic and Gulf coastlines, and then to divide and subdivide the Confederacy by pushing southward along the main water routes: the Mississippi, Tennessee, and Cumberland Rivers. As word leaked out of Scott's plans, the newspapers impatiently derided his "Anaconda" strategy, which they judged far too slow, indicative of the commander's old age and caution. The public and generals began the war in the belief that victory could be achieved quickly and decisively, without the need for Scott's long-term strategy.

BULL RUN   The outbreak of war saw many on both sides predicting a quick and easy victory. Nowhere was this naive optimism more clearly displayed than at the first Battle of Bull Run (or Manassas)*. An eager public pressured both Lincoln and Davis to strike quickly and decisively. Davis allowed the battle-hungry General P. G. T. Beauregard to hurry his main forces in Virginia to the railroad center at Manassas Junction, about twenty-five miles west of Washington. Lincoln decided that General Irvin McDowell's hastily assembled army of some 37,000 might overrun the outnumbered Confederates and quickly march on to Richmond, the Confederate capital. There was a festive mood as hundreds of civilians rode out from Washington to picnic and watch the en-

---

*The Federals most often named battles for natural features, the Confederates for nearby towns, thus Bull Run (Manassas), Antietam (Sharpsburg), Stone's River (Murfreesboro), and the like.

tertaining spectacle of a one-battle war. Instead they witnessed an entangling web of horror.

It was a hot, dry day on July 21, 1861, when McDowell's raw recruits encountered Beauregard's army dug in behind a meandering little stream called Bull Run. The two generals, who had been classmates at West Point, adopted markedly similar plans—each would try to turn the other's left flank. The Federals almost achieved their purpose early in the afternoon, but Confederate reinforcements from canny General Joseph E. Johnston poured in to meet the Union offensive. Amid the fury, a South Carolina officer rallied his men by pointing to Thomas Jackson's brigade of Virginians: "Look, there is Jackson with his Virginians, standing like a stone wall." The reference thereafter served as Jackson's nickname. Jackson, whose coat was torn by bullet holes and whose horse was wounded, ordered his men to hold their fire "until they come within fifty yards! Then fire and give them the bayonet! And when you charge, yell like furies!"

After McDowell's last assault had faltered, his army's frantic retreat turned into a panic as fleeing soldiers and terrified civilians clogged the

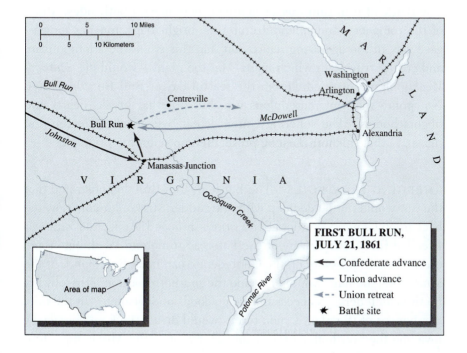

FIRST BULL RUN, JULY 21, 1861
Confederate advance
Union advance
Union retreat
Battle site

Washington road. An Ohio congressman and several colleagues tried to rally the frenzied soldiers. "We called them cowards, denounced them in the most offensive terms, pulled out our heavy revolvers and threatened to shoot them, but in vain; a cruel, crazy, mad, hopeless panic possessed them." Lincoln read a gloomy dispatch from the front: "The day is lost. Save Washington and the remnants of this army. The routed troops will not re-form." Union army veterans remembered their retreat as "the great skedaddle."

Jackson had hoped to pursue the fleeing Federals into Washington. "We must give them no time to think," he stressed in a letter to his wife. "We must bewilder them and keep them bewildered. Our fighting must be sharp, impetuous, continuous. We cannot stand a long war." But the Confederates were about as disorganized and exhausted by the battle as the Yankees were, and they failed to give chase. It would have been futile anyway, for the next day a summer downpour turned roads into quagmires. Jackson later would refer to the failure of the Confederates to follow up their success at Manassas as one of the greatest mistakes of the war.

Although some 4,500 men had been killed, wounded, or captured on both sides, the first major battle of the war was decisive for neither side. The Battle of Bull Run was a sobering experience for both sides. Much of the romance—the splendid uniforms, bright flags, rousing songs—gave way to the agonizing realization that this would be a long, mean, and costly struggle in which many—far too many—would die. *Harper's Weekly* bluntly warned: "From the fearful day at Bull Run dates war. Not polite war, not incredulous war, but war that breaks hearts and blights homes." The sobering Union defeat "will teach us in the first place . . . that this war must be prosecuted on scientific principles."

EMERGING STRATEGIES   The Battle of Bull Run demonstrated that the war would not be decided with one sudden stroke. Lincoln now fell back upon General Winfield Scott's three-pronged "Anaconda" strategy. It called first for the Army of the Potomac to defend Washington and exert constant pressure on the Confederate capital at Richmond. At the same time, the navy would blockade the southern coast and thereby dry up the Confederacy's access to foreign goods and weapons. In the final component of the plan, Union forces would divide the Confederacy by invading the South along the main water routes: the Mississippi, Tennessee, and Cumberland Rivers. This strategy would slowly entwine and crush the southern resistance.

The Confederate strategy was simpler. If the Union forces could be stalemated, Davis and others hoped, then the British or French might be convinced to join their cause, or perhaps public sentiment in the North would force Lincoln to seek a negotiated settlement. So at the same time that armies were forming in the South, Confederate diplomats were seeking assistance in London and Paris, and Confederate sympathizers in the North were urging an end to the North's war effort.

NAVAL ACTIONS   After Bull Run, and for the rest of 1861 into early 1862, the most important military actions involved naval war and blockade. The one great threat to the Union navy proved to be short-lived. The Confederates in Norfolk fashioned an ironclad ship from an abandoned Union steam frigate, the *Merrimack.* Rechristened the *Virginia,* it ventured out on March 8, 1862, and wrought havoc among Union ships at the Chesapeake entrance. But as luck would have it, a new Union ironclad, the *Monitor,* arrived from New York in time to engage the *Virginia* on the next day. They fought to a draw and the *Virginia* returned to port, where the Confederates destroyed it when they had to give up Norfolk soon afterward.

The Merrimack (center, top) *and the* Monitor (center, bottom) *exchange fire at Hampton Roads on March 9, 1862. This print is based on a sketch done at the scene.*

Gradually the Union tightened its grip on the South. In late 1861 a Federal flotilla appeared at Port Royal, South Carolina, pounded the fortifications into submission, and seized the port and nearby sea islands. At Fortress Monroe, Virginia, Union forces held the tip of the peninsula between the James and York Rivers, the scene of much colonial and revolutionary history. The navy extended its bases farther down the coast in the late summer and fall of 1862. Union troops then captured Hatteras Inlet on the Outer Banks of North Carolina in August, a foothold soon extended to Roanoke Island and New Bern on the mainland.

From there the navy's progress extended southward along the Georgia-Florida coast. The Federals first laid siege to Charleston; by 1863 Fort Sumter and the city itself had come under bombardment. In the spring of 1862 Flag Officer David Farragut forced open the lower Mississippi near its mouth and surprised the defenders of New Orleans, who had expected any attack to come downstream. Farragut won a surrender on May 1, then moved quickly to take Baton Rouge in the same way.

FORMING ARMIES   Once the fighting began, the Federal Congress authorized a call for 500,000 more men, and after the Battle of Bull Run added another 500,000. By the end of 1861, the first half million had enlisted as a result mainly of state initiative and in many cases the efforts of groups, towns, and even individuals who raised and equipped regiments. This pell-mell mobilization left the army with a large number of "political" officers, commissioned by state governors or elected by the recruits.

The nineteenth-century army often organized its units along community and ethnic lines. The Union army, for example, included a Scandinavian regiment (the 15th Wisconsin Infantry), a Scottish Highlander unit (the 79th New York Infantry), a French regiment (the 55th New York Infantry), and a mixed unit of Poles, Hungarians, Germans, Spanish, and Italians (the 39th New York Infantry).

In the Confederacy, the first mass enlistment put a great strain on limited means. In March Davis was empowered to call 100,000 twelve-month volunteers and to employ state militia up to six months. In May, once the fighting had started, he was authorized to raise up to 400,000 three-year volunteers "without the delay of a formal call upon the respective states." Thus by early 1862, most of the veteran Confederate soldiers were nearing the end of their terms without having encountered much significant action. They were also resisting the incentives of bonuses and furloughs for reenlistment. The Confederates thus turned to conscription. By act of April 16, 1862, all white male citizens, eighteen to thirty-five, were declared members of the army for three years, and those already in service were required to serve out three years. In 1862 the upper age was raised to forty-five, and in 1864 the age limits were further extended to cover all from seventeen to fifty, with those under eighteen and over forty-five reserved for state defense.

Comprehensive as the law appeared on its face, it included two loopholes. First, a draftee might escape service either by providing an able-bodied substitute not of draft age or by paying $500 in commutation. Second, exemptions, designed to protect key civilian work, were subject to abuse by men seeking "bombproof" jobs. Exemption of state officials, for example, was flagrantly abused by the governors of Georgia and North Carolina, who were in charge of defining the vital jobs. The exclusion of teachers with twenty pupils inspired a sudden educational renaissance, and the exemption of one white man for each plantation with twenty or more slaves led to bitter complaints about "a rich man's war and a poor man's fight."

The Union took nearly another year to decide that volunteers would be too few after the first excitement. In 1863 the government began to draft men aged twenty to forty-five. Exemptions were granted to specified federal and state officeholders and to others on medical or compassionate grounds, but one could still buy a substitute or, for $300, have one's service commuted. In both the North and the South, conscription spurred men to volunteer, either to collect bounties or to avoid the disgrace of being drafted. Eventually the draft in the North produced about 46,000 conscripts and 118,000 substitutes, or only 6 percent of the Union armies.

The draft flouted an American tradition of voluntary service and was widely held to be arbitrary and unconstitutional. In the South the draft also sullied the cause of states' rights by requiring the exercise of a central power. It might have worked better had it operated through the states, some of which had set up their own drafts to meet the calls of President Davis. The governor of Georgia, who had one of the best records for raising troops at first, turned into a bitter critic of the draft, pro-

Enlisting Union soldiers among Irish and German immigrants in New York, 1864.

nouncing it unconstitutional and trying to obstruct its enforcement. Few of the other governors gave it unqualified support, and Vice-President Stephens remained unreconciled to it throughout the war.

Widespread opposition limited enforcement of the draft acts both in the North and South. In New York City, the announcement of a draft lottery on July 11, 1863, led to a week of rioting in which roving bands of immigrant working-class toughs took control of the streets. Although provoked by opposition to the draft, the riots exposed emerging racial and ethnic tensions. The mobs assaulted conscription offices, factories, docks, and the homes of prominent Republicans. But they directed their wrath most furiously at blacks. In their tortured reasoning, they blamed blacks for causing the war and for threatening to take their own unskilled jobs. A white abolitionist watched in horror from her window as the "strange, wretched, abandoned creatures that flocked out from their dens and lairs" fell upon the city's black neighborhoods:

> A child of 3 years of age was thrown from a 4th story window and instantly killed. A woman one hour after her confinement was set upon and beaten with her tender babe in her arms. . . . Children were torn

from their mother's embrace and their brains blown out in the very face of the afflicted mother. Men were burnt by slow fires.

The violence ran completely out of control; 120 people died, and an estimated $2 million in property was destroyed before soldiers brought from Gettysburg restored order.

THE WEST AND THE CIVIL WAR   During the Civil War, western settlement continued unabated. New discoveries of gold and silver along the eastern slopes of the Sierra Nevada and in Montana and Colorado lured thousands of prospectors and their suppliers. As the population grew and dispersed, new transportation and communication networks emerged. Telegraph lines sprouted above the plains, and stagecoach lines fanned out to serve the new communities. Dakota, Colorado, and Nevada gained territorial status in 1861, Idaho and Arizona in 1863, and Montana in 1864. Silver-rich Nevada gained statehood in 1864.

With the firing on Fort Sumter, many of the regular army units assigned to frontier outposts in the West began to head east to meet the Confederate threat. In Texas, the Indian Territory (Oklahoma), and southern New Mexico, Union soldiers left altogether. Elsewhere they left behind skeleton units to man the forts. Texas was the only western state to join the Confederacy. For the most part, the federal government maintained its control of the other western territories during the war.

But it was not easy. Fighting in Kansas and the Indian Territory was widespread and furious. By 1862 Lincoln was forced to dispatch new volunteer units to the West. He had two primary concerns: to protect the shipments of gold and silver and to win over western political support for the war and his presidency. The most intense fighting in the West during the Civil War occurred along the Kansas-Missouri border. There the disputes between proslavery and antislavery settlers of the 1850s turned into brutal guerrilla warfare. The most prominent pro-Confederate leader in the area was William C. Quantrill. He and his proslavery followers, mostly teenagers, fought under a black flag, meaning that they gave no quarter. In destroying Lawrence, Kansas, in 1863, Quantrill ordered his forces to "kill every male and burn every house." They did. By the end of the day, 182 boys and men had been systematically killed. Their opponents—the Jayhawkers—responded in kind. They tortured and hanged prisoners, burned houses, and destroyed livestock.

Quantrill's Raid. *The pro-Confederate leader William C. Quantrill led a raid against Lawrence, Kansas, on August 21, 1863, in which 182 pro-Union men and boys were killed and countless homes were burned and destroyed.*

Many Indian tribes found themselves caught up in the Civil War. Indian regiments fought on both sides, and in the Indian country they fought against each other. Many Indians among the Five Civilized Tribes living in Indian Territory owned black slaves and felt a natural bond with southern whites. Oklahoma's proximity to Texas also influenced the Choctaws and Chickasaws to support the Confederacy.

The Cherokees, Creeks, and Seminoles were more divided in their loyalties. For these tribes, the Civil War served as a wedge that fractured their own unity. The Cherokees, for example, split in two, some supporting the Union and others supporting the South. John Ross, the Principal Chief of the Cherokee Nation, poignantly expressed his dilemma when he responded to a Confederate delegation soliciting an alliance: "I am—the Cherokees are—your friends, but we do not wish to be brought into the feuds between yourselves and your Northern Brethren. Our wish is for peace. Peace at home and peace among you."

Yet eventually Ross acceded to the demands of his followers to align themselves with the Confederacy. A regiment of Cherokee warriors fought with the Confederates during their victory at Wilson's Creek, Missouri, in August 1861. By the end of the year, Confederate and Union Cherokee factions were also at war with one another. During

1862, three Choctaw-Chickasaw regiments, a Creek regiment, a Creek-Seminole regiment, and two Cherokee regiments fought alongside white Confederates in Arkansas. One Cherokee leader attained the rank of brigadier general, and in 1865 he would be the last Confederate officer to surrender his troops, two months after Lee surrendered to Grant at Appomattox.

ACTIONS IN THE WESTERN THEATER   Except for the amphibious thrusts along the southern coast, little happened in the Eastern Theater (east of the Appalachians) before May 1862. On the other hand, the Western Theater (from the mountains to the Mississippi) flared up with several encounters and an important penetration of the Confederate states. In western Kentucky, Confederate general Albert Sidney Johnston had perhaps 40,000 men stretched over some 150 miles, with concentrations at Columbus and Bowling Green, each astride a major north-south railroad. At the center, however, only about 5,500 men held Fort Henry on the Tennessee and Fort Donelson on the Cumberland.

Early in 1862 General Ulysses S. Grant made the first thrust against the weak center of Johnston's overextended lines. Moving out of Cairo and Paducah with a gunboat flotilla, he swung southward up the Tennessee River toward Fort Henry. After a pounding from the Union gunboats, Fort Henry fell on February 6. Grant then moved quickly overland to attack Fort Donelson. On February 16 it gave up with some 12,000 men. Grant's terms, "unconditional surrender," and his quick success sent a thrill through the Union. U. S. "Unconditional Surrender" Grant had not only opened a water route to Nashville, but had thrust his forces between the two strongholds of the western Confederates. Johnston therefore had to give up his foothold in Kentucky and abandon Nashville to Don Carlos Buell's Army of the Ohio (February 25) in order to reunite his forces at Corinth, Mississippi, along the Memphis and Chattanooga Railroad.

SHILOH   Having quickly regained most of Kentucky and western Tennessee, the Union army stood poised in 1862 to strike at the Deep South. On the Mississippi, the Federals under General John Pope took Confederate strongholds at Island No. 10, Fort Pillow, and then Memphis. Meanwhile Grant moved his forces southward along the Tennessee River during the early spring of 1862, hoping to link up with

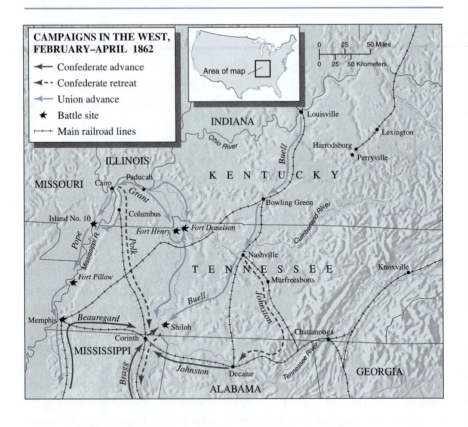

**CAMPAIGNS IN THE WEST,
FEBRUARY–APRIL 1862**

◄── Confederate advance

◄-- Confederate retreat

◄── Union advance

★ Battle site

├──┤ Main railroad lines

Area of map

0 · 25 · 50 Miles

0 · 25 · 50 Kilometers

INDIANA

Louisville

Lexington

Ohio River

Buell

Harrodsburg

ILLINOIS

Perryville

MISSOURI · Cairo · Paducah

K E N T U C K Y

Grant

Bowling Green

Columbus

Cumberland River

Island No. 10

Fort Henry ★★ Fort Donelson

Pope

Polk

Mississippi R.

Nashville

T E N N E S S E E

Knoxville

Fort Pillow

Murfreesboro

Buell

Johnston

Memphis ★ · Beauregard

Shiloh

Chattanooga

Corinth

MISSISSIPPI

Bragg

Johnston · Decatur

Tennessee River

GEORGIA

ALABAMA

Buell's forces. At their rendezvous site, Grant made a costly mistake. While planning his attack on Corinth, Mississippi, he exposed his 42,000 troops on a rolling plateau between two creeks flowing into the Tennessee and failed to dig defensive trenches. General Albert Sidney Johnston shrewdly recognized Grant's oversight, and on the morning of April 6, the Kentuckian ordered an attack on the vulnerable Federals, urging his men to be "worthy of your race and lineage; worthy of the women of the South."

The Confederates struck suddenly at Shiloh, a log church in the center of the Union camp. There amid flowering dogwoods, peach trees, and honeysuckle, they found most of Grant's troops still sleeping or eating breakfast. Many died in their bedrolls. After a day of carnage and confusion, Grant's men were pinned against the river. They may well have been totally defeated had the Confederate commander, General Johnston, not been mortally wounded at the peak of the battle. His second in command called off the attack. Under the cover of gunboats and artillery at Pittsburg Landing, Grant and General William Tecumseh Sherman (who had two horses shot from under him and was himself wounded once) rallied their troops. "We've had the devil's own day," Sherman told Grant that night. "Yes," Grant noted, "but we'll lick them tomorrow." Bolstered by reinforcements from Buell's troops, Grant took the offensive the next day, and the Confederates glumly withdrew to Corinth, leaving the Union army too battered to pursue.

Shiloh, a Hebrew word meaning "place of peace," was the costliest battle in which Americans had ever engaged, although worse was yet to come. Grant observed that the ground was "so covered with dead one could walk across the field without touching the ground." Casualties of nearly 25,000 exceeded the total dead and wounded of the Revolution, the War of 1812, and the Mexican War combined. Like so many battles thereafter, Shiloh was a story of missed opportunities and debated turning points punctuated by lucky incidents and accidents.

The Union lost for a while the full services of its finest general. Grant had been caught napping and many northerners were shocked by the colossal loss of life. His superior, General Henry Halleck, already jealous of Grant's success, spread the false rumor that Grant had been drinking at Shiloh. Some called on Lincoln to fire Grant, but the president refused: "I can't spare this man; he fights." Halleck, however, took Grant's place as field commander, and as a result the Union thrust southward ground to a halt.

Nicknamed "Old Brains," the textbook strategist of offensive war, Halleck proved in the field to be unaccountably timid. Determined not to repeat Grant's mistake, he moved with profound caution on Corinth, taking at face value every inflated report of Rebel strength. But outnumbered better than two to one, P. G. T. Beauregard (Johnston's successor) abandoned Corinth to the Federals on May 30, falling back on Tupelo.

Halleck let slip the chance to overwhelm Beauregard. Grant was left to guard Corinth and Memphis, and Buell withdrew to Nashville. The Confederates under General Braxton Bragg moved via Mobile to Chattanooga. For the remainder of 1862, the chief action in the Western Theater was a series of inconclusive maneuvers and two sharp engagements. Bragg then took his army to Kentucky, threatened Louisville, and was stopped by Buell's Army of the Ohio at Perryville on October 8.

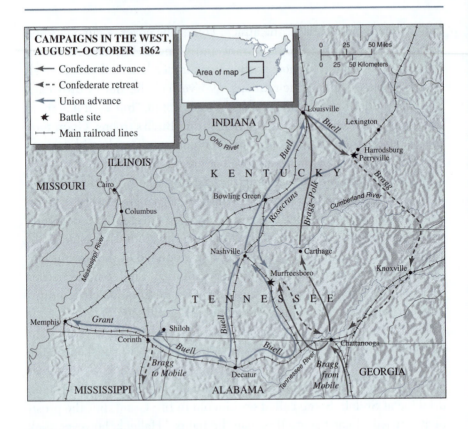

CAMPAIGNS IN THE WEST, AUGUST–OCTOBER 1862

← Confederate advance
◄- - Confederate retreat
← Union advance
✱ Battle site
←⊢⊢→ Main railroad lines

Kentuckians failed to rally to the Confederate flag, and Bragg pulled back into Tennessee. Buell, meanwhile, under pressure to sever the rail line at Chattanooga, proved to be one of the many Union generals who Lincoln said had "the slows." The administration replaced him with William S. Rosecrans, who moved out of Nashville and met Bragg in the costly engagement at Murfreesboro (or Stone's River), December 31 to January 3, after which Bragg cleared out of central Tennessee and fell back on Chattanooga. But Lincoln still coveted eastern Tennessee, both for its many Unionists and for its railroads, which he wanted to cut to get between the Rebels and their "hog and hominy."

MCCLELLAN'S PENINSULAR CAMPAIGN   The Eastern Theater, aside from the coastal operations, remained fairly quiet for nine months after Bull Run. In the wake of the Union defeat, Lincoln had replaced McDowell with General George B. McClellan, Stonewall Jackson's classmate at West Point. As head of the Army of the Potomac, McClellan set about building a powerful, well-trained army that would be ready for its next battle. When General Scott retired in November, Lincoln appointed McClellan as general-in-chief. The wide-shouldered, broad-chested McClellan exuded confidence and poise, as well as a certain flair for parade-ground showmanship. His troops adored him. Yet for all of McClellan's organizational ability and dramatic flair, his innate caution would prove crippling. His foremost concern was to avoid defeat rather than inflict it on the enemy.

Time passed, the army grew, and McClellan kept building his forces to meet the superior numbers that always seemed to be facing him. His intelligence service, headed by the private detective Allan Pinkerton, tended to overestimate enemy forces. Before moving, there was always the need to do this or that, to get 10,000 or 20,000 more men, always something. The president wanted the army to move directly toward

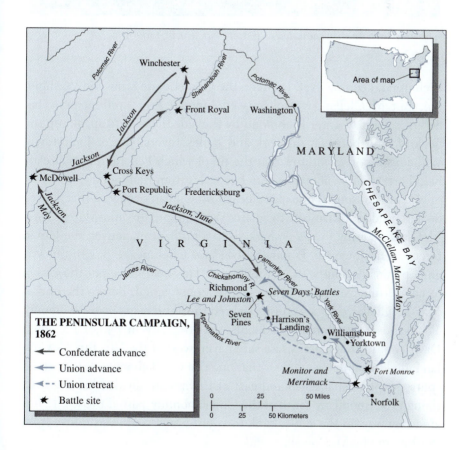

THE PENINSULAR CAMPAIGN, 1862

◄── Confederate advance
◄── Union advance
◄--- Union retreat
★ Battle site

Thirteen-inch mortars mounted at Battery No. 4 near Yorktown.

Richmond, keeping itself between the Confederate army and Washington. But McClellan, who dismissed Lincoln as a "well-meaning baboon," sought to enter Richmond by the side door, so to speak, up the neck of land between the York and James Rivers, site of Jamestown, Williamsburg, and Yorktown, at the tip of which Federal forces already held Fort Monroe, about seventy-five miles from Richmond.

Lincoln consented but specified, to McClellan's chagrin, that a force be left under McDowell to guard Washington. In mid-March 1862 McClellan's army finally embarked. In a brilliant maneuver, the Union forces went down the Potomac River and Chesapeake Bay to the Virginia peninsula southeast of Richmond. This bold move put the Union forces within sixty miles of the Confederate capital. Before the end of May McClellan's advance units sighted the church spires of Richmond. Thousands of Richmond residents fled the city in panic. President Davis sent his own family to a safe haven west of the city. But McClellan failed to capitalize on his situation. The Chickahominy River, which splits the peninsula north and east of Richmond, divided his army. Although Richmond lay south of the Chickahominy, part of the Confederate army was on the north bank to counter any southward move from Washington by McDowell.

McDowell, however, faced more urgent matters, or what seemed so. President Davis, at the urging of military adviser Robert E. Lee, sent Stonewall Jackson into the Shenandoah Valley on what proved to be a brilliant diversionary action. From March 23 to June 9, Jackson and some 18,000 men pinned down two separate Union armies with more than twice their numbers in the western Virginia mountains and at the northern end of the valley. While McDowell braced to defend Washington, Jackson hastened back to defend Richmond.

On May 31 Confederate general Joseph E. Johnston struck at Union forces isolated on the south bank by the flooded Chickahominy River. In the Battle of Seven Pines (Fair Oaks), only the arrival of reinforcements, who somehow crossed the swollen river, prevented a disastrous Union defeat. Both sides took heavy casualties, and General Johnston was severely wounded.

At this point, Robert E. Lee assumed command of the Army of Northern Virginia, a development that changed the course of the war. When McClellan heard the news, however, he declared that he preferred "Lee to Johnston. Lee is too cautious and weak under grave responsibility." He would soon change his opinion.

Tall, erect, and wide-shouldered, Lee, who believed duty to be the "sublimest word in our language," projected a commanding presence. Unlike Johnston, he enjoyed Jefferson Davis's trust. More important, he knew how to use the talents of his superb field commanders: Stonewall Jackson, the pious, fearless mathematics professor from Virginia Military Institute; James Longstreet, Lee's deliberate but tireless "war horse"; sharp-tongued D. H. Hill, the former engineering professor at Davidson College; Ambrose P. Hill, the consummate fighter who challenged one commander to a duel and feuded with Jackson; and J. E. B. Stuart, the colorful young cavalryman who once said: "All I ask of fate is that I may be killed leading a cavalry charge." He would get his wish.

Once in command, Lee launched a desperate attack at Malvern Hill (July 1), where the Confederates suffered heavy casualties from Union artillery and gunboats in the James. This week of intense fighting, labeled the Seven Days' Battles (June 25 to July 1), failed to dislodge the Union forces. McClellan was still near Richmond. On July 9, when Lincoln visited McClellan's headquarters at Harrison's Landing on the James, the general complained that the administration had failed to support him adequately and handed the president a strange document, the "Harrison's Landing Letter," in which, despite his critical plight, he

Lincoln and McClellan in the field, October 1862.

instructed the president at length on war policies. It was ample reason to remove the general. Lincoln returned to Washington and on July 11 called Halleck from the West to take charge as general-in-chief, a post that McClellan had temporarily vacated. Miffed at his demotion, Mc-Clellan angrily dismissed Halleck as an officer "whom I know to be my inferior."

SECOND BULL RUN The new high command ordered McClellan to leave the peninsula and join the Washington defense force, now under John Pope, who had been called back from the West, for a new overland assault on Richmond. In a letter to his wife, McClellan predicted that "Pope will be thrashed and disposed of" by Lee. As McClellan's Army of the Potomac began to pull out, Lee moved northward to strike Pope before McClellan arrived. Dividing his forces, Lee sent Jackson's "foot cavalry" around Pope's right flank to attack his supply lines. At Cedar Mountain, Jackson pushed back an advance party of Federals, and then went on to seize and destroy the Federal supply base at Manassas Junction. At Second Bull Run (or Second Manassas), fought on almost the same site as the earlier battle, Pope assumed that he faced only Jackson, but Lee's main army by that time had joined in. On August 30 a crushing attack on Pope's flank drove the Federals from the field. In the next few days the Union forces pulled back into the fortifications around Washington, where McClellan once again took command and reorganized. He displayed his unflagging egotism in a letter to his wife: "Again I have been called upon to save the country." The disgraced Pope was dispatched to Minnesota to fight in the Indian wars.

ANTIETAM   But Lee gave his adversary little time to prepare. Still on the offensive, determined to move the battlefield out of the South and perhaps thereby gain foreign recognition for the Confederacy, he and his battle-tested troops invaded western Maryland in September 1862, headed for Pennsylvania. But Lee's bold strategy was uncovered when a Union soldier picked up a bundle of cigars and discovered a secret order from Lee wrapped around them. The paper revealed that Lee had again divided his army, sending Jackson off to take Harper's Ferry. McClellan boasted upon seeing the captured document: "Here is a paper with which, if I cannot whip Bobby Lee, I will be willing to go home." Instead of seizing his unexpected opportunity, however, he again delayed for sixteen crucial hours, still worried—as always—about enemy strength, and Lee was thereby able to reassemble most of his tired army behind Antietam Creek. Still, McClellan was optimistic, and Lincoln, too, relished the chance for a truly decisive blow: "God bless you and all with you," he wired McClellan. "Destroy the rebel army if possible."

On September 17, McClellan's forces attacked, commencing the furious Battle of Antietam (Sharpsburg). With the Confederate lines ready to break, A. P. Hill's division arrived from Harper's Ferry, having marched sixteen hot, dusty miles to the battlefield. Bone-weary and foot sore, they nevertheless plunged immediately into the fray, battering the Union army's left flank. It was a ghastly scene. "No tongue can tell, no mind conceive, no pen portray the horrible sights I witnessed this morning," a Pennsylvania soldier reported. Still outnumbered more than two to one, the Confederates forced a standoff in the bloodiest single day of the Civil War, a day participants thought would never end. The Union lost 2,108 dead and counted more than 10,000 wounded or missing. Lee's total losses were fewer, about 10,000, but they represented fully a fourth of his entire army. "God has been very kind to us this day," Stonewall Jackson declared with unintentional irony. The next day the battered Confederates slipped across the Potomac to the safety of Virginia.

The vainglorious McClellan insisted that he "fought the battle splendidly," and that "our victory was complete," but Lincoln thought otherwise. Disgusted by McClellan's failure to follow up his success at Antietam and gain a truly decisive victory, the president sent a curt message to the general: "I have just read your dispatch about sore-tongued and fatigued horses. Will you pardon me for asking what the horses of your army have done . . . that fatigues anything?" Later the president sent his commander a one-sentence letter: "If you don't want to use the army, I should like to borrow it for a while." Failing to receive a satisfactory answer, Lincoln removed McClellan and assigned him to recruiting duty in New Jersey. Never again would he command troops.

FREDERICKSBURG   Lee's invasion had failed and with it hopes of foreign recognition for the Confederacy. Yet the war was far from over. In his search for a fighting general, Lincoln now made the worst choice of all. He turned to Ambrose E. Burnside, whose main achievements to that time had been to capture Roanoke Island and grow his famous side-whiskers. Burnside had twice before turned down the job on the grounds that he felt unfit for so large a command. But if the White House wanted him to fight, he would fight even in the face of oncoming winter.

On December 13, 1862, Burnside sent his men across the icy Rappahannock River to assault Lee's forces, well entrenched west of Fredericksburg on Marye's Heights. Confederate artillery and muskets chewed up the blue columns as they crossed a mile of bottomland outside the town. Fourteen times the Union's suicidal assaults melted under the murderous fire issuing from protected positions above and below them. It was, a Federal general sighed, "a great slaughter-pen." The scene was both awful and awesome, prompting Lee to remark: "It is well that war is so terrible—we should grow too fond of it." After taking more than 12,000 casualties compared to fewer than 6,000 for the Confederates, Burnside wept as he gave the order to withdraw, and his battered forces limped back across the river.

The year 1862 ended with forces in the East deadlocked and the Union advance in the West stalled since midyear. Union morale reached a low ebb. Northern Democrats were calling for a negotiated peace. At the same time Lincoln was under pressure from the Radicals of his own party, who were pushing for more stringent war measures

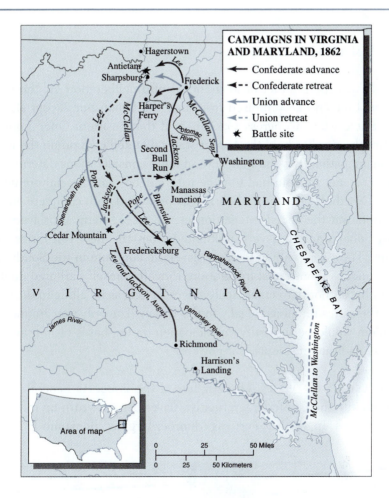

CAMPAIGNS IN VIRGINIA
AND MARYLAND, 1862

◄— Confederate advance

◄- - Confederate retreat

◄— Union advance

◄- - Union retreat

★ Battle site

and questioning the competence of the president. At the same time, Burnside was under fire from his own officers, some of whom were ready to testify publicly to his shortcomings.

But the deeper currents of the war were turning in favor of the Union: in a lengthening war its superior resources began to tell. In both the Eastern and Western Theaters, the Confederate counterattack had been repulsed. And while the armies clashed, Lincoln by the stroke of a pen had changed the conflict from a war for the Union into a revolutionary struggle for abolition. On January 1, 1863, he signed the Emancipation Proclamation.

EMANCIPATION

It was the product of long and painful deliberation. At the war's outset, Lincoln had promised to restore the Union but accept slavery where it existed. Congress too endorsed that position. Once fighting began, the need to hold the border states dictated caution on the issue of emancipation. Beyond that, several other considerations deterred action. For one, Lincoln had to cope with a deep-seated racial prejudice in the North. Where most abolitionists promoted both complete emancipation and the social integration of the races, many antislavery activists only wanted slavery prohibited from the new territories and states. They were willing to allow slavery to continue in the South and were uneasy about racial integration. Lincoln himself harbored doubts about his authority to emancipate slaves so long as he clung to the view that the states remained legally in the Union. The only way around the problem would be to justify emancipation on the bases of military necessity and the president's war powers.

A MEASURE OF WAR   The war forced the issue. As Federal forces pushed into the Confederacy, fugitive slaves began to turn up in Union army camps. In 1861 at Fortress Monroe, Virginia, Benjamin F. Butler

Former slaves, or "contrabands," on a farm in Cumberland Landing, Virginia, 1862.

declared vagabond or captured slaves to be "contraband of war" and put them to work on his fortifications. "Contrabands" soon became a common name for runaways in Union lines. But John C. Frémont pressed the issue one step too far. As commander of the Department of the West, in 1861 he simply liberated the slaves of all who actively helped the Rebel cause, an action that risked unsettling the yet-doubtful border states. Lincoln demanded that Frémont conform to the Confiscation Act of 1861, which freed only those slaves used by Rebel military services, as Butler's first "contrabands" had been. Then in 1862 General David Hunter declared free all slaves in South Carolina, Georgia, and Florida. He had no runaway slaves in his lines, he said, although some runaway masters had fled the scene. Lincoln quickly revoked the order, and took the brunt of the rising outrage among congressional Radicals who saw the war as being fought to eliminate slavery everywhere.

Lincoln himself meanwhile edged toward emancipation. In March 1862 he proposed that federal compensation be offered any state that began gradual emancipation. The plan failed in Congress because of border-state opposition, but on April 16, 1862, Lincoln signed an act that abolished slavery in the District of Columbia, with compensation to owners; on June 19 another act excluded slavery from the territories, without offering owners compensation. A Second Confiscation Act, passed on July 17, liberated the slaves of all persons aiding the rebellion. Still another act forbade the army to help return runaways to their border-state owners.

To save the Union, Lincoln finally decided, complete emancipation would be required for several reasons: slave labor bolstered the Rebel cause, sagging morale in the North needed the lift of a moral cause, and public opinion was swinging that way as the war dragged on. Proclaiming a war on slavery, moreover, would end forever any chance that France or Britain would support the Confederacy. In July 1862 Lincoln first confided to his cabinet that he had in mind a proclamation that under his war powers would free the slaves of the enemy. At the time Seward advised him to wait for a Union victory in order to avoid any semblance of desperation.

The delay lasted through the long weeks during which Lee invaded Maryland and Bragg moved into Kentucky. As late as August 22, 1862, Lincoln responded to editor Horace Greeley's plea for emancipation: "My paramount object in this struggle is to save the Union and is not either to save or destroy slavery." The time to act finally came a month later, after Antietam. It was a dubious victory, but it did result in Lee's withdrawal. On September 22 Lincoln issued a preliminary Emancipation Proclamation, in which he repeated all his earlier stands: that his object was mainly to restore the Union and that he favored proposals for compensated emancipation and colonization. But the main burden of the document was his warning that on January 1, 1863, "all persons held as slaves within any state, or designated part of a state, the people whereof shall be in rebellion against the United States, shall be then, thenceforward and forever free." On January 1, 1863, Lincoln signed the second Emancipation Proclamation, giving effect to his promise of September, again emphasizing that this was a war measure based on his war powers. He also urged blacks to abstain from violence except in self-defense, and added that free blacks would now be received into the armed service of the United States.

REACTIONS TO EMANCIPATION   Among the Confederate states, Tennessee and the occupied parts of Virginia and Louisiana were exempted from the proclamation. It thus freed no slaves who were within Union lines at the time. Moreover, it went little further than the Second Confiscation Act. But these objections missed a point that black slaves readily grasped. "In a document proclaiming liberty," wrote the historian Benjamin Quarles, "the unfree never bother to read the fine print." Though most slaves deemed it safer just to wait for the "day of jubilee" when Union forces arrived, some actively claimed their freedom. One spectacular instance was that of the black harbor pilot Robert Smalls, who one night took over a small Confederate gunboat, the *Planter,* and sailed his family through Charleston Harbor out to the blockading Union fleet. Later he served the Union navy as a pilot and still later became a congressman.

BLACKS IN THE MILITARY   From very early in the war Union commanders found "contrabands" like Smalls useful as guides to unfamiliar terrain and waterways, informants on the enemy, and at the very least common laborers. While menial labor by blacks was familiar enough to whites, military service was something else again. Though not unprecedented, it aroused in whites embedded racial fears. For more than a year, the Lincoln administration warily evaded the issue.

Two views of the Emancipation Proclamation. *The Union view* (top) *shows a thoughtful Lincoln composing the Proclamation with the Constitution and the Holy Bible in his lap. The Confederate view* (bottom) *shows a demented Lincoln with his foot on the Constitution using an inkwell held by the devil.*

Come and Join Us Brothers. *A poster recruiting freed slaves to join the "colored regiments" of the Union forces.*

Even after Congress authorized the enlistment of blacks in the Second Confiscation Act of July 1862, the administration ordered no general mobilization of black troops. Then, on January 1, 1863, Lincoln's Emancipation Proclamation reaffirmed the policy that blacks could enroll in the armed services and sparked new efforts to organize all-black units, to be led by white officers. Massachusetts organized the first northern all-black unit, the Massachusetts Fifty-fourth Regiment under Colonel Robert Gould Shaw. Rhode Island and other states soon followed suit. In May the War Department authorized general recruitment of blacks all over the country. This was a momentous decision, for it transformed a war to preserve the Union into a revolution to overthrow the social, economic, and racial status quo in the South. When one black soldier encountered his former master, now a prisoner of war, the former slave said, "Hello, Massa, bottom rail on top now."

By mid-1863 black units were involved in significant action in both the Eastern and Western Theaters. On July 18, 1863, Colonel Shaw, a Harvard graduate who was the son of a prominent abolitionist, led his black troops in a courageous assault against Fort Wagner, a massive earthwork barrier guarding Charleston, South Carolina. During the battle almost half of the Fifty-fourth Regiment were killed, including Colonel Shaw, who was slain while leading his men over the parapet. Enraged Confederates stripped Shaw's body and threw it into a ditch serving as an unmarked mass grave for his men. When Shaw's father learned of the incident, he told a reporter: "The poor, benighted wretches thought they were heaping indignities upon his dead body, but the act recoils upon them. . . . They buried him with his brave, devoted followers who fell dead over him and around him. . . . We can imagine no holier place than that in which he is . . . nor wish him better company—what a bodyguard he has!"

The Fifty-fourth Regiment's unflinching attack in the face of murderous rifle and cannon fire resolved any doubts about the courage of the black soldier. "Through the cannon smoke of the dark night," went the description in the *Atlantic Monthly,* "the manhood of the colored race shines before many eyes that would not see." When the regiment's flag-bearer was slain, Sergeant William Carney retrieved the colors and carried them safely to the rear despite being shot in the head, chest, arm, and leg. He was the first of twenty-three African Americans to win the Congressional Medal of Honor.

The performance of the Fifty-fourth Regiment, and the use of African-American units in the Vicksburg campaign, did much to win acceptance both for black soldiers and for emancipation, at least as a proper stratagem of war. Commenting on Union victories at Port Hudson and Milliken's Bend, Mississippi, Lincoln reported that "some of our commanders . . . believe that . . . the use of colored troops constitutes the heaviest blow yet dealt to the rebels, and that at least one of

Sergeant J. L. Baldwin, 56th U.S. Colored Infantry, one of the few black officers in the Civil War. Born in Mississippi, Baldwin escaped slavery and went north to St. Louis, Missouri, where he enlisted in 1863. He was wounded in action in Arkansas, but returned to active duty.

these important successes could not have been achieved . . . but for the aid of black soldiers."

Some 178,000 African Americans served in the regiments of the United States Colored Troops, providing around 10 percent of the Union army total. Some 80 percent of the "colored troops" were former slaves or free blacks from the South. "This is the biggest thing that ever happened in my life," one enlistee declared. Of course, the African-American soldiers encountered prejudice and skepticism within the Union ranks. But they persevered. Some 38,000 gave their lives. In the navy the 29,500 blacks accounted for about a fourth of all enlistments; of these more than 2,800 died. Not only black men but black women as well served in the war; Harriet Tubman and Susie King Taylor, for instance, were nurses with Clara Barton in the Sea Islands.

As the war entered its final months, freedom emerged more fully as a legal reality. Three major steps occurred in January 1865, when both Missouri and Tennessee abolished slavery by state action and the House of Representatives passed an abolition amendment introduced by Senator Lyman Trumbull of Illinois the year before. Upon ratification by three-fourths of the reunited states, the Thirteenth Amendment became part of the Constitution on December 18, 1865, and removed any lingering doubts about the legality of emancipation. By then, in fact, slavery remained only in the border states of Kentucky and Delaware.

WOMEN AND THE WAR

While breaking the bonds of slavery, the Civil War also loosened traditional restraints on female activity. "No conflict in history," a journalist wrote at the time, "was such a woman's war as the Civil War." With three out of four white men of military age in the Confederate armed forces, southern women were especially forced to assume new responsibilities. In many southern towns and counties, the home front became a world of white women, children, and slaves. A resident of Lexington, Virginia, reported in 1862 that there were "no men left" in town by mid-1862.

Women on both sides played prominent roles in the conflict, and in the process many saw their outlook and status transformed. Initially the call to arms revived heroic images of female self-sacrifice and domestic skills. Women north and south sewed uniforms, composed uplifting poetry and songs, and raised money and supplies. Thousands of northern women worked with the United States Sanitary Commission, which organized medical relief and other services for soldiers. Others supported the freedmen's-aid movement to help impoverished freed slaves.

In the North alone, some 20,000 women served as nurses or other health-related volunteers. Nursing was as arduous and draining an enterprise as soldiering. A nurse working at a Maryland hospital recorded that she and her peers "endured the cold without sufficient bedding for our hard beds, and with no provision made for our fires. On bitter mornings we rose shivering, broke the ice in our pails, and washed our numb hands and faces, then went out into the raw air, up to our mess room, also without fire, thence to the wards." Perhaps the two most famous nurses were Dorothea Dix and Clara Barton, both untiring volunteers in service to the wounded and dying. Dix, the veteran reformer of the nation's insane asylums, became the Union army's first Superintendent of Women Nurses. She soon found herself flooded with applications from around the country. Dix explained that nurses should be "sober, earnest, self-sacrificing, and self-sustained" women between the ages of thirty-five and fifty who could "bear the presence of suffering and exercise entire self control" and be "calm, gentle, quiet, active, and steadfast in duty."

Such a description fit Clara Barton well. Born in 1821, the fifth child of a Massachusetts family of modest means, she became an itinerant

Clara Barton oversaw the distribution of vital medicines to Union troops, and later founded the American Red Cross.

schoolteacher impatient with the gender discrimination of the day. Barton fought for equal pay and eventually became one of the first female clerks in the United States Patent Office in Washington, D.C. But she remained frustrated by her desire to find "something to do that *was* something." She discovered such fulfilling work as a nurse in the Civil War. Instead of accepting an assignment to a general hospital, she followed the troops on her own, working in makeshift field hospitals. At Antietam she came so close to the fighting that as she worked on a wounded soldier a Confederate bullet ripped through the sleeve of her dress and killed the man.

Confederate Sally Tompkins of Richmond was equally unstinting. She and six others attended to 1,333 wounded men in her private hospital and kept all but 73 of them alive, a performance unmatched by any other hospital, North or South. Tompkins and Barton challenged both male doctors' control of battlefield medicine and male bureaucrats' efforts to restrict the nurses' sphere of operations. In this way the war experience of women helped generate greater confidence in their own abilities and produced female activists such as Annie Wittenmeyer of Iowa, who would become the first president of the Women's Christian Temperance Union, and Josephine Shaw Lowell, who would direct a variety of charitable organizations.

The departure of hundreds of thousands of men for the battlefields forced women to assume the public and private roles the men left behind. Women suddenly found themselves in charge of households, farms, and businesses. They became farmers or plantation managers, clerks, munitions plant workers, and schoolteachers. In North Carolina in 1860, for example, only 7 percent of teachers were women. By the end of the Civil War, a majority of the state's teachers were women. Some 400 women disguised themselves as men and fought in the war; dozens worked as spies; others traveled with the armies, cooking meals, writing letters, and assisting with amputations.

Not all women, however, accepted being cast in the new roles required by the war. Many among the slaveholding elite found themselves woefully unprepared for their new duties. The Confederacy never found enough women willing to serve as nurses. As one historian has recently concluded, "it was not the Confederacy's ladies but its African Americans who cared for the South's fallen heroes." Other genteel women could not cook, sew, or knit, and they balked at the idea of daily cleaning. One of them complained that she "was too delicately raised

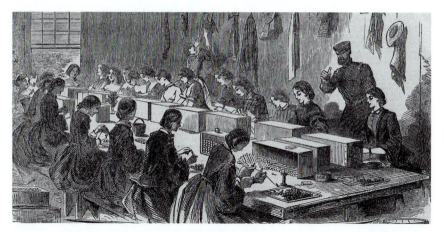

Women workers filling cartridges with gunpowder at the Federal arsenal in Watertown, Massachusetts.

for such work." Those who still owned slaves during the war expressed reluctance at managing them alone. A few slaves took advantage of the departure of their male masters and murdered their white mistresses.

The conflict's unrelenting carnage and demands eventually eroded the martial enthusiasm of some home-front stalwarts. A North Carolina mother lost seven sons in the fighting; another lost four, all at Gettysburg. Women who bore such loss or who witnessed daily suffering while serving as nurses were permanently altered by the experience. Still other women experienced what a West Virginia writer described as the "long, nervous strain" of waiting for news from the front. "No matter how gentle or womanly we might be, we read, we talked, we thought perforce of nothing but slaughter." And the war's effects were enduring. The number of widows, spinsters, and orphans mushroomed. Many bereaved women on both sides came to look on the war with what the poet Emily Dickinson called a "chastened stare." Northerner Julia Ward Howe recalled that after the war ended many battle-scarred women in one way or another refused to revert to their "chimney corner life of the fifties." They struggled to find causes to serve or work to do outside the home.

GOVERNMENT DURING THE WAR

Striking the shackles from 3.5 million slaves was a momentous social and economic revolution. But an even broader revolution began as power in Congress shifted from South to North with secession. Before the war, southern congressmen had been able to frustrate the designs of both Free Soilers and Whigs. But once the secessionists abandoned Congress to the Republicans, a dramatic change occurred. The protective tariff, a transcontinental railroad, and a homestead act—all of which had been stalled by sectional controversy—were adopted before the end of 1862. The National Banking Act followed in 1863. Two other key pieces of legislation were the Morrill Land Grant Act (1862), which provided federal aid to state colleges of "agriculture and mechanic arts," and the Contract Labor Act (1864), which aided the importation of immigrant labor. All of these had great long-term significance.

UNION FINANCES   The more immediate problem for Congress was how to finance the costly war. Three options were available: higher taxes, printing paper money, and borrowing. The higher taxes came chiefly in the form of the Morrill Tariff and excise taxes placed on manufactures and the practice of nearly every profession. A butcher, for example, had to pay 30¢ for every head of beef he slaughtered, 10¢ for every hog, 5¢ for every sheep. On top of the excises came an income tax. In 1861, Congress enacted a halfhearted income tax but postponed any collections until 1863. To collect these, the Internal Revenue Act of 1862 created a Bureau of Internal Revenue.

But tax revenues trickled in so slowly—in the end they would meet only 21 percent of wartime expenditures—that Congress in 1862 resorted to printing paper money. Beginning with the Legal Tender Act of 1862, Congress ultimately authorized $450 million of the notes, which soon became known as "greenbacks" because of their color. The greenbacks helped ease the financial crisis without causing the ruinous inflation that the unlimited issue of paper money caused in the Confederacy.

The federal government also relied on the sale of bonds. A Philadelphia banker named Jay Cooke (sometimes tagged "the Financier of the Civil War") mobilized a nationwide machinery of agents and propaganda for the sale of bonds. Eventually bonds amounting to more than $2 billion were sold, but not all by the patriotic ballyhoo of Jay Cooke and Company. New banks formed under the National Banking Act of 1863 were required to invest one-third of their capital in the bonds and to deposit them with the Treasury Department. They were also encouraged to invest even more of their capital as security for the national bank notes they could issue.

For many businessmen, wartime ventures brought quick riches, which were made visible all too often in vulgar display and extravagance. "The world has seen its iron age, its silver age, its golden age and its brazen age," the *New York Herald* commented. "This is the age of shoddy . . . shoddy brokers in Wall Street, or shoddy manufacturers of shoddy goods, or shoddy contractors for shoddy articles for shoddy government. Six days a week they are shoddy businessmen. On the seventh day they are shoddy Christians." Not all the wartime fortunes, however, were made dishonestly. And they helped promote the capital accumulation with which American businessmen fueled later expansion. Wartime business thus laid the groundwork for the fortunes of tycoons such as J. P. Morgan, John D. Rockefeller, Andrew Mellon, and Andrew Carnegie.

CONFEDERATE FINANCES   Confederate finances were a disaster from the start. In the first year of its existence, the Confederacy levied export and import duties, but exports and imports were low. It enacted a tax of one-half of 1 percent on most forms of property, which should have yielded a hefty income, but the Confederacy farmed out its collection of the taxes to the states, promising a 10 percent rebate on the take. The result was chaos. All but three states raised their quota by floating loans, which only worsened inflation.

In 1863 the Confederate Congress passed a measure that, like Union excises, taxed nearly everything. A 10 percent tax in kind on all agricultural products did more to outrage farmers and planters than to supply the army, however. Enforcement was so poor and evasion so easy that the taxes produced only negligible amounts of depreciated currency.

Altogether, taxes covered no more than 5 percent of Confederate costs, perhaps less; bond issues accounted for less than 33 percent; and Treasury notes for more than 66 percent. The last resort, the printing press, was in fact one of the early resorts. Altogether the Confederacy turned out more than $1 billion in paper money. By 1864 a wild turkey was offered in the Richmond market for $100, flour at $425 a barrel, home calls by doctors at $30, meal at $72 a bushel, and bacon at $10 a pound. Country folk were likely to have enough for subsistence, perhaps a little surplus to barter, but townspeople on fixed incomes were caught in a merciless inflationary squeeze.

CONFEDERATE DIPLOMACY Confederate diplomacy focused on gaining foreign help in the form of supplies, diplomatic recognition, or perhaps even intervention. The Confederates indulged the pathetic hope that diplomatic recognition would prove decisive, when in fact it more likely would have followed decisive victory in the field, which never came. An equally fragile illusion was the conviction that King Cotton would lure military aid and political sympathy from countries around the world dependent upon the fiber.

Indeed, to help foreign leaders make up their minds, the Confederates imposed a voluntary embargo on shipments of cotton, until the Union blockade began to strangle their foreign trade. European textile manufacturers meanwhile subsisted on the carryover from their purchase of the record crops of 1859 and 1860. By the time they needed cotton, it was available from new sources in Egypt, India, and elsewhere. Cotton textiles aside, the British economy was undergoing a boom from wartime trade with the Union and blockade-running into the Confederacy.

The first Confederate emissaries to England and France took hope when the British foreign minister received them informally after their arrival in London in 1861; they even won a promise from France's Napoleon III to recognize the Confederacy if Britain would lead the way. The key was therefore in London, but the British foreign minister refused to receive the Confederates again, partly because of Union pressures and partly out of British self-interest.

One incident early in the war threatened to upset British equanimity. In November 1861 a Union warship stopped a British ship, the *Trent,* and took into custody two Confederate agents, James M. Mason and John Slidell, en route from Havana to Europe. Celebrated as a heroic deed by a northern public still starved for victories, the *Trent* affair roused a storm of protest in Britain. An ultimatum for the captives' release was delivered to Washington, confronting Lincoln and Seward with an explosive crisis. To interfere with a neutral ship on the high seas violated long-settled American principle, and Seward finally decided to face down popular clamor and release Mason and Slidell, much to their own chagrin. As martyrs in Boston, they were more useful to their own cause than they could ever be in London and Paris.

In contrast to the futility of Confederate attempts at King Cotton diplomacy, Confederate agents succeeded in getting supplies. The most spectacular feat was the procurement of raiding ships. Although British law forbade the sale of warships to belligerents, a Confederate commissioner contrived to have the ships built and then, on trial runs, to escape to the Azores or elsewhere for outfitting with guns. In all, eighteen such ships were activated and saw action in the Atlantic, Pacific, and Indian Oceans, where they sank hundreds of Yankee ships and threw terror into the rest. The most spectacular of the Confederate raiders were the first two, the *Florida* and the *Alabama,* which took thirty-eight and sixty-four prizes, respectively.

UNION POLITICS AND CIVIL LIBERTIES   On the home fronts there was no moratorium on partisan politics, north or south. Within his own party Lincoln faced a Radical wing composed mainly of prewar abolitionists. By the end of 1861 they were getting restless with the policy of fighting solely to protect the Union. The congressional Joint Committee on the Conduct of the War became an instrument of their cause. Led by men such as Thaddeus Stevens and George W. Julian in the House, and Charles Sumner, Benjamin F. Wade (the chairman), and Zachariah Chandler in the Senate, the Radical Republicans pushed for confiscation of plantations, emancipation of slaves, and a more vigorous prosecution of the war. The majority of Republicans, however, continued to back Lincoln's more cautious approach. And the party was generally united on economic policy.

The Democratic party suffered the loss of its southern wing and the death of its leader, Stephen A. Douglas, in June 1861. By and large, northern Democrats supported a war for the "Union as it was" before 1860, giving reluctant support to war policies but opposing restraints on civil liberties and the new economic legislation. "War Democrats" such as Senator Andrew Johnson and Secretary of War Edwin M. Stanton fully supported Lincoln's policies, however, while a Peace Wing of the party preferred an end to the fighting, even at risk to the Union. An extreme fringe of the Peace Wing even flirted with outright disloyalty. The "Copperheads," as they were called, were strongest in states such as Ohio, Indiana, and Illinois, all leavened with native southerners, some of whom were pro-Confederate.

Coercive measures against disloyalty were perhaps as much a boost as a hindrance to Democrats, who took up the cause of civil liberty. Early in the war Lincoln assumed the power to suspend the writ of habeas corpus, which entitles people in jail to a speedy hearing. Lincoln

A cartoon lampooning Copperhead Democrats for their subservience to the Confederacy, 1864.

also subjected "disloyal" persons to martial law—often on vague suspicion. The Constitution said only that habeas corpus could be suspended in cases of rebellion or invasion, but congressional leaders argued that Congress alone had authority to act, since the provision fell in Article I, which deals with the powers of Congress. When Congress, by the Habeas Corpus Act of 1863, finally authorized the president to suspend the writ, it required officers to report the names of all arrested persons to the nearest district court, and provided that if the grand jury found no indictment, those arrested could be released upon taking an oath of allegiance.

There were probably more than 14,000 arrests made without recourse to a writ of habeas corpus. Most of those arrested were Confederate citizens accused of blockade-running, or foreign nationals. But Union citizens were also detained. One celebrated case arose in 1863 when Federal soldiers hustled the Democrat Clement L. Vallandigham out of his home in Dayton, Ohio. A military commission condemned Ohio's most prominent Copperhead to confinement for the duration of the war because he had questioned arbitrary arrests. The muzzling of a political opponent proved such an embarrassment to Lincoln that he commuted the sentence, but only by another irregular device, banishment behind the Confederate lines. Vallandigham eventually found his way to Canada. In 1863 he ran as the Democratic candidate for Ohio governor *in absentia,* and in 1864 he slipped back into the country. He was left alone at Lincoln's order, took part in the Democratic national convention, and ultimately his pro-southern stance proved more of an embarrassment to the Democrats than to the president.

At their 1864 national convention in Chicago, the Democrats called for an armistice to be followed by a national convention that would restore the Union. They named General George B. McClellan as their candidate, but he distanced himself from the peace platform by declaring that agreement on Union would have to precede peace.

Radical Republicans, who still regarded Lincoln as soft on treason, tried to thwart his nomination, but he outmaneuvered them at every turn. Lincoln brought about the vice-presidential nomination of Andrew Johnson, a War Democrat from Tennessee, on the "National Union" ticket, so named to minimize partisanship. As the war dragged on through 1864, however, with Grant taking heavy losses in Virginia, Lincoln fully expected to lose the election. Then Admiral Farragut's capture of Mobile in August and General Sherman's capture of Atlanta on September 2 turned the tide. McClellan carried only New Jersey, Delaware, and Kentucky, with 21 electoral votes to Lincoln's 212, and 1.8 million popular votes (45 percent) to Lincoln's 2.2 million (55 percent).

CONFEDERATE POLITICS   Unlike Lincoln, Jefferson Davis never had to contest a presidential election. He and his vice-president, Alexander Stephens, were elected without opposition in 1861 for a six-year term. But discontent flourished as events went from bad to worse, and came very close to home in the Richmond bread riot of April 2, 1863, which ended only when Davis himself persuaded the mob (mostly women) to disperse. After the congressional elections of 1863, the second and last in the Confederacy, about a third of the legislators were anti-administration. Although parties as such did not figure in the elections, it was noteworthy that many ex-Whigs and other opponents of secession were chosen.

Davis, like Lincoln, had to contend with dissenters. Large pockets of Union loyalists appeared in the German counties of Texas, the hill

*Jefferson Davis, president of the
Confederacy.*

country of Arkansas, the North Carolina Piedmont, and most of all
along the Appalachian spine that reached as far south as Alabama and
Georgia. Many Unionists followed their states into the Confederacy reluctantly, and were receptive to talk of peace. They were less troublesome to Davis, however, than the states'-rights men who had embraced
secession and then guarded states' rights against the central government as zealously as they had against the Union. Georgia, and to a
lesser degree North Carolina, were strongholds of such sentiment,
which prevailed widely elsewhere as well. The states'-rights advocates
challenged, among other things, the legality of conscription, taxes on
farm produce, and above all the suspension of habeas corpus. Vice-
President Stephens carried on a running battle against Davis's effort to
establish "military despotism," and left Richmond to sulk at his Georgia
home for eighteen months.

Among other things, the Confederacy died of dogma. Where Lincoln
was the consummate pragmatist, Davis was a brittle dogmatist with a
waspish temper. His fundamental insecurity made him indecisive. But
once he made a decision, nothing could change his mind. One southern
politician said that Davis was "as stubborn as a mule." Davis could
never find it in himself to admit that he had made a mistake. Such a
personality was ill suited to the chief executive of an infant nation.

THE FALTERING CONFEDERACY

In 1863 the hinge of fate began to close the door on the brief career of the Confederacy. After the Union disaster at Fredericksburg, Lincoln's search for a capable general turned to one of Burnside's disgruntled lieutenants, Joseph E. Hooker, whose pugnacity had earned him the name of "Fighting Joe." After the appointment, Lincoln wrote his new commander, "there are some things in regard to which, I am not quite satisfied with you." Hooker had been saying the country needed a dictator, and word had reached Lincoln. "Only those generals who gain successes can set up dictators," the president wrote. "What I now ask of you is military success, and I will risk the dictatorship." But the risk was not great. Hooker was no more able than Burnside to deliver the goods. He failed his test at Chancellorsville, Virginia, May 1–5, 1863.

CHANCELLORSVILLE   With a force of perhaps 130,000, the largest Union army yet gathered, and a brilliant plan, Hooker suffered a loss of control, perhaps a failure of nerve, at the critical juncture. Lee, with perhaps half that number of troops, staged what became a textbook example of daring and maneuver. Hooker's plan was to leave his base, opposite Fredericksburg, on a sweeping movement upstream across the Rappahannock and Rapidan Rivers to flank Lee's position. A diversionary force was to cross below the town. Lee, however, sniffed out the ruse and pulled his main forces back to meet Hooker. At Chancellorsville, after a preliminary skirmish, Lee divided his army again, sending Jackson with more than half the men on a long march to hit the enemy's exposed right flank.

On May 2, toward evening, Jackson surprised the Federals at the edge of a wooded area called the Wilderness, but the fighting died out in confusion as darkness fell. Jackson rode out beyond the skirmish line to locate the Union forces. Fighting erupted in the darkness, and a nervous North Carolina regiment mistakenly opened fire on Jackson, who was struck by three bullets that shattered his left arm and right hand. The next day, a surgeon amputated his arm. He seemed to be recovering well, but then contracted the dreaded pneumonia. Jackson assured his surgeon that "I am not afraid to die." A few hours later he uttered his last words: "Let us cross over the river and rest under the shade of the trees." He had been an utterly fearless general of rapid marches, bold flanking movements, and furious assaults. "I have lost my right arm," Lee lamented, and "I do not know how to replace him."

The next day, Lee forced Hooker's army back across the Rappahannock. It was the peak of Lee's career, but Chancellorsville was his last significant victory—and his costliest: the South suffered some 12,000 casualties, with more than 1,600 killed.

VICKSBURG   While Lee held the Federals at bay in the East, a reinstated Ulysses Grant had been groping his way down the Mississippi River toward Vicksburg in western Mississippi. Grant knew that if he could capture Vicksburg, the Union forces could gain control of the Mississippi River and thereby split the Confederacy in two. Located on a bluff 200 feet above the river, Vicksburg had withstood naval attacks

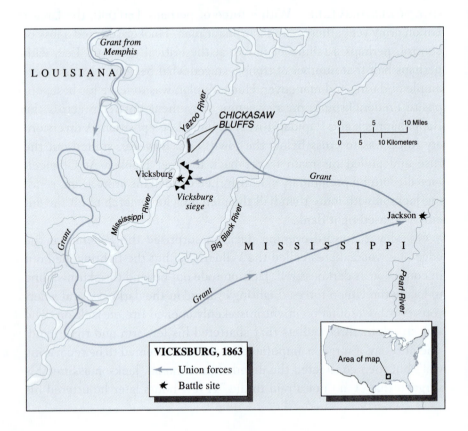

and a downriver expedition led by William T. Sherman, who had attacked at Chickasaw Bluffs. Grant positioned his army about fifteen miles north of the city, but the surrounding bayous baffled efforts to reach the goal. Grant finally gave up the idea of a northern approach. He crossed over to Louisiana and while the navy ran gunboats and transports past the Confederate batteries at Vicksburg, he moved south to meet them, crossed back, and reached dry ground south of Vicksburg at the end of April. From there Grant adopted a new expedient. He would forget supply lines and live off the country. Sherman provided a diversion with another attack on Chickasaw Bluffs. Grant then swept eastward on a campaign that Lincoln later called "one of the most brilliant in the world," took Jackson, Mississippi, where he seized or destroyed supplies, then turned westward and on May 18 pinned the 30,000 Confederates inside Vicksburg. He resolved to wear them down and starve them out.

GETTYSBURG   The plight of Vicksburg put the Confederate high command in a quandary. Joseph E. Johnston, now in charge of the western Confederate forces but with few men under his personal command, would have preferred to focus on the Tennessee front and thereby perhaps force Grant to relax his grip. Lee had another idea for a diversion. If he could win a major battle on northern soil, he might do more than just relieve the pressure at Vicksburg. In June he moved his army into the Shenandoah Valley and northward again across Maryland.

Hooker followed, keeping his forces between Lee's army and Washington, but demoralized by defeat at Chancellorsville and quarrels with Halleck, he turned in his resignation. On June 28 Major-General George G. Meade took command. Neither side chose Gettysburg, Pennsylvania, as the site for the climactic battle, but a Confederate scavenging party entered the town in search of shoes and encountered units of Union cavalry on June 30. The main forces quickly converged on that point. On July 1 the Confederates pushed the Federals out of the town, but into stronger positions on high ground to the south. Meade hastened reinforcements to his new lines along the heights. On July 2 Lee—with uncharacteristic tardiness—mounted furious assaults at both the extreme left and right flanks of Meade's army, but in vain. General Longstreet said that it was the "best three hours' fighting I had seen done by any troops on any battle-field."

On July 3 Lee staked everything on one final assault on the Union center at Cemetery Ridge. His plan suffered from a fatal problem: his generals were not unified in their support of it. Lee, who shrank from confrontation, did not demand their unquestioning obedience. As a result, Longstreet, who remained skeptical of a frontal assault, did not position his forces to assist the division led by General George Pickett that Lee had ordered to take Cemetery Ridge.

About 2 P.M. Pickett's 15,000 troops emerged from the woods into the brilliant sunlight, formed neat ranks, and began their suicidal advance across open ground commanded by Union artillery. It was as hopeless as Burnside's assault at Fredericksburg. Only 5,000 of Pickett's men reached the ridge, and the few who got within range of hand-to-hand combat were quickly overwhelmed. As he watched the few survivors returning from the bloody field, Lee muttered: "All this has been my fault." He then told Pickett to regroup his division to repulse a possible counterattack, only to have Pickett tartly reply, "General Lee, I have no division now." Pickett never forgave Lee. Years later he charged: "That old man had my division slaughtered."

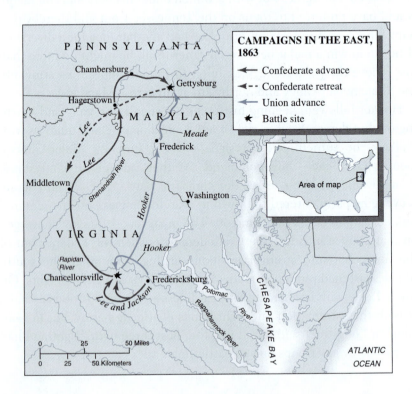

Harvest of Death. *T. H. O'Sullivan's grim photograph of the dead at Gettysburg.*

With nothing left to do but retreat, on July 4 Lee's dejected and mangled army, with about a third of its number gone, began to slog south through a driving rain. They had failed in all their purposes, not the least being to relieve the pressure on Vicksburg. On that same July 4, the Confederate commander at Vicksburg reached the end of his tether and surrendered his entire garrison. Four days later the last remaining Confederate stronghold on the Mississippi, Port Hudson, under siege since May by Union forces, gave up. "The father of waters," Lincoln said, "flows unvexed to the sea." The Confederacy was irrevocably split. Had Meade pursued Lee, he might have delivered the *coup de grace* before the Rebels could get back across the flooded Potomac.

CHATTANOOGA   The third great Union victory of 1863 occurred in fighting around Chattanooga, the railhead of eastern Tennessee and gateway to northern Georgia. In the late summer, a Union army led by General William Rosecrans took Chattanooga and then rashly pursued General Braxton Bragg's forces into Georgia, where they met at Chickamauga. The battle (September 19–20) had the makings of a Union disaster, since it was one of the few times when the Confederates had a numerical advantage (about 70,000 to 56,000). On the second day, Bragg smashed the Federals' right, and only the stubborn stand of Union troops under George H. Thomas (thenceforth "the Rock of Chickamauga") prevented a general rout. The battered Union forces fell back into Chattanooga, while Bragg cut the railroad from the west and held the city virtually under siege from the heights to the south and east.

Rosecrans seemed stunned and apathetic, but Lincoln urged him to hang on: "If we can hold Chattanooga, and East Tennessee, I think rebellion must dwindle and die." The Union command sent reinforcements from Virginia, while Grant and Sherman arrived with more from the West. Grant, given overall command of the Western Theater of operations on October 16, pushed his way into Chattanooga a few days later, forcing open a supply route as he came. He replaced Rosecrans with Thomas. On November 24 the Federals began to move, hitting the Confederate flanks at Lookout Mountain and Signal Hill while Thomas created a diversion at the center. The Union troops took Lookout Mountain in what was mainly a feat of mountaineering, but Sherman's forces stalled at Signal Hill. On the second day of the battle, Grant ordered Thomas forward to positions at the foot of Missionary Ridge. Successful there, but still exposed, the men spontaneously began to move on up toward the crest 400 to 500 feet above. They might well have been cut up badly, but the Rebels were unable to lower their big guns enough. In the face of thousands of Union troops swarming up the hill, the Confederate defenders panicked and fled.

Bragg was unable to regroup his forces until they were many miles to the south, and the Battle of Chattanooga was the end of his active career. Jefferson Davis, who had backed Bragg against all censure, reluctantly replaced him with Johnston and called Bragg back to Richmond as an adviser. Soon after the battle the Federals linked up with Burnside, who had taken Knoxville, and proceeded to secure their control of eastern Tennessee, where the hills were full of native Unionists.

Chattanooga had another consequence. Though the Federals won the battle by rushing up Missionary Ridge, against orders, the victory nonetheless confirmed the impression of Grant's genius. Lincoln had at last found his general. In 1864 Grant arrived in Washington to assume the rank of lieutenant-general and a new position as general-in-chief. Halleck became chief of staff and continued in his role as channel of communication between the president and commanders in the field. Within the Union armies at least, a modern command system was emerging; the Confederacy never had a unified command.

The Confederacy's Defeat

During the winter of 1863–1864, Confederates began to despair of victory. A War Department official in Richmond noted in his diary that his "steadfastness is yielding to a sense of hopelessness." At the same time, Mary Chesnut reported that "gloom and despondency hang like a pall everywhere." Union leaders, sensing the momentum swinging their way, stepped up the pressure on Confederate forces.

Lincoln's main targets now were Lee's army in Virginia and General Joseph Johnston's in Georgia. Grant personally would accompany Meade, who retained direct command over the Army of the Potomac; operations in the West were entrusted to Grant's longtime lieutenant, William T. Sherman. As Sherman put it later, Grant "was to go for Lee, and I was to go for Joe Johnston. That was his plan." Grant brought with him a new strategy against Lee. Where his predecessors had all hoped for the climactic single battle, he adopted a policy of attrition. He would attack, attack, attack, keeping the pressure on the Confederates, grinding down their numbers and taking away their initiative and will to fight. As he ordered Meade, "Wherever Lee goes, there you will go also." Grant would also wage total war, confiscating or destroying any

General Ulysses S. Grant.

and all civilian property of military use. It was a brutal, costly, but ultimately effective plan.

GRANT'S PURSUIT OF LEE   In May 1864, the Army of the Potomac, numbering about 115,000 to Lee's 65,000, moved south across the Rappahannock and the Rapidan into the Wilderness, where Hooker had come to grief in the Battle of Chancellorsville. In the Battle of the Wilderness (May 5–6), the armies fought blindly through the woods, the horror and suffering of the scene heightened by crackling brushfires. Grant's men suffered heavier casualties than the Confederates, but the Rebels were running out of replacements.

Many of the Union officers in the Army of the Potomac whom Grant inherited were still in awe of Lee. They feared another decisive counterattack on their flanks. When one of his officers expressed concern about what Lee might do, Grant exploded: "Oh, I am heartily tired of hearing about what Lee is going to do. Some of you always seem to think he is suddenly going to turn a double somersault, and land in our rear and on both flanks at the same time. Go back to your command,

Civil War Sketch. *Artists like Alfred Waud would travel with the soldiers and render quick and accurate sketches of battle scenes. This Waud drawing shows George Custer and his Union troops moving into the Shenandoah Valley in 1864 after engaging in fierce battle.*

The tattered colors of the 56th and 36th Massachusetts regiments, marching through Virginia, 1864.

and try to think what we are going to do ourselves, instead of what Lee is going to do." Always before when bloodied by Lee's troops, Union forces had pulled back to nurse their wounds, but Grant slid off to his left and continued his relentless advance southward, now toward Spotsylvania Court House.

There Lee's advance guard barely arrived in time to stall the movement, and the armies settled down for five days of bloody warfare, May 8–12. But again Grant slid off to his left, and kept moving. Along the banks of the Chickahominy, the two sides clashed at Cold Harbor (June 1–3). In twenty minutes, 7,000 attacking Federals were killed or wounded. Many of them predicted as much. After the failed assault, Confederates retrieved a diary from a dead Massachusetts soldier. The final entry read: "June 3, 1864, Cold Harbor, Virginia. I was killed." Battered and again repulsed, Grant cut away and headed for Petersburg, at the junction of railroads into Richmond from the south.

Grant dug in for a siege along lines that extended for twenty-five miles above and below Petersburg. Grant telegraphed Lincoln that he intended "to fight it out on this line if it takes all summer." Lincoln replied: "Hold on with a bulldog grip, and chew and choke as much as possible." For nine months the two armies faced each other down while Grant kept pushing toward his left flank to break the railroad arteries

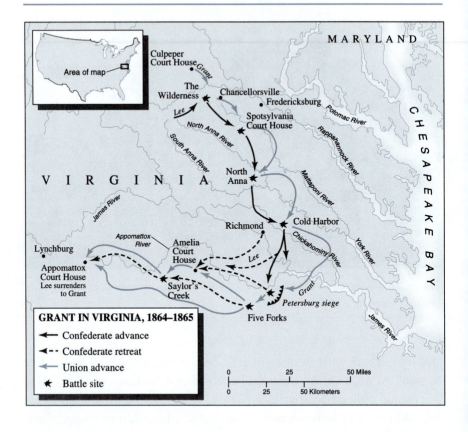

Culpeper Court House
The Wilderness
Chancellorsville
Fredericksburg
Spotsylvania Court House
North Anna
Richmond
Cold Harbor
Lynchburg
Appomattox River
Amelia Court House
Appomattox Court House
Lee surrenders to Grant
Saylor's Creek
Petersburg siege
Five Forks

MARYLAND
VIRGINIA
CHESAPEAKE BAY

Potomac River
Rappahannock River
North Anna River
South Anna River
James River
Mattaponi River
Chickahominy River
York River
James River

Area of map

GRANT IN VIRGINIA, 1864–1865
← Confederate advance
◄- - Confederate retreat
← Union advance
★ Battle site

0		25		50 Miles
0	25		50 Kilometers	

that were Lee's lifeline. During this time, Grant's troops were generously supplied by Union vessels moving up the James, while Lee's forces, beset by hunger, cold, and desertion, wasted away. Petersburg had become Lee's prison while disasters piled up for the Confederacy elsewhere.

SHERMAN'S MARCH   When Grant headed south, so did Sherman— toward the railroad hub of Atlanta, with 90,000 men against Joe Johnston's 60,000. Sherman's campaign, like Grant's, developed into a war of maneuver, but without the pitched battles. Sherman kept moving to his right, but the wily Johnston was always one step ahead of him— turning up in secure positions along the north Georgia ridges, including at Kennesaw Mountain, drawing Sherman farther from his Chattanooga base, harassing the Union supply lines with Joe Wheeler's cavalry, and keeping his own main force intact. But Johnston's skillful de-

William Tecumseh Sherman.

fensive tactics caused an impatient President Davis finally to replace him with the combative but reckless John B. Hood. A towering, blond-bearded Texan, Hood did not know the meaning of retreat. Lee described him as being "all lion." He had "none of the fox" in him. Having had an arm crippled by a bullet at Gettysburg and most of one leg shot off at Chickamauga, he had to be strapped to his horse. Three times in eight days Hood lashed out at the Union lines, each time meeting a bloody rebuff. Sherman at first resorted to a siege of Atlanta, then slid off to the right again, cutting the rail lines below Atlanta. Hood evacuated on September 1, but kept his army intact.

Sherman now laid plans for a march through central Georgia, where no organized armies remained. His intention was to "whip the rebels, to humble their pride, to follow them into their inmost recesses, and make them fear and dread us." Hood meanwhile had hatched an equally audacious plan. He would cut away to northern Alabama and push on into Tennessee, forcing Sherman into pursuit. Sherman refused to take the bait, although he did send a Union force back to Tennessee to keep watch. So the curious spectacle unfolded of the main armies moving off in opposite directions. But it was a measure of the Confederates' plight that Sherman could cut a swath across Georgia with impunity, while Hood was soon outnumbered again.

In the Battle of Franklin (November 30), Hood sent his army across two miles of open ground. Six waves broke against the Union lines, leaving the ground strewn with Confederates. With what he had left, Hood dared not attack Nashville, nor did he dare withdraw for fear of final disintegration. Finally, in the Battle of Nashville (December 15–16), the Federals broke and scattered what was left of the Confederate Army of Tennessee. The Confederate front west of the Appalachians had collapsed, leaving only a few units scattered in the field.

During all this, Sherman's army was marching through Georgia, pioneering the modern practice of total war against a people's resources and against their will to resist. Sherman knew that in a war between democracies the strength of public will was more important than the size of opposing armies. In his effort to demoralize the civilian populace, he was determined to "make Georgia howl." On November 15, 1864, he destroyed Atlanta's warehouses and railroad facilities while spreading fires that consumed about a third of the city. The Union army moved out in four columns over a front twenty to sixty miles wide, living off the land and destroying any provisions that might serve Confederate forces. Bands of stragglers and deserters from both armies joined in looting along the flanks, while Union cavalry destroyed Rebel supplies to keep them out of enemy hands. When, after a month, Sherman arrived in Savannah, he had cut a swath of desolation 250 miles long.

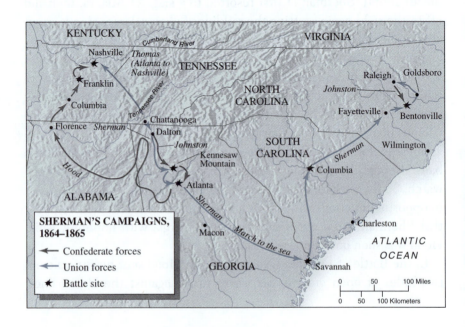

SHERMAN'S CAMPAIGNS, 1864–1865

← Confederate forces
← Union forces
★ Battle site

Ruins of Georgia Railroad Roundhouse at Atlanta, 1864. *In the wake of Sherman's march, abandoned locomotives and twisted rails marked the destruction in Atlanta.*

Pushing across the Savannah River into that "hell-hole of secession," South Carolina, Sherman's men wrought even greater destruction. More than a dozen towns were burned in whole or part, including the state capital of Columbia, captured on February 17, 1865. Meanwhile, Charleston's defenders abandoned the city and headed north to join an army that Joseph E. Johnston was desperately pulling together. Johnston mounted one final attack on Sherman's left wing at Bentonville (March 19–20), but that was his last major battle.

APPOMATTOX   During this final season of the Confederacy, Grant kept pushing, probing, and battering the Petersburg defenses. Raids by Philip H. Sheridan's cavalry had desolated Lee's breadbasket in the Shenandoah Valley, and winter left his men on short rations. News of Sherman's progress through Georgia and South Carolina added to the gloom and the impulse to desert. Lee began to lay plans for his besieged and starving forces to escape and join Johnston's army in North Carolina. At Five Forks (April 1, 1865), Grant finally cut the last rail line to Petersburg, and the next day Lee abandoned Richmond and Petersburg in a desperate flight toward Lynchburg and rails south. President Davis, exhausted but still defiant, gathered what archives and treasure he

Robert E. Lee. *Mathew Brady took this photograph in Richmond eleven days after Lee's surrender at Appomattox.*

could and made it out by train ahead of the advancing Federals, only to be captured in Georgia by Union cavalry on May 10.

By then the Confederacy was already dead. Lee moved out with Grant in hot pursuit, and soon found his escape route cut by Sheridan's cavalry forces. On April 9 (Palm Sunday) he donned a crisp dress uniform and met the mud-spattered Grant in the parlor of the McLean home at Appomattox to tender his surrender, four years to the day after Davis and his cabinet decided to attack Fort Sumter. Grant, at Lee's request, let the Rebel officers keep their sidearms and permitted soldiers to keep personal horses and mules. On April 18, Johnston surrendered to Sherman at the Bennett house near what would soon become the thriving tobacco town of Durham. During May the remaining Confederate forces surrendered as well.

A MODERN WAR

The Civil War was in many respects the first modern war. Its scope was unprecedented. One out of every twelve adult American males served in the war, and few families were unaffected by the event. Over 620,000 Americans died in the conflict, 50 percent more than in World War II. Because battlefield surgeons were constantly overworked and frequently lacked equipment, supplies, and knowledge, almost any stomach or head wound proved fatal, and gangrene was rampant. Fifty thousand of the survivors returned home with one or more limbs amputated. Disease, however, was the greatest threat to soldiers, killing twice as many as were lost in battle.

The Civil War was not neatly self-contained; it was a total war, fought not solely by professional armies but by and against whole societies. Farms became battlefields, cities were transformed into armed encampments, and homes were commandeered for field hospitals. After one battle, a woman recalled that "wounded men were brought into our house and laid side by side in our halls and first-story rooms . . . carpets were so saturated with blood as to be unfit for further use."

The Civil War was also modern in that much of the killing was distant, impersonal, and mechanical. The opposing forces used an array of new weapons and instruments of war: artillery with "rifled" or grooved barrels for greater accuracy, repeating rifles, ironclad ships, observation balloons, and wire entanglements. Men were killed without even knowing who had fired the shot that felled them.

The debate over why the North won and the South lost the Civil War will probably never end, but as in other modern wars firepower and manpower were essential factors. Lee's own explanation of the Confederate defeat retains an enduring legitimacy: "After four years of arduous service marked by unsurpassed courage and fortitude, the Army of Northern Virginia has been compelled to yield to overwhelming numbers and resources."

MAKING CONNECTIONS

- Certain economic and fiscal measures enacted during the Civil War (when southerners were not in Congress to block them) helped fuel the postwar economic growth (see Chapter 20).

- The Confederacy's defeat had a tremendous impact on all dimensions of life in the South, as Chapter 19 (on the New South) demonstrates.

FURTHER READING

The best one-volume overview of the Civil War period is James M. McPherson's *Battle Cry of Freedom: The Civil War Era* (1988). A good introduction to the military events is Herman Hattaway's *Shades of Blue and Gray: An Introductory Military History of the Civil War* (1997). The outlook and experiences of the common soldier are explored in James M. McPherson's *For Cause and Comrades: Why Men Fought in the Civil War* (1997) and Earl J. Hess's *The Union Soldier in Battle: Enduring the Ordeal of Combat* (1997).

For emphasis on the South, turn first to Gary W. Gallagher's *The Confederate War* (1997). For a sparkling account of the birth of the Rebel nation, see William C. Davis's *"A Government of Our Own": The Making of the Confederacy* (1994). The same author provides a fine biography of the Confederate president in *Jefferson Davis: The Man and His Hour* (1992). The best study of Confederate political culture is George C. Rable's *The Confederate Republic: A Revolution Against Politics* (1994).

Insightful biographies of southern military leaders are Emory Thomas's *Robert E. Lee* (1995), Jeffrey D. West's *General James Longstreet: The Confederacy's Most Controversial Soldier* (1992), and James I. Robertson, Jr.'s *Stonewall Jackson: The Man, the Soldier, the Legend* (1997).

Analytical scholarship on the military conflict includes Joseph L. Harsh's *Confederate Tide Rising: Robert E. Lee and the Making of Southern Strategy, 1861–1862* (1998), Steven E. Wordworth's *Jefferson Davis and His Generals: The Failure of Confederate Command in the West* (1990), and Paul D. Casdorph's *Lee and Jackson: Confederate Chieftains* (1992). A cultural interpretation of Confederate military behavior is Grady McWhiney and Perry D. Jamieson's *Attack and Die: Civil War Military Tactics and the Southern Heritage* (1982). Lonnie R. Speer's *Portals to Hell: The Military Prisons of the Civil War* (1997) details the ghastly experience of prisoners of war.

The history of the North during the war is surveyed in Philip S. Paludan's *"A People's Contest": The Union and Civil War, 1861–1865* (1988) and J. Matthew Gallman, *The North Fights the Civil War: The Home Front* (1994). Treatments of northern politics during the war include Harold M. Hyman's *A More Perfect Union: The Impact of the Civil War and Reconstruction on the Constitution* (1973), and Allan G. Bogue's *The Earnest Men: Republicans of the Civil War Senate* (1981).

The central northern political figure, Abraham Lincoln, is the subject of many books. Two good biographies are David H. Donald's *Lincoln* (1995) and Stephen B. Oates's *With Malice toward None* (1977). The election of 1864 is treated in John C. Waugh's *Reelecting Lincoln: The Battle for the 1864 Presidency* (1998). On Lincoln's assassination, see William Hanchett's *The Lincoln Murder Conspiracies* (1983). For a fine biography of Lincoln's wife, see Jean H. Baker's *Mary Todd Lincoln: A Biography* (1987).

Concerning specific military campaigns, see Larry J. Daniel's *Shiloh: The Battle That Changed the Civil War* (1997), Thomas Goodrich's *Black Flag: Guerrilla Warfare on the Western Border, 1861–1865* (1995), Stephen W. Sears's *Landscape Turned Red: The Battle of Antietam* (1983) and *To the Gates of Richmond: The Peninsula Campaign* (1993), James Lee McDonough and James Pickett Jones's *War So Terrible: Sherman and Atlanta* (1992), Robert Garth Scott's *Into the Wilderness with the Army of the Potomac* (1985), and Albert Castel and Laura K. Poracsky's *Decision in the West: The Atlanta Campaign of 1864* (1992).

Biographical studies of the northern military leaders include Michael Fellman's *Citizen Sherman: A Life of William Tecumseh Sherman* (1995), Brooks D. Simpson's *Let Us Have Peace: Ulysses S. Grant and the Politics of War and Reconstruction, 1861–1868* (1991), John F. Marszalek's *Sherman: A Soldier's Passion for Order* (1992), Charles Royster's *The Destructive War: William Tecumseh Sherman, Stonewall Jackson, and the Americans* (1991), and William S. McFeely's *Grant: A Biography* (1981).

The experience of the black soldier is surveyed in Joseph T. Glatthaar's *Forged in Battle: The Civil War Alliance of Black Soldiers and White Officers* (1989); Ira Berlin, Joseph P. Reidy, and Leslie S. Rowland's *Freedom's Soldiers: The Black Military Experience in the Civil War* (1998); and *On the Altar of Freedom: A Black Soldier's Civil War Letters from the Front* (1991), edited by James H. Gooding, James M. McPherson, and Virginia M. Adams. Louis S. Gerteis's *From Contraband to Freedman: Federal Policy toward Southern Blacks, 1861–1865* (1973) traces the federal government's policies dealing with freed slaves during the war. For the black woman's experience, see Susie King Taylor and Patricia W. Romero's: *A Black Woman's Civil War Memoirs: Reminiscences of My Life in Camp with the 33rd U.S. Colored Troops* (1988) and

Jacqueline Jones's *Labor of Love, Labor of Sorrow: Black Women, Work and the Family from Slavery to the Present* (1985).

Recent gender and ethnic studies include *Divided Houses: Gender and the Civil War*, edited by Catherine Clinton and Nina Silber (1992), Drew Gilpin Faust's *Mothers of Invention: Women of the Slaveholding South in the American Civil War* (1997), Shirley Samuels's *The Culture of Sentiment: Race, Gender, and Sentimentality in Nineteenth-Century America* (1992), George C. Rable's *Civil Wars: Women and the Crisis of Southern Nationalism* (1989), and William L. Burton's *Melting Pot Soldiers: The Union's Ethnic Regiments* (2nd ed., 1998). For a fine biography of the North's most famous nurse, see Stephen B. Oates's *A Woman of Valor: Clara Barton and the Civil War* (1994).

18 ✎ RECONSTRUCTION:
NORTH AND SOUTH

CHAPTER ORGANIZER

This chapter focuses on:

- the different approaches to Reconstruction.

- congressional efforts to reshape southern society.

- the role of African Americans in the early postwar years.

- national politics in the 1870s.

*I*n the spring of 1865 the cruel war was over. At the frightful cost of 620,000 lives and the destruction of the southern economy and much of its landscape, American nationalism emerged triumphant, and some 4 million slaves emerged free. Ratification of the Thirteenth Amendment in December 1865 abolished slavery throughout the Union.

But peace had come only on the battlefields. "Cannon conquer," recognized a northern editor, "but they do not necessarily convert." Now the North faced the task of "reconstructing" a ravaged and resentful South.

THE WAR'S AFTERMATH

In the war's aftermath, important questions faced the victors in the North: Should the Confederate leaders be tried for treason? How should new governments be formed? How and at whose expense was the South's economy to be rebuilt? What was to be done with the freed slaves? Were they to be given land? social equality? education? voting rights? Such complex questions required sober reflection and careful planning, but policy makers did not have the luxury of time or the benefits of consensus.

DEVELOPMENT IN THE NORTH   To some Americans the Civil War had been more truly a social revolution than the War of Independence, for it reduced the once-dominant power of the planter elite in the national councils and elevated that of the northern "captains of industry." It is easy to exaggerate the profundity of this change, but government did become subtly more friendly to businessmen and unfriendly to those who would probe into their activities. The wartime Republican Congress had delivered on the major platform promises of 1860, which

The Grand Review of Union Troops in Victory, *Washington, D.C., May 1865.*

had cemented the allegiance of northeastern businessmen and western farmers to the party of free labor.

In the absence of southern members, Congress during the war had seized the opportunity to centralize national power. In this regard, it passed the Morrill Tariff, which doubled the average level of import duties. The National Banking Act created a uniform system of banking and bank-note currency, and helped to finance the war. Congress also passed legislation guaranteeing that the first transcontinental railroad would run along a north-central route from Omaha to Sacramento, and donated public lands and public bonds to ensure its financing. In the Homestead Act of 1862, moreover, Congress voted free homesteads of 160 acres to settlers. They had to occupy the land for five years before gaining title. The Morrill Land Grant Act of the same year conveyed to each state 30,000 acres of public land per member of Congress from the state, the proceeds from the sale of which went to create colleges of "agriculture and mechanic arts." Such measures helped stimulate the North's economy in the years after the Civil War.

DEVASTATION IN THE SOUTH   The postwar South, where most of the fighting had occurred, offered a sharp contrast to the victorious North. Along the path of General Sherman's army, one observer reported in 1866, the countryside "looked for many miles like a broad black streak of ruin and desolation." Columbia, South Carolina, said another witness, was "a wilderness of ruins," Charleston a place of "vacant houses, of widowed women, of rotting wharves, of deserted warehouses, of weed-wild gardens, of miles of grass-grown streets, of acres of pitiful and voiceless barrenness." The border states of Missouri and Kentucky had experienced a guerrilla war that lapsed into postwar anarchy perpetrated by marauding bands of bushwhackers turned outlaws, such as the notorious James boys, Frank and Jesse.

Throughout the South, property values had collapsed. Confederate bonds and money became worthless; railroads were damaged or destroyed. Cotton that had escaped destruction was seized as Confederate property or in forfeit of federal taxes. Emancipation of the slaves wiped out perhaps $4 billion invested in human flesh and left the labor system in disarray. The great age of expansion in the cotton market was over. Not until 1879 would the cotton crop again equal the record harvest of 1860; tobacco production did not regain its prewar level until

The "burned district" of Richmond, Virginia, April 1865.

1880; the sugar crop of Louisiana not until 1893; and the old rice industry of the Tidewater and the hemp industry of the Kentucky Bluegrass never regained their prewar status.

FORCED DOMESTICITY   The defeat of the Confederacy transformed much of southern society. The freeing of slaves, the destruction of property, and the free fall in land values left many among the former planter elite destitute and homeless. Amanda Worthington, a plantation mistress from Mississippi, saw her whole world destroyed. In the fall of 1865, she assessed the damage: "None of us can realize that we are no longer wealthy—yet thanks to the yankees, the cause of all unhappiness, such is the case." Genteel southerners now found themselves forced to rebuild lives and families without the help of slaves. Women accustomed to relying on slaves for their every need were unprepared for the tasks at hand. One girl could not even comb her own hair; a matron cried at night because she had no one to wash her feet. "I did the washing for six weeks," one tired woman wrote, "[and] came near ruining myself for life as I was too delicately raised for such hard work." Those who still had some money after the war often recruited former slaves to work as domestic servants. Now, however, they had to pay for their services.

BITTER IN DEFEAT   After the Civil War many former Confederates were so embittered by defeat and so resistant to the idea of living under northern rule that they abandoned their native region rather than submit to "Yankee rule." Some migrated to Canada, Europe, Mexico, South America, and Asia. Others preferred the western territories and states. Still others moved north, settling in northern and midwestern cities on the assumption that educational and economic opportunities would be better among the victors.

Most of those who remained in the South returned to find their farms and homes and communities transformed. One Confederate army captain reported that on his father's plantation "Our negroes are living in great comfort. They were delighted to see me with overflowing affection. They waited on me as before, gave me breakfast, splendid dinners, etc. But they firmly and respectfully informed me: 'We own this land now. Put it out of your head that it will ever be yours again.'"

As Union troops fanned out across the defeated South, people cursed and spat upon the troops. A Virginia woman expressed a spirited defiance common among her circle of friends: "Every day, every hour, that I live increases my hatred and detestation, and loathing of that race. They [Yankees] disgrace our common humanity. As a people I consider them vastly inferior to the better classes of our slaves." Fervent southern nationalists, both men and women, planted in their children a similar hatred of Yankees and a defiance of northern rule. One mother said that she trained her children to "fear God, love the South, and live to avenge her."

LEGALLY FREE, SOCIALLY BOUND   In the former Confederate states, the newly freed slaves suffered most of all. According to Frederick Douglass, the black abolitionist, the former slave remained dependent: "He had neither money, property, nor friends. He was free from the old plantation, but he had nothing but the dusty road under his feet. . . . He was turned loose, naked, hungry, and destitute to the open sky."

A few northerners argued that what the ex-slaves needed most was their own land. But even dedicated abolitionists shrank from endorsing measures of land reform that might have given the freed slaves more self-support and independence. Citizenship and legal rights were one thing, wholesale confiscation of property and land redistribution quite another. Instead of land or material help, the freed slaves more often got advice and moral platitudes.

According to a former Confederate general, recently freed blacks had "nothing but freedom."

In 1865 Representative George Julian of Indiana and Senator Charles Sumner of Massachusetts proposed to give freed slaves forty-acre homesteads carved out of Rebel lands taken under the Confiscation Act of 1862. But their plan for outright grants was replaced by a program of rentals since, under the law, confiscation was effective only for the lifetime of the offender. Discussions of land distribution, however, fueled rumors that freed slaves would get "forty acres and a mule," a slogan that swept the South at the end of the war. As a black man in Mississippi put it: "Gib us our own land and we take care ourselves; but widout land, de ole massas can hire us or starve us, as dey please." More lands were seized as "abandoned lands" under an act of 1864, and for default on the direct taxes that Congress had levied early in the war, than under the Confiscation Act. The most conspicuous example of confiscation was the estate of Robert E. Lee and the Custis family, which became Arlington National Cemetery, but larger amounts were taken in the South Carolina Sea Islands and elsewhere. Some of these lands were sold to freed blacks, some to Yankee speculators.

THE FREEDMEN'S BUREAU   On March 3, 1865, Congress set up within the War Department the Bureau of Refugees, Freedmen, and

Abandoned Lands, to provide "such issues of provisions, clothing, and fuel" as might be needed to relieve "destitute and suffering refugees and freedmen and their wives and children." The Freedmen's Bureau would also take over abandoned or confiscated land, but the amount of such land was limited. Agents of the Freedmen's Bureau were entrusted with negotiating labor contracts (something new for both blacks and planters), providing medical care, and setting up schools, often in cooperation with northern agencies such as the American Missionary Association and the Freedmen's Aid Society. The bureau had its own courts to deal with labor disputes and land titles, and its agents were further authorized to supervise trials involving blacks in other courts. White intransigence and the failure to grasp the intensity of racial prejudice increasingly thwarted the efforts of Freedmen's Bureau agents to protect and assist the former slaves.

Congress was not willing to strengthen the powers of the Freedmen's Bureau to reflect such problems. Beyond temporary relief measures, no program of Reconstruction ever incorporated much more than constitutional and legal rights for freedmen. These were important in themselves, of course, but the extent to which even these should go was very

The Freedmen's Bureau set up schools such as this throughout the former Confederate states.

uncertain, to be settled more by the course of events than by any clear-cut commitment to equality.

THE BATTLE OVER RECONSTRUCTION

The problem of reconstructing the South involved what governments would constitute authority in the defeated states. This problem arose first in the state of Virginia at the very beginning of the Civil War, when the thirty-five western counties of Virginia refused to go along with secession. In 1861 a loyal state government of Virginia was proclaimed at Wheeling, and this government in turn formed a new state called West Virginia, admitted to the Union in 1863. The loyal government of Virginia then carried on from Alexandria, its reach limited to that part of the state that the Union controlled. As Union forces advanced into the South, Lincoln in 1862 named military governors for Tennessee, Arkansas, and Louisiana. By the end of the following year he had formulated a plan for regular governments in those states and any others that might qualify.

LINCOLN'S PLAN AND CONGRESS'S RESPONSE   Acting under his pardon power, President Lincoln issued in late 1863 a Proclamation of Amnesty and Reconstruction, under which any rebel state could form a Union government whenever a number equal to 10 percent of those who had voted in 1860 took an oath of allegiance to the Constitution and the Union and had received a presidential pardon. Participants also had to swear support for laws and proclamations dealing with emancipation. Certain groups, however, were excluded from the pardon: civil and diplomatic officers of the Confederacy; senior officers of the Confederate army and navy; judges, congressmen, and military officers of the United States who had left their federal posts to aid the rebellion; and those accused of failure to treat captured black soldiers and their officers as prisoners of war. Under this plan, loyal governments appeared in Tennessee, Arkansas, and Louisiana, but Congress recognized them neither by representation nor in counting the electoral votes of 1864.

In the absence of any specific provisions for Reconstruction in the Constitution, politicians disagreed as to where authority properly rested. Lincoln claimed the right to direct Reconstruction under the clause that set forth the presidential pardon power, and also under the constitutional obligation of the United States to guarantee each state a republican form of government. Republican congressmen, however, argued that this obligation implied a power of Congress to act.

A few conservative and most moderate Republicans supported Lincoln's program of immediate restoration. A small but influential group known as Radical Republicans, however, favored a sweeping transformation of southern society based on granting freedmen full-fledged citizenship. The Radicals hoped to reconstruct southern society so as to mirror the North's emphasis on small-scale capitalism. This meant thwarting the efforts of the old planter class to reestablish a caste system and keep the freed blacks in a state of peonage.

The Radicals also maintained that Congress, not the president, should supervise the Reconstruction program. To this end, they helped pass in 1864 the Wade-Davis Bill, sponsored by Senator Benjamin Wade of Ohio and Representative Henry Winter Davis of Maryland. In contrast to Lincoln's 10 percent plan, the Wade-Davis Bill required that a majority of white male citizens declare their allegiance and that only those who could take an "ironclad" oath (required of federal officials since 1862) attesting to their *past* loyalty could vote or serve in the state constitutional conventions. The conventions, moreover, would have to abolish slavery, exclude from political rights high-ranking civil and military officers of the Confederacy, and repudiate debts incurred "under the sanction of the usurping power."

Passed during the closing day of the session, the Wade-Davis Bill never became law. Lincoln exercised a pocket veto. That is, he simply refused to sign it, but he issued an artful statement that he would accept any state that preferred to present itself under the congressional plan. The sponsors responded with the Wade-Davis Manifesto, which accused the president, among other sins, of usurping power and attempting to use readmitted states to ensure his reelection.

Lincoln offered his last public words on Reconstruction in his final public address, on April 11, 1865. Speaking from the White House balcony, he pronounced that the Confederate states had never left the Union. These states were simply "out of their proper practical relation with the Union," and the object was to get them "into their proper practical relation." It would be easier to do this by merely ignoring the abstract issue: "Finding themselves safely at home, it would be utterly immaterial whether they had been abroad." At a cabinet meeting, Lincoln proposed to get state governments in operation before Congress met in December. He described the Radicals as possessing feelings of hate and vindictiveness with which he did not sympathize and could not participate. He wanted "no persecution, no bloody work," no radical restructuring of southern social and economic life.

THE ASSASSINATION OF LINCOLN   That evening Lincoln went to Ford's Theater and his rendezvous with death. With his trusted bodyguard called away to Richmond and with the Metropolitan policeman assigned to his box away from his post watching the play, Lincoln was helpless as John Wilkes Booth slipped into the presidential box. Booth, a crazed actor and Confederate zealot who thought he was helping the South, blocked the door to the box and then fired his derringer point-blank at the president's head, before stabbing Lincoln's aide and jumping from the box onto the stage, crying *"Sic semper tyrannis"* (Thus always to tyrants), the motto of Virginia. The president died nine hours after he had been shot. Accomplices had also targeted Vice-President Andrew Johnson and Secretary of State William Seward. Seward and four others, including his son, were victims of severe but not fatal stab wounds. Johnson escaped injury, however, because his would-be assassin got cold feet and wound up tipsy in the barroom of Johnson's hotel.

The nation extracted a full measure of vengeance from the conspirators. Although he had escaped the night he shot Lincoln, Booth was pursued into Virginia and trapped and shot in a burning barn. His last words were: "Tell Mother I die for my country. I thought I did for the best." Three of Booth's collaborators were convicted by a military commission and hanged, along with the woman at whose boardinghouse they had plotted. Three others got life sentences, including a Maryland doctor who set the leg Booth had broken when he jumped to the stage. President Johnson eventually pardoned them all, except one who died in prison. The doctor achieved lasting fame by making common a once obscure expression. His name was Mudd. Apart from those cases, however, there was only one other execution in the aftermath of war: Henry Wirz, who commanded the infamous prison at Andersonville, Georgia, where Union prisoners were probably more the victims of war conditions than of deliberate cruelty.

City Hall in New York City, on April 24, was thronged with people anxious for a last look at Lincoln.

JOHNSON'S PLAN Lincoln's death suddenly elevated to the White House Andrew Johnson of Tennessee, a man whose state was still in legal limbo and whose party affiliation was unclear. He was a War Democrat who had been put on the Union ticket in 1864 as a gesture of unity. Of humble origins like Lincoln, Johnson had moved as a youth from his birthplace in Raleigh, North Carolina, to Greeneville, Tennessee, where he became proprietor of a tailor shop. Self-educated with the help of his wife, he had made himself into an effective orator of the rough-and-tumble school, served as mayor, congressman, governor, and senator, then as military governor of Tennessee before he became vice-president. In the process he had become an advocate of the small farmers against the privileges of the large planters. He also shared the racial attitudes of most white yeomen. "Damn the negroes," he exclaimed to a friend during the war, "I am fighting those traitorous aristocrats, their masters."

Some of the Radicals at first thought Johnson, unlike Lincoln, to be one of them. Johnson had, for example, once asserted that treason "must be made infamous and traitors must be impoverished." Senator Benjamin Wade loved such language. "Johnson, we have faith in you,"

Andrew Johnson.

he promised. "By the gods, there will be no trouble now in running this government." But Wade would soon find him as unsympathetic as Lincoln, if for different reasons.

Johnson's very loyalty to the Union sprang from a strict adherence to the Constitution. Given to dogmatic abstractions that were alien to Lincoln's temperament, he nevertheless arrived by a different route at similar objectives. The states should be brought back into their proper relation to the Union because the states and the Union were indestructible. And like many other whites, he found it hard to accept the growing Radical movement toward suffrage for blacks. In 1865 Johnson declared that "there is no such thing as reconstruction. Those States have not gone out of the Union. Therefore reconstruction is unnecessary."

Johnson's plan to restore the Union thus closely resembled Lincoln's. A new Proclamation of Amnesty (May 1865) added to those Lincoln had excluded from pardon everybody with taxable property worth more than $20,000. These wealthy planters, bankers, and merchants were the people Johnson believed had led the South into secession. But those in the excluded groups might make special applications for pardon directly to the president, and before the year was out Johnson had issued some 13,000 such pardons. In every case Johnson ruled that pardon, whether by general amnesty or special clemency, restored one's property rights in land. Johnson's rulings nipped in the bud an experiment in land distribution that had barely begun. More than seventy years later, one freed slave, born in Orange County, North Carolina, spoke bluntly of his dashed hopes: "Lincoln got the praise for freeing us, but did he do it? He give us freedom without giving us any chance to live to ourselves and we still had to depend on the southern white man for work, food and clothing, and he held us through our necessity and want in a state of servitude but little better than slavery."

On the same day that Johnson announced his amnesty program, he issued another proclamation to his native state of North Carolina. Within six more weeks, he issued similar edicts for the other Rebel states not already organized. In each a native Unionist became provisional governor with authority to call a convention of men elected by loyal voters. Lincoln's 10 percent requirement was omitted. Johnson called upon the conventions to invalidate the secession ordinances, abolish slavery, and repudiate all debts incurred to aid the Confederacy. Each state, moreover, was to ratify the Thirteenth Amendment. Lincoln had privately advised the governor of Louisiana to consider a grant of suffrage to some blacks, "the very intelligent and those who have fought gallantly in our ranks." In his final public address he had also endorsed a limited black suffrage. Johnson repeated Lincoln's advice. He reminded the provisional governor of Mississippi, for example, that the state conventions might "with perfect safety" extend suffrage to blacks with education or with military service so as to "disarm the adversary"—the adversary being "radicals who are wild upon Negro franchise."

The state conventions for the most part met Johnson's requirements, although South Carolina and Mississippi did not repudiate their debt and the new Mississippi legislature refused to ratify the Thirteenth Amendment. Presidential agents sent to the South reported "that the mass of thinking men of the south accept the present situation of affairs in good faith." But Carl Schurz of Missouri found during his visit to the South "an *utter absence of national feeling* . . . and a desire to preserve slavery . . . as much and as long as possible." The discrepancy between the two reports is perhaps only apparent: southern whites accepted the situation because they thought so little had changed after all. Emboldened by Johnson's indulgence, they ignored his counsels of expediency. Suggestions of black suffrage were scarcely raised in the conventions and promptly squelched when they were.

SOUTHERN INTRANSIGENCE   When Congress met in December 1865, for the first time since the end of the war, it faced the fact that state governments were functioning in the South, and they were remarkably like the old. Southern voters had acted with extreme disregard of northern feelings. Among the new legislative members presenting themselves were Georgia's Alexander H. Stephens, ex-vice-president of the Confederacy, now claiming a seat in the Senate, four Confederate generals, eight colonels, six cabinet members, and a host of lesser Rebels. The Congress forthwith denied seats to all members from the eleven former Confederate states. It was too much to expect, after four bloody years, that Unionists would welcome ex-Confederates like prodigal sons.

Furthermore, the new southern legislatures, in passing repressive "Black Codes" restricting the freedom of blacks, demonstrated that they intended to preserve slavery as nearly as possible. As one white southerner stressed, "the ex-slave was not a free man; he was a free Negro," and the Black Codes were intended to highlight the distinction. The codes extended to blacks certain rights they had not hitherto enjoyed, but universally set them aside as a separate caste subject to special restraints. Details varied from state to state, but some provisions were common. Existing marriages, including common-law marriages, were recognized (although interracial marriages were prohibited), and testimony of blacks was accepted in legal cases involving blacks—and in six states, in all cases. Blacks could own property. They could sue and be sued in the courts. On the other hand, blacks could not own farm lands in Mississippi or city lots in South Carolina; they were required to buy special licenses to practice certain trades in Mississippi; and in some states they could not carry firearms without a license to do so.

The codes' labor provisions confirmed suspicions that whites were seeking to preserve the slave labor system. Blacks were required to enter into annual labor contracts, with provision for punishment in case of violation. Dependent children were subject to compulsory apprenticeship and corporal punishment by masters. Vagrants were punished with severe fines and, if unable to pay, they were forced to labor in the fields for those who paid the courts for this source of cheap labor. To many people it indeed seemed that slavery was on the way back in another guise. The new Mississippi penal code virtually said so: "All penal and criminal laws now in force describing the mode of punishment of crimes and misdemeanors committed by slaves, free negroes, or mulat-

Slavery Is Dead (?) *Thomas Nast's cartoon suggests that, in 1866, slavery was only legally dead.*

toes are hereby reenacted, and decreed to be in full force against all freedmen, free negroes and mulattoes."

Faced with such evidence of southern intransigence, moderate Republicans drifted toward Radical views. Having excluded southern members, the new Congress set up a Joint Committee on Reconstruction, with nine members from the House and six from the Senate, to gather evidence and submit proposals. Initiative on the committee fell to determined Radicals who knew what they wanted: Ben Wade of Ohio, George W. Julian of Indiana—and most conspicuously of all, Thaddeus Stevens of Pennsylvania and Charles Sumner of Massachusetts.

THE RADICALS   Most Radicals had been connected with the anti-slavery cause. While one could be hostile to both slavery and blacks, many whites approached the question of black rights with a humanitarian impulse. Few could escape the bitterness bred by the long and bloody war, however, or remain unaware of the partisan advantage that would come to the Republican party from black suffrage. But the party of Union and freedom, after all, could best guarantee the fruits of vic-

Two leading Radicals: Senator Charles Sumner (left) *and Representative Thaddeus Stevens* (right).

tory, they reasoned, and black suffrage could best guarantee black rights.

The growing conflict of opinion over Reconstruction policy brought about an inversion in constitutional reasoning. Secessionists—and Johnson—were now arguing that their states had in fact remained in the Union, and some Radicals were contriving arguments that they had left the Union after all. Thaddeus Stevens argued that the Confederate states were now conquered provinces, subject to the absolute will of the victors. Charles Sumner maintained that the southern states, by their pretended acts of secession, had in effect committed suicide and reverted to the status of unorganized territories subject to the will of Congress. But few ever took such ideas seriously. Republicans converged instead on the "forfeited-rights theory," later embodied in the report of the Joint Committee on Reconstruction. This held that the states as entities continued to exist, but by the acts of secession and war had forfeited "all civil and political rights under the constitution." And Congress was the proper authority to determine conditions under which such rights might be restored.

JOHNSON'S BATTLE WITH CONGRESS   A long year of political battling remained, however, before this idea triumphed. By the end of 1865, Radical views had gained a majority in Congress, if one not yet large enough to override presidential vetoes. But the critical year 1866 saw the gradual waning of Johnson's power and influence; much of this was self-induced. Johnson first challenged Congress in 1866, when he vetoed a bill to extend the life of the Freedmen's Bureau. The measure, he said, assumed that wartime conditions still existed, whereas the country had returned "to a state of peace and industry." No longer valid as a war measure, the bill violated the Constitution in several ways, he declared. It made the federal government responsible for the care of indigents. It was passed by a Congress in which eleven states were denied seats. And it used vague language in defining the "civil rights and immunities" of blacks. The Congress soon moved to correct that particular defect, but for the time being Johnson's prestige remained sufficiently intact that the Senate upheld his veto.

Three days after the veto, however, Johnson undermined his already weakening prestige with a fiery assault on Radical leaders during an impromptu speech. The Joint Committee on Reconstruction, he charged, was "an irresponsible central directory" that had repudiated the principle of an indestructible Union and accepted the legality of secession by entertaining conquered-province and state-suicide theories. From that point forward, moderate Republicans backed away from a president who had opened himself to counterattack. He was "an alien enemy of a foreign state," Stevens declared. Sumner called him "an insolent drunken brute"—and Johnson was open to the charge because of an incident at his vice-presidential inauguration. Weakened by illness at the time, he had taken a belt of brandy to get him through the ceremony and, under the influence of fever and alcohol, had become incoherent.

In mid-March 1866 Congress passed the Civil Rights Act. A response to the Black Codes, this bill declared that "all persons born in the United States and not subject to any foreign power, excluding Indians not taxed," were citizens entitled to "full and equal benefit of all laws." The grant of citizenship to native-born blacks, Johnson fumed, went beyond anything formerly held to be within the scope of federal power. It would, moreover, "foment discord among the races." Johnson vetoed the bill, but this time, on April 9, 1866, Congress overrode the presidential veto. On July 16 it enacted a revised Freedmen's Bureau Bill, again overriding a veto. From that point on, Johnson steadily lost both public and political support.

THE FOURTEENTH AMENDMENT   To remove all doubt about the constitutionality of the new Civil Rights Act, which was justified as implementing freedom under the Thirteenth Amendment, the Joint Committee recommended a new amendment, which passed Congress on June 16, 1866, and was ratified by the states on July 28, 1868. The Fourteenth Amendment, however, went far beyond the Civil Rights Act. It merits close scrutiny because of its broad impact on subsequent laws and litigation.

The first section asserted four principles: it reaffirmed state and federal citizenship for persons born or naturalized in the United States, and it forbade any *state* (the word "state" was important in later litigation) to abridge the "privileges and immunities" of citizens, to deprive any *person* (again an important term) of life, liberty, or property without "due process of law," or to deny any person "the equal protection of the laws."

The last three of these clauses have been the subject of lawsuits resulting in applications not widely, if at all, foreseen at the time. The "due-process clause" has come to mean that state as well as federal power is subject to the Bill of Rights, and it has been used to protect corporations, as legal "persons," from "unreasonable" regulation by the states. Other provisions of the amendment had less far-reaching effects. One section specified that the debt of the United States "shall not be questioned," but declared "illegal and void" all debts contracted in aid of the rebellion. Another section specified the power of Congress to pass laws enforcing the amendment.

Johnson's home state was among the first to ratify the Fourteenth Amendment. In Tennessee, which had harbored probably more Unionists than any other Confederate state, the government had fallen under Radical control. The state's governor, in reporting the results to the secretary of the Senate, added: "Give my respects to the dead dog of the White House." His words afford a fair sample of the growing acrimony on both sides of the Reconstruction debates. In May and July, bloody race riots in Memphis and New Orleans added fuel to the flames. Both incidents involved indiscriminate massacres of blacks by local police and white mobs. The carnage, Radicals argued, was the natural fruit of Johnson's policy. "Witness Memphis, witness New Orleans," Sumner cried. "Who can doubt that the President is the author of these tragedies?"

RECONSTRUCTING THE SOUTH

THE TRIUMPH OF CONGRESSIONAL RECONSTRUCTION   As 1866 drew to an end, the congressional elections promised to be a referendum on the growing split between Johnson and the Radicals. Johnson sought to influence voters with a speaking tour of the Midwest, a "swing around the circle," which turned into an undignified shouting contest between Johnson and his critics. In Cleveland he described the Radicals as "factious, domineering, tyrannical" men, and he foolishly exchanged hot-tempered insults with a heckler. At another stop, while Johnson was speaking from an observation car, the engineer mistakenly pulled the train out of the station, making the president appear quite the fool. Such incidents tended to confirm his image as a "ludicrous boor" and "drunken imbecile," which Radical papers projected. When the returns of the congressional elections came in, the Republicans had well over a two-thirds majority in each house, a comfortable margin with which to override any presidential vetoes.

The Congress in fact enacted a new program even before new members took office. Two acts passed in 1867 extended the suffrage to African Americans in the District of Columbia and the territories. An-

This cartoon appeared at the time of the 1866 congressional elections. It shows "King Andy I" approving the execution of Radical leaders in Congress.

other law provided that the new Congress would convene on March 4 instead of the following December, depriving Johnson of a breathing spell. On March 2, 1867, two days before the old Congress expired, it passed three basic laws of congressional Reconstruction over Johnson's vetoes: the Military Reconstruction Act, the Command of the Army Act (an amendment to an army appropriation), and the Tenure of Office Act.

The first of the three acts prescribed new conditions under which the formation of southern state governments should begin all over again. The other two sought to block obstruction by the president. The Command of the Army Act required that all orders from the commander-in-chief go through the headquarters of the general of the army, then Ulysses S. Grant, who could not be reassigned outside Washington without the consent of the Senate. The Radicals had faith in Grant, who was already leaning their way. The Tenure of Office Act required the consent of the Senate for the president to remove any officeholder whose appointment the Senate had to confirm in the first place. The purpose of at least some congressmen was to retain Secretary of War Edwin M. Stanton, the one Radical sympathizer in Johnson's cabinet. But an ambiguity crept into the wording of the act. Cabinet officers, it said, should serve during the term of the president who appointed them—and Lincoln had appointed Stanton, although, to be sure, Johnson was serving out Lincoln's term.

The Military Reconstruction Act, often hailed or denounced as the triumphant victory of "Radical" Reconstruction, actually represented a compromise that fell short of a thoroughgoing radicalism. As first reported from the Reconstruction Committee by Thaddeus Stevens, it would have given military commanders in the South ultimate control over law enforcement and would have left open indefinitely the terms of future restoration. More moderate elements, however, pushed through the "Blaine Amendment." Along with programs of land confiscation and education, it scrapped the prolonged national control under which Radicals hoped to put through the far more revolutionary program of reducing the Rebel states to territories. It did require that southern states accept black suffrage and ratify the Fourteenth Amendment.

The act began with a pronouncement that "no legal state governments or adequate protection for life and property now exists in the rebel States. . . ." One state, Tennessee, which had ratified the Fourteenth Amendment, was exempted from the application of the act. The other ten were divided into five military districts, and the commanding officer of each was authorized to keep order and protect the "rights of persons and property." To that end he might use military tribunals in place of civil courts. The Johnson governments remained intact for the time being, but new constitutions were to be framed "in conformity with the Constitution of the United States," in conventions elected by male citizens twenty-one and older "of whatever race, color, or previous condition." Each state constitution had to provide the same universal male suffrage. Then, once the constitution was ratified by a majority of voters and accepted by Congress, other criteria had to be met. The state legislature had to ratify the Fourteenth Amendment, and once the amendment became part of the Constitution, any given state would be entitled to representation in Congress. Persons excluded from office-holding by the proposed amendment were also excluded from participation in the process.

Johnson reluctantly appointed military commanders under the act, but the situation remained uncertain for a time. Some people expected the Supreme Court to strike down the act, and for the time being no machinery existed for the new elections. Congress quickly remedied that on March 23, 1867, with the Second Reconstruction Act, which directed the commanders to register for voting all adult males who swore they were qualified. A Third Reconstruction Act, passed on July 19, directed registrars to go beyond the loyalty oath and determine each person's eligibility to take it, and also authorized district commanders to remove and replace officeholders of any existing "so-called state" or division thereof. Before the end of 1867 new elections had been held in all the states but Texas.

Having clipped the president's wings, the Republican Congress moved a year later to safeguard its program from possible interference by the Supreme Court, which in a series of decisions had shown a readiness to question certain actions related to Reconstruction. With the Court considering *Ex parte McCardle*, the case of a Vicksburg editor arrested for criticizing the administration of the Fourth Military District who now sought release under the Habeas Corpus Act of 1867, Congress acted. On March 27, 1868, it simply removed the power of the Supreme Court to review cases arising under the law, which Congress clearly had the right to do under its power to define the Court's appellate jurisdiction. The Court accepted this curtailment on the same day it affirmed the principle of an "indestructible union" in *Texas* v. *White* (1868). In that case it also asserted the right of Congress to reframe state governments.

THE IMPEACHMENT AND TRIAL OF JOHNSON   Congress's move to restrain the Supreme Court preceded by just a few days the opening arguments in the trial of the president in the Senate on an impeachment brought in by the House. Johnson, though hostile to the congressional program, had gone through the motions required of him. He continued, however, to pardon former Confederates and replaced several district commanders whose Radical sympathies offended him. Nevertheless a lengthy investigation by the House Judiciary Committee, extending through most of 1867, had failed to convince the House that grounds for impeachment existed.

Johnson himself provided the occasion for impeachment when he deliberately violated the Tenure of Office Act in order to test its constitutionality in the courts. Secretary of War Edwin M. Stanton had become a thorn in the president's side, refusing to resign despite his disagreements with the president's Reconstruction policy. On August 12, 1867, during a congressional recess, Johnson suspended Stanton and named General Grant in his place. Grant's political stance was ambiguous at the time, but his acceptance implied cooperation with Johnson. When the Senate refused to confirm Johnson's action, however, Grant returned the office to Stanton. The president thereupon named General Lorenzo Thomas as secretary of war after a futile effort to interest General William T. Sherman. Three days later, on February 24, 1868, the House voted to impeach the president.

Of the eleven articles of impeachment, eight focused on the charge that Johnson had unlawfully removed Stanton and had failed to give the Senate the name of a successor. Article 9 accused the president of issuing orders in violation of the Command of the Army Act. The last two articles in effect charged him with criticizing Congress by "inflammatory and scandalous harangues" and by claiming that the Congress was not legally valid without southern representatives. But Article 11 accused Johnson of "unlawfully devising and contriving" to violate the Reconstruction Acts, contrary to his obligation to execute the laws. At the least, it stated, Johnson had tried to obstruct Congress's will while observing the letter of the law.

House of Representatives managers of the impeachment proceedings and trial of Andrew Johnson. Among them were Benjamin Butler (R-Mass., seated left) and Thaddeus Stevens (R-Pa., seated with cane).

The Senate trial opened on March 5 and continued until May 26, with Chief Justice Salmon P. Chase presiding. Seven managers from the House, including Thaddeus Stevens and Benjamin F. Butler, directed the prosecution. The president was spared the humiliation of a personal appearance. His defense counsel shrewdly insisted on narrowing the trial to questions that would be indictable offenses under the law, and steered the questions away from Johnson's manifest wish to frustrate the will of Congress. Such questions, they contended, were purely political in nature. In the end, enough Republican senators joined their pro-Johnson colleagues to prevent conviction. The vote, first on May 16 and then on May 26, was 35 for guilty and 19 for not guilty, one vote short of the two-thirds needed to convict. Thereupon the Senate dissolved the tribunal.

In a parliamentary system Johnson probably would have been removed as leader of the government long before then. But by deciding the case on the narrowest grounds, the Senate made it unlikely that any future president could ever be removed except for the gravest offenses, and almost surely not for flouting the will of Congress in executing the laws. Impeachment of Johnson was in the end a great political mistake, for the failure to remove the president damaged Radical morale and support. Nevertheless, the Radical cause did gain something. To blunt the opposition, Johnson agreed not to obstruct the process of Reconstruction, named a secretary of war who was committed to enforcing the new laws, and sent to Congress the new Radical constitutions of Arkansas and South Carolina. Thereafter his obstruction ceased and Radical Reconstruction began in earnest.

REPUBLICAN RULE IN THE SOUTH   In June 1868 Congress agreed that seven states had met the conditions for readmission, all but Virginia, Mississippi, and Texas. Congress rescinded Georgia's admission, however, when the state legislature expelled twenty-eight black members and seated some former Confederate leaders. The military commander of Georgia then forced the legislature to reseat the black members and remove the Confederates, and the state was compelled to ratify the Fifteenth Amendment before being admitted in July 1870. Mississippi, Texas, and Virginia had returned earlier in 1870, under the added requirement that they too ratify the Fifteenth Amendment. This amendment, submitted to the states in 1869, ratified in 1870, forbade the states to deny any person the vote on grounds of race, color, or previous condition of servitude.

Long before the new governments were established, Republican groups began to spring up in the South, chiefly sponsored by the Union League, founded at Philadelphia in 1862 to promote support for the Union. Emissaries of the league enrolled African Americans and loyal whites, initiated them into the secrets and rituals of the order, and instructed them "in their rights and duties." Their recruiting efforts were so successful that in 1867, on the eve of South Carolina's choice of convention delegates, the league reported eighty-eight chapters, which claimed to have enrolled almost every adult black male in the state.

THE RECONSTRUCTED SOUTH

THE FREED SLAVES   To focus solely on what white Republicans did to reconstruct the defeated South creates the false impression that the freed slaves were simply pawns in the hands of others. In fact, however, southern blacks were active agents in affecting the course of Reconstruction. Although many of them found themselves liberated but destitute after the fighting ended, the mere promise of freedom raised their hopes about achieving a biracial democracy, equal justice, and economic opportunity. "Most anyone ought to know that a man is better off free than as a slave, even if he did not have anything," said the Reverend E. P. Holmes, a black Georgia preacher and former domestic servant. "I would rather be free and have my liberty."

Participation in the Union army or navy gave many freedmen a training ground in leadership. Black military veterans would form the core of the first generation of African-American political leaders in the postwar South. Military service provided many former slaves with the first opportunities to learn to read and write. Army life also alerted them to alternative social choices and to new opportunities for advancement and respectability. "No negro who has ever been a soldier," reported a northern official after visiting a black unit, "can again be imposed upon; they have learnt what it is to be free and they will infuse their feelings into others." Fighting for the Union cause also instilled a fervent sense of nationalism. A Virginia freedman explained that the United States was "now *our* country—made emphatically so by the blood of our brethren."

Former slaves established independent black churches after the war, churches that would serve as the foundation of African-American community life. In war-ravaged Charleston, South Carolina, the first new building to appear after the war was a black church on Calhoun Street; by 1866 ten more had been built. Blacks preferred Baptist churches over other denominations, in part because of their decentralized structure that allowed each congregation to worship in its own way. By 1890 there were over 1.3 million black Baptists in the South, nearly three times as many as any other black denomination. For many former slaves, churches were the first institutions they owned and controlled. In addition to forming viable new congregations, freed blacks organized thousands of fraternal, benevolent, and mutual-aid societies, clubs, lodges, and associations. Memphis, for example, had over two hundred such organizations; Richmond boasted twice that number.

The freed slaves, both women and men, also hastened to reestablish and reaffirm families. Marriages that had been prohibited were now legitimized through the assistance of the Freedmen's Bureau. By 1870 a preponderant majority of former slaves lived in two-parent households. One white editor in Georgia, lamenting the difficulty of finding black women to serve as house servants, reported that "every negro woman wants to set up house keeping" for herself and her family. To do so they often had little choice but to become tenant farmers, gaining access to land in exchange for a share of their crop. With little money or technical training, freed slaves faced the prospect of becoming wage laborers. Yet in order to retain as much autonomy as possible over their productive energies and those of their children on both a daily and seasonal basis, many husbands and wives chose sharecropping. This enabled mothers and wives to devote more of their time to domestic needs while still contributing to family income.

Black communities in the postwar South also sought to establish schools. The antebellum planter elite had denied education to blacks because they feared that literate slaves would organize uprisings. After the war the white elite worried that education programs would encourage both poor whites and blacks to leave the South in search of better social and economic opportunities. Economic leaders wanted to protect the competitive advantage afforded by the region's low-wage labor market.

The general resistance among the former slaveholding class to new education initiatives forced the freed slaves to rely on northern assistance or take their own initiative. A Mississippi Freedmen's Bureau agent noted in 1865 that when he told a gathering of some 3,000 former slaves that they "were to have the advantages of schools and education, their joy knew no bounds. They fairly jumped and shouted in gladness." Black churches and individuals helped raise the money and often built the schools and paid the teachers. Soldiers who had acquired some reading and writing skills often served as the first teachers, and the students included adults as well as children. A Florida teacher reported that a sixty-year-old former slave woman in her class was so excited by literacy that she "spells her lesson all the evening, then she dreams about it, and wakes up thinking about it."

BLACKS IN SOUTHERN POLITICS   The new role of African Americans in politics caused the most controversy, then and afterward. If largely illiterate and inexperienced in the rudiments of politics, they were little different from millions of whites enfranchised in the age of Jackson or immigrants herded to the polls by political bosses in New York and other cities after the war. Some freedmen frankly confessed their disadvantages. Beverly Nash, a black delegate in the South Carolina convention of 1868, told his colleagues: "I believe, my friends and fellow-citizens, we are not prepared for this suffrage. But we can learn.

Give a man tools and let him commence to use them, and in time he will learn a trade. So it is with voting."

Several hundred black delegates participated in the statewide political conventions. Most had been selected by local political meetings or by churches, fraternal societies, Union Leagues, and black army units from the North, although a few simply appointed themselves. "Some bring credentials," explained a North Carolina black leader, "others had as much as they could to bring themselves, having to escape from their homes stealthily at night" to avoid white assaults. The African-American delegates "ranged all colors and apparently all conditions," but free mulattoes from the cities played the most prominent roles. At Louisiana's Republican state convention, for instance, nineteen of the twenty black delegates had been born free.

By 1867, however, former slaves began to gain political influence and vote in large numbers, and this revealed emerging tensions within the black community. Some southern blacks resented the presence of

Black Suffrage. *The Fifteenth Amendment was passed in 1870 and guaranteed the right of citizens, including the right to vote, regardless of race, color or previous condition of servitude, on the federal level. But former slaves had been registering to vote and voting in large numbers in state elections since 1867, as shown here.*

northern brethren who moved south after the war, while others complained that few ex-slaves were represented in leadership positions. Northern blacks and the southern free black elite, most of whom were urban dwellers, tended to oppose efforts to confiscate and redistribute land to the rural freedmen, and many insisted that political equality did not mean social equality. As an Alabama black leader stressed, "We do not ask that the ignorant and degraded shall be put on a social equality with the refined and intelligent." In general, however, unity rather than dissension prevailed, and blacks focused on common concerns such as full equality under the law.

Brought suddenly into politics in times that tried the most skilled of statesmen, many African Americans served with distinction. Nonetheless, the derisive label "black Reconstruction" used by later critics exaggerates black political influence, which was limited mainly to voting,

A lithograph depicting five of the major black political figures of the Reconstruction period: Hiram Revels (top left) and Blanche K. Bruce (center) served in the U.S. Senate, Joseph H. Rainey (bottom left), John R. Lynch (bottom right), and James T. Rapier (top right) in the House of Representatives.

and overlooks the large numbers of white Republicans, especially in the mountain areas of the upper South. Only one of the new conventions, South Carolina's, had a black majority, 76 to 41. Louisiana's was evenly divided racially, and in only two other conventions were more than 20 percent of the members black: Florida's, with 40 percent, and Virginia's, with 24 percent. The Texas convention was only 10 percent black, and North Carolina's 11 percent—but that did not stop a white newspaper from calling it a body consisting of "baboons, monkeys, mules . . . and other jackasses."

In the new state governments, any African-American participation was a novelty. Although some 600 blacks—most of them former slaves—served as state legislators, no black man was ever elected governor. Only a few served as judges, although in Louisiana Pinckney B. S. Pinchback, a northern black and former Union soldier, won the office of lieutenant-governor and served as acting governor when the white governor was indicted for corruption. Several blacks were elected lieutenant-governors, state treasurers, or secretaries of state. There were two black senators in Congress, Hiram Revels and Blanche K. Bruce, both Mississippi natives who had been educated in the North, and fourteen black members of the House during Reconstruction. Among these were some of the ablest congressmen of the time. African Americans served in every state legislature, and in South Carolina they made up a majority in both houses for two years.

CARPETBAGGERS AND SCALAWAGS The top positions in southern state governments went for the most part to white Republicans, whom the opposition whites soon labeled "carpetbaggers" and "scalawags," depending on their place of birth. The northern opportunists who allegedly rushed South with all their belongings in carpetbags to grab the political spoils were more often than not Union veterans who had arrived as early as 1865 or 1866, drawn South by the hope of economic opportunity and by other attractions that many of them had seen in Union service. Many other so-called carpetbaggers were teachers, social workers, or preachers animated by a missionary impulse.

The "scalawags," or native white Republicans, were even more reviled and misrepresented. A jaundiced editor of a Nashville paper called them the "merest trash that could be collected in a civilized community, of no personal credit or social responsibility." Most "scalawags" had op-

posed secession, forming a Unionist majority in many mountain counties as far south as Georgia and Alabama, and especially in the hills of
eastern Tennessee. Among the "scalawags" were several distinguished
figures, including former Confederate general James A. Longstreet,
who decided after Appomattox that the Old South must change its
ways. He became a successful cotton broker in New Orleans, joined
the Republican party, and supported the Radical Reconstruction program. Other "scalawags" were former Whigs who found the Republican
party's economic program of industrial and commercial expansion in
keeping with Henry Clay's earlier "American System."

THE RADICAL REPUBLICAN RECORD   The new state constitutions
were objectionable to adherents of the old order primarily because of
their provisions for black suffrage and civil rights. Otherwise the documents were in keeping with other state constitutions of the day, their
provisions often drawn from the basic laws of northern states. Most remained in effect for some years after the end of Radical control, and
later constitutions incorporated many of their features. Conspicuous
among Radical innovations were such steps toward greater democracy
as requiring universal manhood suffrage, reapportioning legislatures
more nearly according to population, and making more state offices
elective.

Given the hostile circumstances under which the Radical governments operated, their achievements are remarkable. For the first time
in most of the South they established state school systems, however inadequate and ill-supported at first. The testimony is almost universal
that African Americans eagerly sought education for themselves and
their children. Some 600,000 black pupils were in southern schools by
1877. State governments under the Radicals also gave more attention
than ever before to poor relief and to orphanages, asylums, and institutions for the deaf, dumb, and blind of both races. Public roads, bridges,
and buildings were repaired or rebuilt. Blacks achieved new rights and
opportunities that would never again be taken away, at least in principle: equality before the law and the rights to own property, carry on
business, enter professions, attend schools, and learn to read and write.

Yet several of these Republican regimes also engaged in corrupt practices. Bids for contracts were accepted at absurd prices, and public offi-

cials took their cut. Public money and public credit were often voted to privately owned corporations, notably railroads, under conditions that invited influence peddling. But governmental subsidies—especially for transportation—were common before and after Reconstruction (and still are), and the extension of public aid had general support among all elements, including the Radicals and their enemies. Taxes and public debt rose in every state. Yet the figures of taxation and debt hardly constitute an unqualified indictment of Radical governments, since they then faced unusual and inflated costs for the physical reconstruction of public works in the South. Most states, moreover, had to float loans at outrageous discounts, sometimes at 50 to 75 percent of face value, because of uncertain conditions.

Nor, for that matter, were the breaches of public morality limited to the South or to Republicans. The Democratic Tweed Ring at the time was robbing New York City of more than $75 million, while the Republican "Gas Ring" in Philadelphia was also lining its pockets. Corruption was not invented by the Radical regimes, nor did it die with them. Louisiana's "carpetbag" governor recognized as much: "Why," he said, "down here everybody is demoralized. Corruption is the fashion." In three years Louisiana's printing bill ran to $1.5 million, about half of which went to a newspaper belonging to the young governor, who left office with a tidy nest egg and settled down to a long life as a planter. At about the same time, Mississippi's Democratic state treasurer embezzled over $315,000. During Republican rule in Mississippi, on the other hand, there was no evidence of major corruption.

WHITE TERROR   The case of Mississippi strongly suggests that whites were hostile to Republican regimes less because of their corruption than because of their inclusion of blacks. Most white southerners remained unreconstructed, so conditioned by slavery that they were unable to conceive of blacks as citizens or even free agents. In some places hostility to the new biracial regimes took on the form of white terror. In Grayson County, Texas, three whites murdered three freed slaves because they felt the need to "thin the niggers out and drive them to their holes."

The prototype of terrorist groups was the Ku Klux Klan (KKK), first organized in 1866 by some young men of Pulaski, Tennessee, as a social

This Thomas Nast cartoon chides the Ku Klux Klan and the White League for promoting conditions "worse than slavery" for southern blacks after the Civil War.

club with the costumes, secret ritual, and mumbo-jumbo common to fraternal groups. At first a group devoted to practical jokes, the founders soon turned to intimidation of blacks and white Republicans, and the KKK and imitators like Louisiana's Knights of the White Camellia spread rapidly across the South in answer to the Republican party's Union League. Klansmen rode about the countryside hiding under masks and robes, spreading horrendous rumors, issuing threats, harassing African Americans, and occasionally running amok wreaking violence and destruction.

Klansmen focused their terror on prominent Republicans, black and white. In Mississippi they killed a black Republican leader in front of his family. Three white "scalawag" Republicans were murdered in Georgia in 1870. That same year an armed mob of whites assaulted a Republican political rally in Alabama, killing four blacks and wounding fifty-four. In South Carolina the Klan was especially active. Virtually the entire white male population of York County joined the Klan, and they were responsible for eleven murders and hundreds of whippings. In 1871 some 500 masked men laid siege to the Union County jail and eventually lynched eight black prisoners. Although most Klansmen were poor farmers and tradesmen, middle-class whites—planters, merchants, bankers, lawyers, doctors, even ministers—also joined the group and participated in its brutalities.

Congress struck back with three Enforcement Acts (1870–1871) to protect black voters. The first of these measures levied penalties on persons who interfered with any citizen's right to vote. A second placed the election of congressmen under surveillance by federal election supervisors and marshals. The third (the Ku Klux Klan Act) outlawed the characteristic activities of the Klan—forming conspiracies, wearing disguises, resisting officers, and intimidating officials—and authorized the president to suspend habeas corpus where necessary to suppress "armed combinations." In 1871, the federal government singled out nine counties in upcountry South Carolina as an example, suspended habeas corpus, and pursued mass prosecutions that brought an abrupt halt to the Klan outrages. The program of federal enforcement broke the back of the Klan, whose outrages declined steadily as conservative southerners resorted to more subtle methods.

CONSERVATIVE RESURGENCE   The Klan's impact on politics varied from state to state. In the upper South it played only a modest role in facilitating a Democratic resurgence. But in the Deep South, Klan violence and intimidation had some effect. In Georgia, for instance, Republicans virtually quit campaigning and voting. In overwhelmingly black Yazoo County, Mississippi, vengeful whites used violence to reverse the political balance of power. In the 1873 elections the Republicans cast 2,449 votes and the Democrats 638; two years later the Democrats polled 4,049 votes, the Republicans 7. Throughout the South the activities of the Klan weakened black and Republican morale, and in the North they encouraged a growing weariness with the whole southern question. "The plain truth is," noted the *New York Herald,* "the North has got tired of the Negro."

The erosion of northern interest in civil rights resulted from more than weariness, however. Western expansion, Indian wars, economic opportunities, and political controversy over the tariff and the currency distracted attention from southern outrages. In addition, after a business panic that occurred in 1873 and the ensuing depression, desperate economic circumstances in the North and South created new racial tensions that helped undermine already inconsistent federal efforts to promote racial justice in the former Confederacy. Republican control in the South gradually loosened as "Conservative" parties—Democrats used that name to mollify former Whigs—mobilized the white vote.

RECONSTRUCTION, 1865–1877

States with Reconstruction governments
1868 Date of readmission to the Union
1870 Date of reestablishment of conservative rule
2 Military districts set by Reconstruction Act, 1867
Means by which slavery was abolished
▲ Emancipation Proclamation, 1863
■ State action
◆ Thirteenth Amendment, 1865

Scalawags, and many carpetbaggers, drifted away from the Radical ranks under pressure from their white neighbors. Few of them had joined the Republicans out of concern for black rights in the first place. And where persuasion failed to work, Democrats were willing to use chicanery. As one enthusiastic Democrat boasted, "the white and black Republicans may outvote us, but we can outcount them."

Republican control collapsed in Virginia and Tennessee as early as 1869, in Georgia and North Carolina in 1870, although North Carolina had a Republican governor until 1876. Reconstruction lasted longest in the Deep South states with the largest black population, where whites abandoned Klan masks for barefaced intimidation in paramilitary groups such as the Mississippi Rifle Club and the South Carolina Red Shirts. By 1876 Radical regimes survived only in Louisiana, South Carolina, and Florida, and these all collapsed after the elections of that year. Later the last carpetbag governor of South Carolina explained that "the uneducated negro was too weak, no matter what his numbers, to cope with the whites."

THE GRANT YEARS

THE ELECTION OF 1868   Ulysses S. Grant, who presided over the collapse of Republican rule in the South, brought to the presidency little political experience. But in 1868 the rank-and-file voter could be expected to support "the Lion of Vicksburg" because of his record as a war leader. Both parties wooed him, but his falling-out with President Johnson pushed him toward the Republicans and built trust in him among the Radicals. They were, as Thad Stevens said, ready to "let him into the church." The Republican platform endorsed the Reconstruction policy of Congress, congratulating the country on the "assured success" of the program. One plank cautiously defended black suffrage as a necessity in the South, but a matter each northern state should settle for itself. Another urged payment of the national debt "in the utmost good faith to all creditors," which meant in gold. More important than the platform were the great expectations of a soldier-president and his slogan: "Let us have peace."

The Democrats took opposite positions on both Reconstruction and the debt. The Republican Congress, the platform charged, instead of restoring the Union had "so far as in its power, dissolved it, and subjected ten states, in the time of profound peace, to military despotism and Negro supremacy." As to the public debt, the party endorsed Representative George H. Pendleton's "Ohio idea" that, since most bonds had been bought with depreciated greenbacks, they should be paid off in greenbacks unless they specified payment in gold. With no conspicuously available candidate in sight, the convention turned to Horatio Seymour, war governor of New York and chairman of the convention. His friends had to hustle him out of the hall to prevent his withdrawal. The Democrats made a closer race of it than showed up in the electoral vote. Eight states, including New York and New Jersey, went for Seymour. While Grant swept the electoral college by 214 to 80, his popular majority was only 307,000 out of a total of over 5.7 million votes. More than 500,000 black voters accounted for Grant's margin of victory.

EARLY APPOINTMENTS   Grant had proven himself a great leader in the war, but in the White House he seemed blind to the political forces and influence peddlers around him. He was awestruck by men of

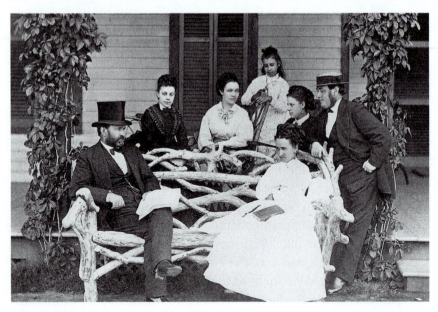

President Grant (seated at left), *with Mrs. Grant next to him, in a family portrait, 1870.*

wealth and unaccountably loyal to some who betrayed his trust. His conception of the presidency was "Whiggish." The chief executive carried out the laws; in the formulation of policy he passively followed the lead of Congress. This approach endeared him at first to party leaders, but it left him at last ineffective and left others disillusioned with his leadership.

At the outset Grant consulted nobody on his cabinet appointments. Some of his choices indulged personal whims; others simply displayed bad judgment. In some cases appointees learned of their nomination from the newspapers. As time went by Grant betrayed a fatal gift for losing men of talent and integrity from his cabinet. Secretary of State Hamilton Fish of New York turned out to be a happy exception; he guided foreign policy throughout the Grant presidency.

THE GOVERNMENT DEBT   Financial issues dominated the political agenda during Grant's presidency. After the war, the Treasury had assumed that the $432 million worth of greenbacks issued during the conflict would be retired from circulation and that the nation would revert to a "hard-money" currency—gold coins. Many agrarian and debtor groups resisted this contraction of the money supply, believing that it would mean lower prices for their crops and would make it harder for them to pay long-term debts. They were joined by a large number of Radicals who thought a combination of high tariffs and inflation would generate more rapid economic growth. In 1868 congressional supporters of such a "soft-money" policy halted the retirement of greenbacks, leaving $356 million outstanding. There matters stood when Grant took office.

The "sound" or hard-money advocates, mostly bankers and merchants, claimed that Grant's election was a mandate to save the country from the Democrats' "Ohio idea" of using greenbacks to repay government bonds. Quite influential in Republican circles, the "sound-money" advocates also had the benefit of a deeply ingrained popular assumption that hard money was morally preferable to paper currency. Grant agreed, and in his inaugural address he endorsed payment of the national debt in gold as a point of national honor. On March 18, 1869, the Public Credit Act endorsing that principle became the first act of Congress that he signed. Under the Refunding Act of 1870, the Treasury was able to replace 6 percent Civil War bonds with a new issue promising 4 to 5 percent in gold.

SCANDALS   The complexities of the "money question" exasperated Grant, but that was the least of his worries, for his administration soon fell into a cesspool of scandal. The first hint of scandal touched Grant in the summer of 1869, when the crafty Jay Gould and the flamboyant Jim Fisk connived with the president's brother-in-law to corner the gold market. Gould concocted an argument that the government should refrain from selling gold on the market because the resulting rise in gold prices would raise temporarily depressed farm prices. Grant apparently smelled a rat from the start, but he was seen in public with the speculators. As the rumor spread on Wall Street that the president had bought the argument, gold rose from $132 to $163 an ounce. When Grant finally persuaded his brother-in-law to pull out of the deal, Gould began quietly selling out. Finally, on "Black Friday," September 24, 1869, Grant ordered the Treasury to sell a large quantity of gold, and the bubble burst. Fisk got out by repudiating his agreements and hiring thugs to intimidate his creditors. "Nothing is lost save honor," he said.

The People's Handwriting on the Wall. *An 1872 engraving comments on the corruption engulfing Grant.*

The plot to corner the gold market was only the first of several scandals that rocked the Grant administration. During the campaign of 1872 the public first learned about the financial buccaneering of the Crédit Mobilier, a construction company that had milked the Union Pacific Railroad for exorbitant fees in order to line the pockets of insiders who controlled both firms. Rank-and-file Union Pacific shareholders were left holding the bag. One congressman had distributed Crédit Mobilier shares at bargain rates where, he said, "it will produce much good to us." This chicanery had transpired before Grant's election in 1868, but it now touched a number of prominent Republicans. The beneficiaries had included Speaker of the House Schuyler Colfax, later vice-president, and Representative James A. Garfield, later president. Of thirteen members of Congress involved, only two were censured by a Congress which, before it adjourned in 1873, voted itself a pay raise from $5,000 to $7,500—retroactive, it decided, for two years. A public uproar forced repeal, leaving only the raises voted the president (from $25,000 to $50,000) and Supreme Court justices.

Even more odious disclosures soon followed, and some involved the president's cabinet. The secretary of war, it turned out, had accepted bribes from merchants who traded with Indians at army posts in the West. He was impeached, but he resigned in time to elude a Senate trial. Post-office contracts, it was revealed, went to carriers who offered the highest kickbacks. The secretary of the treasury had awarded a political friend a commission of 50 percent for the collection of overdue taxes. In St. Louis a "Whiskey Ring" bribed tax collectors to bilk the government of millions in revenue. Grant's private secretary was enmeshed in that scheme, taking large sums of money and other valuables in return for inside information. There is no evidence that Grant himself was ever involved in, or that he personally profited from, any of the fraud, but his poor choice of associates earned him the public censure that was heaped upon his head.

REFORM AND THE ELECTION OF 1872   Long before Grant's first term ended, a reaction against the Reconstruction measures and against incompetence and corruption in the administration had incited mutiny within the Republican ranks. The Liberal Republicans favored free trade, gold to redeem greenbacks, a stable currency, restoring the rights of former Confederates, and civil service reform. Open revolt broke out first in Missouri where Carl Schurz, a German immigrant and war hero, led a group of Liberal Republicans that elected a governor

Horace Greeley, editor of the New York Tribune *and Liberal Republican candidate for president in 1872.*

with Democratic help in 1870 and sent Schurz to the Senate. In 1872 the Liberal Republicans held a national convention at Cincinnati that produced a compromise platform condemning the party's southern policy and favoring civil service reform, but remained silent on the protective tariff. The delegates embraced an anomalous presidential candidate: Horace Greeley, editor of the *New York Tribune,* a longtime champion of just about every reform of his time. His image as a visionary eccentric was complemented by his record of hostility to Democrats, whose support the Liberals needed. The Democrats nevertheless swallowed the pill and gave their nomination to Greeley as the only hope of beating Grant.

The result was a foregone conclusion. Republican regulars duly endorsed Radical Reconstruction and the protective tariff. Grant still had seven carpetbag states in his pocket, generous contributions from business and banking interests, and the stalwart support of the Radicals. Above all, he still evoked the imperishable glory of Appomattox. Greeley, despite an exhausting tour of the country—still unusual for a presidential candidate—carried only six southern and border states and none in the North. Grant won by 3,597,132 votes to Greeley's 2,834,125 votes, and by an electoral college vote of 286 to 66.

PANIC AND REDEMPTION   Economic distress followed close upon the public scandals besetting the Grant administration. Contraction of the money supply brought about by the withdrawal of greenbacks and expansion of the railroads into sparsely settled areas had made investors cautious and helped precipitate a crisis. During 1873 the market for railroad bonds turned sour as some twenty-five railroads defaulted on their interest payments. The investment-banking firm of Jay Cooke and Company, unable to sell the bonds of the Northern Pacific Railroad, financed them with short-term deposits in hope that a European market would develop. But in 1873 the opposite happened when a financial panic in Vienna forced many financiers to unload American stocks and bonds. Caught short, Cooke and Company went bankrupt on September 18, 1873. The ensuing stampede of investors to exchange securities for cash forced the stock market to close for ten days. The Panic of 1873 set off a depression that lasted for six years, the longest and most severe that Americans had yet suffered, marked by widespread bankruptcies, unemployment, and a drastic slowdown in railroad building.

Hard times and scandals hurt Republicans in the midterm elections of 1874. The Democrats won control of the House of Representatives and gained seats in the Senate. The new Democratic House immediately launched inquiries into the scandals and unearthed further evidence of corruption in high places. The panic meanwhile focused attention once more on greenback currency.

Since greenbacks were valued less than gold, they had become the chief circulating medium. Most people spent greenbacks first and held their gold or used it to settle foreign accounts, which drained much gold out of the country. The postwar reduction of greenbacks in circulation from $432 million to $356 million had made for tight money. To relieve deflation and stimulate business, therefore, the Treasury reissued $26 million in greenbacks that had been previously withdrawn.

For a time the advocates of paper money were riding high. But in 1874 Grant vetoed a bill to issue more greenbacks. Then, in his annual message he called for the gradual resumption of specie payments—that is, the redemption of greenbacks in gold. This would make greenbacks "good as gold" and raise their value to a par with the gold dollar. Congress obliged by passing the Resumption Act of 1875. The payment in gold to people who turned in their paper money began on January 1, 1879, after the Treasury had built a gold reserve for that purpose and reduced the value of greenbacks in circulation. This act infuriated those promoting an inflationary monetary policy and provoked the formation of the National Greenback party, which elected fourteen congressmen in 1878. The much-debated "money question" was destined to remain one of the most divisive issues in American politics.

THE COMPROMISE OF 1877 Grant, despite the controversies swirling around him, was eager to run again in 1876, but the recent scandals discouraged any challenge to the two-term tradition. James G. Blaine of Maine, former Speaker of the House, emerged as the Republican front-runner, but he too bore the taint of scandal. Letters in the possession of James Mulligan of Boston linked Blaine to some dubious railroad dealings, and these "Mulligan letters" found their way into print.

A Republican campaign piece from the 1876 election: "Yankee Doodle, that's the talk—/ We've found an honest dealer;/ And o'er the course we ride or walk,/ We'll go for Hayes and Wheeler."

The Republican convention therefore eliminated Blaine and several other hopefuls in favor of Ohio's favorite son, Rutherford B. Hayes. Three times elected governor of Ohio, most recently as an advocate of hard money, Hayes had also made a name as a civil service reformer. But his chief virtue was that he offended neither Radicals nor reformers. As Henry Adams put it, he was "a third rate nonentity, whose only recommendation is that he is obnoxious to no one."

The Democratic convention in St. Louis was abnormally harmonious from the start. The nomination went on the second ballot to Samuel J. Tilden, millionaire corporation lawyer and reform governor of New York who had directed a campaign to overthrow first the notorious Tweed Ring controlling New York City politics and the Canal Ring in Albany, which had bilked the state of millions.

The campaign generated no burning issues. Both candidates favored the trend toward conservative rule in the South. During one of the most corrupt elections ever, both candidates also favored civil service reform. In the absence of strong differences, Democrats waved the Republicans' dirty linen. In response, Republicans waved the bloody shirt, which is to say that they engaged in verbal assaults on former Confederates and the spirit of rebellion, linking the Democratic party with secession and with the outrages committed against black and white Republicans in the South. As one Republican speaker insisted, "Every man that tried to destroy this nation was a Democrat. . . . The man that assassinated Abraham Lincoln was a Democrat. . . . Soldiers, every scar you have on your heroic bodies was given you by a Democrat!" The phrase "waving the bloody shirt" originated at the impeachment trial of President Johnson when Benjamin F. Butler, speaking for the prosecution, displayed the bloody shirt a Mississippi carpetbagger had been wearing when hauled out of bed and beaten by Klansmen.

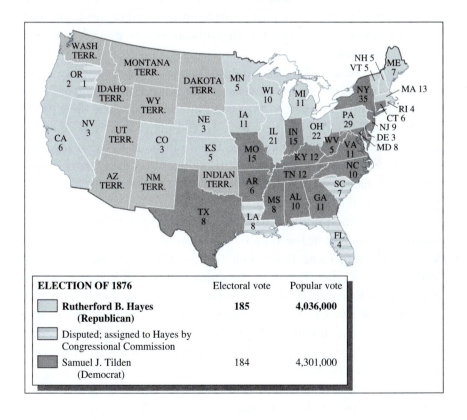

ELECTION OF 1876	Electoral vote	Popular vote
Rutherford B. Hayes (Republican)	185	4,036,000
Disputed; assigned to Hayes by Congressional Commission		
Samuel J. Tilden (Democrat)	184	4,301,000

Early election returns pointed to a Tilden victory. He enjoyed a 300,000 edge in the popular vote and had 184 electoral votes, just one short of a majority. Hayes had 165 electoral votes, but the Republicans also claimed nineteen doubtful votes from Florida, Louisiana, and South Carolina. The Democrats laid a counterclaim to one electoral vote from Oregon. But the Republicans had clearly carried Oregon. In the South the outcome was less certain, and given the fraud and intimidation perpetrated on both sides, nobody will ever know what might have happened if, to use a slogan of the day, "a free ballot and a fair count" had prevailed. As good a guess as any may be, as one writer suggested, that the Democrats stole the election first and the Republicans stole it back.

In all three of the disputed southern states, rival canvassing boards sent in different returns. In Florida, Republicans conceded the state election, but in Louisiana and South Carolina rival state governments also appeared. The Constitution offered no guidance in this unprecedented situation. Even if Congress were empowered to sort things out, the Democratic House and the Republican Senate proved unable to reach an agreement.

Finally, on January 29, 1877, the two houses decided to set up a special Electoral Commission that would investigate and report its findings. It had fifteen members, five each from the House, the Senate, and the Supreme Court. Members were so chosen as to have seven from each major party, with Justice David Davis of Illinois as the swing man. Davis, though appointed to the Court by Lincoln, was no party regular and was in fact thought to be leaning toward the Democrats. Thus, the panel appeared to be stacked in favor of Tilden.

But as it turned out, the panel got restacked the other way. Shortsighted Democrats in the Illinois legislature teamed up with minority Greenbackers to name Davis their senator. Davis accepted, no doubt with a sense of relief. From the remaining justices, all Republicans, the panel chose Joseph P. Bradley to fill the vacancy. The decision on each state went by a vote of 8 to 7, along party lines, in favor of Hayes. After much bluster and threat of filibuster by Democrats, the House voted on March 2 to accept the report and declare Hayes elected by an electoral vote of 185 to 184.

Critical to this outcome was the defection of southern Democrats who, seeing the way the wind was blowing with the composition of the

Electoral Commission, had made several informal agreements with the Republicans. On February 26, 1877, prominent Ohio Republicans (including James A. Garfield) and powerful southern Democrats struck a bargain at the Wormley House, a Washington hotel. The Republicans promised that, if elected, Hayes would withdraw the last federal troops from Louisiana and South Carolina, letting the Republican governments there collapse. In return, the Democrats promised to withdraw their opposition to Hayes, to accept in good faith the Reconstruction amendments, and to refrain from partisan reprisals against Republicans in the South.

Southern Democrats could now justify deserting Tilden because this so-called Compromise of 1877 brought a final "redemption" from the "Radicals" and a return to "home rule," which actually meant rule by white Democrats. Other, more informal promises, less noticed by the public, bolstered the Wormley House agreement. Hayes's friends pledged more support for Mississippi levees and other internal improvements, including a federal subsidy for a transcontinental railroad along a southern route. Southerners extracted a further promise that Hayes would name a white southerner as postmaster-general, the cabinet position with the most patronage jobs at hand. In return, southerners would let Republicans make Garfield Speaker of the new House.

THE END OF RECONSTRUCTION   In 1877 Hayes withdrew federal troops from the state houses in Louisiana and South Carolina, and the Republican governments there collapsed—along with much of Hayes's claim to legitimacy. Hayes chose a Tennessean and former Confederate as postmaster-general. But after southern Democrats failed to permit the choice of Garfield as Speaker, Hayes expressed doubt about any further subsidy for railroad building, and none was voted. Most of the other promises were either renounced or forgotten.

As to southern promises regarding the civil rights of blacks, only a few Democratic leaders, such as the new governors of South Carolina and Louisiana, remembered them for long. Over the next three decades those rights crumbled under the pressure of white rule in the South and the force of Supreme Court decisions narrowing the application of the Reconstruction amendments. Radical Reconstruction never offered more than an uncertain commitment to equality before the law. Yet it left an enduring legacy, the Thirteenth, Fourteenth, and Fifteenth Amendments—not dead but dormant, waiting to be awakened.

MAKING CONNECTIONS

- The political, economic, and racial policies of the conservatives who overthrew the Republican governments in the southern states are described in Chapter 19.

- Several of the political scandals mentioned in this chapter were related to the railroads, a topic discussed in greater detail in Chapter 20.

- This chapter ends with the election of Rutherford B. Hayes; for a discussion of Hayes's administration, see Chapter 22.

FURTHER READING

Reconstruction has long been "a dark and bloody ground" of conflicting interpretations. The most comprehensive treatment is Eric Foner's *Reconstruction: America's Unfinished Revolution, 1863–1877* (1988). More specialized works give closer scrutiny to the aims of the principal political figures. For a study of Andrew Johnson, see Hans L. Trefousse's *Andrew Johnson: A Biography* (1989). Why Johnson was impeached is detailed in Hans L. Trefousse's *Impeachment of a President: Andrew Johnson, the Blacks, and Reconstruction* (1975).

Scholars have been fairly sympathetic to the aims and motives of the Radical Republicans. See, for instance, Herman Belz's *Reconstructing the Union* (1969) and Richard Nelson Current's *Those Terrible Carpetbaggers: A Reinterpretation* (1988). The ideology of these Radicals is explored in Michael Les Benedict's *A Compromise of Principle: Congressional Republicans and Reconstruction, 1863–1869* (1974).

The intransigence of southern white attitudes is examined in Michael Perman's *Reunion without Compromise* (1973), Dan T. Carter's *When the War Was Over: The Failure of Self-Reconstruction in the South, 1865–1867* (1985), and Richard Zuczek's *State of Rebellion: Reconstruction in South Carolina* (1996). Allen W. Trelease's *White Terror* (1971) covers the various organizations that practiced vigilante tactics, chiefly the Ku Klux Klan. The difficulties former laborers had in adjusting to the new labor system are documented in James L. Roark's *Masters without Slaves* (1977). Books on southern politics during Reconstruction include Michael Perman's *The Road to Redemption* (1984), Terry L. Seip's *The South Returns to Congress* (1983), and Mark W. Summer's *Railroads, Reconstruction, and the Gospel of Prosperity* (1984).

Numerous works have appeared on the freed blacks' experience in the South. Start with Leon F. Litwack's *Been in the Storm So Long* (1979), which covers the transition from slavery to freedom. Willie Lee Rose's *Rehearsal for Reconstruction* (1964) examines Union efforts to define the social role of former slaves during wartime emancipation. Joel Williamson's *After Slavery* (1965) argues that South Carolina blacks took an active role in pursuing their political and economic rights. For a work concerning the political activity of freed slaves in other areas of the South, see Howard N. Rabinowitz's *Southern Black Leaders of the Reconstruction Era* (1982). The role of the Freedmen's Bureau is explored in William S. McFeely's *Yankee Stepfather: General O.O. Howard and the Freedmen* (1968). The situation of freed slave women, which was often quite different than that of freed slave men, is discussed in Jacqueline Jones's *Labor of Love, Labor of Sorrow: Black Women, Work, and the Family from Slavery to Present* (1985).

The land confiscation issue is discussed in Eric Foner's *Politics and Ideology in the Age of the Civil War* (1980); Beth Bethel's *Promiseland* (1981), on a South Carolina black community; and Janet S. Hermann's *The Pursuit of a Dream* (1981), on the Davis Bend experiment in Mississippi.

The politics of corruption outside the South is depicted in William S. McFeely's *Grant: A Biography* (1981). The political maneuvers of the election of 1876 and the resultant crisis and compromise are explained in C. Vann Woodward's *Reunion and Reaction* (1951) and William Gillette's *Retreat from Reconstruction, 1869–1879* (1979).

PART FIVE

GROWING

PAINS

The northern victory in 1865 restored the Union and in the process helped to accelerate America's transformation into a modern nation-state. A distinctly national consciousness began to displace the sectional emphases of the antebellum era. During and after the Civil War, the Republican-led Congress pushed through legislation to foster industrial and commercial development and western expansion. In the process, the United States abandoned the Jeffersonian dream of a decentralized agrarian republic and began to forge a dynamic new industrial outlook generated by an increasingly national market.

After 1865, many Americans turned their attention to the unfinished business of settling a continent and completing an urban-industrial revolution begun before the war. Huge new national corporations based upon mass production and mass marketing began to dominate the economic order. As the prominent sociologist William Graham Sumner remarked, the process of industrial development "controls us all because we are all in it. It creates the conditions of our own existence, sets the limits of our social activity, and regulates the bonds of our social relations."

The industrial revolution was not only an urban phenomenon; it transformed rural life as well. Those who got in the way of the new emphasis on large-scale, highly mechanized commercial agriculture and ranching were brusquely pushed aside. Farm folk, as one New Englander stressed, "must understand farming as a business; if they do not it will go hard with them." The friction between new market forces and traditional folkways generated political revolts and social unrest during the last quarter of the nineteenth century. Fault lines appeared throughout the social order, and they unleashed tremors that exerted what one writer called "a seismic shock, a cyclonic violence" upon the body politic.

The clash between tradition and modernity came to a climax during the decade of the 1890s, one of the most strife-ridden in American history. A deep depression, agrarian unrest, and labor violence provoked fears of a class war. This turbulent situation transformed the presidential election campaign of 1896 into a clash between two rival visions of America's future. The Republican candidate, William McKinley, campaigned on behalf of modern urban-industrial values. By contrast, William Jennings Bryan, the nominee of both the Democratic and Populist parties, was an eloquent defender of America's rural past. McKinley's victory proved to be a watershed in American political and social history. By 1900 the United States would emerge as one of the world's greatest industrial powers, and it would thereafter assume a new leadership role in world affairs.

19 NEW FRONTIERS: SOUTH AND WEST

CHAPTER ORGANIZER

This chapter focuses on:

- the economic and political policies of the states in the post-Reconstruction South.

- race relations in the New South.

- the farmers', miners', and cowboys' frontiers.

- late-nineteenth-century Indian policy.

The West and the South of the postwar period provided enticing opportunities for the distinctively American pioneering and entrepreneurial spirit to flourish. Before 1860, most people had viewed the 430 million acres between the Mississippi River and California as a barren landscape unfit for human habitation or cultivation, an uninviting land suitable only for Indians and animals. Half of the state of Texas, for instance, was still not settled at the end of the Civil War. After 1865, however, the federal government encouraged western settlement and economic exploitation. The construction of transcontinental railroads, the military conquest of the Indians, and a liberal land distribution policy combined to help lure thousands of pioneers and expectant capitalists westward. Charles Goodnight, a Texas cattleman, recalled that "we were adventurers in a great land as fresh and full of the zest of darers."

Although the first great wave of railroad building occurred in the 1850s, the most spectacular growth took place during the quarter century after the Civil War. From about 35,000 miles of track in 1865, the network grew to nearly 200,000 miles by 1897. The transcontinental rail lines led the way, and they helped populate the plains and the Far West. During the century after the Civil War, fourteen new states were created out of America's western territories.

In the postwar South, rail lines were rebuilt and supplemented with new branch lines. The defeated Confederacy, although not a frontier in the literal sense of the term, offered capitalists a fertile new ground for investment and industrial development. Proponents of a "New South" after 1865 argued that the region must abandon its single-minded preoccupation with agriculture and pursue industrial and commercial development. As a result, the South as well as the West experienced dramatic social and economic changes during the last third of the nineteenth century. By 1900, these new "frontiers" had been transformed in ways that few could have predicted.

THE NEW SOUTH

A FRESH VISION   Amid the pains of defeat and the ruins of war many southerners looked back wistfully to the plantation life that had dominated their region before the firing on Fort Sumter. A few prominent leaders, however, insisted that the postwar South must liberate itself from such nostalgia and create a modern society of small farms, thriving industries, and bustling cities. The major prophet of a New South emerged in an improbable setting—at New York's most elegant restaurant, Delmonico's—where on December 21, 1886, the New England Society of New York held its annual dinner. The main speaker was Henry W. Grady, thirty-six-year-old editor of the *Atlanta Constitution*. Grady's topic was "The New South," and his eloquent words became the most celebrated statement of what came to be called the New South Creed.

In plain yet almost poetic language, Grady set forth the vision that inspired a generation of approving southerners: "The Old South rested everything on slavery and agriculture, unconscious that these could neither give nor maintain healthy growth. The New South presents a perfect democracy, the oligarchs leading in the popular movement—a social system compact and closely knitted, less splendid on the surface, but stronger at the core—a hundred farms for every plantation, fifty homes for every palace—and a diversified industry that meets the complex need of this complex age."

Many prophets had gone before Grady, and still others stood with him as major spokesmen for the New South Creed. In the aftermath of the Civil War, these men preached with evangelical fervor the gospel of industrial development. The Confederacy, they reasoned, had lost the war because it had relied too much on King Cotton. In the future the South must follow the North's example and industrialize. From that central belief flowed certain corollaries: that a more diversified and efficient agriculture would be a foundation for economic growth, that more widespread education, especially vocational training, would promote material success, and that sectional peace and racial harmony would provide a stable environment for economic growth.

ECONOMIC GROWTH   The chief fruit of the New South ideal was an expansion of the area's textile production that began in the 1880s and overtook its older New England competitors by the 1920s. In the New South, as in New England and Old England, cotton textiles were the advance guard of industrial revolution. Already in the 1870s new cotton mills dotted the landscape of the Carolina Piedmont. From 1880 to 1900 the number of cotton mills in the South grew from 161 to 400, the number of mill workers (among whom women and children outnumbered the men) increased fivefold, and the consumption of cotton went up eightfold, from 182,000 bales to 1,479,000. Initially this development resulted mainly from southern capital and southern labor, though later the decline of the textile industry in New England contributed labor and capital to the South.

Tobacco growth also increased significantly, entering a new era with the development of two new varieties of the weed: burley, which first appeared in southern Ohio, and bright leaf, which was grown on otherwise infertile soils and cured by a charcoal process discovered by a slave in 1839. Knowledge of the bright-leaf type remained chiefly local until, in what seemed a misfortune, Union soldiers swarmed over central North Carolina in 1865.

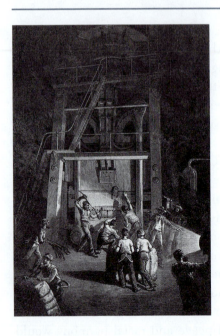

A southern cotton press at night, 1883.

One victim of their looting was John Ruffin Green, whose bright-leaf tobacco factory was ransacked by soldiers loitering around Durham Station. Within a few weeks orders began to pour into Green's factory for the Best Flavored Spanish Smoking Tobacco "that did not bite." With this revival, Green adopted as his trademark a bull's head similar to that on Colman's mustard, made in Durham, England. It did not take long for Green and his successors to make the image of Bull Durham ubiquitous, so much so that years later Mark Twain, notorious for embellishing a good story, claimed that when he visited Egypt he never saw the pyramids because they were obscured by Bull Durham signs.

Even more important in the rise of tobacco and the city of Durham was the Duke family, who inhabited a nearby farm. At the end of the Civil War, the story goes, old Washington Duke had only fifty cents obtained from a Yankee soldier for a souvenir Confederate five-dollar bill. He took a barnful of tobacco and, with the help of his three sons, beat it out with hickory sticks, stuffed it in bags, hitched up two mules to his wagon, and set out across the state, selling tobacco as he went. By 1872 the Dukes had a factory producing 125,000 pounds of leaf annually, and Washington Duke prepared to settle down and enjoy success.

His son Buck (James Buchanan Duke), however, had the same entrepreneurial drive that animated the Carnegies and Rockefellers of that day. Buck Duke recognized early that the tobacco industry was "half smoke and half ballyhoo," and he poured large sums into advertising schemes. Duke also undersold competitors in their own markets and cornered the supply of ingredients. Eventually his competitors agreed to join forces, and in 1890 Duke brought most of them into the American Tobacco Company, which controlled nine-tenths of the nation's cigarette production and, by 1904, about three-fourths of all tobacco production. In 1911 the Supreme Court ruled that the company was in violation of the Sherman Anti-Trust Act and ordered it broken up, but by then Duke had found new worlds to conquer in hydroelectric power and aluminum.

Other natural resources helped revitalize the area along the Appalachian Mountain chain from West Virginia to Alabama. Coal production in the South (including West Virginia) grew from 5 million tons in 1875 to 49 million tons by 1900. At the southern end of the mountains, Birmingham, Alabama, sprang up during the 1870s in the shadow of Red Mountain, so named for its iron ore, and boosters soon tagged the city the "Pittsburgh of the South." Birmingham's proximity to coal, iron, and limestone gave it a strong advantage over Chattanooga, which had a meteoric career as an iron center after the war.

Rapid economic growth spawned a need for housing, and after 1870 lumbering became a thriving industry in the South. Lumber camps sprouted across the mountains and flatlands. By the turn of the century, their product, mainly southern pine, had outdistanced textiles in value. Tree cutting seemed to know no bounds, despite the resulting ecological devastation. In time the industry would be saved only by the warm climate, which fostered quick renewal, and the rise of scientific forestry, which had its beginnings on George Vanderbilt's Biltmore estate near Asheville, North Carolina. Here the nation's first school of forestry opened in 1898.

The South still had far to go to achieve the "diversified industry" that Grady envisioned in the mid-1880s, but a profusion of other products poured from southern plants: phosphate fertilizers from coastal South Carolina and Florida; oysters, vegetables, and fruits from widespread canneries; ships, including battleships, from the Newport News Shipbuilding and Drydock Company; leather products; wagons and buggies;

liquors and beverages; paper in small quantities; and clay, glass, and stone products.

At the turn of the century two great forces that would impel an even greater industrial revolution were already on the horizon: petroleum in the Southwest and hydroelectric power in the Southeast. The Corsicana oil field in Texas had been opened in 1895, and in 1901 the Spindletop gusher would bring a great bonanza. Local power plants dotted the map by the 1890s. Richmond, Virginia, boasted the nation's first electric streetcar system in 1888, and Columbia, South Carolina, opened the first electrically powered cotton mill in 1894. The greatest advance would begin in 1905 when Buck Duke's Southern Power Company set out to electrify entire river valleys in the Carolinas.

AGRICULTURE, OLD AND NEW   At the turn of the century, however, most of the South remained undeveloped, at least by northeastern standards. Despite the optimistic rhetoric of New South spokesmen, the typical southerner was less apt to be tending a loom or forge than, as the saying went, facing the eastern end of a westbound mule. King Cotton survived the Civil War and expanded into new acreage even as its export markets leveled off. The old tobacco belts of Virginia and Kentucky now reached across North Carolina and touched South Carolina. Louisiana cane sugar, probably the most war-devastated of all crops, flourished again by the 1890s.

In 1885 Seaman A. Knapp, an agriculturist from New York by way of Iowa, moved to Louisiana and developed a new rice belt on behalf of an English land company, using machinery imported from the wheatfields. In the process Knapp invented the demonstration method of agricultural education, which showed farmers the most productive practices on selected plots of land with the aim of teaching by example. Knapp later used the demonstration method to fight the boll weevil in Texas. His work led to the national system of farm and home demonstration agents.

In the old rice belt of coastal South Carolina and elsewhere, vegetable and truck farming flourished with the advent of the railroads and refrigerator cars. But the majority of southern farmers were not flourishing. A prolonged deflation in crop prices affected the entire Western world during the last third of the nineteenth century. Sagging prices made it more difficult than ever to own land. Sharecropping and tenancy grew increasingly prevalent. By 1890 most southern farms were

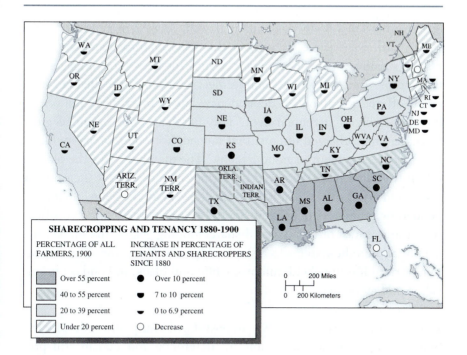

SHARECROPPING AND TENANCY 1880-1900

PERCENTAGE OF ALL FARMERS, 1900

- Over 55 percent
- 40 to 55 percent
- 20 to 39 percent
- Under 20 percent

INCREASE IN PERCENTAGE OF TENANTS AND SHARECROPPERS SINCE 1880

- ● Over 10 percent
- ◕ 7 to 10 percent
- ◡ 0 to 6.9 percent
- ○ Decrease

0   200 Miles

0   200 Kilometers

worked by people who did not own the land. Tenancy rates in the Deep South belied the rosy rhetoric of New South prophets: South Carolina, 61 percent; Georgia, 60 percent; Alabama, 58 percent; Mississippi, 62 percent; and Louisiana, 58 percent.

Sharecropping and tenancy seldom produced the self-sufficiency that advocates envisioned. The sharecropper, who had nothing to offer the landowner but his labor, tilled the land in return for supplies and a share of the crop, generally about half. Tenant farmers, hardly better off, might have their own mule, plow, and line of credit with the country store, and therefore might claim a larger share, commonly three-fourths of the cash crop and two-thirds of the subsistence crop, which was mainly corn. There were, moreover, infinite variations to sharecropping that ranged from cash rental at best to outright peonage at worst. The system was generally inefficient, for the tenant lacked incentive to care for the land, and the owner had little chance to supervise the work. In addition, the system bred a morbid suspicion on both sides. The folklore of the rural South overflowed with stories of tenants who remained stubbornly shiftless and landlords who kept books with crooked pencils.

The crop lien system was equally flawed. At best, it supplied credit where cash was scarce. It worked this way: country merchants furnished supplies to small farmers in return for liens (or mortgages) on their crops. To a few tenants and farmers who seized the chance, such credit offered a way out of dependency, but to most it offered only a hopeless cycle of perennial debt. The merchant, who assumed great risks, generally charged interest that ranged, according to one publication, "from 24 percent to grand larceny." The merchant, like the planter (often the same man), required his farmer clients to grow a cash crop that could be readily sold at harvest time. So for all the wind and ink expended by promoters of a "New South" on preachments of diversification, the routines of tenancy and sharecropping geared the marketing, supply, and credit systems to a staple crop, usually cotton. The stagnation of rural life thus held millions, white and black, in bondage to privation and ignorance.

THE BOURBON REDEEMERS   In post–Civil War politics, despite the South's formal democracy, habits of deference and elitism still prevailed. "Every community," one Union officer noted in postwar South Carolina, "had its great man, or its little great man, around whom his fellow citizens gather when they want information, and to whose monologues they listen with a respect akin to humility." After Reconstruction, southern politics was dominated by small groups of such men, collectively known as Redeemers or Bourbons. The supporters of these postwar leaders referred to them as Redeemers because they supposedly "redeemed," or saved, the South from Yankee domination as well as the straitjacket of a purely rural economy. The Redeemers included a rising class of entrepreneurs who were eager to promote a more diversified economy based on industrial development and railroad expansion.

The opponents of the "Redeemers" labeled them "Bourbons" in an effort to depict them not as progressives but as reactionaries. Like the French royal family which, Napoleon said, forgot nothing and learned nothing in the ordeal of revolution, Bourbons of the postwar South were said to have forgotten nothing and learned nothing in the ordeal of the Civil War. Their Republican, Independent, and Populist adversaries fixed the label so firmly in the vocabulary of the times that Bourbon came to signify the leaders of the Democratic party, whether they were real throwbacks or, more commonly, champions of an industrial New

The Effects of Radical and Bourbon Rule in the South. *This 1880 cartoon shows the South staggering under the oppressive weight of military Reconstruction* (left) *and flourishing under the "Let 'Em Alone Policy" of Hayes and the Bourbons* (right).

South who, if they had forgotten nothing, had at least learned something. They may have worshipped at the shrine of the old order, but they embraced a new order of economic development.

These Bourbons of the New South perfected a political alliance with eastern conservatives and an economic alliance with eastern capitalists. They generally pursued a government policy of laissez-faire, except for the tax exemptions and other favors they offered to business. The Bourbons focused on cutting back the size and scope of government, including the school systems started during Reconstruction. In 1871 the southern Atlantic states were spending $10.27 per pupil; by 1880 the figure was down to $6.00, and in 1890 it stood at $7.63. Illiteracy rates in the South at the time ran at about 12 percent of the native white population and 50 percent of the black population.

Private philanthropy, however, did help to keep southern schools afloat. In 1867 George Peabody, a London banker born in Massachusetts, established the Peabody Fund for Education, which was to spend some $3.6 million on public schools by 1914. Aid from the Peabody Fund was supplemented by the $1 million in the John F. Slater Fund, established in 1882 by a donor in Connecticut and earmarked for black schools. J. L. M. Curry, onetime soldier, preacher, teacher, and politician, became the general agent of both the Peabody and the Slater Funds. Curry pursued an extensive program of speaking and building support for education. He set up teachers' associations and started some of the first summer schools for teachers, and in general tried to foster exemplary schools.

The urge to economize created in the penal system one of the darkest blots on the Bourbon record: convict leasing. Necessity gave rise to the practice immediately after the Civil War. The wartime destruction of prisons and the poverty of state treasuries combined with the demand for cheap labor on the railroads, in the mines, and in lumber and turpentine camps to make the leasing of convict labor a way for southern states to avoid expenses and generate revenues. The burden of detaining criminals grew after the war because freed slaves, who had been subject to the discipline of masters, were now subject to the criminal law. Convict leasing, in the absence of state supervision, allowed inefficiency, neglect, and disregard for human life to proliferate. White political and economic leaders often used a racial argument to rationalize the leasing of convicts, most of whom were black. An "inferior" and "shiftless" race, they claimed, required the regimen of such coercion to elevate it above its idle and undisciplined ways. In only one southern state, Texas, did blacks not constitute a majority either of the total prisoner or leased convict population.

The Bourbons scaled down not only government expenditures but also the public debt, and by a simple means—they repudiated a vast amount of debt in all the former Confederate states except Florida and Mississippi. The corruption and extravagance of Radical rule were commonly advanced as justification for the process, but repudiation did not stop with Reconstruction debts. Altogether nine states repudiated more than half of what they owed. The Bourbons, who respected the sanctity of property, were not of one mind about the process, however. In Virginia their leaders honored the state debt so zealously, and at such cost to public services, that they were temporarily ousted by an Independent rebellion, the Readjuster party.

Despite their penny-pinching ways, these frugal Bourbon regimes, so ardently devoted to laissez-faire, did respond to the demand for commissions to regulate the rates charged by railroads for commercial transport. They also established boards of agriculture and public health, agricultural experiment stations, agricultural and mechanical colleges, teacher-training schools and women's colleges, and even state colleges for African Americans.

Nor can any simplistic interpretation encompass the variety of Bourbon leaders. The Democratic party of the time was a mongrel coalition that threw Unionists, secessionists, businessmen, small farmers, hillbillies, planters, and even some Republicans together in alliance against the Reconstruction Radicals. Democrats therefore, even those who bore the Bourbon label, often marched to different drummers. And once they gained control, the conflicts inherent in any coalition began to erupt, so that Bourbon regimes never achieved complete unity in philosophy or government.

Independent movements cropped up in all the southern states, endorsing a variety of proposals including debt repudiation, inflation, usury laws, and antimonopoly laws. Locally they fought Bourbon Democrats over fencing laws (poor farmers preferred to let their scrub stock forage for itself), patronage, and issues of corruption. On occasion they joined forces with third parties such as the Greenbackers, and sometimes they elected local officials and congressmen. In Tennessee the division became so acute that the Republicans elected a governor in 1880. In Virginia, where the rebels sought reduction of the state debt, a Readjuster party captured the legislature in 1879, elected a governor in 1881, and sent their leader to the United States Senate.

For a brief time there emerged a wholesale collaboration between Republicans and Independents, which Chester A. Arthur, after he became president, promoted in the fall of 1881. The policy failed to make much headway, however, because Republicans had little in common with the Independents except their opposition to the Democrats. Moreover, the Republican machinery in the South had already been devastated by the overthrow of Reconstruction and by President Rutherford B. Hayes's policy of reconciliation with the Bourbons immediately afterward. The Republicans maintained a secure foothold only in the Blue Ridge and Smoky Mountains, "the great spine of Republicanism which runs down the back of the South," where stubborn white Unionists passed the faith on to later generations.

Perhaps the ultimate paradox of the Bourbons' rule was that these paragons of white supremacy tolerated a lingering black voice in politics and showed no haste about raising the barriers of racial separation. A number of them harbored at least some element of patrician benevolence toward blacks. The old slave owner, said a South Carolina editor, "has no desire to browbeat, maltreat, and spit upon the colored man"— clearly in part because the former slave owner saw in freedmen no threat to his status. Blacks sat in the state legislatures of South Carolina until 1900 and of Georgia until 1908; some of these black representatives were Democrats. The South sent black congressmen to Washington in every election until 1900 except one, though they always represented gerrymandered districts into which most of the state's black voters had been placed. Under the Bourbons the disenfranchisement of black voters remained inconsistent, a local matter brought about mainly by fraud and intimidation, but it occurred often enough to ensure white control of the southern states.

A like flexibility applied to other areas of race relations. The color line was drawn less strictly than it would be in the twentieth century. In some places, to be sure, racial segregation appeared before the end of Reconstruction, especially in schools, churches, hotels and rooming houses, and private social relations. In places of public accommodation such as trains, depots, theaters, and soda fountains, however, discrimination was more capricious. In 1885 a black journalist reported from his native state of South Carolina that he rode first-class cars on the railroads and in the streets, was served at saloons and soda fountains, saw blacks dining with whites at train stations, and saw a black policeman arrest a white man on the streets of Columbia. Fifteen years later such events would be rare.

DISENFRANCHISING BLACKS   During the 1890s, the attitudes that permitted such moderation eroded swiftly. One reason was that, despite signs of progress, many white racists held that blacks, freed from the restraints of slavery, were "retrogressing" toward bestiality, especially the younger blacks who had not known slavery.

Another reason was political. The rise of the Populist party in the 1890s divided the white vote to such an extent that in some places the black vote became the balance of power. Populists courted black votes and brought blacks prominently into their leadership councils. In response, the Bourbons revived the race issue, which they exploited with seasoned finesse, all the while controlling for their ticket a good part of the black vote in plantation areas. Nevertheless the Bourbons soon reversed themselves and began arguing that the black vote should be eliminated completely from southern elections. It was imperative, said the governor of Louisiana in 1894, that "the mass of ignorance, vice and venality without any proprietary interest in the State" be denied the vote. Some farm leaders hoped that disenfranchisement of blacks would make it possible for whites to divide politically without raising the specter of "Negro domination."

But since the Fifteenth Amendment made it impossible to disenfranchise blacks as such, the purpose was accomplished indirectly with devices such as poll taxes (or head taxes) and literacy tests. Some opposed such instruments of discrimination because they also trapped poor whites in the net. But this white opposition was neutralized by providing loopholes in the literacy tests through which illiterate whites could slip.

Mississippi led the way to near-total disenfranchisement of blacks. The state called a constitutional convention in 1890 to change the suffrage provisions of the old Radical constitution of 1868. The Mississippi plan set the pattern that seven more states would follow over the next twenty years. First, a residence requirement—two years in the state, one year in the election district—struck at those black tenant farmers who were in the habit of moving yearly in search of a better chance. Second, voters were disqualified if convicted of certain crimes. Third, all taxes, including a poll tax, had to be paid by February 1 of election year, which left plenty of time for white officials to lose the receipt before the fall vote. This proviso fell most heavily on the poor, most of whom were black. Fourth and finally, all voters had to be literate. The alternative, designed as a loophole for whites otherwise disqualified, was an "understanding" clause. The voter, if unable to read the Constitution, could qualify by being able to "understand" it—to the satisfaction of the registrar. Fraud was thus institutionalized rather than eliminated by "legal" disenfranchisement.

In other states, variations on the Mississippi plan added a few flourishes. In 1895 South Carolina tacked on the proviso that owning property assessed at $300 would qualify an illiterate voter. In 1898 Louisiana invented the "grandfather clause," which allowed illiterates to qualify if their fathers or grandfathers had been eligible to vote on January 1, 1867, when blacks were still excluded. Black educator Booker T.

Washington sent the convention a sarcastic telegram expressing hope that "no one clothed with state authority will be tempted to perjure and degrade himself by putting one interpretation upon it for the white man and another for the black man." By 1910 Georgia, North Carolina, Virginia, Alabama, and Oklahoma had adopted the grandfather clause. Every southern state, moreover, adopted a statewide Democratic primary between 1896 and 1915, which became the only meaningful election outside isolated areas of Republican strength. With minor exceptions, the Democratic primaries excluded black voters altogether. The effectiveness of these measures can be seen in a few sample figures. Louisiana in 1896 had 130,000 black voters registered, and in 1900 5,320. Alabama in 1900 had 121,159 literate black males over twenty-one, according to the census; only 3,742 were registered to vote.

SEGREGATION SPREADS "Jim Crow" segregation followed hard on disenfranchisement and in some states came first. The symbolic first target was the railway train. In 1885, the novelist George Washington Cable noted that in South Carolina blacks "ride in first class cars as a right" and "their presence excites no comment." From 1875 to 1883 in

"Jim Crow," a stock character in old minstrel shows, became a synonym for racial segregation in the twentieth century. Dan Rice had developed the character in the 1830s.

fact, any racial segregation violated a federal Civil Rights Act, which forbade discrimination in places of public accommodation. But in 1883 the Supreme Court ruled on seven *Civil Rights Cases* involving discrimination against blacks by corporations or individuals. The Court held, with only one dissent, that the force of federal law could not extend to individual action because the Fourteenth Amendment, which provided that "no State" could deny citizens the equal protection of the laws, stood as a prohibition only against *state* action.

This left as an open question the validity of state laws *requiring* separate facilities under the rubric of "separate but equal," a slogan popular with the New South prophets. In 1881 Tennessee had required railroads in the state to maintain separate first-class cars for blacks and whites. In 1888 Mississippi went a step further by requiring passengers, under penalty of law, to occupy the car set aside for their race. When Louisiana followed suit in 1890, dissidents challenged the law in the case *Plessy v. Ferguson,* which the Supreme Court decided in 1896.

The test case originated in New Orleans when Homer Plessy, an octoroon (a person having one-eighth black ancestry), refused to leave a white railroad car when told to do so. He was convicted, and the case rose on appeal to the Supreme Court. The Court ruled that segregation laws "have been generally, if not universally recognized as within the competency of state legislatures in the exercise of their police power." The sole dissenter was John Marshall Harlan, a former slaveholder and Whig Unionist from Kentucky, who had written the only dissent in the *Civil Rights Cases.* The *Plessy* ruling, he predicted, would "stimulate aggressions, more or less brutal, upon the admitted rights of colored citizens."

Very soon the principle of racial segregation extended into every area of southern life, including street railways, hotels, restaurants, hospitals, recreations, sports, and employment. If an activity was overlooked by the laws, it was not overlooked in custom and practice. The editor of the *Richmond Times* expressed the prevailing view: "It is necessary that this principle be applied in every relation of Southern life. God Almighty drew the color line and it cannot be obliterated. The negro must stay on his side of the line and the white man must stay on his side, and the sooner both races recognize this fact and accept it, the better it will be for both."

As for the "aggressions, more or less brutal," that Justice Harlan foretold, they were already routine when he pronounced his dissent. From the days of slavery, race relations had operated in a context of force and violence. The period of growing discrimination at the turn of the century was one of the worst. In the decade from 1890 to 1899, lynchings in the United States averaged 188 per year, 82 percent of which occurred in the South; from 1900 to 1909 they averaged 93 per year, 92 percent in the South. Whites constituted 32 percent of the victims during the first period, only 11 percent in the latter. A young Episcopal priest in Montgomery said that extremists had proceeded "from an undiscriminating attack upon the Negro's ballot to a like attack upon his schools, his labor, his life—from the contention that no Negro shall vote to the contention that no Negro shall learn, that no Negro shall labor, and (by implication) that no Negro shall live."

WASHINGTON AND DU BOIS   A few brave souls, black and white, spoke out against the new racist measures, but by and large blacks had to accommodate to them as best they could. To be sure, the doctrine of "separate but equal" did open some doors, such as those to black schools, that had once been closed entirely. Some African Americans even began to make a virtue of necessity. The chief spokesman for this accommodationist philosophy was Booker T. Washington, the black prophet of the New South Creed. Born in Virginia of a slave mother and

Booker T. Washington.

a white father, Washington had fought extreme adversity to get an education at Hampton Institute, one of the postwar missionary schools, and then to build at Tuskegee, Alabama, a leading college for African Americans.

Washington argued that blacks should first establish an economic base for their advancement. They should focus "upon the everyday practical things of life, upon something that is needed to be done, and something which they will be permitted to do in the community in which they reside." In his famous speech at the Atlanta Cotton States and International Exposition in 1895, which propelled him to fame, Washington advised fellow blacks: "Cast down your bucket where you are—cast it down in making friends . . . of the people of all races by whom we are surrounded. Cast it down in agriculture, mechanics, in commerce, in domestic service, and in the professions." He conspicuously omitted politics and offered an oblique endorsement of segregation: "In all things that are purely social we can be as separate as the five fingers, yet one as the hand in all things essential to mutual progress."

Some people bitterly criticized Washington, then and since, for making a bad bargain: the sacrifice of broad education and of civil rights for the dubious acceptance of white conservatives and economic opportunities. W. E. B. Du Bois led blacks in this criticism of Washington. A

W. E. B. Du Bois.

native of Massachusetts, Du Bois once said defiantly that he was born "with a flood of Negro blood, a strain of French, a bit of Dutch, but thank God! no 'Anglo-Saxon.'" Du Bois first experienced southern racial practices as an undergraduate at Fisk University in Nashville. Later he earned a Ph.D. in history from Harvard and briefly attended the University of Berlin. In addition to an active career in racial protest, he left a distinguished record as a scholar and author. Trim and dapper in appearance, sporting a goatee, cane, and gloves, Du Bois possessed a combative spirit. Not long after he began his teaching career at Atlanta University in 1897, he began to assault Washington's accommodationist philosophy of black progress and put forward his own program of "ceaseless agitation."

Washington, Du Bois argued, preached "a gospel of Work and Money to such an extent as . . . to overshadow the higher aims of life." The education of blacks, he maintained, should not be merely vocational but should nurture leaders willing to challenge segregation and discrimination through political action. He believed in work, "but work is not necessarily education. Education is the development of power and ideal." He demanded that disenfranchisement and legalized segregation cease and that the laws of the land be enforced. And he provided the formula for attaining such goals: "By voting where we may vote, by persistent, unceasing agitation, by hammering at the truth, by sacrifice and work." Du Bois minced no words in criticizing Washington's philosophy: "We refuse to surrender the leadership of this race to cowards and truck-lers." He called Washington's 1895 speech "the Atlanta Compromise" and argued that it had made Washington the leader of his race only in the eyes of whites.

RECONCILING TRADITION WITH INNOVATION The ultimate achievement of the New South prophets and their allies, the Bourbons, was that they reconciled tradition with innovation. Their relative moderation in racial policy, at least before the 1890s, allowed them to embrace just enough of the new to disarm adversaries and keep control. By promoting the growth of industry, the Bourbons led the South into a new economic era, but without sacrificing a mythic reverence for the Old South. Bourbon rule left a permanent mark on the South. As the historian C. Vann Woodward has noted, "it was not the Radicals nor the Confederates but the Redeemers who laid the lasting foundations in matters of race, politics, economics and institutions for the modern South."

THE NEW WEST

For vast reaches of western America the great epics of Civil War and Reconstruction were remote events hardly touching the lives of Indians, Mexicans, Asians, trappers, miners, and Mormons scattered through the plains and mountains. There the march of Manifest Destiny continued on its inexorable course, propelled by a lust for land and a passion for profits. On one level, the settlement of the West beyond the Mississippi constitutes a colorful drama of determined pioneers overcoming all obstacles to secure their visions of freedom and opportunity amid the region's awesome vastness. But on another level, the colonization of the Far West was a tragedy of shortsighted greed and irresponsible behavior, a story of reckless exploitation that nearly exterminated the culture of Native Americans, scarred the land, and decimated its wildlife. Seen from this perspective, the history of the West is not a grand success story but a tale of hardship, frustration, and failure. Both images of the process of western settlement are accurate in some respects.

In the second tier of trans-Mississippi states—Iowa, Kansas, Nebraska—and in western Minnesota, the last frontier of farmers began spreading across the Great Plains after mid-century. From California the miners' frontier spread east through the mountains at one new strike after another. From Texas the nomadic cowboys migrated northward into the plains and across the Rockies into the Great Basin. Now there were two frontiers of settlement, east and west, and even a third to the south; in another generation there would be none.

As settlement moved west, the environment gradually altered. The Great Plains were arid, swept by dry winds that had surrendered their moisture to the Pacific coastal ranges, the Sierra Nevadas and Cascades, and the Rockies. The scarcity of water and timber rendered useless or impossible the familiar trappings of the pioneer: the axe, the log cabin, the rail fence, and the accustomed methods of tilling the soil.

For a long time the region had been called the Great American Desert, a barrier to cross on the way to the Pacific, unfit for human habitation and therefore, to white Americans, the perfect refuge for Indians. But that pattern changed in the last half of the nineteenth century as a result of new finds of gold, silver, and other minerals, completion of transcontinental railroads, destruction of the buffalo, the collapse of Indian resistance, the rise of the range-cattle industry, and the dawning realization that the arid region need not be a sterile desert. With the use of what water was available, techniques of dry farming and irrigation could make the land fruitful after all.

THE MIGRATORY STREAM   During the second half of the nineteenth century, an unrelenting stream of migrants flowed into the largely Indian and Hispanic West. Newspaper editors described western migration as a "flood tide." Millions of Anglo-Americans, African Americans, Mexicans, and European and Chinese immigrants transformed the patterns of western society and culture. Most of the settlers were relatively prosperous white, native-born farming families. Because of the expense of transportation, land, and supplies, the very poor could not afford to relocate. Three-quarters of the western migrants were men.

The largest number of foreign immigrants came from northern Europe and Canada. In the northern plains, Germans, Scandinavians, and Irish were especially numerous. Not surprisingly, these foreign settlers tended to cluster together according to ethnic and kinship ties. Norwe-

An American family on their way west.

gians and Swedes, for example, often gravitated toward others from the same home province or parish to form cohesive rural communities. In the new state of Nebraska in 1870, a quarter of the 123,000 residents were foreign-born. In North Dakota in 1890, 45 percent of the residents were immigrants. Compared to European immigrants, those from China and Mexico were much less numerous but nonetheless significant. More than 200,000 Chinese arrived in California between 1876 and 1890.

In the aftermath of the collapse of Radical Republican rule in the South, thousands of blacks began migrating west. Most of them left from Kentucky, Tennessee, Louisiana, Arkansas, Mississippi, and Texas. Some 6,000 southern blacks arrived in Kansas in 1879 alone, and as many as 20,000 may have come the following year. They came to be known as "Exodusters," making their exodus out of the South in search of a haven from racism and poverty.

The foremost promoter of black migration to the West was Benjamin "Pap" Singleton. Born a slave in Tennessee in 1809, he escaped and settled in Detroit, where he operated a boardinghouse that became a refuge for other runaway slaves. After the Civil War, he returned to Tennessee, convinced that God was calling him to rescue his black brethren. He decided that the brightest future for African Americans lay not in sharecropping or tenant farming but in farm ownership. When Sin-

Nicodemus, Kansas: a colony founded by southern blacks in the 1860s.

gleton learned that land in Kansas could be had for $1.25 an acre, he began distributing a recruiting pamphlet entitled "The Advantage of Living in a Free State" to former slaves. In 1878 Singleton led the first party of 200 colonists to Kansas, bought 7,500 acres that was formerly an Indian reservation, and established the Dunlop community.

Over the next several years, thousands of African Americans followed Singleton into Kansas, leading many southern leaders to worry about the loss of laborers from the Old South. In 1879 white Mississippians closed access to the river and threatened to sink all boats carrying black colonists to the West. An army officer reported to President Rutherford B. Hayes that "every river landing is blockaded by white enemies of the colored exodus; some of whom are mounted and armed, as if we are at war." One black migrant to Kansas who returned to Mississippi to retrieve his family was seized by whites who cut off his hands and threw them onto his wife's lap, yelling "Now go to Kansas to work!"

The exodus to Kansas and Oklahoma Territory died out by the early 1880s. Many of the settlers encountered terrible hardships. They were unprepared for the quite different living and working conditions on the Plains. Their homesteads were not large enough to be self-sufficient, and most of the black farmers were forced to supplement their income by hiring themselves out to white ranchers in the area. Drought, grasshoppers, prairie fires, and dust storms led to crop failures. The sudden influx of so many people taxed resources and patience. Although sympathizers formed the Kansas Freedmen's Relief Association and collected thousands of dollars for food and clothing, they could not keep up with the needs of the swelling tide of migrants. Many of the black pioneers soon abandoned their land and moved to the few cities in the state. Life on the frontier was not the "promised land" that people had been led to expect. Nonetheless, by 1890, some 520,000 blacks lived west of the Mississippi River. As many as 25 percent of the cowboys who participated in the Texas cattle drives were African Americans.

In 1866 Congress passed legislation establishing two "colored" cavalry units and dispatched them to the western frontier. Nicknamed "Buffalo Soldiers" by the Indians, the soldiers were mostly Civil War veterans from Louisiana and Kentucky. They built and maintained forts, mapped vast areas of the Southwest, strung hundreds of miles of telegraph lines, protected railroad construction crews, subdued hostile Indians, and captured outlaws and rustlers. For this they were paid $13 a month. Eighteen of the "Buffalo Soldiers" won Congressional Medals of Honor for their service in the West.

MINING THE WEST   Miners were also diverse in ethnic background. Every race and nationality was represented in the mining communities. The miners' frontier was in fact not so much a frontier as a scattering of settlements in places unsuitable for farming, such as steep mountainsides, remote highlands, and barren deserts. The California miners of '49 set the typical pattern in which the sudden, disorderly rush of prospectors to the new find was quickly followed by the arrival of the camp followers—a motley crew of peddlers, saloonkeepers, prostitutes, card sharps, hustlers, and assorted desperadoes, out to mine the miners. If the new field panned out, the forces of respectability and more subtle forms of exploitation slowly worked their way in. An era of lawlessness gave way to vigilante rule and, finally, to a stable community.

As mining became more dependent on capital, the day of the individual prospector began to wane. The Forty-niners typically sifted the gold out of the dirt and gravel through "placer" mining or "panning," or by diverting a stream through a "sluice box" or "long tom." But once the rich diggings tailed off, efficient mining required shafts sunk into the ground or crushing mills built to extract the precious metal locked in

Hydraulic mining in the Boise basin in Idaho, circa 1875. Gold, silver, and copper prospectors invaded the West, but only a few made their fortunes.

quartz. The wild rush then gave way to organized enterprise. The miners either moved on, settled down to work for the corporate mines, or took up farming in the vicinity.

The drama of the 1849 gold rush was reenacted time and again in the following three decades. Though the California fever had passed by 1851, and no big strikes were made for seven years, new finds in Colorado and Nevada revived hopes for riches. Along the South Platte River, not far from Pike's Peak in Colorado, a prospecting party found gold in 1858, and stories of success there brought perhaps 100,000 "Fifty-niners" into the country by 1859, only to find that the rumors had been greatly exaggerated.

Wagons that headed west with the legend "Pike's Peak or Bust!" on their sides were soon rumbling back with the sardonic message "Busted, by gosh." Still, a few mines proved out, some new arrivals took up farming to exploit high prices for farm products in Denver and other mining centers, and the census of 1860 showed 35,000 people still in the region. New discoveries kept occurring: near Central City in 1859, at Leadville in the 1870s, and the last important strikes in the West, again gold and silver, at Cripple Creek in 1891–1894. During these years, farming and grazing had given the economy a stable base, and Colorado had become the "Centennial State" in 1876.

While the early miners were crowding around Pike's Peak, the Comstock Lode was discovered near Gold Hill, Nevada. H. T. P. Comstock, a Canadian-born fur trapper, had drifted to the Carson River diggings opened in 1856. Possessed of a glib tongue, he talked his way into a share in a new discovery made by two other prospectors in 1859 and gave it his own name. The lode produced not only gold but a troublesome "blue earth" that turned out to contain silver. Close by, James Finney, known as "Old Virginia," located a lucrative new vein and gave his nickname to nearby Virginia City. Neither man had the foresight to develop his claim; both sold out for tiny sums what proved to be the two richest fields in the West. Within twenty years the Comstock Lode alone had yielded more than $300 million from shafts that reached hundreds of feet into the mountainside. In 1861 Nevada became a territory, and in 1864 the state of Nevada was admitted in time to give its three electoral votes to Lincoln.

The Spaniards had found silver in New Mexico, but mining in Arizona began during the Civil War, when many in a company of California volunteers, going to meet a Confederate foray into New Mexico, deserted to the promising mining country near the Colorado River. In both Arizona and Montana the most important mineral proved to be neither gold nor silver, but copper. The richest copper mines included the Anaconda Mine in Butte, Montana, and the Phelps-Dodge Mine near Bisbee, Arizona.

The last great strike before the Cripple Creek (Colorado) find of the 1890s occurred in 1874–1875 in the Black Hills of South Dakota, which belonged by treaty to the Sioux Indians. Deadwood, the site of the strike, earned brief glory as the refuge of some of the West's most notorious desperadoes: "Calamity Jane," "Wild Bill Hickok," and a host of others. But in Deadwood, as elsewhere, when the gold and silver lodes ran out there was often little to support life in an arid, infertile terrain.

The growing demand for orderly government in the West led to the hasty creation of new territories and eventually the admission of a host of new states. After Colorado was admitted in 1876, however, there was a long hiatus because of the party divisions in Congress. Democrats were reluctant to create states out of territories that were heavily Republican. After the sweeping Republican victory of 1888, however, Congress admitted the Dakotas, Montana, and Washington in 1889,

Creede, Colorado. Towns in Colorado and other Western states were established with the gold rushes of 1849 and 1859.

and Idaho and Wyoming in 1890, completing a tier of states from coast to coast. Utah entered in 1896 (after the Mormons abandoned the practice of polygamy), Oklahoma in 1907, and in 1912 Arizona and New Mexico finally rounded out the forty-eight contiguous states.

THE INDIAN WARS   As the frontier pressed in from east and west, whites pursued the Indians into what was supposed to be their last refuge. Perhaps 250,000 Indians in the Great Plains and mountain regions lived mainly off the buffalo herds, which provided food and, from their hides, clothing and shelter. In 1851 the chiefs of the principal Plains tribes had gathered at Fort Laramie in Wyoming Territory, where they had agreed to accept more or less definite tribal borders and to leave the emigrants unmolested on their trails. The treaty worked for a while, with wagon trains passing safely through Indian lands and the army building roads and forts without resistance from the Indians. Fighting resumed, however, as the emigrants began to encroach upon Indian lands on the Plains rather than merely passing through them.

From the early 1860s until the late 1870s, the frontier was ablaze with Indian wars, and intermittent outbreaks continued through the 1880s. The first serious trouble developed in Minnesota, where a volunteer militia had taken the place of army garrisons fighting in the Civil War. Fighting started in 1862 when a band of Sioux, aroused by recent land cessions, killed five whites. Some of the Sioux fled farther west, but others remained and wrought havoc on the frontier, killing or capturing some 1,000 whites until the militia in overwhelming force drove them back and inflicted a devastating revenge. Out of 400 Indians captured, 300 were sentenced to death. Eventually 38 were hanged in a mass execution.

In Colorado, where Cheyenne and Arapaho chiefs were forced to accept a treaty to abandon land that had been granted to them in treaties ten years earlier and to move westward to other lands, protesting braves began sporadic raids on the trails and mining camps. In 1864 the territorial governor persuaded most of the warring Indians to gather at Fort Lyon on Sand Creek, where they were promised protection. Despite this promise, Colonel J. M. Chivington's militia fell upon an Indian camp flying the American flag and a white flag of truce, slaughtering 450 peaceful Indians—men, women, and children. An army general called it the "foulest and most unjustifiable crime in the annals of

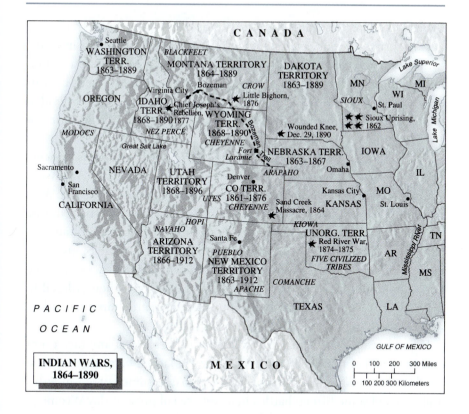

CANADA

Seattle •
WASHINGTON TERR. 1863–1889
BLACKFEET
MONTANA TERRITORY 1864–1889
DAKOTA TERRITORY 1863–1889
MN
WI
MI
Lake Superior

Virginia City
Bozeman
CROW
Little Bighorn, 1876
Sioux Uprising, 1862

OREGON
IDAHO TERR. 1868–1890 1877
Chief Joseph's Rebellion,
WYOMING TERR. 1868–1890
SIOUX
St. Paul •
Lake Michigan

MODOCS
NEZ PERCE
CHEYENNE
Wounded Knee, Dec. 29, 1890

Great Salt Lake
Fort Laramie
NEBRASKA TERR. 1863–1867
IOWA

Sacramento •
NEVADA
UTAH TERRITORY 1868–1896
ARAPAHO
Omaha •
IL

San Francisco •
Denver •
CO TERR. 1861–1876
UTES
CHEYENNE
Kansas City
MO

CALIFORNIA
Sand Creek Massacre, 1864
KANSAS
St. Louis •

HOPI
NAVAHO
Santa Fe •
KIOWA
UNORG. TERR. Red River War, 1874–1875
FIVE CIVILIZED TRIBES
TN

ARIZONA TERRITORY 1866–1912
PUEBLO
NEW MEXICO TERRITORY 1863–1912
APACHE
COMANCHE
AR
MS

PACIFIC
OCEAN
TEXAS
LA

GULF OF MEXICO

INDIAN WARS, 1864–1890
MEXICO

0   100   200   300 Miles
0 100 200 300 Kilometers

America." Chivington, a former Methodist minister, later exhibited his personal collection of 100 scalps in Denver. In 1865 the survivors surrendered unconditionally and gave up their Sand Creek reservation for lands farther west.

With other scattered battles erupting, in 1865 a congressional committee began to gather evidence on the grisly Indian wars and massacres. Its 1867 *Report on the Condition of the Indian Tribes* led to an act to establish an Indian Peace Commission charged with ending the Sioux War and removing the causes of Indian wars in general. Congress decided this was best accomplished at the expense of the Indians, by persuading them to take up life on out-of-the-way reservations. This solution continued the persistent encroachment on Indian hunting grounds.

In 1867 a conference at Medicine Creek Lodge, Kansas, ended with an agreement that the Kiowa, Comanche, Arapaho, and Cheyenne would accept lands in western Oklahoma. Smaller tribes from the southern

Plains were later resettled on reservations in the same area. In the following spring in 1868, a conference at Fort Laramie resulted in peace with the Sioux, who agreed to settle within the Black Hills reservation in Dakota Territory. But Indian resistance in the southern Plains continued until the Red River War of 1874–1875. General Philip Sheridan scattered the Indians and finally brought them to terms in the spring of 1875.

While conflict was being resolved in the south, trouble was brewing once again in the north. In 1874 Lieutenant-Colonel George A. Custer, a reckless, glory-seeking officer who graduated last in his class at West Point in 1861 and then distinguished himself as a cavalry officer during the Civil War, led an exploring expedition into the Black Hills, accompanied by gold seekers. Miners were soon filtering into the Sioux hunting grounds despite promises that the army would keep them out. The army had done little to protect the Indian lands, but when ordered to move against wandering bands of Sioux hunting on the range according to their treaty rights, the army moved vigorously.

What became the Great Sioux War was the largest military event since the end of the Civil War and one of the largest campaigns against the Indians in American history. The war lasted some fifteen months, and entailed some fifteen battles in a vast area of present-day Wyoming, Montana, South Dakota, and Nebraska. In 1876, after several indecisive encounters, Custer found the main encampment of Sioux and their Northern Cheyenne allies on the Little Bighorn River. Separated from the main body of his men, Custer and a detachment of 210, surrounded by a body of warriors numbering about 2,500, were completely annihilated.

But the Battle of the Little Bighorn was only one incident in this war. Instead of following up their victory over Custer and his forces, the Indians celebrated and renewed their hunting. When the army regained the offensive, the Indians began to melt away into the wilderness. Chief Sitting Bull escaped into Canada, only to return to the Sioux reservation several years later. Crazy Horse was captured and later murdered by his guard. The remaining Sioux were forced to give up their hunting grounds and gold fields in return for payments. Forced onto reservations situated on the least valuable lands in the region, the Indians soon found themselves struggling to subsist under harsh conditions. Many of them died of starvation or disease. When a peace commission imposed

The Battle of Little Bighorn in a pictograph by an Oglala Sioux, Amos Bad Heart Bull, 1876.

a settlement, Chief Spotted Tail said: "Tell your people that since the Great Father promised that we should never be removed, we have been moved five times. . . . I think you had better put the Indians on wheels and you can run them about wherever you wish."

In the Rockies and westward the same story of hopeless resistance was repeated. The Blackfoot and Crow had to leave their homes in Montana. In a war along the California-Oregon boundary, the Modocs held out for six months in 1871–1872 before they were overwhelmed. In 1879 the Utes were forced to give up their vast territories in western Colorado after a brief battle. In Idaho the peaceful Nez Percés finally refused to surrender lands along the Salmon River. Chief Joseph tried to avoid war, but when some unruly braves started a fight, he directed a masterful campaign against overwhelming odds, one of the most spectacular feats in the history of Indian warfare. After a retreat of 1,500 miles, through mountains and plains, across the Yellowstone region and through the Bitterroot Mountains of Montana, he was finally caught thirty miles short of the Canadian border, and exiled to Oklahoma.

The heroic Joseph maintained strict discipline among his followers, countenanced no scalpings or outrages against civilians, bought supplies that he could have confiscated, and kept his dignity to the end.

Chief Joseph of the Nez Percé tribe.

His eloquent speech of surrender was an epitaph to the warrior's last stand against the march of empire: "I am tired of fighting. Our chiefs are killed. . . . The old men are all dead. . . . I want to have time to look for my children, and see how many of them I can find. . . . Hear me, my chiefs! I am tired. My heart is sick and sad. From where the sun now stands I will fight no more forever."

A generation of Indian wars virtually ended in 1886 with the capture of Geronimo, a chief of the Chiricahua Apaches, who had fought encroachments in the Southwest for fifteen years. But there would be one tragic epilogue. Late in 1888 Wovoka (or "Jack Wilson"), a Paiute in western Nevada, fell ill and in a delirium imagined he had visited the spirit world where he learned of a deliverer coming to rescue the Indians and restore their lands. To hasten the day, he said, they had to take up a ceremonial dance at each new moon. The Ghost Dance craze fed upon old legends of a coming Messiah and spread rapidly. In 1890 the Sioux took it up with such fervor that it alarmed white authorities. An effort to arrest Chief Sitting Bull led to his death. Shortly afterward, on December 29, 1890, a bloodbath occurred at Wounded Knee, South Dakota. An accidental rifle discharge led nervous soldiers to fire into a group of Indians who had come to surrender. Nearly 200 Indians and 25 soldiers died in the "Battle of Wounded Knee." The Indian wars had ended with characteristic brutality.

Geronimo, a chief of the Chiricahua Apaches.

Over the long run the collapse of Indian resistance resulted as much from the killing off of the buffalo herds on which they subsisted as from direct suppression. White hunters felled buffaloes for sport, sometimes firing from train windows merely for the pleasure of seeing them die. In the 1870s a systematic slaughter served the fashion of buffalo robes and overcoats in the East. By the mid-1880s the herds had reached the verge of extinction.

Most frontiersmen had little tolerance for moralizing on the Indian question. Easterners who were far removed from frontier dangers took a different view. The slaughter of the Indian wars provoked widespread criticism. Politicians and religious leaders spoke out against mistreatment of Indians. In his annual message of 1877 President Hayes echoed the protest: "Many, if not most, of our Indian wars have had their origin in broken promises and acts of injustice on our part." In the 1880s Helen Hunt Jackson, a novelist and poet, focused attention on the Indian cause in *A Century of Dishonor* (1881), which struck a popular chord just as *Uncle Tom's Cabin* had done.

INDIAN POLICY   Indian policy gradually became more benevolent, but this did little to ease the plight of the Indians and actually helped to destroy the remnants of their cultures. The reservation policy inaugurated by the Peace Commission in 1867 did little more than extend a

Issue Day. *Native Americans confined to Pine Ridge Reservation in South Dakota could no longer hunt for themselves and had to wait for government-issued food rations.*

practice that dated from colonial Virginia. Partly humanitarian in motive, this policy also saved money: it cost less to house and feed Indians on reservations than it did to fight them.

Well-intentioned reformers sought to "Americanize" the Indians by dealing with them as individuals rather than as tribes. The fruition of reform efforts came in the Dawes Severalty Act of 1887. Sponsored by Senator Henry M. Dawes of Massachusetts, the act permitted the president to divide the lands of any tribe and grant 160 acres to each head of family and lesser amounts to others. To protect the Indian's property, the government held it in trust for twenty-five years, after which the owner won full title and became a citizen. Under the Burke Act of 1906, Indians who took up life apart from their tribes became citizens immediately. Members of the tribes granted land titles were subject to state and federal laws like all other persons. In 1901 citizenship was extended to the Five Civilized Tribes of Oklahoma, and in 1924 to all Indians.

But the more it changed, the more Indian policy remained the same. Despite the best of intentions, the Dawes Act created opportunities for more plundering of Indian land, and it disrupted what remained of the traditional cultures. The Dawes Act broke up reservations and often led to the loss of Indian lands to whites. Those lands not distributed to Indian families were sold, while others were lost to land sharks because of the Indians' inexperience with private ownership, or simply their weakness in the face of fraud. Between 1887 and 1934, they lost an estimated 86 million of their 130 million acres. Most of what remained was unsuited to agriculture.

CATTLE AND COWBOYS   While the West was being taken from the Indians, cattle entered the grasslands where the buffalo had roamed. The cowboy enjoyed his brief heyday, fading then into the folklore of the Wild West. From colonial times, especially in the South, cattle raising had been a common enterprise just beyond the fringe of settlement. In many cases the early slaves took care of the livestock. Later, in the West, African-American cowboys were a common sight, although they were lost from view in the novels and "horse operas" that pictured a lily-white frontier. Much of the romance of the open-range cattle industry derived from its Mexican roots. The Texas longhorns and the cowboys' horses had in large part descended from stock brought over by the Spaniards, and many of the industry's trappings had been worked out in Mexico first: the cowboy's saddle, chaps (*chaparejos*) to protect the legs, spurs, and lariat.

For many years wild cattle competed with the buffalo in the Spanish borderlands. Natural selection and contact with "Anglo" scrub cattle produced the Texas longhorns: lean and rangy, they were noted more for speed and endurance than for providing a choice steak. They had little value, moreover, because the largest markets for beef were too far away. Occasionally they were driven to market in Austin, Galveston, or New Orleans, and some even to the gold fields of California, Arizona, and Colorado. At the end of the Civil War, perhaps as many as 5 million roamed the grasslands of Texas, still neglected—but not for long. In the upper Mississippi Valley, where herds had been depleted by the war, cattle were in great demand, and the Texas cattle could be had just for the effort of rounding them up.

So the cattle drives began anew after the Civil War, but on a scale far greater than before. In 1866 a large Texas herd set out for Sedalia, Missouri, the western terminus of the Missouri-Pacific Railroad. But that route proved unsuitable because it was subject to raids by postwar bushwhackers (bandits), obstructed by woodlands, and opposed by Arkansas and Missouri farmers. New opportunities arose as railroads

Roundup on the Sherman Ranch, Genesee, Kansas, 1902.

pushed farther west where cattle could be driven through relatively vacant lands.

Joseph G. McCoy, the youngest of three brothers already in the livestock business near Springfield, Illinois, recognized the possibilities for moving the cattle trade west. He turned Abilene into the first successful Kansas cowtown. Located on the Kansas-Pacific Railroad at the northern end of a trail laid out through Indian Territory by the part-Cherokee Jesse Chisholm, Abilene was a "small, dead place, consisting of about one dozen log huts" when McCoy arrived in early 1867.

McCoy bought up 250 acres for a stockyard, laid plans for a barn, an office building, livestock scales, a hotel, and a bank—and sent an agent into Indian Territory to cultivate owners of herds bound north. Over the next few years Abilene developed into a flourishing town. But, as the railroads moved west, so did the cowtowns and the trails: Ellsworth, Wichita, Caldwell, and Dodge City, all in Kansas; and farther north Ogallala, Nebraska; Cheyenne, Wyoming; and Miles City, Montana.

The cattle industry spurred rapid growth. The population of Kansas rose from 107,000 in 1860 to 365,000 ten years later and reached almost a million by 1880. Nebraska witnessed similar increases. During the 1860s, the cattle would be delivered to rail depots, loaded onto freight cars, and shipped east. By the time they arrived in New York or Massachusetts, some would be dead or dying and all would have lost significant weight. The secret to higher profits for the cattle industry was to devise a way to slaughter the cattle in the Midwest and ship the dressed carcasses east and west. That required refrigeration to keep the meat from spoiling. In 1869 G. H. Hammond, a Chicago meat packer, shipped the first refrigerated beef in an air-cooled car from Chicago to Boston. Eight years later, Gustavus Swift developed a more efficient system of mechanical refrigeration, an innovation that earned him a fortune and provided a major stimulus to the growth of the cattle industry.

But it was one thing to develop the processes to produce refrigerated meat; it was another to convince people to eat it. This required a major marketing campaign. Consumers balked at eating beef that had been butchered a thousand miles away. "The idea of eating meat a week or more after it had been killed," Swift's son noted, "met with a nasty-nice horror." What gradually changed public taste was the fact that dressed meat was significantly cheaper than fresh beef. In addition, Swift introduced the practice of displaying various cuts of dressed beef in butcher shops. He urged his agents in eastern cities to cut up the meat "and scatter the pieces," for "the more you cut, the more you sell." The combination of shrewd marketing and low prices soon convinced customers to prefer dressed meat.

During the twenty years after the Civil War, some 40,000 cowboys roamed the Great Plains. They were young—the average age was twenty-four—and from diverse backgrounds. Thirty percent were either Mexican or African American, and hundreds were Indians. Many others were Civil War veterans from North and South who now rode side by side, and a number had come from Europe. The life of a cowboy, for the most part, was rarely as exciting as motion pictures and television shows have depicted. Being a ranchhand involved grueling, dirty, wage labor interspersed with drudgery and boredom.

The flush times of the cowtown soon passed, and the long cattle drives played out too, because they were economically unsound. The dangers of the trail, the wear and tear on men and cattle, the charges levied on drives across Indian Territory, and the advance of farms across the trails combined to persuade cattlemen that they could best function near the railroads. As railroads spread out into Texas and the Plains, the cattle business spread with them over the High Plains as far as Montana and on into Canada.

In the absence of laws governing the range, the cattlemen at first worked out a code of action largely dictated by circumstances. As cattle often wandered onto other people's claims, cowboys would "ride the line" to keep the cattle off the next ranch as well as conducting spring roundups to separate the mixed herds. Each rancher's cattle would be distinguished by distinctive brands. But this changed in 1873 when Joseph Glidden, an Illinois farmer, invented the first effective barbed wire, which ranchers used to fence off their claims at relatively low cost. More often than not these were parts of the public domain to which they had no valid title. In that same year an eastern promoter, John W. "Bet-a-Million" Gates, one of the early agents for Glidden, gave a persuasive demonstration of the barbed wire in San Antonio. Skeptical cattlemen discovered that their meanest longhorns shied away from the fence which, as Gates put it, was light as air, stronger than whiskey, and cheaper than dirt. Orders poured in, and Gates eventually put together a virtual monopoly in the American Steel and Wire Company.

The greatest boom in the range-cattle trade came in the early 1880s, when eastern and European investors began to pour money into the "Beef Bonanza." Cattle growing, like mining, entered a season of wild speculation, and then evolved from a romantic adventure into a prosaic business, often a corporate business.

END OF THE OPEN RANGE   A combination of factors conspired to end the open range. Farmers kept crowding in and laying out homesteads on the open range, waging "barbed-wire wars" with cattlemen by either cutting the cattlemen's fences or policing their own. The boundless range was beginning to be overstocked by 1883, and expenses mounted as stock breeders formed associations to keep intruders out of overstocked ranges, to establish and protect land titles, to deal with railroads and buyers, to fight prairie fires, and to cope with rustlers and predatory beasts. The rise of sheep herding by 1880 caused still another conflict with the cattlemen. A final blow to the open-range industry came with two unusually severe winters in 1886 and 1887, followed by ten long years of drought.

For those who survived all the hazards of the range, the response to these problems was to establish legal title and fence in the lands, restrict the herds to a reasonable size, and provide shelter and hay against the rigors of winter. Moreover, as the long cattle drives ended with the advent of more rail lines and refrigerated cars, the cowboy settled into a more sedentary existence. Within merely two decades, 1866–1886, the era of the cowboy had come and gone.

RANGE WARS   The growth of the cattle industry placed a premium upon land, and conflicting claims over land and water rights ignited violent disputes between ranchers and farmers. Ranchers often tried to drive off neighboring farmers, and farmers in turn tried to sabotage the cattle barons, cutting their fences and spooking their herds. The cattle ranchers also clashed with sheepherders over access to grasslands. A strain of ethnic and religious prejudice heightened the tension between ranchers and herders. In the Southwest, shepherds were usually Mexican Americans; in Idaho and Nevada they were Basques or Mormons. Many Anglo-American cattle ranchers and cowboys viewed these ethnic and religious groups as un-American and inferior. This attitude helped them rationalize the use of violence against the sheepherders. Warfare between defenders of the bovine and ovine species gradually faded, however, as the sheep for the most part found refuge in the high pastures of the mountains, leaving the grasslands of the Plains to the cattlemen.

There also developed a perennial tension over grassland use between large and small cattle ranchers. The large ranchers fenced in huge tracts of public lands, leaving the smaller ranchers with too little pasture. To survive, the smaller ranchers cut the fences. In central Texas this practice sparked the Fence-Cutters' War of 1883–1884. Several ranchers were killed and dozens wounded before the state ended the conflict by passing legislation outlawing fence cutting. An even more violent confrontation between large and small ranchers occurred in Wyoming when members of the Wyoming Stock Association organized an assault against small ranchers, who they charged were rustling their stock. In Johnson County, Wyoming, in 1889, the cattle barons lynched James Averell, a small rancher, and Ella Watson, a prostitute embroiled in the dispute. The vigilantes were brought to trial, but the case was dismissed when the four witnesses to the hanging refused to testify.

Two years later, in 1891, the large ranchers organized a "lynching bee" to eliminate rustlers in Johnson County, and hired gunmen from

Judge Roy Bean's courthouse and saloon, Langtry, Texas, 1900.

Texas to do their bidding. On Tuesday, April 5, 1892, two dozen Texan mercenaries and an equal number of ranchers who dubbed themselves "regulators" set out to wipe out the rustlers. After killing two men, the vigilante group headed north, only to find itself surrounded by a band of small ranchers who had been alerted to their plan. The timely arrival of federal cavalry prevented a massacre. The cattle kings thereupon turned to a bounty hunter, Tom Horn, who murdered "rustlers" until he himself was caught, convicted, and hanged.

FARMERS AND THE LAND   Among the legendary figures of the West, the sodbusters projected an unromantic image in contrast to the cowboys, cavalry, and Indians. Farming has always been a risky and arduous endeavor, and it was made more so on the Great Plains by the unforgiving environment. After 1865, on paper at least, the federal land laws offered favorable terms to the farmer. Under the Homestead Act of 1862 a farmer could either realize the old dream of free land simply by staking out a claim and living on it for five years, or by buying the land at $1.25 an acre after six months. But such land legislation was predicated upon an entirely different environment from that of the Plains, and the laws were never adjusted to the fact that much of the land was suited only for cattle. Cattle ranchers were forced to obtain land by gradual acquisition from homesteaders or land-grant railroads.

The unchangeable fact of aridity, rather than new land laws, shaped institutions in the New West. Where farming was impossible the cattle ranchers simply established dominance by control of the water, regardless of the laws. Belated legislative efforts to develop irrigable lands finally achieved a major success when the Newlands Reclamation Act (after the aptly named Senator Francis G. Newlands of Nevada) of 1901 set up the Bureau of Reclamation. The proceeds of public land sales in sixteen states created a fund for irrigation works, and the Reclamation Bureau set about building such major projects as Boulder (later Hoover) Dam on the Nevada-Arizona line, Roosevelt Dam in Arizona, and Elephant Butte Dam and Arrowrock Dam in New Mexico.

The lands of the New West, as on previous frontiers, passed to their ultimate owners more often from private hands than directly from the government. Many of the 274 million acres claimed under the Homestead Act passed quickly to ranchers or speculators, and thence to settlers. The land-grant railroads got some 200 million acres of the public domain in the twenty years from 1851 to 1871, and sold much of this land to build population centers and traffic along the lines. The New West of ranchers and farmers was in fact largely the product of the railroads.

The first arrivals on the sodhouse frontier faced a grim struggle against danger, adversity, and monotony. Though land was relatively cheap, horses, livestock, wagons, wells, fencing, seed, and fertilizer were not. Freight rates and interest rates on loans seemed criminally high. As in the South, declining crop prices produced indebtedness that soon became a chronic condition that led strapped western farmers to embrace virtually any plan to inflate the money supply. The virgin land itself, although fertile, resisted planting; the heavy sod broke many a plow. Since wood was almost nonexistent on the prairies, pioneer families used buffalo chips (dried dung) for fuel. Farmers and their families also fought a constant battle with the elements: tornadoes, hailstorms, droughts, prairie fires, blizzards, and pests. Swarms of locusts would cloud the horizon, occasionally covering the ground six inches deep and consuming everything in their path. A Wichita newspaper reported in 1878 that the grasshoppers devoured "everything green, stripping the foliage off the bark and from the tender twigs of the fruit trees, destroying every plant that is good for food or pleasant to the eyes, that man has planted."

As the railroads arrived bearing lumber from the wooded regions, farmers could leave their dugouts and sodhouses (homes roofed with sod) to build more familiar frame houses. New machinery helped open fresh opportunities for farmers. Back in 1838 John Deere of Illinois had developed the steel-faced plow and moldboard that conquered the clinging humus of the prairie. But its high cost encouraged further experiments, and in 1868 James Oliver of Indiana made a successful chilled-iron plow. With further improvements his "sodbuster" was soon ready for mass production, easing the task of breaking the shallow but tough grass roots of the Plains. Improvements and new inventions in threshing machines, hay mowers, planters, manure spreaders, cream separators, and other devices lightened the burden of labor but added to the capital outlay for the farmer.

In Minnesota, the Dakotas, and central California, the gigantic "bonanza farms" with machinery for mass production became the marvels of the age. On one farm in North Dakota, 13,000 acres of wheat made a single field. "You are in a sea of wheat," a bedazzled visitor wrote in 1880. "The railroad train rolls through an ocean of grain." Another bonanza farm employed over a thousand migrant workers to tend 34,000 acres.

To get a start on a family homestead required a minimum capital investment of $1,000. While the overall value of farm lands and farm products increased in the late nineteenth century, the small farmers did not keep up with the march of progress. Their numbers grew but decreased in proportion to the population at large. Wheat, like cotton in the antebellum period, provided the great export crop that evened America's balance of payments and spurred economic growth. For a variety of reasons, however, few small farmers prospered. Something was amiss, farmers began to reason, and by the decade of the 1890s they

Harvest on the Dalrymple farm, Red River Valley, Dakota Territory, 1877.

were in open revolt against the "system" of corrupt processors and avaricious bankers who they believed conspired against them.

PIONEER WOMEN   The West remained a largely male society throughout the nineteenth century. In Texas, for example, the ratio of men to women in 1890 was 110 to 1. Women continued to face traditional legal barriers and social prejudice. A wife could not sell property without her husband's approval. In Texas women could not sue except for divorce, nor could they serve on juries, act as lawyers, or witness a will.

But the fight for survival in the trans-Mississippi West made men and women more equal partners than were their eastern counterparts. Many women who lost their mates to the deadly toil of sodbusting thereafter assumed complete responsibility for their farms. In general, women on the prairie became more independent than those living domestic lives back East. One woman declared that she insisted on leaving out the phrasing about "obeying" her husband from their marriage vows. "I had served my time of tutelage to my parents as all children are supposed to. I was a woman now and capable of being the other half of the head of the family." Similar examples of independence abound. Explained one Kansas woman: "The outstanding fact is that the environ-

Woman and her family in front of their sodhouse. The difficult life on the prairie led to more egalitarian marriages.

ment was such as to bring out and develop the dominant qualities of individual character. Kansas women of that day learned at an early age to depend on themselves—to do whatever work there was to be done, and to face danger when it must be faced, as calmly as they were able."

A VIOLENT CULTURE   Although often exaggerated in Hollywood films, the western frontier during the second half of the nineteenth century was indeed a violent place. Guns, rifles, and knives were everywhere evident, and people readily used them to resolve their disputes. The brutal requirements for self-preservation on the frontier or in the mining communities changed the long-standing premise of English common law that required a person to flee or retreat in the face of a violent threat. In 1876 a court ruled that a "true man" was no longer obligated "to fly" from an assailant.

The need to protect one's family or homestead in the face of threats and the frontiersman's obsessive preoccupation with masculine honor helped nourish what came to be called the Code of the West. It stressed the need for a man to stand and fight when threatened or wronged, and this spawned a reckless preoccupation with individual courage. As the famous frontier marshal James Butler ("Wild Bill") Hickok explained, "Meet anyone face to face with whom you disagree," and "if you meet him face to face and took the same risk as he did, you could get away with almost anything [including killing], as long as the bullet was in the front."

Most of the individual violence associated with the "Wild West" occurred in the cattle towns and mining communities where young single men abounded, and liquor was the most popular refreshment. This was not surprising, given that these were societies with shallow roots and populated by so many people on the lookout for the main chance. Bodie, California, in the heart of the mining region, developed a reputation as a "shooter's town." Between 1877 and 1883, there were forty-four shootings, leaving twenty-nine dead. The courts convicted only one man of murder. A few roughnecks in Bodie preferred weapons other than guns. For several months Man Eater McGowan terrorized the town. He gained his nickname from his tendency to chew on his opponents' appendages. Before being run out of town, he bit the sheriff's leg, broke a pitcher over a waiter's head, and chewed or bit off the noses or ears of a dozen others.

Perhaps the most violent region of the West between the 1860s and 1890s was central Texas, an area bounded by Houston, Fort Worth, Dallas, San Antonio, and San Angelo. This huge territory included a volatile mix of peoples—Indians, Hispanics, German immigrants, freed slaves, and former Confederate soldiers. Ethnic and racial tensions, range wars, boundary disputes, outlaw activity, and vigilantism were common. John Wesley Hardin, the West's most prolific gunman, killed over twenty men in political disputes and community feuds. Once, a drunken Hardin fired a bullet through the wall of his hotel room to silence a snoring guest. The man never snored again.

"THE FRONTIER HAS GONE" American life reached an important juncture at the end of the nineteenth century. After the 1890 population count, the superintendent of the census noted that he could no longer locate a continuous frontier line beyond which population thinned out to fewer than two per square mile. This fact inspired the historian Frederick Jackson Turner to develop his influential frontier thesis, first outlined in his paper "The Significance of the Frontier in American History," delivered to the American Historical Association in 1893. "The existence of an area of free land," Turner wrote, "its continuous recession, and the advance of American settlement westward, explain American development." The frontier had shaped the national character in fundamental ways. It was

> to the frontier [that] the American intellect owes its striking characteristics. That coarseness and strength combined with acuteness and acquisitiveness; that practical, inventive turn of mind, quick to find expedients; that masterful grasp of material things, lacking in the artistic but powerful to effect great ends; that restless, nervous energy; that dominant individualism, working for good and for evil, and withal that buoyancy and exuberance which comes with freedom—these are traits of the frontier, or traits called out elsewhere because of the existence of the frontier.

In 1893, Turner concluded, "four centuries from the discovery of America, at the end of a hundred years under the Constitution, the frontier has gone and with its going has closed the first period of American history."

Turner's "frontier thesis" guided several generations of scholars and students in their understanding of the distinctive characteristics of

American history. His view of the frontier as the westward-moving source of America's democratic politics, open society, unfettered economy, and rugged individualism, far removed from the corruptions of urban life, gripped the popular imagination as well. But it left much out of the story. The frontier experience Turner described exaggerated the homogenizing effect of the frontier environment and virtually ignored the role of women, blacks, Indians, Mormons, Hispanics, and Asians in shaping the diverse human geography of the western United States. Turner also implied that the West would be fundamentally different after 1890 because the frontier experience was essentially over. But in many respects that region has retained the qualities associated with the rush for land, gold, timber, and water rights during the post–Civil War decades. The mining frontier, as one historian has recently written, "set a mood that has never disappeared from the West: the attitude of extractive industry—get in, get rich, get out."

MAKING CONNECTIONS

- The problems of southern and western farmers described in this chapter will set the stage for the rise of the Populists as discussed in Chapter 22.

- This is a crucial period in the evolution of race relations in the South, bridging the antebellum period and the twentieth century.

- This chapter closes with the observation that, as of 1890, according to the superintendent of the census and the historian Frederick Jackson Turner, "the frontier has gone." Where would Americans now look to fulfill their expansionist urgings?

FURTHER READING

The classic study of the emergence of the New South remains C. Vann Woodward's *Origins of the New South, 1877–1913* (1951). A more recent treatment of southern society after the end of Reconstruction is Edward L. Ayers's *Southern Crossing: A History of the American South, 1877–1906* (1995).

For Bourbon politics, see Jack P. Maddex's *The Virginia Conservatives, 1867–1879* (1970) and William J. Cooper's *The Conservative Regime: South Carolina, 1877–1890* (1968). On the development of southern politics since Reconstruction, see Dewey W. Grantham's *The Life and Death of the Solid South: A Political History* (1988).

A good survey of industrialization in the South is James C. Cobb's *Industrialization and Southern Society, 1877–1984* (1984). Scholarship on the textile industry, which formed the heart of the New South's aspirations, includes Patrick J. Hearden's *Independence and Empire: The New South's Cotton Mill Campaigns, 1865–1901* (1982), David L. Carlton's *Mill and Town in South Carolina, 1880–1920* (1982), and Jacqueline D. Hall et al.'s *Like a Family: The Making of a Southern Cotton Mill World* (1987). For developments in the tobacco industry, consult Robert F. Durden's *The Dukes of Durham, 1865–1929* (1975). A fine study of convict leasing is Alex Lichtenstein's *Twice the Work of Free Labor: The Political Economy of Convict Labor in the New South* (1996).

C. Vann Woodward's *The Strange Career of Jim Crow* (3rd ed., 1974) remains the standard on southern race relations. Some of Woodward's points are challenged in Howard N. Rabinowitz's *Race Relations in the Urban South, 1865–1890* (1978), Joel Williamson's *The Crucible of Race* (1984), and John W. Cell's *The Highest Stage of White Supremacy* (1982).

Leon Litwack's *Trouble in Mind: Black Southerners in the Age of Jim Crow* (1998) treats the rise of legal segregation. David M. Oshinsky focuses on race relations and convict leasing in Mississippi in *"Worse Than Slavery": Parchman Farm and the Ordeal of Jim Crow Justice* (1996). J. Morgan Kousser's *The Shaping of Southern Politics: Suffrage Restriction and Establishment of the One-Party South, 1880–1910* (1974) handles disenfranchisement. An award-winning study of white women and the race issue is Glenda Gilmore's *Gender and Jim Crow: Women and the Politics of White Supremacy in North Carolina, 1896–1920* (1996).

Several good books discuss developments in southern agriculture. Roger L. Ransom and Richard Sutch's *One Kind of Freedom: The Economic Consequences of Emancipation* (1977) examines the origins of sharecropping. A more recent sociological analysis is Edward Royce's *The Origins of Southern Sharecropping* (1993).

Good overviews of the transformation of the West are Rodman W. Paul's *The Far West and the Great Plains in Transition, 1859–1908* (rev. ed., 1998) and Geoffrey Ward, David Duncan, and Ken Burns's *The West: An Illustrated History* (1996). The Turner thesis is best presented by Frederick Jackson Turner himself in *The Frontier in American History* (1920).

For powerful and provocative reinterpretations of the frontier and the development of the West, see William Cronon's *Nature's Metropolis: Chicago and the Great West* (1991), Patricia Nelson Limerick's *The Legacy of Conquest: The Unbroken Past of the American West* (1987), Richard White's *"It's Your Misfortune and None of My Own": A New History of the American West* (1991), Donald Worster's *Under Western Skies: Nature and History in the American West* (1992), and *Under an Open Sky: Rethinking America's Western Past* (1992), edited by William Cronon, George Miles and Jay Gitlin.

The role of blacks in western settlement is the focus of Willam L. Katz's *The Black West* (1996) and Nell Painter's *Exodusters: Black Migration to Kansas after Reconstruction* (1992). The best account of the conflicts between Indians and whites is Robert Utley's *The Indian Frontier of the American West, 1846–1890* (1984). For a presentation of the Native American side of the story, see Peter Nabokov and Vine Deloria's *Native American Testimony: A Chronicle of Indian-White Relations from Prophecy to the Present, 1492–1992* (1992).

Federal government efforts to facilitate western agriculture are detailed in William D. Rowley's *Reclaiming the Arid West: The Career of Francis G. Newlands* (1996).

20 ∞ BIG BUSINESS AND ORGANIZED LABOR

CHAPTER ORGANIZER

This chapter focuses on:

- factors that fueled the growth of the post–Civil War economy.

- the methods and achievements of major entrepreneurs.

- the rise of large labor unions.

America's rise as an industrial and agricultural giant in the late nineteenth century is a fact of towering visibility. Between 1869 and 1899, the nation's population nearly trebled, farm production more than doubled, and the value of manufactures grew sixfold (in constant prices). Within three generations after the Civil War, the nation, which had long been a predominantly rural society dependent upon household production, governed by the requirements of the land and the rhythms of the seasons, burst forth as the world's preeminent economic power. The United States became a highly structured, increasingly centralized, urban-industrial society buffeted by the imperatives of mass production, mass consumption, and time-clock efficiency. Bigness emerged as the prevailing standard of corporate life, and social tensions worsened with the rising scale of business enterprise.

The Hand of Man, *photogravure by Alfred Stieglitz, 1902.*

The industrial revolution created huge corporations that came to dominate the economy during the late nineteenth century. An older economy dependent upon small business and craftspeople could not satisfy the rapidly growing national market. Entrepreneurs who recognized this fact focused their attention on developing systems of mass production and distribution. To do so, they took advantage of striking technological innovations. As the volume of these businesses grew, the owners sought to integrate all the processes of production and distribution into single companies, thus producing even larger firms. Others joined forces with their competitors in an effort to dominate entire industries. This process of industrial combination and concentration, whether the result of natural economic forces or human machinations, transformed the nation's economy and social order. It also provoked widespread dissent and the emergence of an organized labor movement.

THE POST–CIVIL WAR ECONOMY

ECONOMIC EFFECTS OF THE CIVIL WAR The rise of centralized industry has led all too easily to the judgment that demands created by the Civil War powered a "takeoff" in economic growth. At the same time, the story goes, the legislative program of the Republicans unleashed business enterprise. But the highly visible successes of wartime profiteers in arms and supplies, of speculators in various markets, and of tycoons such as investment banker Jay Cooke, who got rich selling Treasury bonds, have overshadowed the actual setbacks that marked the wartime economy. The decade of the 1860s was the only one in which, on a per-capita basis, economic output actually *decreased,* North and South, during the mid- to late nineteenth century.

The postwar industrial expansion, which started from a relatively high base and moved the economy to even higher levels, may have been fueled *indirectly* by the Civil War. Wartime inflation enhanced the position of those owning property and making profits, while entrepreneurs forced to save by the war contributed to the immediate postwar period of speculation. It is not clear, though, that postwar Republican policies contributed uniquely to economic expansion. The National Banking Act created a sounder currency, but its effects on the economy were ambiguous. Government aid in building the great transcontinental and regional railroads simply continued the encouragement to railroads long offered by state and federal governments. The postwar climate of favoritism to business was but slightly strengthened by the defeat of southern agrarianism. Postwar tariffs also had ambiguous effects, hampering foreign competitors but discouraging American exports. The emotional lift of victory provided an important, if indirect, spur to the northern economy. After the war Senator John Sherman of Ohio wrote to his brother William, the famous general: "The truth is the close of the war with our resources unimpaired gives an elevation, a scope to the ideas of leading capitalists far higher than anything ever undertaken in this country. They talk of millions as confidently as before of thousands."

BUILDING THE TRANSCONTINENTAL RAILROADS   Railroads were the first big business, the first magnet for the great financial markets, and the first industry to develop a large-scale management bureaucracy. The railroads opened the West, connected raw materials to factories and markets, and in so doing created a national market. At the same time, they were themselves gigantic markets for iron, steel, lumber, and other capital goods.

The renewal of railroad building after the Civil War increased the total mileage from 30,600 in 1862 to 53,000 in 1870 and 94,000 by 1880.

During the 1880s, the greatest decade of railroad building, mileage leaped to 167,000, and then to 199,000 by 1900. Most of this construction filled out the network east of the Mississippi, but the most spectacular exploits were the monumental transcontinental lines built across the desolate plains and rugged mountains. Running through sparsely settled lands, the railroads promised little quick return, but they served the national purpose of binding the country together and so received generous government support.

Until 1850 constitutional scruples had constrained federal aid for internal improvements, although many states had subsidized railroads within their borders. But in 1850 Stephen Douglas secured from Congress a grant of public lands to subsidize two north-south railroads connecting Chicago and Mobile. Over the next twenty years, federal land grants, mainly to transcontinentals, amounted to some 129 million acres. In addition to land, the railroads received financial aid from federal, state, and local governments. Altogether the railroads received about $707 million in cash and $335 million in land.

Before the Civil War, sectional differences over the choice of routes held up the start of a transcontinental line. Secession finally permitted passage of the Pacific Railway Bill, which Lincoln signed into law in 1862. The act authorized a line along a north-central route, to be built by the Union Pacific Railroad westward from Omaha and the Central Pacific Railroad eastward from Sacramento. As amended in 1864, the act donated to these two corporations twenty sections of land per mile of track, in alternating blocs of railroad and government property, and loans of $16,000 to $48,000 per mile, depending on the difficulty of the terrain.

Both railroads began construction during the war, but most of the work was done after 1865, as the companies raced to build most of the line and thereby get most of the subsidy. The Union Pacific pushed across the plains at a rapid pace, avoiding the Rockies by going through Evans Pass in Wyoming. The work crews, with large numbers of ex-soldiers and Irish immigrants as laborers, had to cope with bad roads, water shortages, extreme weather, and Indian marauders. The movable encampments with their retinue of peddlers, gamblers, and prostitutes were aptly dubbed "Hell-on-wheels." Construction of the rail line and bridges was hasty and much of it so flimsy that it had to be redone later, but the Union Pacific pushed on to its celebrated rendezvous with the Central Pacific in 1869.

The Central Pacific crews were mainly Chinese workers lured first by the California gold rush and then by railroad jobs. Thousands of Chinese men migrated to America, raising their numbers in the United States from 7,500 in 1850 to 105,000 in 1880. Most of these "coolie" laborers were single males intent upon accumulating money and then returning to their homeland, where they could then afford to marry and buy a parcel of land. Their temporary status and dream of a good life back in China apparently made them more willing than American laborers to endure the dangerous working conditions and low pay of railroad work. Many Chinese died on the job.

The grading and hauling were very dangerous, especially in the rugged mountains. Fifty-seven miles east of Sacramento, the construction crews encountered the towering Sierras, but they were eventually able to cut through to more level country in Nevada. The Union Pacific had built 1,086 miles compared with the Central Pacific's 689 when the race ended on the salt plains of Utah at Promontory. There, on May 10, 1869, California governor Leland Stanford drove a gold spike that

The celebration after the last spike was driven at Promontory, Utah, on May 10, 1869, completing the first transcontinental railroad.

TRANSCONTINENTAL
RAILROAD LINES, 1880s

symbolized the railroad's completion as the telegraph lines signaled the taps of the hammer to a celebrating nation.

The next transcontinental railroad linked the Atchison, Topeka and Santa Fe with the Southern Pacific at Needles in southern California. The Santa Fe completed its line to San Diego by 1884. Meanwhile the Southern Pacific, which had absorbed the Central Pacific, continued on by way of Yuma to El Paso in 1882, where it made connections to St. Louis and New Orleans. To the north, the Northern Pacific had connected Lake Superior with Portland by 1883, and ten years later the Great Northern, which had slowly and carefully been building westward from St. Paul, thrust its way to Tacoma—and without a land grant. Thus before the turn of the century five trunk lines existed, supplemented by connections that afforded other transcontinental routes.

FINANCING THE RAILROADS   The shady financial practices of the railroad men earned them the label of "robber barons," an epithet soon extended to other "captains of industry" as well. The building of both the Union Pacific and Central Pacific—as well as other transcontinentals—induced shameless profiteering through construction companies controlled by insiders, which overcharged the railroad companies. The Crédit Mobilier Company, according to congressional investigators, bought congressmen like sacks of potatoes and charged the Union Pacific $94 million for construction that cost at most $44 million.

In the long run, nevertheless, the federal government recovered much if not all of its investment in transcontinentals and accomplished the purpose of linking the country together. As farms, ranches, and towns sprouted around the rail lines, the value of the alternate sections of government land on either side of the tracks skyrocketed. The railroads also benefited the public by hauling government freight, military personnel and equipment, and the mails at half fare or for free. Moreover, by helping to accelerate the creation of a national market, the railroads spurred economic growth and thereby increased government revenues.

Eastern rail lines, like those in the West, were subject to financial buccaneering, which centered first on the Erie Railroad, the favorite prey of manipulators. The prince of the railroad "robber barons" was Jay Gould, a secretive trickster who mastered the fine art of buying run-

Jay Gould, prince of the railroad buccaneers.

"Commodore" Cornelius Vanderbilt consolidated control of the vast New York Central Railroad in the 1860s.

down railroads, making cosmetic improvements, paying dividends out of capital, and selling out at a profit, meanwhile using corporate funds for personal speculation and judicious bribes. Ousted by a reform group after having looted the Erie Railroad, Gould moved on to richer spoils in western railroads and a variety of other corporations, including Western Union. Nearly every enterprise he touched was either compromised or ruined, while Gould was building a fortune that amounted to $100 million upon his death at age fifty-six.

Few railroad fortunes were built in those freewheeling times by methods of pristine purity, but compared to opportunists such as Gould, most railroad owners were giants of probity. They at least took some interest in the welfare of their companies, if not always in that of the public. Cornelius Vanderbilt, called "Commodore" by virtue of his early exploits in steamboating, stands out among the railroad barons. Already rich before the Civil War, he decided to give up the hazards of wartime shipping and move his capital into land transport. Under his direction, the first of the major eastern railroad consolidations took form.

Vanderbilt engineered the merger of separate trunk lines connecting Albany and Buffalo into a single powerful rail network led by the New York Central. This accomplished, he forged connections to New York City and then tried to corner the stock of his chief competitor, the Erie

Railroad. But the directors of that line beat him there by the simple expedient of printing new Erie stock faster than he could buy it. In 1873, however, he bought the Lake Shore and Michigan Southern Railroad, which gave his lines connections into the lucrative Chicago market. After the Commodore's death in 1877, his son William Henry extended the Vanderbilt railroads to include more than 13,000 miles in the Northeast. The consolidation trend was nationwide: about two-thirds of the nation's railroad mileage fell under the control of only seven major groups by 1900.

MANUFACTURING AND INVENTIONS   The story of manufacturing after the Civil War shows much the same pattern of expansion and merger in both old and new industries. The Patent Office, which had recorded only 276 inventions during its first decade of existence, the 1790s, registered almost 235,000 in the decade of the 1890s. New processes in steel-making and refining were the foundation of the Carnegie and Rockefeller enterprises. The refrigerator car made it possible for the beef, mutton, and pork of the New West to reach a national market, giving rise to great packinghouse enterprises. Corrugated rollers that could crack the hard spicy wheat of the Great Plains provided impetus to the flour milling that centered in Minneapolis under the con-

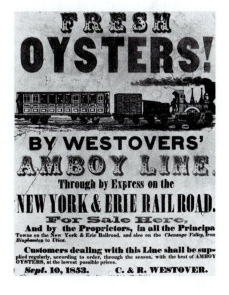

Advertisement for a refrigerator car, 1853. The advent of refrigeration made transcontinental shipment of perishable food such as meat and seafood possible.

trol of the Pillsburys and others. In 1884 tobacco manufacturing moved into a new stage when the Duke interests employed a machine to roll cigarettes.

The list of innovations can be extended indefinitely: barbed wire, farm implements, George Westinghouse's air brake for trains (1868), steam turbines, gas distribution and electrical devices, Christopher Sholes's typewriter (1867), J. W. McGaffey's vacuum cleaner (1869), and countless others. Before the end of the century, the internal-combustion engine and the motion picture, each the work of many hands, were laying the foundations for new industries that would emerge in the twentieth century.

These technological advances altered the lives of ordinary people far more than did activities in the political and intellectual realms. In no field was this more true than in the applications of electricity to power and communications. Few if any inventions of the times could rival the importance of the telephone, which Alexander Graham Bell patented in 1876. To promote the new device the inventor and his supporters formed the National Bell Telephone Company.

Inventions such as the telephone ushered in a new age of competitive battles among companies. Almost from the first the Bell interests had to defend their patent against competitors. The most dangerous threat came from Western Union which, after turning down a chance to buy Bell's "toy," employed Thomas Edison to develop an improved version. Edison's telephone became the prototype of the modern instrument, with its separate transmitter and receiver. But Bell had a prior claim on the basic principle, and Western Union, rather than risk a legal defeat, sold its rights and properties for a tidy sum, clearing the way for the creation of a monopoly. In 1885 the Bell interests organized the American Telephone and Telegraph Company. By 1899 it was a huge holding company in control of forty-nine licensed subsidiaries and itself an operating company for long-distance lines.

In the rise of electrical industries, the name of Thomas Alva Edison stands above that of other inventors. He started his career at an early age, selling papers and candies on trains, soon learned telegraphy, and began making improvements in that and other areas. He invented the phonograph in 1877 and the first successful incandescent light bulb in 1879. Altogether he created or perfected hundreds of new devices and processes, including the storage battery, dictaphone, mimeograph, dy-

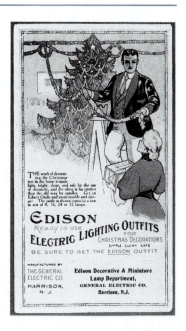

An advertisement for Edison Electric Lighting Outfits, 1890. After Thomas Edison brought basic electricity to homes, extravagances like electric Christmas tree lights became imaginable and obtainable.

namo, electric transmission, and the motion picture. In 1882, with the backing of J. P. Morgan, the Edison Electric Illuminating Company began to supply current to eighty-five customers in New York City, beginning the great electric utility industry. A number of companies making light bulbs merged into the Edison General Electric Company in 1888. Financially secure, Edison retired from business to devote himself full time once again to invention.

The use of direct current limited Edison's lighting system to a radius of about two miles. To cover more distance required an alternating current, which could be transmitted at high voltage and then stepped down by transformers. George Westinghouse, inventor of the air brake, developed the first alternating-current system in 1886 and manufactured the equipment through the Westinghouse Electric Company. Edison resisted the new method as too risky, but the Westinghouse system won the "Battle of the Currents," and the Edison companies had to switch over. After the invention of the alternating-current motor by a Croatian immigrant named Nikola Tesla, Westinghouse acquired and improved the motor and started a revolution by enabling factories to locate wherever they wished. They no longer had to cluster around waterfalls and coal supplies for their energy.

ENTREPRENEURS

Edison and Westinghouse were rare examples of inventors with the luck and foresight to get rich from the industries they created. The great captains of commerce were more often pure entrepreneurs, men skilled mainly in organizing and promoting industry. Several post–Civil War entrepreneurs stand out both for their achievements and for their special contributions: John D. Rockefeller and Andrew Carnegie, for their innovations in organization; J. Pierpont Morgan, for his development of investment banking; and Richard Sears and Alvah Roebuck, pioneers of mail-order retailing.

ROCKEFELLER AND THE OIL TRUST   Born in New York State, the son of a flamboyant, adulterous con man and a frugal, devout Baptist mother, Rockefeller moved as a youth to Cleveland. Soon thereafter, his father abandoned his family and started a new life under an assumed name with a second wife. Raised by his mother, John Rockefeller developed a passion for systematic organization and self-discipline. He was obsessed with precision, order, and tidiness. And early on, he decided to bring order and rationality to the chaotic oil industry.

Cleveland's railroad and ship connections made it a strategic location for servicing the oil fields of western Pennsylvania. The first oil well was struck in 1859 in Titusville, Pennsylvania, and led to the Pennsylvania oil rush of the 1860s. As oil could be refined into kerosene, which could be used in lighting, heating, and cooking, the economic importance of the oil rush soon came to outweigh that of the California gold rush of just ten years before. If it duplicated many of the earlier scenes of disorder, it ended by yielding more wealth. Well before the end of the Civil War, derricks checkered the area, and refineries sprang up in Pittsburgh and Cleveland.

Young Rockefeller, blessed with icy efficiency and tenacious daring, recognized the potential profits in refining oil and backed a refinery in Cleveland started by his friend Samuel Andrews. He then formed a partnership with Andrews, and in 1867 added H. M. Flagler to create the firm of Rockefeller, Andrews, and Flagler. In 1870 Rockefeller incorporated his various interests as the Standard Oil Company of Ohio, capitalized at $1 million.

Wooden derricks crowd the John Benninghoff farm on Oil Creek, Pennsylvania, 1860s.

Although Rockefeller was the largest refiner, he decided to weed out the competition, which he perceived as flooding the market with too much refined oil, which brought down prices and reduced profits. To bring order out of the chaos, in 1872 Rockefeller created the South Improvement Company, which he made the marketing agent for a large percentage of his oil shipments. By controlling this traffic, he gained clout with the railroads, which gave him large rebates (secret discounts) on the standard freight rates in order to keep his high-volume business. In some cases he forced the railroads to provide information on competitors' shipments. Rockefeller then approached his Cleveland competitors and offered to buy them out at his own price. Most of them saw the wisdom of this course. As Rockefeller put it, "the conditions were so chaotic [that is, competitive] that most of the refiners were very desirous to get out of the business." Those who resisted were forced out. As one competitor recalled, we were told that "if we did not sell out, we should be crushed out." In less than six weeks, Rockefeller took over twenty-two of his twenty-six competitors. By 1879 Standard Oil controlled 90 to 95 percent of the oil refining in the country.

Much of Rockefeller's success was based on his determination to "pay nobody a profit." Instead of depending on the products or services of other firms, known as "middlemen," Standard undertook to make its own barrels, cans, staves, and whatever else it needed. In economic

John D. Rockefeller, whose Standard Oil Company dominated the oil business.

terms this is called vertical integration. The company also kept large amounts of cash reserves to make it independent of banks in case of a crisis. In line with this policy, Rockefeller set out also to control his transportation needs. With Standard owning most of the pipelines leading to railroads, plus the tank cars and the oil-storage facilities, it was able to dissuade the railroads from servicing eastern competitors. Those rivals who insisted on holding out then faced a giant marketing organization capable of driving them to the wall with price wars.

Eventually, in order to consolidate scattered business interests under more efficient control, Rockefeller and his friends resorted to a new legal device: the trust. Long established in law to enable one or more people to manage property belonging to others, such as children or the mentally incompetent, the trust now was used for another purpose—centralized control of business. Since Standard Oil of Ohio was not permitted to hold property out of state, it began in 1872 to place properties or companies acquired elsewhere in trust, usually with the company secretary. This was impractical, however, since the death of the trustee would endanger the trust. To solve this problem, in 1882 he organized the Standard Oil Trust. All thirty-seven stockholders in various Standard Oil enterprises would convey their stock to nine trustees, receiving "trust certificates" in return. The nine trustees would thus be empowered to give central direction to all the Standard companies.

The original plan, never fully carried out, was to organize a Standard Oil Company in each state in which the trust did business. But the trust device, widely copied in the 1880s, proved legally vulnerable to prosecution under state laws against monopoly or restraint of trade. In 1892 the supreme court of Ohio ordered the Standard Oil Trust dissolved. For a while the company managed to unify control by the simple device of interlocking directorates, through which the board of directors of one company was made identical or nearly so to the boards of the others. Gradually, however, Rockefeller took to the idea of the holding company: a company that controlled other companies by holding all or at least a majority of their stock. He was convinced that big business was a natural result of capitalism at work. "It is too late," he declared in 1899, "to argue about the advantages of industrial combinations. They are a necessity." That same year Rockefeller brought his empire under the direction of the Standard Oil Company of New Jersey, a holding company. Though less vulnerable to prosecution under state law, some holding companies proved vulnerable to the Sherman Anti-Trust Act of 1890 (see Chapter 22). Meanwhile the term "trust" had become so fixed in the public mind that it was used to describe large combinations under holding companies as well.

CARNEGIE AND THE STEEL INDUSTRY Andrew Carnegie, like Rockefeller, experienced the untypical rise from poverty to riches that came to be known in those days as "the typical American success story." Born in Scotland, he migrated in 1848 with his family to Allegheny,

Andrew Carnegie.

Pennsylvania. Then thirteen, he started out as a bobbin boy in a textile mill at wages of $1.20 per week. At fourteen he was earning $2.50 per week as a telegraph messenger and used his spare time learning to read messages by ear. In 1853 he became personal secretary and telegrapher to Thomas Scott, then district superintendent of the Pennsylvania Railroad and later its president. When Scott moved up, Carnegie took his place as superintendent. During the Civil War, when Scott became assistant secretary of war in charge of transportation, Carnegie went with him, developed a military telegraph system, and personally helped evacuate the wounded from Bull Run.

Carnegie kept on moving—from telegraphy to railroading to bridge building and then to iron- and steel-making and investments. In 1865 Carnegie quit the railroad to devote full time to his own interests. These were mainly in iron and bridge building, but the versatile entrepreneur also made money in oil and sold railroad bonds in Europe. In 1872 he netted $150,000 on one trip, and on that trip met Sir Henry Bessemer, inventor of a new process of steel-making.

The next year Carnegie resolved to concentrate on steel, or as he put it, to put all his eggs in one basket and then watch that basket. Steel was the miracle material of the post–Civil War era, not because it was new, but because it suddenly was cheap. Until the mid–nineteenth century, the only way to make steel was from wrought iron—itself expensive—and in small quantities. Then in 1856 Bessemer invented what became known as the Bessemer converter, a process by which steel could be produced directly and quickly from pig iron. As the volume of steel rose, its price dropped, and its use soared. In 1860 the United States produced only 13,000 tons of steel. By 1880 production had reached 1.4 million tons.

Carnegie launched first the J. Edgar Thompson Steel Works, which he shrewdly named after the head of the Pennsylvania Railroad. As competitors arose, Carnegie picked them off one by one. In 1882, when the Pittsburgh Bessemer Steel Company ran into labor troubles and slackening demand, Carnegie bought out their almost-new Homestead works. When the Duquesne Bessemer Steel Company ran afoul of a smear campaign describing their rails as unsafe, Carnegie bought them out at less than cost.

Carnegie was never a technical expert on steel. He was a promoter, salesman, and organizer with a gift for finding and using men of expert

Carnegie plant at Homestead, Pennsylvania.

ability. He always insisted on up-to-date machinery and equipment, and he used times of recession to expand cheaply. Carnegie retained a large part of his annual profits during good times to tide the business over during lean years. Amid business depressions, when construction costs were low and competitors were forced to the wall, Carnegie used his surplus capital to buy them out and expand. He also preached to his employees a philosophy of constant innovation in order to reduce operating costs. In much of this Carnegie was a typical businessman of the time, if abler and luckier than most.

Carnegie stood out from other businessmen, however, as a thinker who fashioned and publicized a philosophy for big business, a conservative rationale that became deeply implanted in the conventional wisdom of some Americans. He believed that, however harsh their methods at times, he and other captains of industry were on the whole public benefactors. In his best-remembered essay, "The Gospel of Wealth," published in 1889, he argued that in the evolution of society the contrast between the millionaire and the laborer measures the distance society has come. "Not evil, but good, has come to the race from the accumulation of wealth by those who have the ability and energy that produces it." The process had been costly in many ways, but the law of competition was "best for the trade, because it insures the survival of the fittest in every department."

When he retired at age sixty-five, Carnegie devoted himself to dispensing his fortune for the public good, out of a sincere desire to promote social welfare and to further world peace. He called this being a "distributor" of wealth (he disliked the term "philanthropy"). He gave money to universities, libraries, hospitals, parks, halls for meetings and concerts, swimming pools, and church buildings—in that order.

Rockefeller, too, gave many gifts, mainly to education and medicine. A man of simple tastes, who opposed the use of tobacco and alcohol and believed his fortune was a public trust awarded by God, he became the world's leading philanthropist. He donated more than $500 million during his ninety-eight-year life. "I have always regarded it as a religious duty," Rockefeller said late in life, "to get all I could honorably and to give all I could."

J. P. MORGAN, THE FINANCIER   J. Pierpont Morgan was born to wealth and increased it enormously. His father was a partner in a London banking house, which he later came to direct. Young Pierpont at-

J. Pierpont Morgan. *This is the famous portrait by the photographer Edward Steichen, done in 1903.*

tended boarding school in Switzerland and university in Germany. After a brief apprenticeship, he was sent in 1857 to work in a New York firm representing his father's interests, and in 1860 set himself up as its New York agent under the name of J. Pierpont Morgan and Company. This firm, under various names, channeled European capital into America and grew into a financial power in its own right.

Morgan was an investment banker, which meant that he would buy corporate stocks and bonds wholesale and then sell them at a profit. The growth of large corporations put Morgan's and other investment firms in an increasingly strategic position in the economy. Since the investment business depended on the general good health of client companies, investment bankers became involved in the operation of their clients' firms, demanding places on boards of directors and helping to shape their fiscal dealings. By these means bankers could influence company policies. But this often resulted in heavy emphasis on fiscal matters to the detriment of technical innovation. Eventually people were speaking of the "money trust," the greatest trust of all, with its hand in all kinds of other enterprises.

Morgan early realized that railroads were the key to the times, and he acquired and reorganized one line after another. To Morgan, the stability brought by his operations helped the economy and the public. He believed that the railroaders and other businessmen, if unrestrained, would act like anarchists. Morgan's crowning triumph was consolidation of the steel industry, to which he was led by his interests in railroading. After a rapid series of mergers in the iron and steel industry, he bought out Carnegie's huge steel and iron holdings in 1901. Carnegie set his own price, which came to nearly $500 million, of which his personal share was nearly $300 million. In rapid succession, Morgan added other steel interests and the Rockefeller holdings in both Minnesota's Mesabi ore range and a Great Lakes ore fleet. The magnitude of such a fortune was enhanced by the absence of an income tax, a burden Americans would not face until 1914.

Altogether the new United States Steel Corporation, a holding company for these varied interests, was capitalized at $1.4 billion, a total that was heavily "watered" (valued well above the company's actual assets) but was soon made solid by large profits. The new giant was a marvel of the new century, the first billion-dollar corporation, the climactic event in that age of consolidation.

A lavish dinner celebrated the merger of the Carnegie and Morgan interests into U.S. Steel in 1901. These executives are seated at a table that is shaped like a huge rail.

SEARS AND ROEBUCK   American inventors helped manufacturers after the Civil War produce a vast number of new products, but problems of distribution remained acute. The most important challenge was how to extend the reach of modern commerce to the millions of people who lived on isolated farms and in small towns. In the aftermath of the Civil War, a traveling salesman from Chicago named Aaron Montgomery Ward decided that he could reach more people by mail than on foot and in the process could eliminate the "middlemen" whose services increased the retail price of goods. Beginning in the early 1870s, the Montgomery Ward Company began selling goods at a 40 percent discount through mail-order catalogs.

By the end of the century, a new retailer came to dominate the mail-order industry: Sears, Roebuck and Company, founded by two young midwestern entrepreneurs, Richard Sears and Alvah Roebuck, who began offering a cornucopia of goods by mail in the early 1890s. The Sears, Roebuck and Company catalog in 1897 was 786 pages long and was published in German and Swedish as well as in English. It included groceries, drugs, tools, bells, furniture, ice boxes, stoves and household utensils, musical instruments, farm implements, boots and shoes, clothes, books, and sporting goods. Sears and Roebuck claimed that they operated the "cheapest supply house on earth." One of their advertisements proclaimed: "Shop at Sears and Save." Their ability to buy goods in high volumes from wholesalers enabled them to sell items at prices below those offered in rural general stores. For example, Sears offered a sewing machine for $16 in 1897, a third as much as it cost in a retail shop. The company also specialized in fast and efficient service. "Our army of employees," the catalog claimed, "are instructed to handle every order and letter with care, in fact, to treat every customer at a distance just as they would like to be treated were they in the customer's place and the customer in theirs."

In 1895, Sears, Roebuck and Company moved from Minneapolis to Chicago, then the fastest growing city in the nation. As a rail center and busy freshwater port, Chicago was a magnet attracting manufacturers of all kinds. Alvah Roebuck thereupon decided to sell his share of the company to two Chicago businessmen, Aaron Nussenbaum and Julius Rosenwald. Nussenbaum and Rosenwald expanded the company's products to include virtually every item the public desired. By 1907, Sears, Roebuck and Company had become one of the largest business enterprises in the

Sears, Roebuck, and Company, catalog cover, 1897. Sears' extensive mail-order service and discounted prices allowed its many products to reach people in both cities and backcountry.

nation, with annual sales over $500 million. The new mail-order plant that opened in 1906 was the largest business building in the world. Soon there were regional distribution centers scattered across the country.

The Sears catalog helped create a truly national market and in the process transformed the lives of millions of people. With the advent of free rural mail delivery in 1898 and the widespread distribution of Sears catalogs, families on farms and in small towns and villages could purchase by mail the products that heretofore were either prohibitively expensive or available only to city dwellers. By the turn of the century, 6 million catalogs were distributed each year, and the catalog had become the single most widely read book in the nation except for the Bible. Rural schools that lacked readers used the catalog to teach reading and spelling. Students learned arithmetic by adding up lists of orders, and they learned geography by studying the postal zone maps included in the catalog. Some readers of the Sears catalog thought everything pictured was available for purchase. One lonely farmer wrote a letter to the company in which he proposed marriage to the "girl wearing hat number 68 on p. 153 of your catalog."

A Changing Environment for Workers

THE DISTRIBUTION OF WEALTH Accompanying the spread of huge industrial combinations was a rising standard of living for most people. If the rich were still getting richer, a lot of other people were at least better off, and the pre–Civil War trend toward even higher concentrations of wealth slacked off. This, of course, is far from saying that disparities in the distribution of wealth had disappeared. One set of estimates reveals that in both 1860 and 1900 the richest 2 percent of American families owned more than a third of the nation's physical wealth, while the top 10 percent owned almost three-fourths. All the nation's physical assets were in the hands of half its families. Studies of social mobility in towns across the country show, however, that while the rise from rags to riches was rare, "upward mobility both from blue-collar to white-collar callings and from low-ranked to high-ranked manual jobs was quite common."

The continuing demand for unskilled or semiskilled workers, meanwhile, attracted new groups entering the workforce at the bottom: immigrants above all, but also growing numbers of women and children. Because of a long-term decline in prices and the cost of living, real wages and earnings in manufacturing went up about 50 percent between 1860 and 1890, and another 37 percent from 1890 to 1914. By modern-day standards, however, working conditions were dreary indeed. At the turn of the century, the average hourly wage in manufacturing was 21.6¢, and average annual earnings were $490. The average workweek was fifty-nine hours, or nearly six ten-hour days, but that was only an average. Most steelworkers put in a twelve-hour day, and as late as the 1920s, a great many worked a seven-day, or eighty-four-hour, week.

A NEW SOCIAL WORLD   The fact that wages rose in no way discounts the high social costs of industrialization. In the crowded tenements that were built in major cities, the death rates ran substantially higher than in the countryside. Factories maintained poor health and safety conditions. In 1913, for instance, there were some 25,000 factory fatalities and 700,000 job-related injuries that required at least four weeks' disability. In this new bureaucratic world, ever-larger numbers of people were dependent on the machinery and factories of owners whom they seldom if ever saw. In the simpler world of small shops, workers and employers could enter into close personal relationships; the larger corporation, on the other hand, was likely governed by a bureaucracy in which ownership was separate from management. Much of the social history of the modern world in fact turns on the transition from a world of personal relationships to one of impersonal and contractual relationships.

UNION ORGANIZATION

DISORGANIZED PROTEST   Under these circumstances it was far more difficult for workers to organize for mutual benefit than for a few captains of industry to organize for profit. Civic leaders respected property rights more than the rights of labor. Many businessmen believed that a "labor supply" was simply another commodity to be procured at the lowest possible price.

Among workers recently removed from an agrarian world, the idea of permanent unions was slow to take hold. Immigrant workers came from many cultures. They spoke different languages and harbored ethnic animosities. Many, if not most, saw their jobs as transient, the first rung on the ladder to success. They hoped to move on to a homestead, or to return with their earnings to the old farms of their European homelands. With or without unions, though, workers often staged impromptu strikes in response to wage cuts and other grievances. But such action often led to violence, and three incidents of the 1870s colored much of the public's view of labor unions thereafter.

The decade's early years saw a reign of terror in the eastern Pennsylvania coal fields, attributed to an Irish group called the Molly Maguires. Taking their name from an Irish patriot who had directed violent resistance against the British, the group was provoked by the miserable, dangerous working conditions in the mines and the owners' brutal efforts to suppress union activity. Convinced of the justness of their cause, the Molly Maguires used intimidation, beatings, and killings to right perceived wrongs against Irish workers. Later investigations have shown that agents of the mine operators themselves stirred up some of the trouble. The terrorism reached its peak in 1874–1875, and mine owners hired Pinkerton detectives to stop the movement. One of the agents who infiltrated the Mollies produced enough evidence to indict the leaders. At trials in 1876 twenty-four of the Molly Maguires were convicted; ten were hanged. The trials also resulted in a wage reduction in the mines and the final destruction of the Miners' National Association, a weak union the Mollies had dominated.

THE RAILROAD STRIKE OF 1877   Far more significant, because more widespread, was the Great Railroad Strike of 1877, the first major interstate strike. Wage cuts caused the Great Strike. After the Panic of 1873 and the ensuing depression, the major rail lines in the East had cut wages. In 1877 they made another 10 percent cut, which provoked most of the railroad workers at Martinsburg, West Virginia, to walk off the job and block the tracks. Without organized direction, however, their picketing groups degenerated into a mob that burned and plundered railroad property.

Walkouts and sympathy demonstrations spread spontaneously from Maryland to San Francisco. The strike engulfed hundreds of cities and towns, leaving in its wake over a hundred people killed and millions of dollars in property destroyed. Federal troops finally quelled the vio-

The Devastation Wrought by the Railroad Strike of 1877. *Railroad workers in Pittsburgh reacted violently to wage cuts.*

lence. The greatest outbreak began at Pittsburgh, when the Pennsylvania Railroad put on "double-headers" (long trains pulled by two locomotives) in order to reduce crews. Public sympathy for the strikers was so great at first that local militiamen, called out to suppress them, instead joined the workers. Militiamen called in from Philadelphia managed to disperse one crowd at the cost of twenty-six lives, but then found themselves besieged in the railroad's roundhouse, where they disbanded and shot their way out.

Looting, rioting, and burning went on for another day until the frenzy wore itself out. A reporter described the scene as "the most horrible ever witnessed, except in the carnage of war. There were fifty miles of hot rails, ten tracks side by side, with as many miles of ties turned into glowing coals and tons on tons of iron car skeletons and wheels almost at white heat." Public opinion, sympathetic at first, tended to blame the workers for the looting and violence. Eventually the strikers, lacking organized bargaining power, had no choice but to drift back to work. Everywhere the strikes failed.

For many people, the strike raised the specter of a worker-based social revolution like the Paris Commune of 1871, in which disgruntled mobs chanted "Bread or Blood." As a Pittsburgh newspaper warned, "This may be the beginning of a great civil war in this country between labor and capital." Equally disturbing to those in positions of corporate and political power was the presence of many women among the protesters. A Baltimore journalist noted that the "singular part of the disturbances is the very active part taken by the women, who are the wives and mothers of the [railroad] firemen." From the point of view of organized labor, however, the Great Railroad Strike demonstrated potential strength and the need for tighter organization.

THE "SAND LOT" INCIDENT   In California the railroad strike indirectly gave rise to a political movement. At San Francisco's "Sand Lot," a meeting to express sympathy for the strikers ended with attacks on some passing Chinese. Within a few days, sporadic anti-Chinese riots led to a mob attack on Chinatown. Depression had hit the West Coast especially hard, and the Chinese were handy scapegoats for frustrations.

Soon an Irish immigrant, Dennis Kearney, organized the "Workingmen's Party of California." Its platform called for the end of further Chinese immigration. A gifted agitator, himself only recently naturalized, Kearney harangued the "sand lotters" about the "foreign peril" and assaulted the rich for exploiting the poor—sometimes at gatherings beside their mansions on Nob Hill. In 1878 his new party won a hefty number of seats in a state constitutional convention, but managed to incorporate in the state's basic law little more than ineffective attempts to regulate the railroads. The workingmen's movement peaked in 1879 when it elected many members of the new legislature and the mayor of San Francisco. Kearney lacked the gift for building a durable movement, but as his party went to pieces, his anti-Chinese theme became a national issue. In 1882 Congress voted to prohibit Chinese immigration for ten years.

TOWARD PERMANENT UNIONS   Meanwhile, efforts to build a permanent union movement had begun to bear fruit. Earlier efforts, in the 1830s and 1840s, had largely been dominated by reformers with schemes that ranged from free homesteads to utopian socialism. But the 1850s had seen the beginning of "job-conscious" unions in certain skilled trades. By 1860 there were about twenty such craft unions. During the Civil War, because of the demand for labor, such unions grew in strength and numbers.

Until after the war, however, there was no overall federation of these groups. In 1866 some seventy-seven delegates organized the National Labor Union (NLU) at a convention in Baltimore and chose as their leader the head of the Iron Molders. The NLU was composed of congresses of delegates from labor and reform groups more interested in political and social reform, however, than in bargaining with employers. The groups espoused such ideas as the eight-hour workday, workers' cooperatives, greenbackism (the printing of paper money to inflate the currency and thereby relieve debtors), and equal rights for women and blacks. After the head of the union died suddenly, its support fell away quickly. The National Labor Union cannot be labeled a total failure, however. It was influential in persuading Congress to enact an eight-hour workday for federal employees and to repeal the Contract Labor Law, which had been passed during the Civil War to encourage the importation of labor. Employers had taken advantage of the Contract Labor Law to recruit foreign laborers who were willing to work for lower wages than their American counterparts. The National Labor Union, moreover, undertook to encourage the organization of black workers, but with little success.

THE KNIGHTS OF LABOR   Before the National Labor Union collapsed, another group of national standing had emerged: the Noble and Holy Order of the Knights of Labor. The name evoked the aura of medieval guilds. The founder of the Knights of Labor, Uriah S. Stephens, a Philadelphia tailor, was a habitual "joiner" involved with several secret orders, including the Masons. His early training for the Baptist ministry also affected his outlook. Secrecy, he felt, along with a semireligious ritual, would protect members against retaliation and at the same time create a sense of solidarity.

In 1869, with Stephens as leader, nine Philadelphia tailors founded the order. At first it grew slowly, but in 1873 it formed its first district assembly in the Philadelphia area. During the years of depression, as other unions collapsed, it spread more rapidly, and in 1878 its first General Assembly established a national organization. Its preamble and platform endorsed the reforms advanced by previous workingmen's groups, including producers' and consumers' cooperatives, homesteads, bureaus of labor statistics, mechanics' lien laws (to ensure payment of salaries), elimination of convict-labor competition, the eight-hour day, and greenbacks. One plank in the platform, far ahead of the times, called for equal pay for equal work by both men and women.

Throughout its existence the Knights emphasized reform measures and preferred boycotts to strikes as a way to put pressure on employers. The constitution of the order allowed as members all who had ever worked for wages except lawyers, doctors, bankers, and those who sold liquor. Theoretically it was one big union of all workers, skilled and un- skilled, regardless of race, color, creed, or sex. Each local assembly was to be formed on such a basis, but in practice some local and district as- semblies were organized on a craft basis, such as the telegraphers and cigarmakers. Above these stood the General Assembly, a General Exec- utive Board, and at the head, a Grand Master Workman.

Stephens was the first elected to this office, but in 1879 he gave way to Terence V. Powderly, the thirty-year-old mayor of Scranton, Pennsyl- vania. Born of Irish immigrant parents, Powderly had become a railroad switch tender at sixteen but soon moved into the machine shop. In many ways he was unsuited to his new job as head of the Knights. Also, as mayor, county health officer, and part owner and manager of a gro-

Terence V. Powderly in 1885. Powderly led the Knights of Labor at the height of the union's power.

cery store, he had too many irons in the fire. He was physically frail, sensitive to criticism, and indecisive at critical moments. He was temperamentally opposed to strikes, and when they did occur, he did not always back up the local groups involved. Yet the Knights owed their greatest growth to strikes that occurred under his leadership.

In the mid-1880s the Knights grew rapidly. In 1884 a successful strike against wage cuts in the Union Pacific shops at Denver led many railroad workers to form new assemblies. Then, in 1885, the Knights scored a startling victory over Jay Gould. Late in the previous year and early in 1885, Gould had cut workers' wages on his Missouri, Kansas, and Texas and Wabash Railroads. A spontaneous strike on these lines spread to Gould's Missouri-Pacific. As organizers from the Knights of Labor moved in, Gould restored the wage cuts. As a result of this and other successes, the Knights increased from about 100,000 members to more than 700,000 in 1886.

In 1886 the Knights peaked and then went into rapid decline. Taken by surprise in 1885, Jay Gould proceeded to set a trap for the Knights a year later. He spoke favorably of unions and expressed his wish that all railroad workers were organized, but in 1886 he provoked another strike by firing a foreman in the Texas-Pacific shops. When the Knights struck, Gould refused arbitration and hired Pinkerton agents to harass strikers and keep the trains running. The Knights had to call off the strike.

ANARCHISM   The tensions between labor and management during the late nineteenth century in both the United States and Europe helped generate the doctrine of anarchism. The anarchists believed that government, any government, was in itself an abusive device used by the rich and powerful to oppress and exploit the working poor. Anarchists dreamed of the eventual disappearance of government altogether, and many of them believed that the transition to this stateless society could be hurried along by promoting revolutionary action among the masses. One favored tactic was the use of dramatic acts of violence against representatives of the government. Many European anarchists emigrated to the United States during the last quarter of the nineteenth century, and they brought with them this belief in the impact of "propaganda of the deed."

THE HAYMARKET AFFAIR   The Haymarket Affair grew indirectly out of agitation for the eight-hour workday. In 1884 union organizers set May 1, 1886, as the deadline for the institution of the eight-hour workday in all trades. Powderly declined to join in the call for strikes on that day, but some assemblies of the Knights did. Chicago became the center of the movement, and on May 3 the International Harvester plant became the site of an unfortunate clash between strikers and policemen in which one striker was killed.

Leaders of a minuscule anarchist movement in Chicago scheduled an open meeting the following night at Haymarket Square to protest the killing. After listening under a light drizzle to long speeches promoting socialism and anarchism, the crowd was beginning to break up when a group of policemen arrived and called upon the meeting to disperse. At that point somebody threw a bomb at the police, killing one and wounding others. The police then fired into the crowd. In a trial marked by prejudice and hysteria, seven anarchist leaders were sentenced to death despite the lack of any evidence linking them to the bomb-thrower, whose identity was never established. Of these, two were reprieved and some years later pardoned, one committed suicide in prison, but four were hanged. All but one of the group were German-speaking, but that one held a membership card in the Knights of Labor.

The incident at Haymarket Square provoked widespread revulsion against the Knights and labor groups in general. Despite his best efforts, Powderly could never dissociate in the public mind the Knights from the anarchists. He clung to leadership until 1893, but after that the union evaporated. By the turn of the century it was but a memory. A number of problems accounted for the Knights' decline besides fears of their supposed radicalism: a leadership devoted more to reform than to the nuts and bolts of organization, the failure of the Knights' cooperative enterprises, and a preoccupation with politics that led the Knights to sponsor labor candidates in hundreds of local elections. They won a surprising number of races in 1886, but their political efforts proved in the end to be a flash in the pan.

The Knights nevertheless attained some lasting achievements, among them the creation of the federal Bureau of Labor Statistics in 1884 as well as several state bureaus; the Foran Act of 1885, which, though weakly enforced, penalized employers who imported contract labor (an arrangement similar to the indentured servitude of colonial times in which workers were committed to a term of labor in exchange for transportation to America); and a national law enacted in 1880 for the arbitration of labor disputes. The Knights by example also spread the idea of unionism and initiated a new type of union organization: the industrial union, an industrywide union of the skilled and unskilled, begun in special assemblies of railway and telegraph workers. Industrial unions would have the power to match that of the organized concentrations of capital, but not for some time.

The craft unions opposed such industrial unionism. Leaders of the crafts feared that joining with the unskilled would mean a loss of their separate craft identities and a loss of the bargaining power held by skilled workers. They organized workers who shared special skills, such as typographers or cigarmakers. In 1881 the Federation of Organized Trades and Labor Unions came into being as a group similar to the old National Labor Union; it was primarily an association of national craft unions but with representation of state and local assemblies as well.

GOMPERS AND THE AFL   The Knights themselves also began to organize a few special assemblies along craft lines. An effort by the Knights to organize a separate union in the New York cigar trade led the Cigarmakers International Union to call for stronger unity among the existing craft unions. In 1886 delegates from twenty craft unions met in Philadelphia and called on the Knights to cease organizing in trades for which a national union already existed. When the Knights failed to heed the suggestion, a second conference met at Columbus, Ohio, which reorganized the American Federation of Labor (AFL), originally founded in 1881. It differed in structure from the Knights in that it was a federation of national organizations, each of which retained a large degree of autonomy.

Samuel Gompers served as president of the AFL from its start until his death in 1924, with only one year's interruption. Born in London of Dutch-Jewish ancestry, Gompers came to the United States as a teenager, joined the Cigarmakers Union in 1864, and became president of his New York local in 1877. This background was significant. Cigarmakers were the intellectuals of the labor movement. To relieve the tedium of their task, they hired young men to read aloud as they worked, and debated such weighty topics as socialism and Darwinism. Nonetheless, Gompers and other leaders of the union focused on concrete economic gains, avoiding involvement with utopian ideas or politics. "At no time in my life," Gompers once said, "have I ever worked out a definitely articulated economic theory." "We have no ultimate ends," he told a Senate hearing. "We are going on from day to day. We are fighting only for immediate objects—objects that can be realized in a few years."

Such job consciousness became the policy of the AFL under Gompers, whose lifetime concern was the effectiveness of the federation. He hired organizers to spread unionism and worked as a diplomat to prevent overlapping unions and to settle jurisdictional disputes. The federation represented workers in matters of national legislation and acted as a sounding board for their cause. On occasion it exercised its power to request from members dues for the support of strikes. Gompers, it turned out, was temperamentally more fitted than Powderly for the rough-and-tumble world of unionism. He had a thick hide, liked to talk and drink with workers in the back room, and willingly used the strike to achieve favorable trade agreements, including provisos for union recognition in the form of closed shops (which could hire only union members) or union-preference shops (which could hire others only if no union members were available).

One great objective that Gompers achieved at least in principle was making the eight-hour workday standard. In 1889 the AFL voted to revive May Day demonstrations for the eight-hour workday, abandoned after the Haymarket Affair. But gradually the demonstrations under-

Samuel Gompers, head of the American Federation of Labor.

went a curious change. In 1889 the founding congress of the Socialist International in Paris voted to sponsor rallies for the eight-hour workday worldwide. Later, these evolved into demonstrations for general worker demands, labor solidarity, and socialism. Still later, Communists took up the May Day celebrations and paraded through Moscow to observe a holiday that, its origins forgotten, began with an American demand for the eight-hour workday.

The AFL at first grew slowly, but by 1890 it had surpassed the Knights of Labor in membership. By the turn of the century, it claimed 500,000 members in affiliated unions; in 1914, on the eve of World War I, it had 2 million; and in 1920, it reached a peak of 4 million. But even then it embraced less than 15 percent of the nonagricultural workers. All unions, including the unaffiliated railroad brotherhoods, accounted for little more than 18 percent of these workers. Organized labor's strongholds were in transportation and the building trades. Most of the larger manufacturing industries, including steel, textiles, tobacco, and packinghouses, remained almost untouched. Gompers never frowned on industrial unions, and several became important affiliates of the AFL: the United Mine Workers, the International Ladies' Garment Workers, and the Amalgamated Clothing Workers. But the AFL had its greatest success in organizing skilled workers.

THE HOMESTEAD STRIKE Two violent incidents in the 1890s stalled the emerging industrial union movement and set it back for the next forty years—the Homestead Steel Strike of 1892 and the Pullman Strike of 1894. The Amalgamated Association of Iron and Steel Workers, founded in 1876, had by 1891 a membership of more than 24,000 and was probably the largest craft union at that time. But it excluded the unskilled and had failed to organize the larger steel plants. The Homestead Works at Pittsburgh was an important exception. There the union had enjoyed friendly relations with the Carnegie company until H. C. Frick became its president in 1889. A showdown was delayed, however, until 1892, when the union contract came up for renewal. Andrew Carnegie, who had expressed sympathy for unions in the past, had gone to Scotland and left matters in the hands of Frick. Carnegie, however, knew what was afoot: a cost-cutting reduction in the number of workers through the use of labor-saving devices, and a deliberate attempt to smash the union.

As negotiations dragged on, the company announced it would treat workers as individuals unless an agreement was reached by June 29. A strike, or more properly a lockout of unionists, began on that date. Even before the negotiations ended, Frick had hired as plant guards 300 Pinkerton detectives whose specialty was union-busting. On the morning of July 6, 1892, when the Pinkertons floated up the Monongahela River on barges, unionists were waiting behind breastworks on shore. Who fired the first shot remains unknown, but a battle broke out in which six workers and three Pinkertons died. In the end the Pinkertons surrendered and were marched away, subjected to taunts from crowds in the street. Six days later the state militia appeared at the plant to protect the strikebreakers hired to restore production. The strike dragged on until November, but by then the union was dead at Homestead. Its cause was not helped when an anarchist shot and wounded Frick. Much of the local sympathy for the strikers evaporated.

THE PULLMAN STRIKE The Pullman Strike of 1894 was perhaps the most notable walkout in American history. It paralyzed the economies of twenty-seven states and territories making up the western half of the nation. It involved a dispute at the "model" town of Pullman, Illinois, which housed workers of the Pullman Palace Car Company. The town's idyllic appearance was deceptive. Employees were required to live there, pay rents and utility costs higher than those in nearby towns, and buy goods from company stores. During the Depression of 1893, George Pullman laid off 3,000 of 5,800 employees, and cut wages 25 to 40 percent, but not his rents and other charges. When Pullman fired three members of a grievance committee, a strike began on May 11, 1894.

During this tense period, Pullman workers had been joining the American Railway Union, founded the previous year by Eugene V. Debs. The tall, gaunt Debs was a man of towering influence and charismatic appeal. A child of working-class immigrants, he quit school in 1869 at age fourteen and began working for an Indiana railroad. There, he would later write, "I learned of the hardships of the rail in snow, sleet, and hail, of the ceaseless danger that lurks along the iron highway, the uncertainty of employment, scant wages and altogether trying lot of the workingman, so that from my very boyhood I was made to feel the wrongs of labor." He felt these wrongs so deeply that he eagerly accepted an invitation to start a local of the railroad brotherhood, a craft union of skilled workers.

Still, it was not until the Haymarket bombing that Debs saw an inevitable conflict between labor and management. By the early 1890s he had become a tireless spokesman for labor radicalism, and he launched a crusade to organize *all* railway workers—skilled or unskilled—into the American Railway Union. Soon he was in charge of a powerful new labor organization, and he quickly turned his attention to the Pullman controversy.

After Pullman refused Debs's plea for arbitration, the union workers stopped handling Pullman cars. This tied up most of the railroads in the Midwest, which also greatly affected the traffic to the West. Railroad executives then brought strikebreakers from Canada and elsewhere, instructing them to connect mail cars to Pullman cars so that interference with Pullman cars also meant interference with the mails. The U.S. attorney-general, a former railroad attorney himself, swore in 3,400 special deputies to keep the trains running. When clashes occurred between these deputies and some of the strikers, President Grover Cleveland sent federal troops into the Chicago area, where the strike was centered. The Illinois governor insisted that the state could keep order, but Cleveland claimed authority and a duty to ensure delivery of the mails.

Troops guarding the railroads during the Pullman Strike, 1894.

Meanwhile, the attorney-general won an injunction forbidding any interference with the mails or any combination to restrain interstate commerce; the principle was that a strike or boycott violated the Sherman Anti-Trust Act. On July 13 the union called off the strike and on the same day the district court cited Debs for violating the injunction and sentenced him to six months in jail. The Supreme Court upheld the decree in the case of *In re Debs* (1895) on broad grounds of national sovereignty: "The strong arm of the national government may be put forth to brush away all obstructions to the freedom of interstate commerce or the transportation of the mails." Debs served his term, during which time he read deeply in socialist literature, and he emerged to devote the rest of his life to that cause.

SOCIALISM AND THE UNIONS   The major American unions, for the most part, never allied themselves with the socialists, as many European labor movements did. But socialist ideas had been abroad in the country at least since the 1820s. Marxism, one strain of socialism, was imported mainly by German immigrants. Karl Marx's International Workingmen's Association, the First International, founded in 1864, inspired a few affiliates in the United States. In 1872, at Marx's urging, the headquarters was moved from London to New York. In 1876 the First International expired, but the next year followers of Marx in America organized the Socialist Labor party, a group so filled with immigrants that German was its official language in the first years.

The movement gained little notice before the rise of Daniel DeLeon in the 1890s. As editor of its paper, *The People,* he became the dominant figure in the party. A native of the Dutch West Indies, DeLeon had studied law and lectured for some years at Columbia University. He proposed to organize industrial unions with a socialist purpose, and to build a political party that would abolish the state once it gained power, after which the unions of the Socialist Trade and Labor Alliance would become the units of control. His ideas seem to have influenced Lenin, leader of the Bolshevik Revolution of 1917, but DeLeon preached revolution at the ballot box, not by violence.

Debs was more successful at building a socialist movement in America. To many, DeLeon seemed doctrinaire and inflexible. Debs, however, built his new party by following a method now traditional in the

Eugene V. Debs, founder of the American Railway Union and later candidate for president as head of the Socialist Party of America.

United States: he formed a coalition, one that embraced viewpoints ranging from moderate reform to doctrinaire Marxism. In 1897 Debs announced that he was a socialist and organized the Social Democratic party from the remnants of the American Railway Union. He got over 4,000 votes as its candidate for president in 1900. In 1901 his followers joined a number of secessionists from DeLeon's party, led by Morris Hillquit of New York, to set up the Socialist Party of America. In 1904 Debs polled over 400,000 votes as the party's candidate for president and more than doubled that to almost 900,000 votes in 1912, or 6 percent of the popular vote. In 1910 Milwaukee elected a socialist mayor and congressman.

By 1912 the Socialist party seemed well on the way to becoming a permanent fixture in American politics. Thirty-three cities had socialist mayors, including Berkeley, California; Butte, Montana; Flint and Jackson, Michigan; and Milwaukee, Wisconsin. The party sponsored five English daily newspapers, eight foreign-language dailies, and a number of weeklies and monthlies. Its support was not confined to urban workers and intellectuals. In the Southwest the party built a sizable grassroots following among farmers and tenants. Oklahoma, for instance, in 1910 had more paid-up party members than any other state except New York, and in 1912 gave 16.5 percent of its popular vote to Debs, a greater proportion than any other state ever gave. But the Socialist party reached its peak in 1912. During World War I, it was wracked by disagreements over America's participation in the war, and it was split thereafter by desertions to the new Communist party.

THE WOBBLIES   During the years of Socialist party growth, there emerged a parallel effort to revive industrial unionism, led by the Industrial Workers of the World (IWW). The chief base for this group was the Western Federation of Miners, organized at Butte, Montana, in 1893. Over the next decade the Western Federation was the storm center of violent confrontation with unyielding bosses who mobilized private armies against it in Colorado, Idaho, and elsewhere. In 1905 the founding convention of the IWW drew a variety of people who opposed the AFL's philosophy. Debs participated, although many of his comrades preferred to work within the AFL. DeLeon seized this chance to strike back at craft unionism. A radical manifesto issued from the meetings, arguing that the IWW "must be founded on the class struggle, and its general administration must be conducted in harmony with the recognition of the irrepressible conflict between the capitalist class and the working class."

But the IWW waged class war better than it articulated class ideology. Like the Knights of Labor, it was designed to be "One Big Union," including all workers, skilled or unskilled. Its roots were in the mining and lumber camps of the West, where unstable conditions of employment created a large number of nomadic workers, to whom neither the AFL's pragmatic approach nor the socialists' political appeal held much attraction. The revolutionary goal of the Wobblies, as they came to be called, was an idea labeled syndicalism by its French supporters: the ultimate destruction of the state and its replacement by one big union. But just how it would govern remained vague.

Like other radical groups, the IWW was split by sectarian disputes. Because of policy disagreements, all the major founders withdrew, first the Western Federation of Miners, then Debs, then DeLeon. William D. "Big Bill" Haywood of the Western Federation remained, however, and as its leader held the group together. Although since embellished in

Textile workers strike, Lawrence, Massachusetts, 1912. The IWW of this Lawrence mill engaged in a violent strike for increased wages, overtime pay, and other benefits.

myth, Haywood was in fact an imposing figure. Well over six feet tall, handsome and muscular, he commanded the attention and respect of his listeners. This hardrock miner, union organizer, and socialist from Salt Lake City despised the AFL and its conservative labor philosophy. He called Samuel Gompers "a squat specimen of humanity" who was "conceited, petulant, and vindictive." Instead of following Gompers's advice to organize only skilled workers, Haywood promoted the concept of one all-inclusive union whose credo would be the promotion of a socialism "with its working clothes on."

But Haywood and the Wobblies were reaching out to the fringe elements that had the least power and influence, chiefly the migratory workers of the West and the ethnic groups of the East. Always ambivalent about diluting their revolutionary principles, they scorned the usual labor agreements, even when they participated in them. Consequently, they engaged in spectacular battles with capital but scored few victories. The largest was a textile strike at Lawrence, Massachusetts, in 1912, that garnered wage raises, overtime pay, and other benefits. But the next year a strike of silk workers at Paterson, New Jersey, ended in disaster, and the IWW entered a rapid decline.

Branded as anarchists, bums, and criminals, the IWW was effectively destroyed during World War I, when most of its leaders were jailed for conspiracy because of their militant opposition to the war. Big Bill Haywood fled to the Soviet Union, where he married a Russian woman, died in 1928, and was honored by burial in the Kremlin wall. The Wobblies left behind a rich folklore of nomadic working men and a gallery of heroic agitators such as Elizabeth Gurley Flynn, a dark-haired Irish woman who at age eighteen chained herself to a lamppost to impede her arrest during a strike. The movement also bequeathed martyrs such as the Swedish singer and labor organizer Joe Hill, framed (so the faithful assumed) for murder and executed by a Utah firing squad. His last words were written to Haywood: "Goodbye, Bill. I die like a true blue rebel. Don't waste any time mourning. Organize." The intensity of conviction and devotion to a cause shown by Hill, Flynn, and others ensured that the IWW's ideal of a classless society did not die.

MAKING CONNECTIONS

- The Darwinian ideas implicit in the attitudes of many leading entrepreneurs, especially Andrew Carnegie, are described in greater detail in the next chapter.

- In response to the growth of the railroads, reformers in the 1880s and 1890s began to push for regulation, a trend explored in Chapter 22.

- The economic and industrial growth described in this chapter was an important factor in America's "new imperialism" in the late nineteenth century, as shown in Chapter 23.

- The socialist approach to reform was a significant influence on the Progressive movement, covered in Chapter 24.

FURTHER READING

For a masterly synthesis of post–Civil War industrial development, see Walter Licht's *Industrializing America: The Nineteenth Century* (1995). Of more specialized interest are Alfred D. Chandler's *The Visible Hand: The Managerial Revolution in American Business* (1977), and Maury Klein's *The Flowering of the Third America: The Making of an Organizational Society, 1850–1920* (1992).

On the growth of railroads see Albro Martin's *Railroads Triumphant: The Growth, Rejection, and Rebirth of a Vital American Force* (1992). Walter Licht's *Working for the Railroad: The Organization of Work in the Nineteenth Century* (1983) treats the life of the railroad workers. Gabriel Kolko's *Railroads and Regulation, 1877–1916* (1965) argues that the entrepreneurs themselves sought regulation.

On entrepreneurship in the iron and steel sector, see Thomas J. Misa's *A Nation of Steel: The Making of Modern America, 1865–1925* (1995). The best biography of the leading business tycoon is Ron Chernow's *Titan: The Life of John D. Rockefeller, Sr.* (1998).

Nathan Rosenberg's *Technology and American Economic Growth* (1972) documents the growth of invention during the period. For an absorbing biography of the foremost inventor of the era, see Neil Baldwin's *Edison: Inventing the Century* (1995).

Much of the recent scholarship on labor stresses the traditional values and the culture of work that people brought to the factory. Herbert G. Gutman's *Work, Culture, and Society in Industrializing America* (1976) best introduces these themes. The best survey remains David Montgomery's *The Fall of the House of Labor: The Workplace, the State and American Labor Activism, 1865–1925* (1987).

For the role of women in the changing workplace, see Alice Kessler-Harris's *Out to Work* (1983), Susan E. Kennedy's *If All We Did Was to Weep at Home: A History of White Working-Class Women in America* (1979), and S. J. Kleinberg's *The Shadow of the Mills: Working-Class Families in Pittsburgh, 1870–1907* (1989).

As for the labor groups, Gerald N. Grob's *Workers and Utopias* (1961) examines the difference in outlook between the Knights of Labor and the American Federation of Labor. For the Knights, see Leon Fink's *Workingmen's Democracy* (1983). Also useful is Susan Levine's *Labor's*

True Woman (1984), on the role of women in the Knights. To trace the rise of socialism among organized workers, see Nick Salvatore's *Eugene V. Debs: Citizen and Socialist* (1982) and Robert J. Constantine's *Letters of Eugene V. Debs* (1990). Strikes are discussed in Kevin Kenny's *Making Sense of the Molly Maguires* (1998), Paul Avrich's *The Haymarket Tragedy* (1984), and Paul Krause's *The Battle for Homestead, 1880–1892: Politics, Culture, and Steel* (1992).

21 ↬ THE EMERGENCE
OF URBAN AMERICA

CHAPTER ORGANIZER

This chapter focuses on:

- immigration and the growth of the modern city.

- the rise of powerful reform movements.

- the impact of Darwinian thought on the social sciences.

- literary and philosophical trends of the late nineteenth century.

---

*D*uring the second half of the nineteenth century, the United States experienced an urban revolution unparalleled in world history up to that point in time. As factories, mines, and mills sprouted across the landscape, cities grew up around them. The late nineteenth century, declared an economist in 1899, was "not only the age of cities, but the age of great cities." Between 1860 and 1910, the urban population grew from 6 million to 44 million. The United States was rapidly losing its rural flavor. Indeed, by 1920, more than half of the population would be living in urban areas.

The rise of big cities during the nineteenth century created a distinctive urban culture. People from different ethnic and religious back-

The elevator at Lord & Taylor store, 1873.

grounds and representing every walk of life poured into the high-rise apartment buildings and ramshackle tenements springing up in every major city. They came in search of jobs, wealth, and new opportunities. Rising wages and the availability of new consumer goods in the dazzling new downtown department stores improved the material standard of living for millions—while widening the gap between the poor and the affluent. Broadened access to public education and to public health services improved literacy and lowered infant mortality rates (although the death rate for adult black males remained quite high). Break-throughs in medical science eventually brought cures for tuberculosis, typhoid, and diphtheria—although these infectious diseases remained the century's leading killers.

The rise of metropolitan America also created an array of new social problems. Corporations became so powerful that some of their owners decided that they were above the law. When someone warned Cornelius Vanderbilt, the railroad tycoon, that he might be violating the law, he is alleged to have replied, "Law? What do I care about the law. Hain't I got the power?" Rapid urban development also produced wide-spread poverty and political corruption. How to feed, clothe, shelter, and educate the new arrivals taxed the imagination—and patience—of many Americans.

AMERICA'S MOVE TO TOWN

The mushrooming cities served as powerful magnets that lured workers by the millions from the countryside and overseas. This urban-industrial revolution greatly increased the national wealth and transformed the pace and tenor of American life. City people and folks who worked in factories rather than on farms, while differing significantly among themselves, also became distinctively and recognizably urban in demeanor and outlook.

EXPLOSIVE URBAN GROWTH   The frontier was a safety valve, historian Frederick Jackson Turner said in his influential thesis on American development. Its cheap lands afforded a release for the population pressures mounting in the cities. If there was such a thing as a safety valve in his own time, however, he had it exactly backward. The flow of population toward the city was greater than toward the West, and "country come to town" epitomized the American people better than the occasional city "dude" who turned up in cow country.

Much of the westward movement in fact was itself an urban movement, spawning new towns near the mining digs or at the railheads. More often than not, western towns anticipated settlement. They supplied headquarters for the land boomers and services for the hinterlands. On the Pacific coast a greater portion of the population was urbanized than anywhere else; its major concentrations were around San Francisco Bay at first, and then in Los Angeles, which became a boom town after the arrival of the Southern Pacific and Santa Fe Railroads in the 1880s. Seattle grew quickly, first as the terminus of three transcontinental railroad lines, and by the end of the century as the staging area for the Yukon gold rush. Minneapolis, St. Paul, Omaha, Kansas City, and Denver were no longer the mere villages they had been in 1860. The South, too, produced new cities: Durham, North Carolina, and Birmingham, Alabama, which were centers of tobacco and iron manufactures, and Houston, Texas, which handled cotton and cattle, and later oil.

Trade and transportation had been the city builders of the past. Eight of the nine cities that by 1860 had passed 100,000 in population were ports, and the ninth (Brooklyn) was a suburb to the largest port. By the

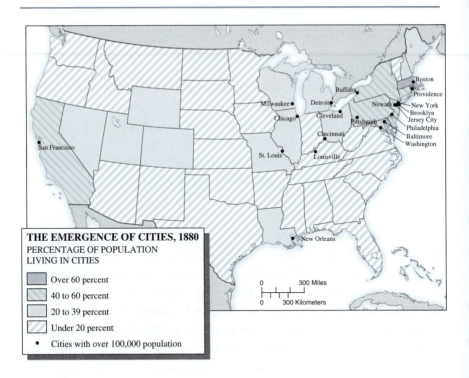

THE EMERGENCE OF CITIES, 1880
PERCENTAGE OF POPULATION
LIVING IN CITIES

▨	Over 60 percent
▨	40 to 60 percent
□	20 to 39 percent
▨	Under 20 percent
•	Cities with over 100,000 population

late nineteenth century no city could hope to thrive without at least one railroad, and most had a cluster of railroads. But it was the explosive rise of industry that powered the growth of new cities during this period. Industry brought huge concentrations of labor, and both required the proliferation of services that became synonymous with city life.

The emergence of the major cities was completed during the years from 1860 to 1910. After that, new cities sprang up only in unusual circumstances: Miami was the product of tourism brought by the coastal railroad, while Tulsa resulted from an oil boom. In those fifty years, population in incorporated towns of 2,500 or more grew from 6 million to 45 million, or from 20 to 46 percent of the nation's total population.

While the Far West had the greatest proportion of urban population, the Northeast had far greater numbers of people in its teeming cities. There the situation that Thomas Jefferson had so dreaded was coming to pass: the people "piled high up on one another in the cities," and worse, these people increasingly were landless, tool-less, and home-less—an urban proletariat with nothing but their labor to sell. By 1900

THE EMERGENCE OF CITIES, 1920
PERCENTAGE OF POPULATION
LIVING IN CITIES

- Over 60 percent
- 40 to 60 percent
- 20 to 39 percent
- Under 20 percent
- • Cities with over 100,000 population

more than 90 percent of the residents in New York's Manhattan lived in rented homes or tenements.

The cities expanded both vertically and horizontally to absorb their huge populations. In either case, transportation innovations played an important role: the elevator, the streetcar, and, before the end of the century, the first automobiles. The first safety elevator, which would not fall if the rope or cable broke, was developed in 1852 by Elisha Graves Otis. In 1889 the Otis Elevator Company installed the first electric elevator, which made possible the erection of taller buildings. Before the 1860s, few structures had gone higher than three or four stories.

Before the 1890s, the chief power sources of urban transport were either animals or steam. Horse- and mule-drawn streetcars had appeared in antebellum cities, but they were slow and cumbersome, and cleaning up after the animals added to the cost. In 1873 San Francisco became the first city to use cable cars that clamped onto a moving underground cable driven by a central power source. Some cities used steam-powered trains on elevated tracks, but by the 1890s electric trolleys were replacing these.

Such systems spread rapidly, and in some places mass-transit companies began to dig underground passages for their cars. Around the turn of the century, subway systems began operation in Boston, New York, and Philadelphia. Advances in bridge building through the use of steel and the perfection of the steel-cable suspension bridge also extended the reach of commuters. The marvels of the age were James B. Eads's cantilevered steel bridge over the Mississippi at St. Louis (1874) and John A. and Washington Roebling's cable-supported Brooklyn Bridge (1883), which linked Brooklyn to Manhattan.

The spread of mass transit allowed large numbers of people to become commuters, and a growing middle class (working folk often could not afford even the nickel fare) retreated to quieter tree-lined "streetcar suburbs" whence they could travel into the central city for business or entertainment. The pattern of urban growth often became a sprawl, since it took place usually without plan, in the interest of a fast buck, and without thought to the need for parks and public services.

The use of horse-drawn railways, cable cars, and electric trolleys helped transform the social characters of cities. Until the implementation of such new transportation systems, people of all classes lived and worked together in the central city. After the Civil War, however, the emergence of suburbs began to segregate people according to their eco-

The Brooklyn Bridge under construction, 1877.

Central Park tunnel, 1903. The subway system helped abate the street-level congestion that plagued cities at the turn-of-the-century.

nomic standing. The more affluent moved outside the city, leaving the working folk, many of whom were immigrants, behind. The poorer districts in the city became more congested and crime-ridden as the population grew, fueled by waves of newcomers from abroad.

CITY POLITICS   The sheer size of cities helped create a new form of politics. Since individuals could hardly provide for themselves such necessary services as transit, paving, water, sewers, street lighting and cleaning, and fire and police protection, they came increasingly to rely on city government. Meanwhile, many city problems were handled by local political bosses who traded in patronage favors and graft. Big-city political machines were not altogether sinister in their effects: they provided food and money for the poor, fixed problems at city hall, and generally helped immigrants in their adjustment to a new life. One ward boss in Boston said: "There's got to be in every ward somebody that any bloke can come to—no matter what he's done—and get help. Help, you understand, none of your law and justice, but help."

In return, the political professionals felt entitled to some reward for having done the grubby work of the local organization. George Washington Plunkitt, for instance, a power in Tammany Hall (New York City's Democratic organization) at the turn of the century, saw nothing wrong with a little honest graft. "Well, I'm tipped off, say, that they're going to lay out a new park at a certain place. . . . I go to that place and buy up all the land I can in the neighborhood. . . . Ain't it perfectly honest to charge a good price and make a profit on my investment and foresight?" Dishonest graft would consist of "robbin' the city treasury or levyin' blackmail on disorderly houses or workin' in with the gamblers and lawbreakers." For his own epitaph Plunkitt proposed: "He Seen His Opportunities, and He Took 'Em."

MOVING FROM COUNTRY TO CITY   But whatever the problems of the cities, the wonder of their glittering new electric lights, their streetcars, telephones, amusements, newspapers and magazines, and a thousand other enticements exerted a magnetic lure on the youth of the farms. Hamlin Garland told in his autobiography, *A Son of the Middle Border,* of his mixed sense of dread and wonder at first visiting Chicago with his brother. The city first appeared from the train window enveloped in clouds of smoke, "the soaring banners of the great and gloomy inland metropolis, whose dens of vice and houses of greed had been so often reported to me." Later the two young men wandered the streets: "Everything interested us. The business section so sordid to others was grandly terrifying to us. . . . Nothing was commonplace, nothing was ugly to us."

The new cities threw into stark contrast the frustration of unending farm toil, the isolation and loneliness of country life. The exodus from the countryside was especially evident in the East, where the census documented the shift in population from country to city, and stories began to appear of entire regions where buildings were abandoned and going to ruin, where the wilderness was reclaiming farms that had been wrested from it during the previous 250 years.

THE NEW IMMIGRATION

The industrial revolution brought to American shores waves of new immigrants from every part of the globe. By the end of the century, nearly 30 percent of the residents of major cities were foreign-born.

These newcomers provided much-needed labor, but their arrival created ugly racial and ethnic tensions.

AMERICA'S PULL   European immigrants not only moved from country to city in their own lands, but increasingly they moved from the great agricultural areas of eastern and southern Europe directly to the foremost cities of America. They gathered in these cities in order to live with others of like language, customs, and religion, and also because they lacked the means to go west and take up farms. Though cities of the South and West (excepting the Far West) drew their populations mainly from the native-born of their regions, American cities as a whole drew more residents from abroad. During the peak decade of immigration, 1900–1910, 41 percent of the urban newcomers arrived from abroad, while 30 percent were American-born, 22 percent were the products of natural increase, and almost 8 percent lived in areas annexed to the cities.

Ethnic neighborhoods, sometimes populated by those from a single province or town, preserved familiar folkways and shielded newcomers from the shocks of a strange culture. In 1890 four out of five New Yorkers were foreign-born, a higher proportion than any other city in the world. New York had twice as many Irish as Dublin, as many Germans as Hamburg, and half as many Italians as Naples. "A map of the city, colored to designate nationalities," Jacob Riis (a native of Denmark) wrote in *How the Other Half Lives* (1890), "would show more stripes than . . . a zebra, and more colors than any rainbow." In 1893 Chicago claimed the largest Bohemian (Czech) community in the world, and by 1910 the size of its Polish population ranked behind only Warsaw and Lodz.

This nation of immigrants continued to draw new inhabitants for much the same reasons as always, and from much the same strata of society. Immigrants took flight from famine or the grinding lack of opportunity in their native lands. They fled racial, religious, and political persecution and compulsory military service. Yet one historian has suggested that "the desire to get cheap labor, to take in passenger fares, and to sell land have probably brought more immigrants than the hard conditions of Europe, Asia, and Africa have sent."

More immigrants probably *were* pulled by America's promise than were pushed out by conditions at home. American industries, seeking

Steerage Deck of the S.S. *Pennland, 1893. These immigrants are about to arrive at New York's Ellis Island.*

cheap labor, kept recruiting agents on watch abroad and at American ports. Railroads, eager to sell land and build up the traffic on their lines, put out tempting propaganda in a medley of languages. Many of the western and southern states set up official bureaus and agents to attract immigrants. Under the Contract Labor Law of 1864, the federal government itself encouraged immigration by helping to pay the immigrant's passage through a lien on his or her wages. The law was repealed in 1868, but not until 1885 did the government forbid companies to import contract labor, which put immigrant workers under the control of their employers. However, domestic service and some skilled occupations were exempted from the ban, and evasion was easy.

From 1820 (when by requirement of Congress official statistics on immigration began to be kept) to 1900, about 20 million immigrants entered American ports, more than half of them coming after the Civil War. The tide of immigration rose from just under 3 million in the 1870s to more than 5 million in the 1880s, then fell to a little over 3.5 million in the depression decade of the 1890s, and rose to its high-water mark of nearly 9 million in the first decade of the new century.

The numbers declined to 6 million in the 1910s and 4 million in the 1920s, after which official restrictions cut the flow of immigration down to a negligible level.

A NEW WAVE   During the 1880s, the continuing search for cheap labor combined with renewed persecutions in eastern Europe to bring a noticeable change in the source of immigration, one fraught with meaning for American social history. Before 1880 immigrants were mainly of Teutonic and Celtic origin, hailing from northern and western Europe. But by the 1870s there were signs of a change. The proportion of Latin, Slavic, and Jewish peoples from southern and eastern Europe rose sharply. After 1890 these groups made up a majority of the newcomers, and by the first decade of the new century they formed 70 percent of the immigrants to this country. Among these new immigrants were Italians, Hungarians, Czechs, Slovaks, Poles, Serbs, Croats, Slovenes, Russians, Romanians, and Greeks—all people of markedly different cultural and language stocks from those of western Europe, and most followers of different religions, including Judaism and Catholicism.

Immigrants, with identification papers, newly arrived at Ellis Island.

ELLIS ISLAND   As the number of immigrants passing through the Port of New York soared during the late nineteenth century, the state-run Castle Garden receiving center overflowed with corruption. Money-changers cheated new arrivals, railroad agents overcharged them for tickets, and baggage handlers engaged in blackmail. With reports of these abuses filling the newspapers, Congress ordered an investigation of Castle Garden, which resulted in the closure of the facility in 1890. Thereafter the federal government's new Bureau of Immigration took over the business of admitting newcomers to New York City.

To launch this effort, Congress funded the construction of a new reception center on a tiny island off the New Jersey coast, a mile south of Manhattan and some 1,300 feet from the Statue of Liberty. The statue, unveiled in 1886, was a centennial gift from the French government commemorating the Franco-American alliance during the Revolutionary War. It soon came to be viewed as a symbol of hope for immigrants passing under "Lady Liberty." In the base of the statue, workers had chiseled the poet Emma Lazarus's tribute to the promise of new life in America:

> Give me your tired, your poor,
> Your huddled masses yearning to breathe free,
> The wretched refuse of your teeming shore.
> Send these, the homeless, tempest-tossed to me,
> I lift my lamp beside the golden door!

In 1892 Ellis Island (named after its late-eighteenth-century owner, Samuel Ellis) opened its doors to the "huddled masses" of the world. Until 1954, when it closed, some 12 million people first touched American soil there. In 1907, the reception center's busiest year, more than a million new arrivals filtered through the cavernous Great Hall, an average of about 5,000 per day; in one day alone immigration officials processed some 11,750 arrivals. These were the immigrants who arrived crammed into the steerage compartments deep in the ships' hulls. Those immigrants who could afford first- and second-class cabins did not have to visit Ellis Island; they were examined on board ship, and most of them simply walked down the gangway onto the docks in lower Manhattan.

Immigrants waiting in the Registry Room for further inspections.

The prevailing atmosphere at Ellis Island was not comforting. Its bureaucratic purpose was to process immigrants, not welcome them. An army of inspectors, doctors, nurses, and public officials questioned, examined, and documented the newcomers. Inspectors asked twenty-nine probing questions, including: Have you money, relatives, or a job in the United States? Are you a polygamist? An anarchist? Doctors and nurses poked and prodded, searching for any sign of debilitating handicap or infectious disease. All the while, the immigrant worried: "Will they let me in?" Although some who were sick or lame were detained for days or weeks, the vast majority of immigrants received stamps of approval and were on their way after three or four hours. "I was jostled and dragged and shoved and shouted at," recalled one immigrant. "I took it philosophically. I had been through the performance many times before—at the Hungarian border, at Vienna, in Germany, in Holland." Only 2 percent of the newcomers were denied entry altogether, usually because they were criminals, anarchists, or carriers of some "loathsome or dangerous contagious disease," such as tuberculosis or trachoma, a contagious eye disease resulting in blindness. These luckless folk were then returned to their places of origin, with the steamship companies picking up the tab.

A health inspector checks immigrants on Ellis Island, 1909. Before being granted entry, each immigrant was examined for contagious diseases, including trachoma, an eye disease that could lead to blindness.

Between 1892 and 1954, 70 percent of all European immigrants circulated through Ellis Island (others landed at Boston, Philadelphia, Baltimore, New Orleans, and Galveston). Among the arrivals at Ellis Island were many youngsters who would distinguish themselves in their new country: songwriter Irving Berlin (Russia), football legend Knute Rockne (Norway), Supreme Court justice Felix Frankfurter (Austria), singer Al Jolson (Lithuania), and comedian Bob Hope (England). But many others found America's opportunities harder to grasp. An old Italian saying expresses the disillusionment that was felt by many: "I came to America because I heard the streets were paved with gold. When I got here, I found out three things: First, the streets weren't paved with gold; second, they weren't paved at all; and third, I was expected to pave them."

MAKING THEIR WAY   Once on American soil in Manhattan or New Jersey, the immigrants felt exhilaration, exhaustion, and usually a desperate need for work. Many were greeted by family and friends who had come over before, others by representatives of the many immigrant aid societies or by hiring agents offering jobs in mines, mills, and sweatshops. Since most knew little if any English and nothing about American employment practices, the immigrants were easy subjects for exploitation. In exchange for providing arrivals with a bit of whiskey and a job, obliging hiring agents claimed a healthy percentage of their wages. Among Italians and Greeks these agents were known as *padrones,* and they came to dominate the labor market in New York. Other contractors provided train tickets for immigrants to travel inland to jobs in cities such as Buffalo, Pittsburgh, Cleveland, Chicago, Milwaukee, Cincinnati, and St. Louis.

Eager to retain a sense of community and to use skills they brought with them, the members of ethnic groups tended to cluster in particular vocations. Poles, Hungarians, Slovaks, Bohemians, and Italians used to the pick and shovel flocked to coal mines, just as the Irish, Cornish, and Welsh had done at mid-century; Slavs and Poles comfortable with muscle work gravitated to the steel mills; Greeks preferred working in textile mills; Russian and Polish Jews peopled the sewing trades and pushcart markets of New York. A few determined peasants uprooted from their agricultural heritage made their way west and were able to find work on farms or even a parcel of land for themselves.

Most of the immigrants, however, settled in the teeming cities. Strangers in a new land, they naturally gravitated to neighborhoods populated by their own kind. These immigrant enclaves—nicknamed Little Italy, Little Hungary, Chinatown, and so on—served as crucial transitional communities between the newcomers' Old World past and their New World future. By 1920 Chicago had some seventeen separate Little Italy colonies scattered across the city representing various home provinces. In such kinship communities the immigrants could practice their religions and native customs, converse in their native tongue, and fill an aching loneliness. But they paid a price for such community solidarity. When the "new immigrants" moved into an area, older residents typically moved out, taking with them whatever social prestige and political influence they had achieved. The quality of living conditions quickly deteriorated as housing and sanitation codes went unenforced.

As the number of new arrivals mushroomed during the last quarter of the nineteenth century, cities grew so cramped and land so scarce that designers were forced to build upward. The result was the "dumbbell"

Mulberry Street, Little Italy. New York, 1906. Immigrants established their own enclaves where old-world traditions could be carried on within their new American homes.

tenement house. These structures, usually six to eight stories in height and jammed tightly against one another, lined street after street. They derived their name from the fact that housing codes required a two-foot-wide air shaft between buildings, giving each structure the appearance of a dumbbell when viewed from overhead. Twenty-four to thirty-two families would cram into each building, meaning that some city blocks housed almost 4,000 people. The tiny air shaft provided little ventilation; instead it proved to be a fire hazard, fueling and conveying flames from building to building. The early tenements were poorly heated and had toilets outside in the yard or alley for communal use. By the end of the century they would feature two toilets on each floor, available to all comers. Shoehorned into such quarters, families had no privacy, free space, or sunshine; children had few places to play except in the city streets; infectious diseases and noxious odors were rampant. Not surprisingly, the mortality rate for urban immigrants was much higher than that of the general population. In one Chicago ethnic ghetto at the end of the century, three babies of every five died before their first birthday.

THE NATIVIST RESPONSE   Not only did immigrants have to face difficult living conditions, they also confronted growing prejudice from native-born Americans. Many saw the new immigration as a threat to their way of life and their jobs. "Immigrants work for almost nothing," groused one American laborer, "and seem to be able to live on wind—something which I cannot do." Others saw in the tide of new immigrants a threat to traditional American culture and values. A Stanford University professor called them "illiterate, docile, lacking in self-reliance and initiative, and not possessing the Anglo-Teutonic conceptions of law, order, and government." The undercurrent of nativism so often present in American culture now surfaced mainly in anti-Catholic, and secondarily anti-Semitic, sentiments. The Catholic church in America, long dominated by the English-speaking Irish, became a polyglot group all the more subject to misunderstanding and persecution. Similarly, Russian and Polish Jews came from a far different tradition than the Sephardic and German Jews who preceded them. The unruly beards and long black coats of the men and the new arrivals' distinctive language, Yiddish, made them seem strange and exotic.

More than religious prejudice underlay hostility toward the latest newcomers. Cultural differences confirmed in the minds of nativists the assumption that the Nordic peoples of the old immigration were superior to the Slavic and Latin peoples of the new immigration. Many of the new immigrants were illiterate, and more appeared so because they could not speak English. Some resorted to crime in order to survive in the new land, encouraging suspicions that criminals were being quietly helped out of Europe just as they had once been transported from England to the colonies. In the early 1890s vendettas among Italian gangs in New Orleans led to the murder of the police chief and the lynching of eleven Italian suspects, an incident that convinced many that the new immigrants were criminals.

The success of the Irish in city politics was emulated by the newer groups, who also thereby offended the sensibilities of well-born natives. Political and social radicals turned up among these immigrant groups in sufficient numbers to encourage nativists to blame labor disputes on alien elements. Such charges harbored a fine irony, however, because mainline labor organizations generally favored restricting immigration to keep down the competition for jobs. Employers sometimes used immigrants as strikebreakers; those who came from peasant origins, and were unfamiliar with strikes, were apt as not to think they were merely taking jobs that others had abandoned. Employers also learned quickly that a babel of foreign tongues could confound unity of action among workers.

A resurgence of nativism in the 1880s spawned groups devoted to saving the country from imaginary papal conspiracies. The most successful of these nativist groups, the American Protective Association (APA), operated mainly in Protestant strongholds of the upper Mississippi Valley. Its organizer harbored paranoid fantasies of Catholic conspiracies, and was especially anxious to keep the public schools free from Jesuit control. The association grew slowly from its start in 1887 until 1893, when leaders took advantage of a severe depression to draw large numbers of the frustrated to its ranks. The APA soon vanished, swallowed up in the Populist and free-silver agitations, but while it lasted it promoted restricted immigration, more stringent naturalization requirements, refusal to employ aliens or Catholics, and the teaching of the "American" language in the schools.

IMMIGRATION RESTRICTION   The movement to restrict immigration had mixed success beyond the exclusion of certain individuals deemed undesirable. In 1875, for instance, a new law refused entry to prostitutes and to convicts whose sentences had been remitted in other countries on condition that they leave. In 1882 a more general law added lunatics, idiots, and persons likely to become public charges, and over the years other specific undesirables joined the list. In 1891 Representative Henry Cabot Lodge of Massachusetts took up the cause of excluding illiterates—a measure that would have affected much of the new immigration even though the language did not have to be English. Bills embodying the restriction were vetoed by three presidents on the ground that they penalized people for lack of opportunity: Cleveland in 1897, Taft in 1913, and Wilson in 1915 and 1917. The last time, however, Congress overrode the veto.

Proponents of immigration restriction during the late nineteenth century did succeed in excluding the Chinese, who were victims of everything the European immigrants suffered, plus color prejudice as well. By 1880 there were some 75,000 Chinese in California, about one-ninth of the state's population. Their nemesis there was himself an immigrant (from Ireland), Dennis Kearney, leader of the Workingmen's party. Many white workers resented the Chinese for accepting lower wages, but their greatest sin, the editor of the *New York Nation* opined,

*Anti-Chinese protest, California, 1880. Widespread prejudice and racism
against the Chinese finally resulted in a ban on Chinese immigration with the
1882 passage of the Chinese Exclusion Act.*

was perpetuating "those disgusting habits of thrift, industry, and self-
denial."

Exclusion of the Chinese was initially prevented by the Burlingame
Treaty, which in 1868 gave China most-favored-nation status (the same
as the best conceded to any other country) with respect to travel and
immigration. But by 1880 the urgent need for railway labor had ebbed,
and a new treaty with China permitted the United States to "regulate,
limit, and suspend" Chinese immigration. In 1882 President Chester A.
Arthur vetoed a twenty-year suspension of immigration from China as
actually a prohibition, but accepted a ten-year suspension, known as
the Chinese Exclusion Act. The legislation closing the doors to Chinese
immigrants received overwhelming support. One congressman explained that because the "industrial army of Asiatic laborers" was increasing the tension between workers and management in the American economy, "the gate must be closed." The Chinese Exclusion Act
was periodically renewed before being extended indefinitely in 1902.
Not until 1943 were such barriers finally removed.

The West Coast counterpart to Ellis Island was the Immigration Station on rugged Angel Island, six miles offshore from San Francisco. Opened in 1910, it served as a processing center for tens of thousands of Asian immigrants, most of them Chinese. Although the Chinese Exclusion Act had sharply reduced the flow of Chinese immigrants, it did not stop the influx completely. Those arrivals who could claim a Chinese-American parent were allowed to enter, as were certain officials, teachers, merchants, and students. The powerful prejudice the Chinese immigrants encountered helps explain why over 30 percent of the arrivals at Angel Island were denied entry. Those who appealed such denials were housed in prison-like barracks for weeks or months. One of the detainees scratched a poignant poem on a wall:

> This place is called an island of immortals,
> When, in fact, this mountainous wilderness is a prison.
> Once you see the open net, why throw yourself in?
> It is only because of empty pockets. I can do nothing else.

EDUCATION

THE SPREAD OF PUBLIC EDUCATION   The spread of public education, spurred partly by the determination to "Americanize" immigrant children, helped quicken the emergence of a new America. The growing importance of public education is evident in statistics compiled by the national commissioner of education, whose office was created in 1867. In 1870 there were 7 million pupils in public schools; by 1920 the number had risen to 22 million. The percentage of school-age children in attendance went from 57 to 78 during these years. City schools quickly became schools of several rooms and separate grades with a teacher for each. In rural areas one-room schools lingered on into the twentieth century, when good roads made it possible to bus children to "consolidated schools." Despite these signs of progress, educational leaders all too often had to struggle against a pattern of political appointments, corruption, and incompetence in the public schools.

The spread of secondary schools accounted for much of the increased enrollment in public schools. In antebellum America private academies prepared those who intended to enter college. At the beginning of the Civil War there were only about 100 public high schools in the whole country, but their number grew rapidly to about 800 in 1880 and 6,000 at the turn of the century. Their curricula at first copied the academies' emphasis on higher mathematics and classical languages, but the public schools gradually accommodated their programs to those not going on to college, devising vocational training in such arts as bookkeeping, typing, drafting, and the use of tools.

VOCATIONAL TRAINING Vocational training was most intensely promoted after the Civil War by missionary schools for African Americans such as Hampton Institute in Virginia, which trained Booker T. Washington, founder of Tuskegee Institute in Alabama. Another major prophet of the vocational training movement was Professor Calvin M. Woodward of St. Louis, who in setting up a school of engineering found his students woefully inept in the use of simple tools. He called on the public schools to teach manual skills as well as more abstract knowledge. Prodded by the National Society for the Promotion of Industrial Education, high schools installed workshops for training in carpentry, printing, drafting, bricklaying, and machine work, and for home management, or "home economics," as well.

Congress had supported vocational training at the college level for many years. The Morrill Act of 1862 granted each state 30,000 acres per representative and senator, the income from which was to be applied to teaching agriculture and the mechanic arts in what came to be known as the "land-grant colleges." Among these new institutions were Clemson University, Pennsylvania State University, and Iowa State Uni-

George Washington Carver at the Tuskegee Institute. Exclusively for African Americans, Tuskegee was one of the leading vocational schools in the country.

versity. In 1890 a Second Morrill Act provided federal grants to these colleges. Their outreach, first attempted in Farmers' Institutes, greatly expanded with the rise of the demonstration technique perfected by Seaman A. Knapp, "schoolmaster to American agriculture." In 1903, about a decade after the Mexican boll weevil crossed the Rio Grande, Knapp set up a demonstration in Texas of the best techniques then known to fight the pest. From this beginning the demonstration technique spread rapidly as a means of getting knowledge into the field.

HIGHER EDUCATION   American colleges at this time, whether church schools or state "universities," sought to instill discipline, morality, and a curriculum stressing mathematics and the classics (and in church schools, theology), along with ethics and rhetoric. History, modern languages and literature, and some science were tolerated, although laboratory work was usually limited to a professor's demonstration to the class. The college teacher was apt to be a young man seeking temporary refuge or a broken-down preacher seeking safe harbor. In 1871 a writer in *The Galaxy,* a literary monthly, called the typical professor "nondescript, a jack of all trades, equally ready to teach surveying and Latin eloquence, and thankful if his quarter's salary is not docked to whitewash the college fence."

The campus of Texas A & M College, 1895, with Ross Hall at the right.

Nevertheless, the demand for higher learning led to an increase in the college student population from 52,000 in 1870 to 157,000 in 1890 and to 600,000 in 1920. During the same years the number of institutions rose from 563 to 998 and then to 1,041, and the number of faculty from 5,553 to 15,809 to 48,615. To accommodate the diverse needs of these growing numbers, colleges moved away from rigidly prescribed courses toward an elective system. In 1866 Washington College in Virginia, under its president, Robert E. Lee, adopted electives, and after 1869 Harvard College did so under its young president Charles W. Eliot. The new approach allowed students to favor their strong points and colleges to expand their scope. But as Henry Cabot Lodge complained, it also allowed students to "escape without learning anything at all by a judicious selection of unrelated subjects taken up only because they were easy or because the burden imposed by those who taught them was light."

Women's access to higher education improved markedly in the period. Before the Civil War, a few male colleges had admitted women, and most state universities in the West were open to women from the start. But colleges in the South and East fell in line very slowly. Vassar, opened in 1865, was the first women's college to teach by the same

Students in the chemistry lab at Mount Holyoke College, 1900.

standards as the best of the men's colleges, though it had to maintain a Preparatory Department for twenty-three years to upgrade poorly pre-pared entrants. In the 1870s, two more excellent women's schools ap-peared in Massachusetts: Wellesley and Smith, the latter being the first to set the same admission requirements as men's colleges. The older women's colleges quickly moved to upgrade their standards in the same way. By the end of the century, women made up more than a third of all college students.

The dominant new trend in American higher education after the Civil War was the rise of the graduate school. The versatile professors of the antebellum era had a knowledge more broad than deep. With some notable exceptions they engaged in little research, nor were they expected to advance the frontiers of knowledge. But gradually more and more Americans experienced a different system at the German univer-sities, where training was more systematic and focused. After the Civil War, the German system became the basis for the modern American university. Yale awarded its first Ph.D. in 1861 and Harvard its first in 1872.

The Johns Hopkins University, opened in Baltimore in 1876, set a new precedent by making graduate work its chief concern. The gradu-ate students gathered in seminar rooms or laboratories, where under the guidance of an experienced scholar they learned a craft, much as journeymen had in the medieval guilds. The crowning achievement, signifying admission to full membership in the craft, was a master-piece—in this case the Ph.D. dissertation, which was expected to make an original contribution to knowledge. Clark University at Worcester, Massachusetts, founded in 1887, followed the model of Johns Hop-kins.

In the early 1890s two more major universities were founded to spread the gospel of Germanic education. The first, established by rail-road magnate Leland Stanford (and named after his son), opened at Palo Alto, California, in 1891, and the following year the University of Chicago, endowed by oil baron John D. Rockefeller, began operation. Meanwhile other established institutions, including Columbia, Cor-nell, Michigan, and Wisconsin, also set up graduate schools. By 1900 American universities annually conferred hundreds of doctorates. The Ph.D. was fast becoming the ticket of admission to the guild of profes-sors.

THE RISE OF PROFESSIONALISM

The Ph.D. revolution was but one aspect of a growing emphasis on professionalism, with its imposition of standards, licensing of practitioners, and accreditation of professional schools. The number of professional schools grew rapidly in fields such as theology, law, medicine, dentistry, pharmacy, and veterinary medicine. While these fields accounted for 60 schools in 1850, there were 146 in 1875 and 283 in 1900. Growth in numbers brought pressures for higher standards. At Harvard in 1870 one could qualify for a medical degree by attending two lecture courses for four months, proving three years of medical experience, and passing a simple examination. Harvard president Charles Eliot then insisted on requiring three years of class attendance, together with laboratory and clinical work. In 1870 the Harvard Law School developed a rough equivalent to the laboratory by introducing the "case method," which required students to dig out the rules for themselves.

Along with advanced schooling went a movement for licensing practitioners in certain fields. The first state licensing law for dentistry, for instance, came in 1868, for pharmacy in 1874, for veterinary medicine in 1886, for accounting in 1896, and for architecture in 1897. By 1894 twenty-one states held standard examinations for doctors, and fourteen others recognized only graduates from accredited medical schools. Licensing benefited the public by certifying competence in a given field, but it also benefited members of the profession by controlling the number of practitioners and thereby limiting competition.

Learned and professional associations began to proliferate after the Civil War. Earlier societies, such as the American Association for the Advancement of Science (1848), which had seemed specialized enough, made way for still more specialized groups such as the American Chemical Society (1876) and the National Statistical Association (1888). Modern-language scholars organized in 1883, American historians in 1884, economists in 1885, political scientists in 1889, folklorists in 1888, and all sponsored meetings and journals to keep members in touch with developments in the field. A host of commonplace and simple jobs entered the ranks of the "professions," including barbering, playing baseball, and planning vacations.

POPULAR CULTURE

As more people moved to large towns and cities, the new urban environment created new patterns of recreation and leisure. Whereas people in rural areas were tied into the rituals of the harvest season and intimately connected to their neighbors and extended families, most middle-class urban whites were mobile and lived in nuclear families (made up of only parents and children), and their affluence enabled them to enjoy greater leisure time and rising discretionary income.

Middle- and upper-class urban families spent much of their leisure time together at home, usually in the parlor, singing around the piano, reading novels, or playing cards, dominoes, backgammon, chess, and checkers. A new invention called the "stereopticon" was all the rage. It was a hand-held device that placed several photographs or paintings at facing angles to one another. When viewed through binocular glasses, it gave the appearance of three-dimensional views.

Where social and economic conditions remained the same as in earlier periods, popular culture remained much the same. For example, most blacks continued to live in rural areas and operated within extended family networks that included cousins, aunts, uncles, and other relatives who provided assistance and emotional support. Popular culture in rural areas included many traditional forms of entertainment, centered on the family and the planting and harvesting of crops, or the arrival of an itinerant evangelist intent upon conducting a revival or camp meeting.

In the towns and cities, however, people were not as dependent upon mobile ministers or harvest rituals and festivities, and popular culture took on new or greatly expanded dimensions that endowed life with a more cosmopolitan quality. For example, traveling circuses brought entertainment to large cities and small towns. Creative promoters such as Phineas T. Barnum and James A. Bailey made the circus the most eclectic form of entertainment. The midwestern writer Hamlin Garland recalled how the circus came to rural hamlets "trailing clouds of glorified dust and filling our minds with the color of romance. . . . It brought to our ears the latest band pieces and taught us the popular songs. It furnished us with jokes. It relieved our dullness. It gave us something to talk about."

In the congested metropolitan areas, politics became as much a form of public entertainment as it was a process of providing civic representation and public services. People flocked to hear visiting candidates give speeches in cavernous halls, outdoor plazas, or from railway cars. Huge crowds regularly attended political rallies, and membership in a political party in cities such as New York, Philadelphia, Boston, and Chicago was akin to belonging to a social club. In addition, labor unions also included activities that were more social than economic in nature, and members often visited the union hall as much to socialize as to discuss working conditions. The sheer numbers of people congregated in cities also helped generate a market for new forms of mass entertainment such as traveling wild West shows, vaudeville shows, and spectator sports.

WILD WEST SHOWS   Another touring extravaganza that enjoyed incredible popularity during the last quarter of the nineteenth century was "Buffalo Bill's Wild West" traveling show. William "Buffalo Bill" Cody was a rugged frontiersman and sharpshooter. Born in Iowa and raised in Kansas, he became a rider for the Pony Express in 1860 and later served as a Union scout during the Civil War. After the war, he operated a hotel and a freight business, but Indians captured his wagons and horses. He thereafter became a renowned buffalo hunter, providing meat for the crews building railroads. His ability earned him the nickname Buffalo Bill. From 1868 to 1872, Cody served as a scout for army troops and was awarded the Congressional Medal of Honor after a ferocious battle with Indians on the Platte River. Four years later, he participated in a skirmish with Cheyennes during which he killed and scalped a young chief, Yellow Hand.

Cody's exploits attracted the attention of writer Ned Buntline, who wrote a series of popular novels that brought international celebrity to Buffalo Bill. Always alert to financial opportunity and ever eager to exaggerate his own accomplishments, Cody took advantage of his popularity to organize a stage show. By 1883 he had broadened its scope into a traveling spectacle that included live elk and buffalo, hundreds of horses, genuine cowboys, authentic Indians, rope tricks, shooting exhibitions, cowgirl Annie Oakley, and Cody himself as the star attraction. One of his advertising promotions heralded him as "young, sturdy, a remarkable specimen of manly beauty, with the brain to conceive and the

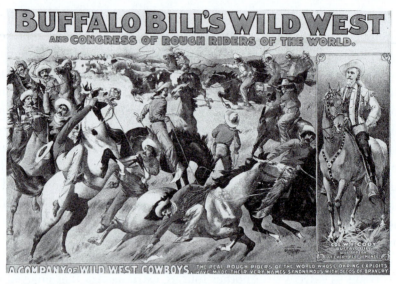

Buffalo Bill's Wild West Show. Although the shows included geniune cowboys and authentic Indians, they romanticized the Amerian West.

nerve to execute, . . . the exemplar of the strong and unique traits that characterize a true American frontiersman."

Indians were prominently featured in the show. In 1885 Cody hired Sitting Bull, the most famous Indian chief, to ride around the arena and sign autographs. One advertisement promised "a horde of war-painted Arapahoes, Cheyenne, and Sioux Indians." Their role in the show was to stage attacks on wagon trains and stagecoaches, as well as to reenact the battle between Indians and soldiers in General George Custer's last stand at the Little Bighorn. The Indians were always portrayed as the aggressors, and the whites as the victims. These images of murderous Indians attacking helpless whites set in motion the mythic depiction of the West that later became the staple of television and movie Westerns.

For three decades, this outdoor spectacle crisscrossed the United States and the world. The Wild West shows visited metropolises such as Chicago and New York as well as smaller cities—Oakland, Memphis, and Raleigh. The shows could accommodate up to twenty thousand people for each performance and promised to present "actual scenes and genuine characters" from the West. When Buffalo Bill died in 1917, his shows died with him, but he bequeathed to Americans a new form of entertainment that has since taken deep root: the rodeo.

VAUDEVILLE   Growing family incomes and innovations in urban transportation—cable cars, subways, electric streetcars and streetlights—enabled more people to take advantage of urban cultural life. Attendance at theaters, operas, and dance halls soared. Those interested in serious music could attend concerts by symphony orchestras appearing in every major city by the end of the nineteenth century.

But by far the most popular—and diverse—form of theatrical entertainment in the late nineteenth century was known as vaudeville. The term derives from a French word meaning a play accompanied by music. It emerged in the United States in saloons whose owners wanted to attract more customers by offering free shows.

Vaudeville "variety" shows featured comedians, singers, musicians, blackface minstrels, farcical plays, animal acts, jugglers, gymnasts, dancers, mimes, and magicians. Because variety shows were held in seedy beer halls populated by drunks and prostitutes and because the entertainers often included vulgar material, they quickly developed a bad reputation. To combat such an image so as to encourage families to attend, promoters of variety shows built elegant new theaters, banned alcoholic beverages, upgraded the performers, hired policemen and bouncers to handle "rowdies," and began to use the more elegant French word "vaudeville" to describe the genre.

Vaudeville houses sprouted like mushrooms in cities across the United States in the 1870s and 1880s. They quickly became popular gathering places for all social classes and types—men, women, and children—all of whom were expected to behave according to middle-class standards of gentility and decorum when attending performances. Ushers walked the aisles and handed out cards to unruly patrons. One of them read: "Gentlemen will kindly avoid the stamping of feet and pounding of canes on the floor, and greatly oblige the Management. All applause is best shown by clapping of hands." Raucous cheering, booing, and tobacco spitting were expressly prohibited. The diverse vaudeville shows would run all day and well into the night. They included something to please every taste and, as such, reflected the heterogeneity of city life. To commemorate the opening of a palatial new Boston theater in 1894, an actress read a dedicatory poem in which she announced that "All are equals here." The vaudeville house was the people's theater; it knew "no favorites, no class." She promised the spectators that the producers would "ever seek the new" in providing entertainers who epitomized "the spice of life, Variety," with its motto, "ever to please—and never to offend."

OUTDOOR RECREATION   The congestion and diseases associated with metropolitan life led many people to participate in forms of outdoor recreation intended to restore their vitality and improve their health. A movement to create city parks flourished after the construction of New York's Central Park in 1858. Its designer, Frederick Law Olmsted, viewed city parks as much more than recreational centers; he sought to create oases of culture that would promote social stability and cohesion. He was convinced that Central Park would exercise "a distinctly harmonizing and refining influence upon the most unfortunate and lawless classes of the city—an influence favorable to courtesy, self-control, and temperance." Olmsted went on to design parks for Boston, Brooklyn, Chicago, Philadelphia, and San Francisco.

Although originally intended as places where people could walk and commune with nature, the parks soon offered more vigorous forms of exercise and recreation—for men and women. During most of the nineteenth century, prevailing social attitudes scoffed at the notion of proper young women participating in even the lightest athletic endeavors. Women were deemed too delicate for such behavior. Before the Civil War, women essentially had only one exercise option: pedestrianism, the formal title for outdoor walking. After the war, however, the growing number of women enrolled in colleges began to participate in physical education, and they in turn demanded access to more vigorous sports.

Croquet and tennis courts were among the first additions to city parks because they took up little space and required little maintenance. Croquet was born in the British Isles in the mid–nineteenth century and soon migrated to most other English-speaking countries. Because croquet could be played by both sexes, it combined the virtues of sport with the opportunities of courtship. Croquet as a public sport suffered a setback in the 1890s, however, when Boston clergymen lambasted the drinking, gambling, and licentious behavior associated with it on the Boston Common, where croquet matches were held.

Lawn tennis was invented by an Englishman in 1873 and arrived in the United States a year later. By 1885 Central Park had thirty courts. Lawn tennis was originally viewed as a leisurely sport best suited for

Croquet, *1886, by Winslow Homer.*

women. The Harvard student newspaper declared in 1878 that the sport was "well enough for a lazy or *weak* man, but men who have rowed or taken part in a nobler sport should blush to be seen playing Lawn Tennis."

Even more popular than croquet or tennis was cycling or "wheeling." In the 1870s, bicycles began to be manufactured in the United States, and by the end of the century, a "bicycle craze" had swept the country. The first bicycles were called "high-wheelers" or "boneshakers" because the front wheel was huge, as much as five feet high, while the rear wheel was tiny, no more than a foot in diameter. The high-wheelers were hard to ride, uncomfortable, and dangerous, as they had no brakes. During the 1880s, an Englishman named J. K. Starley produced the first "safety bicycle." These bicycles had wheels of equal size and axles with ball bearings, which made them easier and safer to ride than high-wheelers. By 1890, bicycles had air-filled rubber tires and brakes. Millions of middle-class Americans (who could afford the new invention) discovered a new mobility and freedom through the bicycle, which had few of the drawbacks of horses. Bicycles went where pointed, did not need to be fed, and did not leave droppings in the road.

Bicycles were especially popular with women who chafed at the restricting conventions of Victorianism. The new vehicles offered exer-

Tandem tricycle. In spite of the danger and discomfort of early bicycles, wheeling became a popular form of recreation and mode of transportation.

cise, freedom, and access to the countryside. Female cyclists were able to discard their cumbersome corsets and full dresses in favor of bloomers and split skirts. Critics feared that the bicycle mania was encouraging young women to grow independent and shun conventional domestic responsibilities. Some guardians of morality believed that cycling was also sexually provocative. In 1899 the Reverend W. W. Reynolds expressed outrage because a "large number of female bicyclists wear shorter dresses than the laws of morality and decency permit, thereby inviting the improper conversations and remarks of the depraved and immoral." He deemed cycling as "detrimental to the advancement of morality."

The working poor in the cities could not afford to acquire a bicycle or join a croquet club. Nor did they have as much free time as the affluent. They toiled long hours, six days a week, and at the end of their long days they eagerly sought recreation and fellowship on street corners or on the front stoops of their apartment buildings. Organ grinders and musicians would perform on the sidewalks among the food vendors. Those with a few extra dollars to spend frequented the saloons and dance halls available in each city. New York City alone had 10,000 sa-

Steeplechase Park, Coney Island, New York. This amusement park attracted working-class patrons who could afford the inexpensive rides.

loons in 1900 featuring five-cent beer and free lunch. In the late nineteenth century, saloons often doubled as gymnasiums. Back rooms housed handball courts, pool tables, bowling alleys, and dart boards.

Many ethnic groups, especially the Germans and the Irish, formed male singing, drinking, or gymnastic clubs. Working folk also attended bare-knuckle boxing matches or baseball games, and on Sundays would gather for picnics. By the end of the century, large-scale amusement parks such as New York's Coney Island provided entertainment for the entire family. Yet many inner-city youth could not afford the trolley fare to visit a suburban amusement park, so the crowded streets and dangerous alleys became their playgrounds.

SPECTATOR SPORTS   In the last quarter of the nineteenth century, horse racing and prizefighting remained popular, but team sports also began to attract legions of fans. New spectator sports such as college football and basketball and professional baseball gained mass popularity, reflecting the growing urbanization of American life. People could gather easily for sporting events in the large cities. And news of the games could be conveyed quickly by newspapers and specialized sporting magazines relying upon telegraph reports. Saloons also posted the scores. Athletic rivalries between distant cities were made possible by the network of railroads spanning the continent and facilitating team travel. Spectator sports became urban extravaganzas, unifying the diverse ethnic groups in the large cities and attracting people with the leisure time and cash to spend (or bet) on watching others perform.

Football emerged as a modified form of soccer and rugby. The College of New Jersey (Princeton) and Rutgers played the first college football game in 1869. Some 200 students and spectators saw Rutgers win 6–4. The teams at first used twenty-five players at a time, and players literally kicked the ball along the ground. By 1880 the number of players had been reduced to eleven, and they carried the ball rather than kicking it. The players wore no protective padding or headgear, and the games often resembled organized fights. In fact, advocates of football portrayed it as a "blood sport" that provided a modern substitute for the frontier experience.

By the end of the century, scores of colleges and high schools had started football teams, and some college games attracted more than 50,000 spectators. Early games featured unregulated mayhem, however, with slugging and kicking commonplace. Scores of players died from injuries. In 1905 alone, 18 players were killed and 150 seriously injured. Gambling on college football games was also widespread, and many college coaches provided cash incentives to lure players to enroll. The president of Cornell University grew so disgusted with the evils infecting the sport that he prohibited the football team from playing the University of Michigan squad, refusing to "permit 30 men to travel 4,000 miles to agitate a bag of wind."

Football became so controversial that President Theodore Roosevelt intervened in 1905. He had long promoted strenuous exercise and "rough, manly sports" as needed antidotes for young Americans leading sedentary lives in cities. With the closing of the frontier, he feared that young boys growing up in urban centers would become effeminate and anemic. Roosevelt championed football as a means of instilling in young men the virtues of "pluck, endurance, and physical address," yet he appealed to coaches, professors, and alumni to "come to a gentlemen's agreement not to have mucker play." His appeal did little good, and the roughness and foul play continued. As a result, Columbia University and the Massachusetts Institute of Technology abolished football. Stanford and the University of California replaced it with rugby. In a further effort to curb injuries and abuses, the National Collegiate Athletics Association (NCAA) was founded in 1910.

Basketball was invented in 1891 when Dr. James Naismith, a physical education instructor, nailed two peach baskets to the walls of the YMCA training school in Springfield, Massachusetts. Naismith wanted to create an indoor winter game that could be played between the fall football and spring baseball seasons. The baskets were ten feet high because that was the height of the balcony at each end of the gym to which the baskets were attached. The first game had nine men on a side, and they used a soccer ball. Basketball quickly grew in popularity among both boys and girls. Vassar and Smith Colleges added the sport in 1892. In 1893, Vanderbilt became the first college to field a men's team.

Baseball laid claim to being America's national pastime at mid-century. Contrary to popular opinion, Abner Doubleday did not invent the game. Instead, Alexander Cartwright, a New York bank clerk and sportsman, is recognized as the father of organized baseball. In 1845 he gathered a group of merchants, stockbrokers, and physicians to form the Knickerbocker Base Ball Club of New York. They began playing a bat-and-ball game on a field at the corner of Twenty-seventh Street and Fourth Avenue in Manhattan. Soon they moved to a field in Hoboken, New Jersey. After their games they would gather at a nearby hotel bar. There they drafted a list of rules that included setting the bases 90 feet apart and allocating nine players to a side. Initially the pitcher stood 45 feet from home plate and threw the ball underhanded. Three strikes resulted in an out, but the batter had to take three swings. There were no called strikes.

The first professional baseball team was the Cincinnati Red Stockings, which made its appearance in 1869. Seven years later, seven other teams joined the Red Stockings in creating the National League. Reporters began to cover the games, and sports sections appeared in every newspaper. With professionalization came changes in the sport. Umpires were added to call balls, strikes, and outs; pitchers threw overhand rather than underhand; fielders began to use gloves; catchers donned protective equipment. Other changes in the late nineteenth century included the addition of a "walk" after four balls and fixing the distance from the pitcher to home plate at 60 feet 6 inches. In 1901 the

Professional baseball game, 1887. The excitement of rooting for the home team united all classes as they watched the athletes who graced the playing field.

American League was organized, and two years later the first World Series was held.

Baseball became the "national pastime" and the most democratic sport in America. People from all social classes (mostly men) attended the games, and ethnic immigrants were among the most faithful fans. The *St. Louis Post-Dispatch* reported in 1883 that "a glance at the audience on any fine day at the ball park will reveal . . . telegraph operators, printers who work at night, travelling men [salesmen] . . . men of leisure . . . men of capital, bank clerks who get away [from work] at 3 P.M., real estate men . . . barkeepers . . . hotel clerks, actors and employees of the theater, policemen and firemen on their day off . . . butchers and bakers." Cheering for a city baseball team gave rootless people a common loyalty and a sense of belonging.

Only white players were allowed in the major leagues. African Americans played on "minor league" teams or in all-black "Negro leagues." In 1867 the National Association of Base Ball Players excluded black clubs from membership. And the National League followed suit when it was organized nine years later. In 1887 black players were banned from minor league teams as well. That same year, the Cuban Giants, a barn-storming team made up of black players, traveled the country. A few major league white teams agreed to play them. An African-American-owned newspaper announced in early 1888 that the Cuban Giants "have defeated the New Yorks, 4 games out of 5, and are now virtually champions of the world." But it added, "the St. Louis Browns, Detroits and Chicagos, afflicted by Negrophobia and unable to bear the odium of being beaten by colored men, refused to accept their challenge."

By the end of the nineteenth century, sports of all kinds had become a major cultural phenomenon in the United States. A writer in *Harper's Weekly* announced in 1895 that "ball matches, football games, tennis tournaments, bicycle races, [and] regattas, have become part of our national life." They "are watched with eagerness and discussed with enthusiasm and understanding by all manner of people, from the day-laborer to the millionaire." One reporter in the 1890s referred to the "athletic craze" that was sweeping the American imagination. Moreover, it was in 1892 that a Frenchman, Pierre de Coubertin, called for the revival of the ancient Olympic games, and the first modern olympiad was held four years later.

THEORIES OF SOCIAL CHANGE

Every field of thought in the post–Civil War years felt the impact of Charles Darwin's *On the Origin of Species* (1859), which argued that existing species, including humanity itself, had evolved through a long process of "natural selection" from less complex forms of life. Those species that adapted to survival by reason of quickness, shrewdness, or other advantages reproduced their kind, while others fell by the way-side. The idea of species evolution shocked people of conventional religious views by contradicting a literal interpretation of the creation stories in Genesis. Heated arguments arose among scientists and clergymen. Some of the faithful rejected Darwin's doctrine, while others found their faith severely shaken not only by evolutionary theory but also by the urging of professional scholars to apply the critical standards of scholarship to the Bible itself, and by the study of comparative religion, which found parallels to biblical stories and doctrines in other faiths. Most of the faithful, however, came to reconcile science and re-

Charles Darwin.

ligion. They viewed evolution as the Divine Will, as one of the secondary causes through which God worked.

SOCIAL DARWINISM   Though Darwin's theory applied only to biological phenomena, other thinkers drew broader inferences from it. The temptation to apply evolutionary theory to the social world proved irresistible. Darwin's fellow Englishman Herbert Spencer became the first major prophet of Social Darwinism and an important influence on American thought. Spencer, whose first works anticipated Darwin, brought forth in eight weighty tomes his *System of Synthetic Philosophy* (1862–1893), an effort to embrace all fields of knowledge within an overall system of Darwinian evolution. He argued that human society and institutions, like organisms, passed through the process of natural selection, which resulted, in Spencer's chilling phrase, in the "survival of the fittest." For Spencer, social evolution implied progress, ending "only in the establishment of the greatest perfection and the most complete happiness."

If, as Spencer believed, society naturally evolved for the better, then individual freedom was inviolable, and governmental interference with the process of social evolution was a serious mistake. This view used biological laws to justify the working of the free market. Social Darwinism implied a governmental policy of hands-off; it decried the regulation of

Herbert Spencer, the first major prophet of Social Darwinism.

business, the graduated income tax, sanitation and housing regulations, and even protection against medical quacks. Such interventions, Spencer charged, would help the "unfit" survive and thereby only impede progress. The only acceptable charity was voluntary, and even that was of dubious value. Spencer warned that "fostering the good-for-nothing at the expense of the good, is an extreme cruelty."

For Spencer and his many American supporters, successful businessmen and corporations were the engines of social progress. If small businesses were crowded out by trusts and monopolies, that too was part of the evolutionary process. John D. Rockefeller told his Baptist Sunday school class that the "growth of a large business is merely a survival of the fittest. . . . This is not an evil tendency in business. It is merely the working-out of a law of nature and a law of God."

The ideas of Darwin and Spencer spread quickly in America. *Popular Science Monthly,* founded in 1872, soon became the chief medium for popularizing Darwinism. That same year Darwin's chief academic disciple, William Graham Sumner, took up the new chair of political and social science at Yale. Trained for the ministry and formerly an Episcopal rector, he preached the gospel of natural selection under titles such as "What Social Classes Owe to Each Other" and "The Absurd Effort to Make the World Over."

Sumner's most lasting contribution, made in his book *Folkways* (1907), was to argue that social conditions were set by the working of tradition, or the customs of a community, and not by reason or natural laws. The implication here too was that it would be a mistake for government to interfere with established customs in the name of ideals of equality or natural rights. Democracy, according to Sumner, was a condition based not on reason but on customs arising from the availability of much free land in America. As available land diminished, customs would slowly change, showing democracy to be merely a temporary condition.

REFORM DARWINISM   The influence of Darwin and Spencer over the American mind did not go without challenge. Reform found its major philosopher in an obscure Washington civil servant, Lester Frank Ward, who had fought his way up from poverty and never lost his empathy for the underdog. Ward's book *Dynamic Sociology* (1883) singled out one product of evolution that previous pundits had neglected: the human brain. People, unlike animals, had minds that could shape social evolution. Far from being the helpless pawn of evolution, Ward argued, humanity could improve its situation by reflecting upon it and then acting. People thus had reached a stage at which they could control the process of evolution. The competition extolled by Sumner was in fact highly wasteful, as was the natural competitive process: plant or cattle

Lester Frank Ward, proponent of Reform Darwinism.

breeding, for instance, could actually improve on the results of natural selection.

Ward's Reform Darwinism challenged Sumner's conservative Social Darwinism, holding that cooperation, not competition, would better promote progress. According to Ward, Sumner's "irrational distrust of government" might have been justified in an earlier day of autocracy, but no longer under a representative system. Government could become the agency of progress by striving to reach two main goals: to ameliorate poverty, which impeded the development of the mind, and to promote the education of the masses. "Intelligence, far more than necessity," Ward wrote, "is the mother of invention," and "the influence of knowledge as a social factor, like that of wealth, is proportional to the extent of its distribution." Intellect, rightly informed by science, could plan successfully. In the benevolent "sociocracy" of the future, legislatures would function mainly to sanction decisions worked out in the sociological laboratory.

REALISM IN FACT AND FICTION

HISTORY AND THE SOCIAL SCIENCES The pervasive effect of Darwinism in late-nineteenth-century America was comparable to the effect of romanticism in the first part of the century. Like the earlier reaction against the Enlightenment's praise of reason, social thought now was turned against abstract logic and toward concrete reality.

In the milieu of Darwinism, the study of history flourished. The historian, like the biologist, studied the process of development, but in the origins and the evolution of society. Under the influence of German scholarship, and the new emphasis on science, history aspired to become "scientific." This meant examining documents and manuscripts critically, using external and internal evidence to determine validity and relevancy. The ideal of the scientific historian was to reproduce history with perfect objectivity, a noble if unreachable goal.

Lester Frank Ward's achievements in *Dynamic Sociology* (1883) qualified him as the father of American sociology, but he, like many others, thought of the book as a broad synthesis of the social studies. It fell to Albion W. Small, head of the department at the University of Chicago, to define the field specifically. In his *General Sociology* (1905), Small confined it to the scientific analysis of social phenomena with emphasis on groups in human society. As founder (1895) and editor of the *American Journal of Sociology,* Small wielded a strong influence in turning sociology from abstract speculation to the study of actual human relations. Theory, once all there was to sociology, gave way to a multitude of special interests: population, the family, ethnic groups, social class, public opinion, and social movements, to name but a few.

Economists made the same transition from abstract theory to the study of actual conditions. The American Economics Association, founded in 1885, turned its attention "not so much to speculation as to historical and statistical study of actual conditions of economic life for the satisfactory accomplishment of [economic] study" and upheld the state "as an agency whose positive assistance is one of the indispensable conditions of human progress." One economist argued that the economic problem would soon no longer be scarcity, since modern technology would make possible a surplus of goods, but distribution: how best to distribute goods and services.

PRAGMATISM   Around the turn of the century, the evolutionary idea found expression in a philosophical principle set forth in mature form by William James in his book *Pragmatism: A New Name for Some Old Ways of Thinking.* James, a professor of philosophy and psychology at

William James (left) *and John Dewey* (right).

Harvard, shared Lester Frank Ward's concern with the role of ideas in the process of evolution. Truth, to James, arose from the testing of new ideas, the value of which lay in their practical consequences. Thus, scientists could test the validity of their ideas in the laboratory and judge their import by their applications. Pragmatism reflected a quality often looked upon as genuinely American: the inventive, experimental spirit.

John Dewey, who would become the chief philosopher of pragmatism after James, preferred the term "instrumentalism," by which he meant that ideas were instruments, especially of social reform. Dewey, unlike James, threw himself into movements for the rights of labor and women, the promotion of peace, and the reform of education. He believed that education was the process through which society would gradually progress toward the goal of economic democracy.

Dewey would become the prophet of what was later labeled "progressive education." He emphasized the teaching of history, geography, and science in order to enlarge the child's personal experience. Dewey also pointed out that social conditions had so changed that schools had to find ways to inculcate values once derived from participation in family and community activities. Another important goal of the schools was to keep habits flexible to prepare children for a changing world. They needed not just knowledge but a critical intelligence to cope with a complex, modern world.

THE LOCAL COLORISTS   Writers of fiction responded in different ways to the changes in American life and thought. The local color movement, which emerged after the Civil War, reflected a reunited nation engrossed with the diversity of its peoples and cultures. This movement also expressed the nostalgia of a people moving from a rural to an urban culture, and longing for those places where the old folkways survived. In California, Bret Harte, the editor of the *Overland Monthly,* burst upon the national consciousness in the late 1860s with colorful stories of the gold country such as "The Outcasts of Poker Flat" and "The Luck of Roaring Camp." Hamlin Garland, in *Main-Traveled Roads* (1891), pictured the hardscrabble existence of farmers and their wives in his native country, the upper Midwest from Wisconsin to the Dakotas.

Sarah Orne Jewett depicted the down-easters of her native Maine, most enduringly in the stories and sketches collected in *The Country of the Pointed Firs* (1896), while Mary Wilkins Freeman wrote stories of village life in Vermont and Massachusetts gathered in *A Humble Romance* (1887) and other works. Jewett's creative glance was always backward-looking and affectionate. She looked upon her parents' "generation as the one to which I really belong—I who was brought up with grandfathers and granduncles and aunts for my best playmates." She told another writer that her head was always full of old women and old houses, and when the two came together the result was a richly textured fiction marked by the essential dignity of a bygone day.

Once the passions of war and Reconstruction were spent, the South became for many northern readers an inexhaustible gallery of quaint types. George Washington Cable exploited the local color of the Louisiana Creoles and Cajuns in *Old Creole Days* (1879), *The Grandissimes* (1880), and other books. Joel Chandler Harris, a newsman and columnist, wove authentic African-American folk tales into the unforgettable stories of Uncle Remus, gathered first in *Uncle Remus: His Songs and His Sayings* (1880). Most Americans are familiar with the wonderful tar baby and the brier patch.

CLEMENS, HOWELLS, AND JAMES   The best of the local colorists could find universal truths in local life, and Samuel Langhorne Clemens (Mark Twain) transcended them all. A native of Missouri, he was forced to work at age twelve, becoming first a printer and then a Mississippi riverboat pilot. When the Civil War shut down the river traffic, he briefly joined a Confederate militia company, then left with his brother, Orion, for Nevada. He moved on to California in 1864 and first gained widespread notice with his tall tale of the gold country, "The Celebrated Jumping Frog of Calaveras County" (1865). In 1867 the San Francisco *Alta Californian* staked him to a tour of the Mediterranean, and his humorous reports on the trip, revised and collected into *Innocents Abroad* (1869), established him as a funny man much in demand on the lecture circuit. With the success of *Roughing It* (1871), an account of his western years, he moved to Hartford, Connecticut, and was able to establish himself as a full-time author and hilarious lecturer.

Clemens was the first great American writer born and raised west of the Appalachians. His early writings accentuated his western background, but for his greatest books he drew heavily upon his boyhood in a border slave state and the tall-tale tradition of southwestern humor. In *The Adventures of Tom Sawyer* (1876) he evoked in fiction the prewar

Mark Twain illustrated in the frontis-piece to his novel, Tramp Abroad, *1880.*

Hannibal, Missouri, where his own boyhood was cut so short. Its story of childhood adventures is firmly etched on the American memory. *Life on the Mississippi* (1883), based on articles written eight years before, drew upon what Clemens remembered as his happiest days as a young riverboat pilot before the war.

Clemens's masterpiece, *The Adventures of Huckleberry Finn* (1884), created unforgettable characters in Huck Finn, his shiftless father, the slave Jim, the Widow Douglas, the "King," and the "Duke." The product of an erratic upbringing, Huck Finn embodied the instinct of every red-blooded American boy to "light out for the territory" whenever polite society set out to civilize him. Huck's effort to help his friend Jim escape bondage expressed well the moral dilemmas imposed by slavery on everyone. Many years later another great American writer, Ernest Hemingway, would claim that "All modern American literature comes from one book by Mark Twain, called *Huckleberry Finn.*"

But it was Twain's friend, William Dean Howells, who dominated the literary scene after the Civil War. Born in Ohio, he went to Boston in 1867 and soon became editor of the influential *Atlantic Monthly.* He left that post to devote himself to novel writing, but later served more than two decades as a columnist and critic for *Harper's Monthly.* How-

William Dean Howells (left) *and Henry James* (right).

ells proclaimed the doctrine of realism, a sort of literary version of scientific history's effort to reproduce the past as it actually happened. He wrote that realism "was nothing more or less than the truthful treatment of . . . the motives, the impulses, the principles that shape the life of actual men and women." The realist commonly wrote of the middle class in a simple and direct language, taking a pragmatic point of view of people and events.

Howells wrote novels, plays, travel books, criticism, essays, biography, and autobiography. Amid the varied output of a long and productive life, *The Rise of Silas Lapham* (1885) stands out as his most famous novel. In it Howells sympathetically portrayed a rags-to-riches paint manufacturer, one of the earliest fictional treatments of an American businessman. Soon after its publication, however, at the height of his career, Howells felt that "the bottom had dropped out" of his life. Converted to socialism by reading Tolstoy, horrified by the "civic murder" of the Haymarket anarchists, he entered a new phase. In *A Hazard of New Fortunes* (1890) he offered less sympathetic views of businessmen, included scenes of squalor and misery in New York City's Bowery district, and introduced a German-American socialist who lost his life in a police beating during a violent streetcar strike.

The third major literary figure of the times, Henry James, moved in a world far different from those of Clemens or Howells. Brother of the pragmatist philosopher William James, Henry spent most of his adult life as a voluntary expatriate in London, where he produced elegant novels that explored the society of Americans in Europe. In novels such as *Daisy Miller* (1878), *Portrait of a Lady* (1881), *The Ambassadors* (1903), and *The Golden Bowl* (1904), James explored the tensions that developed between direct, innocent, and idealistic Americans (most often young women) and sophisticated, devious Europeans. James typically wrote of the upper classes, and his stories turned less on plot than on moral dilemmas. His intense exploration of the inner selves of his characters brought him the titles of "father of the psychological novel" and "biographer of fine consciences."

LITERARY NATURALISM   During the 1890s, a younger generation of writers formed a new literary school known as naturalism. The naturalists imported scientific determinism into literature, viewing people as part of the animal world, prey to natural forces and internal drives without control or full knowledge of them.

Stephen Crane in *Maggie: A Girl of the Streets* (1893) and *The Red Badge of Courage* (1895) portrayed people caught up in environmental situations beyond their control. *Maggie* depicted a tenement girl driven to prostitution and death amid scenes so sordid that Crane had to finance publication himself. *The Red Badge of Courage,* his masterpiece, told the story of a young man going through his baptism of fire in the Civil War, and evoked nobility and courage amid the ungovernable carnage of war.

Two of the naturalists achieved a degree of popular success: Jack London and Theodore Dreiser. London was both a professed socialist and a believer in the German philosopher Friedrich Nietzsche's doctrine of the superman. In adventure stories such as *The Call of the Wild* (1903) and *The Sea Wolf* (1904), London celebrated the triumph of brute force and the will to survive. He reinforced his point about animal force in *The Call of the Wild.* The novel's protagonist is not a superman but a superdog that reverted to the wild in Alaska and ran with a wolf pack.

Theodore Dreiser shocked the genteel public probably more than the others, presenting protagonists who sinned without remorse and without punishment. *Sister Carrie* (1900), a counterpoint to Crane's *Maggie,* departed from it by having Carrie Meeber survive illicit loves and go on to success on the stage. In *The Financier* (1912) and *The Titan*

(1914), Dreiser's main character was a sexual athlete and a man of elemental force who rose to a dominant position in business and society.

SOCIAL CRITICISM   Behind their dogma of determinism, the naturalists harbored intense outrage at human misery. Other writers shared their indignation but addressed themselves more directly to protest and reform. Henry George, a California printer and journalist, was suddenly struck on a visit to New York by the contrast the city offered between wealth and poverty. "Once, in daylight, and in a city street, there came to me a thought, a vision, a call. . . . And there and then I made a vow." The vow was to seek out the cause of poverty in the midst of progress. Back in California, the spectacle of land boomers grabbing choice sites brought George a new insight. The basic social problem, he reasoned, was the "unearned increment" in wealth that came to those who owned the land. The fruit of his thought, *Progress and Poverty* (1879), a thick and difficult book, sold slowly at first, but by 1905 had sold about 2 million copies in several languages.

George held that all people had as much right to the use of the land as to the air they breathed. Nobody had a right to the value that accrued from the land, since that was created by the community, not by its owner. Labor and capital, on the other hand, did have a just claim on the wealth they produced. One justifiable solution to the problem of unearned wealth was to socialize all property in land, but that would have been too disruptive. Better simply to tax the "unearned" increment in the value of the land, or the rent. George's "single-tax" idea was intended to free capital and labor from paying tribute for the land, and to put to use lands previously held out of production by speculators. George's idea was widely propagated and actually affected tax policy here and there, but his influence on the thinking of the day came less from his "single-tax" panacea than from the paradox he posed in his title, *Progress and Poverty*.

The journalist and freelance writer Henry Demarest Lloyd addressed himself to what many found a more vital issue than Henry George's, not the monopoly in land but industrial monopoly. His best-known book, *Wealth Against Commonwealth* (1894), drew on more than a decade of studying the Standard Oil Company. Lloyd, like Lester Frank Ward, saw the key to progress in cooperation rather than competition. Economic activities in their cooperative aspects demonstrated a civilizing process; Lloyd argued that "the spectacle of the million or more employees of the railroads . . . dispatching trains, maintaining tracks, collecting fares and freights . . . is possible only where civilization has reached a high average of morals and culture." But those in charge of the machinery of industry were concerned only with wealth, not with promoting civilization. "Of gods, friends, learning, of the uncomprehended civilization they overrun, they ask but one question: How much? What is a good time to sell? What is a good time to buy?" To avoid destruction, civilization required changes. The cooperative principle should be applied "to all toils in which private sovereignty has become through monopoly a despotism over the public." Where monopoly had developed, it should be transferred to public operation in the public interest. In 1903, just before his death, Lloyd joined the Socialist party.

Thorstein Veblen brought to his social criticism a background of formal training in economics and a purpose of making economics more an evolutionary or historical science. By all accounts he taught miserably, even inaudibly, and seldom held a job for long, but he wrote brilliantly. In his best-known work, *The Theory of the Leisure Class* (1899), he examined the pecuniary values of the middle classes and introduced phrases that have since become almost clichés: "conspicuous consumption" and "conspicuous leisure." With the advent of industrial society, Veblen argued, property became the conventional basis of reputation. For the upper classes, moreover, it became necessary to consume time nonproductively as evidence of the ability to afford a life of leisure. In this and later works Veblen held that the division between industrial experts and business managers was widening to a dangerous point. The businessman's interest in profits combined with his ignorance of efficiency produced wasteful organization and a failure to realize the full potential of modern technology.

Edward Bellamy's *Looking Backward, 2000–1887* (1888) typified another genre of reform literature, the utopian novel. In Bellamy's futuristic story, a Bostonian who falls asleep in 1887 awakens in the year 2000 to find that the millennium has genuinely arrived. More than a hundred years in the future Julian West discovers a society transformed. The revolution that led to political equality has led on, by the democratic method, to a "Nationalist" society of economic equality under socialism. Everybody gets an equal share of the national product, and labor is shared by the simple method of reducing the hours for distasteful jobs until someone is willing to do the work. All this is accomplished by public control under national planning. The book enjoyed a temporary vogue, became a best-seller, and led to the founding of Nationalist Clubs. The popularity of Bellamy's book gave rise to a spate of utopian novels and some anti-utopian ones depicting model societies gone wrong.

THE SOCIAL GOSPEL

RISE OF THE INSTITUTIONAL CHURCH   The churches responded slowly to the mounting social criticism, for American Protestantism had become one of the main props of the established order. The Reverend Henry Ward Beecher, pastor of the fashionable Plymouth Congregational Church in Brooklyn, preached success, Social Darwinism, and the unworthiness of the poor. As the middle classes moved out to the streetcar suburbs, their churches followed. In the years 1868–1888, for instance, seventeen Protestant churches abandoned the areas below Fourteenth Street in Manhattan. In the center of Chicago 60,000 residents had no church, Protestant or Catholic. Where churches became prosperous they fell easily under the spell of respectability and do-nothing Social Darwinism.

A Salvation Army group in Flint, Michigan, 1894.

However, many churches responded to the human needs of the time by devoting their resources to community service and care for the unfortunate. The Young Men's Christian Association had entered the United States from England in the 1850s and grew rapidly after 1870; the Salvation Army, founded in London in 1876, came to the United States four years later. Churches in urban districts began to develop institutional features that were more social than strictly religious in function. After the Civil War, churches acquired gymnasiums, libraries, lecture rooms, and other facilities for social programs. Russell Conwell's Baptist Temple in Philadelphia included, among other features, a night school for working people that grew into Temple University.

RELIGIOUS REFORMERS   Other church leaders preached what came to be called the social gospel. One of the earliest, Washington Gladden of Columbus, Ohio, managed to preach the social gospel from the pulpit of a middle-class Congregational church. The new gospel in fact expressed the social conscience of the middle class. Gladden accepted the new ideas of evolution and textual criticism of the Bible, which he said relieved him of defending the literal truth of the story of Jonah and the whale. In his many books, Gladden argued that true Christianity lies not in rituals, dogmas, or even in the mystical experience of God, but in the principle that "Thou shalt love thy neighbor as thyself." Christian law should govern the operation of industry, with worker and employer united in serving each other's interest. He argued for labor's right to organize and complained that class distinctions split congregations as well.

The acknowledged intellectual leader of the social gospel movement, however, was the Baptist Walter Rauschenbusch, professor at the Colgate–Rochester Theological Seminary. In *Christianity and the Social Crisis* (1907) and other works, he developed a theological basis for the movement in the Kingdom of God. This kingdom existed in the churches themselves, but it embraced far more than these: "It is the Christian transfiguration of the social order. The church is one social institution alongside of the family, the industrial organization of society, and the State. The Kingdom of God is in all these, and realizes itself through them all." The church was indispensable to religion, but "the greatest future awaits religion in the public life of humanity."

THE CATHOLIC CHURCH   In the postbellum years Catholics remained inhibited from supporting the new social movements by the

Syllabus of Errors (1864), issued by Pope Pius IX, which declared erroneous such current ideas as progress, liberalism, rationalism, and socialism. The church's outlook altered drastically in 1891 when Pope Leo XIII issued his encyclical, *Rerum novarum* ("Of modern things"). This new expression of Catholic social doctrine upheld private property as a natural right but condemned capitalism for imposing poverty and degradation on workers. It upheld the right of Catholics to join labor unions and socialist movements insofar as these were not antireligious. But most American Catholics remained isolated from reform movements until the twentieth century, though many of them were among the victims of exploitation.

EARLY EFFORTS AT URBAN REFORM

THE SETTLEMENT HOUSE MOVEMENT While preachers of the social gospel dispensed inspiration, other dedicated reformers attacked the problems of the slums from residential and community centers called settlement houses. The movement sprang from the example of Toynbee Hall, founded in a London industrial district, where an English vicar invited students to join him in "settling" in a deprived section. By 1900 perhaps a hundred settlement houses existed in the United States, some of the best known being Jane Addams's and Ellen Starr's Hull House in Chicago (1889), Robert A. Woods's South End House in Boston (1891), and Lillian Wald's Henry Street Settlement (1895) in New York.

The settlement houses mainly attracted as workers idealistic middle-class young people, a majority of them college-trained women who had few other outlets for meaningful work outside the home. Settlement workers sought to broaden the horizons and improve the lives of slum dwellers in diverse ways. At Jane Addams's Hull House, for instance, workers enrolled the neighborhood children into clubs and kindergartens, and set up a nursery to care for the infant children of working mothers. The program gradually expanded as Hull House sponsored health clinics, lectures, music and art studios, an employment bureau, men's clubs, training in skills such as bookbinding, a gymnasium, and a savings bank.

Jane Addams and other settlement house leaders realized, however, that the spreading slums made their work as effective as bailing out the

Jane Addams.

ocean with a teaspoon. They therefore organized political support for housing laws, public playgrounds, juvenile courts, mothers' pensions, workers' compensation laws, and legislation against child labor. Lillian Wald promoted the establishment of the federal Children's Bureau in 1912, and Jane Addams, for her work in the peace movement, received late in her life the Nobel Peace Prize for 1931.

The settlement house movement, however, was not immune to criticism. Critics accused settlements of subtle and not-so-subtle forms of social control and of attempts to assimilate the ethnic poor to white, middle-class Protestant standards. The cultural gap between middle-class social workers and slum dwellers could often lead to misunderstanding, and in the effort to "Americanize" immigrants, the settlement houses and agencies of education sometimes lacked sensitivity to the values of other cultures. But on balance their contributions were more positive than negative. By the end of the century both the Catholic church and Jewish agencies were taking up the settlement house movement.

WOMEN'S EMPLOYMENT AND SUFFRAGE   Settlement house workers, insofar as they were paid, made up but a fraction of all gainfully employed women. With the growth of population, the number of employed women steadily increased, as did their percentage of the labor force and of the total female population. The greatest leaps forward came in the decades of the 1880s and the 1900s, both of which were also peak decades of immigration, a correlation that can be explained by the immigrant's need for income. The number of employed women went from over 2.6 million in 1880 to 4 million in 1890, then from 5.1 million in 1900 to 7.8 million in 1910. "Between 1880 and 1900 the employment of women in most parts of the economy became an established fact," wrote one historian. "This was surely the most significant event in the modern history of women." Through all those years domestic work remained the largest category of employment for women; teaching and nursing also remained among the leading fields. The main change was that clerical work (bookkeeping, stenographic work, and the like) and sales jobs became increasingly available to women.

These changes in occupational status had little connection with the women's rights movement, which increasingly focused on the issue of suffrage. Immediately after the Civil War, Susan B. Anthony, a seasoned veteran of the movement, demanded that the Fourteenth Amendment guarantee the vote for women as well as black males. She made little impression on the defenders of masculine prerogative, however, who steadfastly insisted that women belonged in the domestic sphere. "Their mission is at home, by their blandishments and their love to assuage the passions of men as they come in from the battle of life," said a New Jersey senator.

In 1869 the unity of the women's movement was broken in a manner reminiscent of the antislavery rift three decades before. The question once again was whether the movement should concentrate on one overriding issue. Anthony and Elizabeth Cady Stanton founded the National Woman Suffrage Association to promote a women's suffrage amendment to the Constitution, but they looked upon suffrage as but one among many feminist causes to be promoted. Later that same year, Lucy Stone, Julia Ward Howe, and other leaders formed the American Woman Suffrage Association, which focused single-mindedly on the suffrage as the first and basic reform.

It would be another half century before the battle could be won, and the long struggle for referenda and state legislation on the issue focused the women's cause ever more on the primary objective of the vote. In 1890, after three years of negotiation, the rival groups united as the National American Woman Suffrage Association, with Elizabeth Cady Stanton as president for two years, to be followed by Susan B. Anthony until 1900. The work thereafter was carried on by a new generation of

Carrie Chapman Catt, a leader in the women's suffrage movement.

activists, led by Anna Howard Shaw and Carrie Chapman Catt. Over the years the movement slogged its way to some local and some partial victories, as a few states granted women suffrage in school board or municipal elections, or bond referenda. In 1869 the Territory of Wyoming granted full suffrage to women, and after 1890 retained women's suffrage when it became a new state. Three other western states soon followed suit: Colorado in 1893, Utah and Idaho in 1896. But women's suffrage lost in a California referendum in 1896 by a dishearteningly narrow margin.

The movement remained in the doldrums thereafter until the cause easily won a Washington state referendum in 1910, and then carried California by a close majority in 1911. The following year three more western states—Arizona, Kansas, and Oregon—joined in to make a total of nine western states with full suffrage. In 1913 Illinois granted women presidential and municipal suffrage. Yet not until New York acted in 1917 did a state east of the Mississippi adopt universal suffrage. In 1878 California's Senator A. A. Sargent introduced the "Anthony Amendment," a women's suffrage provision that remained before Congress until 1896 and then vanished until 1913, when it was finally ratified (see Chapter 26).

Despite the focus on the vote, women did not confine their public work to that issue. In 1866 a Young Women's Christian Association, a

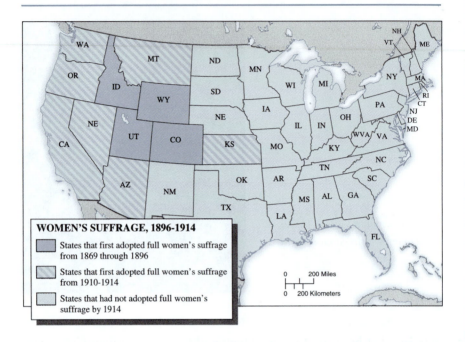

WOMEN'S SUFFRAGE, 1896-1914

- States that first adopted full women's suffrage from 1869 through 1896
- States that first adopted full women's suffrage from 1910-1914
- States that had not adopted full women's suffrage by 1914

0   200 Miles

0   200 Kilometers

parallel to the YMCA, appeared in Boston and spread elsewhere. The New England Women's Club, started in 1868 by Julia Ward Howe and others, was an early example of the women's clubs that then proliferated to the extent that a General Federation of Women's Clubs tied them together in 1890. Many women's clubs confined themselves to "literary" and social activities, but others became deeply involved in charities and reform. The New York Consumers League, formed in 1890, and the National Consumers League, formed nine years later, sought to make the buying public, chiefly women, aware of labor conditions. One of its devices was the "White List" of firms that met its minimum standards. The National Women's Trade Union League, founded in 1903, performed a similar function of bringing educated and middle-class women together with working women for the benefit of women unionists.

These and the many other women's groups of the time may have aroused the fear in opponents to women's suffrage that voting women would tilt toward reform. This was the fear of the brewing and liquor interests, large business interests generally, and political machine bosses. Others, mainly in the South, opposed women's suffrage on the ground that black women would be enfranchised, or because of states'-rights views.

A JUDICIAL HARBOR FOR LAISSEZ-FAIRE   Even without the support of voting women in most places, the states adopted rudimentary
measures to regulate big business and labor conditions in the public interest. By the end of the century, nearly every state had provided for the
regulation of railroads, if not always effectively, and had moved to supervise banks and insurance companies. Between 1887 and 1897, by
one count, the states and territories passed over 1,600 laws relating to
conditions of work, which limited the hours of labor, provided special
protection for women, limited or forbade child labor, required regular
wage payments in cash, called for factory inspections, and outlawed
blacklisting or the importation of "Pinkerton men." Nearly all states had
boards or commissioners of labor, and some had boards of conciliation
and arbitration. Still, conservative judges limited the practical impact of
such new laws.

In thwarting new regulatory efforts, the Supreme Court used a revised interpretation of the Fourteenth Amendment clauses forbidding
the states to "deprive any person of life, liberty or property without due
process of law" or to deny any person "the equal protection of the laws."
Two significant steps of legal reasoning turned the due-process clause
into a bulwark of private property. First, the judges reasoned that the
word "person" in the clause included corporations, which in other connections were legally artificial persons with the right to own property,
buy and sell, sue and be sued like natural persons. Second, the courts
moved away from the old view that "due process" referred only to correct procedures and toward a doctrine of "substantive due process,"
which allowed courts to review the substance of an action. Under this
line of reasoning it was possible for legislatures to pass laws so extreme
(in the view of the judges) as to deprive persons of property to an unreasonable degree, and thereby violate due process.

The Supreme Court first accepted the personality of the corporation
in a tax case, *Santa Clara County* v. *Southern Pacific Railroad Company*
(1886). That same year the Court in *Stone* v. *Farmers Loan and Trust
Company* (1886) recognized the authority of Mississippi to regulate
railroad rates, but declared that there might be cases in which the
Court could review the rates: "Under pretense of regulating fares and
freights, the State cannot require a railroad corporation to carry persons
or property without reward." In *Chicago, Milwaukee and St. Paul Railway Company* v. *Minnesota* (1890) the justices declared unconstitu-

tional a state law that forbade judicial review of rates set by a railroad commission. "The question of the reasonableness of a rate of charge . . . is eminently a question for judicial investigation," the Court ruled, "requiring due process of law for its determination." This was a direct reversal of the ruling in *Munn* v. *Illinois* (1877) that regulation was a legislative prerogative. It remained only for the Court to overturn rates set directly by a state legislature. That it did in *Smyth* v. *Ames* (1898). The case struck down a Nebraska law for setting rates so low as to be, in the Court's view, unreasonable.

From the due-process clause the Court also derived a new doctrine of "liberty of contract," defined as being within the liberties protected by the due-process clause. Liberty, the Court ruled in 1897, involved "not only the right of the citizen to be free from the mere physical restraint of his person, . . . but the term is deemed to embrace the right of the citizen to be free in the enjoyment of all his faculties," and free "to enter into all contracts" proper to carrying out such purposes. When it came to labor laws, this translated into an employee's "liberty" to contract for work under the most oppressive conditions without interference from the state. The courts continued to apply such an interpretation well into the twentieth century.

Judges in some of the lower courts found no need to spin their theories so finely. In 1886 the Pennsylvania Supreme Court overturned an act to protect workers against payment in commodities instead of in cash, declaring it "an insulting attempt to put the laborer under a legislative tutelage, which is not only degrading to his manhood, but subversive of his rights as a citizen of the United States." The high court of West Virginia in 1889 condemned a similar law as an attempt to "foist upon the people a paternal government of the most objectionable character, because it assumes that the employer is a knave, and the laborer an imbecile." At least equally boggling in its blindness to reality was the opinion expressed by a New York judge in 1885, in which he ruled against a law forbidding cigarmaking in tenements. "It cannot be perceived," he said, "how the cigarmaker is to be improved in his health or his morals by forcing him from his home and its hallowed associations and beneficent influences, to ply his trade elsewhere."

As the turn of the century neared, opinion in the country stood poised between such conservative rigidities and a growing sense that new occasions teach new duties. "By the last two decades of the century," wrote one observer, "many thoughtful men had begun to march under various banners declaring that somewhere and somehow the promise of the American dream had been lost—they often said 'betrayed'—and that drastic changes needed to be made to recapture it."

The last two decades of the nineteenth century had already seen a slow erosion of laissez-faire values, which had found their most secure home in the courts. From the social philosophy of the reformers, Social Gospelers, and Populists there emerged a concept of the general-welfare state which, in the words of one historian, sought "to promote the general welfare not by rendering itself inconspicuous but by taking such positive action as is deemed necessary to improve the condition under which its citizens live and work." The reformers supplied no agreed-upon blueprint for a general-welfare utopia, but "simply assumed that government could promote the public interest by appropriate positive action . . . whenever the circumstances indicated that such action would further the common weal." The conflict between this notion and laissez-faire values went on into the new century, but by the mid–twentieth century, after the Progressive movement, the New Deal, and the Fair Deal, the conflict would be "resolved in theory, in practice, and in public esteem in favor of the general-welfare state."

MAKING CONNECTIONS

- As the next chapter shows, the presidential election of 1896 was in many ways a contest between the new urban values discussed in this chapter and those of a more traditional rural American society.

- The reform impulse you've read about in this chapter finds voice again in the discussion of the Progressive movement in Chapter 24.

- The nativist thinking discussed in this chapter fueled the immigration restriction laws enacted in the 1920s (Chapter 26).

Further Reading

The best survey of urbanization remains Charles N. Glaab and A. Theodore Brown's *A History of Urban America* (3rd ed., 1983). Gunther P. Barth discusses the emergence of a new urban culture in *City People: The Rise of Modern City Culture in Nineteenth Century America* (1980). Urban politics is surveyed in Jon C. Teaford's *The Unheralded Triumph: City Government in America, 1870–1900* (1984). Oliver E. Allen's *The Tiger: The Rise and Fall of Tammany Hall* (1994) assesses the significance of New York's famous political machine.

John Bodnar provides a synthesis of the urban immigrant experience in *The Transplanted: A History of Immigrants in Urban America* (1985). Walter Nugent's *Crossings: The Great Transatlantic Migrations, 1870–1914* (1992) provides a wealth of demographic information and insight. John Higham's *Strangers in the Land: Patterns of American Nativism, 1860–1925* (2nd ed., 1988) examines how old-stock residents reacted to the influx of newcomers.

For the growth of urban leisure and sports, see Roy Rosenzweig's *Eight Hours for What We Will: Workers and Leisure in an Industrial City, 1870–1920* (1983) and Steven A. Riess's *City Games: The Evolution of American Urban Society and the Rise of Sports* (1989). Steven A. Riess's *Touching Base: Professional Baseball and American Culture in the Progressive Era* (1980) and Dominick Cavallo's *Muscles and Morals: Organized Playgrounds and Urban Reform, 1880–1920* (1981) link athletics to new forms of organization and socialization.

Richard Hofstadter's *Social Darwinism in American Thought* (rev. ed., 1992) and Cynthia E. Russett's *Darwin in America* (1976) examine the impact of the theory of evolution. On the rise of realism in thought and the arts during the second half of the nineteenth century, see David Shi's *Facing Facts: Realism in American Thought and Culture, 1850–1920* (1995).

William L. O'Neill's *Everyone Was Brave: The Rise and Fall of Feminism in America* (1969) and Eleanor Flexner's *Century of Struggle: The Woman's Rights Movement in the United States* (rev. ed., 1975) survey the condition of women in the late nineteenth century.

22 GILDED-AGE POLITICS AND AGRARIAN REVOLT

*I*n 1873 Mark Twain and Charles Dudley Warner created an enduring label for their times when they collaborated on a novel entitled *The Gilded Age.* The most unforgettable character in the book was an engaging rascal, Colonel Beriah Sellers, who was constantly scheming to profit from political favors. Sellers had enough counterparts in the real politics of the day to enliven that story too, and their humbuggery reinforced the novel's theme that the post–Civil War years were above all an age of corruption, profiteering, and false glitter.

Perspectives on the times would eventually change, but generations of political scientists and historians have since reinforced the two novelists' judgment. As a young college graduate in 1879, Woodrow Wilson described the state of the American political system: "No leaders, no principles; no principles, no parties." Indeed, the real movers and shakers of the Gilded Age were not the men who sat in the White House or the Congress but the captains of industry who crisscrossed the continent with railroads and decorated its cities with plumed smokestacks and gaudy mansions.

PARADOXICAL POLITICS

On the national issues of the day the major parties pursued for the most part a policy of evasion. Only on the tariff were there clear-cut divisions between protectionist Republicans and low-tariff Democrats, but there were individual exceptions even on that. On questions of the currency, regulation of big business, farm problems, civil service reform, internal improvements, and immigration, the parties differed very little.

Two factors, above all, accounted for the muddled politics of this period. Americans feared what had happened in 1860, when parties had taken clear-cut stands on a deeply felt moral issue, with bloody consequences. But the more compelling cause of political inertia was the even division between the parties. From 1869 to 1913, from the presidencies of Ulysses Grant to William Howard Taft, Republicans occupied the White House except during the two nonconsecutive terms of Grover Cleveland, but Republican domination of national politics was more apparent than real. In the years between 1872 and 1896 no president won a majority of the popular vote. In 1888 Benjamin Harrison failed to muster even a plurality over Cleveland, but carried the election anyway because his popular vote was concentrated in the states with the larger electoral votes. And while Republicans usually controlled the Senate, Democrats usually controlled the House. Only during the years 1881–1883 and 1889–1891 did a Republican president have a Republican Congress; and only between 1893 and 1895 did a Democratic president have a Democratic Congress—the only time this occurred between the Civil War and 1913, and that during a severe depression.

No chief executive between Lincoln and Theodore Roosevelt could be described as a "strong" president. None seriously challenged the prevailing view that Congress formulated policy. The function of the chief

The Bosses of the Senate. *This 1889 cartoon bitingly portrays the alliance between big business and politics in this period.*

executive, to these presidents, was simply to administer the government. At the same time, the almost equal strength of the parties in Congress worked against any vigorous new initiatives there, since most bills required bipartisan support to pass both houses, and legislators tended to vote along party lines. Congress thus was caught up in political maneuvers and could not come to grips with national issues.

Under such static conditions, the parties became vehicles for seeking office and dispensing patronage in the form of government jobs and contracts. In the choice of candidates, more than ever, "availability" outweighed ability. The ideal presidential candidate displayed an affable personality, a willingness to cooperate with the party bosses, and an ability to win votes from various factions; he resided in a pivotal state and boasted a good war record. He had no views that might alienate powerful voting blocs, and few or no political enemies. Vice-presidential candidates were chosen to balance the ticket, to placate a disappointed faction, or to improve the party's chances in a key state. This process placed a premium on candidates who were relatively obscure, or at least removed from national party battles capable of arousing opposition.

An alliance between big business and politics characterized the period. This alliance was not necessarily corrupt, since many a politician favored the interests of business out of conviction. Nor was the public as sensitive to conflicts of interest as it would be later. So James G. Blaine of Maine, and hosts of his supporters, saw nothing wrong in his accepting stock commissions from an Arkansas railroad after helping it win a land grant from Congress. It was, they thought, a reward after the event, not a bribe in advance. One Georgia senator freely accepted a retainer fee of $10,000 from the Southern Pacific Railroad, a sum larger than his salary, without losing his reputation with his constituents. Railroad passes, free entertainment, and a host of other favors were freely given to and accepted by politicians, editors, and other leaders in positions to influence public opinion.

POLITICS AND THE VOTERS   But if many observers considered this a time of political futility in which the parties refused to confront such "real issues" as the growth of an unregulated economy and its attendant social injustices, it is nonetheless clear that the voters of the time thought more was at stake. Voter turnout during the Gilded Age was commonly about 70 to 80 percent, even in the South, where the disenfranchisement of blacks was not yet complete. (By contrast, the turnout for the 1996 presidential election was barely 50 percent.) How was it then that leaders who failed to address the real issues presided over the most highly organized and politically active electorate in American history?

The answer is partly that the politicians and the voters deeply believed that they *were* dealing with crucial issues, such as the tariff, monopolies, the currency, civil service reform, and immigration. They turned out in heavy numbers for political rallies and parades. Probably more than any other generation of Americans, they had the patience to follow the intricacies of lengthy debates and heavy tomes on such matters. If the major parties then failed to resolve these issues, no later generation has resolved them either, and they remain live issues, still relevant to American life a century later.

Still another important factor in understanding the nature of Gilded-Age politics is to recognize that most of the significant political activity occurred at the state and local levels. Much more than the national Congress, state governments after the Civil War were dynamic centers of political activity and innovation. Over 60 percent of the nation's spending and taxing was exercised by state and local governments. Then, unlike today, the large cities spent far more on public services than did the federal government. And three-fourths of all public employees worked for local and state governments.

A NEW VIEW OF POLITICAL HISTORY   What most motivated party loyalties and voter turnout in these years were local economic issues and intense cultural conflicts among ethnic and religious groups. Practitioners of what has been called the "new political history" have analyzed the political effects of local, ethnic, cultural, and religious divisions. These historians approach politics less as a simple contest among economic interests, as the "progressive" historians of the earlier twentieth century saw it, than as a complex interplay of motivations, a struggle in which voters follow not simply their pocketbooks but their ethnic prejudices, cultural heritage, and religious convictions as well. According to one of the new political historians: "It has become clear to us . . . that the energies shaping public life are emotional as well as rational, cultural as well as economic."

Far from being like two empty bottles that differed only in their labels, as Woodrow Wilson said of the parties before the turn of the century, each party contained a different mixture of ingredients picked up in the course of its history. The Republican party, legitimate heir to the Whig tradition, attracted political insiders and active reformers. Party members were mainly Protestants of British descent. In their own eyes, and in the eyes of many immigrants, they were prototypical Americans. Their native seat was New England, and their other strongholds were New York and the upper Middle West, both of which they had populated with Yankee stock. Legitimate heirs to the abolitionist tradition, Republicans drew to their ranks a host of reformers and moralists, spiritual descendants of the perfectionists who populated the revivals and the reform movements of the antebellum years. The party's heritage of anti-Catholic nativism, dating from the 1850s when the Republican party had become a haven for former Know-Nothings, also made a comeback in the 1880s. The Republicans could also rely on the votes of blacks and Union veterans of the Civil War.

The Democrats, by contrast, tended to be outsiders, a heterogeneous, often unruly coalition of unlikely allies. What they had in common was that in one way or another they differed from the Republicans. The Democratic party embraced southern whites, immigrants, Catholics of any origin, Jews, freethinkers, skeptics, and all those repelled by the "party of morality." As one Chicago Democrat explained, "A Republican is a man who wants you t' go t' church every Sunday. A Democrat says if a man wants to have a glass of beer on Sunday he can have it." The Democrats were the "party of personal liberty," a combination that sometimes proved volatile. Democratic conventions tended to be more disorderly than Republican gatherings, and often the more interesting for it. There were exceptions to these broad generalizations about party affiliations: black Americans who, though outsiders, clung to the party of Lincoln, and some Protestant immigrants drawn to the Republicans by the party's image of uprightness.

The new immigration of the postbellum years, coming largely from Catholic and Jewish strongholds in eastern and southern Europe, reinforced the Democratic ranks. But the changing ethnic composition of immigrants helped revive a vicious tide of nativism that coursed through the Republican party. As mentioned in Chapter 21, a nativist group called the American Protective Association sprang up in 1887 and spread like a prairie fire through the Middle West, which became its chief stronghold. In that region especially, Republicans pressed nativist causes, calling for tighter naturalization laws, restrictions on immigration and the employment of foreigners, and greater emphasis on the teaching of the "American" language in the schools.

Prohibitionism revived along with nativism in the 1880s. Among the immigrants who crowded into the growing cities were hard-drinking Irish, beer-drinking Germans, and wine-drinking Italians. Democratic constituents in general were more fond of alcohol than Yankees, who increasingly saw saloons as the central social evil around which all others revolved, including vice, crime, political corruption, and neglect of families. Republicans across New England and the Middle West promoted prohibition and were joined after 1869 by a Prohibition party, after 1874 by the Women's Christian Temperance Union, and after 1893 by the Anti-Saloon League. Before the turn of the century, these groups attracted few Democrats to their camp.

CORRUPTION AND REFORM

While grassroots Republicans and Democrats differed over ethnic and cultural issues, their party leaders squabbled over the so-called spoils of office. Each party had its share of corrupt officials willing to buy and sell government appointments or congressional votes, yet each also witnessed the emergence of factions promoting honesty in government. This struggle for clean government soon became one of the foremost issues of the day.

CIVIL SERVICE REFORM   In the aftermath of Reconstruction, Rutherford B. Hayes admirably embodied the "party of morality." He brought to the White House in 1877 a new style of uprightness, a sharp contrast to the graft and corruption of the Grant administration. The son of an Ohio farmer, Hayes entered politics as a Whig but became one of the early Republicans, was wounded four times in the Civil War, and was promoted to major-general. As a member of the House of Representatives for one term, from 1865 to 1867, he supported the congressional Reconstruction program. Elected governor of Ohio in 1867, he served three terms. Honest and respectable, competent and dignified, he lived in a modest style with his wife, nicknamed "Lemonade Lucy" because of her refusal to serve strong drink on social occasions.

Yet Hayes's presidency suffered from the manner of his election. Snide references to him as the *"de facto* President" and "His Fraudulence" dogged his steps and denied him any chance at a second term, which he renounced from the beginning. Hayes's own party was split between so-called Stalwarts and Half-Breeds, led respectively by Senator Roscoe Conkling of New York and Senator James G. Blaine of Maine. The difference between these Republican factions was murkier than that between the parties. The Stalwarts generally supported Grant,

Rutherford B. Hayes and his wife, Lucy Ware Hayes.

a Radical southern policy, and the spoils system. The Half-Breeds took a contrary view on the first two and even vaguely supported civil service reform.

For the most part, however, the factions were loose alliances aimed at advancing the careers of Conkling and Blaine. The two men could not abide each other. Blaine once referred to Conkling as displaying a "majestic, supereminent, overpowering, turkey-gobbler strut." Conkling boasted good looks, fine clothes, and an arrogant manner. He dressed and lived flamboyantly, sporting pastel bow ties, silk scarves, moon-colored vests, and patent-leather shoes. Yet underneath his glamorous facade he was a ruthless power broker. Conkling viewed politics as a brute struggle for control. "Parties," he once declared, "are not built by deportment or by ladies' magazines, or gush." Politics "is a rotten business," he added. "Nothing counts except to win."

Hayes thought otherwise, and he aligned himself with the growing public discontent over the corruption that had prevailed under Grant. American leaders were just learning about the merit system for public employees long established in the bureaucracies of France and Germany, and the new British practice in which civil service jobs were filled by competitive examination. Prominent leaders such as James A. Garfield in the House and Carl Schurz in the Senate embraced civil service reform, and both Hayes and vice-presidential candidate Samuel J. Tilden raised the issue during the campaign of 1876. Hayes repeated his support for reform in his inaugural address.

Although Hayes failed to get legislation on the subject, he did mandate his own rules for merit appointments: those already in office would be dismissed only for the good of the government and not for political reasons; party members would have no more influence in appointments than other respectable citizens; no assessments of government employees for political contributions would be permitted; and no officeholder could manage election campaigns for political organizations, although all could vote and express opinions.

The issue of honest and effective government culminated in a dispute over the federal customs houses. They were notorious centers of corrupt politics, filled with political appointees with little or nothing to do but draw salaries and run political machines. Importers sometimes found that they might gain favor by cooperating with corrupt customs officials, and might be punished for making trouble. An inquiry into operations at the New York Customs House revealed that both collector Chester A. Arthur and naval officer Alonzo Cornell were guilty of "laxity" and of using the customs house for political management on behalf of Senator Roscoe Conkling's organization. When Hayes hinted that resignations would be welcomed, Conkling responded with an attack on reformers in a speech to the state Republican convention: "Their vocation . . . is to lament the sins of other people. Their stock in trade is rancid, canting self-righteousness."

On October 15, 1877, after removing Arthur and Cornell, Hayes named replacements, only to have the nominees rejected when Conkling appealed to the "courtesy of the Senate," an old custom whereby senators might control appointments in their own states. During a recess in the summer of 1878, however, Hayes appointed new replacements. When Congress reassembled, the administration put pressure on senators and, with Democratic support, the nominations were approved. Even this, however, did not end the New York Customs House episode; it would flare up again under the next president.

For all his efforts to clean house, Hayes's vision of government's role remained limited. On the economic issues of the day he held to a conservative line that would guide his successors for the rest of the century. His solution to labor troubles, demonstrated in the Great Railroad Strike of 1877, was to send in troops and break the strike. His answer to demands for an expansion of the currency was to veto the Bland-Allison Act, which required only a limited expansion of silver currency through the government's purchase for coinage of $2 million to $4 million worth of silver per month. (The act passed anyway when Congress overrode Hayes's veto.)

GARFIELD AND ARTHUR   With Hayes unavailable for a second term, the Republicans were forced to look elsewhere in 1880. The Stalwarts, led by Conkling, brought Grant forward for a third time, still a strong contender despite the tarnish of his administration's scandals. For two days the Republican convention in Chicago was deadlocked, with Grant holding a slight lead over Blaine. On the thirty-fifth ballot Wisconsin suddenly switched sixteen votes to Senator-elect James A. Garfield, and on the thirty-sixth ballot the convention stampeded to the dark-horse candidate, carrying him to the nomination. As a sop to the Stalwarts, the convention named Chester A. Arthur, the deposed collector of the New York Customs House for vice-president.

The Democrats selected Winfield Scott Hancock, a Union commander at Gettysburg, to counterbalance the Republicans' Major-General Garfield and thus ward off "bloody-shirt" attacks on their party as the vehicle of Rebellion. Former rebels, nevertheless, advised their constituents to "vote as you shot"—that is, against Republicans. In an election characterized by widespread bribery, Garfield eked out a plurality of only 39,000 votes with 48.5 percent of the vote, but with a comfortable margin of 214 to 155 in the electoral college.

A native of Ohio, Garfield graduated from Williams College, became president of Hiram College in Ohio, was admitted to the bar, and won election to the Ohio Senate as a Republican in 1859. During the Civil War, he distinguished himself at Shiloh and Chickamauga and was mustered out as a major-general when he went to Congress in 1863. Noted for his oratory and parliamentary skills, he became one of the outstanding leaders in the House and eventually its Speaker.

On July 2, 1881, President Garfield started on a vacation in New England to get away from the siege of office seekers. As he walked through the Washington, D.C., rail station, a deranged office seeker named Charles Guiteau shot him in the back. "I am a Stalwart," Guiteau explained to the arresting officers. "Arthur is now President of the United States," an announcement that would prove crippling to the Stalwarts. Garfield lingered near death for two long, hot months, his suffering eased by a contrived air conditioner—a blower rigged up by navy engineers to pass air over a vault of ice into the president's sickroom. Finally, on September 19, Garfield died of complications resulting from the shooting, having been president for a little over six months.

One of the chief henchmen of Stalwart leader Roscoe Conkling was now president. "Chet Arthur, President of the United States?" one of his friends exclaimed, "Good God!" Little in Arthur's past, except for his record as an abolitionist lawyer who had helped secure the freedom of a fugitive slave, raised hopes that he would rise above customs-house politics. A native of Vermont, he had attended Union College, become a lawyer, and made a political career in appointive offices, most notably as New York quartermaster-general during the Civil War and collector of customs from 1871 to 1878.

Chester A. Arthur.

But Arthur demonstrated rare qualities as president. He distanced himself from Conkling and the Stalwarts and established a genuine independence, almost a necessity after Guiteau's announcement. As president, Arthur vigorously prosecuted the Star Route Frauds, a kickback scheme on contracts for postal routes that involved his old political cronies. The president further surprised Washington in 1882 with the veto of an $18 million river and harbors bill, a "pork-barrel" measure that included something for most congressional districts. He also vetoed the Chinese Exclusion Act (1882), which in his view violated the Burlingame Treaty of 1868. Congress proceeded to override both vetoes.

Most startling of all was Arthur's emergence as something of a civil service and tariff reformer. Stalwarts had every reason to expect him to oppose the merit system, but instead he allied himself with the reformers. While the assassin Guiteau had unwittingly added a certain urgency to the public support of reform, the defeat of a reform bill in 1882 sponsored by "Gentleman George" Pendleton, Democratic senator from Ohio, aroused public opinion further.

The Pendleton Civil Service Act finally passed in 1883, setting up a three-member Civil Service Commission independent from the regular cabinet departments, the first such federal agency established on a permanent basis. About 14 percent of all government jobs would now be filled on the basis of competitive examinations rather than political favoritism. What was more, the president could enlarge the class of affected jobs at his discretion. This had important consequences over the years, because after each of the next four presidential elections the "outs" emerged as victors. Each new president thus had a motive to enlarge this category of government jobs, because it would shield his own appointees from political removal.

The high protective tariff, a heritage of the Civil War, had by the early 1880s raised revenues to the point that the government actually enjoyed an embarrassment of riches, a surplus that drew money into the Treasury and out of circulation. Some argued that lower tariff rates would reduce prices and the cost of living, and at the same time leave more money in circulation to fuel economic growth. In 1882 Arthur named a special commission to study the problem. The Tariff Commission recommended a 20 to 25 percent rate reduction, which gained Arthur's support, but Congress's effort to enact the proposal was marred by logrolling (the trading of votes to benefit different legislators' local interests), resulting in the "Mongrel Tariff" of 1883, so called because of its diverse rates for different commodities. The tariff provided for a slight rate reduction, perhaps by 5 percent, but it actually raised the duty on some articles.

SCURRILOUS CAMPAIGN   When the 1884 election campaign began, Arthur's record might have commended him to the voters, but it did not please leaders of his party. So the Republicans dumped Arthur and turned to the glamorous Senator James G. Blaine of Maine, longtime

Senator James G. Blaine of Maine.

leader of the Half-Breeds. Blaine was the consummate politician. He never forgot a name or a face, he inspired the party faithful with his oratory, and at the same time he knew how to wheel and deal in the back rooms. He managed eloquence even when spouting the platitudes of party loyalty, waving the bloody shirt, and twisting the British lion's tail—the last of which held special appeal for the Irish, a group not normally drawn to Republicans. Blaine did have his enemies, however. Democratic newspapers, for example, turned up evidence of his corruption. Based on references in the "Mulligan letters," they claimed that Blaine was in the pocket of the railroad barons, and that he had sold his votes on measures favorable to their interests.

During the campaign, more letters surfaced with disclosures embarrassing to Blaine. For the reform element of the Republican party, this was too much, and one after another, prominent leaders and supporters of the party bolted the ticket. Party regulars scorned them as "goo-goos"—the "good-government" crowd who ignored partisan realities—and the editor of the *New York Sun* jokingly called them Mugwumps, after an Algonquian word meaning a great chieftain. To party regulars, in what soon became a stale joke, Mugwumps were unreliable Republicans who had their "mugs" on one side of the fence and their "wumps" on the other.

The rise of the Mugwumps, however, influenced the Democrats to nominate Stephen Grover Cleveland as a reform candidate. Cleveland rose rapidly from obscurity to the White House. One of many children in the family of a small-town Presbyterian minister, he had been forced by his father's death to go to work at an early age. He won a job as clerk in a law office, read law, passed the bar examination, and became an assistant state attorney-general in New York in 1863 and later sheriff of Erie County. He first attracted national attention as mayor of Buffalo, where he was elected in 1881, for battling graft and corruption. In 1882 he was elected as governor, and he continued to build a reform record by fighting New York's corrupt Tammany Hall organization. As mayor and as governor, he repeatedly vetoed what he considered special-privilege bills serving selfish interests.

A stocky 250-pound man, Cleveland seemed the stolid opposite of Blaine. He possessed little charisma, but impressed the public with his stubborn integrity. One supporter said that "We love him for the enemies he has made."

Then a scandal erupted when the *Buffalo Evening Telegraph* revealed that as a bachelor Cleveland had had an affair with an attractive Buffalo widow, who had named him as the father of a child born to her in 1874, though there was no proof of paternity. Cleveland, it seemed, was only one of several likely fathers, but he took responsibility and provided for the child. When supporters asked Cleveland what to say, he answered "Tell the truth." The respective escapades of Blaine and Cleveland provided some of the most colorful battle cries in American political history. "Blaine, Blaine, James G. Blaine, the continental liar from the state of Maine," Democrats chanted. Republicans countered with "Ma, ma, where's my pa? Gone to the White House, ha, ha, ha!"

Near the end of the campaign, Blaine and his supporters committed two fateful blunders. The first occurred at New York's fashionable Delmonico's restaurant, where Blaine went to a private dinner with several millionaire bigwigs, including John Astor and Jay Gould, to discuss campaign finances. Cartoons and accounts of "Belshazzar's Feast" festooned the opposition press for days. The second fiasco cost Blaine much of the Irish vote when a delegation of Protestant ministers visited

Another Voice for Cleveland. *This 1884 cartoon attacks "Grover the Good" for fathering an illegitimate child.*

Republican headquarters in New York, and one of them referred to the Democrats as the party of "rum, Romanism, and rebellion." The judgment had a certain validity, but the tone was insolent. Blaine, who was present, let pass and perhaps failed to catch the implied insult to Catholics—a fatal oversight, since he had always cultivated Irish-American support with his anti-British talk and public reminders that his mother was Catholic. Democrats spread word that he had let the insult pass, even that he had made it himself.

The incident may have tipped the election. The electoral vote in Cleveland's favor stood at 219 to 182, but the popular vote ran far closer: Cleveland's plurality was fewer than 30,000 votes.

CLEVELAND AND THE SPECIAL INTERESTS   For all of Cleveland's hostility to the spoils system and politics as usual, he represented no sharp break with the conservative policies of his predecessors, except in opposing governmental favors to business. "A public office is a public trust" was one of his favorite mottoes. He held to a strictly limited view of government's role in both economic and social matters, a rigid philosophy illustrated by his 1887 veto of the Texas Seed Bill, an effort to appropriate funds to meet the urgent need of drought victims for seed grain. Back to Congress it went with a lecture on the need to limit the powers and functions of government—"though the people support the government the government should not support the people," Cleveland asserted.

Despite his strong philosophical convictions, Cleveland had a mixed record on the civil service. He had good intentions, but he also had a party hungry for partisan appointments, with the first Democratic president since the election of James Buchanan in 1856. Before his inauguration Cleveland repeated his support for the Pendleton Act; he would not remove able government workers on partisan grounds. But he inserted one significant exception: those who had used federal jobs to forward the interests of the opposition party. In many cases, especially in the post offices, he thus had ample excuse to remove people who had practically made their offices into Republican headquarters.

Party pressures gradually forced Cleveland's hand. To a friend he remarked: "The damned everlasting clatter for office continues . . . and makes me feel like resigning." When he left office about two-thirds of the federal officeholders were Democrats, including all internal revenue

Grover Cleveland made the issue of tariff reform central to the politics of the late 1880s.

collectors and nearly all the heads of customs houses. At the same time, however, Cleveland had extended the number of federal jobs subject to civil service regulation to about 27,000 employees, almost double the number that had been covered when he came in. Yet he satisfied neither Mugwumps nor spoilsmen; indeed, he managed to antagonize both.

On other matters Cleveland's stubborn courage and concern for protecting the public Treasury led him into conflicts with predatory interests, conflicts that eventually cost him the White House. One such dispute arose over misuse of the public domain in the West. Cleveland's secretary of the interior and the commissioner of the General Land Office uncovered one case after another of fraud and mismanagement: bogus surveys by government surveyors, public lands used fraudulently by lumber companies, mine operators, and cattle ranchers with the collusion of government officials, and at least 30 million acres of railroad land grants subject to forfeiture because the required lines were not built.

The administration sued railroads to recover such lands. It nullified exploitive leases of Indian lands, such as that of one cattle company that had leased 6 million acres from the Cherokees for $100,000 and subleased the land for about five times as much. Cattle barons were ordered to remove fences enclosing water holes and grasslands on the open range. In all, during Cleveland's first term about 81 million acres of public lands were restored to the federal government.

Cleveland incurred the wrath of Union military veterans by his firm stand against their pension raids on the Treasury. Congress had passed the first Civil War pension law in 1862 to provide for Union veterans disabled in service and for the widows, orphans, and dependents of veterans. By 1882 the Grand Army of the Republic, an organization of Union veterans and a powerful pressure group, was trying to get pensions paid for any disability, no matter how it was incurred. Meanwhile many veterans succeeded in pushing private pension bills through an obliging Congress. In Washington, lawyers built careers on filing claims and pressing for special laws to benefit veterans.

Insofar as time permitted, Cleveland examined such bills critically and vetoed the dubious ones. Although he signed more than any of his predecessors, running pension costs up from $56 million to $80 million, he also vetoed more. A climax came in 1887 when Congress passed the Dependent Pension Bill, which provided funds for veterans dependent upon manual labor and unable to work for any reason, whether or not the reason was service connected. Cleveland sent it back with a ringing veto, declaring that the pension list would become a refuge for frauds rather than a "roll of honor."

About the middle of his term Cleveland assaulted new special interests, leading to the adoption of an important new policy, railroad regulation. Since the late 1860s, states had adopted railroad regulatory laws, and from the early 1870s, Congress had debated federal legislation. In 1886 a Supreme Court decision finally spurred action. In the case of *Wabash Railroad* v. *Illinois,* the Court denied the state's power to regulate rates on interstate traffic. Cleveland thereupon urged that since this "important field of control and regulation [has] thus been left entirely unoccupied," Congress should act.

It did, and in 1887 Cleveland signed into law an act creating the Interstate Commerce Commission (ICC), the first such independent regulatory commission. The law empowered its five members to investigate carriers and prosecute violators. All rates had to be "reasonable and just." Railroads were forbidden to grant secret rebates to preferred shippers, discriminate against persons, places, and commodities, or enter into pools (secret agreements among competing railroads to fix rates). The commission's actual powers, however, proved to be weak when first tested in the courts. Though creating the ICC seemed to conflict with Cleveland's fear of big government, it accorded with his fear of big business. The Interstate Commerce Act, to his mind, was a legitimate exercise of sovereign power.

THE TARIFF ISSUE Cleveland's most dramatic challenge to special interests focused on tariff reform. Why was the tariff such an important and controversial issue? By the late nineteenth century, many observers had concluded that the formation of huge corporate "trusts" was not a natural development of a maturing capitalist system. Instead, they charged that government policies had fostered big business at the expense of small producers and retailers. Among those policies was an excessively high protective tariff. "The mother of all trusts is the tariff bill," proclaimed one leading business executive. By shielding American manufacturers from foreign competition, the tariff, critics argued, made it easier for them to combine into ever-larger entities. The high tariff also enabled large corporations to restrict production and fix prices. "The heart of the trust problem is in our tariff system of plunder," declared the head of the New England Free Trade League. "The quickest and most certain way of reaching the evils of trusts is not by direct legislation against them, or by constitutional amendment, but by the abolition of tariff duties."

Cleveland agreed. He had entered office as the leader of the traditional low-tariff party, but Democrats were far from unified on the issue, and Cleveland himself confessed at first to limited understanding of the tariff question. Like most politicians of the time, he hesitated to plunge into that tangled thicket. But with greater exposure to the question and further study, he concluded that the rates were too high and included many inequities. Near the end of 1887 Cleveland devoted his entire annual message to the subject. He did so in the full knowledge that he was focusing attention on a political minefield on the eve of an election year, against the warnings of his advisers. "What is the use of being elected if you don't stand for something?" he asked.

Cleveland's message offered a classic summary of the tariff arguments against protection. He noted that tariff revenues had bolstered the surplus, making the Treasury "a hoarding place for money needlessly withdrawn from trade and the people's use." The tariff pushed up prices for everybody, and while it was supposed to protect American workers against the competition of cheap foreign labor, the most recent census showed that of 17.4 million Americans gainfully employed, only 2.6 million were in "such manufacturing industries as are claimed to be benefitted by a high tariff."

It was evident, moreover, that competition produced better prices for buyers. Business combinations could push prices up to the artificial level set by the prices of dutied foreign goods, but prices often fell below that level when domestic producers were in competition, "proof that someone is willing to accept lower prices for such commodity and that such prices are remunerative." Congress, Cleveland argued, should study the more than 4,000 articles subject to tariff duties with an eye to cutting the cost of necessities and of the raw materials used in manufacturing. "Our progress toward a wise conclusion will not be improved by dwelling upon the theories of protection and free trade. . . . It is a condition which confronts us, not a theory." The final sentence became an epigram so infectious that for the next few years public speakers worked it nearly to death.

That did not stop Blaine and other Republicans from denouncing the message as pure "free trade," a doctrine all the more suspect because it was also British policy. The House Ways and Means Committee soon reported a bill calling for modest tariff reductions from an average level of about 47 percent of the value of imported goods to about 40 percent. House Democrats rallied to its support, some of them under assurances that it could not become law. Passed by the House, the bill stalled in the Republican Senate and finally died a lingering death in committee. If Cleveland's talk accomplished his purpose of drawing party lines more firmly, it also confirmed the fears of his advisers. The election of 1888 for the first time in years highlighted a difference between the major parties on an issue of substance.

Cleveland was the obvious nominee of his party. The platform endorsed "the views expressed by the President in his last message to Congress." The Republicans passed up old warhorses such as Blaine and Sherman and turned to the obscure Benjamin Harrison, who had all the attributes of availability. The grandson of President William Henry Harrison, and a flourishing lawyer in Indiana, the diminutive Harrison resided in a pivotal state and also had a good war record. There was little in his political record to offend any voter. He had lost a race for governor and served one term in the Senate (1881–1887). The Republican platform accepted Cleveland's challenge to make the protective tariff the chief issue, and promised generous pensions to veterans.

As insurance against tariff reduction, manufacturers gave generously to the Republican campaign fund, which was used to denounce Cleveland's un-American "free trade" and his pension vetoes. Personal attacks too were leveled against Cleveland. The old charges of immorality had played out. After Cleveland entered the White House he had married young Frances Folsom, who later presented him with a daughter whose name would be immortalized one day by the "Baby Ruth" candy bar. During the campaign, though, the rumor went abroad that a drunken Cleveland had taken to wife-beating. On the eve of the election Cleveland suffered a more devastating blow from the phony "Murchison letter." A California Republican had written British minister Sir Lionel Sackville-West using the false name "Charles F. Murchison." Posing as an English immigrant, he asked advice on how to vote. Sackville-West, engaged at the time in sensitive negotiations over British and American access to Canadian fisheries, hinted that he should vote for Cleveland. The letter aroused a storm of protest against foreign intervention and further linked Cleveland to British free-traders. Democratic explanations never caught up with the public's original sense of outrage.

Still, the outcome was close. Cleveland won the popular vote by 5,538,000 to 5,447,000, but that was poor comfort. The distribution of votes was such that Harrison, with the key states of Indiana and New York on his side by virtue of the sordid, but common practice of paying voters, carried the electoral college by 233 to 168.

REPUBLICAN REFORM UNDER HARRISON   As president, Harrison became a competent and earnest figurehead, overshadowed by his secretary of state, James G. Blaine. He proved something of a cold fish in personal relations. "Harrison can make a speech to ten thousand men and every man of them will go away his friend," said one observer. "Let him meet the same ten thousand in private and every one will go away his enemy." When his campaign manager reported the election returns, Harrison exclaimed fervently: "Providence has given us the victory." The cynical adviser later remarked that Harrison "ought to know that Providence hadn't a damn thing to do with it" and opined that the president "would never know how close a number of men were compelled to approach a penitentiary to make him president."

In an attack on Benjamin Harrison's spending policies, this cartoon shows Harrison pouring Cleveland's huge surplus down a hole.

Harrison had aroused the hopes of civil service reformers when he declared that "fitness and not party service should be the essential and discriminating test" for government employment. Nevertheless he appointed a wealthy Philadelphia merchant as his postmaster-general, allegedly as a reward for a generous contribution. The first assistant postmaster-general announced less than a year later: "I have changed 31,000 out of 55,000 fourth-class postmasters and I expect to change 10,000 more before I finally quit." Harrison made a few feckless efforts to resist partisan pressures, but the party leaders had their way. His most significant gesture at reform was to name young Theodore Roosevelt to the Civil Service Commission.

Harrison owed a heavy debt to the old-soldier vote, which he discharged by naming an officer of the Grand Army of the Republic to the position of pension commissioner. "God help the surplus," the new commissioner reportedly exclaimed. He proceeded to approve pensions with such abandon that the secretary of the interior removed him six months and several million dollars later. In 1890 Congress passed, and Harrison signed, the Dependent Pension Act, substantially the same measure that Cleveland had vetoed. The pension rolls shot up from 490,000 in 1889 to 966,000 in 1893.

During the first two years of Harrison's term, the Republicans controlled the presidency and both houses for only the second time in the twenty years between 1875 and 1895. They were positioned to have pretty much their own way, and they made the year 1890 memorable for some of the most significant legislation enacted in the entire period. In addition to the Dependent Pension Act, Congress and the president approved the Sherman Anti-Trust Act, the Sherman Silver Purchase Act, the McKinley Tariff, and the admission of Idaho and Wyoming as new states, which followed the admission of the Dakotas, Montana, and Washington in 1889.

Both parties had pledged themselves to do something about the growing power of trusts and monopolies. The Sherman Anti-Trust Act, named for Senator John Sherman, chairman of the Senate Judiciary Committee that drafted it, sought to incorporate into federal law a long-standing principle against "restraint of trade." It forbade contracts, combinations, or conspiracies in restraint of trade or in the effort to establish monopolies in interstate or foreign commerce. A broad consensus put the law through, but its passage turned out to be largely symbolic. During the next decade successive administrations expended little effort on enforcement. From 1890 to 1901 only eighteen lawsuits were instituted, and four of those were against labor unions.

Congress meanwhile debated currency legislation against the backdrop of growing distress in the farm regions of the West and South. Hard-pressed farmers were agitating for an increased coinage of silver to inflate the currency, which would raise commodity prices, making it easier for farmers to earn the money with which to pay their debts.

The silverite forces were also strengthened, especially in the Senate, by members from the new western states that had silver-mining interests. Congress passed the new Sherman Silver Purchase Act in 1890, replacing the Bland-Allison Act of 1878. It required the Treasury to purchase 4.5 million ounces of silver each month and to issue in payment Treasury notes redeemable in either gold or silver. But the act failed to satisfy the demands of the silverites. Although the amount of silver purchased doubled, it was still too little to have an inflationary impact on the economy. Eastern business and financial groups, on the other hand, saw a threat to the gold reserve in the growth of paper currency that holders could redeem in gold at the Treasury. The stage was set for the currency issue to eclipse all others in a panic that would sweep the country three years later.

Republicans took their victory over Cleveland as a mandate not just to maintain the protective tariff but to raise it. Piloted through by William McKinley, House Ways and Means chairman, and Senator

Nelson W. Aldrich, the McKinley Tariff of 1890 raised duties on manufactured goods to an average of about 50 percent, the highest to that time. And it included three new departures. First, the protectionists reached out for farmers' votes with high duties on agricultural products. Second, they sought to lessen the tariff's impact on consumers by putting sugar, a universal necessity, on the free list—thus reducing its cost—and then compensating Louisiana and Kansas sugar growers with a bounty of 2¢ a pound out of the federal Treasury. And third, they included a reciprocity section, which empowered the president to hike duties on sugar, molasses, tea, coffee, and hides to pressure countries exporting those items into reducing unreasonably high duties on American goods.

The absence of a public consensus for higher tariffs became clearly visible in the 1890 midterm elections. By the time the November congressional election returns were in, it seemed apparent, at least to Democrats, that the voters had repudiated the McKinley Tariff with a landslide of Democratic votes. In the new House, Democrats outnumbered Republicans by almost three to one; in the Senate, the Republican majority was reduced to eight.

One of the election casualties was McKinley himself, the victim of tricks the Democrats used to reinforce the widespread revulsion against the increased duties. But there was more to the election than the tariff. Voters also reacted against the baldly partisan measures of the Harrison administration and its extravagant expenditures on pensions and other programs. Democrats raised a ruckus about the Republicans' "billion-dollar Congress," to which the Speaker of the House responded with the question: "Isn't this a billion dollar country?" But with expenditures rising and revenues dropping, largely because the tariff was so high as to discourage imports, the nation's Treasury surplus was rapidly shrinking.

The large Democratic vote in 1890 may have also been a reaction to Republican efforts to legislate against alcohol and eliminate funding for state-supported Catholic schools. Between 1880 and 1890, sixteen out of twenty-one states outside the South held referenda on constitutional prohibition of alcoholic beverages. Only six states voted for prohibition, however. With the politics of righteousness, then, Republicans were playing a losing game, arousing wets (anti-Prohibitionists) on the Democratic side. In 1889 Wisconsin Republicans compounded their party's problems by pushing through a law that struck at parochial schools. The law held that a school could be accredited only if it taught the basic subjects in English. That was the last straw: it turned large numbers of outraged immigrants into Democratic activists. In 1889 and 1890 the Democrats swept state after state.

THE PROBLEMS OF FARMERS

Frustrated by the unwillingness of Congress to meet their demands and ease their plight, disgruntled farmers began to organize after the Civil War. Like so many of their counterparts laboring in urban factories, they realized that social change could be provoked only by demonstrations of power, and power lay in numbers. But unlike labor unions, farm organizations faced a more complex array of economic variables affecting their livelihood. They had to deal with more than just management; bankers, processors, railroad and grain elevator operators, and the world market all played a role in affecting the agricultural sector. So too did the unpredictable forces of nature: droughts, blizzards, insects, erosion. Other important obstacles to collective action by farmers included the deeply ingrained tradition of rugged individualism and physical isolation. American farmers had long prided themselves on their self-reliant hardihood, and many balked at sacrificing their independence. Consequently, farm activists discovered that it was often difficult to develop and maintain a cohesive organization. Yet, for all the difficulties, they persevered, and the results were dramatic, if not completely successful. Thus, for example, the deep-seated unrest in the farming communities of the South and West began to find voice in the Granger movement, the Alliance movement, and in the new People's party, agrarian movements of considerable political and social significance.

THE DIVERSITY OF FARM INTERESTS Agricultural interests after the Civil War diverged and in some cases conflicted with one another. In the Great Plains, the railroads were the largest landowners. In addition, there were large absentee landowners, some foreign, who leased out vast tracts of lands. There were also huge "bonanza" farms that employed hundreds of seasonal workers. The majority of rural folk in the

South and West, however, were moderate-size landowners, small land speculators, small landowners, tenant farmers, and hourly wage workers. In 1870, for example, 32 percent of farm laborers in the Great Plains owned no land or implements.

Those farm folk most involved with organized political protest were not the tenants or farm laborers but the middle-size landholding class and the bankers and small merchants in surrounding towns who depended upon the agricultural economy for their livelihoods. The middle-size farmers were the ones who experienced rapidly rising land values and rising indebtedness. They were therefore most concerned about railroad regulation and monetary policy. These farmers, rather than landless workers, were in a position to produce a crop surplus for sale and therefore to benefit from any inflation in commodity prices. Such farmers were thus concerned with land values and crop prices rather than with land redistribution schemes that would have given tenants or croppers or farm hands access to their own land.

ECONOMIC CONDITIONS   For some time, farmers in the South and Midwest had been subject to worsening economic and social conditions. The source of their problems was a long-term decline in commodity prices from 1870 to 1898, the product of domestic overproduction and growing international competition for world markets. The vast new lands brought under cultivation poured an ever-increasing supply of farm products into the market, driving down prices. This effect was reinforced as innovations in transportation and communications brought American farmers ever more into international competition, further increasing the supply of farm commodities. Considerations of abstract economic forces, however, puzzled many farmers. They would never quite understand how want could be caused by plenty. How could one speak of overproduction when so many remained in need? Instead, they reasoned, there must be a screw loose somewhere in the system.

The railroads and the processors who handled the farmers' products were seen as the prime villains. Farmers resented the high railroad rates that prevailed in farm regions with no alternative forms of transportation. Individual farmers could not get the rebates the Rockefellers could extract from railroads, and they could not exert the political influence wielded by the railroad lobbies. In other ways farmers found them-

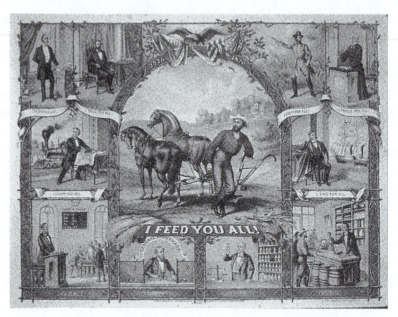

"I Feed You All," a poster showing the farmer at the center of society, first published in Prairie Farmer *in 1869.*

selves with little bargaining power as either buyers or sellers. When they tried to sell wheat or cotton, the buyer set the price; when they went to buy a plow point, the seller set the price.

High tariffs operated to farmers' disadvantage because they protected manufacturers against foreign competition, allowing them to raise the prices of factory goods on which farmers depended. Farmers, however, had to sell their wheat, cotton, and other staples in foreign markets, where competition lowered prices. Tariffs inflicted a double blow on farmers because insofar as they hampered imports, they indirectly hampered exports by making it harder for foreign buyers to get the necessary American currency or exchange to purchase American crops.

Debt, too, had been a perennial problem of agriculture. After the Civil War, farmers became ever more enmeshed in debt—western farmers incurred mortgages to cover the costs of land and machinery, while southern farmers used crop liens. As commodity prices dropped, the burden of debt grew because farmers had to cultivate more wheat or cotton to raise the same amount of money; and by growing more they furthered the vicious cycle of surpluses and price declines.

AN INADEQUATE CURRENCY   Ultimately, farm discontent focused on the currency issue, magnifying this grievance out of proportion to all others. The basic problem with the nation's currency in the late nineteenth century was that it lacked the flexibility to grow along with America's expanding economy. From 1865 to 1890 the amount of currency in circulation actually decreased from about $30 to $27 per capita. Three types of currency existed then: greenbacks, national bank notes, and hard money (gold and silver coins or certificates). The amount of greenback money in circulation had been set at $346 million in 1878, and had remained fixed at that amount, despite agitation for more paper money by debtors (largely farmers) and expansion-minded business leaders. National bank notes, based on government bonds, actually contracted in volume as the government paid off its bonds, which it was able to do rapidly with revenues from tariffs and land sales.

Metallic currency dated from the Mint Act of 1792, which authorized free and unlimited coinage of silver and gold at a ratio of 15 to 1.* The phrase "free and unlimited" simply meant that owners of precious metals could have any quantity of their gold or silver coined free, except for a nominal fee to cover costs. A fixed ratio of values, however, could not reflect fluctuations in the relative market value of the metals. When gold rose to a market value higher than that reflected in the official ratio, owners ceased to present it for coinage. The country was actually on a silver standard until 1837, when Congress changed the ratio to 16 to 1, which soon reversed the situation. Silver became more valuable in the market than in coinage, and the country drifted to a gold standard.

This state of affairs prevailed until 1873, when Congress passed a general revision of the coinage laws and dropped the then-unused provision for the coinage of silver. The action came, however, just when silver production began to increase, reducing its market value through the growth in supply. Under the old laws this would have induced owners of silver to present it at the mint for coinage. Soon advocates of currency inflation began to denounce the "crime of '73," which they had scarcely noticed at the time. Gradually a suspicion, and in some cases a belief, grew that creditor interests had conspired in 1873 to ensure a scarcity of money. But the silverites had little more legislative success than the advocates of greenback inflation. The Bland-Allison Act of 1878 and

---

*The ratio meant that the amount of precious metal in a silver dollar weighed fifteen times as much as that in a gold dollar. This reflected the relative values of silver and gold at the time.

the Sherman Silver Purchase Act of 1890 provided for some silver coinage, but too little in each case to offset the overall contraction of the currency.

THE GRANGER MOVEMENT   When the Department of Agriculture sent Oliver H. Kelley on a tour of the postbellum South in 1866, it was the isolation of farm folk that most impressed him. Resolving to do something about it, Kelley and some government clerks in 1867 founded the Patrons of Husbandry, better known as the Grange (an old word for granary), as each chapter was called. In the next few years the Grange mushroomed, reaching a membership as high as 1.5 million by 1874. The Grange started as a social and educational response to the farmers' isolation, but as it grew it began to promote farmer-owned cooperatives for buying and selling. Their ideal was to free themselves from the conventional marketplace.

The Grange soon became indirectly involved in politics through independent third parties, especially in the Midwest during the early 1870s. The Grangers' chief political goal was to regulate the rates charged by railroads and warehouses. In five states they brought about the passage of "Granger Laws," which at first proved relatively ineffective, but laid a foundation for stronger legislation to follow. Owners subject to their regulation challenged these laws in cases that soon advanced to the

Members of the Crescent Grange, Anoka County, Minnesota, 1880.

Supreme Court, where the plaintiffs in the "Granger Cases" claimed to have been deprived of property without due process of law. In a key case involving warehouse regulation, *Munn v. Illinois* (1877), the high court ruled that the state under its "police powers" had the right to regulate property in the interest of the public good where that property was clothed with a public interest. If regulatory power were abused, the ruling said, "the people must resort to the polls, not the courts." Later, however, the courts would severely restrict state regulatory powers.

The Granger movement gradually declined (but never vanished) as members' energies were drawn off into cooperatives, many of which failed, and into political action. Out of the independent political movements of the time there grew in 1875 a party calling itself the Independent National party, more commonly known as the Greenback party because of its emphasis on that issue. In the 1878 midterm elections it polled over 1 million votes and elected fifteen congressmen. But in 1880 the party's fortunes declined, and it disintegrated after 1884.

FARMERS' ALLIANCES   As the Grange lost energy, other farm organizations grew in size and significance: the Farmers' Alliances. Like the Grange, the Farmers' Alliances offered social and recreational opportunities, but they also emphasized political action. Farmers throughout the South and Midwest, where tenancy rates were highest, rushed to join the Alliance movement. They saw in collective action a way to seek relief from the hardships created by chronic indebtedness, declining prices, and devastating droughts. Unlike the Grange, which was a national organization that tended to attract larger and more prosperous farmers, the Alliance was a grassroots local organization representing marginal farmers.

The Alliance movement absorbed existing farm groups and organized new locals. It swept the cotton belt and established strong positions in Kansas and the Dakotas. In 1886, a white minister in Texas, which had one of the largest and most influential Alliance movements, responded to the appeals of black farmers and organized the Colored Alliance. The white leadership of the Alliance movement in Texas endorsed this development because the Colored Alliance stressed that its objective was economic justice, not social equality. By 1890, the Alliance movement had members from New York to California numbering about 1.5 million, and the Colored Farmers' Alliance claimed over 1 million members.

Members of the Texas Alliance, 1870s. Alliance groups united local farmers, fostered a sense of community, and influenced political policies.

A powerful attraction for many isolated, struggling farmers and their families was the sense of community provided by the Alliance. An Alliance gathering resembled what one observer described as "a religious revival . . . a pentecost . . . in which the tongue of flame sat upon every man, and each spake as the spirit gave him utterance."

The Alliance movement welcomed rural women and men over sixteen years old who displayed a "good moral character," believed in God, and demonstrated "industrious habits." One North Carolina woman expressed her appreciation for the "grand opportunities" the Alliance provided women to emerge from traditional domesticity. "Drudgery, fashion, and gossip," she declared, "are no longer the bounds of woman's sphere." One of the Alliance publications made the point explicitly: "The Alliance has come to redeem woman from her enslaved condition, and place her in her proper sphere." The number of women in the Alliance movement grew rapidly, and many assumed key leadership roles.

The Alliance movement sponsored an ambitious social and educational program, and about 1,000 affiliated newspapers. But unlike the Grange, the Alliance also proposed from the start an elaborate economic program. In 1890 Alliance agencies and exchanges in some eighteen states claimed a business of $10 million, but they soon went the way of the Granger cooperatives, victims of discrimination by wholesalers, manufacturers, railroads, and bankers, and also of their own inexperienced management and overextended credit.

The Alliance movement also was ready to enter the political fray to help farmers. In Texas, for example, in 1886 a devastating drought brought matters to a head. When President Grover Cleveland vetoed a bill to aid Texas farmers, Alliance leaders resolved to challenge the Democratic party at the polls. Although conservative members whose primary allegiance was to the Democratic party left the movement, many members remained who were ready to carry out the fight both locally and nationally.

In 1887 Charles W. Macune, the new Alliance president, announced his intention to exert pressure on Congress to assist southern farmers. In addition, he proposed that Texas farmers create their own Alliance Exchange in an effort to free themselves from their dependence on processors and banks. Members of the Exchange would sign joint notes, borrow money from banks, and purchase their goods and supplies from a new corporation created by the Alliance in Dallas. The Exchange would also build its own warehouses to store and market the crops of members. While their crops were being stored, member farmers could obtain credit from the warehouse cooperative so they could buy goods and supplies.

This grand "cooperative" scheme collapsed when the Texas banks refused to accept the joint notes from Alliance members. This led Macune and others to focus their energies on what Macune called a "subtreasury plan." Under this plan, farmers would be able to store their crops in new government warehouses and obtain government loans for up to 80 percent of their crops' value at 1 percent interest. Besides providing immediate credit, the plan would allow the farmer the leeway to hold a crop for a better price later, since he would not have to sell it at harvest time to pay off debts. The plan would also promote inflation because these loans to farmers would be made in new legal-tender notes.

The subtreasury plan went before Congress in 1890 but was never adopted. Its defeat as well as setbacks to other proposals convinced many farm leaders that they needed political power to secure railroad regulation, currency inflation, state departments of agriculture, antitrust laws, and farm credit.

FARM POLITICS   In the West, where hard times had descended after the blizzards of 1887, farmers were ready for third-party action. In the South, however, white Alliance members hesitated to bolt the Democratic party, seeking instead to influence or control it. Both approaches gained startling success. Independent parties under various names upset the political balance in western states, almost electing a governor under the banner of the People's party (also known as the Populist party) in Kansas (a Populist was elected governor in 1892) and taking control of one house of the legislature there and both houses in Nebraska. In South Dakota and Minnesota, Populists gained a balance of power in the legislatures, while Kansas sent a Populist to the Senate.

The farm movement produced colorful leaders, especially in Kansas, where Mary Elizabeth Lease advised farmers "to raise less corn and more hell." Born in Pennsylvania to parents who were political exiles from Ireland, she grew up within a family traumatized by the Civil War. Her two brothers were killed in battle, and her father died in Georgia's notorious Andersonville Prison. Afterward Lease migrated to Kansas, taught school, raised a family, and finally failed at farming in the mid-1880s. She then studied law for a time, "pinning sheets of notes above her wash tub," and through strenuous effort became one of the state's first female lawyers. At the same time, she took up public speaking on behalf of various causes ranging from Irish nationalism to temperance to women's suffrage. By the end of the 1880s Lease had joined the Al-

Mary Elizabeth Lease, 1890.

liance as well as the Knights of Labor, and she soon applied her gifts as a fiery speaker to the cause of free silver. A tall, proud, and imposing woman, Lease drew attentive audiences. "The people are at bay," she warned in 1894, "let the bloodhounds of money beware."

"Sockless Jerry" Simpson was an equally charismatic agrarian radical. Born in Canada, he had served as a seaman on Great Lakes steamships before buying a farm in northern Kansas. He, his wife, and young daughter made a go of the farm, but when he saw his child crushed to death in a sawmill accident, he and his wife relocated to the southern part of the state. There he raised cattle for several years before losing his herd in a blizzard.

Simpson embraced the Alliance movement, and in 1890 he campaigned for Congress. A shrewd man with huge, callused hands and pale blue eyes, he simplified the complex economic and political issues of the day. "Man must have access to the land," he maintained, "or he is a slave." He warned Republicans: "You can't put this movement down by sneers or by ridicule, for its foundation was laid as far back as the foundation of the world. It is a struggle between the robbers and the robbed." Simpson dismissed his Republican opponent, a wealthy railroad lawyer, as an indulgent pawn of the corporations whose "soft white hands" and "silk hosiery" betrayed his true priorities. His outraged opponent thereupon shouted that it was better to have silk socks than none at all, providing Simpson with his folksy nickname. "Sockless Jerry" won a seat in Congress, and so too did many other friends of "the people" in the Midwest.

In the South, the Alliance won equal if not greater success by forcing the Democrats to nominate candidates pledged to their program. The southern states elected four pro-Alliance governors, seven pro-Alliance legislatures, forty-four pro-Alliance congressmen, and several senators. Among the most respected of the southern Alliance leaders was Tom Watson of Georgia. The son of prosperous slaveholders who lost everything after the Civil War, he became a successful lawyer and orator on behalf of the Alliance cause. Watson took the lead in appealing to black tenant farmers and sharecroppers to join with their white counterparts in ousting the Bourbon white political elite. "You are kept apart," he told black and white farmers, "that you may be separately fleeced of your earnings."

Tom Watson.

THE POPULIST PARTY AND THE ELECTION OF 1892 The success of the Alliances led many to consider the formation of a third political party on the national level. In 1891 a conference in Cincinnati brought together delegates from farm, labor, and reform organizations to discuss strategy. The meeting endorsed a national third party and formed a national executive committee of the People's party. Few southerners were at Cincinnati, but many approved the third-party idea after their failure to move the Democratic party toward the subtreasury plan. In 1892 a larger meeting at St. Louis called for a national convention of the People's party at Omaha to adopt a platform and choose candidates.

The platform focused on issues of finance, transportation, and land. Its financial program demanded implementation of the subtreasury plan, free and unlimited coinage of silver at the 16 to 1 ratio, an increase in the amount of money in circulation to $50 per capita, a graduated income tax, and postal savings banks to protect depositors who otherwise risked disastrous losses in small-town banks vulnerable to farm depression. As to transportation, the time had come "when the railroad corporations will either own the people or the people must own the railroads." Let government therefore nationalize the railroads, and the telephone and telegraph systems as well. The Populists called for the government to reclaim from railroads and other corporations lands "in excess of their actual needs," and to forbid land ownership by aliens. Finally, the platform endorsed the eight-hour workday and restriction of immigration. The party took these last positions to win sup-

A Populist gathering in Callaway, Nebraska, 1892.

port from the urban workers, whom Populists looked upon as fellow "producers."

The party's platform turned out to be more exciting than its candidate. Iowa's James B. Weaver, an able, prudent man, carried the stigma of his defeat on the Greenback ticket twelve years before. To balance Weaver, who had been a Union general, the party named a former Confederate general for vice-president.

The Populist party was the startling new feature of the 1892 campaign. The major parties renominated the candidates of 1888, Democrat Grover Cleveland and Republican Benjamin Harrison. The tariff issue monopolized their attention. Both major candidates polled over 5 million votes, but Cleveland carried a plurality of the popular votes and a majority of the electoral college. Weaver polled over 1 million votes, and carried Colorado, Kansas, Nevada, and Idaho, for a total of twenty-two electoral votes. Alabama was the banner Populist state of the South, with 37 percent of its vote for Weaver.

ECONOMIC DEPRESSION AND THE SILVER SOLUTION

THE DEPRESSION OF 1893 Cleveland's second administration stumbled early. Before it ended, Cleveland had antagonized every major segment of the public: the farmers and silverites opposed his efforts to maintain the gold standard, business groups disliked his attempt to lower the tariff, and a large segment of labor resented his efforts to suppress the Pullman Strike. Worst of all, his second term coincided with one of the most devastating business panics in history, set off just before he took office by the failure of the Philadelphia and Reading Railroad and a panic on Wall Street.

By 1894 many had reached bottom. That year some 750,000 people went out on strike, including the Pullman workers; millions found themselves unemployed; railroad construction workers, laid off in the West, began tramping east and talked of marching on Washington. Few of them made it to the capital.

One group that did was the Army of the Commonweal of Christ, led by Jacob S. Coxey, a wealthy Ohio quarry owner turned Populist who demanded that the federal government provide unemployed people with jobs. Coxey, his wife, and their son, Legal Tender Coxey, rode in a carriage ahead of some 400 hardy protesters as they straggled into Washington. Police arrested Coxey for walking on the grass, but his army as well as the growing political strength of populism struck fear into many Americans. Critics portrayed Populist candidates as "hayseed socialists" whose election would endanger property rights.

The 1894 midterm elections took place amid this climate of anxiety. The outcome disappointed the Populists, who had expected to profit from the discontent. North Carolina's was the only southern legislature lost by the Democrats, and that for only four years. Nationally, the elections amounted to a severe setback for Democrats, and the Republicans were the chief beneficiaries. The Populists emerged with six senators and seven representatives. They had polled 1.5 million votes for their congressional candidates and still expected the festering discontent to carry them to power in 1896.

SILVERITES VS. GOLDBUGS   In the mid-1890s events conspired to focus all concerns on the currency issue. One of the causes of the 1893 depression had been the failure of a British banking house, which led many British investors to unload their American holdings in return for gold. To plug this drain on the Treasury, the president sought repeal of the Sherman Silver Purchase Act to stop the issuance of silver notes redeemable in gold. Cleveland won the act's repeal in 1893, but at the cost of irreparable division in his own party. To further build the gold reserve, the administration struck a deal with banking titan J. P. Morgan in 1895. He and other financiers promised to supply half the gold needed to buy up a series of government bond issues, and to use their influence to stop demands on the Treasury. The deal worked, but it created the unfavorable image of Cleveland and the financial oligarchy working hand in glove.

Meanwhile the American Bimetallic League, heavily financed by silver miners, raised the agitation for silver coinage to a crescendo. The growing importance of the currency issue presented a dilemma for Populists: Should the party promote the whole spectrum of reform it advocated, or should it try to ride the silver issue into power? The latter was the practical choice. So the Populist leaders decided, over the protest of more radical members, to hold their 1896 convention last, confident that the major parties would at best straddle the silver issue and that they would then reap a harvest of bolting silverite Republicans and Democrats.

THE ELECTION OF 1896   Contrary to these expectations, the major parties took opposite positions on the currency issues. The Republicans, as expected, chose William McKinley on a gold-standard platform. McKinley, a former congressman and governor of Ohio, benefited from the political steamroller organized by his campaign manager.

On the Democratic side, the pro-silver forces captured the convention for their platform. William Jennings Bryan arranged to give the closing speech for the silver plank. The son of a judge who was a fervent

William Jennings Bryan, whose "Cross of Gold" speech at the 1896 Democratic convention roused the delegates and secured him the party's presidential nomination.

Baptist moralist, Bryan was a two-term congressman from Nebraska who had been swept out in the Democratic losses of 1894; he had distinguished himself mainly with an exhausting three-hour speech against repeal of the Sherman Silver Purchase Act. In the months before the convention he had traveled the South and West, speaking for free silver. His rehearsed phrases swept the convention into a frenzy:

> I come to speak to you in defense of a cause as holy as the cause of liberty—the cause of humanity. . . . We have petitioned, and our petitions have been scorned. We have entreated, and our entreaties have been disregarded. We have begged, and they have mocked when our calamity came. We beg no longer; we entreat no more; we petition no more. We defy them!

By the time Bryan reached his conclusion, there was little doubt that he would get the nomination: "You shall not press down upon the brow of labor this crown of thorns. You shall not crucify mankind upon a cross of gold!"

The next day Bryan won the nomination on the fifth ballot, and in the process the Democratic party was fractured beyond repair. Disappointed pro-gold Democrats walked out of the convention and nominated their own candidate, Senator John M. Palmer of Illinois. "Fellow Democrats," he announced, "I will not consider it any great fault if you decide to cast your vote for William McKinley."

When the Populists met in St. Louis two weeks later, they faced an impossible choice. They could name their own candidate and divide the silver vote, or they could endorse Bryan and probably lose their identity. In the end they backed Bryan, but chose their own vice-presidential candidate, former representative Thomas E. Watson of Georgia, and invited the Democrats to drop their vice-presidential nominee—an action that Bryan refused to countenance.

The thirty-six-year-old Bryan launched a whirlwind campaign. He crisscrossed the country, exploiting his spellbinding eloquence. McKinley, meanwhile, conducted a "front-porch campaign," receiving selected delegations of supporters at his home in Canton, Ohio, and giving only prepared responses. McKinley's campaign manager, Mark Hanna, shrewdly portrayed Bryan as a radical whose "communistic spirit" would ruin the capitalist system. Many observers agreed with the

"BLOWING HIMSELF AROUND THE COUNTRY." An anti-Populist cartoon of 1896 depicting Bryan blowing hot air at his supporters.

portrait. The *New York Tribune* denounced Bryan as a "wretched rattle-pated boy, posing in vapid vanity and mouthing resounding rottenness." Theodore Roosevelt had equally strong opinions. "The silver craze surpasses belief," he wrote a friend. "Bryan's election would be a great calamity."

By preying upon such fears, Hanna raised a huge campaign chest to finance an army of Republican speakers who traveled the country in support of McKinley. In the end the Democratic-Populist-Silverite candidates were overwhelmed by the well-organized and well-financed Republican campaign. McKinley won the popular vote by 7.1 million to 6.5 million and the electoral college vote by 271 to 176.

Bryan carried most of the West and the South below the border states, but found little support in the metropolitan centers east of the Mississippi and north of the Ohio and Potomac Rivers. In the critical midwestern battleground, from Minnesota and Iowa eastward to Ohio, Bryan carried not a single state. Many Catholic voters, normally drawn to the Democrats, were no doubt repelled by Bryan's Baptist evangelical style. Farmers in the Northeast, moreover, were less attracted to agrarian radicalism than were farmers in the wheat and cotton belts, where there were higher rates of tenancy and a narrower range of crops. Among factory workers in the cities, Bryan found even less support.

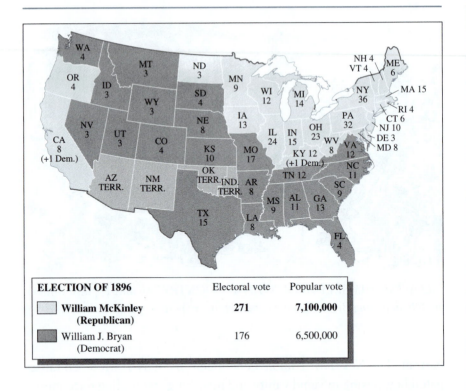

ELECTION OF 1896	Electoral vote	Popular vote
William McKinley (Republican)	271	7,100,000
William J. Bryan (Democrat)	176	6,500,000

They found it easier to identify with McKinley's "full dinner pail" than with Bryan's free silver. Some workers may have been intimidated by business owners' threats to close shop if the "Demopop" heresies triumphed.

A NEW ERA   The election of 1896 had been a climactic political struggle. Urban-industrial values had indeed taken firm hold of the political system. The first important act of the McKinley administration was to call a special session of Congress to raise the tariff again. The Dingley Tariff of 1897 became the highest to that time.

By 1897 economic prosperity was returning, helped along by inflation of the currency, which bore out the arguments of greenbackers and silverites. But the inflation came, in one of history's many ironies, from neither greenbacks nor silver, but from a new flood of gold into the market and into the mints. During the 1880s and 1890s, new discoveries of gold in South Africa, in the Canadian Yukon, and in Alaska led to spectacular new gold rushes. In 1900, Congress passed a Gold Standard Act, which marked an end to the silver movement.

The old issues of tariffs and currency gave way to concerns over the Spanish-American War, which ushered in a new era. "The Spanish War finished us," said Populist Tom Watson. "The blare of the bugle drowned the voice of the Reformer." And yet to compound this irony, most of the Populists' 1892 Omaha platform, which had seemed so radical and controversial at the time, would be in effect within two decades.

MAKING CONNECTIONS

- This chapter concludes with the suggestion that the Spanish-American War, a major event on the horizon, marked the end of the reform spirit of the Populists.

- The laissez-faire policies of the Gilded Age were challenged by Progressive reform activists, discussed in Chapter 24.

- William Jennings Bryan was one of the most prominent figures in American politics and political culture over some thirty years.

FURTHER READING

For overviews of the Gilded Age see Robert H. Wiebe's *The Search for Order, 1877–1920* (1967), John A. Garraty's *The New Commonwealth, 1877–1890* (1968), and Vincent P. DeSantis's *The Shaping of Modern America, 1877–1920* (2nd ed., 1989). Nell Painter's *Standing at Armageddon: The United States, 1877–1919* (1987) focuses on the experience of the working classes.

Party politics is the emphasis of H. Wayne Morgan's *From Hayes to McKinley: National Party Politics, 1877–1896* (1969) and Richard J. Jensen's *The Winning of the Midwest: Social and Political Conflict,*

1888–1896 (1971). Public participation in politics is explained in Paul Kleppner's *Who Voted? The Dynamics of Electoral Turnout, 1870–1980* (1982).

On the Gilded-Age presidents, see William S. McFeely's *Grant: A Biography* (1981), Allan Peskin's *Garfield: A Biography* (1978), Thomas C. Reeves's *Gentleman Boss: The Life of Chester Alan Arthur* (rev. ed., 1991), and Lewis L. Gould's *The Presidency of William McKinley* (1980).

Scholars have also examined various Gilded-Age issues and interest groups. John G. Sproat's *The Best Men: Liberal Reformers in the Gilded Age* (1968) and Gerald W. McFarland's *Mugwumps, Morals, and Politics, 1884–1920* (1975) examine the issue of reforming government service. Tom E. Terrill's *The Tariff, Politics, and American Foreign Policy, 1874–1901* (1973) lends clarity to that complex issue. The finances of the Gilded Age are covered in Irwin Unger's *The Greenback Era: A Social and Political History of American Finance, 1865–1879* (1964) and Walter T. K. Nugent's *Money and American Society, 1865–1880* (1968).

One of the most controversial works on populism is Lawrence Goodwyn's *The Populist Movement: A Short History of the Agrarian Revolt in America* (1978). Goodwyn's emphasis on the cooperative nature of agrarian protest and his criticism of the western branch as a sham movement contradicted the prevailing interpretations. A more judicious account is Robert C. McMath, Jr.'s *American Populism: A Social History, 1877–1898* (1993). Jeffrey Ostler's *Prairie Populism: The Fate of Agrarian Radicalism in Kansas, Nebraska, and Iowa, 1880–1892* (1993) minimizes the role of the financial panic in stimulating the grassroots movement.

PART SIX

MODERN AMERICA

The United States entered the twentieth century in a state of flux. Since the election of Thomas Jefferson in 1800, the country had seen itself relentlessly transformed. A rural, agrarian society largely detached from the concerns of international affairs turned into a highly industrialized, urban culture with a growing involvement in world politics and commerce. In other words, the United States in 1900 was on the threshold of modernity.

The prospect of modernity both excited and scared Americans. Old truths and beliefs clashed with unsettling new scientific discoveries and social practices. People debated the legitimacy of Darwinism, the existence of God, the dangers of jazz, and the federal effort to prohibit alcoholic beverages. The automobile, airplane, and radio helped shrink the distances of time and space and accelerate a national consciousness. In the process, the United States began to emerge from its isolationist shell. Throughout most of the nineteenth century, policy makers had sought to isolate America from the intrigues and conflicts of the great European powers. As early as 1780, John Adams had warned Congress against involving the United States in the affairs of Europe. "Our business with them, and theirs with us," he wrote, "is commerce, not politics, much less war." George Washington echoed this sentiment in his farewell address upon leaving the presidency, warning Americans to avoid "entangling alliances" with foreign governments.

With only a few exceptions, American statesmen during the nineteenth century had followed such advice. Noninvolvement in foreign wars and nonintervention in the internal affairs of foreign governments formed the pillars of American foreign policy until the end of the century. During the 1890s, however, expanding commercial interests around the world led Americans to expand the horizons of their concerns. Imperialism was the order of the day among the great European powers, and a growing number of American expansionists demanded that the United States also adopt a global ambition and join in the hunt for new territories and markets. Such motives helped spark the Spanish-American War of 1898 and helped to justify the resulting acquisition of American colonies outside the continental United States. Entangling alliances with European powers soon followed.

The outbreak of the Great War in Europe in 1914 posed an even greater challenge to the American tradition of isolation and nonintervention. The prospect of a German victory over the French and British threatened the European balance of power, which had long ensured the security of the United States. By 1917 it appeared that Germany might emerge triumphant and begin to menace the Western Hemisphere. Woodrow Wilson's crusade to use American intervention in World War I to transform the world order in accordance with his idealistic principles dislodged American foreign policy from its isolationist moorings. It also spawned a prolonged debate about the role of the United States in world affairs, a debate that World War II would resolve for a time on the side of internationalism.

At the same time that the United States was entering the world stage as a great military power it was also becoming a great industrial power. Cities and factories sprouted across the landscape. An abundance of new jobs served as a magnet attracting millions of immigrants from every corner of the globe. They were not always welcomed nor were they readily assimilated. Ethnic and racial strife, as well as labor agitation, increased at the turn of the century. In the midst of such social turmoil and unparalleled economic development, American reformers made their first sustained attempt to adapt their political and social institutions to the realities of the industrial age. The worst excesses and injustices of urban-industrial development—corporate monopolies, child labor, political corruption, hazardous working conditions, urban ghettos—were finally addressed in a comprehensive way. During the Progressive Era (1900–1917), local, state, and federal governments sought to rein in the excesses of industrial capitalism and develop a more rational and efficient public policy.

A conservative Republican resurgence challenged the notion of the new regulatory state during the 1920s. Free enterprise and corporate capitalism witnessed a dramatic revival. But the stock market crash of 1929 helped propel the United States and many other nations into the worst economic downturn in history. The unprecedented severity of the Great Depression renewed public demands for federal government programs to protect the general welfare. "This nation asks for action," declared President Franklin D. Roosevelt in his 1933 inaugural address. The many New Deal initiatives and agencies instituted by Roosevelt and his Democratic administration created the framework for a welfare state that has since served as the basis for American public policy.

The New Deal helped revive public confidence and put people back to work, but it did not end the Great Depression. It took a world war to restore full employment. The necessity of mobilizing the nation in support of the Second World War also served to accelerate the growth of the federal government. And the unparalleled scope of the war helped catapult the United States into a leadership role in world politics. The creation of a nuclear bomb to help end the war ushered in a new era of atomic diplomacy that held the fate of the world in the balance. For all of the new creature comforts associated with modern life, Americans in 1945 found themselves living amid an array of new anxieties.

23 ∾ AN AMERICAN EMPIRE

CHAPTER ORGANIZER

This chapter focuses on:

- the circumstances that led to America's "new imperialism."

- the causes of the Spanish-American War.

- Theodore Roosevelt's foreign policy in Asia and Latin America.

hroughout most of the late nineteenth century, Americans displayed what one senator called "only a languid interest" in foreign affairs. With the major diplomatic issues stemming from the Civil War having been quickly settled, an isolationist mood swept across the United States, which continued to enjoy what one historian has called "free security": wide oceans as buffers on either side, the British navy situated between America and the powers of Europe, and militarily weak neighbors in the Western Hemisphere.

Yet the notion of America having a "Manifest Destiny" ordained by God to expand its territory and influence remained alive in the decades after the end of the Civil War. Several prominent political and business leaders argued that the rapid industrial development of the United States meant that the nation needed to acquire foreign territories to gain easier access to vital raw materials. In addition, as their exports grew, American companies and farmers would become increasingly intertwined in the world economy. This, in turn, would require an expanded American naval presence to protect the shipping lanes. And a modern steam-powered navy needed bases to replenish the coal and water required for its ships. For these reasons and others, the United States during the last quarter of the nineteenth century began to expand its presence beyond the Western Hemisphere.

TOWARD THE NEW IMPERIALISM

During the last quarter of the nineteenth century, European powers unleashed a new surge of imperialism in Africa and Asia, where they seized colonies, protectorates, and economic privileges. All of Africa except Liberia and Ethiopia fell under outside dominion. Above all, the new imperialism was economic, a quest for markets and raw materials.

Most Americans were concerned about world markets as developments in transportation and communication quickened the pace of commerce and diplomacy. From the first, exports of farm products had been the basis of American economic growth. Now the conviction grew that American manufacturers had matured to the point where they could outsell foreign goods in the world market. But should the expansion of markets lead to territorial expansion as well? Or to intervention in the internal affairs of other countries? On this point Americans disagreed, but a small, yet vocal group of public officials advocated overseas possessions, regardless of the implications. They included Senator Albert J. Beveridge of Indiana and Senator Henry Cabot Lodge of Massachusetts, Theodore Roosevelt, and not least of all, Captain Alfred Thayer Mahan.

NAVAL POWER   During the 1880s, Captain Mahan became the leading proponent of sea power. A graduate of the Naval Academy, he served for years as president of the Naval War College at Newport, Rhode Island. A series of his lectures on naval history grew into a volume published in 1890, *The Influence of Sea Power upon History, 1660–1783*, in which he argued that national greatness and prosperity flowed from sea power, which had a fundamentally economic importance. To Mahan, modern economic development called for a powerful navy, a strong merchant marine, foreign commerce, colonies, and naval bases. The age of steam made a network of coaling stations a new matter of strategic concern. Mahan expounded on his version of America's destiny—to control the Caribbean, build an isthmian canal, and spread Western civilization in the Pacific. He publicized his ideas in popular journals and began to shape public opinion.

Even before Mahan's writings became influential a gradual expansion of the navy had begun. In 1880 the nation had fewer than a hundred seagoing vessels, many of them rusting or rotting at the docks. By the time Cleveland entered office, four new steel vessels had been authorized, and Cleveland's navy secretary got funds for twenty more.

IMPERIALIST THEORY Certain intellectual currents of the day worked to bolster the new spirit of Manifest Destiny. The Darwinian idea of natural selection afforded a handy argument for imperialism. If natural selection worked in the biological realm, would it not apply also in human society? Among nations, as among individuals, the fittest survive and prevail. "There is apparently much truth in the belief that the wonderful progress of the United States, as well as the character of the people, are the results of natural selection," Darwin wrote in *The Descent of Man* (1871).

John Fiske, the historian and popular lecturer on Darwinism, developed racial corollaries from Darwin's idea. In *American Political Ideas* (1885), he stressed the superior character of "Anglo-Saxon" institutions and peoples. The English "race," he argued, was destined to dominate the globe in the institutions, traditions, language, even in the blood of the world's peoples. Josiah Strong, a Congregational minister, added the sanction of religion to theories of racial superiority. In his book *Our Country: Its Possible Future and Its Present Crisis* (1885), Strong argued that "Anglo-Saxons" embodied two great ideas: civil liberty and "a pure spiritual Christianity." The Anglo-Saxon was "divinely commissioned to be, in a peculiar sense, his brother's keeper."

EXPANSION IN THE PACIFIC

For expansionists, Asia offered an especially alluring temptation. President Andrew Johnson's secretary of state, William H. Seward, believed that the United States must inevitably exercise commercial domination "on the Pacific Ocean, and its islands and continents." Eager for American manufacturers to exploit Asian markets, Seward believed the

*In a sardonic comment on Seward's purchase of Alaska in
1866, this cartoon shows Seward and President Andrew
Johnson carting a huge iceberg of "Russian America . . . to
cool down the Congressional majority."*

United States first had to remove all foreign interests from the northern
Pacific coast and gain access to that region's valuable ports. To that end,
he cast covetous eyes on the crown colony of British Columbia, sand-
wiched between Russian America (Alaska) and Washington Territory.

Late in 1866, while encouraging annexation sentiment among the
British Columbians, Seward learned of Russia's desire to sell Alaska,
which had become unprofitable. He leaped at the opportunity, and in
1867 the United States bought Alaska for $7.2 million, thus removing
Russia, the most recent colonial power, from the New World. Critics
scoffed at "Seward's folly" of buying the Alaskan "icebox," but it proved
in time to be the biggest bargain for the United States since the
Louisiana Purchase.

Seward's successors at the State Department sustained his expansionist vision, and key ports in the Pacific Ocean remained the major
focus of overseas activity through the rest of the nineteenth century.
Two island groups occupied especially strategic positions about twenty

degrees from either side of the equator: Samoa on the south and Hawaii (the Sandwich Islands) on the north. Both had major harbors, Pago Pago and Pearl Harbor, respectively. In the years after the Civil War American interest in these islands gradually deepened.

SAMOA   In 1878, the Samoans signed a treaty with the United States that granted a naval base at Pago Pago and extraterritoriality for Americans (meaning that in Samoa they remained subject only to American law), exchanged trade concessions, and called for the United States to extend its good offices in case of a dispute with another nation. The Senate ratified this accord, and in the following year the German and British governments worked out similar arrangements with other islands of the Samoan group. There matters rested until civil war broke out in 1887. The Germans backed a pretender against the native Samoan king and finally installed him under a German protectorate. The sequel to this incident was a conference in Berlin (1889) that established a tripartite protectorate, with Germany, Great Britain, and the United States in an uneasy partnership.

HAWAII   In Hawaii, the Americans had a clearer field. The islands, a united kingdom since 1795, had a sizable settlement of American missionaries and planters and were strategically more important to the United States than Samoa. Occupation by another major power might have posed a threat to American commercial interests and even to American defense.

In 1875 the kingdom entered a reciprocal trade agreement under which Hawaiian sugar would enter the United States duty free and under which Hawaii promised that none of its territory would be leased or granted to a third power. This agreement resulted in a boom in sugar production, and American settlers in Hawaii soon formed an economic elite. The trade agreement was renewed in 1887, when it was amended to grant the United States exclusive right to a fortified naval base at Pearl Harbor near Honolulu.

White planters in Hawaii built their fortunes on cheap immigrant labor, mainly Chinese, Japanese, and Portuguese. By the 1890s, the native population had been reduced to a minority by smallpox and other foreign diseases, and Asians quickly became the most numerous group in Hawaii.

Queen Liliuokalani.

In 1887, the Americans on the islands forced the king to accept a new constitution that created a constitutional government, which they dominated. In 1890, however, the McKinley Tariff destroyed Hawaii's favored position in the sugar trade by putting the sugar of all countries on the free list and granting growers in the continental United States a 2¢ subsidy per pound of sugar. This led to an economic crisis in Hawaii and affected the political situation as well.

In 1891, when the king's sister, Liliuokalani, ascended the throne, she began efforts to reclaim a measure of power and to eliminate white control of the government. Hawaii's white population then staged a revolt against Queen Liliuokalani early in 1893 and seized power. The American minister brought in marines to support the coup. As he cheerfully reported to Washington, "The Hawaiian pear is now fully ripe, and this is the golden hour for the United States to pluck it." Within a month, a committee of the new government turned up in Washington with a treaty of annexation.

The treaty, however, appeared just weeks before President Benjamin Harrison left office, and Democratic senators blocked ratification. President Cleveland withdrew the treaty and sent a special commissioner to investigate. He removed the American marines and reported that the Americans in Hawaii had acted improperly. Most Hawaiians opposed annexation, the commissioner found. He concluded that the revolution had been engineered mainly by the American sugar planters hoping to get the subsidy for sugar grown in the United States. Cleveland proposed to restore the queen to power in return for amnesty to the revolutionists. The provisional government refused to give up power, however, and on July 4, 1894, they proclaimed the Republic of Hawaii, which had in its constitution a standing provision for American annexation. When McKinley became president in 1897, he was looking for an excuse to annex the islands. This excuse was found when the Japanese, also hoping to take over the islands, sent warships to Hawaii. McKinley responded by sending American warships and asked the Senate to approve a treaty to annex Hawaii. When the Senate could not muster the two-thirds majority needed to approve the treaty, McKinley used a joint resolution of the House and Senate to achieve his aims. This resolution passed by simple majorities in both houses, and Hawaii was annexed in the summer of 1898.

DIPLOMATIC INCIDENTS IN THE 1880S AND 1890S

In the 1880s and 1890s, incidents in the Bering Sea and in Venezuela drew Americans into foreign affairs. At issue in the Bering Sea was the practice of pelagic (oceanic) sealing by foreign nationals, mostly Canadians, in offshore waters where the difficulty of distinguishing males and females resulted in the loss of many pups when their mothers were killed.

In 1886 American revenue cutters began seizing Canadian ships engaged in the practice, and three years later Congress declared the Bering a closed sea under United States dominion. In an exchange of notes in 1890, however, the British foreign minister refused to accept the legitimacy of Congress's claim. There was a flurry of bluster in the American press, but never much chance that the two countries would come to blows over what one newspaper called "a few greasy, ill-smelling sealskins." Eventually, an arbitration treaty of 1892 declared that, while the Bering was an open sea, pelagic sealing was forbidden within sixty miles of the Pribilof Islands. Later, in 1911, a treaty with Britain, Russia, and Japan prohibited pelagic sealing throughout the North Pacific and Bering Sea.

Far more serious was the Venezuelan boundary dispute with British Guiana, which had simmered since colonial days but took on new urgency when gold was found in the disputed area. When Venezuela suspended diplomatic relations with Britain in 1887, the American State Department suggested arbitration, but the matter remained unsettled in 1892 when Cleveland was reelected to the White House.

In 1895 Congress passed a Republican-sponsored resolution for arbitration of the dispute, and Cleveland was forced to get tough with the British or see his political opponents do it. He may even have found the occasion a welcome diversion from his domestic problems. His secretary of state, Richard L. Olney, drafted a note in which he invoked the Monroe Doctrine against British interference in the affairs of the New World. Cleveland claimed to have softened the "verbiage" a bit, but still dubbed it a "20 inch gun" note. Olney hoped that the note would provoke a quick reply, but the British minister let it lie for a maddening four months. The British assumed the note was largely for domestic American consumption anyway.

Britain finally rejected the demand for arbitration and noted that the Monroe Doctrine was not recognized international law, and in any case was irrelevant to a boundary dispute. Cleveland pronounced himself "mad clear through" at such a rebuff to the "friendly" suggestion of the United States. Congress, at Cleveland's request, unanimously voted for a commission to run a boundary line in spite of the British. Enthusiasm for war swept the country. Theodore Roosevelt vented his opinion that "this country needs a war." But diplomats on both sides recognized that it was in everyone's interest to negotiate rather than risk the outbreak of war. The British faced more urgent problems in South Africa, and through the good offices of the United States finally came around to an arbitration treaty with Venezuela, signed in 1897. By the time an international commission handed in its findings in 1899, the focus of public attention was elsewhere. The settlement turned out to be almost what the British had offered in the first place.

THE SPANISH-AMERICAN WAR

Until the 1890s, a certain ambivalence about overseas possessions had checked America's drive to expand. Suddenly, in 1898 and 1899,

José Martí, leader of the Cuban revolt against Spanish rule.

the inhibitions collapsed, and American power thrust its way to the far reaches of the Pacific. The occasion for this explosion of imperialism lay neither in the Pacific nor in the quest for bases and trade, but to the south in Cuba. The chief motive was a sense of outrage at another country's imperialism.

"CUBA LIBRE" Throughout the second half of the nineteenth century, Cubans had repeatedly revolted against Spanish rule, only to be ruthlessly suppressed. All the while, American investments in Cuba, mainly in sugar and mining, were steadily rising. The United States in fact traded more with Cuba than Spain did.

On February 24, 1895, insurrection broke out again. Simmering discontent with Spanish rule had been aggravated by the Wilson-Gorman Tariff of 1894, which took sugar off the free list in the midst of a depression already damaging to the market for Cuban sugar. Raw sugar prices collapsed, putting Cubans out of work and thereby rekindling their desire for rebellion. Public feeling in the United States supported the rebels. Many Americans extended help to the Cuban Revolutionary party, which organized the revolt from headquarters in New York. Its leader, José Martí, returned to the island soon after the new outbreak and died in a skirmish with Spanish troops.

The insurrectionists waged guerrilla warfare and sought to damage the economic life of the island, which in turn would excite the concern of American investors. The strategy dictated hit-and-run attacks on trains, railways, and plantations. Americans often compared the insurrection to their own War of Independence. In 1896 Spanish general Valeriano Weyler adopted a policy of gathering Cubans behind Spanish lines, often in detention (*reconcentrado*) centers so that no one could join the insurrections by night and appear peaceful by day. In some of the centers, a combination of tropical climate, poor food, and unsanitary conditions quickly brought a heavy toll of disease and death. The American press promptly christened the Spanish commander "Butcher" Weyler.

Events in Cuba supplied exciting copy for the popular press. William Randolph Hearst's *New York Journal* and Joseph Pulitzer's *New York World* were at the time locked in a monumental struggle for circulation. "It was a battle of gigantic proportions," one journalist later wrote, "in which the sufferings of Cuba merely chanced to furnish some of the most convenient ammunition." Another device of the circulation war was the newfangled comic strip, and one of the most popular was "The Yellow Kid." By association, the sensationalism at which the papers vied came to be called "yellow journalism." Hearst emerged as the undisputed champion, with his *Journal* excelling at invective against "Weyler the brute, the devastator of haciendas, the destroyer of men."

At the outset, the Cleveland administration tried to protect American rights in Cuba but avoided involvement beyond an offer of mediation. Mounting public sympathy for the cause, however, prompted concern in Congress. By concurrent resolution on April 6, 1896, the two houses endorsed official recognition of the Cuban belligerents and urged the president to seek a peace on the basis of Cuban independence. Cleveland, however, denied any designs against Spanish rule and offered to cooperate with Spain in bringing peace on the basis of allowing Cubans a measure of self-governance. The Spanish politely refused.

PRESSURE FOR WAR   America's posture of neutrality changed sharply when McKinley entered office. He had been elected on a platform that endorsed independence for Cuba as well as American control of Hawaii and the construction of an isthmian canal. In 1897 Spain's queen regent offered Cuba autonomy (self-government without formal independence) in return for peace. What the Cubans might once have welcomed, however, they now rejected, insurrectionists and Spanish loyalists alike.

The battleship Maine, *funded in 1886, shown here entering Havana Harbor in 1898.*

Spain was impaled on the horns of a dilemma, unable to end the war and unready to give up Cuba.

Early in 1898 events moved rapidly to arouse opinion against Spain. On January 25, the American battleship *Maine* docked in Havana Harbor, ostensibly on a courtesy call. On February 9 Hearst's *New York Journal* released the text of a letter from Spanish minister Depuy de Lôme to a friend in Havana, stolen from the post office by a Cuban spy. In the letter de Lôme called President McKinley "weak and a bidder for the admiration of the crowd, besides being a would-be politician who tries to leave a door open behind himself while keeping on good terms with the jingoes of his party." This was hardly more extreme than what McKinley's assistant secretary of the navy, Theodore Roosevelt, had said about him: that the "white-livered" president had "no more backbone than a chocolate eclair." But that comment had remained private. De Lôme resigned to prevent further embarrassment to his government.

Six days later, during the night of February 15, 1898, the *Maine* exploded in Havana Harbor and sank with a loss of 266 men, most of whom died in their hammocks. The ship's captain, one of only 84 survivors, scribbled a telegram to Washington: "*Maine* blown up in Havana Harbor at nine forty tonight and destroyed. Many wounded and doubtless more killed or drowned. . . . Public opinion should be suspended until further report."

But those eager for a war with Spain saw no need to withhold judgment; they demanded an immediate declaration. Roosevelt called the

An American cartoon depicts the sinking of the Maine *in Havana Harbor. The uproar created by the incident and its coverage in the "yellow press" edged McKinley toward war.*

sinking "an act of dirty treachery on the part of the Spaniards." A naval court of inquiry reported that an external mine had set off an explosion in the ship's magazine. Lacking hard evidence, the court made no effort to fix the blame, but the yellow press had no need of evidence. The outcry against Spain reached a crescendo in the words "Remember the *Maine!*" Never mind that Spain could have derived little benefit from such an act. A comprehensive study in 1976 concluded that the sinking of the *Maine* was an accident, the result of an internal explosion triggered by a fire in its coal bunker.

Under the mounting pressure of public excitement, McKinley tried to maintain a steady course. But the weight of outraged public opinion and militants in his own party such as Theodore Roosevelt and Henry Cabot Lodge eroded his neutrality. As one congressman remarked, McKinley "keeps his ear to the ground so close that he gets it full of grasshoppers much of the time." On March 9, however, the president coaxed from Congress a $50 million appropriation for defense. Still, McKinley sought to avoid war, as did most business spokesmen. Such caution infuriated Roosevelt. "We will have this war for the freedom of Cuba," he fumed on March 26, "in spite of the timidity of the commercial interests."

The Spanish government, sensing the growing militancy in the United States, announced a unilateral cease-fire in early April 1898. On April 10 the Spanish minister gave the State Department a message that amounted to a surrender: the United States should indicate the nature and duration of the armistice; Cuba would have an autonomous government; and the two countries would submit the question of the sinking of the *Maine* to arbitration. The United States minister to Spain then cabled from Madrid: "I hope nothing will now be done to humiliate Spain, as I am satisfied that the present government is going, and is loyally ready to go, as fast and as far as it can." McKinley, he predicted, could win a settlement by August 1 on any terms: autonomy, independence, or cession of Cuba to the United States.

But the message came too late. The following day McKinley sent Congress what amounted to a war message. He asked for power to use armed forces in Cuba to protect American property and trade. The Cuban situation, McKinley said, was a constant menace to the peace. On April 20 a joint resolution of Congress went beyond endorsing the use of the armed forces: it declared Cuba independent and demanded withdrawal of Spanish forces. The Teller Amendment, added on the Senate floor, disclaimed any American designs on Cuban territory. McKinley signed the resolution, and a copy went off to the Spanish government, with notice that McKinley would execute it unless Spain gave a complete and satisfactory response by noon, April 23. Meanwhile, on April 22 the president announced a blockade of Cuba's northern coast and the port of Santiago. Under international law this was an act of war. Rather than give in to an ultimatum, the Spanish government declared war on April 24. Congress then, determined to be first, declared war on April 25, retroactive to April 21, 1898.

Why such a rush into war after the American minister had predicted that Spain would cave in before the summer was out? Chiefly because too much momentum and popular pressure had already built up for a confidential message to change the course of events. Also, leaders of the business community, which tolerates uncertainty poorly, were now demanding a quick resolution of the problem. Many lacked faith in the willingness or ability of the Spanish government to carry out a moderate policy in the face of a hostile public opinion. Still, it is fair to ask why McKinley did not take a stand for peace, knowing what he did. He might have defied Congress and public opinion, but in the end he decided that the political risk was too high. The ultimate blame for war, if blame must be levied, belongs to the American people for letting themselves be whipped up into such a hostile frenzy.

DEWEY TAKES MANILA   The war itself was short, lasting four months. John Hay, soon to be secretary of state, called it "a splendid little war." The war's end was also the end of Spain's once great New World empire, which had begun with Columbus. It marked as well the emergence of the United States as a world power. If American participation saved many lives by ending the insurrection in Cuba, it also led to American involvement in another insurrection, in the Philippines, and created a host of problems that persisted into the twentieth century.

The war was barely under way before the navy produced a spectacular victory in an unexpected quarter—Manila Bay. While public attention focused on Cuba, young Theodore Roosevelt was thinking of the Philippines. As assistant secretary of the navy, he had Commodore George Dewey appointed commander of the small American squadron in Asia, and had ordered it to engage Spain in the Philippines in case of war. President McKinley had approved those orders.

Arriving late on April 30 with four cruisers and two gunboats, Dewey destroyed or captured all the Spanish warships in Manila Bay. The Spanish force lost 381 men, while Dewey's squadron suffered only 8 wounded. Dewey, without an occupation force, was now in awkward possession of Manila Bay. Promised reinforcements, he stayed while foreign warships hung about the scene like watchful vultures, ready to take over the Philippines if the United States did not do so. Land reinforcements finally arrived, and with the help of Filipino insurrectionists under Emilio Aguinaldo, Dewey's forces entered Manila on August 13.

THE CUBAN CAMPAIGN   While these events transpired halfway around the world, the war reached a surprisingly quick climax closer to home. The U.S. navy blockaded the Spanish navy at Santiago. Although the navy was fit, the army could muster only an ill-assorted guard of 28,000 regulars and about 100,000 militiamen. Altogether during the war about 200,000 more militiamen were recruited, chiefly as state volunteers. The armed forces suffered badly from both inexperience and

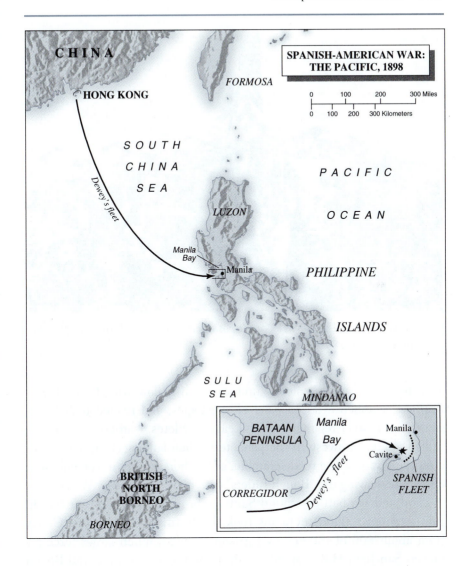

maladministration, with the result that more died from disease than from enemy action. The United States's salvation was that Spanish forces were even worse off.

A force of some 17,000 American troops hastily assembled at Tampa. One significant element of that force was the First Volunteer Cavalry, better known as the "Rough Riders" and best remembered because Lieutenant-Colonel Theodore Roosevelt was second in command. Eager to get "in on the fun," and "to act up to my preachings," Roosevelt had quit the Navy Department soon after war was declared. He ordered

Lieutenant-Colonel Theodore Roosevelt posing with his "Rough Riders" after the battle of San Juan, 1898.

a custom-fitted, fawn-colored uniform with yellow trim from Brooks Brothers, grabbed a dozen pairs of spectacles, and rushed to help organize a volunteer regiment of Ivy League athletes, leathery ex-convicts, Indians, and southwestern sharpshooters. Their landing at the southeastern tip of Cuba was a mad scramble, as the horses were mistakenly sent elsewhere, leaving the "Rough Riders" to become the "Weary Walkers."

Land and sea battles around Santiago broke Spanish resistance. On July 1, about 7,000 Americans took the fortified village of El Caney from about 600 of the enemy garrison. While a much larger force attacked San Juan Hill, a smaller unit, including the dismounted Rough Riders, together with black soldiers from two cavalry units, seized the enemy position atop nearby Kettle Hill. In the midst of the fray, Roosevelt satisfied his bloodlust by seeing a Spaniard he shot double up "neatly as a jackrabbit." He later claimed that he "would rather have led that charge than served three terms in the U.S. Senate." A friend wrote to Roosevelt's wife that her husband was "revelling in victory and gore."

The two battles put American forces atop heights from which to the west and south they could bring Santiago and the Spanish fleet under siege. On July 3 the Spanish navy made a gallant run for it, but its decrepit ships were little more than sitting ducks for the newer American fleet, which included five battleships and two cruisers. The casualties were as one-sided as at Manila: 474 Spanish were killed and wounded and 1,750 were taken prisoner, while only one American was killed and one wounded. Santiago surrendered with a garrison of 24,000 on July 17. On July 25 an American force moved into Spanish-held Puerto Rico against minor resistance.

The next day the Spanish government sued for peace. After discussions lasting two weeks, an armistice was signed on August 12, less than four months after the war's start and the day before Americans entered Manila. The peace protocol specified that Spain should give up Cuba, and that the United States should annex Puerto Rico and occupy Manila pending disposition of the Philippines. Among more than 274,000 Americans who served during the war and the ensuing demobilization, 5,462 died, but only 379 in battle. Most succumbed to malaria, typhoid, dysentery, or yellow fever.

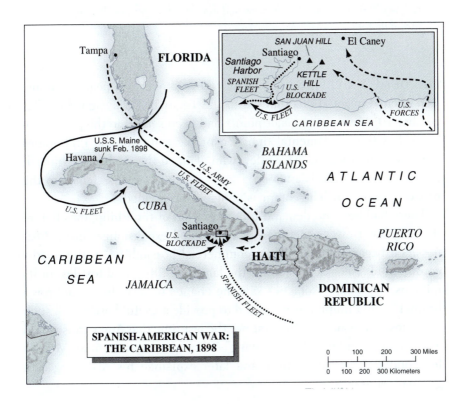

SPANISH-AMERICAN WAR: THE CARIBBEAN, 1898

"Well, I Hardly Know Which to Take First." *At the end of the nineteenth century, it seemed that Uncle Sam had developed a considerable appetite for foreign territory.*

THE DEBATE OVER ANNEXATION   On October 1, a peace commission opened negotiations that led to the Treaty of Paris, signed on December 10. Most of the major points had been settled in the peace protocol, but the fundamental question of the status of the Philippines remained unanswered. McKinley, who claimed that at first he himself could not locate the islands on a map, gave ambiguous signals to the peace commission. The commission itself was divided.

There had been no demand for annexation of the Philippines before the war, but Dewey's victory quickly kindled expansionist fever. Businessmen began thinking of the commercial possibilities in the nearby continent of Asia, such as oil for the lamps of China and textiles for its millions. Missionary societies saw the chance to save the "little brown brother." The Philippines promised to provide a useful base for all such activities. It was neither the first nor the last time that Americans would get caught up in fantasies of "saving" Asia or getting rich there. McKinley pondered the alternatives and later explained his reasoning to a group of Methodists:

And one night late it came to me this way—I don't know how it was, but it came: (1) that we could not give them back to Spain—that would be cowardly and dishonorable; (2) that we could not turn them over to France or Germany—our commercial rivals in the Orient—that would be bad business and discreditable; (3) that we could not leave them to themselves—they were unfit for self-government—and they would soon have anarchy and misrule over there worse than Spain's was; and (4) that there was nothing left for us to do but to take them all, and to educate the Filipinos, and uplift and civilize and Christianize them, and by God's grace do the very best we could by them, as our fellowmen for whom Christ also died. And then I went to bed, and went to sleep and slept soundly.

In one brief statement he had summarized the motivating ideas of imperialism: (1) national honor, (2) commerce, (3) racial superiority, and (4) altruism. Spanish negotiators raised the delicate point that American forces had no claim by right of conquest, and had even taken Manila after the armistice. American negotiators finally offered the Spanish compensation of $20 million. The treaty thus added to American territory Puerto Rico, Guam (a Spanish island in the Pacific), and the Philippines.

Meanwhile Americans had taken other giant steps in the Pacific. Hawaii had been annexed in the midst of the war. Within a year of the peace treaty, in 1899, after another outbreak of fighting over the royal succession in Samoa, Germany and the United States agreed to partition the Samoa Islands. The United States annexed the easternmost islands; Germany took the rest, including the largest island. Britain ceded its claims in Samoa in return for German concessions in the Pacific and in Africa. Meanwhile, in 1898 the United States had laid claim to Wake Island, located between Guam and the Hawaiian islands, which would become a vital link in a future trans-Pacific cable line.

The Treaty of Paris had yet to be ratified in the Senate, where most Democrats and Populists, and some Republicans, opposed it. Anti-imperialists argued that acquisition of the Philippines would undermine democracy. They appealed to traditional isolationism, American principles of self-government, the inconsistency of liberating Cuba and annexing the Philippines, the involvement in foreign entanglements that would undermine the logic of the Monroe Doctrine, and the danger that the Philippines would become an Achilles heel, expensive if not

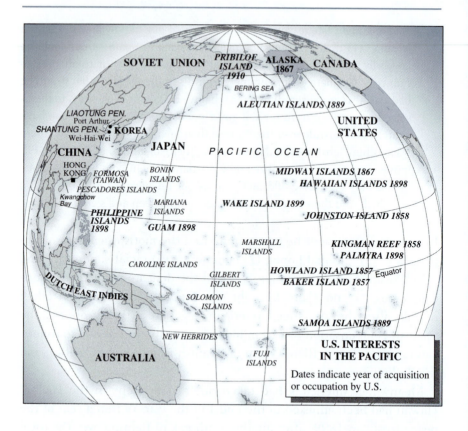

SOVIET UNION
PRIBILOF ISLAND 1910
ALASKA 1867
CANADA
BERING SEA
ALEUTIAN ISLANDS 1889
LIAOTUNG PEN.
Port Arthur
SHANTUNG PEN.
Wei-Hai-Wei
KOREA
CHINA
JAPAN
PACIFIC OCEAN
UNITED STATES
HONG KONG
FORMOSA (TAIWAN)
BONIN ISLANDS
MIDWAY ISLANDS 1867
HAWAIIAN ISLANDS 1898
PESCADORES ISLANDS
Kwangchow-Bay
PHILIPPINE ISLANDS 1898
MARIANA ISLANDS
GUAM 1898
WAKE ISLAND 1899
JOHNSTON ISLAND 1858
MARSHALL ISLANDS
KINGMAN REEF 1858
PALMYRA 1898
CAROLINE ISLANDS
GILBERT ISLANDS
HOWLAND ISLAND 1857
BAKER ISLAND 1857
Equator
DUTCH EAST INDIES
SOLOMON ISLANDS
SAMOA ISLANDS 1889
NEW HEBRIDES
AUSTRALIA
FUJI ISLANDS

U.S. INTERESTS IN THE PACIFIC

Dates indicate year of acquisition or occupation by U.S.

impossible to defend. The prospect of incorporating so many alien peoples into American life was not the least of some people's worries. "Bananas and self-government cannot grow on the same piece of land," one senator claimed.

The opposition might have been strong enough to kill the treaty had not the populist Democrat William Jennings Bryan influenced the vote for approval. Ending the war, he argued, would open the way for the future independence of Cuba and the Philippines. Finally, ratification came on February 6, 1899, by a margin of more than two to one. A week later, the deciding vote of the vice-president defeated a resolution for Philippine independence. That same month in *McClure's* magazine the British poet Rudyard Kipling published "The White Man's Burden," in which he called the American people to a new duty:

> Take up the White Man's burden—
> Send forth the best ye breed—

Go, bind your sons to exile
To serve your captive's need;
To wait in heavy harness
On fluttered folk and wild—
Your new-caught sullen peoples,
Half devil and half child.

By this time Americans had already clashed with Filipino insurrectionists near Manila. The Filipino leader, Emilio Aguinaldo, had been in exile until Commodore Dewey brought him back to Luzon to make trouble for the Spanish. Since Aguinaldo's forces were more or less in control of the islands outside of Manila, what followed was largely an American war of conquest that lasted more than two years. Organized Filipino resistance collapsed by the end of 1899, but even after the capture of Aguinaldo in 1901, sporadic guerrilla action lasted until mid-1902. It was a sordid little war, with massacres and torture on both sides.

Against the backdrop of this nasty guerrilla war the great debate over imperialism continued. The treaty debates inspired a number of anti-imperialist groups, which united in 1899 as the American Anti-Imperialist League. The league attracted members representing many shades

Emilio Aguinaldo (seated third from right) *and other leaders of the Filipino insurgents.*

of opinion; the main thing they had in common was that most belonged to an older generation. Andrew Carnegie footed the bills, but on imperialism at least union leader Samuel Gompers agreed with him. Presidents Charles Eliot of Harvard and David Starr Jordan of Stanford supported the group, along with social reformer Jane Addams. The drive for power, said the philosopher William James, had caused the nation to "puke up its ancient soul."

ORGANIZING THE NEW ACQUISITIONS   Such criticism, however, did not faze the expansionists. Senator Beveridge boasted in 1900: "The Philippines are ours forever. And just beyond the Philippines are China's illimitable markets. We will not retreat from either. . . . The power that rules the Pacific is the power that rules the world. That power will forever be the American Republic."

In the Philippines McKinley had already moved toward setting up a civil government. In 1900 he dispatched a commission under Judge William Howard Taft with instructions to set up a system of government. Unlike some of the Americans on the scene, Taft seemed to like the Filipinos, encouraged them to participate, and eventually convinced Filipino representatives to sit on the commission itself.

On July 4, 1901, military government ended. Under an act of Congress, Taft became the civil governor with appointed provincial governors under his authority. The Philippine Government Act, passed by Congress in 1902, declared the Philippine Islands an "unorganized territory" and made the inhabitants citizens of the Philippines. In 1916 the Jones Act affirmed America's intention to grant the Philippines independence at an indefinite date. Finally, the Tydings-McDuffie Act of 1934 offered independence after a tutelary period of ten more years. A constitution was drafted and ratified, and on September 17, 1934, Manuel Quezon was elected the first president of the Philippines. Independence finally took effect on July 4, 1946.

Puerto Rico had been acquired in part to serve as an American outpost on the approaches to the Caribbean and any future isthmian canal. On April 12, 1900, the Foraker Act established a civil government on the island. The act that was passed two years later for the Philippines would resemble this one. The president appointed a governor and eleven members of an executive council, and an elected House of Delegates made up the lower house of the legislature. Residents of the island were citizens of Puerto Rico but not of the United States until

1917, when the Jones Act granted United States citizenship and made both houses of the legislature elective. In 1947 the governor also became elective, and in 1952 Puerto Rico became a commonwealth with its own constitution and elected officials, a unique status. Like a state, Puerto Rico is free to change its constitution insofar as it does not conflict with the United States Constitution.

The Foraker Act of 1900 also levied a temporary duty on imports from Puerto Rico. The tariff was challenged in the federal courts on the grounds that the island had become part of the United States, but the Supreme Court upheld the tariff. In this and other "Insular Cases" federal judges faced a question that went to the fundamental nature of the American Union and to the civil and political rights of the people in America's new possessions: Does the Constitution follow the flag? The Court ruled in effect that it did not unless Congress extended it.

Having liberated the Cubans from Spanish rule, the Americans found themselves propping up a shaky new Cuban government whose economy was in a state of collapse. Bad relations between American soldiers and Cubans set in almost immediately. When McKinley set up a military government for the island late in 1898, it was at odds with rebel leaders from the start.

Many Europeans expected annexation, and General Leonard Wood, who became Cuba's military governor in 1899, thought this the best solution. But the United States finally did fulfill the promise of independence for Cuba after the military regime had restored order, gotten schools under way, and improved sanitary conditions. The problem of disease in Cuba provided a focus for the work of Dr. Walter Reed, who made an outstanding contribution to the health of people in tropical climates around the world. Named head of the Army Yellow Fever Commission in 1900, he directed experiments with volunteers that proved the theory of a Cuban physician that yellow fever was carried by stegomyia mosquitoes. These experiments led the way to effective control of the disease.

In 1900, at President McKinley's order, General Wood called an election for a Cuban constitutional convention, which drafted a basic law modeled on that of the United States. The Platt Amendment to the Army Appropriations Bill passed by Congress in 1901, however, sharply restricted the independence of the new government. The amendment required Cuba never to impair its independence by treaty with a third power, to maintain its debt within the government's power to repay out of ordinary revenues, and to acknowledge the right of the United States to intervene for the preservation of Cuban independence and the maintenance of "a government adequate for the protection of life, property, and individual liberty." Finally, Cuba was called upon to sell or lease to the United States lands to be used for coaling or naval stations—a proviso that led to an American naval base at Guantanamo Bay, a base still in operation.

Under pressure, the Cuban delegates added the Platt Amendment as an appendix to their own constitution. As early as 1906 an insurrection arose against the new government, and President Theodore Roosevelt responded by sending Secretary of War William Howard Taft to "sit on the lid"—weighing in at more than 300 pounds, he was not a bad choice for the job. Backed up by American armed forces, Taft assumed full governmental authority, as he had in the Philippines, and the American army stayed until 1909, when a new Cuban president was peacefully elected. Further interventions would follow for more than two decades.

IMPERIAL RIVALRIES IN EAST ASIA

During the 1890s, not only the United States but also Japan emerged as a world power. Commodore Matthew Perry's voyage of 1853–1854 had opened Japan to Western ways, and the country began modernization in earnest after the 1860s. Flexing its new muscles, Japan defeated China's stagnant empire in the Sino-Japanese War (1894–1895) and as a result picked up the Pescadores Islands and the island of Taiwan (renamed Formosa). China's weakness, demonstrated in the war, brought the great powers into a scramble for "spheres of influence" on that remaining frontier of imperialist expansion. Russia secured the privilege of building a railroad across Manchuria and established itself in Port Arthur and the Liaotung Peninsula. The Germans moved into Shantung, the French into Kwangchow Bay, the British into Wei-Hai-Wei.

The bright prospect of American trade with China dimmed with the possibility that the great powers would throw up tariff barriers in their own spheres of influence. The British, ensconced at Hong Kong since 1840, had more to lose though, for they already had the largest foreign trade with China. Just before the Spanish-American War, in 1898, the

British suggested joint action with the United States to preserve the integrity of China, and renewed the proposal early in 1899. Both times the Senate rejected the request because it risked an entangling alliance.

CHINA AND THE "OPEN DOOR" In its origins and content, what soon came to be known as the Open Door Policy resembled the Monroe Doctrine. In both cases the United States proclaimed unilaterally a hands-off policy, which the British had earlier proposed as a joint statement. The policy outlined in Secretary of State John Hay's Open Door Note, dispatched in 1899 to London, Berlin, and St. Petersburg, and a little later to Tokyo, Rome, and Paris, proposed to keep China open to trade with all countries on an equal basis. More specifically it called upon foreign powers, within their spheres of influence: (1) not to interfere with any treaty port (a port open to all by treaty) or any vested interest, (2) to permit Chinese authorities to collect tariffs on an equal basis, and (3) to show no favors to their own nationals in the matter of harbor dues or railroad charges. Hay's request that each of the powers accept these principles was, one diplomat later wrote, like asking everyone who believes in truth to stand: the liars would be the first on their feet. As it turned out, none except Britain accepted Hay's principles, but none rejected them, either. The rest gave equivocal answers, usually conditioned on the action of the others. So Hay blandly announced that all powers had accepted the policy. None stood to deny it.

The Open Door Policy, if rooted in the self-interest of American businessmen eager to exploit the markets of China, also tapped the deep-seated sympathies of those who opposed imperialism, especially as it endorsed China's territorial integrity. But it had little more legal standing than a pious affirmation. When the Japanese, concerned about Russian pressure in Manchuria, asked how the United States intended to enforce the policy, Hay replied that America was "not prepared . . . to enforce these views on the east by any demonstration which could present a character of hostility to any other power." So it would remain for forty years, until continued Japanese expansion would bring America to war in 1941.

THE BOXER REBELLION A new crisis arose in 1900, when a group of Chinese nationalists known to the Western world as Boxers ("Fists of Righteous Harmony") rebelled against foreign encroachments on China

The forces of the Western powers and Japan occupying the Forbidden City in Peking after putting down the Boxer Rebellion.

and laid siege to foreign embassies in Peking. An international expedition of British, German, Russian, Japanese, and American forces mobilized to relieve the embassy compound. Hay, fearful that the intervention might become an excuse to dismember China, took the opportunity to further refine the Open Door Policy. The United States, he said in a circular letter of July 3, 1900, sought a solution that would "preserve Chinese territorial and administrative integrity" as well as "equal and impartial trade with all parts of the Chinese Empire."

Six weeks later, the expedition reached Peking and quelled the Boxer Rebellion. The occupying powers then agreed to settle for an indemnity from China of approximately $333 million. Of this total the United States received $25 million, of which nearly $11 million was refunded to China once all claims were paid. Most of this the Chinese government put into a fund to support Chinese students in American colleges.

ROOSEVELT'S BIG STICK DIPLOMACY

More than any other American of his time, Theodore Roosevelt helped transform the role of the United States in world affairs. The country had emerged from the Spanish-American War a world power, and he insisted that this entailed major new responsibilities. To ensure that his country accepted such international obligations, Roosevelt stretched both the Constitution and executive power to the limit. In the process he pushed a reluctant nation onto the center stage of world affairs.

ROOSEVELT'S RISE   Born in 1858, the son of a wealthy New York merchant and a Georgia belle, Roosevelt grew up in Manhattan in cultured comfort, visited Europe as a child, spoke German fluently, and was graduated Phi Beta Kappa from Harvard in 1880. A sickly, scrawny boy with poor eyesight, he built himself up by sheer force of will into a physical and intellectual athlete who became a lifelong practitioner of the "strenuous life." Boxer, wrestler, mountain climber, hunter, and outdoorsman, he was also a dedicated bird watcher, renowned historian and essayist, and outspoken moralist. His energy and fierce competitive spirit were both inexhaustible and infectious, and he was ever willing to express opinions on any and all subjects.

Within two years of graduating from Harvard, Roosevelt won election to the New York legislature and published *The Naval War of 1812,* the first of a number of historical, biographical, and other writings to flow from his pen. But with the world seemingly at his feet, disaster struck. In 1884 his beloved mother, only forty-eight years old, died. Eleven hours later, in the same house, his twenty-two-year-old wife died in his arms, soon after giving birth to their first child. That night Roosevelt drew a large cross over the entry in his diary: "The light has gone out of my life." The double funeral was so wrenching that the officiating minister wept throughout his prayer.

In an attempt to recover from this "strange and terrible fate," Roosevelt sold the family house and moved west to take up the cattle business on the Dakota frontier. There he played the part of a patrician cowboy, adorned in a buckskin shirt, silver spurs, and alligator boots. He told a relative he was "having a glorious time here." The blue-blooded New Yorker relished hunting, leading roundups, capturing outlaws, fighting Indians—and reading Tolstoy by the campfire. When a drunken cowboy, a gun in each hand, tried to bully the tinhorn Roosevelt, teasing him about his glasses, the feisty Harvard dude laid him out with one punch. Although his western career was brief, he never quite got over being a cowboy.

Back in New York City, Roosevelt ran for mayor in 1886 and lost, and later served six years as civil service commissioner and two years as

New York City's police commissioner. In the latter capacity he loved to don a black cloak and broad-brimmed hat and patrol the streets at midnight. When he came upon a sleeping policeman, Roosevelt would rap the man with his nightstick. In 1897, McKinley appointed the conscientious Roosevelt assistant secretary of the navy. After serving in Cuba and hastening into print his own account of the Rough Riders, Roosevelt easily won the governorship of New York, arousing audiences with his impassioned speeches and powerful personality.

In the 1900 presidential contest, the Democrats turned once again to William Jennings Bryan, who sought to make imperialism the "paramount issue" of the campaign. The Democratic platform condemned the Philippine conflict as "an unnecessary war" that had "placed the United States, previously known and applauded throughout the world as the champion of freedom, in the false and un-American position of crushing with military force the efforts of our former allies to achieve liberty and self-government."

The Republicans welcomed the issue. They renominated McKinley and named Roosevelt his running mate. After his role in both the Philippine and Cuban action, Roosevelt had virtually become "Mr. Imperialism." McKinley outpolled Bryan by 7.2 million to 6.4 million in the popular vote and by 292 to 155 in the electoral vote. But less than a year later, on September 6, 1901, while McKinley attended a reception

This 1900 cartoon shows the Republican vice-presidential candidate, Theodore Roosevelt, overshadowing his running mate, President McKinley.

at the Pan American Exposition in Buffalo, a fanatical anarchist named Leon Czolgosz approached him with a gun concealed in a bandaged hand and fired at point-blank range. McKinley died six days later, and Theodore Roosevelt was suddenly elevated to the White House. "Now look," Mark Hanna, the Ohio businessman and politico, erupted, "that damned cowboy is President of the United States!"

Six weeks short of his forty-third birthday, Roosevelt was the youngest man ever to reach the White House, but he brought to it more experience in public affairs than most and perhaps more vitality than any. One observer compared him to Niagara Falls, "both great wonders of nature." Roosevelt's glittering spectacles, glistening teeth, and overflowing gusto were a godsend to the cartoonists, who added another trademark when he pronounced the adage: "Speak softly, and carry a big stick."

Along with Roosevelt's boundless energy went an unshakable righteousness and a tendency to cast every issue in moral and patriotic terms. He considered the presidency his "bully pulpit," and he delivered fist-smacking speeches on the virtues of righteousness, honesty, civic duty, and strenuosity. Yet his boundless energy left a false impression of impulsiveness, and his talk of morality cloaked a cautious pragmatism. Roosevelt could get carried away on occasion, but as he said of his foreign policy steps, this was likely to happen only when "I am assured that I shall be able eventually to carry out my will by force." Indeed, nowhere was President Roosevelt's forceful will more evident than in his conduct of foreign affairs.

BUILDING THE PANAMA CANAL   After the Spanish-American War, the United States became more deeply involved in the Caribbean area. One issue overshadowed every other in the region: the Panama Canal. The narrow isthmus of Panama had excited dreams of an interoceanic canal ever since Balboa's crossing in 1513. Admiral Mahan regarded a canal as important to American commerce and naval power, a point dramatized in 1898 by the long voyage of the battleship *Oregon* around South America's Cape Horn to join the American fleet off Cuba.

Transit across the isthmus had first become a strong concern of the United States in the 1840s, when it became an important route to the California gold fields. Two treaties dating from that period loomed years later as obstacles to construction of a canal. The Bidlack Treaty (1848) with Colombia (then New Granada) guaranteed both Colombia's sovereignty over Panama and the neutrality of the isthmus, so that "free transit . . . not be embarrassed in any future time." In the Clayton-Bulwer Treaty (1850) the British agreed to acquire no more Central American territory, and the United States joined them in agreeing to build or fortify a canal only by mutual consent.

After the Spanish-American War, Secretary of State Hay commenced talks with the British ambassador to establish such consent. The outcome was the Hay-Pauncefote Treaty of 1900, but the Senate rejected it on the grounds that it forbade fortification of the canal and required that the canal be neutral even in time of war. By then a bill was already pending in Congress for a Nicaraguan canal, and the British apparently decided to accept the inevitable. In 1901 the Senate ratified a second Hay-Pauncefote Treaty, which simply omitted reference to the former limitations.

Other obstacles remained, however. From 1881 to 1887 a French company under Ferdinand de Lesseps, who had engineered the Suez

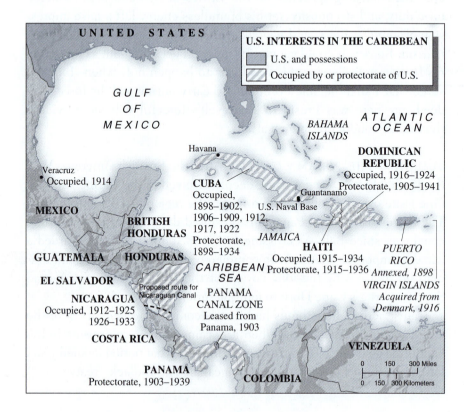

Canal in 1877, had spent nearly $300 million and some 20,000 lives to dig less than a third of the canal through Panama, then under the control of Colombia. The company now wanted $109 million for its holdings. An Isthmian Canal Commission, appointed by McKinley, reported in 1901 that a Nicaraguan route would be cheaper. When the House of Representatives quickly passed an act for construction there, the French company lowered its price to $40 million, and the Canal Commission switched to Panama.

Meanwhile Secretary Hay had opened negotiations with Ambassador Thomas Herrán of Colombia. In return for a Canal Zone six miles wide, the United States agreed to pay $10 million in cash and a rental fee of $250,000 a year. The United States Senate ratified the Hay-Herrán Treaty in 1903, but the Colombian Senate held out for $25 million in cash. At this action of those "foolish and homicidal corruptionists in Bogotá," Theodore Roosevelt, by then president, flew into a rage punctuated by references to "dagoes" and "contemptible little creatures." Meanwhile in Panama, an isolated province long at odds with the remote Colombian authorities in Bogotá, feeling was heightened by Colombia's rejection of the treaty. One Manuel Amador, an employee of the French canal company, then hatched a plot in close collusion with the company's representative, Philippe Bunau-Varilla. He visited Roosevelt and Hay and, apparently with inside information, informed the conspirators that the U.S.S. *Nashville* would call at Colón in Panama on November 2.

With an army of some 500, Amador staged a revolt the next day. Colombian troops, who could not penetrate the overland jungle, found American ships blocking the sea lanes. On November 13 the Roosevelt administration received its first ambassador from Panama, whose name happened to be Philippe Bunau-Varilla, and he signed a treaty that extended the Canal Zone from six to ten miles in width. For $10 million down and $250,000 a year, the United States received "in perpetuity the use, occupation and control" of the zone. The U.S. attorney-general, asked to supply a legal opinion upholding Roosevelt's actions, responded wryly: "No, Mr. President, if I were you I would not have any taint of legality about it."

In 1904 Congress created a new Isthmian Canal Commission to direct construction. Despite sanitary problems, the biggest obstacle at first, Roosevelt instructed the commission to make the "dirt fly." He later explained: "I took the Canal Zone and let Congress debate; and while the debate goes on the Canal does also."

Panama Canal Construction. *The Panama Canal
linked the Atlantic and Pacific, making interoceanic
crossings possible.*

And so did a rankling resentment in Colombia. By needlessly offending Latin American sensibilities, Roosevelt had committed one of the
greatest blunders in American foreign policy. Colombia eventually got
its $25 million from the Harding administration in 1921, but only once
America's interest in Colombian oil had lubricated the wheels of diplomacy. There was no apology, but the payment was made to remove "all
misunderstandings growing out of the political events in Panama, November, 1903." The canal opened on August 15, 1914, less than two
weeks after the outbreak of World War I in Europe.

THE ROOSEVELT COROLLARY   Even without the canal, the United
States would have been concerned about the stability of the Caribbean
area, and particularly with the activities of any hostile power there. A
prime excuse for intervention in those days was to force the collection
of debts owed to foreign nationals. In 1904 a crisis over the debts of the
Dominican Republic gave Roosevelt an opportunity to formulate American policy in the Caribbean. In his annual address to Congress in
1904, he set forth what came to be known as the Roosevelt Corollary to
the Monroe Doctrine: the principle, in short, was that since the Monroe Doctrine prohibited intervention in the region by Europeans, the

The World's Constable. *Theodore Roosevelt, shown here as the world's police-man, wields the "big stick" symbolizing his approach to diplomacy.*

United States was justified in intervening first to forestall the actions of outsiders.

In the president's words, the Roosevelt Corollary held that: "Chronic wrongdoing . . . may in America, as elsewhere, ultimately require intervention by some civilized nation, and in the Western Hemisphere the adherence of the United States to the Monroe Doctrine may force the United States, however reluctantly, in flagrant cases of such wrongdoing or impotence, to the exercise of an international police power." As put into practice by mutual agreement with the Dominican Republic in 1905, the Roosevelt Corollary called for the United States to install and protect a collector of customs who would apply 55 percent of the revenues to debt payments.

THE RUSSO-JAPANESE WAR   In East Asia, meanwhile, the Open Door Policy received a serious challenge when rivalry between Russia and Japan flared into a fight. By 1904 the Japanese had grown convinced that the Russians threatened their own ambitions in China and Korea. On February 8, Japan launched a surprise attack that devastated the Russian fleet. The Japanese then occupied Korea and drove the Russians back into Manchuria. But neither side could score a knockout blow, and neither relished a prolonged war. Roosevelt sought to maintain a balance between the two powers and offered to mediate their conflict. When the Japanese signaled that they would welcome a negotiated settlement, Roosevelt agreed to sponsor a peace conference in Portsmouth, New Hampshire. In the Treaty of Portsmouth, signed on September 5, 1905, the concessions all went to the Japanese. Russia acknowledged Japan's "predominant political, military, and economic interests in Korea" (Japan would annex the kingdom in 1910), and both powers agreed to evacuate Manchuria.

AMERICA'S RELATIONS WITH JAPAN Japan's show of strength against Russia raised doubts among American leaders about the security of the Philippines. During the Portsmouth talks, Roosevelt sent William Howard Taft to meet with the Japanese foreign minister in Tokyo. The two men negotiated the Taft-Katsura Agreement of July 29, 1905, in which the United States accepted Japanese control of Korea and Japan disavowed any designs on the Philippines. Three years later, the Root-Takahira Agreement, negotiated by Secretary of State Elihu Root and the Japanese ambassador, endorsed the status quo and reinforced the Open Door Policy by supporting "the independence and integrity of China" and "the principle of equal opportunity for commerce and industry in China."

Behind the diplomatic facade of goodwill, however, lay mutual distrust. For many Americans the Russian threat in East Asia now gave way to the "yellow peril" of Japan.* Racial animosities on the West Coast helped sour relations with Japan. In 1906 the San Francisco school board ordered students of Chinese, Japanese, and Korean descent to attend a separate public school. The Japanese government sharply protested such prejudice, and President Roosevelt managed to talk the school board into changing its mind after making sure that Japanese authorities would not issue passports to "laborers" except former residents of the United States, the parents, wives, or children of residents, or those who already possessed an interest in an American farming enterprise. This "Gentlemen's Agreement" of 1907, the precise terms of

---

*The term "yellow peril" was apparently coined by Kaiser Wilhelm II of Germany.

which have never been revealed, halted the influx of Japanese immigrants and brought some respite to racial agitations in California.

THE UNITED STATES AND EUROPE   During the years of expansionism, the United States cast its gaze westward and southward. But events in Europe also required attention. While Roosevelt was moving toward mediation of the Russo-Japanese War in 1905, another dangerous crisis began brewing in Morocco. There, on March 31, 1905, German kaiser Wilhelm II stepped ashore at Tangier and gave a saber-rattling speech criticizing French and British interests in North Africa. The kaiser's speech aroused a diplomatic storm of dangerous proportions. Roosevelt felt that the United States had something at stake in preventing the outbreak of a major war. At the kaiser's behest, he talked the French and British into attending an international conference at Algeciras, Spain, with American delegates present. Roosevelt then maneuvered the Germans into accepting his lead.

The Act of Algeciras, signed in 1906, affirmed the independence of Morocco and guaranteed an open door for trade there, but provided for the training and control of Moroccan police by France and Spain. The United States Senate ratified the agreement, but only with the proviso that it was not to be construed as a departure from America's traditional policy of noninvolvement in European affairs. It was a departure, of course, and one that may well have prevented a general war, or at least postponed it until 1914. Roosevelt received the Nobel Peace Prize in 1906 for his work at Portsmouth and Algeciras. For all his bellicosity on other occasions, he had earned it.

Before Roosevelt left the White House, he celebrated America's rise to world power with one great flourish. In 1907 he sent the entire fleet of the United States navy, by then second in strength only to the British, on a grand tour around the world, their commander announcing he was ready for "a feast, a frolic, or a fight." He got mostly the first two, and none of the last. At every port of call the "Great White Fleet" set off rousing celebrations, down the Atlantic coast of South America, up the West Coast, out to Hawaii, and down to New Zealand and Australia. It was the first such show of American naval might in the Pacific, and many feared the reaction of the Japanese, for whose benefit Roosevelt had in fact staged the show. They need not have worried, for in Japan the flotilla got the greatest welcome of all. Thousands of schoolchildren turned out waving tiny American flags and singing "The Star-Spangled Banner" in English. The triumphal procession continued home by way of the Mediterranean and steamed back into American waters in 1909, just in time to close out Roosevelt's presidency on a note of success.

But it was a success that would have mixed consequences. As one insightful student of Roosevelt's role in America's rise to world power wrote: "One comes away from the study with admiration for Roosevelt's ability, his energy, and his devotion to his country's interests as he saw them but with a sense of tragedy that his abilities were turned toward imperialism and an urge for power, which were to have consequences so serious for the future." Roosevelt had influenced the United States "in a direction that . . . was to bring her face to face with grave dangers" before the mid–twentieth century.

MAKING CONNECTIONS

- The Spanish-American War marked a turning point in American foreign policy. America's emergence as a global power is a central theme in the twentieth century.

- Theodore Roosevelt's foreign policy displayed an activist approach to the presidency. In the next chapter, we see the connections between his foreign policies and his approach to domestic affairs.

FURTHER READING

An excellent survey of the diplomacy of the era is Charles Campbell's *The Transformation of American Foreign Relations, 1865–1900* (1976). For background to the events of the 1890s, see Walter LeFeber's *The American Search for Opportunity, 1865–1913* (1993) and David Healy's *U. S. Expansionism: The Imperialist Urge in the 1890s* (1970). The dispute over American policy concerning Hawaii is covered in

Thomas J. Osborne's *"Empire Can Wait": American Opposition to Hawaiian Annexation, 1893–1898* (1981).

Ivan Musicant's *Empire by Default: The Spanish-American War and the Dawn of the American Century* (1998) is the most comprehensive volume on the conflict. Frank Freidel's *The Splendid Little War* (1958) shows what the war was like for those who fought it. Gerald F. Linderman's *The Mirror of War: American Society and the Spanish-American War* (1974) discusses the war at home. For the war's aftermath in the Philippines, see Stuart C. Miller's *"Benevolent Assimilation": American Conquest of the Philippines, 1899–1903* (1982). Robert L. Beisner's *Twelve Against Empire: The Anti-Imperialists, 1898– 1900* (1985) handles the debate over annexation.

A good introduction to American interest in China is Michael H. Hunt's *The Making of a Special Relationship: The United States and China to 1914* (1983). Also useful is Marilyn B. Young's *The Rhetoric of Empire: America's China Policy, 1893–1901* (1968). Kenton J. Clymer's *John Hay: The Gentleman as Diplomat* (1975) examines the role of this key secretary of state in forming policy.

For American policy in the Caribbean and Central America, see Walter LeFeber's *Inevitable Revolutions: The United States in Central America* (1983) and Bruce J. Calder's *The Impact of Intervention: The Dominican Republic During the U.S. Occupation of 1916–1924* (1984). David McCullough's *The Path between the Seas: The Creation of the Panama Canal, 1870–1914* (1977) presents the fullest account of how the United States secured the Panama Canal.

24 ⌘ THE PROGRESSIVE ERA

CHAPTER ORGANIZER

This chapter focuses on:

- the social bases of progressivism.

- the basic elements of progressive reform.

- the presidencies of Theodore Roosevelt, William H. Taft, and Woodrow Wilson.

- the significance of the election of 1912.

heodore Roosevelt's emergence as a national leader coincided with the onset of what historians have labeled the Progressive Era (1900–1917). The rise of the so-called Progressive movement had many causes, the most powerful of which was the devastating depression of the 1890s and its attendant social unrest. The depression brought hard times to the cities and provoked both the fears and consciences of the rapidly growing middle and upper-middle classes. By the turn of the century, so many activists were at work seeking to improve social conditions that people began to speak of a "Progressive Era," a time of fermenting idealism and constructive social, economic, and political change.

ELEMENTS OF REFORM

Progressivism was a reform movement so varied and comprehensive it almost defies definition. The progressives saw themselves as engaged in a crusade against the abuses of urban political bosses and corporate robber barons. Their goals were greater democracy and social justice, honest government, more effective regulation of business, and a revived commitment to public service. They believed that the scope of local, state, and federal government authority should be expanded to accomplish these goals. Doing so, they hoped, would ensure the "progress" of American society. The "real heart of the movement," declared one self-described progressive reformer, was "to use the government as an agency of human welfare."

But the Kansas editor William Allen White hinted at a paradox in the movement when he called progressivism just populism that had "shaved its whiskers, washed its shirt, put on a derby, and moved up into the middle class." As White suggested, urban business and professional leaders brought to progressivism a certain respectability and political savvy that the Populists had lacked. They also brought a more businesslike, efficient approach to reform. While one strand in the varied fabric of progressivism retained the resonant appeal of agrarian democracy and its antitrust traditions, a new emphasis on efficiency soon gained ascendancy.

Another paradox in the movement was that it contained an element of conservatism. In some cases, the regulation of business turned out actually to be regulation proposed *by* business leaders who preferred regulated stability to the chaos and uncertainty of unrestrained competition. Much like the reform spirit of the 1830s and 1840s, once called Jacksonian Democracy, progressivism was diverse in both origins and tendencies. Few people adhered to all of the varied progressive causes.

What reformers shared was a common assumption that the complex social ills and tensions generated by the urban-industrial revolution required new responses. Governments were now called upon to extend a broad range of direct services: schools, good roads (a movement propelled first by cyclists and then by automobilists), conservation, public health and welfare, care of the handicapped, farm loans and demonstration agents, among other things. Such initiatives represented the first tentative steps toward what would become known during the 1930s and after as the welfare state.

ANTECEDENTS TO PROGRESSIVISM   Populism was indisputably one of the catalysts of progressivism. The Populist platform of 1892 outlined many reforms that would be accomplished in the Progressive Era. Many Populists, in addition, believed that their movement achieved vindication in the Progressive Era. Editor William Allen White wrote that populism "was the beginning of a movement that in another decade was to change the politics of the nation: indeed it was a symptom of a worldwide drift to liberalism, which reached its peak . . . twenty-five years later."

After the collapse of the farmers' movement and the revival of the agricultural sector at the turn of the century, the focus of the reform spirit shifted to cities, where middle-class activists had for years attacked the problems of political bossism and urban development. The Mugwumps, those gentlemen reformers who had fought the spoils system and promoted a civil service based on merit, supplied the Progressive movement with an important element of its thinking, the honest-government ideal. Over the years, their ranks had been supplemented and the honest-government outlook broadened by leaders who confronted such new urban problems as crime, vice, and the efficient provision of gas, electricity, water, sewers, mass transit, and garbage collection.

Finally, another significant force in fostering the spirit of progressivism was the growing familiarity with socialist doctrines and their critiques of living and working conditions. The Socialist party of the time served as the left wing of progressivism. Still, most progressives found socialist remedies unacceptable, and the progressive reform impulse grew in part from a desire to counter the growing influence of socialist doctrines. More important in spurring progressive reform were social critics who dramatized the need for reform.

THE MUCKRAKERS   The writers who thrived on exposing scandal got their name when Theodore Roosevelt compared them to a character in John Bunyan's *Pilgrim's Progress:* "A man that could look no way but downwards with a muckrake in his hands." The "muckrakers are often

Lincoln Steffens, whose muckraking articles on municipal corruption were collected in the book The Shame of the Cities.

indispensable to . . . society," Roosevelt said, "but only if they know when to stop raking the muck."

Henry Demarest Lloyd is sometimes cited as the first of the muckrakers for his critical examination of the Standard Oil Company and other monopolies, *Wealth against Commonwealth* (1894). Lloyd exposed the growth of corporate giants responsible to none but themselves, able to corrupt if not control governments. Another early muckraker was Jacob Riis, a Danish immigrant who, as an influential New York journalist, exposed slum conditions in *How the Other Half Lives* (1890). The chief outlets for these social critics were the inexpensive popular magazines that began to flourish in the 1890s, such as the *Arena* and *McClure's* magazine, founded in 1893 by Samuel S. McClure, an Irish immigrant who had begun the first newspaper syndicate in the country.

The golden age of muckraking is sometimes dated from 1902 when *McClure's* began to run articles by the reporter Lincoln Steffens on municipal corruption, later collected into a book: *The Shame of the Cities* (1904). *McClure's* also ran Ida M. Tarbell's *History of the Standard Oil Company* (1904). Tarbell provided a more detailed treatment than the earlier book by Lloyd, but it was all the more damaging in its detail. Other outstanding books that began as magazine articles exposed corruption in the stock market, the meat industry, the life insurance business, and the political world.

Without the muckrakers, progressivism surely would never have achieved the popular support it had. In feeding the public's appetite for facts about their new urban-industrial society, the muckrakers demonstrated one of the salient features of the Progressive movement, and one of its central failures. The progressives were stronger on diagnosis than on remedy. They professed a naive faith in the power of democracy. Let the people know, expose corruption, and bring government close to the people, went the rationale, and the correction of evils would follow automatically. The cure for the ills of democracy, it seemed, was more democracy.

THE FEATURES OF PROGRESSIVISM

DEMOCRACY The most important reform with which the progressives tried to democratize government was the direct primary, or the nomination of candidates by the vote of party members. Under the existing convention system, only a small proportion of the voters attended the local caucuses or precinct meetings that sent delegates to county, and in turn to state and national, conventions. While the system allowed seasoned leaders to sift the candidates, it also lent itself to domination by political professionals who were able to come early and stay late. Direct primaries at the local level had been held sporadically since the 1870s, but after South Carolina adopted the first statewide primary in 1896, the movement spread within two decades to nearly every state.

The primary was but one expression of a broad movement for direct democracy. In 1898 South Dakota became the first state to adopt the initiative and referendum, procedures that allowed voters to enact laws directly. If a designated number of voters petitioned to have a measure put on the ballot (the initiative), the electorate could then vote it up or down (the referendum). Oregon adopted a whole spectrum of reform measures, including a voter registration law (1899); the initiative and referendum (1902); the direct primary (1904); a sweeping corrupt-practices act (1908); and the recall (1910), whereby public officials could be removed by petition and vote. Within a decade nearly twenty states had adopted the initiative and referendum and nearly a dozen the recall.

Most states adopted the party primary even in the choice of United States senators. Nevada was first, in 1899, to let voters express a choice that state legislators of their party were expected to follow in choosing senators. The popular election of senators required a constitutional amendment, and the House of Representatives, beginning in 1894, four times adopted such an amendment, only to see it defeated in the Senate, which came under increasing attack as a "millionaire's club." By 1912 thirty states had provided preferential primaries. The Senate in that year finally accepted the inevitable and agreed to the Seventeenth Amendment, authorizing popular election of senators. The amendment was ratified in 1913.

EFFICIENCY   A second major theme of progressivism was the "gospel of efficiency." In the business world during those years, Frederick W. Taylor, the original "efficiency expert," was developing the techniques he summed up in his book *The Principles of Scientific Management* (1911): efficient management of time and costs, the proper routing and scheduling of work, standardization of tools and equipment, and the like. "Taylorism," as scientific management came to be known, promised to reduce waste through the careful analysis of labor processes. By breaking down the production process into separate steps and by metic-

Poster to encourage on-the-job productivity, 1920s. With a series of posters, the Mather Poster Company aimed to keep workers focused, productive, and loyal.

WHY ROB YOURSELF?

Taking two hours to do an hour's task robs you of an hour's results

Results Win Progress for You

ulously studying the time it took each worker to perform a task, Taylor sought to discover the optimum technique for the average worker and establish performance standards for each job classification. The promise of higher wages, he believed, would motivate workers to exceed the "average" expectations.

As they incorporated Taylor's theories and "time-motion studies" into their operations, American manufacturers highlighted the quest for efficiency and order that characterized the Progressive Era. But many workers resented Taylor's innovations. They saw in scientific management a tool for employers to make them work faster than was healthy or fair. Yet Taylor's system brought concrete improvements in productivity—especially among those industries whose production processes were highly standardized and where jobs were rigidly defined. "In the future," Taylor predicted in 1911, "the system [rather than the individual workers] will be first."

In government, the efficiency movement demanded the reorganization of agencies to prevent overlapping, to establish clear lines of authority, and to fix responsibility. One long-held theory had it that the greater the number of offices chosen by popular vote, the greater the degree of democracy, but progressives considered this inefficient. They believed that voters could make wiser choices if they had a shorter ballot and chose fewer officials in whom power and responsibility were clearly lodged.

Two new ideas for making municipal government more efficient gained headway in the first decade of the new century. The commission system, first adopted by Galveston, Texas, in 1901, when local government there collapsed in the aftermath of a devastating hurricane and tidal wave, placed ultimate authority in a board composed of elected administrative heads of city departments—commissioners of sanitation, police, utilities, and so on. The more durable idea, however, was the city-manager plan, under which a professional administrator ran the government in accordance with policies set by the elected council and mayor. Staunton, Virginia, first adopted the plan in 1908. By 1914 the National Association of City Managers heralded the arrival of a new profession.

When America was a pre-industrial society, Andrew Jackson's notion that any reasonably intelligent citizen could perform the duties of any public office may have been true. In the more complex age of the early

Robert M. La Follette.

twentieth century it was apparent that many functions of government and business had come to require expert specialists. This principle was promoted by Governor Robert M. La Follette of Wisconsin, who advocated progressivism and established a Legislative Reference Bureau to provide research, advice, and help in the drafting of legislation. The "Wisconsin Idea" of efficient government was widely publicized and copied. La Follette also worked for such reforms as the primary, stronger railroad regulation, the conservation of natural resources, and workmen's compensation.

Born in a log cabin and educated at the University of Wisconsin, the short, muscular La Follette possessed an abiding faith in grassroots democracy, in the power and judgment of the people. He was more enlightened about modern trends than William Jennings Bryan, and equally intense, sincere, and determined. He was also Bryan's equal as an orator; La Follette could talk for hours without taxing himself or his listeners.

Progressive counterparts to La Follette also appeared in other states. As counsel to a legislative committee in New York, Charles Evans Hughes became a national figure by uncovering spectacular insurance frauds and won the New York governorship in 1906. Voters in Georgia and Alabama that year elected governors who promised to regulate the railroads. Hiram Johnson, after getting a conviction of the grafting boss of San Francisco in 1908, won the California governorship in 1910 on the promise of reining in the Southern Pacific Railroad.

REGULATION   Of all the problems facing American society at the turn of the century, one engaged a greater diversity of reformers, and elicited more—and more controversial—solutions than any other: the regulation of giant corporations, which became a third major theme of progressivism. Concern over the concentration of economic power had brought bipartisan support to the passage of the Sherman Anti-Trust Act in 1890, but the act had turned out to be more symbolic than effective.

The problem of economic power and its abuse offered a dilemma for progressives. Four broad solutions were available, but of these, two were extremes that had limited support: letting business work out its own destiny under a policy of laissez-faire, or adopting a socialist program of public ownership. At the municipal level, however, the socialist alternative was rather widely adopted in public utilities and transportation—so-called gas and water socialism—but otherwise was not seriously considered as a general policy. The other choices were either to adopt a policy of trust-busting in the belief that restoring old-fashioned competition would best prevent economic abuses, or to accept big business in the belief that it brought economies of scale, but to regulate it to prevent abuses.

Efforts to restore the competition of small firms proved unworkable, partly because breaking up large combinations was complex and difficult. The trend over the years was toward regulation rather than dissolution of big business. To some extent regulation and "stabilization" won acceptance among businessmen who, whatever respect they paid to competition in the abstract, preferred not to face it in practice. As time passed, however, regulatory agencies often came under the influence or control of those they were supposed to regulate. Railroad men, for instance, generally had more intimate knowledge of the intricate details involved in their business, giving them the advantage over the outsiders who might be appointed to the Interstate Commerce Commission.

SOCIAL JUSTICE   A fourth important feature of the progressive spirit was the impulse toward social justice, which motivated diverse ac-

Kohinore Mine, Pennsylvania, 1891. Child labor was rampant until the progressive National Child Labor Committee spearheaded a movement to prohibit employing young children.

tions—from private charities to campaigns against child labor and liquor. The settlement house movement of the late nineteenth century had spawned a corps of social workers and genteel reformers devoted to the uplift of slum dwellers. But with time it became apparent that social evils extended beyond the reach of private charities and demanded the power of the state.

Labor legislation was perhaps the most significant reform to emerge from the drive for social justice. The National Child Labor Committee, organized in 1904, led a movement for laws banning the still widespread employment of young children. Through publicity, the organization of state and local committees, and a telling documentation of the evils of child labor by the photographer Lewis W. Hine, the committee within ten years brought about legislation in most states banning the labor of underage children (the minimum age varied from twelve to sixteen) and limiting the working hours of older children.

Closely linked with the child-labor reform movement was a concerted effort to regulate the hours of work for women. Spearheaded by Florence Kelley, the head of the National Consumers League, this pro-

Triangle Shirtwaist Company Fire, New York City, 1911.

gressive crusade prompted the passage of state laws to ameliorate the distinctive hardships that long working hours imposed on women who were wives and mothers. Many states also outlawed night work and labor in dangerous occupations for both women and children. But numerous exemptions and inadequate enforcement often virtually nullified the laws.

The Supreme Court pursued a curiously erratic course in ruling on state labor laws. It upheld a Utah law limiting the working day in mining and smelting to eight hours as a proper exercise of the state police power to protect the health and safety of workers. In *Lochner v. New York* (1905), however, the Court voided a ten-hour day because it violated workers' "liberty of contract" to accept any terms they chose. But in *Muller v. Oregon* (1908), the high court upheld a ten-hour law for women largely on the basis of sociological data regarding the effects of long hours on the health and morals of women. In *Bunting v. Oregon* (1917), the Court accepted a ten-hour day for both men and women, but held out for twenty more years against state minimum-wage laws.

Legislation to protect workers against avoidable accidents gained impetus from disasters such as the 1911 fire at the Triangle Shirtwaist

Company in New York in which 146 people, mostly women, died for want of adequate exits. They either were trapped on the three upper floors of a ten-story building, or they plunged to the street below. Stricter building codes and factory inspection acts followed. One of the most important advances along these lines was the series of workers' compensation laws enacted after Maryland led the way in 1902. Accident insurance systems replaced the old common-law principle that an injured worker was entitled to compensation only if he could prove employer negligence, a costly and capricious procedure from which the worker was likely to win nothing or, as often happened, excessive awards from overly sympathetic juries.

PROHIBITION   For many progressive activists the cause of liquor prohibition was a fifth area for action. Opposition to strong drink was an ideal cause in which to merge the older private ethics with the new social ethics. Given the moral disrepute of saloons, prohibitionists could equate the "liquor traffic" with progressive suspicion of bossism and "special interests." When reform pressures mounted, prohibition offered an easy outlet, bypassing the complexities of corporate regulation.

A temperance meeting in Kansas, late nineteenth century.

The battle against booze dated far back into the nineteenth century. The Women's Christian Temperance Union had promoted the cause since 1874, and a Prohibition political party had entered the elections in 1876. But the most successful political action followed the formation in 1893 of the Anti-Saloon League, an organization that pioneered the strategy of the single-issue pressure group. Through its singleness of purpose, it forced the prohibition issue into the forefront of state and local elections. At its "Jubilee Convention" in 1913 the Anti-Saloon League endorsed a prohibition amendment to the Constitution, adopted by Congress that year. By the time it was ratified six years later, state and local action already had dried up areas occupied by nearly three-fourths of the nation's population.

Roosevelt's Progressivism

Theodore Roosevelt adopted a cautious version of progressive reform. He cultivated party leaders in Congress, and he steered away from such political thickets as the tariff and banking issues. When he did approach the explosive issue of the trusts, he always took care to reassure the business community. For him, politics was the art of the possible. Unlike the more advanced progressives and the doctrinaire "lunatic fringe," as he called them, he would take half a loaf rather than none at all. Roosevelt acted in large part out of the conviction that reform was needed to keep things on an even keel. He believed that control should rest in the hands of sensible Republicans, and not with irresponsible Democrats or, worse, the growing socialist movement.

EXECUTIVE ACTION   At the outset of his presidency in 1901, Roosevelt took up McKinley's policies and promised to sustain them. He worked with Republican leaders in Congress, against whom the minority of new progressives was as yet powerless. Yet Roosevelt would accomplish more by vigorous executive action than by passing legislation, and in the exercise of executive power he would not be inhibited by points of legal detail. He argued that, as president, he might do anything not expressly forbidden by the Constitution.

Caution suffused Roosevelt's first annual message, delivered in 1901, but he felt impelled to take up the trust problem in the belief that it might be more risky to ignore it. His message carefully balanced argu-

No Lack of Big Game.
A 1905 cartoon shows
Roosevelt going after the
trusts.

ments on both sides of the question. He endorsed the "sincere conviction that combination and concentration should be, not prohibited, but supervised and within reasonable limits controlled." The first essential was "knowledge of the facts—publicity . . . the only sure remedy we can now invoke." Later would follow regulatory legislation, perhaps based on the experience of the Interstate Commerce Commission (ICC).

In 1902 Roosevelt carried the trust issue to the people on a tour of New England and the Midwest. He endorsed a "square deal" for all, calling for enforcement of existing antitrust laws and stricter controls on big business. From the outset, however, Roosevelt believed that wholesale trust-busting was wrongheaded. Effective regulation was better than a futile effort to restore small business, which might be achieved only at a cost to the efficiencies of scale gained in larger operations.

Because Congress boggled at regulatory legislation, Roosevelt sought to force the issue by a more vigorous prosecution of the Sherman Anti-Trust Act. He chose his target carefully. In the case against the sugar trust (*United States* v. *E. C. Knight and Company,* 1895), the Supreme Court had declared manufacturing a strictly intrastate activity. Railroads, however, were beyond question engaged in interstate commerce and thus subject to federal authority.

In 1902 Roosevelt ordered his attorney-general to move against the Northern Securities Company, a firm vulnerable to both the law and public opinion. That company, formed the previous year, had taken shape during a gigantic battle between E. H. Harriman of the Union Pacific and James J. Hill and J. P. Morgan of the Great Northern and Northern Pacific for the stock of the Northern Pacific, which was crucial to shipping in the Northwest. The stock battle raised the threat of a panic on the New York Stock Exchange and led to a settlement in which the chief contenders made peace. They formed Northern Securities as a holding company to control the Great Northern and Northern Pacific. In 1904 the Supreme Court ordered the railroad combination dissolved.

THE COAL STRIKE   Support for Roosevelt's use of the "big stick" against corporations was strengthened by the stubbornness of mine owners in the anthracite coal strike of 1902. On May 12 the United Mine Workers (UMW) walked off the job in Pennsylvania and West Virginia, demanding a 20 percent wage increase, a reduction in daily hours from ten to nine, and official union recognition. The mine operators, having granted a 10 percent raise two years before, dug in their heels against further concessions, and shut down in preparation for a long struggle to starve out the miners. Their spokesman, George F. Baer, the president of the Reading Railroad, helped the union cause more than his own with an arrogant pronouncement: "The rights and interests of the laboring man will be protected and cared for," he said, "not by the labor agitators, but by the Christian men to whom God in his infinite wisdom has given control of the property interests of the country."

Facing the prospect of a nationwide coal shortage, Roosevelt called a conference at the White House. The mine owners, led by Baer, attended but refused even to speak to the UMW leaders. The "extraordinary stupidity and temper" of the "wooden-headed" owners outraged Roosevelt. The president wanted to grab Baer "by the seat of his breeches" and "chuck him out" a White House window. After the conference ended in an impasse, Roosevelt threatened to take over the mines and run them with the army. When a congressman questioned the constitutionality of such a move, an exasperated Roosevelt roared: "To hell with the Constitution when the people want coal!" Militarizing the mines would have been an act of dubious legality, but the owners feared that Roosevelt might actually do it and that public opinion would support him.

The coal strike ended in October 1902 with an agreement to submit the issues to an arbitration commission named by the president. The agreement enhanced Roosevelt's prestige, although it produced only a partial victory for the miners. By the arbitrators' decision in 1903, the miners won a nine-hour day but only a 10 percent wage increase, and no union recognition.

TOWARD A SECOND TERM   Roosevelt continued to use his executive powers to enforce the Sherman Anti-Trust Act, but he drew back from further antitrust legislation. Altogether his administration initiated about twenty-five antitrust suits; the most notable victory came in *Swift and Company* v. *United States* (1905), a decision against the "beef trust" through which most of the meat packers had avoided competitive bidding in the purchase of livestock. In this decision, the Supreme Court put forth the "stream-of-commerce" doctrine, which overturned its previous holding that manufacturing was strictly intrastate. Since both livestock and the meat products of the packers moved in the stream of interstate commerce, the Court reasoned, they were subject to federal regulation. This interpretation of the interstate commerce power would be broadened in later years until few enterprises would remain beyond the reach of federal regulation.

In 1903 Congress passed the Elkins Act, which made it illegal to take as well as to give rebates. In that same year, Congress created a new Bureau of Corporations to study and report on the activities of interstate corporations. Its findings could lead to antitrust suits, but its purpose was rather to help corporations correct malpractices and avoid the need for lawsuits. Many companies, among them United States Steel and International Harvester, worked closely with the bureau, but others held back. When Standard Oil refused to turn over its records, the government brought an antitrust suit that resulted in its breakup in 1911. The Supreme Court broke up the American Tobacco Company at the same time. This approach fell short of the direct regulation that Roosevelt preferred, but without a congressional will to pass such laws, little more was possible. Trusts that cooperated were left alone; others had to run the gauntlet of antitrust suits.

Theodore Roosevelt as an apostle of prosperity (top) *and as a Roman tyrant* (bottom). *Roosevelt's energy, spirit, righteousness, and impulsiveness led people to have distinct reactions to his personality.*

Roosevelt's policies built a coalition of progressive- and conservative-minded voters that assured his election in his own right in 1904. The convention chose him by acclamation. The Democrats, having lost with Bryan twice, turned to Alton B. Parker who, as chief justice of New York, had upheld labor's right to the closed shop (requiring that all employees be union members) and the state's right to limit hours of work. Despite his liberal record, party leaders presented him as a safe conservative, and his acceptance of the gold standard as "firmly and irrevocably established" bolstered such a view. The effort to present a candidate more conservative than Roosevelt proved a futile gesture for the party that had twice nominated Bryan. Despite Roosevelt's trust-busting proclivities, most businessmen, according to the *New York Sun,* preferred the "impulsive candidate of the party of conservatism to the conservative candidate of the party which the business interests regard as permanently and dangerously impulsive." Even J. P. Morgan and E. H. Harriman contributed handsomely to Roosevelt's campaign chest.

An invincible popularity plus the sheer force of his personality swept Roosevelt to an impressive victory by a popular vote of 7.6 million to 5.1 million. Parker carried only the Solid South of the former Confederacy and two border states, Kentucky and Maryland (with an electoral vote of 336 for Roosevelt and 140 for Parker). On election night, Roosevelt announced that he would not run again, a statement he later would regret.

LEGISLATIVE LEADERSHIP Elected in his own right, Roosevelt approached his second term with heightened confidence and a stronger commitment to progressive reform. In 1905 he devoted most of his annual message to the regulation and control of business. This understandably irked many of his corporate contributors. Said steel baron Henry Frick, "We bought the son of a bitch and then he did not stay put." The independent-minded Roosevelt took aim at the railroads first. The Elkins Act of 1903, finally outlawing rebates, had been a minor step. Railroad executives themselves welcomed it as an escape from shippers clamoring for special favors. But a new proposal for railroad regulation endorsed by Roosevelt was something else again. It sought to extend the authority of the ICC and give it effective control over rates.

Enacted in 1906, the Hepburn Act for the first time gave the ICC power to set maximum freight rates. The commission no longer had to go to court to enforce its decisions. While the carriers could challenge the rates in court, the burden of proof now rested on them rather than on the Interstate Commerce Commission. In other ways, too, the Hepburn Act enlarged the mandate of the ICC. Its reach now extended beyond railroads to pipelines, express companies, sleeping-car companies, bridges, and ferries, and it could prescribe a uniform system of bookkeeping to provide uniform statistics.

Railroads took priority, but a growing movement for the regulation of meat packers, food processors, and makers of drugs and patent medicines reached fruition, as it happened, on the very day after passage of the Hepburn Act. Discontent with abuses in these fields had grown rapidly as a result of the muckrakers' revelations. They supplied evidence of harmful preservatives and adulterants in the preparation of "embalmed meat" and other food products. The *Ladies' Home Journal* and *Collier's* published evidence of false claims and dangerous ingredients in patent medicines. One of the more notorious "medicines," Lydia Pinkham's Vegetable Compound, was advertised to work wonders in the relief of "female complaints"; it was no wonder, for the compound was 18 percent alcohol.

But perhaps the most telling blow against such abuses was struck by

Muckraking reports on fraudulent drugs and patent medicines, such as Lydia Pinkham's Vegetable Compound, prompted a growing movement for government regulation.

Upton Sinclair's novel *The Jungle* (1906). Sinclair meant the book to be a tract for socialism, but its main impact came from its portrayal of filthy conditions in Chicago's meat-packing industry: "It was too dark in these storage places to see well, but a man could run his hand over these piles of meat and sweep off handfuls of the dried dung of rats. These rats were nuisances, and the packers would put poisoned bread out for them, they would die, and then rats, bread, and meat would go into the hoppers together." Roosevelt read *The Jungle*—and reacted quickly. He sent two agents to Chicago, and their report confirmed all that Sinclair had said: "We saw meat shovelled from filthy wooden floors, piled on tables rarely washed, pushed from room to room in rotten box carts, in all of which processes it was in the way of gathering dirt, splinters, floor filth, and the expectoration of tuberculous and other diseased workers."

The Meat Inspection Act of 1906 required federal inspection of meats destined for interstate commerce and empowered officials in the Agriculture Department to impose sanitation standards. The Pure Food and Drug Act, enacted the same day, placed restrictions on the makers of prepared foods and patent medicines, and forbade the manufacture, sale, or transportation of adulterated, misbranded, or harmful foods, drugs, and liquors.

CONSERVATION   One of the most enduring legacies of the Roosevelt years was his energetic support for the conservation movement. Concern for protecting the environment grew with the rising awareness that exploitation of natural resources was despoiling the frontier. As early as 1872, Yellowstone National Park had been set aside as a public reserve (the National Park Service would be created in 1916 after other parks had been added). In 1881 Congress had created a Division of Forestry in the Department of Agriculture, and Roosevelt's appointment of Gifford Pinchot, one of the country's first scientific foresters, as chief brought vigorous administration of forests on public lands. The president strove to halt the unchecked destruction of the nation's natural resources and wonders by providing a barrier of federal regulation and protection. To do so, Roosevelt added fifty federal wildlife refuges, approved five new national parks, and initiated the system of designating national monuments such as the Grand Canyon. He also used the Forest Reserve Act (1891) to exclude from settlement or harvest some 172

Gifford Pinchot, chief of the Forestry Service under Roosevelt.

million acres of timberland. Lumber barons were irate, but Roosevelt held firm. As he bristled, "I hate a man who would skin the land."

Forestry chief Pinchot worked vigorously, with the president's support, to develop programs and public interest in conservation. Congressional resistance to their proposals led Pinchot and Roosevelt to publicize the cause through a White House Conference on Conservation in 1908, and later that year by setting up a National Conservation Commission, which proposed a thorough survey of resources in minerals, water, forests, and soil. Within eighteen months, some forty-one state conservation commissions had sprung up, and a number of private groups took up the cause. The movement remained divided, however, between those who wanted to conserve resources for continuous human use and those who wanted to set aside wilderness areas. Pinchot, for instance, won the enmity of naturalist John Muir in 1906 when he endorsed a water reservoir in the wild Hetch Hetchy Valley of Yosemite National Park to supply the needs of San Francisco.

FROM ROOSEVELT TO TAFT

In 1908 Roosevelt declared "I have had a great time as president" and prepared to turn over the mantle. Unlike most presidents, he was strong enough to handpick a successor to carry out "the policies." He decided that the heir to the White House should be Secretary of War William Howard Taft, and the Republican convention ratified the choice on its first ballot in 1908. The Democrats, whose conservative strategy had backfired in 1904, decided to give William Jennings Bryan one more chance at the highest office. Still vigorous at forty-eight, Bryan retained a faithful following, but once again it was not enough. Roosevelt advised Taft: "Do not answer Bryan; *attack* him. Don't let him make the issues." Taft followed Roosevelt's advice, declaring that Bryan's election would result in a "paralysis of business."

The Republican platform declared its support of Roosevelt's policies, including conservation and further strengthening of the ICC. On the tariff and the use of labor injunctions, the platform made vague references to revision but without any specifics. The Democratic platform hardly differed on regulation, but it endorsed a lower tariff and an AFL-supported plank opposing court injunctions against labor actions. In the end, the voters opted for Roosevelt's chosen successor: Taft swept the electoral college by 321 to 162. The real surprise of the election, however, was the strong showing of the Socialist party candidate, labor hero Eugene V. Debs. His 421,000 votes revealed the depth of working-class resentment in the United States.

Once out of office, still only fifty, Roosevelt went on a big-game hunt in Africa, prompting his old foe J. P. Morgan to mutter, "Let every lion do his duty." The new president he left behind was an entirely different kind of political animal, in fact hardly a political animal at all. Offspring of a family long prominent in Cincinnati—his father had been Grant's attorney-general—Taft had progressed through appointive offices, from judge in Ohio to solicitor in the Justice Department, federal judge, commissioner and governor-general in the Philippines, and secretary of war. The presidency was the only elective office he ever held. Later he would be chief justice (1921–1930), a job more suited to his temperament.

Weighing over 300 pounds, Taft had the dubious distinction of being the heaviest president in history. When he cabled a friend that he had just returned from a long horseback ride, the friend asked, "How is the horse?" Taft loved eating and playing golf or poker, but he detested politics. Taft never felt comfortable in the White House. He once observed that whenever someone said "Mr. President," he looked around for Roosevelt. The political dynamo in the family was his wife, Nellie, who had

William Howard Taft.

wanted the White House more than he. One of the major tragedies of Taft's presidency was that Helen "Nellie" Taft suffered a debilitating stroke soon after they entered the White House, and for most of his term she remained unable to serve as his political adviser.

DOLLAR DIPLOMACY In foreign affairs Taft practiced what critics labeled "dollar diplomacy." The policy had its origin in China in 1909, when President Taft personally cabled the Chinese government on behalf of American financiers interested in an international consortium to finance railroad lines in the Yangtze Valley. The American government regarded such cooperation "as best calculated to maintain the Open Door and the integrity of China." In 1911 the Americans were let in on the deal with British, French, and German capitalists, and in 1912 entered an even larger scheme to make a gigantic loan to the new Chinese Republic. Both schemes were repudiated, however, when Woodrow Wilson became president in 1913, and the American investors, lacking support from the government, withdrew.

In Latin America "dollar diplomacy" worked differently and with somewhat more success. The idea was to encourage American bankers to help prop up the finances of shaky governments in the Caribbean region. In 1910 the administration got several lenders to invest in the national bank of Haiti. In 1911 it signed treaties with Nicaragua and Honduras providing them with private loans to bolster their treasuries and ensuring payment by installing American collectors of customs. The Senate refused to go along with the treaties, but the administration continued its private appeals for American bankers to assume debts in the region.

In 1912, however, when the Nicaraguan president asked for help in putting down disorders, American marines entered the country. An American collector of customs was then installed and the government was placed on a monthly allowance doled out by a commission of two Americans and one Nicaraguan. American forces stayed until 1925, then returned in 1926 to stay until 1933. Similar forcible interventions occurred in Haiti in 1915 and the Dominican Republic in 1916.

TARIFF REFORM Taft's domestic policies generated a storm of controversy within his own party. Contrary to Republican tradition, he preferred a lower tariff, and he made this the first important issue of his presidency. But if in pressing an issue that Roosevelt had skirted Taft seemed the bolder of the two, he proved the less adroit.

A tariff bill passed the House with surprising ease. It lowered rates less than Taft would have preferred but made some important reductions and enlarged the free list. But the chairman of the Senate Finance Committee, Nelson W. Aldrich, guided through a bill drastically revised by more than 800 changes. What came out of a conference committee was a measure close to the final Senate version, although Taft did get some reductions on important items: hides, iron ore, coal, oil, cottons, boots, and shoes.

In response to the higher rates in Aldrich's bill, a group of midwestern Republicans took the Senate floor to fight what they considered a corrupt throwback to the days when the Republican party had served big business unquestioningly. In all, ten progressive Republicans joined the Democrats in an unsuccessful effort to defeat the bill. Taft at first agreed with them; then, fearful of a party split, he backed the majority and agreed to an imperfect bill. He lacked Roosevelt's love of a grand battle as well as his gift for working both sides of the street. Temperamentally conservative, inhibited by scruples about interfering too much with the legislative process, he drifted into the orbit of the Republican Old Guard and quickly alienated the progressive wing of his party, whom he tagged "assistant Democrats." He made things worse by labeling the new bill the best tariff the Republican party had ever passed.

BALLINGER AND PINCHOT In 1910 Taft's policies drove the wedge deeper between the Republican factions. What came to be called the Ballinger-Pinchot controversy made Taft appear to be a less reliable custodian of Roosevelt's conservation policies than he actually was. Taft's secretary of the interior, Richard A. Ballinger of Seattle, was well aware that many westerners opposed conservation programs on the ground that they held back full development of the region. The strongest conservation leaders were often easterners such as Roosevelt and Gifford Pinchot of Pennsylvania. Ballinger threw open to commercial use more than a million acres of waterpower sites that Roosevelt had withdrawn in the guise of ranger stations. Ballinger's reasoning was that the withdrawal had "gone far beyond legal limitations," and Taft agreed. At about the same time, Ballinger turned over certain coal lands in Alaska to a group of Seattle men, some of whom he had represented as a lawyer. Apparently without Ballinger's knowledge, this group had already agreed to sell part of the lands to a banking syndicate.

This was too much for one investigator with the General Land Office, who went to Chief of Forestry Pinchot with evidence of the collusion. Pinchot in turn called it to the attention of Taft, who then fired the investigator for his pains. When Pinchot went public with the controversy, he in turn was fired for insubordination early in 1910. A joint congressional investigation exonerated Ballinger from all charges of fraud or corruption, but progressive suspicions created such pressure that he resigned in 1911.

In firing Pinchot, Taft acted on the strictly legal view that his training had taught him to value, but circumstances tarnished his image in the public mind. "In the end," one historian has written, "the Ballinger-Pinchot affair had more impact on politics than it did on conservation." Taft had been elected to carry out the Roosevelt policies, his opponents said, and he was carrying them out—"on a stretcher."

Meanwhile, in the House of Representatives rebellion had broken out among the more progressive Republicans. When the regular session opened in 1910, the insurgents joined Democrats in voting to investigate Ballinger. Flushed with that victory, they resolved to clip the wings of Speaker Joseph G. Cannon (R-Ill.), a conservative who held almost a stranglehold on procedures by his power to appoint all committees and their chairmen, and especially by his control of the Rules Committee, of which he was a member. A coalition of Democrats and progressive Republicans overrode a ruling from the Speaker and proceeded to adopt new rules offered by George W. Norris (R-Neb.) that enlarged the Rules Committee from five to fifteen members, made them elective by the House, and excluded the Speaker as a member. About forty Republicans joined the Democratic minority in the move. In the next Congress the rules would be further changed to make all committees elective.

Events had conspired to cast Taft in a conservative role at a time when progressive sentiment was riding high in the country. The result was a severe rebuke to the president in the congressional elections of 1910, first by the widespread defeat of pro-Taft candidates in the Republican primaries, then by the election of a Democratic majority in the House and of enough Democrats in the Senate that progressive Republicans could wield the balance of power.

TAFT AND ROOSEVELT   In 1910 Roosevelt had returned from his travel abroad. He had been reading news accounts and letters about the Taft "betrayal," but unlike some of his supporters, he refused to break with his successor. With rather severe politeness, however, Roosevelt refused an invitation to visit the White House. But, he wrote Taft: "I shall keep my mind open as I keep my mouth shut." Neither was easy for Roosevelt, whose followers urged him to action. Soon he was rallying support for the Republican gubernatorial candidate in New York, and then he was off on a speaking tour of the West in advance of the congressional elections. In Kansas, he gave a catchy name to his latest principles, the "New Nationalism." Roosevelt issued a stirring call for an array of new federal regulatory laws, a social-welfare program, and new measures of direct democracy, including the old Populist demands for the initiative, recall, and referendum. His purpose was not to revolutionize American life but to save it from the threat of revolution. "What I have advocated," he explained a few days later, "is not wild radicalism. It is the highest and wisest kind of conservatism."

Relations between Roosevelt and Taft remained tense, but it was another year before they came to an open break. It happened in the fall of 1911, when the Taft administration announced an antitrust suit against

United States Steel, citing specifically as cause the company's acquisition of the Tennessee Coal and Iron Company in 1907, a move to which Roosevelt had given tacit approval in the belief that it would avert a panic. In mid-November Roosevelt published a sharp attack on Taft's "archaic" attempt to restore competition. The only sensible response to the problem, he argued, was to accept business combinations under modern circumstances but to enlarge the government's power to regulate them. Roosevelt's entry into the next presidential campaign was now only a matter of time.

Not all progressive Republicans wanted Roosevelt back in the White House. A sizable number proposed to back Senator Robert La Follette in 1912, but some of La Follette's supporters were ready to switch if Roosevelt entered the race. An opening came on February 2, 1912, when La Follette betrayed signs of nervous exhaustion in a rambling speech in Philadelphia. As his following began to drop away, a group of seven Republican governors met in Chicago and called on Roosevelt to become a candidate. On February 24 Roosevelt decided to enter the race. "I hope that so far as possible the people may be given the chance, through direct primaries," Roosevelt wrote the governors, "to express their preference." He had decided that Taft had "sold the Square Deal down the river." He now dismissed Taft as a "hopeless fathead."

The rebuke implicit in Roosevelt's decision to run against Taft, his chosen successor, was in many ways undeserved. During Taft's first year in office one political tempest after another left his image irreparably damaged. The three years of solid achievement that followed came too late to restore its luster or to reunite his divided party. Taft had at least attempted tariff reform, which Roosevelt had never dared. He replaced Ballinger and Pinchot with men of impeccable credentials in conservation matters. He won from Congress the power to protect public lands for any reason, and was the first president to withdraw oil lands from use. Under the Appalachian Forest Reserve Act (1911), he enlarged the national forest by purchase of lands in the East. In the end his administration withdrew more public lands in four years than Roosevelt's had in nearly eight, and brought more antitrust suits, by a score of eighty to twenty-five.

In 1910, with Taft's support, Congress passed the Mann-Elkins Act, which empowered the ICC for the first time to initiate rate changes, extended regulation to telephone and telegraph companies, and set up a

Commerce Court to expedite appeals from the ICC rulings. Taft also established the Bureau of Mines and the Federal Children's Bureau (1912), and he called for statehood for Arizona and New Mexico and territorial government for Alaska (1912). The Sixteenth Amendment (1913), authorizing a federal income tax, was ratified with Taft's support before he left office, and the Seventeenth Amendment (1913), providing for the popular election of senators, was ratified soon after he left office.

Despite this record, Roosevelt now hastened Taft's demise. In all but two of the thirteen states that held presidential primaries, Roosevelt won, even in Taft's Ohio. But the groundswell of popular support was no match for Taft's decisive position as president and party leader. In state conventions the party regulars held the line, so that Roosevelt entered the Republican national convention about 100 votes short of victory. The Taft forces proceeded to nominate their man by the same "steamroller" tactics that had nominated Roosevelt in 1904.

Outraged at such "naked theft," the Roosevelt delegates assembled in a rump convention. "If you wish me to make the fight I will make it," Roosevelt told the delegates, who then issued a call for a Progressive party convention, which assembled in Chicago on August 5. Roosevelt appeared, feeling "fit as a bull moose." He was "stripped to the buff and

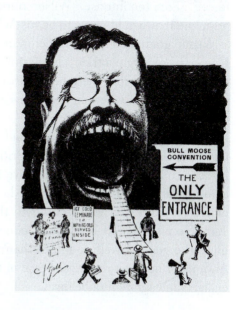

A skeptical view of Roosevelt, the Bull Moose candidate in 1912.

ready for the fight," he said. "We stand at Armageddon and we battle for the Lord." But few professional politicians turned up. Progressive Republicans decided to preserve their party credentials and fight another day. For the time being, with the disruption of the Republican party, the progressive torch was about to be passed on to the Democrats.

WILSON'S PROGRESSIVISM

WILSON'S RISE   The emergence of Thomas Woodrow Wilson as the Democratic nominee climaxed a political rise even more rapid than that of Grover Cleveland. In 1910, before his nomination and election as governor of New Jersey, Wilson had been president of Princeton University, but he had never run for public office. Born in Staunton, Virginia, in 1856, the son of a "noble-saintly mother" and a stern Presbyterian minister, he had grown up in Georgia and the Carolinas during the Civil War and Reconstruction.

Young Wilson, tall, slender, with a lean, long, sharply chiseled face, inherited his father's unquestioning piety, once declaring that "so far as religion is concerned, argument is adjourned." Wilson also developed a consuming ambition to "serve" humankind. Driven by a sense of destiny and duty, as well as by a certain moral fastidiousness, he once confessed: "I am too intense." Wilson nurtured a righteous commitment to principle that would prove to be his Achilles' heel.

Wilson graduated from Princeton in 1879, and after law school at the University of Virginia tried a brief, unfulfilling, and profitless legal practice in Atlanta. From there he went to the new Johns Hopkins University in Baltimore, where he found his calling in the study of history and political science.

Wilson's dissertation, *Congressional Government,* published in 1885, argued that the president, like the British prime minister, should be the leader of party government, as active in directing legislation as in the administration and enforcement of laws. In calling for a strong presidency he expressed views closer to those of Roosevelt than those of Taft. He also shared Roosevelt's concern that politicians should promote the general welfare rather than narrowly serve special interests. And, like Roosevelt, he was critical of big business, organized labor, socialists, and agrarian radicalism.

After Johns Hopkins, Wilson taught at Bryn Mawr and then Wesleyan College before moving to Princeton in 1890. There he quickly earned renown for his scintillating lectures, vigorous mind, and sharp debating skills. In 1902 he was unanimously elected president of the university. In that position he showed the first evidence of reform views. "We are not put into this world to sit still and know," he stressed in his inaugural address. "We are put into it to act." And act he did.

At Princeton Wilson modernized the curriculum, expanded and improved the faculty, introduced the tutorial system, and raised admissions standards. But he failed in his attempts to restructure the social life of Princeton undergraduates and to integrate the new graduate school with the university. He believed that the deeply entrenched system of campus eating clubs (similar to fraternities) was undemocratic, anti-intellectual, and divisive. Wilson proposed to replace the exclusive clubs with residential colleges, or quadrangles, where students would live under the supervision of unmarried faculty members. Unaware of the volatility of this issue, he failed to consult alumni, faculty, and trustees before announcing his intentions. The result was a firestorm of criticism that forced Wilson to withdraw his proposal. In a similar fashion, he failed to marshal a consensus for his proposals regarding the location of the new graduate school. He wanted it integrated with the undergraduate college; others wanted it completely separate. The dean opposed him and won the battle by gaining strong alumni backing. Thereafter Wilson faced a choice of giving up or leaving.

At this juncture, the Democratic boss of New Jersey offered Wilson his support for the 1910 gubernatorial nomination, and Wilson accepted. The party leaders sought a respectable candidate to ward off progressive challengers, but they discovered too late that the supposedly innocent schoolmaster actually had an iron will of his own. Like Roosevelt, Wilson had come to shed some of his original conservatism and to view progressive reform as a necessary expedient in order to stave off more radical social change. Elected as a reform candidate, Governor Wilson promoted progressive measures and pushed them through the legislature. He pressured lawmakers to enact a workers' compensation law, a corrupt-practices law, measures to regulate public utilities, and ballot reforms. Such strong leadership in a state known as the "home of the trusts" for its lenient corporation laws brought Wilson to national attention.

Wilson campaigning from a train platform.

In the spring of 1911 a group of southern Democrats in New York opened a Wilson presidential campaign headquarters, and Wilson set forth on strenuous tours into all regions of the country, denouncing special privilege and political bossism. But by convention time, despite a fast start, the Wilson campaign seemed headed for defeat by Speaker Bennett Champ Clark of Missouri, who garnered supporters among Bryanites, the Hearst newspapers, and party hacks. Clark had enough for a majority in the early ballots, but the Wilson forces combined with supporters of Oscar Underwood of Alabama to prevent a two-thirds majority. On the fourteenth ballot Bryan came over to Wilson. When the Democratic boss of Illinois deserted Clark on the forty-second ballot and the Underwood delegates went over to Wilson on the forty-sixth, he clinched the nomination.

THE ELECTION OF 1912 The 1912 campaign involved four candidates: Wilson and Taft represented the two major parties while Eugene Debs ran as a Socialist and Roosevelt headed the Progressive party ticket. No sooner did the formal campaign open than Roosevelt's candidacy almost ended. While entering a car on his way to deliver a speech in Milwaukee, he was shot by a fanatic. The bullet went through Roosevelt's overcoat, spectacles case, and folded speech, then fractured a rib before lodging just below his right lung. "Stand back, don't hurt the man," he yelled at the crowd as they mobbed the attacker. Roosevelt then demanded that he be driven to the auditorium to deliver his speech. His dramatic sense unhampered, he showed the audience his bloodstained shirt and punctured text and vowed: "It takes more than this to kill a bull moose." He apologized for his halting delivery, but completed his speech before letting doctors remove the bullet.

As the campaign developed, Taft quickly lost ground. "There are so many people in the country who don't like me," he lamented. The campaign settled down to a running debate over the competing ideologies of the two front-runners: Roosevelt's "New Nationalism" and Wilson's "New Freedom." The inchoate ideas that Roosevelt fashioned into his New Nationalism had first been presented systematically in *The Promise of American Life* (1909) by Herbert Croly, a then-obscure New York journalist. Its central point was often summarized in a useful catchphrase: Hamiltonian means to achieve Jeffersonian ends, meaning that Alexander Hamilton's program of governmental intervention, once identified with the business interests, should be used to achieve democratic and egalitarian Jeffersonian goals. The times required people to give up Jeffersonian prejudices against big government and use a strong central government to achieve democratic ends in the interest of the people.

The old nationalism had been used "by the sinister . . . special interests," Roosevelt said. His New Nationalism would enable government to achieve social justice, and more specifically to effect such reforms as graduated income and inheritance taxes, workers' compensation, regulation of the labor of women and children, and a stronger Bureau of Corporations. These and more went into the platform of the Progressive party, which called for a federal trade commission with sweeping authority over business and a tariff commission to set rates on a "scientific basis."

Before the end of his administration, Wilson would be swept into the current of New Nationalism too. But initially he adhered to the decentralizing antitrust traditions of his party. Before the start of the campaign Wilson conferred with Louis D. Brandeis, a progressive lawyer from Boston who focused Wilson's thought much as Croly had focused Roosevelt's. Brandeis's design for the New Freedom differed from Roosevelt's New Nationalism in its belief that the federal government should restore the competition among small economic units rather than regulate huge monopolies. This required a vigorous antitrust policy,

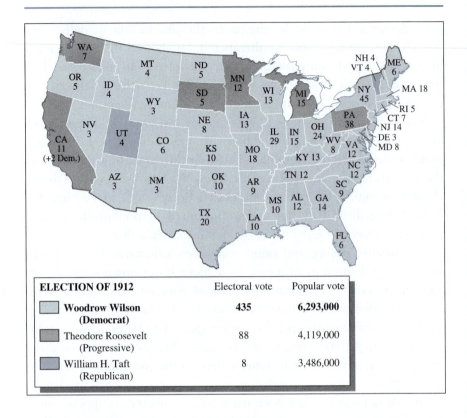

ELECTION OF 1912	Electoral vote	Popular vote
Woodrow Wilson (Democrat)	**435**	**6,293,000**
Theodore Roosevelt (Progressive)	88	4,119,000
William H. Taft (Republican)	8	3,486,000

lowering tariffs to allow competition with foreign goods, and breaking up the concentration of financial power in Wall Street. But Brandeis and Wilson saw the vigorous expansion of federal power as only a temporary necessity, not a permanent condition. Roosevelt, who was convinced that both corporate concentration and an expanding federal government were permanent developments, dismissed the New Freedom as mere fantasy.

The Republican schism between Taft and Roosevelt opened the way for Woodrow Wilson to win by 435 electoral votes to 88 for Roosevelt and 8 for Taft. But in popular votes, Wilson had only 42 percent of the total. Roosevelt received 27 percent, Taft 23 percent, and Debs 6 percent. It was the victory of a minority over a divided opposition. Taft took his loss with grace. When Yale University offered him the Kent Chair of Constitutional Law, the rotund ex-president accepted, noting, however, that a "Sofa of Law" might be more appropriate. In 1921 President

Harding appointed Taft to the Supreme Court, and he served with distinction as chief justice until his death in 1930.

The election of 1912 was significant in several ways. First, it was a high-water mark for progressivism. The election was the first to feature presidential primaries. The two leading candidates debated the basic issues of progressivism in a campaign unique for its focus on vital alternatives and for its high philosophical tone. Taft, too, despite his temperament and associations, showed his own progressive instincts. And the Socialist party, the left wing of progressivism, polled over 900,000 votes for Eugene V. Debs, its highest proportion ever.

Second, the election gave Democrats effective national power for the first time since the Civil War. For two years during the second Cleveland administration, 1893–1895, they had held the White House and majorities in both houses of Congress, but they had fallen quickly out of power during the most severe depression in American history to that time. Now, under Wilson, they again held the presidency and were the majority in both the House of Representatives and the Senate.

Third, the election of Wilson brought southerners back into the orbit of national and international affairs in a significant way for the first time since the Civil War. In Washington, one reporter said, "you feel it in the air . . . you listen to evidence of it in the mellow accent with which the South makes our English a musical tongue." Wilson himself once reported that "the only place in the world where nothing has to be explained to me is the South." Five of his ten cabinet members were born in the South, three still resided there, and William Jennings Bryan, the secretary of state, was an idol of the southern masses. At the president's right hand, and one of the most influential members of the Wilson circle, at least until 1919, was Colonel Edward M. House of Texas. On Capitol Hill southerners, by virtue of their seniority, held the lion's share of committee chairmanships. As a result, much of the progressive legislation of the Wilson era would bear the names of the southerners who guided it through Congress.

Fourth and finally, the election of 1912 had begun to alter the character of the Republican party. Even though most party professionals remained, the defection of the Bull Moose Progressives had weakened the party's progressive wing. The leader of the Republican party that would return to power in the 1920s would be more conservative in tone and temperament.

WILSONIAN REFORM   Wilson's inaugural address voiced in eloquent tones the ideals of social justice that animated many progressives. "We have been proud of our industrial achievements," he said, "but we have not hitherto stopped thoughtfully enough to count the human cost . . . the fearful physical and spiritual cost to the men and women and children upon whom the dead weight and burden of it all has fallen pitilessly the years through." He promised specifically a lower tariff and a new banking system. "This is not a day of triumph; it is a day of dedication. Here muster, not the forces of party, but the forces of humanity."

If Roosevelt had been a strong president by force of personality, Wilson became a strong president by force of conviction. The president, he wrote in *Congressional Government,* "is . . . the political leader of the nation, or has it in his choice to be. The nation as a whole has chosen him, and is conscious that it has no other political spokesman. His is the only national voice in affairs."

Wilson courted popular support, but he also courted members of Congress through personal contacts, invitations to the White House, and visits to the Capitol. He used patronage power to reward friends and punish enemies. He might have acted through a progressive coalition, but chose instead to rely on party loyalty. "I'd rather trust a machine Senator when he is committed to your program," he told his navy secretary, "than a talking Liberal who can never quite go along with others because of his admiration of his own patented plan of reform." Wilson therefore made use of the party caucus, in which disagreements among Democrats were settled.

THE TARIFF   Wilson's leadership faced its first big test on the issue of tariff reform. He summoned Congress into special session and addressed it in person—the first president to do so since John Adams. (Roosevelt was said to have asked, "Why didn't I think of that?") Congress acted vigorously on tariff reductions. Only four Democrats bolted the party line as the new bill passed the House easily.

The crunch came in the Senate, the traditional graveyard of tariff reform. Swarms of lobbyists got so thick in Washington, Wilson said, that "a brick couldn't be thrown without hitting one of them." The president turned the tables with a public statement that focused the spotlight on the "industrious and insidious" tariff lobby. "It is of serious interest to the country," he said, "that the people at large should have no lobby and

"A Near-Futurist Painting." The sponsors of the Underwood-Simmons Tariff look on as Wilson takes the lead on the tariff issue, Chicago Tribune, *April 1913.*

be voiceless in these matters, while great bodies of astute men seek to create an artificial opinion and to overcome the interests of the public for their private profit."

The Underwood-Simmons Tariff became law in 1913. It reduced import duties on 958 items, raised them on only 86, and left 307 the same. It lowered the overall average duty from about 37 percent to about 29 percent. A free list of some 300 items, about 100 of them new to the list, included important consumer goods and raw materials: sugar, wool, iron ore, steel rails, agricultural implements, cement, coal, wood and wood pulp, and many farm products. The act lowered tariffs but raised internal revenues with the first income tax levied under the newly ratified Sixteenth Amendment: 1 percent on incomes over $3,000 ($4,000 for married couples) and a surtax graduated from 1 percent on incomes of about $20,000 to 6 percent on incomes above $500,000. The highest total tax rate thus would be 7 percent.

THE FEDERAL RESERVE   Before the new tariff had cleared the Senate, the administration proposed the first major banking and currency reform since the Civil War. The Glass-Owen Federal Reserve Act of 1913 created a new banking system, with regional reserve banks supervised by a central board of directors. There would be twelve Federal Reserve Banks, each owned by member banks in its district. All national banks became members; state banks and trust companies could join if

Reading the Death Warrant. *Wilson's plan for banking and currency reform spells the death of the "Money Trust," according to this cartoon.*

they wished. Each member bank had to subscribe 6 percent of its capital to the Federal Reserve Bank and deposit a portion of its reserves there, the amount depending on the size of the community.

These "bankers' banks" dealt chiefly with their members and not at all with individuals. Along with other banking functions, the chief service to member banks was to rediscount their loans, that is, to take them over in exchange for Federal Reserve Notes, which member banks might then use to make further loans. The Federal Reserve Notes in turn were based 40 percent on government gold and 60 percent on commercial and agricultural paper (the promissory notes signed by borrowers). This arrangement made it possible to expand both the money supply and bank credit in times of high business activity, or as the level of borrowing increased. A Federal Reserve Board named three of the nine members on each Reserve Bank's board (member banks chose the remaining six) and carried out general supervision, including review of the rediscount rates. These rates might be raised to fight inflation by tightening credit, or lowered to stimulate business by making credit more easily available.

This new system corrected three great defects in the previous arrangements. Now bank reserves could be pooled, affording greater security; both the currency and bank credit became more elastic; and the concentration of reserves in New York was lessened. The system represented a new departure in active governmental intervention and control in one of the most sensitive segments of the economy.

ANTITRUST LAWS   In his campaign Wilson had made trust-busting the central focus of the New Freedom. The concentration of economic power had continued to grow despite the Sherman Anti-Trust Act and the watchdog agency, the Bureau of Corporations. Wilson's solution to the problem was revision of the Sherman Act to define more explicitly what counted as "restraint of trade." He decided to make a strong Federal Trade Commission (FTC) the cornerstone of his antitrust program. Created in 1914, the five-member commission replaced Roosevelt's Bureau of Corporations and assumed new powers to define "unfair trade practices" and to issue "cease-and-desist" orders when it found evidence of unfair competition.

Having now embraced the principle of "controlled competition," Wilson seemed to lose interest in the antitrust bill drafted by Henry D. Clayton (D-Ala.) of the House Judiciary Committee, which followed the president's original idea of defining specific acts in restraint of trade. The Clayton Antitrust Act, passed in 1914, outlawed such practices as price discrimination (charging different customers different prices for the same goods), "tying" agreements that limited the right of dealers to handle the products of competing manufacturers, interlock-

Mr. Wilson Taking Charge of the School. *A cartoon depicting the professorial president taking on big business.*

ing directorates connecting corporations with a capital of more than $1 million (or banks with more than $5 million), and corporations' acquisition of stock in competing corporations. In every case, however, conservative forces in the Senate qualified these provisions by tacking on the weakening phrase "where the effect may be to substantially lessen competition" or words of similar effect. And conservative southern Democrats and northern Republicans amended the act to allow for broad judicial review of the Federal Trade Commission's decisions, thus further weakening its freedom of action. In accordance with the president's recommendation, however, corporate officials were made individually responsible for any violations. Victims of price discrimination and tying agreements could sue for compensation equaling three times the amount of damages suffered.

Agrarian radicals, in alliance with organized labor, won a stipulation that supposedly exempted farm labor organizations from the antitrust laws, but actually only declared them not to be, per se, unlawful combinations in restraint of trade. Injunctions in labor disputes, moreover, were not to be handed down by federal courts unless "necessary to prevent irreparable injury to property." Though hailed by Samuel Gompers as labor's "Magna Carta," these provisions were actually little more than pious affirmations, as later court decisions would demonstrate. Wilson himself remarked that the act did little more than affirm the right of unions to exist by forbidding their dissolution for being in restraint of trade.

Administration of the antitrust laws generally proved disappointing to the more vehement progressives under Wilson. The president reassured business that his purposes were friendly. As his secretary of commerce put it later, Wilson hoped to "create in the Federal Trade Commission a counsellor and friend to the business world." But its first chairman lacked forcefulness, and under its next head, a Chicago industrialist, the FTC practically abandoned its function of watchdog. The Justice Department meanwhile offered help and advice to businessmen interested in arranging matters so as to avoid antitrust prosecutions. The appointment of conservative men to the Interstate Commerce Commission and the Federal Reserve won plaudits from the business world and profoundly disappointed progressives.

SOCIAL JUSTICE Wilson had never been a strong progressive of the social-justice persuasion. He had carried out promises to lower the tariff, reorganize the banking system, and strengthen the antitrust laws. Swept along by the course of events and the pressures of more far-reaching progressives, he was pushed further than he intended to go on some points. The New Freedom was now complete, he wrote late in 1914; the future would be "a time of healing because a time of just dealing." Although Wilson endorsed state action for women's suffrage, he declined to support a suffrage amendment because his party platform had not. He withheld support from federal child-labor legislation because he regarded it as a state matter. He opposed a bill for federal support of rural credits (low-interest loans to farmers) on the ground that it was "unwise and unjustifiable to extend the credit of the government to a single class of the community."

Not until the second anniversary of his inauguration (March 4, 1915) did Wilson sign an important piece of social-justice legislation, the La Follette Seamen's Act. The product of stubborn agitation by the eloquent president of the Seamen's Union, the act strengthened safety requirements, reduced the power of captains, set minimum food standards, and required regular wage payments. Seamen who jumped ship before their contracts expired, moreover, were relieved of the charge of desertion.

PROGRESSIVISM FOR WHITES ONLY   Like many other progressives, Woodrow Wilson showed little interest in the plight of African Americans. In fact, he shared many of the racist attitudes prevalent at the time. Although Wilson denounced the Ku Klux Klan's "reign of terror," he sympathized with its motives to restore white rule in the postwar South and to relieve whites of the "ignorant and hostile" power of the black vote. As a student at Princeton, Wilson had declared that "universal suffrage is the foundation of every evil in this country." He opposed giving the vote to uneducated whites, but he detested the enfranchisement of blacks, arguing that Americans of Anglo-Saxon origin would always resist domination by "an ignorant and inferior race." He believed that white resistance to black rule was "unalterable."

Later, as a politician, Wilson courted black voters, but he rarely consulted African-American leaders and repeatedly avoided opportunities to associate with them in public. Many of the southerners he appointed to his cabinet were uncompromising racists who systematically began segregating the employees in their agencies, even though the agencies had been integrated for over fifty years. Workplaces were segregated by race, as were toilets, drinking fountains, and areas for work breaks. When black leaders protested these actions, Wilson replied that such racial segregation was intended to eliminate "the possibility of friction" in the federal workplace.

PROGRESSIVE RESURGENCE   The need to weld a winning coalition in 1916 pushed Wilson back onto the road of reform. Progressive Democrats were restless, and after war broke out in Europe in August 1914, further divisions arose over defense and foreign policy. At the same time, the Republicans were repairing their own rift, as the Progressive party showed little staying power in the midterm elections and Roosevelt showed little will to preserve it. It was plain to most observers that Wilson could shape a majority only by courting progressives of all parties. In 1916 Wilson scored points with them when he nominated Louis D. Brandeis to the Supreme Court. Conservatives waged a vigorous battle against Brandeis, but Senate progressives rallied to win confirmation of the social-justice champion, the first Jewish member of the Supreme Court.

Meanwhile Wilson began to embrace a broad program of farm and labor reforms. On farm credit, after having first opposed it he reversed himself abruptly, now supporting a proposal to set up land banks to sponsor long-term farm loans. The Federal Farm Loan Act became law in 1916. Under the control of a Federal Farm Loan Board, twelve Fed-

Louis D. Brandeis.

eral Land Banks paralleled the Federal Reserve Banks and offered farmers loans of five to forty years' duration at low interest rates.

Thus the dream of cheap rural credits, sponsored by a generation of Alliance members and Populists, came to fruition. Democrats never embraced the Populist subtreasury plan, but made a small step in that direction with the Warehouse Act of 1916. This measure authorized federal licensing of private warehouses, and federal backing made their receipts for stored produce more acceptable as collateral for short-term bank loans to farmers. Other concessions to farm demands came in the Smith-Lever Act of 1914 and the Smith-Hughes Act of 1917, both of which passed with little controversy. The first provided federal grants-in-aid for farm demonstration agents under the supervision of land-grant colleges. The measure made permanent a program that had started a decade before in Texas and that had already spread to many localities. The second measure extended agricultural and mechanical education to high schools through grants-in-aid.

Farmers with automobiles had more than a passing interest as well in the Federal Highways Act of 1916, which provided dollar-matching contributions to states with highway departments that met certain federal standards. The measure authorized distribution of $75 million over five years, and marked a sharp departure from Jacksonian opposition to internal improvements at federal expense, just as the Federal Reserve System departed from Jacksonian banking principles. Although the argument that highways were one of the nation's defense needs weakened constitutional scruples against the act, it still restricted support to "post roads" used for the delivery of mail. A renewal act in 1921 would mark the beginning of a systematic network of numbered U.S. highways.

The progressive resurgence of 1916 broke the logjam on labor reforms as well. Advocates of child-labor legislation persuaded Wilson that social-justice progressives would regard his stand on the issue as an important test of his humanitarian concerns, and Wilson overcame doubts of its constitutionality to support and sign the Keating-Owen Child Labor Act, which excluded from interstate commerce goods manufactured by children under fourteen. Both the Keating-Owen Act and a later act of 1919 to achieve the same purpose with a prohibitory tax were ruled unconstitutional by the Supreme Court on the ground that regulation of interstate commerce could not extend to the conditions of labor. Effective action against the social evil of child labor had to await the New Deal of the 1930s, although it seems likely that discussion of the issue contributed to the sharp reduction in the number of underage workers during the next few years.

Another important accomplishment was the eight-hour workday for railroad workers, a measure that the Supreme Court upheld. The Adamson Act of 1916 was brought about by a threatened strike of railroad brotherhoods demanding the eight-hour workday and other concessions. Wilson, who objected to some of the union demands, nevertheless went before Congress to request action on the hours limitation. The resulting Adamson Act required an eight-hour workday, with time and a half for overtime, and appointed a commission to study the problem of railroad labor.

In Wilson's first term progressivism reached its zenith. A creative time, the age of progressivism established at the beginning of the twentieth century a framework within which American politics and society would still function, by and large, near the end of the century. Progressivism had conquered the old dictum that the government is best which governs least, whatever political rhetoric might be heard to the contrary. Progressivism, an amalgam of agrarian, business, governmental, and social reform, amounted in the end to a movement for positive government. From two decades of ferment (three, if the Populist years are counted) the great fundamental contribution of progressive politics was the firm establishment and general acceptance of the public-service concept of the state.

THE LIMITS OF PROGRESSIVISM

The Progressive Era was an optimistic age in which reformers of various hues assumed that no problem lay beyond solution. But like all great historic movements, progressivism displayed elements of paradox and irony. Despite its talk of democracy, it was the age of disenfranchisement for southern blacks—an action seen by many whites as progressive. The initiative and referendum, supposedly democratic reforms, proved subject to manipulation by well-financed publicity campaigns. And much of the public policy of the time came to be formulated by experts and members of appointed boards, not by broad segments of the population. There is a fine irony in the fact that the drive to increase the political role of ordinary people moved parallel with efforts to strengthen executive leadership and exalt expertise. This age of efficiency and bureaucracy, in business as well as government, brought into being a society in which more and more of the decisions affecting people's lives were made by unknown policy makers.

Progressivism was largely a middle-class movement in which the poor and unorganized had little influence. The supreme irony was that a movement so dedicated to the rhetoric of democracy should experience so steady a decline in voter participation. In 1912, the year of the Bull Moose campaign, voting dropped off by between 6 and 7 percent. The new politics of issues and charismatic leaders proved to be less effective in turning out voters than party organizations and bosses had been. And by 1916 the optimism of an age that looked to infinite progress was already confronted by a vast slaughter. Europe had already stumbled into war, and America would soon be drawn in. The twentieth century, which dawned with such bright hopes, held in store episodes of unparalleled horror.

MAKING CONNECTIONS

- Many of the progressive reforms described in this chapter—particularly business regulation and the growth of the welfare state—provided the seeds for the New Deal reforms of the 1930s (Chapter 28).

- The progressive impulse carried on after World War I, but was transformed by the new political and social conditions of postwar America. Progressive reforms such as Prohibition and women's suffrage were enacted after the war, but the moralistic strain in progressivism took an ugly turn in the Red Scare and immigration restriction.

- The next chapter shows how Wilson's foreign policy in Latin America and Europe reflected the same moralism that guided his domestic policy.

FURTHER READING

A splendid introduction to the topic of progressivism can be found in Arthur S. Link and Richard L. McCormick's *Progressivism* (1983). Progressivism has been interpreted in many ways. Robert H. Wiebe's *The Search for Order, 1877–1920* (1967) presents the organizational model for reform. Richard Hofstadter's *The Age of Reform: From Bryan to F.D.R.* (1955) examines an emerging middle-class consensus as the basis of reform. Gabriel Kolko sees reform as a means of social control in *The Triumph of Conservatism* (1963). Dewey W. Grantham's *Southern Progressivism: The Reconciliation of Progress and Tradition* (1983) shows the distinctiveness of reform in that region. See also Alan Dawley's *Struggles for Justice: Social Responsibility and the Liberal State* (1991).

Biographers of the three progressive presidents elaborate on the complexity of reform. Edmund Morris's *The Rise of Theodore Roosevelt* (1979) and H. W. Brands's *T.R.: The Last Romantic* (1997) offer compelling portraits. For the Taft years, see Paolo E. Coletta's *The Presidency of William Howard Taft* (1973). Arthur S. Link's multivolume biography *Wilson* (1947–1965)—particularly *The New Freedom* (1956)—is the place to start on that president. John Milton Cooper, Jr., compares Roosevelt and Wilson in *The Warrior and the Priest* (1983).

The evolution of government policy toward business is examined in Martin J. Sklar's *The Corporate Reconstruction of American Capitalism, 1890–1916:The Market, the Law, and Politics* (1988). Roy Lubove's *The Progressives and the Slums* (1962), Mina Carson's *Settlement Folk: Social Thought and the American Settlement Movement, 1885–1930* (1990), and Jack M. Holl's *Juvenile Reform in the Progressive Era* (1971) examine the problem of urban decay.

Robert Kanigel's *The One Best Way: Frederick Winslow Taylor and the Enigma of Efficiency* (1997) highlights the role of efficiency in the Progressive Era. Samuel P. Hays's *Conservation and the Gospel of Efficiency: The Progressive Conservation Movement, 1890–1920* (rev. ed., 1969) and Harold T. Pinkett's *Gifford Pinchot: Private and Public Forester* (1970) cover conservation and the Ballinger-Pinchot controversy.

An excellent study of the role of women in progressivism's emphasis on social justice is Kathryn Kish Sklar's *Florence Kelley and the Nation's Work: The Rise of Women's Political Culture, 1830–1900* (1995).

25 ✒️ AMERICA AND
THE GREAT WAR

---

hroughout the nineteenth century, the United States reaped the benefits of its geographic distance from the wars that plagued Britain and Europe. The Atlantic Ocean provided a welcome buffer. During the early twentieth century, however, events combined to end the nation's comfortable isolation. Spectacular industrial development and ever-expanding world trade entwined American national interests with the fate of Europe. In addition, the development of steam-powered ships and submarines meant that foreign navies could threaten American security. At the same time, the election of Woodrow Wilson brought to the White House a stern moralist determined to impose his standards for right conduct on renegade nations. This combination of circumstances led the outbreak of war in Europe in 1914 to become a profound crisis for Americans, a crisis that in the end would transform the nation's role in international affairs.

WILSON AND FOREIGN AFFAIRS

Woodrow Wilson brought to the presidency little background in the study of diplomacy and none at all in its practice. The former college professor admitted as much when he remarked just before taking office, "It would be an irony of fate if my administration had to deal chiefly with foreign affairs." But events in Latin America and Europe were to make the irony all too real. From the summer of 1914, when the guns of August heralded a catastrophic world war, foreign relations increasingly overshadowed all else, including Wilson's domestic program.

AN IDEALIST'S DIPLOMACY   Although lacking in international experience, Wilson did not lack ideas or convictions in this area. He saw himself as a man of destiny who would help create a new world order governed by morality and idealism rather than by crass national interests. The product of a Calvinist past, he brought to diplomacy a version of progressivism animated by righteousness. His election had put him on a course charted "by no plan of our conceiving, but by the hand of God who led us into this way." Both Wilson and his secretary of state, William Jennings Bryan, believed that America had been called to advance democracy and moral progress in the world. If they did not always follow principle at the expense of national self-interest, they did in many respects try to develop a diplomatic policy based on idealism.

During 1913–1914, Bryan negotiated some thirty "cooling-off" treaties under which participating nations pledged not to go to war over any disagreement for a period of twelve months pending discussion by an international arbitration panel. The treaties, however, were of little consequence, soon forgotten in the revolutionary sweep of world events that would make the twentieth century the bloodiest in recorded history.

One of the first applications of Wilsonian idealism to foreign policy came when the president renounced "dollar diplomacy." The government, he said, was not supporting any "special groups or interest." As good as his word, he withdrew U.S. support of the Six-Power Consortium then preparing to float a large loan to China. Such a monopolistic grant, he said, would compromise China's integrity and possibly involve the United States in a future intervention. Without governmental backing, American bankers withdrew from the project.

INTERVENTION IN MEXICO   Closer to home, Wilson found it harder to take such high ground. Nor did the logic of his "missionary diplomacy" always imply nonintervention. Mexico, which had been in the throes of revolution for nearly three years, presented a thorny problem. For most of the thirty-five years from 1876 to 1911, President Porfirio Díaz had dominated Mexico. As military dictator he had suppressed opposition and showered favors on his followers and on foreign investors, who piled up holdings in Mexican mines, petroleum, railroads, and agriculture. But eventually the dictator's hold slipped, and in 1910 popular resentment boiled over into revolt. A year later, revolutionary armies occupied Mexico City, and Díaz fled.

The leader of the rebellion, Francisco I. Madero, proved unable to manage the tough adversaries attracted by the scramble for power. In 1913 General Victoriano Huerta assumed power, and Madero was murdered soon afterward. Confronted with a military dictator ruling Mexico, Wilson enunciated a new doctrine of nonrecognition: "We hold . . . that just government rests upon the consent of the governed." Recognition, formerly extended routinely to governments that exercised *de facto* power, now might depend on judgments of their legality; an immoral government presumably would not pass muster.

General Victoriano Huerta, whose seizure of power in Mexico in 1913 aroused Wilson's opposition.

Huerta's hold on power remained unsure, and for a while Wilson resisted the impulse to intervene. In 1913 he sought to quiet fears of intervention by declaring that the United States "will never again seek one additional foot of territory by conquest." Nevertheless he obliquely expressed sympathy with the revolutionary movement and began to put diplomatic pressure on Huerta. Early in 1914 he removed an embargo on arms to Mexico in order to help the resurgent revolutionaries under Venustiano Carranza of the Constitutionalist party, and stationed warships off Veracruz to halt arms shipments to Huerta.

On April 9, 1914, several American sailors gathering supplies in Tampico strayed into a restricted area and were arrested. The local commander, a Huertista, quickly released them and sent an apology to the American naval commander. There the incident might have ended, but the naval commander demanded that the Mexicans salute the American flag. Wilson backed him up and got from Congress authority to use force to bring Huerta to terms. Before the Tampico incident could be resolved, Wilson authorized a naval force to enter Veracruz and stop the imminent landing of an arms shipment. American marines and sailors went ashore on April 21, 1914, and occupied the town at a cost of 19 killed. The Mexicans lost at least 200 killed.

In Mexico the American occupation aroused the opposition of all factions, and Huerta tried to rally support against foreign invasion. At this juncture Wilson accepted an offer of mediation by the ABC powers (Argentina, Brazil, and Chile), which proposed withdrawal of United States forces, the removal of Huerta, and installation of a provisional government sympathetic to reform. Huerta refused, but the moral effect of the proposal, his isolation abroad, and the growing strength of his foes forced him to leave office. The Carranzistas entered Mexico City, and the Americans left Veracruz in late 1914. A year later, the United States and several Latin American governments recognized Carranza as president of Mexico.

Still, the troubles south of the border continued. The prolonged disorders had spawned independent bands of bandits, Pancho Villa's among the wildest. All through 1915, fighting between the forces of Villa and Carranza continued sporadically. In 1916 Villa seized a train and murdered sixteen American mining engineers in a deliberate attempt to provoke American intervention, discredit Carranza, and build himself up as an opponent of the "Gringos." That failing, he crossed the border

Pancho Villa (center) *and his followers rebelled against the president of Mexico and antagonized the United States with violent attacks against "gringos."*

on raids into Texas and New Mexico. On March 9 he entered Columbus, New Mexico, burned the town, and killed seventeen Americans.

Wilson then had to abandon his policy of "watchful waiting." With the reluctant consent of Carranza, he sent General John J. Pershing across the border with a force of 11,000 men and mobilized 150,000 National Guardsmen along the frontier. For nearly a year Pershing went on a fruitless chase after Villa through northern Mexico and, missing his quarry, was ordered home in 1917. Carranza then pressed his own war against the bandits and put through a new liberal constitution in 1917. Mexico was by then well on the way to a more orderly government.

PROBLEMS IN THE CARIBBEAN   In the Caribbean, Wilson found it as hard to act on his ideals as in Mexico. The "dollar diplomacy" practiced by the Taft administration encouraged bankers in the United States to aid debt-plagued governments in Haiti, Guatemala, Honduras, and Nicaragua. Despite Wilson's public stand against using military force to back up American investments, he kept the marines in

Nicaragua, where they had been sent by Taft in 1912, to prevent renewed civil war. Then in 1915 he dispatched more marines to Haiti after two successive revolutions and subsequent disorders. "I suppose,"
Wilson told Secretary of State Bryan, "there is nothing to do but to take
the bull by the horns and restore order." The American forces stayed in
Haiti until 1934. Disorders in the Dominican Republic brought American marines to that country in 1916; they remained until 1924. The
presence of these additional U.S. military forces in the region only exacerbated the Yankee phobia among many Latin Americans. And as the
New York Times charged, Wilson's frequent interventions made Taft's
dollar diplomacy look like "ten cent diplomacy."

An Uneasy Neutrality

Problems in Latin America and the Caribbean loomed larger in
Wilson's thinking than the gathering storm in Europe. When the thun-
derbolt of war struck Europe in the summer of 1914, it struck most
Americans, one North Carolinian wrote, "as lightning out of a clear
sky." Whatever the troubles in Mexico, whatever disorders and interventions agitated other countries, it seemed unreal that civilized Europe could descend into such an orgy of destruction. Since the fall of
Napoleon in 1815, Europe had known local wars but only as interrup-
tions of a general peace that contributed to a century of unprecedented
material progress.

But peace ended with the assassination in Sarajevo of Austrian archduke Franz Ferdinand by a Serbian nationalist. Austria-Hungary's determination to punish Serbia provoked Russia to mobilize in sympathy
with its Slavic friends in Serbia. This is turn triggered a European system of alliances: the Triple Alliance or Central Powers (Germany, Austria-Hungary, and Italy) and the Triple Entente or Allied Powers
(France, Great Britain, and Russia). When Russia refused to stop its
mobilization, Germany, which backed Austria-Hungary, declared war
on Russia on August 1, 1914, and on Russia's ally France two days later.
Germany then invaded Belgium to get at France, which brought Great
Britain into the war on August 4. Japan, eager to seize German holdings
in the Pacific, declared war on August 23, and Turkey entered on the
side of the Central Powers in October. Although allied with the Central

Powers, Italy initially stayed out of the war, and then struck a bargain under which it joined the Allied Powers in 1915.

AMERICA'S INITIAL REACTIONS   Shock in the United States gave way to gratitude that an ocean stood between America and the battle-fields. "Our isolated position and freedom from entangling alliances," said the *Literary Digest,* "inspire our press with cheering assurance that we are in no peril of being drawn into the European quarrel." President Wilson repeatedly issued routine declarations of neutrality. He urged the American people to be "impartial in thought as well as action."

That was more easily said than done. In the 1910 population of 92 million, more than 32 million were "hyphenated Americans," first- or second-generation immigrants who retained ties to their old countries.

Among the more than 13 million from the countries at war, by far the largest group was German-American, numbering 8 million. And 4 million Irish-Americans harbored a deep-rooted enmity to England. These groups instinctively leaned toward the Central Powers.

But old-line Americans, largely of British origin, supported the Allied Powers. If, as has been said, Britain and the United States were divided by a common language, they were united by ties of culture and tradition. Americans identified also with France, which had contributed to American culture and ideas, and to independence itself. Britain and France, if not their ally Russia, seemed the custodians of democracy, while Germany more and more seemed the embodiment of autocracy and militarism. If not a direct threat to the United States, Germany would pose at least a potential threat if it destroyed the balance of power in Europe. High officers of the United States government were pro-British in thought from the outset. Robert Lansing, first counselor of the State Department, Walter Hines Page, ambassador to London, and Colonel Edward House, Wilson's close adviser, saw in German militarism a potential danger to America.

Just what effects the propaganda of the warring powers had is unclear. The Germans and the British were most active, but German propaganda, which played on American dislike of Russian autocracy and

Most Americans leaned toward the Allied Powers, but all were shocked at the outbreak of the Great War. In this cartoon, the Samson-like War pulls down the temple of Civilization.

anti-Semitism, fell mainly upon barren ground. Only German-Americans and Irish-Americans responded to a "hate England" theme. From the outset, the British had one supreme advantage in this area. Once they had cut the direct cable from Germany early in the war, nearly all news from the battlefronts had to clear through London. Highly exaggerated reports of German atrocities were convincing to Americans, and there were real atrocities enough in the German occupation of Belgium to affront American feelings.

A STRAINED NEUTRALITY At first the war brought a slump in American exports and the threat of a depression, but by the spring of 1915 the Allies' demand for supplies generated a wartime boom. The Allies at first financed their purchases by disposing of American securities, but ultimately they needed loans. Early in the war, Secretary Bryan informed banker J. P. Morgan that loans to any warring nation were "inconsistent with the true spirit of neutrality." Money, he warned, "is the worst of all contrabands because it commands everything else." Yet Wilson quietly began approving short-term credits to sustain trade with the Allies. When in the fall of 1915 it became apparent that the Allies could no longer carry on without long-term credit, the administration removed all restrictions, and J. P. Morgan soon extended a loan of $500 million to England and France. American investors would advance over $2 billion to the Allies before the United States entered the war, and only $27 million to Germany.

The administration nevertheless clung to the fond hope of neutrality through two and a half years of warfare in Europe and tried to uphold the traditions of "freedom of the seas," which had guided American policy since the Napoleonic Wars. As the German drive through Belgium and toward Paris finally ground down into the stalemate of trench warfare, trade on the high seas assumed a new importance. In a war of attrition, survival depended on access to supplies, and in such a war British naval power counted for a great deal. With the German fleet outnumbered and bottled up almost from the outset, the war in many ways assumed the pattern that had once led America into war with Britain in 1812.

On August 6, 1914, Secretary Bryan called upon the belligerents to accept the Declaration of London, drafted and signed in 1909 by leading powers but never ratified by the British. That document, the culmination of nineteenth-century liberal thought on the rules of warfare, reduced the list of contraband items and specified that a blockade was legal only when effective just outside enemy ports. The Central Powers promptly accepted. The British almost as promptly refused, lest they lose some of their advantage in sea power. Beginning with an Order in Council of August 20, 1914, Britain gradually extended the list of contraband goods to include all sorts of things formerly excluded, such as food, cotton, wood, and certain ores. Wilson protested, but U.S. ambassador Page, personally pro-British, assured British foreign secretary Sir Edward Grey that the two could find ways of getting around the problem. The British consequently gave little serious heed to further protests.

In November 1914 the British declared the whole North Sea a war zone, sowed it with mines, and ordered neutral ships to enter only by the Strait of Dover, where they could be easily searched. In March 1915 they further announced that they would seize ships carrying goods with a presumed enemy destination, ownership, or origin. Previous policies had required search on the high seas and this, combined with Britain's new policy, caused extended delays, sometimes running into months. The same Order in Council also directed British ships to stop vessels carrying German goods via neutral ports. When the State Department protested, Grey reminded the Americans that this was the same doctrine of continuous voyage on which the United States had acted in the 1860s to keep British goods out of the Confederacy.

NEUTRAL RIGHTS AND SUBMARINES British actions, including blacklisting of American companies that traded with the enemy and censorship of the mails, raised some old issues of neutral rights, but the German reaction introduced an entirely new question. With the German fleet bottled up by the British blockade, few surface vessels could venture out to harass the enemy. On February 4, 1915, in response to the "illegal" British blockade, the German government proclaimed a war zone around the British Isles. Enemy merchant ships in those waters were liable to sinking by submarines, the Germans declared, "although it may not always be possible to save crews and passengers." As the chief advantage of U-boat (*Unterseeboot*) warfare was in surprise, it violated the established procedure of stopping enemy vessels on the high seas and providing for the safety of passengers and crews before

"All the News That's Fit to Print"

The New York Times.

THE WEATHER
Fair today and Sunday; fresh to strong southeast to west winds.

VOL. LXIV...NO. 20,923.   NEW YORK, SATURDAY, MAY 8, 1915.—TWENTY-FOUR PAGES.   ONE CENT

LUSITANIA SUNK BY A SUBMARINE, PROBABLY 1,000 DEAD; TWICE TORPEDOED OFF IRISH COAST; SINKS IN 15 MINUTES; AMERICANS ABOARD INCLUDED VANDERBILT AND FROHMAN; WASHINGTON BELIEVES THAT A GRAVE CRISIS IS AT HAND

Americans were outraged when a German torpedo sank the Lusitania *on May 7, 1915.*

sinking the vessel. Since the British sometimes flew neutral flags as a ruse, neutral ships in the zone would also be in danger.

The United States pronounced the German policy "an indefensible violation of neutral rights" and warned that Germany would be held to "strict accountability" for any destruction of American lives and property. If the meaning of the phrase was unclear, the stern tone of the note was unmistakable. On March 28, 1915, one American drowned when the Germans sank the British steamer *Falaba* in the Irish Sea. On May 1 the American tanker *Gulflight* went down with a loss of two lives. The administration was divided on the proper course of action. Bryan wanted to say that American citizens entered the war zone at their own risk; his counselor, Robert Lansing, and Colonel House wanted a possible break in diplomatic relations with Germany. Then, as Wilson pondered the alternatives, the sinking of the British Cunard liner *Lusitania* provoked a crisis.

On May 7, 1915, the captain of the German submarine U-20 sighted a four-stack liner moving slowly through the Irish Sea and fired a torpedo. It hit the mark, and the ship exploded and sank within a few minutes. Only as it tipped into the waves was he able to make out the name *Lusitania* on the stern. Before the ship left New York bound for Liverpool, the German embassy had published warnings in the American press against travel to the war zone, but among the 1,198 persons lost were 128 Americans.

The public was outraged. It was an act of piracy, Theodore Roosevelt declared. Wilson, however, urged patience: "There is such a thing as a man being too proud to fight. There is such a thing as a nation being so right that it does not need to convince others by force that it is right." Bit his previous demand for "strict accountability" forced him to make a strong response. On May 13 Bryan reluctantly signed a note demanding that the Germans abandon unrestricted submarine warfare, disavow the sinking, and pay reparations. The Germans responded that the ship had been armed (which it was not) and carried a cargo of small arms and ammunition (which it did). A second note on June 9 repeated American demands in stronger terms. The United States, Wilson asserted, was "contending for nothing less high and sacred than the rights of humanity." Bryan, unwilling to risk war over the issue, resigned in protest and joined the peace movement as a private citizen. His successor, Robert Lansing, signed the note.

In response to the uproar over the *Lusitania,* the German government had secretly ordered U-boat captains to avoid sinking large passenger vessels. When, despite the order, two American lives were lost in the sinking of the British liner *Arabic,* bound for New York, the Germans paid an indemnity and offered a public assurance on September 1, 1915: "Liners will not be sunk by our submarines without warning and without safety of the lives of non-combatants, provided that the liners do not try to escape or offer resistance." With this *Arabic* pledge, Wilson's resolute stand seemed to have resulted in a victory for his policy.

During the fall of 1915, Wilson's trusted adviser Edward M. House proposed to renew a mediation effort he had explored on a visit to London, Paris, and Berlin the previous spring—before the *Lusitania* sinking. In early 1916 House visited those capitals again, but found neither side ready to begin serious negotiations. The French and British would soon be engaged in destructive battles at Verdun and the Somme, and both were determined to fight until they could bargain from strength.

Peace advocates in Congress now challenged the administration's policy on neutral rights. In 1916 resolutions were introduced in the

House and Senate warning Americans against traveling on armed belligerent vessels. Such surrender to the German threat, Wilson asserted, would be a "deliberate abdication of our hitherto proud position as spokesmen, even amidst the turmoil of war, for the law and the right." He warned that if the United States accepted a single abatement of right, then "the whole fine fabric of international law might crumble under our hands piece by piece." The administration managed to defeat both resolutions by a solid margin. On March 24, 1916, a U-boat torpedoed the French steamer *Sussex,* injuring two Americans. When Wilson threatened to break off relations, Germany renewed its pledge that U-boats would not torpedo merchant and passenger ships. This *Sussex* pledge implied the virtual abandonment of submarine warfare.

THE DEBATE OVER PREPAREDNESS   The *Lusitania* incident, and more generally the quarrels over neutral commerce, contributed to a growing demand for a stronger American army and navy. On December 1, 1914, the champions of preparedness organized the National Security League to promote their cause. After the *Lusitania* sinking, Wilson asked the War and Navy Departments to draft proposals for expansion.

Progressives and pacifists and many from the rural South and West were opposed to military expansion. Their antiwar sentiments tapped into the traditional American suspicion of military establishments, es-

Helping the President. *In this 1915 cartoon, Wilson holds to the middle course between the pacifism of Bryan (shown on left with sign "Let us avoid unnecessary risks") and the belligerence of Roosevelt (shown on right with a sign "Let us act without unnecessary delay").*

pecially of standing armies, which dated back to the colonial period. The new Democratic leader in the House opposed "the big Navy and big Army program of the jingoes and war traffickers." In the East, leaders of the peace movement organized a League to Limit Armament. Jane Addams and suffragist Carrie Chapman Catt organized a Women's Peace party.

The administration's plan to enlarge the regular army and create a national reserve force of 400,000 ran into stubborn opposition in the House Military Affairs Committee. Wilson was forced to accept a compromise between advocates of an expanded force under federal control and advocates of a traditional citizen army. The National Defense Act of 1916 expanded the regular army from 90,000 to 175,000 and permitted gradual enlargement to 223,000. It also expanded the National Guard to 440,000, made provision for their training, and gave federal funds for summer training camps for civilians.

The bill for an increased navy had less trouble because of the general feeling expressed by the navy secretary that there was "no danger of militarism from a relatively strong navy such as would come from a big standing army." The Naval Construction Act of 1916 authorized between $500 million and $600 million for a three-year program of enlargement.

Forced to relent on preparedness, progressives who opposed the action determined that the financial burden should rest on the wealthy people they held responsible for the effort. The income tax became their weapon. Supported by a groundswell of popular support, they wrote into the Revenue Act of 1916 changes that doubled the basic income tax rate from 1 to 2 percent, lifted the surtax to a maximum of 13 percent (for a total of 15 percent) on incomes over $2 million, added an estate tax graduated up to a maximum of 10 percent, levied a 12½ percent tax on gross receipts of munitions makers, and added a new tax on corporation capital, surplus, and excess profits. The new taxes on wealth amounted to the most clear-cut victory of radical progressives in the entire Wilson period, a victory further consolidated and advanced after America entered the war. It was the capstone to the edifice of progressive legislation that Wilson supported in preparation for the election of 1916.

THE ELECTION OF 1916 As the 1916 election approached, Republicans hoped to regain their normal majority, and Roosevelt hoped to be their leader again. But he had committed the deadly sin of bolting his party in 1912 and, what was more, expressed a bellicosity on war issues that would scare off voters. Needing somebody who would draw Bull Moose Progressives back into the fold, the regulars turned to Justice Charles Evans Hughes, who had a progressive record as governor of New York from 1907 to 1910. On the Supreme Court since then, he had neither taken a stand in 1912 nor spoken out on foreign policy. The remnants of the Progressive party gathered in Chicago at the same time as the Republicans. Roosevelt had held out the vain hope of getting both nominations, but he now declined to lead a moribund party. Two weeks later the Progressive National Committee disbanded the party and endorsed Hughes; a minority, including their vice-presidential nominee, came out for Wilson.

The Democrats, as expected, chose Wilson once again, and in their platform endorsed a program of social legislation, neutrality, and reasonable preparedness. The party further commended women's suffrage to the states, denounced groups that placed the interests of other countries above those of the United States, and pledged support for a postwar League of Nations to enforce peace with collective security mea-

Peace with Honor. *Wilson's neutral policies proved popular in the 1916 campaign.*

sures against aggressors. The Democrats found their most popular issue, however, when the keynote speaker, a former New York governor, got an unexpected response to his recital of historic cases in which the United States had refused under provocation to go to war. As he mentioned successive examples, the crowd chanted "What did we do? What did we do?" and the speaker responded: "We didn't go to war! We didn't go to war!" The peace theme, refined into the slogan "He kept us out of war," became the rallying cry of the campaign, one that had the merit of taking credit without making any promises for the future.

Rooseveltians found themselves drawn in large numbers to Wilson. The impression of Democratic purpose and effectiveness was heightened by Republican feuding and ineptitude. On foreign policy, Hughes worked both sides of the street. While trying to keep the votes of German-Americans and other "hyphenates," Hughes refused to disavow Roosevelt, who was going around the country denouncing the kaiser. On social-reform issues Wilson was far ahead of Hughes, and Hughes found himself often the captive of old-line Republican bosses more eager to punish Bull Moose Progressives than to win the election for Hughes.

In the end, Wilson's twin rallying cries of peace and progressivism, a unique combination of issues forged in the legislative and diplomatic crucibles of 1916, brought victory. Early returns showed a Republican sweep in the East and Midwest, signaling a victory for Hughes, but the outcome remained in doubt until word came that Wilson had carried California by 3,772 votes. The final vote showed a Democratic sweep of the Far West and South, enough for victory in the electoral college by 277 to 254, and in the popular vote by 9 million to 8.5 million.

LAST EFFORTS FOR PEACE   Immediately after the election, Wilson began to plan another peace move, whereupon the German government announced on December 12 its readiness to begin discussion of peace terms. Six days later Wilson sent identical notes to the belligerent powers, asking each to state its war aims. The Germans responded promptly that they would state theirs only to a conference of the belligerents at a neutral site (although it soon became clear that they intended to seize new territory along the Baltic Sea, in the Congo of Africa, and in France, Belgium, and Luxembourg). In January 1917 the Allies made it plain that they intended to require reparations, break up the Austro-Hungarian and Ottoman Empires, and destroy German power.

Wilson then decided to make one more appeal, in the hope that public opinion would force the hands of the warring governments. Speaking before the Senate on January 22, 1917, he asserted the right of the United States to a share in laying the foundations for a lasting peace, which would have to be a "peace without victory," for only a "peace among equals" could endure. The peace must be based on the principles of government by the consent of the governed, freedom of the seas, and disarmament, and must be enforced by an international league for peace established to make another such catastrophe impossible. "I would fain believe," the president ended, "that I am speaking for the silent mass of mankind everywhere who have as yet had no place or opportunity to speak their real hearts out concerning the death and ruin they see to have come already upon the persons and homes they hold most dear."

Although Wilson did not know it, he was already too late. Exactly two weeks before he spoke, impatient German military leaders had decided to wage unrestricted submarine warfare. They took the calculated risk of provoking American anger in the hope of scoring a quick knockout. On January 31 the new policy was announced, effective the next day. All vessels in the war zone, belligerent or neutral, would be sunk without warning. "Freedom of the seas," said the *Brooklyn Eagle,* "will now be enjoyed by icebergs and fish."

On February 3, 1917, Wilson told a joint session of Congress that the United States had broken diplomatic relations with the German government. Three weeks later he asked for authority to arm American merchant ships and "to employ any other instrumentalities or methods that may be necessary and adequate to protect our ships and our people." There was little quarrel with arming merchant ships, but bitter opposition to Wilson's vague reference to "any other instrumentalities or methods." A group of eleven or twelve die-hard noninterventionists filibustered the measure until the regular session expired on March 4. Thus, in Wilson's words: "A little group of willful men, representing no opinion but their own, have rendered the great Government of the United States helpless and contemptible." On March 12 the State Department announced that a forgotten law of 1792 allowed the arming of merchant ships regardless of congressional inaction.

Word had reached Wilson on February 25 that the British had intercepted and decoded an important message from German foreign secretary Arthur Zimmermann to his minister in Mexico. The note instructed the envoy to offer an alliance and financial aid to Mexico in case of war between the United States and Germany. In return for diversionary action against the United States, Mexico would recover "the lost territory in Texas, New Mexico, and Arizona."

On March 1, news of the Zimmermann Telegram broke in the American press and outraged the public. Wilson felt it betrayed a trust he had shown in permitting the Germans to use American wireless facilities to transmit the message. Then, later in March, a revolution overthrew Russia's czarist government and established the provisional government of a Russian Republic. The fall of the czarist autocracy allowed Americans the illusion that all the major Allied Powers were now fighting for constitutional democracy. Not until November 1917 was this illusion shattered, when the Bolsheviks seized power in Russia.

AMERICA'S ENTRY INTO THE WAR

In March 1917 German submarines sank five American merchant vessels in the North Atlantic. On March 20 Wilson's cabinet unanimously endorsed a declaration of war, and the following day the president called a special session of Congress. When it met on April 2, Wilson asked Congress to recognize the war that Imperial Germany was already waging against the United States, then turned to a discussion of the issues. The German government had revealed itself as a natural foe of liberty, and therefore "The world must be made safe for democracy. Its peace must be planted upon the tested foundations of political liberty." The war resolution passed the Senate by a vote of 82 to 6 on April 4. The House concurred, 373 to 50, and Wilson signed the measure on April 6, 1917. It was Good Friday.

How had it come to this, less than three years after Wilson's proclamation of neutrality? Prominent among the various explanations of America's entrance into the war were the effects of British propaganda and America's deep involvement in trade with the Allies, which some observers then and later credited to the intrigues of war profiteers and munitions makers. Some Americans thought German domination of Europe would be a threat to American security, especially if it meant the destruction or capture of the British navy. But whatever the influence of such factors, they likely would not have been decisive without the issue of submarine warfare. Once Wilson had taken a stand for the traditional rights of neutrals and noncombatants, he was to some extent at the mercy of decisions by the German high command and was led step by step into a war over what to a later generation would seem a rather quaint, if noble, set of principles.

AMERICA'S EARLY ROLE   The scope of America's role in the European war remained unclear. Few on either side of the Atlantic expected more from the United States than a token military effort. Despite Congress's preparedness measures, the army remained small and rudimentary. The navy also was largely undeveloped. This began to change, however, when Rear Admiral William S. Sims assumed command of American ships in European waters. He then systematically built up the United States Navy, bringing the first contingent of six American destroyers to Queenstown, Ireland, in May 1917, and more later. The Americans, in addition, made two important contributions to Allied naval strategy. Previously, merchant ships had survived through speed and evasive action. Sims persuaded the Allies to adopt a convoy system of escorting merchant ships in groups. The result was a decrease in Allied shipping losses from 881,000 tons in April 1917 to 289,000 in

A Liberty Loan poster with an "honor roll" of ethnic Americans.

November of the same year. Later the United States Navy conceived and laid a gigantic minefield across the North Sea that threatened the U-boats' access to the North Atlantic.

Within a month of the declaration of war, British and French missions arrived in the United States. First they requested money with which to buy supplies, a request Congress had already anticipated in the Liberty Loan Act, which added $5 billion to the national debt in "Liberty Bonds." Of this amount, $3 billion could be loaned to the Allied Powers. The United States was also willing to furnish naval support, credits, supplies, and munitions, but to raise and train a large army, equip it, and send it across a submarine-infested ocean seemed out of the question. Marshal Joseph Joffre, who came with the French mission, nevertheless insisted that the United States send a token force to bolster morale, and on June 26, 1917, the first contingent of Americans, about 14,500 men commanded by General John J. Pershing, began to disembark on the French coast. Pershing and his troops were able to reach Paris by July 4. Pershing soon decided that the war-weary Allies would be unable to mount an offensive by themselves. He advised the War Department that plans should be made to send a million American troops by the following spring. It was done—through strenuous efforts.

When the United States entered the war, the combined strength of the regular army and National Guard was only 379,000; at the end it would be 3.7 million. The need for such large numbers of troops converted Wilson to the idea of conscription. Under the Selective Service Act of 1917, all men aged twenty-one to thirty (later, from eighteen to forty-five) had to register for service. Registrants went into five classes, the first being able-bodied unmarried men without dependents. From this group alone came all the 2.8 million ultimately drafted. All told, about 2 million Americans crossed the Atlantic and about 1.4 million saw some action. Training of the soldiers went on in thirty-two camps, half of them located in the South for climatic reasons. The example of the Spanish-American War was well learned: the camps were for the most part sanitary and equipped with modern plumbing, hospitals, and recreation centers.

Wilson and his secretary of war, Newton D. Baker, as well as many others, saw the mobilization of hundreds of thousands of young men as an opportunity for social engineering. To improve the recruits' character and outlook while preparing them for war, Wilson and Baker created the Commission on Training Camp Activities (CTCA). The idea was to inculcate middle-class "progressive" virtues and values into recruits while they were undergoing their military training. The CTCA produced sex education programs to prevent the spread of venereal diseases, worked with local authorities to police "red-light" districts near the military bases and to arrest prostitutes, and sponsored sporting events and entertainment programs, dances and religious services, all designed to minister to the physical and moral well-being of the trainees.

MOBILIZING A NATION Complete economic mobilization on the home front was also necessary to conduct the war efficiently. Still, a lingering lack of coordination made wartime mobilization in the United States difficult. It was not the Wilson administration's finest hour. The Army Appropriation Act of 1916 had created a Council of National Defense, which in turn led to the creation of other wartime agencies. The Lever Food and Fuel Control Act of 1917 created a Food Administration, headed by Herbert Hoover, a future president. Hoover, a mining engineer and former head of the Commission for Relief in Belgium, sought to raise production while reducing civilian use of foodstuffs.

Food Will Win the War, *the slogan of the Food Administration, appears over the entrance of this "real Bohemian Grill."*

"Food will win the war" was the slogan. Hoover directed a propaganda campaign promoting "Meatless Tuesdays," "Wheatless Wednesdays," "Porkless Saturdays," the planting of victory gardens, and the use of leftovers.

The War Industries Board (WIB), established in 1917, soon became the most important of all the mobilization agencies. It was headed by Bernard Baruch, a brilliant Wall Street speculator, who exercised a virtual dictatorship over the economy. Under Baruch the purchasing bureaus of the United States and Allied governments submitted their needs to the board, which set priorities and planned production. The board could allocate raw materials, tell manufacturers what to produce, order construction of new plants, and, with the approval of the president, fix prices. For the sake of greater efficiency the WIB standardized product styles and designs.

A NEW LABOR FORCE   The closing off of foreign immigration, and the movement of 4 million men from the workforce into the armed services created a labor shortage. To meet it, women, blacks, and other ethnic minorities were encouraged to enter industries and agricultural activities heretofore dominated by white males. Northern businesses sent recruiting agents into the Deep South to find workers for their factories and mills, and over 400,000 southern blacks began the "Great Migration" northward during the war years, a mass movement that continued unabated through the 1920s. Mexican-Americans followed the same migratory pattern. Recruiting agents and newspaper editors portrayed the North as the "land of promise" for southern blacks suffering from their region's depressed agricultural economy and rising racial intimidation and violence. The African-American newspaper *Chicago Defender* exclaimed: "To die from the bite of frost is far more glorious than at the hands of a mob." By 1930 the number of African Americans living in the North had tripled from 1910 levels.

But the newcomers were not always welcomed above the Mason-Dixon line. Many native white workers resented the new arrivals, and racial tensions sparked riots in cities across the country. In 1917 over forty African Americans and nine whites were killed during a riot over employment in a defense plant in East St. Louis. Two years later the toll of a Chicago race riot was nearly as high, with twenty-three black and fifteen white deaths. In these and other incidents of racial violence the pattern was the same. Whites angered by the influx of blacks into

Women taking the place of male work-
ers on the Great Northern Railway,
Great Falls, Montana, 1918.

their communities would seize upon an incident to rampage through black neighborhoods, killing, burning, and looting, while white policemen looked the other way or encouraged the hooliganism.

American intervention in World War I also had a significant impact on women. Initially, women supported the war effort in traditional ways. They helped organize war-bond and war-relief drives, conserved foodstuffs and war-related materials, supported the Red Cross, and joined the Army nurse corps. But as the scope of the war widened, both government and industry sought to mobilize women workers for service on farms, loading docks, and railway crews, as well as in armaments industries, machine shops, steel and lumber mills, and chemical plants. Many women leaders saw such opportunities as a real breakthrough. "At last, after centuries of disabilities and discrimination," said a speaker at a Women's Trade Union League meeting in 1917, "women are coming into the labor and festival of life on equal terms with men." A black woman who exchanged her job as a live-in servant for work in a factory declared: "I'll never work in nobody's kitchen but my own any more. No indeed, that's the one thing that makes me stick to this job."

In fact, however, war-generated changes in female employment were limited and brief. About a million women participated in "war work," but most of them were young and single and already working outside the home. Most returned to their previous jobs once the war ended. In fact, male-dominated unions encouraged women to revert to their stereotypical domestic roles after the war ended. The Central Federated Union of New York baldly insisted that "the same patriotism which induced women to enter industry during the war should induce them to vacate their positions after the war." The anticipated gains of women in the workforce failed to materialize. In fact, by 1920 the 8.5 million working women made up a smaller percentage of the labor force than they had in 1910. Still, one lasting result of women's contributions to the war effort was Woodrow Wilson's decision to endorse female suffrage. In the fall of 1918 he told the Senate that giving women the vote was "vital to the winning of the war."

The wartime emergency placed organized labor in a position to make solid advances in employment and wages, despite the rise in consumer prices. A newly created United States Employment Service placed some 4 million workers in war-related jobs. Labor unions benefited from expanded employment, the increased demand for labor, and government policies favorable to collective bargaining. From 1913 to 1918 AFL membership increased by 37 percent.

WAR PROPAGANDA   The exigencies of winning the war led the government to mobilize more than economic life: the progressive gospel of efficiency suggested mobilizing public opinion as well. On April 14, 1917, eight days after the declaration of war, an executive order established the Committee on Public Information, composed of the secretaries of state, war, and the navy. Its executive head, George Creel, a Denver newsman, sold Wilson on the idea that the best approach to influencing public opinion was "expression, not repression"—propaganda instead of censorship. Creel organized a propaganda machine to convey the Allies' war aims to the people, and above all to the enemy, where it might encourage the forces of moderation. To sell the war, Creel gathered a remarkable group of journalists, photographers, artists, entertainers, and others useful to his purpose. A film division produced such pictures as *The Beast of Berlin*. Hardly any public group escaped a harangue by one of the 75,000 Four-Minute Men, organized to give short speeches on Liberty Bonds, the need to conserve food and fuel, and other timely topics.

CIVIL LIBERTIES   By arousing public opinion to such a frenzy, however, the war effort channeled the zeal of progressivism into grotesque campaigns of "Americanism" and witch-hunting. Wilson had foreseen such consequences. "Once lead this people into war," he said, "and they'll forget there even was such a thing as tolerance." Popular prejudice equated anything German with disloyalty. Symphonies refused to perform Bach and Beethoven, schools dropped courses in the German language, and patriots translated "sauerkraut" into "liberty cabbage," "German measles" into "liberty measles," and "dachshunds" into "liberty pups."

While mobs hunted spies and chased rumors, the federal government stalked bigger game, with results often as absurd. Under the Espionage and Sedition Acts, criticism of government leaders and war policies was in effect outlawed. The Espionage Act of 1917 set penalties of up to $10,000 and twenty years in prison for those who gave aid to the enemy, who tried to incite insubordination, disloyalty, or refusal of duty in the armed services, or who circulated false reports and statements with intent to interfere with the war effort. The postmaster-general could bar from the mails anything that violated the act or advocated treason, insurrection, or forcible resistance to any United States law. The Sedition Act of 1918 extended the penalties to those who did or said anything to obstruct the sale of Liberty Bonds or to advocate cutbacks in production, and—just in case something had been overlooked—for saying, writing, or printing anything "disloyal, profane, scurrilous, or abusive" about the American form of government, the Constitution, or the army and navy.

The Espionage and Sedition Acts generated more than 1,000 convictions. The impact of the acts fell with most severity upon Socialists and other radicals. In Chicago over 100 members of the Industrial Workers of the World went on trial for opposing the war effort. All were found guilty, and the IWW never fully recovered from the blow. Victor Berger, Socialist congressman from Milwaukee, received a twenty-year sentence for editorials in the *Milwaukee Leader* that called the war a capitalist conspiracy. Eugene V. Debs, who had polled over 900,000 votes for president in 1912, ardently opposed American intervention, declaring that "I am opposed to every war but one; I am for that war heart and soul, and that is the world-wide revolution." He repeatedly urged American men to refuse to serve in the military, even though he knew he could be prosecuted for such remarks under the Espionage Act. "I would a thousand times rather be a free soul in jail than a sycophant and a coward in the streets," he told a Socialist gathering in 1918. He received his wish. Two weeks later Debs was arrested and eventually given a twenty-year prison sentence for encouraging draft resistance. In 1920, still in jail, he polled nearly 1 million votes for president.

In two important decisions just after the war, the Supreme Court upheld the Espionage and Sedition Acts. *Schenck v. United States* (1919) upheld the conviction of a man for circulating antidraft leaflets among members of the armed forces. In this case Justice Oliver Wendell Holmes said: "Free speech would not protect a man in falsely shouting fire in a theater, and causing a panic." The act applied where there was "a clear and present danger" that speech in wartime might create evils Congress had a right to prevent. In *Abrams v. United States* (1919) the Court upheld the conviction of a man who circulated pamphlets opposing intervention in Russia. Here Holmes and Louis Brandeis dissented from the majority view. The "surreptitious publishing of a silly leaflet by an unknown man," they argued, posed no danger to government policy.

"THE DECISIVE POWER"

American troops played little more than a token role in the European fighting until early 1918. Before that they were parceled out in quiet sectors mainly for training purposes. All through 1917 the Allies remained on the defensive, and late in the year their situation turned desperate. In October the Italian lines collapsed and were overrun by Austrian forces. With the help of Allied troops from France, the Italians finally held their ground. In November the Bolshevik Revolution overthrew the infant Russian Republic, and the new Soviet government dropped out of the war. With the Central Powers now free to concentrate their forces on the Western Front, the American war effort became a "race for France" to restore the balance of strength. French premier Georges Clemenceau appealed to the Americans to accelerate their mobilization: "A terrible blow is imminent," he predicted to an American journalist. "Tell your Americans to come quickly."

THE WESTERN FRONT On March 21, 1918, Clemenceau's prediction came true when the Germans began the first of several offensives to try to end the war before the Americans arrived in force. On the Somme River they broke through at the juncture of British and French sectors and penetrated thirty-five miles, nearly to Amiens. Farther

Fresh troops moving to an advanced position near the front, France.

north, the Germans struck in Flanders, where the Allies still held a corner of Belgium. At this critical point, on April 14 the Allies made French general Ferdinand Foch the supreme commander of all Allied forces.

On May 27 the Germans began their next drive along the Aisne River, took Soissons, and pushed on to the Marne River along a forty-mile front. By May 1918 there were 1 million fresh American troops in Europe, and for the first time they made a difference. In a counterattack American forces retook Cantigny on May 28 and held it. A week later, on June 2–3, a marine brigade blocked the Germans at Belleau Wood. American army troops took Vaux and opposed the Germans at Château-Thierry. Though these actions had limited military significance, their effect on Allied morale was immense. Each was a solid American success, and together they reinforced Pershing's demand for a separate American army.

Before that could come to pass, the turning point in the western campaign came on July 15, 1918, in the Second Battle of the Marne. On both sides of Reims, the eastern end of a great bulge toward Paris, the Germans commenced their push against the French lines. Within three days, however, they had stalled, and the Allies, mainly with American troops, went on the offensive.

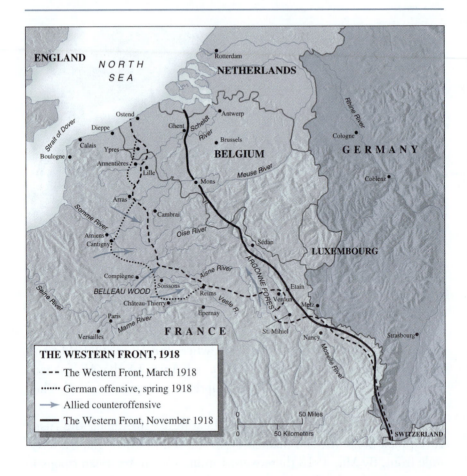

THE WESTERN FRONT, 1918

- - - The Western Front, March 1918

······· German offensive, spring 1918

→ Allied counteroffensive

—— The Western Front, November 1918

Soon the British, French, and Americans began to roll the German front back toward and into Belgium. Then on August 10 the first U.S. Army was organized and assigned the task of liquidating the Germans at St. Mihiel, southeast of Verdun. There, on September 12, an army of more than 500,000 staged the first strictly American offensive of the war. Within three days the Germans had pulled back. The great Meuse-Argonne offensive, begun on September 26, then employed American divisions in a drive toward Sédan and its railroad, which supplied the entire German front. The largest American action of the war, it involved 1.2 million American troops and cost 117,000 American casualties, including 26,000 dead. But along the front from Sédan to Flanders the Germans were in retreat. "America," wrote German general Erich Ludendorff, "thus became the decisive power in the war."

A gun crew firing on entrenched German positions, 1918.

THE BOLSHEVIKS AND THE WAR   When the war broke out in 1914, Russia was one of the Allied Powers. Over the next three years, the Russians suffered some 5.5 million casualties. By 1917, there were shortages of ammunition for Russian troops and food for the Russian people. The czarist government was in disarray, and after the czar's abdication, it first gave way to a provisional republican government, which in turn succumbed in November 1917 to a revolution led by Vladimir Lenin and his Bolshevik party, who promised war-weary Russians "Peace, Land, and Bread."

Once in control of the government, the Bolsheviks unilaterally stopped fighting. With German troops deep in Russian territory, and with armies of "White" Russians (anti-Bolsheviks) organizing resistance to their power, on March 3, 1918, the Bolsheviks concluded a separate peace with Germany in the Treaty of Brest-Litovsk. In an effort to protect Allied supplies and to encourage anti-Bolshevik forces in the developing Russian civil war, Wilson sent American forces into Russia's Arctic ports to prevent military supplies from falling into German hands. On August 2, 1918, some 8,000 American troops landed there and two weeks later in eastern Siberia, where they remained until April 1920 in an effort to curb the growing Japanese ambitions there.

The Allied intervention in Russia failed because the Bolsheviks were able to consolidate their power. Russia took no further part in World War I and did not participate in the peace settlement. The intervention also generated among Soviets long-lasting suspicion of the West.

THE FOURTEEN POINTS   As the war was ending, the question of war aims arose again. Neither the Allies nor the Central Powers, despite Wilson's prodding, had stated openly what they hoped to gain. Wilson repeated that the Americans had no selfish ends. "We desire no conquest, no dominion," he stressed in his war message of 1917. "We seek no indemnities for ourselves, no material compensation for the sacrifices we shall freely make. We are but one of the champions of the rights of mankind." Unfortunately for his purpose, after the Bolsheviks seized power in November 1917, they published copies of secret treaties in which the Allies had promised territorial gains in order to win Italy, Romania, and Greece to their side. When an Interallied Conference in Paris late in 1917 failed to agree on a statement of aims, Colonel House advised Wilson to formulate his own.

During 1917 House had been drawing together an informal panel of American experts called "the Inquiry" to formulate plans for peace. With advice from these experts, Wilson himself drew up a statement that would become the famous Fourteen Points. These he delivered to a joint session of Congress on January 8, 1918, "as the only possible program" for peace. The first five points in general terms called for open diplomacy, freedom of the seas, removal of trade barriers, reduction of armaments, and an impartial adjustment of colonial claims based on the interests of the populations involved. Most of the remainder called on the Central Powers to evacuate occupied lands and to allow self-determination for various nationalities, a crucial principle for Wilson. Point 13 proposed an independent Poland with access to the sea. Point 14, the capstone in Wilson's thinking, championed a general association of nations to secure guarantees of independence and territorial integrity to all countries, great and small.

The Fourteen Points set forth a commitment in which Wilson persisted, but they also served the purposes of psychological warfare. One of their aims was to keep Russia in the war by a more liberal statement of purposes—a vain hope, as it turned out. Another was to reassure the Allied peoples that they were involved in a noble cause. A third was to

*Salvation Army worker writing a letter
home for a wounded soldier.*

drive a wedge between the governments of the Central Powers and
their peoples by the offer of a reasonable peace. Wilson's promise of
"autonomous development" for the subject nationalities of Austria-
Hungary (Point 10) might have weakened the polyglot Hapsburg Empire, though he did not intend to break up the empire. But the chaos
into which central Europe descended in 1918, and the national aspirations of the empire's peoples, took matters out of his hands.

On September 29, 1918, German general Ludendorff advised his
government to seek the best peace terms possible. On October 3, a new
chancellor made the first German overtures for peace on the basis of
the Fourteen Points. A month of diplomatic fencing followed between
Colonel House and Allied representatives. Finally, when he threatened
to pursue separate negotiations, the Allies accepted the Fourteen Points
as a basis of peace, but with two significant reservations: they reserved
the right to discuss freedom of the seas, and they demanded reparations
for war damages.

Meanwhile the German home front was being torn apart by a loss of
morale, culminating in a naval mutiny at Kiel. Germany's allies dropped
out of the war: Bulgaria on September 29, 1918, Turkey on October 30,
and Austria-Hungary on November 3. On November 9, 1918, the kaiser
abdicated, and a German Republic was proclaimed. On November 11,
at 5 A.M., an armistice was signed. Six hours later, at the eleventh hour

Celebration of the Armistice ending World War I, New York City, November 1918.

of the eleventh day of the eleventh month, the guns fell silent. Under the Armistice the Germans had to evacuate occupied territories, pull back behind the Rhine, and surrender their naval fleet, railroad equipment, and other materials. The Germans were assured that the Fourteen Points would be the basis for the peace conference.

THE FIGHT FOR THE PEACE AT HOME AND ABROAD

DOMESTIC UNREST   Wilson made a fateful decision to attend in person the peace conference that convened in Paris on January 18, 1919. It shattered precedent for a president to leave the country for so long, but it dramatized all the more Wilson's messianic vision and his desire to ensure his goal of a lasting peace. From one viewpoint it was a shrewd move, for his prestige and determination made a difference in Paris. But he lost touch with developments at home. His progressive coalition was already unraveling under the pressures of wartime discontent (a state of war officially existed until 1921). Western farmers complained about the government's control of wheat prices while southern cotton producers rode the wartime inflation. Eastern businessmen chafed at revenue policies designed, according to the *New York Sun,* "to pay for the war out of taxes raised north of the Mason and Dixon Line." Organized labor, despite manifest gains, was unhappy with inflation and the problems of reconversion to a peacetime economy.

In the midterm elections of 1918, Wilson made matters worse with a partisan appeal for a Democratic Congress to ensure support of his foreign policies. Republicans, who for the most part had supported war measures, took affront. In elections held on November 5, a week before the Armistice, the Democrats lost control of both houses of Congress. With an opposition majority in the new Congress, Wilson further weakened his standing by failing to involve a single prominent Republican in the peace negotiations. Humorist Will Rogers joked that Wilson was telling the Republicans, "I tell you what, we will split 50-50. I will go and you fellows can stay." Former president Taft groused that Wilson's real intention in going to Paris was "to hog the whole show."

When Wilson reached Europe in December 1918, enthusiastic demonstrations greeted him in Paris. The cheering millions saw in the American idealist a prophet of peace and a spokesman for humanity. Their heartfelt support no doubt strengthened his hand at the conference, but Wilson had to deal with some tough-minded statesmen.

On his way to the Paris Peace Conference, Wilson was welcomed as a hero in Europe. Here he reviews a line of troops at Calais.

The Paris conference comprised a body of delegates from all countries that had declared war or broken diplomatic relations with Germany. It was controlled by the Big Four: the prime ministers of Britain, France, and Italy, and the president of the United States. Japan restricted its interests to Asia and the Pacific. French premier Georges Clemenceau was a stern realist who had little patience with Wilson's utopianism. "God gave us the Ten Commandments and we broke them," Clemenceau sneered. "Wilson gave us the Fourteen Points—we shall see." Clemenceau insisted on harsh measures to weaken Germany and ensure French security. David Lloyd George of England was a gifted politician fresh from electoral victory on the slogan "Hang the Kaiser." Vittorio Orlando of Italy was there to pick up the spoils promised in the secret Treaty of London (1915).

THE LEAGUE OF NATIONS   Wilson carried the point that his cherished League of Nations must come first, in the conference and in the treaty. Whatever compromises he might have to make, whatever mistakes might result, Wilson believed that a permanent agency of collective security would assure international stability. Wilson presided over the commission set up to work out a charter for the League.

Article X of the covenant, which Wilson called "the heart of the League," pledged members to consult on military and economic sanctions against aggressors. The use of arms would be a last (and an improbable) resort. The League, it was assumed, would exercise enormous moral influence that would make military action unnecessary. The League structure allowed each member an equal voice in the Assembly; the Big Five (Britain, France, Italy, Japan, and the United States) and four other nations would make up the Council; the administrative staff in Geneva would make up the Secretariat; and finally, a Permanent Court of International Justice (set up in 1921 and usually called the World Court) could "hear and determine any dispute of an international character."

On February 14, 1919, Wilson reported the finished draft of the League covenant to the plenary session of the conference and departed the next day for a month-long visit home to conduct routine business. Already he faced rumblings of opposition, and shortly before his return to Paris, Henry Cabot Lodge, the chairman of the Senate Foreign Relations Committee, announced that the covenant was unacceptable "in the form now proposed." His statement bore the signatures of thirty-nine Republican senators or senators-elect, more than enough to block ratification. That evening Wilson confidently retorted: "When the treaty comes back, gentlemen on this side will find the covenant not only in it, but so many threads of the treaty tied to the covenant that you cannot dissect the covenant from the treaty without destroying the whole vital structure."

TERRITORY AND REPARATIONS   Back in Paris, Wilson grudgingly conceded to French demands for territorial concessions and reparations from Germany that would keep it weak for years to come. Wilson clashed sharply with Clemenceau, and after the president threatened to leave the conference, they settled on a demilitarized Rhineland (up to 50 kilometers [31 miles] beyond the Rhine River), Allied occupation of this zone for fifteen years, and League administration of the Saar Basin. France could use Saar coal mines for fifteen years, after which a plebiscite would determine the region's status.

In other territorial matters Wilson had to compromise his principle of national self-determination. There was in fact no way to make boundaries correspond to ethnic divisions. The folk wanderings of centuries had left mixed populations scattered throughout central Europe. In some areas, moreover, national self-determination yielded to other interests: the Polish Corridor, for instance, gave Poland its much-needed outlet to the sea through German territory, and the South Tyrol, home for some 200,000 German-speaking Austrians, gave Italy a more defensible frontier at the Brenner Pass. One part of the Austro-Hungarian Empire became Czechoslovakia, which included the German-speaking Sudetenland, an area favored with good defenses. Another part of the empire united with Serbia to create the kingdom of Yugoslavia. Still other substantial parts passed to Poland (Galicia), Romania (Transylvania), and Italy (Trentino and Trieste). All in all, despite aberrations, the new boundaries more nearly followed the ethnic divisions of Europe than the prewar lines.

The discussion of reparations (payments by the vanquished to the victors) was among the longest and most bitter at the conference. Despite a pre-Armistice agreement that Germany would be liable only for civilian damages, Clemenceau and Lloyd George proposed reparations for the entire cost of the war, including veterans' pensions. On this

EUROPE AFTER VERSAILLES

········· 1914 boundaries

New nations

Plebiscite areas

Occupied area

point Wilson made perhaps his most fateful concessions. He accepted in the treaty a clause by which Germany confessed responsibility for the war and thus for its entire costs. The "war guilt" clause offended Germans and caused persistent bitterness.

On May 7, 1919, the victorious powers presented the treaty to the German delegates, who returned three weeks later with 443 pages of criticism protesting that the terms violated the Fourteen Points. A few changes were made, but when the Germans still refused to sign, Marshal Foch prepared to move his army across the Rhine. Finally, on June 28, 1919, the Germans signed the treaty in the Hall of Mirrors at Versailles.

WILSON'S LOSS AT HOME   Wilson returned home with the Versailles Treaty on July 8, 1919. Two days later he called on the Senate to accept "this great duty." The force of Wilson's idealism struck deep, and he returned amid a great clamor of popular support. A third of the state legislatures had endorsed the League, as had thirty-three of forty-eight governors.

Yet, Senator Henry Cabot Lodge, chairman of the Senate Foreign Relations Committee, harbored doubts. He did not want the United States to withdraw from world affairs, but he felt that the outcome at Versailles exhibited the weakness in "the beautiful scheme of making mankind virtuous by a statute or a written constitution." Americans, thought Lodge, were too prone to promise more than they could deliver when great principles entailed great sacrifices. Foreign policy would have to be built up from what the public would sustain rather than be imposed from above. A staunch Republican with an intense dislike for Wilson, Lodge sharpened his partisan knives. He knew the undercurrents already stirring up opposition to the treaty: the resentment of German, Italian, and Irish groups in the United States, the disappointment of liberals at Wilson's compromises on reparations and territories, the distractions of demobilization and the resulting domestic problems, and the revival of isolationism. Lodge's close friend, Theodore Roosevelt, still a popular figure, lambasted the League, noting that he keenly distrusted a "man who cares for other nations as much as his own."

Others agreed. In the Senate a group of "irreconcilables," fourteen Republicans and two Democrats, were unwilling to allow America to enter the League on any terms. They were mainly western or midwestern progressives who feared that foreign commitments threatened domestic reforms. The irreconcilables would be useful to Lodge's purpose, but he belonged to a larger group of "reservationists" who insisted on limiting American participation in the League and its actions. Wilson pointed out to them that the agreement already stipulated that with a veto in the League Council the United States could not be obligated to do anything against its will.

Lodge, who set more store by the old balance of power than by the new idea of collective security, brought forward a set of amendments or reservations. Wilson responded by agreeing to interpretive reservations, but to nothing that would reopen the negotiations. He especially opposed weakening Article X, which provided for collective action against aggression.

By September, with momentum for the treaty slackening, Wilson decided to go to the people and, as he put it, "purify the wells of public

The League of Nations Argument in a Nutshell. *J. N. "Ding" Darling's summation of the League controversy.*

opinion." Against the advice of doctors and friends he set forth on a tour through the Midwest to the West Coast, pounding out speeches on his typewriter between stops. In all he traveled 8,000 miles in twenty-two days, gave thirty-two major addresses and eight informal ones, refuted his opponents, and voiced warnings.

For a while Wilson seemed to be regaining the initiative, but then his body rebelled. On October 2, 1919, Wilson suffered a severe stroke and paralysis on his left side, leaving him an invalid for the rest of his life. For more than seven months he did not meet the cabinet. His protective wife kept him isolated from all but the most essential business. Wilson's disability intensified his stubbornness. He might have done better to stay in the White House and secure the best compromise possible, but now he refused to yield anything. As he scoffed to an aide, "Let Lodge compromise." Wilson ended up committing what one historian called the supreme infanticide, the destruction of his own brain-child.

Lodge was determined to amend the treaty before it was ratified. The Senate adopted fourteen of his reservations, most having to do with the League. Wilson especially opposed the reservation to Article X, which he said, "does not provide for ratification but, rather, for the nullification of the treaty." As a result, the Wilsonians found themselves thrown into an unlikely combination with irreconcilables, who opposed the treaty under any circumstances. The Senate vote was 39 for and 55 against. On the question of taking the treaty without reservations, irreconcilables and reservationists combined to defeat ratification again, with 38 for and 53 against.

In the face of public reaction, however, the Senate voted to reconsider. But the stricken Wilson remained adamant: "Either we should enter the League fearlessly, accepting with responsibility and not fearing the role of leadership which we now enjoy, contributing our efforts toward establishing a just and permanent peace, or we should retire as gracefully as possible from the great concert of powers by which the world was saved." On March 19, 1920, twenty-one Democrats deserted Wilson and joined the reservationists, but the treaty once again fell short of a two-thirds majority by a vote of 49 yeas and 35 nays. The real winner was the smallest of the three groups in the Senate, neither the Wilsonians nor the reservationists but the irreconcilables.

When Congress declared the war at an end by joint resolution on May 20, 1920, Wilson vetoed the action; it was not until July 2, 1921, after he left office, that a joint resolution ended the state of war with Germany and Austria-Hungary. Peace treaties with Germany, Austria, and Hungary were ratified on October 18, 1921, but by then Warren Gamaliel Harding was president of the United States.

Three Senators Refuse the Lady a Seat. *Americans reacted against the Senate's defeat of the Versailles peace treaty.*

LURCHING FROM WAR TO PEACE

The Versailles Treaty, for all the time it took in the Senate, was but one issue clamoring for public attention in the turbulent period after the war. Demobilization proceeded without plan, indeed without much sense that a plan was needed once the war was over. The sudden cancellation of war contracts left workers and business leaders to cope with reconversion on their own. Wilson's leadership was missing. He had been preoccupied by the war and the League, and once broken by his illness, he became strangely grim and peevish. His administration floundered through its last two years.

THE SPANISH FLU   Amid the confusion of postwar life many Americans confronted a virulent menace that produced far more casualties than the war itself. It became known as the Spanish flu, and its contagion spread around the globe. Erupting in the spring of 1918 and lasting a year, the pandemic killed more than 22 million people throughout the world, twice as many as the number who died in World War I. In the United States alone the flu accounted for more than 500,000 deaths, five times the number of combat deaths in France.

American servicemen returning from France brought the flu with them, and it raced through the congested army camps and naval bases. Still, no one seemed alarmed, for the flu remained a common if severe ailment. But then the hospitalized men started dying by the dozens, and it became obvious that this was no ordinary flu virus. In addition to the usual symptoms—coughing, chills, fever, body aches—the afflicted suffered from vomiting, dizziness, labored breathing, nosebleeds, and profuse sweating. Many contracted pneumonia as well, and a startling number of patients died. Some 43,000 American servicemen died of influenza in 1918.

By September 1918 the epidemic had spread to the civilian population. In that month alone 10,000 Americans died from the disease. It was a baffling development. "Nobody seemed to know what the disease was, where it came from or how to stop it," observed the editors of *Science* magazine in 1919. Evangelist Billy Sunday blamed the plague on the Germans, charging that they had brought it across the Atlantic on submarines: "There's nothing short of hell they haven't stooped to do

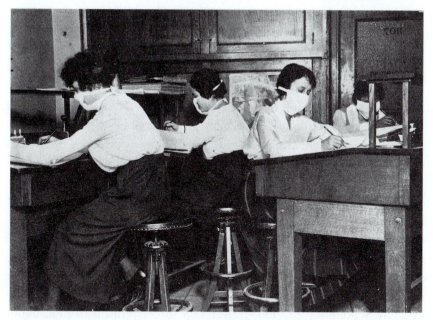

Office workers with gauze masks during the Spanish flu epidemic, 1918.

since the war began. Darn their hides!" Millions of people began wearing surgical masks to work. Phone booths were locked up, as were other public facilities such as dance halls, poolrooms, and theaters. Even churches and saloons in many communities were declared off limits. Still the death toll rose. In Philadelphia 528 people were buried in a single day. From September 1918 to June 1919 some 675,000 Americans died of flu and pneumonia, and fully one-quarter of the population had contracted the illness. Life insurance companies nearly went bankrupt, hospitals were besieged, and cemeteries soon ran out of burial space.

Yet by the spring of 1919 the pandemic had run its course. It ended as suddenly—and as inexplicably—as it had begun. Although another outbreak occurred in the winter of 1920, the population had grown more resistant to its assaults. No disease, plague, war, famine, or natural catastrophe in world history killed so many people in such a short time. The most remarkable aspect of the flu pandemic was that people for the most part took it in stride. People seemed resigned to biological forces beyond their control while issues of war and peace in Europe and the home-front economy continued to dominate the headlines.

THE ECONOMIC TRANSITION   The problems of postwar readjustment were worsened by general labor unrest. Prices continued to rise
after the war, and discontented workers, released from wartime constraints, were more willing to strike for their demands. In 1919, more
than 4 million workers went out in thousands of disputes. Some workers in the East won their demands early in the year, but after a general
strike in Seattle, public opinion began to turn hostile. The Seattle
mayor denounced the walkout of 60,000 workers as evidence of Bolshevik influence. The strike lasted only five days, but public alarm over the
affair damaged the cause of unions across the country.

An AFL campaign to organize steelworkers suffered from charges of
radicalism against its leader, William Z. Foster, who had joined the Socialists in 1900 and later emerged as a Communist. Attention to Foster's radicalism obscured the squalid conditions that had marked the
steel industry since the Homestead Strike of 1892. The twelve-hour
day, often combined with a seven-day week, was common for steelworkers. On September 22, 1919, after U.S. Steel refused to talk, about
340,000 workers walked out. But the union succumbed to a back-to-
work movement and gave up the strike four months later. When information about conditions became widely known, public opinion turned
in favor of the steelworkers, but too late: the strike was over. Steelworkers remained unorganized until the 1930s.

The most celebrated postwar labor dispute was the Boston Police
Strike. Though less significant than the steel strike in the numbers
involved, it inadvertently launched a presidential career. On September 9, 1919, most of Boston's police force went out on strike. Governor
Calvin Coolidge mobilized the National Guard to keep order, and after
four days the strikers were ready to return, but the police commissioner
refused to take them back. When labor leader Samuel Gompers appealed for their reinstatement, Coolidge responded in words that suddenly turned him into a national figure: "There is no right to strike
against the public safety by anybody, anywhere, any time."

RACIAL FRICTION   The summer of 1919 also brought a season of
race riots, both in the North and South. What black leader James Weldon Johnson called "the Red Summer" ("Red" here signified blood) began in July, when whites invaded the black section of Longview, Texas,
in search of a teacher who had allegedly accused a white woman of a li-

A victim of racial rioting in Chicago, July 1919.

aison with a black man. They burned shops and houses and ran several African Americans out of town. A week later in Washington, D.C., reports of attacks on white women aroused white mobs, and for four days gangs of white and black rioters waged race war in the streets until soldiers and driving rains ended the fighting. These were but preliminaries to the Chicago riot of late July in which 38 people were killed and 537 injured. The climactic disorders of the summer occurred in the rural area around Elaine, Arkansas, where black tenant farmers tried to organize a union. According to official reports, 5 whites and 25 blacks died, but whites told one reporter in the area that in reality more than 100 blacks died. Altogether twenty-five race riots took place in 1919, and more threatened.

THE RED SCARE   Public reaction to the wave of labor strikes and race riots was influenced by the impact of the Bolshevik Revolution. A minority of radicals thought America's domestic turbulence, like that in Russia, was the first scene in a drama of world revolution. A much larger public was persuaded that they might be right. After all, a tiny faction in Russia had exploited confusion to impose its will. In 1919 the Socialist party, already depleted by wartime persecution, suffered the further defection of radicals inspired by the Russian example. Left-wing members formed the Communist and the short-lived Communist Labor parties. Wartime hysteria against all things German was readily transformed into a postwar Red Scare.

Fears of revolution might have remained latent except for the actions of a lunatic fringe. In April 1919 the post office intercepted nearly forty bombs addressed to various prominent citizens. One slipped through and blew off the hands of a Georgia senator's maid. In June another destroyed the front of Attorney-General A. Mitchell Palmer's house in Washington. The random violence of these criminals formed no part of Bolshevik tactics, but many Americans saw Red on all sides and condoned attacks on all kinds of minorities in retaliation.

Soon the government itself was promoting witch-hunts. Attorney-General Palmer harbored an entrenched distrust of aliens and a strong desire for the presidency. In 1919 the Justice Department decided to deport radical aliens, and Palmer set up as the head of the new General Intelligence Division the young J. Edgar Hoover, who began to collect an index file on radicals. Raids began on November 7, 1919, when agents swooped down on the Union of Russian Workers in twelve cities. On December 22 the transport ship *Buford,* dubbed the "Soviet Ark," left New York for Finland with 249 people, including assorted anarchists, criminals, and public charges. All were deported to Russia without benefit of a court hearing. On January 2, 1920, a series of police raids in dozens of cities swept up some 5,000 suspects, many taken from their houses without arrest warrants, of whom more than half were kept in custody. That same month the New York legislature expelled five duly elected Socialist members.

Basking in popular approval, Palmer continued to warn of the Red menace, but like other fads and alarms, the mood passed. By the summer of 1920 the Red Scare had begun to evaporate. Communist revolutions in Europe died out, leaving Bolshevism isolated in Russia; bombings tapered off; the wave of strikes and race riots receded. The attorney-general began to seem more threatening to civil liberties than a handful of radicals. By September 1920, when a bomb explosion at the corner of Broad and Wall Streets in New York killed thirty-eight people, Americans were ready to take it for what it was, the work of a crazed mind and not the start of a revolution. The Red Scare nevertheless left a lasting mark on American life. Part of its legacy was the continuing crusade for "100 percent Americanism" and restrictions on immigration. It left a stigma on labor unions and contributed to the anti-union open-shop campaign—the "American Plan," its sponsors called it. But for many Americans the chief residue of the Great War and its disordered aftermath was a profound disillusionment that pervaded American thought in the postwar decades.

MAKING CONNECTIONS

- The Red Scare at the end of World War I led to a wave of nativism and immigration restriction, outlined in the next chapter.

- This chapter ends by noting the "profound disillusionment" Americans felt with efforts to reform the world. The political aspect of that disillusionment—the turn to "normalcy" of the 1920s—is discussed in Chapter 27.

- The treaty ending World War I was designed to cripple Germany's military strength. But as Chapter 29 shows, within two decades Adolf Hitler was leading a rebuilt German military force into World War II.

FURTHER READING

Frederick S. Calhoun's *Power and Principle: Armed Intervention in Wilsonian Foreign Policy* (1986) surveys one aspect of Wilsonian diplomacy. For the Mexican intervention, consult John S. D. Eisenhower's *Intervention!: The United States and the Mexican Revolution, 1913–1917* (1993). A lucid and thoughtful overview of events covered in this chapter is Daniel M. Smith's *The Great Departure: The United States and World War I, 1914–1920* (1965).

A number of scholars have concentrated on the neutrality issue. Arthur S. Link, Wilson's greatest biographer, is sympathetic to the ideals of the president in *Woodrow Wilson: Revolution, War, and Peace* (1979). For a more critical review, see Ross Gregory's *The Origins of American Intervention in the First World War* (1971). A notable recent biography is August Heckscher's *Woodrow Wilson: A Biography* (1991).

Edward M. Coffman's *The War to End All Wars: The American Military Experience in World War I* (1968) is a detailed presentation of America's military involvement. David M. Kennedy's *Over Here: The First World War and American Society* (1980) surveys the impact of the war on the home front. Maurine Weiner Greenwald's *Women, War, and Work: The Impact of World War I on Women Workers in the United States* (1980) discusses the role of women. Ronald Schaffer's *America in the Great War: The Rise of the War Welfare State* (1991) shows the effect of war mobilization on business organization. Richard Polenberg's *Fighting Faiths: The Abrams Case, the Supreme Court, and Free Speech* (1987) examines the prosecution of a case under the 1918 Sedition Act.

How American diplomacy fared in the making of peace has received considerable attention. In addition to the Link book on Wilson, the role of the president is treated in Robert H. Ferrell's *Woodrow Wilson and World War I, 1917–1921* (1985), Arno J. Mayer's *Politics and Diplomacy in Peacemaking: Containment and Counterrevolution at Versailles, 1918–1919* (1967) and N. Gordon Levin, Jr.'s *Woodrow Wilson and World Politics: America's Response to War and Revolution* (1968). Thomas J. Knock interrelates domestic affairs and foreign relations in his explanation of Wilson's peacemaking in *To End All Wars: Woodrow Wilson and the Quest for a New World Order* (1992).

The problems of the immediate postwar years are chronicled by a number of historians. On the Spanish flu, see Alfred W. Crosby's *America's Forgotten Pandemic: The Influenza of 1918* (1990). Labor tensions are examined in David E. Brody's *Labor in Crisis: The Steel Strike of 1919* (1965) and Francis Russell's *A City in Terror: 1919, the Boston Police Strike* (1975). On racial strife, see William Tuttle, Jr.'s *Race Riot: Chicago in the Red Summer of 1919* (1970). The fear of Communists is analyzed in Robert K. Murray's *Red Scare: A Study in National Hysteria, 1919–1920* (rev. ed., 1980).

26 THE MODERN TEMPER

CHAPTER ORGANIZER

This chapter focuses on:

- the reactionary strains of the 1920s.

- the social ferment of the 1920s.

- the influence of modernism in American culture.

The horrors of World War I dealt a shattering blow to the widespread belief that civilization was progressing, a myth that had dominated the public consciousness for a century and that had been so powerful a stimulant to progressivism. The war's unimaginable carnage produced a postwar disillusionment among young intellectuals that challenged old values.

A new "modernist" sensibility emerged among artists, writers, and intellectuals. At once a mood and a movement, modernism emerged first in Europe at the end of the nineteenth century and became a pervasive international force by 1920. It arose out of a widespread recognition that Western civilization had entered an era of bewildering change. New technologies, new modes of transportation and communication, and new scientific discoveries such as quantum mechanics and relativity theory combined to rupture perceptions of reality and generate new forms of artistic expression. "One must never forget," declared Gertrude Stein, the experimentalist poet, "that the reality of the twentieth century is not the reality of the nineteenth century, not at all." Modernism introduced a whole series of intellectual and artistic movements: impressionism, futurism, dadaism, surrealism, Freudianism. As the French painter Paul Gauguin acknowledged, the upheavals of modernism produced "an epoch of confusion."

At the same time that the war and its turbulent aftermath provided an accelerant for modernism, it also stimulated political and social radicalism. The postwar wave of strikes, bombings, Red Scares, and race riots convinced many that America had entered a frightening new era of diversity and change. Defenders of tradition located the germs of radicalism in the polyglot cities teeming with immigrants and foreign ideas. The defensive mood of the 1920s fed on a growing tendency to connect American nationalism with nativism, Anglo-Saxon racism, and militant Protestantism.

REACTION IN THE TWENTIES

NATIVISM   The foreign connections of so many radicals strengthened the sense that the seeds of sedition were foreign borne. The most cele-

Sacco and Vanzetti. *From a series of paintings by Ben Shahn, 1931–1932.*

brated criminal case of the times seemed to prove the connection. It involved two Italian-born anarchists, Nicola Sacco and Bartolomeo Vanzetti. Arrested on May 5, 1920, for a payroll robbery and murder in South Braintree, Massachusetts, they were brought for trial before a judge who privately referred to the defendants as "those anarchist bastards." The question of the two men's guilt remains disputed, and the belief persists in some quarters that they were sentenced for their political ideas and their ethnic origins rather than for any crime they had committed. The case became a great radical and liberal cause célèbre of the 1920s, but despite pleas for mercy and public demonstrations around the world on behalf of the two men, they went to the electric chair on August 23, 1927, their last appeals denied.

The surging postwar nativism generated new efforts to restrict immigration. A pseudo-scientific racism bolstered anti-immigration groups. It found expression in a widely read book, Madison Grant's *The Passing of the Great Race* (1916)—the great race being the Nordics of northern Europe, threatened by the Slavic and Latin people of eastern and southern Europe. The flow of immigrants, slowed by the war, rose again at its end. From June 1920 to June 1921, more than 800,000 persons entered the country, 65 percent of them from southern and eastern Europe; and more were on the way.

An alarmed Congress passed the Emergency Immigration Act of 1921, which restricted new arrivals each year to 3 percent of the foreign-born of any nationality as shown in the 1910 census. A new quota law in 1924 reduced the number to 2 percent based on the 1890 census, which included fewer of the "new" immigrants. This law set a permanent limitation, which became effective in 1929, of slightly over 150,000 per year based on the "national origins" of the American people as of 1920. Since national origins could not be determined with precision, officials were called upon to use available statistics on migration, natural increase, and "such other data as may be found reliable." However inexact the quotas, their purpose was clear: to tilt the balance in favor of immigrants from northern and western Europe, who were assigned about 85 percent of the total. The law completely excluded people from East Asia—a gratuitous insult to the Japanese, who were already kept out of the United States by their "Gentlemen's Agreement" with Theodore Roosevelt.

On the other hand, the law left the gate open to new arrivals from Western Hemisphere countries, so that an ironic consequence was a great increase in the Hispanic Catholic population of the United States. The legal arrivals from Mexico peaked at 89,000 in 1924. Lower figures after that date merely reflect policies of the Mexican government to clamp down on the outflow of labor and stronger American enforcement of old regulations such as the 1882 exclusion of those immigrants likely to become public charges. Waves of illegal immigrants continued to come, however, in response to southwestern agriculture's demand for "stoop" labor. People of Latin American descent (chiefly Mexicans, Puerto Ricans, and Cubans) became the fastest-growing ethnic minority in the country.

THE KLAN   During the postwar years, the nativist tradition took on a new form, a revived Ku Klux Klan modeled on the group founded during Reconstruction. But, in a striking departure from its predecessor, the new Klan was devoted to "100 percent Americanism" and restricted its membership to native-born white Protestants. The new Klan was determined to protect its warped notion of the American way of life not only from African Americans, but also from Roman Catholics, Jews, and immigrants. America was no melting pot, the Klan's founder William J. Simmons warned: "It is a garbage can! . . . When the hordes of aliens walk to the ballot box and their votes outnumber yours, then that alien horde has got you by the throat." A habitual joiner and promoter of fraternal orders, Simmons had gathered a hooded group near Atlanta on Thanksgiving night, 1915. There, "bathed in the sacred glow of the fiery cross, the invisible empire was called from its slumber of half a century to take up a new task."

In going nativist, the Klan had gone national and was no longer restricted to the South. Its appeal reached areas as widely scattered as Oregon and Maine. It thrived in small towns and cities in the North, and especially in the Midwest. It flourished outside the South among the urban social mainstream, attracting clergymen, engineers, accountants, managers and superintendents, small businessmen, and store owners. And it was preoccupied with the defense of white ("native") women and Christian morals. The robes, the flaming crosses, the eerie processionals, the kneeling recruits, the occult liturgies—all tapped a deep urge toward mystery and brought drama into the dreary routine of a thousand communities.

The Klan was a reflex against shifting moral standards, the declining influence of churches, and the broadmindedness of city dwellers and

In 1925 the Ku Klux Klan staged a 40,000-man parade down Pennsylvania Avenue in Washington, D.C.

college students. In the Southwest, it became more than anything else a moral crusade. "It is going to drive the bootleggers forever out of this land," declared a Texan. "It is going to bring clean moving pictures . . . clean literature . . . break up roadside parking . . . enforce the laws . . . protect homes." To achieve such moral goals, the Klan employed night riding intimidation and floggings.

Simmons, always something of a dreamer, betrayed a fatal inability to control the tough customers attracted to the Klan. In 1922 a revolt toppled Simmons who, threatened with violence, abdicated to a new Imperial Wizard, Hiram Wesley Evans, a dentist from Dallas. The hooded order thereafter tried to become a political power. Officeholders either cultivated the Klan or were struck dumb on the subject. But the Klan never achieved much politically. The order had neither a political program nor a dynamic leadership. Unlike kindred movements in postwar Europe, it conjured up no Mussolini, no Hitler.

Estimates of its peak membership, probably inflated, range from 3 million to 8 million, but the Klan's influence evaporated as quickly as its numbers grew. For one thing, the Klan suffered from a decline in nativist excitement after passage of the 1924 immigration law. For another, it suffered recurrent factional quarrels and schisms. And its willing use of violence tarnished its moral pretensions. The "best people" of many towns had joined what they thought was an agency of reform, but they drifted away as the Klan became a cloak for immorality and corruption.

FUNDAMENTALISM   While the Klan saw a threat mainly in the alien menace, many adherents of the old-time religion saw threats from modernism in the churches: new ideas that the Bible should be studied in the light of modern scholarship (the "higher criticism") or that it could be reconciled with biological theories of evolution. Fearing that such notions had infected schools and even pulpits, orthodox Christians took on a militant new fundamentalism. The movement had acquired a name and definition from a series of pamphlets, *The Fundamentals* (1910). The fundamentalists were distinguished less by their belief in a faith that many others shared than by their posture of hostility toward any other belief.

Among rural fundamentalist leaders only William Jennings Bryan had the following, prestige, and eloquence to make the movement a popular crusade. Although advancing age had cost Bryan his commanding physical presence, he remained as optimistic, pious, and silver-tongued as ever. In 1921 Bryan sparked a drive for laws to prohibit the teaching of evolution in the public schools. He denounced Darwin with the same zeal he had once directed against William McKinley. "Evolution," he said, "by denying the need or possibility of spiritual regeneration, discourages all reforms, for reform is always based upon the regeneration of the individual." Anti-evolution bills began to turn up in legislatures, but the only victories came in the South—and there were few of those. Some officials took direct action without legislation. Governor Miriam "Ma" Ferguson of Texas outlawed textbooks upholding Darwinism. "I am a Christian mother," she declared, "and I am not going to let that kind of rot go into Texas schoolbooks."

The climax came in Tennessee, where in 1925 the legislature passed a bill outlawing the teaching of evolution in public schools and colleges. The governor, unwilling to endanger a pending school program, signed the bill with the hope that it would probably never be applied. He was

Courtroom Scene during the Scopes Trial. *The media, food vendors, and other assorted characters flocked to Dayton to hear the case against John Scopes, the teacher who taught evolution.*

wrong. In Dayton, Tennessee, citizens convinced a young high school teacher, John T. Scopes, to accept an offer from the American Civil Liberties Union to defend a test case—chiefly to put their town on the map. They succeeded beyond their wildest hopes: the publicity was worldwide, and enduring. Before the opening day of the "monkey trial" on July 13, 1925, the streets of Dayton swarmed with publicity hounds, curiosity seekers, evangelists and atheists, a blind mountaineer who proclaimed himself the world's greatest authority on the Bible, hot-dog and soda-pop hucksters, and a miscellany of reporters.

The two stars of the show—Bryan, who had offered his services to the prosecution, and Clarence Darrow, renowned trial lawyer of Chicago and confessed agnostic—united at least in their determination to make the trial an exercise in public education. When the judge ruled out scientific testimony, however, the defense called Bryan as an expert witness on biblical interpretation. In his dialogue with Darrow, he repeatedly entrapped himself in literal-minded interpretations and indeed his ignorance of biblical history and scholarship. He insisted that a "great fish" actually swallowed Jonah, that Joshua literally made the sun stand still, that the world was created in 4004 B.C.—all, according to Darrow, "fool ideas that no intelligent Christian on earth believes." It was a bitter scene. At one point the two men, their patience exhausted in the broiling summer heat, lunged at each other, shaking their fists, prompting the judge to adjourn court.

The next day testimony ended. The only issue before the court, the judge ruled, was whether Scopes had taught evolution, and no one denied that he had. He was found guilty, but the Tennessee supreme court, while upholding the act, overruled the $100 fine on a legal technicality. The chief prosecutor accepted the higher court's advice against "prolonging the life of this bizarre case" and dropped the issue. With more prescience than he knew, Bryan had described the trial as a "duel to the death." A few days after it closed, he died suddenly of a heart condition aggravated by heat and fatigue.

After the Dayton trial, the fundamentalists had spent their fury. Their very victories were self-defeating, for they served to publicize evolution, the doctrine they opposed as heresy. The states that went through the fiercest controversies became prime markets for books on evolution, and the movement roused a liberal defense of academic freedom.

PROHIBITION   Prohibition offered another example of reforming zeal channeled into a drive for moral righteousness and social conformity. Around the turn of the century the leading temperance organizations, the Women's Christian Temperance Union and the Anti-Saloon League, had converted from efforts to change individuals to a campaign for legal Prohibition. Building upon the general moral disrepute of saloons, they were able to equate the "liquor traffic" with the trusts and "special interests." At the same time, contrary to certain old-time folk beliefs that alcohol was beneficial, medical and scientific opinion now showed that it did more harm than good. By the 1910s, the Anti-Saloon League had become one of the most effective pressure groups in American history, mobilizing Protestant churches behind its single-minded battle to elect "dry" candidates.

At its "Jubilee Convention" in 1913, the league endorsed a national Prohibition Amendment to the Constitution. The 1916 elections finally produced two-thirds majorities for Prohibition in both houses of Congress. Soon the wartime spirit of sacrifice, the need to use grain for food, and wartime hostility to German-American brewers transformed the cause virtually into a test of patriotism. On December 18, 1917, Congress sent to the states the Eighteenth Amendment which, one year after ratification on January 16, 1919, banned the manufacture, sale, or transport of intoxicating liquors.

By then, however, about three-fourths of the American people already lived in states and counties that were legally dry. In 1919 the Volstead Act defined as "intoxicating" all beverages containing more than 0.5 percent alcohol, which became illegal once the Eighteenth Amendment went into effect in 1920.

But a new law did not convince people to stop drinking. Instead it provoked them to use ingenious—and illegal—ways to satisfy their thirst for alcohol. The Eighteenth Amendment had been in effect fewer than eight months when authorities found a still with a daily capacity of 130 gallons near Austin, Texas, on a farm belonging to Morris Shepard, the "Father of National Prohibition." Congress never supplied adequate enforcement, if such was indeed possible given the public thirst, the spotty support of local officials, and the profits to be made in bootlegging. In Detroit, across the river from Ontario, where liquor was still legal, the liquor industry during the Prohibition Era was second in size only to the auto industry. Speakeasies, hip flasks, and cocktail parties were among the social innovations of the Prohibition Era, along with increased drinking by women.

It would be too much to say that Prohibition gave rise to organized crime, for organized vice, gambling, and extortion had long been prac-

Speakeasy *by Ben Shahn, 1933–1934. After passage of the Eighteenth Amendment, Americans would gather in hidden "speakeasies" to enjoy liquor while avoiding the laws of Prohibition.*

ticed, and often tied in with the saloons. But Prohibition supplied criminals with a new source of enormous income, while the automobile and the submachine gun provided greater mobility and firepower. Gangland leaders showed remarkable gifts for exploiting loopholes in the law, when they did not simply bribe policemen and politicians. One crime boss who operated in the Midwest bought a chain of drugstores so he could order medicinal liquors and then hijack his own trucks as they transported the goods.

The most celebrated gangster and racketeer (a word coined in the 1920s) was "Scarface" Al Capone, who moved from New York to Chicago in 1920 and within a few years became the city's leading bootlegger and gambling and vice lord. In 1927 his bootlegging, prostitution, and gambling empire brought him an income of $60 million, which he flaunted in expensive suits and silk pajamas, a custom-upholstered and bulletproof Cadillac, an entourage of bodyguards, and lavish support for city charities. Capone always insisted that he was merely providing the public with goods and services it demanded: "They say I violate the prohibition law. Who doesn't?" He neglected to say that he himself had also bludgeoned to death several conspiring police lieutenants and ordered the execution of dozens of his rival criminals. Law-enforcement

Al Capone (center) *in 1929.*

officials led by FBI agent Eliot Ness began to smash his bootlegging operations in 1929, but they were unable to pin anything on Capone until a Treasury agent infiltrated his gang and uncovered evidence that nailed him for tax evasion. Tried in 1931, Capone was sentenced to eleven years in prison.

In light of the illegal activities of Capone and other organized-crime members, it came as no great surprise in 1931 when a commission under former attorney-general George W. Wickersham reported evidence that enforcement of Prohibition had broken down. Of the commission's eleven members, only five approved continued efforts to enforce Prohibition without change, four favored modifications, and two personally favored repeal. Still, the commission as a whole voted for further efforts to make Prohibition work, and President Hoover chose to stand by what he called the "experiment, noble in motive and far-reaching in purpose."

THE ROARING TWENTIES

In many ways the defensive temper of the 1920s and the repressive movements it spawned seemed the dominant trends of the times, but they arose in part as reactions to a social and intellectual revolution that seemed about to rip America away from its old moorings. In various labels given to the times, it was an era of excess, the Jazz Age, the Roaring Twenties, the ballyhoo years, the aspirin age. During those years, a new cosmopolitan, urban America confronted an old insular, rural America, and cultural conflict reached new levels of tension.

The smart set of the sophisticated metropolis developed an active disdain for the old-fashioned rural/small-town values of the hinterlands. Sinclair Lewis's novel *Main Street* (1920) portrayed the stifling, mean, cramped life of the prairie town, depicting a "savorless people, gulping tasteless food, and sitting afterward, coatless and thoughtless, in rocking chairs prickly with inane decorations, listening to mechanical music, saying mechanical things about the excellence of Ford automobiles, and viewing themselves as the greatest race in the world."

The banality of small-town life became a pervasive theme in much of the literature of the time. In *Look Homeward, Angel* (1929), Thomas Wolfe scandalized his native Asheville, North Carolina, with his unrelenting drive to escape the encircling hills and flee to the "billion-footed city." Writing for the *Smart Set* and *American Mercury,* the Baltimore journalist H. L. Mencken was the most merciless in his attacks on the American "booboisie." The daily panorama of America, he wrote, had become "so inordinately gross and preposterous . . . that only a man who was born with a petrified diaphragm can fail to laugh himself to sleep every night, and to awake every morning with all the eager, unflagging expectation of a Sunday-school superintendent touring the Paris peep-shows." The hinterlands responded with counterimages of cities infested with vice, crime, corruption, and foreigners.

THE JAZZ AGE   Writer F. Scott Fitzgerald dubbed the postwar era the "Jazz Age" because young people were willing to experiment with new forms of recreation and sexuality. The new jazz music bubbling up in New Orleans, Kansas City, Memphis, New York City, and Chicago blended African and European musical traditions into a distinctive sound characterized by improvisation, "blue notes," and polyrhythms. Its leading performers included King Oliver, Jelly Roll Morton, Louis Armstrong, and Bessie Smith. The syncopated rhythms of jazz were im-

Frankie "Half Pint" Jackson and His Band at the Sunset Cafe, Chicago, 1920s. *Jazz emerged during this period as an especially American expression of the modernist spirit. Black artists bent musical conventions to give fuller rein to improvisation.*

mensely popular among rebellious young adults and helped spawn carefree new dance steps such as the Charleston and Black Bottom, gyrations that shocked guardians of morality.

If people were not listening to "ragtime" or "jazz" music or to the family radio shows that became the rage in the 1920s, they were frequenting movie theaters. By 1930 there were more than 23,000 of them around the country, and they drew more than 95 million customers each week. In Muncie, Indiana, a small city of 35,000 people, there were nine movie theaters operating seven days a week. Movies were by far the most popular form of mass culture in the twenties, and films became even more favored after the introduction of sound in 1927. *The Jazz Singer,* starring Al Jolson, was the first feature-length "talkie."

THE NEW MORALITY   Much of the shock to old-timers during the Jazz Age came from the revolution in manners and morals, evidenced first among young people, and especially on the college campuses. In *This Side of Paradise* (1920), a novel of student life at Princeton, F. Scott Fitzgerald wrote of "the great current American phenomenon, the 'petting party.'" None of the Victorian mothers, he said, "had any idea how casually their daughters were accustomed to be kissed." From such novels and from magazine pieces, the heartland learned about the

The cartoonist John Held's depiction of the modern coed, June 1926.

wild parties, bathtub gin, promiscuity, speakeasies, roadhouses, "shimmy dancers," and the new uses to which automobiles were put on secluded lovers' lanes.

Writers also informed the nation about the "new woman" eager to exercise new freedoms. These independent females discarded corsets, sported bobbed hair, heavy makeup, and skirts above the ankles; they smoked cigarettes and drank beer, drove automobiles, and in general, defied old Victorian expectations for womanly behavior.

Sex came to be discussed with a new frankness during the 1920s. One father said his daughter "would talk about anything; in fact, she hardly ever talked about anything else." Much of the talk derived from a spreading awareness of Dr. Sigmund Freud, the Viennese father of psychoanalysis. When in 1909 Freud visited Clark University in Massachusetts, he was surprised to find himself so well known "even in prudish America." The following year the first English translation of his *Three Contributions to a Theory of Sex* appeared. By the 1920s and 1930s, his ideas had begun to percolate into the popular awareness, and the talk spread in society and literature about libido, inhibitions, Oedipus complexes, transference, sublimation, and repression.

An obsession with sex permeated much of the literature and popular media of the day. Radio singers during the 1920s belted out songs with titles such as "Hot Lips," "I Need Lovin'," and "Burning Kisses." James Branch Cabell, who became famous when his novel *Jurgen* (1919) was banned in Boston, exploited his "phallic candor" in a string of novels, while Eugene O'Neill used Freudian themes onstage in *Desire under the Elms* (1924), *Mourning Becomes Electra* (1931), and other plays. Sex became the stock-in-trade of a prosperous tabloid press, and a new form of literature, the confession magazine, featured lurid stories about women who had gone wrong. In motion pictures "America's Sweetheart," the maidenly Mary Pickford, yielded stardom to the "vamp," Theda Bara. A rising protest over such movie fare as *Up in Mabel's Room, Sinners in Silk,* and *Her Purchase Price* impelled the movie industry to adopt stringent regulations about the content and language in films.

Fashion also reflected the rebellion against prudishness and a loosening of inhibitions. In 1919 women's skirts were typically six inches above the ground; by 1927 they were at the knees, and the "flapper"—with her bobbed hair, rolled stockings, cigarettes, lipstick, and sensuous dancing—was providing a shocking model of the new feminism. The

Women of the 1920s emulated the style of Cotton Club dancers: bobbed hair, short skirts, and lipstick.

name derived from the way fashionable women allowed their galoshes to "flap" about their ankles. Conservative moralists saw the flappers as just another sign of a degenerating society. Others saw in the "new women" an expression of American individualism. "By sheer force of violence," explained the *New York Times* in 1929, the flapper has "established the feminine right to equal representation in such hitherto masculine fields of endeavor as smoking and drinking, swearing, petting, and upsetting the community peace."

By 1930, however, the thrill of rebellion was waning; the revolution against Victorian codes had run its course. Its extreme expressions aroused doubts that the indulgence of lust equaled liberation. Still, some new folkways had come to stay. In *Middletown* (Muncie, Indiana), the subject of Robert and Helen Lynd's classic community study in the mid-1920s, a young man told them on their return in 1935 that young people had "been getting more and more knowing and bold. The fellows regard necking as a taken-for-granted part of a date." In the late 1930s, a survey disclosed that among college women almost half (47 percent) had yielded their virginity before marriage, but of these three-quarters had had sexual relations only with their future spouses.

The most pervasive change brought by the new moral code was in its views of marriage. The old code had made the husband head and mas-

Margaret Sanger (in coat with fur collar) founded the American Birth Control League and opened the first public clinic for counseling on contraception.

ter of the family, responsible for its support, while limiting the wife's "sphere" to the care of the home and children and the nurturing of the husband. By the 1930s, a code exalting romantic love and companionship as the basis for marriage had gained ascendancy. One sociologist announced that the "breaking of the former taboo on sex has made possible for younger men and women a healthier attitude toward marital relationship" and a greater chance for mutual happiness. More important than breaking taboos may have been the social and economic evolution of a century that had taken away functions the family once had and delivered them to the factory, the school, and other institutions. People expressed alarm in the 1920s at the rising divorce rate. The rate declined briefly with the onset of the Great Depression in 1929, but picked up again during the later 1930s and 1940s. The divorce rate reflected perhaps less an increase in unsatisfactory marriages than a greater willingness and ability to abandon an intolerable situation.

THE WOMEN'S MOVEMENT   Voting rights for women arrived in 1920. It had been an unconscionably long time in coming. The suffrage movement, which had been in the doldrums since 1896, sprang back to life in the second decade of the new century. In 1912 Alice Paul, a

Quaker social worker, returned from an apprenticeship with the militant suffragists of England, and became head of the National American Woman Suffrage Association's Congressional Committee. Paul told female activists to picket state legislatures, target and "punish" politicians who failed to endorse suffrage, chain themselves to public buildings, provoke police into arresting them, undertake hunger strikes, and even adopt what the British militants called the "argument of the broken windowpane."

Paul's militant tactics and single-minded focus on the federal amendment increasingly drove a wedge between her and the larger national group. The Congressional Union, formed by her committee in 1913, became a separate organization in 1915 and changed its name to the Woman's party in 1916. This group copied the British suffragists in holding the party in power responsible for failure to act, a reasonable stance under a parliamentary system but one that led them to oppose every Democrat, which the mainline suffragists found self-defeating in America. Alice Paul nevertheless knew how to get publicity for the cause. By 1917 she and her followers were picketing the White House and deliberately provoking arrests, after which they went on hunger strikes in prison. The authorities obligingly cooperated in making martyrs. They arrested them by the hundreds.

A march for women's suffrage, 1915.

Meanwhile, Carrie Chapman Catt became head of the National Suffrage Association once again in 1915 and revived it through her gift for organization. She brought with her a legacy of about $1 million from Mrs. Frank Leslie, publisher of *Leslie's Weekly*, dedicated "to the furtherance of the cause of woman suffrage." The money became available in 1917 and contributed to organizing the final campaigns for voting rights. For several years, President Wilson evaded the issue of an amendment, but he voted for suffrage in a New Jersey referendum and supported a plank in the 1916 Democratic platform endorsing state action for women's suffrage. He also addressed the National Suffrage Organization that year, and thereafter worked closely with its leaders.

Finally, in 1918, after the House had passed the "Anthony Amendment," Wilson went before the Senate to plead for its passage there. The Senate fell short of the needed two-thirds majority by two votes, but the attention centered on the issue helped defeat two antisuffrage senators. On June 4, 1919, the Senate finally adopted the amendment by a bare two-thirds majority. Ratification of the Nineteenth Amendment took another agonizing fourteen months. The Tennessee legislature had the distinction of completing the ratification, on August 21, 1920. It was one of the climactic achievements of the Progressive Era.

Even before ratification, the suffrage organization began transforming itself into the League of Women Voters, founded in 1919, and women thereafter entered politics in growing numbers. But, it was often noted, this did not usher in a sudden release of women from all the trammels of custom and law. What was more, the suffrage victory left the broader feminist movement prey to a letdown that lasted for a generation. A few years after the triumph, Carrie Chapman Catt wrote that suffragists were disappointed "because they miss the exaltation, the thrill of expectancy, the vision which stimulated them in the suffrage campaign. They find none of these appeals to their aspiration in the party of their choice."

One group, however, wanted to take matters further. Alice Paul and the Woman's party set a new feminist goal, first introduced in Congress in 1923: an Equal Rights Amendment that would eliminate any remaining legal distinctions between the sexes—including the special legislation for the protection of working women put on the books in the previous fifty or so years. It would be another fifty years before Alice Paul would see Congress adopt her amendment in 1972; she did not live, however, to see it fall short of ratification.

The sharp increase in the number of women in the workforce during World War I proved short-lived, but in the longer view a steady increase in the numbers of employed women occurred in the 1920s and, surprisingly, continued through the depression decade of the 1930s. Still, this phenomenon represented more evolution than revolution. The greatest breakthroughs had come in the nineteenth century, and by 1900 women had at least a token foothold in most occupations. By 1910 they made up almost a quarter of all nonagricultural workers, and in 1920 they were found in all but 35 of the 572 job categories listed by the census. The continued entry of women into the workforce brought their numbers up from 8 million in the 1920 census to 10 million in 1930, and 13 million in 1940. Still, these women remained concentrated in traditional occupations: domestics, office workers, teachers, clerks, salespeople, dressmakers, milliners, and seamstresses. On the eve of World War II, women's work was little more diversified than it had been at the turn of the century, but by 1940 it was on the verge of a great transformation.

THE "NEW NEGRO" The discriminations that have befallen African Americans and women have many parallels, and the loosening of restraints for both have often coincided. The most significant development in black life during these years was the Great Migration northward. The movement of blacks to the North began in 1915–1916, when rapidly expanding war industries were experiencing a labor shortage at a time when the war prevented replacement by foreign immigrants; legal restrictions on immigration continued the movement in the 1920s. Altogether, between 1910 and 1920, the Southeast lost some 323,000 blacks, or 5 percent of the native black population, and by 1930 it had lost another 615,000, or 8 percent of the native black population in 1920. With the migration, a slow but steady growth in black political influence set in. Blacks were freer to speak and act in a northern setting; they also gained political leverage by concentrating in large cities located in states with many electoral votes.

Along with political activity came a bristling spirit of protest among blacks, a spirit that received cultural expression in a literary and artistic movement known as the "Harlem Renaissance." Claude McKay, a Jamaican immigrant, was the first significant writer of the movement, which was a rediscovery of black folk culture and an emancipation from the genteel tradition. Poems collected in McKay's *Harlem Shadows* (1922)

A Negro Family Just Arrived in Chicago from the Rural South, 1922. *Between 1910 and 1930 almost 1 million blacks left the South in the Great Migration north.*

expressed defiance in such titles as "If We Must Die" and "To the White Fiends." Other emergent writers included the versatile and prolific Langston Hughes, poet, novelist, and columnist; Zora Neale Hurston, folklorist and novelist; Countée Cullen, poet and novelist; and James Weldon Johnson, who portrayed the black mecca in *Black Manhattan.* Perhaps the greatest single creation of the time was Jean Toomer's novel *Cane,* which pictured the lives of simple folk in Georgia's black belt and the sophisticated inhabitants of Washington's brown belt. White writers such as Eugene O'Neill and Sherwood Anderson also took up the theme of what one observer in 1925 called the "New Negro," but more often than not they merely abandoned the old stereotype of the "darkie" for a new stereotype of the exotic primitive, a caricature the more fully alive for its want of inhibitions.

In its extreme expression the spirit of the New Negro found an outlet in what came to be called "Negro nationalism," which exalted black-

Marcus Garvey, founder of the United Negro Improvement Association and a leading spokesman for "Negro nationalism" in the 1920s.

ness, black cultural expression, and black exclusiveness. The leading spokesman for such views was the flamboyant Marcus Garvey. In 1916 he brought to New York the United Negro Improvement Association (UNIA), which he had started in his native Jamaica two years before. His organization grew rapidly under the strains of the postwar years. Racial bias, he said, was so ingrained in whites that it was futile to appeal to their sense of justice. Garvey told American blacks to liberate themselves from the surrounding white culture. "We have outgrown slavery," he declared, "but our minds are still enslaved to the thinking of the Master Race." He saw every white person as a "potential Klansman" and therefore endorsed the "social and political separation of all peoples to the extent that they promote their own ideals and civilization." Such a separatist message appalled other black leaders. W. E. B. Du Bois, for example, labeled Garvey "the most dangerous enemy of the Negro race." Garvey and his aides created their own black version of Christianity, organized their own fraternal lodges and community cultural centers, started their own businesses, and published their own newspaper. Garvey's message of racial pride and self-reliance appealed to many blacks who had arrived in the northern cities during the Great

Migration and grown frustrated and embittered with the hypocrisy of American democracy during the postwar economic slump.

Delivering the keynote address at the first convention of the UNIA in 1920, Garvey declared that the only lasting hope for blacks was to flee America and build their own republic in Africa. Garvey quickly enlisted half a million members and claimed as many as 6 million by 1923. At that point he was charged with fraudulent use of the mails in fund-raising. Found guilty, he went to the Atlanta penitentiary in 1925, where he remained until President Calvin Coolidge pardoned and deported him to Jamaica in 1927. Garvey died in obscurity in London in 1940, but the memory of his movement kept alive an undercurrent of racial nationalism that would reemerge later under the slogan of "black power."

A more lasting and influential force for racial equality was the National Association for the Advancement of Colored People (NAACP), started with one writer's call for a revival of the abolitionist spirit in response to a 1908 race riot in Springfield, Illinois. Plans laid at a meeting in 1909 led to a formal organization in 1910. Black participants came mainly from a group associated with Du Bois and called the Niagara Movement, which had met each year since 1905 at a place associated with antislavery (Niagara Falls, Oberlin, Boston, Harper's Ferry) and issued a defiant statement against discrimination.

Although most white progressives did not embrace the NAACP, the new group took seriously the progressive idea that the solution to social problems began with informing the people, and it planned an active press bureau to accomplish this. Du Bois became its director of publicity and research, and editor of its journal, *The Crisis*. The NAACP's main strategy was to focus on legal action designed to bring the Fourteenth and Fifteenth Amendments back to life. One early victory came with *Guinn v. United States* (1915). The Supreme Court struck down Oklahoma's grandfather clause, used in the state to deprive blacks of the vote. In *Buchanan v. Worley* (1917) the Court invalidated a residential segregation ordinance in Louisville, Kentucky.

In 1919 the NAACP launched a campaign against lynching, a still common form of vicious racism. An anti-lynching bill to make mob murder a federal offense passed the House in 1922, but it lost to a filibuster by southern senators. The bill stayed before the House until 1925, and NAACP field secretary James Weldon Johnson believed the continued agitation of the issue did more than the bill's passage would have to reduce lynchings, which decreased to a third of what they had been in the previous decade.

The emergent black political renaissance found its most important expression in two events: Oscar DePriest's election from a Chicago district in 1928 as the first black congressman since 1901, the first ever from the North; and the fight against the confirmation of Judge John J. Parker for the Supreme Court in 1930. When President Hoover submitted Parker's name, the NAACP found that, as the 1920 Republican candidate for governor of North Carolina, Parker had pronounced Negro suffrage "a source of evil and danger." The NAACP conducted its campaign, Du Bois said, "with a snap, determination, and intelligence never surpassed in colored America." Parker lost by the close vote of 41 to 39; his defeat represented the first instance of a significant black impact on Congress since Reconstruction.

THE CULTURE OF MODERNISM

SCIENCE AND SOCIAL THOUGHT   As the twentieth century advanced, the easy faith in progress and reform expressed by Social Gospelers and other liberals fell victim to a series of frustrations and disasters: the Great War, the failure of the League of Nations, the failure of Prohibition, the Great Depression, the rise of Communist and fascist dictators, and continuing world crises. New currents in science and social thought also challenged the belief in a rational or melioristic universe. Darwin's biology portrayed humans as more akin to apes than to angels. And Darwin's contemporary, Karl Marx, portrayed people as creatures of economic self-interest. In capitalist society, Marx argued, freedom was an illusion: people were actually driven by impersonal economic forces. In Freud's psychology people were also driven, but by needs arising from the depths of the unconscious. Thus Darwin, Marx, and Freud suggested that rational humans did not control their fate.

Startling new findings in physics further shook the verities underlying American life and thought in the progressive period. The conventional wisdom since Sir Isaac Newton had held the universe to be governed by laws that the scientific method could ultimately uncover. A world of such certain order bolstered hopes of infinite progress in human knowledge. But this world of order and certainty disintegrated

Albert Einstein.

when Albert Einstein, a young German physicist working in the Swiss patent office, announced his theory of relativity, which maintained that space, time, and mass were not absolutes but relative to the location and motion of the observer. Newton's mechanics, according to Einstein, worked well enough at relatively slow speeds, but the more nearly one approached the velocity of light (about 186,000 miles per second) the more all measuring devices would change accordingly, so that yardsticks would become shorter, clocks and heartbeats would slow down. An observer on another planet moving at a different speed would see a quite different universe from the one we see. Even more incredibly, people traveling on a spaceship at incredible velocity, and unaware that for them time had slowed relative to earth time, might return to find that centuries had passed in their absence.

Certainty dissolved the farther one reached out into the universe. The same thing happened the farther one reached down into the minute world of the atom. The discovery of radioactivity in the 1890s showed that atoms were not irreducible units of matter but that some of them emitted particles of energy. What this meant, Einstein noted, was that mass and energy were not separate phenomena but interchangeable. In 1907 Einstein quantified this relationship in the famous and deceptively simple formula $E = mc^2$, energy equals mass times the speed of light squared.

Meanwhile the German physicist Max Planck found that electromagnetic emissions of energy, whether as electricity or light, came in little bundles, which he called quanta. The development of the quantum theory suggested that atoms were far more complex than once believed and, as the German physicist Werner Heisenberg stated in his principle of uncertainty in 1927, ultimately indescribable. One could never know both the position and the velocity of an electron, Heisenberg concluded, because the very process of observation would affect the behavior of the particle, altering its position and velocity.

Heisenberg's thesis meant that beyond a certain point things could not possibly be measured, so human knowledge had limits. "The physicist thus finds himself in a world from which the bottom has dropped clean out," a Harvard mathematician wrote in 1929. He had to "give up his most cherished convictions and faith. The world is not a world of reason, understandable by the intellect of man, but as we penetrate ever deeper, the very law of cause and effect, which we had thought to be a formula to which we could force God Himself to subscribe, ceases to have any meaning." Hard for the public to grasp, such findings proved too much even for Einstein, who spent much of the rest of his life in quest of an explanation that would combine electromagnetism and gravitation in one system and unify the relativity and quantum theories. "I shall never believe that God plays dice with the world," Einstein said.

Though few people understood it, Einstein's theory of relativity captured the imagination of a public whose common experience told them that observers differently placed got a different view of things. The ideas of relativity and uncertainty led people to deny absolute values in any sphere of society, and thus undermined the concepts of personal responsibility and absolute standards. Anthropologists aided the process by transforming the word *culture,* which had before meant refinement, into a term for the whole system of ideas, folkways, and institutions within which any group lived. Even the most primitive groups had cultures and, all things being relative, one culture should not impose its value judgments on another. Two students of Columbia University anthropology professor Franz Boas, Ruth Benedict and Margaret Mead, were especially effective in spreading this viewpoint. Benedict's *Patterns of Culture* (1934), a steady seller, introduced millions to the different values of unusual cultures, from the North American Indians to Pacific islanders, and Mead's *Coming of Age in Samoa* (1928) celebrated the healthfulness of the uninhibited sex she observed there.

MODERNIST LITERATURE   The cluster of scientific ideas associated with Darwin and Einstein inspired a revolution in the minds of intellectuals and creative artists, which they expressed in a new "modernism." The modernist world was one in which, as Karl Marx said, "All that is solid melts into air." Where nineteenth-century writers and artists took for granted an accessible world that could be readily observed and accurately represented, self-willed modernists viewed the "real" as something to be created rather than copied, expressed rather than reproduced. They thus concluded that the subconscious regions of the psyche were more interesting and potent than reason, common sense, and logic.

In the various arts, related technical features appeared: abstract painting that represented an inner mood rather than a recognizable image of an object, atonal music, free verse in poetry, stream-of-consciousness narrative, and interior monologues in stories and novels. Writers showed an intense concern with new forms in language in an effort to avoid outmoded forms and structures and to violate expectations and shock their audiences.

The search for the new centered in America's first major artistic bohemias in Chicago and New York, especially the area in lower Manhattan known as Greenwich Village. In 1913 the Armory Show in New York, which went then to Chicago, Philadelphia, and Boston, shocked traditionalists with its display of the latest works by experimental and nonrepresentational artists: post-impressionists, expressionists, primitives, and cubists. Pablo Picasso's work made its American debut there. The show aroused shocked indignation and not a little good-natured ridicule, but it was a huge success. Audiences flocked to the show, and buyers afterward snapped up the pieces for sale.

The chief American prophets of modernism were in neither Chicago nor New York, but were American expatriates in Europe: Ezra Pound and T. S. Eliot in London and Gertrude Stein in Paris, all deeply concerned with creating new and often difficult styles of modernist expression. Pound, as foreign editor for *Poetry,* became the conduit through which many American poets achieved publication in America and Britain. At the same time, he became the leader of the imagist movement, a revolt against the ornamental verbosity of Victorian poetry in favor of the concrete image.

Pound's most important protégé was T. S. Eliot, who in 1915 contributed to *Poetry* his first major poem, "The Love Song of J. Alfred Prufrock," the musings of an ineffectual man who "after tea and cakes and ices" could never find "the strength to force the moment to its crisis." Eliot's *The Waste Land* (1922) made few concessions to readers in its arcane allusions, its juxtaposition of unexpected metaphors, its deep sense of postwar disillusionment and melancholy, and its suggestion of a burned-out civilization; but it became for a generation almost the touchstone of the modern temper, along with the Irishman James Joyce's stream-of-consciousness novel *Ulysses,* published the same year. As poet and critic in the *Criterion,* which he founded in 1922, Eliot became the arbiter of modernist taste in Anglo-American literature.

Gertrude Stein, in voluntary exile since 1903, was with her brother, Leo, an early champion of modern art and a collector of early Cézannes, Matisses, and Picassos. Long regarded as no more than the literary eccentric who wrote "A rose is a rose is a rose is a rose," she came later to

Pablo Picasso's portrait of Gertrude Stein, 1906.

be recognized as one of the chief originators and propagators of modernist prose style, beginning with *Three Lives* (1906). Stein sought to capture interior moods in her writing, developing in words the equivalent of nonrepresentational painting.

But Stein was long known chiefly through her influence on such other expatriates as Ernest Hemingway, whom she told: "All of you young people who served in the war, you are the lost generation." The earliest chronicler of that generation, F. Scott Fitzgerald, blazed up brilliantly and then quickly flickered out, like all the tinseled, sad young people of his novels. Successful and famous at age twenty-four with *This Side of Paradise* (1920), along with his wife, Zelda, he lived in and wrote about the "greatest, gaudiest spree in history," and then both had their crack-up in the Great Depression. What gave depth to the best of his work was what a character in *The Great Gatsby* (1925), his finest novel, called "a sense of the fundamental decencies" amid all the surface gaiety—and almost always a sense of impending doom.

Ernest Hemingway's first novel, *The Sun Also Rises* (1926), pictures an even more desperate search for life. It focuses on a group of Ameri-

The Fitzgeralds Celebrate Christmas. *F. Scott Fitzgerald and his wife, Zelda, lived in and wrote about the "greatest, gaudiest spree in history."*

cans in Europe who careen about frantically from the bistros of Paris to the bullrings of Spain. Young Jake Barnes, emasculated by a war wound, cannot marry his love, Lady Brett Ashley. "Oh, Jake," she says in the poignant ending, "we could have had such a damned good time together." "Yes," he replied. "Isn't it pretty to think so?" Hemingway's second novel, *A Farewell to Arms* (1929), is another tale of lost love. Based on Hemingway's war experience in the ambulance corps in northern Italy, it describes the love affair of a driver and a nurse who abandon the war for Switzerland, where the young woman dies in childbirth.

These novels contain the lively, even frenetic action and the cult of athletic masculinity (epitomized by the bullfighter), which became the stuff of the public image Hemingway cultivated for himself and the hallmark of such novels as *Death in the Afternoon* (1932), *To Have and Have Not* (1937), *For Whom the Bell Tolls* (1940), and *The Old Man and the Sea* (1952). Hundreds of writers tried to imitate Hemingway's terse style, but few had his gift, which lay less in what he had to say than in the way he said it.

THE SOUTHERN RENAISSANCE   As modernist literature arose as a response to the changes taking place in Western civilization, so did southern literature of the twenties reflect a world in the midst of rebirth. A southern renaissance in writing emerged from the conflict between the dying world of tradition and the modern, commercial world struggling to be born in the aftermath of the Great War. While in the South the conflict of values aroused the Ku Klux Klan and fundamentalist furies that tried desperately to bring back the world of tradition, it also inspired the vitality and creativity of the South's young writers. Allen Tate, a talented young poet, novelist, and critic, saw in the South the "curious burst of intelligence that you get at a crossing of the ways, not unlike, on an infinitesimal scale, the outburst of poetic genius at the end of the sixteenth century when commercial England began to crush feudal England."

In Nashville, *The Fugitive: A Journal of Poetry* (1922–1925) announced the arrival of the most influential group in American letters since the New England transcendentalists. The Fugitive poets began as a group of student intellectuals at Vanderbilt University who first gathered for discussions in 1915, then regrouped after the war with young Professor John Crowe Ransom as their dean and mentor. Four of the group eventually stood out in their commitment to literature as a profession: Ransom, Donald Davidson, Allen Tate, and Robert Penn Warren. The Fugitives admired T. S. Eliot and were committed to the new doctrines of modernism in literature. They revolted against the twin images of southern sentimentalists and commercial boosters. *"The Fugitive,"* Ransom wrote, "flees from nothing faster than from the high-caste Brahmins of the Old South."

It dawned on them that they had protested too much, however, when reporters drawn to the Scopes trial mocked the Bible Belt and the Benighted South. In reaction, the Fugitives began to seek a usable past in the southern agrarian tradition. They brought others into the project, and their manifesto, *I'll Take My Stand* (1930), by twelve southerners, appeared just when industrial capitalism seemed on the verge of collapse. The Vanderbilt agrarians championed, in Donald Davidson's words, a "traditional society . . . that is stable, religious, more rural than urban, and politically conservative," a society in which human needs were supplied by "Family, bloodkinship, clanship, folkways, custom, community. . . ." In the end, their agrarianism proved less important as a social-economic force than as a context for creative literature. Yet their image of the agrarian South, as one critic later wrote, provided "a rich, complex metaphor through which they presented a critique of the modern world."

"One may reasonably argue," wrote a critic in 1930, "that the South is the literary land of promise today." Just the previous year two vital figures had emerged: Thomas Wolfe, with *Look Homeward, Angel,* and William Faulkner, with *Sartoris* and *The Sound and the Fury.* Fame rushed in first on Wolfe and his native Asheville, North Carolina, which became in the 1920s a classic example of the scandalized community. "Against the Victorian morality and the Bourbon aristocracy of the South," Wolfe had "turned in all his fury," newspaper editor Jonathan Daniels, a former classmate, wrote. The reaction was not an uncommon response to the works of the southern renaissance, created by authors who had outgrown their "provincial" hometowns and looked back from new perspectives acquired through travel and education.

For all his gargantuan lust for experience and knowledge, his demonic drive to escape the encircling hills for the "fabled" world outside, his agonized search for some "lost lane-end into heaven," Wolfe never completely severed his roots in the South. *Look Homeward, Angel,* his first novel, remained his most successful; it was the lyrical and search-

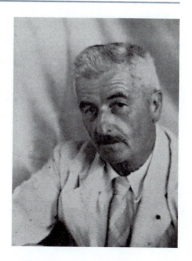

William Faulkner.

ing biography of Eugene Gant's (actually Wolfe's) youth in Altamont (Asheville) and his college days in Pulpit Hill (Chapel Hill). It established him as "the giant among American writers of sensitive youth fiction."

William Faulkner's achievement, more than Wolfe's, was rooted in the coarsely textured social world that produced him. Born near Oxford, Mississippi, he grew up there and transmuted his hometown into the fictional Jefferson, Yoknapatawpha County. After a brief stint with the Royal Canadian Air Force he passed the postwar decade in what seemed to fellow townspeople an aimless drifting. He briefly attended classes at the University of Mississippi, worked at odd jobs, and went to New Orleans where he wrote *Soldiers' Pay* (1926), a novel of postwar disillusionment, and *Mosquitoes* (1927), a caricature of the New Orleans bohemians yachting on Lake Pontchartrain. Between books he shipped out briefly for Europe, and after knocking around the Gulf coast, returned to Oxford.

There, in writing *Sartoris* (1929), he began to discover that his "own little postage stamp of native soil was worth writing about" and that he "would never live long enough to exhaust it." With *Sartoris* and the creation of his mythical land of Yoknapatawpha, Faulkner kindled a blaze of creative energy. Next, as he put it, he wrote his gut into *The Sound and the Fury* (1929). It was one of the triumphs of the modernist style, but most early readers, taking their cue from the title instead of the critics, found it signified nothing.

Modernism and the southern literary renaissance, both of which emerged from the crucible of the Great War and its aftermath, were products of the twenties. But the studied alienation of the artists of the 1920s did not survive the decade. The onset of the Great Depression in 1929 seemed to spark a renewed sense of commitment and affirmation in the arts, as if people could no longer afford the art-for-art's-sake affectations of the 1920s. Alienation would give way to social purpose in the decade to come.

MAKING CONNECTIONS

- The next chapter discusses the growing consumer culture of the 1920s, an economic aspect of the "Roaring Twenties" described here.

- Chapter 28 describes changes in American literary culture wrought by the Great Depression—from the modernism discussed in this chapter to a return of social significance and the cultural "rediscovery of America" in the 1930s.

- The status of women in the workforce remained stable in the 1920s, despite the successes of the women's movement. That status changed, at least temporarily, during World War II. Chapter 30 traces the increase in women in the workforce.

FURTHER READING

For a standard survey of the interwar period, start with William E. Leuchtenburg's *The Perils of Prosperity, 1914–1932* (rev. ed., 1993). The best introduction to the culture of the 1920s remains Loren Baritz's *The Culture of the Twenties* (1970). See also Lynn Dumenil's *The Modern Temper: American Culture and Society in the 1920s* (1995). Paula S.

Fass's *The Damned and the Beautiful: American Youth in the 1920s* (1977) describes the social attitudes of youth.

John Higham's *Strangers in the Land: Patterns of American Nativism, 1860–1925* (rev. ed., 1988) details the story of immigration restriction. Paul Avrich's *Sacco and Vanzetti: The Anarchist Background* (1991) treats the famous case. For analysis of the revival of Klan activity, see Nancy MacLean's *Behind the Mask of Chivalry: The Making of the Second Ku Klux Klan* (1994). Two contrasting views of prohibition are Andrew Sinclair's *Prohibition: The Era of Excess* (1962) and Norman H. Clark's *Deliver Us from Evil: An Interpretation of American Prohibition* (1976).

Women's suffrage is treated extensively in Eleanor Flexner's *Century of Struggle: The Women's Rights Movement in the United States* (rev. ed., 1975). See Charles F. Kellogg's *NAACP: A History of the National Association for the Advancement of Colored People* (1967) for his analysis of the pioneering court cases against racial discrimination. Nathan I. Huggins's *Harlem Renaissance* (1971) assesses the cultural impact of the Great Migration in New York. On the migration to Chicago, see James R. Grossman's *Land of Hope: Chicago, Black Southerners, and the Great Migration* (1989). Nicholas Lemann's *The Promised Land* (1991) is a fine exposition of the changes brought about by the Great Migration in both the South and North.

Much of our treatment of "modernism" comes from Daniel J. Singal's *The War Within: From Victorian to Modernist Thought in the South, 1919–1945* (1982). Stanley Coben's *Rebellion Against Victorianism: The Impetus for Cultural Change in 1920s America* (1991) surveys the appeal of "modernism" among writers, artists, and intellectuals. On developments in physics, see Stanley Goldberg's *Understanding Relativity: Origin and Impact of a Scientific Revolution* (1984). Nathan G. Hale, Jr.'s *Freud and the Americans* (1971) examines the impact of psychoanalysis.

27 ∽ REPUBLICAN RESURGENCE AND DECLINE

> **CHAPTER ORGANIZER**
>
> This chapter focuses on:
>
> • the conservatism in the presidencies of Harding, Coolidge, and Hoover.
>
> • growth in the American economy in the 1920s.
>
> • the causes of the Great Depression.

*T*he progressive coalition that reelected Woodrow Wilson in 1916 proved to be quite fragile, and by 1920 it had fragmented. It unraveled for several reasons. Radicals and other opponents of the war grew disaffected with America's entrance into the conflict and the war's aftermath. Organized labor resented the administration's unsympathetic attitude toward the strikes of 1919–1920. Farmers of the Great Plains and West thought that wartime price controls had discriminated against them. Intellectuals also drifted away from their former support of progressivism. They became disillusioned with the emphases on grassroots democracy because of popular support for Prohibition and the anti-evolution movements. The larger middle class became preoccupied with building a new business civilization "based not upon monopoly and restriction," in the words of one historian, "but upon a whole new set of business values—mass production and consumption, short hours and high wages, full employment, welfare capitalism." Progressivism's final triumphs at the national level were already pretty much foregone conclusions before the war's end: the Eighteenth Amendment, ratified in 1919, which imposed national Prohibition, and the Nineteenth Amendment, ratified in 1920, which extended women's suffrage to the entire country.

Progressivism, however, did not disappear in the 1920s. Progressives dominated Congress during much of the decade even while the White House was in conservative Republican hands. The progressive impulse for "good government" and public services remained strong, especially at the state and local levels, where movements for good roads, education, public health, and social welfare all gained momentum during the decade. Much of the progressive impulse for reform, however, was transformed into the drive for moral righteousness and conformity animating the Ku Klux Klan and the fundamentalist movement. Prohibition, at first a direct outgrowth of the reform spirit, came to be increasingly associated with the narrow intolerance of the times.

"NORMALCY"

HARDING'S ELECTION   Wilson's physical collapse during 1919 symbolized his political deterioration as well. Most Americans had grown weary of idealistic crusades and were suspicious of leaders sounding the trumpet of reform. Wilson himself recognized this fact. "It is only once in a generation," he remarked, "that a people can be lifted above material things. That is why conservative government is in the saddle two-thirds of the time."

When the Republicans met in Chicago in 1920, the Old Guard party regulars found their man in Ohio senator Warren Gamaliel Harding, who had set the tone of his campaign when he told a Boston audience: "America's present need is not heroics, but healing; not nostrums, but normalcy; not revolution, but restoration; not agitation, but adjustment; not surgery, but serenity; not the dramatic, but the dispassionate; not experiment, but equipoise; not submergence in internationality, but sustainment in triumphant nationality." His speeches, said one Democrat, were "an army of pompous phrases moving over the landscape in search of an idea."

Despite his clumsy rhetoric, Harding caught the mood of the times, a longing for "normalcy" rather than government activism and experimentalism. Harding fit the bill for presidential candidate because, though he might not set the pulses pounding, he had few enemies and had all the classic attributes of availability. The vice-presidential choice fell on Calvin Coolidge, who had caught the public fancy with his opposition to the Boston Police Strike.

The Democrats chose James Cox, former newsman and former governor of Ohio, on the forty-fourth ballot. For vice-president the convention named Franklin D. Roosevelt, who as assistant secretary of the navy occupied the same position his Republican cousin Theodore had held before him. The Democratic platform, while broadly endorsing the New Freedom, did not fully endorse the League of Nations. Cox waged an active campaign while the Republicans kept Harding home to conduct a front-porch campaign in the McKinley style—they even redid Harding's porch to look like McKinley's. The Republican platform was a masterpiece of evasion on the League of Nations. It pledged the party to "agreement among the nations to preserve the peace of the world" but "without the compromise of national independence." The phrasing satisfied both reservationists and irreconcilables.

The breakup of the Wilsonian coalition doomed the Democrats. In the words of progressive editor William Allen White, Americans in 1920 were "tired of issues, sick at heart of ideals, and weary of being noble." Wilson therefore became the Republicans' target rather than Cox, who remained a nonentity, and the country voted overwhelmingly for a "return to normalcy." Harding got 16 million votes, about 60 percent of the total, to 9 million for Cox. Harding's electoral vote margin was 404 to 127. Cox carried no state outside the Solid South, even there losing Tennessee.

EARLY APPOINTMENTS AND POLICY   Harding in office had much in common with Ulysses Grant. His cabinet, like Grant's, mixed some of the "best minds" in the party, whom he had promised to seek out, with some of the worst, cronies who sought him out. Charles Evans Hughes, like Grant's Hamilton Fish, became a distinguished secretary of state. Herbert Hoover in the Commerce Department, Andrew W.

Warren Harding "bloviating" on the stump.

Mellon in Treasury, and Henry C. Wallace in Agriculture functioned efficiently and made policy on their own. Among the others, the secretary of the interior landed in prison and the attorney-general narrowly escaped serving time. Many lesser offices went to members of the "Ohio Gang," a group with which Harding met in a "Little House on K Street" to get away from the pressures of the White House.

Until he became president, Harding had loved politics. He was the party hack par excellence, "bloviating" (a verb of his own making, which meant speaking with gaseous eloquence) on the stump, jollying it up in the clubhouse and cloakroom, hobnobbing with the great and near-great in Washington. As president, however, Harding was simply in over his head, and self-doubt overwhelmed him. "I don't think I'm big enough for the Presidency," he confided to a friend. Harding much preferred to get away with the "Ohio Gang," who shared his taste for whiskey, poker, and women. Alice Roosevelt Longworth, Theodore Roosevelt's oldest daughter, witnessed one poker session in the president's study. "Harding wasn't a bad man," she said later. "He was just a slob."

Harding and his friends set about dismantling or neutralizing as many of the social and economic components of progressivism as they could. To that end, Harding took advantage of four Supreme Court vacancies by appointing conservatives, including Chief Justice William Howard Taft, who announced that he had been "appointed to reverse a few decisions." During the 1920s, the Taft Court struck down a federal child-labor law and a minimum-wage law for women, issued numerous injunctions against striking unions, and passed rulings limiting the powers of federal regulatory agencies.

Moreover, Harding established a pro-business tone reminiscent of the McKinley White House. To sustain economic growth, Secretary of the Treasury Mellon instituted a Republican policy of reduced government spending and lower taxes. To get a better handle on expenditures, he persuaded a lukewarm Congress to pass the Budget and Accounting Act of 1921, which created a new Bureau of the Budget, headed by a Chicago banker, to prepare a unified budget, and a General Accounting Office to audit the accounts. This act realized a long-held progressive desire to bring greater efficiency and nonpartisanship to the budget preparation process. General tax reductions from the wartime level were warranted, but Mellon insisted that they should go mainly to the rich, on the Hamiltonian principle that wealth in the hands of the few would augment the general welfare through increased capital investment. Mellon's admirers tagged him "the greatest Secretary of the Treasury since Alexander Hamilton."

In Congress a group of western Republicans and southern Democrats fought a dogged battle to preserve the graduated scale built into wartime taxes, but Mellon, in office through the 1920s, eventually won out. At his behest, Congress in 1921 repealed the wartime excess-profits tax and lowered the maximum rate on personal income from 65 to 50 percent. Subsequent revenue acts lowered the maximum rate to 40 percent in 1924 and 20 percent in 1926. The Revenue Act of 1926 extended further benefits to high-income groups by lowering estate taxes and repealing the gift tax. Unfortunately, much of the tax money released to wealthy people seems to have fueled the speculative excess of the late 1920s as much as it fostered gainful enterprise. Mellon, however, did balance the federal budget for a time. Governmental expenditures fell from $6.4 billion in 1920 to $3.4 billion in 1922, and to a low of $3 billion in 1927. The national debt went down from $25.5 billion in 1919 to $16.9 billion in 1929.

In addition to tax cuts, Mellon favored the time-honored Republican policy of high tariffs, and innovations in the chemical and metal industries revived the argument for protection of infant industries from foreign competition. The Fordney-McCumber Tariff of 1922 increased rates on chemical and metal products as a safeguard against the revival of German industries that had previously commanded the field. To please the farmers, who historically benefited little from tariffs, the new act further extended the duties on farm products.

Higher tariffs, however, had ramifications that had never prevailed before and that were not quickly perceived. During the war, the United States had been transformed from a debtor to a creditor nation. In former years foreign capital had flowed into the United States, playing an important role in the economic expansion of the nineteenth century. But the private and public credits given the Allies during the war had reversed the pattern. Mellon insisted that the European powers must repay all that they had borrowed. But the tariff walls erected around the country made it all the harder for other nations to sell in the United States and thus acquire the dollars or credits with which to repay their war debts. For nearly a decade, further extensions of American loans and investments sent more dollars abroad, postponing the reckoning.

Rounding out the Republican economic program during the 1920s was a more lenient attitude toward government oversight of corporations. Neither Harding nor his successor, Coolidge, could dissolve the regulatory agencies, but they named commissioners who sought to make them more effective for a business constituency that now saw advantages in friendly regulation. Harding named conservative advocates of big business to the Interstate Commerce Commission, the Federal Reserve Board, and the Federal Trade Commission. In 1925 Coolidge's appointee as chairman of the FTC said the commission would not be used "as a publicity bureau to spread socialistic propaganda." He and his colleagues decided to withhold publicity on all cases until they were settled. Senator George Norris characterized the new appointments as "the nullification of federal law by a process of boring from within." Senator Henry Cabot Lodge agreed, boasting that "we have torn up Wilsonism by the roots."

A CORRUPT ADMINISTRATION   Republican conservatives such as Lodge and Mellon were at least operating out of conviction. Members of the "Ohio Gang," however, used White House connections to line their own pockets. In 1923 Harding learned that an official of the Veterans Bureau was systematically looting medical and hospital supplies. The official fled to Europe and resigned. Harding's general counsel then committed suicide in Harding's old house in Washington. Not long afterward, a close buddy of the attorney-general also shot himself. The corrupt crony held no appointment, but had set up an office in the Justice Department from which he peddled influence for a fee. The attorney-general himself was implicated in the fraudulent handling of German assets seized after the war. When discovered, he refused to testify on the ground that he might incriminate himself. Twice brought to court, he was never indicted, for want of evidence, possibly because he had destroyed pertinent records. These were but the most visible among many scandals that touched the Justice Department, the Prohibition Bureau, and other agencies under Harding.

But one major scandal rose above all these petty peculations. Teapot Dome, like Watergate fifty years later, became the catchword for an epoch of corruption. An oil deposit under the sandstone Teapot Rock in Wyoming, Teapot Dome had been set aside as a naval oil reserve administered by the Interior Department under Albert B. Fall. At the time the move seemed a sensible attempt to unify control over public reserves.

Juggernaut. This 1924 cartoon shows the dimensions of the Teapot Dome scandal.

But once Fall had control, he signed contracts letting private interests exploit the oil deposits: Harry Sinclair's Mammoth Oil Company at Teapot Dome, Wyoming, and Edward L. Doheny's Pan-American Petroleum and Transport Company at Elk Hills, California. Fall argued that these contracts were in the government's interest. Yet why did Fall act in secret, without allowing competitive bids?

Suspicion grew when Fall's standard of living suddenly rose. It turned out that he had taken loans of about $400,000 (which came in "a little black bag") from Sinclair and Doheny. As the scandal unraveled, Fall emerged as a figure of tragic weakness. Once wealthy, he had lost extensive mine holdings in the Mexican Revolution, which left him with little more than an expensive dream ranch in New Mexico. Desperate for money, he took loans extended by two old friends—he and Doheny and Sinclair had once worked together in the mines. For the rest of his life, Fall insisted that the loans were unrelated to the oil leases, and that he had contrived a good deal for the government, but at best the circumstances revealed a fatal blindness to his impropriety.

The question of bribery aside, Fall's actions outraged conservationists. A senatorial investigation laid out the whole mess during 1924 to the accompaniment of public outrage. Harding himself avoided the humiliation of public disgrace. How much he knew is unclear, but he knew enough to become visibly troubled. "My God, this is a hell of a job!" he confided to the editor William Allen White. "I have no trouble with my enemies, I can take care of my enemies all right. But my damn friends, my God-damn friends, White, they're the ones that keep me walking the floor nights!" In 1923 Harding left on what would be his last journey, a western speaking tour and a trip to the Alaska Territory. Back in Seattle, he suffered an attack of food poisoning. He recovered briefly, then died in a San Francisco hotel of either coronary or cerebral thrombosis.

Not since the death of Lincoln had there been such an outpouring of grief for a "beloved President," for the kindly, ordinary man with the face of a Roman senator, the man who found it in his heart (as Wilson had not) to pardon Eugene Debs, the Socialist who had been jailed for opposing U.S. entry into World War I. Harding not only received Debs at the White House, but also pressured the steel magnates into giving up their barbarous seven-day workweek. As the black-streamered funeral train moved toward Washington, then back to Ohio, millions stood by the tracks to honor their lost leader. Eventually, however, grief yielded to scorn and contempt. For nearly a decade, the revelations of scandal were paraded before committees and then courts. Harding's long extramarital affair with Nan Britton came to light, first the birth of their illegitimate child, and later their pathetic couplings in a White House closet. Harding's love letters to another man's wife also surfaced. As a result of his amorous detours and corrupt associates, Harding's foreshortened administration came to be widely viewed as one of the worst in American history.

Recent assessments of Harding's presidency, however, suggest that the scandals obscured some real accomplishments. Some historians credit Harding for leading the nation out of the turmoil of the postwar years and creating the foundation for the decade's remarkable economic boom. Revisionists also stress that he was a hardworking president who played a far more forceful role than previously assumed in shaping his administration's economic and foreign policies and in shepherding legislation through Congress. But even Harding's foremost scholarly defender admits that he lacked good judgment and "probably should never have been president."

"SILENT CAL"   Some kind of charmed existence seemed to put Calvin Coolidge in the right place at the right time. The news of Harding's death came when he was visiting his father in the mountain village of Plymouth, Vermont, his birthplace. There at 2:47 on the morning of August 3, 1923, by the light of a kerosene lamp, Colonel John Coolidge administered the oath of office to his son. The rustic simplicity of Plymouth, the very name itself, evoked just the image of roots and solid integrity that the country would long for amid the coming disclosures of corruption. The new first lady, Grace Coolidge, was as unpretentious as her husband, and Alice Roosevelt Longworth found the new atmosphere of the White House "as different as a New England front parlor is from the back room in a speakeasy."

Coolidge brought to the White House a clear conviction that the presidency should revert to its Gilded-Age stance of passive deference to Congress. "Four-fifths of our troubles," Coolidge predicted, "would disappear if we would sit down and keep still." He abided by this rule, insisting on twelve hours of sleep and an afternoon nap. H. L. Mencken asserted that Coolidge "slept more than any other president, whether by day or by night. Nero fiddled, but Coolidge only snored."

Warren Harding (left) *and Calvin Coolidge* (right).

Americans took to their hearts the unflappability of "Silent Cal," his inactivity, and the pictures of him fishing, pitching hay, and wearing Indian bonnets while primly clad in business suit and necktie. His taciturn nature became the subject of affectionate humor, often no doubt apocryphal, as in the story of a dinner guest who bet Coolidge that she could make him say three words. "You lose," he replied.

The image of "Silent Cal," however, distorts as much as it illuminates his character. Although a man of few words, he was not as bland or as dry as critics claimed. Yet he was conservative. Herbert Hoover, the secretary of commerce, once stressed that Coolidge was a "real conservative, probably the equal of Benjamin Harrison. He was a fundamentalist in religion, in the economic and social order, and in fishing, too." (He used live worms for bait.) Even more than Harding, Coolidge embraced the orthodox creed of business. "The chief business of the American people is business," he intoned. "The man who builds a factory builds a temple. The man who works there worships there." Where Harding had sought to balance the interests of labor, agriculture, and industry, Coolidge focused on industrial development at the expense of the other two areas. He sought to unleash the free-enterprise system and, even more than Harding, he strove to end government regulation of business and industry. His pro-business stance led the *Wall Street Journal* to exult: "Never before, here or anywhere else, has a government been so completely fused with business."

THE 1924 ELECTION   Coolidge was also married to politics, and he proved better at it than Harding. He distanced himself from the Harding scandals, and put in charge of the prosecutions two lawyers of undoubted integrity. Coolidge quietly took control of the Republican party machinery and seized the initiative in the campaign for nomination, which he won with only token opposition.

The Coolidge luck held as the Democrats fell victim to internal dissensions. The source of the party's trouble was its uneasy alliance of incongruous elements, which lent much truth to humorist Will Rogers's classic statement: "I am a member of no organized political party. I am a Democrat." The party's divisions illustrated the deep alienation growing up between the metropolis of the Roaring Twenties and the more traditional hinterland, a gap that the Democrats could not bridge. After much factional fighting, it took the Democrats 103 ballots to bestow the tarnished nomination on John W. Davis, a Wall Street lawyer from West Virginia who could hardly outdo Coolidge in conservatism.

Meanwhile a growing farmer-labor coalition was mobilizing a third-party effort. In Minnesota during 1922 and 1923, a new Farmer-Labor party elected two United States senators, a congressman, and some lesser officeholders. In 1922 the railroad unions, smarting from administration opposition, sponsored a Conference for Progressive Political Action that got the support of many farmers who were suffering from price declines at the time. Meeting in Cleveland on July 4, 1924, the conference reorganized as the Progressive party and nominated Robert M. La Follette for president. The Wisconsin reformer also won the support of Minnesota's Farmer-Labor party, the Socialist party, and the American Federation of Labor.

In the campaign Coolidge chose to focus on La Follette, whom he called a dangerous radical who would turn America into a "communistic and socialistic state." The country preferred to "keep cool with Coolidge," who swept both the popular and electoral votes by decisive majorities. Davis took only the Solid South, and La Follette carried only his native Wisconsin. The popular vote went 15.7 million for Coolidge, 8.4 million for Davis, and 4.8 million for La Follette—the largest popular vote ever polled by a third-party candidate. The electoral voting result was 382 to 136 to 13, respectively.

THE NEW ERA

Business executives interpreted the Republican victory as a vindication of their leadership, and Coolidge saw in the surging prosperity of the time a confirmation of his philosophy. In fact, the prosperity and technological achievements of the time known as the New Era had much to do with Coolidge's victory over the Democrats and Progressives. Those in the large middle class who before had formed an important part of the Progressive party coalition were now absorbed instead in the new world created by advances in communications, transportation, and business organization.

More people than ever before had the money and leisure to taste of the affluent society, and a growing advertising industry fueled its appetites. By the mid-1920s advertising had become both a huge enterprise and a major institution of social control. Old-time values of thrift and saving gave way to a new economic ethic that made spending a virtue. The innovation of installment buying made increased consumption feasible for many. A newspaper editorial insisted that the American's "first importance to his country is no longer that of citizen but that of consumer. Consumption is a new necessity."

MOVIES, RADIO, AND THE ECONOMY   Consumer-goods industries fueled much of the boom from 1922 to 1929. Moderately priced creature comforts, including items such as hand cameras, wristwatches, cigarette lighters, vacuum cleaners, washing machines, and linoleum, became increasingly available. Inventions in communications and transportation, such as motion pictures, radio, telephones, and automobiles, not only fueled the boom but also brought transformations in society.

In the 1890s a quick sequence of inventions had made it possible for a New York audience to see the first moving picture show in 1896. By 1905 the first movie house opened in Philadelphia, and within three years there were nearly 10,000 scattered across the nation. By 1915 Hollywood had become the center of movie production, grinding out

Charlie Chaplin in a scene from his classic film, The Kid.

Westerns and the timeless comedies of Mack Sennett's Keystone Studios, where a raft of slapstick comedians, most notably Charlie Chaplin, perfected their art into a form of social criticism.

Birth of a Nation, directed in 1915 by D. W. Griffith, became a triumph of cinematic art that marked the arrival of the modern motion picture and at the same time perpetuated a grossly distorted image of Reconstruction. Based on Thomas Dixon's novel *The Clansman,* the movie featured stereotypes of villainous carpetbaggers, sinister mulattoes, blameless white southerners, and faithful "darkies." The film grossed $18 million and revealed the industry's enormous potential. By the mid-1930s, every large American city and most small towns had theaters, and movies replaced oratory as the chief mass entertainment of Americans. A further advancement in technology came with the "talkies." The first movie with sound accompaniment appeared in 1926, but the success of talking pictures was established by *The Jazz Singer* (1927), starring Al Jolson.

Radio broadcasting had an even more spectacular growth. Except for experimental broadcasts, radio served only for basic communication until 1920. In that year station WWJ in Detroit began transmitting news bulletins from the *Detroit Daily News,* and KDKA in Pittsburgh, owned by the Westinghouse Company, began regular programs. The

Radio Broadcast, *mid-1920s. Radios gained such popularity that within a decade millions would tune into newscasts, soap operas, sporting events, and church services.*

first radio commercial aired in New York in 1922. By the end of that year, there were 508 stations and some 3 million receivers in use. In 1926 the National Broadcasting Company, a subsidiary of RCA, began linking stations into a network; the Columbia Broadcasting System entered the field the next year. In 1927 a Federal Radio Commission was established to regulate the industry; in 1934 it became the Federal Communications Commission, with authority over other forms of communication as well.

AIRPLANES, AUTOMOBILES, AND THE ECONOMY   Advances in transportation were equally startling. Wilbur and Orville Wright of Dayton, Ohio, built and flew the first airplane at Kitty Hawk, North Carolina, in 1903. But the use of planes advanced slowly until the outbreak of war in 1914, after which the Europeans rapidly developed the plane as a military weapon. When the United States entered the war, it still had no combat planes—American pilots did battle in British or French aircrafts. An American aircraft industry developed during the war but foundered in the postwar demobilization. Under the Kelly Act of 1925,

Orville Wright pilots the first flight of a power-driven airplane, while his brother, Wilbur, runs alongside.

however, the government began to subsidize the industry through air-mail contracts. The Air Commerce Act of 1926 started a program of federal aid to air transport and navigation, including aid in establishing airports.

A psychological boost to aviation came in 1927 with the solo flight of Charles A. Lindbergh, Jr., from New York to Paris in thirty-three hours and thirty minutes. The deed, which won him a prize of $25,000, was dramatic. He flew through a dense fog for part of the way and at times

Charles Lindbergh in front of the airplane he piloted across the Atlantic, The Spirit of St. Louis.

dropped to within ten feet of the water before sighting the Irish coast and regaining his bearings. The parade down Broadway in his honor surpassed even the celebration of the Armistice.

By 1930 the industry had forty-three airlines, which carried 385,000 passengers over routes totaling 30,000 miles. Another great impetus came after 1936 when the slow Ford trimotor plane gave way to the more efficient twin-engine Douglas DC-3 as the chief passenger plane. In 1940, nineteen airlines carried 2.8 million passengers over routes of 43,000 miles.

By far the most significant economic and social development of the time was the automobile. The first motor car had been manufactured for sale in 1895, but the founding of the Ford Motor Company in 1903 revolutionized the industry. Ford's reliable Model T (the celebrated "tin lizzie") came out in 1908 at a price of $850 (in 1924 it would sell for $290). Ford vowed "to democratize the automobile. When I'm through everybody will be able to afford one, and about everyone will have one."

He was right. In 1916 the total number of cars manufactured passed 1 million; by 1920 more than 8 million were registered, and in 1929 more than 23 million. The production of automobiles consumed large amounts of the nation's steel, rubber, glass, and textile output, among other materials. It gave rise to a gigantic market for oil products just as the Spindletop gusher (1901) in Texas heralded the opening of vast southwestern oil fields. It quickened the movement for good roads, fi-

Ford Motor Company's Highland Park Plant, 1913. *Gravity slides and chain conveyors aided the mass production of automobiles.*

nanced in large part from a gasoline tax, speeded transportation, encouraged the sprawl of suburbs, and sparked real-estate booms in California and Florida.

By virtue of its size and importance, the automobile industry became the salient example of mass production. When Ford brought out the Model T in 1908, demand ran far ahead of production. Ford then hired a factory expert who, by rearranging the plant and installing new equipment, met his production goal of 10,000 cars in twelve months. The next year Ford's new Highland Park plant was planned with job analysis in mind. In 1910 gravity slides were installed to move parts from one workbench to the next, and by the end of 1913 the system was complete, with endless chain conveyors pulling the parts along feeder lines and the chassis down the final assembly line.

STABILIZING THE ECONOMY   The drive for efficiency, which had been a prominent feature of the progressive impulse, was now powering the wheels of mass production and consumption, and had become a cardinal belief of Republican leaders. Herbert Hoover, who served as secretary of commerce through the Harding-Coolidge years, was himself an engineer who had made a fortune in far-flung mining operations in Australia, China, Russia, and elsewhere. Out of his experiences in business and his management of Belgian relief, the Food Administration, and other wartime activities, Hoover had developed a philosophy that he set forth in his book *American Individualism* (1922). The idea might best be called "cooperative individualism," or in one of his favorite terms, "associationalism." The principle also owed something to his Quaker upbringing, which taught him the virtue of the work ethic and mutual help. When he applied it to the relations of government and business, Hoover prescribed a kind of middle way between the regulatory and trust-busting traditions, a way of voluntary cooperation.

As secretary of commerce, Hoover was a human dynamo who made the trifling Commerce Department into the government's most dynamic agency. During a period of governmental retrenchment, he was engaged in expansion. Through an enlarged Bureau of Foreign and Domestic Commerce he sought out new opportunities and markets for business. A Division of Simplified Practice in the Bureau of Standards sponsored more than a thousand conferences on design, production, and distribution, carried forward the wartime move toward standardization of everything from automobile tires and paving bricks to bedsprings and toilet paper, and reduced in number the different kinds of bolts, nuts, and screws. "When I go to ride in an automobile," Hoover told the author Sherwood Anderson, "it does not matter to me that there are a million automobiles on the road just like mine. I am going somewhere and I want to get there in what comfort I can and at the lowest cost." In 1926 Hoover created a Bureau of Aviation and the next year set out to bring order into the new field of radio with the Federal Radio Commission.

Hoover's priority was the burgeoning trade-association movement. Through trade associations, business leaders in a given field would gather and disseminate information on everything: sales, purchases, shipments, productions, and prices. This information allowed them to make plans with more confidence, the advantages of which included predictable costs, prices, and markets, as well as more stable employment and wages. Sometimes abuses crept in as trade associations engaged in price-fixing and other monopolistic practices, but the Supreme Court in 1925 held the practice of sharing information as such to be within the law.

THE BUSINESS OF FARMING   During the 1920s, agriculture remained a weak sector in the economy, in many ways as weak as its position in the 1890s, when cities flourished and agriculture languished. Briefly after the war, the farmers' hopes soared on wings of prosperity. The wartime boom lasted into 1920, and then prices collapsed. Wheat went in eighteen months from $2.50 a bushel to less than $1; cotton from 35¢ per pound to 13¢. Low prices persisted into 1923, especially in the wheat and corn belts, and after that improvement was spotty. A bumper cotton crop in 1926 resulted only in a price collapse and an early taste of depression in much of the South, where foreclosures and bankruptcies spread.

Yet in many ways farmers shared the entrepreneurial outlook of the New Era. Farms, like corporations, were getting larger, more efficient, and more mechanized. By 1930 about 13 percent of all farmers had tractors, and the proportion was even higher on the western plains. Better plows, drills, cultivators, planters, and other machines were part of the mechanization process that accompanied improved crop yields, fertilizers, and animal breeding.

Farm organizations of the mid- to late 1920s moved away from the alliance with urban labor that marked the Populist Era and toward a new view of farmers as businessmen. During the postwar farm depression, the idea of marketing cooperatives became the farmer's equivalent of the businessman's trade-association movement. Farm groups formed regional commodity-marketing associations that pushed for ironclad contracts with producers to deliver their crops over a period of years. They also promoted "orderly marketing," which required standards and grades, efficient handling of commodities and advertising, and a businesslike setup with professional technicians and executives.

One farm group carried into the twentieth century the old-time gospel of populism. The Farmers' Union, founded in Texas in 1902, emerged in the 1920s mainly as a western wheat-belt group. It was soon overshadowed by the American Farm Bureau Federation, a new group representing the emerging "businesslike" attitude of commercial agriculture in the New Era. Founded in 1920 at a meeting in Chicago, the Farm Bureau was an unexpected outgrowth of the farm demonstration movement. Its philosophy stemmed in part from business leaders who supported the county farm bureaus, but more directly from the larger commercial farmers in its membership. Farm Bureau strength in the Midwest and South represented what by the 1920s was being called a "marriage of cotton and corn."

But if concern with marketing co-ops and other businesslike approaches drew farmers farther away from populism, it was still inevitable that farm problems should invite political solutions. The most effective political response to the falling crop prices of the early 1920s was the formation of the farm bloc, a coalition of western Republicans and southern Democrats that put through an impressive, if fairly moderate, program of legislation from 1921 to 1923. The farm bloc pushed legislation to prevent collusion designed to keep farm prices down. It won an act to exempt farm cooperatives from antitrust laws, and another that set up twelve intermediate credit banks on the model of the Federal Land Banks. The new banks filled the gap of six months to three years between the provisions of short-term loans under the Federal Reserve System and long-term loans by the Federal Land Banks, and could lend to cooperative producing and marketing associations.

Meanwhile a new panacea appeared on the horizon. In 1924 Senator Charles L. McNary of Oregon and Representative Gilbert N. Haugen of Iowa introduced the first McNary-Haugen Bill. It sought to secure "equality for agriculture in the benefits of the protective tariff." Complex as it would have been in operation, it was simple in conception: in short, a plan to dump American farm surpluses on the world market in order to raise prices in the home market. The goal was to achieve "parity"—that is, to raise domestic farm prices to a point where they would have the same purchasing power relative to other prices they had had between 1909 and 1914, a time viewed in retrospect as a golden age of American agriculture.

A McNary-Haugen Bill passed both houses of Congress in 1927, only to be vetoed by President Coolidge. The process was repeated in 1928. Coolidge pronounced the measure an unsound effort at price-fixing, and un-American and unconstitutional to boot. In a broader sense, however, McNary-Haugenism did not fail. The debates made the farm problem into an issue of national policy and defined it as a problem of surpluses. The evolution of the McNary-Haugen plan, moreover, revived the idea of an alliance between the South and West, a coalition that in the next decade became a dominant influence on national farm policy. That policy would follow a different procedure, but its chief focus would be on surpluses and its goal would be "parity."

SETBACKS FOR UNIONS   Urban workers shared more than farmers in the affluence of the times. "A workman is far better paid in America than anywhere else in the world," a French visitor wrote in 1927, "and his standard of living is enormously higher." Non-farm workers gained about 20 percent in real wages between 1921 and 1928, while farm income rose only 10 percent. The benefits of this rise, however, were distributed unevenly. Miners and textile workers suffered a decline in real wages. In these and other trades, technological unemployment followed the introduction of new methods and machines, because technology destroyed as well as created jobs.

Organized labor, however, did no better than organized agriculture in the 1920s. In fact, unions suffered a setback after the growth years of the war. The Red Scare and strikes of 1919 left the uneasy impression that unions practiced subversion, an idea that the enemies of unions promoted. The brief postwar depression of 1921 further weakened the unions, and they felt the severe impact of open-shop associations that proliferated across the country after the war, led by chambers of commerce and other business groups. In 1921 business groups in Chicago designated the open shop the "American Plan" of employment. While the open shop in theory implied only the employer's right to hire anyone, in practice it meant discrimination against unionists and refusal to recognize unions even in shops where most of the workers belonged to one.

Nor were employers always above the use of strong-arm methods, such as requiring "yellow-dog" contracts that forced workers to agree to stay out of unions, using labor spies, exchanging blacklists, and resorting to intimidation and coercion. Some employers tried to kill the unions with kindness. They introduced programs of "industrial democracy" guided by company unions or various schemes of "welfare capitalism" such as profit-sharing, bonuses, pensions, health programs, recreational activities, and the like. The benefits of such programs were often considerable.

Prosperity, propaganda, welfare capitalism, and active hostility combined to cause union membership to drop from about 5 million in 1920 to 3.5 million in 1929. In 1924 Samuel Gompers, founder and longtime president of the AFL, died; William Green of the mine workers, who took his place, embodied the conservative, even timid, attitude of unions during the period. The outstanding exception to the anti-union policies of the decade was passage of the Railway Labor Act in 1926, which abolished the Railway Labor Board and substituted a new Board of Mediation. The act also provided for the formation of railway unions "without interference, influence, or coercion," a statement of policy not extended to other workers until the 1930s.

The Cash Register Chorus *sings of its ties to Coolidge in this 1924 cartoon.*

PRESIDENT HOOVER, THE ENGINEER

HOOVER VS. SMITH   On August 2, 1927, while on vacation in the Black Hills of South Dakota, President Coolidge passed out slips of paper to reporters with the statement: "I do not choose to run for President in 1928." Exactly what he meant puzzled observers then and since. Apparently he at least half hoped for a convention draft, but his statement cleared the way for Herbert Hoover to mount an active campaign. Well before the 1928 Republican convention in Kansas City, Hoover was too far in the lead to be stopped. The platform took credit for prosperity, cost-cutting ("raised to a principle of government"), debt and tax reduction, and the protective tariff ("as vital to American agriculture as it is to manufacturing"). It rejected the McNary-Haugen program, but promised a farm board to promote orderly marketing as a way to manage surpluses.

The Democratic nomination went to Governor Alfred E. Smith of New York. The party's farm plank, while not endorsing McNary-Haugen, did pledge "economic equality of agriculture with other industries." Like the Republicans, the Democrats promised to enforce the Volstead Prohibition Act and, aside from calling for stricter regulation of waterpower resources, promised nothing that departed from the conservative position of the Republicans.

The Democratic party had had its fill of factionalism in 1924, and all remained fairly harmonious until Smith made two controversial decisions. In his acceptance speech he expressed a personal desire to liberalize the Volstead Act, and then he selected for national party chairman a man who was Catholic, "wet," a General Motors executive, and at least until recently a Republican. Hoover by contrast had pronounced Prohibition "a great social and economic experiment, noble in motive and far-reaching in purpose," and called for better enforcement.

The two candidates projected sharply different images that obscured the essential likeness of their programs. Hoover was the Quaker son of middle America, the successful engineer and businessman, the architect of Republican prosperity, while Smith was the prototype of those things rural/small-town America distrusted: the son of Irish immigrants, Catholic, and anti-Prohibition. Outside the large cities all those attributes were handicaps he could scarcely surmount, for all his affability and wit.

In the election Hoover won in the third consecutive Republican landslide, with 21 million popular votes to Smith's 15 million, and an even more top-heavy electoral vote majority of 444 to 87. Hoover even cracked the Solid South, leaving Smith only a hard core of six Deep South states plus Massachusetts and Rhode Island. The election was above all a vindication of Republican prosperity. But the shattering defeat of the Democrats concealed a portentous realignment in the making. Smith had nearly doubled the vote for Davis, the Democratic candidate of four years before. Smith's image, though a handicap in the hinterlands, swung big cities back into the Democratic column. In the farm states of the West there were signs that some disgruntled farmers had switched over to the Democrats. A coalition of urban workers and unhappy farmers was in the making.

HOOVER IN CONTROL   The milestone year 1929 dawned with high hopes. Business seemed good, incomes were rising, and the chief architect of Republican prosperity was about to enter the White House. "I have no fears for the future of our country," Hoover told the audience at his inauguration. "It is bright with hope." For Hoover the presidency crowned a career of steady ascent, first in mining, then in public service. Hoover's image combined the benevolence fitting a director of wartime relief and the efficiency of a businessman and administrator.

Forgotten in the rush of later events would be Hoover's credentials as progressive and humanitarian. Over the objection of Treasury Secretary Mellon, he announced a plan for tax reductions in the low-income brackets. He took action against corrupt patronage practices, and refused to countenance "Red hunts" or interference with peaceful picketing of the White House. He defended his wife's right to entertain the wife of Oscar DePriest, the first black congressman since 1901 and the first ever from the North; sought more federal money for all-black Howard University; and proposed that the membership of the new federal parole board reflect the number of blacks and women in prison.

Hoover's program to stabilize business carried over into his program for agriculture, the most visibly weak sector of the economy. To treat the malady of glutted markets he offered two main remedies: federal help for cooperative marketing and higher tariffs on farm products. In 1929 he pushed through a special session of Congress the Agricultural Marketing Act, which set up a Federal Farm Board with a revolving loan

"I have no fears for the future of our country," Herbert Hoover told his audience at his inauguration in 1929.

fund of $500 million to help farm cooperatives market the major commodities. The act also provided a program in which the Farm Board could set up "stabilization corporations" empowered to buy surpluses off the market. Unluckily for any chance of success the plan might have had, it got under way almost simultaneously with the onset of the depression that fall.

Farmers gained even less from tariff revision. What Hoover won after fourteen months of struggle with competing local interests was in fact a general upward revision of duties on manufactures as well as farm goods. The Hawley-Smoot Tariff of 1930 carried duties to an all-time high. Rates went up on some 70 farm products and more than 900 manufactured items. More than 1,000 economists petitioned Hoover to veto the bill because, they said, it would raise prices to consumers, damage the export trade and thus hurt farmers, promote inefficiency, and provoke foreign reprisals. Events proved them right, but Hoover felt that he had to go along with his party in an election year.

THE ECONOMY OUT OF CONTROL   The tariff did nothing to check a deepening crisis of confidence in the economy. After the slump of 1921, the idea grew that with recovery business had entered a New Era

Miami Beach, *1925. A real-estate boom transformed southern Florida in the early 1920s, but the bubble burst in mid-1926.*

of permanent growth. But real growth propelled an expansive ballyhoo, and a growing contagion of get-rich-quick schemes. Speculative mania fueled the Florida real-estate boom that began when the combination of Coolidge prosperity and Ford's "tin lizzies" gave people extra money and made Florida an accessible playground. By 1925 Miami had become a scene of frantic excitement. In the funfair of fast turnover the reckless speculator was, if anything, more likely to gain than the prudent investor, and the "binder boys" perfected to a fine art the practice of making money at little or no risk. The principle was to pay a small "binder" fee for an option to buy on promise of a later down payment, then reap a profit by selling such binders that might pass through a dozen hands and might or might not convey title. By mid-1926, when there were no more "bigger fools" left to whom one could "pass the baby," the Florida bubble burst.

For the losers it was a sobering lesson, but it proved to be but an audition for the Great Bull Market in stocks. Until 1927 stock values had gone up with profits, but then they began to soar on wings of pure speculation. Mellon's tax reductions had released money that, with the help of aggressive brokerage houses, found its way to Wall Street. Instead of trading binders on real estate, one could buy stock on margin—that is, make a small down payment (the "margin") and borrow the rest from a broker who held the stock as security against a down market. If the stock declined and the buyer failed to meet a margin call for more money, the broker could sell the stock to cover his loan. Brokers' loans more than doubled from 1927 to 1929.

Gamblers in the market ignored warning signs. By 1927 residential construction and automobile sales were catching up to demand, business inventories rose, and the rate of consumer spending slowed. By mid-1929 production, employment, and other measures of economic activity were declining. Still the stock market rose.

By 1929 the market had entered a fantasy world. Conservative financiers and brokers who counseled caution were ignored. Hoover was worried, and he urged stock exchange and Federal Reserve officers to discourage speculation. In August the Federal Reserve Board raised the rate on loans to member banks (the rediscount rate) to 6 percent, but with no effect. On September 4 stock prices wavered, and the day after that they dropped, opening a season of fluctuations. The Great Bull Market staggered on into October, trending downward but with enough good days to keep hope alive. On October 22 a leading bank president told reporters: "I know of nothing fundamentally wrong with the stock market or with the underlying business and credit structure."

THE CRASH AND ITS CAUSES   The next day prices crumbled, and the day after that a wild scramble to unload stocks lasted until word arrived that leading bankers had formed a pool to stabilize prices. Prices steadied for the rest of the week, but after a weekend to think the situation over, stockholders began to unload on Monday. On Tuesday, October 29, the most devastating single day in the market's history, brokers reported sales of 16.4 million shares (at the time 3 million shares traded was a busy day). The plunge in prices fed on itself as brokers sold the shares they held for buyers who failed to meet their margin calls. During October, stocks on the New York Exchange fell in value by 37 percent.

Business and government leaders initially expressed hope. According to President Hoover, "the fundamental business of the country" was sound. Some speculators who got out of the market went back in for

Apprehensive crowds gathered on the steps of the Subtreasury Building, across from the New York Stock Exchange, as news of a stock collapse spread, October 29, 1929.

bargains but found themselves caught in a slow, tedious erosion of values. By March 1933, the value of stocks on the New York Exchange was less than a fifth of the value at the market's peak. The *New York Times* stock average, which stood at 452 in September 1929, bottomed at 52 in July 1932.

Caution became the watchword for consumers and businesspeople. Buyers held out for lower prices, orders fell off, wages fell or ceased altogether, and the decline in purchasing power brought further cutbacks in business. From 1929 to 1932 Americans' personal incomes declined by more than half. Unemployment continued to rise. Farmers, already in trouble, faced catastrophe. More than 9,000 banks closed during the period, hundreds of factories and mines shut down, and thousands of farms were foreclosed for debt and sold at auction.

The crash had revealed the fundamental business of the country to be unsound. Too many businesses had maintained prices and taken profits while holding down wages with the result that about one-third of the personal income went to only 5 percent of the population. By plowing most profits back into expansion rather than wage increases, business brought on a growing imbalance between rising productivity and declining purchasing power. As the demand for goods declined, the rate of investment in the new plants began to decline. For a time the softness of purchasing power was concealed by greater use of installment buying, and the deflationary effects of high tariffs were concealed by the volume of loans and investments abroad that supported foreign demand for American goods. But the flow of American capital abroad began to dry up when the stock market began to look more attractive. Swollen profits and dividends, together with the Mellon tax policies, enticed the rich into market speculation. When trouble came, the bloated corporate structure collapsed.

Governmental policies also contributed to the debacle. Mellon's tax reductions brought oversaving, which helped diminish demand for consumer goods. The growing money supply fed the fever of speculation. Hostility toward labor unions discouraged collective bargaining and may have worsened the prevalent imbalances in income. High tariffs discouraged foreign trade. Lax enforcement of antitrust laws encouraged concentration, monopoly, and high prices.

Another culprit was the gold standard. The world monetary system remained fragile throughout the 1920s. When economic output, prices, and savings began dropping in 1929, policy makers—certain that they

Secretary of the Treasury Andrew Mellon, described by one reporter as "a tired double-entry bookkeeper who is afraid of losing his job."

had to keep their currencies tied to gold at all costs—either did nothing or tightened money supplies, thus exacerbating the downward spiral. The only way to restore economic stability within the constraints of the gold standard was to let prices and wages continue to fall, allowing the downturn, in Andrew Mellon's words, to "purge the rottenness out of the system." What happened instead was that such passivity turned a recession into the world's worst depression.

THE HUMAN TOLL OF DEPRESSION   The devastating collapse of the economy caused immense social hardships. By 1933 there were over 13 million people out of work. As factories shut down, banks closed, farms went bankrupt, and millions of people found themselves not only jobless, but also homeless and penniless. Hungry people lined up at churches and soup kitchens; others rummaged through trash cans behind restaurants. Many slept on park benches or in back alleys. Others congregated in makeshift shelters in vacant lots. Thousands of men in search of jobs "rode the rails." These "hobos" or "tramps," as they were derisively called, sneaked onto empty railway cars and rode from town to town looking for work. During the winter, homeless people wrapped themselves in newspapers to keep warm, referring to them sarcastically as "Hoover blankets." Some grew weary of their grim fate and ended their lives. Suicide rates soared during the 1930s.

HOOVER'S EFFORTS AT RECOVERY   Not only did the policies of public officials help bring on economic collapse, but few public leaders acknowledged the crisis: all that was needed, they thought, was a slight correction of the market. Those who held to the dogma of laissez-faire thought the economy would cure itself. The best policy, Secretary Mellon advised, would be to "liquidate labor, liquidate stocks, liquidate the farmers, liquidate real estate." Hoover himself had little patience with speculators, but he was unwilling now to sit by and let events take their course. Hoover in fact did more than any president had ever done before in such dire economic circumstances. Still, his own philosophy, now hardened into dogma, set limits to governmental action, and he was unready to set it aside even to meet an emergency.

Hoover believed that the nation's fundamental business structure was sound and that the country's main need was confidence. In speech after speech, he exhorted the public to keep up hope, and he asked business owners to keep the mills and shops open, maintain wage rates, and spread the work to avoid layoffs—in short to let the first shock fall on corporate profits rather than on purchasing power. In return, union leaders, who had little choice, agreed to refrain from wage demands and strikes. As it happened, however, words were not enough, and the prediction that good times were just around the corner (actually made by the vice-president, though attributed to Hoover) eventually became a sardonic joke.

Hoover did more than try to reassure the American public. He hurried the building of public works in order to provide jobs, but state and local cutbacks more than offset new federal spending. At Hoover's demand the Federal Reserve returned to an easier credit policy, and Congress passed a modest tax reduction to put more purchasing power in people's pockets. The Federal Farm Board stepped up its loans and its purchases of farm surpluses, only to face bumper crops in 1930 despite droughts in the Midwest and Southwest. The high Hawley-Smoot Tariff, proposed at first to help farmers, brought reprisals abroad, devastating foreign trade.

As always, depression hurt the party in power. Democrats exploited Hoover's predicament for all it was worth, and more. But their role in building the depression image of Hoover has been overblown. In 1930 the floundering president was easy game. During the war, "to Hooverize" had signified patriotic sacrifice; now the president's name signified distress. Near the city dumps, along the railroad tracks, the dispossessed huddled in shacks of tarpaper and galvanized iron, old packing boxes, and abandoned cars. These squalid settlements became known as "Hoovervilles"; a "Hoover flag," was an empty pocket turned inside out. In November 1930 the Democrats gained their first national victory since 1916, winning a majority in the House and enough gains in the Senate to control it in coalition with western agrarians.

One irony of the time was that the great humanitarian of wartime relief was recast as the stubborn opponent of depression relief. But Hoover was still doing business at the same old stand: his answer remained voluntarism. When the head of the Emergency Committee for Employment strongly recommended a governmental spending program for road building and other public works, the president turned it down. His annual message to Congress in December 1930 demanded that each community and state undertake the relief of distress "with that sturdiness and independence which built a great Nation."

In the first half of 1931 economic indicators rose, renewing hope for

Hoovervilles in New York's Central Park, 1931.

an upswing. Then, as recovery beckoned, another shock occurred. In May 1931 the failure of Austria's largest bank triggered panic in central Europe. To halt the domino effect of spreading defaults, President Hoover proposed a one-year moratorium on both reparations and war-debt payments. The moratorium, as it happened, became permanent simply by process of default. The major European nations accepted the moratorium and later also a temporary "standstill" on settlement of private obligations between banks. The general shortage of monetary exchange drove Europeans to withdraw their gold from American banks and dump their American securities. One European country after another abandoned the gold standard and devalued its currency. Even the Bank of England went off the gold standard. The United States meanwhile slid into the third bitter winter of depression.

CONGRESSIONAL INITIATIVES With a new Congress in session, demands for federal action impelled Hoover to stretch his individualistic philosophy to its limits. He was ready now to use governmental resources at least to shore up the financial institutions of the country. In 1932 the new Congress set up the Reconstruction Finance Corporation

(RFC) with $500 million (and authority to borrow $2 billion more) for emergency loans to banks, life insurance companies, building and loan societies, farm mortgage associations, and railroads. Under former vice-president Charles G. Dawes, it authorized $1.2 billion in loans within six months. The RFC staved off bankruptcies, but Hoover's critics found in it favoritism to business, the most damaging instance of which was a $90 million loan to Dawes's own Chicago bank, made soon after he left the RFC in 1932. The RFC nevertheless remained a key agency through the New Deal and World War II.

Further help to the financial structure came with the Glass-Steagall Act of 1932, which broadened the definition of commercial loans that the Federal Reserve would support. The new arrangement also released about $750 million in gold formerly used to back Federal Reserve Notes, countering the effect of foreign withdrawals and domestic hoarding of gold at the same time that it enlarged the supply of credit. For homeowners the Federal Home Loan Bank Act of 1932 created with Hoover's blessing a series of discount banks for home mortgages. They provided for savings and loan and other mortgage agencies a service much like that the Federal Reserve System provided to commercial banks.

Hoover's critics said all these measures reflected a dubious "trickle-down" theory. If government could help banks and railroads, asked New York senator Robert G. Wagner, "is there any reason why we should not likewise extend a helping hand to that forlorn American, in every village and every city of the United States, who has been without wages since 1929?" The contraction of credit devastated debtors such as farmers and those who made purchases on the "installment plan" or who held "balloon-style" mortgages whose monthly payments increased over time. By 1932 members of Congress were filling the hoppers with bills for federal measures to provide relief to individuals. At that point Hoover might have pleaded "dire necessity" and taken the leadership of the relief movement and salvaged his political fortunes.

Instead he held back and only grudgingly edged toward federal relief. On July 21, 1932, Hoover signed the Emergency Relief and Construction Act, which avoided a direct federal dole to individuals but gave the RFC $300 million for relief loans to the states, authorized loans of up to $1.5 billion for state and local public works, and appropriated $322 million for federal public works.

Relief for farmers had long since been abandoned. In mid-1931 the government quit buying surpluses and helplessly watched prices slide. In 1919 wheat had fetched $2.16 a bushel; by 1932 it had sunk to 38¢. Cotton brought 17¢ a pound in 1929; before the 1932 harvest it went to 5¢. Other farm prices declined comparably. Net cash income for farmers dropped more than 55 percent from 1929 to 1932. Between 1930 and 1934, ownership of nearly a million farms passed from the farmers to the mortgage holders.

FARMERS AND VETERANS IN PROTEST   Faced with the loss of everything, some desperate farmers began to defy the law. Angry mobs stopped foreclosures and threatened to lynch the judges sanctioning them. In Nebraska farmers burned corn to keep warm. Iowans formed the militant Farmers' Holiday Association, which called a farmers' strike and forcibly blocked deliveries of produce.

In the midst of the crisis, there was desperate if nebulous talk of revolution. "Folks are restless," Mississippi governor Theodore Bilbo told reporters in 1931. "Communism is gaining a foothold. . . . In fact, I'm getting a little pink myself." Bilbo was doing his usual put-on, but across the country the once-obscure Communist party began to draw crowds to its rallies and willing collaborators into its "hunger marches." In Alabama it formed a Share Croppers Union and reaped a propaganda windfall when the party went to the defense of the Scottsboro Boys, nine black itinerants accused on flimsy evidence of raping two white girls on a freight train in northern Alabama. Around Harlan, Kentucky, desperate coal miners embraced the Communist-run National Mine Workers' Union, which eventually fell victim to guns and whips and ultimately to the rock-ribbed faith of miners who heard leaders "denounce our government and our flag and our religion." Yet, for all the sound and fury, few Americans were converted to the Communist view during the 1930s. Party membership in America never rose much above 100,000.

Fears of mass disorder arose when unemployed veterans converged on Washington in the spring of 1932. The "Bonus Expeditionary Force" grew quickly to more than 15,000. Their purpose was to get immediate payment of the bonus to world-war veterans that Congress had voted in 1924. The House approved a bonus bill, but when the Senate voted it down, most of the veterans went home. The rest, having no place to go,

Unemployed veterans, members of the "Bonus Expeditionary Force," clash with Washington, D.C., police at Anacostia Flats, July 1932.

camped in vacant government buildings and in a shantytown at Anacostia Flats, within sight of the Capitol.

The chief of the Washington police gave the squatters a friendly welcome and won their trust. But a fearful White House fretted. Eager to disperse them, Hoover convinced Congress to pay for their tickets home. More left, but others stayed even after Congress adjourned, hoping at least to meet with the president. Late in July the administration ordered the government buildings cleared. In the ensuing melee, one policeman panicked, fired into the crowd, and killed two veterans. The president then acceded to a request from his secretary of war to move in about 700 soldiers under General Douglas MacArthur, aided by junior officers Dwight D. Eisenhower and George S. Patton, Jr. The soldiers drove out the unarmed veterans and their families, injuring dozens. The one fatality—from tear gas—was an eleven-week-old boy born at Anacostia.

General MacArthur claimed that the "mob," animated by "the essence of revolution," was about to seize control of the government. The administration insisted that the Bonus Army consisted mainly of Communists and criminals, but neither a grand jury nor the Veterans Administration could find evidence to support the charge. One observer wrote before the incident: "There is about the lot of them an atmosphere of hopelessness, of utter despair, though not of desperation. . . . They have no enthusiasm whatever and no stomach for fighting."

Their mood, and the mood of the country, echoed that of Hoover himself. He worked hard, but took no joy from his labors. "I am so tired," he sometimes said, "that every bone in my body aches." News conferences became more strained and less frequent. When friends urged him to seize the reins of leadership he said, "I can't be a Theodore Roosevelt," or "I have no Wilsonian qualities." The gloom, the sense of futility, communicated itself to the country. In a mood more despairing than rebellious, people waited to see what another presidential campaign would produce.

MAKING CONNECTIONS

- This chapter discusses setbacks for labor unions during the Republican administrations of the 1920s. In the next chapter, unions win new protections under Franklin Roosevelt's New Deal.

- An element of the "normalcy" discussed in this chapter was American isolationism from global affairs. Chapter 29 discusses that isolationism in the context of the coming of World War II.

- Compare the characteristics of 1920s American society with the postwar society and culture of the 1950s, discussed in Chapter 32.

FURTHER READING

A fine synthesis of events immediately following the First World War is Ellis W. Hawley's *The Great War and the Search for a Modern Or-*

der: A History of the American People and Their Institutions, 1917–1933 (1979).

For an introduction to Harding, see Francis Russell's *The Shadow of Blooming Grove: Warren G. Harding in His Times* (1968). Robert K. Murray's *The Harding Era: Warren G. Harding and His Administration* (1969) is more favorable to Harding. On Coolidge, see Donald R. Mc-Coy's *Calvin Coolidge: The Silent President* (1967). Studies on Hoover include Joan Hoff Wilson's *Herbert Hoover: Forgotten Progressive* (1975) and George Nash's multivolume work, *The Life of Herbert Hoover* (1983–1987). Other works on politics include Burl Noggle's *Teapot Dome: Oil and Politics in the 1920s* (1962) and David Burner's *The Politics of Provincialism: The Democratic Party in Transition, 1918–1932* (1968).

The impact of transportation is gauged in Reynold M. Wik's *Henry Ford and Grassroots America* (1972). Roland Marchand's *Advertising the American Dream: Making Way for Modernity, 1920–1940* (1985) covers the development of national advertising in the 1920s. Susan J. Douglas's *Inventing American Broadcasting, 1899–1922* (1989) is a cultural history of the formative years of radio. Motion pictures are the subject of Robert Sklar's *Movie-Made America: A Cultural History of American Movies* (1975) and Lary May's *Screening out the Past: The Birth of Mass Culture and the Motion Picture Industry* (1980).

Overviews of the depressed economy are found in Charles P. Kindleberger's *The World in Depression, 1929–1939* (rev. ed., 1986) and Peter Fearon's *War, Prosperity and Depression: The U.S. Economy, 1917–1945* (1987). John Kenneth Galbraith details the fall of the stock market in *The Great Crash, 1929* (1955). A different interpretation is given in Peter Temin's *Did Monetary Forces Cause the Great Depression?* (1976).

John A. Garraty's *The Great Depression: An Inquiry into the Causes, Course, and Consequences of the Worldwide Depression of the Nineteen-Thirties* (1986) describes how people survived the depression. First-hand accounts of the Great Depression can be found in Tom E. Terrill and Jerrold Hirsch's *Such As Us: Southern Voices of the Thirties* (1978), Studs Terkel's *Hard Times* (1970), Robert S. McElvaine's *Down and Out in the Great Depression: Letters from the Forgotten Man* (1983), and *"Slaves of the Depression": Workers' Letters about Life on the Job* (1989), edited by Gerald Markowitz and David Rosner.

28 NEW DEAL AMERICA

*U*pon arriving in the White House Franklin Roosevelt inherited a nation mired in an unprecedented economic depression. He and a supportive Congress immediately adopted bold measures to relieve the human suffering and promote economic recovery. Such initiatives provided the foundation for what came to be called welfare capitalism. A three-pronged strategy guided the New Dealers. They first sought to remedy the financial crisis and provide short-term emergency relief for the jobless. They then tried to promote industrial recovery through increased federal spending and cooperative agreements between management and organized labor. The third prong of the New Deal strategy involved efforts to raise commodity prices (and thereby farm income) by paying farmers to reduce crops and herds, thereby shrinking supply and raising prices. None of these initiatives worked perfectly, but they combined to restore hope and energy to a nation mired in depression and uncertainty.

FROM HOOVERISM TO THE NEW DEAL

FDR'S ELECTION   On June 14, 1932, while the Bonus Army was still encamped in Washington, Republicans gathered in Chicago to renominate Hoover. The delegates went through the motions in a mood of defeat. By contrast, the Democrats converged on Chicago confident that they would nominate the next president. New York governor Franklin D. Roosevelt was already the front-runner with most of the delegates lined up, and he went over the top on the fourth ballot.

In a bold gesture, Roosevelt flew to Chicago and appeared before the convention in person to accept the nomination instead of awaiting formal notification. "Let it . . . be symbolic that . . . I broke traditions," he told the delegates. "Republican leaders not only have failed in material things, they have failed in national vision, because in disaster they have held out no hope. . . . I pledge you, I pledge myself to a new deal for the American people." What the New Deal would be Roosevelt himself had little idea as yet, but unlike Hoover, he was flexible and willing to experiment. What was more, his upbeat personality communicated joy and hope. His campaign song was "Happy Days Are Here Again."

Born in 1882 into a wealthy family, educated by governesses and tutors at Springwood, his father's rambling Hudson River Valley estate, young Franklin led the cosmopolitan life of a young patrician. After attending Groton, an elite Connecticut boarding school, he earned degrees from Harvard and Columbia University Law School. While a law student, he married his distant cousin, Anna Eleanor Roosevelt, the niece of President Theodore Roosevelt.

Franklin Roosevelt began work with a prominent Wall Street law firm, but soon lost interest in legal affairs and decided to enter politics. In 1910 he won a Democratic seat in the New York State Senate. As a freshman legislator he displayed the contradictory qualities that would always characterize his political career: an aristocrat with a sincere affinity for common folk; a traditionalist with a penchant for experiment; an affable charmer with a luminous smile and upturned chin who also harbored profound convictions; and a skilled political tactician with a shrewd sense of timing and a distinctive willingness to listen to and learn from others.

In 1912 Roosevelt backed Wilson, and for both of Wilson's terms he served as assistant secretary of the navy. Then, in 1920, largely on the strength of his name, he became Democrat James Cox's running mate. The following year, at age thirty-nine, his career seemed cut short by an attack of poliomyelitis that left him permanently crippled, unable to stand or walk without braces. But the struggle for recovery transformed the once supercilious young aristocrat into one of the most outgoing political figures of the century. A friend recalled that he emerged from his struggle with polio "completely warm-hearted, with a new humility of spirit" that led him to identify with the poor and suffering. Justice Oliver Wendell Holmes, Jr., later summed up his qualities this way: "A second-class intellect—but a first-class temperament."

For seven years, aided by his talented wife Eleanor, Roosevelt fought his way back to health and in 1928 emerged again on the national scene to nominate Al Smith for the presidency. At Smith's urging, he ran for governor of New York to strengthen the ticket, and he won while Smith was losing the state to Hoover in the race for president. Reelected governor by a whopping majority of 700,000 in 1930, Roosevelt became the favorite for president in 1932.

Partly to dispel doubts about his health, Roosevelt set forth on a grueling campaign tour. He blamed the depression on Hoover and the Republicans, and he began to define what he meant by the "New Deal." Like Hoover, Roosevelt promised to balance the budget, but he was willing to incur short-term deficits to prevent starvation and dire want. On the tariff, he was evasive. On farm policy, he offered several options pleasing to farmers and ambiguous enough not to alarm city dwellers. He did call for strict regulation of utilities and for at least some development of public power, and he consistently stood by his party's pledge to repeal the Prohibition Amendment. Perhaps most important, he recognized that a mature economy would require national planning. "The country needs, and, unless I mistake its temper, the country demands bold, persistent experimentation. . . . Above all, try something."

What came across to voters, however, was less the content of Roosevelt's speeches than the confidence of the man. By contrast, Hoover

Governor Franklin D. Roosevelt, the Democratic nominee, campaigning in Topeka, Kansas. Roosevelt's confidence inspired voters.

lacked assurance. He could turn a neat phrase, but many elegant passages suffered from his pedestrian delivery. Democrats, he argued, ignored the international causes of the depression. They were taking a reckless course. Roosevelt's policies, he warned, "would destroy the very foundations of our American system." Pursue them, and "grass will grow in the streets of a hundred cities, a thousand towns." But few were listening. Amid the persistent depression, the country wanted a new course, a new leadership, a new deal.

Many concerned observers took a dim view of both candidates. Those who believed that only a radical departure would suffice went over to Socialist Norman Thomas, who polled 882,000 votes, and a few preferred the Communist party candidate, who got 103,000. The wonder is that a desperate people did not turn in greater numbers to radical candidates. Instead they swept Roosevelt into office with 22.8 million votes to Hoover's 15.8 million. Hoover carried only four states in New England plus Pennsylvania and Delaware, and lost in the electoral college by 472 to 59.

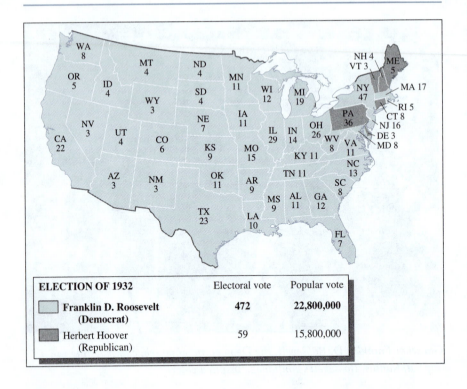

ELECTION OF 1932	Electoral vote	Popular vote
Franklin D. Roosevelt (Democrat)	472	22,800,000
Herbert Hoover (Republican)	59	15,800,000

THE INAUGURATION For the last time the country waited four months, until March 4, for a new president and Congress to take office. The Twentieth Amendment, ratified on February 6, 1933, provided that presidents would thereafter take office on January 20 and the newly elected Congress on January 3.

The bleak winter of 1932–1933 became what one historian called "the interregnum of despair." Amid spreading destitution and misery, unemployment continued to rise, and panic struck the banking system. As bank after bank announced they were closing and did not have adequate cash to repay depositors, people rushed to their own bank to remove their deposits. Many discovered that they, too, were caught short. The "run" on the banks exacerbated the crisis. In Michigan, where automobile production stalled, the threat of runs on the banks impelled the governor to extend the Lincoln's Birthday closing indefinitely. As the panic spread, governors of other states also found excuses for imposing banking holidays. When the Hoover administration ended, four-fifths of the nation's banks were closed, and the country teetered on the brink of economic paralysis.

The profound crisis of confidence that prevailed when Roosevelt took the oath of office on March 4, 1933, gave way to a mood of expectancy. The new president conveyed a confident sense of vigor and action. First, he asserted "that the only thing we have to fear is fear itself—nameless, unreasoning, unjustified terror which paralyzes needed efforts to convert retreat into advance." Roosevelt warned that emergency measures might call for a temporary departure from the normal balance of executive and legislative authority. If need be, he said, "I shall ask the Congress for the remaining instrument to meet the crisis—broad executive power to wage a war against the emergency as great as the power that would be given me if we were in fact invaded by a foreign foe." It was a measure of the country's mood that this call received the loudest applause.

Many people used the nation's mobilization for World War I as a model for dealing with the economic crisis. Many of Roosevelt's appointees had been involved in the wartime mobilization. Other cabinet officers drew upon backgrounds in social work. Frances Perkins, the secretary of labor, was the first female cabinet member. A graduate of Mount Holyoke, she worked with Jane Addams at Chicago's Hull House at the turn of the century. Later she was appointed executive secretary of the Consumers League in New York and became an enormously effective advocate for labor reform.

Franklin Delano Roosevelt (right) *and a glum Herbert Hoover ride to the Capitol on inauguration day.*

COMPETING SOLUTIONS   Roosevelt's "brain trust" of advisers developed conflicting opinions about how best to rescue the economy from depression. Some promoted vigorous enforcement of the antitrust laws as a means of restoring competition; others argued just the opposite, saying that antitrust laws should be suspended so as to enable large corporations to collaborate with the federal government and thereby better manage the overall economy. Still others called for a massive expansion of welfare programs and a prolonged infusion of increased government spending to address the profound human crisis and revive the economy.

For his part, Roosevelt vacillated among these three schools of thought. He was willing to try some elements of each without ever embracing one approach completely. When asked by a reporter to label his philosophy, Roosevelt replied: "Philosophy? I am a Christian and a Democrat—that's all." His willingness to act decisively and to experiment with new programs and policies set his presidency apart. He was a pragmatist rather than an ideologue. As he once explained, "Take a method and try it. If it fails admit it frankly and try another." He liked to say, "I have no expectation of making a hit every time I come to bat. What I seek is the highest possible batting average." Roosevelt's "New Deal," therefore, would take the form of a series of trial-and-error actions.

STRENGTHENING THE MONETARY SYSTEM   The first order of business for the new administration was to free up the channels of finance. On his second day in office, Roosevelt called Congress to meet in special session on March 9, and then declared a four-day banking holiday. It took Congress only seven hours to pass the Emergency Banking Relief Act, which permitted sound banks to reopen and provided managers for those that remained in trouble. On March 12, in the first of his radio "fireside chats," the president insisted that it was safer to "keep your money in a reopened bank than under the mattress." The following day, deposits in reopened banks exceeded withdrawals, and by March 15 banks controlling nine-tenths of the nation's banking resources were once again open. The crisis had ended, and the new administration was ready to get on with its broader program.

In rapid order Roosevelt undertook to meet two specific pledges in the Democratic platform. At his behest, Congress passed an Economy Act granting the executive branch the power to cut salaries, reduce pay-

The Galloping Snail. *A vigorous Roosevelt drives the Congress to action in this* Detroit News *cartoon, March 1933.*

ments to veterans for non-service-connected disabilities, and reorganize federal agencies in the interest of economy. The Beer-Wine Revenue Act amended the Volstead Act to permit sale of beverages with an alcoholic content of 3.2 percent. The Twenty-first Amendment, already submitted by Congress to the states, would be declared ratified on December 5, thus ending the "noble experiment" of Prohibition.

The measures of March were but the beginning. During the session from March 9 to June 16, the so-called Hundred Days, Congress received and enacted fifteen major proposals from the president with a dizzying speed unlike anything seen before in American history:

March 9	The Emergency Banking Relief Act
March 20	The Economy Act
March 31	Establishment of the Civilian Conservation Corps
April 19	Abandonment of the gold standard
May 12	The Federal Emergency Relief Act
May 12	The Agricultural Adjustment Act, including the Thomas Amendment, which gave the president powers to expand the money supply
May 12	The Emergency Farm Mortgage Act, providing for the refinancing of farm mortgages
May 18	The Tennessee Valley Authority Act, providing for the unified hydroelectric development of the Tennessee Valley

May 27	The Federal Securities Act, requiring full disclosure in the issue of new securities
June 5	The Gold Repeal Joint Resolution, which abrogated the gold clause in public and private contracts
June 13	The Home Owners' Loan Act, setting up the Home Owners' Loan Corporation to refinance home mortgages
June 16	The National Industrial Recovery Act, providing for a system of industrial self-regulation under federal supervision and for a $3.3 billion public-works program
June 16	The Glass-Steagall Banking Act, separating commercial and investment banking and establishing the Federal Deposit Insurance Corporation
June 16	The Farm Credit Act, which reorganized the agricultural credit system

With the banking crisis over, there remained an acute debt problem for farmers and homeowners, and a lingering distrust of the banks, which might yet be aroused again. By executive decree, Roosevelt reorganized all farm credit agencies into the Farm Credit Administration (FCA). By the Emergency Farm Mortgage Act and the Farm Credit Act, Congress authorized extensive refinancing of farm mortgages at lower interest rates. Within seven months, the FCA loaned distressed farmers more than $100 million, nearly four times as much as all the land-bank loans made the previous year.

The Home Owners' Loan Act provided a similar service to city dwellers through the new Home Owners' Loan Corporation (HOLC). The HOLC refinanced mortgage loans at lower monthly payments for strapped homeowners. This helped slow the rate of foreclosures. The Glass-Steagall Banking Act further shored up confidence in the banking system. It created the Federal Deposit Insurance Corporation (FDIC) to guarantee bank deposits up to $5,000. To prevent speculative abuses, it separated investment and commercial banking corporations and extended the Federal Reserve's regulatory power over credit. The Federal Securities Act required the full disclosure of information about new stock and bond issues, at first by registration with the Federal Trade Commission, later with the Securities and Exchange Commission (SEC), which was created to regulate the stock and bond markets.

Throughout 1933 Roosevelt tinkered with devaluation of the currency as a way to raise prices and thus ease the debt burden. Having already put an embargo on the withdrawal of gold deposits at the outset of his administration, on April 5 he used powers granted by the Emergency Banking Act to order all gold turned in to the Federal Reserve Banks. On April 19 the government officially abandoned the gold standard: the consequent decline in the value of the dollar increased the prices of commodities and stocks at home. The Gold Repeal Joint Resolution canceled the gold clause in federal and private obligations, made all contracts payable in legal tender, and thus completed the abandonment of the gold standard. The experiment ended when Congress passed the Gold Reserve Act of January 30, 1934, which authorized the president to impound all gold in the Federal Reserve Banks and reduce the theoretical gold value of the dollar. By executive order he set the price of an ounce of gold at $35, which in effect reduced the dollar's gold content. It was done, Roosevelt said, "to make possible the payment of . . . debts at more nearly the price level at which they had been incurred." Prices did rise, and the high price set on gold drew most of the world's supply to the United States, where it was buried in the vaults at Fort Knox, Kentucky.

RELIEF MEASURES   In 1933 relieving the widespread personal distress caused by the Great Depression was an urgent priority, as it would remain until World War II. As Roosevelt once remarked, the "test of our progress is not whether we add to the abundance of those who have much. It is whether we provide enough for those who have too little." As a first step toward such relief Congress created the Civilian Conservation Corps (CCC), which was designed to give work to unemployed and unmarried young men aged eighteen to twenty-five.

Nearly 3 million young men took to the woods to work at a variety of CCC jobs in forests, parks, recreational areas, and soil conservation projects. As part of the CCC, they built roads, bridges, camping facilities, and fish hatcheries, planted trees, taught farmers how to control soil erosion, and fought fires. They were paid a nominal sum of $30 a month, of which $25 went home to their families. The enrollees could also take education courses and earn high school diplomas. Directed by army officers and foresters, they worked under a semimilitary discipline

A CCC camp in the Berkshire Mountains of New England, 1933.

and provided perhaps the most direct analogue of war in the whole New Deal. Like the military at the time, the CCC camps were racially segregated. In Texas, African Americans were initially told that the camps were for whites only, and this falsehood helps explain the low number of blacks enrolled. Only 400 black Texans, less than 5 percent of the total number of men enrolled, participated in the CCC.

The Federal Emergency Relief Administration (FERA), created with an authorization of $500 million, addressed the broader problems of human distress. Harry L. Hopkins, an indefatigable social worker who had directed Roosevelt's state relief efforts in New York, pushed the program with a boundless energy. The FERA expanded the assistance that had begun under Hoover's RFC, but with a difference. Federal monies flowed to the states in grants rather than "loans." While FERA continued to channel aid through state agencies to relief clients mainly in the form of direct cash payments, Hopkins enlarged its scope by gradually developing work programs for education, student aid, rural rehabilitation, and for the many jobless wanderers across the country. He pushed an "immediate work instead of dole" approach on local officials, but they preferred the dole as an easier and quicker way to reach the needy.

The first large-scale experiment with work relief was the Civil Works Administration (CWA), created during the winter of 1933–1934, when it had become apparent that even the largesse of the FERA would not prevent widespread privation. The CWA provided jobs and wages to those able to work. It was implemented hastily, and many of its projects were "make-work" jobs such as leaf-raking and ditch-digging; but it spent over $900 million (mostly in wages) for a variety of useful projects, from highway repairs to teaching jobs that helped keep the schools open. The CWA, unlike the FERA, was a federal operation from top to bottom. The CWA was abandoned in the spring of 1934, having served its purpose of helping people weather the winter; but Roosevelt and Hopkins continued to favor work relief over the dole, which they believed to have a debilitating psychological effect on the unemployed.

RECOVERY THROUGH REGULATION

Beyond rescuing the banks and providing relief to the unemployed lay the long-term goals of recovery for agriculture and business. Members of Franklin Roosevelt's "brain trust" were largely heirs to Theodore Roosevelt's New Nationalism. Like the earlier progressives, they insisted that the trend toward economic concentration was inevitable. They also believed that the mistakes of the 1920s showed that the only way to operate an integrated economy at capacity and in the public interest was through efficient regulation and organized central planning, not through trust-busting. The success of centralized planning during World War I reinforced such ideas. New farm and recovery programs sprang from their beliefs.

AGRICULTURAL RECOVERY: THE AAA   The sharp decline in commodity prices after 1929 meant that many farmers could not afford to plant or harvest their crops. The Agricultural Adjustment Act of 1933 contained nearly every major plan applicable to farm relief, but only some of its provisions were implemented. The act sought to control farm production through compensating farmers for voluntary cutbacks in production in an effort to restore farm prices to "parity," or the same level they had reached relative to other prices during the farmers' golden age of 1909–1914 (1919–1929 for tobacco). The act covered seven "basic commodities," a number later enlarged, and the money for benefit payments came from a processing tax levied on each—at the cotton gin, for example, or the flour mill.

But by the time Congress acted, the growing season was already advanced. The prospect of another bumper cotton crop forced the AAA to sponsor a plow-under program. To destroy a growing crop was a "shocking commentary on our civilization," Agriculture Secretary Henry A. Wallace lamented. "I could tolerate it only as a cleaning up of the wreckage from the old days of unbalanced production." Moreover, given the oversupply of hogs, some 6 million little pink pigs were slaughtered "before they could reach the full hogness of their hogdom." It could be justified, Wallace said, only as a means of helping farmers to do with pigs what steelmakers did with pig iron—cut production to fit the market and therefore raise prices.

It worked temporarily. Cotton farmers received about $112 million in benefit payments, and the crop was reduced by about 4 million bales below the preprogram estimate. Cotton prices rose from 5¢ a pound in May to above 11¢ per pound in July (parity was 12.7¢), but sagged again as the crop came in. In an effort to take up the slack, the president set up the Commodity Credit Corporation (another CCC!), which extended loans first on cotton and later on other crops kept in storage and off the market. In principle, if not in form, it was a revival of the old Farmers' Alliance–Populist subtreasury plan. Loans averaged 10¢ per pound on the 1933 crop and 12¢ per pound in 1934, pegged at those levels because no farmer had to sell for less. But the carryover surplus from the crops of previous years still weighed the market—and prices—down.

Another drastic step was taken in 1934 with passage of the Bankhead Cotton Control Act, which specified that all farmers had to accept cotton production quotas if two-thirds of a county's voters authorized them; farmers who tried to sell more than their share of the quota would be stopped by a prohibitive tax. Almost all of the counties in Texas complied with the Bankhead Act. By 1936 Texans had signed almost 900,000 cotton reduction contracts, more than twice that of any other state. The Kerr-Smith Tobacco Control Act of 1934 applied similar quotas to tobacco.

For a while these farm measures worked. By the end of 1934, Secretary of Agriculture Wallace could report significant declines in wheat,

Dust Storm Approaching, *1930s. When a dust storm blew in, it would bring complete darkness as well as sand and grit that would soon cover every surface, both inside and out.*

cotton, and corn production and a simultaneous increase in commodity prices. Farm income increased by 58 percent between 1932 and 1935. The AAA, however, was only partially responsible for such gains. The devastating drought that settled over the Plains states between 1932 and 1935 played a major role in reducing production and creating the epic "dust bowl" migrations so poignantly evoked in John Steinbeck's *Grapes of Wrath.* Many of these migrant families had actually been driven off the land by AAA benefit programs that encouraged large farmers to take the lands worked by tenants and sharecroppers out of cultivation first.

Although it created unexpected problems, the AAA achieved real successes in boosting the overall farm economy. Then on January 6, 1936, in *United States v. Butler,* the Supreme Court, by a vote of six to three, declared the AAA's processing tax unconstitutional because farm production was intrastate and thus beyond the reach of the power of Congress to regulate interstate commerce. The administration hastily devised a new plan in the Soil Conservation and Domestic Allotment Act, which it pushed through Congress in six weeks. The new act omitted processing taxes and acreage quotas, but provided benefit payments for soil conservation practices that took land out of soil-depleting staple crops, thus indirectly achieving crop reduction. Since the money came out of general funds and not from taxes, this approach was not vulnerable to lawsuits. The act boosted a developing conservation movement directed by the Soil Conservation Service, which had been created in 1935.

The act was an almost unqualified success as an engineering and educational project because it went far to heal the scars of erosion and the plague of dust storms. But soil conservation nevertheless failed as a device for limiting production. With their worst lands taken out of production, farmers cultivated their fertile acres more intensively. In response, Congress passed the Second Agricultural Adjustment Act in 1938, which reestablished the earlier programs but left out the processing taxes. Benefit payments would come from general funds. By the time the second AAA reached a test in the Supreme Court, changes in the Court's personnel had changed its outlook. This time the law was upheld as a legitimate exercise of the interstate commerce power. Agriculture, like manufacturing, was now held to be in the stream of commerce.

INDUSTRIAL RECOVERY: THE NRA   The industrial counterpart to the AAA was the National Industrial Recovery Act (NIRA), passed on June 16, 1933, the two major parts of which dealt with economic recovery and public-works projects designed to put people to work. The latter part, Title II, created the Public Works Administration (PWA) with $3.3 billion for public buildings, highway programs, flood control, and other improvements. Under the direction of Interior Secretary Harold L. Ickes, the PWA indirectly served the purpose of work relief. Ickes directed it toward well-planned permanent improvements rather than the provision of hasty make-work, and he used private contractors rather than placing workers directly on the government payroll. PWA workers built Virginia's Skyline Drive, New York's Triborough Bridge, the Overseas Highway from Miami to Key West, and Chicago's subway system.

The more controversial and ambitious part of the NIRA created the National Recovery Administration (NRA), headed by General Hugh S. Johnson. Its purposes were twofold: first, to stabilize business by reducing competition through the implementation of codes that set wages

In this cartoon employer and employee agree to cooperate in the spirit of unity that inspired the National Recovery Administration.

and prices, and second, to generate more purchasing power by providing jobs, defining labor standards, and raising wages. In each major industry, committees representing management, labor, and government drew up the codes of fair practice. Code Number 1, which dealt with the textile industry, imposed restraints on plant expansion, limited operations to eighty hours a week, and required reports on operations every four weeks. The labor standards featured in every code set a forty-hour workweek and minimum weekly wages of $13 ($12 in the South, where living costs were lower), which more than doubled earnings in some cases. Announcement of a proviso against child labor under the age of sixteen did "in a few minutes what neither law nor constitutional amendment had been able to do in forty years," Johnson said.

As the drafting of other codes began to drag, Johnson proposed a "blanket code" pledging employers generally to observe the same labor standards as applied to cotton textiles. He launched a crusade to whip up popular support for the NRA and its symbol of compliance, the "Blue Eagle," which had been modeled on an Indian thunderbird and embellished with the motto "We do our part." The eagle decal was displayed in shop windows and stamped on products. It was a gamble, but the public responded. Some 2 million employers signed the pledge, and the impact of the campaign broke the logjam in code making.

Labor unions, already hard pressed by the economic downturn and the loss of members, however, were understandably concerned about the NRA's efforts to reduce competition by allowing businesses to cooperate in fixing wages and prices. To gain their support, the NRA included a provision (Section 7a) that guaranteed the right of workers to organize unions. But while prohibiting employers from interfering with labor organizing efforts, the NRA did not create adequate enforcement measures, nor did it require employers to bargain in good faith with labor representatives.

For a time the NRA worked, perhaps because a new air of confidence had overcome the depression blues and the downward spiral of wages and prices had subsided. But as soon as economic recovery began, the honeymoon ended. The daily annoyances of code enforcement inspired growing hostility among business owners. Charges mounted that the larger companies dominated the code authorities and that price-fixing robbed small producers of the chance to compete. In 1934 an investigating committee substantiated at least some of the charges. Limiting production, moreover, had discouraged investment. And because the NRA wage codes excluded agricultural workers and domestic workers, three out of every four employed blacks derived no direct benefit from the program. By 1935 the NRA had developed more critics than friends. When it died in May 1935, struck down by the Supreme Court as unconstitutional, few paused to mourn.

The NRA experiment was generally a failure, but it left an enduring mark. With dramatic suddenness the codes had set new standards, such as the forty-hour workweek and the end of child labor, from which it was hard to retreat. The NRA's endorsement of collective bargaining spurred the growth of unions. The codes, moreover, advanced trends toward stabilization and rationalization that were becoming the standard practice of business at large and that, despite misgivings about the concentration of power, would be further promoted by trade associations.

REGIONAL PLANNING: THE TVA   The philosophy of the New Deal embraced more than the restrictive approaches of the NRA. The cre-

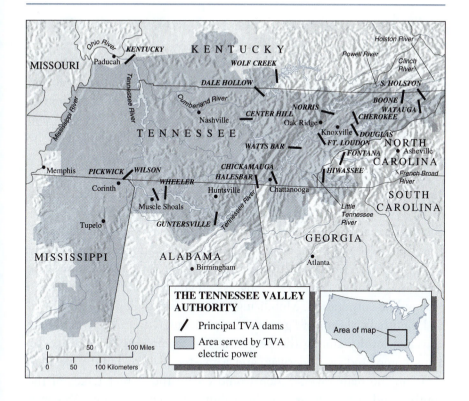

THE TENNESSEE VALLEY
AUTHORITY

/ Principal TVA dams

☐ Area served by TVA
electric power

Area of map

ation of the Tennessee Valley Authority (TVA) was a truly bold venture. Among the measures of Roosevelt's first Hundred Days, most of which were efforts to redress the ills of depression, the TVA refuted the idea that the economy had reached its full measure of mature development. It was the product neither of a single imagination nor of a single concept, but of an unfolding progression of purposes. In 1916, when the government started electric power plants and facilities to produce nitrates for fertilizers and explosives at Muscle Shoals, Alabama, strengthening national defense was the aim. New objectives unfolded in succession: production of nitrate fertilizers as well as nitrate explosives, general industrial development, and cheap public power, to be used as a "yardstick" for private utility rates. Water-power development pointed in turn to navigation, the control of stream flow for both power and flood control, and to conservation of soil and forests to prevent silting. The chain of connections led ultimately to the concept of overall planning for an entire regional watershed, which included a total drainage area of 41,000 square miles overlapping seven states, four-fifths the size of England.

Through the 1920s Nebraska senator George W. Norris had fought off efforts to sell the Alabama project to private companies, but had never won enough support for his goal of public control of the entire electrical power industry. In 1932, however, he backed Roosevelt, and then gained the new president's support for a vast enlargement of the Muscle Shoals project.

Muscle Shoals, Roosevelt said, "gives us the opportunity . . . of setting an example of planning, not just for ourselves but for generations to come, tying in industry and agriculture and forestry and flood prevention . . . over a distance of a thousand miles." The region needed help. The Tennessee River Valley was one of the most underdeveloped and poverty-stricken regions of the country, and illiteracy and disease were rampant. On May 18, 1933, Congress created the TVA as a multipurpose public corporation. Mobilizing local support under Director David E. Lilienthal's slogan of "grassroots democracy," the TVA won almost universal loyalty among the people of the region. By 1936 it had six dams completed or underway, and a master plan to build nine high dams on the main river, which would create the "Great Lakes of the South," and other dams on the tributaries. The agency, moreover, opened the rivers for navigation, fostered soil conservation and forestry, experimented with fertilizers, drew new industry to the region, encouraged the formation of labor unions, improved schools and libraries, and sent cheap power pulsating through the valley.

Cheap public power, Lilienthal's main passion, became more and more the TVA's reason for being—a purpose that would become all the more important during World War II. The TVA's success at generating greater power consumption and lower rates awakened private utilities to the mass consumer markets. Cheap power transported farmers of the valley from the age of kerosene to the age of electricity. "The women went around turning the switches on and off," said a Farm Bureau man who witnessed the transition. "The light and wonder in their eyes was brighter than that from the lamps." The TVA's first rural cooperative, set up at Corinth, Mississippi, in 1934, pointed the way to the electrification of the nation's farms in the decade that followed. The Rural Electrification Administration (REA), formed as a relief agency by presidential order in 1935, achieved a permanent statutory basis in 1936. By

Constructing the Fontana Dam, under the aegis of Roosevelt's TVA.

1940 it had extended loans of more than $321 million to rural electrical cooperatives.

THE SECOND NEW DEAL

During Roosevelt's first year in office his programs and his personal charms aroused massive support. The president's travels and speeches, his twice-weekly press conferences, and his "fireside chats" over the radio generated vitality from a once-remote White House. In the congressional elections of 1934 the Democrats actually increased their strength in both the House and the Senate, an almost unprecedented midterm victory for the party in power. When it was over, only seven Republican governors remained in office throughout the country.

Criticism of the New Deal was muted or reduced to helpless carping. But as the sense of crisis passed, the spirit of unity relaxed. In 1934 a group of conservative businessmen and politicians, including Al Smith and John W. Davis, two previous Democratic presidential candidates, formed the American Liberty League to oppose New Deal measures and to "teach the necessity of respect for the rights of person and property."

THUNDER ON THE LEFT   But the real threat to Roosevelt in those years came from the hucksters of social nostrums, old and new. The most flamboyant of the group, by far, was Louisiana's "Kingfish," Senator Huey P. Long, Jr. A short, strutting man with a round, rosy face and pug nose, Long sported pink suits and pastel shirts, red ties, and two-toned shoes. He loved to make people think he was a country bumpkin, though underneath the carefully calculated image was a shrewd lawyer and consummate demagogue. First as governor of Louisiana, then as political boss of the state, he delivered to its citizens tax favors, roads, schools, free textbooks, charity hospitals, and generally better public services, all at the cost of corruption and personal dictatorship.

Louisiana, however, became only the base from which Long ventured out to conquer other worlds. The vehicle was his Share Our Wealth program, first unveiled in 1932 and refined over the next three years. In one version Long proposed to liquidate large personal fortunes, guarantee every family an allowance of $5,000 and every worker an annual income of $2,500, grant pensions to the aged, reduce the hours of labor, pay veterans' bonuses, and assure a college education for every qualified

The "Kingfish," Huey Long, governor of Louisiana.

student. Whether he had a workable plan or not, his scheme dramatized a fundamental issue in a society that had solved the problem of
production but not that of distribution, an issue few politicians were so
imprudent as to tackle directly. By early 1935 Huey Long was claiming
27,431 Share Our Wealth Clubs and a file of 7.5 million names.

Still another popular scheme appealed to the elderly. A California
doctor, Francis E. Townsend, outraged by the sight of three haggard old
women raking through garbage cans, proposed pensions for the aged. In
1934 he announced the Townsend Plan. It called for payments of $200
a month to every citizen over sixty who retired from employment and
who promised to spend the money within the month. The plan had the
lure of providing both financial security for the aged and job openings
for the young. As the Townsend Club grew, critics noted that the cost
would be more than half the national income. "I'm not in the least interested in the cost of the plan," Townsend blandly told a House committee.

A third huckster of panaceas, Father Charles E. Coughlin, the "radio
priest" of Michigan, founded the National Union for Social Justice in
1934. In broadcasts over the CBS radio network, he promoted schemes
for the coinage of silver and attacks on bankers that carried growing
overtones of anti-Semitism.

Coughlin, Townsend, and Long drew support largely from a desperate lower middle class. Of the three, Long had the widest following. A
survey showed that he could draw 5 million to 6 million votes as a third-
party candidate for president, perhaps enough to undermine Roosevelt's
chances of reelection. Beset by pressures from both ends of the political spectrum, Roosevelt drifted through months of hesitation in 1934
before deciding to "steal the thunder" from the left with new programs
of reform and social security. Political pressures impelled Roosevelt,
but so did the growing influence of Justices Louis Brandeis and Felix
Frankfurter. These men urged Roosevelt to be less cozy with big business and to push for restored competition and heavy taxes on large corporations.

LIGHTNING FROM THE COURT   What finally galvanized the president into action was the behavior of the Supreme Court. In *Schechter
Poultry Corporation v. United States* (1935), quickly tagged the "sick
chicken" case, the defendants, who provided poultry to kosher retailers,

had been convicted of selling an "unfit chicken" and violating other code provisions as well. The high court ruled unanimously that Congress had delegated too much power to the executive branch when it granted the code-making authority under the NRA and had exceeded its power under the commerce clause. Chief Justice Charles Evans Hughes held that the poultry in question had "come to permanent rest within the state," although it had been moved across state lines. The Court's decision outraged Roosevelt. In a press conference soon afterward, he said: "We have been relegated to the horse-and-buggy definition of interstate commerce." The same line of reasoning, he warned, might endanger many other New Deal programs. The Court seemed to be denying the government the authority to deal with the greatest economic calamity in American history.

LEGISLATIVE ACHIEVEMENTS   In an effort to salvage his legislative program, Roosevelt launched the so-called Second New Deal in 1935. The initiative broke the stalemate in Congress, which passed what Roosevelt called "must" legislation:

July 5	The Wagner National Labor Relations Act, guaranteeing the right of labor to organize and bargain collectively
August 14	The Social Security Act, providing unemployment and old-age insurance and public-welfare programs
August 23	The Banking Act of 1935, strengthening the Federal Reserve System
August 28	The Wheeler-Rayburn Public Utility Holding Company Act, preventing the pyramiding of holding companies
August 30	The Revenue Act of 1935, which increased taxes on the wealthy

The National Labor Relations Act, often called the Wagner Act, gave workers the right to bargain through unions of their own choice and prohibited employers from interfering with union activities. A National Labor Relations Board of five members could supervise plant elections and certify unions as bargaining agents where a majority of the workers approved. The board could also investigate the actions of employers and issue "cease-and-desist" orders against specified unfair practices. Under the protection of the law, union activities quickly intensified.

"Yes, You Remembered Me."
*The social legislation of the
Second New Deal prompted this
depiction of FDR as the friend
of "The Forgotten Man."*

The Social Security Act of 1935, Roosevelt announced, was the New
Deal's "cornerstone" and "supreme achievement." Indeed, it has proven
to be the most far-reaching of all the New Deal initiatives. The concept
had its roots in the proposal of progressives early in the 1900s for a federal system of social security for the aged, indigent, disabled, and unemployed. Other nations had already enacted such programs, but the
United States remained steadfast to its deeply rooted tradition of individual self-reliance. The Great Depression, however, revived the idea,
and Roosevelt masterfully guided the legislation through Congress.

The Social Security Act included three major provisions. Its centerpiece was a pension fund for retired people over the age of sixty-five. In
1937, workers and employers began contributing payroll taxes to establish the fund, which three years later started to yield retirees average
payments of $22 per month, a modest sum even for those depressed
times. Roosevelt stressed that the pension program was not intended to
guarantee a comfortable retirement; it was designed to supplement
other sources of income and protect the elderly from some of the
"hazards and vicissitudes of life." Only later did American voters and
politicians come to perceive Social Security as the *primary* source of retirement income for most of the aged. By 1998 the average monthly
payment was about $1,000.

The Social Security Act also set up a shared federal-state unemployment insurance program, financed by a payroll tax on employers. In addition, the new legislation committed the national government to a broad range of social-welfare activities based on the assumption that "unemployables"—people who were unable to work—would remain a state responsibility while the national government would provide work relief for the able-bodied. To that end the law inaugurated federal grants-in-aid for three state-administered public assistance programs—old-age assistance, aid for dependent children, aid for the blind—and further aid for maternal, child welfare, and public health services.

Conservative critics charged that the Social Security system warred against traditions of American individualism. One New Jersey senator lamented that the new law would "take all the romance out of life. We might as well take the child from the nursery, give him a nurse, and protect him from every experience that life affords." But the new federal program was relatively conservative. It was the only government pension program in the world financed by taxes on the earnings of current workers. Most countries funded such programs out of general tax revenues. Moreover, the Social Security payroll tax was regressive: based on a single fixed rate for all, regardless of income level, the tax hurt the poor more than the rich. It also weakened Roosevelt's efforts to revive the economy. The new Social Security tax took money out of workers' pockets and placed it into a trust fund, thus exacerbating the deflation of the money supply that was one of the main causes of the depression. By taking discretionary income away from workers, the government blunted the sharp increase in public consumption needed to restore the health of the economy. Another limit to the Social Security system was its initial exclusion of those classes of workers who needed financial security the most: farm workers, domestics, and the self-employed (these groups have since gained access to the program).

Roosevelt regretted these limitations, but he considered them compromises that would ensure congressional passage of the Social Security Act and enable it to withstand court challenges. As he replied to an aide who criticized funding the pension program through employee contributions, "I guess you're right on the economics, but those taxes were never a problem of economics. They are politics all the way through. We put those payroll contributions there so as to give the contributors a moral, legal, and political right to collect their pensions and their unemployment benefits. With those taxes in there, no damn politician can ever scrap my Social Security program."

In addition to the Social Security Act, the "Second New Deal" included a bill providing work relief for jobless workers. To manage these programs, the Works Progress Administration (WPA), headed by Harry L. Hopkins, replaced the Federal Emergency Relief Administration. The act did not provide a dole, which, Roosevelt told Congress, had been "a narcotic, a subtle destroyer of the human spirit." Rather, the WPA paid people to work, building permanent monuments on the landscape in the form of buildings, bridges, hard-surfaced roads, airports, and schools. The WPA also employed a wide range of talents in the Federal Theater Project, the Federal Art Project, and the Federal Writers' Project. The National Youth Administration, under the WPA, gave part-time employment to students, set up technical training programs,

Artists on WPA *by Moses Soyer, 1935–1936. By sponsoring unemployed artists, the Federal Art Project under the WPA brought original American art to the popular forefront and left a powerful political and cultural legacy.*

and provided aid to jobless youth. Although the WPA took care of only about 3 million out of some 10 million jobless at any one time, in all it helped some 9 million clients before it expired in 1943.

The Banking Act of 1935 strengthened the Federal Reserve Board's ability to regulate member banks and diminished the power of private bankers in the money market. It concentrated in the board's hands all open-market operations—that is, the buying or selling of government securities to increase (by buying) or decrease (by selling) the money supply. The act greatly strengthened the board's control of the whole monetary system.

The Public Utility Holding Company Act struck at financial corruption in the public utility industry. Like railroads in the 1800s, utilities in their early stages of growth had spawned buccaneers interested more in manipulation than in good business. The act passed despite the high-pressure lobbying tactics of the utilities. It limited the sphere of utility holding companies and forbade the pyramiding (separate companies using the same directors on their boards) of such companies.

The last of the major laws passed during this period was the Revenue Act of 1935, sometimes called the Wealth Tax Act, but popularly known as the "Soak the Rich Tax." In asking for the law, Roosevelt told Congress: "Our revenue laws have operated in many ways to the unfair advantage of the few, and they have done little to prevent an unjust concentration of wealth and economic power." The Revenue Act raised surtax rates on incomes above $50,000, and steeply graduated taxes to a maximum of 75 percent on incomes above $5 million. Estate and gift taxes went up, as did the corporate tax on all but small corporations—those with less than $50,000 income. Congress even added to Roosevelt's recommendations an "excess-profits" levy on corporate earnings above 10 percent.

Business owners fumed over Roosevelt's tax and spending policies. The wealthy resented their loss of status and the growing power of government and labor. They vented an intemperate rage against Roosevelt, whom they called "a traitor to his own class," and against all the works of the New Deal. Many landmarks of a once stable and secure world now seemed threatened, from the gold standard itself to one's right to run a business as one saw fit. Hoover called the New Deal an attack on "the whole philosophy of individual liberty." Visitors to the home of

J. P. Morgan, Jr., were cautioned not to mention Roosevelt's name lest it raise his blood pressure.

By "soaking" the rich and enacting Social Security programs, Roosevelt stole much of the thunder from the political left, although the results fell short of the promise. The new tax law failed to increase revenue significantly, nor did it result in a redistribution of income. At the same time, the hoopla over "soaking the rich" obscured the more significant impact of both the Social Security payroll tax—which fell more heavily on lower incomes—and the policy of returning indigents to the care of the states. Most states, insofar as they assumed this burden, raised the needed revenue with sales taxes, which were also regressive. Such taxes impeded economic recovery by reducing total purchasing power.

Roosevelt seemed to have moved in a radical direction, but the extent of the new departure taken by the Second New Deal is easy to exaggerate. Such measures as work relief, Social Security, utility regulation, and progressive income taxes had long been in the works in Congress. The president himself had little use for theoretical speculation. He was still pursuing the bold experiments he had promised before the election. "Roosevelt's program," one historian has written, "rested on the assumption that a just society could be secured by imposing a welfare state on a capitalist foundation."

CONTINUING HARDSHIPS   Although the flurry of New Deal programs helped ease the devastation wrought by the depression, it did not restore prosperity. Nor did it end widespread human suffering. As late as 1939, some 9.5 million workers (17 percent of the labor force) remained unemployed. Prolonged economic hardship continued to create personal tragedies and tremendous social strains. Poverty led desperate people to do desperate things. Petty theft soared during the thirties, as did street-corner begging and prostitution. In Pittsburgh an unemployed father, desperate to feed his starving children, stole a loaf of bread from a neighbor, was arrested, and hanged himself in shame. Although the divorce rate dropped during the thirties, in part because couples could not afford to live separately or pay the legal fees to obtain divorces, all too often husbands down on their luck simply deserted their wives. In 1940 a survey revealed that 1.5 million husbands had

A commodity relief line in San Antonio, Texas, 1939.

left home. A California woman reported to a friend that her husband "went north about three months ago to try his luck. The first month he wrote pretty regularly. . . . For five weeks now we have had no word from him. . . . Don't know where he is or what he is up to."

Many couples decided to postpone marriage because of hard times. Some 800,000 marriages were delayed during the 1930s, and the total number of marriages declined by one-fourth compared to the previous decade. With their own future uncertain, married couples often decided not to have children; the birthrate plummeted during the depression. Those with children sometimes could not support them. In 1933 the Children's Bureau reported that one out of every five children was not getting enough to eat. Often, struggling parents sent their children to live with relatives or friends. Some 900,000 other children simply left home and joined the army of homeless "tramps."

DUST BOWL MIGRANTS   Uprooted farmers and their families joined a migratory stream rushing from the South and Midwest toward California, buoyed by currents of hope and desperation. One couple claimed they had heard "how much money a man could make out there and we wanted to go."

Although frequently lumped together as "Okies," the dust bowl refugees were actually from cotton-belt communities in Arkansas, Texas, and Missouri as well as Oklahoma. During the 1930s and 1940s, some 800,000 people left those four states and headed toward the West. Not all were farmers; many were professionals, white-collar workers, retailers, and farm implement salesmen whose jobs had been tied to the health of the agricultural sector. Ninety-five percent of the dust bowl migrants were white, and most were young adults in their twenties and thirties who relocated with spouses and children. Some traveled on trains or buses, others hopped a freight or hitched a ride; most rode in their own cars, the trip taking four to five days on average.

Many of the dust bowl migrants who had come from cities gravitated to urban areas—Los Angeles, San Diego, or San Francisco. Half the newcomers, however, moved into the San Joaquin Valley, the agricultural heartland of the state. There they discovered that California was no paradise. Only a few of the migrants could afford to buy land. Most men and women found themselves competing with local Hispanics and Asians for seasonal work as pickers in the cotton fields or orchards of large corporate farms. As one local health department report observed, the migrant workers "harvest cotton in the fall, go on relief until May, harvest the potatoes in the spring, work the vegetables and fruits in the summer and rest on relief until cotton harvest again." Living in tents or crude cabins and frequently on the move, they suffered from exposure and from poor sanitation. They also felt the sting of social prejudice. Native Californians scared by the influx of poor newcomers treated them with hostility and called them demeaning names. Steinbeck explained that "Okie us'ta mean you was from Oklahoma. Now it means you're a dirty son-of-a-bitch. Okie means you're scum. Don't mean nothing in itself, it's the way they say it."

Such hostility led a third of the "Okies" to return to their native states. Most of the farm workers who stayed tended to fall back upon their old folkways rather than assimilate themselves into their new surroundings. These gritty "plain folk" brought with them their own prejudices against blacks and ethnic minorities as well as a potent tradition of evangelical Protestantism and a distinctive style of music variously labeled "country," "hillbilly," or "cowboy." This "Okie" subculture remains a vivid part of California society today.

MINORITIES AND THE NEW DEAL   The depression was especially traumatic for those minorities who historically were the most disadvantaged groups in American society. However progressive Roosevelt was on social issues, he refused to assault long-standing patterns of racism and segregation for fear of alienating powerful southern Democrats in Congress. As a result, many of the New Deal programs were for whites only. The Federal Housing Administration (FHA), for example, refused to guarantee mortgages on houses purchased by blacks in white neighborhoods. The Civilian Conservation Corps and the Tennessee Valley Authority both practiced racial segregation. The Social Security Act excluded domestic and migrant workers from its coverage, and the National Labor Relations Act excluded farm workers from its provisions. Moreover, minorities who applied for governmental assistance often were the victims of discrimination. In Houston, Texas, relief payments to blacks and Chicanos averaged 25 percent less than payments to whites. Of 10,344 WPA supervisors hired in the southern states, only 11 were African Americans.

The efforts of the Roosevelt administration to raise crop prices by reducing production proved especially devastating for blacks and Chicanos. To earn the federal payments for reducing crop production as provided by the AAA and other New Deal agricultural programs, many farm owners would first take out of cultivation the marginal lands worked by tenants and sharecroppers. This would drive tenants off farms and cost the jobs of many migrant workers. In Texas, for example, farmers eagerly took advantage of AAA subsidies to destroy 40 percent of the cotton crop. From 1930 to 1940, the number of African-American tenant farmers in Texas decreased from 65,000 to 32,000, while the number of landless black agricultural laborers increased by 25,000; some 20,000 other blacks left the state in search of better opportunities. Over 200,000 black tenant farmers nationwide were displaced by the AAA.

Mexican Americans suffered even more. Thousands of Mexicans had migrated to the United States during the 1920s, most of them settling in California, New Mexico, Arizona, Colorado, Texas, and the midwestern states. But because many Mexican Americans were unable to prove their citizenship, either out of ignorance of the regulations or because their migratory work hampered their ability to meet residency requirements, they were denied access to the many new federal relief programs under the New Deal. As economic conditions worsened, government officials called for the deportation of Mexican-born Americans to avoid the costs of providing them public services and relief. Local governments were even more vigorous in promoting repatriation. By 1935, over 500,000 Mexican Americans and their American-born children had returned to Mexico. The state of Texas alone returned over 250,000 people.

Deportation became such a popular solution in part because of the rising level of involvement among Mexican-American workers in union activities. In 1933 Mexican-American women in El Paso, Texas, formed the Society of Female Manufacturing Workers to protest wages as low as 75 cents a day. The same year some 18,000 cotton pickers went on strike in California's San Joaquin Valley. Police crushed the strike by burning the workers' camps.

Native Americans were encouraged by Roosevelt's appointment of John Collier as the commissioner of the Bureau of Indian Affairs (BIA). As commissioner, Collier steadily increased the number of Native Americans employed by the BIA and lobbied strenuously with the heads of New Deal agencies to ensure that Indians gained access to the various relief programs. In response, the CCC created an Indian Division, and the AAA and other programs employed Indians on projects intended to improve the quality of living on the reservations. Collier also reversed an earlier BIA decision denying the right of Indians to practice their own religions.

Collier's primary objective was passage of the Indian Reorganization Act. He intended the new legislation to revoke the provisions of the Dawes General Allotment Act (1887), which had sought to "Americanize" the Indians by breaking up their tribal lands and allocating them to individuals. Collier insisted that this was a misguided failure. The Dawes Act had produced only widespread poverty and demoralization among the Indians. It had failed because it was based on the faulty assumption that all Americans should conform to a universal cultural norm. Collier hoped to reinvigorate traditional Indian cultural traditions by restoring land to tribes, granting Indians the right to charter business enterprises and establish self-governing constitutions, and providing federal funds for vocational training and economic development.

Because of stiff opposition, both from assimilated Indians who had prospered under the Dawes Plan, and from western congressmen who criticized Collier for restoring Native American cultural traditions and religious practices, the six-page Indian Reorganization Act (also known as the Wheeler-Howard Act) that Congress passed and Roosevelt signed in 1934 was a much diluted version of Collier's original fifty-page proposal. The result was that the "Indian New Deal" brought only a partial improvement in the lives of Native Americans.

COURT DECISIONS AND BLACK VOTERS   During the 1930s, the NAACP's legal campaign gathered momentum. A major setback occurred in *Grovey v. Townsend* (1935), which upheld the Texas Democrats' white primary as the practice of a voluntary association and thus not subject to state action. But the *Grovey* decision held up for only nine years and marked the end of major decisions that for half a century had narrowed application of the Reconstruction Amendments. A trend in the other direction had already set in. Two important precedents rose from the celebrated Scottsboro case in 1931, in which nine black youths were convicted of raping two white women while riding a freight train in Alabama. The first verdict failed, the high court ruled in *Powell v. Alabama* (1932), for want of due process because the judge's appointing "all of the members of the bar" to defend the accused imposed "no substantial or definite obligation upon anyone." Another verdict fell to a judgment in *Norris v. Alabama* (1935) that the systematic exclusion of blacks from Alabama juries had denied the defendants equal protection of the law—a principle that had significant and widespread impact on state courts.

Like Woodrow Wilson, Franklin Roosevelt did not give a high priority to racial issues. As a consequence, many of his New Deal programs failed to help minorities, and in a few instances the new initiatives unintentionally discriminated against those least able to help themselves. Nonetheless, Roosevelt included people in his administration who did care deeply about racial issues. As his first term drew to a close in 1936, Roosevelt found that there was a de facto "Black Cabinet" of some thirty to forty advisers in government departments and agencies, people who were wrestling with racial issues and the plight of African Americans. Moreover, by 1936, many black voters were fast transferring their political loyalty from Republicans to Democrats and would vote accordingly in the coming presidential election.

ROOSEVELT'S SECOND TERM

THE 1936 CAMPAIGN   The popularity of Roosevelt and the New Deal impelled the Republican convention in 1936 to avoid candidates too closely identified with the "hate-Roosevelt" contingent. The party chose Governor Alfred M. Landon of Kansas, a former Bull Moose Progressive, who had fought the Ku Klux Klan and favored regulation of business. While conservative in matters of finance, Landon had endorsed many New Deal programs. The most progressive Republican candidate in years, he was probably more liberal than most of his backers, and clearly more so than the party's platform, which accused the New Deal of usurping power.

The chief hope of the Republicans was that the followers of Coughlin, Townsend, and other dissidents would combine to draw enough votes away from Roosevelt to throw the election to them. But that possibility faded when an assassin gunned down Huey Long. Coughlin, Townsend, and a remnant of the Long movement did support Representative William Lemke of North Dakota on a Union party ticket, but it was a forlorn and foredoomed effort that polled only 882,000 votes.

In 1936 Roosevelt forged a new electoral coalition that would affect national politics for years to come. While holding the support of most traditional Democrats North and South, FDR made strong gains among beneficiaries of the farm program in the West. In the northern cities he held on to the support of ethnic groups pleased by New Deal welfare measures and by greater recognition in federal government appointments. Middle-class voters, whose property had been saved by New Deal measures, flocked to Roosevelt's support, along with intellectuals stirred by the ferment of new ideas in government. The revived labor movement threw its support to Roosevelt, and Socialist voters deserted Norman Thomas for the New Deal coalition.

In perhaps the most seismic and enduring change in the political landscape during the 1930s, a majority of politically active blacks moved away from their traditional adherence to the Republican party.

African-American voters for the first time cast the majority of their ballots for a Democratic president. "My friends, go home and turn Lincoln's picture to the wall," a journalist told black Republicans. "That debt has been paid in full."

On election day Roosevelt carried every state except Maine and Vermont with a popular vote of 28 million to Landon's 17 million, and won what was the closest to a unanimous electoral vote since Monroe's victory in 1820, by 523 to 8. Democrats would dominate Republicans in the new Congress, by 77 to 19 in the Senate and 328 to 107 in the House. Roosevelt said he felt as if he had experienced "baptism by total immersion."

ELEANOR ROOSEVELT   One of the keys to Roosevelt's unprecedented popularity was his wife, Anna Eleanor Roosevelt, an enormous political asset and one of the most influential women of her time. Theodore Roosevelt's favorite niece, she had lost both parents by age ten and was a shy, withdrawn, ungainly youth. But Eleanor grew into a tall, willowy, outgoing woman. After spending three years at a private boarding school in England, she returned to New York and began dating her fifth cousin Franklin. They were very different. Eleanor had grown up in a dysfunctional family. Her father was an alcoholic who had impregnated a servant girl, and her mother was a cold, self-absorbed socialite who viewed

An intelligent, principled, and candid woman, First Lady Eleanor Roosevelt became a political figure in her own right. Here she is waving to delegates at the Democratic convention in 1940.

her daughter as an embarrassment. By contrast, Franklin had been smothered with family affection and attention. As an only child of wealthy and privileged parents, he grew up assuming that he should be the center of attention. Supremely confident of his own power and abilities, he conveyed an air of untroubled ebullience that inspired and delighted people. Perhaps what attracted him to Eleanor was her contrasting qualities. She was intelligent, bookish, and prematurely serious, a person of high ideals and principles.

Yet after their marriage in 1905, the very qualities that attracted Franklin to Eleanor began to irritate and alienate him. Her deeply embedded insecurities and fear of failure kept her from participating in activities that he enjoyed—golf, swimming, driving. She also hated the social requirements of politics. Where he could invoke his natural charm and gregariousness in any setting, she found casual conversation with strangers a painful exercise. She once admitted that "I must have spoiled a good deal of the fun for Franklin because of this inability to feel at ease" in social situations. Still another wedge that served to separate Franklin and Eleanor was the meddling of Roosevelt's indomitable mother, Sara. She refused to relinquish her son to her daughter-in-law. She repeatedly intruded upon Eleanor's efforts to raise her six children, and Franklin steadfastly stayed out of the fray.

Biographers suggest that it was such tensions between Eleanor and Franklin that led him during his thirties to engage in an affair with Lucy Mercer, Eleanor's secretary. When Eleanor discovered a cache of love letters from Mercer to her husband in 1918, "the bottom dropped out of my own particular world & I faced myself, my surroundings, my world honestly for the first time." She told Franklin that he must either renounce Lucy or seek a divorce. He chose to end the affair in order to save his political future and his inheritance (his mother said she would disown him if he ever divorced). Thereafter, Eleanor demanded a separate bedroom. Three years later, in 1921, Franklin contracted polio and was paralyzed from the waist down. Eleanor stepped in to deliver his speeches and attend political gatherings. Her daughter Anna recalled that the onset of polio "was very instrumental in bringing them [her parents] much closer into a very real partnership. They were finding mutual interests on a totally different level."

Now free to pursue new avenues of self-fulfillment, Eleanor Roosevelt in the White House became more of a public figure than any previous First Lady. She had her own staff, held her own press conferences, enjoyed access to Democratic party leaders, and spoke candidly to the president about appointing women to government posts and about his plans for various New Deal programs. As one journalist wrote in 1940, "She never lets the President or his administrators think that all is well, that there is time to rest from advancing their liberal objectives." Eleanor once asked Franklin if he objected to her candor and her activism. "No, certainly not," he replied. "You can say anything you want. I can always say, 'Well, that is my wife; I can't do anything about her.'"

Eleanor's passion was social service. As a teen she had volunteered to work in a New York settlement house, and she remained ardently concerned about issues of human welfare and rights for women and blacks. She convinced Congress to improve housing conditions for the poor in the District of Columbia, and she repeatedly reminded the president of pockets of injustice hidden from public scrutiny. As her secretary recalled, Eleanor Roosevelt "lived to be kind." She came to relish traveling around the country, representing FDR and the New Deal, defying local segregation ordinances by eating with blacks in segregated facilities, supporting women's causes, highlighting the plight of unemployed youth, and imploring Americans to live up to their egalitarian and humanitarian ideals.

Eleanor Roosevelt became her husband's most visible and effective liaison with many liberal groups, brought labor leaders, women activists, and black spokesmen into the White House after hours, and deflected criticism of the president by taking progressive stands and running political risks he himself dared not. He was the politician, she once remarked, she the agitator. A Maine fisherman described her uniquely endearing qualities: "She ain't stuck up, she ain't dressed up, and she ain't afraid to talk."

THE COURT-PACKING PLAN   As Thomas Jefferson and Andrew Jackson had found (and Lyndon Johnson, Richard Nixon, and Ronald Reagan later discovered), some malevolent fate seems to dog presidents who win smashing victories. Roosevelt found himself deluged in a sea of troubles soon after his reelection. His second inaugural address, given on January 20, 1937, suggested that he was ready to move toward even further reform. The challenge of American democracy, he said, was that millions of citizens "at this very moment are denied the greater part of what the very lowest standards of today call the necessities of life. . . . I see one-third of a nation ill-housed, ill-clad, ill-nourished." The election of 1936 had been a mandate for more extensive reforms, he argued; and the overwhelming Democratic majorities in Congress ensured their passage. But one major roadblock stood in the way: the Supreme Court.

By the end of the 1936 term, the Court had ruled against New Deal laws in seven of the nine major cases it reviewed. Having struck down both major accomplishments of the First New Deal, the AAA and the NRA, the Court in 1936 denied that states had the power to fix minimum wages. Since it had already ruled, in 1923, that the federal government had no such power, it had left, as Roosevelt protested, a " 'no-man's land,' where no Government—State or Federal" could act. Suits against the Social Security and Wagner Labor Relations Acts now pended. Given the established trend of rulings, often by margins of five to four or six to three, the Second New Deal seemed in danger of being nullified like the first.

For that reason, Roosevelt and his attorney-general decided to change the Court by enlarging it, a move for which there was ample precedent and power. Congress, not the Constitution, determined the

An editorial cartoon commenting on Roosevelt's grandiose plan to enlarge the Supreme Court.

size of the Court, which at different times had numbered six, seven, nine, and ten justices, and in 1937 numbered nine. Roosevelt sent his plan to Congress without having consulted congressional leaders or more than a few within his administration. He wanted to create up to fifty new federal judges, including six new Supreme Court justices, and to diminish the power of judges who had served ten or more years or had reached the age of seventy.

The "court-packing" maneuver, as opponents quickly tagged it, backfired on Roosevelt. The plan was a shade too contrived. In implying that older judges were impaired by senility, it affronted the elder statesmen of Congress and the Court, especially eighty-year-old Louis D. Brandeis, who was both the oldest and the most liberal of the justices. It also ran headlong into a deep-rooted veneration of the courts and aroused fears that another president might use the precedent for quite different purposes. One Virginia senator feared "the reversal of those decisions of the Court that saved the civilization of the South," by which he meant decisions upholding white supremacy. In the Senate the Republicans shrewdly stood aside while the Democrats plunged into a family squabble.

As it turned out, no direct vote ever tested senatorial convictions on the matter. Unforeseen events blunted Roosevelt's drive to change the Court. A sequence of Court decisions in the spring of 1937 reversed previous judgments in order to uphold a Washington State minimum-wage law, the Wagner Act, and the Social Security Act. What prompted the reversal was the shift of a single vote. Justice Owen Roberts had previously sided with a quartet of conservative justices known as the "Four Horsemen." In 1937 Roberts inexplicably joined the four other members who had been sympathetic to the New Deal. This "switch in time that saved nine" made Roosevelt's court-packing plan irrelevant. Never again did the Supreme Court strike down a New Deal program.

Roosevelt later claimed he had lost the battle but won the war. The Court had reversed itself on important New Deal legislation, and Roosevelt was able to appoint new justices in harmony with the New Deal because of several retirements. But the episode created dissension in his party and blighted Roosevelt's own prestige. For the first time Democrats in large numbers deserted the "champ," and the opposition found an issue on which it could openly take the field. During the first eight months of 1937, the momentum of Roosevelt's great 1936 victory was lost.

A NEW DIRECTION FOR LABOR   Rebellions erupted on other fronts even while the Court bill pended. Under the impetus of the New Deal, the dormant labor movement stirred anew. When Section 7a of the National Industrial Recovery Act demanded in every industry code a statement of the workers' right to organize, alert unionists quickly translated it to mean "The President wants you to join the union."

John L. Lewis of the United Mine Workers was among the first to exploit the spirit of the NIRA. Leading a union decimated by depression, he rebuilt it from 150,000 members to 500,000 within a year. Spurred by the mine workers' example, Sidney Hillman of the Amalgamated Clothing Workers and David Dubinsky of the International Ladies' Garment Workers joined Lewis in promoting a campaign to organize workers in the mass-production industries. As leaders of some of the few *industrial* unions (made up of all workers) in the AFL, they found the more restrictive *craft* unions (made up of skilled male workers) to be obstacles to organizing the basic industries.

In 1934 they persuaded the AFL and its president, William Green, to charter industrial unions in the unorganized industries. But Green and other craft unionists saw these "federal" unions as temporary pools from which to draw members into the crafts. Lewis and the industrial unionists saw them as a chance to organize on a massive scale. In 1935, with passage of the Wagner Act, action began in earnest. The industrial unionists formed a Committee for Industrial Organization (CIO), and craft unionists began to fear submergence by the mass unions. Jurisdictional disputes divided them, and in 1936 the AFL expelled the CIO unions, which then formed a permanent structure called after 1938 the Congress of Industrial Organizations. The rivalry spurred both groups to greater efforts.

The CIO's major organizing drives in the automobile and steel industries began in 1936, but until the Supreme Court upheld the Wagner Act in 1937 there was little compliance with unions on the part of industry. Companies used blacklisting, private detectives, labor spies, vigilante groups, and intimidation. Early in 1937 automobile workers spontaneously adopted a new technique, the "sit-down strike," in which workers refused to leave the workplace until the employers granted collective-bargaining rights.

Led by the fiery young autoworker and union organizer Walter Reuther, thousands of employees at General Motors' assembly plants in Flint, Michigan, occupied the factories and stopped all production. Women workers supported their male counterparts by picketing at the plant entrances. The wives, daughters, and mothers of the strikers formed a Women's Auxiliary to feed the workers who slept at the plants. Management refused to recognize the union efforts. Company officials called in police to harass the strikers, sent spies to union meetings, and threatened to fire the workers. They also pleaded with Roosevelt to dispatch federal troops. He refused, while at the same time expressing his displeasure with the sit-down strike. The standoff lasted over a month. Then, on February 11, the company relented and signed a contract recognizing the United Auto Workers (UAW). Other automotive companies soon followed suit. And the following month, United States Steel capitulated to the Steel Workers Organizing Committee (later the United Steelworkers of America), granting it recognition, a 10 percent wage hike, and a forty-hour workweek.

Having captured two giants of heavy industry, the CIO went on in the next few years to organize much of industrial America: rubber, oil, electronics, and a part of the textile industry, in which unionists had to fight protracted struggles to organize scattered plants. The slow pace of labor organizing in textiles denied the CIO a major victory in the South comparable to its swift conquest of autos and steel, but even there a labor movement appeared that was at last something more than a vehicle for sporadic revolt. Violence punctuated these struggles, most vividly at the Republic Steel plant in Chicago, where police killed ten strikers in 1937. Company guards brutally beat up Walter Reuther and other labor organizers at Henry Ford's River Rouge plant in Detroit. In Harlan County, Kentucky, deputized company hoodlums conducted a reign of terror until the National Labor Relations Board forced operators to bargain with the United Mine Workers late in 1938.

The Wagner Act put the power of the federal government behind the principle of unionization. In the Congress, a Senate subcommittee under Robert M. La Follette, Jr., exposed violent practices against unions. President Roosevelt refused to use force against sit-down strikers, though he was opposed to the tactic. The unions, he said, would soon

CIO pickets jeering at nonstriking workers entering a mill, 1941.

learn that they could not continue to use a "damned unpopular" tactic. Roosevelt himself had come late to the support of unions and sometimes took exception to their behavior. In the fall of 1937 he became so irritated with the warfare between Lewis and Republic Steel that he pronounced "a plague on both your houses." The grandiloquent Lewis, who for a year had been trying to organize a union for steelworkers, responded: "It ill behooves one who has supped at labor's table and who has been sheltered in labor's house to curse with equal fervor and fine impartiality both labor and its adversaries when they become locked in a deadly embrace." In 1940 an angry Lewis would back the Republican presidential candidate, but he would be unable to carry the labor vote with him. As workers became more organized, they more closely identified with the Democratic party.

A SLUMPING ECONOMY   The years 1935 and 1936 had seen steady economic improvement. By the spring of 1937 output had moved above the 1929 level. The prosperity of early 1937 was achieved largely through governmental spending. On top of relief and public-works outlays, Congress in 1936 provided for cash payments of veterans' bonuses upon demand. But in 1937 Roosevelt, worried about deficits and inflation, ordered sharp cuts in spending. At the same time the Treasury began to diminish disposable income by collecting $2 billion in Social Security taxes. Private spending could not fill the gap left by reductions in government spending, and business still lacked the faith to risk large investments. The result was that the economy suddenly stalled, and then slid into a deep business slump sharper than that in 1929. The Dow Jones stock average fell some 40 percent between August and October. By the end of the year 2 million people had been thrown out of work; scenes of the earlier depression reappeared.

The recession provoked a fierce debate within the administration. One group, led by Treasury Secretary Henry Morgenthau, Jr., favored less spending and a balanced budget. The slow pace of recovery, Morgenthau thought, resulted from the reluctance of business to invest, and that resulted in turn from fear that federal spending would bring inflation and heavy taxes. The other group, which included Harry Hopkins and Harold Ickes, argued for renewed government spending. The recession, they noted, had come just when the budget was brought into balance. This view echoed that of the English economist John Maynard Keynes, who had given extended development to the idea in his book *The General Theory of Employment, Interest and Money* (1936). Keynesian economics offered a convenient theoretical justification for what New Dealers had already done in pragmatic response to existing conditions.

ECONOMIC POLICY AND LATE REFORMS   Roosevelt waited as the rival theorists sought his approval. When the spring of 1938 failed to bring recovery, he endorsed the ideas of the spenders. On April 14, 1938, he asked Congress to adopt a large-scale spending program, and Congress voted $3.3 billion, mainly for public works by the PWA and the WPA, with lesser amounts for other programs. In a short time the increase in spending reversed the economy's decline, but the recession and Roosevelt's reluctance to adopt the truly massive, sustained government spending called for in Keynesian theory forestalled the achievement of full recovery. Only during World War II would employment reach pre-1929 levels.

The Court fight, the sit-down strikes, and the recession in 1937 all undercut Roosevelt's prestige and dissipated the mandate of the 1936 elections. When the 1937 congressional session ended, the only major new reforms enacted for the benefit of the "ill-housed, ill-clad, [and] ill-nourished" were the Wagner-Steagall National Housing Act and the Bankhead-Jones Farm Tenant Act. In 1938 the Democratic Congress enacted three more major reforms, the last of the New Deal era: the Second Agricultural Adjustment Act; the Food, Drug and Cosmetic Act; and the Fair Labor Standards Act.

The Housing Act set up the United States Housing Authority (USHA) in the Department of the Interior, which extended long-term loans to local agencies willing to assume part of the cost for slum clearance and public housing. The agency also subsidized low rents. Later, during World War II, it financed housing in connection with defense projects.

The Farm Tenant Act addressed the problem of rural poverty. In some ways the New Deal's larger farm program, the AAA, had aggravated the problem; although tenants were supposed to be kept on in spite of government-sponsored cutbacks in production, landlords often made the most of cutbacks by evicting workers and withholding their shares of benefit payments. The Tenant Act was administered by a new agency, the Farm Security Administration (FSA). The program made available rehabilitation loans to shore up marginal farmers and prevent their sinking into tenancy. It also made loans to tenants for purchase of their own farms. In the end, however, the FSA proved to be little more than another relief operation that tided a few farmers over difficult times. A more effective answer to the problem, sadly, awaited mobilization for war, which took many tenants off into the military services or defense industries, broadened their horizons, and taught them new skills.

The Agricultural Adjustment Act of 1938 was a response to renewed crop surpluses and price declines during the recession. It reenacted the basic devices of the earlier AAA with some new twists. Before the government could apply marketing quotas to a given crop, for instance, it had to hold a plebiscite among the growers and win a two-thirds majority. The new Food, Drug and Cosmetic Act broadened the coverage of the 1906 Pure Food and Drug Act and forbade the use of false or misleading advertising. Enforcement of the advertising provision became the responsibility of the Federal Trade Commission. The Fair Labor Standards Act applied to enterprises that operated in or affected interstate commerce. It set a minimum wage of 40¢ an hour and a maximum workweek of forty hours, to be put into effect over several years. The act also prohibited child labor under the age of sixteen, and prohibited it under eighteen in hazardous occupations.

THE LEGACY OF THE NEW DEAL

SETBACKS FOR THE PRESIDENT   As the New Deal turned its focus from recovery to reform, an effective opposition emerged within the president's party, especially in the southern wing. Local power elites in the South felt that the New Deal jeopardized their position. They felt threatened, too, when in 1936 the Democratic convention eliminated the two-thirds rule for nominations, thereby removing the South's veto power, and seated African-American delegates. Southern Democrats were at best uneasy bedfellows with organized labor and northern blacks. Senator "Cotton" Ed Smith of South Carolina and several other southern delegates walked out of the convention, with Smith declaring that he would not support any party that views "the Negro as a political and social equal." Some disgruntled southern Democrats drifted toward coalition with conservative Republicans. By the end of 1937, a bipartisan conservative bloc had coalesced.

In 1938 the conservative opposition stymied an executive reorganization bill amid cries that it would lead to dictatorship. They also secured drastic cuts in the undistributed-profits and capital gains taxes to help restore business "confidence." The House also set up a Committee on Un-American Activities chaired by Martin Dies of Texas, who took to the warpath against Communists. Soon he began to brand New Dealers as Red dupes. "Stalin baited his hook with a 'progressive' worm," Dies wrote in 1940, "and New Deal suckers swallowed bait, hook, line, and sinker."

As the political season of 1938 advanced, Roosevelt unfolded a new idea as momentous as the Court plan—a proposal to reshape the Democratic party in the image of the New Deal. He announced his purpose to intervene in Democratic primaries as the party leader, "charged with the responsibility of carrying out the definitely liberal declaration of principles set forth in the 1936 Democratic platform." He wanted his own supporters nominated. Instead of succeeding, however, the effort backfired and broke the spell of presidential invincibility, or what was left of it. As in the Court fight, Roosevelt had risked his prestige while handing his adversaries persuasive issues. His opponents tagged his intervention in the primaries an attempted "purge"; the word evoked visions of Adolf Hitler and Joseph Stalin, tyrants who had purged their Nazi and Communist parties in blood.

The elections of November 1938 handed the administration another setback, a result partly of the friction among Democrats. Their majority in the House fell from 229 to 93, in the Senate from 56 to 42. The margins remained large, but the president headed a restive and divided party. In his State of the Union message in 1939, Roosevelt for the first time proposed no new reforms, but spoke of the need "to invigorate the process of recovery, in order to *preserve* our reforms." In the same year, the administration won an extension of Social Security and finally put through its reorganization plan. Under the Administrative Reorganization Act, the president could "reduce, coordinate, consolidate, and reorganize" the agencies of government. With that, Roosevelt's domestic initiatives feebly ended. The conservative coalition and the administration had reached a standoff.

EMERGENCE OF THE BROKER STATE   The New Deal had lost momentum, but it had wrought some enduring changes. By the end of the 1930s, the power of the national government was vastly enlarged over what it had been in 1932. Government had taken on the duty of ensuring the economic and social stability of the country. It had established minimum standards for labor conditions and public welfare. It had helped middle-class Americans hold on to their savings, their homes, and their farms. The protection afforded by deposit insurance, unemployment pay, and Social Security pensions would come to be universally accepted as safeguards against such disasters as the depression.

Roosevelt had steered a course between the extremes of laissez-faire and socialism. The First New Deal had experimented for a time with a managed economy under the NRA, but had abandoned that experiment for a turn toward enforcing competition and priming the economy with government spending. The effect of heavy governmental expenditures, which finally lifted the economy out of the depression during World War II, seemed to confirm the arguments of Keynesians.

Roosevelt himself, impatient with theory, was a pragmatist in developing policy: he kept what worked and discarded what did not. The result was, paradoxically, both profoundly revolutionary and profoundly conservative. The New Deal left America greatly changed in many ways, its economy more managed than before. At the same time, it left the basic capitalistic structure of the economic system in place. "For a permanent correction of grave weaknesses in our economic system," Roosevelt said, "we have relied on new applications of old democratic processes."

CULTURE IN THE THIRTIES

Pragmatism made a comeback not only in government policy during the 1930s, but in artistic expression as well. Artists of all kinds seemed to abandon the alienation of the 1920s in favor of renewed social purpose.

In the early 1930s, a renewed sense of social commitment sometimes took the form of allegiance to revolution. For a time, leftist politics and rhetoric made significant inroads in literary circles. By the summer of 1932, even the "golden boy" of the lost generation, F. Scott Fitzgerald, could declare that "to bring on the revolution, it may be necessary to work within the Communist party." In 1932 fifty-three artists and intellectuals signed an open letter endorsing the Communist party candidate for president. But few writers remained Communists for long. Writers being a notoriously independent lot, they rebelled at demands to hew to a shifting line.

LITERATURE AND THE DEPRESSION   Among the writers who sang songs with social significance, at least two novelists deserve special notice: John Steinbeck and Richard Wright. The single piece of fiction that best captured the ordeal of the depression, John Steinbeck's *The Grapes of Wrath* (1939), was also the most memorable "proletarian" novel of the times because it treated workers as genuine people rather than as cardboard stereotypes. Steinbeck had taken the trouble to travel with displaced "Okies" driven from the Oklahoma dust bowl by foreclosures and farm combines to pursue the illusion of jobs in the fields of California's Central Valley. The story focused on the Joad family as they made their painful journey from Oklahoma west along U.S. 66, enticed by job ads that were actually aimed at producing a labor surplus and depressing wages. Met chiefly with contempt and rejection, caught up in labor agitations, Ma Joad strove to keep hope alive. At the end, even as

Richard Wright, author of Native
Son *and* Black Boy.

the family was breaking up under the pressure, she grasped at a broader
loyalty: "Use'ta be the fambly was fust. It ain't so now. It's anybody.
Worse off we get, the more we got to do."

Among black novelists the supreme genius was Richard Wright. Born
on a plantation near Natchez, Mississippi, the son of a matriarch whose
husband deserted the family, Wright grew up in the course of moving
from town to town, ended his formal schooling with the ninth grade (as
valedictorian of his class), worked in Memphis, and greedily devoured
books he borrowed on a white friend's library card, all the while saving
up to go North and escape the racism of the segregated South. He arrived in Chicago on the eve of the depression, and his period as a Communist from 1934 to 1944 gave him an intellectual framework that did
not, however, overpower his fierce independence. His first book, *Uncle
Tom's Children* (1938), a collection of four novellas, and his autobiographical *Black Boy* (1945) revealed in their very rebellion against racial
injustice his ties to the South, for, he wrote, "there had been slowly instilled into my personality and consciousness, black though I was, the
culture of the South."

Native Son (1940), Wright's masterpiece, is set in the Chicago he
had come to know before moving on to New York. It tells the story of
Bigger Thomas, a product of the black ghetto, a man hemmed in and finally impelled to murder by forces beyond his control. "They wouldn't
let me live and I killed," he said unrepentantly at the end. Somehow
Wright managed to sublimate into literary power his own bitterness and
rage at what he called "The Ethics of Living Jim Crow," an art he never

quite mastered. In the black experience, he wrote, America had "a past tragic enough to appease the spiritual hunger of even a James; and . . . in the oppression of the Negro a shadow athwart our national life dense and heavy enough to satisfy even the gloomy broodings of a Hawthorne."

POPULAR ART AND SOCIAL DOCUMENTARY   In the 1930s, America experienced what *Fortune* magazine called "a sort of cultural revolution," largely through the Works Progress Administration (WPA) projects in writing, arts, music, theater, and historical research. Americans learned that, like it or not, they had a culture and had had one all along—it had simply been overlooked. Now Americans tried to make up for lost time by tracking the culture down, recording, restoring, and celebrating it. They became intrigued with American art of all kinds, and particularly that least influenced by Europe: primitive, folk, or, as it was called most often, "popular" art. American "regionalist" artists, such as Grant Wood and Thomas Hart Benton, turned their attention to their homeland.

The human tragedy of the Great Depression also helped stimulate a new genre: social documentary. The New Deal, through the WPA's Federal Writers' Project, pioneered in the oral history of the "inarticulate." In *These Are Our Lives* (1939), the Writers' Project gathered case histories of workers, sharecroppers, and blacks in North Carolina, Tennessee, and Georgia in a form that the historian Charles A. Beard called "literature more powerful than anything I have read in fiction." *Lay My Burden Down* (1944) presented the life stories of former slaves as recorded by Writers' Project interviewers.

During the 1930s, talented social reporters teamed with photographers: Erskine Caldwell and Margaret Bourke-White, *You Have Seen Their Faces* (1937) and *Say, Is This the USA?* (1941); Paul S. Taylor and Dorothea Lange, *An American Exodus* (1939); and James Agee and Walker Evans, *Let Us Now Praise Famous Men* (1941). The last of these, a sensitive, effective portrait of tenant life in Alabama, got little notice at the time but gradually came to be recognized as a unique masterpiece of documentation and art. The Farm Security Administration built up an enormous photographic documentation of everyday life in America, making familiar in the credits such names as Dorothea Lange and Ben Shahn.

POPULAR CULTURE DURING THE DEPRESSION   While many of America's most talented writers and artists dealt directly with the human suffering and social tensions provoked by the Great Depression, the more popular cultural outlets such as radio programs and movies provided patrons with a welcome "escape" from the decade's grim realities.

By the 1930s, radio had become a major source of family entertainment. More than 10 million families owned a radio, and by the end of the decade the number had tripled. "There is radio music in the air, every night, everywhere," reported a San Francisco newspaper. "Anybody can hear it at home on a receiving set which any boy can put up in an hour."

Millions of housewives listened to formulaic radio "soap operas" during the day. The shows lasted fifteen minutes and derived their name from their sponsors, soap manufacturers. The recipe for a successful soap opera, noted one writer, was to provide "twelve minutes of dialogue, add predicament, villainy, and female suffering in equal measure, throw in a dash of nobility, sprinkle with tears, season with organ music, cover with a rich announcer sauce, and serve five times a week." The soap operas provided struggling people with distractions as well as a sense of comparative well-being. As one female listener explained, "I can get through the day better when I hear they have sorrows, too."

Late afternoon radio programs were directed at children home from school. In the evening after supper, families would gather around the radio to listen to newscasts, comedies such as *Amos 'n Andy* and the husband-and-wife team of George Burns and Gracie Allen, adventure dramas such as *Superman, Jack Armstrong, The Lone Ranger, Dick Tracy,* and *The Green Hornet,* and "big band" musical programs, all interspersed with commercials. On Sundays, most radio stations broadcast church services. Fans could also listen to baseball and football games or boxing matches. Franklin Roosevelt was the first president to take full advantage of the popularity of radio broadcasting. He hosted sixteen "fireside chats" to generate public support for his New Deal initiatives.

In the late 1920s, what had been "silent" films were transformed by the introduction of sound. The "talkies" made the movie industry by far the most popular form of entertainment during the 1930s—much more popular than today. The introduction of double features in 1931 and the construction of outdoor drive-in theaters in 1933 also boosted inter-

Frankenstein. *Popular 1930s movies included the gangster, horror, and animation genres that provided the viewer with pure entertainment and often relieved them from the burdens of the Depression.*

est and attendance. More than 60 percent of the population—70 million people—saw at least one movie each week. Adults paid a quarter and children a dime for their tickets. "The immense influence of Hollywood in our national life," declared a writer in 1936, ". . . seems to be accepted as a matter of fact. Manners, clothes, speech, tastes, all are affected by the actors and actresses of the motion picture screen as they never were by the popular figures of the stage or by any of our popular idols."

Films of the 1930s rarely dealt directly with the hard times of the depression or with racial and ethnic tensions. An exception was the film version of *The Grapes of Wrath* (1940) and classic documentaries by Pare Lorenz entitled *The River* (1937) and *The Plow That Broke the Plains* (1936). Much more common were movies intended for pure entertainment that transported viewers into the realm of adventure, spectacle, and fantasy. People relished "shoot 'em up" gangster films, Walt Disney's animated cartoons, spectacular musicals, "screwball" comedies, and classic horror films such as *Dracula* (1931), *Frankenstein* (1931), *The Werewolf* (1932), and *The Mummy* (1932).

The appeal of gangster films perhaps reflected public sympathy with gritty characters determined to succeed whatever the consequences. *Little Caesar* (1930), *Public Enemy Number One* (1931), and *Scarface* (1932) portrayed the rise and fall of brutal mobsters and in the process made stars of "tough guys" Edward G. Robinson, James Cagney, and Paul Muni. Dozens of similar films followed.

By the time Roosevelt was inaugurated in 1933, theatrical dance musicals choreographed and directed by Busby Berkeley had also captured the popular imagination. Flamboyant, if inane, musicals such as *42nd Street* (1933), *The Gold Diggers* (1933), and *Dames* (1934) reinforced Roosevelt's upbeat assurance that "happy days are here again!" Berkeley used elaborate sets, multiple cameras, flocks of chorus girls, and huge orchestras to produce entertainment extravaganzas.

But the best way to escape the daily troubles of the depression was to watch one of the zany comedies perfected by the Marx Brothers, former vaudeville performers. As one Hollywood official explained, the movies during the 1930s were intended to "laugh the big bad wolf of the depression out of the public mind." *Cocoanuts* (1929), *Animal Crackers* (1930), and *Monkey Business* (1931) introduced Americans to the anarchic antics of Chico, Groucho, Harpo, and Zeppo Marx. These madcap

The Marx Brothers performing one of their many madcap routines.

comedians combined slapstick humor with verbal wit to create plotless masterpieces filled with irreverent satire.

In 1939 the movie version of Margaret Mitchell's historical novel *Gone with the Wind* appeared in Technicolor, then still a novelty. It starred Clark Gable and Vivien Leigh and at 220 minutes was the longest feature film up to that time. It was also the most popular. The Civil War drama captured the romantic imagination of a nation just as a horrific world war was breaking out in Europe and Asia.

MAKING CONNECTIONS

- In the mid-1930s, just as Roosevelt was getting the New Deal into place, the growing conflict in Europe began to assume more and more of his (and America's) attention: Chapter 29 shows how Roosevelt went from combating the depression to leading the United States into World War II.

- Harry Truman, Roosevelt's successor in the White House, tried unsuccessfully to expand the idea of the New Deal into new areas (national health insurance and federal aid to education, for example), a topic covered in Chapter 31.

FURTHER READING

An engaging introduction to the decade of the New Deal is Anthony J. Badger's *The New Deal: The Depression Years, 1933–1940* (1989). Van L. Perkins's *Crisis in Agriculture* (1969) and Sidney Baldwin's *Poverty and Politics: The Rise and Decline of the Farm Security Administration* (1969) look at agricultural reforms. Michael E. Parrish's *Securities Regulation and the New Deal* (1970) and Ellis W. Hawley's *The New Deal and the Problem of Monopoly: A Study in Economic Ambivalence* (1966) analyze government attempts to forestall another market crash.

Alan Brinkley's *The End of Reform: New Deal Liberalism in Recession and War* (1995) suggests that the New Deal reformers did not go far enough in their efforts to curb big business. Bernard Bellush's *The Failure of the NRA* (1977) studies government relations with business. William R. Brock's *Welfare, Democracy, and the New Deal* (1988) describes the development of welfare policy.

For scholarship about the various groups involved in the New Deal, consult Lois Scharf's *To Work and to Wed: Female Employment, Feminism, and the Great Depression* (1980), on women; Nancy J. Weiss's *Farewell to the Party of Lincoln: Black Politics in the Age of FDR* (1983) and Harvard Sitkoff's *A New Deal for Blacks* (1978), on blacks; and John M. Allswang's *A House of All Peoples: Ethnic Politics in Chicago, 1890–1936* (1971), on immigrants.

Works on the critics of the New Deal include T. Harry Williams's *Huey Long* (1969) and Alan Brinkley's *Voices of Protest: Huey Long, Father Coughlin, and the Great Depression* (1982). For leftist reactions to reform, see Harvey Klehr's *The Heyday of American Communism: The Depression Decade* (1984) and David Shannon's *The Socialist Party of America* (1955).

One interest group that both supported and criticized New Deal policies was organized labor. See Sidney Fine's *Sit-down: The General Motors Strike of 1936–1937* (1969) and Jerold S. Auerbach's *Labor and Liberty: The La Follette Committee and the New Deal* (1966).

The fullest introduction to the New Deal in the South remains the relevant chapters in George B. Tindall's *The Emergence of the New South, 1913–1945* (1967). How southern farmers fared is examined in David E. Conrad's *The Forgotten Farmers: The Story of the Sharecroppers in the New Deal* (1965). Dan T. Carter provides an insightful analysis of the influence of reform on race relations in the 1930s in his *Scottsboro: A Tragedy of the American South* (1969).

James M. Gregory's *American Exodus: The Dust Bowl Migration and Okie Culture in California* (1989) describes the migratory movement's effect on American culture. For the cultural impact of the New Deal, consult Richard H. Pells's *Radical Visions and American Dreams: Cultural and Social Thought in the Depression Years* (1973) and Richard D. McKinzie's *The New Deal for Artists* (1973).

29   FROM ISOLATION TO GLOBAL WAR

*I*n the late 1930s, as the winds of war swept across Asia and Europe, the focus of American politics moved abruptly from domestic to foreign affairs. Another Democratic president had to shift attention from social reform to military preparedness and war. And the public again had to wrestle with the painful choice between involving the country in volatile world affairs and remaining aloof and officially neutral.

POSTWAR ISOLATIONISM

THE LEAGUE AND THE UNITED STATES   Between Woodrow Wilson and Franklin Roosevelt lay two decades of isolation from foreign entanglements. The postwar mood expressed in the election of 1920 set the pattern. The voters yearned for a restored isolationism, and President-elect Harding lost little time in disposing of the League of Nations. "You just didn't want a surrender of the United States," he told the people in his victory speech. "That's why you didn't care for the League, which is now deceased." The spirit of isolation found other expressions as well: the higher tariff walls, the Red Scare, the rage for "100 percent Americanism," and restrictive immigration laws by which a nation of immigrants all but shut the door to any more newcomers.

The United States may have felt the urge to leave a wicked world to its own devices, but it could hardly stop the world and get off. American business, despite the tariff walls, now had worldwide connections. American investments and loans abroad put in circulation the dollars that purchased American exports. Overseas possessions, moreover, directly involved the country in world affairs, especially in the Pacific. Even the League of Nations was too great a fact to ignore, although messages from the League at first went unanswered by American diplomats. By the end of 1922, however, the United States had "unofficial observers" at the League's headquarters in Geneva, and after 1924 American diplomats gradually entered into joint efforts on such matters as the international trade in drugs and arms, the criminal traffic in women and children, and a variety of economic, cultural, and technical conferences.

Americans had mixed feelings about adherence to the World Court. The Permanent Court of International Justice (the World Court), established by the League of Nations at The Hague in the Netherlands in 1922, was open to any country, whether a member of the League or not. The idea of bringing foreign disputes before a panel of jurists appealed to legal-minded Americans; the United States had in fact urged the idea in previous years. Still, it smacked too much of extranational authority for isolationists, even though its jurisdiction was always optional. Repeated efforts to join the World Court therefore met with rebuff from the Senate. Franklin D. Roosevelt pressed the issue in 1935, and the Senate voted 52 to 36 in favor, falling short of a two-thirds majority. American judges served on the Court panel, but the United States stayed out.

WAR DEBTS AND REPARATIONS   Probably nothing did more to heighten American isolationism—or anti-American feeling in Europe—than the war-debt tangle. When in 1917 the Allies had begun to exhaust their ability to pay for American military supplies, the United States government had advanced them funds first for the war effort and then for postwar reconstruction. A World War Foreign Debt Commission, created by Congress in 1922, renegotiated the Allied debt to America to a total of about $11.5 billion. Adding the interest payable over sixty-two years to this principal, the Allied debt totaled over $22 billion.

To most Americans it all seemed a simple matter of obligation, but Europeans commonly had a different perception. In the first place, Americans who thought their loan money had flowed to Europe were wrong: most of it went toward purchases of military supplies in the United States, which fueled the wartime boom. Then, too, the Allies held off the enemy at great cost of blood and treasure while the United States was raising an army. American states, the British noted, had repudiated debts to British investors after the Revolution; and the French pointed out that they had never been repaid for help in the American Revolution. But most difficult were the practical problems of repayment. To get dollar exchange, European debtors had to sell their goods to the United States, but American tariff walls went higher in 1921 and 1922, and again in 1930, making debt payment harder. Payment in gold would have undermined the European currencies.

The French and British insisted that they could pay America only as they themselves collected reparations from defeated Germany. Twice during the 1920s the resulting strain on Germany brought the structure of international payments to the verge of collapse, and both times the Reparations Commission called in private American bankers to work out rescue plans.

The whole structure finally did collapse during the Great Depression. In 1931 President Hoover negotiated a moratorium on both German reparations and Allied payment of war debts, thereby indirectly accepting the connection between the two. The purpose, among other things, was to shore up American private loans of several billion dollars in Germany, which for the time had kept the international credit structure intact. Once the United States had accepted the connection between reparations and war debt, the Allies virtually canceled German reparations. At the end of 1932, after Hoover's debt moratorium ended, most of the European countries defaulted on their war debts to the United States; by 1934 all but Finland had defaulted. In retaliation, Congress passed the Johnson Debt Default Act of 1934, which prohibited even private loans to any defaulting government.

ATTEMPTS AT DISARMAMENT   Yet, for all the isolationist sentiment of the time, Wilsonian idealism had struck a responsive chord in many Americans. A lingering doubt, tinged with guilt, haunted many Americans about their rejection of membership in the League. Before long Harding's advisers hit upon a happy substitute—disarmament. The conviction had grown after World War I that excessive armaments had been the war's cause, and that arms limitation would bring lasting peace. The United States had no intention of maintaining a large army, but under the building program begun in 1916, it constructed a navy second only to that of Britain. Neither the British nor the Americans had much stomach for the cost of a naval armaments race with each other, but both shared a common concern with the alarming growth of Japanese power.

During and after the war, Japanese-American relations grew increasingly strained. The United States objected to continued Japanese encroachments in Asia. In 1902 Japan had made a defensive alliance with Great Britain, directed then at Russia but invoked in 1914 against Germany in order to pick up German concessions and territories in East Asia. The Japanese quickly took the Shantung Peninsula and the islands of Micronesia, which Germany had purchased not long before from Spain. The Paris Peace Conference reluctantly confirmed Japanese seizure of the Shantung Peninsula, to the outrage of the Chinese, and the League of Nations authorized a Japanese mandate of Micronesia north of the equator. Occupation of Micronesia put the Japanese squarely athwart eastern approaches to the Philippines.

During the war the Japanese had grabbed the chance for further moves against China. In 1915 the cabinet in Tokyo issued what came to be known as the Twenty-one Demands, which would have brought China virtually under Japanese control. The United States protested, and fortunately the Japanese decided not to force their most rigorous demands. In 1917, after the United States entered the war, Viscount Kikujiro Ishii visited Washington to secure American recognition of Japan's expanding claims in Asia as had France, Britain, and Russia. Secretary of State Lansing entered an ambiguous agreement that recognized Japan's "special interests [translated by the Japanese as 'paramount interests'] in China." Americans were unhappy with the Lansing-Ishii Agreement, but it seemed the only way to preserve the appearance of friendship.

To deal with the growing strains, President Harding invited eight principal foreign powers to the Washington Armaments Conference in 1921. The American secretary of state Charles Evans Hughes, in what was expected to be a perfunctory greeting, announced that "the way to disarm is to disarm." The only way out of an armaments race, he said, "is to end it now." It was one of the most dramatic moments in American diplomatic history. In less than fifteen minutes, one electrified reporter said, Hughes had destroyed more tonnage "than all the admirals of the world have sunk in a cycle of centuries."

The Washington Armaments Conference, 1921. *The Big Five at the conference were* (from left): *Prince Tekugawa (Japan), Arthur Balfour (Great Britain), Charles Evans Hughes (United States), M. Briand (France), and H. E. Carlo Sanchez (Italy).*

Delegates from the United States, Britain, Japan, France, and Italy then reached agreement on a Five-Power Naval Treaty (1922) incorporating Hughes's plan for tonnage limits and a naval hiatus of ten years during which no battleships would be built. These powers also agreed to refrain from further fortification of their Pacific possessions. The agreement in effect partitioned the world: U.S. naval power became supreme in the Western Hemisphere, Japanese power in the western Pacific, British power from the North Sea to Singapore.

Two other major agreements emerged from the Washington Conference. With the Four-Power Treaty, the United States, Britain, Japan, and France agreed to respect each other's possessions in the Pacific, and to refer any disputes or any outside threat to consultation. The Nine-Power Treaty for the first time formally pledged the signers to support the principle of the Open Door enunciated by Secretary of State John Hay at the turn of the century. The Open Door enabled all nations to compete for trade and investment opportunities in China on an equal footing rather than allow individual nations to create economic monopolies in particular regions of the country. The signers of the Nine-Power Treaty also promised to respect the territorial integrity of China. The nations involved, in addition to those signing the Five-Power Treaty, were China, Belgium, Portugal, and the Netherlands.

With these agreements in hand, Harding could boast of a brilliant diplomatic stroke that relieved taxpayers of the need to pay for an enlarged navy, and warded off potential conflicts in the Pacific. A grateful Senate approved the naval treaty with only one dissenting vote. The Four-Power Treaty aroused real opposition, but finally passed with the support of Democrats after the Senate tacked on a reservation that "there is no commitment to armed force, no alliance, no obligation to join in any defense."

There was the rub. Though the agreements tapped a deep urge toward peacemaking, they were uniformly without obligation and without teeth. The signers of the Four-Power Treaty agreed only to consult, not to help each other militarily, a point that was clear even before the Senate tacked on its reservation. The formal endorsement of the Open Door in the Nine-Power Treaty was just as ineffective, and the American people remained unwilling to uphold the principle with anything but pious affirmation. The naval disarmament treaty set limits only on capital ships (battleships and aircraft carriers); the race to build cruisers, destroyers, submarines, and other smaller craft continued. Expansionist Japan withdrew from the agreement in 1934. Thus, twelve years after the Washington Conference, the dream of naval disarmament died.

THE KELLOGG-BRIAND PACT   During and after World War I, the ideal of abolishing war caught the American imagination. Peace societies thrived and spawned innumerable programs. In 1921 a wealthy Chicagoan founded the American Committee for the Outlawry of War. "We can outlaw this war system just as we outlawed slavery and the saloon," said one of the more enthusiastic converts.

The glorious vision of abolishing war at the stroke of a pen culminated in the signing of the Kellogg-Briand Pact in 1928. This unique treaty started with an initiative from French foreign minister Aristide Briand, who had busied himself winning allies against a possible resurgence of German power. In 1927 Briand proposed to Secretary of State Frank B. Kellogg an agreement that the two countries would never go to war against each other. This innocent-seeming proposal was actually a clever ploy to draw the United States into the French security system by the back door. In any future war, for instance, such a pact would inhibit the United States from reprisals against any French intrusions on neutral rights. Kellogg gave the idea a cool reception, and was outraged to discover that Briand had urged leaders of the American peace movements to put pressure on the government to sign.

Finally Kellogg turned the tables on Briand. He countered with a scheme to have all nations sign the pact, an idea all the more acceptable to the peace organizations. Caught in a trap of his own making, the French foreign minister finally relented. The Pact of Paris (its official name), signed on August 27, 1928, solemnly declared that the signatories "condemn recourse to war . . . and renounce it as an instrument of national policy." Eventually sixty-two powers adhered to the pact, but all explicitly or tacitly reserved "self-defense" as an escape hatch. The United States Senate included a reservation declaring the preserving of the Monroe Doctrine necessary to self-defense, and then ratified the agreement by a vote of 85 to 1. One senator who voted for "this worthless, but perfectly harmless peace treaty" wrote a friend later that he feared it would "confuse the minds of many good people who think that peace may be secured by polite professions of neighborly and brotherly love."

*Plans for international disarmament, popular in the 1920s, proved imprac-
tical.*

THE "GOOD NEIGHBOR" POLICY   In Latin America the spirit of
peace and noninvolvement helped allay resentments against "Yankee
imperialism," which had been freely practiced in the Caribbean during
the first two decades of the century. The Harding administration agreed
in 1921 to pay the republic of Colombia the $25 million it had once de-
manded for America's use of Panama Canal rights. In 1924 American
troops left the Dominican Republic, occupied since 1916, although
United States officials continued to collect customs duties there for another twenty-five years.

The marines left Nicaragua in 1925, but returned a year later at the
outbreak of disorders and civil war. There in 1927, the Coolidge administration brought both parties into an agreement for American-super-
vised elections, but one rebel leader, César Augusto Sandino, held out,
and the marines stayed until 1933. The unhappy legacies of this intervention were enmity toward the United States and a ruthless, corrupt
Nicaraguan National Guard, created to keep order after the marines
left, but used in 1936 to set up the dictatorship of Anastasio Somoza.
These legacies continue to have their effects down to the present day.

The troubles in Nicaragua increased strains with Mexico. Relations were already soured by repeated Mexican threats to expropriate American oil properties. In 1928, however, the American ambassador was able to get an agreement protecting American rights acquired before 1917. Expropriation did in fact occur in 1938, but the Mexican government then agreed to reimburse American owners.

In 1928, with problems apparently clearing in Mexico and Nicaragua, President Coolidge traveled to Havana to open the Pan-American Conference. It was an unusual gesture of friendship, and so was the choice of Charles Evans Hughes, the former secretary of state, to head the American delegation. Hughes announced the United States' intention to withdraw its marines from Nicaragua and Haiti as soon as possible, although he did block a resolution declaring that "no state has the right to intervene in the affairs of another."

At the end of 1928 President-elect Hoover began a tour of ten Latin American nations. Once in office he reversed Wilson's policy of refusing to recognize "bad" regimes and reverted to the older policy of recognizing governments in power, regardless of their behavior. In 1930 he generated more goodwill by permitting publication of a memorandum drawn up in 1928 by Undersecretary of State J. Ruben Clark. The Clark Memorandum denied that the Monroe Doctrine justified American intervention in Latin America. It stopped short of repudiating intervention on any grounds, but that fine point hardly blunted the celebration in Latin America. Although Hoover never endorsed the Clark Memorandum, he never intervened in the region. Before he left office, steps had already been taken to withdraw American forces from Nicaragua and Haiti.

Franklin D. Roosevelt likewise embraced "the policy of the good neighbor" and soon advanced it in practice. In 1933, at the Seventh Pan-American Conference, the United States supported a resolution saying "No state has the right to intervene in the internal or external affairs of another." Under Roosevelt the marines completed their withdrawals from Nicaragua and Haiti, and in 1934 the president negotiated with Cuba a treaty that abrogated the Platt Amendment and thus ended the last formal claim to a right of intervention in Latin America. Roosevelt reinforced hemispheric goodwill in 1936, when he opened the Eighth Pan-American Conference with a speech declaring that outside aggressors "will find a Hemisphere wholly prepared to consult together for our mutual safety and our mutual good."

WAR CLOUDS

JAPANESE INCURSIONS IN CHINA   The lessening of irritants in the Western Hemisphere during the 1930s proved an exception in an otherwise dismal world scene, as war clouds thickened over Europe and Asia. Actual conflict erupted first in Asia, where unsettled conditions in China had invited foreign encroachments since before the turn of the century. In 1929 Chinese nationalist aspirations and China's subsequent clashes with Russia convinced the Japanese that their own extensive rights in Manchuria, including the South Manchurian Railway, were in danger.

The Japanese army at the time had a nationalist movement of its own, led by a strong cadre of young officers devoted to ousting corrupt politicians and bringing about a moral regeneration for Japan. Economic pressures strengthened this nationalist movement, for Japan was suffering from the Great Depression and Chinese boycotts of Japanese goods. Manchuria offered both a tempting target and a promising market. Japanese occupation of Manchuria began with the Mukden Incident of 1931, when an explosion destroyed a section of railway track

Japan's seizure of Manchuria in 1931 prompted this American condemnation.

near that city. The Japanese "Kwantung Army," based in Manchuria to guard the railway, blamed the incident on the Chinese and used it as a pretext to begin its occupation, which it extended during the winter of 1931–1932 to all of Manchuria. In 1932 the Japanese converted Manchuria into the puppet empire of "Manchukuo."

The Manchuria Incident, as the Japanese called their undeclared war, was a flagrant breach of the Nine-Power Treaty, the Kellogg-Briand Pact, and Japan's pledges as a member of the League of Nations. But when China asked the League and the United States for help, neither responded. President Hoover was unwilling to invoke either military or economic sanctions. Secretary of State Henry Stimson, who would have preferred to do more, warned in 1932 that the United States refused to recognize any treaty, agreement, or situation that violated American treaty rights, the Open Door, or the territorial integrity of China, or any situation brought about by violation of the Kellogg-Briand Pact. This statement, later known as the Stimson Doctrine, had no effect on Japanese action, for later in the same month the Japanese navy attacked and briefly occupied Shanghai, China's great port city.

Indiscriminate bombing of Shanghai's civilian population aroused indignation but no further Western action. When the League of Nations condemned Japanese aggression in 1933, Japan withdrew from the League. During the spring of 1933, hostilities in Manchuria gradually subsided and ended with a truce. Then an uneasy peace settled upon East Asia for four years, during which time the leaders of Japan's military further extended their political sway.

ITALY AND GERMANY   The rise of the Japanese militarists paralleled the rise of dictators in Italy and Germany. In 1922 Benito Mussolini had seized power in Italy. After returning from World War I as a wounded veteran, he had organized the fascist movement, a hybrid of nationalism and socialism. The movement's name came from the ancient Roman *fasces,* a symbol of authority. The program, and above all Mussolini's promise to restore order and pride in a country fragmented by dissension, enjoyed a wide appeal. Once in power, Mussolini largely abandoned the socialist part of his platform and gradually suppressed all political opposition. By 1925 he wielded dictatorial power as Il Duce (the leader) in a one-party state.

To most Americans there was always something ludicrous about the strutting Mussolini, since Italy afforded but a limited power base in the

Mussolini and Hitler in Munich, Germany, June 1940.

total European picture. But Germany was another matter, and Americans were not amused, even at the beginning, by Il Duce's counterpart, Adolf Hitler. Hitler's National Socialist (Nazi) party duplicated the major features of Italian fascism, including the ancient Roman salute. The impotence of Germany's democratic Weimar Republic in the face of world depression offered Hitler his opening. Made chancellor on January 30, 1933, he swiftly intimidated the opposition, won dictatorial powers from a subservient Reichstag (parliament), and in 1934 assumed the title of Reichsführer (national leader) with absolute powers. The Nazi police state cranked up the engines of tyranny, persecuting socialists and Jews, whom Hitler blamed for all Germany's troubles, and rearming in defiance of the Versailles Treaty. Hitler flouted international agreements, pulled Germany out of the League of Nations in 1933, and frankly proclaimed that he meant to extend control over all German-speaking peoples. Despite one provocation after another, the European democracies lacked the will to resist his bold grab for power.

THE MOOD IN AMERICA Most Americans, absorbed by the problems of the depression, chose to retreat all the more into isolationism during the early 1930s. During the presidential the campaign of 1932, Roosevelt renounced his Wilsonian past and stated that he now opposed joining the League of Nations. Once in office, he rejected an early chance to deal with economic problems on an international basis.

This dealt a severe blow to international cooperation. The epilogue was Europe's final default on the war debts, and further American drift toward isolation.

The chief exception to the administration's isolationism was Secretary of State Cordell Hull's grand scheme of reciprocal trade agreements. Hull, a former Tennessee judge and congressman, believed that free trade among all nations would advance understanding and peace. In 1934 the administration threw its support behind Hull's pet project, and over the objections of business interests and Republicans, Congress adopted the Trade Agreements Act, which authorized the president to lower tariff rates as much as 50 percent for countries that made similar concessions on American products. Agreements were made with fourteen countries by the end of 1935, reaching a total of twenty-nine by 1945. The economic results are hard to measure, since the intervening years were so troubled.

Another scheme for building foreign markets, diplomatic recognition of Soviet Russia, won more support in business quarters than had the reciprocity plan. The vast expanse of Russia stirred fantasies of a trade boom, much as China had at the turn of the century. By 1933 the reasons for American refusal to recognize the Bolshevik regime had grown stale. Japanese expansionism in Asia, moreover, gave Russia and the United States a common concern. Given an opening by the shift of opinion, Roosevelt invited Maxim Litvinov, Soviet commissar for foreign affairs, to visit Washington. After nine days of talks, a formal exchange of notes on November 16, 1933, signaled the renewal of diplomatic relations. Litvinov promised that his country would abstain from propaganda in the United States, extend religious freedom to Americans in the U.S.S.R., and reopen the question of czarist debts to America.

THE EXPANDING AXIS   But a catastrophic chain of events in Asia and Europe sent the world hurtling toward disaster. In 1934 Japan renounced the Five-Power Naval Treaty. In 1935 Mussolini commenced an Italian conquest of Ethiopia. The same year a referendum in the Saar Basin, held in accordance with the Versailles Treaty, delivered that coal-rich region into the hands of Hitler. In 1936 Hitler reoccupied the Rhineland with armed forces, in violation of the Versailles Treaty but without any forceful response from the French. The year 1936 also brought the Spanish Civil War, which began with an uprising of the

Spanish armed forces in Morocco, led by General Francisco Franco. In three years Franco had established a fascist dictatorship with help from Hitler and Mussolini while the democracies stood by and left the Spanish Republic to its fate. On July 7, 1937, Japanese and Chinese troops clashed at the Marco Polo Bridge near Peking. The incident quickly developed into a full-scale war that the Japanese persisted in calling the "China Incident." It was the beginning of World War II in Asia, two years before war came to Europe. That same year Japan joined Germany and Italy in the "Anti-Comintern Pact," allegedly directed at the Communist threat, thus establishing the Rome-Berlin-Tokyo "Axis."

By 1938 the peace of Europe trembled in the balance. Having rebuilt German military force, Hitler forced the *Anschluss* (union) of Austria with Germany in March 1938, and six months later took the Sudeten territory from Czechoslovakia after signing an agreement at Munich under which Britain and France abandoned a country that had probably the second-best army in central Europe. The mountainous Sudetenland, largely German in population, was vital to the defense of Czechoslovakia. Having promised that this was his last territorial demand, Hitler in March 1939 brazenly violated his pledge and occupied the remainder of Czechoslovakia and seized formerly German territory from

German troops entering Prague, the capital of Czechoslovakia, April 1939.

Lithuania. In quick succession the Spanish Republic finally collapsed, and Mussolini seized the kingdom of Albania. Finally, during the summer, Hitler heated up a "war of nerves" over control of the free city of Danzig and the Polish Corridor, and on September 1 launched his conquest of Poland. A few days before, he had signed a nonaggression pact with Soviet Russia. Having deserted Czechoslovakia, Britain and France now honored their commitment to go to war if Poland were invaded.

DEGREES OF NEUTRALITY   During these years of deepening crisis, the Western democracies seemed paralyzed, hoping in vain that each concession would appease the appetites of fascist dictators. The Americans retreated more deeply into isolation. The prevailing mood was reinforced by a Senate inquiry into the role of bankers and munitions makers in World War I. Under Senator Gerald P. Nye of North Dakota, a progressive Republican, the committee sat from 1934 to 1937, and concluded that bankers and munitions makers had made scandalous profits from the war. Although Nye never showed that greed for profit had actually impelled Woodrow Wilson into war, millions of Americans became convinced that Uncle Sam had been duped by the "merchants of death."

Like generals who are said to be always preparing for the last war, Congress occupied itself with keeping out of the last war. Neutrality laws of the 1930s moved the United States toward complete isolation from the quarrels of Europe. Americans wanted to keep out of war, but their sympathies were more strongly than ever with the Western democracies, and the triumph of fascist aggression aroused growing fears for national security.

In 1935 President Roosevelt signed the first in a series of neutrality acts, one that anticipated Italy's invasion of Ethiopia. The Neutrality Act of 1935 forbade the sale of arms and munitions to all belligerents whenever the president proclaimed that a state of war existed. Ameri-

A 1938 cartoon showing U.S. foreign policy entangled by the serpent of isolationism.

cans who traveled on belligerent ships thereafter did so at their own risk. Roosevelt would have preferred discretionary authority to levy an embargo only against aggressors, but reluctantly accepted the act because it would be effective only for six months, and for the time being "meets the need of the existing situation." That is, it would actually be enforced against Italy in its war with Ethiopia. When he signed the act on August 31, Roosevelt nevertheless urged reconsideration of the arms embargo on all belligerents: "History is filled with situations that call for some flexibility of action. It is conceivable that situations may arise in which the wholly inflexible provisions . . . of this act . . . might drag us into war instead of keeping us out."

On October 3, 1935, Italy invaded Ethiopia and the president invoked the Neutrality Act. One shortcoming in its provisions became apparent right away: the key problem was neither arms traffic nor passenger travel, but trade in contraband not covered by the Neutrality Act. While Italy did not need to buy arms, since it had its own arms industry, it did need to buy raw materials, such as oil, which were not covered by the Neutrality Act. Secretary of State Hull warned that citizens trading with the belligerents, meaning in effect Italy since there was little trade with Ethiopia, did so at their own risk. He asked, moreover, for a "moral embargo" on oil and other products. Nonetheless, sanctions imposed under the Neutrality Act had no deterrent effect on Mussolini or his suppliers. In the summer of 1936, Il Duce completed his conquest of Ethiopia.

When Congress reconvened in 1936, it extended the arms embargo and added a provision forbidding loans to belligerents. Then in July 1936, while Italian troops mopped up the last resistance in Ethiopia, the Spanish army led by Franco revolted in Morocco. Ironically, Roosevelt now became more isolationist than some of the isolationists. Although the Spanish Civil War involved a fascist uprising against a recognized, democratic government, Roosevelt accepted the French and British position that only nonintervention would localize the fight. There existed, moreover, a strong bloc of pro-Franco Catholics in America who worried that the Spanish Republic was a threat to the church. They feared an atheistic Communist influence in the Spanish government; intrigues by Spanish Communists did prove divisive and the Soviet Union in fact did supply aid to the Republic, but nothing like the quantity of German and Italian assistance to Franco.

Roosevelt sought another "moral embargo" on the arms trade, and asked Congress to extend the neutrality laws to cover civil wars. Congress did so in 1937 with only one dissenting vote. The Western democracies then stood witness while German and Italian soldiers, planes, and armaments supported Franco's overthrow of Spanish democracy, which was completed in 1939.

In the spring of 1937 isolationist sentiment reached a peak. A Gallup poll found that 94 percent of its respondents preferred efforts to keep out of war over efforts to prevent war. That same spring Congress passed yet another neutrality law. It continued restraints on arms sales and loans, forbade Americans to travel on belligerent ships, and prohibited the arming of American merchant ships trading with belligerents. The president also won discretionary authority to require that goods other than arms or munitions exported to belligerents be placed on a cash-and-carry basis (that is, the purchaser of the goods would have to pay in cash and then carry them away in its own ships). This was an ingenious scheme to preserve a profitable trade without running the risk of war.

The new law faced its first test in July 1937, when Japanese and Chinese forces clashed at the Marco Polo Bridge west of Peking. Since nei-

Japanese troops enter Peking after the clash at the Marco Polo Bridge, July 1937.

ther side declared war, Roosevelt was able to use his discretion about invoking the neutrality law. He decided to wait, and in fact never invoked it. This was because its net effect would have favored the Japanese, since China had greater need of arms but few means to get supplies past the Japanese navy. A flourishing trade in munitions to China flowed around the world as ships carried arms across the Atlantic to England, where they were reloaded onto British ships bound for Hong Kong. Roosevelt, by inaction, had challenged strict isolationism.

Roosevelt soon ventured a step further. On October 5, 1937, he denounced the "reign of terror and international lawlessness" in which 10 percent of the world's population threatened the peace of the other 90 percent. "When an epidemic of physical disease starts to spread, the community approves and joins in a quarantine of the patients in order to protect the health of the community. . . ." There should also be a quarantine against nations "creating a state of international anarchy and instability from which there is no escape through mere isolation or neutrality." On the whole, public reaction to the speech was mixed. The president quickly backed off from its implications and refused to spell out any specific program.

Then, on December 12, 1937, Japanese planes bombed and sank the American gunboat *Panay,* which had been lying at anchor in the Yangtze River and prominently flying the American flag, and then Japan attacked three Standard Oil tankers. Two members of the *Panay* crew and an Italian journalist died; thirty more were injured. Though the Japanese government apologized and paid the reparations demanded—nearly $2.25 million—the incident reinforced American animosity toward Japan. The private boycott of Japanese goods spread, but isolationist sentiment continued strong, as was vividly demonstrated by support for the Ludlow Amendment in Congress. The proposed constitutional amendment would have required a public referendum for a declaration of war except in case of attack on American territory. Only by the most severe pressure from the White House, and a vote of 209 to 188, was consideration of the measure tabled in 1938.

After the German occupation of Czechoslovakia in 1939, Roosevelt no longer pretended impartiality in the impending European struggle. He urged Congress to repeal the embargo and permit the United States to sell arms on a cash-and-carry basis to Britain and France, but to no avail. When the Germans attacked Poland on September 1, 1939, Roosevelt proclaimed neutrality, but in a radio talk said that he did not, like

Wilson, ask Americans to remain neutral in thought because "even a neutral has a right to take account of the facts."

Roosevelt summoned Congress into special session, and asked it once again to amend the Neutrality Act. "I regret the Congress passed the Act," the president said. "I regret equally that I signed the Act." This time he got what he wanted. Under the Neutrality Act of 1939 the Allies could send their own freighters to the United States, buy supplies with cash, and take away arms or anything else they wanted. American ships, on the other hand, were excluded from belligerent ports and from specified war zones. Roosevelt then designated as a war zone the Baltic Sea and the waters around Great Britain and Ireland from Norway south to the coast of Spain. One effect of this move was to relieve Hitler of any inhibitions against using unrestricted submarine warfare to blockade Britain.

American attitudes continued to vacillate. As the war crisis developed, an isolationist policy of "hands off" prevailed. Once the great democracies of western Europe faced war, American public opinion, appalled at Hitler's tyranny, supported measures short of war to help their cause. "What the majority of the American people want," an editor wrote in the *Nation,* "is to be as un-neutral as possible without getting into war." On October 3, while Congress debated repeal of the arms embargo, the foreign ministers of the American republics adopted the Declaration of Panama, which created a "chastity belt" around the Americas, south of Canada, a zone 300 to 1,000 miles wide in which belligerents were warned not to pursue naval action. This unneutral action prohibited German naval activity near North and South American coasts. For a time it seemed that the Western Hemisphere could remain insulated from the war. After Hitler overran Poland in less than a month, the war in Europe settled into an unreal stalemate that began to be called the "phony war." What lay ahead, it seemed, was a long war of attrition in which Britain and France would have the resources to outlast Hitler. The illusion lasted through the winter.

THE STORM IN EUROPE

BLITZKRIEG   In the spring of 1940 the winter's long *Sitzkrieg* suddenly erupted into *Blitzkrieg*—lightning war. At dawn on April 9, without warning, Nazi troops entered Denmark and disembarked along the

French refugees fleeing German troops, June 1940.

Norwegian coast. Denmark fell in a day, Norway within a few weeks. On May 10 Hitler unleashed his dive bombers and panzer tank divisions on neutral Belgium and the Netherlands. On May 21 German troops reached the English Channel, cutting off a British force sent to help the Belgians and French. A desperate evacuation from the beaches at Dunkirk enlisted every available British boat from warship to tug. Some 338,000 men, about a third of them French, escaped to England.

Having outflanked the forts on France's eastern defense perimeter, the Maginot Line, the German forces rushed ahead, cutting the French armies to pieces and spreading panic by strafing refugees in a deliberate policy of terror. On June 10 Italy entered the war as Germany's ally. "I need only a few thousand dead to enable me to take my seat . . . at the peace table," Il Duce said. On June 14 the swastika flew over Paris. On June 22 French delegates, in the presence of Hitler, submitted to his terms in the same railroad car in which German delegates had been forced to sign the Armistice of 1918.

AMERICA'S GROWING INVOLVEMENT   Britain now stood alone, but in Parliament the new prime minister, Winston Churchill, breathed defiance. "We shall go on to the end," he said; "we shall never surrender." Despite the grim resolution of the British, America seemed suddenly vulnerable as Hitler turned his air force against Britain. President Roosevelt, who in his annual budget had requested $1.9 billion for defense, now asked for more, and called for the production of 50,000 combat planes a year. By October 1940, Congress had voted more than $17 billion for defense. In response to Churchill's appeal for military supplies, the War and Navy Departments began releasing stocks of arms, planes, and munitions to the British.

In June 1940 the president set up the National Defense Research Committee to coordinate military research, including a secret look into the possibility of developing an atomic bomb, suggested the previous fall by Albert Einstein and other scientists. To bolster national unity, Roosevelt named two Republicans to the defense posts in his cabinet: Henry L. Stimson as secretary of war and Frank Knox as secretary of the navy.

The summer of 1940 brought the desperate Battle of Britain, in which the Royal Air Force, with the benefit of the new technology of radar, outfought the numerically superior German Luftwaffe and finally forced the Germans to postpone plans to invade England. Submarine warfare meanwhile strained the resources of the battered Royal Navy. To relieve the pressure, Churchill urgently requested the transfer of

St. Paul's Cathedral looms above the destruction wrought by German bombs during the Blitz. Churchill's response: "We shall never surrender."

American destroyers. Secret negotiations led to an executive agreement under which fifty "overaged" American destroyers went to the British in return for ninety-nine-year American leases on naval and air bases in Newfoundland, Bermuda, the Bahamas, Jamaica, St. Lucia, Trinidad, Antigua, and British Guiana. Roosevelt disguised the action as being necessary for hemisphere defense. It was, he declared, "the most important action in the reinforcement of our national defense that has been taken since the Louisiana Purchase." Two weeks later, Congress adopted the first peacetime conscription in American history, requiring the registration of all men aged twenty-one to thirty-five for a year's military service within the United States.

The new state of affairs prompted vigorous debate between "internationalists," who believed national security demanded aid to Britain, and isolationists, who charged that Roosevelt was drawing the United States into a needless war. In 1940 the nonpartisan Committee to Defend America by Aiding the Allies was organized. It drew its strongest support from the East and West Coasts and the South. On the other hand, isolationists formed the America First Committee, which included among its members Herbert Hoover and Charles A. Lindbergh, Jr. Before the end of 1941, the committee had about 450 chapters around the country, but probably two-thirds of its members lived within a 300-mile radius of Chicago. The isolationists argued that the war involved, in Senator William E. Borah's words, "nothing more than another chapter in the bloody volume of European power politics," and that a Nazi victory, while distasteful, would pose no threat to national security.

A THIRD TERM FOR FDR   In the midst of this turbulence, the quadrennial presidential campaign came due. Isolationist sentiment was strongest in the Republican party and both the leading Republican candidates were noninterventionists, but neither loomed as a man of sufficient stature to challenge the "champ," assuming Roosevelt decided to run again. Senator Robert A. Taft of Ohio, son of the former president, lacked popular appeal, and New York district attorney Thomas E. Dewey, who had won fame as a "racket buster," at thirty-eight seemed young and unseasoned. This left an opening for an inspired group of political amateurs to promote the dark-horse candidacy of Wendell L. Willkie of Indiana.

Willkie seemed at first an unlikely choice: a former Democrat who had voted for Roosevelt in 1932, a utilities president who had fought the TVA, but in origins a Hoosier farm boy whose disheveled charm inspired strong loyalty. Unlike the front-runners, he openly supported aid to the Allies, and the Nazi *Blitzkrieg* had brought many other Republicans to the same viewpoint. When the Republicans met at Philadelphia on June 28, six days after the French surrender, the convention was stampeded by the cry of "We Want Willkie" from the galleries.

The Nazi victory in France also ensured another nomination for Roosevelt. The president cultivated party unity behind his foreign policy and kept a sphinx-like silence about his intentions regarding the war. The world crisis reconciled southern conservatives to the man whose foreign policy, at least, they supported. At the July convention in Chicago Roosevelt won nomination for a third term with only token opposition.

Through the summer Roosevelt assumed the role of a man above the political fray, busy rather with urgent matters of defense and diplomacy: Pan-American agreements for mutual defense, the destroyer-bases deal, and visits to defense facilities that took the place of campaign trips. Willkie was reduced to attacks on New Deal red tape and promises to run the programs better. In the end, however, he switched to an attack on Roosevelt's conduct of foreign policy. In October he warned: "If you re-elect him you may expect war in April, 1941." To this Roosevelt responded, "I have said this before, but I shall say it again and again and again: Your boys are not going to be sent into any foreign wars." Neither man distinguished himself with such hollow statements, since both knew the risks of all-out aid to Britain, which both supported.

Roosevelt won the election by a comfortable margin of 27 million votes to Willkie's 22 million, and a wider margin of 449 to 82 in the electoral college. Even so, the popular vote was closer than any presidential vote since 1916. But given the dangerous world situation, a majority of the voters agreed with the Democrats' slogan: "Don't switch horses in the middle of the stream."

THE ARSENAL OF DEMOCRACY   Bolstered by the mandate for an unprecedented third term, Roosevelt moved quickly for greater measures to aid Britain. Since the outbreak of war Roosevelt had corre-

*Women picketing the White House to urge defeat of the lend-lease program.
Like Senator Burton Wheeler they feared that lend-lease would "plow under
every fourth American boy."*

sponded with Winston Churchill, who soon after the election informed
Roosevelt that British cash was fast running out. Since direct American
loans would arouse memories of earlier war-debt defaults—the Johnson
Act of 1934 forbade such loans anyway—the president created an ingenious device to bypass that issue and yet supply British needs, the
"lend-lease" program.

   In a fireside chat, Roosevelt told the nation that it must become "the
great arsenal of democracy" because of the threat of Britain's fall. In his
annual message to Congress on January 6, 1941, he warned that only
the British navy stood between America and the peril of attack. Greater
efforts to bolster British defenses were therefore imperative: "They do
not need manpower. They do need billions of dollars worth of the
weapons of defense." At the end of the speech he enunciated the Four
Freedoms for which the democracies fought: freedom of speech, freedom of worship, freedom from want, and freedom from fear. The Lend-
Lease Bill, introduced in Congress on January 10, authorized the president to sell, transfer, exchange, lend, lease, or otherwise dispose of

arms and other equipment and supplies to "any country whose defense the President deems vital to the defense of the United States."

For two months a bitter debate over the bill raged in Congress and the country. Isolationists saw it as the point of no return. "The lend-lease-give program," said Senator Burton K. Wheeler, "is the New Deal's triple A foreign policy; it will plow under every fourth American boy." Roosevelt pronounced this "the rottenest thing that has been said in public life in my generation." Administration supporters denied that lend-lease would lead to war, but it did manifestly increase the risk. Lend-lease became law in March.

While the nation debated, the war was spreading. In October 1940 when the presidential campaign approached its climax, Mussolini launched attacks on Greece and, from Italian Libya, on the British in Egypt. But he miscalculated, and his forces had to fall back in both cases. In the spring of 1941, German forces under General Erwin Rommel joined the Italians in Libya, forcing the British, whose resources had been drained to help Greece, to withdraw into Egypt. In April 1941 Nazi armored divisions overwhelmed Yugoslavia and Greece, and by the end of May airborne forces subdued the Greek island of Crete, putting Hitler in a position to menace the entire Middle East. With Hungary, Romania, and Bulgaria forced into the Axis fold, Hitler controlled nearly all of Europe.

On June 22, 1941, German armies suddenly fell upon Russia. Frustrated in the purpose of subduing Britain, Hitler sought to eliminate the potential threat on his rear with another lightning stroke. The Russian plains offered an ideal theater for *Blitzkrieg,* or so it seemed. With Romanian and Finnish allies, the Nazis moved on a 2,000-mile front from the Arctic to the Black Sea with seeming invincibility. Then, after four months, the Russian soldiers rallied in front of Leningrad, Moscow, and Sevastopol. During the winter of 1941–1942, Hitler's legions began to learn the bitter lesson the Russians had taught Napoleon and the French in 1812.

Winston Churchill had already decided to offer British support to the Soviet Union in case of such an attack. "If Hitler invaded Hell," he said, "I would make at least a favorable reference to the Devil in the House of Commons." Roosevelt adopted the same policy, offering American aid two days after the attack. Stalinist Russia, so long as it held out, ensured the survival of Britain. American aid was now indispensable to

Europe's defense, and the logic of lend-lease led on to deeper American involvement. To deliver aid to Britain, goods had to be maneuvered through the German U-boat "wolf packs" in the North Atlantic. So in April 1941, Roosevelt informed Churchill that the United States Navy would extend its patrol areas in the North Atlantic nearly all the way to Iceland.

In August 1941 Roosevelt and Churchill held a secret naval rendezvous off Newfoundland, where they drew up a statement of principles that came to be known as the Atlantic Charter. In effect the "common principles" upon which the parties based "their hopes for a better future for the world" amounted to a joint statement of war aims, its eight points a mixture of the idealistic goals of the New Deal and Wilson's Fourteen Points. It called for the self-determination of all peoples, equal access to raw materials, economic cooperation, freedom of the seas, and a new system of general security. In September it was announced that fifteen anti-Axis nations, including the Soviet Union, had endorsed the statement.

Thus Roosevelt had led the United States into a joint statement of war aims with the anti-Axis powers. It was not long before shooting incidents involved Americans in the North Atlantic. The first attack on an American warship occurred on September 4 when a German submarine fired two torpedoes at the destroyer *Greer*. The president announced a week later orders to "shoot on sight" any German or Italian raiders ("rattlesnakes of the Atlantic") that ventured into American defensive waters. Five days later, the United States Navy began convoying merchant vessels all the way to Iceland. Then on October 17, while the destroyer *Kearny* was attacking German submarines, it sustained severe damage and loss of eleven lives from a German torpedo. Two weeks later, a submarine torpedoed and sank the destroyer *Reuben James,* with a loss of ninety-six officers and men, while it was on convoy duty west of Iceland. This action hastened Congress into making the changes in the Neutrality Act already requested by the president. On November 17 the legislation was in effect repealed when the bans on arming merchant vessels and allowing them to enter combat zones and belligerent ports were removed. Step by step the United States had given up neutrality and embarked on naval warfare against Germany. Still, the American people hoped to avoid taking the final step into all-out war. The decision for war came in an unexpected quarter—the Pacific.

THE STORM IN THE PACIFIC

JAPANESE AGGRESSION   After the Nazi victories in the spring of 1940, relations with Japan also took a turn for the worse. Japanese militarists, bogged down in the vastness of China, now eyed new temptations in South Asia: French Indochina, the Dutch East Indies, British Malaya, and Burma. Here they could cut off one of China's last links to the West, the Burma Road. What was more, they could incorporate into their "Greater East Asia Co-Prosperity Sphere" the oil, rubber, and other strategic materials that the crowded homeland lacked. As it was, Japan depended on the United States for important supplies, including 80 percent of its oil. During the summer of 1940, Japan forced the helpless French government at Vichy to permit the construction of Japanese airfields in French-controlled northern Indochina and to cut off the railroad into South China. The United States responded with a loan to China and the Export Control Act of July 2, 1940, which authorized the president to restrict the export of arms and other strategic materials to Japan. Gradually Roosevelt extended embargoes on aviation gas, scrap iron, and other supplies.

On September 27, 1940, the Tokyo government signed a Tripartite Pact with Germany and Italy, by which each pledged to declare war on any nation that attacked any of them. The pact could have been directed against either the United States or the Soviet Union. The Germans hoped to persuade Japan to enter Siberia when Nazi forces entered the Soviet Union from the west. The Soviet presence in Siberia did inhibit the Japanese impulse to move southward, but on April 13, 1941, while the Nazis were sweeping through the Balkans, Japan signed a nonaggression pact with the Soviet Union and, once the Nazis invaded Russia in June, the Japanese were freed of any threat from the north.

In July 1941 Japan announced that it was assuming a protectorate over all of French Indochina. Roosevelt took three steps in response: he froze all Japanese assets in the United States; he restricted exports of oil to Japan; and he merged the armed forces of the Philippines with the Army of the United States and put their commander, General Douglas MacArthur, in charge of all United States forces in East Asia. By September the oil restrictions had tightened into an embargo. The Japanese estimated that their oil reserves would last two years at most,

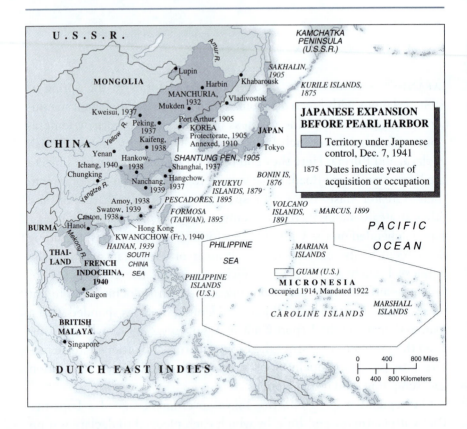

Map labels:

U.S.S.R.

KAMCHATKA
PENINSULA
(U.S.S.R.)

Amur R.

SAKHALIN,
1905

Lupin

MONGOLIA   Harbin   Khabarousk
MANCHURIA,   KURILE ISLANDS,
1932   1875
Mukden   Vladivostok
Kweisui, 1937   1932

Peking,   Port Arthur, 1905
1937   KOREA   JAPAN
Yellow R.   Kaifeng,   Protectorate, 1905
CHINA   1938   Annexed, 1910
Yenan   Tokyo
Ichang, 1940 Hankow, SHANTUNG PEN., 1905
Chungking   1938   Shanghai, 1937
Yangtze R.   Hangchow,   BONIN IS,
Nanchang, 1937   RYUKYU   1876
1939   ISLANDS, 1879
Amoy, 1938   PESCADORES, 1895   VOLCANO
Swatow, 1939   ISLANDS,   MARCUS, 1899
Canton, 1938   FORMOSA   1891
BURMA Hanoi Hong Kong (TAIWAN), 1895
Mekong R.   KWANGCHOW (Fr.), 1940   PACIFIC
HAINAN, 1939   PHILIPPINE   MARIANA   OCEAN
THAI-   SOUTH   SEA   ISLANDS
LAND FRENCH CHINA
INDOCHINA, SEA   GUAM (U.S.)
1940   PHILIPPINE   MICRONESIA
Saigon   ISLANDS   Occupied 1914, Mandated 1922
(U.S.)
MARSHALL
CAROLINE ISLANDS   ISLANDS
BRITISH
MALAYA
Singapore

DUTCH EAST INDIES

**JAPANESE EXPANSION
BEFORE PEARL HARBOR**

Territory under Japanese
control, Dec. 7, 1941

1875 Dates indicate year of
acquisition or occupation

0   400   800 Miles
0 400 800 Kilometers

eighteen months in case of an expanded war. Forced by the embargo to secure other oil supplies, the Japanese army and navy began to perfect plans for attacks on the Dutch and British colonies to the south.

Actions by both sides put the United States and Japan on the way to a war that neither wanted. In his regular talks with the Japanese ambassador, Secretary of State Cordell Hull demanded that Japan withdraw from Indochina and China as the price of renewed trade. A more flexible position might have strengthened the moderates in Japan. The Japanese were not then pursuing a concerted plan of aggression comparable to Hitler's. The Japanese military had stumbled crazily from one act of aggression to another without approval from the government in Tokyo. Premier Fumimaro Konoye, however, while known as a man of liberal principles who preferred peace, caved in to pressures from the militants. Perhaps he had no choice.

The Japanese warlords, for their part, seriously misjudged the United States. The desperate wish of Americans to stay out of war might still have enabled the Japanese to conquer the British and Dutch colonies before an American decision to act. But the warlords decided that they dared not leave the American navy intact and the Philippines un-touched on the flank of their new lifeline to the south.

TRAGEDY AT PEARL HARBOR   Thus a tragedy began to unfold with a fatal certainty—mostly out of sight of the American people, whose at-tention was focused on the war in the Atlantic. Late in August 1941 Premier Konoye proposed a personal meeting with President Roosevelt. Hull advised Roosevelt not to meet unless agreement on fundamentals could be reached in advance. Soon afterward, on September 6, an im-perial conference approved preparations for a surprise attack on Hawaii and gave Premier Konoye six more weeks to reach a settlement. The Japanese emperor's clear displeasure with the risks of an attack af-forded the premier one last chance to pursue a compromise, but the stumbling block was still the presence of Japanese troops in China. In October Konoye urged War Minister Hideki Tojo to consider with-drawal while saving face by keeping some troops in North China. Tojo countered with his "maximum concession" that Japanese troops would stay no longer than twenty-five years if the United States stopped aid-ing China. Faced with this rebuff and with Tojo's threat to resign and bring down the cabinet, Konoye himself resigned on October 15; Tojo became premier the next day. The war party now assumed complete control of the government.

On the very day that Tojo became premier, a special Japanese envoy conferred with Hull and Roosevelt in Washington. His arrival was largely a cover for Japan's war plans, although neither he nor the Japan-ese ambassador knew that. On November 20 they presented Tojo's final proposal. Japan would occupy no more territory if the United States would cut off aid to China, restore trade, and help Japan get supplies from the Dutch Indies. In that case Japan would pull out of southern Indochina immediately and abandon the remainder once peace had been established with China—presumably on Japanese terms. Tojo ex-pected the United States to refuse such demands. On November 26 Hull repeated the demand that Japan withdraw altogether from China.

The Attack on Pearl Harbor. *The view from a Japanese fighter plane shows American battleships in vulnerable positions.*

That same day a Japanese naval force began heading secretly across the North Pacific toward Pearl Harbor.

Washington already knew that war was imminent. Reports of Japanese troop transports moving south from Formosa prompted Washington to send warnings to American commanders in the Pacific, and to the British government. The massive movements southward clearly signaled attacks on the British and the Dutch possessions. American leaders had every reason to expect war in the southwest Pacific, but none expected that Japan would commit most of its carriers to another attack 5,000 miles away at Pearl Harbor.

In the early morning of December 7, 1941, Americans decoded the last part of a fourteen-part Japanese message breaking off the negotiations. Japan's ambassador was instructed to deliver the message at 1 P.M. (7:30 A.M. in Honolulu), about a half hour before the Japanese attack, but delays held up delivery until more than an hour later than scheduled. The War Department sent out an alert at noon that something was about to happen, but the message, which went by commercial telegraph because radio contacts were broken, arrived in Hawaii eight and a half hours later. Even so, the decoded Japanese message had not mentioned Pearl Harbor, and everyone still assumed that any Japanese move would be in Southeast Asia.

It was still a sleepy Sunday morning when the first Japanese planes roared down the west coast and the central valley of Oahu to begin their assault. At 7:53 A.M. the flight commander, Mitsuo Fuchida, sounded the cry "Tora! Tora! Tora!" ("Tiger! Tiger! Tiger!"), the signal that the attackers had taken the American navy by surprise. For nearly two hours the Japanese planes kept up their attack on an unsuspecting Pacific Fleet. Of the eight battleships in Pearl Harbor, three were sunk, one grounded, one capsized, and the others badly battered. Altogether nine-

The Attack on Pearl Harbor. *The view from an American airfield shows the destruction and confusion brought on by the surprise attack.*

teen ships were sunk or disabled. At the adjoining Hickam Field and other airfields on the island the Japanese found planes parked wing to wing, and destroyed in all about 150 of them. Few were able to get airborne, and Japanese losses numbered fewer than thirty planes. Before it was over the raid had killed more than 2,400 American servicemen and civilians, and wounded 1,178 more.

The surprise attack fulfilled the dreams of its planners, but it fell short of total success in two ways. The Japanese ignored the onshore facilities and oil tanks that supported the fleet, without which the surviving ships might have been forced back to the West Coast, and they missed the American aircraft carriers that had fortuitously left a few days earlier. In the naval war to come, these carriers would prove decisive.

Later the same day (December 8 in the western Pacific) Japanese forces began assaults on the Philippines, Guam, and Midway, and on the British forces in Hong Kong and the Malay Peninsula. With one stroke the Japanese had silenced America's debate on neutrality, and a suddenly unified and vengeful nation prepared for the struggle. The next day President Roosevelt delivered his war message to Congress in a speech long remembered by most Americans:

> Yesterday, December 7, 1941—a date which will live in infamy—the United States of America was suddenly and deliberately attacked by naval and air forces of the Empire of Japan. . . .
>
> The facts of yesterday speak for themselves. The people of the United States have already formed their opinions and well understand the implications to the very life and safety of our Nation. . . .

Congress voted for the war resolution unanimously, with the sole exception of Representative Jeanette Rankin, a pacifist who was unable in good conscience to vote for war in 1917 or 1941. For several days it was uncertain whether war with the other Axis Powers would follow. The Tripartite Pact was ostensibly for defense only, and it carried no obligation for them to enter, but Hitler, impatient with continuing American aid to Britain, willingly joined his Asian allies. On December 11, Germany and Italy declared war on the United States. The separate wars that were being waged by armies in Asia and Europe had become one global conflict.

MAKING CONNECTIONS

- The United States tried to stake out a neutral position in the growing world conflict. Compare this to earlier American attempts at neutrality, from the Napoleonic Wars era of Jefferson's administration onward.

- The American alliance with the Soviet Union described in this chapter proved to be temporary: after the war, the Americans and the Soviets would be adversaries in a great cold war, the beginnings of which are outlined in Chapter 31.

- The Japanese conquest of French Indochina (Vietnam) would play an important role in the events leading to American involvement in the region, a topic discussed in Chapter 33.

FURTHER READING

The best overview of interwar diplomacy remains Selig Adler's *The Uncertain Giant: American Foreign Policy between the Wars* (1965). Joan Hoff Wilson's *American Business and Foreign Policy, 1920–1933* (1971) highlights the efforts of Republican administrations during the 1920s to promote international commerce. Robert Dallek's *Franklin D. Roosevelt and American Foreign Policy, 1932–1945* (1979) provides a judicious assessment of Roosevelt's foreign policies during the 1930s.

Other scholars have concentrated on particular diplomatic issues of the 1920s. Thomas H. Buckley's *The United States and the Washington Conference, 1921–1922* (1970) examines disarmament. For a study of the Kellogg-Briand Pact, see Robert H. Ferrell's *Peace in Their Time: The Origins of the Kellogg-Briand Pact* (1968). Relations between the United States and Europe are covered in Frank Costigliola's *Awkward Dominion: American Political, Economic, and Cultural Relations with*

Europe, 1919–1933 (1984). A comprehensive analysis of American responses to Nazi aggression is Arnold Offner's *American Appeasement: United States Foreign Policy and Germany, 1933–1938* (1969).

For American relations in East Asia during the period, see Akira Iriye's *After Imperialism: The Search for a New Order in the Far East, 1921–1931* (1965) and the relevant chapters in Walter LaFeber's *The Clash: A History of U.S.-Japan Relations* (1997). More specific studies are Warren I. Cohen's *America's Response to China: An Interpretive History of Sino-American Relations* (2nd ed., 1981) and Jonathan G. Utley's *Going to War with Japan, 1937–1941* (1985). For relations with Latin America, see Irwin F. Gellman's *Good Neighbor Diplomacy: United States Policies in Latin America, 1933–1945* (1979). The best general account of the onset of World War II is Donald Watt's *How War Came: The Immediate Origins of the Second World War, 1938–1939* (1990).

A noteworthy study of America's entry into World War II is Waldo Heinrichs's *Threshold of War: Franklin D. Roosevelt and American Entry into World War II* (1988). Bruce M. Russett's *No Clear and Present Danger* (1972) provides a critical account of American actions. Other interpretations of Roosevelt's diplomacy include Robert A. Divine's *The Reluctant Belligerent* (2nd ed., 1979) and Patrick Hearden's *Roosevelt Confronts Hitler: America's Entry into World War II* (1986). American relations with Great Britain are detailed in David Reynolds's *The Creation of the Anglo-American Alliance, 1937–1941* (1981).

On Pearl Harbor, see Gordon W. Prange's *Pearl Harbor: The Verdict of History* (1986). The Japanese perspective is given in Robert J. C. Butow's *Tojo and the Coming of War* (1961).

30 ✑ THE SECOND WORLD WAR

The Japanese attack on Pearl Harbor ended a period of tense neutrality for the United States, and launched America into an epochal event that would transform the nation's social and economic life as well as its position in international affairs. The Second World War would become the most destructive and far-reaching war in history. It was a conflict so terrible and capricious, so surreal in its intensity and obscene in its cruelties, that it altered the image of war itself. Devilish new instruments of destruction were invented— plastic explosives, flame throwers, proximity fuses, rockets, jet airplanes, and atomic weapons—and systematic genocide emerged as an explicit war aim of the Nazis. Racist propaganda flourished on both sides, and excited hatred of the enemy caused many military and civilian prisoners to be executed. Over 50 million deaths were attributed to the war, and the physical destruction was incalculable. Whole cities were leveled, nations dismembered, and societies transformed. Latin America was the only region to escape the war's fury. The world is still struggling to cope with its consequences.

AMERICA'S EARLY BATTLES

SETBACKS IN THE PACIFIC   In early December 1941, all attention was focused on halting the Japanese advance and mobilizing the whole nation for war. For months after the attack on Pearl Harbor the news from the Pacific was "all bad," as President Roosevelt frankly confessed. In quick sequence these Allied outposts fell to the enemy before the end of December 1941: Guam, Wake Island, the Gilbert Islands, and Hong Kong. The fall of Rangoon in Burma cut off the Burma Road, the main supply route to Nationalist China. In the Philippines, where General Douglas MacArthur abandoned Manila on December 27, the main American forces, outmanned and outgunned, held out on Bataan Peninsula until April 9, and then on "The Rock," the fortified island of Corregidor. MacArthur slipped away in March, when he was ordered to

American prisoners of war, captured by the Japanese in the Philippines, 1942.

Australia to take command of Allied forces in the southwest Pacific. By May 6, 1942, when American forces surrendered Corregidor, Japan controlled a new empire that stretched from Burma eastward through the Dutch Indies and extending to Wake Island and the Gilberts.

The Japanese might have consolidated an almost impregnable empire with the resources they had seized. But the Japanese navy succumbed to what one of its admirals later called "victory disease." Its leaders resolved to push on into the South Pacific, isolate Australia, and strike again at Hawaii. Japanese planners hoped to draw out and destroy the American navy before the productive power of the United States could be brought to bear on the war effort.

A Japanese mistake and a stroke of American luck, however, enabled the United States Navy to frustrate the plan. Japan's failure to destroy the shore facilities at Pearl Harbor left the base relatively intact, and most of the ships damaged on December 7 lived to fight another day. The aircraft carriers at sea during the attack spent several months harassing Japanese outposts. Their most spectacular exploit, an air raid on Tokyo itself, was launched on April 18, 1942. B-25 bombers took off from the carrier *Hornet* and, unable to land on its deck, proceeded to China. The raid caused only token damage but did much to lift American morale amid a series of defeats elsewhere.

CORAL SEA AND MIDWAY   American forces finally halted the Japanese advances in two decisive naval battles. The Battle of the Coral Sea (May 7–8, 1942) stopped a fleet convoying Japanese troop transports toward New Guinea. Planes from the *Lexington* and *Yorktown* sank one Japanese carrier, damaged another, and destroyed smaller ships. American losses were greater, and included the carrier *Lexington,* but the Japanese advance on Australia was repulsed.

Less than a month after the Coral Sea engagement, Admiral Isoruku Yamamoto, the Japanese naval commander, decided to force a showdown in the central Pacific. With nearly every ship under his personal command, he headed for Midway Island, from which he hoped to render Pearl Harbor helpless. This time it was the Japanese who were the victims of surprise. American cryptanalysts had by then broken the Japanese naval code, and Admiral Chester Nimitz, commander of the central Pacific, knew what was up. He reinforced Midway with planes and carriers.

The first Japanese foray against Midway, on June 4, severely damaged the island, but at the cost of about a third of the Japanese planes. Before another attack could be mounted, American torpedo planes and dive bombers had caught three of the four Japanese carriers in the process of servicing their planes. Most of the first wave of slow American torpedo bombers were shot down, but dive bombers disabled three Japanese carriers and left them to sink. The Japanese lost an additional carrier; the Americans, a carrier and a destroyer. The Japanese navy, having lost its four best aircraft carriers, all veterans of Pearl Harbor, was forced into retreat less than six months after the attack on Hawaii. The Japanese defeat at Midway was the turning point of the Pacific war.

SETBACKS IN THE ATLANTIC   Early American setbacks in the Pacific were matched by setbacks in the Atlantic. Since the *Blitzkrieg* of 1940, German submarine "wolf packs" had wreaked havoc in the North Atlantic. In 1942, after an ominous lull, German submarines suddenly appeared off American shores and began to sink coastal shipping. Nearly 400 ships were lost in American waters before effective countermeasures brought the problem under control. The naval command accelerated the building of small escort vessels, meanwhile pressing into patrol service all kinds of surface craft and planes, some of them civilian. During the second half of 1942, the losses diminished to a negligible number.

MOBILIZATION AT HOME

The Pearl Harbor attack ended not only the long debate between isolation and intervention but also the long depression that had ravaged the country in the 1930s. The war effort would require all of America's huge productive capacity and full employment of the workforce. Soon after Pearl Harbor, Winston Churchill recalled that, thirty years before, one observer had compared the United States to a gigantic boiler: "Once the fire is lighted under it, there is no limit to the power it can generate." Mobilization was in fact already further along than preparedness had been in 1916–1917. The Selective Service had been in effect for more than a year, and the army had grown to more than 1.4 million men by July 1941. With America's entry into the war, men between eighteen and forty-five now became subject to the draft. Altogether more than 15 million men and women would serve in the armed forces over the course of the conflict.

ECONOMIC CONVERSION The economy, too, was already partially mobilized by lend-lease and defense efforts. The War Powers Act of 1941 had given the president a mandate to reshuffle government agencies, and a Second War Powers Act empowered the government to allot materials and facilities as needed for defense, with penalties for those who failed to comply.

The War Production Board (WPB), created in 1942 on the model of its counterpart during the First World War, directed industrial conversion to war production. Auto makers switched to producing tanks, shirt factories began to make mosquito netting, and the manufacturers of refrigerators, stoves, and cash registers began to produce munitions. The Reconstruction Finance Corporation, a New Deal agency, now financed war plants.

The war effort required conservation as well as production. "Use it up, wear it out, make do or do without," became the prevailing slogan.

Mobilization for war deflected many New Deal programs.

People collected scrap metal and grew their own food in backyard "victory gardens." The government named special administrators, or "czars," to promote production of rubber and oil. The president of Union Pacific Railroad, now the rubber "czar," pushed construction of synthetic rubber plants, which by 1944 produced 800,000 tons, or 87 percent of the country's requirements. Tire and gasoline rationing began in earnest. Through the Office of Scientific Research and Development, Dr. Vannevar Bush mobilized thousands of "scientists against time" to create and modify radar, sonar, the proximity fuse, the bazooka, means to isolate blood plasma, and numerous other innovations.

The pressure of wartime needs and the stimulus of government spending sent the gross national product soaring from $100 billion in 1940 to $214 billion in 1945, a rise of 114 percent. The figure for total government expenditures was twice as great as the total of all previous federal spending in the history of the republic, about 10 times what America spent in World War I, and 100 times the expenditures during the Civil War.

FINANCING THE WAR   To cover the war's huge cost the president preferred taxes to borrowing. "I would rather pay one hundred percent of taxes now than push the burden of this war onto the shoulders of my grandchildren," he said. Taxes also relieved upward pressures on prices. The wartime Congress, however, dominated by conservatives, feared taxes more than deficits and refused to go more than halfway with Roosevelt's fiscal prudence. The Revenue Act of 1942 provided for only about $7 billion in increased revenue, less than half that recommended by the Treasury. It also greatly broadened the tax structure. Whereas in 1939 only about 4 million people filed returns, the new act, in the words of a tax historian, "made the Federal income tax a genuine mass tax."

The federal government paid for about 45 percent of its 1939–1946 costs with tax revenues. Roosevelt would have preferred to cover more, but the figure compared favorably with 30 percent for World War I and 23 percent for the Civil War. To cover the rest of its costs, the government borrowed from the public. War-bond drives, including a Victory Drive in 1945, induced citizens to put aside more than $150 billion in bonds. Financial institutions picked up most of the rest of the government's debt. In all, by the end of the war the national debt had grown to about $260 billion, about six times its size at the time of Pearl Harbor.

As the economy finally recovered from the throes of the depression, many became converts to the Keynesian argument that only massive government spending had finally been able to end the depression.

The basic economic problem was no longer finding jobs but finding workers for the booming shipyards, aircraft factories, and gunpowder mills. Millions of people, especially women, who had lived on the margin of the economic system were now brought fully into the economy. Stubborn poverty did not disappear, but for most of those who stayed home the war spelled neither hardship nor suffering but a better life than ever before, despite shortages and rationing.

ECONOMIC CONTROLS Increased incomes and spending during the war conjured up the specter of inflation. Some of the available money went into taxes and war bonds, but even so, more was sent chasing after civilian goods just as production was converting to war needs. Consumer durables such as cars, washing machines, and nondefense housing in fact ceased to be made at all. It was apparent that only strict restraints would keep prices of scarce commodities from soaring out of sight. The administration, having tried in 1933 to raise prices, now reversed its ground and set out to hold them down. In 1942, Congress authorized the Office of Price Administration (OPA) for the first time to set price ceilings. With prices frozen, goods had to be allocated through rationing, with coupons doled out for sugar, coffee, gasoline, automobile tires, and meats.

Wages and farm prices, however, were not controlled, and this complicated things. War prosperity offered farmers a chance to recover from two decades of distress, and farm-state congressmen fought successfully to raise both floors and ceilings on farm prices. Higher food prices reinforced worker demands for higher wages, but the War Labor Board tried to hold the line. Finally, under the Stabilization Act of 1942, the president won new authority to control wages and farm prices. At the same time, he set up the Office of Economic Stabilization under James F. Byrnes, who left his seat on the Supreme Court to coordinate the effort. Stabilization proved to be one of the most complex jobs of the war effort, subject to constant sniping by special interests.

Both business and workers chafed at the wage and price controls. On occasion the government seized industries threatened by strike. The coal mines and railroads both came under government operation for a short time in 1943, and in 1944 the government briefly took over the Montgomery-Ward Company. Soldiers had to carry its chairman bodily out of his office when he stubbornly defied orders of the War Labor Board. Despite these problems, the government effort to stabilize wages and prices was on the whole a success story. By the end of the war, consumer prices had risen about 31 percent, a record far better than the World War I rise of 62 percent.

DOMESTIC CONSERVATISM In domestic politics the wartime period witnessed a growing conservatism. Discontent with price controls, labor shortages, rationing, and a hundred other petty vexations spread. In 1942 the congressional elections registered a national swing against the New Deal. Republicans gained forty-six seats in the House and nine in the Senate, chiefly in the farm areas of the midwestern states. Democratic losses outside the South strengthened the southern delegation's position within the party, and the delegation itself reflected conservative victories in southern primaries. A coalition of conservatives proceeded to eviscerate "nonessential" New Deal agencies. In 1943 Congress abolished the Works Progress Administration, the National Youth Administration, and the Civilian Conservation Corps, began to dismantle the Farm Security Administration, and liquidated the National Resources Planning Board.

Organized labor, despite substantial gains during the war, felt the impact of the conservative trend. In the spring of 1943, when John L. Lewis led the coal miners out on strike, widespread resentment led Congress to pass the Smith-Connally War Labor Disputes Act, which authorized the government to seize plants useful to the war. In 1943 a dozen states adopted laws variously restricting picketing and other union activities, and in 1944 Arkansas and Florida set in motion a wave of "right-to-work" legislation that outlawed the closed shop (requiring that all employees be union members).

SOCIAL EFFECTS OF THE WAR

MOBILIZATION AND THE DEVELOPMENT OF THE WEST The dramatic expansion of defense production after 1940 and the mobilization of millions of men into the armed forces accelerated economic development and the population boom in the western states. Nearly 8 million people moved into the states west of the Mississippi River between 1940 and 1950. The states witnessing the largest population growth during the war were California, Oregon, Washington, Nevada, Utah, Texas, and Arizona. Most of this expansion occurred in metropolitan centers. Indeed, the Far West experienced the fastest rate of urban growth in the country. Small cities such as Phoenix and Albuquerque mushroomed, while Seattle, San Francisco, Los Angeles, and San Diego witnessed dizzying growth. San Diego's population, for example, increased by 147 percent between 1941 and 1945.

Abundant jobs at high wages enticed people to the western states. California alone garnered 10 percent of all the defense contracts during the war years. In Texas, manufacturing employment almost doubled between 1940 and 1945. Los Angeles, which in 1939 was the seventh largest manufacturing center in the nation, had by 1943 become second only to Detroit in industrial activity. City services could not keep up with the influx of workers and military personnel. Employees at Seattle's shipyards and the Boeing airplane plant lived in tents because of a housing shortage. To address the problem, Congress passed the Lanham Act, which authorized the federal government to finance over a million new temporary housing units across the country. Yet this federal housing program did not meet the demand. Some women workers at a San Diego defense plant lived eight to a room in a company dormitory.

The migration of workers to new defense jobs in the West had significant demographic effects. Communities that earlier had few African Americans witnessed an influx of blacks. Lured by news of job openings and higher wages, African Americans from Texas, Oklahoma, Arkansas, and Louisiana headed west. During the war years Seattle's black population jumped from 4,000 to 40,000, Portland's from 2,000 to 15,000.

WOMEN The war marked an important watershed in the changing status of women. The proportion of women working had barely altered from 1910 to 1940, but with millions of men going into military service, the demand for labor shook up old prejudices about sex roles in the workplace—and in the military. Nearly 200,000 women served in the Women's Army Corps (WAC) and the navy's equivalent, Women Accepted for Volunteer Emergency Service (WAVES). Lesser numbers joined the Marine Corps, the Coast Guard, and the Army Air Force.

Women in the Military. *This navy recruiting poster urged women to join the WAVES (Women Accepted for Voluntary Services).*

Even more significant were the over 6 million women who entered the workforce during the war, an increase of over 50 percent and in manufacturing alone of some 110 percent. Old barriers fell overnight as women became toolmakers, machinists, crane operators, lumberjacks, stevedores, blacksmiths, and railroad track workers.

By 1944 women made up 14 percent of all workers in shipbuilding and 40 percent in aircraft plants. The government, desperate for laborers in defense industries, launched an intense publicity campaign to draw women into traditional male jobs. "Do your part, free a man for service," one ad pleaded. "Rosie the Riveter," a beautiful model dressed in overalls, became the cover girl for the recruiting campaign. One striking feature of the new labor scene was the larger proportion of older, married women in the workforce. In 1940 about 15 percent of married women went into gainful employment; by 1945 it was 24 percent. In the workforce as a whole, married women for the first time outnumbered single women. Attitudes sharply changed from those of the depression days, when over 80 percent of Americans opposed work by married women; by 1942 a poll showed 60 percent in favor of hiring married women in war industries. Defense jobs, however, were the ones most vulnerable to postwar cuts.

Women Workers. *These women took the place of men in constructing airplanes for use in the war.*

Still, there were many vocal opponents to this new trend. One disgruntled male legislator asked what would happen to traditional domestic tasks if women were in factories: "Who will do the cooking, the washing, the mending, the humble homey tasks to which every woman has devoted herself; who will rear and nurture the children?" Many women, however, were eager to get away from the grinding routine of domestic life. One female welder remembered that her wartime job "was the first time I had a chance to get out of the kitchen and work in industry and make a few bucks. This was something I had never dreamed would happen." And it was something that many women did not want to relinquish after the war.

BLACKS   The most volatile issue ignited by the war was probably that of African-American participation in the defense effort. From the start black leaders demanded full recognition in the armed forces and defense industries. Eventually about a million African Americans served in the armed forces, in every branch and every theater. But they served usually in segregated units. Every army camp had its separate facilities

Tuskegee Airmen, 1942. *One of the last segregated military training schools, the flight school at Tuskegee trained African-American men for combat during World War II.*

and its periodic racial "incidents." The most important departure was a 1940 decision to give up segregation in officer candidate schools, except those for air force cadets. A separate flight school at Tuskegee, Alabama, trained about 600 black pilots, many of whom distinguished themselves in combat.

War industries were even less accessible to black influence and pressure, although government policy theoretically opposed discrimination. In 1941 A. Philip Randolph, the tall, gentlemanly head of the Brotherhood of Sleeping Car Porters, organized a March on Washington Movement to demand an end to discrimination in defense industries. The administration, alarmed at the prospect of a mass descent on Washington, struck a bargain. The Randolph group called off its march in return for an executive order that forbade discrimination in defense work and training programs by requiring a nondiscrimination clause in defense contracts, and set up the Fair Employment Practices Commission (FEPC). The FEPC's authority was chiefly moral, since it had no power to enforce directives. It nevertheless offered willing employers the chance to say they were following government policy in giving jobs to black citizens, and no doubt persuaded others to go along.

Blacks quickly broadened their drive for wartime participation into a more inclusive social and political front. Early in 1942 the *Pittsburgh*

Courier endorsed the "Double V," which stood for victory at home and abroad. The slogan became immensely popular in black communities, and reflected a growing urge to rid the world not just of Hitler but of Hitlerism, as one editor put it. Blacks began to challenge more openly all kinds of discrimination, including racial segregation itself. "It was as if some universal message had come through to the great mass of Negroes," a sociologist wrote in 1943, "urging them to dream new dreams and to protest against the old order." A foundation was being laid for a great expansion of civil rights efforts after the war. Membership in the NAACP grew during the war from 50,000 to 450,000. Blacks could look forward to greater political participation after the Supreme Court, in *Smith v. Allwright* (1944), struck down Texas's white primary on the ground that Democratic primaries were part of the election process and thus subject to the Fifteenth Amendment.

The growing militancy of blacks aroused antagonism from some whites. Racial violence during this period did not approach the level of that in World War I, but growing tensions on a hot summer afternoon in Detroit sparked incidents at a park. Fighting raged through June 20–21, 1943, until federal troops arrived on the second evening. Twenty-five blacks and nine whites had been killed.

HISPANICS   As rural folk moved to the western cities, the farm counties experienced a labor shortage. In an ironic about-face, local and federal government authorities who before the war strove to force Mexican alien laborers back across the border now recruited them to harvest crops. The Mexican government, however, first insisted that the United States ensure certain minimum work and living conditions before it would assist in providing the needed workers. The result was the creation of the *bracero* program in 1942. Mexico agreed to provide seasonal farm workers in exchange for a promise by the American government not to draft them into military service. The workers were hired on year-long contracts that offered wages at the prevailing rate, and American officials provided transportation from the border to their job sites. Under this *bracero* program, some 200,000 Mexican farm workers entered the western United States. At least that many more crossed the border as illegal aliens.

The influx of peoples created new tensions. The rising tide of Mexican Americans in Los Angeles provoked a growing stream of anti-Hispanic editorials and incidents. Even though Mexican Americans fought in the war with great valor, earning seventeen Congressional Medals of Honor, there was constant conflict between servicemen and Mexican-American gang members and teenage "zoot-suiters" in southern California. "Zoot suits" were the flamboyant clothes worn by some young Chicano men. In 1943, several thousand off-duty sailors and soldiers, joined by hundreds of local white civilians, rampaged through downtown Los Angeles streets, assaulting Hispanics, blacks, and Filipinos. The violence lasted a week and came to be labeled the "zoot suit" riots.

NATIVE AMERICANS Indians may have supported the war effort more fully than any other group in American society. Almost a third of eligible Native American men, over 25,000 people, served in the armed forces. Another one-fourth worked in defense-related industries. Thousands of Indian women volunteered as nurses or joined the Women's Voluntary Service. As was the case with African Americans, Indians benefited from the broadening experiences afforded by the war. Those who left reservations to work in defense plants or to join the military gained new vocational skills as well as a greater awareness of American society and how to succeed within it.

Why did Native Americans fight for a nation that had stripped them of their lands and decimated their heritage? Some felt that they had no choice. Mobilization for the war effort ended many New Deal programs that had provided Indians with jobs. Reservation Indians thus faced the necessity of finding new jobs elsewhere. Many viewed the Nazis and Japanese warlords as threats to their own homeland. Others saw in the war an opportunity to revitalize the warrior tradition. Joseph Medicine Crow remembered that, while fighting in Europe, he "never thought" about the traditional requirements for a young Crow male to earn his status as a warrior, but "afterwards, when I came back and went through this telling of the war deeds ceremony, why, I told my war deeds, and lo and behold I completed the four requirements to become a chief." The most common sentiment, however, seems to have been a genuine sense of patriotism.

Whatever the reasons, Indians distinguished themselves in the military during the war. Unlike their African-American counterparts, Indian servicemen were integrated within the regular units. Perhaps the most distinctive activity performed by Indians was their service as "code talkers." Every military branch used Indians—Oneidas, Chippewas, Sauks,

Foxes, Comanches, and Navajos—to encode and decipher messages so as to prevent enemy discovery. The Dineh (Navajo) developed their own specialized dictionary to convey idiomatic military terms. For example, a submarine became an "iron fish" and a machine gun was a "fast shooter."

JAPANESE AMERICANS   The record on civil liberties during World War II was on the whole better than that during World War I, if only because there was virtually no opposition to the war effort after the attack on Pearl Harbor. Neither German Americans nor Italian Americans faced the harassments meted out to their counterparts in the previous war; few had much sympathy for Hitler or Mussolini. The shameful exception to an otherwise improved record was the treatment given to more than 100,000 Americans of Japanese descent (Nisei), who were forcibly removed from homes and businesses on the West Coast to "War Relocation Camps" in the interior. Caught up in the war hysteria and racial prejudice provoked by the attack on Pearl Harbor, President Roosevelt initiated the removal of Japanese Americans when he issued

Japanese Americans boarding a bus that would take them to War Relocation Camps, 1942.

Executive Order 9066 on February 19, 1942. More than 60 percent of the internees were U.S. citizens; a third were under the age of nineteen. Forced to sell their farms and businesses at great losses, the internees lost not only their liberty but also their property. Few, if any, were disloyal, but all were victims of fear and racial prejudice.

This was especially the case in the months following the attack on Pearl Harbor. A California barbershop offered "free shaves for Japs" but noted that it was "not responsible for accidents." Others were even blunter. Idaho's governor declared: "A good solution to the Jap problem would be to send them all back to Japan, then sink the island." As one Japanese American poignantly complained, "What really hurts most is the constant reference to us evacuees as 'Japs.' 'Japs' are the guys we are fighting. We're on this side and we want to help. Why won't America let us?" Many did support the effort. Japanese-American Hawaiians and mainlanders made up two of the most celebrated infantry units in the war, fighting with distinction on the Italian front. Other thousands of Nisei served as interpreters and translators, the "eyes and ears" of the American armed forces in the Pacific. Not until 1983 did the government finally recognize the injustice of the internment policy. That year it authorized granting those Nisei still living $20,000 each in compensation.

THE ALLIED DRIVE TOWARD BERLIN

By mid-1942, the "home front" began to get news from the war fronts that some of the lines were holding at last. Japanese naval losses at the Coral Sea and Midway had secured Australia and Hawaii. By mid-year a motley fleet of American air and sea sub-chasers was ending six months of happy hunting for German U-boats off the Atlantic coast. This was all the more important because war plans called for the defeat of Germany first.

WAR AIMS AND STRATEGY   There were many reasons for giving top priority to defeating Hitler. Nazi forces in western Europe and the Atlantic posed a more direct threat to the Western Hemisphere; German war potential was greater and German science was more likely to come up with some devastating new weapon. Lose in the Atlantic, General

George Marshall grimly predicted, and you lose everywhere. Despite such assumptions, Japanese attacks involved Americans directly in the Pacific war from the start, and as a consequence, during the first year of fighting more Americans went to the Pacific than across the Atlantic.

The Pearl Harbor attack brought British prime minister Winston Churchill quickly to Washington for lengthy talks about a common war plan. Thus began a wartime alliance between the United States and Great Britain, a partnership marked almost as much by disagreement and suspicion as it was by common purposes. As Churchill later remarked, "There is only one thing worse than fighting with allies, and that is fighting without them." Although he and Roosevelt admired each other, they disagreed about military strategy and the likely makeup of the postwar world. They often pursued the interests of their own country at the expense of the military alliance; they occasionally deceived each other; in a few cases, they lied to each other. Roosevelt worried about Churchill's excessive drinking, and Churchill worried about Roosevelt's "naive" understanding of Soviet behavior and his innocent faith in Stalin's integrity.

Initially, at least, such differences of opinion and outlook were masked by the need to make basic decisions related to the conduct of the war. The meetings in Washington in 1942 produced several major and numerous minor decisions, including the one to name a supreme commander in each major theater of war. Each commander would be subject to orders from the British-American Combined Chiefs of Staff. Other joint boards allotted munitions, raw materials, and shipping.

American and British war plans thereafter proceeded in close concert, and often launched joint operations, especially against Germany. No such coordinated effort was ever effected with Russia, which fought its own war on the eastern front, separate except for the coordinated timing of some major offensives. In Washington on January 1, 1942, representatives of twenty-six governments then at war with the Axis signed the Declaration of the United Nations, affirming the principles of the Atlantic Charter, pledging their full resources to the war, and promising not to make separate peace with the common enemies. Finally, in the course of their talks, the British and American leaders reaffirmed the priority of war against Germany.

Agreement on war aims, however, did not bring agreement on strategy. Roosevelt and Churchill, meeting at the White House again in

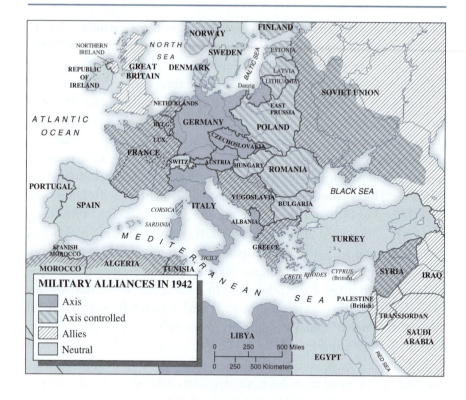

MILITARY ALLIANCES IN 1942

- Axis
- Axis controlled
- Allies
- Neutral

June 1942, could not agree on where to hit first. American military planners wanted to strike directly across the English Channel before the end of 1942, secure a beachhead, and move against Germany in 1943. The British preferred to keep the Germans off balance with hit-and-run raids and air attacks while continuing to build up their forces. With vivid memories of the last war, the British feared a mass bloodletting in trench warfare if they struck prematurely. The Russians, bearing the brunt of the German attack in the east, insisted that the Western Allies must do something to relieve the pressure. Finally, the Americans accepted Churchill's proposal to invade French North Africa.

THE NORTH AFRICA CAMPAIGN On November 8, 1942, Anglo-American forces under the command of American general Dwight D. Eisenhower landed at Casablanca in Morocco and at Oran and Algiers in Algeria. Completely surprised, French forces under the Vichy government (which collaborated with the Germans) had little will to resist. Hitler therefore occupied the whole of France and sent German forces into French Tunisia. By chance Admiral Jean-François Darlan, second to Marshal Pétain in the collaborationist Vichy government, was visiting in Algiers and was persuaded by the Allies to order a cease-fire.

Farther east, General Bernard Montgomery's British forces were pushing the brilliant German tank commander General Erwin Rommel back across Libya, but green American forces confronted seasoned Nazis pouring into Tunisia. Before spring, however, Montgomery had taken Libya, and the Germans were caught in a gigantic pincers. Hammered from all sides, unable to retreat across the Mediterranean, an army of 275,000 surrendered on May 13, 1943, leaving all of North Africa in Allied hands.

While the battle of Tunisia unfolded, in January 1943 Roosevelt and Churchill and the Combined Chiefs of Staff met at Casablanca. Stalin declined to leave Russia for the meeting but continued to press for a second front in western Europe. For the time, however, they decided to postpone the cross-Channel invasion and to carry out Churchill's scheme to attack what he called the "soft underbelly of the Axis" by invading Sicily. Admiral Chester Nimitz and General Douglas MacArthur were authorized meanwhile to start an offensive to dislodge the Japanese from the Pacific islands. Top priority, however, went to an antisubmarine campaign in the Atlantic.

Before leaving Casablanca, Roosevelt announced, with Churchill's endorsement, that the war would end only with the "unconditional surrender" of all enemies. This was designed to reassure Stalin and to quiet suspicions that the Western Allies might negotiate separately with the enemy. The announcement owed a good bit also to the determination that, as Roosevelt put it, "every person in Germany should realize that this time Germany is a defeated nation." This dictum was later criticized for having stiffened enemy resistance, but it probably had little effect; in fact neither the Italian nor the Japanese surrender would be totally unconditional. But the decision did have one unexpected result: it opened an avenue for eventual Soviet control of eastern Europe because it required Russian armies to pursue Hitler's forces all the way to Germany. And as they liberated the countries of eastern Europe, the Soviets created new governments in their own image.

THE BATTLE OF THE ATLANTIC   While fighting raged in North Africa, the more crucial Battle of the Atlantic reached its climax on the

American soldiers catching a last smoke before combat.

high seas. Several factors brought success to the Allied effort. Patrols by land-based planes covered much of the Atlantic from airfields in Britain and the Western Hemisphere, and in 1943 Portugal permitted American planes to operate from the Azores, thereby closing the last gap in coverage in the North Atlantic. Scientists perfected a variety of new detection devices: radar, which the British had already used to advantage in the Battle of Britain, bounced radio waves off objects above the surface and registered their positions on a screen; sonar gear detected sound waves from submerged U-boats, and sonobuoys, dropped from planes, radioed back their findings; advanced magnetic equipment enabled aircraft to detect objects under water. New escort carriers ("baby flat-tops") and improvements in depth charges added to the effectiveness of convoys.

By early 1943 there were in the western half of the North Atlantic at any one time an average of 31 convoys with 145 escorts and 673 merchant ships, and a number of heavily escorted troopships. None of the troopships going to Britain or the Mediterranean was lost, although submarines sank three en route to Greenland and Iceland. The U-boats kept up the Battle of the Atlantic until the war's end; when Germany finally collapsed, at least forty-nine were still at sea. But their commander later admitted that the Battle of the Atlantic was lost by the end of May 1943. He credited the difference largely to radar. What he did not know then was that the Allies had a secret weapon. By early 1943 their cryptanalysts were routinely decoding secret messages and telling their sub-hunters where to look for German U-boats.

SICILY AND ITALY   The North African campaign won, the Allies prepared to attack Sicily. On July 10, 1943, about 250,000 British and American troops landed on Sicily, the largest single amphibious action in the war to that time, scoring a complete surprise. The entire island was in Allied hands by August 17, although some 40,000 Germans escaped to the mainland. Allied success in Sicily ended Mussolini's twenty years of fascist rule. Italians never had had much heart for the war into which he had dragged them. On July 25, 1943, Italy's King Victor Emmanuel III notified the dictator of his dismissal as premier. A new regime startled the Allies when it offered not only to surrender but

Major-General George S. Patton, commander of American invasion forces on Sicily.

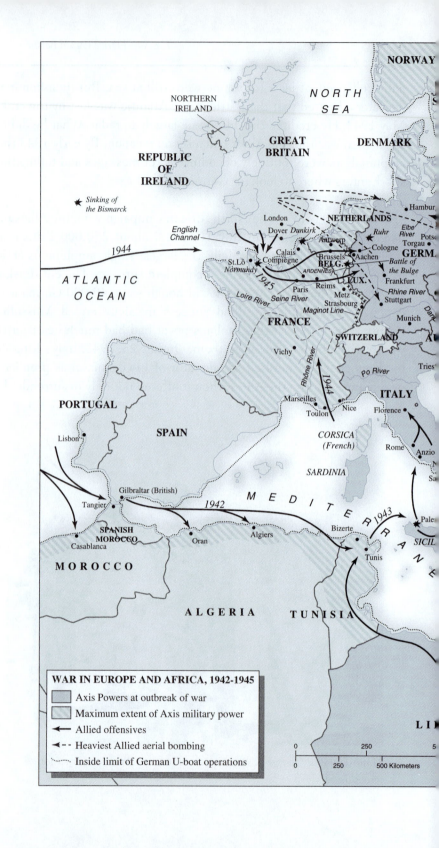

NORWAY

NORTH
SEA

NORTHERN
IRELAND

GREAT
BRITAIN

DENMARK

REPUBLIC
OF
IRELAND

✴ *Sinking of*
the Bismarck

London

English
Channel

Dover *Dunkirk*

NETHERLANDS

• Hambur

Elbe
River   Potsd

Antwerp

Ruhr

Torgau •

1944

Calais
St.Lô • Compiègne
Normandy   1945

Brussels   Aachen
BELG.

Cologne

GERM.

Battle of
the Bulge

ATLANTIC
OCEAN

LUX.

ARDENNES

Frankfurt

Paris

Reims

Metz

Rhine River

Loire River

Seine River

Strasbourg

Stuttgart

FRANCE

Maginot Line

Munich •

Dan

SWITZERLAND

A

Vichy •

Rhône River

Po River

Tries

1944

ITALY

PORTUGAL

SPAIN

Marseilles •
Toulon

Nice

Florence •

CORSICA
(*French*)

Rome •

Anzio

Lisbon •

SARDINIA

Sa

Gilbraltar (British)

M E D I T E R

1942

1943

Pale

Tangier •

Bizerte •

SICIL

SPANISH
MOROCCO

Oran •

Algiers •

R

Casablanca

A

N

E

Tunis •

MOROCCO

ALGERIA

TUNISIA

WAR IN EUROPE AND AFRICA, 1942-1945

Axis Powers at outbreak of war

Maximum extent of Axis military power

◀— Allied offensives

◀-- Heaviest Allied aerial bombing

········· Inside limit of German U-boat operations

L I

0   250   5

0   250   500 Kilometers

to switch sides in the war. Unfortunately, mutual suspicions prolonged talks until September 3, while the Germans poured reinforcements into Italy and seized key points. In the confusion the Italian army disintegrated, although most of the navy escaped to Allied ports. A few army units later joined the Allied effort, and many of the soldiers joined bands of partisans who fought behind the German lines. Mussolini, plucked from imprisonment by a daring German airborne raid, became head of a shadowy puppet government in northern Italy.

Allied landings on the mainland therefore did not turn into a walkover. The main landing at Salerno encountered heavy resistance, but American and British troops nevertheless secured beachheads within a week and soon captured Naples. The Germans had reduced much of the city to rubble, but the bay and port facilities were soon cleared and back in operation.

Rome was the next objective, but fighting stalled in the Appenine Mountains, where the Germans held the Allies through the winter of 1943–1944 in some of the most miserable, mud-soaked, and frostbitten fighting of the war. Finally, on June 4, 1944, the U.S. Fifth Army entered Rome. The capture of Rome provided only a brief moment of glory, however, for the long-awaited cross-Channel landing in France came

"Joe, yestiddy ya saved my life an' I swore I'd pay ya back. Here's my last pair of dry socks." *From Bill Mauldin's "Willie and Joe," a cartoon strip that appeared in the GI newspaper* Yank, *about two infantrymen slogging their way through the Italian campaign.*

two days later. Italy, always a secondary front, faded from the limelight of world attention.

STRATEGIC BOMBING OF EUROPE   Behind the long-postponed landings on the Normandy beaches lay months of preparation. While waiting, the United States Army Air Force (AAF) and the British Royal Air Force (RAF) carried the battle into the German-controlled areas of Europe. Early in 1943 Americans launched their first raid on Germany itself. Thereafter, American strategic bombers were full-fledged partners of the RAF in the effort to pound Germany into submission. The RAF, to cut losses during the hard days after the fall of France, had confined itself mostly to night raids, and continued now to specialize in nocturnal attacks. The Americans believed that they could be more effective with high-level daylight "precision" bombing. Between them the AAF and RAF kept German defenders on watch day and night.

Yet despite the widespread damage it caused, the strategic air offensive failed to cut severely into German production or, some contend, was not able to break civilian morale. German production in fact increased until the last few weeks of the war. Heavy Allied losses persisted through 1943. By the end of that year, however, jettisonable gas tanks permitted escort fighters to go as far as Berlin and back. In the "Big Week" of February 20–25, 1944, almost 4,000 American heavy bombers attacked aircraft plants in Germany. Badly damaged, the German aircraft industry continued to turn out planes to the end, but heavy losses of both planes and pilots forced the German Luftwaffe to conserve its strength and cease challenging every Allied mission.

Berlin, the air strategists assumed, was one target the German fighters would have to protect. But in March the capital became the object of repeated Allied raids, and the resultant losses left German fighters even more reluctant to rise to the bait. The horror at enemy attacks on civilians earlier in the war proved no barrier to a response in kind. Germany, Churchill said, was reaping the whirlwind it had started. With air supremacy assured, the Allies were free to concentrate on their primary urban and industrial targets, and when the time came, to provide cover for the Normandy landings. On April 14, 1944, General Eisenhower assumed control of the Strategic Air Forces for use in the Normandy landings, less than two months away. On D-Day he told the troops: "If you see fighting aircraft over you, they will be ours."

THE TEHERAN MEETING By the summer of 1943, the growing American presence in Britain, combined with successes in the Battle of the Atlantic and the strategic bombing, brought Churchill around on the idea of a cross-Channel invasion. Late in the fall he and Roosevelt finally had their first joint meeting with Joseph Stalin, in Teheran, Iran. Prior to the conference, when England and America gave assurance that a cross-Channel invasion was coming, the Soviets promised to enter the war against Japan after Germany's defeat.

On the way to the Teheran meeting with Stalin, Churchill and Roosevelt met in Cairo with China's General Chiang Kai-shek from November 22 to 26. The resultant Declaration of Cairo (December 1, 1943) affirmed that war against Japan would continue until Japan's unconditional surrender, that all Chinese territories taken by Japan would be restored to China, that Japan would lose the Pacific islands acquired after 1941, and that "in due course Korea shall become free and independent."

From November 28 to December 1, the Big Three leaders conferred in Teheran. Their chief subject was the planned invasion of France and a Russian offensive timed to coincide with it. Stalin repeated his promise to enter the war against Japan, and the three leaders agreed to create an international organization to maintain peace after the war. At further discussions in Cairo (December 4–6) Roosevelt and Churchill decided to put General Eisenhower in command of the cross-Channel invasion.

D-DAY AND AFTER In early 1944 General Dwight D. Eisenhower arrived in London to take command at Supreme Headquarters, Allied Expeditionary Forces (SHAEF). Already battle-tested in North Africa and the Mediterranean, he now faced the supreme test of planning and conducting Operation "Overlord," the cross-Channel assault on Hitler's "Atlantic Wall." Over a million American soldiers were already training along England's southern coast for the cross-Channel invasion. Of course, Hitler had been preparing for such an assault as well. German forces using captive Europeans for laborers had created what seemed to be an impregnable series of fortifications along the French coastline. Huge concrete blockhouses protected their artillery, and trenches and camouflage shielded their machine-gun nests. The Germans also used forced laborers to sow the beaches with 4 million mines interlaced with barbed wire and antitank obstacles.

General Dwight D. Eisenhower instructing paratroopers just before they board their airplanes to launch the D-Day assault.

The prospect of an amphibious assault against such defenses in a single huge battle unnerved some of the Allied planners. Churchill worried about "Channel tides running red with Allied blood." As D-Day approached, Eisenhower's chief of staff predicted only a 50-50 chance of success. Eisenhower had his doubts as well. He kept in his wallet a message for the press in case the invasion failed. It read: "My decision to attack at this time and place was based upon the best information available. If any blame or fault attaches to the attempt, it is mine alone."

Yet Operation Overlord succeeded. It did so largely because Eisenhower and the Allies surprised the Germans. They fooled Hitler's generals into believing that the invasion would come at Pas de Calais, on the French-Belgian border, where the English Channel was narrowest. Instead, the landings occurred in Normandy, almost 200 miles south. In April and May 1944, while the vast invasion forces made final preparations, the Allied air forces disrupted the transportation network of northern France, smashing railroads, bridges, and rolling stock. By early June all was ready, and D-Day fell on June 6, 1944.

On the evening of June 5, Eisenhower visited some of the 16,000 American paratroopers preparing to land behind the German lines to create chaos and disrupt communications. The men noticed his look of grave concern and tried to lift his spirits. "Now quit worrying, General," one of them said, "we'll take care of this thing for you." After the planes took off, Eisenhower returned to his car with tears in his eyes. "Well," he said quietly to his driver, "it's on." He knew that many of his troops would die within a few hours. The day before, Eisenhower's German counterpart, General Erwin Rommel, left his headquarters along the French coast to go to Berlin to see his family and meet with Hitler. As he departed, he confidently asserted that "there's not going to *be* an invasion. And if there is, then they won't even get off the beaches." When the American public learned that the invasion had been launched, routine activities gave way to anxious listening over the radio for reports from the front. Stores closed, baseball games and horse races were canceled, and church bells tolled across the country.

Airborne forces dropped behind the beaches during the night while planes and battleships pounded the coastal defenses. At dawn the invasion fleet of some 4,000 ships and 150,000 men (57,000 Americans)

The array of Allied forces at Normandy, June 1944.

filled the horizon off the Normandy coast. Overhead, thousands of Allied planes supported the invasion force. Sleepy German soldiers awoke to see the vast armada arrayed before them. Lieutenant Hans Heinze, a twenty-one-year-old veteran of the Russian front, could not believe his eyes. Wiping off his binoculars, he peered through the lifting fog and shouted to his messenger: *"Sie kommen!"* [They are coming!] He then scribbled a note for his headquarters and handed it to his messenger, thinking "They'll never believe it." Nearby, another German lookout peered through his binoculars and muttered, "That's not possible! That's not possible!" His aide retreated into their bunker to pray. For several hours, the local German commanders refused to believe that this was the real invasion. They interpreted the Normandy landings as merely a diversion for the "real" attack at Pas de Calais. When Hitler learned of the Allied landings, he boasted that "the news couldn't be better. As long as they were in Britain, we couldn't get at them. Now we have them where we can destroy them."

Despite Eisenhower's meticulous planning and the imposing array of Allied troops and firepower, the D-Day invasion almost failed. Cloud cover and German antiaircraft fire caused many of the paratroopers and glider pilots to miss their landing zones. Oceangoing landing craft delivered their troops to the wrong locations. Low clouds also led the Allied planes assigned to soften up the seaside defenses to drop their bombs too far inland. The naval bombardment was equally ineffective. Rough seas caused many of the soldiers to become seasick and capsized dozens of landing craft. Over a thousand men drowned. On Utah Beach the American invaders made it in against relatively light opposition, but farther east, on a four-mile segment designated Omaha Beach, bombardment had failed to take out German defenders, and the Americans were caught in heavily mined water. They then had to make it across a fifty-yard beach exposed to crossfire from concrete pillboxes before they could huddle under a seawall and begin to root out the defenders. In one rifle company 197 out of 205 men were killed or wounded within ten minutes.

A private remembered that he and his buddies at Omaha Beach were pinned down on the beach by relentless German gunfire. Finally, his colonel stood up and yelled, "There are only two kinds of people on this beach. Those who are dead and those who will die. Move in!" Such bold leadership worked. The private recalled that the colonel's words "had a

The landing at Normandy, D-Day, June 6, 1944.

galvanizing effect on me. I started to repeat them to the men around me. We pulled on our gear. We followed a path around the mines that had been inadvertently laid out for us by the wounded. It took five or six hours to reach the crest of the hill. I had seen a lot of terrible things by the time I got to the top." Still farther east, British forces had less difficulty on Gold, Juno, and Sword Beaches, but found themselves subjected to bitter counterattack by German forces. By nightfall there were some 5,000 killed or wounded Allied soldiers strewn across the sand and surf of Normandy.

German losses were even more incredible. Entire units were decimated or captured. Operation Overlord was the greatest military invasion in the annals of warfare, and the climactic battle of World War II. With the beachhead secured, the Allied leaders knew that victory was now in their grasp. "What a plan!" Churchill exclaimed to the British parliament. Stalin, who had been clamoring for the cross-Channel invasion for years, applauded the Normandy operation and heaped praise on the Allies. He declared that the "history of warfare knows no other like undertaking from the point of view of its scale, its vast conception and its orderly execution."

Within two weeks the Allies had landed a million troops, 556,000 tons of supplies, and 170,000 vehicles. They had seized a beachhead sixty miles wide and five to fifteen miles deep. They continued to pour men and supplies onto the beaches and to edge inland through the Norman marshes and hedgerows. On July 19, 1944, General Omar Bradley's troops took St. Lô, a transportation hub for roads and railroads into the heart of France. The German commanders advised withdrawal to defenses behind the Seine River, but a stubborn Hitler issued disastrous orders to contest every inch of land. General Erwin Rommel, convinced that all was lost, began to intrigue for a separate peace. Other like-minded officers, convinced that the war was hopeless, tried to kill Hitler at his headquarters on July 20, 1944, but the Führer survived the bomb blast, and hundreds of conspirators and suspects were tortured to death. Rommel was granted the option of suicide, which he took.

Meanwhile, the Führer's tactics brought calamity to the German forces in western France. On July 25 American units broke out westward into Brittany and eastward toward Paris. On August 15 a joint American-French invasion force landed on the French Mediterranean coast and raced up the Rhône Valley. German resistance in France collapsed. A Free French division, aided by American forces, had the honor of liberating Paris on August 25. Nazi forces retired pell-mell toward the German border, and by mid-September most of France and Belgium were cleared of enemy troops. By this time, the Americans were in Aachen, the old seat of Charlemagne's empire, the first German town to fall.

SLOWING MOMENTUM   Events had moved so much faster than expected, in fact, that the Allies were running out of gas. Neither their plans nor their supply system could keep up with the rapid movement of tanks and men. British and Canadian forces under General Bernard Montgomery had moved forward into Belgium, where they took Antwerp on September 4. From there, Montgomery argued, a quick fatal thrust toward Berlin could end things. On the right flank, General George Patton was just as sure he could take the American Third Army all the way to Berlin. Eisenhower reasoned, however, that a swift, narrow thrust into Germany would be cut off, counterattacked, and defeated. Instead he advocated advancing along a broad front. Prudence demanded getting his supply lines in order first, which required clearing out stubborn German forces and opening a supply channel to Antwerp—a long, hard battle that lasted until the end of November.

LEAPFROGGING TO TOKYO

Even in the Pacific, relegated to lower priority, Allied forces had brought the war within reach of the enemy homeland by the end of 1944. The war's first American offensive in fact had been in the southwest Pacific. There the Japanese, stopped at the Coral Sea and Midway, had thrust into the southern Solomons, and were building an airstrip on Guadalcanal from which they could attack transportation routes to Australia. On August 7, 1942, two months before the North Africa landings, the First Marine Division landed on Guadalcanal and seized the airstrip.

These quick victories, however, triggered a savage Japanese response. Reinforcements poured in via the "Tokyo Express" down the central channel, the Solomons "Slot," and the opposing navies challenged each other in a confusing series of battles that battered both so badly the sailors named the Savo Island Sound "Iron Bottom Bay." But while the Americans had lost heavily, they delivered such punishment to Japanese carrier groups, already battered at Midway, that the Japanese navy remained on the defensive for the rest of the war. The marines, helped by reinforcements, finally cleared Guadalcanal's steaming jungles of Japanese soldiers.

MACARTHUR IN NEW GUINEA   Meanwhile, American and Australian forces under General MacArthur had begun to push the Japanese out of their positions on the northern coast of New Guinea. These battles, fought through some of the hottest, most humid and mosquito-infested swamps in the world, bought advances at a heavy cost, but by the end of January 1943 the eastern tip of New Guinea was secured.

At this stage, American strategists made a critical decision. MacArthur proposed to move westward along the northern coast of New Guinea toward the Philippines and ultimately to Tokyo. Admiral Nimitz, with headquarters at Pearl Harbor, argued for a sweep through the islands of the central Pacific ultimately toward Formosa and China.

American medics assist a comrade on an island in the Admiralty group, March 1944.

In March 1943 the Combined Chiefs of Staff, meeting in Washington, agreed to MacArthur's plan and allotted resources for the purpose. Soon afterward they agreed that Nimitz should undertake his sweep too, for the central Pacific island complex would expose MacArthur's northern flank to a constant threat if it were left in Japanese hands. Another consideration in this decision was pitifully political: to keep both men satisfied, as well as the services they represented.

A new tactic expedited the movement. During the air Battle of the Bismarck Sea (March 2–3, 1943), American bombers sank eight Japanese troopships and ten warships bringing reinforcements. Thereafter the Japanese dared not risk sending transports to points under siege, making it possible to use the tactic of neutralizing Japanese strongholds with air and sea power, and moving on, leaving them to die on the vine. Some called it "leapfrogging," and Japanese leaders later acknowledged the strategy as a major cause of Allied victory. Meanwhile, in mid-April, before the offensive got under way, American fighter planes shot down a plane that code-breakers knew was carrying Admiral Yamamoto, Japan's naval commander and the planner of the Pearl Harbor attack. His death shattered Japanese morale.

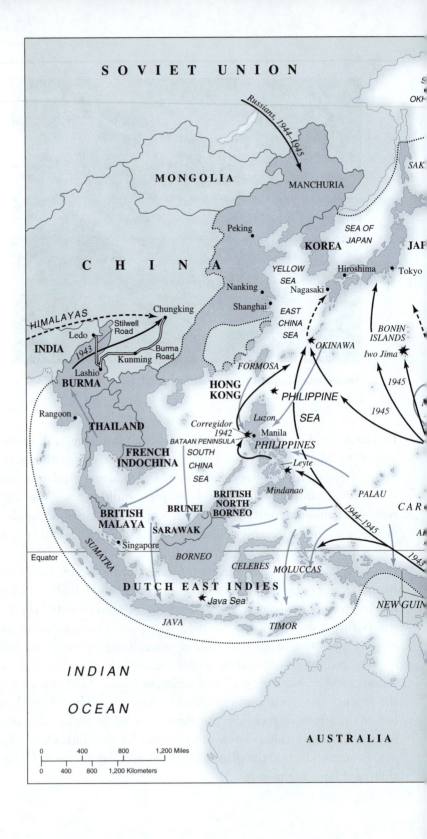

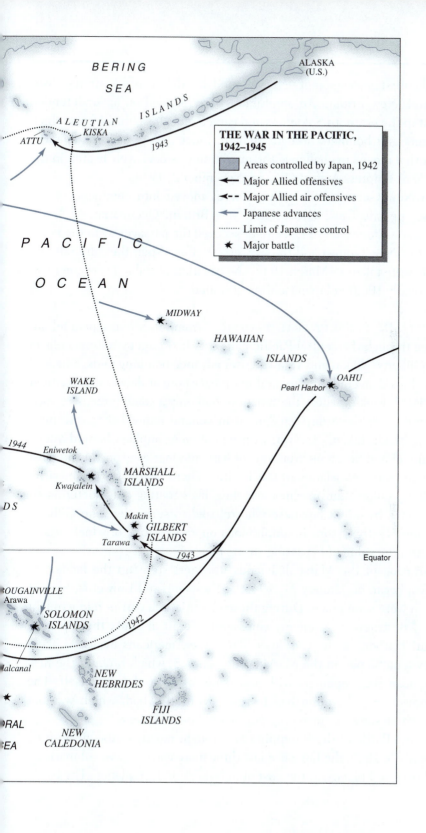

BERING SEA

ALASKA (U.S.)

ALEUTIAN ISLANDS

KISKA
1943

ATTU

THE WAR IN THE PACIFIC, 1942–1945

Areas controlled by Japan, 1942
Major Allied offensives
Major Allied air offensives
Japanese advances
Limit of Japanese control
★ Major battle

PACIFIC

OCEAN

MIDWAY

HAWAIIAN

ISLANDS

OAHU

Pearl Harbor ★

WAKE ISLAND

1944
Eniwetok

MARSHALL ISLANDS

Kwajalein

D S

Makin
★ GILBERT
Tarawa ★ ISLANDS

1943   Equator

BOUGAINVILLE
Arawa

SOLOMON ISLANDS

1942

alcanal

NEW HEBRIDES

FIJI ISLANDS

RAL

NEW CALEDONIA

EA

The first strong point left stranded by the leapfrog strategy was Rabaul, New Britain. An amphibious force landed on an undefended coast in the northern Solomons and carved out a beachhead from which fighters and bombers brought Rabaul under daily attack. A Japanese fleet that moved to challenge the operation was decisively beaten in the Battle of Empress Augusta Bay on November 2, 1943.

In New Guinea, MacArthur's forces moved into command of the coast opposite Cape Gloucester, New Britain. Occupation of Arawe and Cape Gloucester in December secured the passageway to the north coast of New Guinea and the western Pacific. When the Admiralty Islands were taken in March 1944, the isolation of Rabaul was complete and nearly 100,000 Japanese were stranded.

NIMITZ IN THE CENTRAL PACIFIC   Admiral Nimitz's parallel advance through the central Pacific had as its first target two tiny atolls in the Gilberts: Makin and Tarawa. After advance bombing raids, a fleet of 200 ships delivered infantry and marines ashore at dawn on November 20, 1943. Makin, where the Japanese had only a small force, was soon cleared; after three days an American general radioed the terse message, "Makin taken." Tarawa, with its concrete bunkers behind a long coral reef and beach obstructions of wire and logs, was one of the most heavily protected islands in the Pacific. There nearly 1,000 American soldiers, sailors, and marines lost their lives rooting out a determined resistance by 4,000 Japanese who refused to surrender. The Gilberts provided costly lessons in amphibious operations, one of which was to confirm the value of bypassing strong points.

Invasion of the Marshall Islands, the next step "up the ladder" to Tokyo, began on January 31, 1944, at Kwajalein and Eniwetok, both of which were soon taken. During these operations, a carrier raid wrought heavy destruction on enemy ships and aircraft at Truk, the Japanese "Pearl Harbor" in the Carolines. Then the Americans bypassed Truk. They took Saipan in the Marianas on June 15, which brought the new American B-29 bombers within striking distance of Japan itself. The Japanese navy therefore had to resist with all it had, which was not enough, despite its crash program to build new carriers.

In the Battle of the Philippine Sea, fought mostly in the air on June 19 and 20, 1944, the Japanese lost three more carriers, two submarines, and over 300 planes, at the cost of only 17 American planes. The battle secured the Marianas, and soon B-29s were winging their way to the first systematic bombings of the Japanese homeland. Defeat in the Marianas finally brought home to General Tojo the realization that the war was lost. On July 18, 1944, he and his entire cabinet resigned, and General Kuniaki Koiso became the new premier.

THE BATTLE OF LEYTE GULF   With New Guinea and the Marianas all but conquered, President Roosevelt met with General MacArthur and Admiral Nimitz in Honolulu on July 27–28, 1944, to decide the next major step. Previous plans had marked China as the essential springboard for invading Japan, but a Japanese offensive in April 1944 had taken most of the south China airfields from which American air power had operated. This strengthened MacArthur's standing opinion that the Philippines would provide a safer staging area than Formosa. Sentimental and political considerations, as well as military, tipped the decision his way. MacArthur made his move into the Philippines on October 20, landing first on the island of Leyte. Wading ashore behind the first landings, he issued an announcement: "People of the Philippines: I have returned. . . . Rally to me. . . . Let no heart be faint."

General Douglas MacArthur (center) *staging his triumphant return to the Philippines, October 1944.*

The Japanese, knowing that loss of the Philippines would cut them off from the oil and other essential resources of the East Indies, brought in fleets from three directions. The three encounters that resulted on October 25, 1944, came to be known collectively as the Battle of Leyte Gulf. It proved to be the largest naval engagement in history. The Japanese lost most of their remaining sea power and the ability to defend the Philippines. The battle also brought the first of the suicide attacks by Japanese pilots who crash-dived into American carriers, sinking one and seriously damaging others. The "Kamikaze" units, named for the "Divine Wind" that centuries ago had saved Japan from Mongol invasion, inflicted severe damage on the American navy.

A NEW AGE IS BORN

ROOSEVELT'S FOURTH TERM   In 1944, war or no war, the calendar dictated another presidential election. This time the Republicans turned to the former crime-fighter and New York governor, Thomas E. Dewey, as their candidate. Once again no Democratic challenger rose high enough to contest Roosevelt, but a fight did develop over the second spot on the ticket. Vice-President Henry Wallace had earned the enmity of both southern conservative and northern city bosses who feared his ties with labor. Roosevelt finally fastened on the compromise choice of Missouri senator Harry S. Truman.

Dewey ran under the same handicap as Landon and Willkie before him. He did not propose to dismantle Roosevelt's programs, but argued that it was time for younger men to replace the tired old leaders of the New Deal. Roosevelt betrayed decided signs of illness and exhaustion, but nevertheless carried the battle to the enemy. On November 7, 1944, Roosevelt was once again elected, this time by a popular vote margin of 25.6 million to 22 million and an electoral vote of 432 to 99.

CONVERGING FRONTS   After their quick sweep across France, the Allies lost momentum in the fall of 1944 and settled down to slugging at the frontiers of Germany. Along this line the armies fought it out all winter. The Germans sprang a surprise in the rugged Ardennes Forest, where the Allied line was thinnest. Hitting on December 16, 1944, under clouds that prevented air reconnaissance, the Germans advanced

An American infantry regiment marching through the ruins of Bensheim, Germany, March 1945.

along a fifty-mile bulge in Belgium and Luxembourg—hence the Battle of the Bulge. In ten days they penetrated nearly to the Meuse River on their way to Antwerp, but they stalled at Bastogne. Reinforced by the Allies just before it was surrounded, Bastogne held for six days against all the Germans could bring against it. On December 22 American general "Tony" McAuliffe gave his memorable answer to the demand for surrender: "Nuts." When a German major asked what the term meant, an American officer said, "It's the same as 'Go to Hell.' And I will tell you something else—if you continue to attack, we will kill every goddamn German that tries to break into this city." The American situation remained desperate until the next day when the clouds lifted, allowing Allied airpower to hit the Germans and drop in supplies. On December 26, American forces broke through to the relief of Bastogne, but it would be mid-January 1945 before the previous lines were restored.

Germany's sudden thrust upset Eisenhower's timetable, but the outcome shook Nazi power and morale. Their effort had weakened the eastern front, and in January 1945 the Russians began their final offensive. The destruction of Hitler's last reserve units at the Battle of the Bulge had also left open the door to Germany's heartland from the west.

By early March, the Allies had reached the banks of the Rhine nearly all the way from Holland to Switzerland. On March 6 they took Cologne, and the next day, by remarkable luck, the Allies seized the bridge at Remagen before the Germans could blow it up. Troops poured across the Rhine there and soon afterward at other points.

The Allies then encircled the Ruhr Valley, center of Germany's heavy industry. In quick sweeps the army closed the pincers on some 400,000 German soldiers in the region and pounded them into submission. By mid-April resistance there was over. Meanwhile the Soviet offensive had also reached Germany itself, after taking Warsaw on January 17 and Vienna on April 13.

With the British and American armies racing across western Germany and the Soviets moving in from the east, the attention of the war planners turned to Berlin. Churchill had grown suspicious of the Soviets and worried that if they arrived in Berlin first, they would gain dangerous leverage in deciding the postwar map of Europe. He told Eisenhower of his concerns and urged him to get to Berlin first. Eisenhower, however, refused to mix politics with military strategy. Berlin, he said, no longer was of military significance. His purpose remained the destruction of the enemy's ground forces. Churchill disagreed and appealed to Roosevelt, but the American leader, now seriously ill, left the decision to the Supreme Commander. Eisenhower then asked his trusted lieutenant, General Omar Bradley, to estimate what it would take to liberate Berlin before the Soviets. Bradley estimated that it would cost 100,000 Allied casualties, which he described as a "pretty stiff price to pay for a prestige objective." Eisenhower agreed, and they left Berlin for the Soviets to conquer.

YALTA AND THE POSTWAR WORLD   As the final offensives got under way, the Yalta Conference (February 4–11, 1945) brought the Big Three leaders together again in a czar's palace at the Crimean resort. While the focus at Teheran in 1943 had been on wartime strategy, it was now on the shape of the postwar world. Two aims loomed large in Roosevelt's thinking. One was the need to ensure that the Soviet Union join the war against Japan. The other was based on the lessons he drew from the previous world war. Just as the Neutrality Acts of the 1930s were designed with lessons from the previous war in mind, thoughts about the future were now influenced by memories of the interwar years. Chief among the mistakes to be remedied this time were the fail-

The Yalta Conference, *February 1945. Stalin* (right), *FDR* (center), *and Churchill* (left) *confer on the shape of the postwar world.*

ure of the United States to join the League of Nations and the failure of the Allies to maintain a united front against the German aggressors.

The Yalta meeting began by calling for a conference on world organization to be held in the United States, beginning on April 25, 1945. The Yalta conferees decided also that substantive decisions in the Security Council would require the acquiescence of its five permanent members: the United States, Britain, the Soviet Union, France, and China.

GERMANY AND EASTERN EUROPE With Hitler's "Thousand-Year Reich" stumbling to its doom, arrangements for the postwar governance of Germany had to be made. The war map dictated the basic pattern of occupation zones: the Soviets would control the east and the Western Allies would control the rich industrial areas of the west. Berlin, isolated within the Soviet zone, would be subject to joint occupation. At the behest of Churchill and Roosevelt, liberated France received an occupation zone along its border with Germany and also in Berlin. Similar arrangements were made for Austria, with Vienna like Berlin under joint occupation within the Soviet zone. Soviet demands for reparations of $20 billion, half of which would go to the Soviet Union, were referred to a Reparations Commission in Moscow. The commission never reached agreement, although the Soviets appropriated untold amounts of machinery and equipment from their occupation zone.

With respect to eastern Europe, where Soviet forces were advancing on a broad front, there was little the Western Allies could do to influence events. Roosevelt was inhibited by his wish to win Soviet cooperation in the fight against Japan and in the effort to build the proposed United Nations organization. Poland became the main focus of Western concern. Britain and France had gone to war in 1939 to defend Poland and now, six years later, the course of the war had left Poland's fate in the hands of the Soviets.

Events had long foreshadowed the outcome. Controversy over the Katyn Forest massacre of 1940, in which the Soviets had gunned down over 14,000 captured Polish officers, led the Soviets in 1943 to break relations with the Polish government-in-exile in London. When Soviet forces reentered Poland in 1944, they placed civil administration under a Committee of National Liberation in Lublin, a puppet regime representing few Poles. As Soviet troops reached the gates of Warsaw, the underground resistance in the city rose against the Nazi occupiers. The Polish underground, however, supported the Polish government-in-exile in London. The Soviets then stopped their offensive for two months while the Nazis wiped out thousands of Poles, potential rivals to their Lublin puppet government.

That optimism about postwar cooperation could survive such events was a triumph of hope over experience. The attitude was remotely reminiscent of 1919, when Wilson made concessions to win approval of the League of Nations in the hope that the League could later remedy any injustices that had crept into the peace settlement. But in any case the Western Allies at Yalta could do no more than acquiesce or stall. On the Soviet proposal to expand the Lublin Committee into a provisional government together with representatives of the London Poles, they acquiesced. On the issue of Poland's boundaries, they stalled. The Soviets proposed to keep eastern Poland, offering land taken from Germany as compensation. Roosevelt and Churchill accepted the proposal, but considered the western boundary at the Oder–Western Neisse Rivers only provisional. But the peace conference at which the western boundary of Poland was to be settled never took place because of later disagreements. The presence of the London Poles in the provisional government only lent a tone of legitimacy to a regime dominated by the Communists, who soon ousted their rivals.

At Yalta the Big Three promised to sponsor free elections, democratic governments, and constitutional safeguards of freedom throughout the rest of Europe. The Yalta Declaration of Liberated Europe reaffirmed faith in the principles of the Atlantic Charter and the United Nations, but in the end it made little difference. It may have postponed take-overs in eastern Europe for a few years, but before long Communist members of coalition governments had their hands on the levers of power and ousted the opposition. Aside from Czechoslovakia, though, the countries of eastern Europe lacked strong democratic traditions in any case. And Russia, twice invaded by Germany in the twentieth cen-tury, had reason for wanting buffer states between it and the Germans.

YALTA'S LEGACY   The Yalta agreements were later attacked for giving eastern Europe over to Soviet domination. But the course of the war shaped the actions at Yalta. By suppressing opposition in the occupied territories, moreover, the Soviets were not acting under the Yalta ac-cords, but in violation of them.

Perhaps the most bitterly criticized of the Yalta understandings was a secret agreement on the Far East, not made public until after the war. As the Big Three met, fighting still raged in the Philippines and Burma. The Combined Chiefs of Staff still estimated that Japan could hold out for eighteen months after the defeat of Germany. Costly campaigns lay ahead, and the atomic bomb was still an expensive gamble on the un-known. Roosevelt therefore accepted Stalin's demands on postwar arrangements in the Far East, subject technically to later agreement by Chiang Kai-shek. Stalin wanted continued Soviet control of Outer Mongolia through its puppet People's Republic there, acquisition of the Kurile Islands from Japan, and recovery of rights and territory lost after the Russo-Japanese War of 1905. Stalin in return promised to enter the war against Japan two or three months after the German defeat, to rec-ognize Chinese sovereignty over Manchuria, and to conclude a treaty of friendship and alliance with the Chinese Nationalists. Later Roosevelt's concessions would appear in a different light, but given their geograph-ical advantages in Asia as in eastern Europe, the Soviets were in a posi-tion to get what they wanted in any case.

THE THIRD REICH COLLAPSES   The collapse of Nazi resistance was imminent, but President Roosevelt did not live to join the celebra-tions. All through 1944 his health had been declining, and photographs from early 1945 reveal a very sick man. In the spring of 1945 he went to his second home in Warm Springs, Georgia, to rest up for the Charter Conference of the United Nations at San Francisco. On April 12, 1945, he suffered a cerebral hemorrhage, which brought sudden death.

The end of Hitler's Germany came less than a month later. The Allied armies rolled up almost unopposed to the Elbe River, where they met advance detachments of Soviets on April 25. Three days later Italian partisans caught and killed Mussolini and his mistress as they tried to flee. In Berlin, which was under siege by the Soviets, Hitler married his mistress, Eva Braun, in an underground bunker on the last day of April just before killing her and himself in a suicide pact. On May 2 Berlin fell to the Soviets. That same day German forces in Italy surrendered. Hitler's designated successor desperately tried to surrender to the Western Allies, but Eisenhower declined to act except in concert with the Soviets. Finally, on May 7, General Alfred Jodl, Chief of Staff of the German armed forces, signed an unconditional surrender in Allied headquarters at Reims, France. So ended the Thousand-Year Reich, little more than twelve years after its Führer came to power.

Massive celebrations of victory in Europe on V-E Day, May 8, 1945, were tempered by the tragedies that had engulfed the world: mourning

A Russian soldier raises the Soviet flag over the Reichstag after the conquest of Berlin, May 1945.

The celebration in New York's Times Square on V-E Day.

for the lost president and the death and mutilation of untold millions. Most shocking was the discovery of the Holocaust, scarcely believable until the Allied armies came upon the death camps in which the Nazis had sought to apply their "final solution" to the Jewish "problem": the wholesale extermination of some 6 million Jews along with more than 1 million others.

During the war, testimony from underground and neutral relief agencies had piled up growing evidence of the Nazis' systematic genocide against the Jews of Europe. Reports appeared in major American newspapers as early as 1942, but were nearly always buried on inside pages. The falsehoods of World War I propaganda had conditioned too many people to doubt all atrocity stories, and rumors of such horror seemed beyond belief.

American government officials, even some Jewish leaders, dragged their feet for fear that relief for Jewish refugees might stir up latent anti-Semitism at home. Under pressure, Roosevelt set up a War Refugee Board early in 1944, but with few resources at its disposal. It nevertheless managed to rescue about 200,000 European Jews and some 20,000 others. More might have been done by broadcasts warning people in Europe that Nazi "labor camps" were really death traps. The Allies rejected bombing the rail lines into the largest camp, Auschwitz in

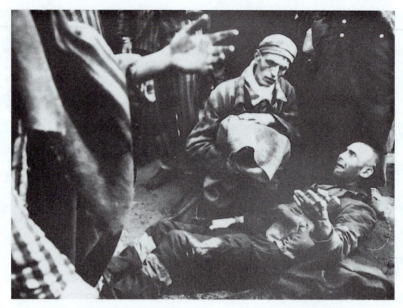

U.S. troops encounter surviving inmates at the Nazi concentration camp at Wobbelin, May 1945.

Poland, although American planes hit industries five miles away. And few refugees were accepted into the United States. The record was hardly one to inspire pride.

A GRINDING WAR   The sobering thought that the defeat of Japan remained to be accomplished cast a further pall over the victory celebrations in Europe. American forces continued to penetrate and disrupt the Japanese Empire in the early months of 1945, but at heavy cost. While fighting went on in the Philippines, on February 19, 1945, marine assault forces invaded Iwo Jima, a speck of volcanic rock 750 miles from Tokyo. It was needed to provide fighter escort for bombers over Japan and a landing strip for disabled B-29s. Nearly six weeks were required to secure an island five miles square from defenders hiding in an underground labyrinth. The cost was more than 20,000 American casualties, including nearly 7,000 dead.

The fight for Okinawa, beginning on Easter Sunday, April 1, was even bloodier. The largest island in the Ryukyu chain, Okinawa was large enough to afford a staging area for an invasion of Japan. It was the largest amphibious operation of the Pacific war, involving some 300,000 troops. From a beachhead on the northern coast the invaders fought their way south through rugged terrain. Desperate Japanese counterattacks inflicted heavy losses on land, by air, and by sea. Kamikaze planes attacked by the hundreds. Finally, the battleship *Yamato,* a survivor of Leyte Gulf, left Kyushu with nine other ships—the remnant of a once-great navy—with fuel only for a one-way trip, all that was available. American seaplanes intercepted the pathetic armada, sank the *Yamato* and two other warships, and badly damaged the rest. It was the end of the Japanese navy, but the fight for Okinawa raged until late June, when the bloody attrition destroyed any further Japanese ability to resist. The Japanese lost an estimated 140,000 dead. Casualties also included about 42,000 Okinawans.

When resistance on Okinawa collapsed, the Japanese emperor instructed his new premier to seek peace terms. Washington had picked this up by decoding Japanese messages, which suggested either an effort to avoid unconditional surrender or perhaps just a stall.

THE ATOMIC BOMB   By this time, however, a new force had changed all strategic calculations: during the summer of 1945 President Truman learned of the first successful test explosion of an atomic bomb, the result of several years of intensive work. The strands of scientific development that led to the bomb ironically ran back to Germany. Except for the Nazi bigotry that drove scientists into exile, Germany might well have developed the atomic bomb first. Early in 1939 a scientific journal revealed that the uranium atom had been split in Berlin; experiments in Denmark and the United States soon confirmed the finding. On October 11, 1939, President Roosevelt learned of the matter when an emissary delivered a letter from Albert Einstein and a memorandum explaining the potential of nuclear fission and warning that the Germans might develop a bomb first. Roosevelt quickly set up a committee to coordinate information in the field, and in 1940 some army and navy funds were diverted into research that grew ultimately into the $2 billion top-secret Manhattan Project.

On December 2, 1942, Dr. Enrico Fermi and other scientists achieved the first atomic chain reaction in a squash-court-turned-laboratory at the University of Chicago, removing any remaining doubts of the bomb's feasibility. Gigantic plants sprang up at Oak Ridge, Tennessee, and

Hanford, Washington, to provide materials for atomic bombs, while a group of physicists under Dr. J. Robert Oppenheimer worked out the scientific and technical problems of bomb construction in a laboratory at Los Alamos, New Mexico. On July 16, 1945, the first atomic fireball rose from the desert. Oppenheimer said later that in the observation bunker "A few people laughed, a few people cried, most people were silent." Colleagues crowded forward with their congratulations: "Oppie," said one, "now we're all sons of bitches."

The question of how to use this awful new weapon had already come before a committee of military and political officials and scientists. Some of the scientists, awed at the ghastly prospect, favored a demonstration in a remote area, but the decision went for military use because only two bombs were available, and even those might misfire. More consideration was given to the choice of targets. Four Japanese cities had been reserved from conventional bombing as potential targets. After Secretary of War Stimson eliminated Kyoto, Japan's ancient capital and center of many national and religious treasures, and Kokura, priority went to Hiroshima, a port city of 400,000 people in southern Japan, which was a major assembly point for Japanese naval convoys and a center of war industries, headquarters of the Second General Army, and command center for the homeland's defenses. This met Truman's guidelines. He had written that only military personnel and installations rather than "women and children" should be targeted. Of course, he had no idea that the bomb would destroy virtually an entire city.

On July 25, 1945, President Truman, then at the Big Three Conference in Potsdam, Germany, ordered the bomb dropped if Japan did not surrender before August 3. Although an intense scholarly debate has emerged over the decision to drop the atomic bomb, Truman never considered not using it at the earliest opportunity. He later stressed: "Let there be no mistake about it. I regarded the bomb as a military weapon and never had any doubt that it should be used." He was convinced that using the atomic bomb would in the end save lives by avoiding an American invasion against defenders who would fight like "savages, ruthless, merciless, and fanatic."

The ferocious Japanese defense of Okinawa had convinced American military planners that an amphibious invasion of Japan itself, scheduled to begin on November 1, 1945, could cost as many as 250,000 Allied casualties and even more Japanese losses. Moreover, some 100,000 Allied prisoners of war being held in Japan were to be executed whenever an invasion began. It is important to remember as well that the bombing of cities and the consequent killing of civilians had become accepted military practice during 1945. Once the Japanese navy was destroyed, American ships were able to roam the Japanese coastline, shelling targets on shore. American planes bombed at will and mined the waters of the Inland Sea. Tokyo, Nagoya, and other major cities were devastated by firestorms created by incendiary bombs. The prevalence of wooden structures in earthquake-prone Japan made the incendiary raids even more deadly. The firebomb raids on Tokyo on a single night in March 1945 killed over 100,000 civilians and left over a million people homeless. By July more than sixty of Japan's largest cities had been firebombed, resulting in 500,000 deaths and 13 million civilians left homeless. The use of atomic bombs on Japanese cities was thus seen as a logical next step in an effort to end the war without an invasion of Japan. As it turned out, American scientists greatly underestimated the physical effects of the atomic bomb. They predicted that 20,000 people would be killed.

On July 26 the heads of the American, British, and Russian governments issued the Potsdam Declaration demanding that Japan surrender or face "prompt and utter destruction." The deadline passed, and on August 6, 1945, a B-29 named the *Enola Gay,* with a crew commanded by Colonel Paul W. Tibbetts, took off at 2 A.M. from the island of Tinian and headed for Hiroshima. At 8:15 in the morning, flying at 31,600 feet, the *Enola Gay* released the five-ton uranium bomb nicknamed "Little Boy." Forty-three seconds later, as the *Enola Gay* turned sharply to avoid the blast, the bomb tumbled to an altitude of 1,900 feet, where it exploded as planned with the force of 15,000 tons of TNT. A blinding flash of light was followed by a fireball towering to 40,000 feet. The tail gunner on the *Enola Gay* described the scene: "It's like bubbling molasses down there . . . the mushroom is spreading out . . . fires are springing up everywhere . . . it's like a peep into hell."

The shock wave, firestorm, cyclonic winds, and radioactive rain killed some 80,000 people, including thousands of Japanese soldiers assigned to the Second General Army headquarters and 23 American prisoners of war housed in the city. Dazed survivors wandered the streets, so painfully burned that their skin began to peel in large strips. By the end of the year, the death toll had reached 140,000 as the effects

A charred watch marks the moment of nuclear conflagration in Hiroshima, August 6, 1945.

of radiation burns and infection took their toll. In addition, 70,000 buildings were destroyed, and four square miles of the city turned to rubble.

In the United States, Americans greeted the first news with elation: it promised a quick end to the long nightmare of war. "No tears of sympathy will be shed in America for the Japanese people," the *Omaha World Herald* predicted. "Had they possessed a comparable weapon at Pearl Harbor, would they have hesitated to use it?" Others were more circumspect. "Yesterday," journalist Hanson Baldwin wrote in the *New York Times*, "we clinched victory in the Pacific, but we sowed the whirlwind." Only later would people realize that it marked the start of a more enduring nightmare, the atomic age.

Two days after the Hiroshima bombing, an opportunistic Russia, eager to share in the spoils of victory, hastened to enter the war. On August 9, the second atomic bomb exploded over the port city of Nagasaki, a shipbuilding and torpedo-factory center, killing 36,000 people. That night the emperor urged his cabinet to accept the inevitable and surrender on the sole condition that he remain as sovereign. The next day the United States government, to facilitate surrender and an orderly transition, announced its willingness to let him keep the throne, but under the authority of an Allied Supreme Commander. Frantic exchanges ended with Japanese acceptance on August 14, 1945, when the emperor himself broke precedent to record a radio message announcing the surrender to his people. Even then a last-ditch palace revolt had to be squashed.

On September 2, 1945, General MacArthur and other Allied representatives accepted Japan's formal surrender on board the battleship *Missouri*. MacArthur then settled in at his headquarters across from the Imperial Palace.

THE FINAL LEDGER

Thus ended the most deadly conflict in human history. No effort to tabulate a ledger of death and destruction can ever take the full measure of the war's suffering, or hope to be more than an informed guess as to the numbers involved. One estimate has it that 70 million in all fought in the war, at a cost in human lives of 25 million military dead and more than 24 million civilian dead. Material costs were also enormous, perhaps $1 trillion in military expenditures and twice that in property losses. The Soviet Union suffered the greatest losses of all, over 13 million military deaths, over 7 million civilians dead, and at least 25 million left homeless. World War II was more costly for the United States than any other of the country's foreign wars: 292,000 battle deaths and 114,000 other deaths. But in proportion to population, the United States suffered a far smaller loss than any of the major Allies or enemies, and American territory escaped the devastation visited on so many other parts of the world.

World War II had profound effects on American life and society. Mobilization for war stimulated a phenomenal increase in American productivity and brought full employment, thus ending the Great Depression and laying the foundation for a new era of unprecedented prosperity. New technologies and products developed for military purposes—radar, computers, electronics, plastics and synthetics, jet engines, rockets, atomic energy—soon began to transform the private sector as well. And new opportunities for women as well as for blacks and other minorities set in motion changes that would culminate in the civil rights movement of the 1960s and the feminist movement of the 1970s.

The Democratic party benefited from the war effort by solidifying its control of both the White House and Congress. The dramatic expansion of the federal government occasioned by the war continued after 1945. Presidential authority and prestige increased enormously at the expense of congressional and state power. The isolationist sentiment in foreign relations that had been so powerful in the 1920s and 1930s fell into disrepute as the United States emerged from the war with global responsibilities and interests.

The war's end opened a new era for the United States in the world arena. It accelerated the growth of American power while devastating all other world powers, leaving the United States economically and militarily the strongest nation on earth. But the Soviet Union, despite its human and material losses, emerged from the war with much new territory and enhanced influence, making it the greatest power on the whole Eurasian landmass. Just a little over a century after Frenchman Alexis de Tocqueville had predicted that western Europe would come to be overshadowed by the power of the United States and Russia, his prophecy had come to pass.

MAKING CONNECTIONS

- Compare the impact of World War II on the home front to that of World War I, especially the effects of war on race and gender relations.

- The growing domestic conservatism of the war years continued into the 1950s, a topic discussed in the next chapter.

- Dwight D. Eisenhower's success as American general and Allied leader led to his nomination and election as president in 1952. Compare Eisenhower's experience to that of General Grant in and after the Civil War, and to the political experiences of other American military leaders.

FURTHER READING

John Keegan's *The Second World War* (1990) surveys the European conflict in its entirety, while Charles B. MacDonald's *The Mighty Endeavor: The American War in Europe* (rev. ed., 1992) concentrates on American involvement. Roosevelt's wartime leadership is analyzed in Eric Larrabee's *Commander in Chief: Franklin Delano Roosevelt, His Lieutenants and Their War* (1987).

Books on specific campaigns in Europe include Stephen E. Ambrose's *D Day, June 6, 1944: The Climactic Battle of World War II* (1994) and Charles B. MacDonald's *A Time for Trumpets: The Untold Story of the Battle of the Bulge* (rev. ed., 1997).

For the war in the Far East, see John Costello's *The Pacific War, 1941–1945* (1983), Ronald H. Spector's *Eagle against the Sun: The American War with Japan* (1984), John Dower's award-winning *War Without Mercy: Race and Power in the Pacific War* (1986), and Dan van der Vat's *The Pacific Campaign: The U.S.–Japanese Naval War, 1941–1945* (1992).

An excellent overview of the war's effects on the home front is Michael C. C. Adams's *The Best War Ever: America and World War II* (1993). The government's effort to use movies to influence public opinion is described in Clayton R. Koppes and Gregory D. Black's *Hollywood Goes to War: How Politics, Profits and Propaganda Shaped World War II Movies* (1987).

Susan M. Hartmann's *The Home Front and Beyond: American Women in the 1940s* (1982) and Karen Anderson's *Wartime Women: Sex Roles, Family Relations, and the Status of Women during World War II* (1981) treat the new working environment for women. Neil Wynn looks at the participation of blacks in *The Afro-American and the Second World War* (rev. ed., 1993). The story of the oppression of Japanese Americans is told in Peter Irons's *Justice at War* (1983) and David J. O'Brien and Stephen S. Fugita's *The Japanese American Experience* (1993).

A sound introduction to American diplomacy during the conflict can be found in Gaddis Smith's *American Diplomacy during the Second World War, 1941–1945* (2nd ed., 1985). To understand the role that Roosevelt played in policy-making, consult Warren F. Kimball's *The Juggler: Franklin Roosevelt as Wartime Statesman* (1991). Diane Shaver Clemens is critical of Roosevelt in *Yalta* (1970).

The issues and events that led to the deployment of atomic weapons are addressed in Gregg Herken's *The Winning Weapon: The Atomic Bomb in the Cold War, 1945–1950* (1980) and Martin J. Sherwin's *A World Destroyed: The Atomic Bomb and the Grand Alliance* (1975). Gar Alperovitz's *Atomic Diplomacy: Hiroshima and Potsdam* (2nd ed., 1995) details how the bomb helped shape American postwar policy.

PART SEVEN

THE AMERICAN AGE

Amid the joyous celebrations of the Allied victory in the Second World War, one commentator announced that the "American era was at hand." Such a declaration was filled with chauvinism, yet it contained a kernel of truth. The United States emerged from World War II the preeminent military and economic power in the world. At the end of the war, the United States enjoyed a commanding position in international trade and was the only nation in possession of the atomic bomb. While much of Europe and Asia struggled to recover from the horrific physical devastation of the war, the United States emerged virtually unscathed, its economic infrastructure intact and operating at peak efficiency. Jobs that were scarce in the 1930s were now available for the taking. By 1955 the United States, with only 6 percent of the world's population, was producing half of the world's goods. American capitalism not only demonstrated its economic strength, it became a dominant cultural force as well. In Europe, Japan, and elsewhere, American products and forms of entertainment and fashion attracted excited attention.

Yet the specter of the "cold war" cast a pall over the buoyant revival of the American economy after World War II. The ideological contest with the Soviet Union and Communist China produced numerous foreign crises and sparked a domestic witch-hunt for Communists that far surpassed earlier episodes of political and social repression in the nation's history.

There was widespread acceptance in both major political parties of the geopolitical assumptions embedded in the ideological cold war with international communism. Both Republican and Democratic presidents affirmed the need to "contain" the spread of Communist influence around the world. This bedrock assumption eventually embroiled the United States in a tragic war in Southeast Asia that destroyed Lyndon Johnson's presidency and revived neo-isolationist sentiments. The Vietnam War also was the catalyst for a countercultural movement in which young idealists of the "baby-boom" generation sought alternatives to a government and a society that in their eyes had become oppressive and corrupt. The youth revolt provided energy for many overdue social reforms, including the civil rights and environmental movements, but it also contributed to an array of social ills, from street riots to drug abuse to sexual license. The social upheavals of the 1960s and early 1970s provoked a conservative backlash that overreached itself as well. In their efforts to restore "law and order," mayors failed to protect civil liberties in their cities. Richard Nixon's para-

noid reaction to his critics led to the destruction of his presidency as a result of the Watergate investigations.

Through all of this turmoil, however, the basic premises of welfare state capitalism that Franklin Roosevelt had instituted with his New Deal programs remained essentially intact. With only a few exceptions, both Republicans and Democrats after 1945 came to accept the notion that the federal government must assume greater responsibility for the welfare of individuals than had heretofore been the case. Even Ronald Reagan, a sharp critic of liberal social-welfare programs, recognized the need for the federal government to provide a "safety net" for those who could not help themselves.

Yet this fragile consensus about public policy began to disintegrate in the late 1980s amid stunning international developments and less visible domestic developments. The internal collapse of the Soviet Union and the disintegration of European communism surprised observers and sent policy makers scurrying to respond to a post–cold war world in which the United States remained the only legitimate superpower. After forty-five years, American foreign policy was no longer keyed to a single adversary, and world politics lost its bipolar quality. During the early 1990s, the European Community finally coalesced, the two Germanies reunited, apartheid in South Africa finally ended, and Israel and the Palestinians signed a heretofore unimaginable peace treaty.

At the same time, American foreign policy began to focus less on military power and more on economic competition and technological development. In those arenas, Japan and a reunited Germany challenged the United States for preeminence. By reducing the public's fear of nuclear annihilation, the ending of the cold war also reduced public interest in foreign affairs. The presidential election of 1992 was the first since 1936 in which foreign policy issues played virtually no role. This was an unfortunate development, for post–cold war world affairs remained volatile and dangerous. The implosion of Soviet communism unleashed a series of ethnic, nationalist, and separatist conflicts. In the face of inertia among other governments and pleas for assistance, the United States found itself being drawn into crises in faraway lands such as Bosnia, Rwanda, Somalia, and Chechnya.

As the new multipolar world careened toward the end of a century and the start of a new millennium, fault lines began to appear in the American social and economic landscape. A gargantuan federal debt and rising *annual deficits threatened to bankrupt a nation that was becoming top-heavy with retirees. Without fully realizing it, much less appreciating its cascading consequences, the American population was becoming disproportionately old. Those aged ninety-five to ninety-nine doubled between 1980 and 1990, and the number of centenarians increased 77 percent. The proportion of the population aged sixty-five and older rose steadily during the 1990s. By the year 2000, half of the elderly population would be over the age of seventy-five. This demographic fact harbored profound social and political implications. It exerted increasing stress on health care costs, nursing home facilities, and the very survival of the Social Security system.*

At the same time that the gap between young and old was increasing, so, too, was the disparity between rich and poor. This trend threatened to stratify a society already experiencing rising levels of racial and ethnic tension. Between 1960 and 1990, the gap between the richest 20 percent of the population and the poorest 20 percent doubled. Over 20 percent of all American children in 1990 lived in poverty, and the infant mortality rate rose. The infant death rate in Japan was less than half that in the United States. Despite the much-ballyhooed "war on poverty" programs initiated by Lyndon Johnson and continued in one form or another by all of his successors, the chronically poor in 1996 were more numerous and more bereft of hope than in 1964. Yet by the end of the century, a prolonged period of economic growth and a runaway stock market revived the myth of perennial prosperity.

31 THE FAIR DEAL AND CONTAINMENT

CHAPTER ORGANIZER

This chapter focuses on:

- the economic, social, and political aftermath of World War II and the origins and early development of the cold war.

- Truman's Fair Deal program.

- U.S. involvement in the Korean War.

- the sources of McCarthyism.

*N*o sooner did the Second World War end than a cold war began. The uneasy wartime alliance between the United States and the Soviet Union collapsed completely by the fall of 1945. The two strongest nations to emerge from the carnage of World War II could not bridge their ideological differences over such basic issues as essential human rights, individual liberties, and religious beliefs. Mutual suspicion and a race to gain influence and control over the so-called Third World countries further polarized the two nations. The defeat of Japan and Germany created power vacuums that sucked the Soviet Union and America into an unrelenting war of words fed by clashing strategic interests. At the same time, the destruction of western Europe and the exhaustion of its peoples led to anticolonial uprisings in Asia and Africa that threatened to strip Britain and France of their once-great empires. The postwar world was thus an unstable one in which international tensions shaped the contours of domestic politics and culture as well as foreign adventures.

Demobilization under Truman

TRUMAN'S UNEASY START   "Who the hell is Harry Truman?" Roosevelt's chief of staff asked the president in the summer of 1944. The question was on more lips when, after less than twelve weeks as vice-president, Harry Truman took the presidential oath on April 12, 1945. Clearly he was not Franklin Roosevelt, and that was one of the burdens he would bear. "With Roosevelt you'd have known he was President even if you hadn't been told," a journalist wrote years later. "He looked imperial, and he acted that way, and he talked that way. Harry Truman, for God's sake, looked and acted and talked like—well, like a failed haberdasher"—which he was.

Roosevelt and Truman came from quite different backgrounds. For Truman there had been no inherited wealth, no early contact with the great and near-great, no European travel, no Groton, no Harvard—indeed, no college at all. Born in 1884 in western Missouri, Truman grew up in Independence, once the staging area for the Oregon and Santa Fe Trails, but by the time of his youth an unglamorous town near Kansas City. Too nearsighted to join in the activities of other boys, Truman became bookish and withdrawn. But after high school he moved to his grandmother's farm, spent a few years working in Kansas City banks, and grew into an outgoing young man.

During World War I, Truman served in France as captain of an artillery battery. Afterward he and a partner went into the clothing business, but it failed in the recession of 1922, and Truman then became a professional politician under the tutelage of Kansas City's Democratic machine. Elected county judge in 1922, he was defeated in 1924 and elected once again in 1926. In 1934 Missouri sent him to the United States Senate, where he remained fairly obscure until he became chairman of the committee to investigate war mobilization.

Something about Harry Truman evoked the spirit of Andrew Jackson: his decisiveness, his feisty character, his family loyalty. But that was a side of the man that the American people came to know only as he settled into the presidency. On his first full day as president, he remained awestruck. "Boys, if you ever pray, pray for me now," he told a group of reporters. "I don't know whether you fellows ever had a load of hay fall on you, but when they told me yesterday what had happened, I felt like the moon, the stars and all the planets had fallen on me."

Truman favored much of the New Deal and was even prepared to extend its scope, but at the same time was uneasy with many New Dealers. "He was not of their clan and kidney," one newsman put it. Within ninety days he had replaced much of the Roosevelt cabinet with his own choices. On the whole they were more conservative in outlook and included several mediocrities. Truman suffered the further handicap of seeming to be a caretaker for the remainder of Roosevelt's term. Few, including Truman himself at first, expected him to run in 1948.

Truman gave one significant clue to his domestic policies on September 6, 1945, when he sent Congress a comprehensive peacetime program that in effect proposed to continue and enlarge the New Deal. Its twenty-one points included expansion of unemployment insurance, a higher minimum wage, a permanent Fair Employment Practices Commission, slum clearance and low-rent housing programs, regional development of the nation's river valleys, and a public-works program. "Not even President Roosevelt asked for so much at one sitting," said the House Republican leader. "It's just a plain case of out-dealing the New Deal." Beset by other problems, Truman soon saw his new domestic proposals mired in disputes over the transition to a peacetime economy.

CONVERTING TO PEACE The raucous celebrations that greeted Japan's surrender signaled the habitual American response to victory: a rapid demobilization and a return to more congenial pursuits. The public demanded that the president and Congress bring the boys home. By 1947 the total armed forces were down from 12 million to 1.5 million. In his memoirs Truman termed this "the most remarkable demobilization in the history of the world, or 'disintegration' if you want to call it that." It was in fact the same pattern that had prevailed since the days of the colonial wars, and it went on for several years, despite mounting

The Eldridge General Store, Fayette County, Illinois. *Postwar America quickly demobilized, turning its attention from rationing to the pursuit of abundance.*

international tensions. By early 1950 the army had fallen to 600,000 men.

The veterans eagerly returned to schools, new jobs, wives, and babies. Population growth, which had dropped off sharply in the depression decade, now soared: the population increase of 9 million during the 1930s exploded to a growth of 19 million in the 1940s. Americans born during this postwar period composed what came to be known as the "baby-boom" generation, and that generation became a dominant force in the nation's social and cultural life.

The end of the war, with its sudden demobilization and reconversion to a peacetime economy, brought sharp dislocations but not the postwar depression that many feared. Several shock absorbers cushioned the economic impact of demobilization: unemployment pay and other Social Security benefits; the Servicemen's Readjustment Act of 1944, known as the "GI Bill of Rights," under which $13 billion was spent for veterans on education, vocational training, medical treatment, unemployment insurance, and loans for building houses or going into business; and, most important, the pent-up demand for consumer goods that was fueled by wartime deprivation. Instead of sinking into depression, businesses seized upon options to buy up properties from the Defense Plant Corporation and began a spurt of private investment in new plants and equipment. The gross national product first exceeded the 1929 level in 1940, when it reached $101 billion, but by annual increases (except in 1946) it had grown to $347 billion by 1952, Truman's last full year in office.

CONTROLLING INFLATION The most acute economic problem Truman faced was not depression but inflation. Released from wartime restraints, the demands of business owners and workers alike combined to frustrate efforts at controlling rising prices. Truman endorsed wage increases to sustain purchasing power. He felt that there was "room in the existing price structure" for business to grant such pay increases, a point management refused to concede. Within six weeks of war's end, corporations confronted a wave of union demands.

A series of strikes followed. The United Automobile Workers walked out on General Motors, with Walter Reuther, head of the union's General Motors division, arguing that the company could afford a 30 percent pay hike without raising car prices. (The company denied this claim.) A strike in the steel industry finally gave rise to a formula for settling most of the disputes. President Truman suggested a pay raise of 18½¢ per hour, which the Steel Workers accepted but management refused. To break the logjam, the administration in 1946 agreed to let the company increase its prices. That pattern then became the basis for settlements in other industries, and also set a dangerous precedent of price-wage spirals that would plague consumers in the postwar world.

Major disputes soon developed in the coal and railroad industries. John L. Lewis of the United Mine Workers wanted more than the 18½¢-per-hour wage increase. He also demanded improved safety regulations and a union health and welfare fund financed by a royalty on coal. Mine owners refused the demands, and a strike followed. The government used its wartime powers to seize the mines; Truman's interior secretary then accepted nearly all the union's demands.

In the rail dispute, the unions and management reached an agreement, but two brotherhoods, the trainmen and locomotive engineers, held out for rule changes as well as higher wages. Truman seized the railroads and won a five-day postponement of a strike. But when the union leaders refused to budge further, the president went before Congress in a burst of fury against their "obstinate arrogance" and demanded authority to draft strikers into the armed forces. In the midst of the speech, he learned that the strike had been settled, but after telling a jubilant Congress, he went on with his message. The House passed a bill including the president's demands, but with the strike settled, it died in the Senate.

Into 1946 the wartime Office of Price Administration (OPA) managed to maintain some restraint on price increases while gradually ending the rationing of most goods, and Truman asked for a one-year renewal of its powers. But during the late winter and spring of 1946, business leaders mounted a massive campaign against price controls and other restraints. Just a week before controls were to expire at the end of June, Congress passed a bill to continue the OPA, but with such cumbersome new procedures as to cripple the agency. Truman vetoed the bill, allowing controls to end. Congress finally extended controls in late July, but by then the cost of living had already gone up by 6 percent. When the OPA restored controls on meat prices, farmers responded by withholding beef from the market until they succeeded in forcing a reversal in October. After the congressional elections of 1946, Truman gave up the battle, ending all price controls except on rents, sugar, and rice.

PARTISAN COOPERATION AND CONFLICT The legislative history of 1946 was not all deadlock and frustration. Amid the turmoil Congress and the administration worked out two new departures, the Employment Act of 1946 and the Atomic Energy Commission. A program of "full employment" had been a Democratic promise in the campaign of 1944, a pledge reaffirmed by Truman in 1945. The administration backed an employment bill proposing that the government make an annual estimate of the investment and production necessary to ensure full employment, and key its spending to that estimate in order to raise production to full-employment levels. Conservatives objected to what they denounced as carte blanche for deficit spending, and proposed a nonpartisan commission to advise the president on the economy. Compromise resulted in the Employment Act of 1946, which dropped the commitment to full employment and set up a three-member Council of

Economic Advisers to make appraisals of the economy and advise the president in an annual economic report. A new congressional Joint Committee on the Economic Report would propose legislation.

With regard to the new force that atomic scientists had released upon the world, there was little question that the public welfare required the control of atomic energy through a governmental monopoly. Disagreements over military versus civilian control were resolved when Congress, in 1946, created the civilian Atomic Energy Commission. The president alone was given power to order the use of atomic weapons in warfare. Subject to "the paramount objective of assuring the common defense and security," the act declared a policy of peaceful development "so far as practicable . . . toward improving the public welfare, increasing the standard of living, strengthening free competition in private enterprise, and promoting world peace." Technical problems and high costs, however, would delay for two decades the construction of nuclear power plants.

As congressional elections approached in the fall of 1946, public discontent ran high, most of it against the administration. Truman caught the blame for labor problems from both sides. A speaker at the CIO national convention tagged Truman "the No. 1 strikebreaker," while much of the public, angry at striking unions, also blamed the strikes on the White House. In 1946 Truman fired Henry A. Wallace as secretary of commerce in a disagreement over foreign policy, thus offending the Democratic left. At the same time, Republicans charged that Communists had infiltrated the government. Republicans had a field day coining slogans. "To err is Truman" was credited to Martha Taft, wife of Senator Robert Taft. But most effective was the simple question, "Had enough?" attributed to a Boston ad agency: their message was that the Democrats had simply been in control too long. In the elections Republicans won majorities in both houses of Congress for the first time since 1928.

Given the head of steam built up against organized labor, the new Republican Congress sought to curb the power of unions. The result was the Taft-Hartley Act of 1947, which banned the closed shop (in which nonunion workers could not be hired) but permitted a union shop (in which workers newly hired were required to join the union), unless banned by state law. It included provisions against "unfair" union practices such as secondary boycotts, jurisdictional strikes (by one union to exclude another from a given company or field), "featherbedding" (pay for work not done), refusal to bargain in good faith, and contributing to political campaigns. Unions' political action committees were allowed to function, but on a voluntary basis only, and union leaders had to take oaths that they were not members of the Communist party. Employers were permitted to sue unions for breaking contracts, to petition the National Labor Relations Board (NLRB) for votes for or against the use of specific unions as collective-bargaining agents, and to speak freely during union campaigns. The act forbade strikes by federal employees, and imposed a "cooling-off" period of eighty days on any strike that the president found to be dangerous to the national health or safety.

Truman's veto of the Taft-Hartley bill, which unions called the "slave-labor act," restored his credit with labor, and many unionists who had gone over to the Republicans in 1946 returned to the Democrats. But the bill passed over Truman's veto. Its most severe impact probably was on the CIO's "Operation Dixie," a drive to win for unions a more secure foothold in the South. By 1954 fifteen states, mainly in the South, had used the Taft-Hartley Act's authority to enact "right-to-work" laws forbidding the union shop and other union security devices.

Truman clashed with the Republicans on other domestic issues, including tax reduction. Congress passed a tax cut but it was vetoed by

"To the Rescue!" Organized labor is being pulled under by the Taft-Hartley Act as Congress, which passed the bill over Truman's veto, makes sure there is no rescue.

The CIO's Operation Dixie aimed to organize workers such as these in a North Carolina lumberyard.

Truman on the principle that in times of high production and employment the federal debt should be reduced. In 1948, however, Congress finally managed to override his veto of a $5 billion tax cut at a time when government debt still ran high. The controversy over the tax cut highlighted a soft point in Keynesian economics. In times of depression, people supported increasing governmental expenditures, but in prosperous times people resisted the taxes needed to reduce the deficits. Truman paid a political price for this weakness in economic theory.

The conflicts between Truman and Congress, so visible in the 1948 campaign, obscured the high degree of bipartisan cooperation marking matters of governmental reorganization and foreign policy. In 1947 Congress passed the National Security Act. It created a National Military Establishment, headed by a secretary of defense with subcabinet departments of army, navy, and air force, and a new National Security Council (NSC), which included the president, heads of the defense departments, and the secretary of state, among others. The act made permanent the Joint Chiefs of Staff, which had been a wartime innovation, and established the Central Intelligence Agency (CIA), descended from the wartime Office of Strategic Service (OSS), to coordinate intelligence-gathering activities.

THE COLD WAR

BUILDING THE U.N.   The hope that the wartime alliance of the United Nations would carry over into the postwar world proved but another great illusion. The pragmatic Roosevelt shared no such hope. To the contrary, he expected that the Great Powers in the postwar world would have spheres of influence, but felt he had to support an organization "which would satisfy widespread demand in the United States for new idealistic or universalist arrangements for assuring the peace."

In the 1941 Atlantic Charter, Roosevelt and Churchill had looked forward to a "permanent system of general security." In the autumn of 1943 both houses of Congress passed a resolution favoring "international machinery with power adequate to establish and to maintain a just and lasting peace." That same autumn the foreign ministers of the "Big Four" (the United States, the Soviet Union, Britain, and China) issued the Moscow Declaration on General Security, which called for an international organization, and in the 1944 elections the platforms of both major parties endorsed the principle.

On April 25, 1945, two weeks after Roosevelt's death and two weeks before the German surrender, delegates from fifty nations at war with the Axis met in San Francisco's Opera House to draw up the Charter of the United Nations (U.N.). Additional members could be admitted by a two-thirds vote of the General Assembly. This body, one of the two major agencies set up by the charter, included delegates from all member nations and was to meet annually in regular session to approve the budget, receive annual reports from U.N. agencies, and choose members of the Security Council and other bodies. The Security Council, the other major charter agency, would remain in permanent session and would have "primary responsibility for the maintenance of international peace and security." Its eleven (after 1965, fifteen) members included six (later ten) members elected for two-year terms and five permanent members: the United States, the Soviet Union, Britain, France, and China. Each permanent member had a veto on any question of substance. The Security Council might investigate any dispute, recommend settlement or reference to an International Court at The Hague, in the Netherlands, and take measures, including a resort to military force.

The Senate ratified the U.N. charter by a vote of 89 to 2 after only six days of discussion. The organization held its first meeting in London in 1946, and the next year moved to temporary quarters at Lake Success, New York, pending completion of its permanent home in New York City.

TRYING WAR CRIMINALS   There was also a consensus that those responsible for the atrocities of World War II should face trial and punishment. Both German and Japanese officials went on trial for crimes against peace, against humanity, and against the established rules of war. At Nuremberg, site of the annual Nazi party rallies, twenty-one major German offenders faced an International Military Tribunal. After a ten-month trial filled with massive documentation of Nazi atrocities, the court acquitted three and sentenced eleven to death, three to life imprisonment, and four to shorter terms. In Tokyo, a similar tribunal put twenty-five Japanese leaders on trial in 1946, and pronounced

Nazi leaders Hermann Goering (standing) *and Rudolf Hess* (seated, arms folded) *at Nuremberg, where they are on trial for war crimes.*

death sentences on seven, life imprisonment on sixteen, and committed two for lesser prison terms. Other international tribunals tried thousands of others, while many accused war criminals were remanded to the courts of the countries in which they had committed their crimes. Well over 2,000 war-crimes trials are estimated to have taken place, not counting those in the Soviet Union and the East-bloc countries.

Critics argued that the trials set an unfortunate precedent of victors' taking revenge on the defeated. They argued as well that the convictions were condemnations *ex post facto,* for crimes against which no law existed at the time they were committed. Supporters responded by pointing to the Pact of Paris outlawing war, to the Geneva Convention for care of the sick and wounded prisoners, to the Hague declarations on the rules of war, and to the fact that crimes against humanity such as murder, rape, and pillage were already crimes under the laws of the countries where they occurred.

DIFFERENCES WITH THE SOVIETS   Since the end of World War II, historians have debated which side was more responsible for the onset of the cold war. The conventional or "orthodox" view declares that the Soviets, led by a paranoid dictator, tried to dominate the globe, and the United States had no choice but to stand firm in defense of democratic capitalist values. By contrast, those scholars known as "revisionists" argue that Truman and American economic imperialists were the culprits. Instead of maintaining Roosevelt's efforts to collaborate with Stalin and ensure the survival of the alliance after the war, these scholars assert, Truman adopted an unnecessarily belligerent stance and activist foreign policy that sought to create American spheres of influence around the world. He and his military advisers exaggerated the Soviet threat, in part to justify an American military buildup. Their provocative policies thus crystallized the tensions between the two countries. Yet such an interpretation fails to recognize that Truman inherited a deteriorating relationship with the Soviets. Events of 1945 made compromise and conciliation more and more difficult, whether for Roosevelt or Truman.

There were signs of trouble in the Grand Alliance as early as the spring of 1945, as the Soviet Union moved to set up compliant governments in eastern Europe, violating the Yalta promises of democratic elections. On February 1 the Polish Committee of National Liberation, a puppet group already claiming the status of provisional government, moved from Lublin to Warsaw. In March the Soviets installed a puppet premier in Romania. Protests against such actions led to Soviet counterprotests that the British and Americans were negotiating German surrender in Italy "behind the back of the Soviet Union" and that German forces were being concentrated against the Soviet Union. A few days before his death, Roosevelt responded to Stalin: "I cannot avoid a feeling of resentment toward your informers . . . for such vile misrepresentations."

Such was the atmosphere when Truman entered the White House. A few days before the San Francisco conference to organize the United Nations, Truman gave Soviet foreign minister Vyacheslav M. Molotov a dressing-down in Washington on the Polish situation. "I have never been talked to like that in my life," Molotov said. "Carry out your agreements," Truman snapped, "and you won't get talked to like that." On May 12, 1945, four days after victory in Europe, Winston Churchill sent a telegram to Truman: "What is to happen about Europe? An iron curtain is drawn down upon [the Russian] front. We do not know what is going on behind [it]. . . . Surely it is vital now to come to an understanding with Russia, or see where we are with her, before we weaken our armies mortally. . . ." Nevertheless, as a gesture of goodwill, and over Churchill's protest, the American forces withdrew from the German occupation zone assigned to the Soviet Union at Yalta. Americans still hoped that the Yalta agreements would be carried out, at least after a fashion, and that the Soviet Union would help against Japan.

Although the Soviets admitted British and American observers to their sectors of eastern Europe, there was little the Western powers could do to prevent Soviet control of the region, even if they had not let their military forces dwindle. The presence of Soviet armed forces frustrated the efforts of non-Communists to gain political influence. Coalition governments appeared temporarily as an immediate postwar expedient, but the Communists followed a long-range strategy of ensconcing themselves in the interior ministries in order to control the police. Opposition political leaders found themselves under accusation, "confessions" were extorted, and the leaders of the opposition were either exiled, silenced, executed, or consigned to prison.

Secretary of State James F. Byrnes struggled on through 1946 with the problems of postwar settlements. As early as September 1945, the first meeting of the Council of Foreign Ministers broke up because of

Byrnes's demand that the governments of Romania and Bulgaria be broadened. A series of almost interminable meetings of the Council of Foreign Ministers wrangled over border lines and reparations from Hitler's satellites, finally producing treaties for Italy, Hungary, Romania, Bulgaria, and Finland. The treaties, signed on February 10, 1947, in effect confirmed Soviet control over eastern Europe, which in Russian eyes seemed but a parallel to American control in Japan and Western control over most of Germany and all of Italy. The Yalta guarantees of democracy in eastern Europe had turned out much like the Open Door Policy in China, little more than pious cant that was subordinate to the pressures of raw power and national interests. Byrnes's impulse to pressure Soviet diplomats by brandishing the atomic bomb only added to the irritations, intimidating no one.

The United States, together with Britain and Canada (partners in developing the atomic bomb), had exclusive possession of atomic weapons at the time, but in 1946 proposed to internationalize the control of atomic energy through a plan presented to the U.N. Atomic Energy Commission. Under the plan an International Atomic Development Authority would have a monopoly of atomic explosives and atomic energy. The Soviets, fearing Western domination of the agency, proposed instead simply to outlaw the manufacture and use of atomic bombs, with enforcement vested in the Security Council and thus subject to a veto. Later they conceded the right of international inspection, but still refused to give up the veto, and the American government rejected the arrangement, which it considered a compromise of international control.

CONTAINMENT   By the beginning of 1947, relations with the Soviet Union had become even more troubled. A year before, Stalin had already pronounced international peace impossible "under the present capitalist development of the world economy." His statement impelled George F. Kennan, counselor of the American embassy in Moscow, to send the secretary of state an 8,000-word dispatch in which he sketched the roots of Soviet policy and warned that the Soviet Union was "committed fanatically to the belief that . . . it is desirable and necessary that the internal harmony of our society be disrupted, our traditional way of life be destroyed, the international authority of our state be broken, if Soviet power is to be secure."

George F. Kennan, whose 1947 For-eign Affairs *article spelled out the doctrine of containment.*

More than a year later, Kennan, now back at the State Department in Washington, spelled out his ideas for a proper response to the Soviets in a 1947 article published anonymously in *Foreign Affairs.* Kennan signed himself "X" so that readers would not mistake the article for an official State Department position. He did not offer a cohesive strategy or an operational plan but instead provided a psychological analysis of Soviet insecurity and intentions. He predicted that the Soviets would try to fill "every nook and cranny available . . . in the basin of world power." Yet their insecurity also meant that, in general, they would act cautiously and seek to reduce their risks. Therefore, he insisted, "the main ele-ment of any United States policy toward the Soviet Union must be that of a long-term, patient but firm and vigilant *containment* of Russian ex-pansive tendencies. . . . Such a policy has nothing to do with outward histrionics: with threats or blustering or superfluous gestures of out-ward 'toughness.'" Americans, he argued, could hope for a long-term moderation of expansionist Soviet ideology and policy, so that in time tensions with the West would lessen. There was a strong possibility "that Soviet power, like the capitalist world of its conception, bears within it the seeds of its own decay, and that the sprouting of those seeds is well advanced."

Kennan's containment concept explained the new departure in for-eign policy that America's political leaders had already decided to take. Behind this shift lay a growing fear that Soviet aims reached beyond eastern Europe, posing dangers in the eastern Mediterranean, the Middle East, and western Europe itself. The first major postwar crisis occurred in Iran, which borders the Soviet Union on the south and provided important trade routes to the U.S.S.R. Soviet troops had been stationed in northern Iran while British-American troops were in the south, and all were supposed to pull out six months after the war. But the Soviets remained beyond the deadline. The crisis finally blew over with a Soviet withdrawal.

Meanwhile the Soviet Union sought a breakthrough into the Mediterranean, long important to Russia for purposes of trade and defense. After the war the Soviet Union began to press Turkey for territorial concessions and the right to build naval bases on the Bosporus, an important gateway between the Black Sea and the Mediterranean. In 1946 civil war broke out in Greece between a government backed by the British and a Communist-led faction that held the northern part of Greece and drew supplies from Yugoslavia, Bulgaria, and Albania. In 1947 the British ambassador informed the American government that the British could no longer bear the economic and military burden of aiding Greece. When Truman conferred with congressional leaders on the situation, the chairman of the Senate Foreign Relations Committee recommended a strong appeal to the American people.

THE TRUMAN DOCTRINE AND THE MARSHALL PLAN   On March 12, 1947, President Truman appeared before Congress to request $400 million for economic aid to both Greece and Turkey and for the authority to send American personnel to train their soldiers. In his speech Truman enunciated what quickly came to be known as the Truman Doctrine. It justified aid to Greece and Turkey in terms more provocative than Kennan's idea of containment and more general than this specific case warranted. "I believe," Truman declared, "that it must be the policy of the United States to support free peoples who are resisting attempted subjugation by armed minorities or by outside pressures."

In 1947 Congress passed the Greek-Turkish aid bill, and by 1950 had spent $659 million on the program. Turkey achieved economic stability, and Greece defeated the Communist insurrection in 1949, partly because President Tito of Yugoslavia had broken with the Soviets in the summer of 1948 and ceased to aid the Greek Communists. But the principles embedded in the Truman Doctrine committed the United States to intervene throughout the world in order to "contain" the

George C. Marshall at the Harvard University commencement where he proposed the "Marshall Plan" for the reconstruction of postwar Europe.

spread of communism, and this global commitment would produce tragic consequences as well as successes in the years to come.

The Truman Doctrine marked the beginning, or at least the open acknowledgment, of a contest that Bernard Baruch named in a 1947 speech to the legislature of his native South Carolina: "Let us not be deceived—today we are in the midst of a cold war." Greece and Turkey were but the front lines of an ideological struggle that would involve western Europe as well. There wartime damage and dislocation had devastated factory production, and severe drought in 1947, followed by a harsh winter, had destroyed crops. Coal shortages in London left only enough fuel to heat and light homes for a few hours each day. In Berlin, people were freezing or starving to death. The transportation system in Europe was in shambles. Bridges were out, canals clogged, and rail networks destroyed. Amid the chaos the Communist parties of France and Italy were flourishing. Aid from the United Nations had staved off starvation, but had provided little basis for economic recovery.

In the spring of 1947, George C. Marshall, who had replaced Byrnes as secretary of state, called for a program of massive aid to rescue western Europe from disaster. The retired chairman of the Joint Chiefs of Staff who orchestrated the Allied victories over Germany and Japan, Marshall had been the highest-ranking army general during World War II. "He is the great one of the age," said Truman. Marshall used the occasion of the Harvard graduation ceremonies in 1947 to outline his plan for the reconstruction of Europe. "Our policy," he said, "is directed not against country or doctrine, but against hunger, poverty, desperation, and chaos." Marshall offered aid to all European countries, including the Soviet Union, and called upon them to take the lead in judging their own needs. On June 27 the foreign ministers of France, Britain, and the Soviet Union met in London to discuss Marshall's overture. Soviet foreign minister Vyacheslav Molotov arrived with eighty advisers, but during the talks he got word from Moscow to withdraw from this "imperialist" scheme. Two weeks later a meeting of delegates from western Europe formed a Committee of European Economic Cooperation (CEEC), which had a plan ready by September.

In December Truman submitted his proposal for the European Recovery Program to Congress. Two months later, a Communist coup d'état in Czechoslovakia ended the last remaining coalition government in eastern Europe. Coming less than ten years after Munich, the seizure of power in Prague assured congressional passage of the Marshall Plan. From 1948 until 1951 the Economic Cooperation Administration (ECA), which managed the Marshall Plan, poured $13 billion into European recovery through the CEEC.

DIVIDING GERMANY The breakdown of the wartime alliance left the problem of postwar Germany unsettled. The German economy had stagnated, requiring the American army to support a staggering burden of relief. Slowly, zones of occupation evolved into functioning governments. In 1948 the British, French, and Americans united their zones. The West Germans then organized state governments and elected delegates to a federal constitutional convention.

Soviet leaders resented the Marshall Plan and the unification of West Germany. In April 1948 the Soviets began to restrict the flow of traffic into West Berlin; on June 23 they stopped all traffic. The Soviets hoped the blockade would force the Allies to give up either Berlin or the plan to unify West Germany. But the American commander in Germany proposed to stand firm. "When Berlin falls, Western Germany will be next," he told the Pentagon. "If we mean . . . to hold Europe against communism, we must not budge."

Truman agreed and, after considering the use of armed convoys to supply West Berlin, opted for a massive airlift. At the time this seemed

NORTH SEA

DENMARK

SWEDEN

BALTIC SEA

U.S.S.R.

To U.S.S.R.

EAST PRUSSIA

Danzig

To Poland

NETHERLANDS

Hamburg

Bremen

Access corridor

Annexed by Poland

Berlin

WEST GERMANY

EAST

Joint occupation by four powers

Warsaw

Oder River

Naisse R.

POLAND

Bonn

BELGIUM

GERMANY

Lublin

Frankfurt

Iron Curtain

LUXEMBOURG

SAAR

FRANCE

Rhine River

Danube River

Munich

CZECHOSLOVAKIA

Vienna

SWITZERLAND

AUSTRIA

HUNGARY

ROMANIA

ITALY

0   50   100 Miles

0 50 100 Kilometers

OCCUPATION OF GERMANY AND AUSTRIA

French zone   U.S. zone

British zone   Soviet zone

YUGOSLAVIA

an enormous and perhaps impossible task, requiring, according to one estimate, 4,500 tons of food and coal a day. But by quick work the Allied air forces brought in planes from around the world, and by October 1948 were flying in nearly 5,000 tons of food and equipment a day. Altogether, from June 1948 to mid-May 1949, the Berlin Airlift provided more than 1.5 million tons of supplies, or well over a half ton for each of the 2.2 million West Berliners.

Finally, on May 12, 1949, after extended talks, the Soviets lifted the blockade in return for a meeting of the Council of Foreign Ministers in Paris. This was purely a face-saving gesture, and the meeting resulted in no important decision on Germany. Before the end of the year the German Federal Republic had a government functioning under Chancellor Konrad Adenauer of the Christian Democratic party. At the end of May 1949, a German "Democratic" Republic arose in the eastern zone, for-

The Berlin Airlift. *An American airplane arrives in West Berlin with much-needed supplies, 1948.*

malizing the division of Germany. West Germany gradually acquired more authority, until the Western powers recognized its full sovereignty in 1955.

BUILDING NATO   As relations between the Soviets and western Europe chilled, transatlantic unity ripened into an outright military alliance. On April 4, 1949, the North Atlantic Treaty was signed at Washington by representatives of twelve nations: the United States, Britain, France, Belgium, the Netherlands, Luxembourg, Canada, Denmark, Iceland, Italy, Norway, and Portugal. Greece and Turkey joined the alliance in 1952, Germany in 1955, Spain in 1982. Senate ratification of the North Atlantic Treaty by a vote of 82 to 13 suggested that the isolationism of the prewar period no longer exerted a hold on the American people.

The treaty pledged that an attack against any one of the signers would be considered an attack against all, and provided for a council of the North Atlantic Treaty Organization (NATO), which could establish other necessary agencies. In 1950 the council decided to create an integrated defense force for western Europe and later named General

NATO, a symbol of renewed strength for a battered Europe.

Dwight Eisenhower to head the Supreme Headquarters of the Allied Powers in Europe (SHAPE). In 1955 the Warsaw Treaty Organization appeared as the eastern European counterpart to NATO.

The eventful year 1948 produced one other foreign policy decision with long-term consequences. Palestine, as the biblical Holy Land had come to be known, was under Turkish rule until the League of Nations made it a British mandate after World War I. Over the early years of the twentieth century, many Zionists, who advocated a Jewish state in the region, had migrated there. More came after the British entered, and a greatly increased number arrived during the Nazi persecution in 1933 and after. Offered a promise by the British of a national homeland, the Jewish inhabitants demanded their own state.

Late in 1947, the U.N. General Assembly voted to partition Palestine into Jewish and Arab states, but this met fierce Arab opposition. Finally, the British mandate expired on May 14, 1948, and Jewish leaders proclaimed the independence of the state of Israel. President Truman, who had been in close touch with Jewish leaders, ordered recognition of the new state within minutes—the United States became the first nation to act. The neighboring Arab states thereupon went to war against Israel, which, however, held its own. U.N. mediators gradually worked out truce agreements with Israel's Arab neighbors, and an uneasy peace was restored by May 11, 1949, when Israel was admitted as a member of the United Nations. But the hard feelings and intermittent warfare between Israel and the Arab states have festered ever since, complicating American foreign policy, which has tried to maintain friendship with both sides.

Harry Gives 'Em Hell

CIVIL RIGHTS DURING THE 1940S   The social tremors triggered by World War II and the onset of the cold war transformed America's racial landscape. The vicious racism of the German Nazis, Italian fascists, and Japanese imperialists focused attention on the need for the United States to improve its own race relations and to provide for equal rights under the law. As a *New York Times* editorial explained in early 1946, "This is a particularly good time to campaign against the evils of bigotry, prejudice, and race hatred because we have witnessed the defeat of enemies who tried to found a mastery of the world upon such cruel and fallacious policy." The postwar confrontation with the Soviet Union also gave Americans an added incentive to improve race relations in the United States. In the ideological contest for influence in Africa, American diplomats were at a disadvantage as long as racial segregation continued in the United States. The Soviets often compared segregation in the American South to the Nazis' treatment of Jews.

For most of his political career, Harry Truman had shown little concern about the plight of African Americans. He had grown up in western Missouri assuming that both blacks and whites preferred to be segregated from one another. As president, however, he began to reassess his convictions. A recent biographer of Truman concludes that he "was magnificently right on what may have been the two most important issues of his time: civil rights and the Soviet challenge."

In the fall of 1946 Truman hosted a delegation of civil rights activists from the National Emergency Committee Against Mob Violence. They urged the president to issue a public statement condemning the resurgence of the Ku Klux Klan and the lynching of blacks. The delegation graphically described incidents of torture and intimidation against blacks in the South. Truman was aghast. "My God," he exclaimed. "I had no idea it was as terrible as that. We've got to do something." Two months later, he appointed a Committee on Civil Rights to investigate violence against African Americans and to recommend preventive measures.

The committee recommended the renewal of the Fair Employment Practices Committee (FEPC) and the creation of a permanent civil rights commission to investigate abuses. It also argued that federal aid be denied to any state that mandated segregated schools and public facilities.

On July 26, 1948, Truman banned racial discrimination in the hiring of federal employees. Four days later, he issued an Executive Order ending racial segregation in the armed forces. The air force and navy quickly complied, but the army dragged its feet until the early 1950s. By 1960 the armed forces were the most racially integrated of all American organizations. Desegregating the military was, Truman claimed, "the greatest thing that ever happened to America."

Meanwhile, racial segregation was being confronted in a much more public field of endeavor—professional baseball. In April 1947, as the baseball season opened, the National League's Brooklyn Dodgers included on their roster the first black player to cross the color line in major league baseball: Jackie Robinson. "This in a way is another Emancipation Day for the Negro race," wrote the sportswriter for the *Montreal Daily Star*, "a day that Abraham Lincoln would like." Another newspaper declared: "Jim Crow Dies at Second Base."

Jackie Robinson, 1949. *Racial discrimination remained widespread through the postwar period. In 1947 Jackie Robinson of the Brooklyn Dodgers became the first black to play major league baseball.*

Born in Georgia but raised in California, Robinson was an army veteran and baseball player in the Negro leagues. He earlier had been a football, basketball, baseball, and track star at UCLA. Branch Rickey, the courageous president of the Dodgers and the son of a Methodist minister, selected Robinson to integrate professional baseball, not only for his athletic potential but because of his willingness to control his temper in the face of virulent racism. Rickey knew that the first black player in the major leagues would face a storm of abuse. Many skeptics, including most of the other team owners, predicted that opposition from players and fans would force Rickey to drop Robinson from the roster. Teammates and opposing players viciously baited Robinson, pitchers threw at him, base runners spiked him, and spectators booed and taunted him in every city. Hotels refused him rooms, and restaurants denied him service. Hate mail arrived by the bucket load. On the other hand, black spectators were electrified by Robinson's courageous example. They turned out in droves to see him play.

What Branch Rickey called his noble experiment provided a public forum for people to confront the charged issue of segregation. The headline in the *Boston Chronicle* trumpeted: "Triumph of Whole Race Seen in Jackie's Debut in Major League Ball." Huge crowds flocked to see Robinson play, and he played well, doing everything necessary to help the Dodgers win games—bunt, sacrifice, draw walks, steal bases, hit for average and for power. His success earned him the Rookie of the Year Award in 1947. Leo Durocher, manager of the Dodgers, declared that Robinson "didn't just come to play. He come to beat ya."

As time passed, Robinson won over many fans and opposing players through his quiet courage, self-deprecating wit, and determined performance. Soon, other teams began to sign black players. In July 1947 the Cleveland Indians added Larry Doby to their roster, thus breaking the color barrier in the American League. That same month the St. Louis Browns signed three players from the Negro leagues. Baseball's path-breaking efforts stimulated other professional sports such as football and basketball to integrate their rosters. Jackie Robinson vividly demonstrated that racism, not inferiority, impeded African-American advancement in the postwar era and that segregation need not be a permanent condition of American life. "When Jackie took the field," the Reverend Jesse Jackson recalled, "something reminded us of our birthright to be free."

I STAND PAT!

YOU MEAN YOU'D RATHER BE RIGHT THAN PRESIDENT?

CIVIL RIGHTS

Truman's support of civil rights for African Americans had its political costs, as this 1948 cartoon suggests.

SHAPING THE FAIR DEAL   The determination Truman projected in foreign affairs did not alter his weak image on the domestic front. By early 1948, after three years in the White House, Truman had yet to shake the impression that he was not up to the job. Rather than go with a loser, New Deal stalwarts and party regulars tried to draft General Eisenhower for the 1948 presidential nomination, but in vain. The Democratic party seemed about to fragment: southern conservatives resented Truman's outspoken support of civil rights, while the left had flared up in 1946 over his firing of Secretary of Commerce Henry Wallace after a speech critical of the administration's policy. "Getting tough [with the Soviet Union]," Wallace had argued, "never brought anything real and lasting—whether for schoolyard bullies or world powers. The tougher we get, the tougher the Russians will get." The left itself was splitting between the Progressive Citizens of America (PCA), formed in 1946, which supported Wallace, and the Americans for Democratic Action (ADA), formed in 1947, which also criticized Truman but took a firm anti-Communist stance.

Truman made an aggressive effort to shore up the New Deal coalition. He needed the midwestern and western farm belts, and had fairly strong support among farmers. In metropolitan areas, he needed to carry the labor and black vote, which he wooed by working closely with unions and liberals, and pressing the cause of civil rights.

Like other presidents, Truman used his State of the Union message in 1948 to set the agenda for an election year. The speech offered something to nearly every group the Democrats hoped to attract. The first goal, Truman said, was "to secure fully the essential human rights of our citizens," and he promised a special message later on civil rights. "To protect human resources," he proposed federal aid to education, increased and extended unemployment and retirement benefits, a comprehensive system of health insurance, more federal support for housing, and extension of rent controls. He continued to pile on the demands: for reclamation projects, more rural electrification, a higher minimum wage, laws to admit thousands of displaced persons to the United States, money for the Marshall Plan, and a "cost-of-living" tax credit.

THE 1948 ELECTION   The Republican Congress for the most part spurned the Truman program, an action it would later regret. At the party convention, New York governor Thomas E. Dewey won the nomination on the third ballot. The platform endorsed most of the New Deal reforms as accomplished fact and approved the administration's bipartisan foreign policy, but as Landon had in 1936 and Willkie had in 1940, Dewey promised to run things more efficiently.

In July a glum Democratic convention gathered in Philadelphia, expecting to do little more than go through the motions, only to find itself doubly surprised: first by the battle over the civil rights plank, and then by Truman's acceptance speech. To keep from stirring southern hostility, the administration sought a platform plank that opposed racial discrimination only in general terms. Liberal Democrats, however, sponsored a plank that called on Congress for specific action and commended Truman "for his courageous stand on the issue of civil rights." Speaking last in favor of the change, Minneapolis mayor Hubert H. Humphrey electrified the delegates and set off a ten-minute demonstration: "The time has arrived for the Democratic party to get out of the shadow of states' rights and walk forthrightly into the bright sunshine of human rights." Segregationist delegates from Alabama and Mississippi walked, instead, out of the convention.

After the convention had nominated Truman, the president showed a new fighting style in his speeches. He pledged to "win this election and make the Republicans like it," he said, "don't you forget it!" He also

The opening of the 1948 Democratic National Convention is marked by demonstrations against racial segregation, led by A. Philip Randolph (left).

vowed to call Congress back into session "to get the laws the people need," many of which the Republican platform had endorsed.

On July 17 a group of rebellious southern Democrats met in Birmingham and nominated South Carolina governor J. Strom Thurmond on a States' Rights Democratic ticket, quickly dubbed the "Dixiecrat" ticket. The Dixiecrats hoped to draw enough electoral votes to preclude a majority for either major party, throwing the election into the House, where they might strike a sectional bargain. A few days later, on July 23, the left wing of the Democratic party gathered in Philadelphia to name Henry A. Wallace on a Progressive party ticket. These splits in the Democratic ranks seemed to spell the final blow to Truman. The special session of Congress petered out in futility.

But Truman, undaunted, set out on a 31,000-mile "whistle-stop" train tour during which he castigated the "do-nothing" Eightieth Congress to the accompaniment of cries from his audiences: "Pour it on, Harry!" and "Give 'em hell, Harry." Truman responded: "I don't give 'em

The "Dixiecrats" nominate South Carolina governor J. Strom Thurmond (center) to lead their ticket in the 1948 election.

hell. I just tell the truth and they think it's hell." Dewey, in contrast, ran a restrained campaign, designed to avoid rocking the boat. By so doing he may have snatched defeat from the jaws of victory.

To the end the polls and the pundits predicted a sure win for Dewey, and most speculation centered on his cabinet choices. But on election day Truman chalked up the biggest upset in American history, taking 24.2 million votes (49.5 percent) to Dewey's 22 million (45.1 percent) and winning a thumping 303 to 189 vote margin in the electoral college. Thurmond and Wallace each got more than a million votes, but the revolt of right and left worked to Truman's advantage. The Dixiecrat rebellion reassured black voters who had questioned the Democrats' commitment to civil rights, while the Progressive movement made it hard to tag Truman as "soft on communism." Thurmond carried four Deep South states (South Carolina, Mississippi, Alabama, and Louisiana) with 39 electoral votes, including one electoral vote from a Tennessee elector who repudiated his state's decision for Truman. Thurmond's success started a momentous disruption of the Democratic Solid South. But Truman's victory also carried Democratic majorities into Congress, where the new group of senators included Hubert

Humphrey and, by eighty-seven disputed votes, "Landslide Lyndon" B. Johnson of Texas.

Truman viewed the outcome as a vindication for the New Deal and a mandate for liberalism. "We have rejected the discredited theory that the fortunes of the nation should be in the hands of a privileged few," he said. His State of the Union message repeated the agenda he had set forth a year previously. "Every segment of our population and every individual," he declared, "has a right to expect from his government a fair deal." Whether deliberately or not he had invented a tag, the "Fair Deal," to set off his program from the New Deal.

Congress passed some of Truman's Fair Deal proposals, but they were mainly extensions or enlargements of New Deal programs already in place: a higher minimum wage, bringing more people under Social Security, extension of rent controls, farm price supports at 90 percent of parity, a sizable slum-clearance and public housing program, and more money for the Reclamation Bureau, the TVA, rural electrification, and farm housing. Despite Democratic majorities, however, the conservative coalition thwarted any drastic new departures in domestic policy. Congress rejected civil rights bills, national health insurance, federal

The Man Who "Done His Damndest." Truman's victory in 1948 was a huge upset.

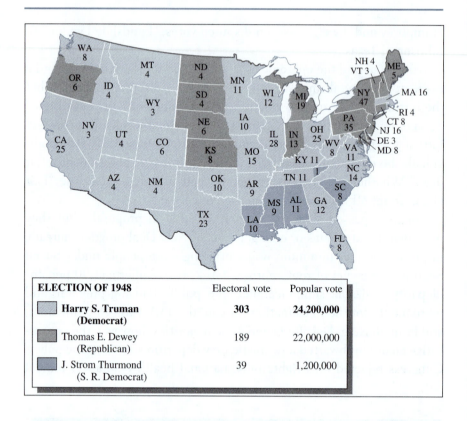

ELECTION OF 1948	Electoral vote	Popular vote
Harry S. Truman **(Democrat)**	**303**	**24,200,000**
Thomas E. Dewey (Republican)	189	22,000,000
J. Strom Thurmond (S. R. Democrat)	39	1,200,000

aid to education, and a plan to provide subsidies that would hold up farm incomes rather than farm prices. Congress also turned down Truman's demand for repeal of the Taft-Hartley Act.

THE COLD WAR HEATS UP

Global concerns, never far from center stage in the postwar world, plagued Truman's second term, as they had his first. People began to live in real fear that the Communists were infiltrating American society and were intent upon world domination. In his inaugural address Truman called for a vigilant anti-Communist foreign policy to rest on four pillars: the United Nations, the Marshall Plan, NATO, and a "bold new plan" for technical assistance to underdeveloped parts of the world, a sort of global Marshall Plan that came to be known simply as "Point Four." This program to aid the postwar world, never accomplished its

Mao Tse-tung on the march with Red Army troops in northern China, 1947.

goals, in part because other international problems soon diverted Truman's attention.

"LOSING" CHINA AND THE BOMB   One of the most intractable problems, the China tangle, was fast coming unraveled in 1949. The Chinese Nationalists (Kuomintang) of Chiang Kai-shek had at first accepted the help of Communists, but expelled them from the ranks in 1927. When a new leader, Mao Tse-tung,* began to rebuild the Communist party by organizing the peasants instead of urban workers, the Nationalists drove him out of his stronghold in the south. After an arduous trek, which the Communists later celebrated as the "Long March" of 1934–1935, they entrenched themselves in northern China at Yenan. The outbreak of war with Japan in 1937 relieved them of pressure from the Nationalists, and at the same time enabled them to assume a patriotic stance by fighting the Japanese. During the war, Roosevelt and Stalin believed that the Nationalists would organize China after the war.

*The traditional (Wade-Giles) spelling is used here. In 1958 the Chinese government adopted the "pinyin" transliterations that became more widely used after Mao's death in 1976, so that, for example, Mao Tse-tung became Mao Zedong, and Peking became Beijing.

But the commanders of American forces in China during World War II concluded that Chiang's government was hopelessly corrupt, tyrannical, and inefficient. After the war, American forces nevertheless ferried Nationalist armies back into the eastern and northern provinces as the Japanese withdrew. U.S. policy during and immediately after the war promoted peace between the factions in China, but sporadic civil war broke out late in 1945.

It soon became a losing fight for the Nationalists, as the Communists radicalized the land-hungry peasantry. By early 1949 Mao's forces were in Peking and headed southward. By the end of the year they had taken Canton, and the Nationalist government had fled to the island of Formosa, which it renamed Taiwan.

From 1945 through 1949 the United States had funneled some $2 billion in aid to the Nationalists, to no avail. Administration critics now asked bitterly: "Who lost China?" A State Department study blamed Chiang for his failure to hold the support of the Chinese people. In fact it is hard to imagine how the United States government could have prevented the outcome short of massive military intervention, which would have been very risky and unpopular. The United States continued to recognize the Nationalist government on Taiwan as the rightful government of China, delaying formal relations with Red China for thirty years. Seeking to shore up friendly regimes in Asia, in 1950 the United States recognized the French-supported regime of Emperor Bao Dai in Vietnam and shortly afterward extended aid to the French in their battle against Ho Chi Minh's guerrillas there.

As the Communists gained control of China, American intelligence in 1949 found an unusual level of radioactivity in the air, evidence that the Soviets had set off an atomic device. The American nuclear monopoly had lasted just four years, but under the umbrella of security that it seemed to offer, the wartime military establishment had been allowed to dwindle. If a crisis had occurred, it would have left American leaders with the choice of doing nothing or cremating millions of people. The discovery of the Soviet bomb provoked an intense reappraisal of the strategic balance in the world, causing Truman in 1950 to end a dispute among his scientific advisers by ordering the construction of a hydrogen bomb, a weapon far more frightful than those dropped on Japan, lest the Soviets make one first. The discovery also led the National Security Council to produce a top-secret document, known as NSC-68, that called for rebuilding conventional military forces to provide options other than nuclear war. This represented a major departure from America's time-honored aversion to keeping large standing armies in peacetime, and was an expensive proposition. But the American public was growing more receptive to the nation's role as world leader, and an invasion of South Korea by Communist forces from the north clinched the issue for most.

WAR IN KOREA   The division of Korea at the end of World War II, like the division of Germany, began as a temporary expedient and ended as a permanent fact. In the hectic days of August 1945, a State-War-Navy Coordinating Committee adopted a hasty proposal to divide Korea at the 38th parallel. The Soviets accepted, to the surprise of American officials involved. Since they bordered on Korea, the Soviets could quickly have occupied the whole country. With the onset of the cold war, it became clear that agreement on unification was no more likely in Korea than in Germany, and by the end of 1948 separate regimes had appeared in the two sectors and occupation forces had withdrawn. The weakened state of the American military contributed to the impression that South Korea was vulnerable. A growing body of evidence later gleaned from Soviet archives reveals that Stalin encouraged the North Koreans to use force to unify their country and oust the Americans from the peninsula. The Soviets helped design and ultimately approved a war plan that called for North Korean forces to seize Seoul within three days and all of South Korea within a week.

North Korean forces crossed the boundary on June 25, 1950, and swept down the peninsula. President Truman responded decisively. He and his advisers assumed that the North Korean attack was directed by Moscow and was a brazen indication of the aggressive designs of monolithic communism. "The attack upon Korea makes it plain beyond all doubt," Truman told Congress, "that communism has passed beyond the use of subversion to conquer independent nations and will now use armed invasion and war."

An emergency meeting of the U.N. Security Council quickly censured the North Korean "breach of peace." The Soviet delegate, who held a veto power, was at the time boycotting the council because it would not seat Red China in place of Nationalist China. On June 27, its first resolution having been ignored, the Security Council called on U.N. members to "furnish such assistance to the Republic of Korea as may be necessary to repel the armed attack and to restore international peace and security in the area." Truman ordered American air, naval, and ground forces into action. In all, some fourteen other U.N. members sent military units, the largest from Britain and Turkey, and five sent medical units. Later, when the U.N. voted a unified command, General Douglas MacArthur was designated to take charge. The defense of South Korea remained chiefly an American affair, and one that set a precedent of profound consequence: war by order of the president rather than by vote of Congress. Yet, it had the sanction of the U.N. Security Council, and could technically be considered a "police action," not a war. To be sure, other presidents had ordered American troops into action without a declaration of war, but never on such a scale.

Truman's conviction that the invasion of South Korea was actually orchestrated by Stalin in Moscow led to two other decisions that had far-reaching consequences. Believing that the Korean action was actually a diversion for a Soviet advance into western Europe, Truman began a major expansion of American forces in NATO. By 1952 there were 261,000 American troops stationed in Europe, three times the number in 1950 and slightly more than the total number of American soldiers in Korea. While dispatching American forces to Korea and Europe, Truman also increased his assistance to the French in Indochina, creating the Military Assistance Advisory Group for Indochina. This was the start of America's deepening involvement in Vietnam.

For three months the fighting in Korea went badly for the Republic of Korea (ROK) and U.N. forces. Soviet pilots battled American planes over South Korea. To mask their identity, the Soviets wore Chinese uniforms and used Chinese phrases over the radio. By September the ROK and U.N. forces were barely hanging on to the Pusan perimeter in the southeast corner of Korea. Then, in a brilliant ploy, on September 15, 1950, MacArthur landed a new force to the North Korean rear at Inchon, the port city for Seoul. Synchronized with a breakout from Pusan, the sudden blow stampeded the enemy back across the border. At this point, MacArthur convinced Truman to allow him to push on and seek to reunify Korea. By now, the Soviet delegate was back in the Security Council, wielding his veto. So on October 7 the United States won approval for this course from the U.N. General Assembly, where the veto did not apply. United States forces had already crossed the boundary by October 1, and now continued northward against minimal resistance.

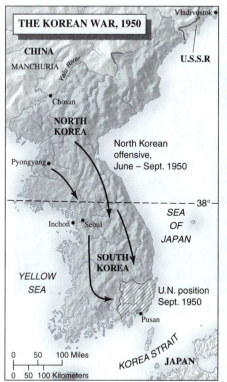

President Truman, concerned about broad hints of intervention by Red China, flew to Wake Island for a conference with General MacArthur on October 15. There the general discounted chances that the Red Chinese Army would act, but if it did, he predicted "there would be the greatest slaughter."

That same day Peking announced that China "cannot stand idly by." On October 20 U.N. forces had entered Pyongyang, the North Korean capital, and on October 26 advance units had reached Chosan on the Yalu River border with China. MacArthur predicted total victory by Christmas. But on the night of November 25 Chinese "volunteers" counterattacked, and massive "human wave" attacks, with the support of tanks and planes, turned the tables on the U.N. forces, sending them into a desperate retreat just at the onset of winter. It had become "an entirely new war," MacArthur said. He began to claim that the fault for the war's continuance lay with the administration for requiring that he conduct a limited war. He proposed air raids on China's "privileged

U.N. forces recapture Seoul from the North Koreans, September 1950.

sanctuary" in Manchuria, a naval blockade of China, and an invasion of the Chinese mainland by the Taiwan Nationalists. MacArthur seemed to have forgotten altogether his onetime reluctance to bog down the country in a major war on the Asian mainland.

Truman stood against leading the United States into the "gigantic booby trap" of war with China, and the U.N. forces soon rallied. By January 1951 U.N. troops under General Matthew B. Ridgway finally secured their lines below Seoul, and then launched a counterattack that in some places carried them back across the 38th parallel in March. When Truman seized the chance and offered negotiations to restore the prewar boundary, MacArthur undermined the move by issuing an ultimatum for China to make peace or be attacked. Truman decided then that MacArthur would have to go. On April 5, on the floor of the House, the Republican minority leader read a letter in which MacArthur criticized the president and said that "there is no substitute for victory." Such an act of open insubordination left the commander-in-chief no choice but to accept MacArthur's policy or fire him. Civilian control of the military was at stake, Truman later said, and he did not let it remain at stake very long. The Joint Chiefs of Staff all backed the decision, and on April 11, 1951, the president removed MacArthur from all his commands and replaced him with Ridgway.

Truman's action ignited an immediate uproar in the country, and a tumultuous reception greeted MacArthur upon his return home for the first time since 1937. MacArthur's speech to a joint session of Congress provided the climactic event. "Once war is forced upon us," he asserted, "there is no alternative than to apply every available means to bring it to a swift end." MacArthur ended the speech in memorable fashion. He recalled a barracks ballad of his youth "which proclaimed most proudly that old soldiers never die, they just fade away." And like the old soldiers of that ballad, he said, "I now close my military career and just fade away, an old soldier who tried to do his duty as God gave him the light to see that duty." A Senate investigation brought out the administration's arguments, best summarized by General Omar Bradley, chairman of the Joint Chiefs of Staff. "Taking on Red China," he explained, would lead only "to a larger deadlock at greater expense." The MacArthur strategy "would involve us in the wrong war at the wrong place at the wrong time and with the wrong enemy." Americans, nurtured on classic Western showdowns in which good always triumphed over evil, found the logic of limited war hard to take, but also found General Bradley's logic persuasive.

On June 24, 1951, the Soviet representative at the United Nations proposed a cease-fire and armistice along the 38th parallel; Secretary of State Dean Acheson accepted in principle a few days later with the consent of the United Nations. China and North Korea responded favorably—at the time General Ridgway's "meat-grinder" offensive was inflicting severe losses—and truce talks started on July 10, 1951, at Panmunjom, only to drag out for another two years while the fighting continued. The chief snags were prisoner exchanges and the insistence of the South Korean president on unification. By the time a truce was finally reached on July 27, 1953, Truman had relinquished the White House to Dwight D. Eisenhower. The truce line followed the front at that time, mostly a little north of the 38th parallel, with a demilitarized zone of two and a half miles separating the forces; repatriation of prisoners would be voluntary, supervised by a neutral commission. No final peace conference ever took place, and Korea, like Germany, remained divided. The war had cost the United States more than 33,000 battle deaths and 103,000 wounded and missing. South Korean casualties, all told, were about 1 million, and North Korean and Chinese casualties an estimated 1.5 million.

ANOTHER RED SCARE   In calculating the costs of the Korean War one must add in the far-reaching consequences of the Second Red Scare, which had grown since 1945 as the domestic counterpart to the cold war abroad and reached a crescendo during the Korean conflict. Since 1938, the House Un-American Activities Committee (HUAC) had kept up a drumbeat of accusations about subversives in government. In 1945 government agents found that secret American documents had turned up in the offices of a Communist-sponsored magazine, and more dramatic revelations came from a Canadian royal commission that uncovered several spy rings in the Canadian bureaucracy. On March 21, 1947, just nine days after he announced the Truman Doctrine, Truman signed an executive order setting up procedures for an employee loyalty program in the federal government. Every person entering civil employ would be subject to a background investigation. By early 1951 the Civil Service Commission had cleared over 3 million people, while over 2,000 had resigned and 212 had been dismissed for doubtful loyalty, but no espionage ring was ever uncovered.

The loyalty program was designed partly if not mainly to protect the president's political flank, but it failed that purpose, mainly because of disclosures of earlier Communist penetrations into government that were few in number but sensational in character. The loyalty review program may in fact have heightened the politically explosive hysteria over Communist infiltration.

Perhaps the single case most damaging to the administration involved Alger Hiss, president of the Carnegie Endowment for International Peace, who had served in several government departments, and while in the State Department, had been secretary-general of the United Nations charter conference. Whittaker Chambers, a former Soviet agent and later an editor of *Time* magazine, told the House Un-American Activities Committee in 1948 that Hiss had given him secret documents ten years earlier, when Chambers worked for the Soviets. Hiss sued for libel, and Chambers produced microfilms of the State Department documents he said Hiss had passed on to him. Hiss denied the accusation, whereupon he was indicted for perjury and, after one mistrial, convicted in 1950. The charge was perjury, but he was convicted of lying about espionage—for which he could not be tried because the statute of limitations on the crime had expired.

Most damaging to the administration was that President Truman, taking at face value the many testimonials to Hiss's integrity, called the charges against him a "red herring." Secretary of State Acheson compounded the damage when, meaning to express compassion, he pledged not "to turn my back on Alger Hiss." The Hiss affair had another political consequence: it raised to national prominence a young California congressman, Richard M. Nixon, who doggedly insisted on pursuing the case and then exploited an anti-Communist stance to win election to the Senate in 1950.

More cases surfaced. In 1949 eleven top Communist party leaders were convicted under the Smith Act of 1940, which outlawed any conspiracy to advocate the overthrow of the government. The Supreme Court upheld the law under the doctrine of a "clear and present danger," which overrode the right to free speech. What was more, in 1950 the government unearthed the existence of a British-American spy network that had fed information about the development of the atomic bomb to the Soviet Union. These disclosures led to the arrest of, among

Ethel and Julius Rosenberg were convicted of passing along American secrets about the atom bomb to the Soviets. They were the only Americans to be executed for espionage during the 1950s Red Scare.

others, Klaus Fuchs in Britain and Julius and Ethel Rosenberg in the United States. The Rosenbergs, convicted of espionage, were executed in 1953.

MCCARTHY'S WITCH-HUNT Such revelations encouraged politicians to exploit public fears. If a man of such respectability as Hiss was guilty, many wondered, who then could be trusted? The United States, which bestrode the world like a colossus in 1945, had since "lost" eastern Europe and Asia, and "lost" its atomic secrets to Russia. Early in 1950 the hitherto obscure Republican senator Joseph R. McCarthy of Wisconsin suddenly surfaced as the shrewdest and most ruthless exploiter of such anxieties. He took up the cause, or at least the pose, of anti-communism. He began with a speech at Wheeling, West Virginia, on February 9, 1950, in which he said that the State Department was infested with Communists and that he held in his hand a list of their names. Later there was confusion as to whether he had said 205, 81, 57, or "a lot" of names, and even whether the sheet of paper carried a list. But such confusion always pursued McCarthy's charges.

Challenged to provide names, McCarthy finally pointed to Owen Lattimore of the Johns Hopkins University, an Asia expert, as head of "the espionage ring in the State Department." A special committee under Maryland senator Millard Tydings looked into the matter and pronounced McCarthy's charges "a fraud and a hoax." McCarthy then turned, in what became his common tactic, to other charges, other names. Whenever his charges were refuted, he loosed a scattershot of new charges. By his hit-and-run tactics, McCarthy planted suspicions without proof and grew ever more impudent. "He lied with wild abandon," one commentator wrote; "he lied without evident fear; . . . he lied vividly and with bold imagination; he lied, often, with very little pretense of telling the truth."

Despite his outlandish claims, McCarthy never uncovered a single Communist agent in government. But with the United States at war with Korean Communists in mid-1950, it was easy for him to mobilize true believers. In the elections of 1950 he intervened in Maryland and helped defeat the conservative Tydings with trumped-up charges that Tydings was pro-Communist. Republicans encouraged him to keep up the game. By 1951 he was riding so high as to list General George C. Marshall among the disloyal. His smear campaign went unchallenged until the end of the Korean War.

Senator Joseph McCarthy (left) *and his aide Roy Cohn* (right) *exchange comments during testimony.*

The anti-Communist hysteria led the Congress in 1950 to pass the McCarran Internal Security Act over President Truman's veto. The act made it unlawful "to combine, conspire, or agree with any other person to perform any act which would substantially contribute to . . . the establishment of a totalitarian dictatorship." Communist and Communist-front organizations had to register with the attorney-general. Aliens who had belonged to totalitarian parties were barred from admission to the United States, a provision that discouraged any temptation for Communists to defect to the United States. The McCarran Act, Truman said in his veto message, would "put the Government into the business of thought control." He might in fact have said as much about the Smith Act of 1940, or even his own program of loyalty investigations.

ASSESSING THE COLD WAR   In retrospect, the onset of the cold war takes on an appearance of terrible inevitability. American and Soviet misunderstanding of each other's motives was virtually unavoidable. America's preference for international principles, such as self-determination and democracy, conflicted with Stalin's preference for international spheres of influence. Russia, after all, had been invaded by Germany twice in the first half of the twentieth century, and Soviet leaders wanted tame buffer states on their borders for protection. The people of eastern Europe, as usual, were caught in the middle. But the Communists themselves held to a universal principle: world revolution. And since the time of President Monroe, Americans had bristled at the thought of foreign intervention in their own sphere of influence, the Western Hemisphere. Thus, to create a defensive shield against the spread of communism, the United States signed mutual defense treaties. Under the Treaty of Rio de Janeiro, the nations of the Western Hemisphere agreed to aid any country in the region that was attacked. In 1951, the United States and Japan signed a treaty that permitted the United States to maintain military forces in Japan. That same year, American negotiators signed other mutual defense treaties with the Philippines, Australia, and New Zealand.

If international conditions set the stage for the cold war, the actions of political leaders and thinkers set events in motion. President Truman may have erred in seeming to include all the world in his 1947 doctrine of Communist containment. The loyalty program, following on the heels of the Truman Doctrine, may have spurred on the anti-Communist hysteria of the times. Containment itself proved hard to contain, its author (George Kennan) later confessed, in part because he failed at the outset to spell out its limits explicitly.

The years after World War II were unlike any other postwar period in American history. Having taken on global burdens, the nation had become, if not a "garrison state," at least a country committed to a major and permanent National Military Establishment, along with the attendant National Security Council, Central Intelligence Agency, and by presidential directive in 1952, the enormous National Security Agency, entrusted with monitoring media and communications for foreign intelligence. The policy initiatives of the Truman years had led the country to abandon its long-standing aversion to peacetime alliances not only in the NATO pact but in the agreements with Japan, the Philippines, and the other American nations. It was a far cry from the world of 1796, when George Washington in his farewell address warned his countrymen against "those overgrown military establishments which . . . are inauspicious to liberty" and advised his country "to steer clear of permanent alliances with any portion of the foreign world." But, then, Washington had warned only against participation in the "ordinary" combinations and collusions of Europe, and surely the postwar years had seen extraordinary events.

MAKING CONNECTIONS

- The cold war had a major impact on American society: among other things, it helped create the "conforming culture" described in the next chapter.

- The New Frontier and Great Society programs of Presidents Kennedy and Johnson accomplished much of what Truman tried to do through his Fair Deal policies. See Chapter 34.

- The world seemed a dangerous place at the height of the cold war, but when seen from the perspective of the post–cold war world of the 1990s (see Chapters 36 and 37), it had a certain stability that discouraged political violence.

FURTHER READING

The cold war remains a hotly debated topic. The traditional interpretation is best reflected in John L. Gaddis's *The United States and the Origins of the Cold War, 1941–1947* (1972). Both superpowers, Gaddis argues, were responsible for causing the cold war, but the Soviet Union was more culpable. The revisionist perspective is represented by Gar Alperovitz's *Atomic Diplomacy* (rev. ed., 1994). He places primary responsibility for the conflict on the United States. Also see H. W. Brands's *The Devil We Knew: Americans and the Cold War* (1993), Michael J. Hogan's *The End of the Cold War: Its Meaning and Implications* (1992), Melvyn P. Leffler's *A Preponderance of Power: National Security, the Truman Administration, and the Cold War* (1992), John Lewis Gaddis's *The Long Peace: Inquiries into the History of the Cold War* (rev. ed., 1993), and Wilson D. Miscamble's *George F. Kennan and the Making of American Foreign Policy, 1947–1950* (1992).

Other scholars concentrate on more specific events in the buildup of international tensions. Lynn Etheridge Davis's *The Cold War Begins:*

Soviet-American Conflict over Eastern Europe (1974) and Bruce Kuk-lick's *American Policy and the Division of Germany* (1972) deal with ini-tial tensions at the close of the war. For the Truman administration's re-liance on the atomic bomb monopoly, see Michael Mandelbaum's *The Nuclear Question: The United States and Nuclear Weapons, 1946–1976* (1979) and Daniel Yergin's *Shattered Peace: The Origins of the Cold War and the National Security State* (1977).

For a positive assessment of Truman's leadership, see Alonzo Ham-by's *Beyond the New Deal: Harry S. Truman and American Liberalism* (1973). The domestic policies of the Fair Deal are treated in William C. Berman's *The Politics of Civil Rights in the Truman Administration* (1970), Richard M. Dalfiumes's *Desegregation of the United States Armed Forces* (1969), and Maeva Marcus's *Truman and the Steel Seizure Case: The Limits of Presidential Power* (rev. ed, 1994). The most compre-hensive biography of Truman is David McCullough's *Truman* (1992).

For an introduction to the tensions in Asia, see Akira Iriye's *The Cold War in Asia* (1974). For the Korean conflict, see Callum A. MacDon-ald's *Korea: The War before Vietnam* (1986) and Max Hasting's *The Ko-rean War* (rev. ed., 1993). The high-command perspective is revealed in Michael Schaller's *Douglas MacArthur: The Far Eastern General* (1989).

The anti-Communist syndrome is surveyed in David Caute's *The Great Fear: The Anti-Communist Purge under Truman and Eisenhower* (1978). Thomas C. Reeves's *The Life and Times of Joe McCarthy* (1982) covers McCarthy himself. For a well-documented account of how the cold war was sustained by superpatriotism, intolerance, and suspicion, see Stephen J. Whitfield's *The Culture of the Cold War* (1990). See also Richard Fried's *Nightmare in Red: The McCarthy Era in Perspective* (1990).

32 ✑THROUGH THE PICTURE WINDOW: SOCIETY AND CULTURE, 1945–1960

CHAPTER ORGANIZER

This chapter focuses on:

- the economic prosperity of America in the postwar period.

- the culture of the 1950s, with its strains of conformity and innovation.

- America's burgeoning consumer culture.

*A*mericans emerged from World War II elated, justifiably proud of their military strength and industrial might. As the editors of *Fortune* magazine proclaimed in 1946, "This is a dream era, this is what everyone was waiting through the blackouts for. The Great American Boom is on." So it was, from babies to Buicks to Admiral television sets. An American public that had known mostly deprivation and sacrifice for the last decade and a half began to enjoy unprecedented prosperity. The postwar era witnessed tremendous economic growth and rising social contentment. Divorce and homicide rates fell, the birthrate soared, and the prevailing mood seemed aggressively upbeat.

Yet in the midst of such rising affluence and comfortable domesticity, many social critics, writers, and artists expressed a growing sense of unease. Was postwar American society becoming too complacent, too conformist, too materialistic? Such questions reflected the perennial tension in American life between idealism and materialism, a tension that arrived with the first settlers and remains with us today. Americans have always struggled to accumulate goods and cultivate goodness. During the postwar era, the nation again tried to do both. For a while, at least, it appeared to succeed.

PEOPLE OF PLENTY

THE POSTWAR ECONOMY The dominant feature of post–World War II American society was its remarkable prosperity. After a surprisingly brief postwar recession, the economy soared to record heights. The gross national product (GNP) nearly doubled between 1945 and 1960, and the 1960s witnessed an even more spectacular expansion of the economy. By 1970 the gap between living standards in the United States and the rest of the world had become a chasm: with 6 percent of the world's population, America produced and consumed two-thirds of the world's goods.

During the 1950s, government officials assured the citizenry that they should not fear another economic collapse. "Never again shall we allow a depression in the United States," President Eisenhower promised. The leading economists of the postwar era agreed that the New Deal safeguards built into the economy would prevent another dramatic downturn. They and others led the public to believe that perpetual economic growth was possible, desirable, and, in fact, essential. The expectation of unending plenty became the reigning assumption of social thought in the postwar era.

Several factors contributed to this prolonged economic surge. The massive federal expenditures for military needs during World War II had catapulted the economy out of the Great Depression. High government spending was sustained in the postwar era, thanks to the tensions generated by the cold war and, in the early 1950s, the increase in defense spending provoked by the Korean conflict. The military budget after 1945 represented the single most important stimulant to the postwar economic boom. Defense research also helped spawn the new glamour industries of the postwar era: chemicals, electronics, and aviation.

Most of the other major industrial nations of the world—England, France, Germany, Japan, the Soviet Union—had been physically devastated during the war, which meant that American manufacturers enjoyed a virtual monopoly over international trade. In addition, technological innovations contributed to the "automation" of the workplace and thereby created spectacular increases in productivity. The widespread use of new and more efficient machinery and computers led to a 35 percent jump in worker productivity between 1945 and 1955. In 1945 it took 310 hours to make a car; in 1960, only 150.

The major catalyst in promoting economic expansion after 1945 was the unleashing of pent-up consumer demand. During the war, Americans had postponed purchases of such major items as cars and houses and in the process had saved over $150 billion. Now they were eager to buy. The United States after World War II thus experienced a purchasing frenzy.

THE GI BILL OF RIGHTS   Part of the purchasing frenzy was financed by the federal government. Fears that a sharp drop in military spending and the sudden influx of veterans as new workers would send the economy into a downward spiral and produce widespread unemployment led Congress to pass by a unanimous vote the Servicemen's Readjustment Act of 1944. Popularly known as the GI Bill of Rights (GI stood for the phrase "government issue" stamped on military uniforms and was slang for a serviceman), it led to the creation of a new government agency, the Veterans Administration, and it included provisions for mustering out pay, unemployment pay for veterans for one year, preference for civil service jobs, loans for home construction, access to government hospitals, and generous subsidies for college or professional training.

Almost 8 million veterans took advantage of $14.5 billion in GI Bill subsidies to attend college or job training programs. Some 5 million used additional monies from the GI Bill to buy new homes. These two programs combined to produce a social revolution. The infusion of funds into the economy provided by the GI Bill helped fuel the postwar prosperity. And the educational benefits encouraged people to consider pursuing higher education. Before World War II, approximately 160,000 Americans graduated from college each year. By 1950 the figure had risen to 500,000. In 1949 veterans accounted for 40 percent of all college enrollments, and the United States could boast the world's best-educated workforce.

The GI Bill democratized higher education. It provided a generation of working-class Americans with an opportunity to earn a college degree for the first time. In turn, a college education served as a lever into the middle class and economic security. But while the GI Bill helped erode class barriers, it was less successful in dismantling racial barriers. Many black veterans could not take equal advantage of the education benefits. Most colleges and universities after the war remained racially segregated, either by regulation or by practice. Of the 9,000 students enrolled at the University of Pennsylvania in 1946, for example, only 46 were African Americans. Those blacks who did manage to gain admission to white colleges or universities were barred from playing on athletic teams, attending dances and other social events, and joining fraternities or sororities.

The historically black colleges, most of which were in the South, could not expand quickly enough to meet the demand. In 1940 black colleges enrolled 43,000 students; in 1950 the number had soared to 77,000. Yet over 20,000 were denied admission because of overcrowded facilities. As a result, most black veterans did not get into a college. In 1946 only one-fifth of the 100,000 who had applied for educational benefits had enrolled. In other cases, black veterans were inadequately prepared for college-level work. As late as 1950, some 70 percent of black adults in the southern states had only a seventh-grade education or below.

The return of some 12 million veterans to private life also helped generate a postwar "baby boom," which peaked in 1957. Many young married couples who had delayed having children were intent on making up for lost time. Between 1945 and 1960, total population grew by some 40 million, an increase of almost 30 percent. Much of America's social history since the 1940s has been the story of the unusually large baby-boom generation and its progress through the stages of life. Initially, the postwar baby boom created a massive demand for diapers, baby food, toys, medicines, schools, books, teachers, furniture, and housing.

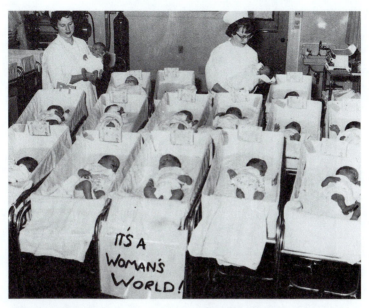

The Baby Boom. *Much of America's social history since the 1940s has been the story of the "baby-boom" generation.*

AN EXPANDING CONSUMER CULTURE   Postwar America soon became a hive of construction activity. The proportion of homeowners in the population increased by 50 percent between 1945 and 1960. And those new homes filled up with the latest appliances—refrigerators, washing machines, sewing machines, vacuum cleaners, freezers, electric mixers, carving knives, shoe polishers.

By far the most popular new household product was the television set. In 1946 there were only 7,000 primitive black-and-white TV sets in the country; by 1960 there were 50 million high-quality sets. Nine out of ten homes had one, and by 1970, 38 percent owned one of the new color sets. *TV Guide* was the fastest-growing new periodical of the 1950s. In 1953 *Business Week* noted that city engineers across the country discovered erratic surges in water consumption during the evening hours, only to discover that Americans, it turned out, were using their bathrooms at the end of television shows and during commercials.

The ubiquitous ownership of television sets not only created a multibillion-dollar industry, it also helped transform the patterns of American social and cultural life. Watching television became an essential daily

I Love Lucy, *starring Lucille Ball* (right), *was one of the most popular television series in the 1950s.*

activity for millions of people. Time previously devoted to reading, visiting, playing, listening to the radio, or movie-going was now spent in front of the "electronic hearth." With the development of "TV dinners" and "TV trays," families no longer had to assemble around a common dinner table; they could eat in silence while watching favorite shows.

What differentiated the affluence of the post–World War II era from earlier periods of prosperity was its ever-widening dispersion. Although rural and urban poverty persisted in every state, and were destined to explode in the 1960s, few commentators noticed such exceptions to the prevailing affluence during the 1950s. Weekly visits to beauty parlors and shopping centers became routine activities for many working-class housewives, and families with two cars were not uncommon. Many boasted a boat or camper as well. When George Meany was sworn in as head of the AFL-CIO in 1955, he proclaimed that "American labor never had it so good."

On the surface many blacks were also beneficiaries of the wave of prosperity that swept over postwar American society. By 1950, African Americans were earning on average more than four times their 1940 wages. One black journalist declared in 1951 that "the progressive improvement of race relations and the economic rise of the Negro in the United States is a flattering example of democracy in action." But while gains had been made, blacks and other minority groups lagged behind whites in their rate of improvement. Indeed, the gap between the average yearly income of whites and blacks widened during the decade of the 1950s. Yet such trends were rarely noticed amid the boosterism of the day. The need to present a united front against communism led commentators to ignore or gloss over issues of racial and economic injustice. Such corrosive neglect would fester and explode during the 1960s, but for now the emphasis was on consensus, conformity, and economic growth.

To perpetuate the postwar prosperity, marketing specialists accelerated their efforts to promote rising expectations and self-gratification. Planned obsolescence became a guiding principle for many manufacturers. Advertising was an even more crucial component of the consumer culture, and during the postwar era advertisers proved adept at exciting consumer desires and social envy. An advertisement for Ford automobiles assured customers that "you'll bask in the envious glances which Ford's Thunderbird styling draws." It then added, "Why not own two?" TV advertising expenditures increased 1,000 percent during the

Mink Coat for Father. *An advertisement for a Ford Thunderbird claims that "What a mink coat does to perk up a lady, a Thunderbird does for a male."*

1950s. Such startling results led the president of the National Broadcasting Company (NBC) to claim in 1956 that the primary reason for the postwar prosperity was that "advertising has created an American frame of mind that makes people want more things, better things, and newer things."

Paying for such "things" was no problem; the age of the credit card had arrived. Between 1945 and 1957, consumer credit soared 800 percent. Where families in other industrialized nations were typically saving 10 to 20 percent of their income, American families by the 1960s were saving only 5 percent. "Never before have so many owed so much to so many," *Newsweek* announced in 1953. "Time has swept away the Puritan conception of immorality in debt and godliness in thrift."

This consumer revolution had far-reaching cultural effects. Shopping became a major recreational activity. In 1945 there were only 8 shopping centers in the entire country; by 1960 there were 3,840. Much as life in a medieval town revolved around the cathedral, life in postwar America seemed to center on the new giant shopping centers and indoor malls.

YOUTH CULTURE   Young people occupied a distinctive place in postwar American life. The children of the postwar baby boom were becoming adolescents during the 1950s, and in the process, a distinctive "teen" subculture began to emerge. Living amid such a prosperous era, teenagers had more money and free time than any previous generation.

Shopping became increasingly important for young Americans. The disproportionate number of adolescents in the population generated a vast new market for goods ranging from transistor radios, Hula-Hoops, and "rock 'n' roll" records to cameras, surfboards, *Seventeen* magazine, and Pat Boone movies. "Today," explained a corporate executive in 1957, "the teenager's income runs to $10 to $15 a week as opposed to $1 to $2 fifteen years ago. It is getting to the point where nearly every teenager has a radio or phonograph, and, in many cases, more than one." Teenagers in the postwar era knew nothing of economic depressions or wartime rationing; immersed in abundance from an early age, the children of prospering parents took the notion of carefree consumption for granted. As a fifteen-year-old Los Angeles girl described her use of a $65 monthly allowance, "I have to save $10, but the rest is mine to do what I want with. I spend about $40 on clothes and the rest on

Hula-Hoop Derby, Brookside Swim Club, New Jersey. *The Hula-Hoop craze was one of many fads of the youth culture.*

records and jewelry. All the teenagers are on that swing. We just find it neat to spend money."

Parents also tended to be more permissive. One commentator described the American family in 1957 as a "child-centered anarchy." To be sure, most young people during the 1950s embraced the values of their parents and the capitalist system. It was "the reassuring truth," reported *Collier's* magazine in 1951, "that the average young American is probably more conservative than you or your neighbor." One critic labeled the college students of the postwar era "the silent generation," content to cavort at fraternity parties and "sock hops" before landing a job with a large corporation, marrying, and settling down into the routine of middle-class suburban life.

Yet such general descriptions masked a great deal of turbulence. During the 1950s, a wave of juvenile delinquency swept across middle-class society. One sociologist went so far as to declare that "no social problem has wrought deeper concern in the United States." By 1956, over a million teens a year were being arrested. Car theft was the leading offense, but larceny, rape, beatings, even murder, were not uncommon. A Boston judge announced that the entire city was being "terrorized" by juvenile gangs.

A Drive-in Movie, *1951. Accessibility to cars gave teenagers in the 1950s mobility and freedom from adult supervision—something that eluded previous generations of adolescents.*

What was causing such delinquency? J. Edgar Hoover, the head of the FBI, insisted that the root of the problem was a lack of religious training in more and more households. Others pointed to the growing number of urban slums. Such "bad" and "brutish" environments almost ensured that children would become criminals. The problem with such explanations was they failed to explain why so many middle-class kids from God-fearing families were becoming delinquents. One contributing factor may have been the unprecedented mobility of young people. Access to automobiles enabled teens to escape parental control, and in the words of a journalist, cars provided "a private lounge for drinking and for petting or sex episodes."

ROCK 'N' ROLL   Many concerned observers blamed the delinquency problem on a new form of music that emerged during the postwar era— rock 'n' roll. Indeed, when the film *The Blackboard Jungle* appeared in 1955, people drew a direct connection between the behavior of the film's juvenile gang members and the rock 'n' roll songs by Bill Haley and the Comets featured in the soundtrack. Rock music combined a strong beat with off-beat accents and repeated harmonic patterns to produce its distinctive sound, and the electric guitar provided the basic instrument. By the mid-1950s it had captured the imagination of young Americans. In 1955 *Life* magazine published a long article about a mysterious new "frenzied teenage music craze," that was creating "a big fuss."

Alan Freed, a Cleveland disc jockey, had coined the term "rock 'n' roll" in 1951. While visiting a record store, he had noticed an interesting new musical trend: white teenagers were buying rhythm and blues (R & B) records that had heretofore been purchased only by African Americans and Chicanos. Freed wanted to take advantage of the new trend, but he realized that few white households would listen to a radio program featuring what was then called "race music." So he began playing R & B records but labeled the music rock 'n' roll (a phrase used in black communities to refer to dancing and sex) to surmount the racial barrier.

Freed's radio program was an immediate success, and its popularity helped bridge the gap between "white" and "black" music. African-American singers such as Chuck Berry, Little Richard, and Ray Charles, and Chicano performers such as Ritchie Valens (Richard Valenzuela) suddenly were the rage among young, white middle-class audiences eager to claim their own cultural style and message. Berry, for example, was distinctive for his biting guitar riffs, inventive vocals, and athletic showmanship. He sang about dating and school life, about alienated teens riding around in cars "with no particular place to go." Valens, whose meteoric career was cut short by his death at age seventeen in a plane crash in 1959 (Buddy Holly was killed in the same accident), wrote a hit song entitled "Donna" about a failed romance with an Anglo classmate whose father ordered her to stop dating "that Mexican" boy. At the same time, Elvis Presley, a young white truck driver and aspiring singer born in Tupelo, Mississippi, and raised in Memphis, Tennessee, began experimenting with "rockabilly" music, his own unique blend of gospel, country-and-western, and R & B rhythms and lyrics.

In 1956 the twenty-one-year-old Presley released his smash hit "Heartbreak Hotel," and over the next two years the sensual baritone garnered fourteen gold records and emerged as the most popular musical entertainer in American history. Presley appeared on numerous television variety shows, starred in movies, and by the end of the decade had captured the attention of the world. His long hair and sideburns,

Elvis Presley, 1956. *The teenage children of middle-class America made rock 'n' roll a thriving industry in the 1950s and Elvis its first star.*

his knowing grins and disobedient sneers, his leather jacket and tight blue jeans—all shouted defiance against adult conventions. His sexually suggestive stage performances featuring twisting hips and a gyrating pelvis drove teenagers wild. Girls attending his performances went into a frenzy, often fainting or throwing themselves at Presley's feet.

Such hysterics prompted cultural conservatives to urge parents to confiscate and destroy Presley's records because they promoted "a pagan concept of life." A Catholic cardinal denounced Presley as a vile symptom of a new teen "creed of dishonesty, violence, lust and degeneration." Patriotic groups claimed that rock music was a tool of Communist insurgents designed to corrupt American youth. One anti-Communist book denounced rock 'n' roll disc jockeys as "Reds, left wingers, or hecklers of social convention." A Buffalo disc jockey was fired for playing Presley's records. And a congressional report concluded that "the gangster of tomorrow is the Elvis Presley type of today." But rock 'n' roll not only survived such assaults, it flourished as an exciting new musical idiom directed at young people experiencing the turbulence of puberty. It gave adolescents a self-conscious sense of being a unique social group with distinctive characteristics. And it represented an unprecedented intermingling of racial, ethnic, and class identities. As such, rock music would become one of the major vehicles of the youth revolt of the 1960s.

THE CRABGRASS FRONTIER   The postwar era witnessed a mass migration to a new frontier—the suburbs. The burgeoning population created new communities and required an array of new services. Almost the entire population increase of the 1950s and 1960s (97 percent) was an urban or suburban phenomenon. Dramatic new technological advances in agricultural production reduced the need for manual laborers and thereby led 20 million Americans to leave the land for the city between 1940 and 1970.

Much of the urban population growth occurred in the South, the Southwest, and the West, in an arc that stretched from the Carolinas down through Texas and into California, diverse states that by the 1970s were being lumped together into the "Sunbelt." Air conditioning, developed by Willis Haviland Carrier in the first decade of the century, became a common household fixture in the 1950s and enhanced the appeal of warm climates. But the Northeast remained the most densely populated area; by the early 1960s, 20 percent of the national population lived in the corridor that stretched from Boston to Norfolk, Virginia.

While more concentrated in cities, post–World War II Americans were simultaneously spreading out within metropolitan areas. In 1950 the Census Bureau redefined the term "urban" to include suburbs as well as central cities. During the 1950s, suburbs grew six times faster than cities. By 1970, more Americans lived in suburbs (76 million) than in central cities (64 million). "Suburbia," proclaimed the *Christian Century* in 1955, "is now a dominant social group in American life." During the 1950s, some 3,000 acres of grassland and forests were bulldozed each day to make room for new suburban housing developments.

William Levitt, a brassy New York developer, led the suburban revolution. Levitt and his brother made a fortune during the depression by building houses. But the Levitts really struck it rich after the war, when the demand for new housing skyrocketed, and they developed an efficient system of mass production. In 1947, on 1,200 acres of Long Island farmland, they built 10,600 houses that were immediately sold and inhabited by more than 40,000 people—mostly young adults under thirty-five and their children. "Everyone is so young," one Levittowner

Levittown. *Identical and affordable housing was built in Levittown, Long Island, to provide homes for veterans and families in the suburbs.*

noted, "that sometimes it's hard to remember how to get along with older people."

Within a few years there were similar Levittowns in Pennsylvania and New Jersey, and other developers soon followed suit in places such as Lakewood, near Long Beach, California, and Park Forest, thirty miles south of Chicago. This suburban revolution benefited greatly from federal government assistance. "If it weren't for the government," one San Francisco developer explained, "the boom would end overnight." By insuring loans for up to 95 percent of the value of a house, the Federal Housing Administration made it easy for a builder to construct low-cost homes. Veterans got added benefits. A veteran could buy a Levitt house with no down payment and monthly mortgage installments of $56.

Expanded automobile production and highway construction also facilitated the rush to the suburbs, as more and more people were able to commute longer distances to work. Car production soared from 2 million in 1946 to 8 million in 1955, and a "car culture" soon transformed social behavior. As one commentator observed, the proliferation of automobiles "changed our dress, manners, social customs, vacation habits, the shape of our cities, consumer purchasing patterns, [and] common tastes." Widespread car ownership also necessitated an improved road network. Local and state governments built many new roads, but the guiding force was the federal government. In 1947 Congress authorized the construction of 37,000 miles of highways, and nine years later it funded over 42,000 additional miles in a new national system of interstate expressways.

Cars and roads provided access to the suburbs, and Americans— mostly middle-class white Americans—rushed to take advantage of the new living spaces. The motives for moving to the suburbs were numerous. The availability of more spacious homes as well as greater security and better educational opportunities for children all played a role. Racial considerations were also a factor. After World War II, African Americans migrated to the cities of the North and Midwest. As they moved in, many white residents moved out. Those engaged in "white flight" were usually eager to maintain residential segregation in their new suburban communities. Contracts for houses in Levittown, Long Island, for example, specifically excluded "members of other than the Caucasian race." Such discrimination, whether explicit or implicit, was widespread; the nation's suburban population in 1970 was 95 percent white.

THE GREAT BLACK MIGRATION   World War II, like World War I, helped spur a mass migration of rural southern blacks to the urban North and Midwest. This second migratory stream was much larger in scope than the first, and its social consequences were much more dramatic. After 1945 more than 5 million southern blacks, mostly farm folk, left their native region in search of better jobs, higher wages, decent housing, and greater social equality. During the 1950s, for example, the black population of Chicago more than doubled. As many as 3,000 migrants a week arrived at the Illinois Central train station. The South Side of Chicago soon became known as the capital of black America. It remains the largest concentration of African Americans in the country. In its scope and effects, this internal migration of blacks from South to North was as significant as the early settlement of the West.

Most of these southern blacks were sharecroppers and farm laborers from the Mississippi Delta, the richest cotton-producing land in the world. For over a century the Delta cotton culture had been dependent on black workers, first as slaves and then as sharecroppers and wage laborers. But a mechanical cotton picker invented in 1944 changed all that. The new machine could do the work of fifty people, thus making many farm workers superfluous. Displaced southern blacks, many of them illiterate and provincial, streamed northward in search of a new promised land, only to see many of their dreams dashed. The great writer Richard Wright, himself a migrant from the Delta to Chicago, observed that "never in history has a more utterly unprepared folk wanted to go to the city." In northern cities such as Chicago, Philadelphia, Newark, Detroit, New York, Boston, and Washington, D.C., rural blacks from the South confronted harsh new realities. Slumlords often gouged them for rent, many employers refused to hire them, and union bosses denied them membership. Soon the promised land had become for many an ugly nightmare of slum housing, joblessness, illiteracy, dysfunctional families, welfare dependency, street gangs, pervasive crime, and racism.

The unexpected tidal wave of black migrants severely taxed the resources of urban governments and the patience of white racists. For several nights during 1951, a white mob in a Chicago suburb assaulted a building into which a black family had moved. The National Guard had to quell the disturbance and disperse the crowd. Like other northern cities, Chicago sought to deal with the migrants and alleviate racial stress by constructing massive, all-black public housing projects to accommodate the newcomers. But these overcrowded racial enclaves were essentially segregated prisons. To be sure, many black migrants and their children did manage through extraordinary determination and ingenuity to "clear," that is, to climb out of the teeming ghettos and into the middle class. But most did not. As a consequence, the great black migration produced a web of complex social problems that in the 1960s would burgeon into a crisis.

A CONFORMING CULTURE

In the 1950s, American social commentators mostly ignored people and cultures outside the middle-class mainstream. As evidenced in many of the new look-alike suburbs sprouting up across the land, much of middle-class social life during the two decades after the end of World War II exhibited an increasingly homogenized character. Fears gener-

Office in a Small City. *Edward Hopper's 1953 painting suggests the alienation associated with white-collar work and a new corporate atmosphere in the 1950s.*

ated by the cold war initially played a key role in encouraging orthodoxy. But McCarthyism was simply the most visible symbol of the many political and social forces promoting common standards of behavior. Suburban life itself encouraged uniformity. In new communities of strangers, people felt a need for companionship and a sense of belonging. "Nobody wants people around who criticize and sit off by themselves and don't take part," observed one resident. Changes in corporate life as well as the influence of the consumer culture also played an important socializing role. "Conformity," predicted an editor in 1954, "may very well become the central social problem of this age."

CORPORATE LIFE   The composition of the American workforce and the very nature of work itself were dramatically changing during the postwar era. More time became available for leisure, as the standard workweek shrank from five and a half days to five days. Fewer people were self-employed, and manual labor was rapidly giving way to mental labor. By the mid-1950s, white-collar (salaried) workers outnumbered blue-collar (hourly-wage) workers for the first time in American history.

Some 60 percent of the population enjoyed a "middle-class" standard of living (defined as annual family incomes of $3,000 to $10,000 in constant dollars). In 1929, before the stock market crash, only 31 percent were so designated. Managers, teachers, professors, researchers, salespeople, government employees, and office workers now constituted the bulk of the workforce, and they tended to work in larger and larger organizations.

This change happened because during World War II big business grew bigger. The government relaxed antitrust activity, and huge defense contracts tended to promote corporate concentration and consolidation. In 1940, for example, 100 companies were responsible for 30 percent of all manufacturing output; three years later, they were providing 70 percent. After the war, a wave of mergers occurred, and dominant corporate giants appeared in every major industry, providing the primary source of new jobs. By 1960, 38 percent of the workforce was employed by organizations with more than 500 employees. In such huge companies, as well as similarly large government agencies and universities, the working atmosphere began to take on a distinctive new cast. The traditional notion of the hardworking, strong-minded individual advancing by dint of competitive ability and creative initiative gave way to the concept of a new managerial personality and an ethic of corporate cooperation and achievement.

WOMEN'S PLACE   Increasing conformity in the middle-class workplace was mirrored in the middle-class home. A special issue of *Life* magazine in 1956 featured the "ideal" middle-class woman, a thirty-two-year-old "pretty and popular" suburban housewife, mother of four, who had married at age sixteen. She was described as an excellent wife, mother, volunteer, and "home manager" who made her own clothes, hosted dozens of dinner parties each year, sang in the church choir, worked with the school PTA and Campfire Girls, and was devoted to her husband. "In her daily round," *Life* reported, "she attends club or charity meetings, drives the children to school, does the weekly grocery shopping, makes ceramics, and is planning to study French." She also exercised on a trampoline in order "to keep her size 12 figure."

Life's description of the middle-class woman was symptomatic of a cult of feminine domesticity that witnessed a dramatic revival in the postwar era. The soaring birthrate reinforced the deeply embedded no-

The Ideal Woman. *A 1956* Life *magazine cover story pronounced the ideal woman a "pretty and popular" suburban housewife who "attends club or charity meetings, drives the children to school, does the weekly grocery shopping, makes ceramics, and is planning to study French."*

tion that a woman's place was in the home as tender of the hearth and guardian of the children. "Of all the accomplishments of the American woman," the *Life* cover story proclaimed, "the one she brings off with the most spectacular success is having babies."

Even though millions of women had responded to wartime appeals and joined the traditionally male workforce, afterward they were encouraged—and even forced—to turn their jobs over to the returning male veterans and resume their full-time commitment to home and family. A 1945 article in *House Beautiful* lectured women on their postwar responsibilities. The returning veteran, it said, was "head man again. . . . Your part in the remaking of this man is to fit his home to him, understanding why he wants it this way, forgetting your own preferences." Women were also to forget wartime-generated thoughts of their own career in the workplace. "Back to the kitchen," was the repeated refrain. "Women must boldly announce," a Barnard College trustee asserted in 1950, "that no job is more exacting, more necessary, or more rewarding than that of housewife and mother." She then pleaded:

"God protect us all from the efficient, go-getter businesswoman whose feminine instincts have been completely sterilized."

Throughout the postwar era, educators, politicians, ministers, advertisers, and other commentators exalted the cult of domesticity and castigated the few feminists who were encouraging women to broaden their horizons beyond crib and kitchen. Two social psychologists, Marynia Farnham and Ferdinand Lundberg, published a best-selling book in 1947 entitled *Modern Woman: The Lost Sex,* in which they invoked the authority of science to reinforce the view that women could achieve fulfillment *only* by accepting their natural functions as wives and mothers. Such notions sound farfetched today, but they were widely embraced in the postwar era. Even such a liberal politician and self-styled progressive intellectual as Adlai Stevenson preached a similar doctrine. He reminded Smith College graduates in 1955 that their heroic purpose in life was to "influence man and boy" in the "humble role of housewife."

SEARCH FOR COMMUNITY Another illustration of the conformist tendencies of middle-class life during the Eisenhower years was the growth of membership in social organizations. Americans were on the move after World War II. Not only were they moving from the central cities to the suburbs, they were moving from suburb to suburb, farm to city, state to state. Some 20 percent of the population changed their place of residence each year. In Levittown an average of 3,000 homes

Moving Day, *1953. A new subdivision opens its doors.*

Sewing Club, Fort Hays, Kansas, 1950. *Club membership provided quick friends and a sense of community for those who frequently moved from place to place.*

per year turned over. A major cause of such mobility was the standard policy of the largest corporations to relocate their sales and managerial employees. IBM executives told friends that the company initials actually stood for "I've Been Moved." Such flux led people to search for a sense of community and rootedness. Hence middle-class Americans, even more than usual, tended to be joiners; they joined civic clubs, garden clubs, bridge clubs, carpools, and babysitting groups.

They also joined churches and synagogues in record numbers. "One comes early to get a seat in suburban churches," a writer observed in 1956; "they overflow, and new ones are being built every day." The postwar era witnessed a massive renewal of religious participation. "Since Communists are anti-God," FBI director J. Edgar Hoover urged, "encourage your child to be active in the church." Many American parents heeded his warning. In 1940 less than half the adult population belonged to churches; by 1960 over 65 percent were official communicants. Sales of Bibles soared during the postwar era, and books, movies, and songs with religious themes were pervasive.

President Eisenhower repeatedly promoted a patriotic crusade to bring Americans back to God. "Recognition of the Supreme Being," he declared, "is the first, the most basic, expression of Americanism. Without God, there could be no American form of government, nor an American way of life." The president had himself first joined a church only in 1953, but he characterized himself as the "most intensely religious man I know." Not to be outdone, Congress in 1954 added the phrase "one nation under God" to the Pledge of Allegiance, and the following year made the statement "In God We Trust" mandatory on all American currency.

Another reason for the increase in popular piety and church membership was that religious groups adopted the same marketing techniques successfully employed by American manufacturers. Billboards across the country urged viewers to "bring the whole family to church," and television commercials declared that the "family that prays together stays together." Catholic bishop Fulton J. Sheen's weekly television show, *Life Is Worth Living,* was a prime-time hit. At another point on the denominational spectrum, Baptist evangelical Billy Graham used both radio and television in promoting his huge crusades. Religious leaders even catered to the new car culture by performing services at drive-in movie theaters.

The prevailing tone of the popular religious revival during the 1950s was upbeat and soothing. Many ministers assumed that people were not interested in "fire-and-brimstone" harangues from the pulpit; they did not want their consciences overly burdened with a sense of personal sin or social guilt over such issues as racial segregation or inner-city poverty. Instead they wanted to be reassured that their own comfortable way of life was indeed God's will. As the Protestant Council of New York City explained to its corps of radio and television speakers, their addresses "should project love, joy, courage, hope, faith, trust in God, goodwill. Generally avoid condemnation, criticism, controversy. In a very real sense we are 'selling' religion, the good news of the Gospel."

By far the best salesman of this gospel of reassuring "good news" was the Reverend Norman Vincent Peale. Drawing on a long tradition of "positive thinking" in American social and religious thought, Peale perfected feel-good theology. No speaker was more in demand during the 1950s, and no writer was more widely read. Peale's book *The Power of Positive Thinking* (1952) was a phenomenal best-seller throughout the decade—and for good reason. It offered a simple "how-to" course in personal happiness. "Flush out all depressing, negative, and tired

Billy Graham Preaches to Thousands, *1955. Encouraged by the president and Congress, radio, television, and billboard advertising, droves of Americans joined churches and synagogues and attended revival meetings.*

thoughts," Peale advised. "Start thinking faith, enthusiasm, and joy." By following this simple formula for success, he pledged, the reader could become "a more popular, esteemed, and well-liked individual."

Peale's message of psychological security and material success was powerfully reassuring, and the psychological needs he addressed were indeed real. By 1957 tranquilizers were the fastest-growing new medication in the country, suggesting that considerable anxiety accompanied America's much-trumpeted affluence. Many people, living uneasily amid the moral and social dilemmas of the postwar period, were profoundly anxious about the meaning of life in general and their lives in particular. Peale offered them peace of mind and soul, assuring them that everything was fine and for the best as long as they believed in God, the American Way, and themselves.

NEO-ORTHODOXY "Stop worrying and start living" was Peale's simple credo. But was it too simplistic? The "peace of mind" and "positive thinking" psychology promoted by Peale and other feel-good ministers struck some members of the religious community as shallow and misleading. In *Protestant–Catholic–Jew* (1955), Will Herberg, professor of Judaic Studies at Drew University, described the popular spiritual revival as representing "religiousness without religion, a religiousness with almost any kind of content or none, a way of sociability or 'belonging,' rather than a way of reorienting life toward God." Such consoling religiosity, he felt, lacked genuine conviction and depth of commitment. Herberg and other theologians steadfastly resisted the dilution of traditional Judeo-Christian beliefs. These advocates of "neo-orthodoxy" especially criticized those who identified the United States as the only truly providential society and who used faith as a sanction for the social status quo.

The most significant spokesman for such "neo-orthodoxy" was Reinhold Niebuhr. A brilliant, penetrating, ironic, and erratic preacher-professor at New York's Union Theological Seminary, Niebuhr lambasted the "undue complacency and conformity" that had settled over American life in the postwar era. Like Herberg, he found the popular religion of self-assurance and psychology of material success woefully inadequate prescriptions for the ills of modern society. "They can not be taken seriously by responsible religious or secular people," he admonished in 1955, "because they do not come to terms with the basic collective problems of our atomic age, and because the peace which they seek to inculcate is rather too simple and neat." True peace, Niebuhr insisted, involves not the cheap comfort and sedating reassurance offered by Peale and other popular evangelists but the reality of pain, a pain "caused by love and responsibility" for the well-being of the entire human race, rather than concern only with one's tortured self. Self-love, he reminded smug Americans, was the very basis of sin.

CRACKS IN THE PICTURE WINDOW

Niebuhr was one of many impassioned disturbers of the peace who challenged the moral complacency and social conformity that he and others felt had come to characterize American social life during the 1950s and early 1960s. The widely publicized evidence of middle-class prosperity masked festering poverty in rural areas and urban ghettos. Moreover, one of the most striking aspects of postwar American life was the sharp contrast between the buoyant public mood and the increasingly bitter criticism of American life coming from intellectuals, theologians, novelists, playwrights, poets, and artists. As the philosopher and editor Joseph Wood Krutch recognized in 1960, "the gap between those who find the spirit of the age congenial and those who do not seems to have grown wider and wider."

THE LONELY CROWD   The criticism of postwar American life and values began in the early 1950s and quickly gathered momentum. Scores of books and articles swollen with mournful righteousness and unsettling truths decried virtually every area of the nation's social life. A common fear unified such fulminations: America in the age of Eisenhower was becalmed in a sea of conformity, content to succumb to the soul-denying demands of the corporate "rat race," and eager to wallow in the consumer culture. In *The Affluent Society* (1958), for example, the economist John Kenneth Galbraith attacked the prevailing notion that sustained economic growth would solve America's chronic social problems. The public sector was starved for funds, Galbraith argued, and public enterprises were everywhere deteriorating. He reminded readers that for all of America's vaunted postwar prosperity, the nation had yet to eradicate poverty.

Commuters on the 5:57, Park Forest, Illinois. *Postwar social critics commented on the overwhelming conformity of middle-class corporate and suburban life.*

Another frequent target of postwar cultural criticism was the supposed serenity of middle-class corporate and suburban life. John Keats, in *The Crack in the Picture Window* (1956), launched the most savage assault on life in the huge new suburban developments. He ridiculed Levittown and other such mass-produced communities as having been "conceived in error, nurtured in greed, corroding everything they touch." In these rows of "identical boxes spreading like gangrene," commuter fathers were always at work and "mothers were always delivering children, obstetrically once and by car forever after." Locked into a monotonous routine, hounded by financial insecurity, and engulfed by mass mediocrity, suburbanites, he concluded, were living in a "homogeneous, postwar Hell."

Mass-produced suburban developments did exhibit a startling sameness. Levittown, for example, encouraged and even enforced uniformity. The houses all sold for the same price—$7,990—and featured the same floor plan and accessories. Each had a picture window, a living room, bath, kitchen, and two bedrooms. Kitchens were equipped with a refrigerator, stove, and Bendix washer, and the living room featured a built-in Admiral television set. A tree was planted every twenty-eight feet. Homeowners were required to cut their grass once a week, fences were prohibited, and laundry could not be hung out on weekends. However, Levittown was in many ways distinctive rather than representative. There were thousands of suburbs by the mid-1950s, and few were as regimented or as unvarying as Keats and other critics implied. Keats also failed to recognize the benefits that the suburbs offered those who would have otherwise remained in crowded urban apartments.

Still, there was more than a grain of truth to the charge that postwar American life was becoming oppressively regimented, and the huge modern corporation was repeatedly cited by social critics as the primary villain. The most comprehensive and provocative analysis of the docile new corporate character was David Riesman's *The Lonely Crowd* (1950). Riesman and his research associates detected a fundamental shift in the dominant American personality from what they called the "inner-directed" to the "other-directed" type. Inner-directed people possessed a deeply internalized set of basic values implanted by strong-minded parents or other elders. This core set of fixed principles, analogous to the traditional Protestant ethic of piety, diligence, and thrift, acted, in Riesman's words, like an internal gyroscope. Once set in mo-

Dr. Benjamin Spock's The Common Sense Book of Baby and Child Care *was enormously influential with the parents of baby boomers.*

tion by parents and other authority figures, inner-directed people had a built-in stabilizer of fixed values that kept them on course.

Such an assured, self-reliant personality, Riesman argued, had been dominant in American life throughout the nineteenth century. But during the mid–twentieth century, an other-directed personality had displaced it. As the emphasis of industrial capitalism shifted from manipulating machines to manipulating workers, the new corporate culture demanded employees who could win friends and influence people rather than rugged individualists indifferent to personal popularity. Other-directed people were more concerned with being well liked than being independent. In the workplace they were always smiling, always glad-handing, always trying to please the boss.

Riesman amassed considerable evidence to show that the other-directed personality was not just an aspect of the business world; its premises were widely dispersed throughout middle-class life. Dr. Benjamin Spock's advice on raising children, Riesman pointed out, had become immensely influential. Spock's popular manual, *The Common Sense Book of Baby and Child Care,* sold an average of 1 million copies a year between its first appearance in 1946 and 1960. Spock said that parents should foster in their children qualities and skills that would enhance their chances in what Riesman called the "popularity market."

By the mid-1950s, social commentators were growing increasingly concerned that such a managerial personality had come to dominate American life. In his influential study, *White Collar Society* (1956), the sociologist C. Wright Mills attacked the attributes and influence of modern corporate life. "When white-collar people get jobs," Mills explained, "they sell not only their time and energy, but their personalities as well. They sell by the week or month their smiles and their kindly gestures, and they must practice the prompt repression of resentment and aggression." William A. Whyte, Jr., the editor of *Fortune,* presented a similar critique in his widely discussed book *The Organization Man* (1956). The new corporate culture, he charged, stressed "a belief in the group as the source of creativity; a belief in 'belongingness' as the ultimate need of the individual."

ALIENATION AND LIBERATION

THE STAGE Many of the best dramatic plays of the postwar period reinforced Riesman's image of modern American society as a "lonely crowd" of individuals without internal values, hollow at the core, groping for a sense of belonging and affection. Arthur Miller's play *Death of a Salesman* (1949), for example, was a powerful exploration of the theme. Willy Loman, an aging, confused salesman in decline, has centered his life and that of his family on the notion that material success is secured through personal popularity, only to be abruptly told by his boss that he is in fact a failure. Loman insists that it is "not what you say, it's how you say it—because personality always wins the day." He had tried to raise his sons, Biff and Happy, in his own image, encouraging them to be athletic, outgoing, popular, and ambitious. As he instructs them: "Be liked and you will never want." Happy followed his father's advice but was anything but happy: "Sometimes I sit in my apartment—all alone. And I think of the rent I'm paying. And it's crazy. But then, it's what I always wanted. My own apartment, a car, and plenty of women. And still, goddammit, I'm lonely." Such vacant loneliness is the play's recurring theme. Willy, for all his puffery about being well liked, admits in a fit of candor that he is "terribly lonely." He has no real

In Arthur Miller's Death of a Salesman, *Willy Loman (center, played by Lee J. Cobb) destroys his life and family with the credo "Be liked and you will never want."*

friends; even his relations with his family are neither honest nor intimate. "He never knew who he was," Biff sighs. When Willy finally realizes that he has been leading a counterfeit existence, he is so dumbfounded that he decides he can endow his life with meaning only by ending it.

Death of a Salesman and many other postwar plays written by Arthur Miller, Edward Albee, and Tennessee Williams portray a central concern of American literature and art during the postwar era: the sense of alienation experienced by sensitive individuals in the midst of an oppressive mass culture. As the novelist Philip Roth, author of *Goodbye Columbus* (1959), observed in 1961: "The American writer in the middle of the twentieth century has his hands full in trying to understand, and then describe, and then make credible much of American reality. It stupefies, it sickens, it infuriates, and finally it is even a kind of embarrassment to one's own meager imagination." Such a gloomy assessment illustrated the revulsion felt by other writers and artists, and many of them were determined to lay bare the conceits and illusions of their times.

THE NOVEL   The most enduring novels of the postwar period display a shared preoccupation with the individual's struggle for survival amid the smothering and disorienting forces of mass society. While the millions were reading heartwarming religious epics such as *The Cardinal*

(1950), *The Robe* (1953), and *Exodus* (1959), critics were praising the more disturbing writings of James Baldwin, Saul Bellow, John Cheever, Ralph Ellison, Joseph Heller, James Jones, Norman Mailer, Joyce Carol Oates, J. D. Salinger, William Styron, John Updike, and Eudora Welty. Their works had few happy endings—and even fewer celebrations of contemporary American life.

A brooding sense of resigned alienation animated the best literature in the two decades after 1945. J. D. Salinger's *The Catcher in the Rye* (1951) was an unsettling exploration of a young man's search for meaning and self in a stifling society. Holden Caulfield finally decides that rebellion against conformity is useless. "If you want to stay alive," he concludes, "you have to say that stuff like 'Glad to meet you' to people you are not at all glad to meet." The characters in novels such as Jones's *From Here to Eternity*, Ellison's *Invisible Man*, Bellow's *Dangling Man* and *Seize the Day*, Styron's *Lie Down in Darkness*, and Updike's *Rabbit, Run*, among many others, tended to be like Willy Loman—restless, tormented, and often socially impotent individuals who can find neither contentment nor respect in an overpowering or uninterested world.

In *From Here to Eternity* (1951) the hero, Private Prewitt, can neither "stomach nor understand nor explain nor change" the world around him. African-American writer Ralph Ellison also explored the theme of

Ralph Ellison, author of Invisible Man.

the lonely individual imprisoned in privacy in his kaleidoscopic novel *Invisible Man* (1952). By using a black narrator struggling to find and liberate himself in the midst of an oppressive white society, Ellison forcefully accentuated the problem of alienation. The narrator opens by confessing: "All my life I had been looking for something, and everywhere I turned someone tried to tell me what it was. I accepted their answers too, though they were often in contradiction and even self-contradictory. I was naive. I was looking for myself and asking everyone except myself questions which I, and only I, could answer."

PAINTING   The artist Edward Hopper also explored the theme of desolate loneliness in urban-industrial American life. His concern grew more acute in the postwar era. Virtually all of his paintings of the period depict isolated individuals, melancholy, anonymous, motionless. A woman undressing for bed, a diner seated at a table in an all-night restaurant, a housewife in a doorway, a businessman at his desk, a lone passerby in the street—these are the characters of Hopper's world. The silence of his scenes is deafening, the monotony striking, the alienation absorbing.

A younger group of painters in New York City decided that postwar society was so chaotic that it precluded any attempt at literal representation. As Jackson Pollock maintained, "the modern painter cannot express this age—the airplane, the atomic bomb, the radio—in the old form of the Renaissance or of any past culture. Each age finds its own technique." The technique Pollock adopted came to be called abstract expressionism, and during the late 1940s and 1950s it dominated not only the American art scene but the international field as well. In addition to Pollock, its adherents included Robert Motherwell, Willem de Kooning, Arshile Gorky, Franz Kline, Clyfford Still, and Mark Rothko. "Abstract art," Motherwell explained, "is an effort to close the void that modern men feel."

In practice this meant that the *act* of painting was as important as the final result. If artists could not bridge the gap between themselves and their contemporary society, they could find meaning through the spontaneous expression of their subjective selves. To do so they adopted a technique called "action painting." Pollock, for example, would place his huge canvases flat on the floor, then walk around each side, pouring and dripping his paints, all in an effort to "literally be *in* the painting." As an approving art critic recognized, a Pollock "canvas was not a pic-

Jackson Pollock at Work. *Pollock poured paint from a can and then dripped and splattered it across the canvas with a stick to create his "action paintings."*

ture but an event. . . . It is the artist's existence . . . he is living on the canvas." Such action paintings were vibrant, frenzied, meditative, disorienting, provocative. Needless to say, the general public found them simply provoking. As one wit observed: "I suspect any picture I think I could have made myself."

THE BEATS   In Saul Bellow's novel *Dangling Man* (1946), a character concludes that the dynamic of life is the "desire for pure freedom." The desire to liberate self-expression, to surmount organizational constraints and discard traditional conventions, was an abiding goal of the abstract expressionists. It was also the central concern of a small but highly visible and controversial group of young writers, poets, painters, and musicians known as the Beats. These angry young men—Jack Kerouac, Allen Ginsberg, Gary Snyder, William Burroughs, and Gregory Corso, among others—rebelled against the regimented horrors of war and the mundane horrors of middle-class life. *Time* called the Beats "a pack of oddballs who celebrate booze, dope, sex, and despair." The Beats, however, were not lost in despair; they strenuously embraced life. But it was life on their own terms, and those terms were shocking to most observers.

The Beats grew out of the bohemian underground in New York's Greenwich Village. They were all unique personalities. Kerouac was a handsome, athletic, working-class kid from Lowell, Massachusetts, who went to Columbia University on a football scholarship. In 1943 he quit school to join the navy. But he soon tired of military discipline, and one day he simply lay down his gun at drill and went to the library. He was arrested and confined in the psychiatric ward, and later was discharged for "indifferent character."

Ginsberg, a skinny New Jersey boy with horn-rimmed glasses, an unstable mother, and an intense love for poetry and ideas, had declared at age fourteen that "I'll be a genius of some kind or another, probably in literature. Either I'm a genius, I'm eccentric, or I'm slightly schizophrenic. Probably the first two." Probably all three, some thought. Ginsberg also studied at Columbia, where he became friends with Kerouac and where a dean directed him to undergo psychotherapy. Ginsberg chose Burroughs as his therapist.

Allen Ginsberg, considered the poet laureate of the Beat generation, reading his uncensored poetry to a crowd in Washington Square Park in New York City.

It was an interesting choice, for Burroughs was the most eccentric of the trio. A graduate of Harvard in 1936, he had studied medicine in Vienna, then worked as an advertising copywriter, detective, bartender, and pest exterminator. He had also cut off one of his fingers during a "Van Gogh kick." Later he would become a heroin addict, kill his wife while trying to shoot an apple off her head, and write the influential experimental novel *Naked Lunch* (1959).

This fervent threesome soon added a fourth member: Neal Cassady, a twenty-year-old ex-convict who arrived in New York from Denver, hoping to enroll at Columbia. Cassady was pure physical and sensual energy. He could throw a football seventy yards and run a hundred yards in less than ten seconds. He claimed he had stolen over 500 cars and had had sex with almost as many people. Ginsberg, Kerouac, and Burroughs were enthralled by Cassady's frenzied sexuality and vital force. They viewed him as a mythic cowboy turned "cool" hipster, free and rootless because he defied both maturity and reason. Soon others joined this quartet in quest of *real* life, and the Beat culture was born. Ginsberg explained that the glue binding them together was their sense of estrangement from a hostile culture and their ability to confess to one another their innermost feelings.

In New York the self-described "Beats" began their quest for a visionary sensibility and spontaneous way of life. Essentially apolitical throughout the 1950s, they were more interested in transforming themselves than in reforming the world. They sought personal rather than social solutions to their anxieties. Kerouac defined the Beat generation as "basically a religious generation. Beat means beatitude, not beat up. You *feel* this. You feel it in a beat, in jazz—real cool jazz or a good gutty rock number." As Kerouac insisted, his friends were not beat in the sense of beaten; they were "mad to live, mad to talk, mad to be saved." Their road to salvation lay in hallucinogenic drugs and alcohol, sex, a penchant for jazz and the street life of urban ghettos, an affinity for Buddhism, and a restless, vagabond spirit that took them speeding back and forth across the country between San Francisco and New York during the 1950s.

This existential mania for intense experience and frantic motion provided the subject matter for the Beats' writings. Ginsberg's long prose-poem *Howl*, published in 1956, featured an explicit sensuality as well as an impressionistic attempt to catch the color, movement, and dynamism of modern life. Ginsberg howled at the "Robot apartments! invincible suburbs! skeleton treasuries! blind capitals! demonic industries!" Kerouac issued his autobiographical novel *On the Road* a year later. In frenzied prose and plotless ramblings, it portrayed the Beats' life of "bursting ecstasies" and maniacal traveling. At one point Dean Moriarty (Neal Cassady) has the following exchange with Sal Paradise (Kerouac): "We gotta go and never stop going till we get there." "Where we going, man?" "I don't know, but we gotta go."

Howl and *On the Road* provoked sarcasm and anger from many reviewers, but the books enjoyed a brisk sale, especially among young people. *On the Road* made the best-seller list, and soon the term "Beat generation" or "beatnik" referred to almost any young rebel who openly dissented from the comfortable ethos of middle-class life. Defiant, unruly actors such as James Dean and Marlon Brando were added to the pantheon of Beat "anti-heroes." In *The Wild One* (1954) a waitress asks Brando what he is rebelling against. He replies: "Whattaya got?" Acid-tongued comedians Mort Sahl and Lenny Bruce displayed affinities with the Beats, and a young folksinger from Minnesota named Bob Dylan was directly inspired by *Howl* and *On the Road*. In this sense, the anarchic gaiety of the Beats played an important role in preparing the way for the more widespread youth revolt of the 1960s.

A PARADOXICAL ERA

For all their color and vitality, the Beats had little impact on the larger patterns of postwar social and cultural life. Nor did most of the other critics who attacked the smug conformity and excessive materialism they saw pervading society. The tone of the nation's social life exuded a sense of tranquil fulfillment and bouncy optimism. By the mid-1960s, however, tensions between innovation and convention would erupt into open conflict. The children of the postwar boom times would become the leaders of the 1960s rebellion against the corporate and consumer cultures. Ironically, the person who would warn Americans of the 1960s about the mounting dangers of the burgeoning "military-industrial complex" was the president who had long symbolized its growth—Dwight D. Eisenhower.

MAKING CONNECTIONS

- The culture of the 1950s laid the groundwork for the counterculture of the 1960s. See Chapters 34 and 35.

- There are fruitful comparisons between American culture in the 1950s and the earlier postwar period, the 1920s. See Chapter 26.

- The women's movement of the 1970s, discussed in Chapter 35, was led by women who rejected the cult of domesticity described in this chapter.

- The baby boom of the postwar period would have continuing economic, social, political, and cultural significance as this generation moved through the life cycle. Follow along in coming chapters.

FURTHER READINGS

Two excellent overviews of social and cultural trends in the postwar era are William H. Chafe's *The Unfinished Journey: America Since World War II* (rev. ed., 1995) and William E. Leuchtenburg's *A Troubled Feast: America Since 1945* (rev. ed., 1983). For fascinating insights into the cultural life of the 1950s, see Douglas T. Miller and Marion Nowak's *The Fifties: The Way We Really Were* (1977), Jeffrey Hart's *When the Going Was Good: American Life in the Fifties* (1982), and David Halberstam's *The Fifties* (1993).

The baby-boom generation and its impact are vividly described in Paul C. Light's *Baby Boomers* (1988). Readers interested in economic trends should consult David P. Calleo's *The Imperious Economy* (1981). A comprehensive history of the advertising industry and its cultural implications can be found in Jackson Lears's *Fables of Abundance: A Cul-*

tural History of Advertising in America (1994). The emergence and impact of the television industry are discussed in Erik Barnouw's *Tube of Plenty: The Evolution of American Television* (1982) and Ella Taylor's *Prime-Time Families: Television Culture in Postwar America* (1989).

A comprehensive account of the process of suburban development is Kenneth Jackson's award-winning study *Crabgrass Frontier: The Suburbanization of the United States* (1985). Michael Danielson examines racial discrimination in the suburbs in *The Politics of Exclusion* (1976). For an analysis of the development of western cities in this century, see Carl Abbott's *The Metropolitan Frontier: Cities in the Modern American West* (1993).

The middle-class ideal of family life in the 1950s is examined in Elaine Tyler May's *Homeward Bound: American Families in the Cold War Era* (1988). Thorough accounts of women's issues in the twentieth century are found in William Chafe's *The American Woman: Her Changing Social, Economic, and Political Roles: 1920–1970* (rev. ed., 1988) and Wini Breines Young's *Young, White and Miserable: Growing Up Female in the 1950s* (1992).

For an overview of the resurgence of religion in the 1950s, see George Marsden's *Religion and American Culture* (1990). For treatments of the two leading religious leaders, see Carol V. R. George's *God's Salesman: Norman Vincent Peale and the Power of Positive Thinking* (1992) and William Martin's *A Prophet with Honor: The Billy Graham Story* (1992).

A lively discussion of movies of the 1950s can be found in Peter Biskind's *Seeing Is Believing: How Hollywood Taught Us to Stop Worrying and Love the Fifties* (1983). The origins and growth of rock 'n' roll music are surveyed in Carl Belz's *The Story of Rock* (1972). Thoughtful interpretive surveys of postwar American literature include Josephine Hendin's *Vulnerable People: A View of American Fiction Since 1945* (1978) and Malcolm Bradbury's *The Modern American Novel* (1984). The colorful Beats are brought to life in Steven Watson's *The Birth of the Beat Generation: Visionaries, Rebels, and Hipsters, 1944–1960* (rev. ed., 1998).

33 CONFLICT AND DEADLOCK: THE EISENHOWER YEARS

CHAPTER ORGANIZER

This chapter focuses on:

- Eisenhower's "dynamic conservatism."

- American foreign policy in the 1950s.

- the civil rights movement in the 1950s.

- the background to the Vietnam War.

*T*he New Deal coalition established by Franklin Roosevelt and sustained by Harry Truman posed a formidable challenge to Republicans after World War II. To counter the unlikely but potent combination of "Solid South" white Democrats, blacks and ethnics, and organized labor, the Grand Old Party turned to General Dwight David Eisenhower, a military hero capable of attracting independent voters as well as tenuous Democrats. His commitment to a "moderate Republicanism" promised to slow the rate of federal government expansion while at the same time retaining many of the coveted social programs established by Roosevelt and Truman. His two terms as president are often characterized as representing a lull between two eras of Democratic activism. But Eisenhower wanted to restore the authority of state and local governments and restrain the executive branch from political and social "engineering." In the process, he sought to revivify traditional virtues and inspire people with a vision of a brighter future.

"TIME FOR A CHANGE"

By 1952 the Truman administration had piled up a heavy burden of political liabilities. Its bold stand in Korea had brought a bloody stalemate abroad, renewed wage and price controls at home, reckless charges of Communist subversion and disloyalty, and the exposure of corrupt lobbyists and influence peddlers who rigged favors in Washington. The disclosure of corruption led Truman to fire nearly 250 employees of the Bureau of Internal Revenue and, among others, an assistant attorney-general in charge of the Justice Department's Tax Division. But doubts lingered that Truman would ever finish the housecleaning.

EISENHOWER'S POLITICAL RISE   It was, Republicans claimed, "time for a change." The Republican field quickly narrowed to two men, Ohio senator Robert A. Taft and General Dwight D. Eisenhower. Taft had become the foremost spokesman for domestic conservatism and for a foreign policy that his enemies branded as isolationist. His conservatism left room for federal aid to education and public housing, and his foreign policy, a "unilateralist" one, favored an active American role in opposing communism but opposed "entangling alliances" such as NATO. In Korea, he felt, the time had come to go all out for victory or to withdraw completely.

But Taft inspired little enthusiasm beyond the party regulars. He projected a lackluster image, and as a leader used to taking controversial stands, he had made enemies. The eastern, internationalist wing of the party turned instinctively to Eisenhower, then the NATO commander. As a war hero he had the glamour that Taft lacked, and his captivating, unpretentious manner inspired confidence. His leadership had been tested in the fires of war, but as a professional soldier he had escaped the scars of political combat. He stood, therefore, outside and above the crass arena of public life, although his political instincts and skills were sharpened during his successful army career.

In 1952 the general affirmed that he was a Republican and permitted his name to be entered in party primaries. He left his NATO post and joined the battle in person. An outpouring of public enthusiasm began to overwhelm Republican party regulars. Bumper stickers across the land announced simply, "I like Ike." Eisenhower won the nomination on the first ballot. He balanced the ticket with a youthful Californian, the thirty-nine-year-old Senator Richard M. Nixon, who had built a career on opposition to left-wing "subversives" and gained his greatest notoriety as the member of the House Un-American Activities Committee most eager in the pursuit of Alger Hiss.

THE 1952 ELECTION   The Twenty-second Amendment, ratified in 1951, forbade any president to seek a third term. The amendment exempted the incumbent, but weary of the war in Korea, harassed by charges of subversion and corruption in government, his popularity declining, Truman chose to withdraw and threw his support to Governor Adlai E. Stevenson of Illinois, who aroused the Democratic delegates with an eloquent speech welcoming them to Chicago.

The campaign matched two of the most magnetic personalities ever pitted against each other in a presidential contest. Both men attracted new followings among people previously apathetic about politics, but the race was uneven from the start. Eisenhower, though a political novice, was a world hero who had been in the public eye for a decade.

Good First Impression. *In the 1952 election the Republican party won significant support in the South for the first time.*

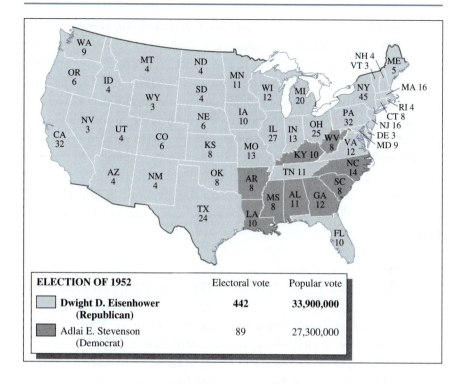

ELECTION OF 1952	Electoral vote	Popular vote
Dwight D. Eisenhower (Republican)	442	33,900,000
Adlai E. Stevenson (Democrat)	89	27,300,000

Stevenson, the politician, was hardly known outside of Illinois and was never able to escape the burden of Truman's liabilities. The genial general, who had led the crusade against Hitler, now opened a domestic crusade to clean up "the mess in Washington." To this he added a promise, late in the campaign, that as president-elect he would go to Korea to secure "an early and honorable" peace. Stevenson possessed a lofty eloquence spiced with a quick wit, but his resolve to "talk sense" and "tell the truth to the American people" came across as just a bit too aloof, a shade too intellectual. The Republicans labeled him an "egghead," an indecisive, latter-day Hamlet, in contrast to Eisenhower, the man of the people, the general of decisive action.

The war hero triumphed in a landslide of 33.9 million votes to Stevenson's 27.3 million, and 442 electoral votes to Stevenson's 89. The election marked a turning point in Republican fortunes in the South: for the first time since the 1850s the South was moving toward a two-party system. Stevenson carried only eight southern states plus West Virginia. Eisenhower picked up five states on the periphery of the Deep South: Florida, Oklahoma, Tennessee, Texas, and Virginia. In the former Confederacy the Republican ticket garnered 49 percent of the votes. The "nonpolitical" Eisenhower had made it respectable, even fashionable, to vote Republican in the South. Elsewhere, too, the former general made inroads in the New Deal coalition, attracting supporters among the ethnic and religious minorities in the major cities.

The voters, it turned out, liked Ike better than they liked his party. Democrats retained most of the governorships, lost control of the House by only eight votes, and broke even in the Senate, where only the vote of the vice-president ensured Republican control. The congressional elections two years later would weaken the Republican grip on Congress, and Eisenhower would have to work with a Democratic Congress until he left office.

EISENHOWER'S HIDDEN-HAND PRESIDENCY

IKE   Born in Denison, Texas, on October 14, 1890, Dwight David Eisenhower grew up in Abilene, Kansas. After finishing West Point, he spent nearly his entire adult life in the military service. After the attack on Pearl Harbor, General George C. Marshall made Brigadier-General Eisenhower his chief of operations. Later, as a major-general, Eisenhower took command of American forces in the European theater and directed the invasion of North Africa in 1942. Two years later he assumed the post of supreme commander of Allied forces in preparation for the invasion of the continent. After the war, by then a five-star general of the army, he became chief-of-staff and supreme commander of NATO forces, with a brief interlude as president of Columbia University.

Eisenhower's inauguration brought a change in style to the White House. The contrast in character between the feisty Truman and the genial Ike was reinforced by a contrast in philosophy and approach to the presidency. Eisenhower's military experience developed in him an instinct for methodical staff work. He met with the cabinet and the National Security Council nearly every week, and he relied heavily on them as consultative bodies.

Far from being a "do-nothing" president, as some have charged, Eisenhower was in fact an effective leader. The art of leadership, he once explained, did not require "hitting people over the head. Any damn fool can do that. . . . It's persuasion—and conciliation—and education—and patience. That's the only kind of leadership I know—or believe in—or will practice."

The public image of Ike was that of a man who rose above partisan politics. He was unpretentious, an ardent golfer, a common man with a winning smile who read little but Western novels, was uninformed about trends in intellectual and artistic life, and was prone to giving folksy advice: "Everybody ought to be happy every day. Play hard, have fun doing it, and despise wickedness." A diplomat labeled him "the nation's number one Boy Scout." But those who were closer to Ike have presented another side to the man. When provoked, he could release a fiery temper and scalding profanity. While Ike talked with genuine feeling about such traditional virtues as duty, honesty, and thrift, he was not above a calculated dissimulation. One student of Eisenhower's techniques has spoken of a "hidden-hand presidency" in which Ike deliberately cultivated a public image of passivity to hide his active involvement in policy decisions.

"DYNAMIC CONSERVATISM" AT HOME   Like Ulysses Grant, Eisenhower betrayed a weakness for hobnobbing with rich men. His cabinet, a columnist in the *New Republic* quipped, consisted of "eight millionaires and a plumber." The plumber, Secretary of Labor Martin Durkin, resigned after eight months, charging that the administration had reneged on a promise to change the Taft-Hartley Act. The president of General Motors became secretary of defense, and two auto distributors became secretary of the interior and postmaster-general, respectively. The New Dealers, Adlai Stevenson wryly remarked, "have all left Washington to make way for the car dealers."

Unaccustomed to the glare of Washington publicity, several cabinet members succumbed to foot-in-mouth disease. It was perhaps innocent enough for the former GM president to say at his confirmation hearings, "I thought what was good for our country was good for General Motors, and vice versa," except that it was readily translated into: "What is good for General Motors is good for the country." The interior secretary put it more baldly: "We're here in the saddle as an Administration representing business and industry."

Eisenhower called his domestic program "dynamic conservatism," which meant being "conservative when it comes to money and liberal when it comes to human beings." In response, Adlai Stevenson conjectured: "I assume what it means is that you will strongly recommend the building of a great many schools to accommodate the needs of our children, but not provide the money." Budget cutting was a high priority for the new administration, which set out to slash both domestic programs and national defense spending. Eisenhower warned repeatedly against the dangers of "creeping socialism," "huge bureaucracies," and budget deficits.

Eisenhower abolished the Reconstruction Finance Corporation, ended wage and price controls, and reduced farm price subsidies. He also moved the government away from the Roosevelt-Truman commitment to public electric power. In fact, had Ike had his way the government would have sold the Tennessee Valley Authority.

In 1954 the administration formulated tax reductions that resembled Republican programs of the 1920s in providing benefits mainly to corporations and individuals in the upper brackets. The new budget slashed expenditures by $6.5 billion, nearly 10 percent, and the Federal Reserve Board reinforced administration policy by tightening credit and raising interest rates to avert inflation. But a business slump followed, which reduced government revenues, making it harder to balance the budget. After that experience, Eisenhower's fiscal and monetary policies became less doctrinaire and more flexible. The government accepted easier credit and deficits as necessary "countercyclical" methods. The Keynesian Age, if not yet acknowledged, endured.

Although Eisenhower chipped away at several New Deal programs, his presidency in the end served rather to legitimate the New Deal by keeping its basic structure and premises intact during an era of prosperity. In a letter to his brother in 1954, Eisenhower observed: "Should any political party attempt to abolish Social Security and eliminate labor laws and farm programs, you would not hear of that party again in our political history." In some ways, the administration not only maintained the New Deal but extended its reach, especially after 1954 when it had the help of Democratic Congresses. Amendments to the Social Security Act in 1954 and 1956 brought coverage to millions in categories formerly excluded: professional people, domestic and clerical workers, farm workers, and members of the armed forces. In 1959 the program's benefits went up 7 percent. The federal minimum wage rose in 1955 from 75¢ to $1 an hour. Federal expenditures for public health rose steadily in the Eisenhower years, and the president went so far as to endorse federal participation in health insurance, but Congress twice refused to act. Low-income housing continued to be built with federal funds, although on a much reduced scale.

Some farm-related aid programs were expanded during the Eisenhower years. The Rural Electrification Administration would announce on its twenty-fifth birthday in 1960 that 97 percent of American farms had electricity. In 1954 the government undertook on a large scale to finance the export of surplus farm products in exchange for foreign currencies. Surpluses were also exported as gifts to needy nations and to provide milk for schoolchildren. In 1959 surpluses became available to Americans by issuing food stamps redeemable at grocery stores.

Despite Eisenhower's general disapproval of public power programs, he continued to support public works for which he saw a legitimate need. Indeed, two such programs left major monuments to his presidency: the St. Lawrence Seaway and the interstate highways. The plan for the St. Lawrence Seaway, designed to open the Great Lakes to oceangoing ships by means of locks and dredging, had languished in Congress since the time of President Hoover because of opposition by eastern business and railroad interests afraid of the competition. In 1954 Eisenhower finally broke the opposition, citing Canadian determination to go ahead anyway and the growing need of American steel producers for Canadian ore as domestic deposits gave out. Congress then approved joint participation with the Canadians, and five years later the seaway opened. In 1956 a new federal highway construction act authorized the federal government to put up 90 percent of the cost of building 42,500 miles of limited-access interstate highways to serve the needs of commerce and defense, as well as private convenience. The states put up the remaining 10 percent. It was only afterward that people realized that the huge national commitment to the automobile might have come at the expense of America's railroad system, already in a state of advanced decay.

CONCLUDING AN ARMISTICE   America's new global responsibilities in the postwar world, however, continued to absorb Eisenhower's attention. The most pressing problem when he entered office was the continuing, painful deadlock in the Korean peace talks. Many prisoners from North Korea wished to remain in South Korea. United Nations negotiators refused to agree to return prisoners of war who did not want to go back to the North. North Korean and Red Chinese negotiators insisted that all prisoners be returned regardless of their wishes. To break the deadlock, Eisenhower resolved upon a bold stand. In mid-May 1953 he stepped up aerial bombardment of North Korea, then had Secretary of State John Foster Dulles make a secret threat to Peking to remove all limits on weapons and targets. It was a thinly veiled warning of atomic warfare. Whether for that reason or others, negotiations then moved quickly toward an armistice along the established border just above the 38th parallel, and toward a complicated arrangement for prisoner exchange that allowed captives to accept or refuse repatriation.

On July 26, 1953, President Eisenhower announced the end of fighting in Korea. Whether Eisenhower had pulled a masterful bluff in getting the armistice has never become clear; no one knows if he would have used atomic weapons. Perhaps the more decisive factors in bringing about a settlement were rising Chinese Communist losses, which they increasingly found unacceptable, and the new spirit of uncertainty and caution felt by Russian Communists after the death of Joseph Stalin on March 5, 1953—six weeks after Ike's inauguration.

CONCLUDING A WITCH-HUNT   The Korean armistice helped to end another dismal episode: the meteoric career of Senator Joseph R. McCarthy, which had flourished amid the anxieties of wartime. Convinced that the government was infested with Communists and spies, the Wisconsin senator launched a one-man crusade to root them out. In the process, he and his aides lied, falsified evidence, and bullied or blackmailed witnesses. During the summer of 1953, he sent two assistants on a junket to Europe to purge American government libraries of "subversive works" such as the writings of Ralph Waldo Emerson and Henry David Thoreau, Theodore Dreiser and John Steinbeck. Eventually McCarthy's unscrupulous tactics led to his self-destruction, but not before he had left still more careers and reputations in ruins. The Republicans thought their victory in 1952 would curb his recklessness, but McCarthy actually grew more outlandish in his charges and his investigative methods. And many Americans caught up in the anti-Communist hysteria viewed him as a heroic knight doing battle against the forces of darkness.

McCarthy finally overreached himself when he made the absurd charge that the United States Army itself was "soft" on communism. From April 22 to June 17, 1954, the Army-McCarthy hearings displayed McCarthy to a large television audience at his capricious worst,

The Army-McCarthy Hearings, June 1954. *Joseph Welch* (hand on head) *listens incredulously after McCarthy's attempt to smear one of Welch's associates.*

bullying witnesses, dragging out lengthy irrelevancies, repeatedly calling "point of order." He became the perfect foil for the army's gentle but unflappable counsel, Joseph Welch of Boston, whose rapier wit repeatedly drew blood. When a witness used the word "pixie," McCarthy demanded a definition and Welch sweetly explained that a pixie was "a kind of fairy." But when McCarthy tried to smear one of Welch's young associates, the counsel went into a cold rage: "Until this moment, Senator, I think I never really gauged your cruelty or your recklessness. . . . Have you no sense of decency, sir, at long last?" When the audience burst into applause, the confused, skulking senator was reduced to whispering, "What did I do?"

McCarthy descended into new depths of scurrility, now directed at his own colleagues, calling one senator "senile" and another "a living miracle . . . the only man who has lived so long with neither brains nor guts." On December 2, 1954, the Senate voted 67 to 22 to "condemn" McCarthy for contempt of the Senate. McCarthy was finished, and increasingly took to alcohol. Three years later, at the age of forty-eight, he was dead.

McCarthyism, Ike joked, had become McCarthywasm, though not for those whose reputations and careers had been wrecked. To the end, Eisenhower kept his resolve not to "get down in the gutter with that guy" and sully the dignity of the presidency, but he did work resolutely against McCarthy behind the scenes. Eisenhower shared, nevertheless, the deeply held conviction of many citizens that espionage posed a real danger to national security. He denied clemency to Julius and Ethel Rosenberg, convicted of transmitting atomic secrets to the Russians, on the grounds that they "may have condemned to death tens of millions of innocent people." The Rosenbergs went to the electric chair on June 19, 1953.

INTERNAL SECURITY   The anti-Communist crusade survived the downfall of McCarthy. Eisenhower stiffened the government security program that Truman had set up six years before. In 1953 an executive order broadened the basis for firing government workers by replacing Truman's criterion of "disloyalty" with the new category of "security risk." Under the new edict, federal workers could lose their jobs because of dubious associations or personal habits that might make them careless or vulnerable to blackmail. In 1953 the Atomic Energy Commission removed the security clearance of the physicist J. Robert Oppenheimer, the "father of the atomic bomb," on the grounds that he had expressed qualms about the hydrogen bomb in 1949–1950 and had associated with Communists or former Communists in the past. Lacking evidence of any disloyalty or betrayal, the AEC nevertheless branded him a "security risk" because of "fundamental defects in his character."

The Supreme Court, however, modified some of the more extreme expressions of the Red Scare. In 1953 Eisenhower appointed former governor Earl Warren of California as chief justice, a decision the president later pronounced the "biggest damnfool mistake I ever made." Warren, who had seemed safely conservative while active in politics, proved to have a social conscience and a streak of libertarianism that another Eisenhower appointee, William J. Brennan, Jr., shared. The Warren Court (1953–1969), under the chief justice's influence, became an important agency of social and political change on through the 1960s.

In connection with security programs and loyalty requirements, the Court veered back in the direction of traditional individual rights. A 1957 opinion narrowly construed the Smith Act of 1940, aimed at conspirators against the government, to apply only to those advocating "revolutionary" action. Merely teaching revolutionary doctrine in the abstract could not be construed as a crime under the act. This, plus other decisions setting rigid standards for evidence, rendered the Smith Act a dead letter.

FOREIGN INTERVENTION

DULLES AND FOREIGN POLICY The Eisenhower administration promised new departures in foreign policy under the direction of Secretary of State John Foster Dulles. Grandson of one former secretary of state and nephew of another, Dulles had pursued a lifetime career as an international lawyer and sometime diplomat. In 1919 he had assisted the American delegates at the Versailles Conference. As counselor to the Truman State Department he had, among other things, negotiated the Japanese peace treaty. Son of a minister and himself an active Presbyterian layman, Dulles, in the words of the British ambassador, resembled those old zealots of the wars of religion who "saw the world as an arena in which the forces of good and evil were continuously at war." Tall, spare, and stooped, he gave the appearance of dour sternness and Calvinist righteousness. But he was also a man of immense energy, intelligence, and experience. As Eisenhower once said of Dulles, "There's only one man I know who has seen *more* of the world, and talked with more people and *knows* more than he does—and that's me."

The foreign policy planks of the 1952 Republican platform, which Dulles wrote, showed both the moralist and the tactician at work. The

Secretary of State John Foster Dulles.

Democratic policy of containment was needlessly defensive, Dulles thought. Containment implied contentment with the status quo. He saw no need for the United States to accept the Soviet presence in eastern Europe. Americans should instead work toward the "liberation" of eastern Europe from Soviet domination. The 1952 Republican platform promised to end "the negative, futile and immoral policy of 'containment' which abandons countless human beings to a despotism and godless terrorism." A new policy of liberation, the platform promised, "will inevitably set up strains and stresses within the captive world which will make the rulers impotent to continue in their monstrous ways and mark the beginning of the end."

The policy came perilously close to proclaiming a holy war, but Dulles took care to explain that he did not intend forcible liberation of Communist-bloc countries. Soon it became apparent that it was less a policy than a web of rhetoric to catch ethnic voters whose homelands had fallen captive to Soviet control. That Dulles's liberation rhetoric rang false became more evident in 1953 when workers in East Germany rebelled against working conditions and food shortages. When Russian tanks rolled over the demonstrators, the administration did nothing except to deplore the situation. For three years more Dulles maintained that his rhetoric was undermining the Communist hold on eastern Europe—until suppression of the 1956 uprising in Hungary underscored the danger of stirring futile hopes among captive peoples.

COVERT ACTIONS Insofar as American interventions occurred abroad, they were covert operations by the Central Intelligence Agency (CIA) in countries outside the Soviet sphere. Under Eisenhower, Allen Dulles, brother of the secretary of state, rose from second in command to chief of the CIA. A veteran of the wartime Office of Strategic Services, he enhanced the CIA's capacity for cloak-and-dagger operations. In two cases early in the Eisenhower years, the CIA actually helped overthrow governments believed hostile to American interests: in Iran (1953) and in Guatemala (1954).

In Iran, Premier Mohammed Mossadegh, a seventy-year-old nationalist, whipped up popular feeling against British control of Iranian oil production and then took over the foreign properties. In challenging Western interests, he had the support of the Tudeh, Iran's Communist party, and left the impression that he either had joined their side or would become their dupe. Under these circumstances, Allen Dulles sent a crack CIA agent along with an adviser to help the shah of Iran organize his secret police. Armed chiefly with about a million dollars, they stirred up street demonstrations against Mossadegh that, reinforced by soldiers loyal to the shah, toppled the premier, sent him to jail, and brought the young shah back from exile in Rome.

In Guatemala, Jacobo Arbenz Guzman had become president in an election in which he had Communist backing. While the administration lacked evidence that Arbenz was a Communist, the American ambassador said "he talked like a Communist, he thought like a Communist, and he acted like a Communist, and if he is not one, he will do until one comes along." Critics of the intervention contended that Arbenz's chief sin was that he had expropriated 225,000 acres of United Fruit Company land. With Eisenhower's consent, the CIA chose a Guatemalan colonel to stage a coup from a base in Honduras.

BRINKSMANSHIP   For all his bold talk of liberation, Dulles made no significant departure from the strategy of containment created under Acheson and Truman. Instead he institutionalized containment in the rigid mold of his cold war rhetoric and extended it into the military strategy of deterrence. He betrayed a fatal affinity for colorful phrases that left him, according to one observer, "perpetually poised between a cliché and an indiscretion." To his lexicon of "liberation" and "roll back," Dulles added two major new contributions while in office: "massive retaliation" and "going to the brink."

"Massive retaliation" was actually a shorthand version of Dulles's phrase "massive retaliatory power," an effort to get, in the slogan soon current, "more bang for the buck" or "more rubble for the ruble." Budgetary considerations lay at the root of military plans, for Eisenhower and his cabinet feared that in the effort to build a superior war power the country could spend itself into bankruptcy. During 1953 members of the Joint Chiefs of Staff began planning a new military posture. The heart of their so-called New Look was the assumption that nuclear weapons could be used in limited-war situations, allowing reductions in conventional forces and thus budgetary savings. Dulles, who announced the policy in early 1954, explained that savings would come "by placing more reliance on deterrent power, and less dependence on local defensive power." No longer could an enemy "pick his time and place and method of warfare." American responses would be "by means and at places of our choosing." No longer would "the Communists nib-

"Don't Be Afraid—I Can Always Pull You Back." *Secretary of State Dulles pushes a reluctant America to the brink of war.*

ble us to death all over the world in little wars," Vice-President Nixon explained.

By this time both the United States and the Soviet Union had exploded hydrogen bombs. With the new policy of deterrence, what Winston Churchill called a "balance of terror" had replaced the old "balance of power." The threat of nuclear holocaust was terrifying, but the notion that the United States would risk such a disaster in response to local wars had little credibility.

Dulles's policy of "brinksmanship" depended for its strategic effect on those very fears of nuclear disaster. Dulles argued in 1956 that in following a tough policy of confrontation with communism, a nation sometimes had to "go to the brink" of war. Such a firm stand had halted further aggression in Korea in 1953 when America threatened to break the stalemate by removing restraints from the armed forces. Dulles had also employed brinksmanship in 1954 in Indochina when the United States sent aircraft carriers into the South China Sea "both to deter any Red Chinese attack against Indochina and to provide weapons for instant retaliation."

INDOCHINA: THE BACKGROUND TO WAR   Dulles's use of brinksmanship in Indochina neglected the complexity of the situation there, which presented a special if not unique case of the nationalism that swept the old colonial world of Asia and Africa after World War II, damaging both the power and prestige of the colonial powers. By the early

1950s, most of British Asia was independent or on the way: India, Pakistan, Ceylon (later Sri Lanka), Burma (later Myanmar), and the Malay States (later the Federation of Malaysia). The Dutch and French, however, were less ready than the British to give up their colonies, which created a dilemma for American policy makers. Americans sympathized with colonial nationalists who sometimes invoked the example of 1776, but Americans also wanted Dutch and French help against communism. The Truman administration felt obliged to answer their pleas for aid. Both the Dutch and the French had to reconquer areas that had passed from Japanese occupation into the hands of local patriots.

In the Dutch East Indies the Japanese had created a puppet Indonesian Republic, which emerged from World War II virtually independent. The Dutch effort to regain control met resistance that exploded into open warfare. Eventually, American pressure persuaded the Dutch to accept self-government under a Dutch-Indonesian Union in 1949, but that lasted only until 1954, when the Republic of Indonesia became independent. In 1955 the Bandung Conference in Indonesia, attended by delegates from twenty-nine independent countries of Asia and Africa, signaled the emergence of a "Third World" of underdeveloped countries, unaligned with either the United States or the Soviet bloc. Among other actions, the conference denounced "colonialism in all its manifestations," a statement that implicitly condemned both the Soviet Union and the West.

French Indochina, created in the nineteenth century out of the old kingdoms of Cambodia, Laos, and Vietnam, offered a variation on Third World nationalism. During World War II, when the Japanese controlled the area, they had supported pro-Vichy French civil servants and had opposed the local nationalists. Chief among the latter were members of the Viet Minh (Vietnamese League for Independence), which fell under the influence of Communists led by Ho Chi Minh. At the end of the war, this group controlled part of northern Vietnam, and on September 2, 1945, Ho Chi Minh proclaimed a Democratic Republic of Vietnam, with its capital in Hanoi.

Ho's declaration of Vietnamese independence borrowed from Thomas Jefferson, opening with the words "We hold these truths to be self-evident. That all men are created equal." American officers were on the reviewing stand in Hanoi and American planes flew over the celebration. Ho had received secret American help against the Japanese during the war, but bids for further aid after the war went unanswered. Viet-

Ho Chi Minh.

nam took low priority in American diplomatic concerns at the time, and Truman could not stomach aiding a professed Communist.

In 1946 the French government, preoccupied with domestic politics, recognized Ho's new government as a "free state" within the French union. Before the year was out, however, Ho's forces challenged French efforts to establish another regime in the southern provinces, and this clash soon expanded into the First Indochina War. In 1949, having set up puppet rulers in Laos and Cambodia, the French reinstated former emperor Bao Dai as head of state in Vietnam. The victory of the Chinese Communists later in 1949 was followed by Red China's diplomatic recognition of the Viet Minh government in Hanoi, and then the recognition of Bao Dai by the United States and Britain.

The Viet Minh movement thereafter became more completely dominated by Ho Chi Minh and his Communist associates, and more dependent on the Soviet Union and Red China for help. In 1950, with the outbreak of fighting in Korea, the struggle in Vietnam became a battleground in the cold war. When the Korean War ended, American aid to the French in Vietnam, begun by the Truman administration, continued. By the end of 1953, the Eisenhower administration was paying about two-thirds of the cost of the French effort, or about $1 billion annually. By 1954 the United States found itself at the edge of the "brink" to which Dulles later referred. A major French force had been sent to Dien Bien Phu, near the Laos border, in the hope of luring Viet Minh guerrillas into a set battle and grinding them up with superior firepower. The French instead found themselves trapped by a Viet Minh force that threatened to overrun their stronghold.

In March 1954 the French government requested an American air strike to relieve the pressure on Dien Bien Phu. As noted earlier, Dulles had U.S. aircraft carriers move into the South China Sea in anticipation of such an air strike. Eisenhower himself seemed to endorse forceful action, but when congressional leaders expressed reservations, he opposed American intervention unless the British lent support. When they refused, he backed away from unilateral action in Vietnam.

On May 7, 1954, the massive attacks loosed by Viet Minh general Vo Nguyen Giap finally overwhelmed the last French resistance at Dien Bien Phu. It was the very eve of the day that an international conference at Geneva took up the question of Indochina. Six weeks later, as French forces continued to suffer defeats in Vietnam, a new French government promised to get an early settlement. On July 20 representatives of France, Britain, the Soviet Union, the People's Republic of China, and the Viet Minh reached agreement on the Geneva Accords. They proposed to neutralize Laos and Cambodia and divided Vietnam at the 17th parallel. The Viet Minh would take power in the north, and the French would remain south of the line until elections in 1956 would reunify Vietnam. American and South Vietnamese representatives refused to join in the accord. This led the Soviet Union and China to back away from their earlier hints that they would guarantee the settlement.

Dulles responded to the growing Communist influence in Vietnam by organizing mutual defense arrangements for Southeast Asia. On September 8, 1954, at a meeting in Manila, the United States joined seven other countries in the Southeast Asia Treaty Organization (SEATO). The impression that it paralleled NATO was false, for SEATO was neither a common defense organization like NATO nor was it primarily Asian. The signers agreed that in case of attack on one, the others would act according to their "constitutional practices," and in case of threats or subversion they would "consult immediately." The members included only three Asian countries—the Philippines, Thailand, and Pakistan—together with Britain, France, Australia, New Zealand, and the United States. India and Indonesia, the two most populous countries in the region, refused to join. A special protocol added to the treaty extended coverage to Indochina. The treaty reflected what

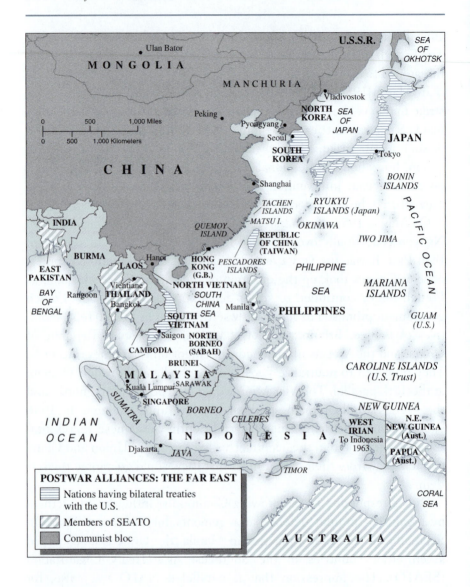

POSTWAR ALLIANCES: THE FAR EAST

▥ Nations having bilateral treaties with the U.S.

▨ Members of SEATO

▦ Communist bloc

Dulles's critics called "pactomania," which by the end of the Eisenhower administration contracted the United States to defend forty-three other countries.

Eisenhower announced that though the United States "had not itself been party to or bound by the decision taken at the [Geneva] Conference," any renewal of Communist aggression "would be viewed by us as a matter of grave concern." (He failed to note that the United States had agreed at Geneva to "refrain from the threat or use of force to disturb" the agreements.) In Vietnam, when Ho Chi Minh took over the north, those who wished to leave for South Vietnam, mostly Catholics, did so with American aid. Power in the south gravitated to a new premier imposed on Emperor Bao Dai by the French at American urging: Ngo Dinh Diem, who had opposed both the French and the Viet Minh. Diem took office during the Geneva talks. Before that he had been in exile at a Catholic seminary in New Jersey. In 1954 Eisenhower offered to assist Diem "in developing and maintaining a strong, viable state, capable of resisting attempted subversion or aggression through military means." In return, the United States expected "needed reforms." American aid took the form of CIA and military cadres charged with training Diem's armed forces and police.

Instead of instituting political and economic reforms, however, Diem tightened his grip on the country, suppressing opposition on both right and left, offering little or no land distribution, and permitting widespread corruption. In 1956 he refused to join in the elections to reunify Vietnam. After French withdrawal from the country, he ousted Bao Dai and installed himself as president. His efforts to eliminate all opposition played into the hands of the Communists, who found recruits and fellow travelers among the discontented. By 1957 guerrilla forces known as the Viet Cong had begun attacks on the Diem government, and in 1960 the resistance coalesced as the National Liberation Front. As guerrilla warfare gradually disrupted South Vietnam, the Eisenhower administration was helpless to do anything but "sink or swim with Ngo Dinh Diem."

PROTECTING TAIWAN   Just before the Manila Conference in 1954, Red Chinese artillery began shelling the South China Sea islands of Quemoy and Matsu, held by Chiang Kai-shek's Nationalists. On his way back from Manila, Dulles stopped in Taipei and worked out a mutual defense treaty that bound the United States to defend Taiwan and the nearby Pescadores Islands, and that bound Taiwan to undertake offensive action only with American consent. The treaty omitted mention of the offshore islands, and the mainland Chinese continued their pressure, occupying one of the Tachens. In 1955 the president secured in Congress a resolution giving him full power to go to the defense of Taiwan and the Pescadores, and also authorizing him to secure and protect "related positions of that area now in friendly hands" in order to defend Taiwan. Congress's endorsement was overwhelming—the resolution drew only three negative votes in each house—for so sweeping a grant of power.

The Red Chinese kept up their provocative activity nonetheless, and under pressure from the American government the Nationalists evacuated the Tachens as indefensible. But Quemoy and Matsu became symbols of the American will to protect Taiwan, and were perhaps strategically useful too. In any case, the American chief of naval operations "leaked" word to journalists that the administration was considering a plan "to destroy Red China's military potential and thus end its expansionist tendencies." Soon afterward the Chinese backed away from the brink. At the Bandung Conference in April, with diplomatic encouragement from other Asian nations, Premier Chou En-lai said Red China was ready to discuss the Formosa Strait issue directly with the United States. In 1955 representatives of the two governments began meetings in Geneva, and the guns fell silent.

REELECTION AND FOREIGN CRISES

As the United States continued to forge postwar alliances and to bring pressure to bear on foreign governments by practicing brinksmanship, a new presidential campaign unfolded. Despite having suffered a coronary seizure in the fall of 1955 and an operation for ileitis (an intestinal inflammation) in early 1956, Eisenhower decided to run for reelection. He retained the support and confidence of the public, although the Democrats controlled Congress. Meanwhile, new crises in foreign and domestic affairs required him to take decisive action.

A LANDSLIDE FOR IKE   In 1956 the Republican convention renominated Eisenhower by acclamation and again named Nixon as the vice-presidential candidate. The party platform endorsed Eisenhower's "modern Republicanism." The Democrats turned again to Stevenson. The platform revived old Democratic issues: less "favoritism" to big business, repeal of the Taft-Hartley Act, parity for farmers, tax relief for those in low-income brackets.

Neither candidate generated much excitement during the campaign. The Democrats centered their fire on the heir apparent, Richard Nixon, a "man of many masks." Stevenson aroused little enthusiasm for two controversial proposals: to drop conscription and rely on an all-volunteer army, and to ban H-bomb tests by international agreement. Both involved military questions that put Stevenson at a disadvantage by pitting his judgment against that of a successful general.

During the last week of the campaign, fighting erupted along the Suez Canal in Egypt and in the streets of Budapest, Hungary. These twin crises were unrelated, but they occurred almost as if placed in malicious juxtaposition by some evil force. The attack on Egypt by Britain, France, and Israel disrupted the Western alliance and damaged any claim to moral outrage at Soviet actions in Hungary. For the Soviets, the Suez War afforded both a smokescreen for the subjugation of Hungary and a chance to enlarge their influence in the Middle East, an increasingly important source of oil.

The two crises led Stevenson to declare the administration's foreign policy "bankrupt." Most voters, however, reasoned that the crises spelled a poor time to switch horses, and they handed Eisenhower a landslide victory. He lost one border state, Missouri, but in carrying Louisiana became the first Republican to win a Deep South state since Reconstruction; nationally, he carried all but seven states. The decision was unmistakably clear: he won more than 35 million popular votes to a little over 26 million for Stevenson, 457 electoral votes to the Democrat's 73.

In the euphoria of his landslide victory on November 6, Eisenhower declared on election night "that modern Republicanism has now proved itself. And America has approved of modern Republicanism." He later defined this as "the political philosophy that recognizes clearly the responsibility of the Federal Government to take the lead in making certain that the productivity of our great economic machine is distributed so that no one will suffer disaster, privation, through no fault of his own." Eisenhower Republicans, it seemed clear, had assimilated the New Deal as an accomplished fact. But Eisenhower's decisive win failed to swing a congressional majority for his own party in either house, the first time this had happened since the election of Zachary Taylor in 1848.

CRISIS IN THE MIDDLE EAST   After 1953 the Eisenhower-Dulles policy in the Middle East had departed from the Truman-Acheson focus on Israel and distanced itself from British-French economic interests in order to cultivate Arab friendship. To forestall Soviet penetration, Dulles in 1955 had completed his line of alliances across the

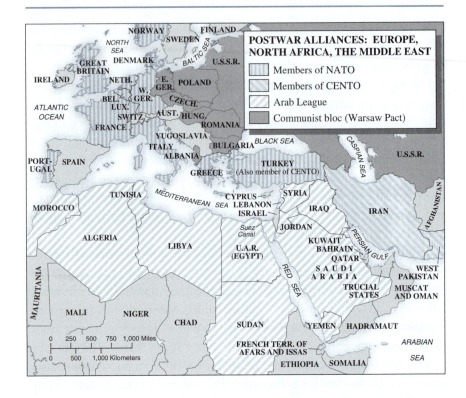

POSTWAR ALLIANCES: EUROPE, NORTH AFRICA, THE MIDDLE EAST

Members of NATO
Members of CENTO
Arab League
Communist bloc (Warsaw Pact)

"northern tier" of the Middle East. Under American sponsorship, Britain had joined the Muslim states of Turkey, Iraq, Iran, and Pakistan in the Middle East Treaty Organization (METO), or Baghdad Pact, as the treaty was commonly called. By linking the easternmost NATO state (Turkey) to the westernmost SEATO state (Pakistan), METO had a certain superficial logic, but after Iraq, the only Arab member, withdrew in 1959, it became clear that the whole thing had been bound to fail from the start. Below the northern tier, moreover, the Arab states remained aloof from the organization. These were the states of the Arab League (Egypt, Jordan, Syria, Lebanon, and Saudi Arabia), which had warred on Israel in 1948–1949 and remained committed to its destruction.

The most fateful developments in the region turned on the rise of Egyptian general Gamal Abdel Nasser after the overthrow of King Farouk in 1952. The bone of contention was the Suez Canal, which had opened in 1869 as a joint French-Egyptian venture. But in 1875 the British government had acquired the largest block of stock, and from 1882 on British forces were posted there to protect the British Empire's "lifeline" to India and other colonies. When Nasser's new nationalist

General Moshe Dayan (center), *commander of Israeli forces during the Sinai campaign, 1956.*

regime pressed for the withdrawal of British forces from the canal zone, Eisenhower and Dulles supported its demand, and in 1954 an Anglo-Egyptian treaty provided for British withdrawal within twenty months. Nasser, like other leaders of the Third World, remained unaligned in the cold war and sought to play both sides off against each other. The United States, meanwhile, courted Egyptian support by offering a loan to build a great hydroelectric plant at Aswan on the Nile River.

From the outset, the administration's proposal was opposed by Jewish constituencies concerned with Egyptian threats to Israel, and by southern congressmen who feared the competition from Egyptian cotton. When Nasser then increased trade with the Soviet bloc and recognized Red China, Dulles abruptly canceled the loan offer in 1956. The outcome was far from a triumph of American diplomacy. The chief victims, it turned out, were Anglo-French interests in the Suez. Unable to retaliate against the United States, Nasser nationalized the Suez Canal Company and earmarked its revenues for the Aswan Dam project, thereby enhancing his prestige in the Arab world. The British and French, faced with loss of control of the crucial Suez Canal, reacted strongly. Fruitless negotiations dragged out through the summer, and finally, on October 29, 1956, Israeli forces invaded the Gaza Strip and the Sinai peninsula. The Israelis invaded ostensibly to root out Arab guerrillas, but actually to synchronize with the British and French, who began bombing Egyptian air bases and occupied Port Said. Their actions, the British and French claimed, were meant to protect the canal against the opposing belligerents.

The Suez War put the United States in a quandary. Either the administration could support its Western allies and see the troublesome Nasser crushed, or it could stand on the United Nations charter and champion Arab nationalism against imperialistic aggression. Eisenhower opted for the latter course, with the unusual result that the Soviet Union sided with the United States. Once the threat of American embargoes had forced Anglo-French-Israeli capitulation, the Soviets capitalized on the situation by threatening to use missiles against the Western aggressors. This belated bravado won for the Soviet Union some of the credit in the Arab world for what the United States had actually accomplished.

REPRESSION IN HUNGARY   In the Soviet Union, Nikita Khrushchev had come out on top in the post-Stalinist power struggles. In 1955, the Soviets had agreed to end the four-power occupation of Austria and to restore its independence as a neutral but Western-oriented state. Khrushchev had delivered a "secret speech" on the crimes of the Stalin era in 1956 before the Communist Party Congress and hinted at relaxed policies and suggestions that different countries might take "different roads to socialism." This new policy of "de-Stalinization" put Stalinist leaders in the satellite countries of eastern Europe on the defensive and emboldened the more independent leaders to take action. Riots in the Polish city of Poznan led to the rise of Wladyslaw Gomulka, a Polish nationalist, to leadership of the Polish Communist party. Gomulka managed to win a greater degree of independence by avoiding an open break with the Soviets.

In Hungary, however, a similar movement got out of hand. On October 23, 1956, fighting broke out in Budapest, followed by the installation of Imre Nagy, a moderate Communist, as head of the government. Again the Soviets seemed content to let "de-Stalinization" follow its course, and on October 28 they withdrew their forces from Budapest. But Nagy's announcement three days later that Hungary would withdraw from the Warsaw Pact brought Soviet tanks back into Budapest. Although Khrushchev was willing to relax relations with the eastern European satellites, he refused to allow them to break with the Soviet

Union or abandon their mutual defense obligations. The Soviets installed a more compliant leader, Janos Kadar, and hauled Nagy off to Moscow, where a firing squad executed him in 1958. It was a tragic ending to a movement that, at the outset, promised the sort of moderation that might have vindicated Kennan's policy of "containment," if not Dulles's notion of "liberation."

DOMESTIC PROBLEMS

THE BUDGET BATTLE   Domestic problems in Eisenhower's second term were first evident in the "great budget battle" of 1957. The president sent up to Capitol Hill the biggest peacetime budget ever. The size of the budget, which increased foreign aid, military spending, and allocations for atomic energy, housing, public works, and education, alarmed even the president, who had little time to cut it back. Eisenhower sent the bill to Congress, still hopeful that continued prosperity and high revenues would supply a surplus.

On the day the budget went to Congress the secretary of the treasury told reporters "there are a lot of places in this budget that can be cut," and suggested that if government could not reduce the "terrific" tax burden "you will have a depression that will curl your hair." Eisenhower claimed to share this desire to reduce the budget, but the spectacle of a treasury secretary's challenging the budget on the day it went to Congress conveyed an impression of divided purpose and conflict in the administration. Both Democrats and Old Guard Republicans declared an open season on the administration's budget request. In the end they hacked out about $4 billion, including heavy cuts in foreign aid, the United States Information Agency, and the Defense Department. By the time the battle was over in August, an economic slump had set in and tax revenues had dropped. In spite of the cuts, the administration projected a $500 million deficit.

U.S. REACTIONS TO SPUTNIK   On October 4, 1957, the Soviets launched the first satellite, called *Sputnik,* an acronym for the Russian phrase "fellow traveler of earth." Sputnik I weighed 194 pounds, but less than a month later the Soviets launched Sputnik II, and it carried a dog wired up for monitoring. Americans, until then complacent about their technical primacy, suddenly discovered an apparent "missile gap."

By the Rocket's Red Glare. *The Soviet success in space shocked Americans.*

If the Soviets were so advanced in rocketry, then perhaps they could hit American cities. *Life* magazine published a cover story entitled "The Case for Being Panicky." A Democratic senator demanded that Eisenhower call a special session of Congress to address the Sputnik crisis. The president refused, not wanting to heighten American anxiety.

All along Eisenhower knew that the "missile gap" was more illusory than real, but he could not reveal that high-altitude American U-2 spy planes were gathering this information. Even so, American missile development was in a state of disarray, with a tangle of agencies and committees engaged in waste and duplication. The launching of Explorer I, the first American satellite, on January 31, 1958, did not quiet the outcry.

The Soviet Union's success with Sputnik led to efforts in America to enlarge defense spending, to offer NATO allies intermediate-range ballistic missiles (IRBMs) pending development of long-range intercontinental ballistic missiles (ICBMs), to set up a new agency to coordinate space efforts, and to establish a crash program in science education. The "Sputnik syndrome," compounded by a sharp recession through the winter of 1957–1958, loosened the purse strings of frugal legislators, who added to the new budget more than Eisenhower wanted for both defense and domestic programs. During 1958, Britain, Italy, and Turkey accepted American missiles on their territory. In 1958 Congress created the National Aeronautics and Space Administration (NASA) to coordinate research and development in the field. Before the end of the year, NASA had a program to put a manned craft in orbit, but the first manned flight, by Commander Alan B. Shepard, Jr., did not take place until May 5, 1961. Finally, in 1958 Congress enacted the National Defense Education Act, which authorized federal grants especially for training in mathematics, science, and modern languages, as well as for student loans and fellowships.

CORRUPT PRACTICES   During the first two years of Eisenhower's second term, public confidence in his performance, as registered by opinion polls, dropped sharply from 79 percent to 49 percent. Emotional issues such as civil rights and defense policy had compounded his troubles. The president's image was further tarnished when congressional investigations revealed that the administration, which had promised to clean up "the mess in Washington," was itself soiled by scandals, one of which involved Sherman Adams, the White House "chief-of-staff." Adams, it seemed, had done little more than open some doors at the Securities and Exchange Commission and the Federal Trade Commission with introductions for a Boston industrialist, but he had taken in return gifts of a fur coat and an Oriental rug. In 1958 the president reluctantly accepted Adams's resignation. Republicans also faced the growing opposition of farmers, angry over cuts in price supports, and of labor, angry because many Republicans had made "right-to-work" (or open-shop) laws a campaign issue in 1958. The Democrats came out of the midterm elections with nearly two-to-one majorities in Congress: 282 to 154 in the House, 64 to 34 in the Senate.

Eisenhower would be the first president to face three successive Congresses controlled by the opposition party, and this meant that he could manage few new initiatives in domestic policy. The most important legislation of the last two years in the Eisenhower presidency were the Landrum-Griffin Labor-Management Act of 1959, the Civil Rights Act of 1960, and the admission of the first states not contiguous to the continental forty-eight. Alaska became the forty-ninth state on January 3, 1959, and Hawaii the fiftieth on August 21, 1959.

The Landrum-Griffin Act, aimed at controlling union corruption, was actually a compromise between the views of its House sponsors and the somewhat less stringent views of Senator John F. Kennedy and some of his colleagues. It reflected, nevertheless, popular feeling against racketeering and monopolistic practices in unions, especially those of the Teamsters, which had been revealed by an extensive Senate probe. The act safeguarded democratic procedures, penalized the misuse of union funds and coercion of members, and excluded from office persons convicted of certain crimes. The act also strengthened restrictions on secondary boycotts and blackmail picketing. Most of its provisions were directed against unfair union practices, but the act also monitored employer payments to union officers or labor-management consultants.

FESTERING PROBLEMS ABROAD

Once the Suez and Hungary crises faded from the front pages, Eisenhower enjoyed eighteen months of smooth sailing in foreign affairs. Nonetheless, a brief flurry occurred in 1958 over hostile demonstrations in Peru and Venezuela against Vice-President Nixon, who was on a goodwill tour of eight Latin American countries.

CRISIS IN THE MIDDLE EAST   In 1958 the Middle East flared up again. By this time the president had secured from Congress authority for what came to be called the Eisenhower Doctrine, which promised to extend economic and military aid to Middle East nations, and to use armed forces if necessary to assist any such nation against armed aggression from any Communist country.

President Nasser of Egypt meanwhile had emerged from the Suez crisis with heightened prestige, and in 1958 he created the United Arab Republic (UAR) by merger (a short-lived one) with Syria. Then on July 14 a leftist coup in Iraq, supposedly inspired by Nasser and the Soviets, threw out the pro-Western government and killed the king, the crown prince, and the premier. In Lebanon, already unsettled by internal conflict, the government appealed to the United States for support against a similar fate. Eisenhower immediately ordered 5,000 marines into Lebanon. British forces meanwhile went into Jordan at the request of King Hussein. Once the situation stabilized, and the Lebanese factions reached a compromise, American forces (up to 15,000 at one point) withdrew in October.

CRISIS IN EAST ASIA   East Asia heated up again when, on August 23, 1958, Red China renewed its shelling of the Nationalists on Quemoy and Matsu. In September the American Seventh Fleet began to escort Nationalist convoys, but stopped short of entering Chinese territorial waters. To abandon the islands, President Eisenhower said, would amount to a "Western Pacific 'Munich.'" But on October 1 he suggested that a cease-fire would provide "an opportunity to negotiate in good faith." Red China ordered such a cease-fire on October 6, and on October 25, which happened to be the day the last American forces left Lebanon, said that it would reserve the right to bombard the islands on alternate days. With that strange stipulation the worst of the crisis passed, but the problem continued to fester.

CRISIS IN BERLIN   The problem of Berlin festered too: Premier Khrushchev called it a "bone in his throat." West Berlin provided a "showplace" of Western democracy and prosperity, a listening post for Western intelligence, and a funnel through which news and propaganda from the West penetrated what Winston Churchill had called "the iron curtain." Although East Germany had sealed its western frontiers, refugees could still pass from East to West Berlin. On November 10, 1958, at a Soviet-Polish friendship rally in Moscow, Khrushchev threatened to give East Germany control of East Berlin and the air lanes into West Berlin. After the deadline he set, May 27, 1959, Western occupation authorities would have to deal with the East German government, in effect recognizing it, or face the possibility of another blockade.

But Eisenhower refused to budge from his position on Berlin. At the same time, he refused to engage in saber-rattling or even to cancel existing plans to reduce the size of the army. Khrushchev, it turned out, was no more eager for confrontation than Eisenhower. In talks with British prime minister Harold Macmillan, he suggested that the main thing was to begin discussions of the Berlin issue, and not the May 27 deadline. Macmillan in turn won Eisenhower's consent to a meeting of the Big Four foreign ministers.

There was little hope of resolving different views on Berlin and German reunification, but the talks distracted attention from Khrushchev's deadline of May 27: it passed almost unnoticed. In September, after the Big Four talks had adjourned, Premier Khrushchev visited the United States, going to New York, Washington, Los Angeles, San Francisco, and Iowa, and dropping in on Eisenhower at Camp David. In talks there Khrushchev endorsed "peaceful coexistence," and Eisenhower

Soviet premier Nikita Khrushchev speaking on the problem of Berlin, 1959.

admitted that the Berlin situation was "abnormal." They agreed that the time was ripe for a summit meeting in the spring.

THE U-2 SUMMIT   The summit meeting blew up in Eisenhower's face. On May 1, 1960, a Soviet rocket brought down an American U-2 spy plane. Such planes had been flying missions over the Soviet Union for three and a half years. Khrushchev set out to entrap Eisenhower and succeeded, by announcing first only that the plane had been shot down. When the State Department insisted that there had been no attempt to violate Soviet airspace, Khrushchev disclosed that the Soviets had pilot Francis Gary Powers, "alive and kicking," and had his pictures of Soviet military installations. On May 11 Eisenhower abandoned his efforts to cover up the incident and finally took personal responsibility—an unprecedented action for a head of state—and justified the action on grounds of national security. "No one wants another Pearl Harbor," he said. In Paris, five days later, Khrushchev withdrew an invitation for Eisenhower to visit the Soviet Union and called on the president to repudiate the U-2 flights and "pass severe judgment on those responsible." When Eisenhower refused, Khrushchev left the meeting. (Later, in 1962, Powers was exchanged for a Soviet spy.)

CASTRO'S CUBA   The greatest thorn in Eisenhower's side was the Cuban regime of Fidel Castro, which came to power on January 1,

1959, after three years of guerrilla warfare against the dictator Fulgencio Batista. In their struggle against Batista, Castro's forces had the support of many Americans who hoped for a new day of democratic government in Cuba. When American television covered trials and executions conducted by the victorious Castro, however, such hopes were dashed. Staged before crowds of howling spectators, the trials vented anger against Batista's corrupt officials and police, but offered little in the way of legal procedure or proof. Castro, moreover, planned a social and agrarian revolution and opposed the widespread foreign control of the Cuban economy. When he began programs of land redistribution and nationalization of foreign-owned property, relations worsened. Some observers believed, however, that by rejecting Castro's requests for loans and other help, the American government lost a chance to influence the direction of the revolution, and by acting on the assumption that Communists already had the upper hand in his movement, the administration may have ensured that fact.

Fidel Castro (center) *became Cuba's first Communist premier in 1959 after three years of guerrilla warfare against the Batista regime.*

Castro, on the other hand, showed little reluctance to accept the Communist embrace. In 1960 he entered a trade agreement to swap Cuban sugar for Soviet oil and machinery. Then, after Cuba had seized three British-American oil refineries that refused to process Soviet oil, Eisenhower cut sharply the quota for Cuban sugar imports. Premier Khrushchev in response warned that any military intervention in Cuba would encounter Soviet rockets. The United States next suspended imports of Cuban sugar and embargoed most shipments to Cuba. One of Eisenhower's last acts as president was to suspend diplomatic relations with Cuba on January 3, 1961. In the hope of creating "some kind of nondictatorial 'third force,' neither Castroite nor Batistiano," as Eisenhower put it, the president authorized the CIA to begin training a force of Cuban refugees (some of them former Castro stalwarts) for a new revolution. But the final decision on its use would rest with the next president, John F. Kennedy.

THE EARLY CIVIL RIGHTS MOVEMENT

While the cold war produced an uneasy stalement by the mid-1950s, race relations in the United States threatened to explode the domestic tranquility masking years of injustice. Eisenhower entered office committed to civil rights in principle, and he pushed the issue in areas of federal authority. During his first three years, public services in Washington, D.C., were desegregated, as were navy yards and veterans' hospitals. Beyond that, however, two aspects of the president's philosophy inhibited vigorous action in enforcing the principle of civil rights: his preference for state or local action over federal involvement, and his doubt that laws could change racial attitudes. "I don't believe you can change the hearts of men with laws or decisions," he said. For the time, then, leadership in the civil rights field came from the judiciary more than from the executive or legislative branch of the government.

In the 1930s, the National Association for the Advancement of Colored People (NAACP) had resolved to test the "separate but equal" doctrine that had upheld racial segregation since the *Plessy* decision in 1896. Charles H. Houston, dean of the Howard University Law School, laid the plans, and his former student, Thurgood Marshall, served as chief NAACP lawyer. They decided to begin with the expensive field of postgraduate study. In *Sweatt* v. *Painter* (1950) the Supreme Court

Racial segregation began to be tested in the courts by the NAACP in the late 1930s.

ruled that a separate black law school in Texas failed to measure up because of intangible factors, such as its isolation from most of the future lawyers with whom its graduates would interact.

THE *BROWN* DECISION   By that time, challenges to state laws mandating segregation in the public schools were rising through the appellate courts. Five such cases, from Kansas, Delaware, South Carolina, Virginia, and the District of Columbia—usually cited by reference to the first, *Brown v. Board of Education of Topeka, Kansas*—came to the Supreme Court for joint argument by NAACP attorneys in 1952. Chief Justice Earl Warren wrote the opinion, handed down on May 17, 1954, in which a unanimous Court declared that "in the field of public education the doctrine of 'separate but equal' has no place." In support of its opinion, the Court cited current sociological and psychological findings—demonstrating that even if separate facilities were equal in quality, the mere fact of separating people by race engendered feelings of inferiority. A year later, after further argument, the Court directed "a prompt and reasonable start toward full compliance," ordering that the process should move "with all deliberate speed."

Eisenhower refused to take any part in leading white southerners toward compliance. Privately he maintained "that the Supreme Court decision *set back* progress in the South *at least fifteen years*. The fellow who tries to tell me you can do these things by *force* is just plain *nuts*." While token integration began as early as 1954 in the border states, hostility mounted in the Deep South and Virginia, led by the newly formed Citizens' Councils. The Citizens' Councils were middle- and upper-class versions of the Ku Klux Klan that spread quickly across the region and eventually enrolled 250,000 members. Instead of physical violence and intimidation, the Councils used economic coercion to discipline blacks who crossed racial boundaries. African Americans who defied white supremacy would lose their jobs, have their insurance policies canceled, or be denied personal loans or home mortgages. The Citizens' Councils grew so powerful that membership in them became almost a prerequisite for an aspiring white politician.

Before the end of 1955, moderate sentiment in the South gave way to surly reaction against desegregation of the schools. Virginia senator Harry F. Byrd supplied a rallying cry: "Massive Resistance." State legislatures sought futilely to interpose their power between the courts and the schools. In 1956, 101 southern members of Congress signed a "Southern Manifesto," which denounced the Court's decision in the *Brown* case as "a clear abuse of judicial power." At the end of 1956, in six southern states, not a single black child attended school with whites. In several others, the degree of desegregation was minuscule.

THE MONTGOMERY BUS BOYCOTT   The essential role played by the NAACP and the courts in providing a legal lever for the civil rights movement often overshadows the courageous contributions of individual African Americans who took great personal risks to challenge segregation. For example, in Montgomery, Alabama, on December 1, 1955, Mrs. Rosa Parks, a black seamstress tired after a day's work, was arrested for refusing to give up her seat on a city bus to a white man. "I'm going to have you arrested," the driver said. "You may do that," Parks replied. As was the case in many southern communities, Montgomery had a local ordinance that required blacks to give up their bus or train seat to a white when asked. The next night black community leaders met in the Dexter Avenue Baptist Church to organize a massive bus boycott under the aegis of the Montgomery Improvement Association.

In Dexter Avenue's twenty-six-year-old pastor, Martin Luther King, Jr., the movement found a charismatic leader. Born in Atlanta, the grandson of a slave and the son of a minister, King was endowed with intelligence, courage, and eloquence. After attending Morehouse College in Atlanta and then receiving a seminary degree, he earned a Ph.D. in philosophy from Boston University before accepting a call to preach in Montgomery. He brought the movement a message of nonviolent disobedience based on the Gospels, the writings of Henry David Thoreau, and the example of Mahatma Gandhi in India. "We must use the weapon of love," he told his people. "We must realize so many people are taught to hate us that they are not totally responsible for their hate." To his antagonists he said: "We will soon wear you down by our capacity to suffer, and in winning our freedom we will so appeal to your heart and conscience that we will win you in the process."

The bus boycott achieved a remarkable solidarity. For months blacks in Montgomery formed carpools, hitchhiked, or simply walked. But the white town fathers held out against the boycott and against the pleas of a bus company tired of losing money. The boycotters finally won a fed-

Martin Luther King, Jr., here facing arrest for leading a civil rights march, advocated nonviolent resistance to racial segregation.

eral case they had initiated against bus segregation, and in 1956 the Supreme Court let stand without review an opinion of a lower court that "the separate but equal doctrine can no longer be safely followed as a correct statement of the law." The next day King and other blacks boarded the buses, but they still had a long way to travel before segregation ended.

Trying to keep alive the spirit of the bus boycott, King and a group of associates in 1957 organized the Southern Christian Leadership Conference (SCLC). Several days later, King found an unexploded dynamite bomb on his front porch. Two hours later, he addressed his congregation: "I'm not afraid of anybody this morning. Tell Montgomery they can keep shooting and I'm going to stand up to them; tell Montgomery they can keep bombing and I'm going to stand up to them. If I had to die tomorrow morning I would die happy because I've been to the mountain top and I've seen the promised land and it's going to be here in Montgomery."

Despite Eisenhower's reluctance to take the lead in desegregating schools, he supported the right of blacks to vote. In 1956, hoping to exploit divisions between northern and southern Democrats and to reclaim some of the black vote for Republicans, Eisenhower proposed legislation that became the Civil Rights Act of 1957. The first civil rights law passed since Reconstruction, it finally got through the Senate, after a year's delay, with the help of Majority Leader Lyndon B. Johnson, who won southern acceptance by watering down the act. Republican Clifford Case of New Jersey dismissed the final bill as a "pitiful remnant" of the original measure, while Georgia Democrat Richard Russell trumpeted it as the "sweetest victory in my twenty-five years as a Senator." The act established for a period of two years the Civil Rights Commission, which was later extended indefinitely, and a new Civil Rights Division in the Justice Department, which could seek injunctions to prevent interference with the right to vote. Yet, by 1959 the Civil Rights Act had not added a single southern black to the voting rolls. Neither did the Civil Rights Act of 1960, which provided for federal court referees to register blacks where a court found a "pattern and practice" of discrimination, and also made it a federal crime to interfere with any court order or to cross state lines to destroy any building. This bill, too, lacked any real teeth and depended upon vigorous presidential enforcement.

DESEGREGATION IN LITTLE ROCK   There had been sporadic violence in resistance to civil rights efforts, but a few weeks after the Civil Rights Act of 1957 passed, Arkansas governor Orval Faubus called out the National Guard to prevent nine black students from entering Little Rock's Central High School under federal court order. A conference between the president and the governor proved fruitless, but on court order Faubus withdrew the National Guard. When the students tried to enter the school, an hysterical white mob forced their removal for their own safety. At that point Eisenhower, who had said two months before that he could not "imagine any set of circumstances that would ever induce me to send federal troops," ordered a thousand paratroopers to Little Rock to protect the students, and placed the National Guard on federal service. The soldiers stayed through the school year.

The following year Faubus closed the high schools of Little Rock rather than allow integration, and court proceedings dragged on into 1959 before the schools could be reopened. In that year, massive resistance to integration in Virginia collapsed when both state and federal courts struck down state laws that had cut off funds from integrated schools. Thereafter, massive resistance for the most part was confined to the Deep South where five states, from South Carolina west through Louisiana, still opposed even token integration.

National Guardsmen were sent to Little Rock, Arkansas, to protect newly enrolled black students who faced violent resistance from those opposed to integration.

Assessing the Eisenhower Years

Until recent years, the Eisenhower administration has not drawn much acclaim from journalists and historians. One journalist called the Eisenhower years "the time of the great postponement," during which the president "lived off the accumulated wisdom, the accumulated prestige, and the accumulated military strength of his predecessors" and left domestic and foreign policies "about where he found them in 1953." Yet even these critics granted that Eisenhower had succeeded in ending the war in Korea and settling the dust raised by McCarthy. But if he had failed to end the cold war and in fact had institutionalized it as a global confrontation, he sensed the limits of American power and kept its application to low-risk situations. If he took few initiatives in addressing the racial and social problems that would erupt in the 1960s, he left the major innovations of the New Deal in place and thereby legitimized them. If he tolerated unemployment of as much as 7 percent at times, inflation remained at a very low rate of 1.6 percent during his terms. His farewell address to the American people, delivered on radio and television three days before he left office, showed his remarkable foresight in his own area of special expertise, the military.

Like Washington, Eisenhower couched his wisdom largely in the form of warnings: that America's "leadership and prestige depend, not merely upon our unmatched material strength, but on how we use our power in the interests of world peace and human betterment"; that the temptation to find easy answers should take into account "the need to maintain balance in and among national problems"; and above all that Americans "must avoid the impulse to live only for today, plundering, for our own ease and convenience, the precious resources of tomorrow."

Eisenhower highlighted the dangers of a military establishment in a time of peace. "This conjunction of an immense military establishment and a large arms industry is new in the American experience," he noted. "In the councils of government we must guard against the acquisition of unwarranted influence, whether sought or unsought, by the military-industrial complex. The potential for the disastrous rise of misplaced power exists and will persist."

Eisenhower confessed great disappointment at his inability to affirm "that a lasting peace is in sight," only that "war has been avoided." But he prayed "that, in the goodness of time, all peoples will come to live together in a peace guaranteed by the binding force of mutual respect and love."

MAKING CONNECTIONS

- The civil rights movement of the 1950s aimed to achieve the racial integration of public services and equal access to political rights. This struggle would continue into the 1960s and then move in several new directions. See Chapter 34.

- American involvement in Vietnam grew in the 1950s, but remained limited to an advisory role. Escalation to an active fighting role came under Lyndon Johnson in 1965, a topic covered in Chapter 34.

- Eisenhower's "hands-off" approach to the presidency was reminiscent of the Gilded-Age presidencies and those of the 1920s. See Chapters 18, 22, and 27.

FURTHER READING

Scholarship on the Eisenhower years is extensive. A carefully balanced overview of the period is Chester Pach, Jr., and Elmo Richardson's *The Presidency of Dwight D. Eisenhower* (1991). For the manner in which Eisenhower conducted foreign policy, see Robert A. Divine's *Eisenhower and the Cold War* (1981).

The conservatism of the 1950s is documented in George H. Nash's *The Conservative Intellectual Movement in America: Since 1945* (1976) and Richard M. Fried's *Nightmare in Red: The McCarthy Era in Perspective* (1990). On the relationship between business and government, see Louis Galambos and Joseph Pratt's *The Rise of the Corporate Commonwealth: United States Business and Public Policy in the Twentieth Century* (1988).

Several specialized studies are illuminating. See Robert A. Divine's *The Sputnik Challenge: Eisenhower's Response to the Soviet Satellite* (1993) and Tom Lewis's *Divided Highways: Building the Interstate Highways, Transforming American Life* (1997).

For the buildup of American involvement in Indochina, consult Lloyd C. Gardner's *Approaching Vietnam: From World War II through Dien Bien Phu, 1941–1954* (1988), and David L. Anderson's *Trapped by Success: The Eisenhower Administration and Vietnam, 1953–1961* (1991). How the Eisenhower Doctrine came to be implemented is traced in Stephen Ambrose and Douglas Brinkley's *Rise to Globalism: American Foreign Policy Since 1938* (rev. ed., 1997). For studies of two important foreign policy topics, see James A. Bill's *The Eagle and the Lion: The Tragedy of American-Iranian Relations* (1988) and Stephen G. Rabe's *Eisenhower and Latin America: The Foreign Policy of Anticommunism* (1988).

Two introductions to the impact wrought by the Warren Supreme Court during the 1950s are Alexander Bickel's *The Supreme Court and the Idea of Progress* (1970) and Paul Murphy's *The Constitution in Crisis Times, 1918–1969* (1972). Also helpful is Archibald Cox's *The Warren Court: Constitutional Decision as an Instrument of Reform* (1968). A masterful study of the important Warren Court decision on school desegregation is Richard Kluger's *Simple Justice: The History of Brown v. Board of Education and Black America's Struggle for Equality* (1975).

For the story of the early civil rights movement, see Taylor Branch's *Parting the Waters: America in the King Years, 1954–1963* (1988), and Robert Weisbrot's *Freedom Bound: A History of America's Civil Rights Movement* (1990).

34 ✑ NEW FRONTIERS: POLITICS AND SOCIAL CHANGE IN THE 1960s

CHAPTER ORGANIZER

This chapter focuses on:

- Kennedy's New Frontier and Johnson's Great Society.

- the achievements of the civil rights movement and ensuing splinter movements.

- America's growing involvement in Vietnam and the rising opposition to it.

- Kennedy's efforts to combat communism in Cuba.

For those who considered the social and political climate of the 1950s dull, the following decade would provide a striking contrast. The 1960s were years of extraordinary social turbulence and innovation in public affairs—as well as sudden tragedy and trauma. Many social ills that had been festering for decades suddenly forced their way onto the national agenda. At the same time, the deeply entrenched assumptions of cold war ideology led the country into the longest, most controversial, and least successful war in the nation's history.

THE NEW FRONTIER

KENNEDY VS. NIXON   In 1960, few sensed such dramatic change on the horizon. The presidential election of that year pitted two candidates—Richard M. Nixon and John F. Kennedy—who seemed to symbolize the unadventurous politics of the 1950s. Though better known than Kennedy because of his eight years as Eisenhower's vice-president, Nixon had also developed the reputation of a cunning chameleon, the "Tricky Dick" who concealed his duplicity behind a series of masks. "Nixon doesn't know who he is," Kennedy told an aide, "and so each time he makes a speech he has to decide which Nixon he is, and that will be very exhausting."

But Nixon could not be so easily dismissed. He possessed a shrewd intelligence and a compulsive love for politics, the more combative the better. His worst flaw was a callous disregard for the rules of political combat, a trait he displayed from his first campaign to his last. Born in suburban Los Angeles in 1913, he grew up amid a working-class Quaker family struggling to make ends meet. In 1946, having completed law school and a wartime stint in the navy, Richard Nixon jumped into the political arena as a Republican, and, with the help of a powerful group of conservative southern California businessmen, he unseated a popular congressman.

Nixon arrived in Washington eager to reverse the tide of New Deal liberalism. "I was elected to smash the labor bosses," he explained. Four years later he won election to the Senate. In his campaigns, Nixon unleashed scurrilous personal attacks on his opponents, employing half-truths, lies, and rumors, and he shrewdly manipulated and fed the growing anti-Communist hysteria. Yet Nixon became both a respected and effective member of Congress, and by 1950 he was the most requested Republican speaker in the country. The reward for his rapid rise to political stardom was the vice-presidential nomination in 1952, which led to successive terms as the partner of the popular Eisenhower.

In comparison to his Republican opponent, Kennedy was inexperienced. Despite an abundance of assets, including a record of heroism in World War II, a glamorous young wife, a bright, agile mind and Harvard education, a rich, powerful family, a handsome face, movie-star charisma, and robust outlook, the forty-three-year-old Kennedy had not distinguished himself in the House or Senate. Indeed, his political rise owed not so much to his abilities or accomplishments as to the effective public relations campaign engineered by his ambitious father, Joseph Kennedy, who was a self-made tycoon. The older Kennedy had made millions on Wall Street in the twenties, gained control of much of the Hollywood film industry in the thirties, and finessed from President Franklin Roosevelt an appointment as ambassador to Great Britain. Ambassador Joseph Kennedy soon developed a consuming ambition to see one of his sons elected president. When the eldest boy, Joseph Jr., was killed in the war, the mantle of paternal expectation fell on John's shoulders.

John F. Kennedy subsequently suffered from criticism that there was more image to him than substance. And there was some truth to the charge. Although he won a Pulitzer Prize for *Profiles in Courage* (1956), a book (ghostwritten by an aide) about past political leaders who had "made the tough decisions," Kennedy, claimed Washington critics, had shown more profile than courage during the McCarthy era of the early 1950s, and he had a weak record on civil rights. Eleanor Roosevelt declined to endorse Kennedy in 1960, noting that presidential authority should not be vested in "someone who understands what courage is and admires it, but has not quite the independence to have it."

During his campaign for the Democratic nomination, Kennedy had shown that he had the energy to match his grace and ambition, even though he suffered from serious spinal problems, Addison's disease (a debilitating disorder of the adrenal glands), recurrent blood disorders, venereal disease, and fierce fevers. He took medicine daily, sometimes hourly. But like Franklin Roosevelt, he and his aides and family members successfully masked such physical ailments from the public.

By the time of the convention in 1960, Kennedy had traveled over 65,000 miles, visited twenty-five states, and made over 350 speeches. In his acceptance speech, he found the stirring, muscular rhetoric that would stamp the rest of his campaign and his presidency: "We stand today on the edge of a New Frontier—the frontier of unknown opportunities and perils—a frontier of unfulfilled hopes and threats." Kennedy and his staff quite consciously fastened upon the frontier metaphor as the label for their domestic program. As an avid student of American history himself, Kennedy knew that the frontier image possessed a special resonance for the American people. Americans had always been ad-

John F. Kennedy's poise and precision in the debates with Richard Nixon impressed viewers and voters.

venturers, eager to conquer and exploit new frontiers, and Kennedy promised to use his administration to continue the process.

Three events shaped the campaign that fall. First, as the only Catholic to run for the presidency since Al Smith, Kennedy strove to dispel the impression that his religion was a major political liability. In a speech before the Houston Ministerial Association in 1960, he directly confronted the political implications of his Catholicism. In America, he told the Protestant clergy, "the separation of church and state is absolute," and "no Catholic prelate would tell the President—should he be a Catholic—how to act and no Protestant minister should tell his parishioners for whom to vote." The religious question thereafter drew little public attention; Kennedy's candor had neutralized it.

Second, Nixon violated one of the cardinal rules of politics when he agreed to debate his less prominent opponent on television. During the first of four debates, few significant policy differences surfaced, allowing viewers to shape their opinions more on matters of style. Some 70 million people watched this first-ever television debate, and they saw an obviously uncomfortable Nixon, still weak from a recent illness, perspiring heavily and sporting his perpetual five-o'clock shadow. He looked haggard, uneasy, and even sinister before the camera. Kennedy, on the other hand, projected a cool poise and offered crisp answers that made him seem equal, if not superior, in his fitness for the office. Kennedy's popularity immediately shot up in the polls. In the words of a bemused southern senator, Kennedy combined "the best qualities of Elvis Presley and Franklin D. Roosevelt."

Still, the momentum created by the first debate was not enough to ensure a Kennedy victory. The third key event in the campaign involved the civil rights issue. Democratic strategists knew that in order to offset the loss of southern conservatives suspicious of Kennedy's Catholicism and strong civil rights positions, they had to woo black voters. To do so they set up a special committee to increase minority voter registration and to attract the black vote.

Perhaps the most crucial incident of the campaign occurred when Martin Luther King, Jr., and some fifty demonstrators were arrested in Atlanta for "trespassing" in an all-white restaurant. Although the other demonstrators were soon released, King was sentenced to four months in prison, ostensibly because of an earlier traffic violation. Robert Kennedy, the candidate's younger brother and campaign manager, called the judge handling King's case, who also happened to be a close friend of the Georgia governor, alerting him "that if he was a decent American, he would let King out of jail by sundown." King was soon released on bail, and the Kennedy campaign seized full advantage of the outcome, distributing some 2 million pamphlets in black neighborhoods extolling Kennedy's efforts on behalf of Dr. King.

When the votes were counted, Kennedy and his running mate, Lyndon B. Johnson of Texas, had won the closest presidential election since 1888. The winning margin was only 118,574 votes out of 68 million cast. Kennedy's wide lead in the electoral vote, 303 to 219, belied the paper-thin margin in several key states, especially Illinois, where Chicago mayor Richard Daley's Democratic machine appeared to have lived up to its legendary campaign motto: "In Chicago we tell our people to vote early and to vote often." Nixon had in fact carried more states than Kennedy, sweeping most of the West, and holding four of the six southern states Eisenhower had carried in 1956. Kennedy's majority was built out of victories in southern New England, the populous Middle Atlantic states, and key states in the South where black voters provided the critical margin of victory. Yet ominous rumblings of discontent ap-

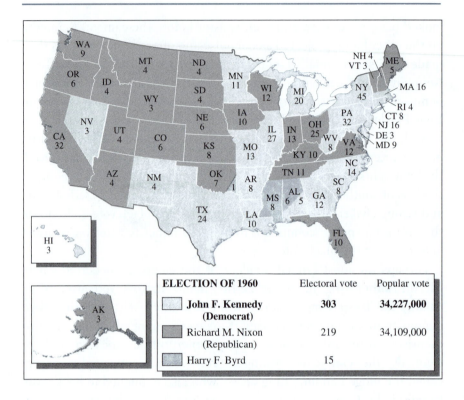

ELECTION OF 1960	Electoral vote	Popular vote
John F. Kennedy (Democrat)	303	34,227,000
Richard M. Nixon (Republican)	219	34,109,000
Harry F. Byrd	15	

peared in the once-solid Democratic South, as all eight of Mississippi's electors and six of Alabama's eleven (as well as one elector from Oklahoma) defied the national ticket and voted for Virginia senator Harry Byrd, the arch-segregationist.

THE NEW ADMINISTRATION   Kennedy was the youngest person ever elected president, and his cabinet appointments put an accent on youth and "Eastern Establishment" figures. As a self-described "idealist without illusions," he was determined to attract the "best and the brightest" minds available, individuals who would inject a tough, pragmatic, and vigorous outlook into governmental affairs. Adlai Stevenson was favored by liberal Democrats for secretary of state, but Kennedy chose Dean Rusk, a career diplomat who then headed the Rockefeller Foundation. Stevenson received the relatively minor post of ambassador to the United Nations. Robert S. McNamara, one of the "whiz kids" who had reorganized the Ford Motor Company with his "systems-

Kennedy and his wife, Jacqueline, at the inauguration, January 20, 1961.

analysis" techniques, was asked to bring his managerial magic to bear on the Department of Defense. C. Douglas Dillon, a Republican banker, was made secretary of the treasury in an effort to reassure conservative business owners. When critics attacked the appointment of Kennedy's thirty-five-year-old brother, Robert, as attorney-general, the president quipped, "I don't see what's wrong with giving Bobby a little experience before he goes into law practice." McGeorge Bundy, whom Kennedy called "the second smartest man I know," was made special assistant for national security affairs, lending additional credence to the impression that foreign policy would remain under tight White House control.

The inaugural ceremonies set the tone of elegance and youthful vigor that would come to be called the "Kennedy style." The glittering atmosphere of snow-clad Washington seemed to symbolize fresh promise. After poet Robert Frost paid tribute to the administration in verse, Kennedy dazzled listeners with uplifting rhetoric. "Let the word go forth from this time and place," he proclaimed. "Let every nation know, whether it wishes us well or ill, that we shall pay any price, bear any burden, meet any hardship, support any friend, oppose any foe, to assure the survival and success of liberty. And so, my fellow Americans: ask not what your country can do for you—ask what you can do for your country." Spines tingled at the time; Kennedy, one journalist wrote, was the first president to be a Prince Charming.

THE KENNEDY RECORD But for all of his idealistic rhetoric, Kennedy had a difficult time launching his New Frontier domestic program. Elected by a razor-thin margin, he did not enjoy a popular mandate. Nor did he show much skill in shepherding legislation through a Congress in the grip of a conservative southern coalition that blocked his efforts to increase federal aid to education, provide health insurance for the aged, and create a new Department of Urban Affairs. The Senate killed his initiatives on behalf of unemployed youth, migrant workers, and mass transit. When Kennedy finally came around to the advice of his Keynesian advisers in 1963 and submitted a drastic tax cut, Congress blocked that as well.

Administration proposals, nevertheless, did win some notable victories in Congress. Those involving defense and foreign policy generally won favor; indeed, defense appropriations exceeded administration requests. On foreign aid there were some cuts, but Congress readily approved broad "Alliance for Progress" programs to help Latin America, and the celebrated Peace Corps, created in 1961 to supply volunteers to provide educational and technical services abroad. Kennedy's greatest legislative accomplishment, however, may have been the Trade Expansion Act of 1962, which eventually led to tariff cuts averaging 35 percent between the United States and the European Common Market.

In the field of domestic social legislation, the administration did score a few victories. They included a new Housing Act, which earmarked nearly $5 billion for urban renewal over four years, a raise in the minimum wage from $1 to $1.25 and its extension to more than 3 million additional workers, the Area Redevelopment Act of 1961, which provided nearly $400 million in loans and grants to "distressed areas," an increase in Social Security benefits, and additional funds for sewage treatment plants. Kennedy also won support for an accelerated space program with the goal of landing on the moon before the end of the decade.

THE WARREN COURT Under Chief Justice Earl Warren, the Supreme Court continued to be a decisive influence on American domestic life during the 1960s. The Court's decisions on civil liberties proved as controversial as its earlier decisions on civil rights. In 1962 the Court ruled that a school prayer adopted by the New York State Board of Regents violated the constitutional prohibition against an established religion. In *Gideon v. Wainwright* (1963) the Court required that every felony defendant be provided a lawyer regardless of the defendant's ability to pay. In 1964 the Court ruled in *Escobedo* v. *Illinois* that a person accused of a crime must also be allowed to consult a lawyer before being interrogated by police. Two years later, in *Miranda* v. *Arizona,* the Court issued perhaps its most bitterly criticized ruling when it ordered that an accused person in police custody must be informed of certain basic rights: the right to remain silent; the right to know that anything said can be used against the individual in court; and the right to have a defense attorney present during interrogation. In addition, the Court established rules for police to follow in informing suspects of their legal rights before questioning could begin.

EXPANSION OF THE CIVIL RIGHTS MOVEMENT

The most important development in American domestic life during the 1960s occurred in civil rights. Kennedy entered the White House reluctant to challenge conservative southern Democrats on the race issue. He was never as personally committed to the cause of civil rights as his brother Robert. Despite a few dramatic gestures of support toward black leaders, John Kennedy only belatedly grasped the moral and emotional significance of the most widespread reform movement of the decade. Eventually, however, his conscience was pricked by the grassroots civil rights movement led by Martin Luther King, Jr.

SIT-INS AND FREEDOM RIDERS   After the Montgomery bus boycott of 1955–1956, King's philosophy of "militant nonviolence" inspired others to challenge the deeply entrenched patterns of racial segregation in the South. At the same time, lawsuits to desegregate the schools got thousands of parents and young people involved. The momentum generated the first genuine mass movement in African-American history when four black college students sat down and demanded service at a "whites-only" Woolworth lunch counter in Greensboro, North Carolina, on February 1, 1960. Within a week, the "sit-in" movement had spread to six more towns in the state, and within two months, demonstrations had occurred in fifty-four cities in nine states.

Sit-in at the Woolworth's Lunch Counter in Greensboro, North Carolina, *February 1, 1960. The four protesters, students at North Carolina A & T College, were* (from left) *Joseph McNeil, Franklin McCain, Billy Smith, and Clarence Henderson.*

In 1960 the student participants, black and white, formed the Student Nonviolent Coordinating Committee (SNCC), which worked with King's Southern Christian Leadership Conference (SCLC) to broaden the movement. The sit-ins at restaurants became "kneel-ins" at churches and "wade-ins" at segregated public pools. Music provided a common source of inspiration and solace to the demonstrators. Drawing upon the tradition of slave spirituals, they developed freedom songs such as "Ain't Gonna Let That Sheriff Turn Me Around" and "We Shall Overcome." A participant in an organizational meeting at a church recalled that after the last speaker concluded, "tears filled the eyes of hard, grown men who had seen with their own eyes merciless atrocities committed. . . . Bertha told of spending Thanksgiving in jail . . . and when we rose to sing 'We Shall Overcome,' nobody could imagine what kept the church on four corners. . . . I threw my head back and closed my eyes as I sang with my whole body."

Everywhere they demonstrated, the protesters refused to retaliate, even when struck with clubs or poked with cattle prods. The conservative white editor of the *Richmond News Leader* conceded his admiration for their courage:

> Here were the colored students, in coats, white shirts, ties, and one of them was reading Goethe, and one was taking notes from a biology text. And here, on the sidewalk, was a gang of white boys come to heckle, a ragtail rabble, slack-jawed, black-jacketed, grinning fit to kill, and some of them, God save the mark, were waving the proud and honored flag of the Southern States in the last war fought by gentlemen.

Words cannot do justice to the suffering, sacrifice, courage, and commitment of the young protesters. During the year after the Greensboro sit-ins, over 3,600 black and white activists spent some time in jail. In many communities they were pelted with rocks, burned with cigarettes, and subjected to unending verbal abuse. In Orangeburg, South Carolina, officers used fire hoses against the demonstrators amid subfreezing temperatures.

In 1961 the Congress of Racial Equality (CORE) sent a group of black and white "freedom riders" on buses to test a federal court ruling that had banned segregation on buses and trains and in terminals. In Alabama mobs attacked the travelers with fists and pipes, burned one of the buses, and assaulted Justice Department observers, but the demonstrators persisted and drew national attention, generating new respect and support for their cause.

FEDERAL INTERVENTION   In 1962 Governor Ross Barnett of Mississippi, who believed that God made the Negro "different to punish him," defied a court order and refused to allow James H. Meredith, a black student, to enroll at the University of Mississippi. Attorney-General Robert Kennedy thereupon dispatched federal marshals to enforce the law. When the marshals were assaulted by a white mob, federal troops had to intervene, but only after two deaths and many injuries. Meredith was finally registered at "Ole Miss" a few days later.

Eugene "Bull" Connor's police unleash attack dogs on civil rights demonstrators in Birmingham, Alabama, May 1963.

Everywhere it seemed black activists and white supporters were challenging deeply entrenched patterns of segregation and prejudice. In 1963 Martin Luther King launched a series of nonviolent demonstrations in Birmingham, Alabama, where Police Commissioner Eugene "Bull" Connor served as the perfect foil for King's tactic of nonviolent civil disobedience. Connor used attack dogs, tear gas, electric cattle prods, and fire hoses on the protesters while millions of outraged Americans watched the confrontations on television.

King, who was arrested and jailed during the demonstrations, took the opportunity to write his "Letter from Birmingham City Jail," a stirring defense of the nonviolent strategy that became a classic of the civil rights movement. "One who breaks an unjust law," he stressed, "must do so openly, lovingly, and with a willingness to accept the penalty." He also signaled a shift in his strategy for social change. Heretofore, King had emphasized the need to educate southern whites about the injustice of segregation and other patterns of discrimination. Now he focused more on gaining federal enforcement and new legislation by provoking racists to display their violent hatreds in public. As King admitted in his "Letter," he sought through organized nonviolent protest to "create such a crisis and foster such a tension that a community which has constantly refused to negotiate is forced to confront the issue." This concept of civil disobedience did not set well with J. Edgar Hoover, the powerful head of the FBI, who labeled King "the most dangerous Negro of the future in this nation." He ordered agents to follow King and authorized the use of wiretaps on his telephones and in his motel rooms.

The sublime courage and resolve that King and many other protesters displayed in carrying out their program of nonviolent coercion helped mobilize national support for their integrationist objectives. (Indeed, in 1964 King would be awarded the Nobel Peace Prize.) Nudged by his brother Robert, a man of passion, compassion, and vision, President Kennedy finally decided that enforcement of existing statutes was not enough; new legislation was needed to deal with the race question. In

Martin Luther King, Jr. (second from left), *and other civil rights leaders at the head of the March on Washington for Jobs and Freedom, August 28, 1963.*

1963 he told the nation that racial discrimination "has no place in American life or law." He then endorsed an ambitious civil rights bill intended to end discrimination in public facilities, desegregate the public schools, and protect black voters. But the bill was quickly blocked in Congress by southern conservatives.

Throughout the Deep South, traditionalists remained steadfast. In the fall of 1963, Governor George Wallace dramatically stood in the doorway of a building at the University of Alabama to block the enrollment of several black students, but he stepped aside in the face of insistent federal marshals. That night President Kennedy spoke eloquently of the moral issue facing the nation: "If an American, because his skin is black, cannot enjoy the full and free life which all of us want, then who among us would be content to have the color of his skin changed and stand in his place? Who among us would be content with the counsels of patience and delay?" Later the same night, NAACP official Medgar Evers was shot to death as he returned to his home in Jackson, Mississippi.

The high point of the integrationist phase of the civil rights movement occurred on August 28, 1963, when over 200,000 blacks and whites marched down the Mall in Washington, D.C., toward the Lincoln Memorial singing "We Shall Overcome." The March on Washington was the largest civil rights demonstration in American history. Standing in front of Lincoln's statue, King delivered one of the memorable public speeches of the century:

> I say to you today, my friends, that in spite of the difficulties and frustrations of the moment I still have a dream. It is a dream deeply rooted in the American dream.
>
> I have a dream that one day this nation will rise up and live out the true meaning of its creed: "We hold these truths to be self-evident; that all men are created equal."
>
> I have a dream that one day . . . the sons of former slaves and the sons of former slaveowners will be able to sit together at the table of brotherhood.

That such racial harmony had not yet arrived, however, became clear two weeks later when a bomb exploded in a Birmingham church, killing four black girls who had arrived early for Sunday school. Yet King's dream—shared and promoted by thousands of other activists—survived. The intransigence and violence that civil rights workers encountered won converts to their cause all across the country.

FOREIGN FRONTIERS

EARLY SETBACKS   Kennedy's record in foreign relations, like that in domestic affairs, was mixed, but more spectacularly so. Although he had made the existence of a "missile gap" a major part of his campaign, he learned upon taking office that there was no "missile gap"—the United States remained far ahead of the Soviets in nuclear weaponry. Kennedy also discovered that there was in the works a CIA operation training 1,500 anti-Castro Cubans for an invasion of their homeland. The Joint Chiefs of Staff assured Kennedy that the plan was feasible in theory; analysts predicted that the invasion would inspire Cubans on the island to rebel against Castro.

In retrospect, it is clear that the scheme, poorly planned and poorly executed, had little chance of succeeding. When the invasion force landed at the Bay of Pigs in Cuba on April 17, 1961, it was brutally subdued in two days and more than 1,100 men were captured. A *New York Times* columnist lamented that the United States "looked like fools to our friends, rascals to our enemies, and incompetents to the rest." It was hardly an auspicious way for the new president to demonstrate his mastery of foreign policy.

Two months after the Bay of Pigs debacle, Kennedy met Soviet premier Khrushchev in Vienna, Austria. It was a tense confrontation during which Khrushchev browbeat the inexperienced Kennedy and threatened to limit Western access to Berlin, the divided city located deep within Communist East Germany. Kennedy was shaken by the aggressive Soviet stand. Upon his return home, he demonstrated American resolve by calling up Army Reserve and National Guard units. The Soviets responded by erecting the Berlin Wall, which cut off movement between East and West Berlin. Although no shooting incident triggered an accidental war, the Berlin Wall plugged the most accessible escape hatch for East Germans, showed Soviet willingness to challenge American resolve in Europe, and became another intractable barrier to the opening of new diplomatic frontiers.

A West Berlin couple climbs up and looks over the newly constructed Berlin Wall to communicate with the woman's mother on the other side. The Berlin Wall both physically divided the city itself and served as a wedge between the United States and the Soviet Union.

THE CUBAN MISSILE CRISIS A year later Khrushchev posed another challenge, this time ninety miles off the coast of Florida. Kennedy's unwillingness to commit the forces necessary to overthrow Castro and his acquiescence to the erection of the Berlin Wall seemed to signify a failure of will, and the Soviets apparently reasoned that they could install their missiles in Cuba with relative impunity. Their motives were to protect Cuba from another American-backed invasion, which Castro believed to be imminent, and to redress the strategic imbalance caused by the presence of American missiles in Turkey aimed at the Soviet Union.

American officials feared that Soviet missiles in Cuba would be placed in areas not covered by radar systems and, if launched, would arrive too quickly for warning. More important to Kennedy was the psychological effect of American acquiescence to a Soviet presence on its doorstep. This might weaken the credibility of the American nuclear deterrent for Europeans and demoralize anti-Castro elements in Latin

America. At the same time, the installation of Soviet missiles served Khrushchev's purpose of demonstrating his toughness to both Chinese and Soviet critics of his earlier advocacy of peaceful coexistence. But he misjudged the American response.

On October 14, 1962, American intelligence experts discovered based on photographs made from high-altitude U-2 flights that Soviet missile sites were under construction in Cuba. From the beginning, the administration decided that they had to be removed; the only question was how. In a series of secret meetings, the Executive Committee of the National Security Council narrowed the options to a choice between a "surgical" air strike and a naval blockade of Cuba. They opted for a blockade, which was carefully disguised by the euphemism "quarantine," since a blockade was technically an act of war. It offered the advantage of forcing the Soviets to shoot first, if it came to that, and left open the further options of stronger action. Monday, October 22, began one of the most anxious weeks in world history. On that day, the president announced to members of Congress and then to the public the discovery of the missile sites in Cuba; he also announced the naval quarantine.

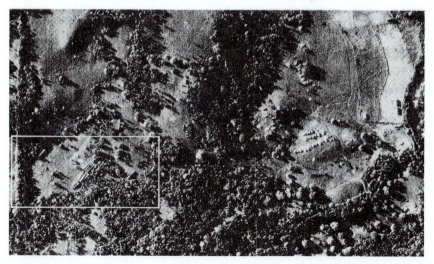

On October 14, 1962, a U2 surveillance plane revealed both missile launchers and shelters in San Cristóbal, Cuba.

Tensions grew as Khrushchev blustered that Kennedy had pushed humankind "to the abyss of a world missile-nuclear war." Soviet ships, he declared, would ignore the quarantine. But on Wednesday, October 24, five Soviet ships, presumably with missiles aboard, stopped short of the quarantine line. Two days later an agent of the Soviet embassy privately approached an American television reporter with a proposal for an agreement: the Soviet Union would withdraw the missiles in return for a public pledge by the United States not to invade Cuba. The reporter was asked to relay the idea to the White House. Secretary of State Dean Rusk replied that the administration was interested, but told the newscaster: "Remember, when you report this, that eyeball to eyeball, they blinked first."

That same evening Kennedy received two messages from Khrushchev, the first repeating the original offer and the second demanding in addition the removal of American missiles from Turkey. The two messages probably reflected divided counsels in the Kremlin. Ironically, Kennedy had already ordered removal of the outmoded missiles in Turkey, but he refused now to act under the gun. Instead he followed Robert Kennedy's suggestion that he respond favorably to the first letter and ignore the second. On Sunday, October 28, Khrushchev agreed to remove the missiles.

In the aftermath of the crisis, tension between the United States and the Soviet Union quickly subsided. Several symbolic steps helped to relax tensions: an agreement to sell the Soviet Union surplus wheat, the installation of a "hot line" telephone between Washington and Moscow to provide instant contact between the heads of government, and the removal of obsolete American missiles from Turkey, Italy, and Britain. On June 10, 1963, the president announced that direct discussions with the Soviets would soon begin, and he called upon the nation to reexamine its attitude toward peace, the Soviet Union, and the cold war. Those discussions resulted in a treaty with the Soviet Union and Britain to stop nuclear testing in the atmosphere. The treaty, ratified in September 1963, did not provide for on-site inspection, nor did it ban underground testing, which continued, but it promised to end the dangerous pollution of the atmosphere with radioactivity. The treaty was an important symbolic and substantive move toward détente. As Kennedy put it: "A journey of a thousand miles begins with one step."

KENNEDY AND VIETNAM   In Southeast Asia events were moving toward what would become within a decade the greatest American foreign policy calamity of the century. During John Kennedy's "thousand days" in office, the turmoil of Indochina never preoccupied public attention for any extended period, but it dominated international diplomatic debates from the time the administration entered office.

The landlocked kingdom of Laos, along with neighboring Cambodia, had been declared neutral in the Geneva Accords of 1954, but had fallen into a complex struggle for power between the Communist Pathet Lao insurgents and the Royal Laotian Army. There matters stood when Eisenhower left office and told Kennedy: "You might have to go in there and fight it out." The chairman of the Joint Chiefs of Staff argued in favor of a stand against the Pathet Lao, even if it meant direct intervention. After a lengthy consideration of alternatives, Kennedy decided to favor a neutralist coalition government including Pathet Lao representatives that would preclude American military involvement in Laos, yet prevent a Pathet Lao victory. The Soviets, who were extending aid to the Pathet Lao, indicated a readiness to negotiate, and in 1961 talks began in Geneva. After more than a year of tangled negotiations, the three factions in Laos agreed to a neutral coalition. American and Soviet aid to the opposing parties was supposed to end, but both countries in fact continued covert operations, while North Vietnam kept open the Ho Chi Minh Trail through eastern Laos, over which it supplied its Viet Cong allies in South Vietnam.

There the situation worsened under the leadership of the Catholic premier Ngo Dinh Diem, despite encouraging reports from the commander of American military "advisers" in South Vietnam. At the time the problem was less the scattered Communist guerrilla attacks than Diem's failure to deliver social and economic reforms and his inability to rally popular support. His repressive tactics, directed not only against Communists but also against the Buddhist majority and other critics, played into the hands of his enemies. In 1961 White House Assistant Walt Rostow and General Maxwell Taylor became the first in a long train of presidential emissaries to South Vietnam's capital, Saigon. Focusing on the military situation, they proposed a major increase in the American military presence. Kennedy refused, but continued to dispatch more military "advisers" in the hope of stabilizing the situation:

South Vietnamese troops in combat with Viet Cong guerrillas in the Mekong River Delta, 1961.

when he took office there had been 2,000; by the end of 1963 there were 16,000, none of whom had been officially committed to battle.

By 1963 sharply divergent reports were coming in from the South Vietnamese countryside. American military advisers, their eyes on the inflated "kill ratios" reported by the Army of the Republic of Vietnam (ARVN), drew optimistic conclusions. On-site political reporters, watching the reactions of the Vietnamese people, foresaw continued deterioration without the promised political and economic reforms. By midyear, growing Buddhist demonstrations made the discontent in South Vietnam more plainly visible. The spectacle of Buddhist monks setting themselves on fire in protest against government tyranny stunned Americans. By the fall of 1963, the Kennedy administration had decided that the autocratic Diem was a lost cause. When dissident generals proposed a coup d'état, U.S. ambassador Henry Cabot Lodge assured them that Washington would not stand in the way. On November 1 they seized the government and murdered Diem, though without explicit American approval. But the generals provided no more stability than earlier regimes, as successive coups set the country spinning from one military leader to another.

KENNEDY'S ASSASSINATION   By the fall of 1963, Kennedy seemed
to be facing up to the intractability of the situation in Vietnam. In September he declared of the South Vietnamese: "In the final analysis it's
their war. They're the ones who have to win it or lose it. We can help
them as advisers but they have to win it." The following month he announced the administration's intention to withdraw United States
forces from South Vietnam by the end of 1965. What Kennedy would
have done thereafter has remained a matter of endless controversy
among historians, endless because it is unanswerable and unanswerable because on November 22, 1963, while visiting Dallas, he was shot
in the neck and head by Lee Harvey Oswald.

Oswald's motives remain unknown. Although a blue-ribbon federal
commission appointed by President Johnson and headed by Chief Justice Earl Warren concluded that Oswald acted alone, debate still swirls
around various conspiracy theories. Kennedy's death and then the murder of Oswald by Jack Ruby, a Dallas nightclub owner, were shown over
and over again on television, the medium that had so helped Kennedy's
rise to the presidency and that now captured his death and the moving
funeral at Arlington Cemetery.

Kennedy's vice-president, Lyndon B. Johnson, takes the presidential oath as Air
Force One *returns from Dallas with Jacqueline Kennedy* (right), *the presidential party, and the body of the assassinated president.*

Shortly after the funeral, Jacqueline Kennedy reminisced for a reporter about their family life. At night they would play records, and the song John Kennedy loved most came from a current Broadway hit, *Camelot,* based on the legends of King Arthur: " 'Don't let it be forgot, that once there was a spot, for one brief shining moment, that was known as Camelot'—and it will never be that way again." This "Camelot mystique" soon enshrouded the fallen president, magnifying his accomplishments and creating an aura of glamour and poignancy around his legacy. A Gallup poll in 1976 showed that a majority of Americans regarded Kennedy as the greatest of all presidents, a judgment that time has since eroded.

LYNDON JOHNSON AND THE GREAT SOCIETY

Texan Lyndon Johnson took the oath as president of the United States on board the plane that took John Kennedy's body back to Washington from Dallas. At age fifty-five he had spent twenty-six years on the Washington scene and had served nearly a decade as Democratic leader in the Senate, where he had displayed the greatest gift for compromise since Henry Clay. Johnson brought to the White House a marked change of style from Kennedy. A self-made man who through gritty determination and shrewd manipulation had worked his way out of a hardscrabble rural Texas background to become one of Washington's most powerful figures, Johnson had none of the Kennedy elegance or charisma. He was a rough-hewn, gregarious, and domineering man who craved both political power and public affection. The first southern president since Woodrow Wilson, he harbored, like another southern president, Andrew Johnson, a sense of being the perpetual "outsider" despite his long experience with legislative power. And indeed he was so regarded by Kennedy "insiders."

Those who viewed Johnson as a stereotypical southern conservative failed to appreciate his long-standing admiration for Franklin Roosevelt, the depth of his concern for poor people, and his commitment to the cause of civil rights. "By political background, by temperament, by personal preference," wrote one journalist, Johnson was "the riverboat man. He was brawny and rough and skilled beyond measure in the full use of tricky tides and currents, in his knowledge of the hidden shoals. He was a swashbuckling master of the political midstreams—but only in the crowded, well-traveled and familiar inland waterways of domestic politics." In foreign affairs, however, he was, like Woodrow Wilson, a novice.

THE JOHNSON MYSTIQUE   Lyndon Johnson was a paradox. He was neither southern nor western but that unique blend of the two regions, a Texan capable of altering himself to fit any occasion. On the one hand, he was a compulsive worker and achiever, animated by greed, ambition, and an all-consuming lust for power, an overbearing man capable of ruthlessness and deceit. On the other hand, he could be warm, caring, and gracious. He made friends easily and displayed genuine concern for the welfare of the disadvantaged.

After a stint in the navy during World War II, which Johnson, like Kennedy, later exaggerated to appear more heroic than it was, he ran for the Senate in 1948. His lieutenants bribed local political bosses to "stuff" ballot boxes in their precincts, and at the last minute Johnson won by eighty-seven votes. Johnson tried to deflect criticism by jokingly referring to himself as "Landslide Lyndon," but a cloud of suspicion hung over him as he assumed his Senate seat. During the early 1950s, Johnson kept his seat by engaging in the required "Red-baiting," catering to the oil and natural gas interests in Texas, and opposing civil rights legislation. In 1951, at age forty-four, he became the youngest Senate minority leader in Democratic party history.

After reelection in 1954, Johnson was elected Senate majority leader when the Democrats recaptured the upper house of Congress. During the next six years he displayed a remarkable ability for manipulating others to get legislation passed, resorting to horse-trading and back-room deals in order to shepherd some 1,300 bills through the Senate. He engineered the censure of Joseph McCarthy and the passage of the Civil Rights Act of 1957. His accomplishments made him a natural contender for the presidency in 1960, but he was unable to project himself as anything more than a regional candidate. Having done all he could as a legislative leader, he eagerly accepted Kennedy's invitation to join the ticket. The invitation resulted not from affection or admiration. Kennedy simply needed Johnson to help carry the South for him.

POLITICS AND POVERTY   Quite naturally, domestic politics became Johnson's first priority as president. Amid the national grief after the assassination, he declared that Kennedy's cabinet and advisers would stay on and that his legislative program, stymied in several congressional committees, would be passed. Johnson loved the kind of political infighting and legislative detail that Kennedy had loathed. Recalcitrant congressmen and senators were brought to the White House for what became famous as "the Johnson Treatment." A journalist described the technique: "He moved in close, his face a scant millimeter from his target, his eyes widening and narrowing, his eyebrows rising and falling. From his pockets poured clippings, memos, statistics. Mimicry, humor, and the genius of analogy made the Treatment an almost hypnotic experience and rendered the target stunned and helpless." The logjam in the Congress that had blocked Kennedy's program broke under Johnson's forceful leadership, and a torrent of legislation poured through.

Before the year 1963 was out Congress had approved the pending foreign aid bill and a plan to sell wheat to the Soviet Union. But Amer-

The Johnson Treatment. *Johnson used powerful body language and facial expressions to intimidate and manipulate anyone who dared to disagree with him.*

ica's commitment to foreign aid pointed up its own people's needs. In 1964 the Council of Economic Advisers reported that 9.3 million American families, about 20 percent of the population, were below the "poverty line" of $3,000 per year for a family of four. "Unfortunately, many Americans live on the outskirts of hope," Johnson told the Congress in his first State of the Union message, "some because of their poverty and some because of their color, and all too many because of both." At the top of his agenda he put the stalled measures for tax reduction and civil rights, then added to his "must" list a bold new idea that bore the LBJ brand: "This Administration today, here and now, declares unconditional war on poverty in America." The particulars of this "war on poverty" were to come later, the product of a task force already at work before Johnson took office.

Americans had suddenly rediscovered poverty in the early 1960s when the social critic Michael Harrington published a powerful exposé titled *The Other America* (1962). Harrington argued that while most Americans had been celebrating their rising affluence during the postwar era, more than 40 million people were mired in a "culture of poverty," hidden from view and passed on from one generation to the next. Unlike the upwardly mobile immigrant poor at the turn of the century, these modern poor were impervious to hope. "To be impoverished," he asserted, "is to be an internal alien, to grow up in a culture that is radically different from the one that dominates the society." Television only exacerbated the problem by accentuating the relative deprivation of the poor. They saw how different they were from middle-class Americans, leaving many fatalistic about their condition.

President Kennedy read *The Other America* in 1963 and asked his advisers to investigate the problem and suggest a plan of attack. Upon taking office, Johnson announced that he wanted an antipoverty package that was "big and bold, that would hit the nation with real impact." When his advisers told him that their research was still incomplete, he declared his determination to act anyway. Money for the program would come from the tax revenues generated by corporate profits that had resulted from the surge in capital investment and increased individual purchasing power made possible by the tax reduction of 1964, which had led to one of the longest sustained economic booms in American history.

The administration's "war on poverty" was embodied in an Economic Opportunity Bill that incorporated a wide range of programs: a Job

Corps for inner-city youths aged sixteen to twenty-one, a Head Start program for disadvantaged preschoolers, work-study jobs for college students, grants to farmers and rural businesses, loans to those willing to hire the chronically unemployed, the Volunteers in Service to America (VISTA, a "domestic Peace Corps"), and the Community Action Program, which would provide "maximum feasible participation" of the poor in directing neighborhood programs designed for their benefit. Speaking at Ann Arbor, Michigan, in 1964, Johnson called for a "Great Society" resting on "abundance and liberty for all. The Great Society demands an end to poverty and racial injustice, to which we are fully committed in our time."

THE 1964 ELECTION   Johnson's liberal social program provoked a Republican counterattack. For years party regulars had come to fear that the party had fallen into the hands of an "Eastern Establishment" that had given in to the same internationalism and big-government policies as liberal Democrats. Ever since 1940, so the theory went, the party had nominated "me-too" candidates who merely promised to run more efficiently the programs that Democrats designed. Offer the voters "a choice, not an echo," they reasoned, and a conservative majority would assert itself. The Republican right thus began to drift toward varieties of dogmatic conservatism, ranging from a kind of "aristocratic" intellectual "new conservatism," which found voice in the *National Review,* edited by William F. Buckley, Jr., to the John Birch Society, founded by Robert Welch, a New England candy manufacturer given to accusing such distinguished citizens as Eisenhower, Dulles, and Chief Justice Earl Warren of supporting a Communist conspiracy.

By 1960 Arizona senator Barry Goldwater, a millionaire department-store magnate, had emerged as the leader of the Republican right. In his book *The Conscience of a Conservative* (1960), Goldwater proposed abolition of the income tax, sale of the TVA, and a drastic overhaul of Social Security. Almost from the time of Kennedy's victory in 1960 a movement to draft Goldwater began, mobilizing right-wing activists to capture party caucuses and contest primaries. In 1964 they took an early lead, and after sweeping the all-important California primary, Goldwater's forces controlled the Republican convention when it gathered in Los Angeles. "I would remind you," Goldwater told the delegates, "that extremism in the defense of liberty is no vice."

Many voters feared that the Republican candidate for president in 1964, Arizona senator Barry Goldwater, was trigger-happy. In this cartoon he wields his book, The Conscience of a Conservative, *in one hand and a hydrogen bomb in the other.*

By the end of the 1964 campaign, Goldwater had achieved a position of splendid isolation on the far right of the political spectrum. He had a gift for frightening voters. Accusing the administration of waging a "no-win" war in Vietnam, he urged wholesale bombing of North Vietnam and left the impression of being trigger-happy. He savaged Johnson's war on poverty and the entire New Deal tradition. At times he was foolishly candid. In Tennessee he proposed the sale of the Tennessee Valley Authority; in St. Petersburg, Florida, a major retirement community, he questioned the value of Social Security. He was on record as opposing both the nuclear test ban and the Civil Rights Act. To Republican campaign buttons that claimed "In your heart, you know he's right," Democrats responded, "In your guts you know he's nuts."

Johnson, on the other hand, moved to the center. He appealed to the great consensus that spanned most of the political spectrum. Having the Democratic nomination from the start, he chose as his running mate Hubert Humphrey from Minnesota, a prominent liberal senator who had long promoted the cause of civil rights. In contrast to Goldwater's bellicose rhetoric on Vietnam, Johnson pledged: "We are not about to send American boys nine or ten thousand miles from home to do what Asian boys ought to be doing for themselves"—a statement reminiscent of the assurance that Johnson's idol, Franklin Roosevelt, had voiced regarding the European war in 1940.

The result was a landslide. Johnson polled 61 percent of the total votes; Goldwater carried only Arizona and five states in the Deep South, where race remained the salient issue. Vermont went Democratic for the first time ever in a presidential election. Johnson won the electoral vote by a whopping 486 to 52. In the Senate the Democrats increased their majority by two (68 to 32) and in the House by thirty-seven (295 to 140). But LBJ was aware that a mandate such as he had received could quickly erode. He shrewdly told aides, "every day I'm in office, I'm going to lose votes. I'm going to alienate somebody. . . . We've got to get this legislation fast. You've got to get it during my honeymoon."

LANDMARK LEGISLATION   Johnson flooded the new Congress with Great Society legislation that, he promised, would end poverty, revitalize the decaying central cities, provide every young American with the chance to attend college, protect the health of the elderly, enhance cultural life, clean up the air and water, and make the highways safer and prettier. The scope of Johnson's legislation was unparalleled since Franklin Roosevelt's Hundred Days.

Priority went to health insurance and aid to education, proposals that had languished since President Truman advanced them in 1945. For twenty years the proposal for a comprehensive plan of medical insurance had been stalled by the steadfast opposition of the American Medical Association (AMA). But now that Johnson had the votes, the AMA joined Republicans in boarding the bandwagon for a bill serving those over age sixty-five. The AMA proposed, in addition to hospital insurance, a program for payment of doctor bills and drug costs, with the government footing half the premium. The act that finally emerged went well beyond the original program. It not only incorporated the new proposal into the Medicare program for the aged, but added another program, dubbed Medicaid, for federal grants to states that would help cover medical payments for the indigent. President Johnson signed the bill on July 30, 1965, in Independence, Missouri, with eighty-one-year-old Harry Truman looking on.

Five days after he submitted his Medicare program, Johnson sent to Congress his proposal for $1.5 billion in federal aid to elementary and secondary education. Such proposals had been ignored since the 1940s, blocked alternately by issues of segregation or separation of church and state. The first issue had been laid to rest, legally at least, by the Civil Rights Act of 1964. Now the Congress devised a means of extending aid to "poverty-impacted" school districts, regardless of their public or parochial character.

The momentum generated by the progress of these measures had already begun to carry others along, and the momentum continued through the following year. Before the Eighty-ninth Congress adjourned, it had established a record in the passage of landmark legislation unequaled since the time of the New Deal. Altogether the tide of Great Society legislation had carried 435 bills through the Congress. Among them was the Appalachian Regional Development Act of 1966, which provided $1 billion for programs in remote mountain coves. The Housing and Urban Development Act of 1965 provided aid for construction of 240,000 housing units and $3 billion for urban renewal. Funds for rent supplements for low-income families followed in 1966, and in that year a new Department of Housing and Urban Development appeared, headed by Robert C. Weaver, the first black cabinet member. Johnson had, in the words of one Washington reporter, "brought to harvest a generation's backlog of ideas and social legislation."

Little noticed in the stream of legislation flowing from the Congress was a major new immigration bill that had originated in the Kennedy White House. Johnson used his 1964 State of the Union address to endorse immigration reform in general and the Kennedy bill in particular. A modified version finally passed the Congress in the fall of 1965.

President Johnson signed the Immigration Act of 1965 in a ceremony held on Liberty Island in New York Harbor, with Ellis Island in the background. In his speech, he stressed that the new law would redress the wrong done to those "from southern and eastern Europe" and the "developing continents" of Asia, Africa, and Latin America. It did so by abolishing the discriminatory quotas based on national origins that had governed immigration policy since the 1920s. The new law, whose provisions were to take full effect in 1968, treated all nationalities and races equally. In place of national quotas it created hemispheric ceilings on visas issued: 170,000 for persons from outside the Western Hemisphere, 120,000 for persons from within. It also stipulated that no more than 20,000 people could come from any one country each year. The new act allowed the entry of immediate family members of American residents without limit. Most of the annual visas were to be given on a first-come-first-served basis to "other relatives" of American residents, and only a small proportion (about 10 percent) were allocated to those with special talents or job skills.

During the prosperous sixties, few western Europeans sought to emigrate to the United States; those living in Communist-controlled eastern Europe could not leave. But Asians and Latin Americans flocked to American consulates in search of visas. And within a few years the new arrivals in turn used the family-preference system to bring their family members as well. This so-called chain immigration quickly filled the annual quotas for nations such as the Philippines, Mexico, Korea, and the Dominican Republic, and Hispanics and Asians became the largest contingent of new Americans.

The Great Society programs included several genuine success stories. The Highway Safety Act and the Traffic Safety Act (1966) established safety standards for automobile manufacturers and highway design, and the scholarships provided for college students under the Higher Education Act (1965) were quite popular. Many Great Society initiatives aimed at improving the health, nutrition, and education of poor Americans, young and old, made some headway against these problems. So, too, did federal efforts to clean up air and water pollution. But several ambitious programs were hastily designed and ill conceived, others were vastly underfunded, and many were mismanaged. Medicare, for example, removed any incentives for hospitals to control costs, and medical bills skyrocketed. Often funds appropriated for various programs never made it through the tangled bureaucracy to the needy. Widely publicized cases of welfare fraud became a powerful weapon in the hands of those who were opposed to liberal social programs. By 1966 middle-class resentment over the cost and waste of the Great Society programs helped to generate a conservative backlash.

FROM CIVIL RIGHTS TO BLACK POWER

CIVIL RIGHTS LEGISLATION   Among the successes of the Great Society were several landmark pieces of civil rights legislation. After Kennedy's death, President Johnson, who had maneuvered through the Senate the Civil Rights Acts of 1957 and 1960, called for passage of a new civil rights bill as a memorial to the fallen leader. With bipartisan support, he finally broke the Senate filibuster mounted by southern segregationists. On July 2 Johnson signed the Civil Rights Act of 1964, the most far-reaching civil rights measure ever enacted by the Congress. The act outlawed discrimination in hotels, restaurants, and other public accommodations. It required that literacy tests for voting be administered in writing, and defined as literate anybody who had finished the sixth grade. The attorney-general could now bring suits for school desegregation, relieving parents of a painful necessity. Federally assisted programs and private employers alike were required to eliminate discrimination. An Equal Employment Opportunity Commission (the old Fair Employment Practices Commission reborn) administered a ban on job discrimination by race, religion, national origin, or sex.

Early in 1965, Martin Luther King, Jr., announced a drive to enroll the 3 million blacks in the South who had not registered to vote. In Selma, Alabama, civil rights protesters began a march to Montgomery, about 50 miles away, only to be violently dispersed by state troopers and a mounted posse. A federal judge agreed to allow the march, and President Johnson provided protection with National Guardsmen and army military police. By March 25, when the demonstrators reached Montgomery, some 35,000 people were with them, and King delivered a rousing address from the steps of the state capitol.

Several days before the march, President Johnson went before Congress with a moving plea that reached its climax when he slowly intoned the words of the movement's hymn: "And we shall overcome." The resulting Voting Rights Act of 1965 was passed to ensure all citizens the right to vote, and authorized the attorney-general to dispatch federal examiners to register voters. In states or counties where fewer than half the adults had voted in 1964, the act suspended literacy tests and other devices commonly used to defraud citizens of the vote. By the end of the year some 250,000 blacks were newly registered.

"BLACK POWER"   In the midst of this success, the civil rights movement began to fragment. On August 11, 1965, less than a week after
the passage of the Voting Rights Act, Watts, a predominantly black and
poor community in Los Angeles, exploded in a frenzy of riots and looting. When the uprising ended, there were thirty-four dead, almost
4,000 rioters in jail, and property damage exceeding $35 million. Lib-
eral commentators were stunned, as the riots occurred in the wake of
the greatest legislative victories for black Americans since Reconstruction.

But events did not stand still to await white liberal comprehension.
Chicago and Cleveland, along with forty other American cities, experienced racial riots in the summer of 1966. The following summer
Newark and Detroit burst into flames. Detroit provided the most graphic
example of urban violence, as tanks rolled through the streets and soldiers used machine guns to deal with snipers in the tenements. Firemen who tried to put out the flames in several of the urban riots were
showered by bricks and bottles thrown by the very people whose houses
were burning.

In retrospect, it was predictable that the civil rights movement would

*During the 1965 riots in Watts, Los Angeles, more than 800 armed guards
were stationed on area streets to quell looting and violence.*

focus on the plight of urban blacks. By the middle 1960s, about 70 percent of America's black population lived in metropolitan areas, most of them in central-city ghettos that had been bypassed by the postwar prosperity. And again it seemed clear, in retrospect, that the nonviolent tactics that had worked in the rural South would not work in the northern cities. In the North the problems were *de facto* segregation resulting from residential patterns, not *de jure* segregation amenable to changes in law. Moreover, northern white ethnic groups did not have the cultural heritage that southern whites shared with blacks. "It may be," wrote a contributor to *Esquire,* "that looting, rioting and burning . . . are really nothing more than radical forms of urban renewal, a response not only to the frustrations of the ghetto but the collapse of all ordinary modes of change, as if a body despairing of the indifference of doctors sought to rip a cancer out of itself." A special Commission on Civil Disorders noted that, unlike earlier race riots, the urban upheavals of the middle 1960s were initiated by blacks themselves; earlier riots had been started by whites, which had then provoked black counterattacks. Now blacks visited violence and destruction on themselves in an effort to destroy what they could not stomach and what civil rights legislation seemed unable to change.

By 1966 "black power" had become the new rallying cry. Radical members of the SNCC had become estranged from Martin Luther King's theories of militant nonviolence. As King became the center of attention from the white media, SNCC members began to refer to him cynically as "de Lawd." When Stokely Carmichael, a twenty-five-year-old graduate of Howard University, became head of the SNCC in 1966, he made the separatist philosophy of black power the official objective of the organization and ousted whites from the organization. "We reject an American dream defined by white people and must work to construct an American reality defined by Afro-Americans," said the author of a SNCC position paper. H. Rap Brown, who succeeded Carmichael as head of the SNCC in 1967, urged blacks to "get you some guns" and "kill the honkies." Meanwhile Carmichael had moved on to the Black Panther party, a self-professed group of urban revolutionaries founded in Oakland, California, in 1966. Headed by Huey P. Newton and Eldridge Cleaver, the Black Panthers terrified the public by wearing bandoleras and carrying rifles, but eventually fragmented in spasms of violence.

Malcolm X, influential spokesman for the Black Muslim movement.

The most articulate spokesman for black power was Malcolm X (formerly Malcolm Little, with the "X" denoting his lost African surname). Malcolm had risen from a ghetto childhood of narcotics and crime to become the chief disciple of Elijah Muhammad, the Black Muslim leader in the United States. "Yes, I'm an extremist," Malcolm acknowledged in 1964. "The black race in the United States is in extremely bad shape. You show me a black man who isn't an extremist and I'll show you one who needs psychiatric attention." By 1964 Malcolm had broken with Elijah Muhammad and founded his own organization committed to the establishment of alliances between African Americans and the nonwhite peoples of the world. But just after the publication of his *Autobiography* in 1965, Malcolm was gunned down in Harlem by assassins representing a rival faction of Black Muslims. With him went the most effective voice for urban black militancy since Marcus Garvey. What made the assassination of Malcolm X especially tragic was that he had just months before begun to abandon his strident antiwhite rhetoric and to preach a biracial message of social change.

Although widely publicized and highly visible, the black power movement never attracted more than a small minority of African Americans. Only about 15 percent of blacks labeled themselves separatists. The preponderant majority continued to identify with the philosophy of nonviolent integration promoted by Martin Luther King, Jr., and organizations such as the NAACP. King dismissed black separatism and the promotion of violent social change as a "nihilistic philosophy." He reminded his followers that "we can't win violently. We have neither the instruments nor the techniques at our disposal, and it would be totally absurd for us to believe we could do it."

Yet the black power philosophy, despite its hyperbole, violence, and the small number of its adherents, had two positive effects upon the civil rights movement. First, it helped African Americans take pride in their racial heritage. As Malcolm X often pointed out, prolonged slavery and institutionalized racism had eroded the self-esteem of many blacks in the United States. "The worst crime the white man has committed," he declared, "has been to teach us to hate ourselves." He and others helped blacks appreciate their African roots and their American accomplishments. In fact, it was Malcolm X who insisted that blacks call themselves African Americans as a symbol of pride in their roots and as a spur to learn more about their history as a people. As the popular singer James Brown urged, "Say it loud—I'm black and I'm proud."

Second, the black power phenomenon forced King and other mainstream black leaders and organizations to launch a new stage in the civil rights movement that would focus attention on the plight of poor inner-city blacks. Legal access to restaurants, schools, and other public accommodations, King pointed out, meant little to people mired in a culture of urban poverty. They needed jobs and decent housing as much as they needed legal rights. To this end, King began to emphasize the economic plight of the black urban underclass. The time had come for radical measures "to provide jobs and income for the poor." Yet as King and others sought to escalate the war on poverty at home, the war in Vietnam was commandeering more and more of America's resources and energies.

THE TRAGEDY OF VIETNAM

As racial violence erupted in America's cities, the war in Vietnam reached new levels of intensity and destruction. In November 1963, when John Kennedy was assassinated, there were 16,000 American military "advisers" in South Vietnam. Lyndon Johnson inherited an Ameri-

can commitment to prevent a Communist takeover there as well as a reluctance on the part of American presidents to assume primary responsibility for fighting the Viet Cong (Communist-led guerrillas in South
Vietnam) and their North Vietnamese allies. Beginning with Truman,
one president after another had done just enough to avoid being
charged with having "lost" Vietnam to communism. Johnson initially
sought to do the same, fearing that any other course of action would undermine his political influence and jeopardize his Great Society programs in Congress. But this path took him and the United States inex-
orably deeper into an expanding military commitment in Southeast
Asia.

During the presidential campaign of 1964, Johnson had opposed the
use of American combat troops and had privately described Vietnam as
"a raggedy-ass fourth-rate country" not worthy of American blood and
money. Nevertheless, by the end of 1965, there were 184,000 American
troops in Vietnam; in 1966 the troop level reached 385,000; and by
1969, the height of the American presence, 542,000. By the time the
last American troops left in March 1973, some 58,000 Americans had
died and another 300,000 had been wounded. The war had cost the
American taxpayers $150 billion, generated economic dislocations that
destroyed many Great Society programs, produced 570,000 draft offenders and 563,000 less-than-honorable discharges from the service,
toppled Johnson's administration, and divided the country as no event
in American history had since the Civil War.

ESCALATION   The official sanction for "escalation"—a Defense Department term coined in the Vietnam era—was the Tonkin Gulf Resolution, voted by Congress on August 7, 1964. Johnson told a national
television audience that two American destroyers, the U.S.S. *Maddox*
and the *C. Turner Joy,* had been attacked by North Vietnamese vessels
on August 2 and 4 in the Gulf of Tonkin off the coast of North Vietnam.
Although Johnson described the attack as unprovoked, in truth the destroyers had been monitoring South Vietnamese attacks against two
North Vietnamese islands—attacks planned by American advisers.
Even though there was no tangible evidence of the attack on the American ships, the Tonkin Gulf Resolution authorized the president to
"take all necessary measures to repel any armed attack against the
forces of the United States and to prevent further aggression." Only

U.S. troops faced a difficult and unfamiliar environment during the Vietnam War. Here two U.S. soldiers take cover in the jungle southwest of Da Nang.

Senator Wayne Morse of Oregon and Senator Ernest Gruening of Alaska voted against the resolution, which Johnson thereafter interpreted as equivalent to a congressional declaration of war.

Soon after his landslide victory over Goldwater in 1964, Johnson made the crucial decisions that shaped American policy in Vietnam for the next four years. On February 5, 1965, the Viet Cong killed 8 and wounded 126 Americans at Pleiku. Further attacks on Americans later that week led Johnson to order operation "Rolling Thunder," the first sustained bombings of North Vietnam, which were intended to stop the flow of soldiers and supplies into the south. Six months later, a task force conducted an extensive study of the bombing's effects on the supplies pouring down the Ho Chi Minh Trail from North Vietnam through Laos. It concluded that there was "no way" to stop the traffic.

In March 1965 the new American army commander in Vietnam, General William C. Westmoreland, received the first installment of combat troops. By the summer, American forces were engaged in "search-and-destroy" operations throughout South Vietnam. As combat operations increased, so did the mounting list of American casualties, announced each week on the nightly news along with the "body count" of alleged Viet Cong dead. "Westy's War," although fought with helicopter gunships, chemical defoliants, and napalm, became like the trench warfare of World War I—a war of attrition.

THE CONTEXT FOR POLICY   Johnson's decision to "Americanize" the Vietnam War, so ill-starred in retrospect, was consistent with the foreign policy principles pursued by all American presidents after World War II. The version of the containment theory articulated in the Truman Doctrine, endorsed by Eisenhower and Dulles throughout the 1950s, and reaffirmed by Kennedy, pledged United States opposition to the advance of communism anywhere in the world. "Why are we in

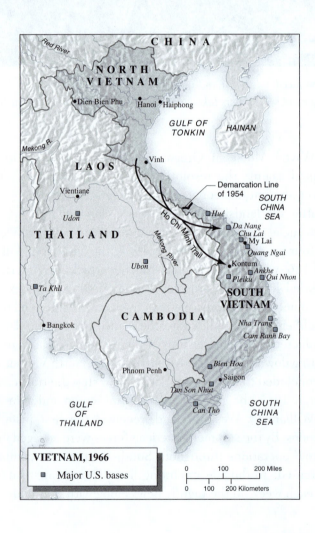

VIETNAM, 1966
■ Major U.S. bases

"How deep do you figure we'll get involved, sir!" Although American soldiers were first sent to Vietnam as noncombatant advisers, they soon found themselves involved in actual fighting.

Vietnam?" Johnson asked rhetorically at Johns Hopkins University in 1965. "We are there because we have a promise to keep. . . . To leave Vietnam to its fate would shake the confidence of all these people in the value of American commitment." Secretary of State Dean Rusk repeated this rationale before countless congressional committees, warning that Thailand, Burma, and the rest of Southeast Asia would fall like dominoes to communism if American forces withdrew. Military intervention in Vietnam was thus a logical culmination of the assumptions that were widely shared by the foreign policy establishment and the leaders of both political parties since the early days of the cold war.

It was clear to Johnson and his advisers from the start that American military involvement must not reach levels that would provoke the Chinese or Soviets into direct intervention. And this meant, in effect, that a complete military victory was never possible. "It was startling to me to find out," said the new secretary of defense, Clark Clifford, in 1968, "that we have no military plan to end the war." The goal of the United States was not to win the war in any traditional sense, but to prevent the North Vietnamese and Viet Cong from winning. This meant that America would have to maintain a military presence as long as the enemy retained the will to fight.

As it turned out, American support for the war eroded faster than the will of the North Vietnamese leaders to tolerate devastating casualties. Systematic opposition to the war on college campuses began in 1965 with "teach-ins" at the University of Michigan. The following year, Senator J. William Fulbright of Arkansas, chairman of the Senate Foreign Relations Committee, began congressional investigations into American policy. George Kennan, the founding father of the containment doctrine, told Fulbright's committee that the doctrine was appropriate for Europe, but not for Southeast Asia. And a respected general testified that Westmoreland's military strategy had no chance of achieving victory. By 1967 antiwar demonstrations in New York and at the Pentagon attracted massive support. Nightly television accounts of the fighting—Vietnam was the first war to receive extended television coverage, and hence has been dubbed "the living room war"—made the official optimism appear fatuous. By May 1967 even Secretary of Defense McNamara was wavering: "The picture of the world's greatest superpower killing or injuring 1,000 noncombatants a week, while trying to pound a tiny backward nation into submission on an issue whose merits are hotly disputed, is not a pretty one."

In a war of political will, North Vietnam had the advantage. Johnson and his advisers grievously underestimated the tenacity of the North Vietnamese commitment to unify Vietnam and expel the United States. Ho Chi Minh had warned the French in the 1940s that "You can kill ten of my men for every one I kill of yours, but even at those odds, you will lose and I will win." He predicted that the Vietnamese Communists would win a war of attrition, for they were willing to sacrifice all for their cause. While the United States fought a limited war for limited objectives, the Vietnamese Communists fought an all-out war for their very survival. Indeed, just as General Westmoreland was assuring Johnson and the American public that the American war effort in early 1968 was on the verge of gaining the upper hand, the Communists again displayed their cunning and tenacity.

THE TURNING POINT   On January 31, 1968, the first day of the Vietnamese New Year (Tet), the Viet Cong defied a holiday truce to launch assaults on American and South Vietnamese forces throughout South Vietnam. The old capital city of Hué fell to the Communists, and

During the 1968 Tet offensive, Viet Cong units temporarily infiltrated the American embassy in Saigon. Here, American military police lead a captured Viet Cong guerrilla away from the embassy.

Viet Cong units temporarily occupied the grounds of the American embassy in Saigon. General Westmoreland proclaimed the Tet offensive a major defeat for the Viet Cong, and most students of military strategy later agreed with him. But while Viet Cong casualties were enormous, the impact of the events on the American public was more telling. *Time* and *Newsweek* soon ran antiwar editorials urging American withdrawal. Walter Cronkite, the dean of American television journalists, confided to his viewers that he no longer believed the war was winnable. "If I've lost Walter," Johnson was reported to say, "then it's over. I've lost Mr. Average Citizen." Polls showed that Johnson's popularity had declined to 35 percent, lower than any president since Truman's darkest days. Civil rights leaders and social activists felt betrayed as they saw federal funds earmarked for the war on poverty siphoned off by the expanding war. In 1968 the United States was spending $322,000 on every Communist killed in Vietnam; the poverty programs at home received only $53 per person.

During 1968 Johnson grew increasingly embittered and isolated. It had become painfully evident that the Vietnam War was a never-ending stalemate. Secretary of Defense Clark Clifford reported to Johnson that a task force of prominent soldiers and civilians saw no prospect for a military victory. Robert Kennedy was reportedly considering a run for the presidency in order to challenge Johnson's Vietnam policy. And Senator Eugene McCarthy of Minnesota had already decided to oppose Johnson in the Democratic primaries. With antiwar students rallying to his candidacy, McCarthy polled 42 percent of the vote to Johnson's 48 percent in New Hampshire's March primary. It was a remarkable showing for a little-known senator. Each presidential primary now promised to become a referendum on Johnson's Vietnam policy. In Wisconsin, scene of the next primary, the president's political advisers forecast a humiliating defeat.

On March 31 Johnson appeared on national television to announce a limited halt to the bombing of North Vietnam and fresh initiatives for a negotiated cease-fire. Then he added a dramatic postscript: "I have concluded that I should not permit the Presidency to become involved in the partisan divisions that are developing in this political year. Accordingly, I shall not seek, and I will not accept the nomination of my party for another term as your President." Although American troops would

The Vietnam War sapped the spirit of Lyndon Johnson, who decided not to run for reelection in 1968.

remain in Vietnam for five more years and the casualties would continue, the quest for military victory had ended. Now the question was how the most powerful nation in the world could extricate itself from Vietnam with a minimum of damage to its prestige.

SIXTIES CRESCENDO

A TRAUMATIC YEAR   History moved at a fearful pace throughout the 1960s, but 1968 was a year of extreme turbulence even for that tumultuous decade. On April 4, only four days after Johnson's announced withdrawal, Martin Luther King, Jr., was gunned down while standing on the balcony of his motel in Memphis, Tennessee. The assassin, James Earl Ray, had expressed hostility toward blacks, but debate still continues over whether he was a pawn in an organized conspiracy. King's death set off an outpouring of grief among whites and blacks. It also ignited riots in over sixty American cities, with the most serious occurring in Chicago and Washington, D.C.

Two months later, on June 6, Robert Kennedy was shot in the head by a young Palestinian, Sirhan Sirhan, who resented Kennedy's strong support of Israel. Kennedy's death occurred at the end of the day on which he had convincingly defeated Eugene McCarthy in the California Democratic primary, thereby assuming leadership of the antiwar forces in the race for the nomination for president. Political reporter David Halberstam of the *New York Times* thought back to the assassinations of John Kennedy and Malcolm X, then the violent end of King, the most influential black leader of the twentieth century, and then Robert Kennedy, the heir to leadership of the Kennedy clan. "We could make a calendar of the decade," Halberstam wrote, "by marking where we were at the hours of those violent deaths."

CHICAGO AND MIAMI   In August 1968 Democratic delegates gathered inside the convention hall at Chicago to nominate Hubert Humphrey, while 24,000 police and National Guardsmen and a small army of television reporters stood watch over an eclectic gathering of protesters herded together miles away in a public park. Chicago mayor Richard Daley, who had given "shoot-to-kill" orders to police during the April riots protesting the King assassination, warned that he would not tolerate disruptions. Nonetheless, riots broke out in front of the Hilton Hotel and were televised nationwide. As police tear gas and billy clubs struck demonstrators, others chanted, "The whole world is watching."

The liberal tradition represented by the Democratic party was clearly in disarray, a fact that gave heart to the Republicans who gathered in Miami to nominate Richard Nixon. Only six years earlier, after he had lost the California gubernatorial race, Nixon had told reporters, "You won't have Nixon to kick around anymore, because, gentlemen, this is my last press conference." But by 1968 he had become a spokesman for all the values of "Middle America." Nixon and the Republicans offered a vision of stability and order that a majority of Americans—soon to be called "the silent majority"—wanted desperately.

George Wallace, the Democratic governor of Alabama who had made his reputation as a defender of segregation, ran as a third candidate in the campaign on the American Independent party ticket. Wallace moderated his position on the race issue, but appealed even more candidly than Nixon to the fears generated by protesters, the welfare system, and the growth of the federal government. Wallace's reactionary candidacy generated considerable appeal outside his native South, especially among white working-class communities, where resentment flourished against Johnson's Great Society liberalism. Although never a possible

Richard Nixon (right) *and Spiro Agnew* (left), *victors in the 1968 election.*

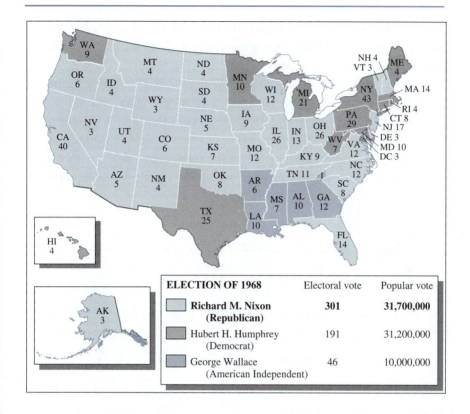

ELECTION OF 1968	Electoral vote	Popular vote
Richard M. Nixon (Republican)	**301**	**31,700,000**
Hubert H. Humphrey (Democrat)	191	31,200,000
George Wallace (American Independent)	46	10,000,000

winner, Wallace did pose the possibility of denying Humphrey or Nixon an electoral majority and thereby throwing the choice into the House of Representatives, which would have provided an appropriate climax to a chaotic year.

NIXON AGAIN It did not happen that way. Nixon enjoyed an enormous lead in the polls, which narrowed as the election approached. Wallace's campaign was hurt by his outspoken running mate, retired air force general Curtis LeMay, who favored expanding the war in Vietnam and using nuclear weapons. In October 1968 Humphrey announced that he would stop bombing North Vietnam "as an acceptable risk for peace."

Nixon and Governor Spiro Agnew of Maryland, his running mate, eked out a narrow victory by about 500,000 votes, a margin of about 1 percentage point. The electoral vote was more decisive, 301 to 191. Wallace received 10 million votes, 13.5 percent of the total, for the best showing by a third-party candidate since Robert La Follette in 1924. All but one of Wallace's 46 electoral votes were from the Deep South. Nixon swept all but four of the states west of the Mississippi. Humphrey's support came almost exclusively from the Northeast.

And so at the end of a turbulent year near the end of a traumatic decade, power passed peacefully to a president who was associated with the complacency of the 1950s. A nation that had seemed on the verge of consuming itself in spasms of violence looked to Richard Nixon to provide what he had promised in the campaign: "peace with honor" in Vietnam and a middle ground on which a majority of Americans, silent or otherwise, could come together.

MAKING CONNECTIONS

- The reform movements of the 1960s galvanized the baby-boom generation into a new youth movement, described in the next chapter, that continued through the early 1970s.

- The conflict in Vietnam, America's longest war, would come to a bitter end for American forces, but the divisions it spawned would echo through the rest of the century.

- The Immigration Act of 1965 would have profound and unexpected consequences on American society: see Chapter 37.

- The success of the civil rights movement in the 1960s led to similar movements for women, gays, Native Americans, and Hispanics, as we will see in the next chapter.

FURTHER READING

Herbert Parmet traces the influence of John F. Kennedy in two volumes, *Jack: The Struggle of John Fitzgerald Kennedy* (1980) and *JFK: The Presidency of John Fitzgerald Kennedy* (1983). Critical assessments can be found in Thomas C. Reeves's *A Question of Character: The Life of John F. Kennedy* (rev. ed., 1998) and Bruce Miroff's *Pragmatic Illusions: The Presidential Politics of John F. Kennedy* (1976). The best study of the Kennedy administration's domestic policies is Irving Bernstein's *Promises Kept: John F. Kennedy's New Frontier* (1991). For details on the assassination, see David W. Belin's *Final Disclosure: The Full Truth about the Assassination of President Kennedy* (1988). A more recent critique of the conspiracy theories is Gerald L. Posner's *Case Closed: Lee Harvey Oswald and the Assassination of John F. Kennedy* (1993).

The most comprehensive biography of LBJ is Robert Dallek's two-volume work, *Lone Star Rising: Lyndon Johnson and His Times, 1908–1960* (1991) and *Flawed Giant: Lyndon B. Johnson, 1960–1973* (1998). An intriguing analysis of the tense relationship between Johnson and Robert Kennedy is Jeff Shesol's *Mutual Contempt: Lyndon Johnson, Robert Kennedy, and the Feud That Defined a Decade* (1997).

Among the works that interpret liberal social policy during the 1960s, John Schwarz's *America's Hidden Success: A Reassessment of Twenty Years of Public Policy* (1983) offers a glowing endorsement of Democratic programs. For a contrasting perspective, see Charles Murray's *Losing Ground: American Social Policy, 1950–1980* (rev. ed., 1995).

On foreign policy, see *Kennedy's Quest for Victory: American Foreign Policy, 1961–1963* (1989), edited by Thomas G. Paterson. To learn more about Kennedy's problems in Cuba, see Mark White's *Missiles in Cuba: Kennedy, Khrushchev, Castro and the 1962 Crisis* (1997). For an understanding of the Alliance for Progress, see Jerome Levinson and Juan de Onis's *The Alliance That Lost Its Way* (1970). On the Peace Corps, see Elizabeth Hoffman's *All You Need Is Love: The Peace Corps and the Spirit of the 1960s* (1998).

American involvement in Vietnam has received voluminous treatment from all political perspectives. For an overview, see Larry Berman's *Planning a Tragedy: The Americanization of the War in Vietnam* (1982) and *Lyndon Johnson's War: The Road to Stalemate in Vietnam* (1989), as well as Stanley Karnow's *Vietnam: A History* (rev. ed., 1991). Tensions between the secretary of defense and the military leadership are detailed in H. R. McMaster's *Dereliction of Duty: Johnson, McNamara, the Joint Chiefs of Staff and the Lies That Led to Vietnam* (1997). Works that portray American policy in a favorable light include Norman Podhoretz's *Why We Were in Vietnam* (1982), Guenter Lewy's *America in Vietnam: Illusion, Myth and Reality* (1978), and Leslie Gelb and Richard Bett's *The Irony of Vietnam: The System Worked* (1979). An excellent analysis of policy making concerning the Vietnam War is David M. Barrett's *Uncertain Warriors: Lyndon Johnson and His Vietnam Advisors* (1994). Former secretary of defense Robert McNamara confesses his mistakes in *In Retrospect: The Tragedy and Lessons of Vietnam* (1995).

Many scholars have dealt with various aspects of the civil rights movement and race relations of the 1960s. See especially Carl Brauer's *John F. Kennedy and the Second Reconstruction* (1977), David Garrow's *Bearing the Cross: Martin Luther King, Jr., and the Southern Christian Leadership Conference* (1986), Adam Fairclough's *To Redeem the Soul of America: The Southern Christian Leadership Conference and Martin Luther King, Jr.* (1987), and David Lewis's *King: A Biography* (2nd. ed., 1978). For the legal turns the civil rights movement took during the 1960s, see J. Harvey Wilkinson's *From Brown to Bakke: The Supreme Court and School Integration, 1954–1978* (1978). William Chafe's *From Civilities to Civil Rights: Greensboro, North Carolina and the Black Struggle for Freedom* (1980) details the original sit-ins. An award-winning study of racial and economic inequality in a representative American city is Thomas J. Sugrue's *The Origins of the Urban Crisis: Race and Inequality in Postwar Detroit* (1996).

35 ⌒ REBELLION AND REACTION IN THE 1960S AND 1970S

CHAPTER ORGANIZER

This chapter focuses on:

- rebellion and struggles for rights in the 1970s.

- ending the war in Vietnam.

- Watergate and Nixon's resignation.

- the Ford and Carter administrations.

*A*s Richard Nixon entered the White House, he faced a nation whose social fabric was in tatters. Everywhere, it seemed, traditional institutions and notions of authority had come under attack. The turbulent events of 1968 revealed how deeply divided American society had become and how difficult a task Nixon faced in carrying out his pledge to restore social harmony. Yet the stability he promised proved to be elusive. His policies and his combative temperament served to heighten rather than reduce the tensions wracking the nation. Those tensions had been long in developing and reflected profound fissures in the postwar consensus promoted by

Eisenhower and inherited by Kennedy and Johnson. What had caused such a seismic breakdown in social harmony? Ironically, many of the same forces that had promoted the flush times of the Eisenhower years helped generate the social upheavals of the 1960s and 1970s.

THE ROOTS OF REBELLION

YOUTH REVOLT   By the 1960s the "baby-boomers" were maturing. Now young adults, they differed from their elders in that they had experienced neither economic depression nor a major war. They also had grown up amid the homogenizing effects of a flourishing consumer culture and television. Moreover, they viewed the cold war primarily as a battle of words and gestures without immediate consequences for them. Record numbers of these young people were attending American colleges and universities during the 1960s: college enrollment quadrupled between 1945 and 1970. At the same time, many universities had become gigantic institutions dependent on research contracts from huge corporations and the federal government. As these "multiversities" grew more bureaucratic and hierarchical, they unknowingly invited resistance from a generation of students wary of involvement in what Eisenhower had labeled the "military-industrial complex."

The success of the Greensboro sit-ins in 1960 not only precipitated a decade of civil rights activism, it also signaled an end to the supposed apathy that had enveloped college campuses and social life during the 1950s. Although most immediately concerned with the rights and status of African Americans, the sit-ins, marches, protests, principles, and sacrifices associated with the civil rights movement provided the model and inspiration for other groups that demanded justice, freedom, and equality as well.

During 1960–1961 a small but significant number of white students joined African Americans in the sit-in movement. They and many others were also inspired by President Kennedy's direct appeals to their youthful idealism. Thousands enrolled in the Peace Corps and VISTA (Volunteers in Service to America, the domestic version of the Peace Corps), and others continued to participate in civil rights demonstrations. But as it became clear that politics was mixed with principle in the president's position on civil rights, and later, as criticism of escalating American involvement in Vietnam mounted, more and more young people grew disillusioned with the government and other institutional bastions of the status quo.

Folksinger Bob Dylan translated the ferment of rebellion into these lyrics in 1963:

> Come mothers and fathers,
> Throughout the land
> And don't criticize
> What you can't understand
> Your sons and your daughters
> Are beyond your command
> There's a battle
> Outside and it's ragin'
> It'll soon shake your windows
> And rattle your walls
> For the times they are a-changin'.

There was a growing feeling among young people that something was fundamentally wrong, not just with the political system but with the entire structure of American life and values. By the mid-1960s, a full-fledged youth revolt had broken out on campuses across the country. Rebellious students began to flow into two distinct, yet frequently overlapping, movements: the New Left and the counterculture.

THE NEW LEFT   The explicitly political strain of the youth revolt had its official origin when Tom Hayden and Al Haber, two University of Michigan students, formed the Students for a Democratic Society (SDS) in 1960. As an ardent critic of American capitalism, Hayden was both charismatic and convincing. A Marxist radical who heard him speak in 1962 rushed home and told his wife, "I've just seen the next Lenin."

In 1962 Hayden and Haber convened a meeting of sixty activists at Port Huron, Michigan. After four days of intense discussion and a final all-night session, Hayden drafted what became known as the Port Huron Statement: "We are the people of this generation, bred in at least moderate comfort, housed in universities, looking uncomfortably to the world we inherit." Hayden's earnest manifesto focused on the absence of individual freedom in modern American life. The country, he insisted, was dominated by huge organizational structures—governments, corporations, unions, universities—all of which conspired to oppress and alienate the individual. Inspired by the example of black activism in the South, Hayden declared that students had the power to restore "participatory democracy" to American life by wresting "control of the educational process from the administrative bureaucracy" and then forging links with other dissident movements. He and others adopted the term "New Left" to distinguish their efforts at grassroots democracy from the Old Left of the 1930s that had espoused an orthodox Marxism and had embraced Stalinism.

In the fall of 1964 students at the University of California at Berkeley took Hayden's program to heart. Many of them had returned to the campus after spending the summer working with hundreds of other students in the SNCC voter registration project in Mississippi. Three volunteers had been killed, dozens shot, and nearly a thousand arrested. The Berkeley student activists returned to school with mixed emotions—exhilarated, frustrated, and embittered. When University Chancellor Clark Kerr announced that political demonstrations would no longer be allowed at the Telegraph Avenue street corner traditionally used for such activity, several hundred students staged a sit-in at the scene. Soon thereafter over 2,000 more joined in. After a tense thirty-two-hour standoff the administration relented. Student groups then formed the Free Speech Movement (FSM).

Led by Mario Savio, a philosophy major and compelling public speaker, the FSM initially protested on behalf of student rights. But it quickly escalated into a more general criticism of the modern university and what Savio called the "depersonalized, unresponsive bureaucracy" infecting American life. In 1964 Savio led hundreds of students into the administration building and organized a sit-in. In the early-morning hours 600 policemen, dispatched by the governor, arrested the protesters. Jerry Rubin, one of the young demonstrators, later observed: "The war against Amerika [*sic*] in the schools and the streets by white middle-class kids thus commenced."

The program and tactics of the FSM and SDS soon spread to colleges throughout the country. Issues large and small became the subject of student protest: unpopular faculty tenure decisions, mandatory ROTC programs, dress codes, curfews, dormitory regulations, appearances by

Johnson administration officials. Michigan students rallied against higher movie prices; at Fairleigh Dickinson in New Jersey students marched for no particular reason but as "an expression of general student discontent."

Escalating American involvement in Vietnam soon changed the student agenda. With the dramatic expansion of the draft after 1965, millions of young American men faced the grim prospect of being drafted to fight in an increasingly unpopular Asian war. In fact, however, the Vietnam conflict, like virtually every other American war, was primarily a poor man's fight. Deferments enabled college students to postpone military service until they received their degree or reached the age of twenty-four; in 1965–1966 they made up only 2 percent of all military inductees. In 1966, however, the Selective Service System modified the provisions so even undergraduates were eligible for the draft.

As the war dragged on and opposition mounted, students and others developed sophisticated ways to evade or resist the draft. Some 200,000 young men simply refused to obey their draft notices, and some 4,000 of those served prison sentences. Those on college campuses or in urban areas took advantage of newly established draft counseling centers that provided legal advice, and hundreds of young men instituted court challenges to the draft. One result was a much broader interpretation of the term "conscientious objector" so as to allow exemptions for those with moral and ethical objections to war rooted in secular rather than religious principles. Some 56,000 men qualified for conscientious-objector status during the Vietnam War, compared with 7,600 during the Korean conflict. Still others left the country altogether—several thousand fled to Canada or Sweden—to avoid military service. The most popular way to avoid the draft was to flunk the physical examination. Many gorged themselves so as to exceed the weight limit; others raised their blood pressure by drinking excessive amounts of coffee; some pretended to be drug addicts or alcoholics; a few feigned homosexuality. Whatever the preferred method, many students succeeded in avoiding military service. Of the 1,200 men in the Harvard class of 1970, only fifty-six served in the military, and just two of those went to Vietnam.

In the spring of 1967, 500,000 war protesters of all ages converged on Manhattan's Central Park, chanting "Hey, hey, LBJ, how many kids did you kill today?" Dozens ceremoniously burned their draft cards, and the so-called resistance phase of the antiwar movement was born. Thereafter a coalition of draft-resistance groups around the country sponsored draft-card-burning rallies and sit-ins that led to numerous arrests. Meanwhile, some SDS leaders were growing even more militant. Inspired by the rhetoric and revolutionary violence of black power spokesmen such as Stokely Carmichael, Rap Brown, and Huey Newton, Tom Hayden abandoned his earlier commitment to participatory democracy and passive civil disobedience. "If necessary," he now could "shoot to kill." Rap Brown told the white radicals to remember the heritage of John Brown: "Take up a gun and go shoot the enemy." As the SDS became more militant, it grew more centralized and authoritarian. Capitalist imperialism replaced university bureaucracy as the primary foe.

Throughout 1967 and 1968, the antiwar movement grew more volatile at the same time that inner-city ghettos were seething with tension and exploding into flames. "There was a sense everywhere, in 1968," the journalist Garry Wills wrote, "that things were giving way. That man had not only lost control of his history, but might never regain it." At the end of March, Lyndon Johnson announced that he would not run for reelection, and in early April Martin Luther King, Jr., was murdered.

During that eventful spring, campus unrest spread across the country. Over 200 major demonstrations took place. The turmoil reached a climax with the disruption of Columbia University. There Mark Rudd, leader of the SDS chapter, who had earlier thrown pies at the faces of Selective Service officials and disrupted speeches at the campus memorial service for King, led a small cadre of radicals in occupying the president's office and classroom buildings. They also kidnapped a dean—all in protest of the university's insensitive decision to displace neighboring black housing in order to build a new gymnasium. During the next week, more buildings were occupied, faculty and administrative offices were ransacked, and classes were canceled. University officials finally called in the New York City police. In the process of arresting the protesters, the police injured a number of innocent bystanders. Their excessive force aroused the anger of many unaligned students, and they staged a strike that shut down the university for the remainder of the semester.

The events at Columbia buoyed the militants. Tom Hayden an-

Mark Rudd, leader of the SDS at Columbia University, talking to the media during student protests over various university policies, April 1968.

nounced: "We are moving toward power." Similar clashes between students, administrators, and police occurred at Harvard, Cornell, and San Francisco State. In response to unrest at Berkeley, Governor Ronald Reagan dispatched a small army of police to evict 5,000 students and activists who had turned a vacant lot into a "people's park." In the melee one student was killed and another blinded.

At the 1968 Democratic convention in Chicago, the polarization of American society reached a tragic and bizarre climax. Inside the tightly guarded convention hall, Democrats nominated Lyndon Johnson's faithful vice-president, Hubert Humphrey. Meanwhile, outside on Chicago's streets, the whole spectrum of antiwar dissenters was gathered, from the earnest supporters of Eugene McCarthy, through the Resistance and SDS to the nihilistic Yippies, members of the new Youth International party. The Yippies were determined to provoke anarchy in the streets of Chicago. Abbie Hoffman, one of their leaders, explained that they were "revolutionary artists. Our conception of revolution is that it's fun." The Yippies distributed a leaflet at the convention calling for the immediate legalization of marijuana and all psychedelic drugs, the abolition of money, student-run schools, and free sex.

The violence at the 1968 Democratic National Convention in Chicago seared the nation.

The outlandish behavior of the Yippies and the other demonstrators did not justify the unrestrained response of Mayor Richard M. Daley and his army of 12,000 police. As a horrified television audience watched, many of the police went berserk, clubbing and gassing demonstrators as well as bystanders caught up in the chaotic scene. The spectacle lasted three days and seriously damaged Humphrey's candidacy. The Chicago riots also generated a wave of anger among many middle-class Americans, anger that Richard Nixon and the Republicans shrewdly exploited at their convention in Miami. At the same time, the riots helped to fragment the antiwar movement. Those groups committed to nonviolent protest, while castigating the reactionary policies of Mayor Daley and the police, also felt betrayed by the actions of the Yippies and other anarchistic militants.

In 1968 SDS began to break up into rival factions, the most extreme of which was the Weathermen, a term derived from one of Bob Dylan's lyrics: "You don't need a weatherman to know which way the wind blows." These hardened young activists embarked on a campaign of violence and disruption, firebombing university buildings and killing innocent people—as well as several of themselves. Government forces responded in kind, arresting most of the Weathermen and sending the rest underground. By 1971 the New Left was dead as a political movement. In large measure it had committed suicide by abandoning the democratic and pacifist principles that had originally inspired participants and given the movement moral legitimacy. The larger antiwar movement also began to fade. There would be a wave of student protests against the Nixon administration in 1970, but thereafter, campus unrest virtually disappeared.

If the social mood was changing during the Nixon years, still a large segment of the public continued the quest for personal fulfillment and social justice. The burgeoning environmental and consumer movements attested to the continuity of sixties idealism. A *New York Times* survey of college campuses in 1969 revealed that many students were transferring their attention from the antiwar movement to the environment. This ecological conscience would blossom in the 1970s into one of the most compelling items on the nation's social agenda.

THE COUNTERCULTURE The numbing events of 1968 led other disaffected activists away from radical politics altogether and toward another manifestation of the sixties youth revolt: the "counterculture." Long hair, jeans, tie-dyed shirts, sandals, mind-altering drugs, rock music, and cooperative living arrangements were more important than revolutionary ideology to the "hippies," the direct descendants of the Beats of the 1950s. These advocates of the counterculture were, like their New Left peers, primarily affluent, well-educated young whites alienated by the Vietnam War, racism, political and parental demands, runaway technology, and a crass corporate mentality that equated the good life with material goods. In their view, a bland materialism and smug complacency had settled over urban and suburban life. But they were uninterested in or disillusioned with organized political action. Instead they eagerly embraced the tantalizing credo outlined by the zany Harvard professor Timothy Leary: "Tune in, turn on, drop out."

For some the counterculture entailed the study and practice of Oriental mysticism. For many it meant the daily use of hallucinogenic drugs. Collective living in urban enclaves such as San Francisco's Haight-Ashbury district, New York's East Village, or Atlanta's Fourteenth Street was the rage for a time among hippies, until conditions grew so crowded, violent, and depressing that residents migrated elsewhere. Rural communes also attracted many of the bourgeois rebels. During the 1960s and early 1970s, thousands of young and inexperi-

This dinner scene with the members of Hog Farm epitomizes the camaraderie of collective living. But communes were rarely able to last as money and food quickly ran out.

enced romantics flocked to the countryside, eager to be liberated from parental and institutional restraints, to live in harmony with nature, and to coexist in an atmosphere of love and openness.

But only a handful of these utopian homesteads survived more than a few months. Rooted in the pleasure principle, rustic hippies often produced more babies than bread. One such "flower child" confessed that "we are so stupid, so unable to cope with anything practical. Push forward, smoke dope. But maintain? Never. We don't know how." Initially intent upon rejecting conventional society, many found themselves utterly dependent on it, and they were soon panhandling on street corners or lined up at government offices, collecting welfare, unemployment compensation, and food stamps to help them survive the rigors of natural living. A participant at Paper Farm in northern California said of its residents: "They had no commitment to the land—a big problem. All would take food from the land, but few would tend it. . . . We were entirely open. We did not say no. We felt this would make for a more dynamic group. But we got a lot of sick people."

Huge outdoor rock music concerts were also a popular source of community for hippies. The largest of these was the Woodstock Music Festival. In August 1969 some 500,000 young people converged on a 600-acre farm near the tiny rural town of Bethel, New York. The musi-

The Woodstock Festival drew nearly a half million people to a farm in Bethel, New York. The concert was billed as three days of "peace, music, . . . and love."

cians—including Joan Baez; Jimi Hendrix; Crosby, Stills, Nash, and Young; Santana; and Richie Havens—were a powerful attraction. So too was the easy availability of drugs. For three days the assembled flower children reveled in good music, cheap marijuana, and free love. "Everyone swam nude in the lake," a journalist reported. He added that the country had never "seen a society so free of repression."

But the Woodstock karma was short-lived. When other promoters tried to repeat the scene four months later, this time at Altamont, California, the counterculture encountered the criminal culture. The Rolling Stones hired Hell's Angels motorcycle gang members to provide the "security" for their show. In the midst of Mick Jagger's performance of "Sympathy for the Devil," the drunken white motorcyclists beat to death a black man wielding a knife in front of the stage. Three other spectators were accidentally killed that night; much of the vitality and innocence of the counterculture died with them.

After 1969 the hippie phenomenon began to wane. "It was good for a time," drug guru Timothy Leary lamented; "then we went so far that we lost it." The counterculture had become counterproductive and had developed both faddish and fashionable overtones. Entrepreneurs were quick to see profits in protest. Retailers developed a banner business in faded blue jeans, surplus army jackets, beads, incense, and sandals.

Health-food stores and "head" shops appeared in shopping malls along-side Nieman Marcus and Sears. Rock music groups, for all their lyrical protests against the capitalist "system," made millions from it. As one wit recognized, the "difference between a rock king and a robber baron [was] about six inches of hair." Many of the flower children themselves grew tired of their riches-to-rags existence and returned to school to become lawyers, doctors, politicians, or accountants. The search on the part of alienated youth for a better society and a good life was strewn with both comic and tragic aspects, and it reflected the deep social ills that had been allowed to fester throughout the post–World War II period.

FEMINISM   The logic of liberation spawned during the sixties helped accelerate a powerful women's rights crusade that aggressively challenged the cult of domesticity. Like the New Left, the new feminism drew much of its inspiration and tactics from the civil rights movement.

The mainstream of the women's movement was led by Betty Friedan. Her immensely influential book, *The Feminine Mystique* (1963), launched the new phase of female protest on a national level. Friedan, a Smith College graduate, had married in 1947. During the 1950s, she raised three children in a New York suburb. Politically active but socially domestic, she mothered her children, pampered her husband, "read *Vogue* under the hair dryer," and occasionally did some freelance

Betty Friedan, author of The Feminine Mystique.

writing. In 1957 she conducted a poll of her fellow Smith alumnae and discovered that, despite all the rhetoric about the happy suburban housewife during the fifties, many—too many—were in fact miserable. This revelation led to more research, which culminated in the publication of *The Feminine Mystique*.

Women, Friedan wrote, had actually lost ground during the years after World War II, when many left wartime assembly lines and settled down in suburbia. A propaganda campaign engineered by advertisers and women's magazines encouraged them to do so by creating the "feminine mystique" of blissful domesticity. This notion that women were "gaily content in a world of bedroom, kitchen, sex, babies, and home" thus served to imprison women. In Friedan's view, the American middle-class home had become "a comfortable concentration camp" where women suffocated in an atmosphere of mindless materialism, daytime television, and neighborhood gossip.

Friedan's book, an immediate best-seller, raised the consciousness of many women who had long suffered from a feeling of being trapped in a rut with no way out. Moreover, Friedan came to realize that there were far more women working outside the home than the pervasive "feminine mystique" suggested. Many of these working women were frustrated by the demands of holding "two full-time jobs instead of just one—underpaid clerical worker and unpaid housekeeper."

In 1967 Syracuse University student Kathy Switzer challenged the Boston Marathon's men-only tradition. Officials tried to pull her from the course, but with the aid of fellow runners she completed the race. Women became official entrants in 1971.

"Well, girls, at least the only way we can go is up."
*Despite support by Congress, the Equal Rights
Amendment failed to muster enough popular support to gain ratification. Equality of rights, regardless
of gender, remained out of reach.*

In 1966 Friedan and a small group of other spirited activists founded
the National Organization for Women (NOW). Soon regarded as the
NAACP of the women's movement, NOW grew rapidly. It initially
sought to end discrimination in the workplace on the basis of sex, and
went on to spearhead efforts to legalize abortion, and to obtain federal
and state support for child-care centers.

In the early 1970s, Congress and the Supreme Court advanced the
cause of sexual equality. Under Title IX of the Educational Amendments Act of 1972, colleges were required to institute "affirmative action" programs to ensure equal opportunity for women. In the same
year Congress overwhelmingly approved the Equal Rights Amendment,

which had been bottled up in a House committee for almost half a century. In 1973 the Supreme Court, in *Roe* v. *Wade,* struck down state laws forbidding abortions during the first three months of pregnancy. Meanwhile the educational bastions of male segregation, including Yale and Princeton, led a new movement for coeducation that swept the country. "If the 1960s belonged to blacks," said one feminist, "the next ten years are ours."

By the end of the 1970s, however, continuing divisions between moderate and radical feminists, as well as the movement's failure to broaden its appeal much beyond the confines of the middle class, caused reform efforts to stagnate. The Equal Rights Amendment, which had once seemed a straightforward assertion of equal opportunity ("Equality of rights under the law shall not be denied or abridged by the United States or by any State on account of sex") and assured of ratification, was stymied in several state legislatures. Despite a congressional extension of the normal time allowed for ratification, by 1982 it died, several states short of passage. And the very success of NOW's efforts to liberalize local and state abortion laws generated a powerful backlash, especially among Catholics and fundamentalist Protestants, who mounted a potent "right-to-life" crusade.

But the success of the women's movement endured long after the militant rhetoric had evaporated. Their growing presence in the labor force assured women of a greater share of economic and political influence. By 1976, over half the married women in America and nine of ten women college graduates were employed outside the home, a development that one economist called "the single most outstanding phenomenon of this century." Yet, many career women did not regard themselves as "feminists"; they took jobs because they and their families needed the money to survive or to achieve higher levels of material comfort. Whatever their motives, traditional sex roles and childbearing practices were being changed to accommodate the two-career family.

HISPANIC RIGHTS   The activism that animated the student revolt, the civil rights movement, and the crusade for women's rights soon spread to various ethnic minority groups. The labor shortages during World War II led defense industries to offer Hispanic Americans their first significant access to industrial and skilled-labor jobs in the cities.

And as was the case with African Americans, service in the military during the war years helped to heighten an American identity among Hispanic Americans and to excite their desire for equal rights and opportunities.

But equality was elusive. After World War II, Hispanic Americans still faced widespread discrimination in hiring, housing, and education. Poverty was widespread. In 1960, for example, the median income of a Mexican-American family was only 62 percent of the median income of a family in the general population. Hispanic-American activists during the 1950s and 1960s mirrored the efforts of black civil rights leaders such as Martin Luther King, Jr. They too denounced segregation, promoted efforts to improve the quality of public education, and struggled to increase Hispanic-American political influence and economic opportunities. Like their black peers, Hispanic college students during the 1960s seized upon ways to heighten their sense of ethnic pride and distinctiveness and to bolster their solidarity.

One of the most popular initiatives was the use of the term *Chicano* as an inclusive label for all Mexican immigrants, Spanish Americans in New Mexico, as well as old *Californios* (descendants of the inhabitants of California before it was seized by the United States, most of whom were Indians or of mixed ancestry), and *Tejanos* (descendants of the inhabitants of Texas before it became independent). The word *Chicano* was originally a Mexican slang term for a clumsy person. Over the years, Anglo Americans had fastened upon the term as a pejorative reference. Now *Chicano* took on a positive connotation. In southern California, students formed Young Chicanos for Community Action, a social service group designed to promote greater self-reliance and local involvement within Chicano neighborhoods. Wearing brown berets, the members protested the disproportionate number of Hispanics being killed in the Vietnam War and demanded improvements in their neighborhood schools. Others promoted Hispanic Studies as a new academic discipline at colleges. In 1968 nearly 10,000 Chicano students walked out of five Los Angeles high schools as a protest against inadequate facilities, racist teachers, and a high dropout rate. Their actions prompted students in other states to stage similar demonstrations.

Unlike their black counterparts, however, Chicano leaders faced an awkward dilemma: what should they do about the continuing stream of

César Chavez (center) *with organizers of the grape boycott.*

illegal Mexican aliens flowing across the border? Many Mexican Americans argued that their own hopes for economic advancement and social equality were put at risk by the influx of Mexican laborers willing to accept low-paying jobs. Mexican-American leaders thus helped to end the *bracero* program (which trucked in *braceros,* Mexican contract day laborers, at harvest time) in 1964 and to form the United Farm Workers (UFW) in 1962 (originally the National Farm Workers Association) to represent Mexican-American migrant workers.

The founder of the UFW was César Chavez. Born in Yuma, Arizona, in 1927 to Mexican immigrant parents, Chavez moved with his parents and four siblings to California in 1939. There they joined thousands of other migrant farm workers traversing the state, moving from job to job, living in tents, cars, or ramshackle cabins. In 1944, at age seventeen, Chavez joined the navy and served for two years in the Pacific. After the war he married and found work, first as a sharecropper raising strawberries and then as a migrant laborer in apricot orchards. In 1952 Chavez joined the Community Service Organization (CSO), a social service group that sought to educate and organize the migrant poor so that they could become more self-reliant. He founded new CSO chapters and was named general director in 1958.

Chavez left the organization in 1962 when it refused to back his proposal to establish a union for farm workers. Other CSO leaders believed that it was impossible to organize migrant workers into an effective union. They thought they were too mobile, too poor, too illiterate, too ethnically diverse, and too easily replaced by *braceros*. Moreover, farm workers did not enjoy protected status under the National Labor Relations Act of 1935 (the Wagner Act). Unlike industrial laborers, they were not guaranteed the right to organize or to receive a minimum wage. Nor did federal regulations govern the safety of their workplaces.

Despite such obstacles, Chavez resolved to organize the migrant farm workers. His fledgling Farm Workers Association gained national attention in 1965 when it joined a strike by Filipino farm workers against the corporate grape farmers in California's San Joaquin Valley. Chavez's personal charisma and Catholic piety, his insistence on nonviolent tactics and his reliance upon college student volunteers, his skillful alliance with organized labor and religious groups, all combined to attract media interest and popular support. Soon the UFW began organizing migrant workers in the lettuce fields of the Salinas Valley.

Still, the grape strike itself brought no tangible gains. So Chavez organized a nationwide consumer boycott of grapes. Contrary to Chavez's own principles and orders, some of the striking workers used violence to express their frustration at the recalcitrant growers. In an effort to break the impasse and defuse the tension among his followers, Chavez began a personal fast in 1968. He explained that "the truest act of courage, the strongest act of manliness, is to sacrifice ourselves for others in a totally nonviolent struggle for justice." After fasting for three weeks, he had lost thirty-five pounds, and doctors began to fear for his life. A week later he ended his fast by taking communion and breaking bread with Senator Robert F. Kennedy.

Two years later, in 1970, the grape strike and consumer boycott finally succeeded in bringing twenty-six grape growers to the bargaining table. They signed formal contracts recognizing the UFW, and soon migrant workers throughout the West were benefiting from Chavez's strenuous efforts on their behalf. Wages increased and working conditions improved. In 1975 the California state legislature passed a bill that required growers to bargain collectively with the elected representatives of the farm workers. As Robert Kennedy had observed, César Chavez was "one of the heroic figures of our time."

But the chief strength of the Hispanic movement lay less in the duplication of civil rights strategies than in the rapid growth of the Hispanic population. In 1960 Hispanics had numbered slightly more than 3 million; by 1970 they had increased to 9 million, and by 1990 they numbered 22.4 million, making them the largest minority in America after African Americans. The most numerous among them were Mexican Americans, who were concentrated in California and the Southwest. Next came the Puerto Rican population, most of whom lived in New York City and the Connecticut Valley. Third largest were the Cubans, many of them refugees from Castro's regime, who were concentrated in southern Florida.

By 1980, aspiring presidential candidates were openly courting the Hispanic vote, promising support for urban renewal projects in New York and amnesty programs for illegal immigrants in Texas, and delivering rousing anti-Castro speeches in Miami. The voting power of Hispanics and their concentration in states with key electoral votes helped give the Hispanic point of view political clout. During the 1960s, four Mexican Americans—Senator Joseph Montoya of New Mexico and Representatives Elizio ("Kika") de la Garza of Texas, Henry B. Gonzalez of Texas, and Edward R. Roybal of California—were elected to Congress. In 1974 two Chicanos were elected governor—Jerry Apodaca in New Mexico and Raul Castro in Arizona. In 1981 Henry Cisneros of San Antonio became the first Mexican-American mayor of a large city. He later served as the secretary of housing and urban development and then as secretary of energy in the Clinton administration.

NATIVE AMERICANS   American Indians—many of whom now called themselves Native Americans—also emerged as a new political force in the late 1960s. Two conditions combined to make Indian rights a priority: first, white Americans felt a deep and persistent sense of guilt for the destructive policies of their ancestors toward a people who had, after all, been here first; second, the plight of the Native American minority was more desperate than that of any other group in the country. Indian unemployment was ten times the national rate, life expectancy was twenty years lower than the national average, and the suicide rate was a whopping one hundred times higher than the rate for whites.

Although President Lyndon Johnson recognized the poverty of the Native Americans and attempted to target federal antipoverty program funds into the reservations, militants within the Indian community became impatient with the slow pace of change and organized protests and demonstrations against local, state, and federal agencies. At first the Indian activists copied the tactics of civil rights and black power activists. In 1968 two Chippewas living in Minneapolis, George Mitchell and Dennis Banks, founded the American Indian Movement (AIM) to promote "red power." The leaders of AIM occupied Alcatraz Island in San Francisco Bay in 1969, claiming the site "by right of discovery." And in 1972, a sit-in at the Department of the Interior's Bureau of Indian Affairs (BIA) in Washington attracted national attention to their cause. The BIA, then and since, has been widely viewed as the worst-managed federal agency. Instead of finding creative ways to promote tribal auton-

Foot soldiers of AIM marched on Wounded Knee, South Dakota, to bring attention to dependence on welfare, poor living conditions, and rampant alcoholism that plagued Indians on reservations nationwide.

omy and economic self-sufficiency, the BIA was a classic example of government inefficiency and paternalism gone awry.

In 1973 AIM led two hundred Sioux in occupying the tiny village of Wounded Knee, South Dakota, the site where the U.S. 7th Cavalry had massacred a Sioux village in 1890. Provoked by the light sentences given a group of local whites who had killed a Sioux in 1972, the organizers also sought to draw attention to the plight of the Indians living on the reservation there. Half of the families were dependent on government welfare checks, alcoholism was rampant, and over 80 percent of the children had dropped out of school. After the Indian militants took eleven hostages, federal marshals and FBI agents surrounded the encampment. For ten weeks, the two sides engaged in a tense standoff. When AIM leaders tried to bring in food and supplies, a shoot-out resulted, and one Indian was killed and another wounded. Soon thereafter, the tense confrontation ended with a government promise to reexamine Indian treaty rights.

Thereafter, Indian protesters discovered a more effective tactic than direct action and sit-ins. They went into federal courts armed with copies of old treaties and demanded that these become the basis for restitution. In Alaska, Maine, South Carolina, and Massachusetts they won significant settlements that provided legal recognition of their tribal rights and financial compensation at levels that upgraded the standard of living on several reservations.

GAY RIGHTS   The liberationist impulses of the sixties also encouraged homosexuals to organize and assert their own right to equal treatment and basic dignity. On June 17, 1969, New York City police raided the Stonewall Inn, a male gay bar in the heart of Greenwich Village. Efforts to close down homosexual gathering places were then commonplace around the country. But this time the patrons fought back and the struggle spilled into the streets. Hundreds of other gays and their supporters joined the fracas against the police. Rioting lasted throughout the weekend. When it ended, gays had forged a new sense of solidarity and a new organization called the Gay Liberation Front (GLF). "Gay is good for all of us," proclaimed one member of the GLF. "The artificial categories 'heterosexual' and 'homosexual' have been laid on us by a sexist society. As gays we demand an end to the gender programming which starts when we are born."

As news of the Stonewall riots spread across the country, the gay rights movement assumed national proportions. One of its main tactics was to encourage people to "come out" and make public their homosexuality. This was by no means an easy decision, for professing gays faced social ostracism, physical assaults, exclusion from the military and civil service, and discrimination in the workplace. Yet despite the risks, thousands of homosexuals did "come out." By 1973 almost 800 gay and lesbian organizations had been formed across the country, and every major city had a visible gay community and cultural life.

But as was the case with the civil rights crusade and the women's movement, the campaign for gay rights soon suffered from internal divisions and a conservative backlash. Gay activists engaged in fractious disputes over tactics and objectives, and conservative moralists and Christian fundamentalists launched a nationwide counterattack against the gay community. In Miami, St. Paul, and Wichita, conservatives managed to repeal new laws banning discrimination against homosexuals. By the end of the 1970s, the gay movement had lost its initial momentum and was struggling to salvage many of its hard-won gains.

NIXON AND VIETNAM

The numerous liberation movements of the 1960s fundamentally changed the tone and texture of American social life. But by the early 1970s, the pendulum of national mood was swinging back. The election of Richard Nixon and Spiro Agnew in 1968 and the rise of George Wallace as a serious political force reflected the emergence of the "silent majority"—those predominantly white working-class and middle-class citizens who were determined to regain control of a society they felt had become awash in permissiveness, anarchy, and tyranny by the minority. Large as the gap was between the silent majority and the forces of dissent, both sides agreed that the Vietnam War remained the dominant event of the time. Until the war was ended and all American troops had returned home, the nation would find it difficult to achieve the equilibrium that the new president had promised.

GRADUAL WITHDRAWAL   During the campaign of 1968, Nixon had claimed to have a secret plan that would bring "peace with honor" in

Vietnam. Peace, however, was long in coming and not very honorable. Although Henry Kissinger, the professor of international relations at Harvard who became Nixon's special assistant for national security affairs, insisted that the war in Indochina was a mere "sideshow" of considerably less significance than American interests in Europe and the Middle East, American withdrawal from Vietnam was agonizingly slow nonetheless. By the time a settlement was finally reached in 1973, another 20,000 Americans had died, the morale of the American army had been shattered, millions of additional Asians were killed or wounded, and fighting continued in Southeast Asia. In the end, Nixon's policy gained nothing he could not have accomplished in 1969.

The new Vietnam policy of the Nixon administration moved along three separate fronts. First, American negotiators in Paris demanded the withdrawal of Communist forces from South Vietnam and the preservation of the American-supported regime of President Nguyen Van Thieu. The North Vietnamese and Viet Cong negotiators insisted on the retention of a military presence in the south and the reunification of the Vietnamese people under a government dominated by the Communists. There was no common ground on which to come together. It required months before the parties could even agree on the shape of the table around which they would meet.

Second, Nixon tried to quell domestic unrest over the war. He reduced the number of American troops in Vietnam, justifying the reduction as the natural result of "Vietnamization"—the equipping and training of the South Vietnamese to assume the burden of ground combat in place of Americans. From a peak of 540,000 in 1969, American combat troops were withdrawn at a gradual and steady pace that matched almost precisely the pace of the American buildup from 1965 to 1969. By 1973 only 50,000 American troops remained in Vietnam. In 1969 Nixon also established a draft lottery system that eliminated many inequities and clarified the likelihood of being drafted—only those nineteen-year-olds with low lottery numbers would have to go—and in 1973 he did away with the draft altogether by creating an all-volunteer military. Nixon was more successful in achieving the goal of reducing antiwar activity than at forcing concessions from the North Vietnamese in Paris.

Third, while reducing the number of American combat troops, Nixon and Kissinger expanded the air war in an effort to persuade the enemy

Even as the Nixon administration began a phased withdrawal of American troops from Vietnam, the war took a heavy toll on Vietnamese and Americans alike.

to come to terms. In March 1969, American planes began a fourteen-month-long bombing campaign aimed at Communist sanctuaries in Cambodia. Congress did not learn of these secret raids until 1970, although the total tonnage of bombs dropped was four times that dropped on Japan during World War II. Then on April 30, 1970, Nixon announced what he called an "incursion" into "neutral" Cambodia by United States troops to "clean out" North Vietnamese staging areas. The head of Cambodia's government for two decades, Prince Norodom Sihanouk, had previously objected to such American raids into his country, but Sihanouk had been replaced in a coup by General Lon Nol earlier in the spring, clearing the way for the American invasion.

DIVISIONS AT HOME   America's slow withdrawal from Vietnam had a devastating effect on the morale and reputation of the military. "No one wants to be the last grunt to die in this lousy war," said one soldier. Between 1969 and 1971, there were 730 reported "fragging" incidents, efforts by American troops to kill or injure their own officers, usually with fragmentation grenades. Drug abuse became a major problem. In 1971 four times as many American troops were hospitalized for drug abuse as for combat-related wounds.

Back on the home front, the public learned of previously suppressed events in Vietnam that caused even the staunchest supporters of the war to wince. Late in 1969 the story of the My Lai massacre broke in the press and plunged the country into two years of exposure to the gruesome tale of Lieutenant William Calley, who ordered the murder of over 200 civilians in My Lai village in 1968. Twenty-five army officers were charged with complicity in the massacre and subsequent cover-up, but only Calley was convicted; Nixon soon granted him parole.

Perhaps the loudest public outcry against Nixon's Indochina policy occurred in the wake of the Cambodian "incursion." Campuses across the country exploded in what the president of Columbia University called "the most disastrous month of May in the history of American higher education." Student protests led to the closing of hundreds of colleges and universities. At Kent State University, the Ohio National Guard was called in to quell rioting in which the campus Reserve Officer Training Corps (ROTC) building was burned down by antiwar protesters. The poorly trained Guardsmen panicked and opened fire on the demonstrators, killing four student bystanders. Eleven days later, on May 15, Mississippi highway patrolmen riddled a dormitory at Jackson State College with bullets, killing two black students. Although an offi-

National Guardsmen shot and killed four student bystanders during antiwar demonstrations on the campus of Kent State University.

"Son . . . !" "Dad . . . !" *The Vietnam War caused vehement divisions between "hawks" and "doves," old and young, even parents and children.*

cial investigation of the Kent State episode condemned the "casual and indiscriminate shooting," polls indicated that the American public supported the National Guard; students had "got what they were asking for." In New York City, antiwar demonstrators who gathered to protest the deaths at Kent State and the invasion of Cambodia were attacked by "hard-hat" construction workers, who forced the student protesters to disperse and then marched on City Hall to raise the flag that had been lowered to half staff in mourning for the Kent State victims.

The following year, in June 1971, the *New York Times* began publishing excerpts from *The History of the U.S. Decision Making Process in Vietnam,* a secret Defense Department study commissioned by Robert McNamara before his resignation as secretary of defense in 1968. The so-called Pentagon Papers, leaked to the press by a former Defense Department official, Daniel Ellsberg, confirmed what many critics of the war had long suspected: Congress and the public had not received the full story on the Gulf of Tonkin incident of 1964, and contingency plans for American entry into the war were being drawn up while Johnson was promising the American people that combat troops would never be sent to Vietnam. Moreover, there was no plan for bringing the war to an end so long as the North Vietnamese persisted. Although the Pentagon Papers dealt with events only up to 1965, the Nixon administration attempted to block their publication, arguing that they endangered national security and that their publication would prolong the war. By a vote of 6 to 3, the Supreme Court ruled against the government. Newspapers throughout the country began publication the next day.

WAR WITHOUT END   The mounting social divisions at home and the approach of the 1972 presidential election combined to produce a shift in the American negotiating position in Paris. In the summer of 1972 Henry Kissinger again began meeting privately with Le Duc Tho, the North Vietnamese negotiator, and he now dropped his insistence on the removal of all North Vietnamese troops from the south before the withdrawal of American troops. On October 26, only a week before the American presidential election, Kissinger announced: "Peace is at hand." But this was a cynical ploy to win votes. Several days earlier the Thieu regime in South Vietnam had rejected the Kissinger plan for a cease-fire, fearful that the presence of North Vietnamese troops in the south virtually guaranteed an eventual Communist victory. The talks broke off on December 16, and two days later the president ordered the saturation bombing of Hanoi and Haiphong, the two largest cities in North Vietnam. These so-called Christmas bombings, and the simultaneous mining of North Vietnamese harbors, aroused worldwide protest.

But the bombings also made the North Vietnamese more flexible at the negotiating table. The "Christmas bombings" stopped on December 29, and the resumption of talks in Paris soon followed. On January 27, 1973, the United States, North and South Vietnam, and the Viet Cong signed an "agreement on ending the war and restoring peace in Vietnam." While Nixon and Kissinger both claimed that the bombing had brought North Vietnam to its senses, in truth the North Vietnamese never altered their basic stance; they kept troops in the south and remained committed to the reunification of Vietnam under one government. What had changed since the previous fall was the willingness of the South Vietnamese to accept these terms, albeit reluctantly, on the basis of Nixon's promise that the United States would respond "with full force" to any violation of the agreement.

On March 29, 1973, the last American combat troops left Vietnam. And on that same day, the last of several hundred American prisoners of war, most of them downed pilots, were released from Hanoi. Within a period of months, however, the cease-fire in Vietnam ended, the war between north and south resumed, and the military superiority of the Communist forces soon became evident. In Cambodia (renamed Kampuchea after it fell to the Communists) and Laos, where fighting had been more sporadic, Communist victory also seemed inevitable. In 1975 the North Vietnamese launched a full-scale armored invasion against the south, and South Vietnamese president Thieu appealed to

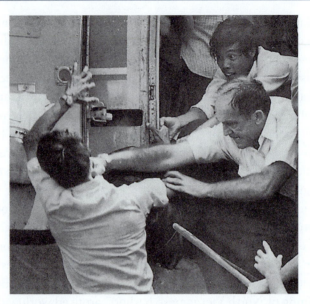

The scramble to board evacuation helicopters on the roof of the American Embassy, Saigon, April 30, 1975.

Washington for assistance. Congress refused. The much-mentioned "peace with honor" had proved to be, in the words of one CIA official, only a "decent interval"—enough time for the United States to extricate itself from Vietnam before the collapse of the South Vietnamese government. On April 30, 1975, Americans watched on television as North Vietnamese tanks rolled into Saigon, soon to be renamed Ho Chi Minh City, and helicopters lifted the officials in the American embassy to ships waiting offshore. In those last desperate moments, terrified South Vietnamese fought to get on the helicopters as they took off.

The longest war in American history was finally over, leaving in its wake a bitter legacy. During the period of American involvement in the fighting, almost 2 million combatants and civilians were killed on both sides. North Vietnam absorbed incredible losses—some 600,000 soldiers and countless civilians killed. More than 58,000 Americans died in Vietnam, 300,000 were wounded, 2,500 were declared missing, almost 100,000 returned missing one or more limbs, and over 150,000 combat veterans suffered drug or alcohol addiction or severe psychological disorders. To be sure, most of the Vietnam veterans readjusted well to civilian life, but even they carried for years the stigma of a "lost war."

The "loss" of the war and revelations of American atrocities such as My Lai eroded respect for the military so thoroughly that many young Americans came to regard military service as corrupting and ignoble. The war, described as a noble crusade on behalf of democratic ideals, instead suggested that democracy was not easily transferable to Third World regions that lacked any historical experience with liberal values and representative government. The war fought to show the world that the United States would be steadfast in containing the spread of communism instead sapped the national will and fragmented the national consensus that had governed foreign affairs since 1947. It also changed the balance of power in domestic politics. Not only did the war cause the downfall of Lyndon Johnson's presidency; it also created enduring fissures in the Democratic party. Said antiwar senator and 1972 Democratic presidential candidate George McGovern: "The Vietnam tragedy is at the root of the confusion and division of the Democratic party. It tore up our souls."

Little wonder that most people at war's end wanted to "put Vietnam behind us" and forget. Although subsequent debates over American foreign policy in the Middle East, Africa, and Latin America frequently referred to "the lessons of Vietnam," the phrase was used by different factions for diametrically opposed purposes, ranging from refusal to commit any American troops and resources in El Salvador and Nicaragua to an insistence on massive military commitments unfettered by any diplomatic restrictions that might preclude outright victory. "In the end, then," one journalist wrote concerning the Vietnam era, "there was no end at all."

NIXON AND MIDDLE AMERICA

Richard Nixon had been elected in 1968 as the representative of "Middle America," those middle-class citizens fed up with the liberal politics and promises of the 1960s. The Nixon cabinet and White House staff reflected their values. The chief figures were John Mitchell, the gruff attorney-general who had made his fortune as a municipal bond lawyer in Nixon's old firm; H. R. Haldeman and John Ehrlichman, advisers on domestic policy whose major experience before their association with the Nixon campaign had been in advertising; William Rogers, the secretary of state, an old-time Nixon friend whose control over foreign policy was quickly preempted by Henry Kissinger; and Melvin Laird, the secretary of defense, who also found his influence undercut by Kissinger's access to the White House. The cabinet was all white, all male, all Republican. "There are no blooded patricians in the lot," said *Time* magazine, "just strivers who have acted out the middle-class dream."

DOMESTIC AFFAIRS   Nixon was the first president since Eisenhower in 1957 to confront a Congress in which both houses were under the control of the opposition party. It followed that he focused his energies on foreign policy, where presidential initiatives were less encumbered and where he, in tandem with Kissinger, achieved several stunning breakthroughs. He also continued to support the American space program and the efforts to beat the Soviets to the moon. In July 1969 American astronaut Neil Armstrong became the first man to walk on the moon. Back on earth, however, Nixon sought to stop social-welfare programs in their tracks. Yet, like Eisenhower before him, he found it difficult to dismantle liberal programs.

In July 1969, a program begun by President Kennedy reached its goal: putting a man on the moon.

White teenagers march on City Hall Plaza, Boston, 1975, to protest the busing of students to racially integrate their school system.

Despite the efforts of the Nixon administration, the civil rights legislation enacted during the Johnson years continued to take effect. "There are those who want instant integration and those who want segregation forever," said Nixon in 1969. "I believe we need to have a middle course between these extremes." In practice this "middle course" took the shape of a concerted effort in 1970 to block congressional renewal of the Voting Rights Act of 1965 and to delay implementation of court orders requiring the desegregation of school districts in Mississippi. "For the first time since Woodrow Wilson," said the head of the NAACP, "we have a national administration that can be rightly characterized as anti-Negro." Sixty-five lawyers in the Justice Department signed a letter of protest against the administration's stance. Congress then extended the Voting Rights Act over Nixon's veto. The Supreme Court, in the first decision made under the new chief justice, Warren Burger—a Nixon appointee—ordered the integration of the Mississippi public schools. In *Alexander v. Holmes County Board of Education* (1969), a unanimous Court ordered a quick end to segregation. During Nixon's first term and despite his wishes, more schools were desegregated than in all the Kennedy-Johnson years combined.

Nixon's attempts to block desegregation efforts in urban areas also failed. The Burger Court ruled unanimously in *Swann* v. *Charlotte-Mecklenburg Board of Education* (1971) that school systems must bus students out of their neighborhoods if necessary to achieve integration. Protest over desegregation now began to manifest itself more in the North than in the South, as white families in Boston, Denver, and other cities denounced the destruction of "the neighborhood school," and angry parents in Pontiac, Michigan, firebombed school buses.

Nixon asked Congress to impose a moratorium on all busing orders by the federal courts. The House of Representatives, equally attuned to voter outrage at busing to achieve racial integration, went along. But a Senate filibuster blocked the president's antibusing bill. Busing opponents won a limited victory when the Supreme Court ruled, in *Milliken* v. *Bradley* (1974), that desegregation plans in Detroit requiring the transfer of students from the inner city to the suburbs were unconstitutional. This landmark decision, along with the *Bakke* v. *Board of Regents of California* (1978) decision, which restricted the use of quotas to achieve racial balance, marked the transition of desegregation from an issue of simple justice to a more tangled thicket of conflicting group and individual rights.

Fate and the aging of the justices on the Warren Court gave Nixon the chance to make four new appointments. His first, Warren Burger, caused no dissent. But Nixon's next two nominations generated opposition in the Senate. Clement F. Haynsworth, a federal appeals court judge from South Carolina, had the support of the American Bar Association but drew fire from civil rights groups and labor unions for his conservative record. There was no question of Haynsworth's integrity, but the Senate rejected him when it learned that he had heard a case involving a subsidiary of a corporation in which he owned a small amount of stock.

The nomination of G. Harrold Carswell, a judge of the Florida appeals court, created far more trouble. Carswell had not only been an out-and-out defender of white supremacy, but he was acknowledged by all parties to be singularly lacking in distinction. By a vote of 51 to 45, the Senate rejected Carswell. Nixon condemned the Senate rejection as "an act of regional discrimination." But he took care thereafter to nominate jurists of stature for the Supreme Court: Harry Blackmun, a compatriot of Burger from Minnesota; Lewis F. Powell, Jr., a respected conservative judge from Virginia; and William Rehnquist, an articulate, conservative lawyer in the Justice Department. None encountered serious opposition in the Senate. And none, save perhaps Rehnquist, would consistently support Nixon's interpretation of the Constitution.

Nixon invented several names for his domestic program. At one point it was called the "New Federalism," which would "start resources and power flowing back from Washington to the States and to the people." To that end, in 1972 he pushed through Congress a five-year revenue-sharing plan that would distribute $30 billion of federal revenues to the states for use as they saw fit. At another point Nixon called for a "New American Revolution" to revive traditional values. These catchphrases never caught on, as had the "New Frontier" or the "Great Society," because Nixon's domestic program was mostly defensive and negative.

Meanwhile, the Democratic Congress moved forward with new legislation: the right of eighteen-year-olds to vote in national elections (1970), and in all elections under the Twenty-sixth Amendment (1971); increases in Social Security benefits indexed to the inflation rate and a rise in food-stamp funding; the Occupational Safety and Health Act (1970); the Clean Air Act (1970); new bills to control water pollution (1970 and 1972); and the Federal Election Campaign Act (1972), which modified the rules of campaign finance. These measures accounted for a more rapid rise in spending on social programs than Johnson's Great Society programs had.

ECONOMIC MALAISE   The economy continued to prove troublesome. Overheated by the expense of the Vietnam War, the annual inflation rate began to rise in 1967, when it was 3 percent. By 1973 it was at 9 percent; a year later it was at 12 percent, and it remained in double digits for most of the 1970s. The Dow Jones average of major industrial stocks fell by 36 percent between 1968 and 1970, its steepest decline in more than thirty years. Meanwhile unemployment, at a low of 3.3 percent when Nixon took office, climbed to 6 percent by the end of 1970 and threatened to keep rising. Somehow the American economy was undergoing a recession and inflation at the same time. Economists coined the term "stagflation" to describe the syndrome that defied the orthodox laws of economics.

The economic malaise had at least three deep-rooted causes. First, the Johnson administration had attempted to pay for both the Great Society social-welfare programs and the war in Vietnam without a major tax increase, generating larger federal deficits, a major expansion of the money supply, and price inflation. Second, and more important, by the late 1960s, American goods faced stiff competition in international markets from West Germany, Japan, and other emerging industrial powers. No longer was American technological superiority unquestioned. Third, the American economy had depended heavily on cheap sources of energy; no nation was more dependent on the automobile and the automobile industry, and no nation was more careless in its use of fossil fuels in factories and homes.

Just as domestic petroleum reserves began to dwindle and dependence on foreign sources increased, the Organization of Petroleum Exporting Countries (OPEC) combined to use their oil as a political and economic weapon. In 1973, when the United States sent massive aid to Israel after a devastating Syrian-Egyptian attack during Yom Kippur, the holiest day in the Jewish calendar, OPEC announced that it would not sell oil to nations supporting Israel and that it was raising its prices by 400 percent. Motorists thereafter faced long lines at gas stations and factories cut production.

Another condition leading to stagflation was the flood of new workers—mainly baby-boomers and women—entering the labor market. From 1965 to 1980 the workforce grew by 40 percent, almost 30 million workers, a number greater than the total labor force of France or West Germany. The number of new jobs could not keep up, leaving many unemployed. At the same time, worker productivity declined, pushing up inflation in the face of rising demand.

Stagflation posed a new set of economic problems, but Nixon responded erratically and ineffectively, trying old remedies for a new problem. First, he tried to reduce the federal deficit by raising taxes and cutting the budget. When the Democratic Congress refused to cooperate with this approach, he encouraged the Federal Reserve Board to reduce the money supply by raising interest rates. The stock market immediately collapsed, and the economy plunged into the "Nixon recession."

In 1969, when asked about government restrictions on wages and prices, Nixon had been unequivocal: "Controls. Oh, my God, no! . . . We'll never go to controls." But in 1971, he reversed himself. He froze all wages and prices for ninety days and announced that the United

States would no longer convert dollars into gold for foreign banks. The dollar, its link to gold cut, now drifted lower on world currency exchanges. After ninety days, Nixon established mandatory guidelines for subsequent wage and price increases under the supervision of a federal agency. Still the economy floundered. By 1973 the wage and price guidelines were made voluntary, and therefore almost entirely ineffective.

ENVIRONMENTAL PROTECTION   The widespread recognition that America faced limits to economic growth fueled broad support for environmental protection in the early 1970s. The realization that cities and industrial development were damaging the physical environment and altering the earth's ecology was not new: Rachel Carson's book *Silent Spring* (1962) had sounded the warning years earlier. But in Nixon's first term the Democratic-controlled Congress took concerted action, passing several acts to protect and clean up the environment. The administration also created by executive order the Environmental Protection Agency, a consolidation of existing agencies, to oversee federal guidelines for controlling air pollution, toxic wastes, and water quality.

The Arab oil boycott and the OPEC price increase led to an energy crisis in the United States. People began to realize that natural resources were not infinitely expendable. "Although it's positively unAmerican to think so," said one sociologist, "the environmental move-

An Earth Day demonstration dramatizing the dangers of air pollution, April 1972.

ment and energy shortage have forced us all to accept a sense of our limits, to lower our expectations, to seek prosperity through conservation rather than growth."

Although the environmental movement cut across class, racial, and ethnic lines by appealing to the collective interests of all Americans in clean air and water, it simultaneously aggravated the competition between regional vested interests. In Texas, where the oil lobby resented controls on gas prices and speed limits, bumper stickers read: "Drive fast, freeze a Yankee." In Tennessee, where a federal dam project was halted because it threatened the snail darter—a species of fish—with extinction, local developers took out ads asking residents to "tell the government that the size of your wallet is more important than some two-inch-long minnow."

As stagflation persisted into the middle and late 1970s, corporate criticism that environmental regulations were cutting into jobs and profit margins began to sound more persuasive, especially when the staggering cost of cleaning up accumulated toxic wastes became known. "Why worry about the long run," said one unemployed steelworker in 1976, "when you're out of work right now." Polls showed that protection of the environment remained a high priority among a majority of Americans, but that few were willing to suffer a cutback in their standard of living to achieve that goal. "It was," bemoaned one journalist, "as if passengers knew they were boarding the *Titanic,* but preferred to jostle with one another for first class accommodations so they might enjoy as much of the voyage as possible."

NIXON TRIUMPHANT

CHINA   If the ailments of the economy proved more than Nixon could remedy, in foreign policy his administration managed to diagnose and improve American relations with the major powers of the Communist world—China and the Soviet Union—and to shift fundamentally the pattern of the cold war. In 1971 Nixon's diplomatic adviser Henry Kissinger made a secret trip to Beijing (Peking) to explore the possibility of American recognition of China. Since 1949, when Mao Tse-tung's revolutionary movement established control in China, the United States had refused to recognize Communist China, preferring to regard Chiang Kai-shek's exiled regime on Taiwan as the legitimate govern-

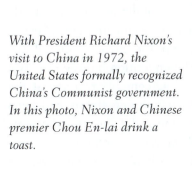

With President Richard Nixon's visit to China in 1972, the United States formally recognized China's Communist government. In this photo, Nixon and Chinese premier Chou En-lai drink a toast.

ment of China. In one simple but stunning stroke, Nixon and Kissinger ended two decades of diplomatic isolation for the People's Republic of China and drove a wedge between the two chief bastions of communism in the world.

In 1972 Americans watched on television as their president visited famous Chinese landmarks, which had been invisible to Americans for over two decades, and drank toasts with Premier Chou En-lai and Mao Tse-tung. The United States and China agreed to scientific and cultural exchanges, steps toward the resumption of trade, and the eventual reunification of Taiwan with the mainland. A year after the Nixon visit, "liaison offices" were established in Washington and Beijing (Peking) that served as unofficial embassies, and in 1979 diplomatic recognition was formalized. Richard Nixon, the former anti-Communist crusader who had condemned the State Department for "losing" China in 1949, had accomplished a diplomatic feat that his Democratic predecessors could not.

DÉTENTE   In truth, China welcomed the breakthrough in relations with the United States because its rivalry with the Soviet Union, with which it shared a long border, had become more bitter than its rivalry with the West. The Soviet leaders, troubled by the Sino-American agreements, were also anxious for an easing of tensions with the United

States now that they had, as the result of a huge arms buildup following the Cuban missile crisis, achieved virtual parity with the United States in nuclear weapons. Once again the president surprised the world, by announcing that he would visit Moscow in 1972 for discussions with Leonid Brezhnev, the Soviet premier. The high theater of the China visit was repeated in Moscow, with toasts and elegant dinners between world leaders who had previously regarded each other as incarnations of evil.

What became known as "détente" with the Soviets offered the promise of a more orderly and restrained competition between the two superpowers. Nixon and Brezhnev signed agreements reached at the Strategic Arms Limitation Talks (SALT), which negotiators had been working on since 1969. The SALT agreement did not end the arms race, but it did limit both the number of intercontinental ballistic missiles (ICBMs) and the construction of antiballistic missile systems (ABMSs). In effect, the Soviets were allowed to retain a greater number of missiles with greater destructive power, while the United States retained a lead in the total number of warheads. No limitations were placed on new weapons systems, though each side agreed to work toward a permanent freeze on all nuclear weapons. The Moscow summit also produced new trade agreements, including an arrangement whereby the United States sold almost one-quarter of its wheat crop to the Soviets at a favorable price. American farmers rejoiced, since the wheat deal assured them a high price for their crop, but domestic critics grumbled that the deal would raise food prices in the United States and rescue the Soviets from troublesome economic problems.

SHUTTLE DIPLOMACY   The Nixon-Kissinger initiatives in the Middle East were less dramatic and less conclusive than the agreements with China and the Soviet Union, but they did show that America recognized Arab power in the region and its own dependence on the oil from Islamic states fundamentally opposed to Israel. After the Six-Day War of 1967, in which Israeli forces routed the armies of Egypt, Syria, and Jordan, Israel seized territory from all three Arab nations. Moreover, the number of Palestinian refugees, many of them homeless since the creation of Israel in 1948, increased after the Israeli victory in 1967. When Israel recovered from the initial shock of the surprise Yom Kippur War of 1973, Kissinger negotiated a cease-fire and exerted pressure to prevent Israel from taking additional Arab territory. American reliance on Arab oil led to closer ties with Egypt and its president, Anwar el-Sadat, and more restrained support for Israel. Though Kissinger's "shuttle diplomacy" among the capitals of the Middle East won acclaim from all sides, he failed to find a comprehensive formula for peace in the troubled region and ignored altogether the Palestinian problem. But he did lay groundwork for the subsequent accord between Israel and Egypt in 1977.

THE 1972 ELECTION   Nixon's foreign policy achievements allowed him to stage the campaign of 1972 as a triumphal procession. The main threat to his reelection came from Alabama's Democratic governor George Wallace, who had the potential to deprive the Republicans of conservative votes and thereby throw the election to the Democrats or the Democratic-controlled Congress. But on May 15, 1972, Wallace was shot and left paralyzed below the waist by a white midwesterner anxious to achieve a grisly brand of notoriety. Wallace was forced to withdraw from the campaign.

Meanwhile, the Democrats were further ensuring Nixon's victory by nominating Senator George S. McGovern of South Dakota, a crusading liberal who embodied antiwar and social-welfare values associated with the turbulence of the 1960s. At the Democratic convention in Miami Beach, McGovern benefited from party reforms that increased the representation of women, blacks, and minorities. But such changes alienated party regulars. Mayor Richard Daley of Chicago was actually ousted from the convention, and the AFL-CIO refused to endorse the liberal Democratic candidate. McGovern also suffered from his handling of the crisis that developed when it was revealed that his running mate, Senator Thomas Eagleton of Missouri, had undergone shock treatments for depression. McGovern first announced complete support for Eagleton, then bowed to critics and dropped him, leaving an impression of vacillation and indecisiveness.

The campaign was an exercise in futility for McGovern, while Nixon made only a few formal political trips and cast himself in the role of "global peacekeeper." Nixon won the greatest victory of any Republican presidential candidate in history, capturing 520 electoral votes to only 17 for McGovern. The popular vote was equally decisive: 46 million to 28 million, a proportion of the total vote (60.8 percent) that was second only to Johnson's victory over Goldwater in 1964.

During the course of the campaign McGovern complained about the "dirty tricks" of the Nixon administration, most especially the curious incident in which a group of burglars was caught breaking into the Democratic National Committee headquarters in the Watergate apartment complex in Washington, D.C. McGovern's accusations seemed shrill and biased at the time, the lamentations of an obvious loser. Nixon and his staff made plans for "four more years" as the investigation of the fateful Watergate break-in proceeded apace.

WATERGATE

During the trial of the accused Watergate burglars, the relentless prodding of Judge John J. Sirica led one of the accused to tell the full story of the Nixon administration's complicity in the Watergate episode. James W. McCord, a former CIA agent and security chief for the Committee to Re-elect the President (CREEP), was the first in a long line of informers and penitents in a melodrama that unfolded over the next two years. It ended in the first resignation of a president in American history, the conviction and imprisonment of twenty-five officials of the Nixon administration, including four cabinet members, and the most serious constitutional crisis since the impeachment trial of President Andrew Johnson.

UNCOVERING THE COVER-UP The trail of evidence pursued first by Judge Sirica, then by a grand jury, and then by a Senate investigation committee headed by Senator Samuel J. Ervin, Jr., of North Carolina, led directly to the White House. Republican senator Howard Baker of Tennessee, a member of the Ervin Committee, put the crucial questions succinctly: "What did the President know and when did he know it?" There was never any evidence that Nixon ordered the break-in or that he was aware of plans to burglarize the Democratic National Committee. But from the start, Nixon was personally involved in the cover-up of the incident. He used his presidential powers to discredit and block the investigation. And, most alarming, the Watergate burglary was merely one small part of a larger pattern of corruption and criminality sanctioned by the Nixon White House.

The White House had become committed to illegal tactics in 1970 when the *New York Times* disclosed that the secret American bombings in Cambodia had been going on for years. Nixon had ordered illegal telephone taps on several journalists and government employees suspected of leaking the story. The covert activity against the press and critics of Nixon's Vietnam policies increased in 1971 during the crisis generated by the publication of the Pentagon Papers, when a team of burglars under the direction of White House adviser John Ehrlichman had broken into Daniel Ellsberg's psychiatrist's office in an effort to obtain damaging information on Ellsberg, the man who had given the Pentagon Papers to the press. By the spring of 1972, Ehrlichman commanded a team of "dirty tricksters" who performed various acts of sabotage against prospective Democratic candidates for the presidency, including falsely accusing Hubert Humphrey and Senator Henry Jackson of sexual improprieties, forging press releases, setting off stink bombs at Democratic rallies, and associating the opposition candidates with racist remarks. By the time of the Watergate break-in, the money to finance such "pranks" was being illegally collected through the Committee to

Senator Sam Ervin, chairman of the Senate Watergate Committee, swears in the ex–White House counsel John Dean, whose testimony linked President Nixon to the cover-up.

Re-elect the President and placed under the control of the White House staff.

The cover-up began to unravel as various people, including John Dean, legal counsel to the president, began to believe they were being set up as fall guys, and began to cooperate with prosecutors. It unraveled further in 1973 when L. Patrick Gray, acting director of the FBI, resigned after confessing that he had confiscated and destroyed several incriminating documents. On April 30 Ehrlichman and Haldeman resigned, together with Attorney-General Richard Kleindienst. A few days later the president nervously assured the public in a television address, "I am not a crook." But then John Dean, whom Nixon had dismissed because of his cooperation with prosecutors, testified to the Ervin Committee that there had been a cover-up and that Nixon had approved it. In another "bombshell" disclosure, a White House aide told the committee that Nixon had installed a taping system in the White House and that many of the conversations about Watergate had been recorded.

A year-long battle for the "Nixon tapes" began. Harvard law professor Archibald Cox, who had been appointed as special prosecutor to handle the Watergate case, took the president to court in October 1973 in order to obtain the tapes. Nixon, pleading "executive privilege," refused to release the tapes and ordered Cox fired. In what became known as the "Saturday Night Massacre," Attorney-General Elliot Richardson and Deputy Attorney-General William Ruckelshaus resigned rather than execute the order. Solicitor-General Robert Bork finally fired Cox. Cox's replacement as special prosecutor, Leon Jaworski, proved no more pliable than Cox, and he also took the president to court. In March 1974 the Watergate grand jury indicted Ehrlichman, Haldeman, and Mitchell for obstruction of justice, and it named Nixon as an "unindicted co-conspirator."

On July 24, 1974, the Supreme Court ruled unanimously that the president must surrender the tapes. No sooner were the tapes handed over than investigators learned that sections of certain recordings were missing, including eighteen minutes of a key conversation during which Nixon first mentioned the Watergate burglary. The president's loyal secretary tried to accept blame for the erasure, claiming she accidentally pushed the wrong button. But experts later concluded that the missing segments had been intentionally deleted.

Having resigned his office, Richard Nixon waves farewell outside the White House, August 9, 1974.

A few days later the House Judiciary Committee dramatically voted to recommend three articles of impeachment: obstruction of justice through the payment of "hush money" to witnesses and the withholding of evidence; abuse of power through using federal agencies to deprive citizens of their constitutional rights; and defiance of Congress by withholding the tapes. But before the House of Representatives could meet to vote on impeachment, Nixon handed over the complete set of White House tapes. On August 9, 1974, fully aware that the evidence on the tapes implicated him in the cover-up, Richard Nixon resigned from office, the only president ever to do so.

EFFECTS OF WATERGATE Spiro Agnew did not succeed Nixon because he himself had been forced to resign in October 1973 when it became known that he had accepted bribes from contractors before and during his term as vice-president. In a plea bargain with prosecutors he agreed to resign and to a single charge of tax evasion. The vice-president at the time of Nixon's resignation was Gerald Ford, the former House minority leader from Michigan whom Nixon had appointed, with the approval of Congress, under provisions of the Twenty-fifth Amendment. Ratified in 1967, the amendment provided for the appointment of a vice-president when the office became vacant. Ford insisted that he had no intention of pardoning Nixon, who was still liable for criminal prosecution. "I do not think the public would stand for it," said Ford. But a month after Nixon's resignation, the new president did issue the pardon, explaining that it was necessary to end the national obsession with the Watergate scandals. Many suspected that Nixon and Ford had made a deal, though there was no evidence to confirm the speculation. President Ford testified personally to a congressional committee: "There was no deal, period."

If there was a silver lining in the dark cloud of Watergate, it was the vigor and resiliency of the institutions that had brought a president down—the press, Congress, the courts, and an aroused public opinion. Congress responded to the Watergate revelations with several pieces of legislation designed to curb executive power. Already nervous about possible efforts to renew American military assistance to South Vietnam, the Democratic-led Congress passed the War Powers Act (1973), which required the president to inform Congress within forty-eight hours if U.S. troops were being deployed in combat abroad and to withdraw troops after sixty days unless Congress specifically approved their stay. In an effort to correct abuses of campaign funds, Congress enacted legislation in 1974 that set new ceilings on political contributions and expenditures. And in reaction to the Nixon claim of "executive privilege" as a means of withholding evidence, Congress strengthened the 1966 Freedom of Information Act to require prompt responses to requests for information from government files and to place on government agencies the burden of proof for classifying information as secret.

With Nixon's resignation, the nation had weathered a profound constitutional crisis, but the aftershock of the Watergate episode produced a deep sense of disillusionment with the so-called imperial presidency. Apart from Nixon's illegal actions, the scurrilous language used in the White House and made public on the tapes stripped away the veils of mystery surrounding national leaders and left even the die-hard defenders of presidential authority shocked at the crudity and duplicity of Nixon and his subordinates. Coming on the heels of the erosion of public confidence generated by the Vietnam War, the Watergate affair renewed public cynicism toward a government that had systematically lied to the people and violated their civil liberties. Said one bumper sticker of the day: "Don't vote. It only encourages them."

Nixon's resignation pleased his critics but also initiated a prolonged crisis of confidence. A poll taken in 1974 asked people how much faith they had in the executive branch of government. Only 14 percent answered "a great deal"; 43 percent said "hardly any." Restoring credibility and respect thus became the primary challenge facing Nixon's successors. Unfortunately a new array of economic and foreign crises would make that task doubly difficult.

AN UNELECTED PRESIDENT

During Richard Nixon's last year in office the Watergate crisis so dominated the Washington scene that major domestic and foreign problems received little executive attention. The perplexing combination of inflation and recession worsened, as did the oil crisis. At the same time, Henry Kissinger, who assumed control over the management of foreign policy, watched helplessly as the South Vietnamese forces began to crumble before North Vietnamese attacks, attempted with limited success to establish a framework for peace in the Middle East, and supported a CIA role in overthrowing Salvador Allende, the popularly elected Marxist president of Chile. Allende was subsequently murdered and replaced by General Augusto Pinochet, a military dictator supposedly friendly to the United States.

THE FORD YEARS   Gerald Ford inherited these simmering problems when he assumed office after Nixon's resignation. An amiable, honest man, Ford candidly admitted upon becoming vice-president, "I am a Ford, not a Lincoln." He enjoyed widespread popular support for only a short time. His pardon of Nixon on September 8, 1974, generated a storm of criticism. The *New York Times* called it "an unconscionable act."

As president, Ford soon adopted the posture he had developed as a conservative minority leader in the House: nay-saying leader of the opposition who believed that the federal government exercised too much power over domestic affairs. In his fifteen months as president, Ford vetoed thirty-nine bills, thereby outstripping Herbert Hoover's veto record in less than half the time. By resisting congressional pressure to reduce taxes and increase federal spending, he succeeded in plummeting the economy into the deepest recession since the Great Depression. Unemployment jumped to 9 percent in 1975, and the federal deficit hit a record the next year. When New York City announced that it was near bankruptcy, unable to meet its payrolls and bond payments, Ford vowed "to veto any bill that has as its purpose a federal bailout." The headline in the *New York Daily News* was: "Ford to New York: Drop Dead." But the president relented after the Senate and House banking committees voted to guarantee a loan; New York was saved from insolvency. Ford rejected wage and price controls to curb inflation, preferring voluntary restraints that he tried to bolster by passing out "WIN" buttons, symbolizing his campaign to "Whip Inflation Now." The WIN buttons instead became a national joke and a popular symbol of Ford's ineffectiveness in the fight against stagflation.

In foreign policy, Ford retained Henry Kissinger as secretary of state and attempted to pursue Nixon's goals of stability in the Middle East, rapprochement with China, and détente with the Soviet Union. Late in 1974, Ford met with Soviet leader Leonid Brezhnev at Vladivostok in Siberia and accepted the framework for another arms-control accord that was to serve as the basis for SALT II. Meanwhile Kissinger's tireless shuttling between Cairo and Tel Aviv produced an agreement: Israel promised to return to Egypt most of the Sinai territory captured in the 1967 war, and the two nations agreed to rely on negotiations rather than force to settle future disagreements. These limited but significant achievements should have enhanced Ford's image, but they were drowned in the sea of criticism and carping that followed the collapse of South Vietnam to Communists in May 1975.

Not only had a decade of American effort in Vietnam proved futile, but the Khmer Rouge, the Cambodian Communist movement, had also won a resounding victory, plunging that country into a bloodbath. Meanwhile, the OPEC oil cartel was threatening another worldwide boycott while other Third World nations denounced the United States as a depraved and declining imperialistic power. Ford lost his patience when he sent in the marines to rescue the crew of the American merchant ship *Mayaguez,* which had been captured by the Cambodian Communists. This vigorous move won popular acclaim until it was disclosed that the Cambodians had already agreed to release the captured Americans: the forty-one Americans killed in the operation had died for no purpose.

THE 1976 ELECTION   In the midst of such turmoil, the Democrats could hardly wait for the 1976 election. At the Republican convention Ford managed to fend off a powerful challenge for the nomination from the former California governor and Hollywood actor, Ronald Reagan, whose robust appearance belied his sixty-five years. Because even the Republicans were divided over Ford's leadership, and because Ford's failure to solve the economic and energy problems was beyond dispute, the Democratic nominee seemed a shoo-in for the presidency. "We could run an aardvark this year and win," predicted one Democratic leader.

The Democrats chose an obscure former naval officer and engineer turned peanut farmer who had served one term as governor of Georgia. Jimmy Carter campaigned harder than any of the other Democratic hopefuls; he capitalized on the post-Watergate cynicism by promising "I will never tell a lie to the American people" and by citing his inexperience in the byways of Washington politics as an asset. Carter promised to revive the moral presidency of Woodrow Wilson. In the midst of the continuing revulsion against the political corruption unearthed by the Watergate inquiries, he preached the need for national repentance and personal self-sacrifice. Facing the prospect of the first president from the Deep South since 1849, and the first ever born and bred in that particular briar patch, reporters marveled at a Baptist candidate who claimed to be "born again," and began to speculate that Carter's native region harbored some forgotten virtues after all.

To the surprise of many pundits, Carter revived the New Deal coalition of southern whites, blacks, urban labor, and ethnic groups to win 41 million votes to Ford's 39 million, and a narrow electoral vote majority of 297 to 241. A heavy turnout of blacks in the South enabled Carter to sweep every state in the region except Virginia. Carter also benefited from the appeal of Walter F. Mondale, his liberal running mate and a favorite among blue-collar workers and the urban poor. Carter lost most of the trans-Mississippi West, but no other Democratic candidate had made much headway there since Harry Truman in 1948. The big story of the election was the low voter turnout. "Neither Ford nor Carter won as many votes as Mr. Nobody," said one reporter, commenting on the fact that almost half the eligible voters, apparently alienated by Watergate and the lackluster candidates, chose to sit out the election.

THE CARTER INTERREGNUM

POLICY STALEMATE   Once in office, Carter suffered the fate of all American presidents since Kennedy: after an initial honeymoon, during which Carter displayed folksy charm by walking down Pennsylvania Avenue after his inauguration rather than riding in a limousine, and wearing cardigan sweaters during televised "fireside chats," his popularity and political effectiveness waned. Soon *Newsweek* was referring to the "corn bread-and-cardigan atmospherics." The truth was that, like Ford before him, Carter faced an almost insurmountable set of domestic and international problems. He was expected to cure the economic recession and inflation at a time when all industrial economies were shaken by a shortage of energy and confidence. He was expected to reassert America's global power at a time of waning respect for America's international authority. And he was expected to do this, as well as buoy the national spirit, through a set of political institutions in which many Americans had lost faith.

Yet, during the first two years of his term, Carter enjoyed several successes, most reflecting the values of moderate liberalism. His administration included more blacks and women than ever before; his appoint-

President Jimmy Carter and wife, Rosalynn, forgo the traditional limousine and walk down Pennsylvania Avenue after the inauguration, January 20, 1977.

ment of Andrew Young, a former protégé of Martin Luther King, as ambassador to the United Nations attracted the most attention. Carter created a federal task force to study the problem of Vietnam-era draft evaders and eventually offered amnesty to the thousands of young Americans who had fled the country rather than serve in Vietnam. He reformed the civil service to provide rewards for merit, and he created new cabinet-level Departments of Energy and Education. He also pushed several significant environmental initiatives through Congress, including a bill to establish controls over strip mining, a "superfund" of $1.6 billion to clean up chemical waste sites, and a proposal to protect over 100 million acres of Alaskan land from development.

But success was short-lived. Carter's political predicament surfaced in the protracted debate over energy policy. Carter, like Hoover, served at a time of diminishing resources, and like that other engineer-businessman, he had a distaste for stroking legislators or wheeling and dealing to get legislation through. The energy bill passed in 1978 was a gutted version of the original proposed by the administration, reflecting the power of both conservative and liberal special-interest lobbies. One Carter aide said that the energy bill looked like it had been "nibbled to death by ducks." The clumsy political maneuvers that plagued Carter and his inexperienced aides repeatedly frustrated efforts to remedy the energy crisis. Moreover, with party discipline in the Congress a shambles and each special-interest group clamoring for its own program, the White House was repeatedly forced to create what one Carter aide described as a "roll-your-own majority" for each presidential proposal.

In the summer of 1979, when renewed violence in the Middle East produced a second fuel shortage in the United States, motorists were again forced to wait in long lines for limited supplies of gas that they regarded as excessively expensive. Opinion polls showed Carter with an approval rating of only 26 percent, lower than Nixon during the worst moments of the Watergate crisis. During July Carter called his advisers to an extraordinary retreat at Camp David, Maryland, and emerged ten days later proclaiming a need for "a rebirth of the American spirit." He also called for a "new and positive energy program." But Congress only partially funded the major feature of his new plan—a federal agency to encourage development of synthetic fuels.

Several of Carter's early foreign policy initiatives also got caught in political crossfires. Soon after his inauguration, Carter vowed that "the soul of our foreign policy" should be the defense of human rights abroad. This human rights campaign, however, provoked attack from two sides: those who feared it sacrificed a detached appraisal of national interest for high-level moralizing, and those who believed that human rights were important but that the administration was applying the standard inconsistently.

Similarly, Carter's successful negotiation of treaties to turn over control of the Panama Canal to the government of Panama generated intense criticism. Republican Ronald Reagan claimed that the Canal Zone was sovereign American soil purchased "fair and square" in Theodore Roosevelt's administration. (In the congressional debate one senator quipped, "We stole it fair and square, so why can't we keep it?") Carter argued that the limitations on American influence in Latin America, and the deep resentment toward American colonialism in Panama left the United States with no other choice. The Canal Zone would revert in stages to Panama by 1999. The Senate ratified the treaties by a paper-thin margin (68 to 32, two votes more than the required two-thirds), but conservatives lambasted Carter for surrendering American authority in a strategically critical part of the world.

THE CAMP DAVID ACCORDS   Carter's crowning foreign policy achievement, which even his most bitter critics applauded, was the arrangement of a peace agreement between Israel and Egypt. In 1977 Egyptian president Anwar el-Sadat flew to Tel Aviv at the invitation of Israeli prime minister Menachem Begin. Sadat's bold act, and his accompanying announcement that Egypt was now willing to recognize the legitimacy of the Israeli state, opened up diplomatic opportunities that Carter and Secretary of State Cyrus Vance quickly pursued.

In 1978 Carter invited Sadat and Begin to the presidential retreat at Camp David for two weeks of difficult negotiations. The first part of the eventual agreement called for Israel to return all land in the Sinai in exchange for Egyptian recognition of Israel's sovereignty. This agreement was successfully implemented in 1982 when the last Israeli settler vacated the Sinai. But the second part of the agreement, calling for Israel to negotiate with Sadat to resolve the Palestinian refugee dilemma, began to unravel soon after the Camp David summit.

By March 26, 1979, when Begin and Sadat returned to Washington to sign the formal treaty, Begin had already made clear his refusal to

Egyptian president Anwar Sadat (left), *Jimmy Carter* (center), *and Israeli prime minister Menachem Begin* (right) *at the announcement of the Camp David accords, September 1978.*

block new Israeli settlements on the West Bank of the Jordan River, which Sadat had regarded as a prospective homeland for the Palestinians. In the wake of the Camp David accords, most of the Arab nations condemned Sadat as a traitor to their Islamic cause. Still, Carter and Vance were responsible for a dramatic display of high-level diplomacy that, whatever its limitations, made an all-out war between Israel and the Arab world less likely in the foreseeable future.

MOUNTING TROUBLES   Carter's crowning failure, which even his most avid supporters acknowledged, was his management of the economy. In effect he inherited a bad situation and left it worse. Carter employed the same economic policies as Nixon and Ford to fight stagflation, but he reversed the order of the federal "cure," preferring first to fight unemployment with a tax cut and increased public spending. Unemployment declined slightly, from 8 to 7 percent in 1977, but inflation soared; at 5 percent when he took office, it reached 10 percent in 1978 and kept going. During one month in 1980 it measured at an annual rate of no less than 18 percent. Like previous presidents, Carter then reversed himself to fight the other side of the economic malaise.

By midterm he was delaying tax reductions and vetoing government spending programs that he had proposed in his first year. The result, however, was the worst of both possible worlds: a deepened recession with unemployment at 7.5 percent in 1980, mortgage rates at 15 percent, interest rates at an all-time high of 20 percent, and a runaway inflation averaging between 12 and 13 percent.

The signing of a controversial new Strategic Arms Limitation Treaty (SALT II) with the Soviets put Carter's leadership to the test just as the mounting economic problems made him the subject of biting editorial cartoons nationwide. Like SALT I, the new agreement did not do much to slow down the nuclear arms race. It placed a ceiling of 2,250 bombers and missiles on each side and set limits on the number of warheads and new weapons systems. To pacify his conservative critics, who charged that SALT II would give the Soviets a decided advantage in the number and destructive power of land-based missiles, Carter announced that the United States would build a new missile system, called the MX, that would be housed in a vast maze of underground tunnels connected by railroad, creating a sort of "nuclear shell game" that would prevent Soviet planners from knowing where to strike. Liberal critics called the MX plan "a combination of Disney World and Armageddon" and criticized the SALT II agreement as "a step sideways rather than backwards in the arms race." Conservatives questioned the whole idea of détente, arguing that the Soviets would never have signed the agreement if it did not guarantee them nuclear superiority. Whether SALT II would pass the Senate became an open question.

The question became moot in 1979 when the Soviet army invaded Afghanistan to rescue the faltering Communist government there, which was being challenged by Muslim rebels. Carter immediately shelved SALT II, suspended grain shipments to the Soviet Union, and began a campaign for an international boycott of the 1980 Olympics, which were to be held that summer in Moscow.

IRAN Then came the Iranian crisis, a year-long cascade of unwelcome events that epitomized the inability of the United States to control world affairs. The crisis began with the fall of the shah of Iran in 1979. The revolutionaries who toppled the shah rallied around Ayatollah Ruhollah Khomeini, a Muslim religious leader who symbolized the Islamic values the shah had tried to replace with Western ways. Khomeini's hatred of the United States dated back to the CIA-sponsored overthrow of Iran's Mossadegh government in 1953. Nor did it help the American image that the CIA had trained SAVAK, the shah's ruthless secret police force. Late in 1979 the exiled shah was allowed to enter the United States in order to undergo treatment for cancer. A few days later, a frenzied mob stormed the American embassy in Teheran and seized the diplomats and staff inside. Khomeini endorsed the mob action and demanded the return of the shah along with all his wealth in exchange for the release of the fifty-three American hostages. In the meantime, the Iranian militants staged daily demonstrations for the benefit of worldwide news and television coverage in which the American flag and effigies of the American president were burned and otherwise desecrated.

Indignant Americans demanded a military response to such outrages, but Carter's range of options was limited. He appealed to the United Nations, protesting what was a clear violation of diplomatic immunity and international law. Khomeini scoffed at U.N. requests for the release of hostages. Carter then froze all Iranian assets in the United States and appealed to American allies for a trade embargo of Iran. The trade restrictions were only partially effective—even America's most

Iranian militants stormed the U.S. Embassy in Teheran in 1979, taking 53 Americans hostage for over a year. Here one of the hostages (face covered) is paraded before a camera.

loyal European allies did not want to lose their access to Iranian oil—so a frustrated and besieged Carter authorized a risky rescue attempt by American commandos in 1980. Secretary of State Vance resigned in protest against the rescue attempt, and against Carter's sharp turn toward a more hawkish foreign policy. The commando raid was aborted because of helicopter failures, and ended with eight fatalities when another helicopter collided with a transport plane in the desert.

Nightly television coverage of the taunting Iranian rebels generated widespread popular craving for action and a near obsession with the falling fortunes of the United States and the fate of the hostages. The end came after 444 days of captivity when Carter released several billion dollars of Iranian assets to ransom the kidnapped hostages. A plane carrying them left Teheran for Algiers, and Carter then flew to Wiesbaden, West Germany, to greet the released hostages at an American base. Few noted the irony that Algiers was one of the Barbary states that had extorted tribute from the early republic by holding American prisoners until 1815.

MAKING CONNECTIONS

- Foreign affairs in the 1970s show the changing patterns of the cold war. The next chapter details the end of both the cold war and the Soviet Union.

- Presidents Nixon and Ford tried, with limited success, to decrease the power of the federal government over domestic affairs. President Reagan was much more successful at advancing the conservative agenda, a topic covered in the next chapter.

- The rebellion and turbulence of the 1960s and 1970s became less apparent in the following decade: as Chapter 37 shows, however, that turbulence reappeared, in a somewhat different form, in the 1990s.

FURTHER READING

Engaging overviews of the cultural trends of the 1960s include William L. O'Neill's *Coming Apart: An Informal History of America in the 1960s* (1972) and Godfrey Hodgson's *America in Our Time* (1976). The scholarly literature on the New Left includes Irwin Unger's *The Movement: A History of the American New Left 1959–1972* (1974). On the Students for a Democratic Society, see Kirkpatrick Sale's *SDS* (1973) and Allen J. Matusow's *The Unraveling of America: A History of Liberalism in the 1960s* (1984). Also useful is Todd Gitlin's *The Sixties: Years of Hope, Days of Rage* (rev. ed., 1993).

Two influential assessments of the counterculture by sympathetic commentators are Theodore Roszak's *The Making of a Counterculture: Reflections on the Technocratic Society and Its Youthful Opposition* (1969) and Charles Reich's *The Greening of America* (1970). A good scholarly analysis of the hippies that takes them seriously is Timothy Miller's *The Hippies and American Values* (1991). On the communal movement, see Keith Melville's *Communes in the Counter Culture* (1972).

There is a wealth of good books dealing with the women's liberation movement. Among the most powerful accounts are those by participants. See Shulamith Firestone's *The Dialectic of Sex* (1972), Betty Friedan's *It Changed My Life: Writings on the Women's Movement* (1976), Kate Millett's *Sexual Politics* (1971), and *Sisterhood Is Powerful* (1970), edited by Robin Morgan. Sara Evans explains the ambivalent relationship of feminism with the civil rights movement in *Personal Politics: The Roots of Women's Liberation in the Civil Rights Movement and the New Left* (1980).

The organizing efforts of César Chavez are detailed in Ronald Taylor's *Chavez and the Farm Workers* (1975). The struggles of Native Americans for recognition and power are sympathetically described in Stan Steiner's *The New Indians* (1968). On the shifting cultural mood of the 1970s, see Christopher Lasch's influential critique, *The Culture of Narcissism* (1978). Peter Clecak convincingly questions the stereotypic notion of the seventies as an age of apathy and narcissism in *America's Quest for the Ideal Self* (1983).

On Nixon, see Stephen Ambrose's *Nixon: The Triumph of a Politician, 1962–1972* (1989) and *Nixon: Ruin and Recovery, 1973–1990* (1991). Equally valuable is Herbert S. Parmet's *Richard Nixon and His America* (1990). For a solid overview of the Watergate scandal, see

Stanley Kutler's *The Wars of Watergate: The Last Crisis of Richard Nixon* (1990).

For the way the Republicans handled affairs abroad, consult Tad Szulc's *The Illusion of Peace: Foreign Policy in the Nixon Years* (1978). Secretary of State Henry Kissinger recounts his role in policy formation in *The White House Years* (1978). A less favorable report of the Kissinger role appears in Seymour M. Hersh's *The Price of Power: Kissinger in the Nixon White House* (1983).

The loss of Vietnam and the end of American involvement are traced in Allan E. Goodman's *The Lost Peace: America's Search for a Negotiated Settlement of the Vietnam War* (1978), Frank Snepp's *Decent Interval: An Insider's Account of Saigon's Indecent End Told by the CIA's Chief Strategy Analyst in Vietnam* (1977), and Gareth Porter's *A Peace Denied: The United States, Vietnam and the Paris Agreement* (1975). William Shawcross's *Sideshow: Kissinger, Nixon, and the Destruction of Cambodia* (1978) deals with the broadening of the war, while Larry Berman's *Planning a Tragedy: The Americanization of the War in Vietnam* (1982) assesses the final impact of American involvement. The most comprehensive treatment of the antiwar movement in the United States is Tom Wells's *The War Within: America's Battle over Vietnam* (1994). A recent effort to reflect upon the lingering impact of the Vietnam War is Arnold R. Isaacs's *Vietnam Shadows: The War, Its Ghosts, and Its Legacy* (1997).

To examine the rise of Jimmy Carter, consult Betty Glad's *Jimmy Carter: In Search of the Great White House* (1980). The best overview of the Carter administration is Burton I. Kaufman's *The Presidency of James Earl Carter, Jr.* (1993). A work more sympathetic to the Carter administration is John Dumbrell's *The Carter Presidency: A Re-Evaluation* (1993). Also useful is Kenneth E. Morris's *Jimmy Carter: American Moralist* (1997). Gaddis Smith's *Morality, Reason, and Power* (1986) provides an overview of American diplomacy in the Carter years. Zbigniew Brzezinski's *Power and Principle: Memories of the National Security Advisor, 1977–1981* (1983) and Cyrus Vance's *Hard Choices: Critical Years in America's Foreign Policy* (1983) lend insight into the Carter approach to foreign policy. Background on how the Middle East came to dominate much of American policy is found in William B. Quandt's *Decade of Decisions: American Policy toward the Arab-Israeli Conflict, 1967–1976* (1977).

36 ⌒ A CONSERVATIVE
INSURGENCY

CHAPTER ORGANIZER

This chapter focuses on:

- the demographic, social, and economic reasons for the rise of Ronald Reagan and Republican conservatism.

- changing relations with the Soviet Union, including the end of the cold war.

- the economic and social aspects of the 1980s.

- the cause and aftermath of the Gulf War.

*P*resident Jimmy Carter and his embattled Democratic administration hobbled through 1979. The economy remained sluggish, double-digit inflation continued unabated, and failed efforts to free the American hostages in Iran made the administration appear indecisive. Carter's inability to mobilize the nation behind his ill-fated energy program revealed mortal flaws in his reading of the public mood and his understanding of legislative politics. In July 1979, a much ballyhooed presidential address to the nation aroused more criticism than support. Carter's claim that a "crisis of confidence" was paralyzing the nation and his insistence that the days of dramatic economic growth were over fell on deaf or indignant ears. As a Phoenix newspaper editorial declared, the nation did not want "sermons" from the president; it wanted "action."

While the lackluster Carter administration was foundering, Republican conservatives were forging a plan to win the White House in 1980 and to assault the "New Deal welfare state" mentality in Washington. Those plans centered on the popularity and charisma of Ronald Reagan, the Hollywood actor turned California governor and prominent political commentator. Reagan was not a deep thinker, but he was a superb analyst of the public mood, an unabashed patriot, and a committed advocate of conservative principles. He was also charming and cheerful, a likable politician renowned for his relentless anecdotes. Where the dour Carter denounced the evils of free enterprise capitalism and tried to scold Americans into reviving long-forgotten virtues of frugality, a sunny Reagan promised a "revolution of ideas" designed to unleash the capitalist spirit, restore national pride, and regain international respect.

During the late 1970s, Reagan's simple message promoting a grass-roots political revolution and a restoration of American pride and prosperity offered an uplifting alternative to Carter's strident moralism. More specifically, Reagan wanted to increase military spending, dismantle the "bloated" federal bureaucracy, reduce taxes and regulations, and in general, undo the welfare state. He also wanted to affirm old-time morality by ending abortions and reinstituting school prayer. Reagan's appeal derived from his remarkable skills as a public speaker and his dogmatic commitment to a few overarching ideas and simple themes. As a true believer and an able compromiser, he combined the fervor of a revolutionary with the pragmatism of a diplomat.

Such attributes won Reagan two presidential terms in 1980 and 1984 and ensured the election of his successor, George Bush, in 1988. Just how revolutionary the Reagan era was remains a subject of intense partisan debate. What cannot be denied, however, is that Reagan's actions and beliefs set the tone for the decade and continue to affect American political and economic life.

THE REAGAN REVOLUTION

THE MAKING OF A PRESIDENT   Ronald Reagan seemed at first a more remote presidential possibility than Carter, if longer in the public

President Ronald Reagan, "the Great Communicator."

eye as a screen and television personality. A small-town boy from Dixon, Illinois, Reagan became a radio sports announcer in Iowa after gradua- tion in 1932 from Eureka College. In 1937 he went west and wangled a screen test, the start of a movie career. As president of the Screen Ac- tors Guild, Reagan was at first a liberal and a New Dealer. But he bounced to the far right on the political spectrum during the 1950s. Re- pelled by Communist infiltrators in liberal groups, he said, "I was be- ginning to see the seamy side of liberalism." He campaigned for both Eisenhower (1952, 1956) and Nixon (1960), switched his registration to Republican in 1962, then achieved political stardom in 1964 when he delivered a rousing speech on national television on behalf of Barry Goldwater.

The Republican right had a new idol whose appeal survived the Goldwater debacle. Those who discounted Reagan as a minor actor and a mental midget underrated his many virtues, including the importance of his years in front of the camera. Politics had always been a perform- ing art, the more so in an age of television, and few, if any, others in public life had Reagan's stage presence. He had, moreover, a contagious zest for life and a genuine instinct for the witty one-liner. Drawn by wealthy admirers into the campaign for governor of California in 1966, Reagan moderated his rawest rhetoric, and won the governorship by a landslide.

Reagan appealed especially to middle-class and lower-middle-class voters resentful of "high" taxes, welfare programs for the dependent, the "neurotic vulgarities" of university students running wild, crime in the streets, and challenges to traditional values in general. In the forefront of the counterculture, California was in the forefront of reaction against it as well.

From the start of his gubernatorial term, Reagan had his eye on the presidency, but in the mid-1970s his rhetoric still seemed too extreme for the mainstream, and his "back-to-basics" speeches provoked barbed jokes from journalists: "Ronald Reagan wants to take us back to the fifties," wrote one reporter, "back to the 1950s in foreign policy and back to the 1850s in economic and domestic policy."

By the eve of the 1980 election, however, Reagan had become the beneficiary of a development that made his conservative vision of America more than a harmless flirtation with nostalgia. The 1980 census revealed that the elderly proportion of the nation's population was increasing and moving to the "Sunbelt" states of the South and West. This dual development—an increase in the numbers of senior citizens and the steady transfer of population to regions of the country where hostility to "big government" was endemic—meant that demographics were carrying the United States toward Reagan's political philosophy.

THE MORAL MAJORITY   Reagan's presidential aspirations also benefited from a major revival of evangelical religion, not unlike the Great Awakenings of the eighteenth and nineteenth centuries. No longer a local or provincial phenomenon that could be easily dismissed, Christian evangelicals now owned their own television and radio stations and operated their own schools and universities. A survey in 1977 revealed that more than 70 million Americans described themselves as born-again Christians who had a personal relationship with Jesus.

During the previous two decades, widely publicized Supreme Court decisions had stirred fundamentalist indignation and thus unwittingly helped arouse a political backlash. Among these were rulings for abortion, against prayer in public schools, for the right to teach Darwinism, and for narrower definitions of pornography.

The Reverend Jerry Falwell's "Moral Majority" (later the Liberty Lobby) expressed the sentiments of the religious right wing: the economy should operate without "interference" by the government, which should be reduced in size; the Supreme Court decision in *Roe* v. *Wade* (1973) legalizing abortion should be reversed; Darwinian evolution should be replaced in schoolbooks by the biblical story of creation; and Soviet expansion should be opposed as a form of pagan totalitarianism. "Our task is not to Christianize America," said Falwell, "but to bring about a moral and conservative revolution." By not focusing on divisive theological questions, he and others sought to use "traditional morality" to create an interdenominational political force drawing upon millions of evangelical Christians. The moralistic zeal and financial resources of the religious right made them formidable opponents of liberal political candidates and programs. By 1980 Falwell's Moral Majority organization claimed over 4 million members, including 72,000 ministers, priests, and rabbis. Its base of support was in the South and was strongest among Baptists, but its appeal extended across the country.

A curiosity of the 1980 campaign was that the religious right opposed Jimmy Carter, a self-professed born-again Christian, and supported Ronald Reagan, a man who was neither conspicuously pious nor even often in church. His divorce and remarriage, once an almost automatic disqualification for the presidency, got little mention. Nor did the fact that as governor he had signed one of the most permissive abortion laws in the country. That Ronald Reagan became the Messiah of the Religious Right, God's man for the hour, was a tribute both to the force of social issues and the candidate's political skills.

THE 1980 ELECTION   Reagan, who had lost a last-minute try for the Republican nomination in 1968 and had failed to wrest it from Gerald Ford in 1976, easily won the nomination in 1980. Reagan was an adept campaigner who presented a consistent message to the voters: Carter and the Democrats, he insisted, believed that the United States had entered an era of permanent limits on economic growth and personal initiative. On the contrary, he asserted, the Republicans believed that America's greatest economic accomplishments were just around the corner. Reagan pledged that his recovery plans would restore prosperity and public confidence. He used folksy maxims and jokes to punctuate his themes. For instance, at one campaign stop he quipped: "A recession is when your neighbor loses his job. A depression is when you lose yours. A recovery is when Jimmy Carter loses his."

On November 4, before the polls had closed on the West Coast, Carter conceded the election. Reagan won a bare majority (50.7 per-

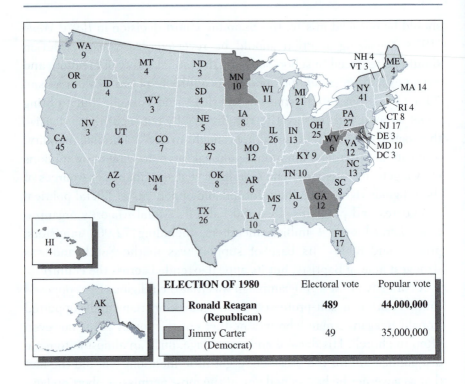

ELECTION OF 1980	Electoral vote	Popular vote
Ronald Reagan (Republican)	489	44,000,000
Jimmy Carter (Democrat)	49	35,000,000

cent) of the popular vote, but that was well ahead of Carter's 41 percent. John Anderson, a liberal Republican congressman running as an independent, got most of the rest. In the electoral college, Reagan's victory was overwhelming—489 to 49. Carter carried only six states and the District of Columbia.

More than a victory for the conservative policies Reagan championed, the election may have reflected the triumph of what one political scientist called the "largest mass movement of our time"—nonvoting. Almost as striking as Reagan's one-sided victory was the fact that his vote total represented only 28 percent of the potential electorate. Only 53 percent of eligible voters cast ballots in the 1980 election; in western European countries such as France and Germany, voter participation hovered at 85 percent in national elections during the 1970s.

Where had all the voters gone? Political analysts noted that most of the nonvoters were working-class Democrats in the major urban centers. Voter turnout was lowest in poor inner-city neighborhoods such as New York's Bedford-Stuyvesant district, which had a 19 percent voter participation rate. Turnout was highest, by contrast, in the affluent suburbs of large cities, areas where the Republican party was experiencing a dramatic surge in popularity. Such trends meant that American office-holders were being selected during the 1970s by an electorate increasingly dominated by middle- and upper-class voters.

Explanations for the high levels of voter apathy among working-class Americans vary. Some argue that they reflected the continuing sense of disillusionment with government itself, growing out of the Watergate affair. Another widespread perception influencing voting behavior was that the Democratic party had turned its back on its traditional blocs of support among common folk. Democratic leaders no longer spoke eloquently on behalf of those at the bottom of America's social scale. By embracing a fiscal conservatism indistinguishable from that of the Republicans, as Carter had done, Democrats lost their appeal among blue-collar workers and ghetto dwellers. And so the largest group of nonvoters in the 1980 election were former Democrats who had decided that neither party served their interests. When viewed in this light, Ronald Reagan's victory represented less a resounding victory for conservative Republicans than a self-inflicted defeat by a fractured Democratic party. But for the moment, at least, such results were masked by the Republicans' euphoric victory celebrations. Flush with a sense of power and destiny, Ronald Reagan headed toward Washington with a blueprint for dismantling the welfare state.

REAGAN'S FIRST TERM

REAGANOMICS   Reagan's inaugural address prescribed full-strength conservative medicine for the decade-long stagflation. "Government is not the solution to our problem," Reagan insisted; "government is the problem." Reagan credited Calvin Coolidge and his treasury secretary, Andrew Mellon, with demonstrating that by reducing taxes and easing government regulation of business, the elixir of free-market capitalism would revive the economy. Like his Republican predecessors of the 1920s, he wanted to unleash entrepreneurial energy as never before. By cutting taxes and domestic federal spending, he claimed, a surging economy would produce *more* government revenues that would help reduce the budget deficit. This "supply-side" economic program, soon dubbed "Reaganomics," derived from a group of economists who challenged the Keynesian doctrine that the problems of the economy were mainly on the demand side. Supply-siders contended, to the contrary, that these problems resulted from governmental intrusions into the marketplace and from excessive taxes that reduced incentives to work, save, and invest.

One of Reagan's first steps was to abandon price controls on oil; another was to call off the embargo on wheat exports to the Soviet Union. But the administration's energies focused on the tax reform plan advanced during the election campaign. Reagan had become entranced by the idea of the "Laffer curve," named for economist Arthur Laffer of the University of Southern California. Derived from the truism that neither a tax of 0 nor a tax of 100 percent would produce revenue, the theory held that somewhere in between these two extremes tax rates reached a point beyond which they began to reduce a person's incentive to seek more income.

For a while, during his first two months in office, Reagan's popularity declined in the polls and doubts arose that he could get his economic program through a Democratic House. Then on March 30, 1981, a tragic event, an attempted assassination, fortuitously boosted support of Reagan's program. The troubled young assailant, obsessed by the hope of impressing a movie actress, fired several shots as Reagan's party emerged from a speech in a Washington hotel. A bullet hit Reagan in the chest, another inflicted permanent brain damage on his press secretary, and other bullets wounded a policeman and a Secret Service agent. While recovering from his wound, Reagan aroused universal admiration for his courage and wit.

Reagan's economic program gained ground along with his physical recovery. Enough Democrats—sympathetic southern "boll weevils" or centrists and liberals frightened by his popularity—went along to pass it by overwhelming majorities. On August 4, 1981, Reagan signed the Economic Recovery Tax Act, which cut personal income taxes 25 percent across the board over thirty-three months, lowered the maximum rate from 70 to 50 percent for 1982, cut the capital gains tax from a 28 percent maximum to 20 percent, and offered a broad array of other tax concessions.

Reaganomics departed from the Coolidge record mainly in the mounting deficits of the 1980s and in their major cause—growing expenditures for the armed forces. While Republican administrations of the 1920s had steadily reduced the national debt by holding the line on government expenditures, the Republican administration of the 1980s built ever-larger deficits, debts larger than those under all its predecessors put together. To be sure, the congressional Democrats were even more reluctant to cut domestic spending. Most items other than defense were deemed politically inviolable. The biggest category in the projected $700 billion budget involved payments to individuals: Social Security checks, pension checks, reimbursements for Medicare and Medicaid services, veterans' checks, and welfare checks. About 48 cents of every dollar the government spent thus went to well-organized social groups capable of capturing attention in Congress.

BUDGET CUTS   Reagan staffers discovered that there was not enough waste and fraud to make the substantial budget cuts that had been so easily promised in the campaign. Along with the 1981 tax cuts went budget cuts of $35 billion, while defense spending in 1982 went up $12 billion. Despite Democratic opposition, budget cuts were aimed at educational programs, along with health, housing, urban aid, food stamps, school meals, the National Endowments for the Arts and Humanities, and the Corporation for Public Broadcasting. Synthetic fuel projects were completely canceled as oil imports continued to rise.

Amid his budget cutting, Reagan clarified his assault on the welfare state. He wanted to eliminate aid to those who could presumably help themselves through their own efforts. He promised to retain a "safety net" for the "truly needy" and not to eliminate all federal aid programs. This new approach targeted for aid only those who could not work because of disability or child care. This, in fact, had been the original purpose of New Deal welfare, but during the 1930s the government had provided WPA jobs for those able to work.

In 1981 the administration declared that support from the Aid for Dependent Children (AFDC) program should last only four months after one joined the working poor, and that every dollar earned should reduce one's welfare payments by that amount. As a consequence, more than 400,000 people lost AFDC coverage, many of whom also lost the benefits of Medicaid. The administration argued that the working poor would keep working despite the loss of AFDC-Medicaid, and studies confirmed this in many cases. Still, a determination to work proved costly. Many working mothers, however eager to be self-reliant, refused to penalize their children and returned to welfare full time.

While publicly proclaiming a great accomplishment in making such cuts in domestic spending, Reagan and his advisers knew privately that the figures were not adding up to those they had pledged. David Stockman, the whiz-kid head of the Office of Management and Budget, realized that the cuts in domestic spending were far short of what would be needed to balance the budget in four years as Reagan had promised. He pleaded with Reagan to cut back on new defense spending and to slow the proposed tax cuts. But the president refused. The result was a soaring budget deficit and the worst economic recession since the 1930s.

Wall Street, perversely fearful that a rising public debt would send interest rates up, responded to the most pro-business president in years with sagging bond and stock markets. A business slump and rising unemployment carried through most of 1982. Government economic policy was strangely out of sync, a combination of fiscal stimulus (tax cuts) and monetary restraint (interest rates kept high by an independent Federal Reserve to control inflation).

Aides persuaded the president that to reassure the public about deficits and the threat of inflation the government needed "revenue enhancements," a fine euphemism for tax increases. With Reagan lending support, Congress and the administration cobbled together the Tax Equity and Fiscal Responsibility Bill of 1982, which would raise an estimated $98 billion. Nonetheless, the economic slump persevered through November, with unemployment standing at 10.4 percent, and the Republicans experienced moderate losses in the midterm elections.

NEW PRIORITIES   Like Coolidge and Harding in the 1920s, Reagan named to government posts people who were less than sympathetic to the regulatory functions for which they were responsible. The most visible early example was Interior Secretary James Watt, who had a gift for provocative denunciations of environmentalists. A Colorado champion of the "Sagebrush Rebellion," which proposed to turn federal lands over to the states, he breezily proposed to encourage commercial development of public resources. He was finally forced out of office by the uproar over an offensive remark about affirmative action appointments.

From the start, the Reagan administration failed to comprehend potential conflicts of interest in offices of public trust and showed a dangerous insensitivity to borderline ethics and outright scandals that one pundit soon labeled the "sleaze factor." Yet the president himself remained so totally untouched by hints of impropriety that Reagan was tagged the "Teflon president," since the buck never stopped because the blame never stuck.

As in the 1920s, organized labor encountered severe setbacks during the Reagan years. Nearly half of all union members, entranced by Reagan's personality and showmanship, had voted for him against the advice of their leaders. Reagan's smashing electoral victories in 1980 and 1984 broke the political power of the AFL-CIO, a longtime pillar of support for the Democratic party. Reagan himself made much of being the only president to have headed a national union (the Screen Actors Guild), but his appointees to the National Labor Relations Board tended to favor management. In 1981, early in his term, Reagan fired members of the Professional Air Traffic Controllers who organized an illegal strike. Reagan's public criticism of unions reflected a general trend in public opinion. Although a record number of new jobs were created during the 1980s, union membership steadily dropped. In 1979 unions represented 24 percent of the workforce. By 1987 union membership was down to 17 percent, and in 1995 it reached 15.5 percent.

Reagan also went on the offensive against feminism. He cut welfare programs, which especially affected impoverished women and their children, and opposed the Equal Rights Amendment and abortion on demand, as well as the idea of requiring equal pay for jobs of comparable worth. Women critics were little mollified by his naming the first female justice to the Supreme Court, Sandra Day O'Connor. Polls consistently reported a "gender gap" in opinion on Reagan, who had less support among women than among men.

Blacks and other minorities shared with women aggravation at the administration's limited support for affirmative action programs in employment. In the administration itself the Civil Rights Commission reported in 1982 that only 8 percent of its appointments had gone to females and 8 percent to minorities, in contrast to 12 and 17 percent, respectively, under Carter. Because of the commission's criticisms, the president in 1983 fired three of its members and tried to fire two more.

Funds for civil rights enforcement were among those targeted for reduction, and the Equal Employment Opportunity Commission's staff was sharply reduced. The administration supported in the courts the action of its Internal Revenue Service in granting tax exemptions to fundamentalist schools that practiced racial segregation. On that it was overruled by the Supreme Court, 8 to 1.

THE DEFENSE BUILDUP   Reagan's conduct of foreign policy reflected his belief that world troubles stemmed mainly from Moscow. He also feared that Americans had overlearned the lessons of Vietnam and forgotten the lessons of Munich in 1938. At times, he insisted, the United States must use military force to protect its interests around the globe. As a consequence of these assumptions, he promoted a major buildup of nuclear and conventional weapons, to close the gap that he claimed had developed between Soviet and American forces.

In 1983 Reagan escalated the nuclear arms race by authorizing the Defense Department to develop a Strategic Defense Initiative (SDI). It involved a complex anti-missile defense system using super-secret laser and high-energy particles weapons to destroy enemy missiles in outer space well before they reached their targets. To Reagan its great appeal was the ability to destroy weapons rather than people, thereby freeing defense strategy from the concept of mutually assured destruction that had long governed Soviet and American attitudes toward nuclear war. Journalists quickly dubbed the program "Star Wars" in reference to the popular science fiction film. Despite skepticism among the media and many scientists that such a "foolproof" celestial defense system could be built, it forced the Soviets to launch an expensive research and development program of their own to keep pace. As a West German defense analyst commented, "I have never seen Soviets so emotional as they are over Star Wars."

Reagan borrowed the rhetoric of John Foster Dulles and the Kennedy inaugural to express American resolve in the face of "Communist aggression anywhere in the world." At his first news conference, he pronounced the Soviet rulers men who "reserved unto themselves the right to commit any crime, to lie, to cheat." Someday, however, the West would "transcend Communism," leaving it "a sad, bizarre chapter in human history whose last pages are even now being written." Few at the time realized how accurate his prediction would become.

THE AMERICAS   Reagan's foremost international concern was in Central America. In 1981 an endemic guerrilla war in El Salvador intensified. Reagan's State Department believed it was a textbook case of indirect Soviet aggression. Many of the weapons reaching the Salvadoran rebels were American arms earlier seized in Vietnam and Ethiopia. The administration abandoned Jimmy Carter's efforts to promote a

"Shhhh. It's top secret." *A comment on Reagan administration covert operations in Nicaragua.*

compromise and sent in more arms and advisers to help the government of President José Napoleón Duarte defeat the rebels. The fighting persisted on through the 1980s, but after elections in 1982 showed heavy turnouts in support of moderate candidates, Duarte's government gained a tenuous stability, but one still threatened from both the left and right.

Reagan also confronted trouble in Nicaragua. Carter had believed that a rebel victory over the corrupt regime of dictator Anastasio Somoza in Nicaragua was inevitable, even though Cuban-sponsored "Sandinistas" were part of the rebel National Liberation Front (FSLN). He argued that America should help democratic elements in the Front. Nonetheless, when the Somoza government fell, it was the Sandinistas who gradually emerged as the dominant power in the new government.

The Reagan State Department claimed that the Sandinista government in Nicaragua was funneling Soviet and Cuban arms to Salvadoran rebels. In response, the administration set the CIA and the American ambassador in Honduras to mobilizing guerrilla bands of disgruntled Nicaraguans, soon tagged "Contras." The administration's hidden agenda, it soon became clear, was not only to prevent arms from reaching the rebels in El Salvador but to overthrow the Sandinistas, to make them "cry uncle," in Reagan's words.

Fearing a military tinderbox in Central America, neighboring countries pressed for a negotiated settlement. Representatives of Mexico, Panama, Colombia, and Venezuela began the Contadora Process (after the Panamanian island where they first met). By late 1983, the Contadora countries had advanced the first of many proposals for a compromise peace, the withdrawal of foreign advisers, and an end to imports of foreign arms. Drawn into the talks, the Reagan administration raised so many technical objections as to suggest that it would settle for nothing less than an overthrow of the Sandinistas.

THE MIDDLE EAST   In the Middle East, no peaceable end seemed possible for the prolonged, bloody Iran-Iraq war, entangled as it was with the passions of Islamic fundamentalism. In 1984 both sides began to attack tankers in the Persian Gulf, a major source of the world's oil. (The main international response was the sale of arms to both sides.) Nor was any settlement in sight for Afghanistan, where the Soviets had bogged down as badly as the Americans had in Vietnam.

American governments continued to see Israel as the strongest and most reliable ally in the region, all the while seeking to encourage moderate Arab groups. But the forces of moderation were dealt a blow during the mid-1970s when Lebanon, long an enclave of peace despite its ethnic complexity, collapsed into an anarchy of warring groups. The capital, Beirut, became a battleground for Sunni and Shi'ite Muslims, the Druze, the Palestine Liberation Organization (PLO), Arab Christians, Syrian invaders cast as peacekeepers, and Israelis responding to PLO attacks across the border.

In 1982 Israeli forces pushed the PLO out of southern Lebanon all the way north to Beirut and then the Israelis began heavy shelling of PLO strongholds in Beirut. The United States neither endorsed nor condemned the invasion, but sent a special ambassador to negotiate a settlement. Israeli troops moved into Beirut and looked the other way when Christian militiamen slaughtered Muslim women and children in Palestinian refugee camps. French, Italian, and American forces then moved into Lebanon as "peacekeepers," but in such small numbers as to become only targets. Angry Muslims kept them under constant harassment. American warships and planes responded by shelling and bombing Muslim positions in the highlands behind Beirut, which only increased Muslim resentment. On October 23, 1983, an Islamic suicide bomber drove a truck laden with explosives into the U.S. Marine headquarters at Beirut airport; the explosion left 241 Americans dead. Reagan declared that a continued American presence was "central to our credibility," but soon began preparations to pull out. In early 1984, he announced that the marines would be "redeployed" to warships offshore. The Israelis pulled back to southern Lebanon, while the Syrians remained in eastern Lebanon. And bloody anarchy remained a way of life in a formerly peaceful country.

GRENADA   Fortune, as it happened, presented Reagan the chance for an easy triumph closer to home, a "rescue mission" that eclipsed news of the debacle in Lebanon. On the tiny island of Grenada, the smallest independent country in the Western Hemisphere, a leftist government had admitted Cuban workers to build a new airfield and signed military agreements with Communist countries. In 1983 an even more radical military council seized power.

Appeals from the governments of neighboring islands led Reagan to order 1,900 marines to invade the island, depose the new government, and evacuate a small group of American students at Grenada's medical school. The U.N. General Assembly condemned the action, and many Latin Americans saw it as a revival of gunboat diplomacy, but it was popular among Grenadans and their neighbors, and immensely popular in the United States. Although a lopsided affair, the action made Reagan look decisive, and served notice on Latin American revolutionaries to beware of American force.

REAGAN'S SECOND TERM

By 1983, prosperity had returned, and the Reagan economic program seemed to be working as touted. Contradictory policies of fiscal stimulus (tax cuts and heavy expenditures for defense) and monetary restraint (high interest rates) brought at least in the short run an economic recovery without inflation. The gradual unraveling of the OPEC cartel and resultant decline in oil prices was the greatest stroke of luck for Reagan and the economy.

THE ELECTION OF 1984 Republican strategy for the presidential election worked on the old principle that if you have a good thing, you should stick with it. By contrast, the nominee of the Democrats, former vice-president Walter Mondale, never quite got his act together. Endorsed by the AFL-CIO, the National Organization for Women, and many blacks despite a serious challenge from Jesse Jackson, Mondale was tagged the candidate of the "special interests." He set a precedent by choosing as his running mate New York representative Geraldine Ferraro. Unhappily for the Democratic campaign, she was quickly placed on the defensive by the need to explain her spouse's complicated finances, something no male candidate had been called upon to do. One politician observed that "the pioneers take all the arrows."

A fit of frankness in his acceptance speech further complicated Mondale's campaign. "Mr. Reagan will raise taxes, and so will I," he told the convention. "He won't tell you. I just did." Remembered as a political blunder, it was a brilliant opportunity missed. Mondale seemed unaware that just the previous day, while attention was focused on the Democratic convention, Reagan had quietly signed a bill that raised taxes $50 billion, the Deficit Reduction Act of 1984. Nor did he mention that Reagan had signed tax increases in each of the two previous years. Reagan responded by vowing never to approve a tax increase, and by chiding Mondale for his candid stand. Mondale never caught up. In the end, Reagan took 59 percent of the popular vote and lost only Minnesota and the District of Columbia. His coattails were not as strong, however. Republicans had a net gain of only fifteen seats in the House, and lost two in the Senate. Entering his second term, Reagan faced several political time bombs ticking away. They were planted around the world from Nicaragua to Afghanistan.

DOMESTIC CHALLENGES Although Reagan had won an overwhelming victory, domestic problems that he had tried to ignore demanded his attention and shook his complacency. Episodes of borderline ethics and outright scandals that had emerged during his first term could not be ignored forever. Strains seemed bound to arise as well in a political coalition of the indulgent rich and the ultra-righteous.

Still, for a while, the Reagan luck held out. OPEC continued to lower oil prices, sending inflation down and the stock market up. In his State of the Union message, Reagan called for "a Second American

Revolution of hope and opportunity." He dared Congress to raise taxes. His veto pen was ready: "Go ahead and make my day," he said in echo of a movie line.

Through much of 1985 the president drummed up support for a tax simplification plan to eliminate loopholes and set only two or three brackets. It was a retreat from the principle of a progressive tax, which levied higher rates on high incomes, but that principle had long since been eroded by a variety of complex tax dodges within the reach mainly of the rich.

After vigorous debate that ran nearly two years, Congress passed, and in 1986 the president finally signed, a comprehensive Tax Reform Act. The new measure would reduce the number of tax brackets from fourteen to two and reduce rates from the maximum of 50 percent to 15 and 28 percent—the lowest since Coolidge. Tax shelters were also sharply limited. Economists were cautious about predicting the effects of the tax "simplification." One pundit noted that the "simplified" tax law remained a good bit longer than the Constitution and a good bit harder to understand.

ARMS CONTROL   Meanwhile Reagan, for all his bluff talk about the Soviet Union being an "evil empire," seemed unwilling to be the first president since World War II to arrive at no agreement on arms with the Soviets. In 1985, for the first time in six years, an American president met with the leader of the Soviet Union. After much preliminary maneuvering, Reagan and Mikhail Gorbachev, the recently elected Soviet president, met in Geneva on November 19 for a series of talks. They soon signed six agreements on cultural and scientific exchanges and other matters. They also issued statements, but reached no agreements, on arms limitations.

Nearly a year later, on sudden notice and with limited preparation, Gorbachev and Reagan met in Reykjavik, Iceland, for two days. Reagan subsequently said that the United States put forward the "most sweeping and generous arms-control proposal in history," but the talks collapsed over disagreement about Reagan's SDI.

THE IRAN-CONTRA AFFAIR   The year 1986 opened with a terrible tragedy when the space shuttle *Challenger* exploded minutes after liftoff, killing its seven crew members, including a teacher. Then came

Soviet premier Mikhail Gorbachev (left) *and U.S. president Ronald Reagan* (right) *during a light moment at the Geneva summit, November 1985.*

a double blow to Reagan's agenda on November 4, 1986. In the midterm elections the Senate went from a Republican majority of 53 to 47 to Democratic control by 55 to 45. Senators elected in 1980 on Reagan's coattails lacked that advantage this time. All seven Senate races in the South went to Democrats. Farm problems in the Midwest damaged Republicans there. The Democrats picked up only six seats in the House, but they increased their already comfortable margin there to 259 to 176. For his last two years as president Reagan would face an opposition Congress.

What was worse, on election day one of the administration's political time bombs went off. Reports arrived from an obscure publication in Beirut that the United States had been secretly selling arms to Iran in hopes of securing the release of American hostages held in Lebanon by extremist groups sympathetic to Iran. Such actions contradicted Reagan's repeated public insistence that his administration would never negotiate with terrorists. The disclosures angered America's allies as well as many Americans who vividly remembered the 1979 Iranian takeover of their country's embassy in Teheran.

There was even more to the sordid story. Over the next several months, a series of revelations reminiscent of the Watergate affair disclosed a more complicated and even more incredible series of covert activities carried out by administration officials. At the center of the Iran-Contra affair was the much-decorated Marine lieutenant-colonel Oliver North. A swashbuckling aide to the National Security Council who specialized in counterterrorism, North had been running secret operations from the basement of the White House involving many governmental, private, and foreign individuals. His most farfetched scheme sought to use the profits gained from the secret sale of military hardware to Iran to subsidize the Contra rebels fighting in Nicaragua, at a time when Congress had voted to ban such aid.

North's activities, it turned out, had been approved by National Security Adviser Robert McFarlane, his successor Admiral John Poindexter, and CIA Director William Casey. Secretary of State George Shultz and Secretary of Defense Caspar Weinberger both criticized the arms sale to Iran, but their objections were ignored, and they were thereafter kept in the dark about what was going on. Later, on three occasions, Shultz threatened to resign over the continuing operation of the "pathetic" scheme. As information about the secret (and illegal) dealings surfaced in the press, McFarlane attempted suicide, Poindexter resigned, North was fired, and Casey, who denied any connection, left the CIA for health reasons. Casey died shortly thereafter from a brain tumor.

The White House, meanwhile, assumed a siege mentality as the president's popularity plummeted. Worse was yet to come. During the spring and summer of 1987, a joint House-Senate investigating committee began holding televised hearings into the Iran-Contra affair. The sessions dominated public attention for months and revealed a tangled web of inept financial and diplomatic transactions, the shredding of incriminating government documents, crass profiteering, and misguided patriotism.

The investigations of the independent counsel led to six indictments in 1988. A Washington jury found Oliver North guilty of three relatively minor charges but innocent of nine more serious counts, apparently reflecting the jury's reasoning that he acted as an agent of higher-ups. His conviction was later overturned on appeal. Of those involved in the affair, only John Poindexter got a jail sentence—six months for his conviction on five felony counts of obstructing justice and lying to Congress.

CENTRAL AMERICA   The Iran-Contra affair showed the lengths to which members of the Reagan administration would go to support the rebels fighting the ruling Sandinistas in Nicaragua. Fearing heightened Soviet and American involvement in Central America, neighboring countries pressed during the mid-1980s for a negotiated settlement to the unrest in Nicaragua. In 1988 Daniel Ortega, the Nicaraguan president, pledged to negotiate directly with the Contra rebels. In the spring of 1988 these negotiations produced a cease-fire agreement, ending nearly seven years of fighting in Nicaragua. Secretary of State George Shultz called the pact an "important step forward," but the settlement surprised and disappointed hardliners within the Reagan administration who saw in it a Contra surrender. The Contra leaders themselves, aware of the eroding support for their cause in the United States Congress, saw the truce as their only chance for tangible concessions such as amnesty for political prisoners, the return of the Contras from exile, and "unrestricted freedom of expression."

Meanwhile, in neighboring El Salvador, the Reagan administration's attempt to shore up the centrist government of José Napoleón Duarte through economic and military aid suffered a body blow when the far-right ARENA party scored an upset victory at the polls during the spring of 1988.

LEVERAGED BUYOUTS AND S&L'S   Throughout the 1980s, social commentators repeatedly bemoaned the virus of greed and self-absorbed materialism that seemed to infect the nation. One prominent symptom was the largest outbreak of corporate mergers and acquisitions ever. Hijacking corporations was nothing new, but by the mid-1980s an innovative technique had come into play: using the value of the company itself as a means of taking it over. The corporate "raiders" would buy out the target company's public stockholders with borrowed money, to be repaid from the future earnings of the company. They then used its value to underwrite voluminous "junk bonds"—speculative issues that drew investors into risky investments with the promise of very high returns. Given this magic act, no company was out of reach now, no matter how big.

The charm of the device was that the takeover targets got stuck with the debts, while stockholders could bail out at handsome prices driven up by the acquisition. Commonly, the company was then broken up and sold piece by piece on the principle that components could be sold off separately for more than the whole. A character in a popular movie of 1990 likened the process to stealing cars and selling the parts.

These shenanigans were not unusual during the 1980s. Other financial buccaneers pursued quick profits within the "thrift institutions"— the savings and loan banks (S&L's) designed at first to serve aspiring homeowners. In 1982 Congress permitted S&L's to invest up to 40 percent of their assets in nonresidential real estate. High-rise office buildings began to clutter the landscape. California, not to be outdone, then permitted state-chartered S&L's to invest 100 percent of their assets in any venture, and other states followed suit. From a conservative industry designed to encourage homeowning, many of the S&L's became major customers for junk bonds, among other risky ventures.

The opportunities for outrageous profits, with regulators and Congress reducing capital reserve requirements and looking the other way, brought hustlers flocking into the business, often with borrowed capital. Vernon Savings and Loan, which served a town of 12,000 in Texas, at one time kept a fleet of six jets; company funds also bought expensive homes for its head and provided $5.5 million to decorate the walls.

DEBT AND THE PLUNGE IN THE STOCK MARKET The getting and spending of more money seemed to become the pervasive concern throughout the 1980s. Debt, all kinds of debt—personal, corporate, and governmental—increased dramatically during the decade. Whereas in the 1960s Americans on average saved 10 percent of their income, in 1987 the figure was less than 4 percent. The Reagan budget deficits also reached record levels as legislators reluctant to offend constituents by raising taxes or cutting popular programs engaged in talk and symbolic action with a president ideologically resistant to taxes. The federal debt more than tripled from $908 billion in 1980 to $2.9 trillion at the end of the 1989 fiscal year.

Then, on October 19, 1987, the bill collector suddenly arrived at the nation's doorstep. On that "Black Monday," the stock market, already buffeted by sharp declines the previous week, experienced a tidal wave of selling reminiscent of the 1929 crash. The Dow Jones industrial average plummeted 508 points, or an astounding 22.6 percent. The market plunge nearly doubled the record 12.8 percent fall on October 28, 1929. Almost $560 billion in paper value disappeared, an amount larger than the gross national product of France. With cyclonic suddenness, the nation's financial mood went from boom to gloom during the fall of 1987. Wall Street's selling frenzy reverberated throughout the capitalist world, sending stock prices plummeting in Tokyo, London, Paris, and Toronto.

What caused the goring of the bull market? Some analysts argued that the runaway market of the 1980s had become artifically high, driven by excessive greed and hope rather than by the economy's actual performance. Others blamed new computerized trading programs that distorted market activity. But most agreed that the fundamental problem was the nation's spiraling indebtedness and chronically high trade deficits. Americans were consuming more than they were producing, importing the difference, and paying for imported goods with borrowed money and dollars whose value had sharply declined. Foreign investors had lost confidence in Reaganomics and were no longer willing to finance America's spending binge.

In the aftermath of the calamitous selling spree on Black Monday, President Reagan insisted that the "underlying economy remains sound," an unsettling echo of Herbert Hoover's equally sunny assurances in 1929. Few observers actually feared a depression of the magnitude of the 1930s; there were too many safeguards built into the system to allow that. But there was real concern of an impending recession, and this led business leaders and economists to attack the president for glossing over such a profound warning signal. Within a few weeks, Reagan agreed to work with Congress in developing a deficit reduction package, and for the first time indicated that he was willing to include increased taxes in such a package. But the eventual compromise plan was so modest that it did little to restore investor confidence. As one Republican senator lamented, "There is a total lack of courage among those of us in the Congress to do what we all know has to be done."

THE POOR, THE HOMELESS, AND AIDS VICTIMS   Against the picture that the president's supporters envisioned of roaring prosperity,

Despite the nation's prosperity and some efforts to build low-cost housing, the number of homeless people continued to increase during the 1980s.

burgeoning new technology, and 19 million new jobs in the Reagan years could be set the picture of uncounted beggars in the streets and homeless people sleeping in doorways, in cardboard boxes, and on heat grates—street scenes once associated with Calcutta. A variety of causes could be adduced for the shortage of low-cost housing: government had given up on building public housing; with the best of intentions, urban renewal had demolished blighted areas but provided no housing for the displaced; and owners had abandoned unprofitable buildings in poor neighborhoods or converted them into expensive condominiums. The last was called "gentrification." Other causes of homelessness included family disorganization, and the deinstitutionalization of the mentally ill thanks to new medications for treatment and based on the promise of community mental health services that failed to materialize—a program started under President Kennedy but never adequately funded. By the summer of 1988, the *New York Times* estimated, more than 45 percent of the city's adult residents constituted an underclass totally outside the labor force for lack of skills, lack of motivation, drug use, and other problems.

Still another group cast aside were those suffering from a strange new malady known as AIDS (acquired immune deficiency syndrome). At the beginning of the decade, public health officials had begun to re-

A quilt commemorating the deaths of many thousands of Americans from AIDS, is stretched out and displayed before the White House in October 1988, so that friends and family can walk amidst the entire quilt and view the various sections up close.

port that gay men and intravenous drug users were especially at risk for this syndrome. Those infected with AIDS showed signs of fatigue, developed a strange combination of infections, and eventually died. Researchers struggled to discern the origins of the new malady. Eventually they linked it to a virus (HIV) originating in Africa and spread from there to Europe and America. People contracted it by coming into contact with the blood or body fluids of an infected person. One reason the Reagan administration showed little interest in AIDS was that it initially was viewed as a "gay" disease. Patrick Buchanan, the conservative spokesman who served as White House director of communications, said that homosexuals had "declared war on nature, and now nature is extracting an awful retribution."

By 1998, however, AIDS had claimed over 270,000 American lives and was spreading among the larger population. Nearly a million Americans were estimated to be carrying the deadly HIV virus, and it had become the leading cause of death among men aged twenty-five to forty-four. The potential for exponential spread of HIV, owing to the very long incubation period before the onset of symptoms, provoked the surgeon general to launch a controversial public education program that included encouraging "safe sex" through the use of condoms. With no prospect for an early cure and with skyrocketing treatment costs,

AIDS emerged as one of the nation's most horrifying and intractable problems.

A HISTORIC TREATY   In the midst of a weak, unpredictable economic situation, the main prospect for positive achievement before the end of Reagan's second term seemed to lie in arms-reduction agreements with the Soviet government. Under Mikhail Gorbachev, the Soviets pursued renewed détente in order to free their energies and financial resources to address pressing domestic problems. The logjam that had impeded arms negotiations since the summit at Reykjavik suddenly broke in 1987, when Gorbachev announced that he was willing to deal separately on a medium-range missile treaty. After nine more months of strenuous, highly technical negotiations, Reagan and Gorbachev met amid much fanfare in Washington on December 9, 1987, and signed a treaty to eliminate intermediate-range (300–3,000 miles) nuclear forces (INF).

It was an epochal event, not only because it marked the first time that the two nations had agreed to destroy a whole class of weapons systems, but because it represented a key first step toward the eventual end of the arms race altogether. Under the terms of the treaty, the United States would destroy 859 missiles, and the Soviets would eliminate 1,752. On-site inspections by each side would verify compliance. Still, this winnowing would represent only 4 percent of the total nuclear missile count on both sides. Arms-control advocates thus looked toward a second and more comprehensive treaty dealing with long-range strategic missiles.

Gorbachev's successful efforts to liberalize Soviet domestic life and improve East-West foreign relations cheered Americans. The Soviets suddenly began stressing cooperation with the West in dealing with "hot spots" around the world. They urged the Palestine Liberation Organization to recognize Israel's right to exist and advocated a greater role for the U.N. in the volatile Persian Gulf. Perhaps the most dramatic symbol of a thawing cold war was the phased withdrawal of 115,000 Soviet troops from Afghanistan, which began in 1988.

THE REAGAN LEGACY   Historians are just beginning to assess the legacy of the nation's fortieth president. Although Reagan had declared in 1981 his intention to "curb the size and influence of the federal establishment," the New Deal welfare state remained intact when Reagan left office. Neither the Social Security system nor Medicare nor other major welfare programs were dismantled or overhauled. And the federal agencies that Reagan threatened to abolish, such as the Department of Education, not only remained in place in 1989, their budgets grew. The federal budget as a percentage of the gross domestic product (GDP) was actually higher when Reagan left office than when he had entered. Moreover, he did not try to push through Congress the incendiary social issues championed by the religious right such as school prayer and a ban on abortions.

Yet Ronald Reagan nonetheless succeeded in redefining the national political agenda and accelerated the conservative insurgency that had been developing for over twenty years. His greatest successes were in renewing America's soaring sense of possibilities, bringing inflation under control and stimulating the longest sustained period of peacetime prosperity in history, and negotiating the nuclear disarmament treaty and helping to light the fuse of democratic freedom in eastern Europe. By redirecting the thrust of both domestic and foreign policy, he put the Democratic party on the defensive and forced conventional New Deal "liberalism" into a panicked retreat. The fact that Reagan's tax policies widened the gap between the rich and poor and created huge budget deficits for future presidents to confront did not diminish the popularity of the "Great Communicator."

THE 1988 ELECTION In 1988 a gaggle of eight Democratic presidential candidates entered a wild scramble for their party's nomination. As the primary season progressed, however, it soon became a two-man race between Massachusetts governor Michael Dukakis and Jesse Jackson, the charismatic black civil rights activist who had been one of Martin Luther King, Jr.'s chief lieutenants. Dukakis eventually won out and managed a difficult reconciliation with the Jackson forces that left the Democrats unified and confident as the fall campaign began.

The Republicans nominated Reagan's two-term vice-president, George Bush, who after a bumpy start had easily cast aside his rivals in the primaries. As Reagan's handpicked heir, Bush claimed credit for the administration's successes, but like all dutiful vice-presidents, he also faced the challenge of asserting his own political identity. Although a veteran government official, having served as a Texas congressman, en-

George Bush (right) *at the 1988 Republican National Convention with his newly chosen running mate, Dan Quayle, a former senator from Indiana.*

voy to China, ambassador to the U.N., and head of the CIA, Bush projected none of Reagan's charisma or rhetorical skills. Cartoonists caricatured the patrician vice-president, the son of a rich Connecticut senator, schooled at Andover and Yale, as a well-heeled "wimp," and one Democrat described him as a man born "with a silver foot in his mouth." Early polls showed Dukakis with a surprisingly wide lead.

Yet Bush, a genuinely decent and honorable man with a distinguished record of heroism in World War II, delivered a surprisingly forceful convention address that sharply enhanced his stature. Although pledging to continue the Reagan agenda, he also recognized that "things aren't perfect" in America, an admission his boss rarely acknowledged. Bush promised to use the White House to fight bigotry, illiteracy, and homelessness. Humane sympathies, he insisted, would guide his conservatism. "I want a kinder, gentler nation," Bush said softly in his acceptance speech. But the most memorable line was a defiant statement on taxes: "Congress will push me to raise taxes, and I'll say no, and they'll push, and I'll say no, and they'll push again. And all I can say to them is, read my lips: *no new taxes.*"

In a campaign given over to mudslinging, Bush and his aides fastened on an effective strategy: they attacked Dukakis as a camouflaged liberal in the mold of McGovern, Carter, and Mondale. The Republican on-

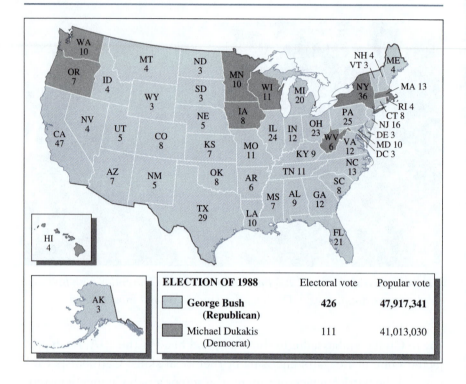

ELECTION OF 1988	Electoral vote	Popular vote
George Bush (Republican)	426	47,917,341
Michael Dukakis (Democrat)	111	41,013,030

slaught took its toll against the less organized, less focused Dukakis campaign. In the end, Dukakis took only ten states plus the District of Columbia, with clusters in the Northeast, Midwest, and Northwest. Bush carried the rest, with a margin of about 54 percent to 46 percent in the popular vote and 426 to 111 in the electoral college.

Generally speaking, the more affluent and better-educated voters preferred the Republican ticket. While Dukakis won the inner-city vote, garnering 86 percent of the black vote, Bush scored big in the sub-urbs and in rural areas, especially in the once-Democratic South, where his margins of white voters ranged from a low of 63 percent in Florida to a high of 80 percent in Mississippi. More significant was Bush's success among blue-collar workers. He captured 46 percent of these typically Democratic voters.

Hidden among the election returns was a long-term trend that did not bode well for the American political system: voter turnout continued to decline. In the 1988 election, only 50 percent of the voting-age population cast ballots, the lowest in any presidential election since

Calvin Coolidge defeated Democrat John W. Davis in 1924. The most important third party emerging in national politics were those so disengaged from the process that they did not vote at all. Voting was highest among affluent whites (52 percent), while 46 percent of eligible blacks and only 23 percent of eligible Hispanics turned out. But the most alarming statistic was that two-fifths of all the nonvoters were under thirty years of age. Apparently, many young adults no longer viewed the political process as significant enough to participate in.

THE BUSH YEARS

George Bush viewed himself as a guardian president rather than an activist. Lacking Reagan's visionary outlook and his skill as a speaker, Bush was a prudent patrician, a pragmatist caretaker eager to avoid "stupid mistakes" and to find a way to get along with the Democratic majority in Congress. "We don't need to remake society," he announced. As a consequence, Bush sought to consolidate and nurture the programs that Reagan had put in place rather than launch his own array of new programs and policies.

DOMESTIC INITIATIVES The Reagan administration left some issues that demanded immediate attention from the Bush White House. In 1989 Bush tackled the most pressing of these, the savings and loan crisis, with a rescue plan to close or sell ailing thrifts and bail out the depositors. Congress consolidated the insurance fund for savings and loan deposits with the fund covering banks, the Federal Deposit Insurance Corporation (FDIC). A new agency, the Resolution Trust Corporation (RTC), was created to sell off failed thrifts—or at least their assets. At the time, the cost to taxpayers of the bailout was put at $300 billion over thirty years, although in 1990 the General Accounting Office estimated the cost at $500 billion.

The biggest hangover from the binge years of the 1980s was the national debt, which stood at $2.6 trillion by the time Bush was elected, nearly three times its 1980 level. Bush's taboo on tax increases (meaning, mainly, income taxes) and his insistence upon lowering capital gains taxes—on profits from the sales of stocks and other property—made it more difficult to reduce the annual deficit or trim the long-term debt. By 1990 the country faced "a fiscal mess." Bipartisan budget talks between administration and congressional leaders spawned "rancorous partisanship [and] deep divisions within the two parties." Eventually, Bush decided "that both the size of the deficit problem and the need for a package that can be enacted" required a number of measures, including "tax revenue increases." Then he claimed that the Democrats had forced him to accept such language, a message that did not convey strong leadership. These elaborate partisan dances continued through the summer, until a budget plan was announced in September 1990. Through a combination of tax hikes and spending cuts, the measure promised to reduce the budget deficit by $43 billion in 1991 and by $331 billion in 1991–1995.

Another domestic initiative was Bush's war on drugs. During the 1980s, cocaine addiction spread through sizable segments of American society, luring those with money to spend and—in its smokable form, known as crack—those with little money to spare. Bush vowed to make drug abuse his number-one domestic priority, and appointed William J. Bennett, former education secretary, as "drug czar," or head of a new Office of National Drug Control Policy, with cabinet status but no department. Total outlays in the war on drugs would amount to $8 billion in fiscal 1990, although only $716 million represented new spending. The message, on this and on education, housing, and other social problems, was that more of the burden should fall on state and local authorities.

THE DEMOCRACY MOVEMENT ABROAD Bush entered the White House with more foreign policy experience than most presidents, and he found the spotlight of the world stage more congenial than wrestling with the intractable problems of the inner cities, drug abuse, or the deficit. Within two years of his inauguration, George Bush would lead the United States into two wars, a record unequaled by any of his predecessors. Throughout most of 1989, however, he merely had to sit back and observe the dissolution of one totalitarian or authoritarian regime after another. For the first time in years, democracy was suddenly on the march in a sequence of mostly bloodless revolutions that surprised most of the world.

Although a suddenly risen democracy movement in China came to a tragic end in 1989 when government forces mounted a deadly assault on demonstrators in Beijing's (Peking's) Tiananmen Square, eastern Europe had an entirely different experience. With a rigid economic system failing to deliver the goods to the Soviet peoples, Mikhail Gorbachev responded with policies of "perestroika" (restructuring) and "glasnost" (openness), a loosening of central economic planning and censorship. His foreign policy sought rapprochement and trade with the West, and to relieve the Soviet economy of burdensome military costs.

Gorbachev also backed off from Soviet imperial ambitions. Early in 1989, Soviet troops left Afghanistan, after nine years of being bogged down in civil war there. Gorbachev then repudiated the "Brezhnev doctrine," which had asserted the right of the Soviet Union to intervene in the internal affairs of Communist countries. The days when Soviet tanks rolled through Warsaw and Prague were over, and hardline leaders in the East-bloc countries found themselves beset by demands for reform from their own peoples. With opposition strength building, the old regimes fell in rapid order, and with surprisingly little bloodshed. Communist party rule ended first in Poland and Hungary, then in hardline Czechoslovakia and in Bulgaria. In Romania, the year of peaceful revolution ended in a bloodbath when the Romanian people joined the army in a bloody uprising against the brutal dictator Nicolae Ceausescu. He and his wife were captured, tried, and then executed on Christmas Day. But lacking experienced opposition leaders, as did all the eastern European countries, the new government fell under the control of members of the old Communist establishment.

The most spectacular event in the collapse of the Soviet empire in eastern Europe came on November 9, when the chief symbol of the cold war—the Berlin Wall—was torn down by Germans using small tools and even their hands. With the borders to the West now fully open, the Communist government of East Germany collapsed, a freely elected government came to power, and on October 3, 1990, the five states of East Germany were united with those of West Germany. The unified German nation remained in NATO, and the Warsaw Pact alliance was dissolved.

The democratic movement also reached other parts of the world. During 1990, the Communist party of Mongolia—strategically located on the borders of the Soviet Union and China—voted to give up its monopoly on power, and in Nicaragua, where the ruling Sandinista party avowed Marxism, President Daniel Ortega was defeated in a presidential

West Germans hacking away at the Berlin Wall on November 11, 1989, two days after all crossings between East and West Germany were opened.

election in February. Even in isolated Albania, the ruling party yielded to demands for an election in 1991.

Democratic change overtook authoritarian regimes of a different stripe as well. In Chile, Augusto Pinochet, who had become military dictator in a bloody coup in 1973, yielded to a popular vote in 1988 against his remaining in office, and was defeated in presidential elections the following year. And in South Africa, to which the U.S. Congress had applied trade sanctions in protest of its apartheid (racial segregation) policies since 1986, a new prime minister, Frederik W. DeKlerk, came to office in 1989, released black nationalist Nelson Mandela from twenty-seven years in prison, and announced plans to abandon apartheid gradually.

The reform impulse that Gorbachev helped unleash in the East-bloc countries began to career out of control within the Soviet Union itself. Gorbachev proved unusually adept at political restructuring, yielding the Communist monopoly of government but building a new presidential system that gave him, if anything, increased powers. His skills in the Byzantine politics of the Kremlin, though, did not extend to an antiquated economy that resisted change. The revival of old ethnic allegiances added to the instability. Although Russia proper included slightly over half the Soviet Union's population, it was only one of fifteen constituent republics, most of which began to seek autonomy, if not independence. Along the fringes of the Russian republic, to the west and south, lay a jigsaw puzzle of about a hundred nationalities and languages.

Gorbachev's popularity shrank in the Soviet Union as it grew abroad. It especially eroded among the Communist hardliners, who saw in his reforms the unraveling of their bureaucratic and political empire. Once the genie of freedom was released from the Communist lamp, however, it took on a momentum of its own. On August 18, 1991, a cabal of political and military leaders suddenly tried to seize the reins of power. They accosted Gorbachev at his vacation retreat in the Crimea and demanded that he sign a decree proclaiming a state of emergency and transferring his powers to them. He replied: "Go to hell," whereupon he was placed under house arrest.

The coup, however, was doomed from the start. Poorly planned and clumsily implemented, it lacked effective coordination. The plotters failed to arrest popular leaders such as Boris Yeltsin, the populist president of the Russian republic, they neglected to close the airports or cut off telephone and television communications, and they were opposed by key elements of the military and KGB (secret police). But most important, the plotters failed to recognize the strength of the democratic idealism unleashed by Gorbachev's reforms. Upon learning of the attempted overthrow, tens of thousands of Muscovites poured into the streets outside Yeltsin's headquarters to act as human shields against efforts to arrest him. Three were killed in the process. Yeltsin himself clambered atop a menacing tank and publicly defied the conspirators, calling them a "gang of bandits."

As the drama unfolded in the Soviet Union, a crescendo of indignation welled up from foreign leaders around the world. On August 20 President Bush, after a day of indecision, responded favorably to Yeltsin's request for support and convinced world leaders to join him in refusing to recognize the legitimacy of the new Soviet government. Siberian coal miners went on strike to oppose the coup. The next day word began to seep out that the plotters had given up and were fleeing. Several committed suicide, and a newly released Gorbachev ordered the others arrested. Yet, things did not go back to the way they had

As a final act against the Communist regime, people toppled the statues that had been erected to honor their former leaders.

been. Although Gorbachev reclaimed the title of president, he was forced to resign as head of the Communist party and admit that he had made a grave mistake in appointing the men who had turned against him. Yeltsin emerged as the most popular political figure in the country.

What began as a reactionary coup turned into a powerful accelerant for stunning new changes in the Soviet Union, or the "Soviet Disunion," as one wag termed it. No sooner had the plotters been arrested than most of the fifteen republics proclaimed their independence, with the Baltic republics of Latvia, Lithuania, and Estonia regaining the status of independent nations. The Communist party apparatus was dismantled, prompting celebrating crowds to topple statues of Lenin and other mythic Communist heroes.

A chastened Gorbachev could only acquiesce in the breakup of the Soviet empire. The man who had put reform into motion was now buffeted by the whirlwind of change. In the midst of the political turmoil, the systemic problems burdening the Soviet Union before the coup remained intractable. The economy was stagnant, languishing between the promise of free-market principles and the gridlock of state collectivism. Food and coal shortages loomed on the horizon, and consumer goods remained scarce. It would take decades before the economies of the fifteen republics would approach Western standards of production and efficiency. The reformers had won, but they had yet to establish deep roots in a country with no democratic tradition. Leaping into the unknown, they faced years of hardship and uncertainty ahead.

The aborted coup also accelerated Soviet and American efforts to reduce the stockpiles of nuclear weapons. In late 1991 President Bush stunned the world by announcing that the United States would destroy all its tactical nuclear weapons on land and at sea in Europe and Asia, take its long-range bombers off twenty-four-hour alert status, and initiate discussions with the Soviet Union for the purpose of instituting sharp cuts in ICBMs with multiple warheads. Bush explained that the prospect of a Soviet invasion of western Europe was "no longer a realistic threat," and this presented an unprecedented opportunity for reducing the threat of nuclear holocaust. President Gorbachev responded by announcing reciprocal Soviet cutbacks.

PANAMA   The end of the cold war did not spell the end of international tensions and conflict, however. Indeed, before the end of 1989, American troops were engaged in battle in Panama, where a petty tyrant provoked the first of America's military engagements under George Bush. In 1983 General Manuel Noriega had maneuvered himself into the leadership of the Panamanian Defense Forces—which made him head of government in fact if not in title. Earlier, as chief of intelligence, Noriega had developed a profitable business of supplying information on the region to the CIA, including during the period when Bush headed the agency. At the same time, he was developing avenues in the region for drug smuggling and gunrunning, laundering the money through Panamanian banks. For a time, American intelligence analysts looked the other way, regarding him as too useful a contact, but eventually he became too great an embarrassment. In 1987 a rejected associate published charges of Noriega's drug activities and accused him further of rigged elections and political assassination.

In 1988 federal grand juries in Miami and Tampa indicted Noriega and fifteen others on drug charges. The Panamanian president tried to fire Noriega, but the National Assembly ousted the president instead and named Noriega "maximum leader." It then proclaimed that Panama "is declared to be in a state of war" with the United States. The next day, December 16, 1989, four off-duty American servicemen were stopped at a roadblock, and as they tried to proceed, one marine was shot and killed. President Bush thereupon ordered an invasion of Panama with the purpose of capturing Noriega for trial on the American indictments and installing a government headed by President Guillermo Endara.

The 12,000 American military personnel in Panama were quickly joined by 12,000 more, and in the early morning of December 20, five military task forces struck at strategic targets in the country. Noriega surrendered to American forces. Twenty-three American servicemen were killed in the action, and estimates of Panamanian casualties ranged up to 4,000, including many civilians caught in the crossfire. In April 1992 Noriega was convicted in the United States on eight counts of racketeering and drug distribution.

THE GULF WAR   Months after Panama had moved to the background of public attention, Saddam Hussein, dictator of Iraq, focused attention on the Middle East when his army suddenly fell upon his tiny, wealthy neighbor Kuwait on August 2, 1990. Kuwait had raised its production of oil, contrary to agreements with the Organization of Petroleum Exporting Countries (OPEC). The resultant drop in oil prices offended Saddam, deep in debt and heavily dependent on oil revenues. Complaining of "economic aggression" against Iraq, he demanded that Kuwait reduce its oil production and, with Saudi Arabia, cancel Iraqi debts of $30 million.

Saddam did not expect the sudden storm his invasion of Kuwait provoked. The U.N. Security Council quickly voted 14–0 to condemn the invasion and demand withdrawal. American secretary of state James Baker and Soviet foreign minister Eduard Shevardnadze issued a joint statement of condemnation. On August 6, the Security Council endorsed Resolution 661, an embargo on trade with Iraq, by a vote of 13–0, with Cuba and Yemen abstaining. Such unanimity, of course, would have been unlikely during the cold war era.

On August 2, Bush condemned Iraq's "naked aggression" and said he was not ruling any options out. He vowed to reporters: "This aggression will not stand." Asked how it would be undone, he replied: "Just wait, watch, and learn." On August 6–7, the United States responded to Saddam's threats against Saudi Arabia by dispatching planes and troops to Saudi Arabia on a "wholly defensive" mission—to protect Saudi Arabia. British forces soon joined in, as did Arab troops from Egypt, Morocco,

Syria, Oman, the United Arab Emirates, and Qatar. On August 22, Bush began to order the mobilization of American reserve forces for the operation now dubbed "Desert Shield." Later in September, after meeting with Gorbachev in Helsinki, Bush told Congress that dictators could no longer find comfort in East-West divisions, and proclaimed a "New World Order," which he described as "A world where the strong respect the rights of the weak."

On November 8, Bush announced that he was doubling American forces in the Middle East from about 200,000 to 400,000, to build up "an adequate offensive military capability." Bush asserted that he already had authority to take such action under the Security Council resolutions. Congress erupted in debate, with many arguing that the embargo should have a chance to work, and that it would be ill advised to go to war without formal congressional support. Bush's position was strengthened on November 29 by U.N. Resolution 678, which authorized the use of force to dislodge Iraq from Kuwait, and set a deadline for Iraqi withdrawal of January 15, 1991.

A flurry of peace efforts sent diplomats scurrying all over, but without result. Saddam refused to yield. On January 10, Congress began to debate a resolution authorizing the use of U.S. armed forces. Senate Majority Leader George Mitchell warned, "A grave decision for war is being made prematurely. There has been no clear rationale, no convincing explanation for shifting American policy from one of sanctions to one of war." Others insisted on the need to present a united front behind the president. The outcome was uncertain to the end, but on January 12 the resolution for the use of force passed the House by 250–183, and the Senate by 52–47.

By January 1991, a twenty-eight-nation allied force was committed to Operation Desert Shield. Some nations sent only planes, ships, or support forces, but sixteen committed ground combat forces, ten of these Islamic countries. Desert Shield became Operation Desert Storm when the first missiles and planes began to hit Iraq at about 2:30 A.M., January 17, Baghdad time, or about 6:30 P.M., January 16, Washington time.

With the allies in control of the air from the beginning, Saddam's only recourse was to fire off lumbering Soviet-made SCUD missiles, which he aimed from the first day into Israel with the hope of provoking Israeli retaliation and undermining the Arab coalition against him. But the resulting damage and casualties were light, and the Israelis showed remarkable restraint in the face of the continuing attacks. The Iraqis responded also with desperation moves, which did more damage to the environment than to enemy forces: releasing oil into the Persian Gulf from tankers and loading platforms in Kuwait and setting fire to Kuwaiti oil wells.

Saddam's key strategy of digging in and prolonging the war into a costly land struggle, as he did in his war with Iran, never had a chance. Saddam concentrated his forces in Kuwait and expected an allied attack northward into Kuwait and a landing on the coast. But the Iraqis were outflanked when 200,000 allied troops, largely American, British, and French, vanished with much of their heavy armor and turned up on the undefended border with Saudi Arabia 100–200 miles to the west. The allied ground assault began on February 24 and lasted only four days. Iraqi soldiers surrendered in wholesale lots.

On February 28, six weeks after the fighting began, President Bush called for a cease-fire, the Iraqis accepted, and the shooting ended. American fatalities were 137. The lowest estimates of Iraqi fatalities, civilian and military, were around 100,000. The coalition forces occu-

An American soldier watches a burning Kuwaiti oil well, which was set on fire by desperate Iraqi troops.

pied about one-fifth of Iraq. In late March, after a quick survey, a U.N. official reported: "Bombing had wrought near apocalyptic results upon the infrastructure of what had been, until January 1991, a rather highly urbanized and mechanized society." The Persian Gulf War, the "mother of all battles" in Saddam Hussein's words, had been intense and deadly and had left consequences to be played out far into the future. Despite all the destruction, Saddam Hussein remained in power.

The Middle East, as it had for centuries, still resisted any quick fix. There was an understanding—details to be worked out—that the United States would maintain a military presence in the Persian Gulf. It was, ironically, an American missionary who said to one of the British planners carving up the former Ottoman territory after World War I: "You are flying in the face of four millenniums of history." The words retain their haunting quality.

THE COMPUTER REVOLUTION

Among the most important factors promoting the surge in productivity and prosperity during the 1980s was a dramatic revolution in information technology. Cellular phones, laser printers, VCRs, fax machines, and personal computers became commonplace at work and in homes. The computer age had arrived.

The idea of a programmable machine that would rapidly perform mental tasks had been around since the eighteenth century, but it took the crisis atmosphere of World War II to bring to bear the intellectual and financial resources needed to create such a "computer." The Allies needed machines to decipher the complex German and Japanese military codes and to calculate the ballistics for new artillery systems. They also needed sophisticated mathematical tools to aid in the development of the atomic bomb.

Funding for such priorities enabled a team of engineers at the University of Pennsylvania to create ENIAC (Electronic Numerical Integrator and Computer), the first all-purpose, all-electronic digital computer. Unveiled in 1944, it could perform 5,000 operations per second. ENIAC, however, was so large that it was almost impractical. It took up 3,000 cubic feet of space and included 18,000 vacuum tubes (glass canisters designed to amplify electrical current), 70,000 resistors, 10,000

The Electronic Numerical Integrator and Computer (ENIAC), *1946. Developed for the army, the ENIAC was cumbersome but could perform complex calculations in minutes.*

capacitors, and 6,000 switches. John Von Neumann, a Hungarian-born American mathematician at the Institute for Advanced Study at Princeton, where he was a colleague of Albert Einstein, volunteered his services to help solve some of ENIAC's weaknesses—too little memory storage, too many tubes, and too lengthy programming. His insights led to a new machine, EDVAC (Electronic Discrete Variable Automatic Computer), unveiled in 1949, which became the model for the worldwide computer industry.

During the 1950s and 1960s, corporations (such as International Business Machines—IBM) and government agencies transformed computers from being mathematical calculators to electronic data-processing machines. The key development in facilitating such a transformation occurred in 1947 when three physicists at Bell Laboratories in central New Jersey invented the transistor (so named because it *trans*fers electric current across a re*sistor,* which is a conductor used to control voltage in an electrical circuit). Transistors were a dramatic breakthrough because they took the place of the much larger and more fragile, glass vacuum tubes. Like the vacuum tube, the transistor could amplify an electric signal. Unlike the vacuum tube, however, transistors were cheap, durable, required less power and, as future research would demonstrate, they could be made almost infinitely tiny. The availability of transistors led to the development of hearing aids and portable radios.

They also led to faster and more reliable, smaller and less expensive, mainframe computers. These "second-generation" computers were ten times as fast as EDVAC, but programming remained slow, requiring the use of punch cards fed into the machines. The next major breakthrough was the invention in 1971 of the microprocessor—literally a computer on a silicon chip—by Ted Hoff of Intel Corporation. The functions that had once been performed by computers taking up an entire room could now be performed by a microchip circuit the size of a postage stamp. Microchips were incorporated into television sets, wristwatches, automobiles, kitchen appliances, and the spacecraft being developed by NASA.

The use of such microchips enabled computers not only to be smaller but also cheaper. These "third-generation" computers were so much faster that a new word had to be created to measure their processing speeds: *nanoseconds* (billionths of a second). High-performance computers heightened efficiency throughout the American economy and helped fuel an information revolution that affected virtually every aspect of life.

The invention of the microchip made possible the idea of a personal computer. In 1975 Ed Roberts, an engineer, made the first prototype of a "personal computer." The Altair 8800, which cost $397, was imperfect and cumbersome, with no display, no keyboard, and not enough memory to do anything useful. But its potential excited a young Harvard sophomore named Bill Gates. He was a self-described "computer nerd," a student lacking in social skills and addicted to computing, willing to skip his classes in order to work night and day on programming projects.

Gates offered his software programming services for the Altair 8800 and formed a new company called Microsoft. Against the objections of his parents, Gates dropped out of Harvard to devote all his time to the new venture. "We realized that the revolution had started," Gates recalled, "and there was no question of where life would focus." By 1977 he and others had helped to transform the personal computer from a hobby machine to a mass consumer product. In 1986 Gates became a billionaire at the age of thirty-one.

Hundreds of new firms sprang up to produce the hardware and software for the burgeoning new industry. The infant personal computer industry soared into the 1980s, offering word processing, games, and perhaps most important, the capacity to calculate financial spreadsheets. This last feature convinced the corporate community that personal computers could indeed become a mass-production commodity. By the end of the decade, there were 60 million personal computers in the United States, and people began to talk about an "information superhighway," a worldwide network of linked computers and databases connected by fiber-optic lines that facilitated high-speed transmission. "We're all connected," declared a telephone company commercial.

During the 1990s, the development of the Internet and electronic mail enabled anyone with a personal computer and modem the opportunity to travel on the information superhighway. Such advances had the effect of shrinking the globe and facilitating almost instantaneous communication across the continents. Yet those too poor to gain easy access to the information revolution faced a bleak future. To the extent

Students at Mansfield University in Pennsylvania work on laptop computers in the school libary. Rapid developments in technology have made computers, e-mail, and the Internet readily accessible and affordable.

that computers become essential tools for educational and economic success, they threaten to widen the gap between rich and poor. As always, it seems, technological progress provides uneven benefits.

MAKING CONNECTIONS

- Much of what happened in the 1980s, from economic and social policy to presidential leadership style, was reminiscent of the late nineteenth century as well as the 1920s and 1950s.

- Another parallel between the late nineteenth century and the 1980s was a rise in immigration and a change in immigration patterns. This is discussed in the next chapter.

- Chapter 37 shows how the economic and political conservatism of the 1980s became much more ideological in the early 1990s.

FURTHER READING

It is too early for a definitive scholarly analysis of the Reagan administration, but two brief accounts are David Mervin's *Ronald Reagan and the American Presidency* (1990) and Michael Schaller's *Reckoning with Reagan: America and Its President in the 1980s* (1992).

On Reaganomics, see David Stockman's *The Triumph of Politics: How the Reagan Revolution Failed* (1986) and Robert Lekachman's *Greed Is Not Enough: Reaganomics* (1982). On the issue of arms control, see Strobe Talbott's *Deadly Gambits: The Reagan Administration and the Stalemate in Nuclear Arms Control* (1984).

For Reagan's foreign policy in Central America, see James Chace's *Endless War: How We Got Involved in Central America and What Can Be Done* (1984) and Walter LaFeber's *Inevitable Revolutions: The United States in Central America* (2nd ed., 1993). Insider views of Reagan's foreign policy are offered in Alexander M. Haig, Jr.'s *Caveat: Realism, Reagan, and Foreign Policy* (1984) and Caspar W. Weinberger's *Fighting for Peace: Seven Critical Years in the Pentagon* (1990).

On Reagan's second term, see Jane Mayer and Doyle McManus's *Landslide: The Unmaking of the President, 1984–1988* (1988). For a masterful work on the Iran-Contra affair, see Theodore Draper's *A Very Thin Line: The Iran Contra Affair* (1991). Several collections of essays include varying assessments of the Reagan years. Among these are *The Reagan Revolution* (1988), edited by B. B. Kymlicka and Jean V. Matthews; *The Reagan Presidency: An Incomplete Revolution* (1990), edited by Dilys M. Hill, et al.; and *Looking Back on the Reagan Presidency* (1990), edited by Larry Berman.

On the 1988 campaign see Jack Germond and Jules Witcover's *Whose Broad Stripes and Bright Stars? The Trivial Pursuit of the Presidency, 1988* (1989) and Sidney Blumenthal's *Pledging Allegiance: The Last Campaign of the Cold War* (1990). Major issues in economic and social policy are addressed in Robert Reich's *The Work of Nations: Preparing Ourselves for Twenty-first Century Capitalism* (1991) and William Julius Wilson's *The Truly Disadvantaged: The Inner City, the Underclass, and Public Policy* (1987).

37   CULTURAL POLITICS

CHAPTER ORGANIZER

This chapter focuses on:

- demographic patterns from the 1990 census and the "new immigrants" of the 1980s and 1990s.

- the Democratic resurgence of the early 1990s; the Republican landslide of 1994; and the Contract with America.

- the remarkable performance of the economy and stock market during the 1990s.

- the revelations of scandal that recall earlier sexual escapades during the Harding administration.

*D*uring the 1980s and 1990s, various cultural and political developments combined to transform American society and institutions. The makeup of the population shifted as the baby-boomers entered middle age. Immigrants to America were now primarily from Asia and Latin America rather than from Europe. In the 1980s and 1990s, the political landscape also began to be transformed, as many conservative politicians won election to local, state, and federal government offices, and many conservative judges were appointed or elected to the courts. In an effort to become more productive and competitive, American businesses engaged in "reengineering" efforts that often brought widespread job cuts. As corporations began to downsize, people began to lose faith in company loyalty and job security. At the same time, a backlash against racial preferences created new social tensions. Whites in large numbers began to argue that affirmative action would limit their access to the nation's colleges and business contracts. They supported a balanced budget, feared for their jobs, and yearned for an end to corruption in government and a revival of "traditional" moral values.

America's Changing Face

DEMOGRAPHIC SHIFTS   During the 1980s, the nation's population grew by 10 percent, or some 23 million people, boosting the total to almost 250 million. The median age of the quarter-billion Americans rose from thirty to thirty-three, and the much-discussed baby-boom generation—the 43 million people born between 1946 and 1964—entered middle age. Because of its disproportionate size, the baby-boom generation magnifies changes in American society as it moves through the life cycle. As one demographer noted, it resembles a "pig in a python." Political analysts suggested that this generation's maturation and preoccupation with practical concerns such as raising families, paying for college, and buying houses helped explain the surge of political conservatism during the 1980s. Surveys revealed that baby-boomers wanted stronger family and religious ties and promoted a greater respect for authority. Yet having come to maturity during the turbulent sixties and early seventies, the baby-boomers also displayed more tolerance of social and cultural diversity than their parents.

The "Sunbelt" states of the South and West continued to lure residents from the Midwest and Northeast. Fully 90 percent of the nation's total population growth during the 1980s occurred in southern or western states. California gained more people than any other state during the eighties, boosting its total to 30 million, 5 million more than in 1980. Texas and Florida each added more than 3 million new residents, while West Virginia, Iowa, and the District of Columbia experienced a net loss of residents. The Northeast became the nation's least populous region. These population shifts forced a massive redistricting of the House of Representatives, with Florida and California gaining three more seats each and Texas two, while states such as New York lost seats.

Americans in the 1980s tended to settle in large communities. Almost 90 percent of the decade's population growth occurred in large metropolitan areas. The number of cities with 100,000 people or more increased by 29 to a total of 195, with 18 of the new metropolises in California alone. In 1990 some 78 percent of the population lived in a metropolitan area, and for the first time, a majority of Americans lived in cities of a million or more people. This move to the cities largely reflected trends in the job market, as the "postindustrial" economy continued to shift from manufacturing to professional service industries, particularly those specializing in telecommunications and information processing. By 1990 fewer than 5 million people out of a total population of 250 million—or 2 percent—lived on farms.

Women continued to enter the workforce in large numbers. Indeed, one of the most significant sociological developments in American life since 1970 was the accelerated entry of women into the world of work outside the home. In 1970, 38 percent of the workforce was female; in 1990 the figure was almost 50 percent. Women workers accounted for 60 percent of labor force growth since 1980, and fully 58 percent of all adult women were gainfully employed. A third of the new medical doctors during the eighties were women (4 percent in 1970); 40 percent of new lawyers were female (8.4 percent in 1970); and 23 percent of new dentists were women (less than 1 percent in 1970).

The decline of the traditional family unit—two parents with children—continued during the 1980s. The proportion of the nation's households in that category dropped from 31 percent in 1980 to 26 percent in 1990. And more people were living alone than ever before, largely as a result of high divorce rates or a growing practice of delaying marriage until well into the twenties. One out of every four households in 1990 was made up of a person living alone, a 26 percent increase over 1980. The number of single mothers increased 35 percent during the decade. The rate was much higher for African Americans: in 1990 less than 38 percent of black children lived with both parents, down from 67 percent in 1960.

Young blacks burdened by the absence of one or both parents faced shrinking economic opportunities in the 1980s. The 1990 census documented a slight rise in the proportion of Americans living in poverty but a substantially heightened inequality in the distribution of income. By 1992, roughly 14.5 percent of the American people were living at or below the official poverty level, pegged at $14,335 in annual income for a family of four. The urban poor were particularly victimized by a developing underclass culture, with young black males suffering the most. In 1990 the leading cause of death among black males between the ages of fifteen and twenty-four was homicide. Twenty-five percent of black males aged twenty to twenty-nine were in prison, on parole, or on probation, while only 4 percent were enrolled in college. Forty percent of black adult males were functionally illiterate.

THE NEW IMMIGRANTS   The racial and ethnic composition of the country also changed rapidly during the 1980s, with nearly one in every four Americans claiming African, Asian, Hispanic, or American Indian ancestry. Among an overall population of 250 million, blacks represented 12 percent of the total, Hispanics 9 percent, Asians about 3 percent, and American Indians almost 1 percent. The rate of increase

Increased numbers of Chinese risked their money and their lives trying to gain entry into the United States. These illegal immigrants from China are trying to keep warm after being captured when the freighter carrying them to the United States ran aground in Rockaway, New York City.

among those four groups was twice as fast as it had been during the 1970s.

The primary cause of this dramatic change in the nation's ethnic mix was a surge of immigration. During the 1980s, legal immigration into the United States totaled over 7 million people, 30 percent higher than the previous decade and more than in any other decade except 1901–1910. These figures do not include the hundreds of thousands of illegal aliens, mostly Mexicans and Haitians. In 1990 the United States welcomed more than twice as many immigrants as all other countries in the world put together.

Even more significant than the overall number of newcomers were their places of origin. For the first time in the nation's history, the majority of immigrants came not from Europe but from other parts of the world. The percentage of European immigrants to the United States declined from 53 percent of the total in the 1950s to 12 percent in the 1980s and 1990s. Asian Americans were the fastest-growing segment of the population in the eighties, with their numbers increasing by 80 percent, a rate seven times as great as the general population. Among the legal immigrants during the decade, Mexicans made up the largest share, averaging about 60,000 a year. The second-highest number came from the Philippines (46,000), while immigrants from mainland China, Taiwan, and Hong Kong totaled 45,000 annually. The next largest groups were Vietnamese and Koreans, followed by Dominicans, Asian Indians, Jamaicans, Iranians, Cubans, Cambodians, and Laotians.

Heightening the social impact of these new immigrants was their tendency to cluster in a handful of states and cities. Most of them gravitated to New York, Illinois, and New Jersey, as well as Florida, Texas, Hawaii, California, and other Sunbelt states. By 1990, California had 64 percent of the Asian Americans in the country and 34 percent of the Hispanics. The population of Miami, Florida, was 64 percent Hispanic, and San Antonio, Texas, boasted 55 percent. Los Angeles contained 2 million Mexican Americans.

The wave of new immigration brought rising conflict between old and new ethnicities. African-American leaders worried that the newcomers were gaining an economic foothold at the expense of poor blacks. And many native whites resented the influx of newcomers into their communities.

Such reactions recall earlier chapters in American immigrant history, a story marked from the start by ambivalence about the nation's tradi-

RESIDENT POPULATION DISTRIBUTION FOR THE UNITED STATES BY RACE AND ETHNIC ORIGIN: 1980 AND 1990

	1980		1990		
	Number	%	Number	%	Change
Total population	**226,545,805**	**100.0**	**248,709,873**	**100.0**	**9.8**
White	188,371,622	83.1	199,686,070	80.3	6.0
Black	26,495,025	11.7	29,986,060	12.1	13.2
American Indian, Eskimo, or Aleut	1,420,400	0.6	1,959,234	0.8	37.9
Asian or Pacific Islander	3,500,439	1.5	7,273,662	2.9	107.8
Other race	6,758,319	3.0	9,804,847	3.9	45.1
Hispanic origin	14,608,673	6.4	22,354,059	9.0	53.0

Source: U.S. Bureau of the Census, 1991.

tion of inclusiveness. With rhetoric reminiscent of the nativist movement a century earlier, critics of the new tide of immigration charged that America was being "overrun" with foreigners; they questioned whether Hispanics and Asians could be "assimilated" into American culture. In 1994 a large majority of California voters approved Proposition 187, a controversial initiative that denied the state's estimated 4 million illegal immigrants access to public schools, nonemergency health care, and other social services. It also required teachers, doctors, and government officials to report anyone suspected of being an undocumented immigrant. Proponents of the new measure claimed it would save taxpayers billions of dollars. Critics labeled Proposition 187 racist in motive and effect. In 1998 California voters passed a referendum ending bilingual education.

The bitter irony of this new nativism was that it targeted recent immigrants for bringing with them to the United States virtues long prized by Americans—hope, energy, persistence, and an aggressive work ethic. Like most of their predecessors who braved tremendous hardships to make their way to America, they toiled long and hard for a slice of the American dream, and most economic studies concluded that their presence was beneficial to the nation. They created more wealth than they consumed, and many of them compiled an astonishing record of achievement. The median household income of Asian Americans, for example, exceeded every other group, including native whites, and

IMMIGRANTS ADMITTED BY
TOP 15 COUNTRIES OF BIRTH
IN FISCAL YEAR 1990

Country of Birth	1990
Total	**656,111**
Mexico	56,549
Philippines	54,907
Vietnam	48,662
Dominican Republic	32,064
Korea	29,548
China (mainland)	28,746
India	28,679
Soviet Union	25,350
Jamaica	18,828
Iran	18,031
Taiwan	13,839
United Kingdom	13,730
Canada	13,717
Poland	13,334
Haiti	11,862
Other	248,265

Source: U.S. Immigration and Naturalization Service, 1991.

Asian Americans were disproportionately represented in the nation's most prestigious colleges and universities. Although constituting only 1.6 percent of the total population in 1985, Asian Americans made up over 11 percent of Harvard's freshman class and almost 20 percent at Berkeley and the California Institute of Technology. Yet the very success of the new immigrants contributed to the resentment they encountered from other groups.

CULTURAL CONSERVATISM

Cultural conservatives helped elect Reagan and Bush in the 1980s, but they were disappointed in the results. Once in office, neither president had, in their eyes, adequately addressed their moral agenda, including a complete ban on abortions and the restoration of prayer in public schools. By the 1990s, a new generation of young conservative activists, mostly political independents or Republicans, began to emerge as a force to be reckoned with in national affairs. They were more ideological, more libertarian, more partisan, and more impatient than their predecessors.

ATTACKS ON THE LIBERAL AGENDA   The new breed of cultural conservatives abhorred the excesses of cultural and political liberalism. They lamented the disappearance of basic forms of decency and propriety, and believed that fundamental liberties were at risk. They attacked affirmative action programs designed to redress historic injustices against women and minorities. During the 1990s, powerful groups inside and outside the Republican party mobilized to roll back government programs giving preferences to specified social groups. Prominent black conservatives supported such efforts, arguing that racially based preferences were demeaning and condescending remedies. They argued that preferential government treatment of African Americans raised doubts in the minds of both blacks and whites about the inherent worth of any black achievement.

THE RELIGIOUS RIGHT   Although quite diverse, cultural conservatives tended to be evangelical Christians or orthodox Catholics who joined together to exert increasing pressure on the political process. In 1989 the television evangelist Pat Robertson organized the Christian Coalition to replace Jerry Falwell's Moral Majority as the flagship organization of the resurgent religious right. The Christian Coalition encouraged religious conservatives to vote, run for public office, and support only those candidates who shared the organization's views.

With a well-organized grassroots movement in every state, the Christian Coalition chose the Republican party as the best vehicle for transforming its pro-family campaign into new public policies. It encouraged its supporters to withhold political support from any candidate who did not provide an ironclad promise to support the Coalition's school prayer, anti-abortion, anti–gay rights positions. In addition to promoting "traditional family values," it urged politicians to "radically downsize and delimit government."

As a centrist professional politician, George Bush initially tried to keep the cultural conservatives at arm's length, only to find himself the target—and victim—of their in-your-face attacks and take-no-prisoners tenacity. His Democratic successor, Bill Clinton, also underestimated the growing strength of organized groups such as the Christian Coalition. In the 1994 congressional elections, religious conservatives went to the polls in record numbers, and 70 percent of them voted Republican tickets. A third of the voters identified themselves as "white, evangelical, born-again Christians." In many respects, they took control of the political and social agendas in the nineties. As one journalist acknowledged in 1995, "the religious right is moving toward center stage in American secular life."

BUSH TO CLINTON

For months after the Gulf War, George Bush seemed unbeatable. In the polls his approval rating rose to 91 percent. But the aftermath of Desert Storm was mixed, with Saddam Hussein's grip on Iraq still intact. Despite his image of strength abroad, the president began to look weak even on foreign policy. The Soviet Union meanwhile stumbled on to its surprising end. On December 25, 1991, the Soviet flag over the Kremlin was replaced by the flag of the Russian Federation. The cold war had ended with not just the collapse but the dismemberment of the Soviet Union into its fifteen constituent republics. As a result, the United States was now the world's only superpower.

"Containment" of the Soviet Union, the bedrock of American foreign policy for more than four decades, had lost its reason for being. Bush, the ultimate cold war careerist—ambassador to the U.N., envoy to China, head of the CIA, vice-president under Reagan—struggled to interpret the fluid new international scene. He spoke of a "New World Order" but never defined it. By his own admission he had trouble with the "vision thing." The situation, in fact, did not lend itself to a simple vision—unless the answer was to drift into isolation, a great temptation, with foreign dangers seemingly lessened. By the end of 1991, Bush faced a primary challenge from the Republican commentator and former White House aide Patrick Buchanan, who adopted the slogan "America First" and called on Bush to "bring home the boys." As the Gulf War victory euphoria wore off, a popular bumper sticker reflected the growing public frustration with the Bush administration: "Saddam Hussein still has his job. What about you?"

RECESSION AND DOWNSIZING   In November 1988, a few days after George Bush was elected president, a journalist observed that the most important issue to be addressed by the new administration was the nation's deepening financial debt. "It is the issue that probably will determine the fate of the President. Indeed, it could also be his ultimate undoing." It was an accurate prediction. For the Bush administration and for the nation, the most devastating development in the early nineties was a prolonged economic recession that began in 1990. The first economic setback in more than eight years, it grew into the longest, if not the deepest, since the Great Depression. By early 1992, over 2 million jobs had dried up. During 1991, 25 million workers—about 20 percent of the labor force—were unemployed at some time.

What made this recession unusual was that its victims included large numbers of white-collar workers. In 1991, for instance, General Motors, Xerox, and IBM cut 100,000 salaried employees from their payrolls. In the corporate world, terms such as "restructuring" and "downsizing" ruled the day. Companies began reducing personnel, switching employees to part-time status to reduce benefits, and finding other ways to cut labor costs.

Prosperity gave way to firings, growing unemployment, declining sales and profits, the continuing imbalance in foreign trade, and the lack of a plan for the demobilization of the military-industrial complex after the cold war. With soaring expenditures on defense and social entitlement programs, a $150 billion annual deficit had become a $450 billion shortfall during 1991.

A Senate committee analysis of the stagnant economy confirmed a chilling fact. Under the Bush administration "the average standard of living has actually declined." Some critics with a historical bent compared Bush to Hoover: both presidents and their aides initially denied that there was a problem with the economy and then assured the nation that the recession would be short and self-correcting. The euphoria over the Allied victory in the Gulf War quickly gave way to anxiety and resentment generated by the depressed economy. At the end of 1991, *Time* magazine declared that "no one, not even George Bush" could deny "that the economy was sputtering."

Whatever the reasons for recession, the cure remained elusive. Although the Federal Reserve Board began cutting interest rates, the economy remained in the doldrums through 1992. The Democratic Congress and the Republican president squabbled over legislation to promote economic recovery but little was done to prod new growth or to reduce the hemorrhaging deficits. With his domestic policies in disarray and his foreign policy abandoned, George Bush tried a clumsy balancing act in addressing the recession, on the one hand acknowledging that "people are hurting" while on the other urging Americans that "this is a good time to buy a car."

THE COURT VEERS RIGHT   Other developments affected the president's popularity, among them the retirement in 1991 of the first black Supreme Court justice, Thurgood Marshall, after twenty-four years on the bench. To succeed him Bush named Clarence Thomas, a black federal judge who had been raised in poverty in the segregated South and educated in Catholic schools. After graduating from Yale Law School, Thomas had worked as an aide to a Republican senator before serving as chairman of the Equal Employment Opportunity Commission (EEOC) from 1982 to 1990. Then, after sixteen months on the U.S. Court of Appeals, he was tapped for the Supreme Court.

Despite Thomas's limited time in the judiciary, his views delighted conservative senators. He had questioned the wisdom of the minimum wage, school busing for desegregation, and affirmative action hiring programs, and he had preached "black self-help," once declaring that all civil rights leaders ever did was "bitch, bitch, bitch, moan, and whine."

Such opinions promised trouble in the Democratic Senate, but the real explosion occurred when Anita Hill, a soft-spoken law professor at the University of Oklahoma, charged that Thomas had sexually harassed her when she worked for him at the EEOC. Pro-Thomas senators orchestrated an often savage and sometimes absurd cross-examination of Hill. Some accused her of mental instability. An indignant Thomas denied her charges and called the hearings a "high-tech lynching for uppity blacks." He implied that Hill had fabricated the charges at the behest of civil rights groups determined to thwart his confirmation.

The televised hearings revealed that either Hill or Thomas had lied, and the committee's tie vote reflected the doubt: seven to recommend confirmation and seven against. The full Senate then narrowly confirmed Thomas by a 52–48 margin.

The hearings marked a new surge in the women's movement. Before the galvanizing effects of Anita Hill's rough treatment at the hands of male senators, feminism as an organized political movement had been in disarray. As early as 1975 Betty Friedan had broken away from the National Organization for Women (NOW), the organization she had started less than a decade before, claiming that its radical leaders had abandoned the core constituency of working women. By 1992 many claimed that NOW had reached a dead end. Columnist Sally Quinn charged that "many women have come to see the feminist movement as anti-male, anti-child, anti-family, anti-feminine. And therefore it has nothing to do with us."

In the ambiguous aftermath of the Thomas hearings, many women grew incensed at the treatment of Hill, and an unprecedented number of women ran for national and local offices in 1992. The Thomas confirmation struggle thus widened the gender gap for a Republican party already less popular with women than with men. As one political commentator put it: "The war with Anita Hill was not a war Bush needed."

REPUBLICAN TURMOIL The president had already set a political trap for himself when he declared in his 1988 convention address: "Read my lips. No new taxes!" Fourteen months into his term, he had decided that the deficit was a greater risk than violating his "no tax" pledge. After intense negotiations with congressional Democrats, Bush had announced that reducing the federal deficit required "tax revenue increases." He had not exactly said "new taxes," but as one House Democrat put it, "the charade is over." Bush's backsliding set off a revolt among House Republicans, but a bipartisan majority (most Republicans opposing) finally approved a tax measure raising the top personal rate from 28 to 31 percent, disallowing certain deductions to the upper brackets, and raising various excises. Conservative Republicans would not let George Bush forget his abandoned pledge.

Social issues had been one of the adhesives in the Reagan coalition, keeping the focus away from divisive economic issues, but as hardships crowded in on the attention of blue-collar workers, the economy surged to the fore. Moreover, social issues strengthened the force of the new "Christian Right" and grated on traditional Republicans. Reagan had been adept at exploiting moral issues, especially abortion, while doing little or nothing about them in practice. Bush's efforts to talk up such issues eventually ran out of control when right-wing militants seized the podium and the attention of the TV cameras at the 1992 convention. Patrick Buchanan, who had won about a third of the votes in the Republican primaries, used the occasion for a defense of "family values." Pat Robertson, the television evangelist, insisted that the proposed

Equal Rights Amendment represented "a socialist, anti-family, political movement that encourages women to leave their husbands, kill their children, practice witchcraft, destroy capitalism and become lesbians."

DEMOCRATIC RESURGENCE   In contrast to such strident rhetoric, the Democrats presented an image of centrist forces in control. For several years the Democratic Leadership Council (DLC), in which Arkansas governor William Jefferson Clinton figured prominently, had pushed the party to the center. Clinton strove to move the Democrats closer to the mainstream of political opinion. A graduate of Georgetown University, he had won a Rhodes scholarship to Oxford, and then earned a law degree from Yale, where he met and married Hillary Rodham. By 1979, at age thirty-two, he was back in his native Arkansas as the youngest governor in the country. He served three more terms as governor and in the process emerged as a dynamic young leader within the national Democratic party committed to winning back the middle-class white voters who had voted Republican during the eighties. Democrats had grown so liberal, he argued, that they had alienated their key constituencies.

A self-described moderate, Clinton promised to cut the defense budget, provide tax relief for the middle class, and create a massive economic aid package for the former republics of the Soviet Union. He was less precise about how such initiatives would be funded. Handsome, witty, intelligent, and a compelling speaker, Clinton reminded many political observers of John F. Kennedy. But underneath the veneer of Clinton's charisma were several flaws. He often seemed so determined to become president that he was willing to sacrifice consistency and principle. He made extensive use of polls to shape his stance on issues, pandered to special-interest groups, and flip-flopped on controversial issues, leading critics to label him "Slick Willie." Said one former opponent in Arkansas, "He'll be what people want him to be. He'll do or say what it will take to get elected." Even more enticing to the media and more embarrassing to Clinton were unending reports that he was a chronic adulterer and that he had manipulated the ROTC program during the Vietnam War to avoid the draft. Clinton's denials of both allegations could not dispel a lingering distrust of his personal character.

After a series of bruising party primaries, Clinton emerged as the front-runner by the time of the nominating convention in the summer of 1992. The Clinton forces dominated the convention, where Clinton chose Albert Gore, Jr., of Tennessee as his running mate. So the candidates were two southern Baptists from adjoining states.

Flushed with their convention victory, sporting a ten-point lead in the polls, the Clinton-Gore team stressed economic issues to win over working-class white and black voters. This strategy worked. Exit polls showed that the most important issue had been the economy. Clinton won with 370 electoral votes and about 43 percent of the vote; Bush had 168 electoral votes and 39 percent of the vote; and off-and-on independent candidate H. Ross Perot of Texas garnered 18 percent of the popular vote but no electoral votes. A feisty billionaire, Perot found a big audience for his simplified explanations of public problems and his offers to just "get under the hood and fix them." Yet during the Democratic convention, Perot withdrew, explaining that the Democratic party had "revitalized itself." Later he got back in the race as a third-party candidate and stayed for a surprisingly strong finish, one that suggested a widespread disillusionment with politics-as-usual.

DOMESTIC POLICY IN CLINTON'S FIRST TERM

Once inaugurated and faced with the realities of governing, Clinton alienated many who had voted for him when he reneged on several of his campaign promises. His infant presidency lurched from one cliffhanger to another. He abandoned his promised middle-class tax cut in order to keep down the federal deficit. When his attempt to allow professed homosexuals in the military provoked strong opposition among military commanders and in Congress, he backed down nine days into office and later announced an ambiguous new policy concerning gays in the military that came to be summed up in the words "Don't ask, don't tell." These inconsistent actions at the start of his administration had a negative effect on public impressions of the president, whom opponents accused on the one hand of putting a leftist agenda first and on the other hand of being too quick to cave in to criticism. In Clinton's first two weeks in office, his approval ratings dropped 20 percent.

Clinton had no traditional honeymoon of bipartisan support as he assumed office, partly because he seemed to live life as a perpetual campaign, partly because his critics permitted no letup. He therefore failed to enlarge substantially the narrow margin of support he had won during the election. He also failed to receive deserved credit for his achievements, such as the Family and Medical Leave Act, which enabled government workers and workers in companies with more than fifty employees to take off twelve weeks (unpaid leave) each year to deal with birth or adoption or an illness in the family. During the campaign, Clinton had promised to submit to Congress within 100 days a comprehensive economic program and a health care reform plan. In both cases, he failed to muster the necessary support of Congress and the public.

THE ECONOMY   Clinton entered office determined to reduce the federal deficit without damaging the economy. To this end, on February 17, he laid out a program of tax hikes and spending cuts. He proposed higher taxes for corporations and for individuals in higher tax brackets and called for an economic stimulus package for "investment" in public works (transportation, utilities, and the like) and in "human capital" (education, skills, health, and welfare). The Republican minority in the Senate used a filibuster to block the stimulus package, which they described as a "budget buster" that would fail to pep up the economy. The Democrats were unable to muster enough votes to cut off debate, and the stimulus package lay dead in the water. In response to Clinton's deficit reduction package of spending cuts and tax hikes on upper incomes, both Republicans and conservative Democrats who favored even deeper spending cuts opposed the package. The hotly contested bill finally passed by 218–216 in the House and 51–50 in the Senate, with Vice-President Gore breaking the tie.

The major scuffle of the fall also concerned the economy and was over approval of the North American Free Trade Agreement (NAFTA), which the Bush administration had negotiated with Canada and Mexico. The debate revived old arguments on the tariff, pro and con. Clinton stuck with his party's tradition of low tariffs and urged approval of NAFTA, which would make North America the largest free trade area in the world. He and his supporters argued that tariff reductions would open up foreign markets to American industries. Opponents of the bill like wealthy gadfly Ross Perot and organized labor favored barriers against cheaper foreign products and believed that with NAFTA the country would hear a "giant sucking sound" of American jobs being drawn to Mexico. Yet Clinton prevailed with solid Republican support while losing a sizable minority of Democrats, mostly from the South.

The final vote in the House was 234–200, with 102 Democrats and 132 Republicans making up the majority. The Senate approved NAFTA on November 21, 1993.

HEALTH CARE REFORM   Clinton's major public policy initiative was a new health care plan. Government-subsidized health insurance was not a new idea. Other industrial countries had long since started national health insurance programs, Germany as early as 1883, Britain in 1911. Off and on the idea had been a subject of political discussion in the United States throughout the twentieth century. Medicare, initiated in 1965, provided insurance for people sixty-five and older, and Medicaid supported state medical assistance for the indigent. These programs had grown enormously in the years since, as had business spending on private health insurance.

Sentiment for health care reform spread as annual medical costs approached the trillion-dollar mark, and some 39 million Americans went without insurance either by choice or out of necessity. The administration argued that universal medical insurance would reduce the overall costs of health care. Medicare covered older people, the most vulnerable to medical expenses, and the costs were soaring. Many of the working poor could not afford insurance, and many younger, healthier people took a chance on doing without. When they got in trouble, they reported to emergency rooms, which were reluctant to reject desperate people. As a result, those who could pay covered the others' costs in higher fees.

Universal medical coverage as proposed by Clinton would entitle every American and legal immigrant to health insurance. Government would subsidize all or part of the payments for small businesses and the poor, the latter from funds that formerly went to Medicaid, and would collect a "sin tax" on tobacco and perhaps on alcoholic beverages to pay for the program. Hillary Clinton chaired the health care plan task force and became the administration's lead witness on the plan before congressional committees. In January 1994, in his first State of the Union address, Clinton promised to veto any health care bill that "does not guarantee every American private health insurance that can never be taken away." For the remainder of 1994, a comprehensive health insurance plan remained the centerpiece of the Clinton agenda.

Hillary Clinton testifying before a congressional committee on the administration's health care legislation, September 1993.

But the bill aroused opposition from vested interests, especially the pharmaceutical and insurance industries. Drug companies insisted that they needed large profits to support expensive research. Insurance interests funded TV advertisements that questioned the bill's benefits. Small-business groups attacked the requirements that employers share the cost of medical insurance, already a common practice in old-age, unemployment, and health insurance, even though government would provide subsidies to small business. By midsummer 1994, the health insurance plan was pretty well doomed. Republican senators began a filibuster to prevent a vote on the bill. Lacking the votes to stop the filibuster, the Democrats acknowledged defeat and gave up the fight for universal medical coverage.

HANDGUNS AND THE CRIME BILL   During Clinton's first year in office, fear of violent crime prompted legislators to limit the availability of unregistered guns. In 1993, Congress passed the Brady Bill, which required a five-day wait to buy a handgun. Clinton called for passage of a crime bill in his State of the Union message. The bill had been passed in both houses in 1993, but when a conference committee reported back a compromise bill, a coalition of unlikely bedfellows—black Democrats who objected to expanding use of the death penalty, pro-gun Democrats who objected to a ban on assault weapons, and Republicans who dismissed crime-prevention programs as "pork" and who sought to embarrass the administration—joined together to oppose the legislation. After Congress voted 225–210 to postpone consideration of the bill, the Clinton administration pulled out all the stops to win its approval, and the new vote in the House in favor of the bill was 235–195. When the Senate passed the bill, people characterized it as one of Clinton's greatest victories. Ironically, however, it damaged the chances for health care legislation, as Clinton was preoccupied with the crime bill for ten days and used up much of his political leverage in the final moves to win its approval. This meant that there were fewer favors he could pull in to overcome the growing opposition to universal health care.

MISTRUST OF GOVERNMENT AND THE MILITIA MOVEMENT While Clinton sparred with Republicans in Washington, a burgeoning "militia" or "patriot" movement spread across the country in the 1990s. It represented the paranoid and populist strain in cultural politics. Convinced that the federal government was conspiring against individual liberties (especially the right to bear arms), thousands of mostly working-class folk joined well-armed militia organizations. Some militias harkened back to the origins of the Ku Klux Klan and fomented racial and ethnic hatred. Others aligned themselves with right-wing Christian groups, particularly the militant wing of the anti-abortion movement. In the Far West, several of the militias challenged the federal control of public lands, refused to pay taxes, and threatened to arrest and execute local government officials and judges.

Militia groups grew in numbers in reaction to dramatic government actions at Ruby Ridge, Idaho, and Waco, Texas. In Idaho in 1992, white supremacist Randy Weaver held off federal agents when they laid siege to his mountain cabin because he had failed to appear in federal court on weapons charges. Crossfire at the cabin killed Weaver's wife and son and convinced many people that the government intended to confiscate all weapons and to start a war against the radical right.

In Waco, Texas, another siege also resulted in catastrophic consequences. Responding to reports and rumors about the stockpiling of weapons, false imprisonment, child abuse, and the violation of immigration laws by the Branch Davidians, an apocalyptic sect headed by David Koresh, agents from the Treasury Department's Bureau of Alcohol, Tobacco, and Firearms (BATF) tried to serve a warrant on the sect on February 28, 1993. When the agents entered the sect's compound, they were met with gunfire. Four agents and two Branch Davidians were killed, and twenty or so people were injured. The next day, the FBI took over the siege of the compound. After fifty days of fruitless psychological warfare against the Branch Davidians, the FBI yielded to frustration and hints of child abuse, and on April 19, the fifty-first day of the siege, agents attacked the compound with armored vehicles and tear gas. Amid the commotion, the compound caught fire and quickly burned to the ground. The fire was so intense that no one could be certain of the number dead, but at least seventy-seven people died in the inferno.

On the second anniversary of the Waco incident, April 19, 1995, a massive truck bomb exploded in front of the federal office building in

The Murrah Federal Building in Oklahoma City after it was bombed, April 19, 1995.

Oklahoma City, Oklahoma. The entire front portion of the nine-story building collapsed, killing 168 people, 19 of them children in a day-care center that was in the building. Six hundred others were injured. Within days, the FBI arrested Timothy McVeigh and Terry Nichols and charged them with the bombing. A third man pleaded guilty to separate charges of conspiring to produce explosives. All three men were militia members who hated the federal government and who had been incensed by the way the BATF and FBI had dealt with the Branch Davidians at Waco.

The Oklahoma City bombing shocked and saddened the nation. It brought to public attention the rise of right-wing militia groups and also revealed the depth of anti-government sentiment among such fringe groups. A year later, in the spring of 1996, the FBI lay siege to a dozen members of the Freemen, a heavily armed militia group that kept federal authorities at bay outside a remote Montana homestead. The Freemen refused to pay taxes or be evicted from the property, which had been foreclosed upon eighteen months earlier. They declared their right to exercise governmental authority, posted bounties for the capture of local police and judges, and threatened to shoot their neighbors' livestock. Unlike the incident at Waco, this time federal officials resolved to wait out the fugitives. "The FBI," said Attorney-General Janet Reno, "has gone to great pains to ensure that there is no armed confrontation, no siege, no armed perimeter, and no use of military-assault-type tactics or equipment. The FBI is trying to negotiate a peaceful solution." The tactics succeeded, and eventually the Freemen were arrested.

FOREIGN POLICY CHALLENGES

Foreign policy under Clinton initially took a low priority. Yet, like Woodrow Wilson, Lyndon Johnson, and Jimmy Carter before him, Clinton was a Democratic president who came into office determined to focus on the nation's domestic problems, only to find himself mired down in foreign entanglements that had no easy resolution. In the search for a new rationale or paradigm of foreign policy, however, the Clinton administration faced a more complex situation than before.

Attention focused on the transition in eastern Europe from a politics of Communist party rule into one of ethnic loyalties and clashes. With the collapse of Communist power, old ethnic and religious enmities quickly resurfaced in eastern Europe and elsewhere, often leading to violent clashes that were difficult to resolve quickly. The Clinton administration struggled to find a consistent vision of its role in international affairs. In the meantime, it operated mostly on an ad hoc basis, often failing to win international backing for its initiatives. As one of Clinton's own ambassadorial appointees admitted, "We're always too ramshackle, we've never been smooth."

In 1993 Clinton aides defined the administration's foreign policy doctrine. National Security Adviser Anthony Lake announced that "the successor to a doctrine of containment must be a strategy of . . . enlargement of the world's free community of market democracies." That had a distinct echo of Woodrow Wilson's dictum: "The world must be made safe for democracy."

One place to expand democratic capitalism was in Russia itself. On this, as on other issues, Clinton continued the Bush administration policy of support for Russian president Boris Yeltsin, a position articulated in Secretary of State Warren Christopher's statement that "helping to consolidate democracy in Russia is not a matter of charity but a security concern of the highest order." Yet American assistance continued to be centered on the exchange of goods, expertise, and training instead of financial assistance. And for want of a better candidate, Clinton stuck with Yeltsin through his brutal invasion of Chechnya, a crime-ridden ethnic region on the Caucasus border with Georgia, to prevent its secession. The struggle dragged on until October 1996, when an agreement was reached to give Chechnya an autonomy that amounted to independence in all but name.

Clinton also continued the Bush policy of sponsoring patient negotiations between Arabs and Israelis. After the Gulf War, an Arab-Israeli Peace Initiative with American and Russian sponsorship led to an ongoing conference in Madrid attended by most Arab countries plus, in a new departure, the Palestine Liberation Organization (PLO), accepted by Israel as part of Jordan's delegation. The meetings were dogged by bloody incidents between Israelis and Palestinians, and interrupted when Israel expelled some 400 Palestinians. But none of the parties deemed it wise to abandon the talks.

On August 30, 1993, word leaked out that secret talks had been going on between Israeli and Palestinian representatives in Oslo, with the Norwegian foreign minister as intermediary. A draft agreement between

Israel and the PLO provided for the restoration of Palestinian self-rule in the occupied Gaza Strip and in Jericho on the West Bank, in an exchange of land for peace as provided in U.N. Security Council resolutions. A formal signing was quickly arranged at the White House where on September 13, with President Clinton presiding, Prime Minister Yitzhak Rabin and PLO leader Yasir Arafat exchanged handshakes and their foreign ministers signed the agreement.

In the aftermath of this dramatic agreement, talks continued by fits and starts, punctuated by violent incidents provoked by extremist Jewish settlers and Palestinian factions. But a movement toward peace seemed to be proceeding deliberately when on October 26, 1994, Israel and the kingdom of Jordan signed an agreement at ceremonies on their border, which were attended by President Clinton. The Middle East peace process suffered a terrible blow in early November 1995, however, when Israeli prime minister Yitzhak Rabin was assassinated at a peace rally in Tel Aviv. The gunman was an Israeli Jewish zealot who resented Rabin's efforts to negotiate with the Palestinians.

Some observers feared that the assassin had killed the peace process as well when seven months later conservative hardliner Benjamin Netanyahu narrowly defeated the U.S.-backed Shimon Peres in the election for a new prime minister. Netanyahu campaigned against the Rabin-Peres peace efforts, arguing that returning land to Arab control endangered Israeli security. In the face of a flurry of suicide bombings conducted by Islamic extremists against Israelis, he promised to slow the peace process, build new Jewish settlements along the West Bank, block the creation of a Palestinian state in the West Bank and Gaza, and retain control of the Golan Heights, captured from Syria in 1967.

Arab leaders responded to Netanyahu's election by threatening to reconsider the concessions they had made over the previous five years. Finally, in October 1998, Clinton brought together Arafat and Netanyahu at Wye Mills, Maryland, and with the ailing King Hussein of Jordan, brokered an agreement whereby Israel would surrender land in return for security guarantees by the Palestinians. As hardliners attempted to derail the tenuous peace, however, stability in the Middle East remained a dream rather than a reality.

Clinton continued the Bush administration's intervention in Somalia, on the northeastern horn of Africa, where collapse of the government early in 1991 had left the country in anarchy, prey to tribal marauders. The televised scenes of starvation horrified American viewers, many of whom demanded action. President Bush in December 1992 had gained U.N. sanction for a military force led by American troops to relieve hunger and restore peace. In January 1993, U.S. troop levels peaked and began to shrink with the arrival of international forces. Clinton inherited this situation. The Somalia operation proved successful at its primary mission, but never solved the political problems that lay at the root of the starvation.

Bush had gone into Somalia in part to counter criticism that he had failed to act decisively in the former Yugoslavia, now a volatile, fractious mixture of warring ethnic groups, chiefly Eastern Orthodox Serbs, Catholic Croats, and Bosnian Muslims. Many of them took pride in how well they got along, but when Yugoslavia imploded in 1991, fanatics and tyrants set out to stir ethnic conflict as four of its six republics seceded. Serb minorities, backed by Serbia itself, stirred up civil wars in Croatia and Bosnia. In Bosnia especially, the war involved "ethnic cleansing"—driving Muslims from their homes and towns—and mass rape of Muslim women. The options facing the United States were sobering: to ignore the butchery, to accept the refugees, to use American airpower, or to risk introducing ground troops.

Once in the White House, Clinton backed off from his hawkish campaign statements about using force in Yugoslavia. Western European countries dispatched "peacekeeping" forces and put an embargo on arms shipments—which favored Serbs who had fallen heir to the equipment of the Yugoslav army. Clinton started with the apparent purpose of acting vigorously, but confronted by European reluctance, he settled for dropping food and medical supplies to besieged Bosnians and sending planes to retaliate a few times for attacks on places designated "safe havens" by the United Nations. Serb forces soon learned that by alternating defiance and parleys, they could avoid any real deterrence except by Bosnian forces.

Despite a cease-fire agreement at the end of 1994, fighting continued in many parts of the faction-ridden country. In September 1995 American negotiators finally convinced the foreign ministers of Croatia, Bosnia, and Yugoslavia to agree to a comprehensive peace plan. Bosnia would remain a single nation but would be divided into two states: a Muslim-Croat federation controlling 51 percent of the territory and a Bosnian Serb republic controlling the remaining 49 percent. Basic human rights would be restored and free elections held to appoint a parliament and joint presidency. To enforce the agreement, 20,000 American troops would be dispatched to Bosnia as part of a 60,000-person NATO peacekeeping operation. A cease-fire went into effect in October, and a final agreement confirming these provisions was signed in Paris in December 1995. Yet in 1998, events seemed to replay yet again, this time in the Yugoslav province of Kosovo, where Serbian-led troops attacked ethnic Albanians and destroyed their villages. Faced with threats of air strikes by NATO, however, some Serbian forces withdrew from Kosovo.

The U.S. Congress had given only grudging support to the use of American forces in the Balkans. "I was opposed" to the Bosnian policy, explained Senator John McCain, an Arizona Republican and Vietnam veteran. "But if the president made a commitment and if we reversed it, it would be a terrible blow to the credibility of the United States."

The most successful new departure in foreign policy for the Clinton administration came in Haiti. The end of the cold war had removed any threat of Soviet infiltration in the Caribbean, and brought a new emphasis on Wilsonian themes of democracy. Haiti had emerged suddenly from a cycle of coups with a rebellion in the army rank and file and a democratic election in 1990, which brought to the top a popular priest, Jean-Bertrand Aristide. Old habits returned, however, when a Haitian army general ousted Aristide. The United States immediately announced its intention to bring back Aristide.

Another new element in the situation was the appearance of thousands of Haitian refugees desperate to reach Florida in leaky wooden boats. Coast Guard vessels began to pick them up and take them back to Haiti or to Guantanamo Bay in Cuba, denying that they were refugees. Public reaction to the flood of new immigrants put the Clinton administration under even greater pressure to resolve the situation.

With drawn-out negotiations leading nowhere, Clinton eventually moved in July 1994 to get a U.N. resolution authorizing force as a last resort. At this juncture, former president Jimmy Carter asked permission to negotiate. He went to Port-au-Prince and convinced the military leaders to quit by October 15. The first American forces were already in the air and landed September 19, without opposition and to a cordial welcome from the people.

Clinton had promised that the bulk of American forces would be quickly withdrawn and replaced by an international force of peacekeepers, and in November the American withdrawal began. Aristide returned to Haiti and on March 31, 1995, the occupation was turned over to a U.N. force commanded by an American general. Only about 2,400 American troops remained to retrain Haitian military and police in orderly procedures. They had a tough assignment, maybe an impossible one, but there was occasion for hope. Aside from Haiti, the status of American foreign policy remained in 1995 without drastic change from that of 1992.

REPUBLICAN INSURGENCY

During 1994, Clinton began to see his presidency unravel. Unable to get either health care reform or welfare reform bills through the Democratic Congress, and having failed to carry out his campaign pledge for middle-class tax relief, he and his party found themselves on the defensive. This opened up opportunities for the Republicans to capture control of Congress.

In the midterm elections of 1994, the Democrats suffered a humbling defeat. It was the first election since 1952 in which Republicans captured both houses of Congress at the same time. In both, the majority was solid: 52–48 in the Senate, a majority that soon increased when two Democrats switched parties, and 230–204 in the House. Not a single Republican incumbent was defeated. Republicans also won a net gain of eleven governorships and fifteen state legislatures. It was a thorough repudiation of the Democratic party, one that occurred in all regions.

There could be little question that the returns signaled a repudiation of Clinton and the Democratic Congress. Squabbling between the president and congressional Democrats did not help matters. Nor did Clinton's response to the Republican takeover of Congress in 1994 endear him to party loyalists. Initially, he and his aides decided to adopt a passive role, letting the Republicans initiate policies and programs and then hoping that they would be decimated by the affected interest groups. He offered no deficit reduction plan, no welfare reform proposal, no new health reform initiative.

Clinton's waffling on major issues began to convince many in his own party that he was a politician rather than a leader, someone who thrived as a campaigner but was bereft of genuine convictions. Said Democratic congressman David Obey: "I think most of us learned some time ago that if you don't like the president's position on a particular issue, you simply need to wait a few weeks." When Clinton joined the chorus of conservatives calling for a scaling back of affirmative action plans designed to remedy historic patterns of racial discrimination in hiring and the awarding of government contracts, liberals felt betrayed.

CONTRACT WITH AMERICA   A Georgian named Newton Leroy Gingrich led the Republican insurgency in Congress. In early 1995 he became the first Republican Speaker of the House in forty-two years. Most of the new Republicans in Congress credited "Newt" Gingrich for their election. In the late 1980s he had launched a series of attacks on the ethics of the Democratic leadership in the House, ultimately leading to the resignation of both Democratic Speaker Jim Wright and Democratic Whip Tony Coelho. Gingrich had also helped mobilize religious and social conservatives associated with the Christian Coalition.

In 1995 Gingrich assaulted the "welfare state" and sought to restore conservative values and principles. He was aided by the freshman Republicans, who came to Washington filled with ardor for Gingrich. More than half of all the House members and more than 60 percent of the Republicans had been first elected in the 1990s. Now the majority in the House, freshman Republicans promoted what Gingrich called the "Contract with America." The ten-point contract outlined an anti-big-government program with less regulation, less conservation, term limits for members of Congress, a line-item veto for the president, welfare reform, and a balanced-budget amendment. New members hailed their electoral victory as a mandate to enact the "Contract."

By April 13, exactly 100 days after taking office, the Republicans had passed twenty-six bills growing out of the Contract with America, and had failed to pass only two: a proposal for an anti-missile ("Star Wars") defense system and term limits for Congress. Nonetheless, twenty-two of these bills did not become law. The four bills that did become law were: a law mandating that all laws applicable to ordinary Americans should also apply to members of Congress; a law in which Congress agreed to stop imposing mandated programs on local and state governments without footing the bill; a large defense spending bill, which Clinton reluctantly accepted, lest Republicans rebel on foreign policy; and a new crime bill providing for stiff penalties for child abuse and pornography. The line-item veto would not pass until a year later.

Thereafter, the much ballyhooed GOP revolution and the "Contract with America" fizzled out. The revolution that Gingrich touted was far too ambitious to carry out in so limited a time, with so slim a majority, and with so little sense of crisis. What is more, many of the Republican freshmen were scornful of compromise and amateurs at the rules of order, and they limited the Speaker's room for maneuver. The Senate rejected many of the bills that had been passed in the House, as senators were less under Gingrich's spell and not party to the Contract with America anyway. And beyond them, a presidential veto stood in the path. Finally, President Clinton shrewdly moved to the political center and co-opted much of the Republican agenda. His distinctive strength—at least in the eyes of his supporters—resided in his agile responsiveness to changing public moods. To Clinton, the Republican victory in the 1994 congressional elections and in the passage of the Contract with America initiatives bore a simple message: he must recapture the political center by radically changing his agenda.

The Republicans' Contract with America succeeded in focusing public and presidential attention on basic questions of governmental philosophy. But Gingrich and other House Republican insurgents had overestimated the public's interest in dismantling the federal government and many of its social programs. To be sure, voters wanted to reduce the size and intrusiveness of the Washington bureaucracy, but they did not want to return to the laissez-faire approach of Calvin Coolidge and Herbert Hoover. By the end of 1995, it seemed clear that Clinton's fortunes were back on the rise as the Gingrich revolution petered out, leaving Gingrich with a bag of unfilled promises and with low ratings in the polls. If the American people had voted a mandate for anything, it may have been a mandate for the status quo. Said one contrite Republican freshman in 1996: "We scared too many people in the last year talking with such revolutionary fervor. I think we showed more guts than brains sometimes."

LEGISLATIVE BREAKTHROUGH   In the late summer of 1996, as lawmakers were preparing to adjourn and participate in the presidential nominating conventions, the 104th Congress broke through its partisan gridlock and passed a flurry of important legislation that President Clinton quickly signed.

Two of the bills increased the minimum wage and broadened access to health insurance. The $4.25 per hour minimum wage was increased by 90¢ over thirteen months. In exchange for their support of the wage increase, Republicans obtained $21 billion in tax cuts over ten years for small businesses. The health care measure, sponsored by Senator Nancy Kassebaum, a Kansas Republican, and Senator Edward Kennedy, a Massachusetts Democrat, allowed workers to keep their insurance coverage even if they changed jobs. The Kennedy-Kassebaum bill also made it harder for insurers to deny coverage to patients with a history of illness.

Even more significant was a comprehensive welfare reform measure that ended the federal government's open-ended guarantee of aid to the poor, a guarantee that had been in place since 1935. The Personal Responsibility and Work Opportunity Act turned over the major federal welfare programs to the states. In exchange, the states would receive federal grants to fund the programs. The bill also limited the amount of time a person could receive welfare benefits funded by federal money and required that at least half of a state's welfare recipients have jobs or be enrolled in job training programs by the year 2002. Those states failing to meet the deadline would have their federal funds cut.

The Republican-sponsored welfare reform legislation passed the Senate by a vote of 74–24. It had the effect of cutting $56 billion over six years from Aid to Families with Dependent Children, food stamps, and other programs, several of which dated back to Franklin Roosevelt's New Deal. In total budgets of about $1.5 trillion, that amounted to less than 1 percent. Senator Patrick Moynihan, the New York Democrat who had been a champion of federal social-welfare programs since the 1960s, predicted that over 3.5 million children would be thrown into poverty as a result of the bill. He and other liberals charged that Clinton was abdicating Democratic social principles in order to gain reelection amid the conservative climate of the times. Democratic senator Christopher Dodd of Connecticut called the president's action "unconscionable."

Clinton and his centrist advisers, however, dismissed such criticisms. With his reelection bid at stake, he was determined to live up to his 1992 campaign pledge to "end welfare as we know it." Clinton also knew that most voters in both parties were eager to see major cuts in federal entitlement programs.

THE 1996 CAMPAIGN   After clinching the Republican nomination in March 1996, Majority Leader Bob Dole resigned his Senate seat in order to devote his attention to defeating Bill Clinton. "I will seek the

Former Republican Senate Majority Leader Bob Dole on the campaign trail.

presidency," he said, "with nothing to fall back on but the judgment of the people, and nowhere to go but the White House or home."

Born in Kansas in 1923, the product of a hardscrabble existence in a small prairie town, Dole enrolled in the University of Kansas in 1941, only to be drawn into military service during World War II. During a battle in Italy, a piece of shrapnel shattered his right shoulder and fractured his neck. It took thirty-nine months and seven separate operations before he could leave the hospital. His right arm and hand remained permanently paralyzed.

Driven by a gritty determination to succeed despite his physical setback, Dole graduated from college and law school and then entered local politics. By 1960 he was a member of the House of Representatives, and nine years later he gained election to the Senate. In 1976 Dole served as Gerald Ford's running mate, only to return to the Senate after the Carter-Mondale victory. Dole developed a reputation as a brilliant legislative tactician and a tough, smart, and honest leader known for his ability to build consensus and forge coalitions. An unsuccessful candidate for the presidential nomination in 1980 and 1988, Dole was officially nominated at the Republican convention in San Diego in mid-August 1996.

As the 1996 presidential campaign unfolded, Clinton maintained a large lead in the polls. With a generally healthy economy and with no major foreign policy crises to confront, cultural and personal issues surged into prominence. Concern about Dole's age (seventy-three) and his acerbic manner, as well as rifts in the Republican party between economic and social conservatives over issues such as abortion and gun control, hampered Dole's efforts to generate widespread support.

To jump-start his lagging campaign, Dole announced a surprise choice for his running mate: Jack Kemp, the former pro football star for the Buffalo Bills, a congressman, secretary of Housing and Urban Development under Bush, and presidential candidate himself. On economic issues, Kemp and Dole had been poles apart. Dole represented the Eisenhower wing of the Republican party in promoting deficit reduction and a balanced budget. Kemp was a Reaganite in his commitment to supply-side economic theory and large tax cuts. Yet Dole now embraced not only Kemp but his economics, proposing a 15 percent income tax cut across the board coupled with increased tax credits for dependent children and capital gains tax cuts and a balanced budget. This program assumed that people would spend the estimated $600 billion from tax cuts over the next six years and thereby generate record economic growth that in turn would raise tax revenues.

Clinton scorned Dole's tax cut and responded with smaller targeted tax reductions. Democrats claimed that Republicans wanted to "pay for" the tax cut with cuts in Medicare. Republicans had come to rely heavily on cultural issues, largely under the rubric of "family values," but Clinton had co-opted much of that with his Family and Medical Leave Act, student loans, and increase in the minimum wage.

Late in the campaign, Dole charged that the Democrats had raised unprecedented sums of money by dubious means. The role of people with foreign connections in the fund-raising even gave rise to suspicions that money from abroad had found its way into Democratic accounts. Yet while Clinton excited extreme animosity in his enemies, he was also like Reagan, the "Teflon president," to whom none of their charges stuck. The polls favored Clinton so heavily that a pall of depression seemed to fall over the Dole campaign.

On November 5 Clinton won again with an electoral vote of 379 to 159 and 49 percent of the popular vote. He lost Georgia, Colorado, and Montana, but added Arizona and Florida to his column. Dole received

President Bill Clinton and Vice-President Al Gore at the 1996 Democratic National Convention in Chicago.

41 percent and Perot got 8 percent of the popular vote. Thus Clinton would remain a minority president, and once again he would be denied a Democratic majority in Congress. The Republicans lost eight seats in the House, but suspicions of Democratic money scandals may have helped them hold control of Congress. They held a 227–207 edge over the Democrats in the House; in the Senate Republicans gained two seats for a 55–45 majority. The resulting deadlock reflected the conservative mood of the times.

CLINTON'S SECOND TERM

After the election, Clinton reshuffled his cabinet and other posts. Madeleine Albright, ambassador to the United Nations, became the first woman to head the State Department, and Senator William Cohen, a Republican from Maine, took over at the Defense Department. The overall direction of his changes was a move to the right.

THE "NEW ECONOMY"   As the twentieth century comes to a close, the United States has benefited from a prolonged period of unprecedented prosperity. Buoyed by low inflation, high employment, declining federal budget deficits, dramatic improvements in productivity, the rapid "globalization" of economic life, and the firm and astute leadership of Federal Reserve Board Chairman Alan Greenspan, American business and industry have witnessed record profits.

The stock market soared during the late 1990s. In 1993 the Dow Jones industrial average hit 3,500. By 1996 it had topped 6,000. During 1998, it reached 9,000, defying the predictions of experts that the economy could not sustain such performance. In 1998 unemployment was only 4.3 percent, the lowest since 1970. Inflation was a measly 1.7 percent. "The current economic performance," observed Greenspan, ". . . is as impressive as any I have witnessed." He and others began to talk of a "new economy" that defied the boom-and-bust cycles of the previous hundred years. "It is possible," Greenspan suggested, "that we have moved 'beyond history.'"

By 1998 swelling tax revenues generated a federal budget surplus. Such sustained prosperity seemed to support the "monetarist" philosophy of the Nobel Prize–winning economist Professor Milton Friedman. Keynesian economics, which had emerged against the background of deflation and prolonged depression in the 1930s, had favored fiscal remedies (deficit spending) to stimulate economic growth. Monetarists such as Friedman believed that economic growth would best be promoted by a stable monetary supply (cash plus bank accounts), and they feared inflation more than unemployment. To them, the key to economic stability was the Federal Reserve's power to regulate interest rates.

Before President Clinton took office, he was persuaded to support Greenspan's monetarist policies and was convinced that a balanced budget was necessary to keep government borrowing from putting inflationary pressure on interest rates. Clinton chose to reduce deficits in part by spending cuts, in part by a tax hike on upper income brackets. At the same time, he abandoned promised tax cuts for middle income brackets. His supporters claimed, however, that he had put the country on the way to a balanced budget and financial stability.

In the past, invention and innovation had been basic to economic booms. Much of this had been in electronics, ever since the transistor replaced the vacuum tube in 1947 and created the television revolution at mid-century. Yet, in the 1990s, much of the surging economy resulted from "globalization." The "new" classical economics of Friedman and Greenspan favored free markets on a world scale—markets without tariffs and other barriers. More and more gigantic corporations such as International Business Machines or General Electric had become international in scope. This encouraged free trade agreements such as NAFTA or most-favored-nation treatment for China and other countries. American companies might then "outsource" much of their production to plants in countries with lower labor costs. This led to a decline of the labor union movement and to corporate moves toward "downsizing," which worked wonders with stock prices, whether or not it served business efficiency. Blue-collar labor lost ground to cheap labor in assembly plants or "sweatshops" elsewhere in the world. Part-time labor became popular because employers could avoid paying for expensive benefits—whether for flipping hamburgers or for teaching. At the same time, it became notorious for chief executives to win extravagant rewards for downsizing workers, even for sheer arrogance, it sometimes seemed, as in the case of Albert J. Dunlop, a.k.a. "Chain Saw Al," "the Shredder," "Rambo in Pinstripes."

RACE INITIATIVE   Since the triumphs of the civil rights movement in the 1960s, the momentum for minority advancement had run out—except for gains in college admissions and employment under the rubric of "affirmative action." The principle of affirmative action, as stated by President Lyndon Johnson in 1965, involved an effort to overcome the effects of past discrimination. "We seek not just equality as a right and theory," Johnson said, "but equality as a fact and equality as a result." Affirmative action covered a variety of devices, but mainly involved the inclusion of race among other criteria for jobs and admissions. Such measures were extended under Richard Nixon.

Despite moves by Reagan and Bush staff members to limit such measures, the outcry from minority leaders caused both administrations to back away from outright opposition to affirmative action. The Supreme Court, as well, accepted such measures, including voluntary programs of corporations and other institutions. Race could be a factor among others, but racial quotas were ruled out.

In the 1980s and 1990s, however, the outlook of the federal courts began to shift to the right. The conservative mood during the mid-

1990s also manifested itself in the Supreme Court. One consequence was a challenge to the legality of gerrymandering (redrawing) congressional and legislative districts to create black or Hispanic majorities. Minorities had favored gerrymandering to increase minority officeholding, and Republicans had favored it because such districts would draw minority votes from other districts. But in *Thaw* v. *Reno* (1993), the Court ruled that such districts in North Carolina violated equal protection of the law.

In 1995, a conservative Court again ruled against election districts redrawn to create black or Hispanic majorities, narrowed federal affirmative action programs, and limited the legal remedies for segregated public schools. All were decided by the same vote of 5–4 (Chief Justice Rehnquist, and Justices Kennedy, O'Connor, Scalia, and Thomas deciding against Justices Breyer, Ginsburg, Souter, and Stevens).

In one of the cases, *Adarand Constructors* v. *Peña* (1995), the Court assessed a program that gave some advantages to businesses owned by "disadvantaged" minorities. An Hispanic-owned firm had won a highway guard rail contract over a lower bid by a white-owned company. The white-owned company sued on the ground of "reverse discrimination." For the majority, Justice O'Connor said that such programs had to be "narrowly tailored" to serve a "compelling national interest." O'Connor did not define what the Court meant by a "compelling national interest," but the implication of her language was clear: the Court had come to embrace the growing public suspicion of the value and legality of such race-based programs.

Conservatives found a new battle cry in "racial preferences." In the area of college admissions, especially, this would mean falling back on such criteria as scores on the Scholastic Aptitude Test (SAT), high school grades, and special consideration for children of alumni or those talented at playing the oboe or basketball—none of which is above suspicion of racial bias one way or the other.

In 1996 two major new steps were taken against affirmative action in college admissions. In *Hopwood* v. *Texas* (1996), the Fifth Circuit Court ruled that considering race to achieve a diverse student body at the University of Texas was "not a compelling interest under the Fourteenth Amendment." In November, the state of California, while voting for Clinton, also passed Proposition 209, an initiative that ruled out race, sex, ethnicity, or national origin as criteria for preferring any group.

These rulings eviscerated affirmative action programs and drastically reduced black enrollments, something that caused second thoughts. In Texas, for instance, a new state law guaranteed admission to the state university for 10 percent of any high school class—some argued for high school grades as a better predictor of college performance than SAT scores—and in Houston voters rejected a proposition to abandon an affirmative action program adopted by the city.

Programs of affirmative action, which had gained widespread acceptance over a quarter of a century, remained under siege. And affirmative action still did not address intractable problems that lay beyond civil rights, that is, problems of dependency—illiteracy, poverty, unemployment, urban decay, and slums.

THE SCANDAL MACHINE   Since before his first election in 1992, Clinton had faced allegations of both sexual and financial scandal that grew into a relentless inquiry such as no previous president had ever before encountered. In the 1970s, the Watergate scandal had provoked the Ethics in Government Act of 1978, which created an office of "special prosecutor" (renamed "independent counsel" in 1988) to investigate allegations against high officials in the government. The law, renewed in 1982 and 1988, was allowed to lapse in 1992, but it was renewed early in 1994.

During his first term, Clinton was dogged by allegations of improper involvement in the Whitewater Development Company. In 1978, as governor of Arkansas, he had invested in a resort project on the White River in northern Arkansas. The project turned out to be a fraud and a failure, and the Clintons took a loss on their investment. James MacDougal, the promoter of the project, also took over a small savings and loan, Madison Guaranty, and turned it into one of the go-go ventures of the flush years of wildcat banking in the 1980s. It collapsed in 1989, but in the fall of 1993, reports surfaced that Madison money had gone into the foundering Whitewater project and that Madison Guaranty had misused funds in the Clinton campaign. Robert Fiske was named as independent counsel to investigate the allegations of improper Clinton involvement in Whitewater. While revealing that Hillary Clinton had handled some legal work for the Whitewater Development Company, Fiske did not uncover evidence that the Clintons were involved in the fraud.

The ongoing Whitewater investigation threatened to derail important initiatives as it occupied the attention of the president and Congress.

In 1994, Fiske was replaced with another Republican independent counsel, Kenneth Starr, who continued to investigate the Whitewater case. Although Starr had a reputation for fairness, many believed that his unwillingness to end the investigation and his former subcabinet position in the Bush administration suggested a taint of partisanship. After nearly four years of expensive investigation, Starr found no criminal involvement by the Clintons, although a number of their close associates had been caught in the web and convicted of various charges, some related to Whitewater and some not.

The office of independent counsel, created to insure investigations free from conflict of interest, instead contributed to a political culture of scandal. Every president after Nixon saw at least one of his subordinates, if not himself, under criminal investigation. By early 1998, some $50 million had been spent investigating Clinton and his administration. Besides Whitewater, these investigators looked into Paula Jones's allegations that Clinton had sexually harassed her while he was governor and she was a state employee in Arkansas. Clinton's lawyers sought postponement of the Paula Jones case until 2001 on the principle that such spiteful actions against a sitting president could foster enough lawsuits to disable the presidency. But in May 1997 the Supreme Court unanimously dismissed that claim. Clinton's lawyers then sought to invoke executive privilege to prevent the questioning of aides and secret service personnel, but that too was rejected by the Court.

In the course of the investigation, it surfaced that the president may have had a sexual affair with a former White House intern, Monica Lewinsky, and may have pressed her to lie about it under oath. The public was titillated by the initial allegations of the alleged affair as expressed by Lewinsky in phone conversations that a coworker had taped without her knowledge. By the spring of 1998, some Republicans in Congress were even discussing the possibility of impeachment proceedings. Meanwhile, the Paula Jones case was dismissed by a judge in Arkansas on the ground that, even if everything charged against the president were true, Paula Jones still did not have a legal claim to sexual harassment under the law, which required that the claimant must have suffered discrimination in her employment. At the same time, polls suggested that a majority did not care whether Clinton had had an affair with Lewinsky. This seemed to imply the public's contentment with the way things were going, especially the soaring economy—and perhaps a wish that the scandal would simply go away and not become a constitutional crisis.

But the tawdry scandal would not disappear. In August 1998, in the face of a possible subpoena from the independent counsel, President Clinton agreed to testify before the grand jury investigating the allegations about him. He was the first president in history to do so. On August 17, with the nation anxiously awaiting the results, the federal grand jury watched on closed-circuit television while Clinton testified using a video hookup from the White House. During his six hours of closed-door testimony, the president recanted his earlier denials and acknowledged having had "inappropriate intimate physical contact" with White House intern Monica Lewinsky.

That evening Clinton delivered a four-minute televised address to the nation in which he admitted that he did, in fact, have an inappropriate and "wrong" relationship with Lewinsky, but insisted he had done nothing illegal. "I know that my public comments and my silence about this matter gave a false impression. I misled people, including even my wife," Clinton said. "I deeply regret that."

Clinton's admission was a stunning reversal from his insistent public denials over the previous seven months. His dishonesty, he explained, was motivated by a desire to protect his family and "myself from the embarrassment of my own conduct." Had Clinton stopped there, he might have avoided much of the angry criticism that greeted his disclosure. But he went on to attack the "politically inspired" investigation.

Public reaction to Clinton's remarkable about-face was mixed. A majority of Americans expressed sympathy for the president because of his public humiliation and wanted the entire matter dropped. But polls also showed that Clinton's credibility had suffered a serious blow.

Meanwhile, Starr continued his tenacious investigation, trying to determine if Clinton had obstructed the investigation and had encouraged Lewinsky to lie about their affair. On September 9, 1998, Starr submitted to Congress his 445-page report and eighteen boxes of supporting evidence. The report found "substantial and credible" evidence of wrongdoing by the president. The Republican-controlled House Judiciary Committee voted to recommend a full impeachment inquiry into perjury and obstruction of justice allegations against Clinton, and on October 8, the House of Representatives voted 258–176 to begin the inquiry. Yet, with a surprisingly strong Democratic showing in the November elections, the Republicans found their majority in Congress eroded, perhaps as a result of public disgust with the continuing investigation. Republican dismay at their losses prompted Speaker of the House Newt Gingrich to resign. He announced that he could no longer effectively lead congressional Republicans. As House Judiciary Committee hearings got underway in the late fall, the fate of the Clinton presidency still hung in the balance.

FIN-DE-SIÈCLE AMERICA

The approach of the year 2000 has prompted contradictory reflections upon American life at the end of a millennium and the start of the twenty-first century. As at the close of the last century, referred to as the *fin-de-siècle* (a French term for "end of the century"), many people are celebrating the unprecedented prosperity and amazing technological breakthroughs of the times. But, as in 1900, other observers are more gloomy. Skeptical of material notions of perpetual progress and worried about the cohesion of an increasingly diverse population, they have expressed an anxious foreboding about societal dissolution and decay.

As the twentieth century draws to a close, the United States seems to be experiencing the best and worst of times. The economy remains on the crest of a wave of record-setting productivity and profits, inflation is dormant, and the federal government is enjoying balanced budgets for the first time in over a generation. The cold war is over, the nuclear arms race has ended, and the digital revolution is in full swing. Americans are enjoying their personal freedoms, their cornucopia of consumer goods, and their sophisticated technologies. They are also living longer than ever.

Yet a *Times Mirror* survey portrays a prosperous nation awash in anxiety and self-doubt, with some 73 percent of Americans expressing dissatisfaction with "the way things are going." Soaring rates of teenage drug use, violence, and suicide provide conspicuous evidence of social problems. Moreover, people express growing concern about job security and job-related stress, rising health care costs, the adequacy of savings for college and retirement, and turmoil in the world economy—especially Asia and South America—and the resulting tremors in the American stock market, which threaten the stability of the U.S. economy. New technologies are improving productivity and efficiency, but many people are working harder and longer than ever before to keep up with the "wired" workplace and a culture of rising expectations.

The most acute concern is the ability of our multicultural society to get along in the midst of our seductive freedoms. Seemingly intractable issues threaten to unravel the social fabric. Religious, racial, and ethnic-related tensions are growing, and the gap between rich and poor is widening. Our obsession with individual rights is eroding our ability to behave socially. In-your-face confrontation, narrow group loyalties, and bipartisan moral arrogance have displaced respectful dialogue and civic virtue. As the perceptive cartoonist Walt Kelly once observed in his Pogo comic strip, "We have met the enemy and he is us."

Some cultural analysts worry that the ferocious, take-no-prisoners nature of public discourse and political campaigns is undermining the consensus needed for democracy to work. Divisive issues such as abortion, gun control, doctor-assisted suicide, affirmative action, prayer in schools, political correctness, and gay rights, to name a few, have fostered a special-interest sectarianism that has disrupted and divided communities, political parties, and churches.

In 1995 Harvard political scientist Robert Putnam addressed such issues in a provocative essay entitled "Bowling Alone: The Decline of Social Capital" in which he declared that the "social fabric is becoming visibly thinner, our connections among each other are becoming visibly thinner. We don't trust one another as much, and we don't know one another as much. And, of course, this is behind the deterioration of the political dialogue, the deterioration of public debate." Putnam highlighted plummeting membership in organizations such as the PTA, Red Cross, Boy Scouts, and the League of Women Voters, as well as civic clubs and labor unions. He blamed such declining civic involvement on many aspects of popular culture—television, VCRs, and personal computers—for distracting people from their social responsibilities. Technological change, Putnam noted, is privatizing leisure time by promoting solitary forms of entertainment.

But Putnam's influential thesis overlooks contrary evidence of civic energy and social interaction. Today Americans engage with each other in many different forms of association. Voluntarism is soaring, as are other group activities. Youth soccer leagues and spectator sports, fitness centers and social clubs, for instance, are examples of popular culture activities that generate a shared discourse and bring people together.

Yet more needs to be done to strengthen the social fabric. "Our greatest responsibility," said President Clinton in his second inaugural address, "is to embrace a new spirit of community for a new century." It is an old ideal. In 1630 Governor John Winthrop told the Puritan colonists settling near Boston that "We must delight in each other, make others' conditions our own, rejoice together, mourn together, labor and suffer together, having always before our eyes our community as members of the same body." *E pluribus unum*—one out of many. At the start of a new century, it remains the best definition of what the unique American experiment in self-government means. It also remains America's greatest hope—and its greatest challenge.

FURTHER READING

On the Bush presidency, see Ryan J. Barilleaux and Mary E. Stuckey's *Leadership and the Bush Presidency: Prudence or Drift in an Era of Change* (1992), Charles Tiefer's *The Semi-Sovereign Presidency: The Bush Administration's Strategy for Governing without Congress* (1994). Among the journalistic accounts of the presidential election of 1992, the best narrative is Jack Germond and Jules Witcover's *Mad as Hell: Revolt at the Ballot Box, 1992* (1993). The best scholarly study is Theodore J. Lowi and Benjamin Ginsberg's *Democrats Return to Power: Politics and Policy in the Clinton Era* (1994).

On Bill Clinton, up to his presidency, the best treatment is David Maraniss's *First in His Class: A Biography of Bill Clinton* (1995). The early months of the Clinton presidency are most thoroughly covered in Elizabeth Drew's *On the Edge: The Clinton Presidency* (1994). Bob Woodward's *The Agenda: Inside the Clinton White House* (1994) focuses on financial policies and the economy. For a psychoanalytic assessment of Clinton, see Stanley A. Renshon's *High Hopes: The Clinton Presidency and the Politics of Ambition* (1996). Recent analysis of the Clinton years can be found in *The Clinton Presidency: First Appraisals* (1995), edited by Colin Campbell and Bert A. Rockman, and *Back to Gridlock?: Governance in the Clinton Years* (1996), edited by James L. Sundquist. For a Republican perspective, see Haley Barbour's *Agenda for America: A Republican Direction for the Future* (1996).

On social and cultural problems and issues of the times, a good account is Haynes Johnson's *Divided We Fall: Gambling with History in the Nineties* (1994), based on street interviews around the country during 1992. Collections of magazine and newspaper articles are in John Leo's *Two Steps Ahead of the Thought Police* (1994), Molly Ivins's *Nothin' But Good Times Ahead* (1993), and George F. Will's *The Leveling Wind: Politics, the Culture, and Other News, 1990–1994* (1994). The onset and growth of the AIDS epidemic are traced in *And the Band Played On: Politics, People, and the AIDS Epidemic* (1987) by Randy Shilts, a journalist who reported much of the story, and in essays edited by historians Elizabeth Fee and Daniel M. Fox, *AIDS: The Burdens of History* (1988) and *AIDS: The Making of a Chronic Disease* (1992).

Aspects of fundamentalist and apocalyptic movements are the subject of Paul L. Boyer's *When Time Shall Be No More: Prophecy and Belief in Modern American Culture* (1992), George M. Marsden's *Understanding Fundamentalism and Evangelicalism* (1991), and Ralph Reed's *Politically Incorrect: The Emerging Faith Factor in American Politics* (1994).

Aspects of recent cultural debates can be found in *Culture Wars: Documents from the Recent Controversies in the Arts* (1992), edited by Richard Bolton; Gerald Graff's *Beyond the Culture Wars: How Teaching the Conflicts Can Revitalize American Education* (1992); and *The Politics of Liberal Education* (1992), edited by Darryl Gless and Barbara Herrnstein Smith.

On the banking and other scandals, see L. William Seidman's *Full Faith and Credit: The Great S & L Debacle and Other Washington Sagas* (1993). Aspects of corporate restructuring and downsizing are the subject of Bennett Harrison's *Lean and Mean: The Changing Landscape of Corporate Power in the Age of Flexibility* (1994). The story of the Whitewater affair is the subject of Martin L. Gross's *The Great Whitewater Fiasco: An American Tale of Money, Power, and Politics* (1994).

For further treatment of the end of the cold war, see Michael R. Beschloss's *At the Highest Levels: The Inside Story of the End of the Cold War* (1993), Thomas J. McCormick's *America's Half Century: United States Foreign Policy in the Cold War and After* (2nd ed., 1995), Richard Crockatt's *The Fifty Years War: The United States and the Soviet Union in World Politics, 1941–1991* (1995), and Zbigniew Brzezinski's *Out of Control: Global Turmoil on the Eve of the Twenty-first Century* (1994). On the Panama and Persian Gulf conflicts, see Edward W. Flanagan's *Battle for Panama: Inside Operation Just Cause* (1993), Bruce W. Jentleson's *With Friends Like These: Reagan, Bush, and Saddam, 1982–1990* (1994), and Lester H. Brune's *America and the Iraqi Crisis, 1990–1992: Origins and Aftermath* (1993).

APPENDIX

THE DECLARATION
OF INDEPENDENCE

WHEN IN THE COURSE OF HUMAN EVENTS, it becomes necessary for one people to dissolve the political bands which have connected them with another, and to assume among the Powers of the earth, the separate and equal station to which the Laws of Nature and of Nature's God entitle them, a decent respect to the opinions of mankind requires that they should declare the causes which impel them to the separation.

We hold these truths to be self-evident, that all men are created equal, that they are endowed by their Creator with certain unalienable rights, that among these are Life, Liberty, and the pursuit of Happiness. That to secure these rights, Governments are instituted among Men, deriving their just powers from the consent of the governed. That whenever any Form of Government becomes destructive of these ends, it is the Right of the People to alter or to abolish it, and to institute new Government, laying its foundation on such principles and organizing its powers in such form, as to them shall seem most likely to effect their Safety and Happiness. Prudence, indeed, will dictate that Governments long established should not be changed for light and transient causes; and accordingly all experience hath shown, that mankind are more disposed to suffer, while evils are sufferable, than to right themselves by abolishing the forms to which they are accustomed. But when a long train of abuses and usurpations, pursuing invariably the same Object evinces a design to reduce them under absolute Despotism, it is their right, it is their duty, to throw off such Government, and to provide new Guards for their future security.— Such has been the patient sufferance of these Colonies; and such is now the necessity which constrains them to alter their former Systems of Government. The history of the present King of Great Britain is a history of repeated injuries and usurpations, all having in direct object the establishment of an absolute Tyranny over these States. To prove this, let Facts be submitted to a candid world.

He has refused his Assent to Laws, the most wholesome and necessary for the public good.

He has forbidden his Governors to pass Laws of immediate and pressing importance, unless suspended in their operation till his Assent should be obtained; and when so suspended, he has utterly neglected to attend to them.

He has refused to pass other Laws for the accommodation of large districts of people, unless those people would relinquish the right of Representation in the Legislature, a right inestimable to them and formidable to tyrants only.

He has called together legislative bodies at places unusual, uncomfortable, and distant from the depository of their public Records, for the sole purpose of fatiguing them into compliance with his measures.

He has dissolved Representative Houses repeatedly, for opposing with manly firmness his invasions on the rights of the people.

He has refused for a long time, after such dissolutions, to cause others to be elected; whereby the Legislative powers, incapable of Annihilation, have returned to the People at large for their exercise; the State remaining in the mean time exposed to all dangers of invasion from without, and convulsions within.

He has endeavoured to prevent the population of these States; for that purpose obstructing the Laws of Naturalization of Foreigners; refusing to pass others to encourage their migrations hither, and raising the conditions of new Appropriations of Lands.

He has obstructed the Administration of Justice, by refusing his Assent to Laws for establishing Judiciary powers.

He has made Judges dependent on his Will alone, for the tenure of their offices, and the amount and payment of their salaries.

He has erected a multitude of New Offices, and sent hither swarms of Officers to harass our People, and eat out their substance.

He has kept among us, in times of peace, Standing Armies without the Consent of our legislatures.

He has affected to render the Military independent of and superior to the Civil Power.

He has combined with others to subject us to a jurisdiction foreign to our constitution, and unacknowledged by our laws; giving his Assent to their Acts of pretended Legislation:

For quartering large bodies of armed troops among us:

For protecting them, by a mock Trial, from Punishment for any Murders which they should commit on the Inhabitants of these States:

For cutting off our Trade with all parts of the world:

For imposing taxes on us without our Consent:

For depriving us in many cases, of the benefits of Trial by jury:

For transporting us beyond Seas to be tried for pretended offences:

For abolishing the free System of English Laws in a neighbouring Province, establishing therein an Arbitrary government, and enlarging its Boundaries so as to render it at once an example and fit instrument for introducing the same absolute rule into these Colonies:

For taking away our Charters, abolishing our most valuable Laws, and altering fundamentally the Forms of our Governments:

For suspending our own Legislatures, and declaring themselves in vested with Power to legislate for us in all cases whatsoever.

He has abdicated Government here, by declaring us out of his Protection and waging War against us.

He has plundered our seas, ravaged our Coasts, burnt our towns, and destroyed the lives of our people.

He is at this time transporting large armies of foreign mercenaries to compleat the works of death, desolation, and tyranny, already begun with circumstances of Cruelty & perfidy scarcely paralleled in the most barbarous ages, and totally unworthy the Head of a civilized nation.

He has constrained our fellow Citizens taken Captive on the high Seas to bear Arms against their Country, to become the executioners of their friends and Brethren, or to fall themselves by their Hands.

He has excited domestic insurrections amongst us, and has endeavoured to bring on the inhabitants of our frontiers, the merciless Indian Savages, whose known rule of warfare, is an undistinguished destruction of all ages, sexes, and conditions.

In every stage of these Oppressions We have Petitioned for Redress in the most humble terms: Our repeated Petitions have been answered only by repeated injury. A Prince, whose character is thus marked by every act which may define a Tyrant, is unfit to be the ruler of a free people.

Nor have We been wanting in attention to our British brethren. We have warned them from time to time of attempts by their legislature to extend an unwarrantable jurisdiction over us. We have reminded them of the circumstances of our emigration and settlement here. We have appealed to their native justice and magnanimity, and we have conjured them by the ties of our common kindred to disavow these usurpations, which, would inevitably interrupt our connections and correspondence. They too must have been deaf to the voice of justice and of consanguinity. We must, therefore, acquiesce in the necessity, which denounces our Separation, and hold them, as we hold the rest of mankind, Enemies in War, in Peace Friends.

WE, THEREFORE, the Representatives of the UNITED STATES OF AMERICA, in General Congress, Assembled, appealing to the Supreme Judge of the world for the rectitude of our intentions, do, in the Name, and by Authority of the good People of these Colonies, solemnly publish and declare, That these United Colonies are, and of Right ought to be FREE AND INDEPENDENT STATES; that they are Absolved from all Allegiance to the British

Crown, and that all political connection between them and the State of Great Britain, is and ought to be totally dissolved; and that as Free and Independent States, they have full Power to levy War, conclude Peace, contract Alliances, establish Commerce, and to do all other Acts and Things which Independent States may of right do. And for the support of this Declaration, with a firm reliance on the Protection of Divine Providence, we mutually pledge to each other our Lives, our Fortunes, and our sacred Honor.

The foregoing Declaration was, by order of Congress, engrossed, and signed by the following members:

John Hancock

NEW HAMPSHIRE
Josiah Bartlett
William Whipple
Matthew Thornton

MASSACHUSETTS BAY
Samuel Adams
John Adams
Robert Treat Paine
Elbridge Gerry

RHODE ISLAND
Stephen Hopkins
William Ellery

CONNECTICUT
Roger Sherman
Samuel Huntington
William Williams
Oliver Wolcott

NEW YORK
William Floyd
Philip Livingston
Francis Lewis
Lewis Morris

NEW JERSEY
Richard Stockton
John Witherspoon
Francis Hopkinson
John Hart
Abraham Clark

PENNSYLVANIA
Robert Morris
Benjamin Rush
Benjamin Franklin
John Morton
George Clymer
James Smith
George Taylor
James Wilson
George Ross

DELAWARE
Caesar Rodney
George Read
Thomas M'Kean

MARYLAND
Samuel Chase
William Paca
Thomas Stone
Charles Carroll, of Carrollton

VIRGINIA
George Wythe
Richard Henry Lee
Thomas Jefferson
Benjamin Harrison
Thomas Nelson, Jr.
Francis Lightfoot Lee
Carter Braxton

NORTH CAROLINA
William Hooper
Joseph Hewes
John Penn

SOUTH CAROLINA
Edward Rutledge
Thomas Heyward, Jr.
Thomas Lynch, Jr.
Arthur Middleton

GEORGIA
Button Gwinnett
Lyman Hall
George Walton

Resolved, That copies of the Declaration be sent to the several assemblies, conventions, and committees, or councils of safety, and to the several commanding officers of the continental troops; that it be proclaimed in each of the United States, at the head of the army.

ARTICLES OF
CONFEDERATION

To ALL TO WHOM these Presents shall come, we the undersigned Delegates of the States affixed to our Names send greeting.

Whereas the Delegates of the United States of America in Congress assembled did on the fifteenth day of November in the Year of our Lord One Thousand Seven Hundred and Seventy-seven, and in the Second Year of the Independence of America agree to certain articles of Confederation and perpetual Union between the States of Newhampshire, Massachusetts-bay, Rhodeisland and Providence Plantations, Connecticut, New York, New Jersey, Pennsylvania, Delaware, Maryland, Virginia, North-Carolina, South-Carolina and Georgia in the Words following, viz.

Articles of Confederation and perpetual Union between the States of Newhampshire, Massachusetts-bay, Rhodeisland and Providence Plantations, Connecticut, New-York, New-Jersey, Pennsylvania, Delaware, Maryland, Virginia, North-Carolina, South-Carolina and Georgia.

ARTICLE I. The stile of this confederacy shall be "The United States of America."

ARTICLE II. Each State retains its sovereignty, freedom and independence, and every power, jurisdiction and right, which is not by this confederation expressly delegated to the United States, in Congress assembled.

ARTICLE III. The said States hereby severally enter into a firm league of friendship with each other, for their common defence, the security of their liberties, and their mutual and general welfare, binding themselves to assist each other, against all force offered to, or attacks made upon them, or any of them, on account of religion, sovereignty, trade or any other pretence whatever.

ARTICLE IV. The better to secure and perpetuate mutual friendship and intercourse among the people of the different States in this Union, the free inhabitants of each of these States, paupers, vagabonds and fugitives from justice excepted, shall be entitled to all privileges and immunities of free citizens in the several States; and the people of each State shall have free ingress and regress to and from any other State, and shall enjoy therein all the privileges of trade and commerce, subject to the same duties, impositions and restrictions as the inhabitants thereof respectively, provided that such restrictions shall not extend so far as to prevent the removal of property imported into any State, to any other State of which the owner is an inhabitant; provided also that no imposition, duties or restriction shall be laid by any State, on the property of the United States, or either of them.

If any person guilty of, or charged with treason, felony, or other high misdemeanor in any State, shall flee from justice, and be found in any of the United States, he shall upon demand of the Governor or Executive power, of the State from which he fled, be delivered up and removed to the State having jurisdiction of his offence.

Full faith and credit shall be given in each of these States to the records, acts and judicial proceedings of the courts and magistrates of every other State.

ARTICLE V. For the more convenient management of the general interests of the United States, delegates shall be annually appointed in such manner as the legislature of each State shall direct, to meet in Congress on the first Monday in November, in every year, with a power reserved to each State, to recall its delegates, or any of them, at any time within the year, and to send others in their stead, for the remainder of the year.

No State shall be represented in Congress by less than two, nor by more than seven members; and no person shall be capable of being a delegate for more than three years in any term of six years; nor shall any person, being a delegate, be capable of holding any office under the United States, for which he, or another for his benefit receives any salary, fees or emolument of any kind.

Each State shall maintain its own delegates in a meeting of the States, and while they act as members of the committee of the States.

In determining questions in the United States, in Congress assembled, each State shall have one vote.

Freedom of speech and debate in Congress shall not be impeached or questioned in any court, or place out of Congress, and the members of Congress shall be protected in their persons from arrests and imprisonments, during the time of their going to and from, and attendance on Congress, except for treason, felony, or breach of the peace.

ARTICLE VI. No State without the consent of the United States in Congress assembled, shall send any embassy to, or receive any embassy from, or enter into any conference, agreement, alliance or treaty with any king, prince or state; nor shall any person holding any office of profit or trust under the United States, or any of them, accept of any present, emolument, office or title of any kind whatever from any king, prince or foreign state; nor shall the United States in Congress assembled, or any of them, grant any title of nobility.

No two or more States shall enter into any treaty, confederation or alliance whatever between them, without the consent of the United States in Congress assembled, specifying accurately the purposes for which the same is to be entered into, and how long it shall continue.

No State shall lay any imposts or duties, which may interfere with any stipulations in treaties, entered into by the United States in Congress assembled, with any king, prince or state, in pursuance of any treaties already proposed by Congress, to the courts of France and Spain.

No vessels of war shall be kept up in time of peace by any State, except such number only, as shall be deemed necessary by the United States in Congress assembled, for the defence of such State, or its trade; nor shall any body of forces be kept up by any State, in time of peace, except such number only, as in the judgment of the United States, in Congress assembled, shall be deemed requisite to garrison the forts necessary for the defence of such State; but every State shall always keep up a well regulated and disciplined militia, sufficiently armed and accoutred, and shall provide and constantly have ready for use, in public stores, a due number of field pieces and tents, and a proper quantity of arms, ammunition and camp equipage.

No State shall engage in any war without the consent of the United States in Congress assembled, unless such State be actually invaded by enemies, or shall have received certain advice of a resolution being formed by some nation of Indians to invade such State, and the danger is so imminent as not to admit of a delay, till the United States in Congress assembled can be consulted: nor shall any State grant commissions to any ships or vessels of war, nor letters of marque or reprisal, except it be after a declaration of war by the United States in Congress assembled, and then only against the kingdom or state and the subjects thereof, against which war has been so declared, and under such regulations as shall be established by the United States in Congress assembled, unless such State be infested by pirates, in which case vessels of war may be fitted out for that occasion, and kept so long as the danger shall continue, or until the United States in Congress assembled shall determine otherwise.

ARTICLE VII. When land-forces are raised by any State of the common defence, all officers of or under the rank of colonel, shall be appointed by the

Legislature of each State respectively by whom such forces shall be raised, or in such manner as such State shall direct, and all vacancies shall be filled up by the State which first made the appointment.

ARTICLE VIII. All charges of war, and all other expenses that shall be incurred for the common defence or general welfare, and allowed by the United States in Congress assembled, shall be defrayed out of a common treasury, which shall be supplied by the several States, in proportion to the value of all land within each State, granted to or surveyed for any person, as such land and the buildings and improvements thereon shall be estimated according to such mode as the United States in Congress assembled, shall from time to time direct and appoint.

The taxes for paying that proportion shall be laid and levied by the authority and direction of the Legislatures of the several States within the time agreed upon by the United States in Congress assembled.

ARTICLE IX. The United States in Congress assembled, shall have the sole and exclusive right and power of determining on peace and war, except in the cases mentioned in the sixth article—of sending and receiving ambassadors—entering into treaties and alliances, provided that no treaty of commerce shall be made whereby the legislative power of the respective States shall be restrained from imposing such imposts and duties on foreigners, as their own people are subjected to, or from prohibiting the exportation or importation of and species of goods or commodities whatsoever—of establishing rules for deciding in all cases, what captures on land or water shall be legal, and in what manner prizes taken by land or naval forces in the service of the United States shall be divided or appropriated—of granting letters of marque and reprisal in times of peace—appointing courts for the trial of piracies and felonies committed on the high seas and establishing courts for receiving and determining finally appeals in all cases of captures, provided that no member of Congress shall be appointed a judge of any of the said courts.

The United States in Congress assembled shall also be the last resort on appeal in all disputes and differences now subsisting or that hereafter may arise between two or more States concerning boundary, jurisdiction or any other cause whatever; which authority shall always be exercised in the manner following. Whenever the legislative or executive authority or lawful agent of any State in controversy with another shall present a petition to Congress, stating the matter in question and praying for a hearing, notice thereof shall be given by order of Congress to the legislative or executive authority of the other State in controversy, and a day assigned for the appearance of the parties by their lawful agents, who shall then be directed to appoint by joint consent, commissioners or judges to constitute a court for hearing and determining the matter in question: but if they cannot agree, Congress shall name three persons out of each of the United States, and from the list of such persons each party shall alternately strike out one, the petitioners beginning, until the number shall be reduced to thirteen; and from that number not less than seven, nor more than nine names as Congress shall direct, shall in the presence of Congress be drawn out by lot, and the persons whose names shall be so drawn or any five of them, shall be commissioners or judges, to hear and finally determine the controversy, so always as a major part of the judges who shall hear the cause shall agree in the determination: and if either party shall neglect to attend at the day appointed, without reasons, which Congress shall judge sufficient, or being present shall refuse to strike, the Congress shall proceed to nominate three persons out of each State, and the Secretary of Congress shall strike in behalf of such party absent or refusing; and the judgment and sentence of the court to be appointed, in the manner before prescribed, shall be final and conclusive; and if any of the parties shall refuse to submit to the authority of such court, or to appear or defend their claim or cause, the court shall nevertheless proceed to pronounce sentence, or judgment, which shall in like manner be final and decisive, the judgment or sentence and other proceedings being in either case transmitted to Congress, and lodged among the acts of Congress for the security of the parties concerned: provided that every commissioner, before he sits in judgment, shall take an oath to be administered by one of the judges of the supreme or superior court of the State where the case shall be tried, "well and truly to hear and determine the matter in question, according to the best of his judgment, without favour, affection or hope of reward:" provided also that no State shall be deprived of territory for the benefit of the United States.

All controversies concerning the private right of soil claimed under different grants of two or more States, whose jurisdiction as they may respect such lands, and the states which passed such grants are adjusted, the said grants or either of them being at the same time claimed to have originated antecedent to such settlement of jurisdiction, shall on the petition of either party to the Congress of the United States, be finally determined as near as may be in the same manner as is before prescribed for deciding disputes respecting territorial jurisdiction between different States.

The United States in Congress assembled shall also have the sole and exclusive right and power of regulating the alloy and value of coin struck by their own authority, or by that of the respective States—fixing the standard of weights and measures throughout the United States—regulating the trade and managing all affairs with the Indians, not members of any of the States, provided that the legislative right of any State within its own limits be not infringed or violated—establishing and regulating post-offices from one State to another, throughout all of the United States, and exacting such postage on the papers passing thro' the same as may be requisite to defray the expenses of the said office—appointing all officers of the land forces, in the service of the United States, excepting regimental officers—appointing all the officers of the naval forces, and commissioning all officers whatever in the service of the United States—making rules for the government and regulation of the said land and naval forces, and directing their operations.

The United States in Congress assembled shall have authority to appoint a committee, to sit in the recess of Congress, to be denominated "a Committee of the States," and to consist of one delegate from each State; and to appoint such other committees and civil officers as may be necessary for managing the general affairs of the United States under their direction—to appoint one of their number to preside, provided that no person be allowed to serve in the office of president more than one year in any term of three years; to ascertain the necessary sums of money to be raised for the service of the United States, and to appropriate and apply the same for defraying the public expenses—to borrow money, or emit bills on the credit of the United States, transmitting every half year to the respective States an account of the sums of money so borrowed or emitted,—to build and equip a navy—to agree upon the number of land forces, and to make requisitions from each State for its quota, in proportion to the number of white inhabitants in such State; which requisition shall be binding, and thereupon the Legislature of each State shall appoint the regimental officers, raise the men and cloath, arm and equip them in a soldier like manner, at the expense of the United States; and the officers and men so cloathed, armed and equipped shall march to the place appointed, and within the time agreed on by the United States in Congress assembled: but if the United States in Congress assembled shall, on consideration of circumstances judge proper that any State should not raise men, or should raise a smaller number of men than the quota thereof, such extra number shall be raised, officered, cloathed, armed and equipped in the same manner as the quota of such State, unless the legislature of such State shall judge that such extra number cannot be safely spared out of the same, in which case they shall raise officer, cloath, arm and equip as many of such extra number as they judge can be safely spared. And the officers and men so cloathed, armed and equipped, shall march to the place appointed, and within the time agreed on by the United States in Congress assembled.

The United States in Congress assembled shall never engage in a war, nor grant letters of marque and reprisal in time of peace, nor enter into any treaties or alliances, nor coin money, nor regulate the value thereof, nor ascertain the sums and expenses necessary for the defence and welfare of the United States, or any of them, nor emit bills, nor borrow money on the credit of the United

States, nor appropriate money, nor agree upon the number of vessels to be built or purchased, or the number of land or sea forces to be raised, nor appoint a commander in chief of the army or navy, unless nine States assent to the same: nor shall a question on any other point, except for adjourning from day to day be determined, unless by the votes of a majority of the United States in Congress assembled.

The Congress of the United States shall have power to adjourn to any time within the year, and to any place within the United States, so that no period of adjournment be for a longer duration than the space of six months, and shall publish the journal of their proceedings monthly, except such parts thereof relating to treaties, alliances or military operations, as in their judgment require secresy; and the yeas and nays of the delegates of each State on any question shall be entered on the Journal, when it is desired by any delegate; and the delegates of a State, or any of them, at his or their request shall be furnished with a transcript of the said journal, except such parts as are above excepted, to lay before the Legislatures of the several States.

ARTICLE X. The committee of the States, or any nine of them, shall be authorized to execute, in the recess of Congress, such of the powers of Congress as the United States in Congress assembled, by the consent of nine States, shall from time to time think expedient to vest them with; provided that no power be delegated to the said committee, for the exercise of which, by the articles of confederation, the voice of nine States in the Congress of the United States assembled is requisite.

ARTICLE XI. Canada acceding to this confederation, and joining in the measures of the United States, shall be admitted into, and entitled to all the advantages of this Union: but no other colony shall be admitted into the same, unless such admission be agreed to by nine States.

ARTICLE XII. All bills of credit emitted, monies borrowed and debts contracted by, or under the authority of Congress, before the assembling of the United States, in pursuance of the present confederation, shall be deemed and considered as a charge against the United States, for payment and satisfaction whereof the said United States, and the public faith are hereby solemnly pledged.

ARTICLE XIII. Every State shall abide by the determinations of the United States in Congress assembled, on all questions which by this confederation are submitted to them. And the articles of this confederation shall be inviolably observed by every State, and the Union shall be perpetual; nor shall any alteration at any time hereafter be made in any of them; unless such alteration be agreed to in a Congress of the United States, and be afterwards confirmed by the Legislatures of every State.

And whereas it has pleased the Great Governor of the world to incline the hearts of the Legislatures we respectively represent in Congress, to approve of, and to authorize us to ratify the said articles of confederation and perpetual union. Know ye that we the undersigned delegates, by virtue of the power and authority to us given for that purpose, do by these presents, in the name and in behalf of our respective constituents, fully and entirely ratify and confirm each and every of the said articles of confederation and perpetual union, and all and singular the matters and things therein contained: and we do further solemnly plight and engage the faith of our respective constituents, that they shall abide by the determinations of the United States in Congress assembled, on all questions, which by the said confederation are submitted to them. And that the articles thereof shall be inviolably observed by the States we respectively represent, and that the Union shall be perpetual.

In witness thereof we have hereunto set our hands in Congress. Done at Philadelphia in the State of Pennsylvania the ninth day of July in the year of our Lord one thousand seven hundred and seventy-eight, and in the third year of the independence of America.

THE CONSTITUTION OF
THE UNITED STATES

WE THE PEOPLE OF THE UNITED STATES, in order to form a more perfect Union, establish Justice, insure domestic Tranquility, provide for the common defence, promote the general Welfare, and secure the Blessings of Liberty to ourselves and our Posterity, do ordain and establish this Constitution for the United States of America.

ARTICLE. I.

Section. 1. All legislative Powers herein granted shall be vested in a Congress of the United States, which shall consist of a Senate and House of Representatives.

Section. 2. The House of Representatives shall be composed of Members chosen every second Year by the People of the several States, and the Electors in each State shall have the Qualifications requisite for Electors of the most numerous Branch of the State Legislature.

No Person shall be a Representative who shall not have attained to the Age of twenty five Years, and been seven Years a Citizen of the United States, and who shall not, when elected, be an Inhabitant of that State in which he shall be chosen.

Representatives and direct Taxes shall be apportioned among the several States which may be included within this Union, according to their respective Numbers, which shall be determined by adding to the whole Number of free Persons, including those bound to Service for a Term of Years, and excluding Indians not taxed, three fifths of all other Persons. The actual Enumeration shall be made within three Years after the first Meeting of the Congress of the United States, and within every subsequent Term of ten Years, in such Manner as they shall by Law direct. The Number of Representatives shall not exceed one for every thirty Thousand, but each State shall have at Least one Representative; and until such enumeration shall be made, the State of New Hampshire shall be entitled to chuse three, Massachusetts eight, Rhode-Island and

Providence Plantations one, Connecticut five, New-York six, New Jersey four, Pennsylvania eight, Delaware one, Maryland six, Virginia ten, North Carolina five, South Carolina five, and Georgia three.

When vacancies happen in the Representation from any state, the Executive Authority thereof shall issue Writs of Election to fill such Vacancies.

The House of Representatives shall chuse their Speaker and other Officers; and shall have the sole Power of Impeachment.

Section. 3. The Senate of the United States shall be composed of two Senators from each State, chosen by the legislature thereof, for six Years; and each Senator shall have one Vote.

Immediately after they shall be assembled in Consequence of the first Election, they shall be divided as equally as may be into three Classes. The Seats of the Senators of the first Class shall be vacated at the Expiration of the second Year, of the second Class at the Expiration of the fourth Year, and of the third Class at the Expiration of the sixth Year, so that one third may be chosen every second Year; and if Vacancies happen by Resignation, or otherwise, during the Recess of the Legislature of any State, the Executive thereof may make temporary Appointments until the next Meeting of the Legislature, which shall then fill such Vacancies.

No Person shall be a Senator who shall not have attained to the Age of thirty Years, and been nine Years a Citizen of the United States, and who shall not, when elected, be an Inhabitant of that State for which he shall be chosen.

The Vice President of the United States shall be President of the Senate, but shall have no Vote, unless they be equally divided.

The Senate shall chuse their other Officers, and also a President pro tempore, in the Absence of the Vice President, or when he shall exercise the Office of President of the United States.

The Senate shall have the sole Power to try all Impeachments. When sitting for that Purpose, they shall be on Oath or Affirmation. When the President of the United States is tried, the Chief Justice shall preside: And no Person shall be convicted without the Concurrence of two thirds of the Members present.

Judgment in Cases of Impeachment shall not extend further than to removal from Office, and disqualification to hold and enjoy any Office of honor, Trust or Profit under the United States: but the Party convicted shall nevertheless be liable and subject to Indictment, Trial, Judgment and Punishment, according to Law.

Section. 4. The Times, Places and Manner of holding Elections for Senators and Representatives, shall be prescribed in each State by the Legislature thereof; but the Congress may at any time by Law make or alter such Regulations, except as to the Places of chusing Senators.

The Congress shall assemble at least once in every Year, and such Meeting shall be on the first Monday in December, unless they shall by Law appoint a different Day.

Section. 5. Each House shall be the Judge of the Elections, Returns and Qualifications of its own Members, and a Majority of each shall constitute a Quorum to do Business; but a smaller Number may adjourn from day to day, and may be authorized to compel the Attendance of absent Members, in such Manner, and under such Penalties as each House may provide.

Each House may determine the Rules of its Proceedings, punish its Members for disorderly Behaviour, and, with the Concurrence of two thirds, expel a Member.

Each House shall keep a Journal of its Proceedings, and from time to time publish the same, excepting such Parts as may in their Judgment require Secrecy; and the Yeas and Nays of the Members of either House on any question shall, at the Desire of one fifth of those Present, be entered on the Journal.

Neither House, during the Session of Congress, shall, without the Consent of the other, adjourn for more than three days, not to any other Place than that in which the two Houses shall be sitting.

Section. 6. The Senators and Representatives shall receive a Compensation for their Services, to be ascertained by Law, and paid out of the Treasury of the United States. They shall in all Cases, except Treason, Felony and Breach of the Peace, be privileged from Arrest during their Attendance at the Session of their respective Houses, and in going to and returning from the same; and for any Speech or Debate in either House, they shall not be questioned in any other Place.

No Senator or Representative shall, during the Time for which he was elected, be appointed to any civil Office under the Authority of the United States, which shall have been created, or the Emoluments whereof shall have been encreased during such time; and no Person holding any Office under the United States, shall be a Member of either House during his Continuance in Office.

Section. 7. All Bills for raising Revenue shall originate in the House of Representatives; but the Senate may propose or concur with Amendments as on other Bills.

Every Bill which shall have passed the House of Representatives and the Senate shall, before it become a Law, be presented to the President of the United States; If he approve he shall sign it, but if not he shall return it, with his Objections to that House in which it shall have originated, who shall enter the Objections at large on their Journal, and proceed to reconsider it. If after such Reconsideration two thirds of that House shall agree to pass the Bill, it shall be sent, together with the Objections, to the other House, by which it shall likewise be reconsidered, and if approved by two thirds of that House, it shall become a Law. But in all such Cases the Votes of both Houses shall be determined by yeas and Nays, and the Names of the Persons voting for and against the Bill shall be entered on the Journal of each House respectively. If any Bill shall not be returned by the President within ten Days (Sundays excepted) after it shall have been presented to him, the Same shall be a Law, in like Manner as if he had signed it, unless the Congress by their Adjournment prevent its Return, in which Case it shall not be a Law.

Every Order, Resolution, or Vote to which the Concurrence of the Senate and House of Representatives may be necessary (except on a question of Adjournment) shall be presented to the President of the United States; and before the Same shall take Effect, shall be approved by him, or being disapproved by him, shall be repassed by two thirds of the Senate and House of Representatives, according to the Rules and Limitations prescribed in the Case of a Bill.

Section. 8. The Congress shall have Power To lay and collect Taxes, Duties, Imposts and Excises, to pay the Debts and provide for the common Defence and general Welfare of the United States; but all Duties, Imposts and Excises shall be uniform throughout the United States;

To borrow Money on the credit of the United States;

To regulate Commerce with foreign Nations, and among the several States, and with the Indian Tribes;

To establish an uniform Rule of Naturalization, and uniform Laws on the subject of Bankruptcies throughout the United States;

To coin Money, regulate the Value thereof, and of foreign Coin, and fix the Standard of Weights and Measures;

To provide for the Punishment of counterfeiting the Securities and current Coin of the United States;

To establish Post Offices and Post Roads;

To promote the Progress of Science and useful Arts, by securing for limited Times to Authors and Inventors the exclusive Right to their respective Writings and Discoveries;

To constitute Tribunals inferior to the supreme Court;

To define and punish Piracies and Felonies committed on the high Seas, and Offences against the Law of Nations;

To declare War, grant Letters of Marque and Reprisal, and make Rules concerning Captures on Land and Water;

To raise and support Armies, but no Appropriation of Money to that Use shall be for a longer Term than two Years;

To provide and maintain a Navy;

To make Rules for the Government and Regulation of the land and naval Forces;

To provide for calling forth the Militia to execute the Laws of the Union, suppress Insurrections and repel Invasions;

To provide for organizing, arming, and disciplining, the Militia, and for governing such Part of them as may be employed in the Service of the United States, reserving to the States respectively, the Appointment of the Officers, and the Authority of training the Militia according to the discipline prescribed by Congress.

To exercise exclusive Legislation in all Cases whatsoever, over such District (not exceeding ten Miles square) as may, by Cession of Particular States, and the Acceptance of Congress, become the Seat of the Government of the United States, and to exercise like Authority over all Places purchased by the Consent of the Legislature of the State in which the Same shall be, for the Erection of Forts, Magazines, Arsenals, dock-Yards, and other needful Buildings;—And

To make all Laws which shall be necessary and proper for carrying into Execution the foregoing Powers, and all other Powers vested by this Constitution in the Government of the United States, or in any Department or Officer thereof.

Section. 9. The Migration or Importation of such Persons as any of the States now existing shall think proper to admit, shall not be prohibited by the Congress prior to the Year one thousand eight hundred and eight, but a Tax or duty may be imposed on such Importation, not exceeding ten dollars for each Person.

The Privilege of the Writ of Habeas Corpus shall not be suspended, unless when in Cases of Rebellion or Invasion the public Safety may require it.

No Bill of Attainder or ex post facto Law shall be passed.

No Capitation, or other direct, Tax shall be laid, unless in Proportion to the Census or Enumeration herein before directed to be taken.

No Tax or Duty shall be laid on Articles exported from any State.

No Preference shall be given by any Regulation of Commerce or Revenue to the Ports of one State over those of another: nor shall Vessels bound to, or from, one State, be obliged to enter, clear, or pay Duties in another.

No Money shall be drawn from the Treasury, but in Consequence of Appropriations made by Law; and a regular Statement and Account of the Receipts and Expenditures of all public Money shall be published from time to time.

No Title of Nobility shall be granted by the United States: And no Person holding any Office of Profit or Trust under them, shall, without the Consent of the Congress, accept of any present, Emolument, Office, or Title, of any kind whatever, from any King, Prince, or foreign State.

Section 10. No State shall enter into any Treaty, Alliance, or Confederation; grant Letters of Marque and Reprisal; coin Money; emit Bills of Credit; make any Thing but gold and silver Coin a Tender in Payment of Debts; pass any Bill of Attainder, ex post facto Law, or Law impairing the Obligation of Contracts, or grant any Title of Nobility.

No State shall, without the Consent of the Congress, lay any Imposts or Duties on Imports or Exports, except what may be absolutely necessary for executing its inspection Laws: and the net Produce of all Duties and Imposts, laid by any State on Imports or Exports, shall be for the Use of the Treasury of the United States; and all such Laws shall be subject to the Revision and Controul of the Congress.

No State shall, without the Consent of Congress, lay any Duty of Tonnage, keep Troops, or Ships of War in time of Peace, enter into any Agreement or Compact with another State, or with a foreign Power, or engage in War, unless actually invaded, or in such imminent Danger as will not admit of delay.

Article. II.

Section. 1. The executive Power shall be vested in a President of the United States of America. He shall hold his Office during the term of four Years, and, to-gether with the Vice President, chosen for the same Term, be elected, as follows:

Each State shall appoint, in such Manner as the Legislature thereof may direct, a Number of Electors, equal to the whole Number of Senators and Rep-resentatives to which the State may be entitled in the Congress: but no Sena-tor or Representative, or Person holding an Office of Trust or Profit under the United States, shall be appointed an Elector.

The Electors shall meet in their respective States, and vote by Ballot for two Persons, of whom one at least shall not be an Inhabitant of the same State with themselves. And they shall make a List of all the Persons voted for, and of the Number of Votes for each; which List they shall sign and certify, and transmit sealed to the Seat of the Government of the United States, directed to the President of the Senate. The President of the Senate shall, in the Presence of the Senate and House of Representatives, open all the Certificates, and the Votes shall then be counted. The Person having the greatest Number of Votes shall be the President, if such Number be a Majority of the whole Number of Electors appointed; and if there be more than one who have such Majority, and have an equal Number of Votes, then the House of Representatives shall im-mediately chuse by Ballot one of them for President; and if no Person have a Majority, then from the five highest on the List the said House shall in like Manner chuse the President. But in chusing the President, the Votes shall be taken by States, the Representation from each State having one Vote; A quo-rum for this Purpose shall consist of a Member or Members from two thirds of the States, and a Majority of all the States shall be necessary to a Choice. In every Case, after the Choice of the President, the Person having the greatest Number of Votes of the Electors shall be the Vice President. But if there should remain two or more who have equal Votes, the Senate shall chuse from them by Ballot the Vice President.

The Congress may determine the Time of chusing the Electors, and the Day on which they shall give their Votes; which Day shall be the same throughout the United States.

No Person except a natural born Citizen, or a Citizen of the United States, at the time of the Adoption of this Constitution, shall be eligible to the Office of President; neither shall any Person be eligible to that Office who shall not have attained to the Age of thirty five Years, and been fourteen Years a Resident within the United States.

In Case of the Removal of the President from Office, or of his Death, Resignation, or Inability to discharge the Powers and Duties of the said Office, the Same shall devolve on the Vice President, and the Congress may by Law provide for the Case of Removal, Death, Resignation or Inability, both of the President and Vice President, declaring what Officer shall then act as President, and such Officer shall act accordingly, until the Disability be removed, or a President shall be elected.

The President shall, at stated Times, receive for his Services, a Compensation, which shall neither be encreased or diminished during the Period for which he shall have been elected, and he shall not receive within that Period any other Emolument from the United States, or any of them.

Before he enters on the Execution of his Office, he shall take the following Oath or Affirmation:—"I do solemnly swear (or affirm) that I will faithfully execute the Office of President of the United States, and will to the best of my Ability, preserve, protect and defend the Constitution of the United States."

Section. 2. The President shall be Commander in Chief of the Army and Navy of the United States, and of the Militia of the several States, when called into the actual Service of the United States; he may require the Opinion, in writing, of the principal Officer in each of the executive Departments, upon any Subject relating to the Duties of their respective Offices, and he shall have Power to grant Reprieves and Pardons for Offences against the United States, except in Cases of Impeachment.

He shall have Power, by and with the Advice and Consent of the Senate, to make Treaties, provided two thirds of the Senators present concur; and he shall nominate, and by and with the Advice and Consent of the Senate, shall appoint Ambassadors, other public Ministers and Consuls, Judges of the supreme Court, and all other Officers of the United States, whose Appointments are not herein otherwise provided for, and which shall be established by Law;

but the Congress may by Law vest the Appointment of such inferior Officers, as they think proper, in the President alone, in the Courts of Law, or in the Heads of Departments.

The President shall have Power to fill up all Vacancies that may happen during the Recess of the Senate, by granting Commissions which shall expire at the End of their next Session.

Section. 3. He shall from time to time give to the Congress Information of the State of the Union, and recommend to their Consideration such Measures as he shall judge necessary and expedient; he may, on extraordinary Occasions, convene both Houses, or either of them, and in Case of Disagreement between them, with Respect to the Time of Adjournment, he may adjourn them to such Time as he shall think proper; he shall receive Ambassadors and other public Ministers; he shall take Care that the Laws be faithfully executed, and shall Commission all the Officers of the United States.

Section. 4. The President, Vice President and all civil Officers of the United States, shall be removed from Office on Impeachment for, and Conviction of, Treason, Bribery, or other high Crimes and Misdemeanors.

ARTICLE. III.

Section. 1. The judicial Power of the United States, shall be vested in one supreme Court, and in such inferior Courts as the Congress may from time to time ordain and establish. The Judges, both of the supreme and inferior Courts, shall hold their Offices during good Behavior, and shall, at stated Times, receive for their Services, a Compensation, which shall not be diminished during their Continuance in Office.

Section. 2. The judicial Power shall extend to all Cases, in Law and Equity, arising under this Constitution, the Laws of the United States, and Treaties made, or which shall be made, under their Authority;—to all Cases affecting Ambassadors, other public Ministers and Consuls;—to all Cases of admiralty and maritime Jurisdiction;—the Controversies to which the United States shall be a Party;—to Controversies between two or more States;—between a State and Citizens of another State;—between Citizens of different States;—between Citizens of the same State claiming Lands under Grants of different States, and between a State, or the Citizens thereof, and foreign States, Citizens or Subjects.

In all cases affecting Ambassadors, other public Ministers and Consuls, and those in which a State shall be Party, the supreme Court shall have original Jurisdiction. In all the other Cases before mentioned, the supreme Court shall have appellate Jurisdiction, both as to Law and Fact, with such Exceptions, and under such Regulations as the Congress shall make.

The Trial of all Crimes, except in Cases of Impeachment, shall be by Jury; and such Trial shall be held in the State where the said Crimes shall have been committed; but when not committed within any State, the Trial shall be at such Place or Places as the Congress may by Law have directed.

Section. 3. Treason against the United States, shall consist only in levying War against them, or in adhering to their Enemies, giving them Aid and Comfort. No Person shall be convicted of Treason unless on the Testimony of two Witnesses to the same overt Act, or on Confession in open Court.

The Congress shall have Power to declare the Punishment of Treason, but no Attainder of Treason shall work Corruption of Blood, or Forfeiture except during the Life of the Person attainted.

Article. IV.

Section. 1. Full Faith and Credit shall be given in each State to the public Acts, Records, and judicial Proceedings of every other State. And the Congress may by general Laws prescribe the Manner in which such Acts, Records and Proceedings shall be proved, and the Effect thereof.

Section. 2. The Citizens of each State shall be entitled to all Privileges and Immunities of Citizens in the several States.

A Person charged in any State with Treason, Felony, or other Crime, who shall flee from Justice, and be found in another State, shall on Demand of the executive Authority of the State from which he fled, be delivered up, to be removed to the State having Jurisdiction of the Crime.

No Person held to Service or Labour in one State, under the Laws thereof, escaping into another, shall, in Consequence of any Law or Regulation therein, be discharged from such Service or Labour, but shall be delivered up on Claim of the Party to whom such Service or Labour may be due.

Section. 3. New States may be admitted by the Congress into this Union; but no new State shall be formed or erected within the Jurisdiction of any other State; nor any State be formed by the Junction of two or more States, or Parts of States, without the consent of the Legislatures of the States concerned as well as of the Congress.

The Congress shall have Power to dispose of and make all needful Rules and Regulations respecting the Territory or other Property belonging to the United States; and nothing in this Constitution shall be so construed as to Prejudice any Claims of the United States, or of any particular States.

Section. 4. The United States shall guarantee to every State in this Union a Republican Form of Government, and shall protect each of them against Invasion; and on Application of the Legislature, or of the Executive (when the Legislature cannot be convened) against domestic Violence.

Article. V.

The Congress, whenever two thirds of both Houses shall deem it necessary, shall propose Amendments to this Constitution, or, on the Application of the Legislatures of two thirds of the several States, shall call a Convention for proposing Amendments, which, in either Case, shall be valid to all Intents and Purposes, as Part of this Constitution, when ratified by the Legislatures of three fourths of the several States, or by Conventions in three fourths thereof, as the one or the other Mode of Ratification may be proposed by the Congress; Provided that no Amendment which may be made prior to the Year One thousand eight hundred and eight shall in any Manner affect the first and fourth Clauses in the Ninth Section of the first Article; and that no State, without its Consent, shall be deprived of its equal Suffrage in the Senate.

Article. VI.

All Debts contracted and Engagements entered into, before the Adoption of this Constitution, shall be as valid against the United States under this Constitution, as under the Confederation.

This Constitution, and the Laws of the United States which shall be made in Pursuance thereof; and all Treaties made, or which shall be made, under the Authority of the United States, shall be the supreme Law of the Land; and the Judges in every State shall be bound thereby, any Thing in the Constitution or Laws of any State to the Contrary notwithstanding.

The Senators and Representatives before mentioned, and the Members of the several State Legislatures, and all executive and judicial Officers, both of the United States and of the several States, shall be bound by Oath or Affirmation, to support this Constitution; but no religious Test shall ever be required as a Qualification to any Office or public Trust under the United States.

Article. VII.

The Ratification of the Conventions of nine States, shall be sufficient for the Establishment of this Constitution between the States so ratifying the Same.

Done in Convention by the Unanimous Consent of the States present the Seventeenth Day of September in the Year of our Lord one thousand seven hundred and Eighty seven and of the Independence of the United States of America the Twelfth. In witness thereof We have hereunto subscribed our Names,

G°. WASHINGTON—Presd^t.
and deputy from Virginia.

New Hampshire	{ John Langdon Nicholas Gilman		
		Delaware	{ Geo: Read Gunning Bedford jun John Dickinson Richard Bassett Jaco: Broom
Massachusetts	{ Nathaniel Gorham Rufus King		
Connecticut	{ Wm Saml Johnson Roger Sherman	Maryland	{ James McHenry Dan of St Thos Jenifer Danl Carroll
New York: ...	Alexander Hamilton		
		Virginia	{ John Blair— James Madison Jr.
New Jersey	{ Wil: Livingston David A. Brearley. Wm Paterson. Jona: Dayton		
		North Carolina	{ Wm Blount Richd Dobbs Spaight. Hu Williamson
Pennsylvania	{ B Franklin Thomas Mifflin Robt Morris Geo. Clymer Thos FitzSimons Jared Ingersoll James Wilson Gouv Morris	South Carolina	{ J. Rutledge Charles Cotesworth Pinckney Charles Pinckney Pierce Butler.
		Georgia	{ William Few Abr Baldwin

AMENDMENTS TO THE CONSTITUTION

ARTICLES IN ADDITION TO, and Amendment of the Constitution of the United States of America, proposed by Congress, and ratified by the Legislatures of the several States, pursuant to the fifth Article of the original Constitution.

AMENDMENT I.

Congress shall make no law respecting an establishment of religion, or prohibiting the free exercise thereof; or abridging the freedom of speech, or of the press; or the right of the people peaceably to assemble, and to petition the Government for a redress of grievances.

AMENDMENT II.

A well regulated Militia, being necessary to the security of a free State, the right of the people to keep and bear Arms, shall not be infringed.

AMENDMENT III.

No Soldier shall, in time of peace be quartered in any house, without the consent of the Owner, nor in time of war, but in a manner to be prescribed by law.

AMENDMENT IV.

The right of the people to be secure in their persons, houses, papers, and effects, against unreasonable searches and seizures, shall not be violated, and no Warrants shall issue, but upon probable cause, supported by Oath or affirmation, and particularly describing the place to be searched, and the persons or things to be seized.

AMENDMENT V.

No person shall be held to answer for a capital, or otherwise infamous crime, unless on a presentment or indictment of a Grand Jury, except in cases arising in the land or naval forces, or in the Militia, when in actual service in time of War or public danger; nor shall any person be subject for the same offence to be twice put in jeopardy of life or limb; nor shall be compelled in any criminal case to be a witness against himself, nor be deprived of life, liberty, or property, without due process of law; nor shall private property be taken for public use, without just compensation.

AMENDMENT VI.

In all criminal prosecutions, the accused shall enjoy the right to a speedy and public trial, by an impartial jury of the State and district wherein the crime shall have been committed, which district shall have been previously ascertained by law, and to be informed of the nature and cause of the accusation; to be confronted with the witnesses against him; to have compulsory process for obtaining witnesses in his favor, and to have the Assistance of Counsel for his defence.

AMENDMENT VII.

In Suits at common law, where the value in controversy shall exceed twenty dollars, the right of trial by jury shall be preserved, and no fact tried by a jury, shall be otherwise re-examined in any Court of the United States, than according to the rules of the common law.

AMENDMENT VIII.

Excessive bail shall not be required, nor excessive fines imposed, nor cruel and unusual punishments inflicted.

AMENDMENT IX.

The enumeration in the Constitution, of certain rights, shall not be construed to deny or disparage others retained by the people.

AMENDMENT X.

The powers not delegated to the United States by the Constitution, nor prohibited by it to the States, are reserved to the States respectively, or to the people. [The first ten amendments went into effect December 15, 1791.]

AMENDMENT XI.

The Judicial power of the United States shall not be construed to extend to any suit in law or equity, commenced or prosecuted against one of the United States by Citizens of another State, or by Citizens or Subjects of any Foreign State. [January 8, 1798.]

AMENDMENT XII.

The Electors shall meet in their respective States, and vote by ballot for President and Vice-President, one of whom, at least, shall not be an inhabitant of the same state with themselves; they shall name in their ballots the person voted for as President, and in distinct ballots the person voted for as Vice-President, and they shall make distinct lists of all persons voted for as President, and of all persons voted for as Vice President, and of the number of votes for each, which lists they shall sign and certify, and transmit sealed to the seat of the government of the United States, directed to the President of the Senate;—The President of the Senate shall, in the presence of the Senate and House of Representatives, open all the certificates and the votes shall then be counted;—The person having the greatest number of votes for President, shall be the President, if such number be a majority of the whole number of Electors appointed; and if no person have such majority, then from the persons having the highest numbers not exceeding three on the list of those voted for as President, the House of Representatives shall choose immediately, by ballot, the President. But in choosing the President, the votes shall be taken by states, the representation from each state having one vote; a quorum for this purpose shall consist of a member or members from two-thirds of the states, and a majority of all the states shall be necessary to a choice. And if the House of Representatives shall not choose a President whenever the right of choice shall devolve upon them, before the fourth day of March next following, then the Vice-President shall act as President, as in the case of the death or other constitutional disability of the President.—The person having the greatest number of votes as Vice-President, shall be the Vice-President, if such number be a majority of the whole number of Electors appointed, and if no person have a majority, then from the two highest numbers on the list, the Senate shall choose the Vice-President; a quorum for the purpose shall consist of two-thirds of the whole number of Senators, and a majority of the whole number shall be necessary to a choice. But no person constitutionally ineligible to the office of President shall be eligible to that of Vice-President of the United States. [September 25, 1804.]

Amendment XIII.

Section 1. Neither slavery nor involuntary servitude, except as a punishment for crime whereof the party shall have been duly convicted, shall exist within the United States, or any place subject to their jurisdiction.

Section 2. Congress shall have power to enforce this article by appropriate legislation. [December 18, 1865.]

Amendment XIV.

Section 1. All persons born or naturalized in the United States, and subject to the jurisdiction thereof, are citizens of the United States and of the State wherein they reside. No State shall make or enforce any law which shall abridge the privileges or immunities of citizens of the United States; nor shall any State deprive any person of life, liberty, or property, without due process of law; nor deny to any person within its jurisdiction the equal protection of the laws.

Section 2. Representatives shall be apportioned among the several States according to their respective numbers, counting the whole number of persons in each State, excluding Indians not taxed. But when the right to vote at any election for the choice of electors for President and Vice President of the United States, Representatives in Congress, the Executive and Judicial officers of a State, or the members of the Legislature thereof, is denied to any of the male inhabitants of such State, being twenty-one years of age, and citizens of the United States, or in any way abridged, except for participation in rebellion, or other crime, the basis of representation therein shall be reduced in the proportion which the number of such male citizens shall bear to the whole number of male citizens twenty-one years of age in such State.

Section 3. No person shall be a Senator or Representative in Congress, or elector of President and Vice President, or hold any office, civil or military, under the United States, or under any State, who, having previously taken an oath, as a member of Congress, or as an officer of the United States, or as a member of any State legislature, or as an executive or judicial officer of any State, to support the Constitution of the United States, shall have engaged in insurrection or rebellion against the same, or given aid or comfort to the enemies thereof. But Congress may by a vote of two-thirds of each House, remove such disability.

Section 4. The validity of the public debt of the United States, authorized by law, including debts incurred for payment of pensions and bounties for services in suppressing insurrection or rebellion, shall not be questioned. But neither the United States nor any State shall assume or pay any debt or obligation incurred in aid of insurrection or rebellion against the United States, or any claim for the loss or emancipation of any slave; but all such debts, obligations and claims shall be held illegal and void.

Section 5. The Congress shall have power to enforce, by appropriate legislation, the provisions of this article. [July 28, 1868.]

AMENDMENT XV.

Section 1. The right of citizens of the United States to vote shall not be denied or abridged by the United States or by any State on account of race, color, or previous condition of servitude—

Section 2. The Congress shall have power to enforce this article by appropriate legislation.—[March 30, 1870.]

AMENDMENT XVI.

The Congress shall have power to lay and collect taxes on incomes, from whatever source derived, without apportionment among the several States, and without regard to any census or enumeration. [February 25, 1913.]

AMENDMENT XVII.

The Senate of the United States shall be composed of two senators from each State, elected by the people thereof, for six years; and each Senator shall have one vote. The electors in each State shall have the qualifications requisite for electors of the most numerous branch of the State legislatures.

When vacancies happen in the representation of any State in the Senate, the executive authority of such State shall issue writs of election to fill such vacancies: *Provided,* That the legislature of any State may empower the executive thereof to make temporary appointments until the people fill the vacancies by election as the legislature may direct.

This amendment shall not be so construed as to affect the election or term of any senator chosen before it becomes valid as part of the Constitution. [May 31, 1913.]

AMENDMENT XVIII.

After one year from the ratification of this article, the manufacture, sale, or transportation of intoxicating liquors within, the importation thereof into, or the exportation thereof from the United States and all territory subject to the jurisdiction thereof for beverage purposes is hereby prohibited.

The Congress and the several States shall have concurrent power to enforce this article by appropriate legislation.

This article shall be inoperative unless it shall have been ratified as an amendment to the Constitution by the legislatures of the several States, as provided in the Constitution, within seven years from the date of the submission thereof to the States by Congress. [January 29, 1919.]

AMENDMENT XIX.

The right of citizens of the United States to vote shall not be denied or abridged by the United States or by any State on account of sex.

The Congress shall have power by appropriate legislation to enforce the provisions of this article. [August 26, 1920.]

AMENDMENT XX.

Section 1. The terms of the President and Vice-President shall end at noon on the twentieth day of January, and the terms of Senators and Representatives at noon on the third day of January, of the years in which such terms would have ended if this article had not been ratified; and the terms of their successors shall then begin.

Section 2. The Congress shall assemble at least once in every year, and such meeting shall begin at noon on the third day of January, unless they shall by law appoint a different day.

Section 3. If, at the time fixed for the beginning of the term of the President, the President-elect shall have died, the Vice-President-elect shall become President. If a President shall not have been chosen before the time fixed for the beginning of his term, or if the President-elect shall have failed to qualify, then the Vice-President-elect shall act as President until a President shall have qualified; and the Congress may by law provide for the case wherein neither a President-elect nor a Vice-President-elect shall have qualified, declaring who shall then act as President, or the manner in which one who is to act shall be selected, and such person shall act accordingly until a President or Vice-President shall have qualified.

Section 4. The Congress may by law provide for the case of the death of any of the persons from whom the House of Representatives may choose a President whenever the right of choice shall have devolved upon them, and for the case of the death of any of the persons from whom the Senate may choose a Vice-President whenever the right of choice shall have devolved upon them.

Section 5. Sections 1 and 2 shall take effect on the 15th day of October following the ratification of this article.

Section 6. This article shall be inoperative unless it shall have been ratified as an amendment to the Constitution by the legislatures of three-fourths of the several States within seven years from the date of its submission. [February 6, 1933.]

AMENDMENT XXI.

Section 1. The eighteenth article of amendment to the Constitution of the United States is hereby repealed.

Section 2. The transportation or importation into any State, Territory or possession of the United States for delivery or use therein of intoxicating liquors, in violation of the laws thereof, is hereby prohibited.

Section 3. This article shall be inoperative unless it shall have been ratified as an amendment to the Constitution by convention in the several States, as provided in the Constitution, within seven years from the date of the submission thereof to the States by the Congress. [December 5, 1933.]

AMENDMENT XXII.

Section 1. No person shall be elected to the office of the President more than twice, and no person who has held the office of President, or acted as President, for more than two years of a term to which some other person was elected President shall be elected to the office of the President more than once. But this Article shall not apply to any person holding the office of President when this Article was proposed by the Congress, and shall not prevent any person who may be holding the office of President, or acting as President, during the term within which this Article becomes operative from holding the office of President or acting as President during the remainder of such term.

Section 2. This article shall be inoperative unless it shall have been ratified as an amendment to the Constitution by the legislatures of three-fourths of the several states within seven years from the date of its submission to the States by the Congress. [February 27, 1951.]

AMENDMENT XXIII.

Section 1. The District constituting the seat of government of the United States shall appoint in such manner as the Congress may direct:

A number of electors of President and Vice-President equal to the whole number of Senators and Representatives in Congress to which the District would be entitled if it were a State, but in no event more than the least populous State; they shall be in addition to those appointed by the States, but they shall be considered, for the purposes of the election of President and Vice-President, to be electors appointed by a State; and they shall meet in the District and perform such duties as provided by the twelfth article of amendment.

Section 2. The Congress shall have the power to enforce this article by appropriate legislation. [March 29, 1961.]

AMENDMENT XXIV.

Section 1. The right of citizens of the United States to vote in any primary or other election for President or Vice President, for electors for President or Vice President, or for Senator or Representative in Congress, shall not be denied or abridged by the United States or any State by reason of failure to pay any poll tax or other tax.

Section 2. The Congress shall have power to enforce this article by appropriate legislation. [January 23, 1964.]

AMENDMENT XXV.

Section 1. In case of the removal of the President from office or of his death or resignation, the Vice President shall become President.

Section 2. Whenever there is a vacancy in the office of Vice President, the President shall nominate a Vice President who shall take office upon confirmation by a majority vote of both Houses of Congress.

Section 3. Whenever the President transmits to the President pro tempore of the Senate and the Speaker of the House of Representatives his written declaration that he is unable to discharge the powers and duties of his office, and until he transmits to them a written declaration to the contrary, such powers and duties shall be discharged by the Vice President as Acting President.

Section 4. Whenever the Vice President and a majority of either the principal officers of the executive departments or of such other body as Congress may by law provide, transmit to the President pro tempore of the Senate and the Speaker of the House of Representatives their written declaration that the President is unable to discharge the powers and duties of his office, the Vice President shall immediately assume the powers and duties of the office as Acting President.

Thereafter, when the President transmits to the President pro tempore of the Senate and the Speaker of the House of Representatives his written declaration that no inability exists, he shall resume the powers and duties of his office unless the Vice President and a majority of either the principal officers of the executive departments or of such other body as Congress may by law provide, transmit within four days to the President pro tempore of the Senate and the Speaker of the House of Representatives their written declaration that the President is unable to discharge the powers and duties of his office. Thereupon Congress shall decide the issue, assembling within forty-eight hours for that purpose if not in session. If the Congress, within twenty-one days after receipt of the latter written declaration, or, if Congress is not in session, within twenty-one days after Congress is required to assemble, determines by two-thirds vote of both Houses that the President is unable to discharge the powers and duties of his office, the Vice President shall continue to discharge the same as Acting President; otherwise, the President shall resume the powers and duties of his office. [February 10, 1967.]

Amendment XXVI.

Section 1. The right of citizens of the United States, who are eighteen years of age or older, to vote shall not be denied or abridged by the United States or by any State on account of age.

Section 2. The Congress shall have power to enforce this article by appropriate legislation [June 30, 1971.]

Amendment XXVII.

No law, varying the compensation for the services of the Senators and Representatives shall take effect, until an election of Representatives shall have intervened. [May 8, 1992.]

PRESIDENTIAL ELECTIONS

Year	Number of States	Candidates	Parties	Popular Vote	% of Popular Vote	Electoral Vote	% Voter Participation
1789	11	**GEORGE WASHINGTON**	No party designations			69	
		John Adams				34	
		Other candidates				35	
1792	15	**GEORGE WASHINGTON**	No party designations			132	
		John Adams				77	
		George Clinton				50	
		Other candidates				5	
1796	16	**JOHN ADAMS**	Federalist			71	
		Thomas Jefferson	Democratic-Republican			68	
		Thomas Pinckney	Federalist			59	
		Aaron Burr	Democratic-Republican			30	
		Other candidates				48	
1800	16	**THOMAS JEFFERSON**	Democratic-Republican			73	
		Aaron Burr	Democratic-Republican			73	
		John Adams	Federalist			65	
		Charles C. Pinckney	Federalist			64	
		John Jay	Federalist			1	
1804	17	**THOMAS JEFFERSON**	Democratic-Republican			162	
		Charles C. Pinckney	Federalist			14	

Year	Number of States	Candidates	Parties	Popular Vote	% of Popular Vote	Electoral Vote	% Voter Participation
1808	17	**JAMES MADISON**	Democratic-Republican			122	
		Charles C. Pinckney	Federalist			47	
		George Clinton	Democratic-Republican			6	
1812	18	**JAMES MADISON**	Democratic-Republican			128	
		DeWitt Clinton	Federalist			89	
1816	19	**JAMES MONROE**	Democratic-Republican			183	
		Rufus King	Federalist			34	
1820	24	**JAMES MONROE**	Democratic-Republican			231	
		John Quincy Adams	Independent			1	
1824	24	**JOHN QUINCY ADAMS**	Democratic-Republican	108,740	30.5	84	26.9
		Andrew Jackson	Democratic-Republican	153,544	43.1	99	
		Henry Clay	Democratic-Republican	47,136	13.2	37	
		William H. Crawford	Democratic-Republican	46,618	13.1	41	
1828	24	**ANDREW JACKSON**	Democratic	647,286	56.0	178	57.6
		John Quincy Adams	National-Republican	508,064	44.0	83	

Year	Number of States	Candidates	Parties	Popular Vote	% of Popular Vote	Electoral Vote	% Voter Participation
1832	24	**ANDREW JACKSON**	Democratic	688,242	54.5	219	55.4
		Henry Clay	National-Republican	473,462	37.5	49	
		William Wirt	Anti-Masonic	101,051	8.0	7	
		John Floyd	Democratic			11	
1836	26	**MARTIN VAN BUREN**	Democratic	765,483	50.9	170	57.8
		William H. Harrison	Whig			73	
		Hugh L. White	Whig	739,795	49.1	26	
		Daniel Webster	Whig			14	
		W. P. Mangum	Whig			11	
1840	26	**WILLIAM H. HARRISON**	Whig	1,274,624	53.1	234	80.2
		Martin Van Buren	Democratic	1,127,781	46.9	60	
1844	26	**JAMES K. POLK**	Democratic	1,338,464	49.6	170	78.9
		Henry Clay	Whig	1,300,097	48.1	105	
		James G. Birney	Liberty	62,300	2.3		
1848	30	**ZACHARY TAYLOR**	Whig	1,360,967	47.4	163	72.7
		Lewis Cass	Democratic	1,222,342	42.5	127	
		Martin Van Buren	Free Soil	291,263	10.1		
1852	31	**FRANKLIN PIERCE**	Democratic	1,601,117	50.9	254	69.6
		Winfield Scott	Whig	1,385,453	44.1	42	
		John P. Hale	Free Soil	155,825	5.0		
1856	31	**JAMES BUCHANAN**	Democratic	1,832,955	45.3	174	78.9
		John C. Frémont	Republican	1,339,932	33.1	114	
		Millard Fillmore	American	871,731	21.6	8	

Year	Number of States	Candidates	Parties	Popular Vote	% of Popular Vote	Electoral Vote	% Voter Participation
1860	33	**ABRAHAM LINCOLN**	Republican	1,865,593	39.8	180	81.2
		Stephen A. Douglas	Democratic	1,382,713	29.5	12	
		John C. Breckinridge	Democratic	848,356	18.1	72	
		John Bell	Constitutional Union	592,906	12.6	39	
1864	36	**ABRAHAM LINCOLN**	Republican	2,206,938	55.0	212	73.8
		George B. McClellan	Democratic	1,803,787	45.0	21	
1868	37	**ULYSSES S. GRANT**	Republican	3,013,421	52.7	214	78.1
		Horatio Seymour	Democratic	2,706,829	47.3	80	
1872	37	**ULYSSES S. GRANT**	Republican	3,596,745	55.6	286	71.3
		Horace Greeley	Democratic	2,843,446	43.9	66	
1876	38	**RUTHERFORD B. HAYES**	Republican	4,036,572	48.0	185	81.8
		Samuel J. Tilden	Democratic	4,284,020	51.0	184	
1880	38	**JAMES A. GARFIELD**	Republican	4,453,295	48.5	214	79.4
		Winfield S. Hancock	Democratic	4,414,082	48.1	155	
		James B. Weaver	Greenback-Labor	308,578	3.4		
1884	38	**GROVER CLEVELAND**	Democratic	4,879,507	48.5	219	77.5
		James G. Blaine	Republican	4,850,293	48.2	182	
		Benjamin F. Butler	Greenback-Labor	175,370	1.8		
		John P. St. John	Prohibition	150,369	1.5		
1888	38	**BENJAMIN HARRISON**	Republican	5,477,129	47.9	233	79.3
		Grover Cleveland	Democratic	5,537,857	48.6	168	
		Clinton B. Fisk	Prohibition	249,506	2.2		
		Anson J. Streeter	Union Labor	146,935	1.3		

Year	Number of States	Candidates	Parties	Popular Vote	% of Popular Vote	Electoral Vote	% Voter Participation
1892	44	**GROVER CLEVELAND**	Democratic	5,555,426	46.1	277	74.7
		Benjamin Harrison	Republican	5,182,690	43.0	145	
		James B. Weaver	People's	1,029,846	8.5	22	
		John Bidwell	Prohibition	264,133	2.2		
1896	45	**WILLIAM McKINLEY**	Republican	7,102,246	51.1	271	79.3
		William J. Bryan	Democratic	6,492,559	47.7	176	
1900	45	**WILLIAM McKINLEY**	Republican	7,218,491	51.7	292	73.2
		William J. Bryan	Democratic; Populist	6,356,734	45.5	155	
		John C. Wooley	Prohibition	208,914	1.5		
1904	45	**THEODORE ROOSEVELT**	Republican	7,628,461	57.4	336	65.2
		Alton B. Parker	Democratic	5,084,223	37.6	140	
		Eugene V. Debs	Socialist	402,283	3.0		
		Silas C. Swallow	Prohibition	258,536	1.9		
1908	46	**WILLIAM H. TAFT**	Republican	7,675,320	51.6	321	65.4
		William J. Bryan	Democratic	6,412,294	43.1	162	
		Eugene V. Debs	Socialist	420,793	2.8		
		Eugene W. Chafin	Prohibition	253,840	1.7		
1912	48	**WOODROW WILSON**	Democratic	6,296,547	41.9	435	58.8
		Theodore Roosevelt	Progressive	4,118,571	27.4	88	
		William H. Taft	Republican	3,486,720	23.2	8	
		Eugene V. Debs	Socialist	900,672	6.0		
		Eugene W. Chafin	Prohibition	206,275	1.4		

Year	Number of States	Candidates	Parties	Popular Vote	Electoral Vote	Percentage of Popular Vote	Percentage of Voter Participation
1916	48	**WOODROW WILSON**	Democratic	9,127,695	277	49.4	61.6
		Charles E. Hughes	Republican	8,533,507	254	46.2	
		A. L. Benson	Socialist	585,113		3.2	
		J. Frank Hanly	Prohibition	220,506		1.2	
1920	48	**WARREN G. HARDING**	Republican	16,143,407	404	60.4	49.2
		James M. Cox	Democratic	9,130,328	127	34.2	
		Eugene V. Debs	Socialist	919,799		3.4	
		P. P. Christensen	Farmer-Labor	265,411		1.0	
1924	48	**CALVIN COOLIDGE**	Republican	15,718,211	382	54.0	48.9
		John W. Davis	Democratic	8,385,283	136	28.8	
		Robert M. La Follette	Progressive	4,831,289	13	16.6	
1928	48	**HERBERT C. HOOVER**	Republican	21,391,993	444	58.2	56.9
		Alfred E. Smith	Democratic	15,016,169	87	40.9	
1932	48	**FRANKLIN D. ROOSEVELT**	Democratic	22,809,638	472	57.4	56.9
		Herbert C. Hoover	Republican	15,758,901	59	39.7	
		Norman Thomas	Socialist	881,951		2.2	
1936	48	**FRANKLIN D. ROOSEVELT**	Democratic	27,752,869	523	60.8	61.0
		Alfred M. Landon	Republican	16,674,665	8	36.5	
		William Lemke	Union	882,479		1.9	
1940	48	**FRANKLIN D. ROOSEVELT**	Democratic	27,307,819	449	54.8	62.5
		Wendell L. Willkie	Republican	22,321,018	82	44.8	
1944	48	**FRANKLIN D. ROOSEVELT**	Democratic	25,606,585	432	53.5	55.9
		Thomas E. Dewey	Republican	22,014,745	99	46.0	

Year	Number of States	Candidates	Parties	Popular Vote	% of Popular Vote	Electoral Vote	% Voter Participation
1948	48	**HARRY S. TRUMAN**	Democratic	24,179,345	49.6	303	53.0
		Thomas E. Dewey	Republican	21,991,291	45.1	189	
		J. Strom Thurmond	States' Rights	1,176,125	2.4	39	
		Henry A. Wallace	Progressive	1,157,326	2.4		
1952	48	**DWIGHT D. EISENHOWER**	Republican	33,936,234	55.1	442	63.3
		Adlai E. Stevenson	Democratic	27,314,992	44.4	89	
1956	48	**DWIGHT D. EISENHOWER**	Republican	35,590,472	57.6	457	60.6
		Adlai E. Stevenson	Democratic	26,022,752	42.1	73	
1960	50	**JOHN F. KENNEDY**	Democratic	34,226,731	49.7	303	62.8
		Richard M. Nixon	Republican	34,108,157	49.5	219	
1964	50	**LYNDON B. JOHNSON**	Democratic	43,129,566	61.1	486	61.9
		Barry M. Goldwater	Republican	27,178,188	38.5	52	
1968	50	**RICHARD M. NIXON**	Republican	31,785,480	43.4	301	60.9
		Hubert H. Humphrey	Democratic	31,275,166	42.7	191	
		George C. Wallace	American Independent	9,906,473	13.5	46	
1972	50	**RICHARD M. NIXON**	Republican	47,169,911	60.7	520	55.2
		George S. McGovern	Democratic	29,170,383	37.5	17	
		John G. Schmitz	American	1,099,482	1.4		

Year	Number of States	Candidates	Parties	Popular Vote	Percentage of Popular Vote	Electoral Vote	Percentage of Voter Participation
1976	50	**JIMMY CARTER**	Democratic	40,830,763	50.1	297	53.5
		Gerald R. Ford	Republican	39,147,793	48.0	240	
1980	50	**RONALD REAGAN**	Republican	43,901,812	50.7	489	52.6
		Jimmy Carter	Democratic	35,483,820	41.0	49	
		John B. Anderson	Independent	5,719,437	6.6		
		Ed Clark	Libertarian	921,188	1.1		
1984	50	**RONALD REAGAN**	Republican	54,451,521	58.8	525	53.1
		Walter F. Mondale	Democratic	37,565,334	40.6	13	
1988	50	**GEORGE H. BUSH**	Republican	47,917,341	53.4	426	50.1
		Michael Dukakis	Democratic	41,013,030	45.6	111	
1992	50	**BILL CLINTON**	Democratic	44,908,254	43.0	370	55.0
		George H. Bush	Republican	39,102,343	37.4	168	
		H. Ross Perot	Independent	19,741,065	18.9	0	
1996	50	**BILL CLINTON**	Democratic	47,401,185	49.0	379	49.0
		Bob Dole	Republican	39,197,469	41.0	159	
		H. Ross Perot	Independent	8,085,295	8.0	0	

Candidates receiving less than 1 percent of the popular vote have been omitted. Thus the percentage of popular vote given for any election year may not total 100 percent.

Before the passage of the Twelfth Amendment in 1804, the Electoral College voted for two presidential candidates; the runner-up became vice-president.

ADMISSION OF STATES

Order of Admission	State	Date of Admission	Order of Admission	State	Date of Admission
1	Delaware	December 7, 1787	26	Michigan	January 26, 1837
2	Pennsylvania	December 12, 1787	27	Florida	March 3, 1845
3	New Jersey	December 18, 1787	28	Texas	December 29, 1845
4	Georgia	January 2, 1788	29	Iowa	December 28, 1846
5	Connecticut	January 9, 1788	30	Wisconsin	May 29, 1848
6	Massachusetts	February 7, 1788	31	California	September 9, 1850
7	Maryland	April 28, 1788	32	Minnesota	May 11, 1858
8	South Carolina	May 23, 1788	33	Oregon	February 14, 1859
9	New Hampshire	June 21, 1788	34	Kansas	January 29, 1861
10	Virginia	June 25, 1788	35	West Virginia	June 30, 1863
11	New York	July 26, 1788	36	Nevada	October 31, 1864
12	North Carolina	November 21, 1789	37	Nebraska	March 1, 1867
13	Rhode Island	May 29, 1790	38	Colorado	August 1, 1876
14	Vermont	March 4, 1791	39	North Dakota	November 2, 1889
15	Kentucky	June 1, 1792	40	South Dakota	November 2, 1889
16	Tennessee	June 1, 1796	41	Montana	November 8, 1889
17	Ohio	March 1, 1803	42	Washington	November 11, 1889
18	Louisiana	April 30, 1812	43	Idaho	July 3, 1890
19	Indiana	December 11, 1816	44	Wyoming	July 10, 1890
20	Mississippi	December 10, 1817	45	Utah	January 4, 1896
21	Illinois	December 3, 1818	46	Oklahoma	November 16, 1907
22	Alabama	December 14, 1819	47	New Mexico	January 6, 1912
23	Maine	March 15, 1820	48	Arizona	February 14, 1912
24	Missouri	August 10, 1821	49	Alaska	January 3, 1959
25	Arkansas	June 15, 1836	50	Hawaii	August 21, 1959

POPULATION OF THE UNITED STATES

Year	Number of States	Population	% Increase	Population per Square Mile
1790	13	3,929,214		4.5
1800	16	5,308,483	35.1	6.1
1810	17	7,239,881	36.4	4.3
1820	23	9,638,453	33.1	5.5
1830	24	12,866,020	33.5	7.4
1840	26	17,069,453	32.7	9.8
1850	31	23,191,876	35.9	7.9
1860	33	31,443,321	35.6	10.6
1870	37	39,818,449	26.6	13.4
1880	38	50,155,783	26.0	16.9
1890	44	62,947,714	25.5	21.1
1900	45	75,994,575	20.7	25.6
1910	46	91,972,266	21.0	31.0
1920	48	105,710,620	14.9	35.6
1930	48	122,775,046	16.1	41.2
1940	48	131,669,275	7.2	44.2
1950	48	150,697,361	14.5	50.7
1960	50	179,323,175	19.0	50.6
1970	50	203,235,298	13.3	57.5
1980	50	226,504,825	11.4	64.0
1985	50	237,839,000	5.0	67.2
1990	50	250,122,000	5.2	70.6
1995	50	263,411,707	5.3	74.4

IMMIGRATION TO THE UNITED STATES, FISCAL YEARS 1820–1990

Year	Number	Year	Number	Year	Number	Year	Number
1820–1989	**55,457,531**	**1871–80**	**2,812,191**	**1921–30**	**4,107,209**	**1971–80**	**4,493,314**
1820	8,385	1871	321,350	1921	805,228	1971	370,478
1821–30	**143,439**	1872	404,806	1922	309,556	1972	384,685
1821	9,127	1873	459,803	1923	522,919	1973	400,063
1822	6,911	1874	313,339	1924	706,896	1974	394,861
1823	6,354	1875	227,498	1925	294,314	1975	386,914
1824	7,912	1876	169,986	1926	304,488	1976	398,613
1825	10,199	1877	141,857	1927	335,175	1976	103,676
1826	10,837	1878	138,469	1928	307,255	1977	462,315
1827	18,875	1879	177,826	1929	279,678	1978	601,442
1828	27,382	1880	457,257	1930	241,700	1979	460,348
1829	22,520	**1881–90**	**5,246,613**	**1931–40**	**528,431**	1980	530,639
1830	23,322	1881	669,431	1931	97,139	**1981–90**	**7,338,062**
1831–40	**599,125**	1882	788,992	1932	35,576	1981	596,600
1831	22,633	1883	603,322	1933	23,068	1982	594,131
1832	60,482	1884	518,592	1934	29,470	1983	559,763
1833	58,640	1885	395,346	1935	34,956	1984	543,903
1834	65,365	1886	334,203	1936	36,329	1985	570,009
1835	45,374	1887	490,109	1937	50,244	1986	601,708
1836	76,242	1888	546,889	1938	67,895	1987	601,516
1837	79,340	1889	444,427	1939	82,998	1988	643,025
1838	38,914	1890	455,302	1940	70,756	1989	1,090,924
1839	68,069	**1891–1900**	**3,687,564**	**1941–50**	**1,035,039**	1990	1,536,483
1840	84,066	1891	560,319	1941	51,776		
1841–50	**1,713,251**	1892	579,663	1942	28,781		
1841	80,289	1893	439,730	1943	23,725		
1842	104,565	1894	285,631	1944	28,551		
		1895	258,536	1945	38,119		
		1896	343,267	1946	108,721		

Year	Number	Year	Number	Year	Number
1843	52,496	1897	230,832	1947	147,292
1844	78,615	1898	229,299	1948	170,570
1845	114,371	1899	311,715	1949	188,317
1846	154,416	1900	448,572	1950	249,187
1847	234,968	**1901–10**	**8,795,386**	**1951–60**	**2,515,479**
1848	226,527	1901	487,918	1951	205,717
1849	297,024	1902	648,743	1952	265,520
1850	369,980	1903	857,046	1953	170,434
1851–60	**2,598,214**	1904	812,870	1954	208,177
1851	379,466	1905	1,026,499	1955	237,790
1852	371,603	1906	1,100,735	1956	321,625
1853	368,645	1907	1,285,349	1957	326,867
1854	427,833	1908	782,870	1958	253,265
1855	200,877	1909	751,786	1959	260,686
1856	200,436	1910	1,041,570	1960	265,398
1857	251,306	**1911–20**	**5,735,811**	**1961–70**	**3,321,677**
1858	123,126	1911	878,587	1961	271,344
1859	121,282	1912	838,172	1962	283,763
1860	153,640	1913	1,197,892	1963	306,260
1861–70	**2,314,824**	1914	1,218,480	1964	292,248
1861	91,918	1915	326,700	1965	296,697
1862	91,985	1916	298,826	1966	323,040
1863	176,282	1917	295,403	1967	361,972
1864	193,418	1918	110,618	1968	454,448
1865	248,120	1919	141,132	1969	358,579
1866	318,568	1920	430,001	1970	373,326
1867	315,722				
1868	138,840				
1869	352,768				
1870	387,203				

Source: U.S. Immigration and Naturalization Service, 1991.

IMMIGRATION BY REGION AND SELECTED COUNTRY OF LAST RESIDENCE, FISCAL YEARS 1820–1989

Region and Country of Last Residence[1]	1820	1821–30	1831–40	1841–50	1851–60	1861–70	1871–80	1881–90
All countries	8,385	143,439	599,125	1,713,251	2,598,214	2,314,824	2,812,191	5,246,613
Europe	7,690	98,797	495,681	1,597,442	2,452,577	2,065,141	2,271,925	4,735,484
Austria-Hungary	—[2]	—[2]	—[2]	—[2]	—[2]	7,800	72,969	353,719
Austria	—[2]	—[2]	—[2]	—[2]	—[2]	484[3]	63,009	226,038
Hungary	—[2]	—[2]	—[2]	—[2]	—[2]	7,124[3]	9,960	127,681
Belgium	1	27	22	5,074	4,738	6,734	7,221	20,177
Czechoslovakia	—[4]	—[4]	—[4]	—[4]	—[4]	—[4]	—[4]	—[4]
Denmark	20	169	1,063	539	3,749	17,094	31,771	88,132
France	371	8,497	45,575	77,262	76,358	35,986	72,206	50,464
Germany	968	6,761	152,454	434,626	951,667	787,468	718,182	1,452,970
Greece	—	20	49	16	31	72	210	2,308
Ireland[5]	3,614	50,724	207,381	780,719	914,119	435,778	436,871	655,482
Italy	30	409	2,253	1,870	9,231	11,725	55,759	307,309
Netherlands	49	1,078	1,412	8,251	10,789	9,102	16,541	53,701
Norway-Sweden	3	91	1,201	13,903	20,931	109,298	211,245	568,362
Norway	—[6]	—[6]	—[6]	—[6]	—[6]	—[6]	95,323	176,586
Sweden	—[6]	—[6]	—[6]	—[6]	—[6]	—[6]	115,922	391,776
Poland	5	16	369	105	1,164	2,027	12,970	51,806
Portugal	35	145	829	550	1,055	2,658	14,082	16,978
Romania	—[7]	—[7]	—[7]	—[7]	—[7]	—[7]	11	6,348
Soviet Union	14	75	277	551	457	2,512	39,284	213,282
Spain	139	2,477	2,125	2,209	9,298	6,697	5,266	4,419
Switzerland	31	3,226	4,821	4,644	25,011	23,286	28,293	81,988
United Kingdom[5,8]	2,410	25,079	75,810	267,044	423,974	606,896	548,043	807,357
Yugoslavia	—[9]	—[9]	—[9]	—[9]	5	8	—[9]	—[4]
Other Europe	—	3	40	79			1,001	682

Asia	6	30	55	141	41,538	64,759	124,160	69,942
China[10]	1	2	8	35	41,397	64,301	123,201	61,711
Hong Kong	—[11]	—[11]	—[11]	—[11]	—[11]	—[11]	—[11]	—[11]
India	1	8	39	36	43	69	163	269
Iran	—[12]	—[12]	—[12]	—[12]	—[12]	—[12]	—[12]	—[12]
Israel	—[13]	—[13]	—[13]	—[13]	—[13]	—[13]	—[13]	—[13]
Japan	—[14]	—[14]	—[14]	—[14]	—[14]	186	149	2,270
Korea	—[15]	—[15]	—[15]	—[15]	—[15]	—[15]	—[15]	—[15]
Philippines	—[16]	—[16]	—[16]	—[16]	—[16]	—[16]	—[16]	—[16]
Turkey	1	20	7	59	83	131	404	3,782
Vietnam	—[11]	—[11]	—[11]	—[11]	—[11]	—[11]	—[11]	—[11]
Other Asia	3	—	1	11	15	72	243	1,910
America	387	11,564	33,424	62,469	74,720	166,607	404,044	426,967
Canada & Newfoundland[17,18]	209	2,277	13,624	41,723	59,309	153,878	383,640	393,304
Mexico[18]	1	4,817	6,599	3,271	3,078	2,191	5,162	191,319
Caribbean	164	3,834	12,301	13,528	10,660	9,046	13,957	29,042
Cuba	—[12]	—[12]	—[12]	—[12]	—[12]	—[12]	—[12]	—[12]
Dominican Republic	—[20]	—[20]	—[20]	—[20]	—[20]	—[20]	—[20]	—[20]
Haiti	—[20]	—[20]	—[20]	—[20]	—[20]	—[20]	—[20]	—[20]
Jamaica	—[21]	—[21]	—[21]	—[21]	—[21]	—[21]	—[21]	—[21]
Other Caribbean	164	3,834	12,301	13,528	10,660	9,046	13,957	29,042
Central America	2	105	44	368	449	95	157	404
El Salvador	—[20]	—[20]	—[20]	—[20]	—[20]	—[20]	—[20]	—[20]
Other Central America	2	105	44	368	449	95	157	404
South America	11	531	856	3,579	1,224	1,397	1,128	2,304
Argentina	—[20]	—[20]	—[20]	—[20]	—[20]	—[20]	—[20]	—[20]
Colombia	—[20]	—[20]	—[20]	—[20]	—[20]	—[20]	—[20]	—[20]
Ecuador	—[20]	—[20]	—[20]	—[20]	—[20]	—[20]	—[20]	—[20]
Other South America	11	531	856	3,579	1,224	1,397	1,128	2,304
Other America	—[22]	—[22]	—[22]	—[22]	—[22]	—[22]	—[22]	—[22]
Africa	1	16	54	55	210	312	358	857
Oceania	1	2	9	29	158	214	10,914	12,574
Not specified[22]	300	33,030	69,902	53,115	29,011	17,791	790	789

Region and Country of Last Residence[1]	1891–1900	1901–10	1911–20	1921–30	1931–40	1941–50	1951–60	1961–70
All countries	3,687,564	8,795,386	5,735,811	4,107,209	528,431	1,035,039	2,515,479	3,321,677
Europe	3,555,352	8,056,040	4,321,887	2,463,194	347,566	621,147	1,325,727	1,123,492
Austria-Hungary	592,707[23]	2,145,266[23]	896,342[23]	63,548	11,424	28,329	103,743	26,022
Austria	234,081[3]	668,209[3]	453,649	32,868	3,563[24]	24,860[24]	67,106	20,621
Hungary	181,288[3]	808,511[3]	442,693	30,680	7,861	3,469	36,637	5,401
Belgium	18,167	41,635	33,746	15,846	4,817	12,189	18,575	9,192
Czechoslovakia	—[4]	—[4]	3,426[4]	102,194	14,393	8,347	918	3,273
Denmark	50,231	65,285	41,983	32,430	2,559	5,393	10,984	9,201
France	30,770	73,379	61,897	49,610	12,623	38,809	51,121	45,237
Germany	505,152[23]	341,498[23]	143,945[23]	412,202	114,058[24]	226,578[24]	477,765	190,796
Greece	15,979	167,519	184,201	51,084	9,119	8,973	47,608	85,969
Ireland[5]	388,416	339,065	146,181	211,234	10,973	19,789	48,362	32,966
Italy	651,893	2,045,877	1,109,524	455,315	68,028	57,661	185,491	214,111
Netherlands	26,758	48,262	43,718	26,948	7,150	14,860	52,277	30,606
Norway-Sweden	321,281	440,039	161,469	165,780	8,700	20,765	44,632	32,600
Norway	95,015	190,505	66,395	68,531	4,740	10,100	22,935	15,484
Sweden	226,266	249,534	95,074	97,249	3,960	10,665	21,697	17,116
Poland	96,720[23]	—[23]	4,813[23]	227,734	17,026	7,571	9,985	53,539
Portugal	27,508	69,149	89,732	29,994	3,329	7,423	19,588	76,065
Romania	12,750	53,008	13,311	67,646	3,871	1,076	1,039	2,531
Soviet Union	505,290[23]	1,597,306[23]	921,201[23]	61,742	1,370	571	671	2,465
Spain	8,731	27,935	68,611	28,958	3,258	2,898	7,894	44,659
Switzerland	31,179	34,922	23,091	29,676	5,512	10,547	17,675	18,453
United Kingdom[5,8]	271,538	525,950	341,408	339,570	31,572	139,306	202,824	213,822
Yugoslavia	—[9]	—[9]	1,888[9]	49,064	5,835	1,576	8,225	20,381
Other Europe	282	39,945	31,400	42,619	11,949	8,486	16,350	11,604

Asia	74,862	323,543	247,236	112,059	16,595	37,028	153,249	427,642
China[10]	14,799	20,605	21,278	29,907	4,928	16,709	9,657	34,764
Hong Kong	—[11]	—[11]	—[11]	—[11]	—[11]	—[11]	15,541[11]	75,007
India	68	4,713	2,082	1,886	496	1,761	1,973	27,189
Iran	—[12]	—[12]	—[12]	241[12]	195	1,380	3,388	10,339
Israel	—[13]	—[13]	—[13]	—[13]	—[13]	476[13]	25,476	29,602
Japan	25,942	129,797	83,837	33,462	1,948	1,555	46,250	39,988
Korea	—[15]	—[15]	—[15]	—[15]	—[15]	107[15]	6,231	34,526
Philippines	—[16]	—[16]	—[16]	—[16]	528[16]	4,691	19,307	98,376
Turkey	30,425	157,369	134,066	33,824	1,065	798	3,519	10,142
Vietnam	—[11]	—[11]	—[11]	—[11]	—[11]	—[11]	335[11]	4,340
Other Asia	3,628	11,059	5,973	12,739	7,435	9,551	21,572	63,369
America	38,972	361,888	1,143,671	1,516,716	160,037	354,804	996,944	1,716,374
Canada & Newfoundland[17,18]	3,311	179,226	742,185	924,515	108,527	171,718	377,952	413,310
Mexico[18]	971[19]	49,642	219,004	459,287	22,319	60,589	299,811	453,937
Caribbean	33,066	107,548	123,424	74,899	15,502	49,725	123,091	470,213
Cuba	—[12]	—[12]	—[12]	15,901[12]	9,571	26,313	78,948	208,536
Dominican Republic	—[20]	—[20]	—[20]	—[20]	1,150[20]	5,627	9,897	93,292
Haiti	—[20]	—[20]	—[20]	—[20]	191[20]	911	4,442	34,499
Jamaica	—[21]	—[21]	—[21]	—[21]	—[21]	—[21]	8,869[21]	74,906
Other Caribbean	33,066	107,548	123,424	58,998	4,590	16,874	20,935[21]	58,980
Central America	549	8,192	17,159	15,769	5,861	21,665	44,751	101,330
El Salvador	—[20]	—[20]	—[20]	—[20]	673[20]	5,132	5,895	14,992
Other Central America	549	8,192	17,159	15,769	5,188	16,533	38,856	86,338
South America	1,075	17,280	41,899	42,215	7,803	21,831	91,628	257,954
Argentina	—[20]	—[20]	—[20]	—[20]	1,349[20]	3,338	19,486	49,721
Colombia	—[20]	—[20]	—[20]	—[20]	1,223[20]	3,858	18,048	72,028
Ecuador	—[20]	—[20]	—[20]	—[20]	337[20]	2,417	9,841	36,780
Other South America	1,075	17,280	41,899	42,215	4,894	12,218	44,253	99,425
Other America	—[22]	—[22]	—[22]	31[22]	25	29,276	59,711	19,630
Africa	350	7,368	8,443	6,286	1,750	7,367	14,092	28,954
Oceania	3,965	13,024	13,427	8,726	2,483	14,551	12,976	25,122
Not specified[22]	14,063	33,523[25]	1,147	228	—	142	12,491	93

Region and Country of Last Residence[1]	1971–80	1981–89	1984	1985	1986	1987	1988	1989	Total 170 Years 1820–1989
All countries	4,493,314	5,801,579	543,903	570,009	601,708	601,516	643,025	1,090,924	55,457,531
Europe	800,368	637,524	69,879	69,526	69,224	67,967	71,854	94,338	36,977,034
Austria-Hungary	16,028	20,152	2,846	2,521	2,604	2,401	3,200	3,586	4,338,049
Austria	9,478	14,566	2,351	1,930	2,039	1,769	2,493	2,845	1,825,172[2]
Hungary	6,550	5,586	495	591	565	632	707	741	1,666,801[3]
Belgium	5,329	6,239	787	775	843	859	706	705	209,729
Czechoslovakia	6,023	6,649	693	684	588	715	744	526	145,223
Denmark	4,439	4,696	512	465	544	515	561	617	369,738
France	25,069	28,088	3,335	3,530	3,876	3,809	3,637	4,101	783,322
Germany	74,414	79,809	9,375	10,028	9,853	9,923	9,748	10,419	7,071,313
Greece	92,369	34,490	3,311	3,487	3,497	4,087	4,690	4,588	700,017
Ireland[5]	11,490	22,229	1,096	1,288	1,757	3,032	5,121	6,983	4,715,393
Italy	129,368	51,008	6,328	6,351	5,711	4,666	5,332	11,089	5,356,862
Netherlands	10,492	10,723	1,313	1,235	1,263	1,303	1,152	1,253	372,717
Norway-Sweden	10,472	13,252	1,455	1,557	1,564	1,540	1,669	1,809	2,144,024
Norway	3,941	3,612	403	386	367	372	446	556	800,672[6]
Sweden	6,531	9,640	1,052	1,171	1,197	1,168	1,223	1,253	1,283,097[6]
Poland	37,234	64,888	7,229	7,409	6,540	5,818	7,298	13,279	587,972
Portugal	101,710	36,365	3,800	3,811	3,804	4,009	3,290	3,861	497,195
Romania	12,393	27,361	2,956	3,764	3,809	2,741	2,915	3,535	201,345
Soviet Union	38,961	42,898	3,349	1,532	1,001	1,139	1,408	4,570	3,428,927
Spain	39,141	17,689	2,168	2,278	2,232	2,056	1,972	2,179	282,404
Switzerland	8,235	7,561	795	980	923	964	920	1,072	358,151
United Kingdom[5,8]	137,374	140,119	16,516	15,591	16,129	15,889	14,667	16,961	5,100,096
Yugoslavia	30,540	15,984	1,404	1,521	1,915	1,793	2,039	2,464	133,493
Other Europe	9,287	7,324	611	719	771	708	785	741	181,064

Asia	1,588,178	2,416,278	247,775	255,164	258,546	248,293	254,745	296,420	5,697,301
China[10]	124,326	306,108	29,109	33,095	32,389	32,669	34,300	39,284	873,737
Hong Kong	113,467	83,848	12,290	10,795	9,930	8,785	11,817	15,257	287,863[11]
India	164,134	221,977	23,617	24,536	24,808	26,394	25,312	28,599	426,907
Iran	45,136	101,267	11,131	12,327	12,031	10,323	9,846	13,027	161,946[12]
Israel	37,713	38,367	4,136	4,279	5,124	4,753	4,444	5,494	131,634[13]
Japan	49,775	40,654	4,517	4,552	4,444	4,711	5,085	5,454	455,813[14]
Korea	267,638	302,782	32,537	34,791	35,164	35,397	34,151	33,016	611,284[15]
Philippines	354,987	477,485	46,985	53,137	61,492	58,315	61,017	66,119	955,374[16]
Turkey	13,399	20,028	1,652	1,690	1,975	2,080	2,200	2,538	409,122
Vietnam	172,820	266,027	25,803	20,367	15,010	13,073	12,856	13,174	443,522[11]
Other Asia	244,783	557,735	55,998	55,595	56,179	51,793	53,717	74,458	940,099
America	1,982,735	2,564,698	208,111	225,519	254,078	265,026	294,906	672,639	12,017,021
Canada & Newfoundland[17,18]	169,939	132,296	15,659	16,354	16,060	16,741	15,821	18,294	4,270,943
Mexico[18]	640,294	975,657	57,820	61,290	66,753	72,511	95,170	405,660	3,208,543
Caribbean	741,126	759,416	68,368	79,374	98,527	100,615	110,949	87,597	2,590,542
Cuba	264,863	135,142	5,699	17,115	30,787	27,363	16,610	9,523	739,274[12]
Dominican Republic	148,135	209,899	23,207	23,861	26,216	24,947	27,195	26,744	468,000[20]
Haiti	56,335	118,510	9,554	9,872	12,356	14,643	34,858	13,341	214,888[20]
Jamaica	137,577	184,481	18,997	18,277	18,916	22,430	20,474	23,572	405,833[21]
Other Caribbean	134,216	111,384	10,911	10,249	10,252	11,232	11,812	14,417	762,547
Central America	134,640	321,845	27,626	28,447	30,086	30,366	31,311	101,273	673,385
El Salvador	34,436	133,938	8,753	10,093	10,881	10,627	12,043	57,628	195,066[20]
Other Central America	100,204	187,907	18,873	18,354	19,205	19,739	19,268	43,645	478,319
South America	295,741	375,026	38,636	40,052	42,650	44,782	41,646	59,812	1,163,482
Argentina	29,897	21,374	2,287	1,925	2,318	2,192	2,556	3,766	125,165[20]
Colombia	77,347	99,066	10,897	11,802	11,213	11,482	10,153	14,918	271,570[20]
Ecuador	50,077	43,841	4,244	4,601	4,518	4,656	4,736	7,587	143,293[20]
Other South America	138,420	210,745	21,208	21,724	24,601	26,452	24,201	33,541	623,454
Other America	995	458	2	2	2	11	9	3	110,126
Africa	80,779	144,096	13,594	15,236	15,500	15,730	17,124	22,485	301,348
Oceania	41,242	38,401	4,249	4,552	4,352	4,437	4,324	4,956	197,818
Not specified[22]	12	582	295	12	8	63	72	86	267,009

Source: U.S. Immigration and Naturalization Service, 1991.

[1]Data for years prior to 1906 relate to country whence alien came; data from 1906–79 and 1984–89 are for country of last permanent residence; and data for 1980–83 refer to country of birth. Because of changes in boundaries, changes in lists of countries, and lack of data for specified countries for various periods, data for certain countries, especially for the total period 1820–1989, are not comparable throughout. Data for specified countries are included with countries to which they belonged prior to World War I.

[2]Data for Austria and Hungary not reported until 1861.

[3]Data for Austria and Hungary not reported separately for all years during the period.

[4]No data available for Czechoslovakia until 1920.

[5]Prior to 1926, data for Northern Ireland included in Ireland.

[6]Data for Norway and Sweden not reported separately until 1871.

[7]No data available for Romania until 1880.

[8]Since 1925, data for United Kingdom refer to England, Scotland, Wales, and Northern Ireland.

[9]In 1920, a separate enumeration was made for the Kingdom of Serbs, Croats, and Slovenes. Since 1922, the Serb, Croat, and Slovene Kingdom recorded as Yugoslavia.

[10]Beginning in 1957, China includes Taiwan.

[11]Data not reported separately until 1952.

[12]Data not reported separately until 1925.

[13]Data not reported separately until 1949.

[14]No data available for Japan until 1861.

[15]Data not reported separately until 1948.

[16]Prior to 1934, Philippines recorded as insular travel.

[17]Prior to 1920, Canada and Newfoundland recorded as British North America. From 1820 to 1898, figures include all British North America possessions.

[18]Land arrivals not completely enumerated until 1908.

[19]No data available for Mexico from 1886 to 1893.

[20]Data not reported separately until 1932.

[21]Data for Jamaica not collected until 1953. In prior years, consolidated under British West Indies, which is included in "Other Caribbean."

[22]Included in countries "Not specified" until 1925.

[23]From 1899 to 1919, data for Poland included in Austria-Hungary, Germany, and the Soviet Union.

[24]From 1938 to 1945, data for Austria included in Germany.

[25]Includes 32,897 persons returning in 1906 to their homes in the United States.

—represents zero.

NOTE: From 1820 to 1867, figures represent alien passengers arrived at seaports; from 1868 to 1891 and 1895 to 1897, immigrant aliens arrived; from 1892 to 1894 and 1898 to 1989, immigrant aliens admitted for permanent residence. From 1892 to 1903, aliens entering by cabin class were not counted as immigrants. Land arrivals were not completely enumerated until 1908. For this table, fiscal year 1843 covers 9 months ending September 1843; fiscal years 1832 and 1850 cover 15 months ending December 31 of the respective years; and fiscal year 1868 covers 6 months ending June 30, 1868.

PRESIDENTS, VICE-PRESIDENTS, AND SECRETARIES OF STATE

President	*Vice-President*	*Secretary of State*
1. George Washington, Federalist 1789	John Adams, Federalist 1789	Thomas Jefferson 1789 Edmund Randolph 1794 Timothy Pickering 1795
2. John Adams, Federalist 1797	Thomas Jefferson, Dem.-Rep. 1797	Timothy Pickering 1797 John Marshall 1800
3. Thomas Jefferson, Dem.-Rep. 1801	Aaron Burr, Dem.-Rep. 1801 George Clinton, Dem.-Rep. 1805	James Madison 1801
4. James Madison, Dem.-Rep. 1809	George Clinton, Dem.-Rep. 1809 Elbridge Gerry, Dem.-Rep. 1813	Robert Smith 1809 James Monroe 1811
5. James Monroe, Dem.-Rep. 1817	Daniel D. Tompkins, Dem.-Rep. 1817	John Q. Adams 1817
6. John Quincy Adams, Dem.-Rep. 1825	John C. Calhoun, Dem.-Rep. 1825	Henry Clay 1825
7. Andrew Jackson, Democratic 1829	John C. Calhoun, Democratic 1829 Martin Van Buren, Democratic 1833	Martin Van Buren 1829 Edward Livingston 1831 Louis McLane 1833 John Forsyth 1834
8. Martin Van Buren, Democratic 1837	Richard M. Johnson, Democratic 1837	John Forsyth 1837
9. William H. Harrison, Whig 1841	John Tyler, Whig 1841	Daniel Webster 1841

President	Vice-President	Secretary of State
10. John Tyler, Whig and Democratic 1841	None	Daniel Webster 1841 Hugh S. Legaré 1843 Abel P. Upshur 1843 John C. Calhoun 1844
11. James K. Polk, Democratic 1845	George M. Dallas, Democratic 1845	James Buchanan 1845
12. Zachary Taylor, Whig 1849	Millard Fillmore, Whig 1849	John M. Clayton 1849
13. Millard Fillmore, Whig 1850	None	Daniel Webster 1850 Edward Everett 1852
14. Franklin Pierce, Democratic 1853	William R. King, Democratic 1853	William L. Marcy 1853
15. James Buchanan, Democratic 1857	John C. Breckinridge, Democratic 1857	Lewis Cass 1857 Jeremiah S. Black 1860
16. Abraham Lincoln, Republican 1861	Hannibal Hamlin, Republican 1861 Andrew Johnson, Unionist 1865	William H. Seward 1861
17. Andrew Johnson, Unionist 1865	None	William H. Seward 1865
18. Ulysses S. Grant, Republican 1869	Schuyler Colfax, Republican 1869 Henry Wilson, Republican 1873	Elihu B. Washburne 1869 Hamilton Fish 1869
19. Rutherford B. Hayes, Republican 1877	William A. Wheeler, Republican 1877	William M. Evarts 1877

	President	Vice-President	Secretary of State
20.	James A. Garfield, Republican 1881	Chester A. Arthur, Republican 1881	James G. Blaine 1881
21.	Chester A. Arthur, Republican 1881	None	Frederick T. Frelinghuysen 1881
22.	Grover Cleveland, Democratic 1885	Thomas A. Hendricks, Democratic 1885	Thomas F. Bayard 1885
23.	Benjamin Harrison, Republican 1889	Levi P. Morton, Republican 1889	James G. Blaine 1889 John W. Foster 1892
24.	Grover Cleveland, Democratic 1893	Adlai E. Stevenson, Democratic 1893	Walter Q. Gresham 1893 Richard Olney 1895
25.	William McKinley, Republican 1897	Garret A. Hobart, Republican 1897 Theodore Roosevelt, Republican 1901	John Sherman 1897 William R. Day 1898 John Hay 1898
26.	Theodore Roosevelt, Republican 1901	Charles Fairbanks, Republican 1905	John Hay 1901 Elihu Root 1905 Robert Bacon 1909
27.	William H. Taft, Republican 1909	James S. Sherman, Republican 1909	Philander C. Knox 1909
28.	Woodrow Wilson, Democratic 1913	Thomas R. Marshall, Democratic 1913	William J. Bryan 1913 Robert Lansing 1915 Bainbridge Colby 1920
29.	Warren G. Harding, Republican 1921	Calvin Coolidge, Republican 1921	Charles E. Hughes 1921
30.	Calvin Coolidge, Republican 1923	Charles G. Dawes, Republican 1925	Charles E. Hughes 1923 Frank B. Kellogg 1925

	President	Vice-President	Secretary of State
31.	Herbert Hoover, Republican 1929	Charles Curtis, Republican 1929	Henry L. Stimson 1929
32.	Franklin D. Roosevelt, Democratic 1933	John Nance Garner, Democratic 1933 Henry A. Wallace, Democratic 1941 Harry S. Truman, Democratic 1945	Cordell Hull 1933 Edward R. Stettinius, Jr. 1944
33.	Harry S. Truman, Democratic 1945	Alben W. Barkley, Democratic 1949	Edward R. Stettinius, Jr. 1945 James F. Byrnes 1945 George C. Marshall 1947 Dean G. Acheson 1949
34.	Dwight D. Eisenhower, Republican 1953	Richard M. Nixon, Republican 1953	John F. Dulles 1953 Christian A. Herter 1959
35.	John F. Kennedy, Democratic 1961	Lyndon B. Johnson, Democratic 1961	Dean Rusk 1961
36.	Lyndon B. Johnson, Democratic 1963	Hubert H. Humphrey, Democratic 1965	Dean Rusk 1963
37.	Richard M. Nixon, Republican 1969	Spiro T. Agnew, Republican 1969 Gerald R. Ford, Republican 1973	William P. Rogers 1969 Henry Kissinger 1973
38.	Gerald R. Ford, Republican 1974	Nelson Rockefeller, Republican 1974	Henry Kissinger 1974
39.	Jimmy Carter, Democratic 1977	Walter Mondale, Democratic 1977	Cyrus Vance 1977 Edmund Muskie 1980

	President	Vice-President	Secretary of State
40.	Ronald Reagan, Republican 1981	George Bush, Republican 1981	Alexander Haig 1981 George Schultz 1982
41.	George Bush, Republican 1989	J. Danforth Quayle, Republican 1989	James A. Baker 1989 Lawrence Eagleburger 1992
42.	William J. Clinton, Democrat 1993	Albert Gore, Jr., Democrat 1993	Warren Christopher 1993 Madeleine Albright 1997

CREDITS

CHAPTER 1: p. 9, Peabody Museum, Harvard University; **p. 10,** Milwaukee Public Museum; **p. 12** Denver Convention & Visitors Bureau; **p. 16,** Library of Congress; **p. 18,** The New York Public Library, Rare Book Division, Astor, Lenox and Tilden Foundations; **p. 22,** © The British Museum; **p. 24,** Neg. No. 286821, courtesy Department of Library Services, American Museum of Natural History; **p. 27,** Neg. No. 330880 Photo. Rota., Courtesy Department of Library Services, American Museum of Natural History; **p. 28,** Newberry Library, Chicago, **p. 35,** Royal Library, Copenhagen; **p. 37,** Scala/Art Resource, NY; **p. 38,** Musée Historique de la Reformation; **p. 39,** Corbis-Bettman; **p. 42,** National Maritime Museum, London; **p. 44,** Corbis-Bettman.

CHAPTER 2: p. 49, By courtesy of the National Portrait Gallery, London; **p. 51,** *(top)* By courtesy of the National Portrait Gallery, London, and *(bottom)* Photo Bulloz; **p. 52,** By courtesy of the National Portrait Gallery, London; **p. 56,** The Huntington Library, Art Collection and Botanical Gardens (San Marino, CA); **p. 57,** Library of Congress; **p. 58,** Corbis-Bettman; **p. 59,** Society of Antiquaries, London; **p. 66,** Stadelschen Kunstinstituts Frankfurt, photo © Ursula Edelmann; **p. 68,** Courtesy of the Pilgrim Society, Plymouth, MA; **p. 69** Courtesy, American Antiquarian Society; **p. 72,** Courtesy, American Antiquarian Society; **p. 74,** The Warder Collection; **p. 78,** Courtesy of the John Carter Brown Library at Brown University; **p. 80,** The Library Company of Philadelphia; **p. 81,** Courtesy, Massachusetts Historical Society, Boston; **p. 87,** Courtesy of the John Carter Brown Library at Brown University; **p. 88,** The South Carolinian Library; **p. 90,** The New York Public Library, Astor, Lenox and Tilden Foundations; **p. 92,** National Archives of Canada, Negative # PA124105; **p. 93,** Cranbrook Institute of Science; **p. 96,** The Historical Society of Pennsylvania; **p. 95,** Bequest of Maxim Karolik. Courtesy, Museum of Fine Arts, Boston; **p. 99,** Courtesy, The Mariners Museum, Newport News, Virginia.

CHAPTER 3: p. 108, Beinecke Rare Book and Manuscript Library, Yale University; **p. 111,** The Worcester Art Museum; **p. 112,** *The Cheney Family*, Gift of Edgar William and Bernice Chrysler Garbisch, photograph © Board of Trustees, National Gallery of Art, Washington; **p. 114,** Connecticut Historical Society; **p. 116,** Colonial Williamsburg Foundation; **p. 118,** All rights reserved, The Metropolitan Museum of Art, Gift of Edgar William and Bernice Chrysler Garbisch, 1963; **p. 119,** Swem Library, The College of William and Mary; **p. 120,** Swem Library, The College of William and Mary; **p. 123,** Statue of Liberty National Monument; **p. 124,** The Abby Aldrich Rockefeller Folk Art Center, Williamsburg, Virginia; **p. 126,** National Museum of American History, Smithsonian Institution; **p. 127,** Courtesy, Henry Francis du Pont Winterhur Museum; **p. 128,** Historic Christ's Church, Virginia; **p. 130,** Corbis-

CHAPTER 8: p. 328, Library of Congress; **p. 330,** Print Collection, Miriam and Ira D. Wallach Division of Art, Prints and Photographs, The New York Public Library, Astor, Lenox and Tilden Foundations; **p. 332,** Collection of the Albany Institute of History & Art, 1971.12.17; **p. 334,** Corbis-Bettman; **p. 338,** Corbis-Bettman; **p. 341,** The Library Company of Philadelphia; **p. 343,** Independence National Historical Park Collection; **p. 348,** Detroit Public Library; **p. 350,** The Warder Collection; **p. 353,** Rare Book Division, The New York Public Library, Astor, Lenox and Tilden Foundations; **p. 355,** Collection Washington University, St. Louis; **p. 357,** Collection of the Maryland Historical Society, Baltimore; **p. 360,** Collection of the Boston Athenaeum, **p. 362,** The Henry E. Huntington Library, Art Gallery and Botanical Gardens (San Marino, CA); **p. 365,** Print Collection, Miriam and Ira D. Wallach Division of Art, Prints and Photographs, The New York Public Library, Astor, Lenox and Tilden Foundations.

CHAPTER 9: p. 372, The Warder Collection; **p. 374,** The New York Public Library, Astor, Lenox and Tilden Foundations; **p. 376,** The Cincinnati Historical Society; **p. 379,** Corbis-Bettman; **p. 382,** Beinecke Rare Book and Manuscript Library, Yale University; **p. 385,** National Portrait Gallery, Smithsonian Institution/Art Resource, NY; **p. 390,** The New York Public Library, Astor, Lenox and Tilden Foundations; **p. 391,** © Collection of the New-York Historical Society; **p. 393,** American Museum of Natural History; **p. 394,** Indiana Historical Society; **p. 398,** © Collection of the New-York Historical Society; **p. 401,** The Peale Museum, Baltimore; **p. 402,** Courtesy of the Massachusetts Historical Society, Boston; **p. 405,** Collection of Davenport West, Jr.

CHAPTER 10: p. 409, Collection of the Maryland Historical Society, Baltimore; **p. 410,** The Historical Society of Pennsylvania; **p. 414,** National Portrait Gallery, Smithsonian Institution, transfer from the National Gallery of Art, Gift of Andrew W. Mellon; **p. 418,** Historical Museum of Southern Florida; **p. 419,** National Archives; **p. 424,** Henry Clay Memorial Foundation; **p. 425,** Library of Congress; **p. 427,** All rights reserved, The Metropolitan Museum of Art, Rogers Fund, 1942 (42.95.7); **p. 432,** © Collection of the New-York Historical Society; **p. 434,** © Collection of the New-York Historical Society; **p. 437,** © Collection of the New-York Historical Society; **p. 438,** © Collection of the New-York Historical Society.

CHAPTER 11: p. 449, The Historical Society of Pennsylvania; **p. 451,** National Museum of American History, Smithsonian Institution; **p. 452,** National Portrait Gallery, Smithsonian Institution; **p. 453,** Library of Congress; **p. 456,** Boston Art Commission; **p. 458,** Courtesy, American Antiquarian Society; **p. 464,** Western Historical Collections, University of Oklahoma Library; **p. 468,** © Collection of the New-York Historical Society; **p. 469,** Collection of the Boatmen's National Bank of Saint Louis; **p. 471,** Library of Congress; **p. 475,** © Collection of the New-York Historical Society; **p. 476,** Library of Congress; **p. 477,** Library of Congress; **p. 479,** © Collection of the New-York Historical Society; **p. 482,** Library of Congress.

CHAPTER 12: p. 487, Merrimack Valley Textile Museum; **p. 490,** Hudson's Bay Company Archives, Provincial Archives of Manitoba; **p. 491,** V & A Picture Library; **p. 493,** Minnesota Historical Society; **p. 496,** All rights reserved, The Metropolitan Museum of Art, Harris Brisbane Dick Fund, 1941 (41.51); **p. 500,** Library of Congress; **p. 502,** © New York State Historical Association, Cooperstown, New York; **p. 504,** © New York State Historical Association, Cooperstown, New York; **p. 506,** Library of Congress/Corbis; **p. 507,** Library of Congress; **p. 510,** From *Memoir of Samuel Slater*, Davis Library, University of North Carolina Library at Chapel Hill; **p. 512,** Smithsonian Institution; **p. 514,** © Collection of the New-York Historical Society; **p. 515,** Museum of the City of New York, The Harry T. Peters Collection

58.300.52; **p. 516,** *Bare Knuckles,* Gift of Edgar William and Bernice Chrysler Garbisch, © 1998 Board of Trustees, National Gallery of Art, Washington; **p. 518,** © Collection of the New-York Historical Society; **p. 521,** Courtesy, National Park Service, Ellis Island Collection; **p. 524,** The Warder Collection; **p. 526,** Courtesy, American Antiquarian Society; **p. 528,** Library of Congress; **p. 530,** The Historical Society of Pennsylvania; **p. 533,** The Bancroft Library, University of California, Berkeley.

CHAPTER 13: p. 540, Old Dartmouth Historical Society, New Bedford Whaling Museum; **p. 545,** © 1998 by Intellectual Reserve, Inc., Courtesy of Historical Department, used by permission; **p. 548,** Wadsworth Athenaeum, Hartford, Bequest of Daniel Wadsworth; **p. 549,** New England Magazine; **p. 551,** Thoreau Institute; **p. 553,** Courtesy, Peabody Essex Museum, Salem, Mass; **p. 555,** Courtesy, American Antiquarian Society; **p. 556,** The Chrysler Museum of Art, Norfolk, Gift of Edgar William and Bernice Chrysler Garbisch, 76.53.25; **p. 557,** Amon Carter Museum, Fort Worth, Texas; **p. 559,** William Sidney Mount, *The Herald in the Country,* 1853, The Museums at Stony Brook; **p. 564,** University of Virginia Manuscript Department; **p. 565,** All rights reserved, The Metropolitan Museum of Art, Gift of I. N. Phelps Stokes, Edward S. Hawes, Alice Mary Hawes, Marion Augusta Hawes, 1937 [37.14.22]; **p. 568,** Library of Congress; **p. 570,** The New York Public Library, Astor, Lenox and Tilden Foundations; **p. 572,** From Catharine Beecher, *The American Woman's Home,* 1869; **p. 574,** The Warder Collection; **p. 575,** All rights reserved, The Metropolitan Museum of Art, Gift of I. N. Phelps Stokes, Edward S. Hawes, Alice Mary Hawes, Marion Augusta Hawes, 1937 [37.14.10]; **p. 576,** The Huntington Library, Art Collection and Botanical Gardens (San Marino, CA) LS 14 (2)2.

CHAPTER 14: p. 586, *Buffalo Lancing in the Snow Drifts*—Sioux, Paul Mellon Collection, © 1998 Board of Trustees, National Gallery of Art, Washington; **p. 589,** Courtesy of the Museum of New Mexico; **p. 591,** All rights reserved, The Metropolitan Museum of Art, Morris K. Jesup Fund, 1933; **p. 593,** The Henry E. Huntington Library, Art Gallery, and Botanical Gardens (San Marino, CA); **p. 595,** The Bancroft Library, University of California, Berkeley; **p. 598,** The Bancroft Library, University of California, Berkeley; **p. 599,** Kansas State Historical Society, Topeka, Kansas; **p. 601,** Library of Congress; **p. 604,** Library of Congress; **p. 607,** In the Collection of the Corcoran Gallery of Art, Museum Purchase, Gallery Fund; **p. 610,** Library of Congress; **p. 614,** Library of Congress; **p. 615,** The Warder Collection.

CHAPTER 15: p. 629, Library of Congress; **p. 633,** Photographs and Prints Division, Schomburg Center for Research in Black Culture, The New York Public Library, Astor, Lenox and Tilden Foundations; **p. 634,** Library of Congress; **p. 637,** *(top and bottom)* Library of Congress; **p. 645,** *Harper's Weekly,* July 14, 1886; **p. 647,** The Historical Society of Pennsylvania; **p. 648,** The Charleston Museum, Charleston, South Carolina; **p. 650,** Library of Congress; **p. 651,** Abby Aldrich Rockefeller Folk Art Center, Williamsburg, VA; **p. 652,** Peabody Museum, Harvard University; **p. 656,** Abby Aldrich Rockefeller Folk Art Center, Williamsburg, VA; **p. 657,** South Carolina Historical Society; **p. 662,** All rights reserved, The Metropolitan Museum of Art, Gift of I. N. Phelps Stokes, Edward S. Hawes, Alice Mary Hawes, Marion Augusta Hawes, 1937 (37.14.37); **p. 663,** Library of Congress/Corbis; **p. 666,** *(left)* © Collection of the New-York Historical Society, and *(right)* National Portrait Gallery, Smithsonian Institution/ Art Resource, NY.

CHAPTER 16: p. 678, Amon Carter Museum, Fort Worth, Texas; **p. 679,** William Sidney Mount, *California News,* 1850, The Museums at Stony Brook; **p. 680,** Amon Carter Museum, Fort Worth, Texas; **p. 684,** All rights reserved, The Metropolitan Museum of Art, Gift of I. N. Phelps Stokes, Edward S. Hawes, Alice Mary Hawes, Marion Augusta Hawes, 1937; **p. 686,** Library of Congress; **p. 689,** Library of Congress;

p. 690, © Collection of the New-York Historical Society; **p. 692,** © Collection of the New-York Historical Society; **p. 694,** National Portrait Gallery, Smithsonian Institution/Art Resource, NY; **p. 699,** Library of Congress; **p. 700,** Print Collection, Miriam and Ira D. Wallach Division of Art, Prints and Photographs, The New York Public Library, Astor, Lenox and Tilden Foundations; **p. 704,** *(left)* Missouri Historical Society, St. Louis, and *(right)* National Archives; **p. 706,** Library of Congress; **p. 711,** Collection of the Boston Athenaeum; **p. 713,** Library of Congress; **p. 716,** Chicago Historical Society; **p. 718,** Rare Book Division, The New York Public Library, Astor, Lenox and Tilden Foundations.

CHAPTER 17: p. 728, Library of Congress; **p. 729,** Library of Congress; **p. 732,** *The Gun Foundry,* by John Ferguson Weir, Courtesy of Putnam County Historical Society & Foundry School Museum, Cold Spring, NY; **p. 737,** Prints Division, The New York Public Library, Astor, Lenox and Tilden Foundations; **p. 740,** Library of Congress; **p. 742,** Kansas State Historical Society, Topeka, Kansas; **p. 748,** Library of Congress; **p. 750,** Library of Congress; **p. 754,** Library of Congress; **p. 757,** *(top and bottom)* Library of Congress; **p. 758,** Library of Congress; **p. 759,** Chicago Historical Society; **p. 761,** Library of Congress; **p. 763,** Library of Congress; **p. 768,** Library of Congress; **p. 770,** National Archives; **p. 775,** Library of Congress; **p. 777,** Chicago Historical Society, J. W. Cumberland, ICHI-10484; **p. 778,** Library of Congress; **p. 779,** Massachusetts Commandery Military Order of the Loyal Legion and the U. S. Army Military History Institute; **p. 781,** Massachusetts Commandery Military Order of the Loyal Legion and the U. S. Army Military History Institute; **p. 783,** Library of Congress; **p. 784** Library of Congress.

CHAPTER 18: p. 790, Courtesy, Massachusetts Historical Society, Boston; **p. 792,** Library of Congress; **p. 794,** Library of Congress; **p. 795,** Library of Congress/Corbis; **p. 799,** Courtesy George Eastman House; **p. 800,** Library of Congress; **p. 803,** *Harper's Weekly*; **p. 804,** *(left)* Library of Congress, and *(right)* U. S. Signal Corps photo no. 111-B-1084 (Brady Collection) in the National Archives; **p. 807,** National Portrait Gallery, Smithsonian Institution/Art Resource, NY; **p. 811,** U. S. Signal Corps photo no. 111-B-4371 (Brady Collection) in the National Archives; **p. 815,** Corbis-Bettman; **p. 816,** National Archives; **p. 820,** Library of Congress; **p. 824,** National Portrait Gallery, Smithsonian Institution/Art Resource, NY; **p. 826,** Library of Congress; **p. 827,** Library of Congress; **p. 830,** Library of Congress.

CHAPTER 19: p. 842, *Harper's Weekly,* March 1883, photo courtesy of Davis Library, University of North Carolina Library at Chapel Hill; **p. 847,** The Granger Collection, New York; **p. 852,** The Warder Collection; **p. 854,** Library of Congress; **p. 855,** The Warder Collection; **p. 858,** Courtesy Denver Public Library, Western History Collection; **p. 859,** Library of Congress; **p. 861,** Idaho State Historical Society #349; **p. 865,** Courtesy Colorado Historical Society; **p. 869,** Princeton University Press; **p. 870,** The Smithsonian Institution; **p. 871,** Amon Carter Museum, Fort Worth, Texas; **p. 872,** National Archives; **p. 874,** National Archives; **p. 878,** National Archives; **p. 880,** Haynes Foundation Collection, Montana Historical Society, Helena; **p. 881,** Western History Collections, University of Oklahoma Libraries.

CHAPTER 20: p. 888, Amon Carter Museum, Fort Worth, Texas; **p. 891,** Union Pacific Museum Collection; **p. 893,** © Collection of the New-York Historical Society; **p. 894,** National Archives; **p. 895,** © Collection of the New-York Historical Society; **p. 897,** Courtesy, Gotham Book Mart, NY; **p. 899,** Courtesy of American Petroleum Institute Historical Photo Collection; **p. 900,** The Warder Collection; **p. 901,** Carnegie Library, Pittsburgh; **p. 903,** Keystone-Mast Collection (WX 13101), UCR/California Museum of Photography, University of California, Riverside; **p. 904,** The Pierpont Morgan Library; **p. 906,** Carnegie Library, Pittsburgh; **p. 907,** Courtesy of Sears, Roebuck and Co.; **p. 911,** Carnegie Library, Pittsburgh; **p. 914,** Chicago Historical Society; **p. 918,** Library of Congress; **p. 921,** Library of Congress; **p. 923,** Collection of The Archives of Labor and Urban Affairs, University Archives, Wayne State University; **p. 925,** Brown Brothers.

CHAPTER 21: p. 930, Library of Congress; **p. 934,** © Collection of the New-York Historical Society; **p. 935,** New York Transit Museum Archives, Brooklyn; **p. 938,** Museum of the City of New York; **p. 939,** The New York Public Library, Astor, Lenox and Tilden Foundations; **p. 941,** The New York Public Library, Astor, Lenox and Tilden Foundations; **p. 942,** Museum of the City of New York; **p. 944,** Library of Congress; **p. 947,** Courtesy Denver Public Library, Western History Collection; **p. 949,** Library of Congress; **p. 950,** Texas A&M University Archives; **p. 951,** Mount Holyoke College Library; **p. 956,** Library of Congress; **p. 959,** Winslow Homer, American, 1869–1910, *Croquet Scene,* oil on canvas, 15 7/8 x 26 1/16 in, Friends of American Art Collection, 1942.35, photograph © 1998, The Art Institute of Chicago, All rights reserved; **p. 960,** Brown Brothers; **p. 961,** Old York Library; **p. 964,** Library of Congress; **p. 966,** Negative No. 326662, Courtesy Department of Library Services, American Museum of Natural History; **p. 967,** The Warder Collection; **p. 968** Courtesy of the John Carter Brown Library at Brown University; **p. 970,** *(left)* National Library of Medicine, and *(right)* The Warder Collection; **p. 973,** Mansell/TIME Inc.; **p. 974,** *(left)* Library of Congress, and *(right)* The Warder Collection; **p. 978,** The Salvation Army; **p. 981,** University of Illinois at Chicago, University Library, Jane Addams Memorial Collection; **p. 983,** Nebraska State Historical Society.

CHAPTER 22: p. 991, Library of Congress; **p. 995,** Rutherford B. Hayes Presidential Center; **p. 999,** The Warder Collection; **p. 1000,** The Warder Collection; **p. 1002,** The Warder Collection; **p. 1004,** United Press International Photo; **p. 1009,** The Warder Collection; **p. 1014,** Corbis-Bettman; **p. 1016,** Photo by John Wesley Rand, from the Collection of the Minnesota Historical Society; **p. 1018,** Wooten Studios; **p. 1020,** Kansas State Historical Society, Topeka, Kansas; **p. 1022,** University of North Carolina, Chapel Hill; **p. 1023,** Nebraska State Historical Society; **p. 1025,** Library of Congress; **p. 1027,** Kansas State Historical Society, Topeka, Kansas.

CHAPTER 23: p. 1038, Library of Congress; **p. 1040,** Hawaii State Archives; **p. 1043,** Brown Brothers; **p. 1045,** National Archives; **p. 1046,** Library of Congress; **p. 1050,** National Archives; **p. 1052,** Library of Congress; **p. 1055,** National Archives; **p. 1060,** National Archives; **p. 1062,** *The New York Times;* **p. 1066,** Library of Congress/Corbis-Bettman; **p. 1067,** Library of Congress.

CHAPTER 24: p. 1075, AP/Wide World Photos; **p. 1077,** Valdis Kupris; **p. 1079,** Library of Congress; **p. 1081** Library of Congress; **p. 1082,** Underwood & Underwood/Corbis-Bettman; **p. 1083,** Kansas State Historical Society, Topeka, Kansas; **p. 1085,** Library of Congress; **p. 1088,** *(top)* © Collection of the New-York Historical Society, and *(bottom)* Library of Congress; **p. 1090,** Schlesinger Library, Radcliffe College; **p. 1092,** The Warder Collection; **p. 1094,** Library of Congress; **p. 1099,** Library of Congress; **p. 1102,** Library of Congress; **p. 1107,** Library of Congress; **p. 1108,** The Warder Collection; **p. 1109,** Historical Picture Service; **p. 1112,** Library of Congress.

CHAPTER 25: p. 1119, Library of Congress; **p. 1121,** Corbis-Bettman; **p. 1124,** The Warder Collection; **p. 1127,** *The New York Times;* **p. 1129,** Princeton University Libraries; **p. 1131,** UPI/Corbis-Bettman; **p. 1135,** National Archives; **p. 1137,** National Archives; **p. 1139,** National Archives; **p. 1143,** National Archives; **p. 1145,** National Archives; **p. 1147,** National Archives; **p. 1148,** The Warder Collection; **p. 1149,** National Archives; **p. 1154,** Ding Darling Foundation; **p. 1155,** Library of Congress; **p. 1157,** Corbis-Bettman; **p. 1159,** Chicago Historical Society.

CHAPTER 26: p. 1164, Shahn, Ben, *Bartolomeo Vanzetti and Nicola Sacco*, From the Sacco-Vanzetti series of twenty-three paintings, Tempera on paper over composition board, 10.5 x 14.5", Collection, The Museum of Modern Art, New York, Gift of Abby Aldrich Rockefeller; p. 1167, UPI/ Corbis-Bettman; p. 1169, Corbis-Bettman; p. 1171 Ben Shahn, *Speakeasy Scene, Interior*, Mural Project for Central Park Casino, © Museum of the City of New York, L1226.3G; p. 1172, Chicago Historical Society; p. 1174, Ramsey Archive; p. 1175, Henry Rockwell; p. 1177, Photographs and Prints Division, Schomburg Center for Research in Black Culture, The New York Public Library, Astor, Lenox and Tilden Foundations; p. 1178, Library of Congress; p. 1179, Brown Brothers; p. 1182, University of Chicago Press; p. 1183, AP/Wide World Photos; p. 1186, The Warder Collection; p. 1189, Pablo Picasso, *Portrait of Gertrude Stein*, All rights reserved, The Metropolitan Museum of Art/© 1999 Estate of Pablo Picasso/Artists Rights Society (ARS), New York; p. 1190, Brown Brothers; p. 1193, Brown Brothers.

CHAPTER 27: p. 1199, Brown Brothers; p. 1202, Library of Congress; p. 1205, Library of Congress; p. 1208, Brown Brothers; p. 1209, The National Broadcasting Company; p. 1210, (*top*) National Archives, and (*bottom*) Library of Congress; p. 1211, From the Collections of the Henry Ford Museum & Greenfield Village; p. 1216, The Warder Collection; p. 1219, Herbert Hoover Presidential Library; p. 1220, Historical Association of Southern Florida; p. 1222, AP/Wide World Photos; p. 1223, Ohio Historical Society; p. 1226, Museum of the City of New York; p. 1229, *New York Daily News* Photo.

CHAPTER 28: p. 1235, AP/Wide World Photos; p. 1237, UPI/Corbis-Bettman; p. 1239, National Archives; p. 1242, UPI/Corbis-Bettman; p. 1245, National Archives; p. 1247, Library of Congress; p. 1251, Courtesy, Tennessee Valley Authority; p. 1252, Corbis-Bettman; p. 1255, Library of Congress; p. 1257, Moses Soyer, *Artists on WPA*, National Museum of American Art, Washington, DC/Art Resource, NY; p. 1260, Library of Congress; p. 1266, UPI/Corbis-Bettman; p. 1269, National Archives; p. 1273, Library of Congress; p. 1279, AP/Wide World Photos; p. 1282, Corbis-Bettman; p. 1283, Corbis-Bettman.

CHAPTER 29: p. 1290, AP/Wide World Photos; p. 1293, The Warder Collection; p. 1295, The Granger Collection, New York; p. 1297, National Archives; p. 1299, The Warder Collection; p. 1301, Library of Congress; p. 1303, Imperial War Museum, London; p. 1306, National Archives; p. 1307, British Information Services; p. 1310, UPI/Corbis-Bettman; p. 1316, National Archives; p. 1317, National Archives.

CHAPTER 30: p. 1322, The Warder Collection; p. 1325, The Granger Collection, New York; p. 1330, Library of Congress; p. 1331, Culver Pictures; p. 1332, AP/Wide World Photos; p. 1335, Library of Congress; p. 1340, National Archives; p. 1341, AP/Wide World Photos; p. 1344, Bill Mauldin and Wil-Jo Associates, Inc.; p. 1347, Army Photographic Agency; p. 1348, UPI/Corbis-Bettman; p. 1350, National Archives; p. 1353, The Warder Collection; p. 1357, National Archives; p. 1359, National Archives; p. 1361, National Archives; p. 1364, Globe Photos; p. 1365, National Archives; p. 1366, National Archives; p. 1370, Yuichiro Sasaki, UN Photo 149443.

CHAPTER 31: p. 1382, University of Louisville, Photographic Archives; p. 1386, The New York Public Library, Astor, Lenox and Tilden Foundations; p. 1387, The George Meany Memorial Archives; p. 1389, Library of Congress; p. 1393, © Herman Landshoff; p. 1395, AP/Wide World Photos; p. 1398, U.S. Information Agency; p. 1399, Courtesy *Hartford Courant*; p 1401, Life Picture Service; p. 1403, C. K. Berryman,

INDEX

Page numbers in *italics* refer to illustrations.

AAA, *see* Agricultural Adjustment Act
Abenakis, 78, 79
abolition movement, 578–79, 624, 661–69
  African Americans in, 665–67
  African colonization proposed in, 661–62,
    664
  free press and, 668
  Fugitive Slave Act and, 687–89, 696
  legacy of, 993
  Polk on, 609
  radicalization of, 662–64
  reactions to, 667–68
  split in, 664–65
  women in, 572, 664–65
abortion issue, 1563, 1609, 1615, 1655, 1660
Abrams v. United States, 1142
abstract expressionism, 1453
Acadia, 178, 179, 183, 186, 191
  see also Nova Scotia
Acheson, Dean, 1415, 1417
Acomas, 587
acquired immune deficiency syndrome
    (AIDS), 1627–28, *1628*
Act for the Impartial Administration of Justice
    (1774), 223
Act of Settlement (1701), 52
Act of Union (1707), 52
ADA (Americans for Democratic Action),
    1403
Adams, Abigail, 282–83, 286
  on Shays's Rebellion, 307–8
Adams, Charles Francis, 677
Adams, Henry, 830
Adams, John, 226, 272, 289, 311, *360*, 373,
    389, 1032
  in Boston Massacre case, 218
  committee work of, 292
  and Declaration of Independence, 234–35
  domestic discontent and, 364–66
  in election of 1789, 330
  in election of 1792, 345
  in election of 1796, 359
  in election of 1800, 366, 367, *367*
  foreign policy under, 360–63
  French conflict and, 361, 362
  on Hamilton's death, 385
  lame-duck judicial appointments of, 368,
    374–75
  on peace commission, 270, *270,* 331
  political philosophy of, 360
  Revolution and, 270, 272, 283
  as vice-president, 331
  on women's rights, 283
Adams, John Quincy, 291, 383, 403, 416,
    419–20, *434,* 474, 608
  abolitionism and, 668
  as congressman, 459
  on Eaton Affair, 452
  in election of 1824, 431–34, *432,* 437
  in election of 1828, 436–40, *439,* 524
  Indian lands and, 464
  on Mexican War, 612
  Monroe Doctrine and, 429, 430
  named secretary of state, 415
  Oregon Country issue and, 428–29
  presidency of, 434–36
  Transcontinental Treaty and, 420, 428
  on Tyler, 583
Adams, Samuel, *215,* 216, 222, 229, 288
  and Boston Tea Party, 222
  in Committee of Correspondence, 220
  in ratification debate, 321, 323
  as revolutionary agitator, 214–16, 218, 222
  warned by Paul Revere, 229
Adams, Sherman, 1487
Adamson Act (1916), 1114
Adarand Constructors v. Peña, 1682
Addams, Jane, 980–81, *981,* 1056, 1130, 1237
Adena-Hopewell culture, 10
Adenauer, Konrad, 1397
Administrative Reorganization Act (1939),
    1277

Admiralty courts, vice-admiralty courts, 172, 206, 208, 213, 218
Admiralty Islands, 1356
Adventures of Huckleberry Finn, The (Twain), 973
Adventures of Tom Sawyer, The (Twain), 972–73
advertising, 1429–30
AFDC (Aid for Dependent Children), 1613
affirmative action, 1562, 1615, 1650, 1656, 1659, 1673–74, 1681–83
Affluent Society, The (Galbraith), 1447
Afghanistan, 1600, 1618, 1629, 1635
AFL (American Federation of Labor), 917–19, 924, 1158, 1206, 1271
AFL-CIO (American Federation of Labor-Congress of Industrial Organizations), 1428, 1587, 1615, 1620
Africa:
    European exploration of, 17, 25
    imperialism in, 1036
    slaves in return to, 661–62, 664
African Americans, 145, 1652, 1654
    in abolition movement, 665–67
    African roots of, 121–23, 654
    affirmative action and, 1615, 1656, 1681–83
    in agriculture, 813–14, 1262, 1437–38
    in antebellum southern society, 646–48
    in baseball, 964–65
    Black Code restrictions on, 802, 805
    black power and, 1532–35, 1554
    in Boston Massacre, 217–18
    under Bourbon rule, 849–50
    and B. T. Washington's vs. Du Bois's views, 854–56
    in Carter administration, 1596
    citizenship of, 316, 805
    Civil War attacks on, 740–41
    as Civil War soldiers, 756–60, 758, 813, 815
    constitutional rights, lack of, 313–15, 333
    as cowboys, 873, 875
    crime and, 1652
    in Democratic party, 850, 1265–66, 1276
    desegregation and, 1401, 1492–97, 1509–15
    disenfranchisement of, in South, 850–52, 992, 1114, 1264
    in early twentieth century, 1181–85
    in early U.S., 328–29
    education of, 814, 818, 848, 856, 1426
    in election of 1948, 1405, 1406
    in election of 1960, 1505
    in election of 1976, 1595
    in election of 1984, 1620
    in election of 1988, 1632
    as "Exodusters," 859–60
    first, 60
    folklore of, 655
    free blacks, 646–47
    gerrymandered districts and, 1682
    Great Migration of, 1138, 1181, 1437–38
    immigration and, 1653
    as indentured servants, 119–20
    Irish Americans' animosity toward, 523
    land policy and, 793, 794, 800–801, 816
    literature and, 972, 1452–53
    lynchings of, 854, 1184, 1400
    marriage of, 125, 656, 802, 813
    in military, 232, 279, 756–60, 758, 813, 815, 860–61, 1331–32, 1401
    minstrel shows and, 517, 519
    mulattoes, 646
    music of, 124, 655, 656, 1433
    Negro nationalism and, 1182–84, 1183
    in New Deal programs, 1242, 1262
    population of, 121, 328–29
    in post–Civil War South, 849–50
    post–World War II economy and, 1428–29
    proslavery arguments, 668–69
    Reagan and, 1615
    in Reconstruction South, 793–96, 800–801, 802, 812–17, 816
    in Reconstruction politics, 812, 813, 814–17, 816
    religion of, 124, 629, 654–55, 656, 813
    in religious revivals, 542
    in Republican party, 994, 1265–66
    as Revolutionary soldiers, 232, 279
    segregation and, 852–54, 1262, 1331–33, 1492–97, 1509–15
    separatist, 1533, 1534–35
    single mothers and, 1651
    and slave culture, 123–26
    slaves owned by, 646, 647–48
    and slave trade, 648–51
    Underground Railroad and, 667, 689
    violence against, 854, 860, 1184, 1400
    in West, 858, 859–60
    in World War I, 1138–39
    in World War II, 1329, 1331–33
    see also civil rights and liberties; civil rights movement; racial riots; segregation, desegregation; slavery; slaves; slave trade; voting rights
Agee, James, 1280
Age of Reason, The (Paine), 537
Agnew, Spiro, 1544, 1545, 1570
Agricultural Adjustment Act (AAA) (1933), 1239, 1243–44, 1262, 1263, 1269
Agricultural Adjustment Act, Second (1938), 1246, 1275
Agricultural Marketing Act (1929), 1218
agriculture, farmers, 116, 299, 301, 1036, 1586, 1612
    in Africa, 122
    African Americans and, 813–14, 1262, 1437–38
    Alliance movement and, 1017–19, 1020–23
    biological exchange in, 22–23

"bonanza" farms in, 1012
cattle ranchers in conflict with, 876–78
Civil War and, 732–33
in colonial era, 55, 115–17, 131–32, 135, 143
cooperatives and, 1019
crop lien system in, 846
currency and, 1010, 1015–16, 1024
diversity of interests in, 1012–13
in early nineteenth century, 409, 486–91
in early U.S., 305, 328
economic conditions and, 1013–14
education and, 844
electrification and, 1250
Granger movement and, 1016–17
in Great Depression, 1228, 1234
growth of (early 1800s), 486–91, 494
of Indians, 7, 12, 78, 79, 86, 108, 587
in Kentucky, 356
land policy and, 878–81
in late nineteenth century, 1012–23
Mexican farm workers in, 1333
in mid-twentieth century, 1467
in New Deal, 1243–46, 1262, 1275–76
in New England, 131–32
in New West, 878–82
in 1920s, 1213–15, 1217, 1218–19
plantations and, 636–39, 637, 651–53
in pre-Columbian cultures, 7, 12
railroads and, 844, 1013
rural credit and, 1112–13
sharecropping and, 844–45, 845
size of holdings in, 1013
in South, 115–17, 629–32, 636–39, 640, 651–53, 658, 732–33, 844–46
steamboats' influence on, 494
tariffs and, 1010, 1011, 1014, 1214–15
technology of, 487, 490–91, 879–80, 896, 1438
trust laws and, 1110
UFW and, 1565–67
in Virginia colony, 55
in West, 485, 488–91, 633
Agriculture Department, U.S., 1091
Aguinaldo, Emilio, 1048, 1055, 1055
AIDS (acquired immune deficiency syndrome), 1627–28, 1628
Aid to Families with Dependent Children (AFDC), 1613, 1676
AIM (American Indian Movement), 1568, 1568
Air Commerce Act (1926), 1210
air conditioning, 1435
airplanes, 1209–11
Aix-la-Chapelle, Treaty of (1748), 185, 188
Alabama, 86, 181, 380, 488, 1511
agriculture in, 448, 486, 632, 845
cotton in, 486
Indian conflicts in, 399
migration to, 659

progressivism in, 1080
secession of, 718
segregation in, 1494, 1511, 1514
slave trade in, 651
Union Loyalists in, 770, 818
voting rights in, 852
War of 1812 in, 398
Yazoo Fraud and, 384
Alabama, University of, desegregation of, 1514
Alabama Platform, 705
Alamance, Battle of (1771), 219
Alamo, 603–4
Alaska:
    gold rush in, 1028
    protected land in, 1597
    purchase of, 1038, 1038
    Russian claim to, 428, 1038
    statehood for, 1099, 1487
Albania, Albanians, 1300, 1394, 1672
Albany Congress (1754), 190–91
Albee, Edward, 1451
Albright, Madeleine, 1679
Alcatraz Island, Indian occupation of (1969), 1568
alcohol abuse:
    in colonial era, 151–52
    in Old Southwest, 660
    Puritans on, 136
    temperance and, 567–69, 568
Alcott, Bronson, 549
Alden, John, 66
Aldrich, Nelson W., 1011, 1095
Alexander I, czar of Russia, 402, 437
Alexander v. Holmes County Board of Education, 1579
Algeciras, Act of (1906), 1069
Algeria, 361, 362, 363
    in World War II, 1338
Algiers, 377, 405, 1339
Algonquians, 78, 81, 91, 179
Alien Act (1798), 364, 365, 366
Alien Enemy Act (1798), 364
Allen, Ethan, 219, 230
Allen, Gracie, 1281
Allende, Salvador, 1593
Alliance for Progress, 1508
Allied Powers (Triple Entente), 1122–23, 1124, 1147
Alliance movement, 1017–19, 1020–23
Altamont, Calif., music festival in (1969), 1559
AMA (American Medical Association), 1528
Amador, Manuel, 1065
Amalgamated Association of Iron and Steel Workers, 919
Amalgamated Clothing Workers, 919, 1271
America First Committee, 1308
American and Foreign Anti-Slavery Society, 665
American Anti-Imperialist League, 1055–56

American Anti-Slavery Society, 663, 665, 666, 668
American Association for the Advancement of Science, 504, 953
American Birth Control League, *1178*
American Chemical Society, 953
American Civil Liberties Union, 1169
American Colonization Society, 661, 662
American Committee for the Outlawry of War, 1292
American Crisis, The (Paine), 247–48
American Economics Association, 970
American Farm Bureau Federation, 1214
American Federation of Labor (AFL), 917–19, 924, 1158, 1206, 1271
American Federation of Labor-Congress of Industrial Organizations (AFL-CIO), 1428, 1587, 1615, 1620
American Historical Association, 883
American Indian Movement (AIM), 1568, *1568*
American Indians, *see* Indians, American
American Individualism (Hoover), 1212
American Journal of Sociology, 970
American Liberty League, 1252
American Medical Association (AMA), 1528
American Mercury, 1173–74
American Missionary Association, 795
American (Know-Nothing) party, 527–28, *528*, 697, 701
American Philosophical Society, 155
American Political Ideas (Fiske), 1037
American Protective Association (APA), 946, 994
American Railway Union, 921, 923
American Renaissance (Mathiessen), 552
American Revolution, 228–72
   African-American soldiers in, 232, 279
   American nationalism and, 197, 285–89
   American society in, 249–53
   backcountry in, 250, 252, 259, 266
   Boston Tea Party and, 221–23
   British strategies in, 254–55, 258–59, 263
   British surrender in, 269
   causes of, 237–39
   Committees of Correspondence and, 220
   coup attempt in, 294
   events leading to, 205–27
   finance and supply of, 252–53, 259, 293–94
   first battles of, 228–30
   France and, 233, 242, 253, 257–58, 260, 268, 269, 270, 271
   frontier in, 260–63
   Hessians in, 233, 249, 250
   independence issue in, 234–39, 246, 275, 286
   Indians in, 233, 256–57, 260, 261–63, *261*, 298
   Loyalists in, 228, 232–33, 250–51, 252, 255, 256, 259, 260, 261, *261*, 262, 263, 265, 266, 279
   mercenaries in, 233
   militias in, 228, 230, 249–50, 251, 252, 257, 263, 266
   naval warfare in, 267–68
   Patriot forces in, 228–33, 251–52, 253, 256–57, 259–60
   peace efforts in, 232, 258–59, 269–72, *270*
   Peace of Paris and, 271–72
   political revolution and, 272–76
   slavery and, 278–81
   slaves in, 232, 251, 347, 348
   social revolution and, 276–84
   South in, 263–69
   Spain and, 233, 257, 258, 270, 271
   spreading conflict in, 230–33
   supporters, 242, 350
   women in, 281–83
"American Scholar, The" (Emerson), 550
Americans for Democratic Action (ADA), 1403
American Society for the Promotion of Temperance, 567
American Steel and Wire Company, 876
American System, *432*, 432, 433, 437, 474, 479, 582, 609, 818
American Telephone and Telegraph, 896
American Temperance Union, 567
American Tobacco Company, 843, 1087
American Unitarian Association, 538
American Woman Suffrage Association, 982
Amherst, Jeffrey, 192–93, *192*
Amish, 37
Amos 'n Andy, 1281
Anabaptists, 37
"Anaconda" strategy, 734, 736–37
Anacostia Flats, shantytown at, 1228–29, *1229*
anarchism, 915–17
Anasazis, 12–13
Anderson, John, 1610
Anderson, Robert, 719–20, 725–26
Anderson, Sherwood, 1182, 1213
Andersonville, Ga., Confederate prison at, 798
Andover Seminary, 539
André, John, 267
Andrews, Samuel, 898
Andros, Sir Edmund, 170, 171
Angel Island, 948
Anglican Church (Church of England), 39–40, 50, 51, 106, *128*, 160
   Andros's support of, 170
   education and, 161
   Puritan views of, 70, 73, 136
   in South, 106, 127–29
   state support of, 283
   see also Episcopal church
animals, domesticated, 13, 22, 26, 632
Annapolis Convention (1786), 309
Anne, queen of England, 52, 171, 173
Anschluss, 1299

Anthony, Susan B., 573, 574, 982
Anti-Comintern Pact (1937), 1299
anti-communism:
  Eisenhower and, 1470–71
  McCarthyism and, 1416–19, 1439,
    1468–70, 1503
  Nixon and, 1502
  Reagan and, 1607, 1616
  Truman and, 1408–9, 1416, 1419
  after World War II, 1385
  see also cold war
Antietam (Sharpsburg), Battle of (1862),
  751–52, 756
Antifederalists:
  Bill of Rights and, 321, 332
  in ratification debate, 319, 321
Anti-Masonic party, 468–69, 474, 475, 479
Anti-Saloon League, 994, 1084
anti-Semitism, 945
antislavery movement, *see* abolition movement
antitrust laws, 843
  and American Tobacco Company, 843, 1087
  and Bureau of Corporations, 1087, 1103,
    1109
  Clayton Antitrust Act, 1109–10
  and Federal Trade Commission, 1109, 1110
  passage of, 1010, 1080
  and rebates, 1087
  and regulation, 1080, 1085
  and Roosevelt, Theodore, 1085–86
  Sherman Anti-Trust Act, 843, 901, 922,
    1010, 1080, 1085, 1087
  and Standard Oil, 901, 1087
  and Taft, 1097–98
  and Wilson, 1109–10
APA (American Protective Association), 946,
  994
Apaches, 13, 36, 587, 590, 870
Apalachees, 86, 87
apartheid, 1636
Apodaca, Jerry, 1567
Appalachian Forest Reserve Act (1911), 1098
Appalachian mountain people, 642
Appalachian Regional Development Act
  (1966), 1529
Appeal to the Christian Women of the South
  (Grimké), 665
Appomattox, Va., surrender at, 783–84
apprentices, 529
Arab countries, 1481–82, 1484, 1583, 1586,
  1669
  Camp David accords opposed by, 1599
Arabic, sinking of, 1128
Arab-Israeli conflicts, 1399, 1483–84, 1586,
  1618–19, 1669–70
Arab League, 1482
Arafat, Yasir, 1670
Arapahoes, 587, 866, 867, 956
Arawaks, 19
Arbella, 70

Arbenz Guzman, Jacobo, 1473
archeology, 6
architecture, 953
  Georgian ("colonial"), 126
  Jefferson and, 343
  in New England, 130–31
  in pre-Columbian cultures, 12
  southern, 638
  of Virginia Capitol, *175*
Area Redevelopment Act (1961), 1508
Arena, 1075
ARENA party, 1624
Argentina, 1120
Aristide, Jean-Bertrand, 1672
Arizona, 587, 741
  copper in, 864–65
  Gadsden Purchase and, 693
  in Spanish Empire, 590
  statehood for, 866, 1099
  voting rights in, 983
  in World War II, 1329
Arkansas, 596, 770
  Civil War fighting in, 729
  cotton in, 486
  dust bowl in, 1261
  labor movement in, 1328
  military government of, 796
  Reconstruction in, 812
  secession of, 726
  segregation in, 1497
Arkansas Peace Society, 730
Arkansas Territory, 422
Arkwright, Richard, 503
Armory Show (1913), 1188
arms control negotiations, 1586, 1594, 1600,
  1621, 1629, 1639
Armstrong, Louis, 1174
Armstrong, Neil, 1578
Army, U.S., 363, 410
  in Constitution, 313
  after War of 1812, 406
  see also military, U.S.; *specific wars*
Army Air Force, U.S., 1345
Army Appropriation Act (1916), 1137
Army-McCarthy hearings (1954), 1468–69,
  1469
Army of the Commonweal of Christ, 1024
Army Yellow Fever Commission, 1057
Arnold, Benedict, 232, 256, 267, *267*
Arrowrock Dam, 879
Arthur, Chester A., 849, 947, 997, 998–99,
  999, 1000
Articles of Confederation (1781), 242,
  275–76, 291, 292–309
  amendment process for, 308–9, 319
  calls for revision of, 308–9
  debt under, 292–93, 294
  finance under, 292–94
  unanimity required under, 319
  see also Confederation Congress

arts:
  in early U.S., 285–86
  in Great Depression, 1280–81
  in mid-twentieth century, 1450–57
  in New Deal, 1257, *1257*
  in nineteenth century, 516–17
  in pre-Columbian cultures, 10–11
  romanticism in, 547
  see also architecture; literature; movies;
    painting; poetry
Asbury, Francis, 284, 541
Ashburton, Lord, 585
Ashley-Cooper, Lord, 85
Asia:
  exploration and, 18, 24
  imperialism in, 1036, 1037–38
  trade with, 17, 1037
  see also specific countries
Asian Americans, 1530, 1649, 1652, 1653,
    1654–55, *1654*
assembly, freedom of, 333
Astor, John Jacob, 532, 1002
Aswan Dam, 1483
asylums, 570–71
Atchison, Topeka and Santa Fe Railroad, 892
Atlanta, Ga., capture of, 769, 781, 782, 783
Atlanta Confederacy, 713
Atlanta Constitution, 840
Atlantic, Battle of the, 1339–41
Atlantic Charter (1941), 1312, 1337, 1363,
    1388
Atlantic Monthly, 759, 973
atomic bombs, *see* nuclear weapons
Atomic Energy Commission, 1384, 1385,
    1392
Attucks, Crispus, 217–18
Auburn Penitentiary, 569–70
Auschwitz death camp, 1365–66
Austin, Stephen F., 602–3
Australia:
  defense treaties with, 1420
  Forty-niners from, 679
  in SEATO, 1477
  in World War II, 1323
Austria, 31
  in colonial wars, *185,* 191–92
  French Revolution and, 345
  German annexation of, 1299
  in Napoleonic Wars, 387
  in Quintuple Alliance, 429
  U.S. peace with, 1155
  after World War II, 1484
Austria-Hungary:
  Versailles treaty and, 1151
  in World War I, 1122, 1132, 1142, 1147,
    1155
automobiles, 1211–12, 1582
  in Great Depression, 1271–72
  mass production and, 1211–12

in 1950s, 1432, 1436–37
  suburban revolution and, 1436–37
  see also highways and roads
Averell, James, 877
Aztecs, 7, 9, *24,* 27, 28, 31

"baby-boom" generation, 1382, 1426, *1427,*
    1650
backcountry, 144, 146–47, 218–20
  in American Revolution, 250, 252, 259, 266
  and conflict with Indians, 202–5, 219,
    349–50, 355, 393–99
  education in, 156
  Hamilton opposed in, 342
  and lack of organized government, 218–20
  popular culture in, 954
  ratification debate and, 323
  religion in, 157
  underrepresentation of, 278
  Whiskey Rebellion in, 350–51
  see also frontier
Bacon, Nathaniel, 62
Bacon's Rebellion, 62–64
Baer, George F., 1086
Baez, Joan, 1559
Baffin Island (Helluland), 14
Baghdad Pact, 1482
Bagot, Charles, 416
Bailey, James A., 954
Baker, Howard, 1588
Baker, James, 1640
Baker, Newton D., 1136–37
Bakke v. Board of Regents of California, 1580
Balboa, Vasco Núñez de, 25, 32
Baldwin, Hanson, 1370
Baldwin, James, 1452
Baldwin, J. L., 759
Balfour, Arthur, *1290*
Ball, Lucille, *1428*
Ballard, Martha, 114–15
Ballinger, Richard A., 1096–97, 1098
Baltimore, Cecilius Calvert, second Lord, 64,
    65, 83, 117
Baltimore, fourth Lord, 171
Baltimore, Md., 512, 514
  War of 1812 in, 400–401
Baltimore, Sir George Calvert, first Lord, 64
Baltimore and Ohio (B&O) Railroad, 497
Baltimore Republican, 480
Bandung Conference (1955), 1475, 1480
Bankhead Cotton Control Act (1934), 1244
Bankhead-Jones Farm Tenant Act (1937),
    1275
Banking Act (1935), 1254
banking industry:
  1837 runs on, 473
  in Great Depression, 1236, 1238–41
  investment bankers in, 905
  regulation of, 985, 1240, 1625, 1658

saving and loan crisis and, 1625, 1633
state-chartered banks and, 421
banking system, *see* Federal Reserve System
Bank of North America, 293
Bank of the United States (national bank), 337–40, *338*, 421, 432, 583
constitutionality of, 338–39, 411, 466
expiration of first charter of, 395
Hamilton's recommendation for, 336, 337–40
Jackson and, 449, 465–74, *468*, 474, 482
Jefferson's acceptance of, 376
McCulloch v. Madison and, 426–27
and Panic of 1819, 421
removal of government deposits from, 470–72
second charter of, 410–12, 413
and speculative binge (1834), 471–72
Tyler on, 582
Banks, Dennis, 1568
Bao Dai, emperor of Vietnam, 1410, 1476, 1479
Baptists, 38, 129, 139, 144, 160, 161, 813
in revivals, 541, 542
in split over slavery, 669, 696–97
in Whig party, 474
Bara, Theda, 1176
Barbados, 70, 85, 86, 116
Barbary pirates, 377, 405
barbed wire, 876, 896
barley, 23, 143
"Barnburners," 677, 690
Barnett, Ross, 1511
Barnum, Phineas T., 954
Barras, comte de, 268
Barton, Clara, 760, 761–62, *761*
Bartram, John, 154
Baruch, Bernard, 1138, 1395
baseball, 963–65, *964*, 1401–2
basketball, 963
Bataan Peninsula, 1322
Bates, Edward, 725
BATF (Bureau of Alcohol, Tobacco, and Firearms), 1667, 1668
Batista, Fulgencio, 1491
Battle of Bunker Hill, The (Trumbull), 285
Battle-Pieces (Melville), 557
Bayard, James, 402–3
Bay of Pigs invasion (1961), 1515
Bean, Roy, 878
beans, 7, 22, 78, 109
Beard, Charles A., 320, 1280
Beats, 1454–57
Beauregard, Pierre G. T., 725, 734
at Shiloh, 745
Beecher, Catharine, 571, 572, 665
Beecher, Henry Ward, 515, 978
Beecher, Lyman, 527, 538, 539, 542, 664
beef trust, 1087

Beer-Wine Revenue Act (1933), 1239
Beethoven, Ludwig van, 155
Begin, Menachem, 1598–99, *1599*
Beirut bombing (1983), 1619
Belgium, 1291
in NATO, 1398
in World War I, 1122, 1143, 1144
in World War II, 1306, 1351, 1359
Bell, Alexander Graham, 896
Bell, John, 715, 717, *717*
Bellamy, Edward, 977
Bell Laboratories, 1644
Bellow, Saul, 1452, 1454
Benedict, Ruth, 1187–88
Bennett, James Gordon, 559
Bennett, William J., 1634
Bennington, Battle of (1777), 257
Benton, Thomas Hart (painter), 1280
Benton, Thomas Hart (Senator), 399, 411, 459, 466, 490, 601, 613, 675, 706
and Compromise of 1850, 682, 686
Berger, Victor, 1141
Bering, Vitus, 428
Bering Sea, sealing in, 1041
Bering Strait and Beringia, 5
Berkeley, Busby, 1283
Berkeley, Lord John, 94
Berkeley, Sir William, 61, 62, 63, 83, 127–28
Berlin, Irving, 942
Berlin Airlift (1948–1949), 1396–98, *1398*
Berlin Conference (1889), 1039
Berlin crises, 1396–97, *1398*, 1489–90, 1515
Berlin Decree (1806), 388, 392
Berlin Wall, 1515, *1516*, 1635, *1636*
Bermuda, 56, 57, 81
Berry, Chuck, 1433
Beveridge, Albert J., 1036, 1056
BIA (Bureau of Indian Affairs), 1263, 1568–69
Bibb, Henry, 666
Bible, 541, 965
bicycles, 959–60, *960*
Biddle, Nicholas, 421, 466, 467–68, 470, 471, *471*, 474
Bidlack Treaty (1848), 1063–64
Bienville, Jean Baptiste le Moyne, sieur de, 182
Bigelow, Jacob, 504
Bilbo, Theodore, 1228
Bill for the More General Diffusion of Knowledge (Virginia), 288
Bill of Rights, English (1689), 52, 171
Bill of Rights, U.S.:
debate on, 332–33
in ratification of Constitution, 321, 324
states subject to, 806
bills of attainder, 319
bills (declarations) of rights, state, 274, 275
Bingham, George Caleb, *355*, *469*, *591*
biological exchange, 21–24

Birch, William, *300*
John Birch Society, 1526
Birmingham, Ala.:
  church bombing in (1963), 1514
  civil rights demonstrations in (1963), 1512
  coal mining and, 843
Birney, James G., 668
Birth of a Nation, 1208
birthrates, in colonial period, 110–11
Bismarck Sea, Battle of the (1943), 1353
Blackboard Jungle, The, 1432
Black Boy (Wright), 1279
Black Codes, 802, 805
Blackfoot Indians, 587, 869
Black Hawk, Sauk and Fox chief, 462
Black Hawk, Sioux chief, 589
Black Hawk War, 462
Black Hills, 868
  mining in, 865
Black Legend, 30
Black Manhattan (Johnson), 1182
"Black Monday" (1987), 1625–26
Blackmun, Harry, 1580
Black Muslims, 1534
Black Panther party, 1533
black power, 1532–35, 1554
blacks, *see* African Americans
Blackwell, Elizabeth, 574
Blaine Amendment (1867), 808–9
Blaine, James G., 829, 992, 995, 996, 997,
  1000–1001, *1000*, 1002–3, 1007, 1008
Blair, James, 161
Bland-Allison Act (1878), 997, 1010, 1015–16
Blithedale Romance, The (Hawthorne), 578
Blitzkrieg, 1305–6, 1309, 1311, 1324
blockades, *see* embargoes and blockades
"Blue Back Speller" (Webster), 288
Board of Customs Commissioners, 213, 215,
  218
Board of Mediation, 1216
Board of Trade (Lords of Trade and
  Plantations), 168, 169, 172–73, 174, 190,
  204
  functions of, 172–73
Boas, Franz, 1187
Bohemian Americans, 146, 937, 943
Boleyn, Anne, 39
Bolshevik Revolution, 922, 1142, 1145–46,
  1158, 1159–60
"bonanza" farms, 1012
Bonnie Prince Charlie (Charles Edward
  Stuart), 146
Bonus Expeditionary Force, 1228–30, *1229*,
  1233
Book of Common Prayer, 40
Boone, Daniel, 204, 262, 354–55, 492, 601
Boone, Rebecca Bryan, 354
Boonesborough, Ky., 355
  Revolutionary fighting at, 262
Booth, John Wilkes, 798

bootlegging, during Prohibition, 1171–73
Borden, Gail, 506
Bork, Robert, 1590
"born-again" Christians, 1608–9, 1656
Bosnia, 1377, 1671
Boston, Mass.:
  antislavery demonstrations in, 696
  Boston Tea Party, 221–23
  class stratification in, 149
  in colonial period, 70, 140, 148, 149, 150,
    169
  customs officials in, 169, 209–10, 213,
    215–16, 222
  disciplined by Parliament, 1774, 223–24
  Great Awakening in, 161
  Irish Americans in, 522
  in nineteenth century, 512, *512*, 514
  police strike in (1919), 1158, 1198
  poverty in, 149
  redcoats quartered in, 216, 217–18
  school desegregation in, 1579–80
  shipyards in, 133
  siege of (1775–1776), 232, 254
  subways in, 934
  tax protests in, 209–10, 216, 221–23
  unitarianism in, 538
Boston Associates, 510–11
Boston English High School, 562
Boston Manufacturing Company, 507
Boston Marathon, *1561*
Boston Massacre, 217–18, *217*
Boston Pilot, 523
Boston Port Act (1774), 224, *224*
Boston Tea Party, 221–23, *222*
  reprisals for, 223–24
Boudinot, Elias, *464*
Boulder (Hoover) Dam, 879
Bourbon Redeemers, 846–50, *847, 851*,
  856–57
Bourke-White, Margaret, 1280
Bowie, Jim, 604
Boxer Rebellion (1900), 1059–60, *1060*
boxing, 515–16, *516*
boycotts, 226
  of grapes, 1566
bracero program, 1333, 1565
Braddock, Edward, 191
Bradford, William, 66, 67, 73, 79
Bradley, Joseph P., 832
Bradley, Omar, 1351, 1360, 1415
Brady, Mathew, 784
Brady Bill (1993), 1665–66
Bragg, Braxton, 746, 755
  background of, 620
  at Chattanooga, 775–76
Branch Davidians, 1667
Brandeis, Louis D., 1103, 1112, *1112*, 1253,
  1270
Brando, Marlon, 1457
Brandywine Creek, Battle of (1777), 255

Brant, Joseph (Thayendanegea), 261, *262*
Braun, Eva, 1364
Brazil, 26, 120, 1120
Breckinridge, John C., 714, 715, 717, *717*
Breed's Hill, Battle of (1775), 230–32
Brennan, William J., Jr., 1470
Brest-Litovsk, Treaty of (1918), 1145
Breyer, Stephen, 1682
Brezhnev, Leonid, 1586, 1594
Brezhnev Doctrine, 1635
Briand, Aristide, *1290, 1292*
Bridger, Jim, 597
Brief Relation of the Destruction of the Indies, A
    (las Casas), 30
brinksmanship, 1473–74
British Empire, 13, 26, 31, 41, 120
    colonization in, 36, 43–45
    French Empire compared with, 77–78, 102,
        165, 178, 182
    maps of, *194, 195*
    Reformation in, 38
    Spanish Empire compared with, 30, 53,
        77–78, 102, 165, 178, 182
    trade in, 33
    see also American Revolution; colonial
        period; Great Britain
British Guiana, 1042
British military:
    American criticism of, 200
    quartering of, 207
    as standing army, 208, 216
    see also American Revolution; War of 1812
British navy, 267, 388, 389, 429
British Rule (1756), 388
Britton, Nan, 1204
Brock, Isaac, 396
Brook Farm, 578
Brooklyn Bridge, 934, *934*
Brooklyn Dodgers, 1401, *1401*
Brooklyn Heights, Battle of (1776), 247
Brooks, Preston S., 700–701, *700*
Brotherhood of Sleeping Car Porters, 1332
Brown, Frederick, 698
Brown, H. Rap, 1533, 1554
Brown, John, 698–99, 701, 711–13, *711*, 715
    death of, 712–13
    Harper's Ferry raided by, 711–12
    Kansas violence led by, 698–99
Brown, Watson, 712
Brown, William Wells, 666
Brownson, Orestes, 549
Brown University (College of Rhode Island),
    161, 565
Brown v. Board of Education of Topeka, Kansas,
    1493–94
Bruce, Blanche K., *816*, 817
Bruce, Lenny, 1457
Bry, Theodor de, 78, 87
Bryan, William Jennings, 1054
    as fundamentalist, 1168

in presidential elections, 838, 1025–27,
    1025, 1027, 1028, 1062, 1093
at Scopes trial, 1169–70
as secretary of state, 1105, 1118, 1122,
    1125, 1127, 1128, *1129*
as silverite, 1025–26
Buchanan, Franklin, 730
Buchanan, James, 582, 610, *706*, 711
    and *Dred Scott* decision, 705
    in election of 1856, 702
    and election of 1860, 714
    in Kansas crisis, 706–7
    after Lincoln's election, 719–20, 725
    and Panic of 1857, 707–8
    and secession, 719
    and support of Lecompton constitution,
        706–7
Buchanan, Patrick, 1628, 1660
Buchanan v. Worley, 1184
Buckley, William F., Jr., 1526
Budget and Accounting Act (1921), 1200
Buell, Don Carlos, 743, 745
Buena Vista, Battle of (1847), 617, 676
buffalo, 586–87, 588
    decimation of, 871
Buffalo Lancing in the Snow Drifts (Catlin),
    586
Buffalo soldiers, 860–61
Buford, deportation of radical aliens on (1919),
    1160
Bulgaria, 1147, 1394
    fall of communism in, 1635
    Soviet domination of, 1392
    in World War II, 1311, 1392
Bulge, Battle of the (1944), 1359
"Bull Moose" (Progressive) party, 1099–1100,
    1102, 1103, 1105, 1115, 1131
Bull Run (Manassas), first Battle of (1861),
    734–36
Bull Run (Manassas), second Battle of (1861),
    750–51
Bunau-Varilla, Philippe, 1065
Bundy, McGeorge, 1507
Bunker Hill, Battle of (1775), 230–32, *231*
Bunting v. Oregon, 1082
Buntline, Ned, 955
Bureau of Alcohol, Tobacco, and Firearms
    (BATF), 1667, 1668
Bureau of Aviation, 1213
Bureau of Corporations, 1087, 1103, 1109
Bureau of Foreign and Domestic Commerce,
    1212
Bureau of Immigration, 940
Bureau of Indian Affairs (BIA), 1263, 1568–69
Bureau of Internal Revenue, 764, 1461
Bureau of Labor Statistics, 916
Bureau of Mines, 1099
Bureau of the Budget, 1200
Burger, Warren, 1580
Burgoyne, John, 230, 254, 255, *255*, 257

Burke, Edmund, 173, 213, 223
  on American Revolution, 227
Burke Act (1906), 872
Burlingame Treaty (1868), 947, 999
Burma (Myanmar), 1313, 1322, 1363, 1475
"Burned-Over District," 542–44
Burns, Anthony, 696
Burns, George, 1281
Burnside, Ambrose E., 752, 771, 774, 776
Burr, Aaron, 344, 383, 385–87, 385, 436
  in election of 1796, 359
  in election of 1800, 366, 367, 367
  Hamilton's duel with, 383, 385, 644
Burr Conspiracy, 385–87
Burroughs, William, 1454, 1455–56
Bush, George, 1633–43, 1669
  affirmative action and, 1681
  cultural conservatives and, 1655
  deficits and, 1633–34, 1658
  domestic initiatives of, 1633–34
  economy and, 1657–59, 1660
  in election of 1988, 1630–33, 1631, 1632
  in election of 1992, 1660–61, 1662
  and fall of communism, 1634, 1637, 1639
  foreign policy of, 1657
  Hoover compared with, 1658
  nuclear weapons and, 1639
  Panama invasion of, 1639
  Persian Gulf War and, 1640–43, 1657
  Somalia and, 1670–71
  tax policy of, 1631, 1633–34, 1660
  Thomas appointed by, 1659
Bush, Vannevar, 1326
business:
  entrepreneurs, 898–905
  and Great Depression, 1219–24
  and growth in 1990s, 1680–81
  mail order, 906–8
  regulation of, 1080, 1085
  and technological innovations, 504–6,
    507–10, 895–97
  see also antitrust laws; corporations,
    business; labor movement
Business Week, 1427
busing, in school desegregation, 1579, 1659
Butler, A. P., 700
Butler, Benjamin F., 754–55, 811, 811, 831
Byrd, Harry F., 1494, 1506, 1506
Byrd, Lucy Parke, 113
Byrd, William, II, 110, 113, 127
Byrnes, James F., 1327, 1391–92, 1395

Cabell, James Branch, 1176
Cabeza de Vaca, Núñez, 32
cabinet, British, 173, 201, 218
cabinet, U.S., 331
Cable, George Washington, 852, 972
cable cars, 933
Cabot, John, 24

Cadore, duc de, 392
Cagney, James, 1283
Cairo Conference (1943), 1346
Cajuns, 191
"Calamity Jane" (Martha Jane Burke), 865
Caldwell, Erskine, 1280
Calhoun, Floride, 452
Calhoun, John C., 366, 395, 412, 413, 415,
    419, 430–31, 452, 682, 696, 704–5
  Calhoun Resolutions (1847), 674–75
  in Compromise of 1850, 682, 683
  Eaton Affair and, 452
  on economic growth, 486
  in election of 1824, 431, 432, 433, 434
  on Independent Treasury, 478
  Indian conflicts and, 418, 462
  internal improvements and, 453
  Jackson's rift with, 457–59
  on Mexican War, 675–76
  national bank issue and, 411, 466, 470
  nullification issue and, 454–60
  and slavery on frontier, 674–76
  tariff issue and, 435–36
  Texas annexation and, 606
  Van Buren's rivalry with, 450–53
  vice-presidency resigned by, 460
Calhoun Resolutions (1847), 674–75
California, 33, 42, 430, 592–95
  affirmative action in, 1682
  agriculture in, 880, 1566–67
  annexation of, 602, 609, 614–16
  anti-Asian sentiment in, 1068–69
  Chicanos in, 1564
  Chinese in, 859, 946, 947
  and Compromise of 1850, 682, 683, 687
  gold rush in (1848), 501, 588, 597, 678–81,
    678, 864
  in Great Depression, 1260–62
  immigrants in, 1653
  Indian conflicts in, 869
  Indians in, 587
  Mexican Americans in, 1567
  Mexican independence and, 593
  Mexican War and, 611, 614–16, 619
  migration to, 859
  mining in, 861
  "Okies" in, 1260–62
  Polk and, 609
  population of, 1650, 1651
  S&L industry in, 1625
  slavery and, 676, 681–82, 683, 687
  in Spanish Empire, 34, 36, 592
  statehood for, 681–82, 683, 687
  U.S. settlers in, 590, 596, 599
  voting rights in, 983
  workingmen's movement in, 912
  in World War II, 1329
California, University of, at Berkeley, 1552
California Trail, 592, 595

Calley, William, 1573
Call of the Wild, The (London), 975
Calvert, Leonard, 115
Calvin, John, 38, 38
Calvinism, 38, 39, 74, 137, 144, 146, 160, 537, 538, 539, 541, 543
Cambodia, 1475, 1476, 1477, 1519
  immigration from, 1653
  Khmer Rouge in, 1594
  U.S. bombing of (1969), 1572, 1573, 1574, 1575, 1589
Cambridge Agreement (1629), 70, 137, 172
Camden, S.C., Revolutionary fighting at, 265
Cameron, Simon, 725
campaign finance:
  in election of 1996, 1678
  unions and, 1386
campaigns, *see* elections and campaigns
Campbell, Alexander, 544
Campbell, Archibald, 263
Campbell, Thomas, 544
Camp David accords (1978), 1598–99
Canada:
  in American Revolution, 232, 254, 255–56
  British acquisition of, 186, 196
  in colonial wars, 186, 188, 192–93, 196
  immigration to, 521, *1655*
  Indian conflicts and, 349, 394–95
  Maine border with, 478, 585
  NAFTA and, 1663–64, 1681
  nationalism in, 584
  in NATO, 1398
  nuclear weapons and, 1392
  Quebec Act and, 223–24, 278
  sealing dispute and, 1041
  War of 1812 and, 393, 396
  in World War II, 1351
Canal Ring, 830
canals, *494*, 495–96, 501, 522
Cane (Toomer), 1182
Canning, George, 430
Cannon, Joseph G., 1096–97
Cape Verde, 17, 19
capitalism:
  Catholic views on, 980
  Hamilton and, 341–42, 344
  Marx on, 1185
Capone, Al, 1172, *1172*
Caribs, 19, 40
Carmichael, Stokely, 1533, 1554
Carnegie, Andrew, 765, 895, 898, *901*, 905, *906*, 1056
  philosophy of, 903–4
Carnegie Endowment for International Peace, 1416
Carney, William, 759
Caroline incident (1837), 584
carpetbaggers, 817–18, 822
Carranza, Venustiano, 1120, 1121

Carrier, Martha, 141, 142
Carrier, Willis Haviland, 1435
Carroll, Charles, 497
Carroll, John, 284
Carson, Christopher "Kit," 601, 615–16
Carson, Rachel, 1583
Carswell, G. Harrold, 1580
Carter, Jimmy, 1596–1602, 1615
  Camp David accords and, 1598–99, *1599*
  economy and, 1599–1600, 1605
  in election of 1976, 1595
  in election of 1980, 1609–11, *1610*
  foreign policy of, 1597–98
  Haiti negotiations of, 1672
  inauguration of, 1596, *1596*
  Iran hostages and, 1600–1602, *1601*, 1605
  Latin America policy of, 1616–17
Carter, Rosalynn, *1596*
Carteret, Sir George, 94
Cartier, Jacques, 40
Cartwright, Peter, 541, 963
Carver, George Washington, *949*
Casablanca Conference (1943), 1339
Case, Clifford, 1496
Casey, William, 1623
Cass, Lewis, 589, 675, 676, 678
Cassady, Neal, 1456, 1457
Castle Garden, 940
Castro, Fidel, 1515
  rise of, 1490–92, *1491*
Castro, Raul, 1567
Catawbas, 86
Catcher in the Rye, The (Salinger), 1452
Catherine of Aragon, 39
Catholicism, Catholic Church:
  in Canada, 224
  and Democratic party, 474, 993, 994, 1027
  education and, 1012
  in England, 42–43, 51, 52, 64
  first U.S. bishop in, 284
  in French colonies, 179
  German Americans in, 525
  immigrant ties with, 945
  Indians and, 29, 30, 34, 35–36, 87, 178, 180, 182, 590, 593, 594
  Irish Americans in, 523, 524
  James II and, 170–71
  Kennedy and, 1504
  in late nineteenth century, 979–80
  Maryland as a refuge for, 64–65
  missionaries of, 34, 35–36, 87, 180, 182, 590, 592–94
  prejudice against, 523, 527, 528, *528*, 945
  Reformation attacks on, 37
  Religious Right and, 1656
  in Spanish Empire, 29, 30, 34–35, 178, 195, 590
Catt, Carrie Chapman, 983, *983*, 1130, 1180

cattle, 22, 26, 86, 109, 116, 132, 632, 873–78
    drives of, 873–74
    farmers and, 876–78
    meat refrigeration and, 875
    range wars and, 877–78
Cavaliers, 51
Cayugas, 91, 262
CBS, 1253
CCC (Civilian Conservation Corps), 1239,
    1241–42, *1242,* 1262, 1263, 1328,
    1441–42
CCC (Commodity Credit Corporation), 1244
Ceausescu, Nicolae, 1635
CEEC (Committee of European Economic
    Cooperation), 1396
Celia (slave), 660–61
censorship, in World War I, 1140–42
Central Federated Union, 1140
Central Intelligence Agency (CIA), 1387–88,
    1420, 1472, 1479, 1576
    Central America and, 1617–18
    Chile and, 1593
    Cuba and, 1492, 1515
    Iran and, 1600–1601
    Noriega and, 1639
Central Pacific Railroad, 890, 891, 893
Central Park (New York City), 958
Central Powers (Triple Alliance), 1122–23,
    1124, 1142, 1147
Century of Dishonor, A (Jackson), 871–73
Ceylon (Sri Lanka), 1475
Challenger, explosion of (1986), 1621
Chambers, Whittaker, 1416
Champlain, Samuel de, 40, 178–79, *179*
Chancellorsville, Battle of (1863), 771–72,
    778
Chandler, Phoebe, 141
Chandler, Zachariah, 767
Channing, William Ellery, 538, 573
Chaplin, Charlie, 1208, *1208*
Charles I, king of England, 50–51, *51,* 64, 69,
    115, 166, 168
    colonial administrators under, 166, 168
    execution of, 51, 83
Charles II, king of England, 51, 62, 83, 84, 89,
    96, 167
    colonial administration under, 62, 167, 168
    death of, 169
    France policy of, 183–84
Charles V, king of Spain, 31, 39
Charles, Ray, 1433
Charleston (dance), 1175
Charleston, S.C.:
    in Civil War, 783, 791
    in colonial period, 85, 146, 148, 150
    founding of, 85
    in Revolutionary War, 233, 263–65
    and secession of South, 717–18, 725–26
Charleston and Hamburg Railroad, 497

Charlestown peninsula, during Revolution,
    230
Chase, Salmon P., 725, 811
Chase, Samuel, 375
Chattanooga, Battle of (1863), 775–76
Chauncey, Charles, 161
Chavez, César, 1565–66, *1565*
Chechnya, 1377, 1669
checks and balances, 312
Cheever, John, 1452
Cherokee Nation v. Georgia, 463
Cherokee Phoenix, 464
Cherokees, 86, 88, 89, 187, 193, *261,* 262–63,
    329, 351
    in Civil War, 742–43
    government of, 462, 463
    lands ceded by, 298–99
    in Ohio land disputes, 204
    post–Revolutionary weakness of, 298–99
    removal of, 462, 463–65
    Tecumseh and, 393
Chesapeake, U.S.S., 389
Chesnut, Mary Boykin, 639, 726, 777
Cheves, Langdon, 421
Cheyennes, 587, 866, 867, 868, 955, 956
Chiang Kai-shek, 1346, 1409, 1410, *1410,*
    1479, 1584
Chibchas, 9
Chicago, Ill.:
    African Americans in, 1437
    Democratic Convention in (1968),
        1543–44, 1555, *1556*
    growth of, 513–14
    Haymarket Affair in (1886), 916–17
    Pullman Strike in (1894), 920–22
    racial riot in (1919), 1138–39, *1159*
    racial riot in (1966), 1532
    Sears and Roebuck in, 907
*Chicago, Milwaukee and St. Paul Railway
    Company v. Minnesota,* 985–86
Chicago, University of, 952
Chicago Defender, 1138
Chicanos, 1433, 1564
Chickasaws, 86, 89, 303, 329, 351
    in Civil War, 742, 743
    removal of, 462, 464, 487
    Tecumseh and, 393
child labor, 510, 531, 1081, *1081,* 1111,
    1113–14, 1200, 1247, 1248, 1276
    progressive campaign against, 1081, 1113–14
Children's Bureau, U.S., 981, 1099, 1260
Chile, 29, 1120, 1593, 1636
China, 89
    American plants in, 23
    Boxer Rebellion in, 1059–60, *1060*
    Communist takeover of, 1409–11, 1476
    dollar diplomacy and, 1094
    foreign domination of, 1058–60, 1067,
        1118–19

Forty-niners from, 679, 681
immigration restrictions and, 946–47
Japanese aggression in, 1289–90, 1295–96, *1295*, 1299, 1303–4, *1303,* 1313, 1314, 1315, 1409
Open Door Policy and, 1059, 1067, 1068, 1094, 1291, 1296
Protestant missionaries to, 692
in Sino-Japanese War, 1058
Soviet conflicts with, 1295
trade with, 301, 473, 501, 691–92, 1058–59, 1291
China, Nationalist:
Communist defeat of, 1409–11, 1476
United Nations and, 1361, 1388, 1411
in World War II, 1322, 1352, 1357
see also Taiwan
China, People's Republic of, 1483
cold war and, 1376
democracy movement in, 1634–35
Indochina and, 1477
Korean War and, 1413–14, 1415, 1467, 1468
"loss" of China to, 1409–11, 1476
Nixon's visit to, 1584–86, *1585*
Taiwan and, 1479–80, 1488–89
trade with, 1681
United Nations and, 1411
Vietnam War and, 1539
Chinese Americans, 526, 858, 859, 912, 946–48, 1068, *1652, 1655*
railroads and, 891
violence against, 912
Chinese Exclusion Act (1882), *947,* 999
Chinooks, 587
Chippewas, 349, 1334, 1568
Chiricahua Apaches, 870, *871*
Chisholm, Jesse, 874
Chivington, J. M., 866
Choctaws, 86, 88, 89, 303, 329, 351
in Civil War, 742, 743
removal of, 462, 464, 487
Tecumseh and, 393
Chou En-lai, 1480, 1585, *1585*
Christian Coalition, 1656
Christianity and the Social Crisis (Rauschenbusch), 979
Christian right, 1608–9, 1630, 1656–57, 1660
Christopher, Warren, 1669
Christy Minstrels, 518
Churchill, Winston, 1306–8, *1307,* 1310, 1311, 1312, 1324, 1345, 1360, 1489
Atlantic Charter and, 1312, 1388
at Cairo and Teheran, 1346
at Casablanca, 1339
cold war and, 1391
D-Day and, 1347, 1350
French occupation zone and, 1361
nuclear weapons and, 1474

Roosevelt's 1941 meeting with, 1312
war aims and, 1337–38
at Yalta, 1360–61, *1361*
Church of England, *see* Anglican Church
Church of Jesus Christ of Latter-Day Saints (Mormons), 544–47, 877
CIA, *see* Central Intelligence Agency
Cigarmakers Union, 917
Cincinnati, Ohio, *376,* 512, 531
CIO (Congress of Industrial Organizations), 1271, 1272, *1273,* 1385, 1386, *1387*
"circuit riders," 541
Cisneros, Henry, 1567
Citadel, 733
cities and towns:
amenities in, 505
in colonial period, 147–52
early factories in, 507–10
in early nineteenth century, 512–14, *513*
in early twentieth century, *933*
employment in, 149
and growth of industry, 932
immigrants in, 937, 943–44
industrialization as impetus to, 512–14
in late nineteenth century, 929–36, *932*
in late twentieth century, 1651
and mass transit, 933–35
politics of, 935–36
poverty in, 149–50
recreation in, 515–16
reform movements in, 980–87
rise of, 16
rural migration to, 936
settlement house movement in, 980–81, 1081, 1268
transportation between, 150, 512–14
Citizen Genêt, 346
Citizens' Councils, 1494
citizenship and naturalization:
of African Americans, 316, 805
Constitutional Convention and, 315–16
of Indians, 316, 872
of Puerto Ricans, 1056–57
city-manager plan, 1078
City of Philadelphia As It Appeared in the Year 1800, The (Birch), *300*
"Civil Disobedience" (Thoreau), *551,* 552
Civilian Conservation Corps (CCC), 1239, 1241–42, *1242,* 1262, 1263, 1328, 1441–42
civil liberties, *see* civil rights and liberties
Civil Rights Act (1866), 805, 806
Civil Rights Act (1957), 1496, 1523, 1531
Civil Rights Act (1960), 1487, 1531
Civil Rights Act (1964), 1529, 1531
civil rights and liberties:
Alien and Sedition Acts and (1798), 364–66
in Civil War, 767–68
in colonial period, 176, 208, 216, 272

civil rights and liberties (continued)
in election of 1948, 1403, 1404
Johnson and, 1522, 1531
Reagan and, 1615
Red Scare and (1919–1920), 1159–61
Truman and, 1400–1402, 1403, 1403
in World War I, 1140–42
Civil Rights Cases, 853
Civil Rights Commission, 1496, 1615
civil rights movement:
black power and, 1532–35, 1554
Brown decision and, 1493–94
colleges and, 1550
early period of, 1492–97
in election of 1960, 1505
expansion of, 1509–15
federal intervention in, 1511–15
Little Rock crisis and, 1497
massive resistance and, 1494, 1497
Montgomery bus boycott and, 1494–96,
1509
Civil Service Commission, 999, 1009, 1416
civil service reform, 827, 828, 831, 995–97,
999–1000
Cleveland and, 1003–4
Harrison and, 1009
merit system and, 996
Roosevelt, Theodore, and, 1009, 1061
Civil War, English, 82–84, 95, 96, 167
Civil War, Spanish, 1298–99, 1300, 1302
Civil War, U.S., 723–85
African-American soldiers in, 756–60, 758,
813, 815
aftermath of, 790–96
"Anaconda" strategy in, 734, 736–37
balance of force in, 731–33
bond sales in, 764–65
as "brothers' war," 729–30
calls for peace in, 752, 767, 770
casualties in, 624, 745, 760, 784–85
choosing sides in, 718–19, 726–29
civil liberties and, 767–68
compromise attempted before, 720
Confederate command structure in, 749,
773, 776
Congress in, 658, 720, 726–27, 754, 755,
760, 764, 790–91
conscription in, 739–41
coverage of, 560
diplomacy and, 766–67
economic effects of, 888–89
economy in, 731–33, 765, 766
emancipation in, 753–63
financing of, 764–65
government during, 763–70
Indians in, 648, 742
Mexican War and generals of, 620
military advantages in, 733
naval warfare in, 730, 737–38
outbreak of fighting in, 725–26

peninsular campaign in, 746–50, 747
presidential transition and, 719–20, 723–24
recruitment and draft in, 738–41, 758
and secession of South, 717–19, 726–29,
727
southern blockade in, 733, 734, 736
strategies in, 734, 736–37, 777
technology in, 785
as total war, 777, 782, 784–85
Union command changes in, 745, 746–47,
749–50, 751, 752, 771, 773, 776
veterans of, 1004–5, 1007, 1009
West in, 741–43, 744
women in, 760–63
see also Confederate States of America;
Reconstruction
Civil Works Administration (CWA), 1243
Clansman, The (Dixon), 1208
Clark, Bennett Champ, 1102
Clark, George Rogers, 260–61, 346, 380
Clark, J. Ruben, 1294
Clark, William, 380–82, 381, 382
Clarke, James Freeman, 549
Clark Memorandum, 1294
Clark University, 952
Clay, Henry, 395, 403, 415, 424, 435, 437,
453, 461, 474, 532, 582, 708
African colonization and, 661
American system of, 432, 432, 433, 437,
474, 479, 582, 609, 818
in Compromise of 1850, 682–83
in duel, 644–45
in election of 1824, 432, 432, 433, 437,
474, 479, 582, 609
in election of 1832, 469, 470
in election of 1840, 479
in election of 1844, 606, 607, 608
and election of 1848, 676
Missouri Compromise and, 423
national bank debate and, 411, 467, 470,
472
nullification and, 461
tariff policy of, 472, 583
Tyler administration and, 582, 583
Clayton, Henry D., 1109
Clayton Antitrust Act (1914), 1109
Clayton-Bulwer Treaty (1850), 1064
Clean Air Act (1970), 1581
Cleaver, Eldridge, 1533
Clemenceau, Georges, 1142, 1150, 1151–52
Clemens, Samuel (Mark Twain), 646, 972–73,
973, 989
Clermont, U.S.S., 493
Cleveland, Frances Folsom, 1008
Cleveland, Grover, 921, 946, 990, 1002, 1019,
1023–24, 1025, 1044
and civil service reform, 1003–4
in election of 1884, 1001–3
in election of 1888, 1008
in election of 1892, 1023, 1042

first term of, 1003–5
Hawaii and, 1040–41
navy under, 1037
tariff issue and, *1002*, 1006–8
Cleveland, Ohio, racial riot in (1966), 1532
Clifford, Clark, 1539, 1542
Clinton, Bill:
Bosnia and, 1671
community promoted by, 1688
deficits and, 1662, 1663–64, 1680
draft issue and, 1661
economy and, 1680–81, 1687
in election of 1992, 1661–62
and election of 1994, 1673–74, 1675
in election of 1996, 1676–79, *1679*
foreign policy of, 1668–73
Haiti and, 1672
health care effort of, 1664–65
infidelity issue and, 1661
Lewinsky matter and, 1685–86
Middle East policy of, 1670–71
race issues and, 1681–83
Religious Right and, 1656–57
Republican Congress and, 1673–76
scandals under, 1683–86
second-term cabinet of, 1679
Whitewater case and, 1683–84
Clinton, De Witt, 495
Clinton, George, 344, 345, 346
in election of 1804, 383
in election of 1808, 390–91
in ratification debate, 321
Clinton, Hillary Rodham, 1661, 1664, *1665*, 1683
Clinton, Sir Henry, 230, 231, 233, 259, 260, 263, 265
clipper ships, 500–501, *500*
closed shop, 1089, 1385
coal industry, 843, 1383
Cobbett, William, 567
cocaine, 1634
Code of the West, 882
"code talkers," 1334–35
Cody, William "Buffalo Bill," 955–56, *956*
Coelho, Tony, 1674
Coercive (Intolerable) Act (1774), 223–25
Coffin, Levi, 667
Cohen, William, 1679
Cohens v. Virginia, 425
Colbert, Jean Baptiste, 180
Cold Harbor, Battle of (1864), 779
cold war, 1388–99, 1408–21
brinkmanship and, 1473–74
China and, 1409–11, 1584–86
containment in, 1392–94, 1420, 1472, 1473, 1540, 1657
détente and, 1585–86
end of, 1377
Marshall Plan and, 1395–96
origins of, 1376, 1379–80, 1390–92

segregation and, 1400
and spheres of influence, 1419–20
Truman Doctrine and, 1394–96, 1416, 1538
see also Korean War; Vietnam War
Cole, Thomas, 547, *547*
Colfax, Schuyler, 826
colleges and universities, 161, 563–66, 950–52
in early U.S., 287–88
football at, 962–63
GI Bill of Rights and, 1425–26
graduate schools in, 952
land-grant, 764, 791
in late nineteenth century, 950–52, 962–63
in 1920s, 1175
in 1960s, 1550, 1552–54
religious movements and, 158, 161, 538, 539
segregation at, 1426, 1492–93, 1511–12
social sciences at, 969–70
women's, 566
see also education
Collier, John, 1263
Colombia, 29
in Contadora Process, 1618
Panama Canal and, 1064, 1065, 1066, 1293
colonial governments:
assemblies' powers in, 72–73, 175–77, 208–9, 225–27
charters in, 69, 70, 72, 84, 137, 166–67, 169, 172, 174
in Connecticut, 170, 173, 174
covenant theory in, 137
in Delaware, 173
and Dominion of New England, 169–71
in Dutch colonies, 90
English administration and, 166–73
in Georgia, 102, 166, 171
governors' powers in, 174–75, 177
in Maryland, 64–65, 171, 173
in Massachusetts, 69, 70–73, 84, 166–67, 168–69, 170, 171, 174
in New Hampshire, 169
in New Jersey, 171
in New York, 170, 171
in North Carolina, 171
in Pennsylvania, 98, 173
in Plymouth, 68
in Rhode Island, 84, 137, 170, 173, 174
self-government developed in, 173–77
in South Carolina, 85–86, 171, 175
of towns, 150
in Virginia, 59, 61, 62, 175
colonial period:
agriculture in, 55, 115–17, 131–32, 135, 143
alcoholic beverages in, 151–52
architecture in, 126, 130–31
assemblies' powers in, 175–77
backcountry in, 144, 146–47

colonial period *(continued)*
  birthrates and death rates in, 110–11
  British folkways in, 106–7
  cities in, 147–52
  class stratification during, 148–50
  colonial wars in, 183–96
  craft guilds in, 529
  currency shortage in, 134–35
  education in, 155–56
  employment in, 149
  Enlightenment in, 152–56
  ethnic mix in, 144–46
  European settlement in, 53–77
  Great Awakening during, 156–62
  indentured servants in, 62, 118–20
  Indian conflicts in, 60, 61, 62–63, 75,
    80–82, *80*, 83, 88, 92, 94, 187, 193, 202,
    204
  land policy in, 117–18, 143
  manufactures in, 502–3
  mercantile system in, 167–68
  newspapers in, 152
  population growth in, 109–13
  postal service in, 152
  prisons and punishment in, 569
  religion in, 136–38, 139, 140, 144, 156–62
  sex ratios in, 112–13
  slavery in, 119–26
  social and political order in, 148–50
  society and economy in, 115–47
  taverns in, 150–52
  taxation in, 72, 128, 170, 177, 206–17,
    223–27
  trade and commerce in, 43, 53, 55, 62, 79,
    86–89, 98, 116–18, 131–35, *135*, 138,
    167–69, 179, 200
  transportation in, 150
  triangular trade, 134
  ways of life in, 105–64
  westward expansion and, 180, 188, 202–5,
    260–63, 354–55
  witchcraft in, 140–43
colonial wars, 183–96
  French and Indian War, 188–96
  with Indians, 60, 61, 62–63, 75, 80–82, *80*,
    83, 88, 92, 94, 187, 193, 202, 204
  King George's War, 187–88
  King William's War, 184–86
  Queen Anne's War, 186–87
Colorado:
  Indian conflicts in, 869
  labor movement in, 924
  statehood for, 865
  voting rights in, 983
Colorado Territory, 596, 741, 864, *865*
  Indian conflicts in, 866
Colored Farmers' Alliance, 1017
Columbia, S.C., 783, 791, 844
Columbia Broadcasting System, 1209

Columbia University (King's College), 161,
    952, 1554–55, *1555*
Columbus, Christopher, 2, 6, 15
  background of, 18
  Marco Polo read by, 17
  voyages of, 17–21, *18*, *20*
Comanches, 587, 590, 867, 1335
Coming of Age in Somoa (Mead), 1188
Command of the Army Act (1867), 808, 810
commerce, *see* economy; trade and commerce
Commerce Court, 1099
Commercial Convention (1815), 417
Commission for Relief, 1137–38
Commission on Civil Disorders, 1533
Commission on Training Camp Activities
    (CTCA), 1137
Committee of Correspondence, 220, 221–22,
    224
Committee of European Economic
    Cooperation (CEEC), 1396
Committee of National Liberation, 1362
Committee of Safety (Boston), 229
Committee on Civil Rights, 1400
Committee on Public Information, 1140
Committee to Defend America by Aiding the
    Allies, 1308
Committee to Re-elect the President
    (CREEP), 1588, 1589–90
Commodity Credit Corporation (CCC), 1244
common law, 48–49
Common Sense (Paine), 233–34, 247
Common Sense Book of Baby and Child Care,
    The (Spock), 1449–50, *1449*
Commonwealth v. *Hunt,* 529
communes, 1557–58, *1558*
communism, 919
  in Cuba, 1491–92
  Eisenhower Doctrine and, 1488
  fall of, 1634–39, 1668–69
  in Guatemala, 1473
  Indochina and, 1474–79
  and Red Scare after World War I, 1159–60,
    1215
  in Spain, 1302
  see also anti-communism; cold war; Soviet
    Union; Vietnam War
Communist Labor party (U.S.), 1160
Communist party (China), 1409, 1476
Communist party (France), 1395
Communist party (Italy), 1395
Communist party (U.S.), 1160, 1417
  in Great Depression, 1228, 1276, 1278
  in presidential elections, 1235
Community Action Program, 1526
Community Service Organization (CSO),
    1565–66
Compromise of 1850, 682–91, 687
Compromise of 1877, 829–33
computer revolution, 1643–47

ENIAC in, 1643–44
Internet and, 1646–47
transistor in, 1644–45
Comstock, H.T.P., 864
Comstock Lode, 864
Conciliatory Resolution (1775), 227
Concord, Battle of (1775), 228–30, 228, 229
Conestogas, 219
Confederate States of America (Confederacy):
agriculture in, 732
command structure of, 749
constitution of, 718
devastation in, 791–92
diplomacy of, 766–67
finances of, 765
formation of, 717–19, 726–29
industry in, 731–32
navy of, 733, 767
politics in, 769–70
recruitment in, 738–39
states' rights in, 739, 770
Union Loyalists in, 730, 769–70, 806, 818
Union soldiers from, 730
see also Civil War, U.S.
Confederation Congress, 276, 292, 293–94, 296
accomplishments of, 292
Articles of Confederation revision endorsed by, 309
diplomacy and, 301–3
end of, 324–25
land policies of, 294–99
Loyalist property and, 302–3
paper currency issued by, 305
powers of, 275–76, 292–93
trade and commerce regulated by, 276, 299–301
weaknesses of, 303–6, 308–9
Conference for Progressive Political Action (1922), 1206
Confiscation Act (1861), 755
Confiscation Act (1862), 755, 756, 758, 794
Congregationalists, 69, 157, 160, 161, 284, 527, 538
Presbyterians' union with, 540–41
in Whig party, 474
Congress, Confederate, 765
Congress, U.S., 288, 561, 562–63
African Americans in, 817
and Barbary pirates, 405
Bush and, 1660
Carter and, 1597
in Civil War, 658, 720, 726–27, 754, 755, 760, 764, 790–91
Clinton impeachment and, 1685, 1686
commerce regulated by, 428
in Constitution, 313, 314, 316, 317, 319
currency policy of, 829
education promoted by, 563–64

Eisenhower and, 1464, 1485, 1487
and election of 1876, 832–33
and election of 1948, 1404–8
and election of 1994, 1657
emancipation and, 754, 755
environmentalism and, 1583
Equal Rights Amendment and, 1562–63
executive departments established by, 331
first meeting of, 330
Ford and, 1593
gerrymandering and, 1682
Grant's relations with, 824
in Great Depression, 1226–28
Great Society and, 1529
immigration investigated by, 940
immigration policy of, 528, 1165
Independent Treasury voted by, 478
Indian conflicts investigated by, 867
Indian policy and, 462
internal improvements and, 413, 415, 501–2
Johnson's (Andrew) conflict with, 804–5
Johnson's (Andrew) impeachment and, 810–12
Kennedy and, 1508
in Korean War, 1412
land policy and, 352, 353–54, 490, 583
McCarthyism and, 1419
Mexican War and, 612
Napoleonic Wars and, 391
national bank issue in, 337, 339, 411, 426, 467
Nixon and, 1578, 1591, 1592
Persian Gulf War and, 1641
policy role of, 990–91
railroads and, 693
Reagan and, 1622, 1626
in Reconstruction, 794–95, 797, 801–10, 812, 821, 829
religion promoted by, 1444
slavery issue and, 674–75, 676, 681, 705, 707, 760
and suspension of habeas corpus, 768
Taiwan and, 1479–80
tariff policy of, 460, 461
taxation power of, 313
Texas annexation and, 605
trade policy of, 391–92, 417
Truman and, 1385, 1386–87
Tyler's conflicts with, 583
Vietnam War and, 1572
War of 1812 and, 392, 395
welfare reform and, 1676
West Virginia admitted to Union by, 726–27
see also House of Representatives, U.S.; Senate, U.S.
Congressional Government (Wilson), 1100, 1106
Congressional Union, 1179

Congress of Industrial Organizations (CIO), 1271, 1272, *1273*, 1385, 1386, *1387*
Congress of Racial Equality (CORE), 1511
Congress of Vienna (1814–1815), 403, 429
Conkling, Roscoe, 995, 996, 997, 998, 999
Connecticut:
  Constitution ratified by, 322
  disestablishment in, 439
  divorce in, 283
  government of, 274
  at Hartford Convention, 404
  land claims of, 295
  Revolutionary troops from, 230
  slave trade halted by, 279
  voting rights in, 438–39
Connecticut colony, 79–80, 82, 83
  charter of, 84, 174
  in colonial taxation disputes, 219
  European settlement of, 76
  government of, 170, 173, 174
  Indian conflicts in, 80–81, *80*, 83
  in land disputes, 224
Connecticut (Great) Compromise, 313–14
Connor, Eugene "Bull," 1512, *1512*
Conscience of a Conservative, The (Goldwater), 1526–27, *1527*
conservation, 1091–92, 1096, 1098
Considerations on the Nature and Extent of the Legislative Authority of the British Parliament (Wilson), 226
Constellation, U.S.S., 363
Constitution, U.S.S., 363
Constitution, U.S., 291, 309–25, 455
  amendment process and, 319
  Congress in, 313, 314, 316, 317, 319
  foreign policy in, 317
  habeas corpus in, 768
  implied powers and, 339, 379, 412, 426
  internal improvements and, 453, 890
  judicial review principle and, 375
  Louisiana Purchase and, 379
  motivation of advocates of, 320
  national bank issue and, 338–39, 466, *468*
  nullification issue and, 455, 457, 460
  presidency in, 316–18
  ratification of, 319–25
  Reconstruction and, 796–97, 800, 804, 805
  separation of powers and, 316–19
  slavery in, 313–15, 377
  state-compact theory of, 365
  strict construction of, 379, 384, 387, 412, 432, 582
  Theodore Roosevelt's view of, 1084
  treason in, 387
  see also Constitutional Convention
Constitution, U.S.S., 363
constitutional amendments, U.S.:
  First, 668
  Fifth, 675, 704–5
  Ninth, 333

Tenth, 319, 333, 339
Thirteenth, 315, 760, 789, 801, 806, 834
Fourteenth, 625, 806, 808–9, 834, 853, 985, 1184
Fifteenth, 625, 812, *815*, 834, 851, 1184
Sixteenth, 1099
Seventeenth, 1077, 1099
Eighteenth, 319, 1171, 1197, 1234
Nineteenth, 1180, 1197
Twentieth, 1236
Twenty-first, 1239
Twenty-second, 1462
Twenty-fifth, 1591–92
Twenty-sixth, 1581
proposed Equal Rights Amendment, 1180, 1562–63, *1562*, 1615, 1661
Constitutional Convention (1787), 242, 309–19, *310*, *318*
  call for, 308–9
  delegates to, 309–12
  Madison at, 310, 311, *312*, 316, 317, 320, 344
  political philosophy of, 311–12
  representation issue in, 313, 316
  separation of powers at, 316–19
  slavery issue at, 313–15
  trade and commerce issue, 313–15
  women's rights ignored by, 315
Constitutional Union party, 715
constitutions:
  British, 48, 50, 200–201, 208
  state, 274–75, 278, 279, 283, 316, 375, 809, 818
  see also Constitution, U.S.
Consumers League, 1237
Contadora Process, 1618
containment, 1392–94, 1420, 1472, 1473, 1540, 1657
Continental army, 252
  desertions from, 252, 259
  recruitment to, 252, 253, 253
  supply problems of, 252–53, 259
  winter quarters of, 253, 255, 256, 259
  see also American Revolution
Continental Association, 226
Continental Congress, First (1775), 205, 225–27, 228, 263–65, 285
  call for, 224–25
  financial problems and, 252
  plan of union considered by, 225
Continental Congress, Second, 230, 246, 252–53, 260
  on African-American soldiers, 279
  extralegal nature of, 275
  governmental functions taken by, 233
  independence voted by, 234–38, *236*, 286
  peace efforts and, 232, 259, 270
  supply problems and, 259, 293–94
  Washington's resignation before, 272
Continental System, 388

Contract Labor Act (1864), 764, 913, 938
contract rights, 425–26
contract theory of government, 172, 237, 273
Contract with America, 1674–75
Contras, 1617–18, 1624
  Iran-Contra affair and, 1621–24
Convention of 1800, 363
Convention of 1818, 416, 417, 591
convict leasing, 848
Conwell, Russell, 979
Cooke, Jay, 764, 828, 889
Coolidge, Calvin, 1158, 1184, 1201, 1204–6,
  1205, 1207, 1215, 1217, 1611
  in election of 1920, 1198
  in election of 1924, 1206–7
  Latin American policy of, 1293, 1294
Coolidge, Grace, 1204
Coolidge, John, 1204
Cooper, James Fenimore, 554
Cooper, Peter, 563
cooperatives, labor movement and, 531
Copernicus, Nicolaus, 153
Copley, John Singleton, 285
Copperheads, 767, 768
copper mining, *861*, 865
Coral Sea, Battle of (1942), 1323, 1336, 1352
Corbin, Margaret, 282
CORE (Congress of Racial Equality), 1511
Corey, Giles, 142
corn (maize), 7, 22, 23, 67, 78, 109, 356, 632
Cornell, Alonzo, 997
Cornell University, 952, 962
Cornish Americans, 642, 943
Cornwallis, Lord, 233, 255, 263, 265, 266–67,
  268, 269
Coronado, Francisco Vásquez de, 32
Corporation for Public Broadcasting, 1613
corporations, business, 510–11, 991–92
  downsizing in, 1650, 1658, 1681
  in Europe, 16, 49
  in Great Depression, 1227
  growth of, 905
  Harding and, 1201
  leveraged buyouts and, 1624–25
  Muckrakers and, 1075
  in New Deal, 1243, 1246–48, 1258
  in 1920s, 1201, 1205–6, 1287
  as persons in judicial reasoning, 806, 985
  in post–World War II era, 1439–40
  progressivism and regulation of, 1073, 1080,
    1089
  see also industry; trusts; *specific corporations*
Corps of Discovery, 380–82
corruption, 994–95
  Arthur's efforts against, 999
  civil service reform and, 827, 828, 831,
    995–97, 999–1000, 1003–4, 1009
  Harding administration and, 1201–4
  Hayes's efforts against, 996
  Granat's administration and, 825–27, 995

Corsicana oil field, 844
Corso, Gregory, 1454
Cortés, Hernando, 27–29, *27*, *28*, *32*
Cosmography (Ptolemy), 21
cotton, 328, 409, 448, 474, 486–88, 629–30,
    630, 631, *631*, 632, *842*, 1437–38
  British trade in, 389–90, 454, 473, 624,
    631, 634, 636
  in Civil War, 732, 766, 791
  French trade in, 454, 473, 631
  in Great Depression, 1244
  in Old Southwest, 659
  in Panic of 1857, 708
  in Southwest, 676
  see also textile industry
Cotton, John, 137
cotton gins, 487–88, *487*, 502, 505
Coubertin, Pierre de, 965
Coughlin, Charles E., 1253, 1265
Council for New England, 65, 68, 69, 76
Council of Economic Advisers, 1384–85, 1525
Council of Foreign Ministers, 1391–92, 1397
Council of National Defense, 1137
Council of the Indies, 30
counterculture, 1557–60
Country of the Pointed Firs, The (Freeman),
    971–72
courts, *see* Admiralty courts, vice-admiralty
    courts; legal system; Supreme Court, U.S.
covenant theory, 137
cowboys, 873–76
  African Americans as, 860, 873
Cowpens, Battle of (1781), 266
Cox, Archibald, 1590
Cox, James, 1198, 1234
Coxey, Jacob S., 1024
crack cocaine, 1634
Crack in the Picture Window, The (Keats),
    1448
Crane, Stephen, 975
Crawford, William, 415, 431, 432, 433, 434,
    476, 644
Crazy Horse, chief of Sioux, 868
Crédit Mobilier, 826, 893
Creeks, 86, 88, 89, 186, 187, 299, 303, 329,
    351, 361, 418, 464
  in Civil War, 742, 743
  Jackson's campaign against, 399, 462
  removal of, 462, 464, 487
  Tecumseh and, 393
Creel, George, 1140
CREEP (Committee to Re-elect the
    President), 1588, 1589–90
Creole incident (1841), 584
crime:
  Clinton and bills on, 1665–66, 1674
  in colonial era, 149
  immigration and, 118
  juvenile delinquency and, 1431–32
  in late twentieth century, 1652

crime (continued)
Prohibition and, 1172
in West, 882, 883
see also prisons
Crimean War, 707
Cripple Creek, Colo., mining at, 865
Crisis, The, 1184
Criterion, 1189
Critique of Pure Reason (Kant), 547
Crittenden, John J., 720, 730
Croatia, 1671
Crockett, Davy, 603–4
Crompton, Samuel, 503
Cromwell, Oliver, 51, 53, 82, 83–84, 167
Cronkite, Walter, 1541
crop lien system, 846
croquet, 958
Crosby, Stills, Nash, and Young, 1559
Crown Point, Battle of (1775), 230
Crows, 589, 869, 1334
cruel and unusual punishment, 52, 333
Cruikshank, Robert, 449
CSO (Community Service Organization),
1565–66
CTCA (Commission on Training Camp
Activities), 1137
C. Turner Joy, U.S.S., 1536
Cuba, 26, 32, 194, 195, 429, 430, 1294
Bay of Pigs invasion of, 1515
Castro's rise in, 1490–92
Columbus in, 19, 20
Grenada invasion and, 1619
immigration from, 1653
missile crisis in (1962), 1516–18, 1517
Ostend Manifesto and, 691
in Spanish-American War, 1043–47,
1048–51, 1054
trade with, 1492
U.S. role in, 1057–58
Cuban Americans, 1166, 1567
Cuban Revolutionary party, 1043
Cudahy, Michael, 522
Cudahy Packing Company, 522
Cullen, Countée, 1182
culture, U.S.:
emergence of, 285–89
in nineteenth century, 514–19
see also arts; popular culture
Cumberland (National) Road, 413, 413, 415,
453, 492
Cumberland Road Bill (1822), 415
currency:
agriculture and, 1010, 1015–16, 1024
in American Revolution, 252, 294
in Civil War, 764, 765
after Civil War, 824–25, 889
in colonial era, 135, 207, 219
Constitution and, 320
in early twentieth century, 1089, 1107

in early U.S., 303, 304, 305, 305, 308, 337,
338
gold, 829, 1015, 1024–25, 1028–29, 1089,
1226, 1227, 1239, 1241, 1258, 1583
Great Depression and, 1223–24, 1226,
1239, 1241
greenbacks and, 764, 823, 824–25, 827,
1015, 1028
"In God We Trust" on, 1444
in late nineteenth century, 997, 1000, 1010,
1015, 1024–26
national bank issue and, 466, 467, 472, 473
shortages of, 134–35, 304–6, 330
silver, 997, 1010, 1015, 1024–25, 1028
in War of 1812, 410
Currency Act (1764), 207, 218
Curry, J.L.M., 848
Custer, George A., 778, 868, 956
Custis family, 794
customs, 206, 215–16
customs houses, 996–97
Cutler, Manasseh, 296–97
CWA (Civil Works Administration), 1243
Czech Americans, 937, 939
Czechoslovakia, 1151
fall of communism in, 1635
German invasion of, 1299, 1304
Soviet domination of, 1363, 1396
Czolgosz, Leon, 1063

Dakota Territory, 741, 868
Dale, Thomas, 57–58
Daley, Richard, 1505, 1543–44, 1556, 1587
dams, 879
dance, 1175, 1176–77
African-American, 655, 656
in 1920s, 1174–75, 1176, 1177
Dangling Man (Bellow), 1454
Daniel Boone Escorting Soldiers through the
Cumberland Gap (Bingham), 355
Daniels, Jonathan, 1192
Dare, Elinor, 45
Dare, Virginia, 45
Darlan, Jean-François, 1339
Darrow, Clarence, 1169–70
Dartmouth College, 161, 425–26
Dartmouth College v. Woodward, 425
Darwin, Charles, 965–66, 966, 968, 1037,
1168, 1185, 1188, 1609
Darwinism:
banned from public schools, 1168–70
effect on American society, 969
natural selection in, 965, 1037
reform, 968–69
religious opposition to, 1168–70, 1608
social, 966–68
Davenport, James, 160
Davidson, Donald, 1192
Davis, David, 832

Davis, Henry Winter, 797
Davis, Jefferson, 681, 693, 748, 749
  in Black Hawk War, 463
  capture of, 783–84
  Civil War strategy of, 737
  and Compromise of 1850, 682, 683
  as Confederate president, 718, 769
  enlistment efforts and, 738–39
  and first Battle of Bull Run, 734
  Fort Sumter and, 725
  Lee's relationship with, 749
  in Mexican War, 617–18
  stubbornness of, 770
Davis, John W., 1206, 1251–52
Dawes, Charles G., 1227
Dawes, Henry M., 872–73
Dawes, William, 229
Dawes Severalty (General Allotment) Act
  (1887), 872–73, 1263–64
Dayan, Moshe, *1483*
Dean, James, 1457
Dean, John, *1589, 1590*
Dearborn, Henry, 396–97
Death of a Salesman (Miller), 1450–51,
  1451
death rates, during colonial period, 110–11
Debs, Eugene V.:
  and American Railway Union, 921
  imprisonment of, 922, 1141–42
  pardon of, 1203
  in presidential elections, 923, 924, 1093,
    1102, 1105, 1141, 1142
  and Pullman Strike, 920–22
  as socialist, 923–24
  in World War I, 1141–42
debt:
  agricultural, 879, 1010, 1014, 1015, 1017,
    1227
  after American Revolution, 302, 305–6,
    308, 348
  for Confederate cause, repudiation of, 801,
    806
  European, from World War I, 1201,
    1288–89
  issuance of paper currency and, 304–5
  in 1980s, 1625
  Shays's Rebellion and, 306–8
  state, federal assumption of, 335, 336–37,
    342, 343
debt, national:
  under Articles of Confederation, 292–93,
    294
  Bush and, 1633–34, 1658
  after Civil War, 823, 824–25
  Clinton and, 1662, 1663–64, 1680
  in early U.S., 335, 336–37, 341, 343, 353
  elimination of (1830s), 472
  gold vs. greenbacks in repayment of, 823,
    824–25

Jackson on, 449, 472
  in Jefferson administration, 376
  Reagan and, 1612–13, 1625, 1630
  Truman and, 1387
debtors, imprisonment for, 530–31, 570
Decatur, Stephen, 377, 405
Declaration of American Rights (1775), 225
Declaration of Cairo (1943), 1346
"Declaration of Causes" (Texas) (1836), 603
Declaration of Independence (1776), 234–38,
  235, 242, 329, 536
  Independence Day and, 286–87
  slavery in draft of, 278
  sources of, 235
Declaration of London (1909), 1125–26
Declaration of Panama (1939), 1305
Declaration of Rights, Virginia (1776), 236,
  283–84, 311, 333
Declaration of Sentiments (1848), 573
Declaration of the Causes and Necessity of
  Taking Up Arms (1775), 232
Declaration of the Causes of Secession (South
  Carolina) (1860), 717–18
Declaration of the Rights and Grievances of
  the Colonies (1765), 211
Declaration of the United Nations (1942),
  1337, 1363
Declaratory Act (1766), 212
Deere, John, 491, 879–80
defendants' rights, 1264, 1509
Defense Plant Corporation, 1383
Deficit Reduction Act (1984), 1620
deficits, federal, *see* debt, national
Defoe, Daniel, 118
deism, 153, 537–38
DeKlerk, Frederik W., 1636
de Kooning, Willem, 1453
de la Garza, Elizio "Kika," 1567
DeLancey family, 344
Delaware:
  Constitution ratified by, 322
  disestablishment in, 439
  in early interstate cooperation, 309
  free blacks in, 648
  secession rejected by, 727
  segregation in, 1493
  voting rights of, 278, 439
Delaware and Hudson Canal, 495
Delaware colony, 84, 98, 143, 202
  European settlement of, 106
  government of, 173
Delawares, 192, 262, 696
De La Warr (Delaware), Thomas West, Lord,
  56, 57
DeLeon, Daniel, 92, 922, 924
de Lôme, Depuy, 1045
Democratic Leadership Council (DLC), 1661
Democratic National Committee, Watergate
  and, 1588

Democratic party, 345
  African Americans in, 850, 1265–66, 1276
  "Barnburners" vs. "Hunkers" in, 677, 690
  Bourbons and, 846–47, 849
  budget deficits and, 1613
  Bush and, 1633, 1634, 1660
  in Civil War, 752, 767, 768–69, 768
  in Cleveland's presidency, 1003–4
  cold war and, 1376
  corruption and, 994–95
  in election of 1832, 469
  in election of 1836, 475
  in election of 1840, 479
  in election of 1844, 606
  in election of 1848, 676–78
  in election of 1852, 690
  in election of 1856, 702
  in election of 1860, 713–14
  in election of 1864, 769
  in election of 1868, 823
  in election of 1874, 829
  in election of 1876, 830–33
  in election of 1880, 998
  in election of 1894, 1024
  in election of 1896, 1026
  in election of 1900, 1062
  in election of 1904, 1089
  in election of 1908, 1093
  in election of 1918, 1149
  in election of 1920, 1198
  in election of 1924, 1206
  in election of 1928, 1217
  in election of 1948, 1403, 1404
  in election of 1956, 1480
  in election of 1958, 1487
  in election of 1964, 1527–28
  in election of 1968, 1543–44, 1555, 1556
  in election of 1980, 1611
  in election of 1988, 1630
  in election of 1992, 1661–62
  in election of 1994, 1673
  ethnic groups in, 523–24, 993–94, 1011–12
  Farmers' Alliances and, 1020, 1021
  in formation of Republican party, 697
  in formation of Whigs, 474
  Free Soil party and, 677
  in Great Depression, 1225
  immigration issue and, 1012
  Independent Treasury and, 478
  Irish Americans in, 474, 523
  in Kansas-Nebraska crisis, 696
  labor and, 530
  late nineteenth-century components of,
    993–94
  New Deal and, 1377
  new states resisted by, 865
  origins of, 435
  in Reconstruction South, 821–22, 846–47
  reshaped by Roosevelt, Franklin, 1276–77
    slavery issue in, 609, 697, 713–14
    in South, 1406
    Spanish-American War and, 1053
    in split over slavery, 713–14
    in Taft administration, 1097
    tariff issue and, 990, 1006
    Vietnam War and, 1577
    voting rights and, 1264
    in Wilson's presidency, 1106
    World War II and, 1372
Democratic-Republicans, 435
    see also Democratic party
Democratic Review, 481
Denmark:
    in NATO, 1398
    in World War II, 1305
dentistry, 953
Dependent Pension Act (1890), 1009
Dependent Pension Bill (1887), 1005
Depression, Great, 1033
    banking industry in, 1236, 1238–41
    congressional initiatives in, 1226–28
    culture in, 1278–84
    currency and, 1223–24, 1226, 1239, 1241
    dust bowl in, 1245–46, 1260–62, 1278
    farmers and, 1222, 1225, 1227, 1228, 1240,
      1243–46
    hardships of, 1224, 1225, 1228, 1236,
      1259–60, 1261, 1262–64
    Hoover's efforts at recovery, 1224–26
    human toll of, 1224, 1225, 1226, 1259–60,
      1260–62, 1262–64
    isolationism in, 1297–98
    labor movement in, 1225, 1248, 1250,
      1254–55, 1265, 1271–73, 1275–76
    market crash and, 1221–24
    unemployment in, 1222, 1224, 1228–29,
      1232, 1236, 1242, 1259
    World War I veterans in, 1228–30, 1229,
      1273–74
    see also New Deal
depression of 1893, 1023–24
DePriest, Oscar, 1185, 1218
Descent of Man, The (Darwin), 1037
desegregation, see civil rights movement;
    segregation, desegregation
Deseret, 682
Desert Shield, Operation, 1641
Desert Storm, Operation, 1641–43, 1657
Desire under the Elms (O'Neill), 1176
détente, 1585–86
Detroit, Mich.:
    racial riot in (1943), 1333
    racial riot in (1967), 1532
Dewey, George, 1048, 1055
Dewey, John, 970, 971
Dewey, Thomas E., 1308, 1358, 1404, 1406,
    1408
Dial, The, 549, 575

Diaz, Bartholomew, 17–18
Díaz, Porfirio, 620, 1119
Dickens, Charles, 509
Dickinson, Emily, 553–54, 763
Dickinson, John, 214, 232, 275
Diedrich Knickerbocker's A History of New York
    (Irving), 554
Diem, Ngo Dinh, 1479, 1519, 1520
Dien Bien Phu, Battle of (1954), 1476–77
Dies, Martin, 1276
Dillon, C. Douglas, 1507
Dingley Tariff (1897), 1028
direct primaries, 1076
disarmament and arms reduction:
    and détente, 1629
    SALT and, 1586, 1594, 1600
    after World War I, 1289
Disciples of Christ, 544
Discourse of Western Planting, A (Raleigh), 43
discovery and explorations:
    of Americas, 14–15, 17–36
    of Africa, 17–18
    biological exchange from, 21–24
    Dutch, *41*
    English, *41, 43–44
    European visions of America, 13–15
    French, 18, 25, 40, *41*, 178–79, 180–81
    Norse, 14–15
    Spanish, 18–21, *18*, 25, 31–34, *32*
    technology in, 15–16
    see also Columbus, Christopher
Discovery of the Asylum, The (Rothman), 569
disease:
    AIDS, 1627–28, *1628*
    colonists die from, 57, 110–11
    Indian susceptibility to, 23–24, 29, 79,
        86–87, 91, 94, 593
    influenza, 1156–57
    measles, 23
    and Overland Trail, 597
    among slaves, 651
    smallpox, 23, 24, 79, 94, 111
    among southern poor whites, 641
    on Southwest frontier, 658
    and voyage to America, 521
    yellow fever, 1057
disenfranchisement of blacks, in South,
        850–52, 992, 1114, 1264
Disney, Walt, 1282
Distribution Act (1836), 472
District of Columbia, *see* Washington, D.C.
divine right of kings, 50, 172
divorce, 281, 283, 1178, 1259
Dix, Dorothea Lynde, 571, 761
Dixiecrats, 1405–6, *1406*
Dixon, George Washington, 518
Dixon, Jeremiah, 96
Dixon, Thomas, 1208
DLC (Democratic Leadership Council), 1661

Doby, Larry, 1402
documentaries, 1280
Dodd, Christopher, 1676
Doegs, 62
Doheny, Edward L., 1203
Dole, Bob, 1676–79, *1677*
dollar diplomacy, 1094–95, 1118, 1121–22
Dominica, 196
Dominican Republic, 19
    immigration from, 1530, 1653, *1655*
    U.S. intervention in (1916–1925), 1067,
        1095, 1122, 1293
Dominion of New England, 169–71
dominion theory, 226
Donner, George, 600–601
Donner Party, 600–601
Doubleday, Abner, 963
Doughty, Thomas, 547
Douglas, Stephen A., 502, *694*, 710, 890
    and Compromise of 1850, 682, 686
    death of, 767
    in election of 1860, 714, 715, 716, 717, *717*
    Kansas-Nebraska issue and, 694–96
    Lecompton constitution and, 707
    Lincoln's debates with, 708–11
    and popular sovereignty on slavery, 675
Douglass, Frederick, 655, 659, 666–67, *666*,
        793
Downing, Lucy Winthrop, 113
downsizing, 1650, 1658, 1681
draft:
    in Civil War, 739–41
    in Vietnam War, 1553, 1571, 1597
    in World War I, 1136, 1142
    in World War II, 1324–25
Drake, Francis, 42, 43
Drake, Mary, 660
Drayton, Percival, 730
Dred Scott v. Sandford, 703–5, 708, 710
Dreiser, Theodore, 975–76
drugs:
    Bush's policy on, 1634
    from Americas, 23
    illegal, 1555, 1557, 1572, 1628, 1634, 1639
    patent medicines, 1090, *1090*
Duane, William J., 470
Duarte, José Napoleón, 1617, 1624
Dubinksy, David, 1271
Du Bois, W. E. B., 855–56, *855*, 1183, 1184
duels, 644–45, *645*
"due-process clause," 806, 985, 986, 1017
Dukakis, Michael, 1630–33, *1632*
Duke, James Buchanan "Buck," 842, 843, 844
Duke, Washington, 842–43
Dulany, Daniel, 209
Dulles, Allen, 1472–73
Dulles, John Foster, 1468, 1471–72, *1471*,
        1473–74, *1474*, 1476, 1478, 1479,
        1481–82, 1483, 1485, 1616

Dunkers, 37, 144
Dunlop, Albert J., 1681
Dunmore, John Murray, Lord, 232–33, 279
Duquesne, Marquis, 188
Durand, John, *148*
Durkin, Martin, 1465
Durocher, Leo, 1402
dust bowl, 1245–46, 1260–62, 1278
Dutch Americans, 94, 96, 144, *145,* 146, 156
Dutch East India Company, 89
Dutch East Indies, 1313, 1315, 1323, 1358, 1475
Dutch Empire, 26, 41, 82, 83, 89, 92, 143, 179
Dutch Reformed Church, 38, 144, 161
Dutch Republic, 41, 184
Dutch West India Company, 90
Dwight, Timothy, 539
Dylan, Bob, 1457, 1551, 1556
Dynamic Sociology (Ward), 968, 969
dysentery, 111

Eads, James B., 934
Eagleton, Thomas, 1587
Earth Day, *1583*
East India Company, 221
East St. Louis, Ill., racial riot in (1917), 1138
Eaton, John, 452
Eaton, Peggy, 452
Eaton Affair, 452
Economic Cooperation Administration (ECA), 1396
Economic Interpretation of the Constitution, An (Beard), 320
Economic Opportunity Bill (1964), 1525–26
Economic Recovery Tax Act (1981), 1612
economics, 970, 977
    Keynesian, 1274, 1277, 1327, 1387, 1466, 1612, 1680
    Reaganomics, 1611–13
    Veblen, Thorstein, on, 977
economy:
    agriculture and, 1013–14
    airplanes and automobiles in, 1209–12
    in antebellum South, 634–36
    Bush and, 1657–59, 1660
    Carter and, 1599–1600, 1605
    in Civil War, 731–33, 765, 766
    Civil War influence on, 888–89
    Clinton and, 1680–81, 1687
    in Confederation, 292–94
    consumer goods and, 1207
    in early nineteenth century, 409–14, 485–514
    in early U.S., 303–4, 334–42
    entrepreneurs in, 898–908
    Ford and, 1594
    globalization in, 1681
    Hamilton's views on, 334–42

Hayes's views on, 997
immigration as spur to, 519–20
Independent Treasury and, 478–79
investment bankers in, 905
in Jacksonian era, 448, 471, 473–74
and laissez-faire policies, 482, 985–87
in late nineteenth century, 887–97
in 1920s, 1201, 1205–6, 1207–16, 1219–21
Nixon and, 1581–83
of North vs. South, 624
and Panic of 1819, 420
"postindustrial," 1651
planned, in World War I, 1138
Reagan and, 1611–13, 1619, 1624–25, 1626–27
sea power in, 1036–37
social criticism and, 976–77
in South, 634–36, 840–41, 847–49
of Soviet Union, 1636–37, 1638–39
stock market and, 1221–24, 1625–26, 1680, 1687
transportation improvements and, 492–502
trusts in, 900–901, 1010, 1084–85, *1085,* 1087, 1097–98, 1103–4, 1109–10
Van Buren and, 478–79
after War of 1812, 405–6
of West, 581
in World War I, 1137–38
after World War I, 1158
in World War II, 1325–28, 1329, 1371
after World War II, 1376, 1383–85, 1424–25
see also agriculture; antitrust laws; banking industry; corporations, business; currency; debt; Depression, Great; industry; manufactures; tariffs and duties; trade and commerce; *specific panics and depressions*
Economy Act (1933), 1238–39
Edison, Thomas, 896, 897, *898*
Edison General Electric Company, 897
education:
    affirmative action in, 1562, 1650, 1682
    of African Americans, 814, 818, 848, 856, 1426
    agricultural, 844, 1113
    Alliance movement and, 1018
    of Asian Americans, 1068
    bilingual, 1654
    busing and, *1579,* 1659
    colleges and universities, 950–52, 1425–26
    in colonial era, 155–56
    Dewey's views on, 971
    in early U.S., 287–89
    evolution in, 1168
    federal aid to, 296, 764, 791
    of gentry, during colonial period, 127
    GI Bill of Rights and, 1425–26
    Great Society and, 1528, 1529, 1530

higher, 563–66, 950–52
immigration and, 948, 1654
in nineteenth century, 561–66, 930, 948–52
parochial, 1012
professional schools, 953
public schools, 288, 530, 561–63, 948–49
in Reconstruction, 814, 818
religion and, 161, 563, 564
school prayer and, 1508–9, 1655
secondary, 948–49
segregation and desegregation in, 1068,
    1401, 1426, 1492–94, 1509, 1511–12,
    1531, 1579–80, 1615, 1682
in social reform, 543–44, 561
in South, 157, 847, 849
space program and, 1487
teaching profession and, 562
technical, 564–65
township support of, 296
vocational training, 949–50
women and, 565–66, *565*, 571, 951–52
see also colleges and universities
Educational Amendments Act, Title IX of
    (1972), 1562
Education Department, U.S., 1597, 1630
EDVAC (Electronic Discrete Variable
    Automatic Computer), 1644, 1645
Edwards, Jonathan, 157–58, *157*, 159–60,
    289, 539
EEOC (Equal Employment Opportunity
    Commission), 1615, 1659
Egypt, 1586–87, 1594
    in Arab League, 1482
    Camp David accords and, 1598–99
    in Persian Gulf War, 1640
    in Six-Day War, 1586
    Suez War in, 1481, 1482–84
    in World War II, 1311
Ehrlichman, John, 1577, 1589, 1590
Eighteenth Amendment, 319, 1171, 1197,
    1234
Einstein, Albert, 1186–87, *1186*, 1188, 1307,
    1367, 1644
Eisenhower, Dwight D., 1424
    background of, 1464–65
    Bonus Army and, 1229–30
    brinksmanship under, 1473–74
    budget battle of, 1485
    civil rights movement and, 1492, 1494,
        1496, 1497
    Congress and, 1464, 1485, 1487
    corruption under, 1487–88
    covert actions under, 1472–73
    Cuba and, 1490–92
    dynamic conservatism of, 1465–67
    economic policy of, 1466
    and election of 1948, 1403
    in election of 1952, 1460–61, 1462–64,
        1463, 1502

in election of 1956, 1480–81
farewell address of, 1498–99
foreign alliances and, 1481–82
foreign policy of, 1471–72
Indochina and, 1476, 1477, 1478, 1479,
    1519
internal security under, 1470–71
Khrushchev's summit with, 1490
Korean War and, 1415, 1468
Little Rock crisis and, 1497
McCarthyism and, 1469–70
Middle East policy of, 1481–84
on military-industrial complex, 1457
NATO and, 1399
New Deal and, 1481
political rise of, 1461–62
religion promoted by, 1443
Sputnik and, 1486
Suez War and, 1483, 1484
U-2 summit and, 1490
Vietnam and, 1477–79
in World War II, 1338, 1346, 1347–48,
    1347, 1359, 1364
Eisenhower Doctrine, 1488
Elaine, Ark., racial riot in (1919), 1159
elderly, aging population and, 1378
elections and campaigns:
    congressional mechanisms for, 316
    fraud and intimidation in, 821–22
    gerrymandering and, 1682
    nomination process in, 431–32
    of 1789, 330–31
    of 1792, 345
    of 1796, 359
    of 1800, 243, 366–68, *367*, 373
    of 1804, 373, 383
    of 1808, 390–91
    of 1816, 414
    of 1820, 415–16, 431
    of 1824, 431–34, *432*, 437, 476
    of 1828, 436–37, *437*, *438*, 439, 444, 449,
        455, 462, 476, 524
    of 1832, 460, 467, 468–70
    of 1836, 475–76
    of 1840, 479–81, *479*, *480*, 582, 668
    of 1844, 606–8, *608*, 668
    of 1848, 676–78
    of 1852, 690–91
    of 1854, 527–28
    of 1856, 701–2, *703*
    of 1858, 709–11
    of 1860, 624, 713–17
    of 1864, 769, 796, 799, 864
    of 1868, 823
    of 1872, 827–28
    of 1874, 829
    of 1876, 829–33, *831*, 996
    of 1878, 1017
    of 1880, 997–98, 1017

elections and campaigns (*continued*)
of 1884, 997–98, 1000–1003, 1017
of 1888, 990, 1007
of 1890, 1011
of 1892, 1022, 1042, 1074
of 1894, 1024, 1026
of 1896, 838, 1024, 1025–28, *1027, 1028*
of 1900, 923, 1062, *1062*
of 1904, 923, 1089
of 1908, 1093–94
of 1910, 1097, 1101
of 1912, 923, 924, 1098–1100, 1102–5, *1104,* 1141
of 1916, 1112, 1130–32, *1131*
of 1918, 1149
of 1920, 1142, 1197–98
of 1924, 1206–7
of 1928, 1217–18
of 1930, 1225
of 1932, 1233–35, *1235, 1236*
of 1934, 1251
of 1936, 1265–66
of 1938, 1277
of 1940, 1308–9
of 1944, 1358, 1384
of 1946, 1384, 1385
of 1948, 1387, 1403, 1404–8, *1408,* 1523
of 1950, 1418
of 1952, 1460–61, 1462–63, *1463,* 1471, 1502, 1462–64
of 1954, 1523
of 1956, 1480–81
of 1958, 1487
of 1960, 1502–6, *1506*
of 1964, 1526–28, 1536, 1607
of 1966, 1607
of 1968, 1542–46, *1544,* 1555, *1556,* 1570
of 1972, 1575, 1577, 1587–88
of 1976, 1595, 1677
of 1980, 1608, 1609–11, *1610,* 1615, 1677
of 1984, 1615, 1620
of 1988, 1630–33, *1631, 1632,* 1677
of 1992, 1377, 1660–61
of 1994, 1657, 1673–75
of 1996, 992, 1676–79
platforms introduced into, 469
precinct-level organization in, 481
primaries, direct, 1076
progressive reforms in, 1076–77
voter registration drives and, 1496, 1531
voter turnout, 992, 1115, 1595, 1610–11, 1632–33
voting rights protected, 821
electoral college:
and Constitution, 317
and "corrupt bargain," 433
and election of Washington, 330
see also elections and campaigns
Electoral Commission (1877), 832
electrical motors, 504

electricity, 844, 896, 897, 1407, 1466
TVA and, 1248–51
Electronic Discrete Variable Automatic Computer (EDVAC), 1644, 1645
Electronic Numerical Integrator and Computer (ENIAC), 1643–44, *1644*
Elephant Butte Dam, 879
elevators, 930, 933
Eliot, Charles W., 951, 953, 1056
Eliot, John, 81
Eliot, T. S., 1188, 1192
Elizabeth I, Queen of England, 39, *39,* 42, 43, 44, 48, 50, 53
Elkins Act (1903), 1087, 1089
Ellis Island, *938, 939,* 940–42, *941, 942*
Ellison, Ralph, 1452–53, *1452*
Ellison, William, 647
Ellsberg, Daniel, 1574, 1589
El Salvador, 1577, 1616, 1624
emancipation:
early proposals for, 662–63
freedmen's plight after, 793–94
in northern states, during Revolutionary War, 279–80
southern economy and, 791
as war measure, 754–56
Emancipation Proclamation (1863), 753, 756, 757, 758
Embargo Act (1807), 389, 503
embargoes and blockades:
of Arab oil (1973), 1582, 1583
in Civil War, 736, 737–38, 766
against Iraq, 1640, 1641
against Iran, 1601–2
in Napoleonic Wars, 387–92
before Revolutionary War, 209–10
against South Africa, 1636
in World War I, 1125–29
in World War II, 1301–2, 1313–14
Emergency Banking Relief Act (1933), 1238, 1239, 1241
Emergency Committee for Employment, 1225
Emergency Farm Mortgage Act (1933), 1239, 1240
Emergency Immigration Act (1921), 1165
Emergency Relief and Construction Act (1932), 1227
Emerson, Ralph Waldo, 444, 445, 549–50, *549,* 551, 552, 573
Brook Farm supported by, 578
on Fugitive Slave Act, 688
on John Brown, 712–13
lectures of, 509, 515, 550
on Mexican War, 620, 673–74
transcendentalism and, 549–50
employment, *see* labor, employment
Employment Act (1946), 1384–85
Employment Service, U.S., 1140
Empress Augusta Bay, Battle of (1943), 1356
Empress of China, 301

enclosure movement, 50
encomenderos, 35
encomienda, 29, 30
Endara, Guillermo, 1640
energy crisis, 1582, 1583–84, 1597
Energy Department, U.S., 1597
Enforcement Acts (1870–1871), 821
England:
  background on, 48–52
  Catholics in, 42–43, 51, 52, 64
  Civil War in, 82–84, 95, 96, 167
  colonial administration and, 102, 165,
    166–73, 205–13, 215–16
  constitution of, 48, 50, 200–201, 208
  explorations of, 18, 24–25, *41*, 43–44
  government of, 48–49, 52, 165, 173, 201–2,
    272
  landownership in, 50, 138–39
  liberties in, 48–49, 50
  monarchy of, 50, 165, 166
  nobles in, 48, 49
  privateers from, 42, 84
  Reformation in, 39–40
  Scotland joined with, 52
  Spanish Armada defeated by, 42–43, *42*
  taxation in, 48, 50, 52, 176, 206
  traders from, 33
  after Wars of the Roses, 17
  see also Great Britain
English Civil War (1642–1646), 82–84, 95,
  96, 167
ENIAC (Electronic Numerical Integrator and
  Computer), 1643–44, *1644*
Enlightenment, 152–56, 537–38, 547
Enola Gay, 1369
entail, 344
entrepreneurs, 898–908
  see also specific entrepreneurs
environment, 1583–84, 1597
  conservation and, 1091–92, 1096, 1098
  Persian Gulf War and, 1642
  pollution and, 1581
  Watt and, 1614
Environmental Protection Agency (EPA), 1583
Episcopal church, 284, 538
Equal Employment Opportunity Commission
  (EEOC), 1615, 1659
equality:
  American Revolution and, 277–78
  Jacksonian era and, 448
  racial, 710
"equal protection" clause, 806
Equal Rights Amendment (ERA), 1180,
  1562–63, *1562*, 1615, 1661
Equal Rights party, 530
Erie Canal, 495, *496*, 522
Erie Railroad, 893, 894–95
Eries, 92
Eriksson, Thorvald, 14
Erik the Red, 14

Erskine, David, 391
Ervin, Samuel J., Jr., 1588, *1589*
Escobedo v. *Illinois*, 1509
Eskimos, 14
Espionage Act (1917), 1141
Essay on Calcareous Manures (Ruffin), 633
Essay on Human Understanding (Locke),
  153
Essex Junto, 383, 404
Estonia, 1638
Ethics in Government Act (1978), 1683
Ethiopia, 1298, 1301, 1302
European Community, 1377
European Recovery Program (Marshall Plan),
  1395–96, 1408
evangelism, 156–62, 276–77, 539–47
Evans, Hiram Wesley, 1167
Evans, Walker, 1280
Evers, Medgar, 1514
evolution, 965, *1169; see also* Darwinism
executive branch:
  constitutional separation of powers and,
    316–18
  departments established in, 331
  see also presidency
executive privilege, 349, 386–87
"Exodusters," 859–60
Ex parte McCardle, 809
explorations, *see* discovery and explorations
Explorer I, 1486
Export Control Act (1940), 1313
ex post facto laws, 319

factories:
  conditions in, 909
  electrification and, 897
  the Lowell System, 507–10
  Taylorism in, 1077–78
  see also manufactures; working class
Fair Deal, 1403–4, 1407
Fair Employment Practices Commission
  (FEPC), 1332, 1381, 1400–1401
Fair Labor Standards Act (1938), 1275
Fair Oaks (Seven Pines), Battle of (1862),
  749
Fall, Albert B., 1202–3
Fallen Timbers, Battle of (1794), 349–50
Fall River (Rhode Island) system, 509–10
Falwell, Jerry, 1608–9, 1656
Familists, 37
family:
  in colonial period, 110, 112–13
  in late twentieth century, 1651
  and life on trail, 599
  in 1930s, 1177–78
  in 1940s and 1950s, 1430–31, 1449–50
  in 1980s, 1651
  slave, 656–57
  Spock and, 1449–50
  see also marriage

Family and Medical Leave Act (1993), 1663, 1678
Farewell to Arms, A (Hemingway), 1191
farm bloc, 1214–15
Farm Bureau, U.S., 1214, 1250
Farm Credit Act (1933), 1240
Farm Credit Administration (FCA), 1240
Farmer-Labor party, 1206
farmers, *see* agriculture, farmers
Farmers' Alliances, 1017–21
Farmers' Holiday Association, 1228
Farmers' Institutes, 950
Farmers' Union, 1214
Farm Security Administration (FSA), 1275, 1280, 1328
Farm Tenant Act (1937), 1275
Farnham, Marynia, 1442
Farouk, king of Egypt, 1482
Farragut, David, 738, 769
fascism, 1296–97
fashion, 1176–77
Faubus, Orval, 1497
Faulkner, William, 1192–93, *1193*
FBI (Federal Bureau of Investigation), 1513, 1590, 1667, 1668
FCA (Farm Credit Administration), 1240
FDIC (Federal Deposit Insurance Corporation), 1240, 1633
Federal Art Project, 1257, *1257*
Federal Bureau of Investigation (FBI), 1513, 1590, 1667, 1668
Federal Communications Commission, 1209
Federal Deposit Insurance Corporation (FDIC), 1240, 1633
Federal Emergency Relief Act (1933), 1239
Federal Emergency Relief Administration (FERA), 1242, 1257
Federal Farm Board, 1218–19, 1225
Federal Farm Loan Act (1916), 1112
Federal Farm Loan Board, 1112–13
Federal Highways Act (1916), 414, 1113
Federal Home Loan Bank Act (1932), 1227
Federal Housing Administration (FHA), 1262, 1436
Federalist, The (Hamilton, Madison and Jay), 321–22, 332
Federalists, 243, 309, 416
    Alien and Sedition Acts of, 364
    and *Dartmouth College* v. *Woodward,* 425
    decline of, 384
    in election of 1796, 359
    in election of 1800, 366–68
    in election of 1808, 391
    in election of 1816, 414
    in election of 1824, 431
    Essex Junto and, 383
    French Revolution and, 347
    land policy of, 353
    Louisiana Purchase as seen by, 379
    military spending of, 377
    Napoleonic Wars and, 390
    national bank and, 411
    officeholder conflicts and, 374, 375–76
    in ratification debate, 319, 321, 322
    Republican opposition to, 342
    Republicans' role reversal with, 406, 410
    1798 army authorization and, 363
    War of 1812 and, 404, 406
Federal Land Banks, 1214
Federal Radio Commission, 1213
Federal Reserve System, 1107–9, 1110, 1201, 1214, 1258, 1466, 1658, 1680
    creation of, 1107–8
    Glass-Owen Act and, 1107–8
    Glass-Steagall Banking Act, 1227, 1240
Federal Securities Act (1933), 1240
Federal Theater Project, 1257
Federal Trade Commission (FTC), 1109, 1110, 1201, 1240, 1275, 1487
Federal Writers' Project, 1257, 1280
Federation of Organized Trades and Labor Unions, 917
Feminine Mystique, The (Friedan), 1560–61, *1560*
feminism, 1180, 1442, 1560–63, 1615, 1659–60
Fence-Cutters' War, 877
FEPC (Fair Employment Practices Commission), 1332, 1381, 1400–1401
FERA (Federal Emergency Relief Administration), 1242, 1257
Ferdinand II, king of Aragon, 17, 18, *18*, 19
Ferguson, Miriam "Ma," 1168
Ferguson, Patrick, 265
Fermi, Enrico, 1367
Ferraro, Geraldine, 1620
feudalism, 50, 90
FHA (Federal Housing Administration), 1262, 1436
Fifth Amendment, 675, 704–5
Fifteenth Amendment, 625, 812, *815*, 834, 851, 1184
Fillmore, Millard, *686*, 692
    and Compromise of 1850, 686–88
    in election of 1856, 701, 702
Finance Department, U.S., 292
Financier, The (Dreiser), 975–76
Finland, 1289, 1311, 1392
Finney, Charles Grandison, 543, 577, 664
Finney, James "Old Virginia," 864
Finnish Americans, 94, 144
firearms:
    Brady Bill and, 1665–66
    interchangeable parts for, 505
    right to bear, 333, 1666
First Amendment, 668
First Report on the Public Credit (Hamilton), 335
Fish, Hamilton, 824

fishing, in New England, 132, *132,* 134, 138, 417
Fisk, Jim, 825
Fiske, John, 1037
Fiske, Robert, 1683–84
Fitzgerald, F. Scott, 1175, 1190, *1190,* 1278
Fitzgerald, Zelda, 1190, *1190*
Five-Power Naval Treaty (1922), 1291, 1298
Flagler, H. M., 898
Fletcher v. Peck, 384, 425
Florida, 33, 36, 86, 98, 299, 346, 378, 385, 590
  acquisition of, 417–20
  after American Revolution, 271
  British colonies established in, 202
  Civil War fighting in, 738
  in colonial wars, 186, 195, 196
  Cuban Americans in, 1567
  in election of 1876, 832
  emancipation in, 755
  exploration of, 32
  Huguenots in, 33
  immigrants in, 1653
  labor movement in, 1328
  Louisiana Purchase and, 379, 380
  population of, 1650, 1651
  real-estate boom in, 1220
  Reconstruction in, 817, 822
  secession of, 718
  Seminoles in, 463
  Spanish exploration and colonization of, 32, 87, 590
  War of 1812 and, 393, 395, 401
Florida Rangers, 263
Floyd, John, 470
flying shuttle, 503
Flynn, Elizabeth Gurley, 926
Foch, Ferdinand, 1143, 1152
folklore, African-American, 655
Folkways (Sumner), 968
Foner, Eric, 701–2
food:
  in colonial times, 131, 132, 137
  on Overland Trail, 598
  reform movements and, 566–67
  safety of, 1090–91
  of slaves, 651
  technology and, 505–6, 522, 895
Food, Drug and Cosmetic Act (1938), 1275
Food Administration, 1137, *1137*
food stamps, 1467, 1676
Foot, Samuel A., 455
Foot Resolution, 455, 457
football, 962–63
Foote, Henry S., 619
Foraker Act (1900), 1056, 1057
Foran Act (1885), 916
Forbes Road, 492
Force Bill (1833), 461, 470
Ford, Gerald, 1593–95
  appointed vice-president, 1591
  in election of 1976, 1595, 1677
  Nixon pardoned by, 1592, 1593
  presidency assumed by, 1591
  vetoes of, 1593
Ford, Henry, 1211, 1272
Ford Motor Company, 1211, *1211*
Fordney-McCumber Tariff (1922), 1201
Foreign Affairs, 1393
Foreign Affairs Department, U.S., 292
foreign policy:
  and annexation of California, 614–16
  and annexation of Texas, 605–6
  and Barbary pirates, 405
  brinksmanship, 1473–74
  containment, 1392–94, 1420, 1472, 1473, 1540, 1657
  covert actions, 1472–73
  détente, 1585–86
  dollar diplomacy, 1094–95, 1118, 1121
  good neighbor policy, 1293–94
  human rights in, 1597–98
  isolationism, 1287–94, 1297–98, 1303
  and Louisiana Purchase, 377–80
  Marshall Plan, 1394–96, 1408
  and Mexican War, 611–20
  Monroe Doctrine, 429–31, 1042
  mutual defense treaties, 1477–78
  in Napoleonic Wars, 387–92
  Open Door policy in, 1067, 1068, 1094, 1291, 1296
  progressive idealism in, 1117–18, 1146–47, 1150
  reciprocal agreements, 1298
  after Revolutionary War, 301–3
  shuttle diplomacy, 1586–87, 1594
  Truman Doctrine, 1394–96
  after War of 1812, 416–20
  see also imperialism; *specific foreign powers, presidents, treaties, wars*
Forest Reserve Act (1891), 1091–92
forfeited-rights theory, 804
Formosa, *see* Taiwan
Fort Detroit, 180, 348
Fort Donelson, 743
Fort Duquesne (Pittsburgh, Pa.), 189, 192, 204, 512
Fort Henry, 743
Fort Jackson, Treaty of (1814), 399
Fort Laramie conference (1851), 866
Fort Laramie conference (1868), 868
Fort Laramie Treaty (1851), 588–89
Fort Le Boeuf, 189
Fort McHenry, 400–401, *401*
Fort Michilimackinac, 180
Fort Necessity, 189
Fort Niagara, 192
Fort Pitt, 202
Fort Rémy, *180*
Fort Stanwix, Battle of (1777), 256

Fort Stanwix, Treaty of (1768), 204
Fort Stanwix, Treaty of (1784), 298
Fort Sumter, 719–20
  fall of (1861), 725–26
Fort Ticonderoga, Battle of (1775), 230
Fort Ticonderoga, Battle of (1777), 256
Fortune, 1280, 1423, 1450
Fort Wagner, 758–59
Foster, Stephen, 519
Foster, William Z., 1158
Four Freedoms, 1310
Fourier, Charles, 578
Four-Power Treaty (1922), 1291
Fourteen Points, 1146–48
Fourteenth Amendment, 625, 806, 808–9,
  834, 853, 982, 1184
  private property and, 985
Fox, George, 95
Foxes, 92, 462–63, 1335
France, 133, 385
  American Revolution and, 233, 242, 253,
    257–58, 260, 268, 269, 270, 271
  California and, 602
  in China, 1058, 1094
  Citizen Genêt and, 346
  in colonial wars, 183–96, 198, 199
  communism in, 1395
  cotton trade with, 454, 473, 631
  1823 Spanish incursion of, 429
  explorations of, 18, 24, 40, *41,* 178–79,
    180–81
  food technology in, 505–6
  Forty-niners from, 679
  Germany occupied by, 1396, *1397*
  after Hundred Years' War, 17
  in Indochina, 1313, 1410, 1412, 1474–79
  in Kellogg-Briand Pact, 1292
  late eighteenth-century conflict with,
    360–63, 364
  in League of Nations, 1150
  in Lebanon, 1618
  Louisiana purchased from, 378–80, 422
  Marshall Plan and, 1396
  Monroe Doctrine and, 430
  Morocco crisis and (1905–1906), 1069
  in Munich agreement, 1299
  in Napoleonic Wars, 387–92, *390,* 429, 590
  in NATO, 1398
  navy of, 268
  New World explorations and colonies of, 40,
    178–83
  Normandy invasion in, 1346–51, *1348,*
    1350
  Paris Peace Conference and, 1150
  in Persian Gulf War, 1642
  in post–World War I treaties, *1290,* 1291
  privateers from, 40, 346, 347
  in Quintuple Alliance, 429
  Revolution in, 345–47
  in SEATO, 1477

  Spanish Civil War and, 1302
  Statue of Liberty given by, 940
  in Suez War, 1481, 1483, 1484
  Texas Republic recognized by, 605
  traders from, 33
  in United Nations, 1361, 1388
  U.S. Civil War and, 737, 755, 766
  U.S. trade with, 334, 387–88, 389–90, *390,*
    391–92, 454, 473, 631
  Vichy government of, 1313, 1338, 1475
  in World War I, 1122, 1124, 1125, 1128,
    1136, 1142, 1144
  World War I debt of, 1288–89
  World War II and, 1298, 1300, 1302, 1304,
    1305, *1306,* 1309, 1338–39, 1344–45,
    1346–51, 1358–59, 1425
  XYZ Affair and, 361–62, *362*
  see also French Empire
Franciscans, 34, 35–36, 592–94
Franco, Francisco, 1299, 1302
Frankfurter, Felix, 942, 1253
Frank Leslie's Illustrated Newspaper, 560
Franklin, 298
Franklin, Battle of (1864), 781–82
Franklin, Benjamin, 119, 138, 152, *154,* 158,
  190, 196, 233, 324, 343
  at Albany Congress, 190, 191
  background of, 154–55
  Boston Tea Party condemned by, 223
  on British in Philadelphia, 255
  in colonial taxation disputes, 212
  on Constitution, 325
  at Constitutional Convention, 310
  and Declaration of Independence, 234
  as deist, 537
  land speculation of, 204
  Paxton Boys and, 219
  on peace commission, 270, *270,* 331
  Plan of Union of, 190
  on population growth, 110
  as postmaster-general, 233
Franklin, William Temple, 270
Franz Ferdinand, archduke of Austria, 1122
Frederick II (the Great), king of Prussia, 192
Fredericksburg, Battle of (1862), 752–53, 771,
  774
Frederick Turnpike, 492
Freed, Alan, 1433
Freedmen's Aid Society, 795
Freedmen's Bureau, Mississippi, 814
Freedmen's Bureau, U.S., 794–95, *795,* 805,
  813
freedom from fear, 1310
freedom from want, 1310
freedom of assembly, 333
Freedom of Information Act (1966), 1592
freedom of petition, 52, 275
freedom of religion, *see* religious freedom
freedom of speech, 275, 333, 364, 1310
freedom of the press, 364

abolitionism and, 668
in Bill of Rights, 333
in colonial era, 152
and Reconstruction, 809
freedom riders, 1511
Freeman, Mary Wilkins, 971–72
Freemen, 1668
Freeport Doctrine, 710
Free Soil party, 676–78, 690, 697, 701, 764
Free Speech Movement (FSM), 1552
free trade, *see* tariffs and duties
Frémont, John Charles, 601–2, *601*, 701
    captured slaves and, 755
    in election of 1856, 702
    Mexican War and, 614, 615
French Americans, *145*, 146, 364
    in Civil War, 738
French and Indian War (Seven Years' War),
    185, 188–92, *189*
    American soldiers in, 200
    legacy of, 199–201
French Empire, 13, 31, 82, 90, 120
    British Empire compared with, 30, 77–78,
        102, 165, 178, 182
    colonization in, 33, 40
    fur trade in, 78, 90, 179, 180, 182
    in Indian conflicts, 88, 89, 94, *179*
    Indian relations with, 178, 182, 184–85,
        202
    map of, *181, 194*
    missionaries in, 87, 180, 182
    religious restrictions in, 179
    trade in, 33, 178, 179, 182, 186–87
    see also France
French Revolution, 345–47
Freud, Sigmund, 1176, 1185
Frick, Henry C., 919, 1089
Friedan, Betty, 1560–61, *1560*, 1562, 1659–60
Friedman, Milton, 1680
Friendly Sons of St. Patrick, 523
From Here to Eternity (Jones), 1452–53
Frontenac, Louis de Baude, Count, 180
frontier, 581
    American Revolution and, 260–63
    in Civil War period, 741–43
    closing of, 883–84
    in colonial period, 146–47
    in early nineteenth century, 485
    in early U.S., 349–50
    Indian conflicts on, 866–71
    internal improvements and, 412
    in Jefferson administration, 376
    manifest destiny and, 444, 585, 607, 612
    and mountain men, 591
    Northwest Ordinance and, 297–99
    and Overland Trail, 596–600
    religious revivals on, 540–42
    and settlements, 356–57
    in 1760s, *203*
    slavery in, 674–82

southern, 657–61
statehood procedures for, 296
transportation links to, 492–93
Turner's thesis of, 883–84, 931
War of 1812 and, 393, 394
westward expansion and, 202–5, 278,
    294–97, 329, 352–57, 376, 839–40
Wilderness Road and, 204–5, 354–55
see also backcountry; West
Frost, Robert, 1507
FSA (Farm Security Administration), 1275,
    1280, 1328
FSLN (National Liberation Front)
    (Nicaragua), 1617
FSM (Free Speech Movement), 1552
FTC (Federal Trade Commission), 1109,
    1110, 1201, 1240, 1275, 1487
Fuchida, Mitsuo, 1317
Fuchs, Klaus, 1418
Fugitive, The: A Journal of Poetry, 1191, 1192
Fugitive Slave Act (1850), 687–89
    protests against, 696
fugitive slave laws, 664, 683, 687–88, 696
Fulbright, J. William, 1540
Fuller, Margaret, 549, 574–75, *575*, 578
Fulton, Robert, 427, *427*, 493
Fundamental Constitutions of Carolina,
    85–86
fundamentalism, 1168–70, 1608–9, 1615
Fundamental Orders of Connecticut (1639),
    76, 137, 172
fur trade, 81, 86–89, 91, 116, 143, 183, 187,
    188, 202, 302, 514, 590
    Dutch, 78, 89, 90, 91
    French, 78, 90, 179, 180, 182
    and mountain men, 590–91
    rendez-vous system in, 591

Gable, Clark, 1284
Gadsden, Christopher, 209, 285
Gadsden Purchase, 620, 693, *693*
Gage, Thomas, 223, 228, 231, 254
Galbraith, John Kenneth, 1447
Gallatin, Albert, 374, 376, 395, 402–3
Galloway, Joseph, 225
Galveston, Tex., 1078
Gama, Vasco da, 18, 25
gambling, 644
Gandhi, Mohandas K., 552, 1495
Garfield, James A., *564*, 826, 833, 996, 997,
    998
Garfield, Lucretia Randolph, *564*
Garland, Hamlin, 936, 954, 971
Garrison, William Lloyd, 573, 662, *662, 663*,
    667, 713
Garvey, Marcus, 1183–84, *1183*
Gaspee incident (1772), 220, 222
Gates, Bill, 1645–46
Gates, Horatio, 256, *256*, 257, 265
Gates, John W. "Bet-a-Million," 876

Gates, Sir Thomas, 56, 57
Gauguin, Paul, 1164
Gay Liberation Front (GLF), 1569
gays:
  AIDS and, 1628
  in military, 1662
  rights of, 1569–70
Gaza Strip, 1670
gender gap, 1615, 1660
General Accounting Office, 1200
General Assembly of Virginia, 59
General Court, Massachusetts, 71, 72, 74, 75
General Federation of Women's Clubs, 984
General Land Office, 1096
Generall Historie (Smith), 58
General Motors, 1383, 1465
General Sociology (Small), 969–70
General Theory of Employment, Interest and
  Money, The (Keynes), 1274
Genêt, Edmond Charles, 346
Geneva Accords (1954), 1477–79, 1519
Geneva Conventions, 1390
Geneva summit (1985), 1621, *1622*
"Gentlemen's Agreement" (1907), 1068–69,
  1165
gentrification, 1627
gentry, in southern colonies, 126–29
George I, king of England, 173
George II, king of England, 98, 166, 173, 194
George III, king of England, *199*, 201, 259, 263
  accession of, 194, 198
  on Boston Tea Party, 223
  mercenaries recruited by, 233
  ministerial changes of, 211, 212, 216
  Paine on, 234
  peace efforts and, 232, 258
George, Henry, 976
Georgia:
  African Americans in legislature of, 850
  African-American soldiers outlawed by, 279
  agriculture in, 486, 487, 630, 845
  Civil War fighting in, 738, 775, 780–83, 783
  Confederacy and states' rights in, 770
  Confederate troops from, 739–40
  Constitution ratified by, 322, *322*
  cotton in, 486, 487
  and Declaration of Independence, 278
  education in, 287–88
  emancipation in, 755
  Indian conflicts in, 299, 399
  Indians removed from, 463–64
  land claims of, 275, *295*, 298
  mining in, 635
  paper currency in, 305
  progressivism in, 1079–80
  Reconstruction in, 821, 822
  secession of, 718
  Sherman's march through (1864–1865),
    780–83
  slave trade to, 279
  suffrage in, 278, 438
  Union Loyalists in, 770, 818
  voting rights in, 278, 438, 852
  Yazoo Fraud in, 384
Georgia colony:
  backcountry of, 147
  in colonial wars, 188
  creation of, 187
  ethnic groups in, 99
  European settlement of, 98–102
  government of, 102, 166, 171
  Indians in, 86–87, 98
German Americans, 98, 99, 118, 144, *145*,
    146, 147, 186, 444, 449, 521, 525–26,
    526, 532, 642, 937
  in Civil War, 730, 738, 740, 769
  clubs of, 961
  in Democratic party, 474
  in middle colonies, 98, 144, 146
  prejudice against, 524, 527
  Prohibition and, 994, 1170
  in Socialist Labor party, 922
  westward migration and, 858
  in World War I, 1124–25, 1141, 1153
  in World War II, 1335
German Reformed Church, 38
Germantown, Battle of (1777), 255
Germany:
  American scholarship influenced by, 969
  in China, 1058, 1060, 1094
  in Morocco crisis, 1069
  occupation of, after World War II, 1396–98
  Paris Peace Conference and, 1150–52
  Reformation in, 37
  reparations from, 1151–52, 1288–89
  rise of Nazism in, 1297
  in Samoa, 1039, 1053
  Weimar Republic in, 1297
  in World War I, 1033, 1122, 1125,
    1126–29, 1132–33, 1134, 1142–44,
    1145, *1145*, 1148, 1155, 1289
Germany, East, 1397–98, 1472, 1489, 1635,
    1636
Germany, Nazi:
  Anschluss and, 1299
  atomic bombs and, 1367
  Blitzkrieg tactics of, 1305–6
  Czechoslovakia invaded by, 1299, 1304
  early aggression of, 1298–99
  Hitler's rise and, 1297
  Poland invaded by, 1304–5
  Rhineland reoccupied by, 1298
  Spanish Civil War and, 1299, 1303
  in Tripartite Pact, 1313
  war criminals of, 1389
  see also World War II
Germany, West, 1396–98
  East Germany reunified with, 1635, *1636*
  in NATO, 1398
  wartime damage in, 1425

Geronimo, Chiricahua Apache chief, 870, *871*
Gerry, Elbridge:
  at Constitutional Convention, 310–11, 316
  in ratification debate, 321
  and XYZ Affair, 361
gerrymandering, 1682
Gettysburg, Battle of (1863), 773–75
Ghent, Treaty of (1814), 402–3, 405, 416
Ghost Dance, 870
Giap, Vo Nguyen, 1477
Gibbons, Thomas, 428
Gibbons v. Ogden, 427–28
GI Bill of Rights (1944), 1382, 1425–26
Gideon v. Wainright, 1509
Gilbert, Sir Humphrey, 43–44
Gilbert Islands, 1322, 1323, 1356
Gilded Age, The (Twain and Warner), 989
Gingrich, Newt, 1674
Ginsberg, Allen, 1454, 1455, *1455*, 1456
Ginsburg, Ruth Bader, 1682
Gladden, Washington, 979
glasnost, 1635
Glass-Owen Federal Reserve Act (1913), 1107–8
Glass-Steagall Act (1932), 1227, 1240
Glidden, Joseph, 876
globalization, 1681
Glorious Revolution, 52, 166, 170–72, 176, 184, 201, 208
Goering, Hermann, *1389*
gold:
  currency and, 829, 1015, 1024–25, 1028–29, 1089, 1226, 1227, 1239, 1241, 1258, 1583
  market in, under Grant, 825–26
  in mercantile system, 167
  national debt repayments in, 823, 824–25
  paper currency redeemed in, 829
  Spanish Empire and, 19, 31, 33, 35, 36, 177
Gold Repeal Joint Resolution (1933), 1240, 1241
Gold Reserve Act (1934), 1241
gold rushes, 741, 861, *861*
  California (1848), 501, 588, 597, 678–81, *678*, 864
  Yukon, 931
Gold Standard Act (1900), 1029
Goldwater, Barry, 1526–28, *1527*, 1607
Gompers, Samuel, 917–19, *918*, 925, 1056, 1110, 1158, 1216
Gomulka, Wladyslaw, 1484
Gone with the Wind, 1284
Gonzalez, Henry B., 1567
Good, Sarah, 141
Goodbye Columbus (Roth), 1451
"good neighbor" policy, 1293–94
Goodnight, Charles, 840
Goodyear, Charles, 506
Gorbachev, Mikhail, 1621, *1622*, 1629, 1635, 1636–39, 1641

Gore, Albert, Jr., 1662, *1679*
Gorges, Sir Ferdinando, 76, 167
Gorky, Arshile, 1453
Gosiutes, 587
"Gospel of Wealth, The" (Carnegie), 903
Gould, Jay, 825, 893–94, *893*, 915, 1002
government:
  of Cherokees, 462
  during Civil War, 763–70
  Cleveland's limited view of, 1003
  contract theory of, 172, 237, 273
  of early U.S., 330–32
  English, 48–49, 52, 165, 173, 201–2, 272
  federal, strengthening of, 426–27
  of Indians, 91–92, 462, 587
  in Iroquois League, 91–92
  Locke on, 172
  New Deal and role of, 1277
  new state constitutions and, 274–75
  in occupied South, 796, 808–9
  post–Revolutionary debates on, 272–76
  progressive reforms in, 1078–79
  progressive view of, 1073
  separation of powers and, 316–19
  social change and, 969
  Theodore Roosevelt's views on, 1103
  transportation role of, 501–2
  of Transylvania colony, 204–5
  World War II and, 1372
graduate schools, 952
Graduation Act (1854), 490
Grady, Henry W., 840–41, 843
Graham, Billy, 1444, *1445*
Grand Army of the Republic, 1005, 1009
Grand Canyon National Monument, 1091
"grandfather clause," 851, 1184
Grandissimes, The (Cable), 972
Grange (Patrons of Husbandry), 1016–17
Grant, Madison, 1165
Grant, Ulysses S., 728, 769, 777, *824*
  background of, 620
  at Chattanooga, 776
  early appointments of, 823–24
  economic policy of, 824–25, 829
  in election of 1868, 823
  in election of 1872, 827–28
  in election of 1880, 997
  at Gettysburg, 773
  Lee pursued by, 777–80
  Lee's surrender to, 783–84
  in post–Civil War army, 808, 810
  scandals under, 825–27, 995
  at Shiloh, 743, 745
  at Vicksburg, 772–73
Grapes of Wrath, The (Steinbeck), 1245, 1278, 1282
Grasse, Admiral de, 268
Gray, L. Patrick, 1590
Grayson, William, 644
Great Awakening, 156–62, 276–77, 537

Great Awakening, Second, 539–47
Great Britain:
  in Bering Sea sealing dispute, 1041
  Burr Conspiracy and, 386
  California and, 602
  Canadian border and, 478
  Canadian nationalism and, 584
  Caroline incident and, 584
  in China, 1058–59, 1060, 1094
  colonial administration of, 166–73
  colonial trade with, 117, 134, 200
  in colonial wars, 183–96, 198
  cotton trade with, 389–90, 454, 473, 624,
    631, 634, 636
  and dominion theory of empire, 226
  early U.S. relations with, 302
  eighteenth-century politics of, 201–2
  French Revolution and, 345, 347
  Germany occupied by, 1396, *1397*
  and Greek civil war, 1394
  improving relations with, 416–17
  independence movements and, 1475
  Indian conflicts and, 329, 348, 394–95
  Indochina and, 1477
  industry in, 503
  Israel and, 1399
  Japanese pact with, 1289
  Jay's Treaty with, 347–49, *348*, 359, 361,
    388
  Jordan intervention of, 1488
  in Korean War, 1412
  in League of Nations, 1150
  Marshall Plan and, 1396
  in METO, 1482
  military of, 200, 207, 208, 216
  Monroe Doctrine and, 430
  Morocco crisis and, 1069
  in Munich Agreement, 1299
  in Napoleonic Wars, 345, 387–89, *390*,
    391–92
  in NATO, 1398
  navy of, 267, 388, 389, 429
  nuclear weapons and, 1392, 1518
  Oregon Country and, 429, 591, 609–11
  Panama Canal and, 1064
  Paris Peace Conference and, 1150
  in Persian Gulf War, 1642
  in post–World War I treaties, *1290*, 1291
  in Quintuple Alliance, 429
  in Samoa, 1039, 1053
  in SEATO, 1477
  slave trade and, 584
  Spanish Civil War and, 1302
  in Suez War, 1481, 1482–83, 1484
  Texas Republic relations with, 605, 606
  tribute payments by, 377
  in United Nations, 1361, 1388
  U.S. Civil War and, 737, 755, 766–67
  U.S. missiles in, 1486, 1518
  U.S. trade with, 300, 303, 304, 333–34,
    347–48, 361, 387–88, *390*, 391–92, 403,
    416, 420, 449, 454, 473, 474, 476, 630
  in War of 1812, 399, 417–18
  in World War I, 1122, 1125, 1126–27,
    1128, 1133, 1134, 1136, 1142, 1144
  World War I debt of, 1288–89
  in World War II, 1300, 1304, 1305, 1306,
    1309–13, 1318, 1336–38, 1339, 1340,
    1345, 1346, 1350, 1351, 1360, 1369,
    1425
  see also American Revolution; British
    Empire; England; War of 1812; *specific
    colonies*
Great (Connecticut) Compromise, 313–14
Great Depression, *see* Depression, Great; New
  Deal
Greater East Asia Co-Prosperity Sphere, 1313
Great Gatsby, The (Fitzgerald), 1190
Great Migration of 1630s, 70
Great Migration of African Americans, 1138,
  1181, 1437–38
Great Northern Railroad, 1086, *1139*
Great Plains, seen as desert, 857–58
Great Railroad Strike of 1877, 910–12, *911*,
  997
Great Society, 1522–30, 1544, 1581–82
Great White Fleet tour, 1069–70
Greece:
  in NATO, 1398
  U.S. post–World War II aid to, 1394, 1395
  in World War II, 1311
Greek Americans, 939, 943
Greeley, Horace, 560, 575, 578, 755–56, 827,
  828
Green, John Ruffin, 842
Green, William, 1216, 1271
Greenbackers, 849
Greenback (Independent National) party,
  1017, 1023
greenbacks, 764, 823, 824–25, 827, 1015,
  1028
Greene, Catharine, 487
Greene, Nathanael, 252, 259, 265–66, 486
Green Mountain Boys, 219, 230
Greensboro, N.C., sit-in in (1960), 1509–10,
  1510, 1511, 1550
Greenspan, Alan, 1680
Greenville, Treaty of (1795), *349*, 350, 352
Grenada invasion (1983), 1619
Grenville, George, 205, *205*, 207, 211, *212*
Grey, Sir Edward, 1126
Griffith, D. W., 1208
Grimké, Angelina, 664–65
Grimké, Sarah, 664–65
Griswald, Roger, *365*
Grovey v. Townsend, 1264
Gruening, Ernest, 1537
Grundy, Felix, 395

Guadalcanal, 1352
Guadalupe Hidalgo, Treaty of (1848), *616,* 619
Guam, 25, 1053, 1318, 1322
Guatanamo Bay, 1058
Guatemala, 29, 1121, 1473
Guinn v. United States, 1184
Guiteau, Charles, 998, 999
Gulf of Tonkin incident (1964), 1574
Gullah, 654–55
Gutenberg, Johann, 15
Gutérrez, Diego, *16*

habeas corpus, 821
   Lincoln's suspension of, 727, 767–68
Habeas Corpus Act (1863), 768
Habeas Corpus Act (1867), 809
Haber, Al, 1551
hacienda, 30
Hague declarations, 1390
Haight-Ashbury, 1557
Haiti (Saint Domingue), 19, 378, 379, 630, 1095, 1121
   immigration from, 1653, *1655*
   U.S. interventions in, 1095, 1122, 1294, 1672–73
Hakluyt, Richard, 43
Halberstam, David, 1543
Haldeman, H. R., 1577, 1590
Hale, John P., 677, 690
Haley, Bill, 1432
Half-Breeds, 995–96, 1001
"Half-Way Covenant" (1662), 140
Halleck, Henry, 745, 750, 773, 776
Hamilton, Alexander, 243, 269, 294, 316, 411, 426
   Adams administration and, 361
   Burr's duel with, 383, 385, 644
   Constitutional Convention and, 309, 311, 317, 335
   economic vision of, 334–42
   in election of 1796, 359
   and election of 1800, 366, 367
   Federalist and, 321, 332
   French Revolution and, 345, 346–47
   Jefferson compared with, 343–45
   Jefferson's continuation of programs of, 376
   land policy of, 353
   national bank promoted by, 337–40
   in ratification debate, 321, 322
   as secretary of the treasury, 331, 334–42, *334*
   1798 army authorization and, 363
   Washington's farewell and, 358
Hamilton, William, 260
Hammond, G. H., 875
Hammond, James H., 636
Hancock, John, 209, 216, 222, 229, 287
   and British customs' agents, 216

   in ratification debate, 322
   in tax protests, 209, 222
Hancock, Winfield Scott, 998
handgun regulation, 1665–66
Hanna, Mark, 1026, 1027, 1063
Hannibal and St. Joseph Railroad, 497
Hanoverian succession, 201
Hardin, John Wesley, 883
Harding, Warren G., 1066, 1105, 1155, *1199, 1205*
   appointments and policy of, 1198–1201
   corruption under, 1201–4
   death of, 1203
   in election of 1920, 1197–98
   Latin American policy of, 1293
   Washington Armaments Conference and, 1290, 1291
Hard Labor, Treaty of (1768), 204
Hargreave, James, 503
Harlan, John Marshall, 853–54
Harlem Renaissance, 1181–82
Harlem Shadows (McKay), 1181–82
Harper's Ferry, Va., 711–13
Harper's Illustrated Weekly, 560
Harper's Magazine, 560
Harper's Monthly, 973–74
Harper's Weekly, 645, 736, 965
Harriman, E. H., 1086
Harrington, Michael, 1525
Harris, Joel Chandler, 972
Harris, Townsend, 692
Harrison, Benjamin, 990, 1008–9, *1009,* 1011, 1040
   civil servant appointments of, 1009
   in election of 1888, 1007, 1008
   in election of 1892, 1023
Harrison, William Henry, 393–94, 398, 1007
   in election of 1836, 475, *475*
   in election of 1840, 479–81, *480,* 582
Harte, Bret, 971
Hartford, Treaty of (1638), 81
Hartford Convention (1814), 403–4, 456
Harvard University, 161, 951, 952, 953
hatmaking, 507
Haugen, Gilbert N., 1214
Havens, Richie, 1559
Hawaii, 1039–41, 1044, 1053
   annexation by United States, 1041
   Forty-niners from, 679
   immigrants in, 1653
   reciprocal trade agreement with United States, 1039
   statehood for, 1487
Hawkins, John, 42
Hawley-Smoot Tariff (1930), 1219, 1225
Hawthorne, Nathaniel, 536, 549, 552–53, *553, 578,* 724
Hay, John, 1059, 1060, 1064, 1065
Hayden, Tom, 1551–52, 1554–55

Hayes, Lucy Ware, 995, *995*
Hayes, Rutherford B., 830–33, *830, 831, 847,*
    849, 860, 871, 995–97, *995*
    and civil service reform, 995–97
Hay-Herrán Treaty (1903), 1065
Haymarket Affair, 916–17, 918
Hayne, Robert Y., 455, 460, 632–33
Haynes, Lemuel, *284*
Haynsworth, Clement F., 1580
Hay-Pauncefote Treaty (1900), 1064
Hays, Mary Ludwig (Molly Pitcher), 282
Haywood, William D. "Big Bill," 924
Hazard of New Fortunes, A (Howells), 974
headright system, 117, 143
Head Start, 1526
health and medicine:
    AIDS, 1627–28, *1628*
    in Civil War, 761
    in colonial era, 110–11
    education and, 565, 953
    in late nineteenth century, 930
    in Old Southwest, 659
    patent medicines and, 1090, *1090*
    of slaves, 651–52
    yellow fever and, 1057
    see also disease; drugs
health insurance, 1467–68
    health care reform and, 1664–65
    and Johnson, Lyndon, 1528–29
    Kennedy-Kassebaum bill and, 1676
    Medicaid, 1528–29, 1613, 1664
    Medicare, 1528–29, 1530, 1613, 1630,
        1664
    proposed by Truman, 1404
Hearst, William Randolph, 1044, 1045
Heisenberg, Werner, 1187
Heller, Joseph, 1452
Hell's Angels, 1559
Helluland (Baffin Island), 14
Helsinki summit (1990), 1641
Hemingway, Ernest, 973, 1190–91
hemp, 631, 792
Henderson, Clarence, *1510*
Henderson, Richard, 204
Hendrix, Jimi, 1559
Henrietta Maria, queen of England, 64
Henry VII, king of England, 17, 24, 42–43, 50
Henry VIII, king of England, 39
Henry, Joseph, 504
Henry, Patrick, 208, 211, 343
    Constitutional Convention avoided by, 309,
        321
    at Continental Congress, 225
    on national identity, 285
    in ratification debate, 321, 323–24
    as slaveholder, 280
    Virginia Resolves and, 211
Henry, prince of Portugal, 17–18
Henry Street Settlement, 980

Hepburn Act (1906), 1089, 1090
Herberg, Will, 1446
Herbert, Victor, 522
Herrán, Thomas, 1065
Hess, Rudolf, *1389*
Hessians, 233, 249, 250
Hickok, James Butler "Wild Bill," 865, 882
Hidalgo y Costilla, Miguel, 590
Higher Education Act (1965), 1530
Highway Safety Act (1966), 1530
highways and roads, 150, 355, 413, 414, 415,
    453, 492, *494,* 501
    in colonial period, 147, 150, 152, 355
    Cumberland Road, 413, 415
    in early twentieth century, 1113
    federal funding for, 410, 412, 413–14, 501,
        1436–37, 1467
    to frontier regions, 147, 204, 355, 492
    interstate highway system, 1437, 1467,
        1528, 1530
    Maysville Road, 453
    National Road, 413, 453, 492
    safety on, 1530
    state funding for, 472, 501, 1437
    turnpike boom and (1820s), 492, 501
    Wilderness Road, 204, 354–57, 492
    after World War II, 1437, 1467
Hill, Ambrose P., 749, 751
Hill, Anita, 1659
Hill, D. H., 749
Hill, James J., 1086
Hill, Joe, 926
Hillman, Sidney, 1271
Hillsborough, earl of, 215
Hine, Lewis W., 1081
Hirohito, emperor of Japan, 1315
Hiroshima, atomic bombing of (1945), 1369–70
Hispanics, 1530
    gerrymandered districts and, 1682
    gold rush and, 681
    in late twentieth century, 1652, *1654*
    rights of, 1563–67
    in Spanish America, 30, 31–32, 589,
        593–94
    westward expansion and, 858
    in World War II, 1333–34
Hispaniola, 19, 26
Hiss, Alger, 1416, 1417, 1462
History of the Standard Oil Company (Tarbell),
    1075
History of the U.S. Decision Making Process in
    Vietnam, The (McNamara), 1574
Hitler, Adolf, 1297, *1297,* 1349
    assassination attempt on, 1351
    death of, 1364
    rise of, 1297
    see also Germany, Nazi
Ho Chi Minh, 1410, 1475, 1476, *1476,* 1479,
    1540

Ho Chi Minh Trail, 1519, 1537
Hoe, Richard, 558–59
Hoe rotary press, 559
Hoff, Ted, 1645
Hoffman, Abbie, 1555
HOLC (Home Owners' Loan Corporation),
  1240
Holly, Buddy, 1433
Holmes, E. P., 813
Holmes, Oliver Wendell, Jr., 1142, 1234
Holmes, Oliver Wendell, Sr., 553
Holocaust, 1365
Holy Roman Empire, 31
homelessness, 1627
Home Owners' Loan Act (1933), 1240
Home Owners' Loan Corporation (HOLC),
  1240
Homer, Winslow, *959*
Homestead, Pa., 902, *903*
  steel strike in (1892), 919–20, 1158
Homestead Act (1862), 791, 878
homesteading, 878–82
homosexuals, *see* gays
Honduras, 1095, 1121
Hong Kong, 1058, 1653
  in World War II, 1318, 1322
Hood, John B., 781–82
Hooker, Joseph E., 771
  at Chancellorsville, 771
  at Gettysburg, 773
Hooker, Thomas, 76
Hoover, Herbert, 1173, *1219*, *1237*, 1242
  in America First Committee, 1308
  Bush compared with, 1658
  in election of 1928, 1217–18
  in election of 1932, 1234–35, *1236*
  Latin American policy of, 1294
  Manchuria invasion and, 1296
  on New Deal, 1258–59
  recovery efforts of, 1224–26, 1227
  reparations and, 1288–89
  as secretary of commerce, 1198–99, 1205,
    1212–13
  stock-market crash and, 1221
  in World War I, 1137
Hoover, J. Edgar, 1160, 1432, 1443, 1513
Hoover (Boulder) Dam, 879
Hope, Bob, 942
Hopewell, Treaty of (1785), 298
Hopewell culture, 10–11, *10*
Hopis, 12, 587
Hopkins, Harry L., 1242, 1257, 1274
Hopper, Edward, 1453
Hopwood v. Texas, 1682
Horn, Tom, 878
horses, 109, 632
  Spanish introduction of, 13, 22, 26–27, 28
House, Edward M., 1105, 1124, 1128, 1146,
  1147

House Judiciary Committee, 810
House of Commons, British, 48, *49*, 201
  American Revolution and, 258, 269
House of Lords, British, 48
House of Representatives, U.S.:
  and Bill of Rights, 333
  in Constitution, 316
  election of 1800 decided by, 368
  Jay's Treaty opposed in, 348–49
  Johnson's impeachment in, 810, *811*
  see also Congress, U.S.
House of the Seven Gables, The (Hawthorne),
  552
House Un-American Activities Committee
  (HUAC), 1276, 1416, 1462
housing:
  in antebellum South, *637*, *638*, 640
  in colonial era, 130–31, 150–51
  on frontier, 147, 356–57
  gentrification and, 1627
  GI Bill of Rights and, 1425
  in Great Depression, 1268, 1275
  for immigrants, 944
  in late nineteenth century, 933
  in 1960s, 1508, 1529
  in 1980s, 1627
  public, 1438
  segregation in, 1262, 1437
  of slaves, 637, 651
  in suburbs, 1435–36, 1448
  technological advances to, 505
  tenements, 944
  in World War II, 1329
  after World War II, 1381, 1407, 1427,
    1435–36
Housing Act (1961), 1508
Housing and Urban Development Act (1965),
  1529
Housing and Urban Development
  Department, U.S., 1529
Housing Authority, U.S. (USHA), 1275
Houston, Charles H., 1492
Houston, Sam, *604*, 605, 643, 644, 706
  and Compromise of 1850, 683
  Kansas-Nebraska Act denounced by, 696
  secession resisted by, 718
Howard University, 1218
Howe, Elias, 506
Howe, Julia Ward, 763, 982, 984
Howe, Richard, Lord, 246
Howe, Sir William, 230, 232, 246, *247*,
  248–49, 253, 254–55, 259
Howells, William Dean, 973, 974, *974*
Howl (Ginsberg), 1456, 1457
How the Other Half Lives (Riis), 937, 1075
HUAC (House Un-American Activities
  Committee), 1416, 1462
Hudson, Henry, 89, 179
Hudson Bay, 186

Hudson Bay Company, 183
Huerta, Victoriano, 1119–20, *1119*
Hughes, Charles Evan, 1079–80, 1131–32,
  1198, 1254, 1290, *1290*, 1291, 1294
Hughes, Langston, 1182
Huguenots, 33, 38, 40, 84, *145*, 146, 179
Huitzilopochtli, 9
Hull, Cordell, 1298, 1302, 1314, 1315
Hull, William, 396
Hull House, 980, 1237
human rights, 1598
  see also civil rights and liberties
Humble Romance, A (Freeman), 972
Humphrey, Hubert H., 1404, 1406–7, 1589
  in election of 1964, 1527–28
  in election of 1968, 1543–46, *1545*, 1555,
    1556
Hundred Years' War, 17
Hungarian Americans, 738, 939, 943
Hungary:
  fall of communism in, 1635
  Soviet domination of, 1472, 1481, 1484–85
  U.S. peace with, 1155
  in World War II, 1311, 1392
"Hunkers," 677
Hunt, Harriet, 574
Hunter, David, 755
hunters and gatherers, 7, 12, 27, 78
Hurons, 92, 179
Hurston, Zora Neale, 1182
Hussein, king of Jordan, 1488
Hussein, Saddam, 1640–43, 1657
Hutchinson, Anne, 74–75, 77, 548
Hutchinson, Thomas, 210, 218, 220, *221*, 222
hydrogen bomb, 1410, 1470, 1474, 1481

Iberville, Pierre le Moyne, sieur d,' 181
IBM, 1644
ICC (Interstate Commerce Commission),
  1005, 1085, 1089–90, 1098, 1110, 1201
Iceland, in NATO, 1398
Ickes, Harold L., 1246, 1274
Idaho, 741, 869
  labor movement in, 924
  sheep in, 877
  statehood for, 866, 1010
  voting rights in, 983
Illinois:
  agriculture in, 632
  German Americans in, 526
  immigrants in, 1653
  Indian conflicts in, 462, 463
  Revolutionary fighting in, 260–61
Illinois Central Railroad, 502
I'll Take My Stand, 1192
I Love Lucy, *1428*
immigration, 144–46, *145*, 1165
  and Alien Act, 364, 365, 366
  attraction of U.S. for, 937–39
  British regions in, 106–7

Constitutional Convention and, 315
of convicts, 118
Democratic party and, 1012
in early twentieth century, 1033, 1160–61,
  1164–66
Eastern European wave of, 939–40
economic growth and, 519–20
education and, 1654
Ellis Island and, *938*, *939*, 940–42, *941*,
  942
Great Migration and, 70
illegal, 1166, *1652*, 1653, 1654
in late nineteenth century, 936–48, 994
in late twentieth century, 1652–55, *1655*
nativism and, 527–28, 944–46, 994,
  1164–66
in 1960s, 1529–30
in nineteenth century, 519–28
occupations of, 942–44
Populist call for restriction on, 1022
rates of, 938–39
restrictions on, 946–48, 1160–61, 1165
  see also specific ethnic groups and countries
Immigration Act (1965), 1529–30
impeachment, 317, 318, 375
  Clinton and, 1685, 1686
  Johnson, Andrew, and 810–12, 831
  Nixon and, 1591
imperialism, 1032, 1036–41
  in East Asia, 1058–60
  European model of, 1036
  independence movements and, 1474–79
  naval power in, 1036–37, 1069–70
  Open Door policy and, 1059, 1067, 1068,
    1094, 1291, 1296
  in Pacific, 1037–41
  as quest for markets, 1036, 1052
  theory of, 1037
  trade and, 1036
  see also Spanish-American War
implied powers, 339, 379, 412, 426
impressment, 388, 402, 403
Incas, 7, 9–10, 13, 29, 31
income tax, 764, 1099, 1130
indentured servants, 62, 118–20
  Africans as, 119–20
Independence Day, 286–87
independence movements, 1474–79
independent counsels, 1683
Independent National (Greenback) party,
  1017, 1023
Independents (post–Civil War), 846, 849
Independents (religious group), 51
Independent Treasury, 478, 583, 609
India, 17, 188, 193, 473, 1475, 1477
  European voyages to, 18, 25
  immigration from, 1653, *1655*
  trade with, 416
Indiana, 350, 479, 501
Indian Bureau, U.S., 588

Indian conflicts:
  and Bacon's rebellion, 62–64
  Black Hawk War, 462
  Canada and, 349, 394–95
  in colonial period, 60, 61, 62–63, 75,
    80–82, *80,* 83, 88, 92, 94, 187, 193, 202,
    204
  in Connecticut colony, 80–81, *80,* 83
  in early U.S., 302, 329, 349–50
  French in, 88, 89, 94, *179*
  in Georgia, 299
  Great Britain and, 329, *348,* 394–95
  Jackson in, 399, 418–20, 462, 603
  in Kentucky, 355
  King Philip's War, 81–82, 187
  in New York colony, 75
  Opechancanough's campaign, 60
  Pequot War, 79–81
  Pontiac's campaigns, 193–94, 202, 208, 219
  in South, 187, 193
  Spain and, 299, 329, 351–52
  Tecumseh and, 393–95, 398
  in Virginia colony, 60, 61, 204
  War of 1812 and, 393, 396
  in West, 866–71, *867*
  Yamasee War, 187
Indian Peace Commission, 867, 871–72
Indian Removal Act (1830), 462
Indian Reorganization Act (1934), 1263–64
Indians, American, *1654*
  agriculture of, 7, 12, 78, 79, 86, 108, 587
  Americanization of, 872
  in American Revolution, 233, 256–57, 260,
    261–63, *261,* 298
  Americas settled by, 2, 5–7, *6*
  buffalo herds and, 866, 871, 873
  Catholicism and, 29, 30, 34, 35–36, 87,
    178, 180, 182, 590, 593, 594
  Christian, 219
  citizenship of, 316, 872
  in Civil War, 648, 742
  colonial trade with, 53, 79, 86–89, 98, 179
  in colonial wars, 184–85, 186
  Connecticut colony and, 76
  as cowboys, 875
  and diseases contracted from Europeans,
    23, 29, 79, 86–87, 91, 593
  Dutch relations with, 90
  in early U.S., 329
  education and, 161
  environment influenced by, 107–8
  Europeans joining societies of, 13
  forced labor of, 2, 28
  in French and Indian War, 191
  French relations with, 77–78, 178, 182,
    184–85, 202
  French vs. English relations with, 77–78,
    182
  in fur trade, 78, 86–89, 91, 94, 134,
    178–80, 590–91
  gold rush and, 681
  Jackson's policy toward, 449, 461–65
  Kansas-Nebraska Act and, 696
  language, 23
  in late twentieth century, 1652, *1654*
  and Lewis and Clark expedition, 380, *382*
  map of, *101*
  massacres of, 30, 60, 79–80, 219, 866–67,
    870
  missionaries to, 34, 35–36, 81, 87, 180,
    182, 593, 594
  in Native American movement, 1568
  in New Deal, 1263–64
  in New England, 77–82
  in New York colony, 91, 143
  Old Northwest land of, 296, 298–99
  in Old Southwest, 659
  in Pennsylvania colony, 143
  Plymouth colony and, 67
  poverty of, 1263, 1567–69
  pre-Columbian civilizations of, 7–13, *8, 11*
  Quakers' relations with, 97
  religious beliefs of, 30, 32, 34, 79
  removal of, 462–65, *465*
  reservations and, 588–89, 867–68, 871–73
  rights of, 1567–69
  as slaves, 20, 81, 82, 86, 87–88, *87,* 125,
    186
  slaves owned by, 648
  in South, 642
  technology of, 23
  and Trail of Tears, from Georgia, 463–65
  Virginia colony and, 55, 58–59, 60, 61, 63,
    204
  wagon trains and, 597
  wars on Great Plains, 866–71
  westward migration and, 858, 866
  in Wild West shows, 955, 956
  in World War II, 1334–35
  see also specific tribes
Indian Territory, 696
  see also Oklahoma
indigo, 116, 265, 630
individualism, 445, 547, 550
Indochina, 1314, 1519–20
  French in, 1313, 1410, 1412, 1474–79
  Japanese aggression in (1940–1941),
    1313–14, 1315
  nationalist movement in, 1474–79
  see also Vietnam War
Indonesia, 1475, 1477
  in World War II, 1313, 1315, 1323, 1358
Industrial Workers of the World (IWW),
    924–26, 1141
industry:
  cities and, 512–14
  in Civil War, 731–32
  corporations and, 510–11
  in early nineteenth century, 502–14, *511*
  family system in, 509–10

industry (continued)
  German Americans in, 525
  innovations in business organizations and,
    510–12, 888, 899–901, 905
  Irish Americans in, 522
  in late nineteenth century, 887–88, 930
  Lowell System in, 507–10
  mass production in, 505
  in New South, 856
  technological innovations in, 502–6, 888,
    895–897
  see also corporations, business;
    manufactures; specific industries
inflation, 889, 1010, 1015, 1028, 1581, 1582
  control of, after World War II, 1383–84
  and discovery of gold, 1028–29
  silver coinage and, 1010, 1015
  in the 1950s, 1466
  in the 1970s, 1581–83
Influence of Sea Power upon History,
    1660–1783, The (Mahan), 1036
influenza, 1156–57
initiative, right of, 1076
Innocents Abroad (Twain), 972
In re Debs, 922
Institutes of the Christian Religion, The
    (Calvin), 38
instrumentalism, 971
"Insular Cases," 1057
Intel Corporation, 1645
Interallied Conference (1917), 1146
Interior Department, U.S., 435
internal improvements, 412–14, 415, 432,
    501–2
  Constitution and, 453, 890
  Jackson on, 449, 453, 453
  John Quincy Adams's promotion of, 435
  Polk on, 609
  Tyler on, 582
  Whigs on, 474
Internal Revenue Act (1862), 764
Internal Revenue Service, 1615
International Atomic Development Authority,
    1392
International Harvester, 916, 1087
International Ladies' Garment Workers, 919,
    1271
International Workingmen's Association, 922
Internet, 1646–47
interposition, see nullification and
    interposition
Interstate Commerce Commission (ICC),
    1005, 1085, 1089–90, 1098, 1110, 1201
interstate highways
  building of, 1437, 1467
  safety of, 1528, 1530
Intolerable (Coercive) Act (1774), 223–25
inventions, 895–97
investment bankers, 905
Invisible Man (Ellison), 1452, 1452, 1453

Iowa, population of, 1650
Iran:
  CIA covert actions in, 1472–73
  immigration from, 1653, 1655
  in METO, 1482
  Soviet troops in, 1394
  U.S. hostages in, 1600–1602, 1601, 1605
Iran-Contra affair, 1621–24
Iran-Iraq war, 1618
Iraq, 1488, 1657
  in METO, 1482
  in Persian Gulf War, 1640–43
Ireland, 53
  Forty-niners from, 679
Irish Americans, 118, 144, 146, 351, 642, 937,
    943, 1001
  African Americans' animosity with, 523
  associations of, 523
  city politics and, 945
  in Civil War, 730, 740
  clubs of, 961
  in Democratic party, 474, 523
  and election of 1884, 1002–3
  immigration by, 520–24, 937
  in labor force, 522
  in nineteenth century, 516, 517, 520–24,
    521, 532
  prejudice against, 364, 522–23, 524, 527,
    528
  prohibitionism and, 994
  reasons for migration of, 520
  westward migration of, 858
  in World War I, 1124, 1153
Irish Rifles, 523
iron industry, 634
Iroquois League, 88, 89, 91–94, 92, 143, 182,
    186, 187, 191, 192, 275
  "adoption" in, 93–94
  Albany Congress and, 190
  in American Revolution, 21, 256
  in colonial wars, 183, 186–87, 192
  French conflict with, 179
  in Ohio land dispute, 204
  post–Revolutionary weakness of, 298
  Tuscaroras in, 88, 91, 186
Irving, Washington, 509, 554
Isabella I, queen of Castile, 17, 18, 18, 19
Ishii, Kikujiro, 1290
isolationism:
  disarmament and, 1289
  in Great Depression, 1297–98, 1302–3
  Kellogg-Briand Pact, 1292
  neutrality acts and (1930s), 1300–1305
  after World War I, 1287–94
Israel, 1582, 1587, 1594, 1618
  Camp David accords and, 1598–99
  founding of, 1399
  Lebanon invaded by, 1618
  Oslo accords and, 1669–70
  in Persian Gulf War, 1641–42

in Six-Day War, 1586
in Suez War, 1481, 1483–84, *1483*
Wye accords, 1670
Isthmian Canal Commission, 1065
Italian Americans, 146, 937, 939, 943, 1153
in Civil War, 738
prohibitionism and, 994
in World War II, 1335
Italy, 429
Albania seized by, 1300
communism in, 1395
Ethiopia conquered by, 1298, 1301, 1302
explorers from, 24
Greece and Libya attacked by, 1311
in League of Nations, 1150
in Lebanon, 1618
Mussolini's rise to power in, 1296–97
in NATO, 1398
Paris Peace Conference and, 1150, 1151
in post–World War I treaties, *1290,* 1291
rise of fascism in, 1296–97
in Tripartite Pact, 1313
U.S. missiles in, 1486, 1518
in World War I, 1122, 1123, 1142
in World War II, 1306, 1311, 1318, 1339,
1341–42, 1364, 1391, 1392
Iwo Jima, 1366
IWW (Industrial Workers of the World),
924–26, 1141

Jackson, Andrew, *419, 451, 458, 482,* 1078
abolitionist literature and, 668
appointments of, 450–51
assessment of presidency of, 481–82
background of, 449–50
Calhoun's rift with, 457–59
California annexation and, 602
on debt, 449, 472
in duel, 644
Eaton Affair and, 452
in election of 1824, 432, *432*
in election of 1828, 436–40, *437, 438, 439,*
444, 449, 462, 476, 524
in election of 1832, 468–70
and election of 1836, 475
and election of 1844, 606
in Florida campaign, 418
Houston and, 605
inauguration of, 448–50, *449*
in Indian conflicts, 399, 418–20, 462, 603
Indian policy of, 449, 461–65
internal improvements and, 449, 453, *453*
Irish-American support of, 523
land policy of, 472–73
national bank issue and, 449, 465–74, *468,*
474, 482
nullification issue and, 457, 460, 470, 474,
582–83
Polk compared with, 608
tariff issue and, 435–36, 449, 460, 461, 470

ten-hour workday and, 531
in War of 1812, 398–99, 401–2, *402,* 404
Jackson, Frankie "Half Pint," *1174*
Jackson, Helen Hunt, 871
Jackson, Henry, 1589
Jackson, Jesse, 1402, 1620, 1630
Jackson, Rachel, 436–37, 448, 452
Jackson, Thomas "Stonewall," 749
at Antietam, 751
background of, 620
at Chancellorsville, 771–72
at first Bull Run, 735, 736
nickname given to, 735
at second Bull Run, 750
Jackson State College, 1573
Jacobins, 346
Jacobs, George, 142
Jacobs, Harriet, 652
Jagger, Mick, 1559
Jamaica, 20, 83–84
immigration from, 1653, *1655*
James I, king of England, 48, 50, *51,* 53, 66,
173
James II, king of England (duke of York), 52,
91, *170*
accession of, 169
colonization and, 91, 96, 97, 169, 170
France policy of, 183–84
overthrow of, 170–72, 201
James, Frank, 791
James, Henry, 974–75, *974*
James, Jesse, 791
James, William, 970–71, *970,* 974, 1056
Jamestown colony, 36, 55, 57, 58, 119, 126,
144
Japan:
Asian expansion of, 1289–90, 1292, 1298,
1313–15
atomic bombing of, 1367–71
in Bering Sea sealing dispute, 1041
in China, 1058, 1059, 1060, 1067
China invaded by, 1289–90, 1295–96, *1295,*
1299, 1303–4, *1303,* 1313, 1314, 1315,
1409
early twentieth-century relations with,
1068–69
Great White Fleet in, 1069–70
immigration from, 1165
Kamikaze units from, 1358
in League of Nations, 1150
opening of, 692, *692,* 1058
Paris Peace Conference and, 1289
Pearl Harbor attack of, 1315–18, *1316,*
1317, 1323, 1337
in post–World War I treaties, *1290,* 1291,
1298
in Russo-Japanese War, 1067–68, *1069,*
1363
in Sino-Japanese War, 1058
surrender of, 1370–71, 1381

Japan (continued)
  trade with, 1315
  in Tripartite Pact, 1313
  U.S. occupation of, 1392, 1420
  war criminals of, 1389–90
  in World War I, 1122, 1145, 1339
  in World War II, 1322–24, 1336, 1339,
    1352–58, 1360, 1362, 1363, 1366–67,
    1475, 1643
Japanese Americans, 1068
  in World War II, 1335–36, 1335
Jasper Greens, 523
Jaworski, Leon, 1590
Jay, John, 332
  background of, 331–32
  Federalist and, 321, 332
  land policy of, 353
  on peace commission, 270, 270, 331
  in ratification debate, 321, 322
  treaty negotiated by, 347–49
  Washington's farewell and, 358
Jayhawkers, 741
Jay's Treaty (1795), 347–49, 348, 359, 361,
  388
Jazz Age, 1173, 1174–75
Jazz Singer, The, 1175, 1208
Jefferson, Thomas, 224, 226, 227, 242, 243,
  289, 308, 343, 344, 374, 391, 409, 424,
  486, 503, 508, 669, 932, 1475
  and Alien and Sedition Acts, 365
  background of, 343
  Barbary pirates and, 377
  Burr Conspiracy and, 386
  in colonial protests, 224, 227
  on Constitutional Convention, 310, 318
  debt issue and, 337
  on debt of gentry, 127
  Declaration of Independence drafted by,
    234–38, 235, 278, 536
  as deist, 537
  domestic reforms of, 376–77
  as early Republican leader, 342, 343
  economic policies of, 339, 344, 376–77, 503
  education efforts of, 288, 564
  in election of 1796, 359
  in election of 1800, 243, 366, 367, 367, 373
  in election of 1804, 373
  exploration of West promoted by, 380–83
  on foreign alliances, 358
  French Revolution and, 345, 346, 347
  Hamilton compared with, 343–45
  inauguration of, 371–73
  internal improvements and, 413
  land policy and, 296, 297, 353
  Louisiana Purchase and, 377–80
  on Missouri Compromise, 424
  on Monroe, 415
  Monroe Doctrine and, 430
  Napoleonic Wars and, 387, 388, 389, 390
  national bank and, 339, 376

  on religious freedom, 284
  second Washington term urged by, 345
  as secretary of state, 331
  on Shays's Rebellion, 307–8
  as slaveholder, 280
  on territories, 296
  on Whiskey Rebellion, 351
  on women's rights, 283
Jeremiah, Thomas, 279
Jericho, 1670
Jesuits, 34, 180
Jewett, Sarah Orne, 971
Jews, 86, 99, 125, 145, 146, 525, 939, 943,
  945
  in Democratic party, 993, 994
  Holocaust and, 1365
  immigration of, 939, 943, 945
Jim Crow (minstrel character), 518
"Jim Crow" policies, 852, 852
  see also segregation, desegregation
Job Corps, 1525–26
Jodl, Alfred, 1364
Joffre, Joseph, 1136
John Birch Society, 1526
John F. Slater Fund, 847–48
Johns Hopkins University, 952
Johnson, Andrew, 767, 800, 1522
  assassination plot on, 798
  congressional conflicts with, 804–5
  in election of 1864, 769, 799
  impeachment and trial of, 810–12, 831
  Pacific policy and, 1037, 1038
  Radical Republicans' conflict with, 799,
    806, 807, 807, 810–12
  Reconstruction plans of, 799–803, 804
Johnson, Hiram, 1080
Johnson, Hugh S., 1246
Johnson, James Weldon, 1158, 1182, 1184–85
Johnson, Lyndon B., 1496, 1524
  affirmative action and, 1681
  antipoverty efforts of, 1378, 1522, 1525–26,
    1528–30, 1544, 1568, 1581
  background of, 1522–23
  civil rights and, 1522, 1531
  elected to Senate, 1407
  in election of 1960, 1505
  in election of 1964, 1526–28
  and election of 1968, 1542, 1554, 1555
  Great Society and, 1522–30
  Kennedy assassination and, 1521, 1521
  Vietnam War and, 1376, 1535–43, 1542,
    1577, 1582
  war on poverty of, 1525–26, 1528
Johnson, Natchez William, 646
Johnson, Richard M., 395
Johnson Debt Default Act (1934), 1289, 1310
Johnston, Albert Sidney, 644, 743, 744–45
Johnston, Joseph E., 735, 773, 776, 783
  at Chattanooga, 776
  at Seven Pines, 749

Sherman's march countered by, 780–81
surrender of, 784
Joint Chiefs of Staff, 1473, 1515, 1519
Joint Committee on Reconstruction, 803, 804, 805, 806
Joint Committee on the Conduct of the War, 767
Joint Committee on the Economic Report, 1385
joint-stock companies, 49–50
Jolliet, Louis, 180, *181*
Jolson, Al, 942, 1208
Jones, James, 1452
Jones, Jehu, 646
Jones, John Paul, 267–68
Jones, Paula, 1684–85
Jones Act (1916), 1056, 1057
Jordan:
    in Arab League, 1482
    in Six-Day War, 1586
Jordan, David Starr, 1056
Joseph, Nez Percé chief, 869–70, *870*
Joyce, James, 1189
Jubilee Convention (1913), 1084
judicial review, 306, 318, 319, 425
Judiciary Act (1789), 375
Judiciary Act (1801), 368, 374
Julian, George W., 767, 794, 803
Jungle, The (Sinclair), 1091
Jurgen (Cabell), 1176
juries, 1264
Justice Department, U.S., Civil Rights Division of, 1496
juvenile delinquency, 1431–32

Kadar, Janos, 1485
Kamikaze units, 1358
Kanagawa, Treaty of (1854), 692
Kansas:
    African Americans in, 859, 860
    agriculture in, 1017
    cattle industry in, 874
    Civil War fighting in, 741
    populists in, 1020
    segregation in, 1493
    voting rights in, 983
Kansas Freedmen's Relief Association, 860
Kansas-Nebraska Act (1854), 694–96, 695, 697, 702, 705
    proposed by Douglas, 694–96
    violence in Kansas and, 697–99
    violence in Senate and, 699–701
    Whig party destroyed over, 697
Kansas Territory, 33
    Civil War fighting in, 741
    creation of, 693–94
    Lecompton constitution in, 705–7, 711
    settlement of, 697–99
    slavery issue and, 694–96, 697–99, 705–7

statehood for, 698
violence in (1856), 698–99
Kant, Immanuel, 547
Kassebaum, Nancy, 1676
Katyn Forest massacre (1940), 1362
Kay, John, 503
Kearney, Dennis, 912, 946
Kearny, Stephen, 615, 616
Keating-Owen Child Labor Act (1916), 1113
Keats, John, 1448
Kelley, Florence, 1081–82
Kelley, Oliver H., 1016
Kellogg, Frank B., 1292
Kellogg-Briand Pact (Pact of Paris) (1928), 1292, 1296, 1390
Kelly, Walt, 1687
Kelly Act (1925), 1209–10
Kemp, Jack, 1678
Kennan, George F., 1392–94, *1393*, 1420, 1485, 1540
Kennedy, Anthony, 1682
Kennedy, Edward M., 1676
Kennedy, Jacqueline, *1507, 1521, 1522*
Kennedy, John F., 1487, 1492, 1550, *1578*, 1616, 1627, 1661
    assassination of, 1521–22, 1543
    background of, 1502–3
    cabinet of, 1506
    civil rights and, 1509, 1513, 1514
    Cuban missile crisis and, 1516–18
    in election of 1960, 1502–6, *1506*
    foreign policy of, 1515–20
    health of, 1503
    inauguration of, *1507, 1507*
    New Frontier and, 1503–4, 1508
    Nixon's debate with, 1504–5, *1504*
    poverty and, 1525
Kennedy, Joseph, 1503
Kennedy, Joseph, Jr., 1503
Kennedy, Robert, 1505
    assassination of, 1543
    as attorney general, *1507*, 1509, 1511, 1513, 1518
    Chavez and, 1566, 1567
    in election of 1968, 1542, 1543
Kent State University, 1573–74, *1573*
Kentucky, 204, 262, 298, 303, 329, 349, 354, 356, 492
    admitted to union, 357
    agriculture in, 630, 631, 844
    Civil War fighting in, 743, 745–46, 755
    debtors in, 570
    Indian conflicts in, 355
    Indian lands ceded in, 299
    Indian removal and, 462
    post–Civil War anarchy in, 791
    religious revivals in, 541
    secession debate in, 727–28
    settlement of, 354–57
    slavery referendum in, 641

Kentucky (continued)
  statehood for, 357
  tariff issue and, 435
  voting rights in, 438
Kentucky Resolutions (1798 and 1799), 365, 366, 456
Kerouac, Jack, 1454, 1455, 1456, 1457
Kerr, Clark, 1552
Kerr-Smith Tobacco Control Act (1934), 1244
Key, Francis Scott, 401
Keynes, John Maynard, 1274, 1277, 1327
Keynesian economics, 1274, 1277, 1327, 1387, 1466, 1612, 1680
Keystone Studios, 1208
KGB, 1637
Khmer Rouge, 1594
Khomeini, Ayatollah Ruhollah, 1600–1601
Khrushchev, Nikita, 1484, 1489–90, 1490, 1492, 1515, 1517, 1518
  and crises in Berlin, 1489–90, 1515
  and Cuban missile crisis, 1516–18
  and U-2 summit, 1490
Kickapoos, 92
King, Martin Luther, Jr., 552, 1495, 1505, 1531, 1535, 1564, 1597, 1630
  assassination of, 1543, 1554
  background of, 1495
  economic issues and, 1535
  "Letter from Birmingham City Jail" of, 1512–13
  in March on Washington, 1513, 1514–15
  in Montgomery bus boycott, 1495–96, 1509
  SNCC estrangement from, 1533
  and Southern Christian Leadership Conference (SCLC), 1496, 1510
King, Rufus, 383, 391, 414
King George's War (War of the Austrian Succession) (1744–1748), 184, 185, 187–88
King Philip's (Metacomet's) War, 82, 187
King's College (Columbia University), 161, 952, 1554–55, 1555
King's Mountain, Battle of (1780), 265
King William's War (War of the League of Augsburg) (1689–1697), 184–86, 185
Kiowas, 587, 589, 867
Kipling, Rudyard, 1054–55
Kissinger, Henry, 1578, 1586
  Vietnam and, 1571–72, 1575, 1578, 1593
KKK (Ku Klux Klan), 819–20, 820, 1111, 1166–68, 1167, 1400, 1494, 1666
Kleindienst, Richard, 1590
Kline, Franz, 1453
Knapp, Seaman A., 844, 950
Knight, Amelia, 597
Knights of Labor, 913–15, 916, 919, 1021
Knights of the White Camellia, 820
Know-Nothing (American) party, 527–28, 528, 697, 701

Knox, Frank, 1307
Knox, Henry, 363
Knoxville Road, 492
Koiso, Kuniaki, 1357
Konoye, Fumimaro, 1314, 1315
Korea:
  division of, 1411
  immigration from, 1530, 1653, 1655
  independence of, 1346
  Japan in, 1067, 1068
  Russo-Japanese rivalry over, 1067–68
Korean Americans, 1068
Korean War, 1411–15, 1413, 1424, 1474, 1476, 1498, 1553
  armistice in, 1467–68
  casualties of, 1416
  and election of 1952, 1461, 1463
  Red Scare and, 1416
Koresh, David, 1667
Kosovo, 1672
Krutch, Joseph Wood, 1447
Ku Klux Klan (KKK), 819–20, 820, 1111, 1166–68, 1167, 1400, 1494, 1666
Ku Klux Klan Act (1871), 821
Kuomintang, see China, Nationalist
Kurile Islands, 1363
Kuwait, 1640–43, 1642

labor, employment:
  American Revolution and, 277–78
  child, 510, 531, 1081, 1081, 1111, 1113–14, 1200, 1247, 1248, 1276
  in colonial cities, 149
  currency issue and, 1024
  in early nineteenth century, 509
  eight-hour workday, 914, 916, 918, 1022, 1082, 1114
  of immigrants, 522, 942–44
  professionalism and, 953
  in southern colonies, 118–19
  ten-hour workday, 531, 1082
  of women, 114–15, 508–9, 510, 574, 762, 981–82, 1081–82, 1138, 1139–40, 1181, 1330–31, 1331, 1441–42, 1563, 1582, 1651
  working conditions of, 508–10
  in World War I, 1138–40
  after World War II, 1384–85
  see also indentured servants; slaves; working class
labor movement, 909–26
  anarchism and, 915–17
  Catholic views on, 980
  and Clayton Anti-Trust Act, 1109
  closed shop in, 1089, 1385
  corruption in, 1487–88
  disorganized protest and, 909–10
  in early nineteenth century, 529–32
  eight-hour workday and, 914, 916, 918, 1022, 1082, 1114

in Great Depression, 1225, 1248, 1250, 1254–55, 1265, 1271–73, 1275–76
and Great Railroad Strike of 1877, 910–12
Hayes's policies toward, 997
Haymarket Affair, 916–17, 918
Knights of Labor in, 913–15, 916, 919, 1021
minimum-wage laws and, 1082, 1200, 1269, 1270, 1275, 1381, 1407, 1466, 1659, 1675
NAFTA opposed by, 1663
in 1920s, 1215–16
in 1980s, 1615
in 1990s, 1681
open shop and, 1215–16
permanent unions and, 912–13
Pullman Strike and, 919, 920–22, *921*, 1024
"right-to-work" laws and, 1328, 1386, 1487
"Sand Lot" incident in, 912
socialism and, 922–24
strikes and, 529, 910–12, 915, 919–20, *921*, 925, *925*, 1058, 1086–87, 1271–72, 1383, 1566
ten-hour workday and, 531, 1082
trust laws and, 1110
UFW and, 1565–67
violence and, 910–11, 916–17, 924
Wobblies in, 924–26, 1141
women in, 912
in World War I, 1140
after World War I, 1158
in World War II, 1328
after World War II, 1383–84, 1385–86
see also working class; *specific unions*
Labrador (Markland), 14, 417
Lafayette, marquis de, 267
Laffer, Arthur, 1612
La Follette, Robert M., 1079, *1079*, 1098, 1206–7
La Follette, Robert M., Jr., 1272
La Follette Seamen's Act (1915), 1111
Lagunas, 587
Laird, Melvin, 1578
Lake, Anthony, 1669
Lakota Sioux, 589
Lamar, Mirabeau Bonaparte, 605
Land Act (1796), 353–54
Land Act (1800), 354, 420–21, 488
Land Act (1804), 354
Land Act (1820), 488
land grants:
    for colleges, 764, 791
    for railroads, 502, 791, 890
Landon, Alfred M., 1265–66, 1404
landownership:
    and confiscation of Loyalist estates, 272, 278, 302–3, 425
    in England, 50, 138–39
    European view of, 108

in late nineteenth century, 1012–13, 1014
in New England, 138–39
in North Carolina, 640
in Virginia colony, 59, 62
land policy, 583
    African Americans and, 793, 794, 800–801, 816
    agriculture and, 878–81
    under Articles of Confederation, 294–97
    in California, 593, 594
    under Cleveland, 1004
    in colonial period, 117–18, 143
    in Confederation, 294–99
    Congress and, 352, 353–54, 490, 583
    in early nineteenth century, 488–90
    in early U.S., 352–57
    Foot Resolution on, 455
    for freedmen, 793–95, 800–801, 816
    headright system and, 117, 143
    Homestead Act and, 791
    Indians and, 871–73
    under Jackson, 472–73
    Morrill Land Grant Act and, 764, 791
    in New England, 129–30
    railroads and, 502, 791, 879, 890, 1004
    range wars and, 876–77
    Reconstruction and, 793, 794, 800–801, 808, 816
    Revolution and, 278
    in southern colonies, 117–18
    in Southwest, 659
    for surveys and sales, 117, 353–54, 472–73, 488, 659
    in Texas, 603
    under Van Buren, 478
Landrum-Griffin Labor-Management Act (1959), 1487
land speculators, 188, 202, 353, 354, 421, 472–73
Lane Theological Seminary, 527, 664
Lange, Dorothea, 1280
Lanham Act (1940), 1329
L'Anse-aux-Meadows, 14
Lansing, Robert, 1124, 1127, 1128, 1290
Lansing-Ishii Agreement (1917), 1290
Laos, 1475, 1476, 1477, 1519, 1537, 1575
    immigration from, 1653
Larkin, Thomas O., 594, 611
La Salle, Robert Cavalier, sieur de, 181, *181*
las Casas, Bartolomé de, 30
Latin America:
    Alliance for Progress, 1508
    dollar diplomacy in, 1094–95, 1121–22
    "good neighbor" policy with, 1293–94
    immigration from, 1649
    liberation of, 429
    Monroe Doctrine, 429–31, 1042, 1066, 1067
    Reagan and, 1616–18
    see also specific countries

Latrobe, Benjamin, 277, 357
Lattimore, Owen, 1418
Latvia, 1638
Laud, William, 50, 166
Laud Commission (Lords Commissioners for Plantations in General), 166
Laurens, Henry, 270
Lawrence, Kans.:
  Civil War destruction of, 741, 742
  proslavery violence in (1856), 698
Lawrence, Mass., textile strike in (1912), 925
Lazarus, Emma, 940
League of Nations, 1131–32, 1146, 1150–51, 1154, 1198, 1287, 1289, 1296, 1297, 1361, 1399
League of Women Voters, 1180
League to Limit Armament, 1130
Leary, Timothy, 1557, 1559
Lease, Mary Elizabeth, 1020–21, 1020
Leather-Stocking Tales, The (Cooper), 554
Leaves of Grass (Whitman), 552, 557–58
Lebanon:
  in Arab League, 1482
  Iran-Contra affair and, 1622
  U.S. interventions in, 1488, 1618
Lecompton Constitution, 705–7, 711
Le Duc Tho, 1575
Lee, Charles, 260, 265
Lee, Henry, 259, 351
Lee, Richard Henry:
  and Bill of Rights, 332
  at Continental Congress, 234, 275
  in ratification debate, 321
Lee, Robert E., 749, 755, 777, 784, 951
  at Antietam, 751
  background of, 620
  at Chancellorsville, 771–72
  Confederate side chosen by, 729
  estate of, 794
  at Fredericksburg, 752
  at Gettysburg, 773–75
  Grant's pursuit of, 777–78
  at Harper's Ferry, 712
  surrender of, 783–84
legal system:
  Admiralty courts in, 172, 206, 208, 213, 218
  in colonial period, 174
  in Constitution, 318
  education and, 565, 953
  English, 48–49
  judicial nationalism in, 424–28
  judicial review in, 306, 318, 319, 425
  and Judiciary Act of 1801, 368
  testimony of African Americans in, 802
  U.S., establishment of, 331
  see also Supreme Court, U.S.
Legal Tender Act (1862), 764
legislatures, in colonial period, 174

Leigh, Vivien, 1284
Leisler, Jacob, 171
LeMay, Curtis, 1545
Lemke, William, 1265
lend-lease program, 1310–11, *1310*
Lenin, V. I., 922, 1145
Leopard incident, 389
Leslie, Frank, 560
Leslie, Mrs. Frank, 1180
Lesseps, Ferdinand de, 1064–65
"Letter from Birmingham City Jail" (King), 1512–13
Letter on the Equality of the Sexes and the Condition of Women (Grimké), 665
Letters of a Pennsylvania Farmer (Dickinson), 214
leveraged buyouts, 1624–25
Lever Food and Fuel Control Act (1917), 1137
Levitt, William, 1435–36
Levittowns, 1435–36, 1443
Lewinsky, Monica, 1685–86
Lewis, John L., 1271, 1328, 1383
Lewis, Meriwether, 380–82, *381*, 382
Lewis, Sinclair, 1173
Lexington, Battle of (1775), 228, *228*, 229, 229
Lexington, U.S.S., 1323
Leyte Gulf, Battle of (1944), 1357–58
Liberator, The, 662, 663
Liberia, 662
Liberty Loan Act (1917), 1136
liberty of contract, 986
Liberty party, 607, 668, 677
  Free Soil party and, 677
Libya, 1311, 1339
licensing, professional, 953
Life, 1440, *1441*, 1486
Life and Adventures of a Female Soldier (Snell), 282
Life Is Worth Living, 1444
Life on the Mississippi (Twain), 973
Lilienthal, David E., 1250
Liliuokalani, queen of Hawaii, *1040*
Lincoln, Abraham, 709–10, *750*
  assassination of, 798
  background of, 708–9
  and Battle of Petersburg, 779
  in Black Hawk War, 463
  border states held by, 727, 728
  cabinet and appointments of, 725, 808
  on Chattanooga, 776
  civil liberties curtailed by, 767–68
  Douglas's debates with, 708–11
  between election and inauguration, 719, 723
  in election of 1860, 624, 714–17, *716*, *717*
  in election of 1864, 769
  emancipation and, 754–56, 757
  and first Battle of Bull Run, 734, 736

first inauguration of, 724–25
McClellan's antagonism with, 748, 749–50, 752
Mexican War opposed by, 612
military strategy of, 736, 741, 745, 776
and outbreak of Civil War, 726
railroads and, 890
Reconstruction plans of, 796, 797–98, 801
secession and, 719
in senatorial election (1858), 708–11
slavery issue and, 674, 708–11, 714–15, 720, 724, 754–56
Union command structure and, 745, 746–47, 749–50, 752, 771, 776
on Union control of Mississippi, 775
on use of African-American soldiers, 759
and western fighting, 741
on Wilmot Proviso, 674
Lincoln, Benjamin, 263, 306
Lincoln, Mary Todd, 730
Lindbergh, Charles A., Jr., 1210–11, *1210*, 1308
line-item veto, 1674
literacy tests, 851, 1531
literature:
  antislavery, 689
  in Great Depression, 1278–80
  Harlem Renaissance and, 1181–82
  local colorists in, 971–72
  in mid-twentieth century, 1451–53, 1454–57
  modernist, 1188–91
  naturalism in, 975–96
  in nineteenth century, 547, 552–60
  realism, 969–76
  romanticism in, 547–52
  southern, 554–55
  Southern Renaissance, 1191–94
  transcendentalism and, 548–49
  women and, 558
Lithuania, 1300, 1638
Little Bighorn, Battle of (1874), 868–69, *869*
Little Richard, 1433
Little Rock, Ark., desegregation in, 1497, *1497*
Litvinov, Maxim, 1298
Livingston, Edward, 470
Livingston, Margaret, 281
Livingston, Robert R., 234, 378, 379, 427, *427*, 493
Livingston family, 344
Lloyd, Henry Demarest, 976–77, 1075
Lloyd Georges, David, 1150, 1151–52
local colorists, 971–72
Lochaber, Treaty of (1770), 204
Lochner v. New York, 1082
Locke, John, 85, 153, 161, 172, 208, 237, 310
Locofocos, 530
Lodge, Henry Cabot, 946, 951, 1036, 1046, 1150–51, 1153, 1154–55, 1201, 1520

Logan, George, 362
Logan Act (1799), 362
Log College, 158, 161
London, Jack, 975
London, Treaty of (1915), 1150
London School of Medicine for Women, 574
Lonely Crowd, The (Riesman), 1448
Long, Huey P., Jr., 1252–53, *1252*, 1265
Longfellow, Henry Wadsworth, 553
"Long Parliament," 50–51
Longstreet, James A., 749, 773, 774, 818
Longview, Tex., racial riot in (1919), 1158–59
Longworth, Alice Roosevelt, 1199, 1204
Lon Nol, 1572
Look Homeward, Angel (Wolfe), 1173, 1192–93
Looking Backward, 2000–1887 (Bellamy), 977
Lords Commissioners for Plantations in General (Laud Commission), 166
Lords of Trade and Plantations (Board of Trade), 168, 169, 172–73, 174, 190, 204
Lords Proprietors, 84, 85
Lorenz, Pare, 1282
Los Angeles, Calif., 931, 1329, 1333, 1653
lost generation, 1190
Louis XI, king of France, 17
Louis XIV, king of France, 180, 181, *184*, 186
Louis XVI, king of France, 345
Louisbourg, attack on, 192, *192*
Louisiana, 422
  agriculture in, 486, 844, 845
  in election of 1876, 832
  Reconstruction in, 796, 801, 815, 817, 822, 833
  secession of, 718
  segregation in, 853
  slave trade in, 651
  voting rights in, 851
Louisiana Purchase (1803), 377–80, 462, 512, 694
  boundaries of, 378–79, 417, 419–20
  exploration of, 380–83
  slavery in, 422
Louisiana territory, 33, 180–83, 191, 346, 378, 422, 462
  border of, 420
  Burr Conspiracy and, 386
  French settlement of, 181–82
  Jefferson's purchase of, 377–80
  name of, 181
  northern border of, 417
  in Peace of Paris, 195–96
  Texas and, 378–79
  War of 1812 and, 401–2
Louisville and Portland Canal, 513
Lovejoy, Elijah P., 667
"Love Song of J. Alfred Prufrock, The" (Eliot), 1189
Lowell, Francis Cabot, 507, 563

Lowell, James Russell, 325, 553
Lowell, Josephine Shaw, 762
Lowell system, 507–10
Low Horn, Blackfoot chief, 587
Loyalists (Tories), 221
  in American Revolution, 228, 232–33,
    250–51, 252, 255, 256, 259, 260, 261,
    261, 262, 263, 265, 266, 279
  after American Revolution, 273
  confiscated estates of, 272, 278, 302–3, 425
Lublin Committee, 1362
Lucas (Pinckney), Eliza, 116
Ludendorff, Erich, 1144, 1147
Ludlow Amendment (1938), 1304
Lundberg, Ferdinand, 1442
Lusitania, 1127–28, 1127, 1129
Luther, Martin, 37, 37, 39
Lutheranism, 37, 144, 525
Luxembourg, 1359, 1398
lyceum movement, 563
Lynch, John R., 816
lynchings:
  of African Americans, 854, 1184, 1400
  in range wars, 877
Lynd, Helen, 1177
Lynd, Robert, 1177
Lyon, Mary, 566
Lyon, Matthew, 364, 365, 365

MacArthur, Douglas:
  Bonus Army and, 1229–30
  firing of, 1414–15
  in Korean War, 1412–15
  in World War II, 1313, 1322–23, 1339,
    1352–56, 1357, 1357, 1371
McAuliffe, "Tony," 1359
McCain, Franklin, 1510
McCain, John, 1672
McCarran Internal Security Act (1950), 1419
McCarthy, Eugene, 1542, 1543, 1555
McCarthy, Joseph R., 1418–19, 1419,
    1468–70, 1469, 1498, 1523
McCarthyism, 1416–19, 1439, 1468–70, 1503
McClellan, George B., 750
  at Antietam, 751–52
  background of, 620
  in election of 1864, 769
  in formation of West Virginia, 726–27
  Lincoln's antagonism with, 748, 749–50,
    752
  peninsular campaign of, 746–50, 747
  at second Bull Run, 750–51
McClure, Samuel S., 1075
McClure's, 1054, 1075
McCord, James W., 1588
McCormick, Cyrus Hall, 491, 491, 632
McCoy, Joseph G., 874
McCulloch v. Maryland, 425, 426, 466
Macdonough, Thomas, 400

MacDougal, James, 1683
McDowell, Irvin, 746, 748, 749
  at first Bull Run, 734–36
McFarlane, Robert, 1623
McGaffey, J. W., 896
McGovern, George S., 1577, 1587–88
McGowan, Man Eater, 882
McHenry, Joseph, 361
McKay, Claude, 1181
McKean, Thomas, 287
McKinley, William, 1010–11, 1062, 1065,
    1084, 1168
  assassination of, 1062–63
  Cuban government and, 1057
  in election of 1896, 838, 1025–28, 1028
  in election of 1900, 1062–63, 1062
  Philippines and, 1052–53, 1056
  Spanish-American War and, 1044–47, 1046,
    1052
McKinley Tariff (1890), 1010, 1011, 1040
McLane, Louis, 470
Macmillan, Harold, 1489
McNamara, Robert S., 1506–7, 1540, 1574
McNary, Charles L., 1214
McNary-Haugen Bill (1927), 1214, 1215,
    1217
McNeil, Joseph, 1510
Macon, Nathaniel, 391–92, 412
Macune, Charles W., 1019
McVeigh, Timothy, 1668
Maddox, U.S.S., 1536
Madeira, 134
Madero, Francisco I., 1119
Madison, James, 243, 308, 311, 312, 366,
    406, 414, 453
  African colonization and, 661
  Alien and Sedition Acts opposed by, 365
  Bill of Rights and, 332
  at Constitutional Convention, 310, 311,
    312, 316, 317, 320, 344
  debt issue and, 336, 337
  as early Republican leader, 342, 343
  in election of 1808, 390–91
  Federalist and, 321–22
  government strengthening recommended by,
    317, 410
  on Indians, 461–62
  internal improvements and, 414
  land policy and, 353
  in Marbury v. Madison, 375
  Monroe Doctrine and, 430
  Napoleonic Wars and, 391, 392
  national bank and, 338–39, 411
  in ratification debate, 321, 322
  as secretary of state, 374
  tariff policy and, 333
  Virginia Plan and, 312–13
  War of 1812 and, 392, 395, 402, 403
Madison Guaranty, 1683

magazines, proliferation of (1800–1850), 560
Magellan, Ferdinand, 25–26
Maggie: A Girl of the Streets (Crane), 975
Magna Carta (1215), 48
magnetic compass, 15–16
Mahan, Alfred Thayer, 1036, 1063
Mahicans, *see* Mohegans
Mailer, Norman, 1452
Maine, 147
   Canadian border with, 478, 585
   in colonial period, 65, 76, 78, 168, 183
   disestablishment in, 439
   Indians in, 78
   statehood for, 422
   temperance in, 569
   in War of 1812, 404
Maine, U.S.S., explosion of (1898), 1045–46,
   1045, 1046
Main Street (Lewis), 1173
Main-Traveled Roads (Garland), 971
maize (corn), 7, 22, 23, 67, 78, 109, 356, 632
Malaya, 1313
Malay Peninsula, 1318, 1475
Malaysia, 1475
Malcolm X, 1534, *1534*, 1543
Malvern Hill, Battle of (1862), 749
Mammoth Oil Company, 1203
Manassas (Bull Run), first Battle of (1861),
   734–36
Manassas (Bull Run), second Battle of (1862),
   750–51
Manchuria, Japanese in, 1295–96, *1295*
Mandan Sioux, 380
Mandela, Nelson, 1636
Manhattan Project, 1367
manifest destiny, 444, 585, 607, 612, 1035,
   1037
Manila, 194
Manila Conference (1954), 1479
Mann, Horace, 561
Mann-Elkins Act (1910), 1098–99
manufactures:
   and cities, 512–14
   corporate organization of, 510–11
   in early nineteenth century, *409*, 412, 435,
     436, 502–3
   in early U.S., 304, 333, 336, 340–41
   in handicraft stage, 502–3, 507
   Jefferson's embargo and, 409
   in late nineteenth century, 895–97
   Lowell system, 507–10
   Oneida, 577
   of Shakers, 576
   in South, 634–35, 642
   War of 1812 and, 405, 412
   see also factories; industry
Mao Tse-tung, 1409, *1409*, 1584, 1585
Marbury, William, 374–75
Marbury v. Madison, 374–75, 425, 705

March on Washington (1963), *1513*, 1514–15
Marco Polo Bridge, 1299, 1303, *1303*
Marcy, William L., 450
Mariana Islands, 1357
Maria Theresa, empress of Austria, 191–92
Marine Corps, U.S., 233
Marion, Francis, 265
Markland (Labrador), 14, 417
Marquette, Jacques, 180, *181*
marriage:
   African, 121
   of African Americans, 125, 656, 802, 813
   of clergy, 40
   in colonial period, 110, 113
   and cult of domesticity, 571–72
   divorce and, 281, 283, 1178, 1259
   in Great Depression, 1259–60
   interracial, 802
   Mormon, 545
   in 1920s, 1177–78
   in Oneida Community, 577
   in West, 881
   women's rights and, 572
Marshall, George C., 1337, 1395–96, *1395*,
   1418, 1464
Marshall, John, 285, 339, 372, 385, 425, 448,
   466
   African colonization and, 661
   Burr Conspiracy and, 386
   Indian lands and, 463, 464
   judicial nationalism of, 424–28
   in *Marbury v. Madison,* 375
   named as chief justice, 368
   and XYZ Affair, 361
Marshall, Thurgood, 1492
Marshall Islands, 1356
Martí, José, 1043, *1043*
Martin, Luther, 311, 321
Martin v. Hunter's Lessee, 425
Marx, Karl, 1185, 1188
Marx Brothers, 1283–84, *1283*
Marxism, 922, 923
Mary, queen of Scots, 42–43, 50
Mary I, queen of England, 169
Mary II, queen of England, 52, 171, 172
Maryland:
   agriculture in, 630
   Civil War fighting in, 751–52, 753, 755
   constitution of, 375
   Constitution ratified by, 322
   free blacks in, 280, 648
   Know-Nothing party in, 528
   labor laws in, 1083
   land claims of, 275
   secession debate in, 727
   at 1785 navigation meeting, 309
   voting rights in, 438
   War of 1812 in, 400

Maryland colony, 62, 64–65, *64*, 83, 84, 115
  charter of, 64–65
  European settlement of, 64–65
  government of, 64–65, 171, 173
  land policy in, 117
  tobacco in, 115
Maryland Toleration Act (1649), 83
Mason, Charles, 96
Mason, George, 235–36
  and Bill of Rights, 332, 333
  at Constitutional Convention, 311, 314,
    316–17
  in ratification debate, 321
Mason, James M., 766
Mason, John, 76
Mason-Dixon line, 96
Masonic order, 468
Massachusetts:
  asylums in, 571
  Civil War troops from, 758, 779
  constitution of, 274–75, 279
  Constitution ratified by, 322–23, *322*, 323
  disestablishment in, 439
  education in, 288, 561, 562–63
  at Hartford Convention, 404
  Know-Nothing party in, 528
  Revolutionary fighting in, 228–32
  Revolutionary troops from, 230, 279
  Shays's Rebellion in, 306–8
  slavery in, 279
  taxation in, 306, 307
  temperance in, 568–69
  voting rights in, 439
  War of 1812 and, 404
Massachusetts Bay Company, 70
Massachusetts colony, 2–3, 82, 115
  in border disputes, 77
  charter of, 69, 70, 72, 84, 166–67, 169, 174
  in colonial taxation disputes, 211, 215, 216,
    227
  in colonial wars, 184, 186
  education in, 155
  European settlement of, 69–75, 106
  government of, 69, 70–73, 84, 166–67,
    168–69, 170, 171, 174
  governors' salary in, 220
  heresy repressed in, 139
  Plymouth combined with, 171
  postal system in, 152
  religious freedom in, 140
  taxation in, 72, 170
  trade and commerce in, 168–69
  see also Plymouth colony
Massachusetts Government Act (1774), 223,
    258–59
Massachusetts Indians, 78
Massasoit, Wampanoag chief, 68, 82
massive resistance, 1494, 1497
massive retaliation, 1473

Mather, Cotton, 80, 141
Mather, Increase, 136
Mathiessen, F. O., 552
Matsu, 1479, 1480, 1488–89
Mauldin, Bill, *1344*
Mayaguez incident (1975), 1594
Mayas, 7, 8–9, *9*
Mayflower, 66
Mayflower Compact (1620), 67, 68, 137, 172
Mayhew, Jonathan, 161
Maysville Road Bill (1830), 453, *453*, 459
Mead, Margaret, 1187–88
Meade, George, 777
  background of, 620
  at Gettysburg, 773
Meany, George, 1428
Meat Inspection Act (1906), 1091
meat-packing industry:
  abuses in, 1090–91
  antitrust suit against, 1087
  regulation of, 1087, 1090, 1091
mechanics' lien laws, 531
media, *see* press
Medicaid, 1528–29, 1613, 1664
Medicare, 1528–29, 1530, 1613, 1630, 1664
medicine, *see* health and medicine
Medicine Creek Lodge conference (1867),
    867
Medicine Crow, Joseph, 1334
Mellon, Andrew W., 765, 1198–99,
    1200–1201, 1218, 1220–21, 1223, *1223*,
    1224, 1611
"melting pot," 107
Melville, Herman, 552, 554, 555–57, *556*,
    579, 618
Memphis, Tenn.:
  Irish Americans in, 522
  racial riot in (1866), 806
Mencken, H. L., 1174, 1204
Mennonites, 37, 144
mentally ill, 570–71, *571*
  deinstitutionalization of, 1627
mercantile system, 167–68, 299, 333
Mercer, Lucy, 1267
Meredith, James H., 1511–12
merit system, 996
Merrick, Caroline, 643
Merrimack (*Virginia*), 730, 737, *737*
Metacomet (Philip), Wampanoag chief, 81–82
Metacomet's (King Philip's) War, 82, 187
Methodists, 160, 284
  in revivals, 541–42
  in split over slavery, 669, 696–97
METO (Middle East Treaty Organization),
    1482
Mexican Americans, 589–90, 858, 859, 1166,
    1653
  Chicanos and, 1564
  as cowboys, 873, 875

in New Deal, 1262–63
northward migration of, 1138
as shepherds, 877
UFW and, 1565–67
Mexican Revolution, 589–90
Mexican War (1845–1848), 551, 610, 611–20, 616, 675–76
California annexation and, 611, 614–16
casualties in, 619
legacies of, 619–20
opposition to, 612
outbreak of, 611–12
peace treaty in, 619
Polk's intrigue with Santa Anna in, 617
preparations for, 613–14
slavery issue and, 551, 612
U.S. capture of, 618–19
Mexico, 33, 177–78, 195
in Contadora Process, 1618
European diseases in, 23–24
exploration of, 33
Gadsden Purchase from, 693
as heart of Spanish Empire, 31
immigration from, 1166, 1262–63, 1333–34, 1530, 1564–65, *1655*
independence of, 177, 590, 593, 603
NAFTA and, 1663–64, 1681
pre-Columbian, 7, 8
seasonal worker agreement with, 1333
Texas independence from, 590, 603–5, 606
and U.S. efforts to annex California, 602
U.S. expansion and, 582
U.S. oil properties in, 1294
U.S. trade with, 473, 596
Wilson's intervention in, 1119–21
in World War I, 1134
Mexico City (Tenochtitlán), 9, 27, 28, *28*, 30
battle of, 617–19
Miami, Fla., 1220, 1653
Miamis, 696
Michigan, University of, 952
Michigan State University, 565
microprocessors, 1645
Microsoft, 1645–46
middle class:
in antebellum South, 640–41
in Ku Klux Klan, 1494
in late nineteenth century, 934, 954
New Deal and, 1265, 1277
in 1950s, 1433, 1440
Nixon and, 1577
progressivism and, 1073, 1074, 1115
Reagan and, 1608, 1611
reform movement and, 530–31, 979, 980
at theater, 517
women's rights in, 571
Middle Colonies, 143–47
ethnic mix in, 144–46

Middle East Treaty Organization (METO), 1482
Middletown (Lynd and Lynd), 1177
Midway Island, 1318, 1323–24, 1336, 1352
Milan Decree (1807), 388, 392
military, U.S.:
African Americans in, 232, 279, 756–60, 758, 813, *815*, 860–61, 1331–32, 1401
conscription into, 739–41, 1136, 1308, 1480–81
in Constitution, 313, 317
Eisenhower on, 1498
gays in, 1662
Hispanics in, 1563–64
in Jefferson administration, 376–77
massive retaliation strategy and, 1473
in Mexican War, 613
post–World War II budget of, 1424–25
segregation in, 1331–32, 1401
see also Army, U.S.; *specific wars*
Military Academy, U.S. (West Point), 564, 734
Military Assistance Advisory Group, 1412
Military Reconstruction Act (1867), 808
militia movement, 1666–68
militias, 171, 396, 399, 531
in American Revolution, 228, 230, 249–50, 251, 252, 257, 263, 266
in War of 1812, 399, 400
Miller, Arthur, 1450–51, *1451*
Miller, Perry, 137
Miller, Phineas, 487
Milliken v. Bradley, 1580
Mills, C. Wright, 1450
Miners' National Association, 910
minimum-wage laws, 1082, 1200, 1269, 1270, 1275, 1381, 1407, 1466, 1659, 1675
mining, 635, 680–81
coal, 843, 1383
copper, *861*, 865
silver, 741, *861*, 864
in West, 861–66
Minnesota, 526
agriculture in, 880
farmer-labor coalition in, 1206
Indian conflicts in, 866
Populists in, 1020
minstrel shows, 517–19, *518*
Mint Act (1792), 1015
Minuit, Peter, 89
Miranda v. Arizona, 1509
missionaries:
Catholic, 34, 35–36, 87, 180, 182, 590, 592–94
French, 87, 180, 182
to frontier, 540
in Philippines, 1052
Puritan, 81
Spanish, 34, 35–36, 87, 590, 592–94
U.S., to China, 692

Mississippi, 86, 380, 488
  agriculture in, 448, 632, 845
  Civil War fighting in, 759, 772–73
  cotton in, 486
  migration to, 659
  railroads in, 985
  Reconstruction in, 801, 812, 821
  secession of, 718
  segregation in, 853, 1511–12, 1579
  temperance in, 569
  voting rights in, 851
  women's rights in, 574
  Yazoo Fraud and, 384
Mississippi, University of, desegregation of,
    1511–12
Mississippian culture, 10, 11
Mississippi Rifle Club, 822
Mississippi River, 180–81, 188
  in Civil War, 736–37, 738, 743, 772–73,
    775
  navigation rights to, 303, 351, 352, 378
  Pike's exploration of, 382–83
  steamboats on, 493–94
  U.S. access to, 303, 351–52, 378
  in War of 1812, 399
Missouri:
  agriculture in, 630, 631
  Civil War fighting in, 728, 741, 742
  dust bowl in, 1261
  emancipation in, 760
  German Americans in, 526
  post–Civil War anarchy in, 791
  secession debate in, 727, 728
Missouri, Kansas, and Texas Railroad, 915
Missouri, U.S.S., 1371
Missouri Compromise (1820), 421–24, 423,
    454, 629, 674, 676, 684, 686, 694, 701,
    705
Missouri-Pacific Railroad, 915
Missouri Territory, 422
Mitchell, George, 1568, 1641
Mitchell, John, 1577, 1590
Mitchell, Margaret, 1284
Mobile, Ala., capture of, 769
Mobile and Ohio Railroad, 502
Moby-Dick (Melville), 552, 556, 556
"Model of Christian Charity, A" (Winthrop), 70
modernism, 1185–94
  literature of, 1188–91
Modern Woman: The Lost Sex (Farnham and
    Lundberg), 1442
Modocs, 869
Mohammed Reza Pahlavi, shah of Iran, 1600
Mohawk and Genesee Turnpike, 492
Mohawks, 89, 91, 179, 262
Mohegans (Mahicans), 82
Molasses Act (1733), 206, 208
Molly Maguires, 910
Molotov, Vyacheslav, 1396

Moluccas (Spice Islands), 25, 26
monarchy:
  English, 50, 165, 166
  Locke on, 172
Mondale, Walter F.:
  in election of 1976, 1595
  in election of 1984, 1620
Mongolia, 1635
"Mongrel Tariff" (1883), 1000
Monitor, 737, 737
Monmouth Court House, Battle of (1778),
    260
Monroe, James, 378, 385, 388, 414–16, 414,
    453, 1420
  African colonization and, 661
  as ambassador to France, 361
  in American Revolution, 249
  background of, 414–15
  in election of 1816, 415
  in election of 1820, 415–16, 431
  Florida and, 418
  foreign policy under, 416–20, 428–31
  Missouri Compromise and, 424
  and relations with Britain, 416
  War of 1812 and, 402
Monroe Doctrine, 429–31, 1042, 1066, 1067
  Clark Memorandum and, 1294
  Kellogg-Briand Pact and, 1292
  Roosevelt Corollary to, 1066–67
  Venezuelan border dispute and, 1042
Montana, 741, 865
  cattle industry in, 874
  Indian conflicts in, 868, 869
  statehood for, 865, 1010
Montcalm, Louis Joseph de, 193
Montesquieu, 310
Montezuma II, Aztec emperor, 9, 27, 28
Montgomery, Bernard, 1339, 1351
Montgomery, Richard, 232
Montgomery bus boycott (1955–1956),
    1494–96, 1509
Montgomery Improvement Association, 1494
Montgomery-Ward Company, 1328
Montoya, Joseph, 1567
Montréal, 40, 183
Montserrat, 70
Moore's Creek Bridge, Battle of (1776), 233
Moral Majority, 1608, 1656
Moravian Indians, 219
Moravians, 99, 144
Morgan, Daniel, 266
Morgan, J. Pierpont, 765, 897, 898, 904–5,
    904, 906, 1025, 1086, 1093, 1125
Morgan, J. Pierpont, Jr., 1259
Morgenthau, Henry, Jr., 1274
Mormons (Church of Jesus Christ of Latter-
    Day Saints), 544–47, 877
Morocco, 377, 1302
  in Persian Gulf War, 1640

trade with, 301
  in World War II, 1338
Morocco crisis (1905), 1069
Morrill Act (1890), 950
Morrill Land Grant Act (1862), 764, 791, 949
Morrill Tariff (1861), 764, 791
Morris, Gouverneur, 307, 311
Morris, Robert, 292, 293, *293*, 336
Morristown, winter quarters at (1776–1777), 253, 256
Morse, Jedidiah, 539
Morse, Samuel F. B., 504, 506, *506*, 527
Morse, Wayne, 1537
Morton, Jelly Roll, 1174
Moscow Declaration on General Security (1945), 1388
Moscow Olympics (1980), 1600
Mosquitoes (Faulkner), 1193
Mossadegh, Mohammed, 1472, 1601
Mother Ann (Ann Lee Stanley), 575–76
Motherwell, Robert, 1453
Mott, Lucretia, 573
Moultrie, William, 233
Mount, William Sidney, *559*
mountain men, 591, 601, 614–15
Mourning Becomes Electra (O'Neill), 1176
movable type, 15
movies, 1175, 1176, 1207–8, *1432*
  documentaries, 1280
  in Great Depression, 1281–84
  in 1920s, 1175, 1176, 1207–8
Moynihan, Daniel Patrick, 1676
Mozart, Wolfgang Amadeus, 155
Muckrakers, 1074–76
Mugwumps, 1001, 1074
Muhammad, Elijah, 1534
Muir, John, 1092
Mukden Incident (1931), 1295–96
mulattoes, 646
Muller v. Oregon, 1082
Mulligan, James, 829
"Mulligan letters," 1001
Muni, Paul, 1283
Munich Agreement (1938), 1299
Munn v. Illinois, 986, 1017
"Murchison letter," 1008
Murfreesboro (Stone's River), Battle of (1862), 746
Murray, John, 538
Murray, Judith Sargent, 282
Murray, William Vans, 363
music:
  African-American, 124, 655, *656*, 1433
  Jazz Age and, 1174–75
  rhythm and blues, 1433
  rock 'n' roll, 1432–35, 1558–59
Mussolini, Benito, 1296, *1297,* 1298, 1300, 1311, 1341, 1364
  Spanish Civil War and, 1299, 1303

Myanmar (Burma), 1313, 1322, 1363, 1475
My Lai massacre (1969), 1573, 1577

NAACP (National Association for the Advancement of Colored People), 1184–85, 1262, 1264, 1333, 1492–93, 1514, 1535
NAFTA (North American Free Trade Agreement), 1663–64, 1681
Nagasaki, atomic bombing of (1945), 1370–71
Nagy, Imre, 1484
Naismith, James, 963
Naked Lunch (Burroughs), 1456
Napoleon I, emperor of France, 345, 363, 378, 380, 387, 399, 404, 734
Napoleon III, emperor of France, 766
Napper Tandy Light Artillery, 523
Narragansets, 74, 78, *80,* 82
Narragansett Bay, 44
Narrative of the Life of Frederick Douglass (Douglass), 666–67
Narváez, Pánfilo de, 32, *33*
NASA (National Aeronautics and Space Administration), 1486–87
Nash, Beverly, 814
Nashville, Battle of (1864), 782
Nashville, U.S.S., 1065
Nasser, Gamal Abdel, 1482, 1483, 1488
National Aeronautics and Space Administration (NASA), 1486–87
National American Woman Suffrage Association, 982, 1179, 1180
National Association for the Advancement of Colored People (NAACP), 1184–85, 1262, 1264, 1333, 1492–93, 1514, 1535
national bank, *see* Bank of the United States
National Banking Act (1863), 764, 791, 889
National Bell Telephone Company, 896
National Broadcasting Company (NBC), 1209, 1430
National Child Labor Committee, 1081, *1081*
National Collegiate Athletics Association (NCAA), 963
National Consumers League, 984, 1081–82
national conventions, 469
National Defense Act (1916), 1130
National Defense Research Committee, 1307
National Emergency Committee Against Mob Violence, 1400
National Endowments for the Arts and Humanities, 1613
National Greenback party, 829
National Industrial Recovery Act (NIRA) (1933), 1240, 1246–48, 1271
nationalism, American, 454, 474
  arts and, 285–86
  Clay's "American System" and, 432, 474, 582
  development of, 199, 285, 288

nationalism, American (continued)
  in diplomacy, 428–31
  economic, in early nineteenth century,
    409–14, 415
  education and, 287–88, 561
  of John Quincy Adams, 435
  judicial, 424–28
  Tyler and, 582
  after War of 1812, 406
  of Webster, 457
National Labor Relations (Wagner) Act (1935),
    1254–55, 1262, 1269, 1270, 1271, 1272,
    1566
National Labor Relations Board (NLRB),
    1386, 1615
National Labor Union (NLU), 913, 917
National Liberation Front (Nicaragua)
    (FSLN), 1617
National Liberation Front (Vietnam), 1479
National Military Establishment, 1387, 1420
National Mine Workers' Union, 1228
national mint, 336
National Organization for Women (NOW),
    1562, 1620, 1659–60
National Park Service, 1091
National Recovery Administration (NRA),
    1246–47, 1247, 1269
National-Republicans, 435, 467, 469, 474
National Resources Planning Board, 1328
National Review, 1526
National (Cumberland) Road, 413, 413, 415,
    453, 492
National Security Act (1947), 1387
National Security Agency, 1420
National Security Council (NSC), 1387,
    1410–11, 1420, 1464, 1517
National Security League, 1129
National Society for the Promotion of
    Industrial Education, 949
National Statistical Association, 953
National Trades' Union, 529
National Typographical Union, 532
National Union for Social Justice, 1253
National Woman Suffrage Association, 982
National Youth Administration, 1257–58, 1328
Native American Association, 527
Native Americans, see Indians, American
Native Son (Wright), 1279–80
nativism, 527–28, 944–46, 994, 1164–66
  anti-Catholic strain in, 527–28, 944–46
  in 1830s, 527–28
  in 1980s and 1990s, 1653–54
  of Klan, 1166–68
  and Know-Nothing party, 527–28, 697, 901
  after World War I, 1160–61
NATO, see North Atlantic Treaty Organization
naturalism, 975–96
naturalization, see citizenship and
    naturalization

Naturalization Act (1798), 364
Nausets, 78
Navajos, 13, 36, 587, 1335
Naval Academy, U.S., 564
Naval Construction Act (1916), 1130
naval stores, 116, 265
Naval War of 1812, The (Roosevelt), 1061
Navigation Act (1651), 167
Navigation Act (1660), 167
Navigation (Staple) Act (1663), 168
Navigation (Plantation Duty) Act (1673), 168,
    206
Navigation Act (1696), 172
Navigation Act (1817), 417
navigation acts, British enforcement of,
    168–69, 172–73
Navy, U.S., 267, 362, 377, 410, 416
  in Civil War, 733, 737–38
  in Constitution, 313
  formation of, 233
  Great White Fleet tour of, 1069–70
  in late nineteenth century, 1036–37
  and Quemoy and Matsu, 1488–89
  in Spanish-American War, 1048–49
  in War of 1812, 395–96, 398, 399
  after War of 1812, 406
  in World War I, 1130, 1135–36
  after World War I, 1291–92
  in World War II, 1312
Navy Department, U.S., 363, 1129
Nazism, 1297
  see also Germany, Nazi
NBC (National Broadcasting Company),
    1209, 1430
NCAA (National Collegiate Athletics
    Association), 963
Nebraska:
  cattle industry in, 874
  Indian conflicts in, 868
  migration to, 859
  Populists in, 1020
  railroads in, 986
Nebraska Territory, 590
  slavery issue and, 694, 697
"necessary and proper" clause, 426
Negro nationalism, 1182–84, 1183
Nelson, Horatio, 387
neo-orthodoxy, 1445–46
Ness, Eliot, 1173
Netanyahu, Benjamin, 1670
Netherlands, 31, 43, 1291
  American Revolution and, 258
  colonial trade with, 133
  in colonial wars, 185
  colonization by, 89–91, 143
  Dutch Republic and, 41, 184
  empire of, 26, 41, 82, 83, 89, 92, 143, 179
  in fur trade, 78, 89, 90, 91
  independence movements and, 1475

in NATO, 1398
privateers from, 41–42
Puritans in, 66
in rebellion against Spain, 41
Reformation in, 38
trade with, 301
in World War II, 1306
Neutrality Act (1935), 1301–2
Neutrality Act (1939), 1305
Nevada:
  election reforms in, 1077
  gold rush in, 864
  Indians in, 587
  sheep in, 877
  statehood for, 741
  in World War II, 1329
New Amsterdam, 89, 90
Newark, N.J., racial riot in (1967), 1532
Newburgh Conspiracy, 294
New Deal, 1033–34, 1113, 1232–78
  agriculture in, 1243–46, 1262, 1275–76
  banking industry and, 1236, 1238–41
  business in, 1243, 1246–48, 1258
  conservative criticism of, 1251–52, 1256
  currency in, 1239, 1241
  Eisenhower and, 1466
  electoral coalition of, 1265, 1403, 1460,
    1464, 1595
  industrial recovery program in, 1240,
    1246–48
  Keynesian theory and, 1274
  labor unions and, 1271–73
  late-1930s opposition to, 1276–78
  left-wing ideas coopted into, 1252–53
  legacy of, 1377
  minorities and, 1262–64
  Reagan and, 1630
  and recession of 1937, 1273–74
  regional planning in, 1248–51
  regulation in, 1243–51
  and role of government, 1277
  Social Security in, 1255–57
  Supreme Court and, 1245, 1248, 1253–54,
    1268–71
  taxation in, 1255–57
  three-pronged strategy of, 1232–33
  Truman's support of, 1381
  work relief in, 1241–43, 1246, 1257–58
  in World War II, 1328
  see also Depression, Great; Roosevelt,
    Franklin D.
New England:
  colonial life in, 129–43
  in colonial wars, 183, 186, 200
  currency in, 207
  divorce in, 283
  Dominion of, 169–71
  dwellings in, 130–31
  education in, 155, 561, 562–63

European settlement of, 65–77, 67
in French and Indian War, 200
Great Awakening in, 157, 159–60
Hartford Convention and, 404
Indians in, 77–82
industry in, 504, 506, 507–10, 511
Know-Nothing party in, 528
landownership in, 138–39
literature in (1800–1850), 549–54
Lousiana Purchase as seen in, 379
Mexican War as seen in, 612
post–Revolutionary debt in, 337
religion in, 136–38, 139, 159–61; *see also*
  Puritans
secession considered by, 383, 404
settling of, 65–77
sex ratios in, 112
social distinctions in, 533–34
society and economy in, 129–43
South compared with, 134
and Tariff of 1816, 412
temperance in, 567–69
trade and commerce in, 131–35, 138, 328,
  435, 503
transcendentalist movement in, 548–49
turnpikes in, 501
utopian communities in, 578
in War of 1812, 399
water transportation in, 500
New England Anti-Slavery Society, 663
New England Company, 69
New England Confederation, 82
New England Free Trade League, 1006
New England Primer, The, 156
New England Protective Union, 531
New England Women's Club, 984
Newfoundland (Vinland), 14, 32, 44, 134,
  183, 184, 186, 417
New France, 178–83
New Freedom, 1103, 1111
New Frontier, 1503–4, 1508
New Guinea, 1323, 1352–56
New Hampshire:
  in Constitutional Convention, 309
  Constitution ratified by, 322, 323, 324
  Dartmouth's charter altered by, 425–26
  disestablishment in, 439
  at Hartford Convention, 404
  Revolutionary troops from, 230
  voting rights in, 438
New Hampshire colony, 76, 77, 147, 168
  government of, 169
  in land disputes, 219
New Jersey:
  constitution of, 283
  Constitution ratified by, 322, 322
  Gibbons v. *Ogden* and, 427–28
  immigrants in, 1653
  paper currency in, 305

New Jersey (continued)
  Revolutionary fighting in, 247, 248–49, 248,
    253, 260
  voting rights in, 283, 438
  Wilson's governorship in, 1101–2
New Jersey, College of (Princeton University),
  158, 161
New Jersey colony, 84
  ethnic mix in, 144
  European settlement of, 94–95, 106
  government of, 171
New Jersey Plan, 313, 318
Newlands, Francis G., 879
Newlands Reclamation Act (1901), 879
New Left, 1551–57
New Light faction, 158
New Mexico, 33, 587, 589
  Chicanos in, 1564
  in Civil War, 741
  Gadsden Purchase and, 693
  Mexican War and, 616, 619
  silver in, 864
  slavery and, 676, 682, 685, 687
  in Spanish Empire, 34–36, 590
  statehood for, 682, 685, 866, 1099
New Morality, 1175–77
New Nationalism, 1103
New Netherland colony, 89, 146, 156
New Orleans, La., 195, 494, 512
  Battle of (1815), 401–2, 402, 523
  in Civil War, 738
  Irish Americans in, 522
  racial riot in (1866), 806
  segregation in, 853
  in War of 1812, 399, 401–2, 404
Newport, R.I., 144, 148, 150
Newsom, Robert, 660–61
newspapers:
  in colonial period, 152
  proliferation of (1800–1850), 558–60
New Sweden, 89–90
Newton, Huey P., 1533, 1554
Newton, Sir Isaac, 153, 161, 537, 1185–86
New View of Society, A (Owen), 577
New York:
  canals in, 495
  Civil War troops from, 738
  at Constitutional Convention, 311
  Constitution ratified by, 322, 323, 324
  and election of 1800, 367
  and election of 1844, 607
  Essex Junto and, 383
  in Gibbons v. Ogden, 427–28
  immigrants in, 937, 1653
  Indian lands ceded in, 298
  Jeffersonian Republicans in, 344, 345
  Know-Nothing party in, 528
  land claims of, 275, 295
  paper currency in, 305
  population of, 1651

prisons in, 569–70
  progressivism in, 1079–80
  Revolutionary fighting in, 230, 246, 247–49,
    248, 255–57, 260, 268
  Revolutionary Loyalists in, 250
  school prayer and, 1508–9
  slavery in, 280
  spoils system in, 450
  temperance in, 569
  voting rights in, 439, 524, 983
  in War of 1812, 396
  workers' rights in, 986
New York Central Railroad, 497, 894, 894
New York City, N.Y.:
  Civil War draft riots in, 740–41
  in colonial period, 146, 148, 149–50, 149
  demonstrations in, 1553–54
  education in, 561
  ethnic mix in, 146
  housing in, 933
  immigrants in, 520, 937, 940, 942–44
  insolvency crisis in, 1594
  Irish Americans in, 522
  in nineteenth century, 512, 514, 520
  Panic of 1837 in, 477
  poverty in, 149–50
  subways in, 934
  Tammany Hall in, 530, 936, 1001
  tenements in, 944
  Tweed Ring in, 819, 830
  Vietnam protests in, 1574
New York colony, 84, 152
  in colonial taxation disputes, 211, 213
  Dutch origins of, 89–91, 144, 146, 156
  education in, 156
  ethnic mix in, 144, 146
  government of, 170, 171
  Indians in, 91, 143
  in land disputes, 204, 219
  Leisler government in, 171
  quartering of British in, 207
New York Consumers League, 984
New York Customs House, 997
New York Herald, 559, 765, 821
New York Infirmary for Women and Children,
  574
New York Journal, 1044, 1045
New York militia, 171, 396
New York Sun, 559, 1001, 1089, 1148–49
New York Times, 1177, 1515, 1574, 1588,
  1593, 1627
New York Tribune, 523, 560, 575, 827, 828,
  1026–27
New York World, 1044
New Zealand:
  defense treaties with, 1420
  in SEATO, 1477
Nez Percés, 587, 870
Ngo Dinh Diem, 1479, 1519, 1520
Nguyen Van Thieu, 1571, 1575–76

Niagara Movement, 1184
Nicaragua, 1095, 1121, 1624, 1635
  Iran-Contra affair and, 1621–24
  proposed canal in, 1064, 1065
  U.S. interventions in, 1095, 1122, 1293, 1294, 1617–18
Nichols, Terry, 1668
Niebuhr, Reinhold, 1446
Nietzsche, Friedrich, 975
Niles, Hezekiah, 560
Niles' Weekly Register, 560
Nimitz, Chester, 1323, 1339, 1352, 1353, 1356–57
Niña, 18
Nine-Power Treaty (1922), 1291, 1296
Nineteenth Amendment, 1180, 1197
"Ninety-five Theses" (Luther), 37
Ninth Amendment, 333
NIRA (National Industrial Recovery Act) (1933), 1240, 1246–48, 1271
Nisquallys, 587
Nixon, Richard M., 1376–77, 1474, 1488, 1557, 1681
  background of, 1502
  China policy of, 1584–86, *1585*
  domestic policy of, 1578–81
  economy under, 1581–83
  in election of 1952, 1462, 1502
  in election of 1956, 1480–81
  in election of 1960, 1502–6, *1506*
  in election of 1968, 1544–46, *1544, 1545,* 1556
  in election of 1972, 1587–88
  Ford's pardon of, 1592, 1593
  Hiss affair and, 1417
  Kennedy's debate with, 1504–5, *1504*
  on Latin American tour (1958), 1488
  resignation of, 1591, *1591,* 1593
  segregation and, 1579–80
  Supreme Court appointments of, 1580
  as vice-president under Eisenhower, 1462, 1480–81, 1488, 1502
  Vietnam War and, 1570–77, *1572*
  wage freeze under, 1582–83
  Watergate and, 1588–93, *1589,* 1683
NLRB (National Labor Relations Board), 1386, 1615
NLU (National Labor Union), 913, 917
Nobel Peace Prize, 981, 1069, 1513
nobles, English, 48, 49
Non-Aggression Pact (1939), 1300
Non-Intercourse Act (1809), 391
Noriega, Manuel, 1639–40
Norris, George W., 1097, 1201, 1250
Norris v. Alabama, 1264
Norse explorers, 14–15
North, Frederick, Lord, 216–17, 223, 224, 227, 258, 269, 270
North, Oliver, 1623–24
North, Simeon, 505

North American Free Trade Agreement (NAFTA), 1663–64, 1681
North American Review, 560
North Atlantic Treaty Organization (NATO), 1408, 1420, 1635
  building of, 1398–99
  former Yugoslavia and, 1671–72
  missiles to, 1486
North Carolina:
  agriculture in, 630, 632, 640, 844
  Civil War fighting in, 738
  Civil War troops from, 771
  Confederacy and states' rights in, 770
  Constitution ratified by, 322, 324
  education in, 562
  free blacks in, 423
  Indian lands ceded in, 299
  Indians removed from, 299, 463, 464
  land claims of, 298
  migration from, 658
  mining in, 635
  paper currency in, 305
  Reconstruction in, 817, 822
  redistricting in, 1682
  Revolutionary fighting in, 233, 262, 263, 265, 266
  Revolutionary Loyalists in, 250
  Revolutionary troops from, 266
  secession of, 726
  segregation in, 1509–10, *1510*
  Union Loyalists in, 770
  voting rights of, 278, 852
North Carolina, University of, 288
North Carolina colony, 144
  backcountry of, 147, 219
  in colonial wars, 186
  colonization of, 44–45
  European settlement of, 84
  government of, 171
  Indians in, 86, 87, 88
  in land disputes, 204
  naval stores in, 116
North Dakota:
  agriculture in, 880, 1017
  migration to, 859
  statehood for, 865, 1010
Northern Pacific Railroad, 828, 1086
Northern Securities Company, 1086
North Star, 666
Northwest Ordinance (1787), 297–99, 676, 684
Norway:
  in NATO, 1398
  in World War II, 1306
Norwegian Americans, 526, 858–59
Notes on Virginia (Jefferson), 280, 669
Novanglus Letters (Adams), 226
Nova Scotia, 178, 186, 191
NOW (National Organization for Women), 1562, 1620, 1659–60

Noyes, John Humphrey, 577
NRA (National Recovery Administration), 1246–47, *1247*, 1269
NSC (National Security Council), 1387, 1410–11, 1420, 1464, 1517
nuclear energy, 1385
nuclear weapons:
  AEC and, 1392
  hydrogen bomb and, 1410, 1470, 1474, 1481
  Korean War and, 1468
  limited use of, 1473–74
  "missile gap" in, 1515
  Reagan and, 1616
  Soviet acquisition of, 1410
  treaties on, 1518, 1527, 1586, 1600, 1621, 1629, 1639
  in World War II, 1367–71
nullification and interposition, 365–66, 436, 454–61
  Calhoun and, 436, 454–55, 459
  Jackson and, 457, 460, 470, 474, 582–83
  South Carolina Ordinance and, 460
  theory of, 365–66
  Webster-Hayne debate on, 455–57
Nullification Proclamation (1832), 460
Nuremberg trials, 1389–90
Nurse, Rebecca, 142
Nussenbaum, Aaron, 907
Nye, Gerald P., 1301

Oakley, Annie, 955
Oates, Joyce Carol, 1452
oats, 23, 132, 143, 632
Oberlin College, 543–44, 566, 664
Obey, David, 1673
Observations Concerning the Increase of Mankind (Franklin), 110
Occupational Safety and Health Act (1970), 1581
ocean transportation, 500–501
O'Connor, Sandra Day, 1615, 1682
Office of Economic Stabilization, 1327
Office of National Drug Control Policy, 1634
Office of Price Administration (OPA), 1327, 1384
Office of Scientific Research and Development, 1326
Office of Strategic Services, 1472
Ogden, Aaron, 427–28
Oglethorpe, James E., 98, 99, 102, 188
Ohio, 350, 413
  education in, 563–64
  German Americans in, 525, 526
  Indian lands ceded in, 299
  land dispute in, 204
  statehood for, 376, 413, 563–64
Ohio Company, 188, 296
Ohio Life Insurance and Trust Company, 707
Ohio River, transportation on, 492–93

Ohio Valley:
  French and British penetration of, 188
  Indian troubles in, 202–4
  Revolutionary fighting in, 260
Ohio Women's Rights Convention (1851), 667
oil industry, 844, 898–901, 1211–12, 1612
Okinawa, 1366–67, 1368
Oklahoma, 33
  African Americans in, 860
  in Civil War, 741, 742
  dust bowl in, 1261, 1278
  Indians moved to, 867, 869, 872
  socialism in, 924
  statehood for, 866
  voting rights in, 852, 1184
  see also Indian Territory
Oklahoma City bombing (1995), 1667, *1668*
Old Creole Days (Cable), 972
older Americans, 1378
Old Northwest, 297–99, *297*
Old Southwest, 657–61
Old Walton Road, 492
Olive Branch Petition (1775), 232
Oliver, James, 880
Oliver, John, 491
Oliver, King, 1174
Olmsted, Frederick Law, 958
Olney, Richard L., 1042
Olympic games, 965
  of 1980, 1600
Oman, 1641
Omoo (Melville), 556
Oñate, Juan de, 34–36
Oneida Community, 577
Oneidas, 91, 1334
O'Neill, Eugene, 1176, 1182
Onondagas, 91, 93
"On the Equality of the Sexes" (Murray), 282
On the Origin of Species (Darwin), 965
On the Road (Kerouac), 1457
OPA (Office of Price Administration), 1327, 1384
OPEC (Organization of Petroleum Exporting Countries), 1582, 1583, 1594, 1619, 1620, 1640
Opechancanough, Powhatan chief, 60, 61
Open Door Policy, 1059, 1067, 1068, 1094, 1291, 1296
open shops, 1215–16
Operation Desert Shield, 1641
Operation Desert Storm, 1641–43, 1657
Operation Dixie, 1386, *1387*
Operation Rolling Thunder, 1537
opium, 473
Oppenheimer, J. Robert, 1368, 1470
Order of the Star Spangled Banner, 527
Orders in Council (Great Britain) (1806–1807), 388, 402
Ordinance of Secession (South Carolina) (1860), 717

Ordinance of Secession (Virginia) (1861), 726
Oregon:
  election reforms in, 1076
  voting rights in, 983
  in World War II, 1329
Oregon Country, 417, 428–29, 590, 591–92
  and election of 1844, 607
  Indian conflicts in, 869
  Polk and, 609
  Russia and, 428
  slavery issue and, 676
  U.S.-British border in, 609–11
  U.S. settlement of, 596, 599
Oregon (Overland) Trail, 588, 592, 596–600,
  599, 601
Oregon, U.S.S., 1063
Organization Man, The (Whyte), 1450
Organization of Petroleum Exporting
  Countries (OPEC), 1582, 1583, 1594,
  1619, 1620, 1640
Oriskany, Battle of (1777), 256
Orlando, Vittorio, 1150
Ortega, Daniel, 1624, 1635–36
Osborne, Sarah, 141
Osceola, 463
Oslo accords (1993), 1669–70
Ostend Manifesto (1854), 691
O'Sullivan, T. H., 775
Oswald, Lee Harvey, 1521
Other America, The (Harrington), 1525
Otis, Elisha Graves, 933
Otis, Harrison Gray, 404
Otis, James, 200–201, 208, 215
Otis Elevator Company, 933
Ottawas, 193–94, 202, 349
*Our Country: Its Possible Future and Its Present
  Crisis* (Strong), 1037
Overland (Oregon) Trail, 588, 592, 596–600,
  599, 601
"Over-soul, The" (Emerson), 550
Owen, Robert, 577–78
Oxbow Route, 592

Pacific Railway Bill (1862), 890
Page, Walter Hines, 1124
Paine, Thomas, 247–48, 537
  in American Revolution, 247
  background of, 233–34
painting:
  in Revolutionary era, 285–86
  romanticism and, 548
  in twentieth century, 1188, 1453–54
Paiutes, 587, 870
Pakenham, Richard, 610
Pakenham, Sir Edward, 401–2
Pakistan, 1475
  in METO, 1482
  in SEATO, 1477, 1482
Palestine Liberation Organization (PLO),
  1618, 1629, 1669–70

Palestinians, 1586, 1598
Palmer, A. Mitchell, 1160
Palmer, John M., 1026
Palmerston, Henry John Temple, Lord, 584
Palo Alto, Battle of (1846), 613
Pamaunkees, 56
Panama, 7, 25, 187
  in Contadora Process, 1618
  U.S. invasion of (1989), 1639–40
Panama Canal, 1063–66, *1066*, 1293, 1598
Pan-American Conference (1928), 1294
Pan-American Conference, Seventh (1933),
  1294
Pan-American Conference, Eighth (1936),
  1294
Pan-American Petroleum and Transport
  Company, 1203
Panay incident, 1304
Panic of 1819, 413, 420, 435, 466, 488
Panic of 1837, 473, 476–78, *477*, 496, 501,
  531, 591–92, 632
Panic of 1857, 707–8
Panic of 1873, 828–29, 910
Paris, Pact of (Kellogg-Briand Pact) (1928),
  1292, 1296, 1390
Paris, Peace of (1763), *185*, 195–96, 198
Paris, Peace of (1783), 271–72, 292, 302, 303,
  331
Paris, Treaty of (1898), 1052, 1053
Paris Peace Conference (1919), 1148–52,
  1149, 1289
Parker, Alton B., 1089
Parker, John, 229
Parker, John J., 1185
Parker, Theodore, 549
Parkman, Francis, 182
Parks, Rosa, 1494
Parliament, British, 118
  American Revolution and, 258–59
  Charles I's conflict with, 50–51
  in colonial taxation disputes, 211, 212, 213,
    218, 223, 234
  colonies' undefined relationship with, 176
  Continental Congress on, 225, 226, 227
  currency policies of, 135, 207
  elections of, 216
  kings' conflict with, 165, 174, 176
  Leisler government and, 171
  Restoration and, 51
  taxation and, 48, 176
  trade regulated by, 167
Parris, Samuel, 141
Partisan, The (Simms), 555
party system, 342, 435
  cultural-ethnic identity and, 474, 523–24
  establishment of, 342
  Jefferson's role in, 373–74
  patronage and, 991
  third parties and, 468–69, 527–28, 697
  Washington on, 358, 359

Passing of the Great Race, The (Grant), 1165
patent medicines, 1090, *1090*
Patent Office, U.S., 895
Paterson, N.J., silk strike in (1912), 926
Pathet Lao, 1519
patriot movement, 1666–68
Patrons of Husbandry (Grange), 1016–17
Patterns of Culture (Benedict), 1188
Patton, George S., Jr.:
  Bonus Army and, 1229–30
  in World War II, *1341,* 1351
Paul, Alice, 1178–79, *1180*
Paxton Boys, 219
Paz, Octavio, 30
PCA (Progressive Citizens of America), 1403
Peabody, Elizabeth, 549
Peabody, George, 563, 847, 848
Peabody, Sophia, 549
Peabody Fund for Education, 847
Peace Corps, 1508, 1550
Peale, Charles Willson, *249,* 285–86, *293,*
  312, 343, 647
Peale, Norman Vincent, 1444–45
Pea Ridge, Battle of (1862), 729
Pearl Harbor attack (1941), 1315–18, *1316,*
  1317, 1323, 1337
penal system, 569–70
Pendleton, George H., 823, 999
Pendleton Civil Service Act (1883), 999, 1003
penitentiaries, 569–70
Penn, Sir William, 96
Penn, William, 94, 96–98, *96,* 156, 219, 525
  Pennsylvania colony founded by, 96–98
Pennsylvania:
  canals in, 495
  Civil War fighting in, 773–75
  Constitution ratified by, 322
  divorce in, 283
  in early interstate cooperation, 309
  German Americans in, 525
  government of, 275
  Indian lands ceded in, 298
  land claims of, 295
  paper currency in, 305
  Revolutionary fighting in, 247, *254, 255,*
    261, 267–69
  slavery in, 279
  spoils system in, 450
  voting rights in, 278, 438
  Whiskey Rebellion in, 350–51
  workers' rights in, 986
Pennsylvania, University of (Philadelphia
  Academy), 155, 161
Pennsylvania Chronicle, 214
Pennsylvania colony, 84, 86, 98, 119, 144,
  171, 196
  backcountry of, 96–98, 146–47
  discontent on frontier of, 219
  education in, 156

ethnic groups in, 98, 144, 146–47
European settlement of, 96–98, 106
government of, 98, 173
Indians in, 143
in land disputes, 204, 219, 224
postal system in, 152
and protests against British, 214, 219, 222,
  225, 233
and Quakers, 96–98, 106
religion in, 95, 144
Pennsylvania Dutch, 144
Pennsylvania Gazette, 154
Pennsylvania Hospital, 570–71, *570*
Pennsylvania Journal, 210
Pennsylvania Railroad, 497
Pennsylvania State University, 565
Pentagon Papers, 1574, 1589
People's party, *see* Populist party
Pequots, 76, 78, 79, 80–81, *80,* 91
Pequot War, 79–81
Peres, Shimon, 1670
perestroika, 1635
Perkins, Frances, 1237
Perot, H. Ross, 1662, 1663, 1678
Perry, Matthew, 692, *692*
Perry, Oliver H., 397–98
Pershing, John J., 1121, 1136, 1143
Persian Gulf War, 1640–43, 1657, 1658
personal computers, 1645–46
Personal Responsibility and Work Opportunity
  Act (1996), 1676
Peru, 7, 177, 1488
Pescadores Islands, 1058
Pétain, Philippe, 1339
Petersburg, Battle of (1864), 779
petition, freedom of, 52, 275
Philadelphia, 377
Philadelphia, Pa., 512
  Battle of (1777), *254, 255*
  in colonial period, 97, 146, 148, 149, 150
  Declaration of Independence written in,
    234–37
  and First Continental Congress, 225–27
  founding of, 97
  Irish Americans in, 522
  labor in, 530
  nativist clashes in (1844), 527
  and Second Continental Congress, 230,
    234–37
  subways in, 934
  as U.S. Capital, 337
  and Whiskey Boys, 351
Philadelphia Academy (University of
  Pennsylvania), 155, 161
Philadelphia-Lancaster Turnpike, 492
Philip (Metacomet), Wampanoag chief, 81–
  82
Philip II, king of Spain, 26, 43
Philippine Government Act (1902), 1056

Philippines, 25, 26, 194
  annexation debate about, 1052–56
  defense treaties with, 1420
  immigration from, 1530, 1653, *1655*
  Japan and, 1068, 1289
  in SEATO, 1477
  in Spanish-American War, 1048
  U.S. conquest of, 1055–56, 1062
  in World War II, 1318, 1322, *1322*,
      1357–58, *1357*, 1363, 1366
Philippine Sea, Battle of (1944), 1356–57
Phips, William, 186
photography, 1280
physics, 1185–87
Picasso, Pablo, 1188, 1189, *1189*
Pickering, John, 375
Pickering, Thomas, 383
Pickering, Timothy, 361, 404
Pickett, George:
  background of, 620
  at Gettysburg, 774
Pickford, Mary, 1176
Pierce, Franklin:
  in election of 1852, 690–91
  in election of 1856, 702
  foreign policy under, 691–92
  Kansas-Nebraska Act and, 696
pigs, 22, 26, 109, 132, 632
Pike, Zebulon, *381,* 382–83, 422
Pilgrims, 65–68, 136
Pinchback, Pinckney B. S., 817
Pinckney, Charles, 116
Pinckney, Charles Cotesworth, 361
  in election of 1800, 366, 367, *367*
  in election of 1804, 383
  in election of 1808, 391
  1798 army authorization and, 363
Pinckney, Eliza Lucas, 116
Pinckney, Thomas, 351, 352, 361
  in election of 1796, 359
  and treaty with Britain, 351–52
Pinckney family, 127
Pinckney Treaty (1795), 351–52, *352,* 418
Pine Ridge Reservation, 872
Pinkerton, Allan, 747
Pinochet, Augusto, 1593, 1636
Pinta, 18
Pioneers, The (Cooper), 554
pirates:
  Barbary, 377, 405
  see also privateers
Pitcairn, John, 228, 229–30
Pitcher, Molly (Mary Ludwig Hays), 282
Pitt, William, 192, 200, 211–12, 213
Pittsburgh, Pa. (Fort Duquesne), 189, 192,
      204, 512
Pittsburgh Courier, 1332–33

Pius IX, Pope, 980
Pizarro, Francisco, 29, 32
Planck, Max, 1187
Plan of Union (1801), 540
Plantation Duty (Navigation) Act (1673), 168,
      206
plantations, 636–39, *637,* 651–53
Platt Amendment (1901), 1057–58, 1294
"Pledge of Allegiance," 1443
Plessy, Homer, 853
Plessy v. Ferguson, 853, 1492
PLO (Palestine Liberation Organization),
      1618, 1629, 1669–70
Plow That Broke the Plains, The, 1282
Plunkitt, George Washington, 935–36
Plymouth colony, 53, 65–68, 82, 84, 108–9
  division of Virginia Company, 53, *54,* 65
  government of, 68
  Indian relations with, 67
  Massachusetts combined with, 171
  population of, 109
Pocahontas, 58, *58,* 59
Poe, Edgar Allan, 554–55, *555*
poetry, 1181–82, 1188–89, 1191–92, 1456
Poindexter, John, 1623, 1624
Point Four, 1408
Poland:
  fall of communism in, 1635
  immigration from, *1655*
  Soviet domination of, 1362, 1390–91, 1484
  in World War I, 1146, 1151
  in World War II, 1300, 1304–5, 1362
Polish Americans, 146, 738, 937, 939, 943,
      945
Polk, James K., 588, 606–11, *607,* 691
  background of, 608
  in election of 1844, 606–8, *608*
  gold discovery confirmed by, 678, *678*
  Jackson compared with, 608
  Mexican War and, 611, 612, 613, 614, 617,
      619, 620
  reelection bid eschewed by, 676
  slavery issue and, 674, 675, *676*
  western expansion under, 608–11, 620
Pollock, Jackson, 1453–54, *1454*
poll taxes, 851
pollution, 1581
Polo, Marco, 17
polygamy, 545
Ponce de León, Juan, 32
Pontiac, Ottawa chief, 193–94, 202, 208, 219
Poor Richard's Almanac, 154
Popé, 36
Pope, John, 743, 750, 751
popular culture:
  advertising in, 1429–30
  in colonial times, 150–52, 514–15
  and community, 1687–88
  and conforming culture, 1438–46

popular culture (*continued*)
dueling in South, 642–46
in early nineteenth century, 515–16
on the frontier, 356–57, 660
and German immigrants, 526
in Great Depression, 1281–84
and Independence Day, 286–87
in late nineteenth century, 954–65
and lonely crowd, 1447–50
and minstrel shows, 517–19
and movies, 1281–84
and 1960s counterculture, 1557–60
and popular press, 558–60
and post–World War II consumer culture,
1427–30
and radio, 1281
and rock 'n' roll, 1432–35, 1558–59
and slaves, 124, 654–55
and southern planters, 126–27
and sports, 515–16, 958–61, 1401–2
in suburbs, 1435–37
and taverns, 150–51
and theater, 516–17
and urban recreation, 515–16
vaudeville, 957–58
Wild West shows, 955–56, *956*
and youth culture, 1430–32
Popular Science Monthly, 967
population:
aging of, 1378
"baby-boom" generation and, 1382, 1426,
1427, 1650
of cities, 512
in colonial period, 109–13
in early U.S., 328–29
of Indians, 29
in late twentieth century, 1650–55, *1654*
Mayan, 9
in nineteenth century, *489*
post–World War II growth in, 1382
in South, *631*
Populist party (People's party), 1020, 1024,
1025
agriculture and, 1213–14
in election of 1892, 1022–23, 1029
in election of 1896, 1026
progressivism and, 1073, 1074
Spanish-American War and, 1053
Populists, Reconstruction and, 846
Port Huron statement (1962), 1551–52
Portsmouth, Treaty of (1905), 1068
Portugal, 1291
colonial trade with, 133, 186
colonial wars and, 186
exploration and discovery by, 17–18, 25
Jews in, 146
in Napoleonic Wars, 390
in NATO, 1398
in slave trade, 125
in World War II, 1340

Portuguese Americans, 146
Portuguese Empire, 26
in Treaty of Tordesillas, 19
postal service, in colonial period, 152
Post Office Department, U.S., 233
potatoes, 22, 23, 632, *633*
Potawatomis, 349
Potsdam conference (1945), 1368
Potsdam Declaration (1945), 1369
Pottawatomie Massacre (1856), 698, 711
Pound, Ezra, 1188, 1189
poverty:
alcoholism and, 567
among American Indians, 1263, 1567–69
in antebellum South, 641
in colonial era, 149
in Depression, 1259–60
education and, 561
Hispanics and, 1564
homelessness and, 1627
Internet and, 1646–47
Johnson's efforts against, 1378, 1522,
1525–26, 1528–30, 1544, 1568, 1581
in late twentieth century, 1378
in 1990s, 1652
in post–Civil War South, 791
in post–World War II era, 1428, 1446, 1447
Reagan and, 1613, 1630
recreation and, 960–61
"safety net" and, 1613
urban, 930, 1652
war on, 1525–26
see also Depression, Great; welfare
Powderly, Terence V., 914, *914,* 916, 918
Powell, Lewis F., Jr., 1580–81
Powell v. Alabama, 1264
Power of Positive Thinking, The (Peale),
1444–45
Powers, Gary, 1490
Powhatans:
and assistance to colonists, 55
and conflicts with settlers, 60
and Pocahontas, 58–59
pragmatism, 970–71
*Pragmatism: A New Name for Some Old Ways of
Thinking* (James), 970–71
Pratt, Daniel, 635
predestination, 38
Preemption Act (1830), 490
Preemption Act (1841), 490
Presbyterians, 38, 42, 50, 51, 144, 158, 160,
161, 284, 538
in Civil War split, 669
Congregationalists' union with, 540–41
in revivals, 540–41, 542
in Whig party, 474
Prescott, Samuel, 229
presidency:
in Constitution, 316–18
electors for, 317–18, 439

executive privilege of, 349, 386–87
  nominations for, 431–32, 469
  powers of, 316–17
  war powers of, 1412, 1592
  see also executive branch
presidios, 34
Presley, Elvis, 1433–34, *1434*
press:
  and antislavery, 662–63, 668
  and colonial newspapers, 152
  freedom of, 152, 333, 364, 668, 809
  Muckrakers in, 1074–76
  popular, in early nineteenth century, 558–60
  and Reconstruction, 809
  in Spanish-American War, 1044
Preston, Levi, 238
Prevost, Augustin, 263
Prevost, George, 399–400
primaries, direct, 1076
primogeniture, 49, 344
Princeton, Battle of (1777), 249
Princeton University (College of New Jersey), 158, 161, 1101
Principia (Newton), 153
Principles of Scientific Management, The (Taylor), 1077–78
printing technology, 558–59
prisons:
  convict leasing and, 848
  debtors in, 530–31, 570
  reform movements and, 569–70
privateers:
  American, 267
  Dutch, 41–42
  English, 42, 84
  French, 40, 346, 347
Privy Council, 166, 173, 201
Proclamation Line, 202
Proclamation of 1763, 202–4, 205, 278
Proclamation of Amnesty (1865), 800
Proclamation of Amnesty and Reconstruction (1863), 796
Professional Air Traffic Controllers, 1615
professionalism, 953
Profiles in Courage (Kennedy), 1503
Progress and Poverty (George), 976
Progressive Citizens of America (PCA), 1403
Progressive National Committee, 1131
Progressive ("Bull Moose") party, 1099–1100, 1102, 1103, 1105, 1115, 1131
Progressive party (1924), 1206
Progressive party (1948), 1405, 1406
progressivism, 1033, 1072–1116, 1196–97
  antecedents to, 1074
  corporate regulation and, 1073, 1080, 1089
  democratic reforms in, 1076–77
  efficiency and, 1077–78
  features of, 1076–84
  income tax and, 1130
  limits of, 1114–15

Muckrakers and, 1074–76
  NAACP and, 1184
  populism compared with, 1073, 1074
  resurgence of, 1112
  social justice promoted in, 1080–83
  Theodore Roosevelt and, 1084–92
  Wilson and, 1100–1114
  see also Prohibition movement
Prohibition movement, 319, 567–69, 994, 1011, 1083–84, 1170–73
  bootlegging and, 1171–73
  Eighteenth Amendment and, 319, 1171, 1197, 1234
  temperance and, 567–69, *568,* 984
  World War I and, 1170–71
Prohibition party, 1084
Prohibitory Act (1775), 233, 259
Promise of American Life, The (Croly), 1103
property:
  African-American ownership of, 802
  Catholic views on, 980
  Fourteenth Amendment and, 985
  voting rights and, 176, 278, 438–39, 523–24, 530–31
  women and, 113, 115, 572
Proposition 187 (California), 1654
Proposition 209 (California), 1682
prostitution, 517
Protestant-Catholic-Jew (Herberg), 1446
Protestantism, 640, 642
  anti-Catholic feeling and, 527
  rationalism in, 538
  Reformation and, 36–40
  see also Anglican Church; Baptists; Calvinism; Huguenots; Methodists; Pilgrims; Presbyterians; Puritans; Quakers
Prussia:
  in colonial wars, *185,* 192
  French Revolution and, 345
  in Quintuple Alliance, 429
  trade with, 301
Ptolemy, 21
Public Credit Act (1869), 825
public schools, 288, 530, 561–63, 948–49
Public Utility Holding Company Act (1935), 1254, 1258
Public Works Administration (PWA), 1246, 1274
Pueblo-Hohokam culture, 10
Pueblos, 32, 35, 587, 590
Puerto Ricans, 1166, 1567
Puerto Rico, 26, 32, 429
  acquisition of, 1053, 1056
Pulitzer, Joseph, 1044
Pullman, George, 920
Pullman Strike (1894), 919, 920–22, *921,* 1024
Pure Food and Drug Act (1906), 1091, 1275

Puritans, 81, 83, 84, 129, 136–38
  Andros's conflict with, 170
  Anglican Church as viewed by, 70, 73, 136
  communitarian standards of, 139
  in Connecticut, 76, 80
  Cromwell and, 82
  dissension among, 73–75, 160–61
  education and, 155
  in England, 38, 50
  evolving doctrines of, 538
  Great Awakening and, 160
  Harvard founded by, 161
  lifestyle of, 136
  in Maine, 76–77
  in Massachusetts, 69, 70, 73, 74–75, 106,
    115
  missionaries of, 81
  in New Hampshire, 76–77
  Newtonian science accepted by, 153
  in Rhode Island, 73–76
  Separatists, 40, 65–66, 69, 136
  transcendentalism and, 548
  in Virginia, 128
  witchcraft and, 140–43
Putnam, Robert, 1687–88
"putting-out" system, 503, 506, 507
PWA (Public Works Administration), 1246,
  1274
Pythagoreans, 15

Qatar, 1641
Quadruple Alliance, 429, 430
Quakers (Society of Friends), 38, 95–96, 95,
    97, 106, 129, 139, 140, 144, 219
  educational efforts of, 156
  and founding of Pennsylvania, 96–98, 106
  transcendentalism and, 548
  in Virginia, 128
Quantrill, William C., 741, 742
Quarles, Benjamin, 756
Quartering Act (1765), 207, 213, 218
Quartering Act (1774), 223
quartering of military, 207, 333
Quayle, Dan, 1631
Quebec, 40, 179, 183, 183, 193, 193
  attack on, during American Revolution, 232
  battle of (1759), 193
  established as British colony, 202
  founding of, by French, 179
  land claims of, 224
  in War of 1812, 396
Quebec Act (1774), 223–24, 278
Quechuas, see Incas
Queen Anne's War (War of the Spanish
    Succession) (1701–1713), 184, 185,
    186–87
Queen's College (Rutgers University), 161
Quemoy, 1479, 1480, 1488–89
Quezon, Manuel, 1056

Quinn, Sally, 1660
Quintuple Alliance, 429, 430

Rabin, Yitzhak, 1670
racial riots:
  in Chicago (1919), 1138, 1159
  in Chicago (1966), 1532
  in Cleveland (1966), 1532
  in Detroit (1943), 1333
  in Detroit (1967), 1532
  in East St. Louis (1917), 1138
  in Elaine, Ark. (1919), 1159
  in Longview, Tex. (1919), 1158–59
  in Memphis (1866), 806
  in Newark (1967), 1532
  in New Orleans (1866), 806
  in Washington, D.C. (1919), 1159
  in Watts (1965), 1532
racism, 1165
  against Asians, 1335–36
  Darwin and, 1037
  see also segregation, desegregation
Radical Republicans:
  assessment of, 818–19
  in Civil War, 752–53, 755, 767, 769
  corruption charges against, 818–19
  Johnson's relations with, 799, 806, 807,
    807, 810–12
  presidential elections and, 431
  in Reconstruction, 797, 798, 799, 803–4,
    805, 818–19, 821, 849
radio, 1208–9, 1209
radioactivity, 1186
RAF (Royal Air Force), 1345
railroads, 522, 840, 992, 1114
  agriculture and, 844, 1013
  building of, 889–90
  cattle drives and, 873–74
  in Civil War, 732, 733
  in early nineteenth century, 496–500, 498,
    499, 501–2
  economic benefits of, 499–500
  financing of, 893–95
  Gadsden Purchase and, 693
  in growth of cities, 932
  ICC and, 1005
  immigration encouraged by, 938
  Indian relocation and, 696
  Kansas-Nebraska Act and, 694–95, 695
  labor disputes and, 915, 920–22, 1383
  land policy and, 502, 791, 879, 890, 1004
  Morgan and, 905
  in Panic of 1873, 828
  Populists and, 1022
  progressivism and, 1080
  regulation of, 985–86
  segregation in, 853
  in South, 848–49
  steam power introduced to, 496

Theodore Roosevelt's actions against, 1085–86, 1089–90
transcontinental, 693, 791, 889–92, *891, 892*
travel on, 498–500
Railway Labor Act (1926), 1216
Railway Labor Board, 1216
Rainbow, 500–501
Rainey, Joseph H., *816*
Raleigh, Sir Walter, 23, 43, 44–45
R & B (rhythm and blues), 1433
Randolph, A. Philip, 1332, *1405*
Randolph, Edmund, 324, 331
Randolph, Edward, 168–69, 172, 216
Randolph, John, 375, 384–85, 395, 436, 644, 645
Randolph, Peyton, 225
Rankin, Jeanette, 1318
Ransom, John Crowe, 1191–92
Rapier, James T., *816*
Rauschenbusch, Walter, 979
RCA, 1209
REA (Rural Electrification Administration), 1250–51, 1467
Reading Railroad, 1086
Readjuster party, 848, 849
Reagan, Ronald, 1377, 1555, 1598, *1607*
  affirmative action and, 1681
  attempted assassination of, 1612
  background of, 1606–8
  budget cuts of, 1613–14
  cultural conservatives and, 1655
  defense buildup under, 1616
  deficits and, 1612–13, 1625, 1630
  economy and, 1611–13, 1619, 1624–25, 1626–27
  in election of 1976, 1595
  in election of 1980, 1608, 1609–11, *1610*
  in election of 1984, 1620–21
  inaugural addresses of, 1611
  Iran-Contra affair and, 1621–24
  legacy of, 1629–30
  Middle East and, 1618–19
  regulation under, 1614
  scandals under, 1614
  Soviet Union and, 1621
  at summit meetings, 1621, *1622,* 1629
realism, 974
"Real Whigs," 207–8
recall elections, 1076
recessions, 1274, 1581–83, 1593–94, 1599–1600, 1626, 1657–59
Reclamation Bureau, U.S., 879, 1407
Reconstruction, 789–834
  African Americans in, 793–96, 800–801, 802, 812–17, *816*
  Black Codes in, 802, 805
  Bourbon Redeemers in, 846–50, 847, 851, 856–57

carpetbaggers in, 817–18, 822
civil rights legislation in, 805, 806, 814, 820–21
Congress in, 794–95, 797, 801–10, 812, 821, 829
conservative resurgence in, 821–22
constitutional debates over, 796–97, 800, 804, 805
corruption and abuses in, 818–19
education in, 814, 818
end of, 833–34
Johnson's plans on, 799–803, 804
land policy in, 793, 794, 800–801, 808, 816
Radical Republicans and, 797, 798, 799, 803–4, 805, 818–19, 821, 849
scalawags in, 817–18, 820, 822
southern intransigence over, 801–3
Supreme Court in, 809–10, 833
white terror in, 819–21
Reconstruction Act, Second (1867), 809
Reconstruction Act, Third (1867), 809
Reconstruction Finance Corporation, 1226–27, 1325, 1466
Red Badge of Courage, The (Crane), 975
Redeemers, Bourbon, 846–50, *847,* 851, 856–57
Red Scare (1919), 1159–60, 1215
Reed, Esther, 282
Reed, Walter, 1057
referenda, 1076
Reformation, 36–40
  in England, 39–40
Reform Darwinism, 968–69, *968*
reform movements, 530–31, 566–79
  and antislavery, 662–67, 689
  churches in, 979–80
  for civil service, 827, 828, 831, 995–97, 999–1000, 1003–4, 1009
  Cleveland and, 1001
  dietary, 566–67
  education, 561–62
  and labor, 531
  for prisons and asylums, 569–70
  Prohibition movement, 567–69
  utopian, 575–79
  women's rights and, 571–75, 667, 984
  see also progressivism
refrigeration, 895, *895*
Refunding Act (1870), 825
regulation, governmental:
  of agriculture, 1243–46, 1275
  of atomic energy, 1385
  of banking industry, 1107–9, 1109–10, 1227, 1240–41, 1258, 1633
  of child labor, 985, 1081, 1099, 1113–14
  of communications, 1098–99, 1209, 1213
  of corporations, 985, 1073, 1080, 1085, 1087, 1089, 1109–10, 1246
  of drugs, 1090, 1275

regulation, governmental (continued)
  of electric power, 1249–51, 1407, 1466
  of housing, 1275, 1381, 1407
  of liquor, 1011, 1081, 1083–84, 1170–73
  of meat packers, 1087, 1091
  progressivism and, 1080
  pollution restricted by, 1581, 1583–84
  of public utilities, 1258
  of railroads, 985–86, 1005, 1080, 1089,
    1114, 1327
  of wages and prices, 1327–28, 1384, 1466,
    1582–83, 1594
  of wartime industry, 1137–38, 1325–26
  of worker safety, 1082
Regulators (Carolinas), 219, 233, 250
regulators (Texas), 878
Rehnquist, William, 1581, 1682
relativity, 1186, 1187
religion:
  African, 122
  African-American, 124, 629, 654–55, 656,
    813
  American Indian, 30, 32, 34, 79
  in backcountry, 157
  in colonial period, 136–38, 139, 140, 144,
    156–62
  deism and, 537–38
  denominational colleges and, 158, 161, 538,
    539
  denominational splits in, 160
  education and, 161, 563, 564
  Enlightenment and, 153
  freedom of, 37, 51, 52, 73, 74, 75–76, 83,
    86, 95, 144, 175, 179, 283–84, 333, 439
  on frontier, 540–42, 581
  fundamentalism and, 1168–70, 1608–9,
    1615
  Great Awakening in, 156–62, 276–77, 537
  institutional churches in, 978–79
  in Massachusetts, 140
  neo-orthodoxy and, 1445–46
  in New England, 136–38, 139, 159–61
  in post–World War II era, 1443, 1444
  rational, 537–39
  Religious Right and, 1608–9
  revival meetings and, 540–42, 540
  school prayer and, 1508–9, 1655
  Second Great Awakening in, 539–47
  segregation and, 1615
  slavery justified through, 668–69
  in South, 629, 642
  in southern colonies, 127–29
  temperance and, 567
  transcendentalism and, 548–49
  unitarianism and, 538
  universalism and, 539–40
  utopian communities and, 575–76
  witchcraft and, 140–43
  see also revivals, religious; specific religions
    and denominations

religious freedom, 37, 51, 52, 144
  after American Revolution, 283–84
  in Bill of Rights, 333
  disestablishment and, 439
  in Four Freedoms, 1310
  French colonies and, 179
  in Maryland, 83
  in Massachusetts, 140
  in Pennsylvania, 95, 144
  Roger Williams and, 73, 74, 75–76
  and separation of church and state, 73
  in South Carolina, 86
  voting rights and, 175
Religious Right, 1608–9, 1630, 1656–57, 1660
rendez-vous system, 591
Reno, Janet, 1668
Reparations Commission, 1288, 1361
Report on Manufactures (Hamilton), 335,
    336, 340, 341
Report on the Condition of the Indian Tribes,
    867
Representative Men (Emerson), 552
Republican party:
  African Americans in, 1265–66
  anti-Catholicism in, 528
  in Civil War, 764
  cold war and, 1376
  and Contract with America, 1674–75
  corruption and, 994–95
  cultural conservatives and, 1655–57
  in election of 1856, 701–2
  in election of 1860, 713–14
  in election of 1868, 823
  in election of 1872, 827–28
  in election of 1876, 830–33, 830
  in election of 1884, 1000–1001
  in election of 1888, 1007–8
  in election of 1894, 1024
  in election of 1908, 1093
  in election of 1912, 1098, 1104
  in election of 1916, 1112, 1131
  in election of 1918, 1149
  in election of 1920, 1197–98
  in election of 1928, 1217–18
  in election of 1932, 1233
  in election of 1936, 1265
  in election of 1940, 1308–9
  in election of 1948, 1404
  in election of 1952, 1461, 1471
  in election of 1956, 1480
  in election of 1964, 1526–27
  in election of 1968, 1544, 1556
  in election of 1972, 1587
  in election of 1976, 1595
  in election of 1980, 1611
  in election of 1992, 1660–61
  in election of 1994, 1673–75
  emergence of, 696–97
  KKK intimidation of, 820
  late nineteenth-century components of, 993

Lincoln's early involvement with, 709
Mugwumps in, 1001, 1074
nativism in, 994
New Deal and, 1377
new states approved by, 865–66
in 1920s, 1033, 1105
1960s conservatism of, 1526
nineteenth-century dominance of, 1009
nineteenth-century economy and, 889
Reagan's rise in, 1607
in Reconstruction, 821, 822, 846
scalawags in, 817–18, 820, 822
slavery compromise sought by, 720
in South, 849, *1462*, 1463–64
Spanish-American War and, 1053
Stalwarts vs. Half-Breeds in, 995–96,
    997–98, 999, 1001
in Taft administration, 1095–96, 1097
tariff issue and, 990, 1007, 1010
see also Radical Republicans
Republicans, Jeffersonian, 243, 416
Adams criticized by, 360
Alien and Sedition Acts and, 364
and *Dartmouth College* v. *Woodward,* 425
in election of 1796, 359
in election of 1800, 366–68
in election of 1816, 414
in election of 1824, 431
Federalists' role reversal with, 406, 410
formation of, 342–45
French conflict and, 362, 364
French Revolution and, 347
Hartford Convention and, 404
Jay's Treaty and, 348
Jefferson's party role with, 373–74
land policy of, 353
Louisiana Purchase and, 379
national bank and, 376, 411
officeholder conflicts and, 374, 375–76
split among, 384–85
War of 1812 and, 406
Washington criticized by, 359
Whiskey Rebellion and, 351
Republic Steel, 1273
Rerum novarum (Leo XIII), 980
Resaca de la Palma, Battle of (1846), 613
reservations (Indian), 588–89, 867–68,
    871–72
Resignation of General Washington, The
    (Trumbull), 285
Resolution Trust Corporation (RTC), 1633
Restoration, English, 51
Resumption Act (1875), 829
retail, 906–8
Reuther, Walter, 1272, 1383
Revels, Hiram, *816,* 817
Revenue (Sugar) Act (1764), 206, 207, 209,
    210, 213, 216, 218
Revenue Act (1767), 213, 214
Revenue Act (1916), 1130–32

Revenue Act (1926), 1200
Revenue Act (1935), 1254, 1258
Revenue Act (1942), 1326
revenue sharing, 1581
Revere, Paul, *217*
at Continental Congress, 225
warning ride of, 229
revivals, religious, 1444
and "burned-over" district, 542–44
on the frontier, 540–42
Great Awakening, 156–62
and Mormons, 544–47
Second Great Awakening, 540–44
Reykjavik Summit (1987), 1621, 1629
Reynolds, W. W., 960
Rhea, John, 418
Rhett, Robert Barnwell, 688
Rhineland, 1298
Rhode Island:
Civil War troops from, 758
Constitutional Convention avoided by, 309
Constitution ratified by, 322, 324
government of, 274
at Hartford Convention, 404
paper currency in, 305–6
Revolutionary troops from, 230, 279
slavery in, 279–80
Rhode Island, College of (Brown University),
    161, 565
Rhode Island colony, 44, 86
charter of, 84, 137, 174
European settlement of, 73–76
in events before American Revolution, 220
government of, 84, 137, 170, 173, 174
as refuge, 146
and Roger Williams, 73–74, 75–76
Rhode Island (Fall River) system, 509–10
rhythm and blues (R & B), 1433
Ricard, Cyprien, 646
rice, 23, 86, 116, 409, 630, 792, 844
Rice, Thomas "Daddy," 518, *518*
rich:
in colonial period, 126–29, 149
in early nineteenth century, 532–33, *533*
housing of, 505
in late nineteenth century, 908–9, 954
in late twentieth century, 1378
in post–World War II era, 1428
and profits from wartime ventures, 765
recreation of, 515
social origins of, 532–33
in South, 126–27, 635–36, 636–39
at theater, 517
Richardson, Elliot, 1590
Richmond, Va., 792
bread riot in (1863), 769
capture of (1865), 783–84
as Confederate capital, 734, 736
as military goal of Union army, 734, 736,
    747–48, 779, 783

Richmond (continued)
  streetcars in, 844
  Tredegar Iron Works in, 732
Rickey, Branch, 1402
Ridgway, Matthew B., 1414, 1415
Riesman, David, 1448, 1449
Rights of the British Colonists Asserted and
    Proved, The (Grenville), 208
"right-to-work" laws, 1328, 1386, 1487
Riis, Jacob, 937, 1075
Rio de Janeiro, Treaty of, 1420
Ripley, George, 549, 578
Rise of Silas Lapham, The (Howells), 974
Rittenhouse, David, 154
River, The, 1282
river transportation:
  federal funding for, 410, 412, 414, 453, 501
  to frontier regions, 492–96, 498
  Gibbons v. Ogden, 427–28
  state funding for, 472, 495, 501
  steamboats on, 427–28, 493–94, 505
roads, see highways and roads
Roanoke Island, 23, 44–45, 44
Roaring Twenties, 1173–85
Roberts, Ed, 1645
Roberts, Owen, 1270
Robertson, Pat, 1656, 1660–61
Robinson, Edward G., 1283
Robinson, Jackie, 1401–2, 1401
Rochambeau, comte de, 268
Rockefeller, John D., 765, 895, 898–901, 900,
    905, 952, 967
Rockingham, marquis of, 211, 212, 213, 270
Rockne, Knute, 942
rock 'n' roll, 1432–35, 1558–59
rodeos, 956
Roebling, John A., 934
Roebling, Washington, 934
Roebuck, Alvah, 898, 906
Roe v. Wade, 1563, 1609
Rogers, Will, 1149, 1206
Rogers, William P., 1577–78
Rolfe, John, 58–59, 60
Rolfe, Thomas, 59
Rolling Stones, 1559
Rolling Thunder, Operation, 1537
Romania, 1151
  fall of communism in, 1635
  Soviet domination of, 1391
  in World War II, 1311, 1392
Romanian Americans, 939
romanticism, 547–52
  in art and architecture, 547
  flowering of American literature and,
    552–60
  transcendentalism and, 548–49
romantic movement, 445
Rommel, Erwin, 1311, 1339, 1348, 1351
Roosevelt, Anna, 1267

Roosevelt, Eleanor, 1233, 1234, 1260–68,
    1266, 1267, 1503
Roosevelt, Franklin D., 1033
  Atlantic Charter and, 1312, 1388
  atomic bombs and, 1367
  background of, 1233–34
  brain trust of, 1238
  at Cairo and Teheran, 1346
  at Casablanca, 1339
  China and, 1409
  Churchill's 1941 meeting with, 1312
  court-packing plan of, 1268–71, 1269
  death of, 1363–64
  Democratic primary intervention of,
    1276–77
  in election of 1932, 1233–35, 1235, 1236
  in election of 1936, 1265–66
  in election of 1940, 1308–9
  in election of 1944, 1358
  fireside chats of, 1281
  first inauguration of, 1236–38, 1237
  Four Freedoms articulated by, 1310
  French occupation zone and, 1361
  growing war involvement and, 1307,
    1309–12
  Japanese Americans relocated by, 1335–36
  Japanese assets frozen by, 1313
  Johnson's admiration of, 1522, 1528
  Joseph Kennedy and, 1503
  labor movement and, 1272–73
  Latin American policy of, 1294
  leftward movement of, 1253
  legacy of, 1377
  postwar world as seen by, 1388
  racial issues ignored by, 1264
  Truman compared with, 1380
  U.S. neutrality and, 1301, 1302, 1303, 1304
  war aims and, 1337–38
  war financing and, 1326
  World Court and, 1288
  in Yalta, 1360–61, 1361
  see also Depression, Great; New Deal
Roosevelt, Sara, 1267
Roosevelt, Theodore, 541, 962, 1009, 1027,
    1036, 1074, 1088, 1100, 1165
  assassination attempt on, 1102–3
  big stick diplomacy of, 1060–70, 1067
  coal strike and, 1086–87
  conservation promoted by, 1091–92
  Cuban insurrection and, 1058
  in election of 1900, 1062, 1062
  in election of 1904, 1089
  in election of 1912, 1098–1100, 1102–5,
    1104
  in election of 1916, 1130–31, 1132
  executive action favored by, 1084–86
  food safety and, 1091
  Japan relations and, 1068
  Panama Canal and, 1063–66, 1066

progressivism of, 1084–92
rise of, 1061–63
and Rough Riders, 1049–50
Spanish-American War and, 1045–46, 1048,
    1049, *1050,* 1062
Taft's break with, 1097–98
Taft selected as successor by, 1092–93
trusts and, 1084–85, *1085,* 1087
Venezuela border and, 1042
Versailles Treaty opposed by, 1153
World War I and, 1128, *1129*
Roosevelt Corollary, 1066–67
Roosevelt Dam, 879
Root, Elihu, 1068
Rosecrans, William S., 746, 775, 776
Rosenberg, Ethel, *1417,* 1418, 1470
Rosenberg, Julius, *1417,* 1418, 1470
Rosenwald, Julius, 907
Ross, John, 742
Ross, Robert, 400
Rossiter, Thomas Pritchard, *318*
Rostow, Walt, 1519
Roth, Philip, 1451
Rothko, Mark, 1453
Rothman, David, 569
Roughing It (Twain), 972
Rough Riders, 1049, 1050, *1050,* 1062
Roundheads, 51
Royal Air Force (RAF), 1345
Royal Navy, 1307, 1310
Royal Proclamation (1763), 202–3, 278
Roybal, Edward R., 1567
RTC (Resolution Trust Corporation), 1633
Rubin, Jerry, 1552
Ruby, Jack, 1521
Ruby Ridge, Idaho, stand-off at (1992),
    1666–67
Ruckelshaus, William, 1590
Rudd, Mark, 1554, *1555*
Ruffin, Edmund, 633, 688
rugby, 963
Rule of 1756, 347
Rump Parliament, 51
Rural Electrification Administration (REA),
    1250–51, 1467
Rush, Benjamin, 288, 289, 567
Rush, Richard, 416
Rush-Bagot Agreement (1817), 416
Rusk, Dean, 1518, 1539
Russell, Jonathan, 403
Russell, Richard, 1496
Russia:
    Alaska and, 428, 1038
    in Bering Sea sealing dispute, 1041
    Bolshevik Revolution in, 922, 1142,
        1145–46, 1158, 1159–60
    California and, 592
    in China, 1058, 1059
    in colonial wars, *185,* 192

Monroe Doctrine and, 430
in Napoleonic Wars, 387
Oregon Country and, 428–29, 591
in Quintuple Alliance, 429
in Russo-Japanese War, 1067–68, 1069,
    1363
seal traders from, 33, 592
after Soviet era, 1657, 1661, 1669
in World War I, 1122, 1134, 1142, 1145
see also Soviet Union
Russian-American Company, 428
Russian Americans, 939, 943, 945
Russo-Japanese War, 1067–68, 1069, 1363
Rutgers University (Queen's College), 161
Rutledge, John, 313–14
Rwanda, 1377
Ryswick, Treaty of (1697), *185,* 186

Saar Basin, 1151, 1298
Sacajawea, 381
Sacco, Nicola, *1164,* 1165
Sackville-West, Sir Lionel, 1008
Sadat, Anwar el-, 1586–87, 1598–99, *1599*
Sagadahoc, Maine, 65
Sahl, Mort, 1457
St. Augustine, Fla., 33–34, 177, 202
St. Christopher, 70, 186
St. Domingue, *see* Haiti
St. Lawrence Seaway, 1467
St. Leger, Barry, 256
St. Louis, Mo., 514, 934, 1022
St. Marks, Fla., 202
St. Mary's, Md., 109
St. Vincent, 196
Saipan, 1356
Salem, Mass., 139, *139,* 140, 142–43
Salinger, J. D., 1452
SALT (Strategic Arms Limitation Talks), 1586,
    1594, 1600
Salvation Army, 978
Samoa, 1039, 1053
Sampson, Deborah, 282
San Antonio, Tex., 177, 1653
Sanchez, H. E. Carlo, *1290*
Sand Creek massacre, 866–67
San Diego, Calif., 1329
Sandinistas, 1617, 1624, 1635
Sandino, César Augusto, 1293
S&L (savings and loan) crisis, 1625, 1633
"Sand Lot" incident, 912
Sandys, Sir Edwin, 59, 61
San Francisco, Calif., 931, 933, 1329
    anti-Chinese violence in, 912
    gold rush and, *679*
San Francisco *Alta Californian,* 972
San Francisco conference (1945), 1388–89,
    1391
Sanger, Margaret, *1178*
San Salvador, 19

Santa Anna, Antonio López de, 603, 604–5, 617
Santa Clara County v. Southern Pacific
    Railroad Company, 985
Santa Fe, N. Mex., 36, 177, 596
Santa Fe Railroad, 892, 931
Santa Fe Trail, 592, 596
Santa María, 18, 19
Santana, 1559
Santo Domingo, 26, 429
Saratoga, Battle of (1777), 254, 255–57, 258,
    259
Saratoga, U.S.S., 400
Sargent, A. A., 983
Sartoris (Faulkner), 1192, 1193
Sassacus, Pequot chief, 80
Sassamon, 82
Saudi Arabia:
    in Arab League, 1482
    Persian Gulf War and, 1640
Sauks, 92, 462–63, 1334–35
SAVAK, 1601
Savannah, Ga., 99
    Battle of (1778), 263
    fall of (1864), 782
savings and loan (S&L) crisis, 1625, 1633
Savio, Mario, 1552
sawmills, 133
scalawags, 817–18, 820, 822
Scalia, Antonin, 1682
Scandinavia, Reformation in, 37
Scandinavian Americans, 144, 526, 858
    in Civil War, 738
Scarlet Letter, The (Hawthorne), 552, 553, 553
Schechter Poultry Corporation v. United States,
    1253–54
Schenck v. United States, 1142
Schmacher, Ferdinand, 525
school prayer, 1508–9, 1655
Schurz, Carl, 525–26, 801, 827–28, 996
Schuyler, Philip, 344
Schwenkfelders, 38
science:
    in colonial era, 152–55
    in early nineteenth century, 504–5
    in twentieth century, 1185–88
Scioto Company, 297
SCLC (Southern Christian Leadership
    Conference), 1496, 1510
Scopes, John T., 1169, 1169, 1192
Scotch-Irish Americans, 22, 98, 144, 145, 146,
    147, 158, 355, 540, 642, 643
Scotland, 38, 50, 52
Scots, Highland, 99, 146
Scott, Dred, 703–5, 704, 708, 710
Scott, Thomas, 902
Scott, Winfield, 395, 461, 478, 479
    in Civil War, 729, 734, 736, 747
    in election of 1852, 690, 702
    in Mexican War, 613, 617, 618–19, 620

Scottish Americans, 94, 99, 144, 145, 146,
    351, 642
    in American Revolution, 233
    in Civil War, 738
Scottsboro case, 1228, 1264
Screen Actors Guild, 1607, 1615
SDI (Strategic Defense Initiative), 1616, 1621
SDS (Students for a Democratic Society),
    1551, 1554, 1555, 1555
Seamen's Union, 1111
search warrants, 200–201
Sears, Richard, 898, 906
Sears and Roebuck, 906–8
SEATO (Southeast Asia Treaty Organization),
    1477
Seattle, Wash., 1329
    strikes in, 1158
Sea Wolf, The (London), 975
secession, considered by New England, 383,
    403–4
secession of South, 717–19, 726–29, 727
    Buchanan's response to, 719–20
    choosing sides, 726–29
    efforts at compromise, 720
    forfeited-rights theory and, 804
    Lincoln's response to, 719, 724–25, 727,
        728
    movement for, 717–19
Second Great Awakening, 539–47
    and "burned-over" district, 542–44
    on frontier, 540–42
    and Mormons, 544–47
    and New England colleges, 539
    and salvation, 543
Second Report on Public Credit (Hamilton),
    336
Securities and Exchange Commission (SEC),
    1240, 1487
Sedition Act (1798), 364, 365, 365, 366
Sedition Act (1918), 1141
segregation, desegregation:
    in armed forces, 1331–32, 1401
    of Asian Americans, 1068
    under Bourbon Redeemers, in New South,
        850, 852–54
    busing and, 1579, 1659
    cold war and, 1400
    in early twentieth century, 1184
    in education, 1068, 1401, 1426, 1492–94,
        1509, 1511–12, 1531, 1579–80, 1615,
        1682
    Eleanor Roosevelt and, 1268
    and election of 1948, 1405
    and election of 1968, 1544
    freedom riders, 1509, 1511
    in housing, 1262, 1437
    "Jim Crow" laws, 852–53
    Montgomery bus boycott and, 1494–96,
        1509

in New Deal programs, 1242, 1262
in nineteenth century, 850, 852–56
in public accommodations, 853
of schools, 1492–93, 1496, 1497, 1511,
    1531, 1579–80
"separate but equal" rubric, 853, 854,
    1492–93
suburbanization and, 1437
in transportation, 853, 1494–96
Wilson's endorsement of, 1111–12
in World War II, 1331–1333
see also African Americans; civil rights
    movement
Selective Service Act (1917), 1136
self-incrimination, 275, 333
"Self-Reliance" (Emerson), 550
Seminoles, 329, 418, *418*, 462
    in Civil War, 742, 743
    Creek refugees take name of, 418
    removal of, 462, 463, 464–65
Senate, U.S.:
    Compromise of 1850 in, 682–88
    in Constitution, 316, 317
    Convention of 1800 ratified by, 363
    Jay's Treaty approved by, 348
    Johnson's trial in, 811–12
    Louisiana Purchase approved by, 380
    violence on floor of (1856), 699–701
    see also Congress, U.S.
Seneca Falls Convention (1848), 573
Senecas, 91, 262
Sennett, Mack, 1208
"separate but equal," 853, 854, 1492, 1496
separation of church and state, 73
separation of powers, 275, 316–19
separatists, African-American, 1533, 1534–35
Separatists, Puritan, 40, 65–66, 69, 136
Serbia, 1671, 1672
    in World War I, 1122, 1151
serfdom, 50
Sergeant, John, 469
Serra, Junipero, 592
servants, *see* indentured servants
settlement house movement, 980–81, 1081,
    1268
Seven Days' Battles (1862), 749
Seven Pines (Fair Oaks), Battle of (1862), 749
Seventeenth Amendment, 1077, 1099
Seven Years' War, *see* French and Indian War
Seward, William H.:
    appointed secretary of state, 725
    assassination attempt on, 798
    and Compromise of 1850, 682, 685
    and election of 1856, 701
    in election of 1860, 715
    Pacific policy and, 1037–38, *1038*
sewer systems, 505
sewing machines, 506
sex ratios, 112–13

sexual relations:
    in 1920s, 1176–77, 1178
    AIDS and, 1628
    Puritans on, 136
    slavery and, 639, 656–66
Seymour, Horatio, 823
Shahn, Ben, *1164, 1171*, 1280
shah of Iran (Mohammed Reza Pahlavi),
    1600
Shakers (United Society of Believers in
    Christ's Second Coming), 575–76, *576*
Shakespeare, William, 56
Shame of the Cities, The (Steffens), 1075,
    1075
Share Croppers Union, 1228
sharecropping, 844–45, *845*
Share Our Wealth program, 1252–53
Sharpsburg (Antietam), Battle of (1862),
    751–52, 756
Shaw, Anna Howard, 983
Shaw, Robert Gould, 758, 759
Shawnees, 202, 204, 262, 349, 393, *393*, 394,
    479, 696
Shays, Daniel, 306, *307*
Shays's Rebellion, 306–8
Sheen, Fulton J., 1444
sheep, 22, 109, 132, 632
    in nineteenth-century West, 876, 877
Shelburne, Lord, 270
Shepard, Alan B., Jr., 1487
Shephard, Morris, 1171
Sheridan, Philip H., 783, 784, 868
Sherman, John, 889, 1010
Sherman, Roger, 234, 311, 313
Sherman, William Tecumseh, 777, *781*, 810,
    889
    Atlanta destroyed by, 782
    at Chattanooga, 776
    Johnston's surrender to, 784
    in march to sea, 780–83, *782*, 791
    at Shiloh, 745
    at Vicksburg, 773
Sherman Anti-Trust Act (1890), 843, 901, 922,
    1010, 1080, 1085, 1087, 1109
Sherman Silver Purchase Act (1890), 1010,
    1016, 1024, 1026
Shevardnadze, Eduard, 1640
shipbuilding, 132, 133
Shirley, William, 188
shoemakers' strike (1860), 532
shoemaking, 507
Sholes, Christopher, 896
Shultz, George, 1623, 1624
Siberia, 5
"Significance of the Frontier in American
    History, The" (Turner), 883–84
Signing the Constitution (Rossiter), *318*
Sihanouk, Prince Norodom, 1572
Silent Spring (Carson), 1583

silver:
    currency and, 997, 1010, 1015, 1024–25,
        1028
    in mercantile system, 167
    mining of, 741, *861*, 864
    Spanish Empire and, 31, 35, 36, 177
Simmons, William J., 1166, 1167
Simms, William Gilmore, 555
Simpson, "Sockless Jerry," 1021
Sims, William S., 1135
Sinai, 1594
Sinclair, Harry, 1203
Sinclair, Upton, 1091
Singer, Isaac Merritt, 506
Singleton, Benjamin "Pap," 859–60
"Sinners in the Hands of an Angry God"
        (Edwards), 159–60
Sino-Japanese War, 1058
Sioux, 380, 462–63, 586, 587, 588, 589, 597,
        865, 866, 868–69, 869, 870, 956
Sioux War (1860s–1870s), 868–69
Sirhan, Sirhan, 1543
Sirica, John J., 1588
Sister Carrie (Dreiser), 975
Sitting Bull, chief of Sioux, 868, 870, 956
Six-Day War (1967), 1586
Six-Power Consortium, 1118–19
Sixteenth Amendment, 1099
Sketch Book, The (Irving), 554
"slash-and-burn" techniques, 79, 108
Slater, Samuel, 503, 526
Slater, John F., Fund, 847–48
slave codes, 120, 652
slavery, 454, 461, 629
    American Revolution and, 278–81
    banned from Old Northwest, 298, 674, 675,
        676, 684
    California and, 676, 681–82, 683, 687
    Civil War as crusade against, 754–56
    in colonial period, 60, 86, 98, 117, 119–21,
        123–26, 134
    and Compromise of 1850, 682–91, 687
    in Constitution, 313–15, 377
    defense of, 668–69
    in District of Columbia, 478
    Dred Scott case and, 703–5, 708, 710
    economics of, 635–36
    and election of 1844, 607
    emancipation and, 754–63, 791
    Kansas-Nebraska crisis over, 693–702
    Lincoln-Douglas debates on, 708–11
    Mexican War and, 612
    Missouri Compromise and, 421–24, *423*,
        454, 629, 674, 676, 684, 686, 694, 701,
        705
    New Mexico and, 676, 682, 685, 687
    northern end to, 279
    origins of, 119–21, 125
    religious justification of, 668–69

    southern defense of, 627, 628, 667–69
    in territories, 674–82
    Texas annexation and, 605–6, 609
    Thirteenth Amendment and, 315, 760, 789,
        801, 806, 834
    Tyler and, 583
    Wilmot Proviso and, 674–75, 684
    see also abolition movement
slaves, 98, 99, 106, 132, 148, 186–87
    African roots of, 121–23
    in American Revolution, 232, 251, 347, 348
    after American Revolution, 299
    baptism and status of, 124
    black ownership of, 646, 647–48
    community of, 653–54
    as "contrabands," 755, 756
    culture of, 123–26
    emancipation of, 278–81, 298, 625, 646,
        661–69, 754–63, 791
    escaped, 418, 652
    freed, 646–48
    fugitive slave laws and, 664, 683, 687–88,
        696
    Indian ownership of, 648
    Indians as, 20, 81, 82, 86, 87–88, 87, 125,
        186
    in industry, 634, 635
    infant mortality of, 652
    insurrections of, 123, 454, 652–53, 663,
        712, 733
    management of, 640
    manumission of, 280
    marriage of, 125, 656
    middle-class southerners and, 640–41
    in Old Southwest, 659
    plantations and, 636–38, 639, 651–53
    population of, 638, *649*
    prices of, 648
    religion and, 654–55, *656*
    sexual exploitation of, 639, 656–66
    in southern mythology, 627–28
    southern white culture and, 636
    in West, 488
    slave trade, 3, 86, 91, *122*, 123, 134, 313–15,
        314, 648–51
    constitutional provisions on, 314, 315
    in District of Columbia, 478, 688
    end of, 279, 377, 584, 585, 648, 650
    foreign, outlawing of, 377, 584, 585, 658
    within U.S., 650–51, 683, 688, 755
Slavic Americans, 943
Slavs, 125–26
Slidell, John, 612, 766
Sloat, John D., 614
Slovak Americans, 939, 943
Slovene Americans, 939
Small, Albion W., 969
smallpox, 23, *24*, 79, 94, 111
Smalls, Robert, 756

Smart Set, 1173–74
Smith, Adam, 299
Smith, Alfred E., 1217, 1234, 1251–52, 1504
Smith, Bessie, 1174
Smith, Billy, *1510*
Smith, "Cotton" Ed, 1276
Smith, Francis, 228–29
Smith, Hyrum, 545
Smith, John, *56, 58,* 60
  background of, 55
  and Pocahontas, 58
Smith, Joseph, Jr., 544–45
Smith Act (1940), 1417, 1419, 1470–71
Smith College, 952, 963
Smith-Connally War Labor Disputes Act
  (1943), 1328
Smith-Hughes Act (1917), 1113
Smith-Lever Act (1914), 1113
Smithson, James, 504
Smithsonian Institution, 504
Smith v. Allwright, 1333
smuggling, 133, 187, 206, 213, 216, 220, 299,
  768
Smyth v. Ames, 986
snail darter, 1584
SNCC (Student Nonviolent Coordinating
  Committee), 1510, 1533
Snyder, Gary, 1454
social change, theories of, 965–69
social criticism, 976–78
Social Darwinism, 966–68, *967,* 978
Social Democratic party, 923
Social Gospel, 978–80
socialism:
  Fourieristic, 578
  labor movement and, 922–24
  public utilities and, 1080
Socialist International, 919
Socialist Labor party, 922
Socialist party, 923, 977, 980, 1074, 1206
  in presidential elections, 1093, 1102, 1105,
    1235
  in World War I, 1141
  after World War I, 1159–60
Socialist Trade and Labor Alliance, 922
social sciences, study of, 969–70
Social Security, 1274, 1277, 1407, 1466,
  1508, 1527, 1613, 1630
  inflation and, 1581
  Supreme Court and, 1269
Social Security Act (1935), 1254, 1255–57,
  1262, 1270
Society of Female Manufacturing Workers,
  1263
sociology, 969
Soil Conservation and Domestic Allotment Act
  (1936), 1245–46
Soil Conservation Service, 1246
Soldier's Pay (Faulkner), 1193

Solomon Islands, 1352
Somalia, 1377, 1670–71
Somoza Debayle, Anastasio, 1617
Somoza García, Anastasio, 1293
Son of the Middle Border, A (Garland), 936
Sons of Liberty, 209, 215, *215*
Sons of Temperance, 567
Soto, Hernando de, *32, 33*
Soulé, Pierre, 691
Sound and the Fury, The (Faulkner), 1192,
  1193
Souter, David, 1682
South, 624–72, 840–57
  African-American culture in, 123–26,
    653–57
  African Americans in politics of, 850
  agriculture in, 115–17, 629–32, 636–39,
    640, 651–53, 658, 732–33, 844–46
  in American Revolution, 263–69, *264*
  architecture of, 638
  Bourbon Redeemers in, 846–50, *847,* 851,
    856–57
  in colonial period, 115–29
  cotton in, 486–87
  devastation of, by Civil War, 782–83,
    791–92
  distinctiveness of, 628–36
  dueling in, 644–46
  economy of, 634–36, 840–41, 847–49
  education in, 157, *847,* 849
  free persons of color in, 646–48
  in French and Indian War, 193
  frontier of, 657–61
  gentry in, 125–29
  honor and violence in, 642–46
  Indian conflicts in, 187, 193
  Irish Americans in, 522
  land policies in, 117–18
  literature of, 554–55
  manufactures in, 634–35, 642
  masculine culture in, 643–44, 660
  middle class in, 640–41
  Middle Colonies' trade with, 143
  migration to Southwest, 658–60
  military tradition in, 733
  mythology of, 629–30, 643
  New Deal and, 1276
  New England compared with, 134
  plantations in, 636–39, *637,* 651–53
  poor whites in, 629–30, 641
  post–Civil War devastation in, 791–92
  professionals in, 642
  railroads in, 848–49
  after Reconstruction, 840–57
  religion in, 629, 642
  Republican party in, 849, *1462, 1463–64*
  secession of, 717–19, 726–29, *727*
  sex ratios in, 112
  slaves in, 119–21, 123–26, 648–57

South (*continued*)
society and economy in, 115–29
soil exhaustion in, 632
and Tariff of 1816, 412
trade and commerce in, 634–35
voting rights in, 642
War of 1812 in, 398–99, 399
Whigs in, 474, 475
white society in, 636–46
under Wilson, 1105
see also Civil War, U.S.; Confederate States
of America; Reconstruction
South Africa, 1636
South Carolina:
African Americans in legislature of, 850
agriculture in, 630, 632–33, 844, 845
Civil War fighting in, 725–26, 730, 738,
758–59, 783
Constitution ratified by, 322
cotton in, 486, 487
and Declaration of Independence, 278
disestablishment in, 439
education in, 561
in election of 1800, 367
in election of 1876, 832
emancipation in, 755
government of, 85–86, 171, 175
Indian lands ceded in, 299
land claims of, 295
migration from, 658
nullification and, 436, 454, 457, 459, 461
paper currency in, 305
post–Revolutionary debt in, 337
primaries adopted in, 1076
Reconstruction in, 801, 812, 817, 822, 833
Revolutionary fighting in, 233, 262, 265,
266
Revolutionary loyalties in, 250
Revolutionary troops from, 263, 266, 279
secession of, 717
segregation in, 852, 1493, 1511
slave trade to, 279, 377
turnpikes in, 501
voting rights in, 438, 439, 851
South Carolina colony, 87–88, 144
agriculture in, 116
backcountry of, 147, 219
in colonial wars, 186
gentry of, 126
Huguenots in, 33
Indians in, 86
as refuge, 146
Regulators in, 219
settlement of, 85–86
sex ratios in, 112
slaves in, 121
trade and commerce in, 116–17
South Carolina Exposition and Protest
(Calhoun), 436, 454, 456

South Carolina Ordinance, 460
South Carolina Red Shirts, 822
South Dakota:
agriculture in, 880, 1017
election reforms in, 1076
Indian conflicts in, 868
mining in, 865
Populists in, 1020
statehood for, 865, 1010
Southeast Asia Treaty Organization (SEATO),
1477
South End House, 980
Southern Christian Leadership Conference
(SCLC), 1496, 1510
Southern Manifesto (1956), 1494
Southern Pacific Railroad, 892, 931, 1080
Southern Power Company, 844
Southern Renaissance, 1191–94
South Improvement Company, 899
Southwest, Old, 657–61
Soviet Union, 1142, 1584
Afghanistan invaded by, 1600, 1618, 1629,
1635
Berlin crises and, 1396–97, *1398*, 1489–90,
1515
Chinese conflicts with, 1295
containment and, 1392–94, 1420, 1472,
1473, 1540, 1657
Cuba and, 1492
Cuban missile crisis and, 1516–18, *1517*
détente with, 1585–86
dissolution of, 1636–39, 1657
Dulles's alliances and, 1481–82
Eastern Europe dominated by, 1362,
1390–91, 1396, 1472, 1484–85, 1635
economy of, 1636–37, 1638–39
Germany occupied by, 1396, *1397*
immigration from, *1655*
Indochina and, 1477, 1519
Korean War and, 1411, 1412, 1415
Latin America and, 1616, 1624
liberalization in, 1629, 1635
Nasser and, 1488
1991 coup attempt in, 1637
nuclear arms treaties with, 1518, 1527,
1586, 1600, 1621, 1629, 1639
nuclear weapons of, 1410, 1474
Reagan and, 1616
SALT, 1586, 1594, 1600
Spanish Civil War and, 1302
Sputnik launched by, 1485–87
Suez War and, 1481
trade with, 1298, 1586
in United Nations, 1361, 1388
Vietnam War and, 1539
in World War II, 1311, 1312, 1337, 1338,
1346, 1359, 1360, 1361, 1362, 1364,
1364, 1369, 1370, 1371, 1372, 1425
see also cold war; Russia

space program, 1486–87, 1578
Spain, 378, 380, 385, 417–20
    American Revolution and, 233, 257, 258,
        270, 271
    Civil War in, 1298–99, 1300, 1302
    colonial trade with, 133, 186
    in colonial wars, *185*, 186–87, 188, 194,
        195
    decline of, 418
    early U.S. relations with, 302, 349
    explorations of, 18–21, *18*, 25, 31–34, *32*
    Indian conflicts and, 299, 329, 351–52
    Mexican independence from, 177, 590, 593,
        603
    in Napoleonic Wars, 387–88, 390, 429, 590
    in NATO, 1398
    Oregon Country claim of, 428, 591
    Pinckney Treaty with, 351–52
    in slave trade, 125
    in Spanish-American War, 1029, 1032,
        1042–58, *1051*
    and U.S. Mississippi access, 303
    and War of 1812, 395, 401
Spanish Americans, 146, 738
Spanish-American War, 1029, 1032, 1042–58,
    1051
    annexation debate after, 1052–56
    casualties in, 1051
    Cuba in, 1043–47, 1048–51, 1054
    Maine incident and, 1045–46
    Manila Bay taken, 1048
    organizing acquisitions from, 1056–58
    Philippines in, 1048, 1051
    pressure for, 1044–48
    Rough Riders in, 1049–50
Spanish Empire, 13, 26–36, 88, 89, 178,
    589–90, 592
    Aztecs defeated by, 9
    British Empire compared with, 30, 53,
        77–78, 102, 165, 178, 182
    California as territory of, 34, 592–93
    Catholicism and, 29, 30, 34–35, 178, 195,
        590
    challenges to, 40–45
    colonization in, 33–34
    conquests of, 27–29
    Cromwell's conflicts with, 83–84
    decline of, 177–78, 418
    decolonization of, 429
    European diseases spread in, 24
    Florida as territory of, 31, 32, 195, 378, 395,
        418–20, 590
    Louisiana as territory of, 195, 351, 378
    maps of, *181*, *194*, *195*
    Mexico as territory of, 31, 593
    missionaries in, 34, 35–36, 87, 590, 592–94
    privateers' attacks against, 41–42
    silver mining and, 864
    in Treaty of Tordesillas, 19
Spanish flu, 1156–57
special prosecutors, 1683
Specie Circular, 472
speculators:
    in bonds, 335–36
    in gold, 825–26
    in land, 188, 202, 353, 354, 421, 422–73,
        1220
speech, freedom of, 275, 333, 364
speedy trial, right to, 333
Spencer, Herbert, 966, 967, *967*, 968
Spice Islands (Moluccas), 25, 26
Spindletop gusher (1901), 844, 1211
spinning jenny, 503
spinning mule, 503
Spock, Benjamin, 1449–50, *1449*
spoils system, patronage, 450–51, 991
    Cleveland and, 1003
    Harrison and, 1009
    Hayes's efforts against, 996
Spokanes, 587
sports:
    baseball, 963–65, 1401–2
    basketball, 963–65
    bicycling, 959–60
    boxing, 961
    croquet, 958, 959
    football, 962–63
    in nineteenth century, 515–16, 958–65
    segregation in, 1401–2
    spectator, 961–65
    tennis, 958–59
    women in, 958, 959–60
Spotsylvania Court House, Battle of (1864),
    779
Spotted Tail, chief of Sioux, 869
Sputnik, 1485–87
Spy, The (Cooper), 554
Squanto, 67
squatters' rights, 355
Sri Lanka (Ceylon), 1475
Stabilization Act (1942), 1327
stagecoaches, 150, 492, 499
stagflation, 1581, 1582, 1594, 1611
Stalin, Joseph:
    containment and, 1392
    death of, 1468
    denunciation of, 1484
    Korean War and, 1411
    and spheres of influence, 1419
    in World War II, 1337, 1339, 1346, 1350,
        1360–61, 1363, 1390, 1391, 1409
Stalwarts, 995–96, 997–98, 999
Stamp Act (1765), 207–13, *210*, 216, 270, 285
    colonial protests against, 209–11
    repeal of, 211–13
Stamp Act Congress (1765), 211
Standard Oil Company, 898, *900*, 901, 976,
    1075, 1087

Standard Oil Trust, 900–901
Standish, Miles, 66
Stanford, Leland, 891–92, 952
Stanford University, 952
Stanley, Ann Lee (Mother Ann), 575–76
Stanton, Anthony, 982
Stanton, Edwin M., 767, 808, 810
Stanton, Elizabeth Cady, 573, 574, 982
Staple (Navigation) Act (1663), 168
Stark, John, 257
Starley, J. K., 959
Star of the West, 720
Starr, Ellen, 980
Starr, Kenneth, 1684, 1686
Star Route Frauds, 999
"Star-Spangled Banner, The," 401
Star Wars, see Strategic Defense Initiative (SDI)
state-compact theory, 365, 457
State Department, U.S., 331
  McCarthyism and, 1418
state power:
  civil rights movement and, 1492
  after Civil War, 992–93
  in Constitution, 313
  Granger Laws and, 1017
  interstate commerce and, 1005
  Jeffersonian Republicans and, 342
  and paper currency, 304–6
states' rights, 384, 432, 474, 582
  Confederacy and, 739, 770
  at Constitutional Convention, 311, 318
  Webster-Hayne debate on, 455–57
  see also nullification and interposition
States' Rights Democratic (Dixiecrat) party, 1405–6, 1406
Statue of Liberty, 940
steamboats, 493–94, 493
  Gibbons v. Ogden and, 427–28
steam engine, 503
steel industry, 901–4, 905
Steel Workers Organizing Committee, 1272
Steffens, Lincoln, 1075, 1075
Stein, Gertrude, 1163–64, 1188, 1189–90, 1189
Stein, Leo, 1189
Steinbeck, John, 1245, 1261, 1278
Steinway, Heinrich, 525
Stephens, Alexander, 718, 740, 769, 770
Stephens, Uriah S., 913
stereopticons, 954
Stevens, John Paul, 1682
Stevens, Thaddeus, 767, 803, 804, 805, 808, 811, 811, 823
Stevenson, Adlai, 1442, 1465–66
  in election of 1952, 1462–63, 1463
  in election of 1956, 1480–81
  at United Nations, 1506
Stewart, Alexander T., 522

Stieglitz, Alfred, 888
Still, Clyfford, 1453
Stimson, Henry L., 1296, 1307, 1368
Stimson Doctrine, 1296
Stockman, David, 1614
stock market:
  in late 1990s, 1680, 1687
  1929 crash of, 1221–24
  1987 crash of, 1625–26
Stockton, Robert F., 615, 616
Stone, Lucy, 573, 982
Stone's River (Murfreesboro), Battle of (1862), 746
Stone v. Farmers Loan and Trust Company, 985
Stonewall Inn, 1569
Stono uprising (1739), 123
Stowe, Harriet Beecher, 689
Strategic Arms Limitation Talks (SALT), 1586, 1594, 1600
Strategic Defense Initiative (SDI), 1616, 1621
Strauss, Levi, 525
Strong, George Templeton, 523, 726
Strong, Josiah, 1037
Stuart, Charles Edward (Bonnie Prince Charlie), 146
Stuart, J. E. B., 730, 749
  at Harper's Ferry, 712
Student Nonviolent Coordinating Committee (SNCC), 1510, 1533
Students for a Democratic Society (SDS), 1551, 1554, 1555, 1555
Stuyvesant, Peter, 90–91
Styron, William, 1452
submarines:
  in World War I, 1126–29, 1133, 1135
  in World War II, 1307, 1312, 1324, 1336, 1340–41
suburbs, 934–35, 1435–37, 1439
  criticisms of, 1448
  housing in, 1435–36, 1448
  streetcars in growth of, 934
subway systems, 934, 935
Suez War, 1481, 1482–84
Suffolk Resolves (1775), 225
suffrage, see voting rights
Sufis, 549
sugar, 116, 630–31, 792, 844, 1040
  in Cuba, 1492
  and tariffs, 1011, 1039, 1040
  trust, 1085
Sugar (Revenue) Act (1764), 206, 207, 209, 210, 213, 216, 218
Sullivan, John, 261–62
Summary View of the Rights of British America (Jefferson), 226
Sumner, Charles, 677, 767, 794, 803, 804, 805, 806
  Brooks's attack on, 699–701, 700
Sumner, William Graham, 838, 967–68

Sumter, Thomas, 265
Sun Also Rises, The (Hemingway), 1190–91
Sunday, Billy, 1156
"superfund" sites, 1597
Supreme Court, U.S.:
  on abortions, 1563
  in *Adarand Constructors* v. *Peña,* 1682
  on affirmative action, 1681–82
  on anti-communism, 1417, 1470
  antitrust cases and, 843
  appointments to, 331, 368, 1199–20, 1580, 1659
  in *Bakke* v. *Board of Regents of California,* 1580
  in *Brown* v. *Board of Education,* 1493–94
  on busing, 1580
  in *Cherokee Nation* v. *Georgia,* 463–64
  in *Civil Rights Cases,* 853
  civil rights decisions of, 833–34
  on Civil War, 726
  in Constitution, 318
  on defendants' rights, 1509
  in *Dred Scott* case, 703–5
  on Espionage and Sedition Acts, 1142
  establishment of, 331
  FDR's court-packing plan for, 1268–71, *1269*
  in *Gibbons* v. *Ogden,* 427–28
  in *Gideon* v. *Wainwright,* 1509
  on Granger Laws, 1017
  implied powers broadened by, 339
  Indian lands and, 463
  in "Insular Cases," 1057
  on interstate commerce, 1005
  judicial nationalism and, 424–28
  judicial review, 425, 704–5
  on labor issues, 922, 1082, 1113, 1200
  laissez-faire and, 985–87
  legislative power reduced by, 985–86
  in *McCulloch* v. *Maryland,* 426–27
  in *Marbury* v. *Madison,* 374–75
  in *Miranda* v. *Arizona,* 1509
  in New Deal, 1245, 1248, 1253–54, 1268–71
  Nixon's appointments to, 1580
  on Paula Jones suit, 1685
  Pentagon Papers case and, 1574
  in Reconstruction, 809–10, 833
  Religious Right and, 1608, 1609
  in *Roe* v. *Wade,* 1563, 1609
  school prayer and, 1508–9
  segregation and, 853, 1492–94, 1496, 1579, 1615
  in *Swann* v. *Charlotte-Mecklenburg Board of Education,* 1580
  on sexual equality, 1562
  Thomas appointed to, 1659
  on trade associations, 1213
  on trusts, 1085–86, 1087

  on voting rights, 1184, 1264–65, 1333
  Watergate and, 1590
Surrender of General Burgoyne, The (Trumbull), 285
Surrender of Lord Cornwallis (Trumbull), 285, 286
Susquehannocks, 62
Sussex, sinking of, 1129
Sutter, John A., 594–95
Swann v. *Charlotte-Mecklenburg Board of Education,* 1580
Sweatt v. *Painter,* 1492–93
Sweden, trade with, 301
Swedish Americans, 94, 96, 144, *145,* 526, 859
Swedish colonies, 89
Swift, Gustavus, 875
Swift and Company v. *United States,* 1087
Swiss Americans, 99, 146, 186
Switzer, Kathy, *1561*
Switzerland, Reformation in, 38
Syllabus of Errors (Pius IX), 980
Sylvania Phalanx, 578
syndicalism, 924
Syria, 1488
  in Arab League, 1482
  in Lebanon, 1618, 1619
  in Persian Gulf War, 1641
  in Six-Day War, 1586
System of Synthetic Philosophy (Spencer), 966

Taft, Helen "Nellie," 1093–94
Taft, Martha, 1385
Taft, Robert A., 1308, 1385, 1461
Taft, William Howard, 946, *1094*
  and antitrust action, 1097–98
  Ballinger-Pinchot controversy and, 1096–97
  Cuba and, 1058
  dollar diplomacy of, 1094–95, 1121
  in election of 1908, 1093–94
  in election of 1912, 1098–1100, 1102–5, *1104*
  and federal income tax ratification, 1099
  Philippines and, 1056, 1068
  and regulation of communications, 1098–99
  Roosevelt's break with, 1097–98
  selected as Roosevelt's successor, 1092–93
  as Supreme Court chief justice, 1105, 1200
  tariff reform of, 1095–96
Taft-Hartley Act (1947), 1385–86, *1386,* 1465
Taft-Katsura Agreement (1905), 1068
Taiwan (Formosa), 1058, 1316, 1352
Taiwan (Nationalist China), 1411, 1414, 1584
  Chinese threats against, 1479–80, 1488–89
  immigration from, 1653
  Nationalist flight to, 1410
  see also China, Nationalist
Talleyrand, 361, 363, 378
Tallmadge, James, Jr., 422

Tammany Hall, 530, 936, 1001
Taney, Roger B., 470, 704, *704*
   Dred Scott decision and, 704–5
Taos Indians, 587
Tappan, Arthur, 663, 664, 665
Tappan, Lewis, 663, 664, 665
Tarbell, Ida M., 1075
Tariff Commission, 1000
Tariff of 1816, 412, 420
Tariff of 1824, 435
Tariff of 1828 (Tariff of Abominations), 454,
   455, 460
Tariff of 1832, 459, 460
Tariff of 1833, 461
Tariff of 1842, 583
Tariff of 1846, 583, 609
Tariff of 1857, 708
tariffs and duties, 206, 215, 276, 432, 472,
   583, 624
   Adams's view on, 435–36
   agriculture and, 1010, 1011, 1014, 1214–15
   in Civil War, 764, 765
   under Cleveland, *1004,* 1006–8
   Constitution and, 455
   under Coolidge, 1214–15
   Dingley Tariff (1897), 1028
   in early twentieth century, 1095–96,
     1106–7, *1107,* 1200–1201, 1214–15
   in early U.S., 303, *304,* 333–34, 340, *341*
   and economic nationalism, 406, 409, 410,
     412
   Fordney-McCumber Tariff (1922), 1201
   in Great Depression, 1219, 1225, 1234,
     1298
   in Hamiltonian program, 335, 340–41
   under Harding, 1200–1201
   Hawley-Smoot Tariff (1930), 1219
   Jackson on, 435–36, 449, 460, 461, 470
   under Jefferson, 376
   under Kennedy, 1508
   in late nineteenth century, 990, 1000,
     1010–11, 1014, 1028, 1040, 1043
   McKinley Tariff (1890), 1010, 1011, 1040
   Mellon and, 1200–1201, 1223
   Morrill (1861), 764, 791
   NAFTA and, 1663–64, 1681
   under Polk, 609
   with Puerto Rico, 1057
   in South Carolina nullification crisis, 454
   and Taft, 1095–96
   Tyler on, 582
   after War of 1812, 412
Tarleton, Banastre, 265, 266
Tate, Allen, 1191, 1192
taverns, 150–51, *151*
taxation:
   under Articles of Confederation, 276, 293
   British, 48, 50, 52, 176, 206
   Bush and, 1631, 1633–34, 1660

   Carter and, 1599, 1600
   churches supported by, 283
   in Civil War, 764, 765
   Clinton and, 1662, 1675–76
   in colonial period, 72, 128, 170, 177,
     206–17, 223–27
   congressional power of, 313
   in Constitution, 313
   Dole and, 1678
   in early U.S., 333–34, 336, 343
   estate, 1258
   in events before American Revolution,
     206–17, 223–27
   "external" vs. "internal," 212
   gift, 1258
   Grenville's program of, 205–8
   in Hamiltonian program, 336
   Harding and, 1200–1201
   Hoover and, 1218
   income, 764, 1099, 1130
   Johnson, Lyndon, and, 1525, 1581
   in Massachusetts, 72, 170, 306, 307
   Mellon and, 1200–1201, 1220–21, 1223
   national bank and, 426–27
   in New Deal, 1255–57, 1258, 1259, 1274
   in 1950s, 1466, 1485
   Reagan and, 1608, 1612, 1614, 1619, 1621,
     1630
   in Reconstruction, 819
   representation and, 208–9
   and revenue sharing with states, 1581
   "single-tax" idea and, 976
   Stamp Act, 207, 209–13
   Townshend's program of, 213–14
   Truman and, 1386–87
   in Virginia, 128
   voting rights and, 278, 438–39
   on whiskey, 343, 350–51, 376
   in World War II, 1326
Tax Equity and Fiscal Responsibility Bill
   (1982), 1614
Tax Reform Act (1986), 1621
Taylor, Frederick W., 1077–78
Taylor, John, 384
Taylor, Maxwell, 1519
Taylor, Paul S., 1280
Taylor, Susie King, 760
Taylor, Zachary:
   California statehood and, 681
   and Compromise of 1850, 683, 685
   death of, 685–86
   in election of 1848, 676, 677, 678
   in Mexican War, 611–12, 613–14, 616–18,
     620
Taylorism, 1077–78
tea, trade in, 501
Tea Act (1773), 221
Teamsters, 1488
Teapot Dome scandal, 1202–3, *1202*

technology:
  agricultural, 487, 490–91, 879–80, 896, 1438
  in early nineteenth century, 504–6
  education and, 564–65
  exploration aided by, 15–16
  food and, 505–6, 522, 895
  growth of industry and, 502–14
  Indian, 23, 26
  in late nineteenth century, 895–96
  post–World War II automation and, 1425
  of printing, 558–59
  of Spanish vs. Indians, 26
  transportation and, 492, 496, 500–501, 896
  in World War II, 1340
Tecumseh, Shawnee chief, 393–95, *393*, 398
Teheran Conference (1943), 1346
Tekugawa, Prince, *1290*
telegraph, 504, *506*, 527, 741, 902
telephone, 896
television, 1427–28, 1429–30, 1433, 1504–5, 1521
Teller Amendment (1898), 1047
temperance, 567–69, *568*
  women's suffrage and, 984
  see also Prohibition movement
Tempest, The (Shakespeare), 56
tenancy, 50
tenements, 944
Tennent, Gilbert, 158
Tennent, William, 158, 161
Tennessee, 303, 492
  admitted to union, 357
  Civil War fighting in, 743–46, 773, 775–76, 782
  emancipation in, 760
  free blacks in, 423
  Indian conflicts in, 351
  Indian lands ceded in, 299
  Indian removal and, 299, 462
  migration to, 659
  military government of, 796
  in Reconstruction, 806, 808–9, 822
  Republicans in, 849
  secession of, 726
  segregation in, 853
  and teaching of evolution, 1168–69
  Union loyalists in, 806, 818
  voting rights in, 438
Tennessee Coal and Iron Company, 1098
Tennessee militia, 399
Tennessee Valley Authority (TVA), 1248–51, *1251*, 1262, 1407, 1466, 1527
Tennessee Valley Authority Act (1933), 1239
tennis, 958–59
Tenochtitlán (Mexico City), 9, 27, 28, *28*, 30
Tenskwatawa, 393
Tenth Amendment, 319, 333, 339
Tenure of Office Act (1867), 808, 810

Tertium Quid, 384–85
Tesla, Nikola, 897
Tet offensive (1968), 1540–41
Texas, 33, 34, 36, 420, 430, 590, 596, 602–6
  agriculture of, 631, 632, 1017, 1019
  annexation by U.S., 605–6, 609
  border of, 683, 685, 687
  Chicanos in, 1564
  in Civil War, 741
  and Compromise of 1850, 683, 685, 687
  dust bowl in, 1261
  in election of 1844, 606, 607
  European diseases in, 24
  evolution teaching and, 1168
  German Americans in, 526
  immigrants in, 1653
  independence from Mexico of, 590, 603–5, 606
  Louisiana territory and, 378–79
  Mexican War and, 611, 612, 619, 620
  oil industry in, 1211, 1584
  population of, 1650, 1651
  Reconstruction in, 812, 817
  secession of, 718
  segregation in, 1493
  slavery issue and, 674, 683, 685, 687
  Unionist sentiment in, 730, 769–70
  U.S. settlers in, 602–3
  violence in, 883
  voting rights in, 1333
  in World War II, 1329
Texas, University of, 1682
Texas and New Mexico Act (1850), 687
Texas Seed Bill (1887), 1003
Texas v. White, 810
textile industry, *409*, 448, 502–3, *510*, 624, 634, 766, 844
  corporations in, 511
  Lowell system in, 507–10
  mechanization of, 503
  in South, 841
  see also cotton
Thailand, 1477
Thames, Battle of the, *393*, 398
Thaw v. Reno, 1682
Thayendanegea (Joseph Brant), 261, *262*
theater, 516–17, 1176
  antebellum, 516–17
  in mid-twentieth century, 1450–51
  minstrel shows at, 517–19
Theory of the Leisure Class, The (Veblen), 977
These Are Our Lives, 1280
Thieu, Nguyen Van, 1571, 1575–76
third parties:
  Anti-Masonic party, 468–69, 474, 475, 479
  Dixiecrats, 1405–6, *1406*
  and emergence of Republican party, 696–97
  introduction of, 468–69
  Know-Nothing party, 527–28, *528*, 697, 701

third parties (continued)
  Progressive ("Bull Moose") party,
    1099–1100, 1102, 1103, 1105, 1115,
    1131
  Progressive party (1924), 1206
  Progressive party (1948), 1405, 1406
Third World, independence movements and,
  1474–79
Thirteenth Amendment, 315, 760, 789, 801,
  806, 834
Thirty Years' War, 89
This Side of Paradise (Fitzgerald), 1175, 1190
Thomas, Clarence, 1659, 1682
Thomas, George H., 775
Thomas, Lorenzo, 810
Thomas, Norman, 1235
Thomson, Charles, 225, 292
Thoreau, Henry David, 445, 549, 550–52,
  551, 552, 1495
Three Lives (Stein), 1190
Thurmond, J. Strom, 1405, 1406, 1406, 1408
Tiananmen Square massacre (1989), 1635
Tibbetts, Paul W., 1369
Tientsin, Treaty of (1858), 692
Tilden, Samuel J., 830–33, 831, 996
timber industry, 109, 843
Timucuas, 86, 87
Tippecanoe, Battle of, 394, 394, 479
Titan, The (Dreiser), 975–76
Title IX of the Educational Amendments Act
  (1972), 1562
Tito (Josip Broz), 1394
Tituba (slave), 141
Titusville, Pa., 898
tobacco, 23, 53, 116, 126, 128, 265, 299, 409,
  630, 632, 634
  cigarette rolling and, 896
  Civil War and, 791–92
  in early U.S., 328
  increase in, 841
  in Maryland colony, 65
  Rolfe's experiment with, 58
  soil depleted by, 117
  in Virginia colony, 58, 60, 61, 62, 115
Tocqueville, Alexis de, 504, 539, 1372
Tojo, Hideki, 1315, 1357
Toleration Act (1689), 52, 171, 175
Toltecs, 7, 9
Tompkins, Sally, 762
Tonkin Gulf Resolution (1964), 1536–37
Tonnage Act (1789), 334
Toombs, Robert, 685
Toomer, Jean, 1182
Tordesillas, Treaty of (1494), 19, 25
Tories, see Loyalists
Toussaint l'Ouverture, Pierre Dominique, 378,
  379
Townsend, Francis E., 1253, 1265
Townshend, Charles, 213

Townshend Acts (1767), 213, 217, 218,
  258–59
  colonial protest against, 214–17
  modification and repeal of, 217, 258
townships, 296
Trade Agreements Act (1934), 1298
trade and commerce:
  agriculture and, 299, 301
  after American Revolution, 299–301
  American Revolution and, 233, 258, 299
  in California, 594
  with China, 301, 473, 501, 691–92,
    1058–59, 1291
  in Civil War, 766
  in colonial period, 43, 53, 55, 62, 79,
    86–89, 98, 116–18, 131–35, 135, 138,
    167–69, 179, 200
  colonization and, 53
  in Confederation period, 299–301, 303–6
  congressional power over, 276
  in Constitution, 313, 315
  Continental Congress and, 226
  in cotton, 389–90, 454, 473, 488, 624, 631,
    634, 636
  with Cuba, 1043–44
  in Dutch colonies, 179
  in early U.S., 303–5, 309
  in events before American Revolution,
    206–17, 223–27
  exploration and, 25
  with France, 334, 387–88, 389–90, 390,
    391–92, 454, 473, 631
  in French colonies, 33, 178, 179, 182,
    186–87
  globalization and, 1681
  with Great Britain, 300, 303, 304, 333–34,
    347–48, 361, 387–88, 390, 391–92, 403,
    416, 420, 449, 454, 473, 474, 476, 630
  imperialism and, 1036
  with Indians in colonial period, 53, 79,
    86–89, 98, 179
  interstate, regulation of, 427–28
  with Iran, 1601–2
  in late nineteenth century, 931
  mercantile system in, 167–68, 299, 333
  with Mexico, 473, 596
  NAFTA and, 1663–64, 1681
  Napoleonic Wars and, 387–91
  in New England colonies, 131–35, 138
  of Portugal, 186
  in pre-Columbian cultures, 9, 10
  in South Carolina colony, 86
  in southern colonies, 116–18
  with Soviet Union, 1298, 1586
  in Spanish Empire, 33, 178, 179, 182,
    186–87
  with Texas, 605
  urban growth and, 931
  in Virginia colony, 55

with West Indies, 102, 132, 133, 134, 143, 200, 206, 299, 300, 347, 348, 387, 417
in World War I, 1125, 1126–29, 1134
see also boycotts; fur trade; tariffs and duties; taxation; transportation
trade associations, 1213
Trade Expansion Act (1962), 1508
Traffic Safety Act (1966), 1530
Trail of Tears, 463–65
Tramp Abroad (Twain), 973
Transcendental Club, 549
transcendentalism, 445, 548–49, 566
transcontinental railroads, 693, 791, 889–92, *891, 892*
Transcontinental Treaty (1819), 420, 428
transistors, 1644–45
transportation, 485
   in colonial era, 150
   in early nineteenth century, 492–502, *494*
   government role in, 501–2
   internal improvements to, 412–14
   ocean, 500–501
   in post–Civil War era, 819
   technology of, 492, 496, 500–501, 896
   urban growth and, 931, 933–34
   water, 309, 427–28, 492–96, 500–501
   see also highways and roads; railroads
Transylvania, 205
Transylvania Company, 204
Travis, William B., 603, 604
treason, 387
Treasury Department, U.S., 331, 764, 824, 829
   Hamilton's program for, 341–42
   under Van Buren, 478–79
Treatise on Domestic Economy, A (Beecher), 571
Treaty of Alliance (1778), 257
Treaty of Amity and Commerce (1778), 257
Tredegar Iron Works, 634, *634, 732*
Trent affair, 766
Trenton, Battle of (1776), 249
trial by jury, 208, 275, 333
Triangle Shirtwaist Company fire (1911), 1082–83, *1082*
"trickster tales," 655
Triple Alliance (Central Powers), 1122–23, 1124, 1142, 1147
Triple Entente (Allied Powers), 1122–23, 1124, 1147
Tripoli, 377, 405
Trist, Nicholas P., 619
Truman, Harry S., 1528, 1529
   anti-communism and, 1408–9, 1416, 1419
   atomic bomb and, 1367
   background of, 1380–81
   Berlin blockade and, 1396–97
   civil rights supported by, 1400–1402, *1403*
   demobilization under, 1380–88

in election of 1948, 1404–8, *1407, 1408*
and election of 1952, 1461
Fair Deal of, 1403–4, 1407
foreign policy of, 1387–88, 1390–91
and health insurance, 1404
Hiss and, 1418
Indochina and, 1475, 1476, 1536
Israel recognized by, 1399
Korean War and, 1411, 1412, 1414–15
labor movement and, 1385, 1386
MacArthur fired by, 1414–15
at Potsdam, 1368
Roosevelt compared with, 1380
social agenda of, 1407
as vice-president, 1358
Truman Doctrine, 1394–96, 1416, 1538
Trumbull, John, 285, 286
Trumbull, Lyman, 760
trusts, 900–901, 1010
   Taft and, 1097–98
   Theodore Roosevelt and, 1084–85, *1085,* 1087
   Wilson and, 1103–4, 1109–10
   see also antitrust laws
Truth, Sojourner, *666, 667*
Tryon, William, 219
Tubman, Harriet, 667, 760
Tucker, William, 60
Tudeh, 1472
Tunis, 377, 405
Tunisia, 1339
Turkey, 1399
   in Korean War, 1412
   in METO, 1482
   in NATO, 1398, 1482
   U.S. missiles in, 1486, 1516, 1518
   U.S. post–World War II aid to, 1394, 1395
   in World War I, 1122, 1132, 1147
turkeys, 7, 13, 22
Turner, Frederick Jackson, 883–84, 931
Turner, Nat, 653, 663
turnpikes, 492, 502
Tuscany, 378
Tuscaroras, 86, 88, 91, 186
Tuscarora War (1711–1713), 88, 186
Tuskegee Airmen, *1332*
Tuskegee Institute, *949*
TVA (Tennessee Valley Authority), 1248–51, *1251, 1262,* 1407, 1466, 1527
Twain, Mark (Samuel Clemens), 646, 972–73, *973, 989*
Tweed Ring, 819, 830
Twentieth Amendment, 1236
Twenty-one Demands (1915), 1290
Twenty-first Amendment, 1239
Twenty-second Amendment, 1462
Twenty-fifth Amendment, 1591–92
Twenty-sixth Amendment, 1581
Twice-Told Tales (Hawthorne), 552

Two Treatises on Government (Locke), 172, 208
Tydings, Millard, 1418
Tydings-McDuffie Act (1934), 1056
Tyler, John, 479, 582, 602, 609, 720
Typee (Melville), 556

U-2 spy planes, 1486, 1490, 1517
UAR (United Arab Republic), 1488
UAW (United Auto Workers), 1272, 1383
UFW (United Farm Workers), 1565–67
Ulysses (Joyce), 1189
UMW (United Mine Workers), 919, 1086–87, 1272, 1383
U.N., *see* United Nations
uncertainty principle, 1187
Uncle Remus: His Song and His Sayings (Harris), 972
Uncle Tom's Cabin (Stowe), 689, 690
Uncle Tom's Children (Wright), 1279
unemployment
  in Great Depression, 1222, 1224, 1228–29, 1232, 1236, 1242, 1259
  in 1970s, 1581, 1599–1600
  in 1980s, 1614, 1650
  in 1990s, 1658
unemployment insurance, 1255, 1256, 1257
Underground Railroad, 667, 689
Underwood, Oscar, 1102
Underwood-Simmons Tariff (1913), 1107, *1107*
UNIA (United Negro Improvement Association), 1183–84, *1183*
Union League, 812, 815, 820
Union Manufactories, *409*
Union of Russian Workers, 1160
Union Pacific Railroad, 826, 890, 891, 893, 1086, 1326
Union party, 1265
unions, *see* labor movement
Unitarians, 52, 161, 538–39, 549
United Arab Emirates, 1641
United Arab Republic (UAR), 1488
United Auto Workers (UAW), 1272, 1383
United Farm Workers (UFW), 1565–67
United Fruit Company, 1473
United Mine Workers (UMW), 919, 1086–87, 1272, 1383
United Nations (U.N.), 1395, 1399, 1408, 1506, 1629
  China in, 1411
  Grenada invasion condemned by, 1619
  Haiti and, 1672
  Iran hostages and, 1601
  Korean War and, 1411–12, 1467–68
  origins of, 1361, 1388–89, 1391
  Persian Gulf War and, 1640, 1641, 1643
  Somalia and, 1670–71
  Young at, 1597
United Negro Improvement Association (UNIA), 1183–84, *1183*

United States, U.S.S., 363
United States Sanitary Commission, 761
United States Steel Corporation, 905, 1087, 1098, 1272
United States v. Butler, 1245
United States v. E. C. Knight and Company, 1085
Universalists, 161, 538–39
universities, *see* colleges and universities
unreasonable search and seizure, 333
Updike, John, 1452
USHA (Housing Authority, U.S.), 1275
Utah:
  and Compromise of 1850, 687
  Indians in, 587
  labor laws in, 1082
  Mormons in, 545–46
  statehood for, 866
  voting rights in, 983
  in World War II, 1329
Utah Act (1850), 687
Utes, 869
utopian communities, 575–79
utopian ideas, 977
Utrecht, Peace of (1713), *185,* 186

Valens, Ritchie, 1433
Vallandigham, Clement L., 768
Valley Forge, Pa., winter quarters at (1777–1778), 255, 259
Van Buren, Martin, 434, 436, 458, 474–81, *476*
  background of, 476
  Calhoun's rivalry with, 450–53
  Canadian nationalists and, 584
  Eaton Affair and, 452
  in election of 1832, 469
  in election of 1836, 475–76, *475*
  in election of 1840, *480,* 481
  in election of 1844, 606–7
  in election of 1848, 677, 678, 690
  Great Britain post denied to, 459
  Independent Treasury under, 478–79
  national bank issue and, 467
  slavery issue and, 674
  ten-hour workday and, 531
Vance, Cyrus, 1598, 1602
Vandalia, 204
Vanderbilt, Cornelius, 894–95, *894,* 930
Vanderbilt, George, 843
Van Rensselaer, Stephen, 396
Van Rensselaer family, 344
Vanzetti, Bartolomeo, *1164,* 1165
Vassar College, 566, 951–52, 963
vaudeville, 957–58
Veblen, Thorstein, 977
Venezuela, 1488
  in British Guiana border dispute, 1042
  in Contadora Process, 1618
Verdict of the People (Bingham), *469*
Vergennes, comte de, 257

Vermont, 147, 219
  admitted to union, 357
  constitution of, 279
  disestablishment in, 439
  at Hartford Convention, 404
  Revolutionary fighting in, 257
  Revolutionary troops from, 230
  slavery in, 279
  voting rights in, 278, 438
Verrazano, Giovanni da, 40
Versailles Treaty (1919), 1152, 1156, 1297, 1298
  ratification debate on, 1152–54
vertical integration, 900
Vesey, Denmark, 454, 653
Vespucci, Amerigo, 21
Veterans Administration, 1425
Veterans Bureau, 1201–2
veterinary medicine, 953
veto, line-item, 1674
vice-presidency, 991
Vicksburg, Miss.:
  Battle of (1863), 759, 772–73, *772*, 775
  Irish Americans in, 522
Victor Emmanuel III, king of Italy, 1341
Vienna Summit (1961), 1515
Viet Cong, 1479, *1520*, 1536, 1538, 1540–41, *1541*, 1571, 1575
Viet Minh, 1475, 1476–77
Vietnam, 1410, 1412, 1475–79, *1520*
  gradual withdrawal from, 1570–72
  immigration from, 1653, *1655*
  Kennedy and, 1519–20
  see also Indochina
Vietnam War, 1376, 1535–43, 1582, 1592, 1593
  amnesty for draft evaders of, 1597
  bombing of North in, 1537, 1542
  Cambodian incursion in, 1571–72
  casualties in, 1576
  Clinton and, 1661
  collapse of South Vietnam in, 1594
  conscientious objectors in, 1553
  context for policy in, 1538–40
  domestic opposition to, 1540, 1553–54, 1557, 1571, 1572–74
  draft in, 1553, 1571, 1597
  in election of 1964, 1527, 1528, 1536
  end of, 1575–77
  escalation of, 1536–38
  Geneva Accords and, 1477–79, 1519
  Hispanics in, 1564
  My Lai massacre, 1573, 1577
  negotiations in, 1571, 1575
  Nixon and, 1570–77, *1572*
  Tet offensive in, 1540–41
  Tonkin Gulf Resolution and, 1536–37
  Vietnamization of, 1571
vigilantes, 219, 221–23, 306–8, 350–51, 490, 680

Vikings, 14
Villa, Pancho, 1120–21, *1121*
Vincennes, Ill., 260
Vindication of the Rights of Woman, A (Wollstonecraft), *281*
Vinland (Newfoundland), 14, 32, 44, 134, 183, 184, 186, 417
Virginia:
  agriculture in, 630, 632, 844
  Civil War fighting in, 734–36, 738, 748–50, 752–53, *753*, 771–72, 779, *779*, *780*
  Constitution ratified by, 322, 323, 324
  and Declaration of Independence, 235
  education in, 288
  emancipation in, 668, 756
  land claims of, 275, 295, *295*, 298, 329
  Loyalist property in, 425
  migration from, 658
  post–Revolutionary debt in, 337
  Readjuster party in, 849
  Reconstruction in, 812, 817, 822
  religious freedom in, 283–84
  Revolutionary fighting in, 233, 262, 263, 268
  Revolutionary troops from, 266
  secession of, 726
  segregation in, 1493, 1497
  at 1785 navigation meeting, 309
  slave trade in, 314
  voting rights in, 852
Virginia (Merrimack), 730, 737, *737*
Virginia, University of, 564
Virginia colony, *64*, 83, 84, 144
  Anglican church in, 127–29
  Bacon's Rebellion in, 62–64
  Capitol of, *175*
  charter of, 53, 56, 275
  in colonial taxation disputes, 216, 219, 224
  Committees of Correspondence in, 220–21
  European settlement of, 53–64, 106
  first permanent settlement in, 53–55
  gentry of, 126
  government of, 59, 61, 62, *175*
  Indians in, 55, 58–59, 60, 61, 63, 204
  in land disputes, 224
  landownership in, 59, 62
  Loyalists in, 232–33
  in organization of Kentucky, 205
  population of, 109
  religion in, 127–29
  Roanoke colony, 23, 44–45, 59–60
  as royal colony, 61
  Sandys's reforms in, 59
  slavery in, 120–21, 124, 125
  Smith's administration of, 55–56
  Stamp Act and, 211
  "starving time" in, 57
  taxes in, 128
  tobacco in, 58, 61, 62, 115
  voting rights in, 176

Virginia Company, 47, 54, 56, 57, 59, 65, 117, 166
  origins of, 53
Virginia Declaration of Rights (1776), 236, 283–84, 311, 333
Virginia Military Institute, 733
Virginia Plan, 312–13, 318
Virginia Resolutions (1798), 365, 366, 404, 456
Virginia Resolves (1765), 211, 216
Virginia Statute of Religious Freedom (1786), 284
VISTA (Volunteers in Service to America), 1526, 1550
Vladivostok Summit (1974), 1594
vocational training, 949–50
Volstead Act (1919), 1171, 1217, 1239
Voltaire, 153
voluntarism, 1688
Volunteers in Service to America (VISTA), 1526, 1550
Vo Nguyen Giap, 1477
Von Neumann, John, 1644
von Steuben, Frederick William Augustus Henry Ferdinand, baron, 259–60, 267
voter turnout, 1115, 1595
  in election of 1840, 481
  in election of 1980, 1610
  in election of 1988, 1632–33
  in late nineteenth century, 992
voting rights:
  for African Americans, 423, 800, 801, 803, 807, 808, 812, 814–15, 815, 818, 821, 823
  for eighteen-year-olds, 1581
  Eisenhower and, 1496
  grandfather clauses and, 851, 1184
  literacy tests and, 851, 1531
  poll taxes and, 851
  property qualifications and, 176, 278, 438–39, 523–24, 530–31
  religion and, 175
  in South, 642
  southern disenfranchisement of African Americans, and, 850–52, 992, 1114, 1264
  Supreme Court and, 1184, 1264–65, 1333
  taxation and, 278, 438–39
  voter registration and, 1531
  Wilson and, 1111
  women and, 283, 572, 982–84, 984, 1131, 1140, 1178–81
Voting Rights Act (1965), 1531, 1579

Wabash Railroad, 915
Wabash Railroad v. Illinois, 1005
WAC (Women's Army Corps), 1329
Waco, Tex., standoff at (1993), 1666
Wade, Benjamin F., 767, 797, 799–800, 803
Wade-Davis Bill (1865), 797

Wagner, Robert G., 1227
Wagner National Labor Relations Act (1935), 1254–55, 1262, 1269, 1270, 1271, 1272, 1566
Wagner-Steagall National Housing Act (1937), 1275
Wahunsonacock, Powhatan chief, 55, 58, 60
Wake Island, 1053, 1322, 1323
Wald, Lillian, 980, 981
Walden (Thoreau), 551, 551, 552
Waldseemüller, Martin, 21
Walker, Robert J., 705–6, 707
Walker Tariff (1846), 609
Wallace, George, 1514, 1544–46, 1545, 1570, 1587
Wallace, Henry A., 1358, 1385, 1403
  in election of 1948, 1405, 1406
  in New Deal, 1244–45
Wallace, Henry C., 1199
Walloon Americans, 146
Walpole, Horace, 213
Walpole, Robert, 173
Wampanoags, 67, 68, 78, 81–82
wampum, 92, 92
Wanghsia, Treaty of (1844), 691–92
Ward, Aaron Montgomery, 906
Ward, Lester Frank, 968–69, 968, 971, 976
War Department, U.S., 292, 1129
Warehouse Act (1916), 1113
War Industries Board (WIB), 1138
War Labor Board, 1327
Warner, Charles Dudley, 989
War of 1812, 392–406, 397, 398, 405, 417–18, 503
  aftermath of, 404–6
  Baltimore attacked in, 400–401
  causes of, 392–95
  in Chesapeake, 400–401
  coverage of, 560
  Hartford Convention and, 403–4
  Indian troubles in, 393–95
  and naval warfare, 396, 397–98
  New Orleans, battle of, 401–2
  northern front of, 396–98, 399–400
  peace treaty in, 402–3
  preparations for, 395–96
  southern front in, 398–99, 399
  Washington, D.C., captured in, 400
War of Independence, *see* American Revolution
War of Jenkins' Ear, 187
War of the Austrian Succession (King George's War) (1744–1748), 184, 185, 187–88
War of the League of Augsburg (King William's War) (1689–1697), 184–86, 185
War of the Palatinate, *see* War of the League of Augsburg
War of the Spanish Succession (Queen Anne's War) (1701–1713), 184, 185, 186–87

War Powers Act (1941), 1325
War Powers Act (1973), 1592
War Production Board (WPB), 1325
War Refugee Board, 1365
Warren, Earl, 1470, 1493, 1508–9, 1521
Warren, Joseph, 231
Warren, Robert Penn, 1192
wars, *see specific conflicts*
Warsaw Treaty Organization, 1399, 1484–85, 1635
Washington (state):
  statehood for, 865, 1010
  in World War II, 1329
Washington, Booker T., 851–52, 854–55, *854*
Washington, D.C.:
  and Compromise of 1850, 683
  first inauguration in, 371, *372*
  march on (1963), *1513*, 1514–15
  population of, 1650
  racial riot in (1919), 1159
  segregation in, 1493
  slaves in, 478, 668, 683, 688, 755
  voting rights in, 807
  in War of 1812, 400
Washington, George, 289, 308, *324*, 335, 360–61, *391*
  Algerian conflict and, 363
  in American Revolution, 230, 242, 249, *249*, 253, 259, 261, 265, 267, 268–69, 272, 279, 293
  called from retirement, 363
  chosen as commander-in-chief, 230
  on Constitution, 325
  at Constitutional Convention, 310, *310*, 312, *318*
  at Continental Congress, 225
  on economy, 341
  farewell address of, 358–59, 1032, 1420
  on foreign alliances, 358
  in French and Indian War, 188, 189–90, 191
  French Revolution and, 345, 346
  inauguration of, *330*
  Jay's Treaty and, 348
  on national bank issue, 338–39
  parties opposed by, 343
  in presidential elections, 330–31, 345
  on Shays's Rebellion, 307
  as slaveholder, 280
  Whiskey Rebellion and, *350*, 351
Washington, Lawrence, 187
Washington Armaments Conference (1921), 1290–92, *1291*
Washington College, 951
Washington Territory, 590
"Waste Land, The" (Eliot), 1189
Watauga colony, 204
Watauga Compact (1772), 204
Watauga country, 265

water frame, 503
Watergate scandal, 1588–93, 1683
  effect of, 1591–93
Watertown Protest (1632), 72
water transportation, 309, 427–28, 500–501
  canals as, 494, 495–96, 501, 522
  in early nineteenth century, 492–96, *494*
Watson, Ella, 877
Watson, Tom, 1021, *1022*, 1026, 1029
Watt, James, 503
Watt, James G., 1614
Watts riot (1965), 1532, *1532*
Waud, Alfred, 778
WAVES (Women Accepted for Volunteer Emergency Service), 1329, *1330*
Wayne, Anthony, 267, 349
Wealth against Commonwealth (Lloyd), 976, 1075
Wealth of Nations, The (Smith), 299
Weathermen, 1556
Weaver, James B., 1023
Weaver, Randy, 1666–67
Weaver, Robert C., 1529
Webster, Daniel, 426, 436, 474, *684*
  African colonization and, 661–62
  in Compromise of 1850, 682, 683, 684–85
  in debate with Hayne, 455–57
  in election of 1836, 475
  on Independent Treasury, 478
  national bank issue and, 411, 465
  on nullification issue, 455–57, *456*
  in Tyler administration, 582, 583, 584
Webster, Noah, 288
Webster-Ashburton Treaty (1842), *584*, 585
Webster-Hayne Debate, 455–57
Weimar Republic, 1297
Weinberger, Caspar, 1623
Welch, Joseph, *1469*
Welch, Robert, 1526
Weld, Theodore Dwight, 664, 665, 667, 668
welfare, 1530, 1578
  AFDC, 1613
  Clinton and, 1676
  Gingrich and, 1674
  Reagan and, 1613, 1615, 1630
  see also specific programs
Welles, Gideon, 733
Wellesley College, 952
Wellington, duke of, 618
Welsh Americans, 99, 144, *145*, 146, 642, 943
Welty, Eudora, 1452
Wesleyan College, 566
West, 595–602, 857–84
  African Americans in, 858, 859–60
  agriculture in, 485, 488–91, 633
  cattle and cowboys in, 873–78
  in Civil War, 741–43, *744*
  farmers and, 878–82

West (continued)
  gold rushes and mining in, 501, 588, 597,
    678–81, 741, 861–66, 861, 931
  growth of, 857–58
  Indian conflicts in, 866–71, 867
  Indian policy, 871–73
  map of, 862
  migratory stream to, 858–61, 931
  North and South in conflict over, 624
  range wars in, 877–78
  trails through, 596–602
  urbanization in, 931, 932
  violence in, 882–83
  Whigs in, 474
  women in, 881–82
  in World War II, 1328–31
  see also frontier
West, Benjamin, 270, 285
West Bank, 1670
Western Reserve Eclectic Institute, 564
Western Union, 894, 896
West Indies, 26, 29, 120, 200
  French-U.S. conflict in, 363
  Napoleonic Wars and, 387
  trade with, 102, 132, 133, 134, 143, 200,
    206, 299, 300, 347, 348, 387, 417
Westinghouse, George, 896, 897, 898
Westinghouse Company, 897, 1208
Westmoreland, William C., 1537, 1540, 1541
West Virginia, 204, 796, 986
  formation of, 726–27
  population of, 1650
Weyler, Valeriano, 1044
whaling, 132, 556, 556
wheat, 23, 143, 632, 732, 1612
Wheeler, Burton K., 1310, 1311
Wheeler, Joe, 780
Wheeler, William, 830
Wheeler-Howard Indian Reorganization Act
    (1934), 1263–64
Wheeler-Rayburn Public Utility Holding
    Company Act (1935), 1254, 1258
Wheelwright, John, 76–77
Whig party, 583, 764
  as coalition against Andrew Jackson, 474
  "Conscience" vs. "Cotton" members of, 677
  destruction of, 697
  divisions over slavery, 677, 685, 697
  economic policies of, 477–79, 582, 583
  in election of 1840, 479–81, 479, 582
  in election of 1844, 607
  in election of 1848, 676–78
  in election of 1852, 690
  in election of 1856, 701
  in election of 1860, 715
  formation of, 474
  in formation of Republican party, 697
  Free Soil party and, 677
  on Independent Treasury, 478

  legacy of, 993
  Mexican War and, 612, 620
  reorganized into Constitutional Union party,
    715
  scalawags and, 818
  Taylor supported by, 682
Whigs (Great Britain), 201, 237
whiskey, tax on, 343, 350–51, 376
Whiskey Rebellion, 350–51, 350
Whiskey Ring, 827
White, Hugh Lawson, 475
White, John, 22, 45, 78, 87
White, William Allen, 1073, 1074, 1198, 1203
White Collar Society (Mills), 1450
Whitefield, George, 158–59, 159
White House Conference on Conservation
    (1908), 1092
White League, 820
"White Man's Burden" (Kipling), 1054–55
Whitewater scandal, 1683–84
Whitman, Walt, 552, 557–58, 557, 620
Whitney, Eli, 487, 487, 503, 505
Whittier, John Greenleaf, 553
Whyte, William A., Jr., 1450
WIB (War Industries Board), 1138
Wickersham, George W., 1173
Wilderness, Battle of the (1863), 771, 778
Wilderness Road, 204, 354–57, 492
Wild One, The, 1457
Wild West shows, 955–56, 956
Wiley, Calvin H., 562
Wilhelm II, kaiser of Germany, 1069
Wilkinson, Eliza, 315
Wilkinson, James, 303, 386
Willard, Emma, 565–66
William III, king of England, 52, 171, 172, 184
William and Mary, College of, 161
Williams, Roger, 73–74, 75–76, 80, 306
Williams, Tennessee, 1451
Willkie, Wendell L., 1308–9, 1404
Wills, Garry, 1554
Wilmot, David, 674, 675, 676, 677
Wilmot Proviso, 674–75, 684, 688
Wilson, Jack (Wovoka), 870
Wilson, James, 226, 311
  at Constitutional Convention, 311, 317
Wilson, Woodrow, 946, 1033, 1094, 1234,
    1301, 1669
  background of, 989–90, 1100–1102
  Debs and, 1203
  dollar diplomacy rejected by, 1118
  in election of 1912, 1102–5, 1104
  in election of 1916, 1112, 1130–32, 1131
  Federal Reserve and, 1107–9
  foreign policy of, 1118–22
  Fourteen Points of, 1146–48
  Latin American policy of, 1294
  League of Nations and, 1146, 1150–51,
    1153, 1155

Mexican intervention of, 1119–21
at Paris Peace Conference, 1148–52, *1149*
preparedness issue and, 1129–30
progressivism of, 1100–1114
social justice and, 1110–11
stroke suffered by, 1154, 1156, 1197
tariff policy of, 1106–7, *1107*
trusts and, 1103–4, 1109–10
and U.S. entry into World War I, 1134–42
U.S. neutrality and, 1123, 1125, 1126–29,
    1129, 1131
Versailles Treaty promoted by, 1152–55
women's suffrage supported by, 1180
World War I and, 1145
Wilson-Gorman Tariff (1894), 1043
Wilson's Creek, Battle of (1861), 742
Winthrop, John, 69–70, *69, 72,* 74, 75, 113,
    137, 537, 1688
Winthrop, John, Jr., 154
Winthrop, John, IV, 154
Wirt, William, 469, 470
Wirz, Henry, 798
Wisconsin:
    Civil War troops from, 738
    education in, 1011–12
    migration to, 526
    progressivism in, 1079
Wisconsin, University of, 952
Wisconsin Territory, Indian conflicts in, 462,
    463
witchcraft, 140–43
Wittenmeyer, Annie, 762
Wobblies (Industrial Workers of the World),
    924–26, 1141
Wolcott, Oliver, 361
Wolfe, James, 193
Wolfe, Thomas, 1173, 1192–93
Wollstonecraft, Mary, *281*
Woman in the Nineteenth Century (Fuller),
    575
Woman's party, 1179, 1180
women:
    in abolition movement, 572, 664–65
    in armed forces, 1329, 1330
    in Alliance movement, 1018
    American Revolution and, 281–83
    in Carter administration, 1596
    in Civil War, 760–63
    as Civil War soldiers, 762
    in colonial period, 110, 112–15
    Constitutional Convention and, 315
    domestic role of, 114–15, 282, 571–72, 639,
        640
    education and, 565–66, *565,* 571, 951–52
    employment of, 114–15, 508–9, *510,* 574,
        762, 981–82, 1081–82, 1138, 1139–40,
        1181, 1330–31, *1331,* 1441–42, 1563,
        1582, 1651
    equal pay for, 914

gender gap and, 1615, 1660
Iroquois, 92
in labor movement, 912
legal status of, 114, 271–83, 572
literature and, 558
in Lowell system, 508–9
marriage and child-bearing patterns of, 110,
    113–14, 115, 281–83, 571–72, 639
on mining frontier (California), 681
in 1920s, 1175–77
in 1950s, 1440–42
in Old Southwest, 658, 659, 660
on Overland Trail, 598–99
Quaker, *95, 95*
in Reconstruction, 792
in religious revivals, 542
slave, 125, 652–53
slave, sexual exploitation of, 639, 656–66
southern honor and, 643
on southern plantations, 638–39
in sports, 958, 959–60
theater and, 516–17
voting rights and, 283, 572, 982–84, *984,*
    1111, 1140, 1178–81
in West, 881–82
witchcraft and, 142
in World War I, 1138, 1139–40, 1181
in World War II, 1329–31, *1330, 1331*
see also feminism
Women Accepted for Volunteer Emergency
    Service (WAVES), 1329, *1330*
Women's Army Corps (WAC), 1329
Women's Christian Temperance Union, 762,
    994, 1084, 1170
women's clubs, 984
Women's Peace Party, 1130
women's rights, 283, 571–75, 982
    abolitionism and, 572, 664–65
    in Civil War, 762
    and property, 283, 572, 881
    Sojourner Truth on, 667
women's suffrage movement, 573–75, 981–84,
    1020, 1111, 1140, 1178–81
Women's Trade Union League, 1139
Women's Voluntary Service, 1334
Wood, Grant, 1280
Wood, Jethro, 490–91
Wood, Leonard, 1057
Woods, Robert A., 980
Woodstock Music Festival (1969), 1558–59,
    1559
Woodward, C. Vann, 856–57
Worcester v. Georgia, 464
working class:
    conditions for, 909, 910
    and distribution of wealth, 908–9
    in early nineteenth century, 509, *533*
    and election of 1896, 1027–28
    housing of, 505

working class (continued)
  Irish Americans as, 522
  legislative protection of, 986
  in Panic of 1837, 477
  recreation of, 515, 960–61, 961
  religion of, 538
  Taylorism and, 1077–78
  at theater, 517
  see also labor, employment; labor movement
Working Men's party, 530, 561, 912, 946
Works Progress Administration (WPA),
    1257–58, 1274, 1280, 1328
World Court, 1150, 1287–88, 1389
World War I, 1032–33, 1117–62
  airplanes in, 1209
  armistice in, 1147–48
  conscription in, 1136
  decisive role of U.S. in, 1142–48
  disarmament efforts after, 1289–92
  domestic unrest in, 1148–50
  labor movement in, 926
  loans to Europe in, 1125, 1201, 1226,
    1288–89, 1298
  Paris conference after, 1148–52, 1149, 1289
  Prohibition and, 1170–71
  propaganda in, 1140
  reparations after, 1151–52, 1288–89
  Socialist Party and, 924
  submarines and neutral rights in, 1126–29,
    1133, 1135
  U.S. entry into, 1134–42
  U.S. isolationism after, 1287–94
  U.S. mobilization in, 1137–38
  U.S. neutrality in, 1122–34
  U.S. preparedness in, 1129–30
  veterans of, 1228–30, 1229, 1273–74
  women in, 1138, 1139–40, 1181
World War II, 1321–74, 1390–91
  African Americans in, 1329, 1331–33
  air conflicts in, 1307, 1345
  atomic bombs in, 1367–71
  Battle of the Atlantic in, 1339–41
  Blitzkrieg in, 1305–6
  computers and, 1643
  conscription in, 1308
  D-Day in, 1346–51, 1348, 1350
  debt in, 1326–27
  demobilization after, 1380–88
  domestic mobilization in, 1324–28
  drive toward Berlin in, 1336–52
  economy in, 1325–28, 1329, 1371
  ethnic minorities in, 1331–36
  final ledger from, 1371–72
  financing of, 1326–27
  growing U.S. involvement in, 1306–8
  Holocaust in, 1365
  Indonesia in, 1475
  Leyte Gulf in, 1357–58
  maps of, 1342, 1355

New Deal programs eliminated in, 1328
North Africa fighting in, 1338–39
Pacific fighting in, 1322–24, 1336, 1339,
    1352–58, 1366–67
Pearl Harbor attack in, 1315–18, 1316,
    1317, 1323, 1337
selective service in, 1324
social effects of, 1328–36
strategic bombing in, 1345
submarines in, 1307, 1312, 1324, 1336,
    1340–41
U.S. arms aid in, 1309–13
U.S. neutrality in, 1300–1305, 1312
veterans of, 1382, 1425–26
war aims and strategy in, 1336–38, 1352–
    53
war criminals of, 1389–90
women in, 1329–31, 1330, 1331
World War Foreign Debt Commission, 1288
Wormley House agreement (1877), 833
Worthington, Amanda, 792
Wounded Knee, S. Dak.:
  FBI-AIM standoff at (1973), 1568, 1569
  massacre at (1890), 870
Wovoka (Jack Wilson), 870
WPA (Works Progress Administration),
    1257–58, 1274, 1280, 1328
WPB (War Production Board), 1325
Wright, Jim, 1674
Wright, Orville, 1209, 1210
Wright, Richard, 1278, 1279, 1438
Wright, Wilbur, 1209, 1210
writs of assistance, 200
Wyatt-Brown, Bertram, 642
Wye accords (1998), 1670
Wyoming:
  cattle industry in, 874, 877
  Indian conflicts in, 868
  statehood for, 866, 1010
  voting rights in, 983

XYZ Affair (1797), 361–62, 362

Yakimas, 587
Yale College, 161, 539, 952
  religious revival at, 539
Yalta Conference (1945), 1360–61, 1361,
    1362–63, 1390, 1391, 1392
Yamamoto, Isoruku, 1323, 1353
Yamasees, 186, 187
Yamasee War, 88, 89, 187
Yancey, William Lowndes, 688, 714
Yazoo Fraud, 384
yellow fever, 1057
yellow journalism, 1044, 1046
Yellowstone National Park, 1091
Yeltsin, Boris, 1637, 1638, 1669
Yemassee, The (Simms), 555
"ye old deluder Satan" Act (1647), 155

Yippies (Youth International Party), 1555, 1556
YMCA (Young Men's Christian Association), 979, 984
Yom Kippur War (1973), 1582, 1586
York, duke of, 94, 98
Yorktown, Battle of (1781), *264, 269, 269*
Yosemite National Park, 1092
Young, Andrew, 1597
Young, Brigham, 545–47
Young Chicanos for Community Action, 1564
Young Men's Christian Association (YMCA), 979, 984
Young people, 1430–32
  juvenile delinquency and, 1431–32

in 1960s, 1550–51
  voting rights for, 1581
Young Women's Christian Association, 983–84
Youth International Party (Yippies), 1555, 1556
Yugoslavia, 1151, 1311, 1394, 1671
Yukon gold rush, 931
Yumas, 590

Zenger, John Peter, 152
Zias, 587
Zimmermann, Arthur, 1133–34
Zionism, 1399
"zoot suit" riots (1943), 1334
Zunis, 12, 587

THE WORLD